ENCYCLOPEDIA OF
SCIENCE AND RELIGION

ENCYCLOPEDIA OF
SCIENCE AND RELIGION

VOLUME 2
J-Z

J. Wentzel Vrede van Huyssteen,
Editor in Chief

MACMILLAN
REFERENCE
USA™

THOMSON

GALE

New York • Detroit • San Diego • San Francisco • Cleveland • New Haven, Conn. • Waterville, Maine • London • Munich

Encyclopedia of Science and Religion

J. Wentzel Vrede van Huyssteen

© 2003 by Macmillan Reference USA.
Macmillan Reference USA is an imprint of
The Gale Group, Inc., a division of
Thomson Learning, Inc.

Macmillan Reference USA™ and
Thomson Learning™ are trademarks used
herein under license.

For more information contact
Macmillan Reference USA
300 Park Avenue South, 9th Floor
New York, NY 10010
Or you can visit our Internet site at
http://www.gale.com

For permission to use material from this
product, submit your request via Web at
http://www.gale-edit.com/permissions, or you
may download our Permissions Request form
and submit your request by fax or mail to:

Permissions Department
The Gale Group, Inc.
27500 Drake Rd.
Farmington Hills, MI 48331-3535
Permissions Hotline:
248-699-8006 or 800-877-4253 ext. 8006
Fax: 248-699-8074 or 800-762-4058

Cover image reproduced by permission of
Corbis (Shooting Stars Over the Meteor
Crater).

Macmillan Reference USA
300 Park Avenue South, 9th Floor
New York, NY 10010

Macmillan Reference USA
27500 Drake Road
Farmington Hills, MI 48331-3535

LIBRARY OF CONGRESS CATALOGING-IN-PUBLICATION DATA

Encyclopedia of science and religion / J. Wentzel Vrede van Huyssteen,
editor in chief. — 2nd ed.
   p. cm.
  Includes bibliographical references and index.
    ISBN 0-02-865704-7 (alk. paper) — ISBN 0-02-865705-5 (v. 1 : alk. paper)
    — ISBN 0-02-865706-3 (v. 2 : alk. paper)
    1. Religion and science—Encyclopedias. I. Van Huyssteen, Wentzel.

  BL240.3 .E43 2003
  291.1'75—dc21

                       2002152471

Printed in the United States of America
10 9 8 7 6 5 4 3 2

J

JUDAISM

Judaism is a monotheistic, scriptural religion that evolved from the religion of ancient Israel during the Second Temple period (516 B.C.E.–70 C.E.). Two core beliefs shaped the attitude of Judaism toward nature and toward the systematic study of nature (i.e., science): that God is the creator of the universe and that God revealed God's will in the form of Law—the Torah (literally "instruction")—to the chosen people, Israel.

The doctrine of creation facilitates an interest in the natural world that God brought into existence, even though the details of the creative act remain beyond the ken of human knowledge. Several Psalms express the notion that the more one observes nature, the more one comes to revere its creator, since the world manifests order and wise design. Awareness of nature's orderliness leads the observer to praise and thanksgiving and evokes awe and reverence. The study of nature, then, did not conflict with love of and obedience to God. Indeed, in the Middle Ages, Jewish philosophers regarded the study of God's created nature as a religious obligation. Nonetheless, the natural world was not to be worshiped for its own sake; that is the form of idolatry against which Judaism rails. In Judaism, nature always points, rather, to the divine creator who governs and sustains nature and who intervenes in human affairs, making God's will known through the performing of miracles, the greatest of which is the revelation of the Torah to Israel.

Rabbinnic attitudes

Even though in principle there is no theological impediment to study the natural world, the degree to which Jews should engage in scientific inquiry has always been debated in traditional Jewish society. Since philosophy and science originated in ancient Greece, the debate pertained to the cultural boundaries of Judaism, especially because Jews encountered Hellenistic culture as the culture that occasionally oppressed them, curtailing Jewish political independence and threatening Jewish mores. Since immersion in Greek culture could conceivably lead one away from commitment to God's Torah and the life it prescribed, rabbinic literature contains suspicious attitudes toward "alien wisdoms" (hochmot hitzoniyot) and issues a call to avoid teaching "Greek wisdom" to children. This caution is found side by side with information about rabbis who promoted the Greek *paideia* or who were themselves learned in the natural sciences. More problematically, the primacy of Torah study itself was justified by the claim that the revealed Torah, identical with God's wisdom, encompasses all true knowledge. If so, Jews have no need to pursue knowledge outside the perimeters of Torah. It is difficult, then, to generalize about the rabbinic attitude toward the study of nature and determine the precise scope of rabbinic knowledge of the science in their day.

The main scientific data in rabbinic literature pertains to astronomy and human physiology. Several rabbis (e.g., R. Yohanan ben Zakkai, Gamaliel II, and Joshua ben Hananya) were expert astronomers, using observed data for the calculation and adjustment of the lunar-solar calendar. The rabbinic corpus is also replete with information about the motions of celestial bodies, the four seasons, the planets, the zodiac, and even comets. The picture of the universe in Talmudic texts has the Earth in the center of creation with heaven as a hemisphere spread over it. The Earth is usually described as a disk encircled by water. Interestingly, cosmological and metaphysical speculations were not to be cultivated in public nor were they to be committed to writing. Rather, they were considered as "secrets of the Torah not to be passed on to all and sundry" (Ketubot 112a). While study of God's creation was not prohibited, speculations about "what is above, what is beneath, what is before, and what is after" (Mishnah Hagigah: 2) were restricted to the intellectual elite.

Within the created world, the human body was of utmost interest to the rabbis, although their information about human anatomy was shaped by religious concern for ritual purity. Rich in details about the skeleton, the digestive organs, the respiratory system, the heart, the genitals and other organs, the rabbinic corpus also includes rather fanciful material and is totally lacking in graphic illustration. The discussion is concerned primarily with physical disfigurements that disqualify men from the priesthood, with rules concerning menstruating women, and with other sources of ritual pollution. The rabbinic corpus also includes informative claims about embryology, diagnosis of diseases, and a host of medications and hygienic strategies for prevention of disease. Indeed, the physician is viewed as an instrument of God, treated with utmost respect, and several Talmudic scholars were themselves physicians. Nonetheless, the rabbinic discourse about scientific matters was unsystematic, primarily because it was embedded in the interpretation of Scriptures. Whether the rabbinic legal reasoning as a whole could be considered "science" is debated in contemporary times, reflecting twentieth-century changes in the philosophy of science.

Scientific learning in the Middle Ages

The cultivation of science as a public, albeit elitist, activity began in earnest in the ninth century, when most of world Jewry lived in the orbit of Islam. Greek and Hellenistic philosophy and science were translated into Arabic and stimulated the rise of Islamic rationalist theology. Writing in

Arabic, Jews emulated Islamic scholars, reinterpreting rabbinic Judaism in rationalist categories derived from Muslim neo-Platonism and Aristotelianism. Jewish scholars studied all branches of the sciences and a few Jews (e.g., Isaac Israeli, Moses Maimonides, and Levi ben Gershom, known as Gersonides) achieved distinction in the non-Jewish world. Jews participated in astronomy at the court of Alphonso X and were largely responsible for the construction of the Alphonsine Tables for computing planetary positions that remained popular until the mid-seventeenth century. Lacking an institutional setting, Jewish scientific learning was an autodidactic, bookish activity of translating texts of the liberal arts and natural philosophy from Arabic into Hebrew and occasionally from Hebrew into Latin, writing commentaries on them, and working out the theological implications of the apparent conflict between revealed knowledge ("religion") and knowledge discovered by human reason ("science"). One primarily exception was the astronomical observations of Gersonides (1288–1344), who built an instrument to study the distance between the stars, the Jacob Staff remained in use by European navigators until the mid-eighteenth century.

Moses Maimonides (1135–1204) articulated the most sophisticated synthesis of science and Judaism. In principle, he held, there can be no contradiction between the inner, nonliteral meaning of the Torah and what is true in the sciences of physics and metaphysics. Apparent conflicts emerge either because a nondemonstrable scientific theory is adopted (for example, Aristotle's view that the world is eternal and his explanation of celestial motions), or because the biblical text is not interpreted in light of philosophy and science. For Maimonides, who accepted Aristotelian science in regard to processes of the sublunar world, possessing knowledge about the physical world was a religious obligation, because accurate knowledge about the physical world leads one to understand how God governs the world (i.e., God's attributes of action). However, Maimonides's radical negative theology, according to which scientific knowledge does not yield valid knowledge about God's essence, placed a limit on science and made the intellectual perfection (the goal of human life according to Maimonides) unattainable.

For the subsequent four centuries, Maimonides's followers translated scientific literature into Hebrew and interpreted Scripture as an esoteric text that contains scientific-philosophic truths. To disseminate philosophic-scientific knowledge Jewish scholars composed encyclopedias that summarized known scientific data in the linguistic sciences (logic, rhetoric, and grammar), the mathematical sciences (arithmetic, geometry, optics, astronomy, music, mechanics, algebra), the physical sciences (based on the eight books of Aristotle's *Organon*), metaphysics, and politics (including ethics and economics). This vast knowledge was deemed necessary for the attainment of intellectual perfection, resulting in immortality of the intellect. Whether it was also sufficient knowledge for immortality was vigorously debated, especially after Maimonides's theory of divine attributes was modified by Gersonides to mean that scientific knowledge does yield positive knowledge about God's essence. For Jewish philosophers to attain religious perfection, they had to be philosopher-scientists.

Jewish scientific learning during the Middle Ages was broad in scope and ambitious in aim but it was not unproblematic. First, scientific learning was cultivated only by Jews in Mediterranean communities of Spain, Southern France, Italy, and North-Africa but did not penetrate the Jewish communities north of the Alps. Second, the Jewish scientists-philosophers did not have an institutional setting and did not receive official support for their inquiries. Unlike their Christian neighbors, Jews did not create universities, and the scientific curriculum was not incorporated into the rabbinic academies for higher learning. Third, scientific knowledge was cultivated by a very small number of experts and did not engage the community at large. Finally, there was organized opposition to the cultivation of the sciences, spearheaded not just by rabbis who regarded secular knowledge to be irrelevant or even undermining to the authority of the Jewish tradition, but sometimes by Jews who were themselves quite knowledgeable in the sciences. The Maimonidean controversy that engulfed world Jewry during the thirteenth century and resurfaced in the fifteenth and sixteenth centuries indicated that the cultivation of science remained problematic even in the Middle Ages.

Early modern period

In the early modern period (sixteenth through eighteenth centuries), the Maimonidean tradition lost its interpretative power and was replaced by *Kabbalah,* the Jewish mystical tradition, as the official theology of Judaism. In a way, the turn to Kabbalah was an attempt to overcome the restrictions of Maimonides's radical negative theology. For the kabbalists, knowledge of God's essence and intimacy with God were to be attained not through observation of the material world interpreted by Aristotelian scientific theories, but through fathoming the symbolic meaning of God's revealed Torah. Constructed out of the building blocks of the Hebrew alphabet, nature mirrors God's essence and the primordial Torah is the key to decipher nature's symbolic structures. The kabbalists regarded nature not as observable, measurable mass, but as an information system that has to be decoded. Their elaborate speculations about the origins of the universe were ultimately a hermeneutic activity, framed by the very language of Jewish canonic texts. This approach to nature was in accord with trends in Renaissance culture and usually went hand in hand with preoccupation with magic, astrology, and alchemy, but it did not necessarily prevent the Jewish scholar from also being informed about new scientific discoveries in astronomy, human physiology, botany, zoology, and mineralogy.

While Kabbalah did not preclude one from interest in nature, on the whole, Kabbalah probably retarded the involvement of Jews in the scientific revolution of the seventeenth century. Jewish scholars played a marginal role in the development of early modern science, although a small number of Jews were aware of the emerging new sciences. David Ganz (1541–1613), for example, corresponded with the astronomer Johannes Mueller and was personally familiar with Johann Kepler and Tycho Brahe. The first Jew to mention Copernicus and praise him, Ganz nonetheless adapted Brahe's model, which reconciled the Copernican and Ptolemaic systems on the basis of actual observations. For Brahe, Ganz translated the Alphonsine Tables from the Hebrew into German, and for his Jewish audience Ganz composed in Hebrew the history of Jewish involvement in astronomy. That book, however, was printed only in 1743, indicating a relative lack of interest in the subject among Jews. A typical Jewish response to the heliocentric theory was voiced by Isaac Cardozo (1604-1681), the most scientifically informed Jew of his day, who rejected it on religious grounds and adduced nineteen biblical verses against the theory. By contrast, Joseph Solomon Delmedigo (1591–1655), who had contacts with Galileo Galilei and who was the first Jewish scholar to use the recently invented logarithmic tables, parted company with the followers of Ptolemy to espouse the Copernican system. Delmedigo was also a student of Kabbalah, which he proceeded to criticize, but he promoted knowledge of the empirical sciences as a way to alleviate the miserable conditions of Jewish life in Europe's ghettos. The small cadre of Jews who earned doctoral degrees from European universities, especially in medicine from the University of Padua, did not change the fact that interest in the natural sciences was marginal in Jewish culture during the early modern period. Instead, the study of Halachah and Kabbalah—both are elaborate, textual, self-referential, abstract edifices—preoccupied Jewish intellectual interests. The ethos of Jewish traditional life in eighteenth-century Europe remained largely uninformed by the scientific revolution.

In the late eighteenth century, a small group of Jewish intellectuals in Germany began to agitate for change. Inspired by the Enlightenment, these Jews insisted that Judaism must embrace scientific knowledge or else stagnate. Desiring social integration and an end to Jewish segregation and persecution, the advocates of Jewish Enlightenment (*Haskalah*) were very critical of traditional Jewish education and encouraged Jews to study the sciences in order to become fit to enter modern society. The proponents of Haskalah worked tirelessly to persuade European states to grant Jews equal civil rights.

France was the first country to grant citizenship to Jews (1791), as the logical consequence of the Declaration of the Rights of Man (1789). Yet the struggle for legal emancipation lasted until the 1870s in central Europe and was achieved in Russia only with the revolution of 1917. As citizens, Jews who flocked to the universities of western and central Europe embraced the natural sciences as secular pursuits that promised social progress and modernization. Some even converted to Christianity in order to be able to hold academic positions, and for those who remained nominally Jewish, science replaced traditional Jewish Torah-study and was devoid of religious meaning. In the nineteenth century, individual Jews contributed immensely to a plethora of natural sciences, but they

did so as individuals and not as members of Israel, God's chosen priestly nation. The secularization of Western (Christian) culture, which privatized religion, and the prevailing scientific theories of classical physics exacerbated the perception that science and religion were diametrically opposed. The main Jewish responses to modernity—Reform, Conservative, and Orthodoxy—articulated distinctive approaches to the perceived tension.

Strands of modern Judaism

Reform Judaism essentially denies that there is a conflict between Judaism and science. Reform thinkers assume that Judaism is a rational religion that welcomes the scientific, ongoing sequence of observation, hypothesis, experimentation, and conclusion, with each conclusion subject to further investigation by the same method. The rationalist spirit of Reform Judaism intended to strip Judaism from the morass of ossifying, legalistic minutiae and bring to the fore the timeless, universal truths of Judaism. The rationalist temper, which led Reform Judaism to discard many traditional practices or invent new rituals, did not necessarily mean endorsing the most challenging scientific theory of the nineteenth century—Darwinism. In the United States, the radical reformer David Einhorn (1809–1879) sneered at the idea that humans descended from lower animals, and his opponent, Isaac Mayer Wise (1819–1900), also took a dim view of Darwinian thought. However, by the 1880s several Reform rabbis attempted to reconcile religion with the new science and defended Judaism's superiority over other religions because of its nondogmatic, ever-evolving character. Reform rabbis accepted biblical criticism and viewed the Bible itself, and not only rabbinic Judaism, as a product of history. To their chagrin, however, Reform rabbis had to contend with Protestant biblical criticism that used the Darwinian model to prove that Judaism was a primitive religion out of which evolved the superior religion of Christianity.

Interest in the relationship between science and religion is stronger in Conservative Judaism because it takes the rabbinic tradition to be obligatory, while acknowledging that it evolved over time. More than the natural sciences, the academic discipline of history was the scientific inquiry that concerned Conservative Judaism. In the nineteenth century, Conservative scholars accepted the evolutionary model and applied it to the history of Jewish law, leaving the Bible untouched. In the twentieth century, the critical method has been applied to the biblical text and the perceived challenge by science is rebuffed by saying that the revealed biblical text did not intend itself to be understood literally but as a poetic statement of certain truths: that the world was created by God, and that God planned it carefully and designed it to be hospitable to human beings. These conclusions are consistent with contemporary scientific theories in physics and cosmology. Indeed, the twentieth-century move away from classical physics to a new model of the universe explained by relativity theory or by quantum mechanics enabled some Conservative rabbis to make the biblical narrative more intelligible. Rabbi Lawrence Troster, for example, argued that the Anthropic Principle shows that the universe is not a neutral entity, empty of purpose and meaning, and that partnership between science and religion is possible and desirable. For him the Big Bang theory can lead to an intellectual or emotional enthusiasm for the creator. Conversely, contemporary physics should lead to rethinking the meaning of the doctrine of creation, especially creation in the image of God, and of the problem of evil. Troster's studies are consistent with the work of Norbert Samuelson, the only Reform rabbi who has made a significant contribution to the dialogue of science and religion.

The main area for the confluence of science and religion in Conservative Judaism is bioethics. Conservative legal thinkers such as Elliot Dorff maintain that scientific research is both possible and potentially fruitful and that contemporary interpretation of Halachah must be informed of advances in science and technology. Yet, scientific activity cannot be taken for its own sake: Scientific means and ends have to be evaluated by religious values. Science, and especially its application in technology, can be used to solve legal problems or to alleviate legal restrictions. Though rabbis must be informed about science, the scientific facts of every disputed issue do not settle anything since how one construes the facts is crucial, and this is determined by one's religious and moral values. Biomedical issues of most concern to Conservative thinkers are issues of human sexuality (e.g., fertility and homosexuality) as well as questions of the beginning and end of life (i.e., abortion and euthanasia). Conservative legal thinkers legitimize the consultation with science by insisting that Jewish law itself presupposes the existence of knowledge and morality independent of Jewish law.

Of all variants of modern Judaism, Modern Orthodoxy (in contradistinction from Ultra Orthodoxy) is most preoccupied in the dialogue between science and religion, precisely because on the surface the two may appear to be contradictory. Founded by Samson Raphael Hirsch (1808–1888) in Germany, Modern Orthodoxy was also a response to the challenges of modernity, even though it rejected the radical ritual changes of Reform Judaism or the historical approach of the positive-historical school, the ideological foundation of Conservative Judaism. For Hirsch, a "Torah-True Judaism" meant that the Torah is eternal and unchanged, but that Judaism must be informed about and selectively involved in the secular world. His slogan, *Torah im Derekh Eretz*" (Torah combined with secular knowledge), became the institutional credo of Yeshiva College in New York City, which was founded in 1928 and became a university in 1946. This institution was committed to the synthesis of "Torah U-Mada" (Torah and science), although the precise meaning of this ideal is repeatedly questioned. The faculty and graduates of Yeshiva University publish essays about the interplay of science and religion in their academic magazines—*Tradition: A Journal of Orthodox Thought* and *The Journal of Halacha and Contemporary Society*—and even founded a magazine devoted solely to that issue: *The Torah U-Mada Journal*. Precisely because Orthodoxy understands Judaism as truth, it takes note of seemingly competing truth claims in science.

For Modern Orthodoxy the affirmation of the dialogue between science and Judaism is based on the following assumptions: first, Halachah is binding and all-encompassing and no aspect of human life is irrelevant to it, including science. Second, since halachic discourse exposes the true meaning of divine revelation, there can be no contradiction between what is true in science and what is true in Judaism. Third, scientific and technological advances can help resolve many practical details of religious practice, especially in matters that concern the human body. Medical ethics is thus a primary area in which a fruitful interaction between science and Judaism can take place.

Fourth, science is not the source of value, and science requires a framework of values whose authority is other than human. Judaism's moral values are absolute and immutable because they are revealed by God.

Orthodox scholars reject biblical criticism and treat the halachic tradition as an eternally valid legal system that has its internal mechanisms of self-interpretation. In terms of the doctrine of creation, Orthodox Jews, who tend to pursue the study of the natural sciences but shun the humanities and social sciences, argue, not without a tinge of apologetics, that the Big Bang theory validates even the details of biblical narrative of creation, although science still fails to explain why the world was created. That explanation is available only to the believing Jew who ascribes the creative act to God's will. In regard to bioethics, Orthodox jurists such as Rabbi J. David Bleich and Rabbi Immanuel Jakobovits, who are informed in contemporary medicine, bring their extensive knowledge of the halachic tradition to bear on a host of medical problems. These include dwarfism, transsexual surgery, egg donation, and implantation, Tay-Sachs disease, dental practices, skin grafting, organ transplantation, hazardous medical procedures, establishment of death, the treatment of human corpses, eugenics, sterilization, contraception, the proper conduct of physicians, gene therapy, and cloning technology. Though no medical issue is outside the scope of Halachah, it is the halachic corpus itself that defines the principles that enable the Modern Orthodox jurist to determine what is permissible. To the extent that this endeavor requires a theological justification, the model is found in medieval Jewish philosophy of Maimonides and his disciples. Ultra-Orthodox Jews, however, do not accept the Maimonidean synthesis, are not interested in accommodation to modern life, and take a literalist approach to Scripture. For them, science and Judaism belong to different realms and their truth-claims are of unequal epistemic value.

In sum, while there is no theological impediment to the study of nature in Judaism, there has been some unease about the pursuit of science in traditional Jewish society. Either because scientific knowledge originated outside Jewish society, or because scientific inquiry could divert Jews focusing exclusively on Torah, premodern Jewish culture harbored suspicion toward the study of nature,

classified as "secular learning." In the Middle Ages, especially in Spain and Southern France, Jews cultivated the natural sciences and excelled in mathematics, astronomy, and medicine, but these achievements were overshadowed by the preoccupation with law and with Kabbalah in the early-modern period. In the modern period, the dialogue between science and religion has been configured in the context of Jewish social integration into Western society and the need to rethink the authority of Halachah. Reform Judaism, which champions full integration and denies the authority of the rabbis, takes for granted that Judaism is rational, and does not see science as a challenge to Judaism at all. Conservative Judaism, which promotes allegiance to the Jewish tradition along with admission that Halachah evolved over time, is aware of the challenge but considers scientific theories useful for a deeper understanding of Scripture and legal decision-making. Finally, modern Orthodoxy, which insists on the eternal validity of Halachah while being open to modern life, is most creative in attempting to respond to new scientific theories and technological advances. Most modern Jews, who define themselves religiously, and not only ethnically or culturally, regard scientific study of God's created world positively, while insisting that scientific means and ends be judged and/or complemented by Jewish religious and moral values.

See also JUDAISM, CONTEMPORARY ISSUES IN SCIENCE AND RELIGION; JUDAISM, HISTORY OF SCIENCE AND RELIGION, MEDIEVAL PERIOD; JUDAISM, HISTORY OF SCIENCE AND RELIGION, MODERN PERIOD; MAIMONIDES

Bibliography

Bleich David J. *Contemporary Halakhic Problems,* Vols. 1–3. New York: Ktav, 1977–1989.

Borowitz, Eugene B. "The Autonomous Jewish Self." *Modern Judaism* 4, no. 1 (1984): 39–56.

Cohen, Naomi W. "The Challenges of Darwinism and Biblical Criticism to American Judaism." *Modern Judaism* 4, no. 2 (1984): 121–158.

Dorff, Elliot N. "Artificial Insemination, Egg Donation, and Adoption." *Conservative Judaism* 49 (1996): 3–60.

Dorff, Elliot N. "A Methodology for Jewish Medical Ethics." In *Contemporary Jewish Ethics and Morality: A Reader,* ed. Elliot N. Dorff and Louis E. Newman. New York: Oxford University Press, 1995.

Fisch, Menachem. *Rational Rabbis: Science and Talmudic Literature.* Bloomington: Indiana University Press, 1997.

Goldstein, Bernard R., "Scientific Traditions in Late Medieval Jewish Communities," in *Les juifs au regard de l'histoire: Melanges en l'honneur de Bernard Blumenkranz* (Picard: Paris, 1985), pp. 235-247.

Harvey, Steven, ed. *The Medieval Hebrew Encyclopedias of Science and Philosophy.* Dordrecht, Boston, and London: Kluwer, 2000.

Jakobovits, Immanuel. *Jewish Medical Ethics: A Comparative and Historical Study of the Jewish Religious Attitude to Medicine and Its Practice.* New York: Bloch, 1959.

Lamm, Norman. *Torah Umadda: The Encounter of Religious Learning and Worldly Knowledge in the Jewish Tradition.* Northvale N.J.: J. Aronosn, 1990.

Langermann, Tzvi Y. *The Jews and the Sciences in the Middle Ages.* Aldershot, UK: Ashgate/Variorium, 1999.

Luxemburg, Jack. "Science, Creationism, and Reform Judaism." *Journal of Reform Judaism* 29, no. 3 (1982): 42–49.

Plaut, Gunther W. *Judaism and the Scientific Spirit.* New York: Union of American Hebrew Congregations, 1962.

Ruderman, David B. *Kabbalah, Magic, and Science: The Cultural Universe of a Sixteenth-Century Jewish Physician.* Cambridge, Mass.: Harvard University Press, 1988.

Samuelson, Norbert M. *Judaism and the Doctrine of Creation.* Cambridge, UK: Cambridge University Press, 1994.

Schacter, Jacob J. "Torah u-Madda Revisited: The Editor's Introduction." *The Torah U-Madda Journal* 1 (1989): 1–22.

Tigay, Jeffrey H. "Genesis, Science, and Scientific Creationism." *Conservative Judaism* 40, no. 2 (1987/1988): 20–27.

Tirosh-Samuelson, Hava. "Theology of Nature in Sixteenth-Century Italian Jewish Philosophy." *Science in Context* 10, no. 4 (1997): 529–570.

Troster, Lawrence. "Love of God and the Anthropic Principle." *Conservative Judaism* 40, no. 2 (1987/1988): 43–51.

Troster, Lawrence. "From Big Bang to Omega Point: Jewish Response to Recent Theories to Modern Cosmology." *Conservative Judaism* 49, no. 4 (1997): 17–31.

HAVA TIROSH-SAMUELSON

JUDAISM, CONTEMPORARY ISSUES IN SCIENCE AND RELIGION

Although the pace of the scientific inquiry has increased tremendously since 1800 and the hegemony with which scientific veracities shape culture has surely increased as well, for religious systems, texts, and communities, the challenges and questions posed by science are classic ones. Science as a theory and practice makes several claims: that the natural world has order, laws, and causality; that such order can be apprehended and explained by human beings; and that the manipulation of the nameable, quantifiable, and discernable elements of that natural and tangible world can be achieved to organize human social and cultural life.

Science and ethics in Judaism: discernment and discourse

In Jewish thought and tradition, this search for understanding, the discernment of order, and the re-ordering of the natural world are not only achievable, but a divinely commanded part of a larger imperative to heal and to repair the world. For Jewish philosophers, the freely entered Covenant that assigns these tasks to an elected people is what makes ethical norms possible (Hartman 1985). However, moral norms cannot be established without reference to a complex legal system that draws on centuries of case law and textual interpretation. For over two centuries, this system has been applied in reflection on the dilemmas of science and of modernity. Science, in particular natural science, has been wholeheartedly embraced as allowing the fullest understanding of the events and cases in the world in which the community practices its religion.

Unlike faith traditions that reify the natural world as essentially sacred and unchangeable, Jewish thought affirms the human ability to alter the natural world, seeing in this alteration the ability to create justice and healing as acts of faith and obligation. The relationship between Jewish thought and scientific understanding varies over different historical periods. In fact, the intellectual attention of Jewish tradition had been largely focused on the moral and social task rather than the actual achievements of science until well into the Enlightenment (H. Levine 1972; Samuelson 2001).

The structure of Jewish ethics and Halachah

Jewish ethical norms are established via a legal system called *Halachah*. (The root of this word in Hebrew is related to the word "to walk"; the same root is also found in Islamic law or *sharia*.) Bounded by this system of religio-legal behavior, the individual Jew, once past the age of thirteen (twelve for women), is responsible for the performance of *mitzvot* or divine commandments of activity and response to God and to the community. There are 613 such commandments in the traditional reckoning, a metaphorical number that stands for the completeness of obligation. Many commandments are concerned with the daily details of ritual and familial life, many are employed in the service of civil codes, and others set the perimeters of response to newly arising dilemmas, such as how to regard cloning, nuclear fission, and space travel. At stake in the system is not only whether the intended act is regarded as a prohibited, permissible, or exemplary activity, but how the activity ought to be carried out, using what criteria for assessment. Jewish ethics is a complex negotiation with procedural questions and substantive ones.

The first procedural question that the system of Jewish ethics addresses is the problem of how to achieve good ends in a nonteleological system. Judaism answers this in a way that is the unique hallmark of the method; it is a method that, while based in law, draws on a variety of sources both to create the cases for the law and to resist and query its assumptions. The basic procedure for the evaluation of norms is the mode of argumentation—commentary, debate, and discussion. Essentially casuistic, the halachic system uses the encounter with the Torah text, and the encounter with the other's encounter with the text, to create a continuous discursive community. Cases are raised to illustrate points of law and then to illustrate alternate interpretations of the law. Narrative, in a variety of literary forms (metaphor, allegory, historical reference, intertextual mirroring) called *aggadah,* are embedded in the text. While the details of the *aggadah* did not create binding laws, the form was used to grapple with and embellish the discussion of the details of the Halachah. The casuistic account attempts to decipher the particular and specific human ways the principle has been, or theoretically could be, applied. In fact, it is essential to remember that much of the case law turns on elaborate constructs that never happened, or could never be expected to happen, as well as actual cases that arose in community practice.

Judaism is both a deontological and a casuistic system, rooted in rules, duties, and normative conduct and concerned with motive and process. But it is unlike a purely deontological system because the real world, and the context and outcome of each case, count in their assessment. Judaism is a modified casuistic deontology. Consequences, once enacted, are reexamined and debated. The real world matters: knowledge of precedence, historicity, the tactile, and the theoretical all count in this system. Human reason is needed both to negotiate the system and to interpret intelligently the sensory natural world. Talmudic methodology was argument structured by text, history, and community. These three elements, and the use of reason to decipher them, modify the deontological method of Jewish ethics. It was *deontological* because it assumed Torah law as motivational, commanded, central, and binding; it was *casuistic* because it was also inductive and case (context) modified.

The central claim of Jewish ethics is that truth is found in the house of discursive study—the *bet midrash*. Such a public discourse is created when Jews argue, face to face, about the meaning and relevance of the narrative, symbols, and referents. Embedded in the problem are issues of context, causation, agency, norm, and assessment. Each of these issues must be addressed by whomever is describing whatever methodology of ethics they use, with the assumption that methodology in ethics involves not only a general theory of morality, authority, and value, but also "middle axioms," or the middle ground between general principles and the details of policy. James Childress and John Macquarrie, however, consider this a "misleading term" in the *Westminster Dictionary of Christian Ethics* (1967). Perhaps a better description would be a coinage: "middle processes." Methodology in any integral ethical system must address both the *why* and the *how* of a "right act" if it is to have coherency and if it can be used in the human hands and heart of the world, and Jewish ethics is no exception. Jewish ethics presumes public choices; it assumes community, human sociability, and embodied dailiness, and that ordinary human acts have a weight and meaning that ought to be the subject of urgent discourse.

A central question: Is there an ethics independent of Halachah?

The idea that rules and laws form the base of the system can be agreed on, yet the methodology of argumentation creates nuances of interpretation. Since about the mid-nineteenth century, four branches of Judaism have developed. All acknowledge the role of Halachah, but each gives it different weight in the setting of normative standards for their tradition. For the Orthodox Jew, Halachah is interpreted by his or her rabbi, who then consults with leading scholars if the issue is difficult, and that decision is considered halachically binding. For the Conservative Jew, Halachah has a strong voice in the determination of *din* (Judgment) by the rabbinic community. The Conservative *minhag* (custom) is determined by the community. Jewish law is then integrated with insights from the social sciences and Western philosophic norms in making a decision. For Reform Jews, the individual is autonomously responsible for his or her own choices, in light of the "tradition" and the primary ethical stance of the tradition. This entry will describe the traditional or *halachically* grounded position, although it is crucial to remember that among Jews there is considerable variance. It is arguable that, even for Jews not bound by its restraint, Halachah wields a strong methodological influence.

The central procedural question for all branches of Judaism stands in tension with the praxis. For example, the dilemma of the achievement of justice is *not* resolved, and the quest itself proves key to opening the method. The multivocity of the form itself insists on the questioning of the solidity of the text: To name as definitive one personal interpretation is a violation of the Talmudic method. For many of the proof texts there are countervailing premises and correspondent inimitable truths, and rabbinic decisors who defend differing positions.

Marvin Fox, writing in *Modern Jewish Ethics, Theory, and Practice* (1975), one of the central works in English on this topic, argued that the halachic system itself includes an accountability to a variety of sources. His insight was that the basic method incorporates science, philosophy, and natural reality into the traditional texts. The rabbis used exegesis and interpretation as the most important device to reconcile the basic and sacred text with the reality of exile, change, and science.

Fox further noted that the incorporation of "external to Sinitic" sources was always a part of the discourse. He argued that Maimonides (c. 1135–1204) assumes math, astronomy, and "speculative realities" are better known by the Arabic world than by the rabbinic sages and that Jews need to "accept truth from any source." Fox noted Judah HaNasi's confession that, in some arguments, the Gentile sages "vanquished the sages of Israel." This was cited in the tradition as a case of how best evidence and best argument from whatever source ought to prevail.

Saadya Gaon made this point, according to Fox, even more forcefully by insisting that reason existed both prior to and after Sinai. Further, Fox noted that interpretation has always varied widely, even at the heart of basic texts (like the Moses story, the Ruth story, the view of the Nazarite vow, and the problem of creation itself). Additionally, he pointed to the flexibility of the *aggadah* as indicative of the freedom at the heart of Jewish method itself. Fox reminded us that tradition has each Jew at Sinai now and for eternal generations and noted the rabbinic *Midrash* that says each Jew hears the revelation through his or her own body and experience.

Rabbi Joseph Soleveitchik, the late leading contemporary halachist, wrote extensively regarding the relationship between the method of ethical discernment and the scientific method itself, finding in physics a way of understanding the structure of human understanding. He argued that physics and the theory of relativity teach that truth can be viewed from many perspectives, and that the universe is not a Newtonian machine, but a complex of related happenings. One's perspective, then, will determine the "true" view of the object. One can see a stream and note its beauty, its physical properties, or its ritual use, for example. All are "real" views of the same phenomena. Further, Soleveitchik understood that human perception is a function of the truth that each person perceives, as each person individually views the "real" from the perspective of a particular and chosen order. What is seen as actual is a chosen fact pattern based on a system of value and belief. Soleveitchik posited the notion that to be religious or to be scientific, while they may represent radically different worldviews, was not only to value the world differently, but to experience and to see the phenomena of the world differently as well. That notion was entirely consistent with the concept of truth understood as "plural truth," and it served to explain how specific events could be seen as miracles or a function of the events of the causative natural world.

Science: the epistemic questions

Scientific inquiry is based on the application of human observation and human reasoning to events in the observable world. As such, it might seem that science offers a primal threat to faith traditions due to the unseen and unprovable truth claims of faith. However, Jewish tradition has long been able to incorporate secular knowledge from medicine and science into ethical norms. New insights are evaluated as cases to be compared to historically precedential ones. Scientific insights and achievements can thus be incorporated. Hence, post-Darwinian writings reinterpreted the "six days of Creation" as occurring in "six periods," or six divine "days," and electricity became legally bound by the rules of the Sabbath by understanding it as a form of "fire-making." "Science" or secular knowledge in general was often used to represent "a vehicle for a certain cluster of liberal, democratic values" argued as central to Western, or American values, a metaphor for the use of objectivity, impartiality, and civic order (Holliger). The methods of science, the use of clinical trials and controls and the use of animal models were also strongly embraced by Jews. In general, Judaism makes the assumption that the order of nature is accessible to human reason, and that nature, while offering some suggestive models for human behavior, is not the source of moral authority.

While social conditions, exclusion from the developing academy, constraints on employment, and isolation in European ghettos left Jewish intellectuals behind in the development of science in the early modern period, the nineteenth and twentieth centuries were marked by an enthusiastic embrace of and a mastery of many fields of scientific inquiry.

Science: substantive questions

Astronomy and cosmology dominated early reflections in Jewish thought because of the importance in calculations of calendar holidays, and, as Hillel Levine notes, because of the rabbinic attention to time rather than space after the destruction of the Second Temple (Levine, p 856). Levine further remarks that Jews, in their capacity as traders between different Jewish communities, acted as interpreters of the insights from Islamic and renaissance Christian civilizations. Medicine, as a commanded obligation of Jewish communities, was often a venue for investigation in science. Jewish physicians were often called upon to assume the relatively high-risk activity of caring for the sick, in part because they had a access to the large armamentarium of knowledge. Scientific discovery came later to the large Jewish community. A complex interest in kabbalistic beliefs and rituals, a renewed emphasis on spirituality, and compelling disputes about how to resist persecution and about how to engage modernity politically or communally, dominated Jewish views on the "new science" of the Enlightenment in the sixteenth through the eighteenth centuries. To the extent that science was posited as opposed to faith, it was regarded in traditional communities as suspect. It is Levine's contention that Jews in that period did not view science as "universally valid, but simply as the source of religious persecution in a new key" (p. 860).

But the search for the truth grounds moral reasoning. By the nineteenth century, the truth claims of science had been well established. Descriptive science such as the cataloging of species, germ theory, and the use of instruments of observation were eagerly taken on by the Jewish intelligentsia. In the twentieth century, Jewish commentators turned their attention to the problems of intervention, prevention, and cure, as well as the search for origins. Finding little to prohibit basic research, and reasoning from principles that stressed stewardship and ordering of the natural world, Jews were easily able to reconcile new discoveries, supporting the sense not only that the natural world was knowable, but that it ought to be. It should be mentioned here, of course, that Nobel Prizes in the sciences and medicine have been won by Jews in numbers far greater then their presence in the world population.

Halachah, too, has advanced to address new science. Science disrupts categories of being. An essential premise of the method is that events are best understood by disassembly into knowable parts—ever smaller, ever more essential. For a halachic system, this offers an opportunity to renegotiate the borders of permissibility at each component piece, commodity, or event. Modern halachic authorities such as Orthodox rabbi Faitel Levine openly struggle with the challenge that new science brings to a textual tradition governed by law. Levine, a traditional rabbinic *poskim* (a rabbi to whom specific legal questions are directed) specializing in new technology, writes in *Halacha, Medical Science, and Technology* (1987): "Once reality was relatively constant, unchanging . . . in the objective world in which halachah operates . . . But things have changed. In today's world, reality itself is undergoing repeated, fundamental changes. Objects which have little in common with traditional objects are constantly produced . . . consequently, our contemporary world in evading the control of traditional terms and concepts. But Torah is eternal!"

Recent controversies in the field of reproductive health and genetic medicine have often dominated the debate between religious communities and scientific investigators. In these debates one can see how the concern for healing, the obligation to repair the world, and the view that human life is fully ensouled only in developmental stages, rather than at the moment of conception, has allowed for a robust acceptance of basic research in biological sciences.

The acts of practice in traditional Judaism revolved around two centralities. The first is study of text, and the second is commanded acts that create a just society. Central to Jewish texts is the recognition of the as yet unredeemed quality of the world—even the natural world as understood by science. Just as circumcision is one mark of the covenant, a mark of a human response to birth, and a refinement of the natural world, so too is the notion that advanced scientific inquiry is a part of *tikkun olam*, the mandate to be an active partner in the world's repair and perfection. In the world of suffering and injustice, much, although not all, of clinical and business scientific research can be understood as an opportunity to address this injustice. This justice consideration is made actual by a support for science, medical advance, and the freedom of inquiry, all ways that human work to perfect the world can be fully embraced. While texts warn of the possibility of hubris, and there are many texts that teach of the danger of confusing the quest for learning with the temptation to control, the struggle to understand and to interpret the covenantal relationship includes extending the duty to heal. In this way, Jewish thought has long turned to science as

a critical way to lay the groundwork for the study and the repair of the world.

See also JUDAISM; JUDAISM, HISTORY OF SCIENCE AND RELIGION, MEDIEVAL PERIOD; JUDAISM, HISTORY OF SCIENCE AND RELIGION, MODERN PERIOD

Bibliography

Childress, James, and Macquarrie, John, eds. *The Westminster Dictionary of Christian Ethics*. Philadelphia: Westminster Press, 1967.

Fox, Marvin, ed. *Modern Jewish Ethics, Theory, and Practice*. Columbus: Ohio State University Press, 1975.

Holliger, David. *Science, Jews, and Secular Culture: Studies in Mid-Twentieth Century American Intellectual History*. Princeton, N.J.: Princeton University Press, 1995.

Levine, Faitel. *Halacha, Medical Science, and Technology: Perspectives on Contemporary Halacha Issues*. New York: Maznaim, 1987.

Levine, Hillel. "Science." In *Contemporary Jewish Religious Thought*, ed. Arthur A. Cohen and Paul Mendes-Flor. New York: Free Press, 1972.

Samuelson, Norbert M. "Rethinking Ethics In the Light of Jewish Thought and the Life Sciences." *Journal of Religious Ethics* 20, no. 2 (2001): 209–234.

Soloveitchik, Joseph B. *The Halakhic Mind: An Essay on Jewish Tradition and Modern Thought*. New York: Seth Press, 1986.

LAURIE ZOLOTH

JUDAISM, HISTORY OF SCIENCE AND RELIGION, MEDIEVAL PERIOD

Interest in science among medieval Jews, which began in the ninth century, was a consequence of the unprecedented rise of a scientific culture within Islamic civilization a century earlier. Traditionally, Jewish intellectual life was self-contained. It revolved around a canonic corpus of texts, notably the Talmud and the *midrash* in Hebrew and Aramaic; cultural goods existing beyond this corpus were considered as threatening "foreign sciences." But having adopted Arabic (or rather

Judeo-Arabic) as their cultural language, Jews became acquainted with the surrounding Arabic culture. This set in motion a process of reception, assimilation, and transmission of knowledge, leading to the constitution of the medieval Jewish rationalist culture, first in Arabic and then in Hebrew.

The first influential Jewish writers to discuss philosophy in Arabic were Saadia Gaon (882–942) in Baghdad, and Isaac Israeli (855–955) in Kairouan (present-day Tunisia). Both drew heavily on contemporary scientific theories and thereby introduced their Jewish readers to them, *ipso facto* also legitimizing them. In the next century, the center of gravity of the philosophic-scientific activity of Jews switched to Spain: Salomon Ibn Gavirol (c.1020–1057), the well-known poet, was followed by a number of scholars who wrote books on religious Jewish philosophy: Baya Ibn Paqudah (second half of the eleventh century), Juda ha-Levi (c.1075–1141), Joseph Ibn Zaddik (d.1149), Abraham Ibn Daud (c.1110—1180), and others. Beyond their great ideological differences, all these works naturally drew on contemporary scientific and philosophical theories, testifying that these theories were familiar to, and accepted by, the educated Jewish reader. These same works were translated into Hebrew a century or two later for the benefit of readers not knowing Arabic, thereby introducing Greek and Arabic science into the traditionalist communities of Southern France.

Maimonides

Moses Maimonides (1135–1204), the central medieval figure of both Jewish thought and Law, was born in Córdoba, Spain. Owing to persecutions by the Almohads, who forbade Jews or Christians to profess their religion openly, Maimonides left Córdoba and eventually arrived in Egypt, where he settled in the 1160s. Maimonides's two most important writings are the monumental *Mishne Torah,* a code of the Jewish law composed in Hebrew, and the *Guide for the Perplexed,* the major Jewish work of religious philosophy, written in Arabic. Maimonides possessed charisma, a natural, unquestioned authority accepted near and far. The opinions Maimonides expressed with respect to the value of the study of science and philosophy are therefore of crucial importance for an adequate understanding of the Jewish attitudes toward them from the thirteenth century onward.

The Aristotelian sciences and philosophy are an integral part of Maimonides's worldview. The *Mishenh Torah,* although a legal work, opens with a concise account of the Aristotelian cosmology, in which Maimonides indicates that the first commandment is to *know*—not believe—that there exists a First Being who endows with existence all beings. In the *Guide for the Perplexed,* scientific theories are woven into the very substance of most arguments. Maimonides also repeatedly states explicitly that the study of the sciences and of philosophy is strictly indispensable for a knowledge of God, which is the goal of human existence.

Maimonides regards a contradiction between the truths established by the philosophers (i.e., Arab Aristotelianism) and the Scriptures as an impossibility. He holds that the scientifically established tenets of Aristotelian philosophy being necessarily true, whatever statements in the Scriptures appear to be at variance with them must be interpreted so as to make the Scriptures conform. This means that whoever naïvely reads the Scriptures without the input of science and philosophy necessarily errs and ends up in heresy; only the student of Aristotle can correctly grasp the meaning of the Scriptures. For Maimonides, acquiring scientific knowledge is therefore a religious obligation: "listen to the truth from whoever says it," Maimonides repeatedly urged. Only reason, not tradition, was to determine which knowledge-claims were to be accepted within Judaism and which not. Maimonides thus deserves the credit for having opened the gates widely to the study of the "foreign sciences" within Judaism.

This statement must be qualified, however. For Maimonides, the study of the sciences is never an end in itself: It is always propaedeutic, preparing the student for something more noble, namely, the metaphysical knowledge of God. In this respect, Maimonides's stance differs fundamentally from that of the Muslim scientists and philosophers of his day, with whom he is often compared: Maimonides and his Muslim contemporaries construe the social role of the man of knowledge in very different terms.

The place that Maimonides assigns to science is limited also on the epistemological plane, for he sets severe limits on the possible bearing of the sciences. Maimonides thus argues that, contrary to what Aristotle himself believed, Aristotle did not succeed in demonstrating that the world was eternal. Maimonides also argues that upholders of creation *ex nihilo* have not been able to demonstrate their own claims either. For Maimonides, the question of the eternity of the world is thus undecidable (i.e., it cannot be scientifically decided). Maimonides then says that he himself opts for the thesis of creation, but for theological and social, not scientific, reasons. Thus, although Maimonides affirms that without science the Scriptures cannot be correctly understood, in the end he assigns to science a severely curtailed scope. Maimonides is thus fundamentally ambivalent about the role of science.

This ambiguity of Maimonides's message was exacerbated by the fact that Maimonides affirmed that his *Guide* was an "esoteric text," one comprising certain "secrets" that only the wise and learned reader would be able to uncover. Some readers took this statement as signaling that Maimonides's true beliefs were the opposite of those he ostensibly affirmed, and that in truth he held radical theses—notably that of the eternity of the world—which he did not wish to state openly. Some Maimonideans therefore found in the *Guide* messages that were the precise opposite of the literal messages.

Maimonides's philosophy was a decisive turning point: It legitimized the study of the Greek-Arabic sciences as a permissible, indeed, an obligatory activity. Still, at the same time, the scope of the sciences and their authority relative to that of the traditional disciplines was not defined unequivocally. This remained a subject of controversy for the centuries to come.

Transmission of science and philosophy into and Northern Spain and Southern France

The reception of science and philosophy within the Jewish communities of Northern Spain and Southern France, whose only cultural tongue was Hebrew, can usefully be divided into three phases, The first phase of the transmission began early in the twelfth century when Spanish scholars composed in Hebrew (or translated from Arabic) scientific works for Jews living north of the Pyrénées. During the first half of the twelfth century, Abraham bar Hiyya (died c. 1145) of Barcelona, a political leader and scholar who was very well versed in the sciences of his day, wrote a number of works summarizing the sciences in Hebrew. He offered basic courses in such immediately useful disciplines as practical geometry and astronomy, and also composed an encyclopedia affording "general culture" with no immediate practical utility. Also influential was the poet Abraham Ibn Ezra (1089–1164), who left Spain and traveled throughout France, Italy, and England, spreading his ideas and writings. In addition to his astronomical and astrological works, Ibn Ezra composed numerous Biblical commentaries that often invoked scientific, philosophical, and astrological notions. Ibn Ezra thereby suggested that these scientific theories were indispensable to uncover the true meaning of the Scriptures. Owing to the great popularity of these commentaries throughout Europe, they contributed much to the spread and legitimization of "Greek learning."

The second phrase of the process gathered momentum when, in the second half of the twelfth century, Andalusian Jewish scholars immersed in Arabic culture fled to Provence to escape the Almohad persecutions in Spain, enhancing considerably the process of translation into Hebrew of philosophical works. A number of erudite Jewish families settled in Provence during the late 1140s, bringing with them a culture that was altogether different from that of their brethren. Whereas the latter were absorbed in traditional, Talmudic learning, the immigrants were comfortable with Arabic poetry, literature, grammar, philosophy, and science. This led to a massive translation movement that was to last for some two centuries, during which the newcomers and their descendants rendered a rich body of literature from Arabic into Hebrew. The first translated works were mostly Jewish religious philosophy, but gradually works of general philosophy and science by pagan and Muslim writers were translated as well.

The third phrase began after the transmission process got a new and decisive impetus when Maimonides's writings, notably the Hebrew translation of the *Guide of the Perplexed* (1204), became influential in southern France. Jewish scholars imbued in Arabic culture composed a number of encyclopedic works with the aim of affording Jews who could read only Hebrew an overview of the sciences of the day. In parallel, scientific and philosophical works were translated systematically and professionally. Many of the translators were scholars belonging to the Tibbonid family: Yehudah Ibn Tibbon (c. 1120–1190); his son Samuel (1150–1230), the translator of the *Guide*; and Samuel's son Moses (c. 1240–1285). A number of other translators of scientific and philosophical texts were active too. Together, these scholars created the Jewish medieval philosophical-scientific bookshelf. This bookshelf includes the basic works of the exact sciences, beginning with Euclid (mathematics) and Ptolemy (astronomy), and numerous further mathematical and astronomical texts. It also comprises the basic works of the "qualitative" sciences (natural philosophy, biology, medicine, psychology, metaphysics, etc.). Most important in this respect are Averroës's systematized presentations of the Aristotelian doctrines, which became for the centuries to come the standard textbooks studied by Jewish scholars.

Assessment of scientific contributions of medieval Judaism

The introduction of these works of Greek and Arabic science into Judaism triggered a production of scientific works in Hebrew. This movement developed on the basis of texts available in Hebrew, for it was fairly (although not totally) isolated from the Latin scholastic university culture. Whereas, from a cultural point of view, this literature had great significance for Jewish intellectual life, it is not comparable in terms of originality and intrinsic importance qua science to the literature of medieval Arabic or Latin cultures. Astronomy is, however, a significant exception to this rule, and Jewish astronomers performed as well as (and occasionally better than) their contemporaries. The reason for this relative underdevelopment of medieval Hebrew science was arguably the social role that Maimonides had assigned to science as (merely) propaedeutic to the study of God. Two towering figures stand out as exceptions, however. Levi ben Gershom, or Gersonides (1288–1344), lived in Provence and wrote treatises on logic, mathematics, biblical exegesis, philosophy, and astronomy. In all these domains his contributions are eminently original, and the fact that he made numerous astronomical observations, using instruments he himself invented, must be particularly emphasized. Gersonides also had disciples who studied commentaries by Averroës with him and engaged in a written debate over purely scientific issues. The second

figure is Hasdai Crescas (c. 1340–1412), who regarded Jewish adherence to the philosophical doctrines as a threat to the coherence and very existence of the community. This stance motivated Crescas toward a radical and highly insightful criticism of Aristotle's physics, which contributed to the rejection of Aristotelian philosophy during the Renaissance.

The introduction of the study of the sciences into the Jewish discourse did not go unchallenged. Even before Maimonides, Juda ha-Levi's *Kuzari* (1140) had criticized the philosophical project and contrasted the traditional "God of Abraham" with the philosophers' "God of Aristotle." Maimonides was vehemently attacked during his lifetime and the split, indeed the confrontation, between traditionalists and their adversaries over the study of the profane sciences was to continue during the centuries to come.

The thirteenth through the fifteenth centuries were the heyday of Hebrew science and of the rationalist Jewish culture in general. The rise of Kabbalah and the expulsion of the Jews from the Iberian peninsula in the 1490s were followed by a long period in which few Jews engaged in science or philosophy. The influential astronomer Abraham Zacut (late fifteenth century) is an exception. Still, here and there during the sixteenth and seventeenth centuries, some Ashkenazi rabbis in Germany and Poland continued to study the texts of the medieval Hebrew bookshelf. In the early eighteenth century, this dormant tradition was to bear new fruit and provide an important impetus to the *Haskalah* (Jewish enlightenment movement).

The cultural dimension of the reception of the sciences

The reception of science and philosophy within medieval Judaism had implications far beyond the mere sphere of science: It was nothing less than a theological upheaval. On the one hand, Maimonides's consequential synthesis legitimized the profane books as a source of knowledge, in addition to the traditional, sacred ones. On the other, the espousal of philosophy and science implied the acceptance of formerly unheard-of religious teachings: The Maimonidean God had very little in common with that of the Talmudists or the kabbalists, and, in addition, the intellectual activity of those who sought felicity (immortality of the soul) through philosophical knowledge was incommensurable with that of the fideists, for whom the Jews' afterlife depended solely on respecting the commandments and on erudition in the Talmud. In *Even Bohan* (*The Touchstone*), his satirical *maqâmah,* the early fourteenth-century scientist, translator and poet Qalonimos ben Qalonimos acutely noted: "Our Gods are as numerous as our towns." This upheaval thus implied a profound transformation of the definition of what it meant to be Jewish. The depth of the resulting fragmentation of Jewish society is perhaps comparable to that of the contemporary split of Judaism between Reformist, Conservative, and Orthodox.

See also JUDAISM; JUDAISM, CONTEMPORARY ISSUES IN SCIENCE AND RELIGION; JUDAISM, HISTORY OF SCIENCE AND RELIGION, MODERN PERIOD; MAIMONIDES

Bibliography

Chabás, José, and Goldstein, Bernard R. *Astronomy in the Iberian Peninsula: Abraham Zacut and the Transition from Manuscript to Print.* Philadelphia: American Philosophical Society, 2000.

Drory, Rina. *Models and Contacts: Arabic Literature and Its Impact on Medieval Jewish Culture.* Leiden, Netherlands, and Boston: Brill, 2000.

Freudenthal, Gad. "Les sciences dans les communautés juives médiévales de Provence: Leur appropriation, leur rôle." *Revue des études juives* 152 (1993): 29–136.

Freudenthal, Gad. "Science in the Medieval Jewish Culture of Southern France." *History of Science* 33 (1995): 23–58.

Freudenthal, Gad. "Levi ben Gershom (Gersonides): 1288–1344." In *The Routledge History of Islamic Philosophy,* eds. Seyyed Hossein Nasr and Oliver Leaman. London and New York: Routledge, 1996.

Glasner, Ruth. "Levi ben Gershom and the Study of Ibn Rushd in the 14th Century: A New Historical Reconstruction." *Jewish Quarterly Review* 86 (1995): 51–90.

Goldstein, Bernard R. *Theory and Observation in Ancient and Medieval Astronomy.* London: Variorum, 1985.

Guttmann, Julius. *The Philosophy of Judaism: The History of Jewish Philosophy from Biblical Times to Franz Rosenzweig,* trans. David W. Silverman. New York: Holt, 1964. Reprint: Northvale, N.J., and London: Aronson, 1988.

Harvey, Steven, ed. The *Medieval Hebrew Encyclopedias of Science and Philosophy.* Amsterdam: Kluwer, 2000.

Langermann, Y. Tzvi. *The Jews and the Sciences in the Middle Ages.* Aldershot, UK, and Brookfield, Vt.: Ashgate, 1999.

Lévy, Tony. "Hebrew Mathematics in the Middle Ages: An Assessment." In *Tradition, Transmission, Transformation,* eds. F. Jamil Ragep and Sally P. Ragep. Leiden, Netherlands, and New York: Brill, 1996.

Lévy, Tony. "The Establishment of the Mathematical Bookshelf of the Medieval Hebrew Scholar: Translations and Translators." *Science in Context* 10 (1997): 431–451.

Sirat, Colette. *A History of Jewish Philosophy in the Middle Ages,* trans. Mira Reich. Cambridge, UK: Cambridge University Press; Paris: La Maison des Sciences de l'Homme, 1985.

Steinschneider, Moritz. *Die Hebraeischen ⸀bersetzungen des Mittelalters und die Juden als Dolmetscher* (1893). Graz, Austria: Akademische Druck-u. Verlagsanstalt, 1956.

Wolfson, Harry Austryn. *Crescas' Critique of Aristotle: Problems of Aristotle's Physics in Jewish and Arabic Philosophy* (1929). Cambridge, Mass.: Harvard University Press, 1971.

Zonta, Mauro. *La filosofia antica nel Mediovo ebraico.* Brescia, Italy: Paideia Editrice, 1996.

Zonta, Mauro. "Mineralogy, Botany, and Zoology in Hebrew Medieval Encyclopedias." *Arabic Sciences and Philosophy* 6 (1996): 263–315.

GAD FREUDENTHAL

JUDAISM, HISTORY OF SCIENCE AND RELIGION, MODERN PERIOD

Moses Maimonides (1135–1204) wrote at the beginning of his comprehensive code of Jewish law, the *Mishneh Torah,* that the most fundamental commandment in Judaism is to believe in the creator deity, that no one can believe in the creator who does not understand creation, and to understand creation requires knowledge of the sciences, especially physics and astronomy. All medieval rabbis agreed that the proper worship of God involves commandments to do what is good and to believe what is true, and many of them agreed with Maimonides that scientific knowledge was a critical way to fulfill this religious obligation.

The early modern period (sixteenth to early nineteenth centuries)

As is clear from the example of religious scientists such as the astronomer Levi Ben Gershom (Gersonides, 1288–1344), Jews followed Maimonides's directives and made first-rate contributions to the advancement of scientific knowledge in the late middle ages. However, this consensus on the symbiosis of religion and science disappeared by the early modern period in European civilization. The level of Jewish studies in the sciences as of the middle of the fourteenth century was the peak of this development. Jews continued to study science, but there was little growth. While the level of Jewish achievements in the field of medicine remained high by comparison with the level of medical sciences in Christian Europe, the same cannot be said for the other sciences, even in the case of astronomy and physics.

From the sixteenth through the early nineteenth centuries the focus of Jewish spiritual practice turned away from natural philosophy (from science) towards a concentration on Jewish law (*Halachah*) and mysticism (*Kabbalah*). Still, there were many Jews who continued the Maimonidean tradition of scientific inquiry, especially in astronomy. Among their notable tractates were Judah Loew ben Bezalel's *Torat ha-Olah* (Prague, 1569), Mordecai ben Abraham Jaffe's Levush's *Or Yekarot* (Lubin, 1594), David Gans's *Nechmad ve-Na'im* (1613), Joseph Solomon Delmedigo's *Elim (Amsterdam, 1629),* Tobias Cohen's *Ma'aseh Turiyyah* (Venice, 1707/8), Jonathan ben Joseph from Ruchim's *Yeshu'ah be-Yisrael* (Frankfurt 1720), Raphael ha-Levi of Hannover's *Tekhumat ha-Shamayim* (Amsterdam, 1756), Israel ben Moses ha-Levi of Zamosc's *Netzach Yisrael* (Frankfurt am Oder, 1741), and Israel David ben Mordecai Jaffe-Margoliot's *Chazon Mo'ed* (Pressburg, 1843).

In general, by the second half of the sixteenth century Jewish students of astronomy were familiar with Copernicus's heliocentric theory. However, their attitudes to it were no more enlightened than that of the Roman Catholic Church, for in general all of these books were written as an apologetic defense of Maimonides's Aristotelian geocentric theory.

What happened that so dramatically altered the status of scientific learning in traditional Jewish communities between the twelfth and the sixteenth centuries? This is a question that scholars continue to debate. Critical factors include the increase of Jewish persecution in Christian Europe, which is conjoined to the increase of interest in Kabbalah and the decline of interest in the kind of natural philosophy that would develop into modern science.

The dramatic focus of this competition between legal studies, Kabbalah, and philosophic/scientific studies to win the hearts of intelligent Jews was the so-called "Maimonidean Controversies" that began in Europe during Maimonides's own lifetime, broke out again in Provence between 1230 and 1232, and spread from Provence into Christian Spain between 1300 and 1306. One of the important consequences of these controversies occurred in fifteenth-century Spain, where the curriculum of Jewish studies was revised to intensify the emphasis on law and all but eliminate the sciences as something identifiably "Jewish." (The critical exception to this generalization was the study of medicine and, as part of medicine, the study of what would become chemistry.) Whatever the causes, Jews who identified themselves primarily as Jews, as opposed to as members of a particular nation state, ceased to make any significant contributions to science. The same can also be said of Jews as human beings. However, this situation changed dramatically in the second half of the nineteenth century.

The modern period (late nineteenth and twentieth centuries)

When the philosopher Baruch Spinoza (1632–1677) was offered a professorship at the University of Heidelberg, he became, as far as we know, the first Jew ever to be offered a teaching position in a Christian European university. However, this was not a proper beginning, for Spinoza was a Dutch Jew who, as such, represented a most atypical Jewish community that had only recently emerged from its secret Jewish life as *conversos* in Spain. Moreover, Spinoza was a heretic. That a Jew could enter a Christian university if he left Judaism and became a Christian was not uncommon. However, Spinoza did not become a believing Christian even though he ceased to be a believing Jew. In the end, Spinoza did not accept the position in Heidelberg, and his thought had no significant impact on Jews until the late nineteenth century.

Excluding Spinoza, the first Jew to complete a doctorate in a Christian university was Joseph ben

Judah Chamitz, who earned a degree in philosophy and medicine from the University of Padua in 1624. Other Jews followed his example throughout western Europe after Joseph II of Austria issued his Edit of Toleration in 1782, after the Jews were emancipated in France in 1791, and after the Congress of Vienna created an union of German states to replace the Holy Roman Empire in 1815 and Italy was unified in 1861. The Jews were emancipated in Switzerland in 1866 and in Austria-Hungary in 1867. The Franco-Prussian War of 1870 to 1871 resulted in William I of Prussia becoming emperor of all the German states, and Germany became unified in 1871 under Otto von Bismarck. Two other, related critical events occurred in 1871: the new German constitution gave full rights to Jews, and the term anti-Semitism was used for the first time. The former event opened the doors to Jews throughout Germany, and from Germany throughout the Western world, from the late nineteenth through the early twentieth centuries. The latter event closed the doors of the university, culminating in the Nazi German attempt to "eliminate" Jews altogether.

The achievements of Jews as individuals (as citizens of their nation states and not especially as Jews) from the late nineteenth through the early twentieth centuries are impressive. By 1910, 2.5 percent of all full professors in Germany were Jewish, and 7.5 percent of all German students and 9.4 percent of all students (including foreigners) at Prussian universities were Jewish. Furthermore, by 1933 Jews constituted thirty percent of academic staff in natural sciences, over forty percent in medical faculties, and almost fifty percent of the mathematicians in German universities.

In general, the achievements of Jews as individuals in every academic field are even more dramatic. The originality that Jews failed to achieve in the early modern period was more than compensated for in late modern times. Notable Jewish astronomers include Hermann Goldschmidt (1802–1866, in France) who from 1852 to 1861 discovered fourteen asteroids between mars and Jupiter; Maurice Loewy (1857–1938, in Austria) who invented the Coudé telescope at the Paris Observatory; and Richard Prager (1883–1945, in Germany) who made major discoveries about variable stars at Berlin. In the United States, Frank Schlesinger (1871–1943) devised photographic methods for making parallax-determinations; Martin Schwarzschild (1912-1997) researched stellar evolution and designed satellite-born telescopes at Princeton University in New Jersey; and Herbert A. Friedman (1916–2000) studied outer-space spectroscopy at the U. S. Naval Research Laboratory in Washington, D.C.

Jewish involvement in chemistry was a natural outgrowth of earlier Jewish interest in medicine. In this respect it is notable that between 1905 and 2000 twenty-two Jews received the Nobel Prize in chemistry: Adolph Von Baeyer (1905), Henri Moissan (1906), Otto Wallach (1910), Richard Willstaetter (1915), Fritz Haber (1918), George Charles de Hevesy (1943), Melvin Calvin (1961), Max Ferdinand Perutz (1962), William Howard Stein (1972), Ilya Prigogine (1977), Herbert Charles Brown (1979), Paul Berg (1980), Walter Gilbert (1980), Ronald Hoffmann (1981), Aaron Klug (1982), Albert A. Hauptman (1985), Jerome Karle (1985), Dudley R. Herschbach (1986), Robert Huber (1988), Sidney Altman (1989), Rudolph Marcus (1992), and Alan J. Heeger (2000).

Jews even excelled in physics, which had ceased to be part of the Jewish curriculum in the early modern period. For example, during the twentieth century, Jews received thirty one Nobel prizes in physics: Albert Abraham Michelson (1907), Gabriel Lippmann (1908), Albert Einstein (1921), Niels Bohr (1922), James Franck (1925), Gustav Hertz (1925), Gustav Stern (1943), Isidor Issac Rabi (1944), Felix Bloch (1952), Max Born (1954), Igor Tamm (1958), Emilio Segre (1959), Donald A. Glaser (1960), Robert Hofstadter (1961), Lev Davidovich Landau (1962), Richard Phillips Feynman (1965), Julian Schwinger (1965), Murray Gell-Mann (1969), Dennis Gabor (1971), Brian David Josephson (1973), Benjamin Mottleson (1975), Burton Richter (1976), Arno Allan Penzias (1978), Peter L Kapitza (1978), Stephen Weinberg (1979), Sheldon Glashow (1979), Leon Lederman (1988), Melvin Schwartz (1988), Jack Steinberger (1988), Jerome Friedman (1990), and Martin Perl (1995).

The works of these physicists include: the perfection of the electromagnetic theory of radiation; quantum theory and its experimental confirmation; relativity concepts and their universal impact; atomic structure and its implication for electronics; and nuclear physics with its applications and implications for the study of high energy particles. Of these Jewish physicists, the most famous is Albert Einstein (1879–1955), who is especially known for his work on relativity theory. Many of the mathematicians who provided the foundation for Einstein's contributions to physics were also Jews. Of special note were Karl Gustav Jacob Jacobi (1804–1851) for his work on elliptic functions, Herman Minkowski (1864–1909) for his work on four dimensional space, and Tullio Levi-Cività (1873–1941) for fundamental mathematics of relativity theory.

The least surprising area of Jewish excellence in science was medicine, since this was the one scientific subject Jews continued to study into the modern period in their traditional Jewish community schools. It is the area of scientific research whose application to Judaism is most evident, since it raises any number of questions concerning morality and Jewish law. For example, what is the role of sex in marriage independent of reproduction? Under Jewish law are any of the modern methods of treating infertility (including cloning, artificial insemination, and the use of surrogate mothers) permissible? The same questions apply to applications of genetic engineering and screening. Conversely, are any of the ways of preventing pregnancy (especially contraception, sterilization, and abortion) permissible? Furthermore, as modern science impacts on Jewish law and ethics with respect to life, it has implications for ways of dying, including questions about assisted suicide, cremation, autopsies, and organ donations. Finally, modern medicine raises questions for social ethics, from issues about a fair distribution of health care to issues about cosmetics (tattooing, body piercing, and cosmetic surgery).

By the middle of the seventeenth century European medical schools (notably in Germany, Poland, and Russia) began to admit Jews. One of the first was the University of Frankfurt on the Oder in Germany. One of its first students was Tobias ben Moses Cohen of Metz. Although he did not complete his studies there, he received his M.D. degree later from the University of Padua. Eventually he became a court physician to five successive sultans in Constantinople. Among the notable Jewish physicians of the eighteenth century were Marcus Eliezer Bloch in Berlin and Gumpertz Levison in England and Sweden, as well as Elias Henschel, who was a pioneer of modern obstetrics.

Jewish involvement in medical practice and research grew exponentially after the 1782 Edit of Tolerance in Austria. Still Jews tended to be held back, rarely rising academically beyond the titular professorial position of *privatdocent*. Jews tended to prefer new fields that were less attractive to non-Jewish competitors. An example is the pioneering work of Moritz Kaposi, Isador Neumann, and Heinrich Auspits in dermatology-venereology in Austria. In Germany dermatology came to be known as *Judenhaut* (Jews' skin). German specialists in this study included Paul Unna, Oskar Lassar, and Josef Jadassohn, and in Switzerland, Bruno Bloch.

Jews tended to dominate biochemistry, immunology, psychiatry, heatology, histology, and microscopic pathology. Among the leaders of microscopy were Ludwig Traube; of neuropathology is Moritz Romberg; and of neurology were Leopold Auerbach, Ludwig Edinger, and Hermann Oppenheim. In the twentieth century Jews entered freely into all fields of medicine and made major contributions to them, especially chemotherapy, immunology, hematology, heart disease research, lung and kidney disease research, gastroenterology, dermatology, pediatrics, surgery, obstetrics, gynecology, radiology, pathology, public health, and medical education.

In this respect it is notable that between 1908 and 1995, forty-four Jews received the Nobel Prize in medicine: Elie Metchnikoff (1908), Paul Erlich (1908), Robert Barany (1914), Otto Meyerhof (1922), Karl Landsteiner (1930), Otto Warburg (1931), Otto Loewi (1936), Joseph Erlanger (1944), Herbert Spencer Gasser (1944), Ernst Boris Chain (1945), Hermann Joseph Muller (1946), Tadeus Reichstein (1950), Selman Abraham Waksman (1952), Hans Krebs (1953), Fritz Albert Lipmann (1953), Joshua Lederberg (1958), Arthur Kornberg (1959), Konrad Bloch (1964), Francois Jacob (1965), Andre Lewoff (1965), George Wald (1967), Marshall W. Nirenberg (1968), Salvador Luria (1969), Julius Axelrod (1970), Sir Bernard Katz (1970), Gerald Maurice Edelman (1972), David Baltimore (1975), Howard Martin Temin (1975), Baruch S. Blumberg (1976), Rosalyn Sussman Yalow (1977), Daniel Nathans (1978), Baruj Benacerraf (1980), Cesar Milstein (1984), Michael Stuart Brown (1985), Joseph L. Goldstein (1985), Stanley Cohen [& Rita Levi Montalcini] (1986), Gertrude Elion (1988), Harold Varmus (1989), Erwin Neher (1991), Bert

Sakmann (1991), Richard J. Roberts (1993), Phillip Sharp (1993), Alfred Gilman (1994), and Edward B. Lewis (1995)

Of special importance within the discipline of medicine is psychology, within psychology is psychiatry, and within psychiatry is the work of Sigmund Freud (1856–1939) and his followers in psychoanalysis. As psychology emerged at the end of the nineteenth century, there were few Jews involved, G. F. Heymans at Louvain in Belgium being a notable exception. Modern psychiatry began with the work of Phillipe Pinel in France after the French revolution. The first Jewish psychiatrists to join this movement were Cesare Lombroso and Hippolyte Bernheim. Freud's own study began as an observer of Bernheim's work with hypnosis on mental patients. Freud published *Interpretation of Dreams* in 1900. Those initially associated with psychoanalysis in Freud's "inner circle" included the Jews Sandor Ferenczi, Karl Abraham, Max Eitingon, Otto Rank, and Hans Sachs. Most notable among those who followed Freud were Alfred Adler, Hans Sachs, Paul Federn, Theodor Reik, Helene Deutsch, Melanie Klein, and Freud's daughter Anna. Leading psychiatrists in the United States included Erik Homberber Erikson, Margarert Mahler, Leo Kanner, Lauretta Bender, Moritz Tramer, Paul Schilder, Beata Rank, and Rene Spitz.

Jewish science

One must be careful to distinguish the role of Jews in modern science as individuals from their role as Jews. Jews have been scientists in the modern period not as members of a Jewish community (as they were in the Middle Ages) but as free citizens in secular nation states. The schools where they studied, did research, published, and taught were sponsored by the secular state and not by any agency of the Jewish community. Is it legitimate to ask about these Jews whether or not their being Jewish in any way contributed to their science? Those most likely to give an affirmative answer to this question would be anti-Semites, especially those who dominated German culture in the 1930s and 1940s. Certainly most of these scientists themselves would make a sharp distinction between who they are as Jews (if anything) and who they are as scientists.

The most obvious names that people associate with Jews are Baruch Spinoza, Karl Marx, Henri Bergson, Albert Einstein, and Sigmund Freud. All five would have strongly denied that their Jewish ethnic identity had any bearing on their contributions to science. Spinoza was a product of a *converso* community, and furthermore, he was excommunicated; the excommunication did not seem to matter much to him, for he could live as easily among his Christian friends as he had lived in a Jewish community. Karl Heinrich Marx (1818–1883) can hardly be called Jewish at all. His father converted with his children to Christianity in 1824 (when Karl six years old). The case is almost the same with Henri Louis Bergson (1859–1941). He was raised in Paris by a father from Warsaw and mother from England, and Henri himself did the best that he could to conceal his upbringing, including the fact that he was Jewish.

There are many other Jews who could be listed in the category of those whose Jewish identity, even on cultural terms, was so tenuous that to call them "Jewish" is seriously misleading. Notable in this category are the sociologist Emile Durkheim (1859–1917) and the philosopher Edmund Husserl (1859–1938). Others include Karl Gustav Jacob Jacobi (1801–1851), who developed the generalization of Hamilton's theory in mechanics, and Georg Cantor (1845–1910), who made major contributions to the theory of the functions of real numbers. Felix Klein (1849–1925), who in 1882 published a paper on Riemann's theory of algebraic functions, developed the *Erlangen program*. which classified geometries in mathematical group theory. Ferdinand Cohn (1828–1898) identified several bacteria as agents of disease. Eugen Goldstein (1850–1930), together with Cromwell Varley (1828–1883), developed the leading hypothesis (waive interpretation) of the nature of cathode radiation. Finally, Paul Ehrlich (1854–1915) created chemotherapy.

The only notable modern Jewish scientist who understood his major work to be specifically Jewish was Hermann Cohen (1848–1918). Cohen is known primarily as a leading German philosopher of the neo-Kantian Marburg School and as a theologian of Reform Judaism. However, his career began as a philosopher of mathematics with the 1883 publication of his *Das Prinzip der infinitesimal methode und seine Geschichte* (The Principle of the infinitesimal method and its History), in which he developed an account of the meaning of differentiation and integration in calculus that served later as the foundation of his Marburg philosophy and his liberal Jewish theology. Cohen's colleague Paul Natorp (1854–1924) and his first pupil Ernst Cassirer (1874–1945) were both distinguished Jewish philosophers in the first half of the twentieth century. Both were oppressed for being Jewish and both shared the widespread view, in opposition to Hermann Cohen, that their Jewish identity was a sheer accident, of no relevance to their work as intellectuals.

The most interesting scientist in this respect was Albert Einstein (1879–1955). Jewishness played an important part in his life in terms of secular politics because he was a lifelong Zionist who was offered the first presidency of the modern secular state of Israel. Similarly, religious belief of some sort seemed to play a role in his speculations as a scientist. However, the role of religion in his life was always a private form of religiosity that he consciously dissociated from any traditional or conservative form of historical rabbinic Judaism. To the extent that Einstein was religious it was more like the religion of Spinoza, whose work he first read in 1920, when he was already forty-one years old.

The religion of Einstein was a religion that identified the highest form of divine worship with the uncompromising pursuit of the truth about the universe in general. Einstein identified this religious quest with Spinoza, who arrived at his distinctive conception of science as worship through his study of the Jewish philosophy of Maimonides. So we end where we began—with a symbiosis of science and religion, one that was clearly Jewish and religious in the medieval period and became increasingly universalist and secular in the modern period.

See also EINSTEIN, ALBERT; JUDAISM; JUDAISM, CONTEMPORARY ISSUES IN SCIENCE AND RELIGION; JUDAISM, HISTORY OF SCIENCE AND RELIGION, MEDIEVAL PERIOD; MAIMONIDES

Bibliography

Bleach, J. David. *Bioethical Dilemmas: A Jewish Perspective.* Hoboken N.J.: Ktav, 1998.

Dorff, Elliot N. *Matters of Life and Death: A Jewish Approach to Modern Medical Ethics.* Philadelphia: Jewish Publication Society of America, 1998.

Jammer, Max. *Einstein and Religion.* Princeton, N.J.: Princeton University Press, 1999.

Kaku, Michio, and Trainer, Jennifer. *Beyond Einstein: The Cosmic Quest for the Theory of the Universe.* New York: Bantam, 1987.

Poma, Andrea. *The Critical Philosophy of Hermann Cohen.* Albany: State University of New York Press, 1997.

Robertson, Ritchie. *The "Jewish Question" in German Literature: 1749–1939.* Oxford: Oxford University Press, 2001.

Ruderman, David B. *Jewish Thought and Scientific Discover in Early Modern Europe.* New Haven, Conn., and London: Yale University Press, 1995.

Volkov, Shulamit. "Jewish Scientists in Imperial Germany (Parts I and II)." *Aleph: Historical Studies in Science and Judaism* 1 (2000): 215–281.

Yerushalmi, Yosef Hayim. *Freud's Moses: Judaism Terminable and Interminable.* New Haven, Conn.: Yale University Press, 1991.

NORBERT M. SAMUELSON

K

KANT, IMMANUEL

Immanuel Kant, it is said, never traveled more than fifty miles from his native city of Königsberg in East Prussia. Nevertheless, there are few thinkers who have had as wide an influence as Kant in the history of Western thought. His importance for discussions about science and religion stems from his reasoned defense of the position that religion and science should be kept clearly separated from one another.

Life and writings

Born in 1724, Kant was the son of humble pietistic parents who wished for him to have an education. At sixteen he entered the University of Königsberg, where he studied Christian Wolff's interpretation of Gottfried Wilhelm von Leibniz's (1646–1716) philosophy. Kant's encounter with Isaac Newton's (1642–1727) work during his student years encouraged in him an independent attitude toward Leibniz's thought, with the additional result that he developed a profound interest in the natural sciences. When his father died during his university training, Kant left the university and served as a tutor in private families near Königsberg between 1748 and 1754. After returning to the university he completed a thesis in June of 1755 and, on finishing a second thesis in September, was granted permission to lecture. Prior to the age of thirty-six, Kant's writings dealt primarily, although not exclusively, with the natural sciences. His most famous work from this period, the *Universal Natural History and Theory of the Heavens*, was published in 1755 and contained Kant's ideas on the how a cosmos subject to Newton's laws of motion might have formed.

After Kant received a professorship in logic and metaphysics at Königsberg in 1770 it took some time before his writings reflected the turn his appointment marked from a precritical stance to what he himself labeled critical philosophy. Once Kant began publishing, the works came thick and fast. The first edition of his most famous book, the *Critique of Pure Reason,* did not appear until 1781. When it did so it was largely misunderstood, moving Kant to restate its main arguments two years later in his *Prolegomena to Every Future Metaphysics*. He also expanded the *Critique* in a second edition in 1787, and in the following year he published the first of two new critiques, the *Critique of Practical Reason*. This second critique picked up on a concern with moral philosophy Kant had initially addressed in another work from the 1780s. The *Critique of Judgment,* which appeared in 1790, dealt with reasoning about the realms of the aesthetic and the purposeful. Earlier in 1786 Kant returned to his reflections on science and its methods in a work entitled *The Metaphysical Foundations of Natural Science*. Finally, his *Religion Within the Boundaries of Pure Reason,* which appeared in 1793, provoked King Frederick William II to forbid him from publishing anything more on religion, a mandate he honored until the king's death in 1797. Kant died February 12, 1804.

Impact on science and religion discussion

Kant's impact on the subject of natural science and religion is best understood in his relation to the

Scottish thinker David Hume (1711–1776), whom Kant claimed awakened him from his dogmatic slumber. Exactly when this was to have occurred is unclear; however, among other things Hume represented for Kant the possibility that the use of reason in fact undermined the essential truths of religion, morality, and common sense. Kant faced squarely Hume's skepticism about causality and other conclusions of common sense that haunted the thinkers of the late eighteenth century. The fear was that if Hume's reasoning was correct about these matters, then how was one to retain one's belief in God? As Kant's contemporary Friedrich Jacobi (1743–1819) put it, "Nothing frightens man so much, nothing darkens his mind to such a degree as when God disappears from nature … when purpose, wisdom, and goodness no longer seem to reign in nature, but only a blind necessity of dumb chance."

In *Dialogues Concerning Natural Religion* (1779) Hume exposed the inadequacy where the relationship of God to nature was concerned of both classical metaphysical rationalism, in which one reasoned from principles accepted apart from or before experience (a priori), and empiricism, where reasoning was undertaken only after one experienced the world (a posteriori). In the *Critique of Pure Reason,* Kant attempted to forge a new path between both rationalism and empiricism by introducing what he called in the preface to the second edition a "Copernican" viewpoint in philosophy. The astronomer Nicolaus Copernicus (1483–1543) had shown that the way to think about the relationship of the earth and the sun was to reverse their traditional roles. Kant demanded that to understand the relationship of the world of experience and the mind one must also reverse the way in which roles were traditionally assigned. It is not that the mind is shaped by experience of the world (empiricism); rather, the world of experience is shaped by "categories" associated with the mind's operation. But in shaping our experience of the world the categories themselves prescribe only the structure for objects of possible experience (not the content of actual experience, as in metaphysical rationalism). Human minds dictate in advance, for example, that experience can only be apprehended in accordance with causal relationships between events, but they cannot determine prior to a person's experiencing the world which specific causal relationships actually obtain.

Without content supplied by sense experience, the mind, even equipped as it is by its categories, would still be blind. But without the ordering impact of the categories, experience would be chaos. This is why Kant said at the beginning of the introduction to the *Critique* that "although all our knowledge begins with experience, it does not follow that it all arises out of experience."

This middle way contained important implications for the understanding of scientific knowledge. If the mind contributes in a formative way to the manner in which people experience the world, then they can no longer claim that the world they experience is necessarily the world that exists apart from the mind. Regularities in one's experience of the world, even those so repetitive as to earn the label of scientific laws, cannot be known as regularities in nature that one discovers; rather, they bear the touch of one's mind. People are, as Kant says in his *Prolegomena to Every Future Metaphysics,* "lawgivers of reason." Scientific knowledge, then, refers to the world of experience, the world of phenomena apprehended with the senses, not to a reality lying behind human experience. Gone is the possibility of conceiving truth as the correspondence of one's ideas to the way things are, a common conception of many scientists. One cannot be sure of the way things are, so there is no possibility of checking that against one's ideas.

If Kant's critique of reason introduced a radical limitation of what could be known, he was adamant that there was a realm that lay beyond cognition. "I have therefore found it necessary to deny *knowledge* in order to make room for *faith,*" he wrote in the preface to the second edition of the *Critique.* The object of faith, however, could not by definition be articulated or expressed in terms of knowledge. Religion for Kant did not and could not have to do with cognitive propositions about nature. In his 1793 book, *Religion within the Boundaries of Reason Alone,* he made clear that he accepted Hume's negative conclusions about the so-called argument from design, according to which one reasoned from evidence of design in the world to the existence of a designer. Religion did not commence with nor have to do with one's knowledge of the world. Religion had to do with the purity of one's heart. To be religious is to view one's duties as if they are divine commands. It should be noted that Kant's religious stance was purely intellectual. In spite of the fact that his philosophy made room for the possibility of eternal life, it was clear to those close to him that he scoffed at prayer and other religious practices and that he had no faith in a personal God.

Kant's position, then, radically separated science from religion, as if the two subjects contained no common ground. It took some time for this position to gain a hearing since in the Romantic period, which dominated in the first decades of the nineteenth century, there was great dissatisfaction with Kant's severe restriction of reason's scope to the realm of phenomena. Even one of the earliest neo-Kantian thinkers from this era, Jakob Fries (1773–1843), added *Ahndung* (aesthetic sense) to knowledge and faith as a third possible way in which people may relate to that which exists outside of them. Fries believed that through aesthetic sense people could intimate the infinite that was present in the finite.

It was not until the neo-Kantian revival of the late nineteenth century that Kant's radical separation of science from religion emerged in earnest. In the works of the Marburg theologian Wilhelm Herrmann (1846–1922), composed during the heyday of debates about biological evolution, one recognizes the attempt to cede to natural science the freedom to investigate natural phenomena without restriction while at the same time stressing religion's right to address questions of value and right. If religion must surrender nature to natural science, natural science, in turn, must along with religion renounce any claim to have arrived at metaphysical reality. Religion becomes morality while science becomes *Naturbeherrschung,* mastery of the world.

In the twentieth century the separation of natural science and religion continued to mark much of German theology, especially the works of well-known existential theologians who wrote in the decades following World War I. Most recently something of a Kantian position on the relationship between science and religion has been advocated by the noted American paleontologist Stephen Jay Gould (1941–2000) who, without ever naming Kant, introduced the notion of non-overlapping *magisteria* (NOMA) as a means of dealing with the realities of science, which is concerned with the factual construction of nature, and religion, which concerns itself with moral issues about the value and meaning of life. Gould acknowledge more than classical neo-Kantians, however, that

while magisteria do not overlap, they are everywhere interlaced in a complex manner that often makes it extremely challenging to keep the two separate. Critics of the Kantian position maintain that in practice it is impossible to retain a rigid separation of science and religion.

See also METAPHYSICS; MORALITY; NATURAL THEOLOGY

Bibliography

Beiser, Frederick. *The Fate of Reason: German Philosophy from Kant to Fichte.* Cambridge, Mass.: Harvard University Press 1987.

Fries, Jakob. *Knowledge, Belief, and Aesthetic Sense* (1805), trans. Kent Richter, ed. Frederick Gregory. Cologne, Germany: Dinter Verlag, 1989.

Gould, Stephen Jay. *Rocks of Ages: Science and Religion in the Fullness of Life.* New York: Ballantine, 1999.

Gregory, Frederick. *Nature Lost? Natural Science and the German Theological Traditions of the Nineteenth Century.* Cambridge, Mass.: Harvard University Press, 1992.

Kant, Immanuel. *Cambridge Edition of the Works of Immanuel Kant,* eds. Paul Guyer et al. Cambridge, UK: Cambridge University Press, 1992-2001.

Kuehn, Manfred. *Kant: A Biography.* Cambridge, UK: Cambridge University Press, 2001.

FREDERICK GREGORY

KARMA

Hinduism has many different definitions of karma, some making karma appear quite deterministic. A clear classical description is found in the *Yoga Sutras* of Patanjali (c. 200 B.C.E.–c. 200 C.E.) (sutras II: 12–14 and IV: 7–9). This description has been widely influential and makes room for free will. Every time one does an action or thinks a thought, a memory trace or karmic seed is laid down in one's unconscious. There it waits for circumstances conducive to it sprouting forth as an impulse or predisposition to do the same action or think the same thought again. This impulse is not mechanistic in nature, rather, it simply predisposes a person to do an action or think a thought. Through the use of free choice one decides either to go with the karmic impulse, in which case it is reinforced and strengthened, or to say "no" and negate it, in which case its strength is diminished until it is removed from the unconscious. Karmas can be either good or bad as defined by Hindu scripture. Good actions and thoughts lay down good karmic traces in the unconscious for the predisposing of future good karmic impulses. Evil actions or thoughts do the reverse. Karmic impulses do not disappear at death but are carried forward into the next life as one is reborn (*samsara*).

See also DETERMINISM; HINDUISM

Bibliography

The Yoga Sutras of Patanjali, trans. J. H. Woods. Harvard Oriental Series, Vol. 17. Varanasi, India: Motital Banarsidass, 1966.

HAROLD COWARD

KENOSIS

Literally "emptying" in Greek, kenosis is a theological notion signifying the Christian belief that in the life and death of Jesus of Nazareth God empties out the divine selfhood in humble self-giving love to the world. This interpretation of deity has been inspired especially by reflection on the life and crucifixion of Jesus in whom Christians believe the fullness of God resides. In a letter to the Philippians, St. Paul cites an early Christian hymn that pictured Jesus as being "in the form of God," yet as one who forsook this lofty status and became a "slave" (Phil 2:5-11). Through the humiliation of being crucified, Jesus emptied *(ekenosen)* himself completely; for this reason, Philippians continues, "at the name of Jesus every knee should bow." Here Lordship somehow coincides with absolute self-emptying love.

Subsequent theological reflection has often, though not always or consistently, interpreted the text of Philippians to imply that in Jesus the very being of God is what is "emptied out." At times theologies have even gone to the extreme of interpreting the notion of kenosis to mean that God, in pouring out the divine substance, literally ceases to be God. The more accepted view, however, is that in God's self-abandoning incarnation in Jesus, who for Christians became the crucified and risen Christ, the ultimate ground and sustainer of the universe is revealed decisively as absolute selflessness and limitless compassion (co-suffering).

The image of a self-empting God in Christian tradition

This biblically inspired picture of a God who from all eternity foregoes any crudely domineering power in order to relate intimately to the created world has emerged more conspicuously than ever in contemporary theological reflection on the roots of Christian faith. While the image of God as self-emptying love has always been present in Christian tradition, it has often been subordinated to pictures of God as potentate, designer, or even dictator. However, to a theology that views the crucified Christ as part of the revelation of reality's underlying depths, it would seem that God renounces any claims to coercive omnipotence. It is to this God of actual religious experience, rather than to philosophically abstract portraits of deity, that an increasing number of theologians today hope to connect their conversations with science, and especially with evolutionary biology.

The theme of God's self-humbling has been present, though often nearly invisible, from the very beginnings of Christian tradition. However, in the nineteenth and twentieth centuries it began to emerge more explicitly. The theme of the "descent of God" can be found in many early Christian writers, and it is present in Martin Luther's (1483–1546) focus on the crucified God. Later it breaks out in the German philosopher George Friedrich Hegel's (1770–1831) interpretation of the divine incarnation. But it began to become a more prominent feature of Christian theology especially in the late nineteenth century and increasingly throughout the twentieth century. German theologian Dietrich Bonhoeffer wrote from prison, prior to his execution by the Nazis in 1943, that only a "weak" God could be truly effective in the world. His ideas, though undeveloped, became an important stimulus to the contemporary recovery of a kenotic theology. Likewise, British mathematician and philosopher Alfred North Whitehead (1861–1947) and process theologians have emphasized that God is a "fellow sufferer" who participates in the world's struggle and pain.

Thus for many contemporary Christian thinkers the image of a self-emptying, fully relational God seems to lie at the heart of a religiously coherent and pastorally acceptable theology. God's self-emptying is the underlying dynamism of the doctrine of the Trinity, which the Swiss theologian Karl Barth (1886–1968) held to be the distinguishing content of Christian revelation. The Roman Catholic theologian Karl Rahner (1904–1984) insisted that the primary message of Christian faith is the self-emptying of God. In Section 93 of his 1998 encyclical *Fides et Ratio* (Faith and Reason) Pope John Paul II stated that "the prime commitment of theology is seen to be the understanding of God's kenosis, a grand and mysterious truth for the human mind, which finds it inconceivable that suffering and death can express a love which gives itself and seeks nothing in return."

A self-emptying God as explanation for the creation and evolution of the universe

For some theologians the idea of a self-emptying God allows us to explain in an ultimate way, and in a manner that does not compete or interfere with scientific explanation, both the creation and the evolution of the cosmos and life. Uniting the idea of kenosis with Jewish cabalistic reflections, the Protestant theologian Jürgen Moltmann (b. 1926), for example, speculates in *God in Creation* (1985) that

> God "withdraws himself from himself to himself" in order to make creation possible. His creative activity outwards is preceded by this humble divine self-restriction. In this sense God's self-humiliation does not begin merely with creation, inasmuch as God commits himself to this world: it begins beforehand, and is the presupposition that makes creation possible. God's creative love is grounded in his humble, self-humiliating love. This self-restricting love is the beginning of that self-emptying of God that Philippians 2 sees as the divine mystery of the Messiah. Even in order to create heaven and earth, God emptied himself of all his all-plenishing [i.e., pervasive] omnipotence, and as Creator took upon himself the form of a servant. (p. 88)

Today, especially in discussions of religion and evolution, reflection on the idea of divine kenosis allows theologians to embrace the scientific picture of life without reservation. Emergent complexity, chaos, and nature's generically self-organizing tendencies fit more comfortably a universe grounded less in coercive power than nurturing love that allows the universe some degree of self-creativity. After all, it is in the very nature of self-sacrificing, kenotic love to long for the freedom and self-determination of the beloved. We may assume, then, that an infinitely self-emptying divine love would will that the created universe become something "other" than God. God could not be said to love unreservedly a universe that is not allowed to be distinct from the divine. Since kenotic love requires an "other," any conceivable creator who refused to risk allowing the world to be, at least to some degree, independent of God could not truly love it.

So, according to this line of theological speculation, it is because God is infinite self-emptying love that the universe is not constituted as perfect and complete at the beginning in one instantaneous act of divine magicianship. It is because a kenotic God wills the otherness of the world that it is not frozen into finished perfection from the moment of its origins, but is invited to emerge in patterns of self-organization that contemporary science has begun to notice so clearly.

To those who follow a kenotic theology any conceivable world must likewise allow for the kind of spontaneity that occurs in biological evolution. Any universe grounded in a divine kenotic love must possess a vein of indeterminacy from the moment of its most primitive physical origins. In the light of the divine kenosis it would not be surprising, then, to discover that the cosmos is not fixed in an immobile pattern of eternal sameness, but that it always has an inherent openness to novel and unpredictable outcomes. In the light of a kenotic understanding of the creator, it makes good theological sense that modern physics has disclosed a domain of "uncertainty" or indeterminacy in the elusive realm of subatomic energy events. It is consonant also with the notion of a kenotic deity that evolutionary biologists would encounter another kind of indeterminacy in the "accidental," undirected genetic mutations and many other contingencies of natural history that allow for the serendipitous emergence of life's prodigious variety. And, finally, the fact that humans apprehend in their own subjectivity an undeniable capacity for free choice appears especially consistent with the belief that the cosmos to which they are linked is rooted in a self-emptying principle of being intent upon the emergence of what is truly and deeply "other" than itself. A universe of emergent evolution is more or less what should be expected when people begin reflecting on nature with a belief in the kenotic nature of ultimate reality.

The seemingly aimless meandering of biological evolution may be incompatible with a divine designer, but not with a creative power that takes the form of defenseless love. If the deity were powerful only in the vulgar sense of having the capacity to overwhelm, then evolution might be theologically troubling. But a divine power that manifests itself in infinite self-giving love does not manipulate that which it enfolds. According to advocates of a kenotic theology, therefore, the unqualified religious claim that God is primarily a "designer" would be quite problematic. A designing deity could not permit the world any real independence. A kenotic understanding of divine creation, on the other hand, would allow that life and eventually mind may blossom indeterminately, and over a long period of time, in a universe that is in some sense self-creative from the outset. A kenotic deity would be the ultimate source of the possibilities for novel patterning made available to an evolving cosmos, but in such a way as to allow for a great measure of spontaneity in the evolution of life, mind, and freedom.

See also CHRISTOLOGY; EVOLUTION, THEOLOGY OF; WHITEHEAD, ALFRED NORTH

Bibliography

Balthasar, Hans Urs Von. *Mysterium Paschale,* trans. Aidan Nichols. Edinburgh, UK: T&T Clark, 1990.

Hallmann, Joseph M. *The Descent of God: Divine Suffering in History and Theology.* Minneapolis, Minn.: Fortress Press, 1991.

Haught, John F. *God After Darwin: A Theology of Evolution.* Boulder, Colo.: Westview Press, 2000.

John Paul II. Encyclical Letter *Fides Et Ratio* (September 14, 1998). Washington, D.C.: United States Catholic Conference, 1998.

Jüngel, Eberhard. *The doctrine of the Trinity: God's being is in becoming,* trans. Horton Harris. Grand Rapids, Mich.: Eerdmans, 1976.

Macquarrie, John. *The Humility of God.* Philadelphia, Pa.: Westminster Press, 1978.

Moltmann, Jürgen. *The Crucified God,* trans. R. A. Wilson and John Bowden. New York: Harper, 1974.

Moltmann, Jürgen. *God in Creation,* trans. Margaret Kohl. San Francisco: Harper, 1985.

Murphy, Nancey, and Ellis, George F. R. *On the Moral Nature of the Universe: Theology, Cosmology, and Ethics.* Minneapolis, Minn.: Fortress Press, 1996.

Polkinghorne, John, ed. *The Work of Love.* Grand Rapids, Mich.: Eerdmans, 2001.

Richard, Lucien J. *Christ: The Self-Emptying of God.* New York: Paulist Press, 1997.

JOHN HAUGHT

LAMARCKISM

Jean-Baptiste Pierre Antoine de Monet de Lamarck was born in Picardy, France, on August 1, 1744. He received a Jesuit education at Amiens and briefly pursued a military career before turning to science. Lamarck's interests ranged widely from natural history to meteorology, and with the reorganization of the Jardin du Roi into the Muséum d'Histoire Naturelle in 1793, he was appointed to the professorship of invertebrates. Lamarck's central concern, reflecting his Enlightenment values, was to present a thoroughly naturalistic and developmental account of all aspects of the natural world. His developmental geology followed uniformitarian principles, and his deism rendered irrelevant the optimism of natural theology and dissolved the distinction between humans and other animals. Lamarck believed that "life" is a force imposed on the universe by the creator, but he rejected any idea of a plan for the development of species. His early interest in botanical classification led to his conversion to a transformationist position after 1800, allowing him to explain a wide range of biological phenomena in one coherent system. Lamarck died in relative obscurity on December 18, 1829. His most influential works were his *Hydrogéologie* (1802), *Recherches sur l'organisation des corps vivants* (1802), *Philosophie zoologique* (1809), and *Histoire naturelle des animaux sans vertèbres* (1815–1822).

Although Lamarck himself founded no school of thought, his ideas became a standard point of reference and controversy during the century that followed. His failure to develop a convincing theory of the transmutation of species—in an era increasingly favorable to biological mutability—can be traced to his inability to articulate a credible mechanism for such change. He rejected the idea of species extinction, and evolution through the natural selective pressures never occurred to him. Lamarck's own theory about the transmission of acquired traits from parents to offspring lacked empirical support, and he seems not to have appreciated the significance of biogeography or the fossil record offered by paleontology for developing a complete evolutionary account of life. His posthumous reputation suffered substantially from the campaign of Georges Cuvier (1769–1832) against the insufficiencies of his theory of the inheritance of acquired characteristics. Nevertheless, Lamarck played a seminal role in broaching the basic idea of species change and in supporting it with a justification that rivaled natural selection in plausibility until the integration of Mendelian genetics with the theory of Charles Darwin (1809–1882) after 1900.

Neo-Lamarckism was a late-nineteenth-century movement with variants in France, Britain, and North America. Following the publication Darwin's *Origin of Species* (1859), naturalists who were skeptical of Darwin's insistence on natural selection drew upon Lamarck's theory to elaborate an evolutionary science of life driven by an alternate mechanism. In France his main ideas were preserved through the efforts of his colleague Etienne Geoffroy Saint-Hilaire (1772–1844), and elaborated a generation later by biologists such as Alfred Giard (1846–1908). The neo-Lamarckian school in the United States was led by paleontologist

Edward Cope (1840–1897) and other scientists who combined diligent fieldwork with a distinctive theistic metaphysic. Their journal *The American Naturalist* called for a new natural theology built upon perceived evidence of divine purpose in the environmental adaptation of organisms. In contrast, the French neo-Lamarckian school was secular in flavor, rejecting any intent of discovering divine purpose in nature, illustrating how neo-Lamarckism as a scientific theory was compatible with a wide variety of conflicting theological and metaphysical interpretations.

See also DARWIN, CHARLES; EVOLUTION; NEO-
  DARWINISM

Bibliography

Bowler, Peter J. *Evolution: The History of an Idea.* Berkeley: University of California Press, 1984.

Bowler, Peter J. "Lamarckism." In *Keywords in Evolutionary Biology,* ed. Evelyn Fox Keller and Elisabeth A. Lloyd. Cambridge, Mass.: Harvard University Press, 1992.

Burkhardt, Richard W. *The Spirit of System: Lamarck and Evolutionary Biology* (1977). Cambridge, Mass.: Harvard University Press, 1995.

Corsi, Pietro. *The Age of Lamarck: Evolutionary Theories in France, 1790–1830.* Berkeley: University of California Press, 1988.

Jordanova, L. K. *Lamarck.* Oxford: Oxford University Press, 1984.

Moore, James R. *The Post-Darwinian Controversies: A Study of the Protestant Struggle to Come to Terms with Darwin in Great Britain and America, 1870-1900.* Cambridge, UK: Cambridge University Press, 1979.

Persell, Stuart M. *Neo-Lamarckism and the Evolution Controversy in France, 1870–1920.* Lewiston, N.Y.: Edwin Mellen Press, 1999.

PETER M. J. HESS

LANGUAGE

Human mental life includes biologically unprecedented ways of experiencing and understanding the world, from aesthetic experience to spiritual contemplation. Nevertheless, the origins of many of the most distinctive human mental attributes are likely intertwined with the origins of language. Language is without doubt the most distinctive human adaptation. There is almost no realm of human cognition unaffected by it. Yet there is still debate over even the most basic aspects of its nature, including the degree to which linguistic competence can be coaxed from other species (e.g., apes, dolphins, and parrots); what the neural basis for this distinctive capacity is; and when exactly in human ancestry this capacity emerged and matured to its modern level. There is little doubt that some substantial role is played by distinctive aspects of human biology. Both the special adaptations for language and language itself have played important roles in the origins of human moral and spiritual capacities.

The evolution of language ability in humans

The relative contributions of biological versus cultural aspects of language cognition depend on its evolutionary antiquity. If languages have a shallow prehistory (less than one hundred thousand years), we can expect little correlated biological restructuring of cognition as a result, except insofar as required to get this capacity off the ground. In this case, most of its influence will be traced through cultural processes. If languages have a deep prehistory (on the order of a million years), however, then we can expect that human cognitive and emotional systems have been substantially shaped by its ubiquitous presence in all aspects of human social life. This also should correlate with the extent to which human ethical and spiritual sentiments have become a part of human nature, as opposed to mere cultural overlays on ape nature.

Assessing the origins of these abilities is complicated by the fact that no direct consequences of language use are preserved in the fossil record. Paleolithic archeological evidence for symbolic expression that may signal well-developed linguistic and spiritual activities is well known from European cave paintings and carvings and Australian rock paintings, and from evidence of intentional burials (possibly including Neanderthal burials, as well as the burials of anatomically modern humans). Though the creation of icons and burial of the dead are not guarantees of shamanistic or religiouslike activities, they do suggest the existence of sophisticated symbolic reasoning, and this is a crucial correlation. The first sculpted and pictorial forms can be dated to no earlier than about sixty thousand years ago, and the most well known date to within thirty thousand years ago. This is quite recent, considering that hominids have been on a separate evolutionary track from other African apes for at least five million years, that members of species similar enough to be included in the genus *Homo* have been around for 1.8 million years, and that the human species *Homo sapiens* is at least two hundred thousand years old. In general, these earliest samples of expressive symbolism must be understood not as evidence for the initial evolution of symbolic abilities but rather for their first expression in durable media. They likely had long been incorporated into conventionalized social activities by that time. The origins of the symbolic traditions that these works express in material form could easily anticipate this data by an order of magnitude.

To get some idea of the possible extremes of this range of possible dates consider the following. The earliest direct archeological evidence of language is, of course, in the form of early forms of writing, which are all less than ten thousand years old, and most considerably more recent (about five thousand years ago). Since not even the most radical theorists among archeologists and paleontologists would date the appearance of modern languages more recently than about fifty thousand years ago, this late externalization of language offers a curious challenge: Why did it take so long for this most important means of communication to exhibit direct external expression? The same question can be asked of the first evidence of pictorial and carved forms, which date back about sixty thousand years in Europe and Australia and possibly earlier in Africa (though this African evidence is currently less well known). Assuming some comparable difficulties in externalizing these different modes of symbolic expression, we might suggest that, most conservatively, the corresponding distinctively human symbolic communication must be at least ten times as old; that is, 5,000 to 50,000 years for modern language, and 50,000 to 500,000 years for some form of language.

At the other end of the spectrum, there is a series of apparently linked paleontological transitions evident between 1.6 and 2.4 million years ago in Africa that suggest that the beginnings of symbolic communications in some form may date to this fossil epoch. The first clear evidence for the regular production of stone choppers, at a site called Gona, can be dated to about 2.4 million years ago. These are associated with fossil species of the genus *Australopithecus* (possibly *A. garhi*). Australopithecines exhibited ape-sized brains, relatively large jaws with heavy dentition (evidence of a vegetarian dietary adaptation), relatively modern bipedal locomotion, and also a characteristic sexual dimorphism (males much larger on average than females), which is indicative of male competition over females in a polygynous mating system that is fairly typical of monkeys and great apes. By 1.8 million years ago a number of fossil sites begin to demonstrate hominid species with larger brains and reduced dentition, correlated with extensive stone tool assemblages. These features have prompted paleontologists to cite this as the point where our genus, *Homo,* begins. By 1.6 million years ago members of our genus, with brains beginning to cross into the low end of the modern range, had left Africa to spread into Asia, Southeast Asia, and possibly throughout more temperate Asian regions as well, taking with them more sophisticated tools. Given these unprecedented features, there can be little doubt that some significant changes in communication and cognition also are contemporaneous with these transitions—the first forms of crude symbolic communication—though it is likely that the evolution of modern forms of linguistic communication took much longer to develop.

If symbolic communication has been around in some form for as much as two million years then we can expect it to have had significant consequences not just for human culture but also for human brain function. The evolutionary biological effect of a behavioral adaptation such as this may be usefully compared to that of dam building in North American beavers. The evolution of this ability has changed the niche in which beavers mature and live, and this has changed the natural selection forces affecting beaver physiology and behavioral propensities in succeeding generations. Thus, beavers exhibit extensive aquatic adaptations as a feed-forward result of beaver behaviors. This evolutionary process has been called *niche construction*. The effects of human symbolic communication and culture can also be understood as a form of niche construction, though symbolic culture is in many ways a far more all-encompassing niche than a beaver pond. This niche likely favored the evolution of certain cognitive capacities and social predispositions relevant to symbolic learning and communication, but also, as in the case of beavers, there may be many special features of this artificial niche that are idiosyncratic to it. Thus, there is good reason to expect that human brains have been reorganized in response to language, a reorganization that included changes affecting emotional, social, and communicative tendencies, as well as mnemonic, attentional, and motor capacities supportive of symbolic communication. Anatomical hints of this effect are evident in the changes in regional brain proportions (e.g., disproportionately expanded prefrontal cortex), cortical vocal control (unprecedented among mammals), and lowered laryngeal position. Hints from behavior are even more extensive. These include the convergent contributions of many systems to this capacity, its robustness in the face of variations in learning conditions and the effects of early brain damage, its highly predictable developmental progression, the remarkable universality of many of the structural features of languages, and its unprecedented efficiency. These effects need to be understood also with respect to the complex cultural dynamic of language change, which itself is a kind of quasi-evolutionary process. The ways different languages carve up the meaning and reference "space" and the syntactic systems that organize linguistic expression clearly change and evolve over historical time, and probably with respect to these biological predispositions and abilities as background.

Consequences of language ability for religious and spiritual development

The consequences of this unprecedented evolutionary transition for human religious and spiritual development must be understood on many levels as well. There are reasons to believe that the way language refers to things—symbolic reference—provides the crucial catalyst that initiated the transition from species with no inkling of meaning in life to a species where questions of ultimate meaning have become core organizers of culture and consciousness. Symbolic reference is reference to things and ideas that is mediated by an intervening system of symbol-symbol relationships, as well as conventions of use that allow there to be considerable conceptual "distance" between a sign vehicle and its object of reference. Unlike *icons,* which refer by means of structural similarities between a sign vehicle and its object, or *indices,* which refer via their physical contiguity or invariant causal correlation with their object, this conceptual "distance" is an intermediate referential step that allows the form of symbols to be entirely independent of the objects to which they refer. Symbolic reference is thus both arbitrary and capable of providing considerable displacement and abstraction. *Displacement* refers to the capacity to refer to things distant in space or time, and *abstraction* refers to the ability to represent only the more spare and skeletal features of things, including their logical features, such as whether they are even ontologically existent. So it is with the evolution of this symbolic capacity that it first becomes possible to represent the possible future, the impossible past, the act that should or shouldn't take place, the experience that is unimaginable even though representable. These capacities are ubiquitous for humans and largely taken for granted when it comes to spiritual and ethical realms, but this is precisely where crucial differences in ability mark the boundary that distinguishes humans from other species.

Consider the ethical dimension of humanness. Though the family cat may gleefully torment a small animal causing its terrifying and painful death, few among us would consider this a moral issue concerning the cat, though whether to intervene may be a moral dilemma for us. Even when a large predator, say dog or bear, happens to maul and kill a human being, efforts to destroy the animal are not accompanied by moral outrage, just a desire to prevent further harm. But the situation is very different in cases where humans perform similar actions. It is not merely that we consider nonhuman predators to be guiltless because it is in their nature to kill. We hold them guiltless because we believe they lack a critical conception of the consequences of their actions on their victim's experience. This ability to anticipate and to some extent imagine the experience of another are critical ingredients in this moral judgment.

This does not mean that other creatures are merely selfish robots. Selfless behaviors of a sort are not at all uncommon in other species. Caregiving behaviors by parents are nearly ubiquitous in birds and mammals, and what we might call prosocial emotional responses and predispositions that cause individuals to behave in ways conducive to social solidarity are especially widespread among social mammals. However, there need be little or no role played by intersubjective considerations in the generation of these emotions and their associated care-giving, protective, and comforting behaviors. And if that is so, then it may not be appropriate to consider these as moral or ethical, even incipiently.

There is good reason to believe that the capacity to represent the intentions and experiences of others is deeply dependent on human symbolic capacity. This is because it is a difficult cognitive task. It involves generating something like a simulation of oneself in different circumstances (i.e., projected from another individual's point of view), and it must include the emotional experiences this would invoke as well. This representation is perhaps supported by recall of images from analogous past experiences, juxtaposed against the images and emotions of current experience. But the salience of direct experience, especially one's current emotional state, poses a difficult impediment to simultaneously representing the perspective of this other simulated emotional experience. Holding such mutually contradictory representations in mind at once is a difficult task, even when there is little emotion involved, but it becomes deeply challenging when the exclusive states are heavily emotion-laden.

All such cognitive tasks depend critically on the prefrontal lobes of the cerebral cortex. This brain region is essential to any mental process that requires holding the traces of alternative associations and behavioral options in mind to be compared, so that one can act with respect to likely consequences and not merely with respect to their general reinforcement value or their stimulus salience. Reduction of such stimulus drives allows the most effective sampling of options. It is suggested that the prefrontal lobes are disproportionately enlarged in human brains as an evolutionary adaptation to the demands imposed by symbol learning and use. The indirectness of symbolic reference demands a shift of attention away from immediately associated features and to the relational logic behind the symbols, which binds them into a system. So this neuro-anatomical divergence from the ancestral condition likely contributes to the capacity and perhaps even a predisposition to generate the "simulations" required for the representation of others' experiences.

But it is the referential displacement provided by symbols themselves that is probably critical to reducing the differential in salience of competing emotional state representations to make this mental comparison possible. Studies with primates and children have shown, for example, that failures to make optimal choices when highly arousing stimuli (e.g., candy) are presented can be overcome by substituting representations for the actual thing. By a somewhat ironic logic, then, it may be the capacity to use representations to reduce the emotional salience of particular experiences that has enabled the development of intersubjective empathic abilities.

Symbolic reference also provides a critical support for an additional element of ethical cognition: the need to project forward the consequences of different possible alternative actions. Projecting the plausible physical consequences with respect to one's own needs and desires is difficult enough, but simultaneously projecting the likely affect on another's experience is doubly complicated. This is the mental equivalent of running simulations of the effects of simulated actions on simulated emotions, all in conflict with current experiences and emotional states. As the numbers of potentially interfering images and the intensities of the potentially conflicting emotions increase, the importance of symbolic support grows. For this reason, not only do we recognize that young children have difficulty performing anything beyond simple moral assessments, but all cultures actively provide narrative and ritual exemplars for guiding its members in handling ethical matters. The symbolic traditions that constitute cultures almost universally transmit the expectation that one is responsible for considering experiential consequences for others before acting—a moral imperative. Of course, it is also this capacity for imagining the experiences of others that makes possible the most heinous of human acts, such as extortion and torture. The emergence of good and evil are not, then, just mythically linked. Both are implicit in the symbolic transfiguration of emotional experience and the gift of intersubjectivity that results.

Ultimately, humanness may be most clearly marked by this transformation of the merely physical and physiological into the meaningful and implicitly value-laden by virtue of symbolic reference. Under the influence of the generalizing power of symbols this experience of ethical significance can be extended well beyond the social sphere, to recognize an ethical dimension implicit in all things. This suggests a way to think about two additional features that are characteristic of most spiritual traditions: the ubiquitous assignment of symbolic meaning, purpose, and value to things outside human affairs (e.g., origins, places, natural phenomena, and life and death itself), and the presumption that there is something like intentionality or intelligence behind the way that things are and the unfolding of worldly events.

Both of these nearly universal tendencies reflect a complex interaction between the cognitive predispositions that have evolved to ease the acquisition of symbolic communication and the implicit power of symbols to alter conditions of life in the world. Since a prerequisite to symbolic reference is the "discovery" of the logic of the system of inter-symbolic relationships that supports any individual symbolic reference, there are reasons to believe that the changes in prefrontal proportions contributed not just an ability to sample these non-overt relational features, but also a predisposition to look for them. With symbols, what matters is not surface details, but a hidden logic derived from the complex topologies of semantic relationships that constrain symbol use.

So the neuropsychological propensity to incessantly, spontaneously, and rapidly interpret symbols should express itself quite generally as a predisposition to look beyond surface correlations among things to find some formal systematicity, and thus meaning, behind them, even things that derive from entirely nonhuman sources. Everything is thus a potential symbol—trees, mountains, star patterns, coincidental events—and if the systematicity and intentionality is not evident it may mean merely that one has not yet discovered it. Symbolic meaning is a function of consciousness and symbols are produced to communicate. So if the world is seen as full of potential symbols, it must implicitly be part of some grand effort of communication, and the product of mind. Whether this projected subjectivity is experienced as different personalities resident in hills, groves of trees, or rivers, or as some single grand infinite mind, this personification also taps into the intersubjective drive that is also fostered by symbolic projection.

In summary, the role of symbolic communication, and especially language, in moral cognition is ubiquitous. It has played a role in the evolution of a brain more capable of the cognitive operations required; it has provided critical tools for easing the implicit cognitive strain of performing these mental operations; and it has made it possible for

societies to evolve means for developing these abilities (as well as opening the door for the horrors of their abuse). Moreover, the capacity for spiritual experience itself can be understood as an emergent consequence of the symbolic transfiguration of cognition and emotions. Human predispositions seem inevitably to project this ethical perspective onto the whole world, embedding human consciousness in vast webs of meaning, value, and intersubjective possibilities.

See also SEMIOTICS

Bibliography

Deacon, Terrence. *The Symbolic Species: The Coevolution of Language and the Brain*. New York: Norton, 1997.

Deacon, Terrence. "How I Gave Up the Ghost and Learned to Love Evolution." In *When Worlds Converge: What Science and Religion Tell Us about the Story of the Universe and our Place in it,* ed. Clifford Matthews, Mary Evelyn Tucker, and Philp Hefner. Chicago: Open Court, 2002.

Dennett, Daniel. *Darwin's Dangerous Idea: Evolution and the Meaning of Life*. New York: Touchstone, 1995.

Katz, Leonard, ed. *Evolutionary Origins of Morality: Cross-Disciplinary Perspectives*. Thorverton, UK: Imprint Academic, 2000.

Langer, Susanne. *Mind: An Essay on Human Feeling,* Vol. 2. Baltimore, Md.: Johns Hopkins University Press, 1972.

Wilson, David Sloan. *Darwin's Cathedral: Evolution, Religion, and the Nature of Society*. Chicago: University of Chicago Press, 2002.

TERRENCE W. DEACON

LAWS OF NATURE

It is generally held that the search for laws is part and parcel of natural science. Statements of the laws of nature provide the most systematic and unified account of phenomena; they are used to make predictions, and they figure centrally in explanation. But are the laws of nature real? Do they belong to the world or do they rather reflect the way people speak about it? Do they merely describe the facts and processes in nature or do they govern them? In other words, do laws possess a modal force, the force of nomological necessity, not attaching to merely contingent facts? And if they do, how does one get a handle on this important distinction between laws and nonlawful accidental generalizations? These questions continue to be widely debated and there is no generally accepted philosophical theory of the laws of nature. It is also unclear whether any single theory could do justice to the diverse kinds of laws used in different scientific disciplines (physics, chemistry, biology, psychology, etc.). Finally, it is a matter of controversy how the laws of various disciplines are related to each other.

Do laws describe or prescribe? Some historical background

The question of whether laws describe or prescribe the course of nature has always been given particular emphasis in the debates. Most historians agree that the concept of scientific law as it is used today did not become widely accepted until the scientific revolution marking the birth of modern science. The ancestors of this concept, however, are old and include the ideas of social, legal, and moral order, which themselves can be traced to the notion of divine legislation. This notion is clearly associated with the prescribing force various laws (*lex, regula*) possess due to their origin in God's will—be they the natural laws of moral conduct or the laws of mechanics. The mathematician and philosopher René Descartes (1596–1650), in particular, explicitly related his law of inertia to the sustaining power of God. Even as late as the Enlightenment age, philosophers such as Montesquieu (1689–1755) attributed the order of nature to the hand of God. But alongside this divine-necessitation understanding, natural scientists and philosophers as different as Roger Bacon (c. 1220–1292) and Johannes Kepler (1571–1630) advanced a quite different conception of law that was free of theological connotations and had to do with observable and measurable regularities in nature. The view of laws as regularities capable of being inductively inferred (or even "deduced," as Isaac Newton [1642–1727] thought) from phenomena and then used in prediction and explanation became firmly entrenched in the new science of mechanics and in many other disciplines in the decades following the scientific revolution. Such regularities were widely interpreted as being descriptive, not prescriptive. Rather than being imposed on phenomena, they simply reflected the way things are. This interpretation received

a stamp of approval in the empiricist tradition and especially in the philosophy of David Hume (1711–1776). In was, however, challenged in twentieth-century philosophy, especially after the demise of logical positivism, the rise of scientific realism, and the revival of metaphysics.

A taxonomy of scientific laws

The sciences display a wide variety of laws. Some laws are deterministic, the paradigm example being the laws of Newtonian mechanics, which prompted the astronomer Pierre Simon Laplace (1749–1827) to invoke his famous image of a demon capable of performing an arbitrary number of calculations in a finite amount of time. If the demon knew all the laws pertaining to the interaction of matter particles and the exact configuration of all the matter in the universe at a certain moment of time, he would be able to predict with absolute accuracy the state of the entire world at any future moment, as well as retrodict its past states. Given the deterministic laws and initial conditions, there is only one way for the phenomena and processes to occur. Probabilistic or statistical laws, in contrast, only attribute a certain probability to such occurrences. The laws of statistical mechanics, of Mendelian genetics, and of social and economic development are in this category. Since such laws are not the most fundamental laws of reality, however, their probabilistic character may not be irreducible. But if the currently dominant interpretation of quantum mechanics is correct, then indeterminism is a feature of even the most basic laws of nature.

Laws pertaining to natural processes (deterministic or not) and relating their earlier and later stages (e.g., a putative chemical law to the effect that putting together substances X and Y results in an explosive reaction) are often referred to as causal laws. The relationship between causal laws and causation (in particular, whether the former are constitutive of the latter) is a matter of dispute. Far from all laws are causal, however. Some laws assert a synchronic dependence among several quantities (e.g., the ideal gas law relating pressure, volume, and temperature). Still other laws state that an entity of a certain kind has a certain property (e.g., water's boiling point is 100° C).

Finally, there are conservation laws (of matter, momentum, energy, etc.), other basic principles such as relativistic and gauge invariance, and prohibitions such as Pauli's exclusion principle and the principle ruling out superluminal signals. How should they be classified? Are they on the same footing with other laws? Or are they rather second-order constraints on first-order laws? In any case, they are of paramount importance. Thus the invariance of some physical quantities with respect to coordinate and other kinds of transformation is bound up with the concept of symmetry and has been a powerful heuristic tool in the search for the fundamental forces of nature.

This classification of various types of laws can be extended in many directions. The diversity of laws calls into question any attempt to provide their universal form.

Philosophical theories of laws

Philosophical theories of laws are focused on the ontological status of the latter. In many ways, the ongoing debate about this status is a successor of the older dispute between the descriptive and prescriptive views of laws. It is hard to get rid of the feeling that when water boils at 100° C (under normal atmospheric conditions), it does so not simply as a matter of fact but out of necessity. Moreover, if no samples of water were ever heated to 100° C, it would still be true that, were an arbitrary water sample so heated, it would boil. Advocates of necessitarian theories attribute this necessity to nature and hold some facts about the world responsible for the modal power inherent in natural laws. Philosophers in the empiricist tradition, however, have always thought otherwise. Instead of attributing nomological necessity to nature, they have attempted to achieve the effect of this necessity by working in rather barren metaphysical landscapes. In spite of the sustained critique leveled against this attitude beginning in the early 1960s, it remains very influential, under the name of the *regularity theory*.

According to this theory, laws of nature are nothing but universal truths of spatio-temporally unlimited scope that can, in many cases, be expressed by quantified material conditionals involving only qualitative and local predicates: $(\forall x)(Px \supset Qx)$; for example, "All frogs are green," "All metals expand when heated," "All electrons have a unit electric charge." Laws, in other words, are cosmic regularities. On this view, being such a regularity is necessary and sufficient for being a law. What makes it a matter of law that water boils at 100° C is the cosmic fact about the instantiation of first-order properties—the fact that all actual samples of water at 100° C found in the history of the universe have boiled, are boiling, and will boil. The manifestly Humean character of this concept of lawhood made it one of the cornerstones of logical positivism.

The regularity theory confronts many problems. First of all, being a cosmic regularity is neither necessary nor sufficient for being a law. Some laws are probabilistic (e.g., those of quantum mechanics) and hence compatible with any actual degree of correlation between the relevant P's and Q's. There are also uninstantiated laws. For example, Newton's first law, which states that an object will remain at rest or in uniform motion in a straight line unless acted upon by a net external force, probably has no instances at all. It is (arguably) a genuine law of nature nonetheless. Thus being a (cosmic) regularity is not necessary for being a law.

It is also not sufficient for it. To use the renowned example of the philosopher Karl Popper (1902–1994), suppose every moa (an extinct species of bird in New Zealand) that ever lived died before age fifty as a result of some ubiquitous disease, thus giving an instance of cosmic regularity. There is, however, no law corresponding to this regularity. Every moa could have lived longer but, as a matter of fact, has not. The regularity in question is merely accidental, not genuinely lawful. But the theory is incapable of distinguishing these two cases.

This has prompted a modification in the regularity account based on the notion of counterfactual conditional. Genuine laws of nature, but not accidental uniformities, can be said to support (that is, imply) the relevant counterfactuals. Thus the regularity from Popper's example does not imply "If something were a moa, it would have died before age fifty." On the other hand, a genuine law that moa have a certain number n of chromosomes does imply the counterfactual "If something had been a moa, it would have had n chromosomes." To be able to use this criterion, however, one needs an independent account of truth conditions for the relevant sort of counterfactuals, namely, those that are not also counterlegals violating the laws of nature. But it is hard to see how one could know which counterfactuals are true and which of them are not counterlegals without already knowing what laws of nature there are.

It has been argued that laws, but not mere regularities, possess considerable explanatory power. While this is true, it can hardly serve as a criterion of lawhood. Something is not made into a law when its statement becomes explanatorily powerful. It is powerful because it is already a statement of law. A similar objection applies to the best version of the regularity theory, which was anticipated by John Stuart Mill (1806–1873) and Frank Ramsey (1903–1930) and elaborated in the 1970s and 1980s by David Lewis (1941–2001). According to Lewis, "a contingent generalization is a law of nature if and only if it appears as a theorem (or axiom) in each of the true deductive systems that achieves the best combination of simplicity and strength" (p. 73). This account makes lawhood relative to merely epistemic (hence subjective) standards of simplicity and strength pulling in opposite directions.

These and other problems have led to the emergence of necessitarian alternatives to the regularity theory. One such alternative, widely known as the Dretske-Tooley-Armstrong theory, takes laws to be grounded in relations between universals. A lawful regularity, such as the fact that all metals are electric conductors, obtains because *being a metal* nomologically necessitates *being an electric conductor.* Although such a relation between the two universals, *metallicity* and *conductivity,* is itself contingent (could have failed to take place), its actual presence confers on particular facts falling under it the right sort of necessity (i.e., the nomological of physical necessity), which sustains the relevant countarfactuals and accounts for the explanatory power of this law. On the contrary, no relation of necessitation obtains between *being moa* and *dying before age fifty.* The corresponding cosmic regularity is still there but only as a matter of historical accident, not as a matter of nomological necessity.

To uphold such a theory, however, one has to accept, not only real universals (entities such as *metallicity,* in addition to actual metals) but also contingent relations of nomic necessitation between them. Such relations must then translate into the relations among particulars. Some authors have argued that these commitments create serious difficulties (Bas van Fraassen's problems of identification and of inference).

The second major type of necessitarian theory states that laws derive from causal powers (dispositions and propensities) of objects. The possession of such powers by natural kinds of objects (e.g., elementary particles, chemical elements) disposes their bearers to behave in specific ways or to exemplify other characteristic properties. On this account, most properties—and especially those of the fundamental objects—are ultimately dispositional in nature. For example, the electric charge possessed by the electron disposes the latter to interact in a certain way with the electromagnetic field. Laws of nature, on this account, simply codify the natural behavior of things enforced by their intrinsic causal powers. Moreover, natural kinds possess their dispositional properties essentially: Nothing counts as an electron unless it has a unit electric charge, a specific mass, spin 1/2, and perhaps other essential dispositional properties. The major difference of this account from the relations-between-universals view is erasing the boundary between what things are and how they behave. On the former view, all electrons have a certain charge because of the relation between the two universals: *electronhood* and a determinate *chargehood.* On the latter view, part of what makes something an electron is having a certain charge. Instead of being imposed "from above," in the form of the necessitation relation between universals, lawhood emerges "from below," from the ascription of essential dispositional properties to particulars.

One difficulty with this view is that it raises the specter of *virtus dormitiva*: Causal powers of fundamental objects turn out to be their irreducible dispositional properties that must be possessed even when they are not manifested. But what exactly is involved in saying that a certain substance has an irreducible disposition that is not currently manifested? What keeps such a pure disposition in existence? Other questions arise: Do fundamental objects, such as electrons, have one disposition or many? If many, what accounts for their connection?

Thus all major philosophical accounts of laws have their difficulties. This has led some authors to skepticism about the possibility of a satisfactory analysis of lawhood or even to the view that the notion of law must be rejected altogether as being empty, obsolete, and having no important role to play in contemporary science. This, however, remains a minority view. Most philosophers (and probably all scientists) continue to think that laws are important, even if their ontological nature is elusive.

Laws and explanation

Even if explanatory potential does not by itself make something into a law, the ubiquitous role of laws in scientific explanations is beyond doubt. This observation has formed the basis of the covering-law model of explanation introduced in 1948 by the philosophers Carl Hempel (1905–1997) and Paul Oppenheim (1885–1977) and further elaborated by Hempel in the 1950s and 1960s. To explain a particular phenomenon is to answer a why-question, and this requires an account of how the phenomenon was brought about. Hempel has construed deterministic explanation as a deductive argument of the form:

$$\frac{C_1, C_2, \ldots, C_n \quad L_1, L_2, \ldots, L_m}{E}$$

Here $C_1, C_2, \ldots, C_n$ are statements describing the initial conditions and $L_1, L_2, \ldots, L_m$ are statements of laws (together constituting the *explanans*), while E is a statement describing the event to be explained (the *explanandum*). Thus to explain why a particular sample of metal expanded when heated, one invokes a law to the effect that all metals do so when heated and the initial condition stating that the sample in question was heated. The above deductive-nomological schema has a probabilistic (statistical) counterpart to account for explanations involving indeterministic laws.

Since its inception the covering-law model has been the target of many objections. But it is still the starting point of any informed discussion of explanation. It is plausible that most deficiencies of Hempel's model are ultimately due to its implicit reliance on a broadly Humean (i.e., regularity) conception of laws.

Laws and reductionism

Whether higher-level laws of nature (chemical, biological, psychological, etc.) are reducible to the fundamental physical laws—and if so, in what exact sense—is part of the problem of reductionism. However natural it may seem to think that chemistry is eventually just a chapter of physics, many authors have resisted this line of thought. Even physicists have always doubted that the irreversibility inherent in the second law of thermodynamics can be explained on the basis of time-reversal invariant laws of mechanics. Developments in chaos theory have all but deepened such doubts.

See also CAUSATION; DETERMINISM; SYMMETRY

Bibliography

Armstrong, David *What Is a Law of Nature?* Cambridge, UK: Cambridge University Press, 1983.

Ayer, A. J. "What is a Law of Nature?" *Revue Internationale de Philosophie* 10 (1956):144–165.

Bigelow, John, and Pargetter, Robert. *Science and Necessity.* Cambridge, UK: Cambridge University Press, 1990.

Carroll, John. *Laws of Nature.* Cambridge, UK: Cambridge University Press, 1994.

Cartwright, Nancy. *How the Laws of Physics Lie.* Oxford: Clarendon Press, 1983.

Dretske, Fred. "Laws of Nature." *Philosophy of Science* 44 (1977): 248–268.

Earman, John. "Laws of Nature: The Empiricist Challenge." In *D. M. Armstrong,* ed. Radu Bogdan. Dordrecht, Netherlands: Reidel, 1984.

Ellis, Brian. *Scientific Essentialism.* Cambridge, UK: Cambridge University Press, 2001.

Harré, Rom, and Madden, Edward H. *Causal Powers: A Theory of Natural Necessity.* Totowa, N.J.: Rowman and Littlefield, 1975.

Hempel, Carl. *Aspects of Scientific Explanation.* New York: Free Press, 1965.

Lange, Marc. *Natural Laws in Scientific Practice.* Oxford and New York: Oxford University Press, 2000.

Lewis, David. *Counterfactuals.* Cambridge, Mass.: Harvard University Press, 1973.

Mellor, D. H. "Necessities and Universals in Natural Laws." In *Science, Belief, and Behavior: Essays in Honour of R. B. Braithwaite,* ed. D. H. Mellor. Cambridge, UK: Cambridge University Press, 1980.

Rube, Jane. "The Origins of Scientific 'Law.'" *Journal of the History of Ideas* 47 (1986): 341–359.

Shoemaker, Sidney. "Causality and Properties." In *Time and Cause: Essays Presented to Richard Taylor,* ed. Peter van Inwagen. Dordrecht, Netherlands: Reidel, 1980.

Skyrms, Brian. "Physical Law and the Nature of Physical Reduction." In *Induction, Probability and Confirmation*, Vol. 7: Minnesota Studies in the Philosophy of Science, eds. Grover Maxwell and Robert M. Anderson, Jr. Minneapolis: University of Minnesota Press, 1975.

Swartz, Norman. *The Concept of Physical Law*. Cambridge, UK: Cambridge University Press, 1985.

Swoyer, Chris. "The Nature of Natural Laws." *Australasian Journal of Philosophy* 60 (1982): 203–223.

Tooley, Michael. "The Nature of Laws." *Canadian Journal of Philosophy* 7 (1977): 667–698.

Urbach, Peter. "What is a Law of Nature? A Humean Answer." *British Journal for the Philosophy of Science* 39 (1988): 193–210.

Vallentyne, Peter. "Explicating Lawhood." *Philosophy of Science* 55 (1988): 598–613.

Van Fraassen, Bas. *Laws and Symmetries*. Oxford: Clarendon Press, 1989.

Weinert, Friedel, ed. *Laws of Nature: Essays on the Philosophical, Scientific and Historical Dimensions*. Berlin and New York: Walter de Gruyter, 1995.

YURI V. BALASHOV

LEVEL THEORY

Level theories are used to explain the relationship between different academic disciplines and the realities that they describe. Drawing on concepts of emergence and supervenience, level theories seek to counter the claim that all of reality can be explained as nothing but a collection of atoms. Various scholars in science and religion have argued that reality should be understood in terms of increasing levels of complexity, each level emergent from, but not reducible to, the levels below.

See also COMPLEXITY; EMERGENCE; HIERARCHY

GREGORY R. PETERSON

LIBERATION

Liberation is a central religious notion both in South Asian religious traditions and in contemporary Christian theology, but in what way are South Asian meanings of liberation (*mokṣa, mukti,*

nirvāṇa) comparable to liberation as understood by contemporary Christian theologians? This entry will highlight significant differences regarding the meanings of liberation across traditions, then draw conclusions about the meaning of those differences for how each tradition engages the sciences. The discussion will focus on those traditions that seem most philosophically unlike Western religious traditions, namely the nondualism of Advaita Vedānta (constituted as a school by the eighth-century theologian, Śaṇkara) and Buddhism, particularly the Madhyamaka tradition (inaugurated by first-century C.E. Buddhist philosopher Nāgārjuna).

Success in cross-cultural comparison requires examining what South Asian religious traditions seek to be liberated from. There is greater agreement about the nature of the predicament that makes liberation necessary than about how to escape. The reason for this wide divergence is plain: Each South Asian tradition (indeed each subtradition) has a unique understanding about the nature of the ultimate reality to which liberation leads. Nevertheless, nearly all concur in their assessment that all beings are beginninglessly bound to *saṃsāra,* the wheel of rebirth or transmigration, by the force of karma. The question about just what causes karmic bondage quickly reintroduces serious debate both within and across South Asian religious traditions.

South Asian traditions, although they have typically maintained that all sentient beings are in bondage, have traditionally been anthropocentric in focus. Even if all beings are in bondage, it is primarily human beings who can be liberated. Moreover, only individual human beings, not communities, are liberated from the cycle of transmigration. Human bondage is rarely construed in sociopolitical terms. Liberation is understood largely as a matter of freedom from afflictions of the heart and ignorance of the mind, the root causes of bondage to the process of rebirth. Liberation from craving, ignorance, and delusion (the three poisons in Buddhism and also in Śaṇkara's Advaita) does lead to more compassionate living, but the essential locus of transformation is the person.

Until contemporary attention to ecological matters transformed Western religious thinking, Western traditions have also been anthropocentric in character. And, like South Asian traditions, the religious goal has most often been understood as salvation for individual human beings. Salvation was understood as healing, as a reunion with God that brings about the reintegration of the divided self and reconciliation with neighbor. A comparison that focused on salvation as healing would find important similarities with the South Asian goal to be free from craving, ignorance, and delusion.

However, for nearly the entire history of Western monotheism, the predicament from which one needs to escape has always included a sociopolitical component, even when that component has been muted by the quest for personal salvation. The sociopolitical character of Western religious anthropologies has meant that communities qua communities, and not just individual persons, can and must be healed. Communal healing requires doing justice. Doing justice in turn has concretely meant the liberation of persons from oppressive socioeconomic and political structures that disfigure human flourishing. This is the meaning of liberation that finds vital expression in contemporary Christian liberation theology.

Here, communities are liberated and their collective well-being is the focus. Liberation is not construed as individual escape from the threat of an otherworldly judgment but freedom from a this-worldly hell. This particular kind of communal liberation is not commonly found in South Asian religious reflection. The compassionate presence of liberated individuals can and does have social and political consequences, but groups and communities are not liberated in their collectivity. This deep difference has important ramifications for thinking about the scientific implications of the notion of liberation in Western and South Asian thought.

The human predicament in South Asian religions

The human predicament in South Asian religions is construed as bondage to a beginningless process of rebirth. That process is fueled by karma, which generates consequences for all human actions, consequences that exert their presence across multiple lifetimes. That law-like process is driven by some fundamental affective cause, usually described as craving. Craving leads persons to act, and action in turn generates the consequences that insure rebirth.

But craving itself is analyzed as deriving from a cognitive factor, namely ignorance. What exactly one is ignorant of depends on the specific tradition in question. Ignorance is always the failure to know or realize what each tradition takes to be ultimately true. For example, whereas Advaita Vedāntins argue that persons are ignorant of their true, infinite, and unchanging Self (ātman), South Asian Buddhist schools concur in arguing that ignorance consists in entertaining the very idea of any substantial, enduring or permanent self (anātman).

This analysis of the root causes of transmigration indicates yet another meaning of liberation in South Asian traditions. Liberation is not understood merely as a post-mortem escape from the cycle of rebirth. Liberation is also the cessation of ignorance and the elimination of the three poisons in and through which ignorance is expressed and perpetuated.

Action, karma, craving, and ignorance are all crucial links in a complex chain of causes and conditions that extend over multiple lifetimes by which the process of transmigration operates. The Buddhist term for this complex cycle of causes and conditions (hetupratyaya) is pratitya-samutpāda, best translated as "dependent co-origination." Buddhist and Hindu reflection on liberation focuses precisely on those cognitive, affective, volitional tendencies that generate karma because the cycles can be interrupted precisely at these points. But the vision of complex causality and interdependence evinced in the chain of links that both perpetuates and is the process and reality of transmigration is worthy of attention to those interested in the implications of Hindu and especially Buddhist thinking about science.

Despite radical disagreements about the object of ignorance, these traditions do agree that "ignorance" does not refer to matters of everyday experience. There are all sorts of things that an enlightened person may not know about the empirical world which do not imperil liberation. Because liberating knowledge is knowledge about ultimate matters and not conventional ones, religious knowledge is not contingent on, nor does it need to control, what counts as knowledge in conventional matters. Cosmology or quantum mechanics, theories about how the world works, either at the macroscopic or the subatomic realm, are not directly relevant to liberating knowledge. There is, therefore, the possibility of a comprehensively hands-off attitude about scientific ventures. The working and operation of the world are matters of conventional truth (vyavahāra satya).

The term "ignorance" refers to the failure to apprehend the ultimate truth (*paramārtha satya*) about the underlying nature of reality, about the being of things and not about how things work. A radical distinction is made between the operation of the world as it is ordinarily experienced and the ultimate truth about the being of things, even if, as it turns out later, these two perspectives turn out to be profoundly interrelated, as is the case in the Madhyamaka Buddhism of Nāgārjuna.

Ultimate truth and scientific truth: South Asian approaches

The possibility of radically severing religious truth from conventional truths that are the objects of scientific inquiry is far easier for Hindu nondualists than Buddhist nondualists. For the classical Hindu Advaitins like Śaṅkara, the empirical world, the experienced world, is not ultimately real. Nothing given in experience endures. It is intrinsically impermanent and doomed to perish.

The fleeting realities of everyday experience need a basis, a substratum, apart from which they would not be. That basis or substratum itself is free from change, beyond temporality, indivisible, self-identical, and intrinsically real. Because it is free from fragility, it is radically transcendent, but because it is the being of all things, it is also radically immanent as the ground and basis of the conventional world of experience. This reality is pure being (*sat*) and is known as *brahman*. Only this underlying reality is truly real and thus this tradition qualifies as nondualistic. From the point of view of persons, liberation consists in coming to know that one is in truth this ultimate reality and not the finite self of ordinary experience.

The Buddhist nondualism of Nāgārjuna is strikingly different from Advaita Vedanta. Nāgārjuna's nondualism is a radical reinterpretation of early Buddhist insights regarding the impermanent dependent co-arising of things. Nāgārjuna argues that the pluralistic view of reality in which each thing is a stream or a flow of momentary arisings does not represent the deepest truth taught by the Buddha. The ultimate truth taught by the Buddha is to be found in the affirmation that everything arises in dependence on the causes and conditions that give it rise. If everything arises through the causes and conditions that give it rise, then no thing has any intrinsic being or self-existence (*svabhāva*). Indeed, if anything did possess intrinsic being that

did not arise dependently on causes and conditions, it would be unconditioned and therefore eternal. But no such things are given in experience. Nothing, in that sense, exists. Thus, the fundamental notion at the heart of Nāgārjuna's system is emptiness (*śūnyatā*), the affirmation that all is empty of self-existence.

Buddhist nondualism of Nāgārjuna's variety is different from the Hindu nondualism of Śaṅkara. Nāgārjuna's nondualism does not affirm a single nondual reality that lies beneath the unreal world of experience. Rather, Nāgārjuna's nondualism argues that conventional reality is nondual because it is fundamentally interrelated or relational. The reifying conceptual processes that lead one to believe that reality is thing-like, composed of a plurality of unrelated entities, is produced by craving and ignorance. Liberation here means removing those affective and cognitive afflictions that obscure persons from understanding the interrelatedness of all reality.

The implications of these two different kinds of nondualism for the relationship between science and religion are intriguing. Nondualist Hindus are freer to say that religion and science are unrelated and independent ventures because religious persons seek to know the infinite reality of *brahman* that undergirds all things but is itself beyond all particulars. Scientists are free to pursue their own investigations as are the religious because both attend to different dimensions of reality. Science explores conventionality but religion inquires about the ultimate truth of *brahman*. In the terms used by the philosopher Harold H. Oliver (1984), it is possible to read Advaitins as subscribing to a "compartment theory" of the relationship between religious and scientific truth because each has for its object a different "domain."

Unlike Advaitins, Buddhist nondualists of Nāgārjuna's variety cannot say that science and religion are inquiring about different domains. For Madhyamaka, there is no ultimate reality that lies beneath the conventional realm. Ultimate truth is simply seeing that everything conventional is empty of own-being. Emptiness is not an ultimate reality behind the world of phenomena. Thus science and religion must be two "complementary" ways of interrogating the same domain of conventional experience.

Buddhist nondualists, therefore, can more strongly expect that scientific knowledge should disclose that the world of experience is fundamentally relational. Just how and where this relationality will show itself is not the concern of Buddhist thinkers, although Buddhists do point to the strong parallels between Madhyamaka Buddhism and quantum mechanics. At a still deeper level, Buddhist thinkers can be suspicious of scientific models that imagine reality to be particulate, composite, and unrelated. Such models cannot falsify Buddhist intuitions because Buddhists maintain that spiritual transformation is required before persons are capable of experiencing reality as radically relational. Scientists are not themselves committed to these technologies of transformation but rather to technologies of experimentation. Consequently, Buddhists can have robust expectations about what the sciences are likely to discover and can celebrate those discoveries that seem consonant with Buddhist intuitions, but they need not predict or control scientific research.

Ultimate truth and scientific truth: comparative judgments

Christian liberation theologians and others committed to particular conceptions of the just social order called for by God may be constrained to be more intrusive in their stance towards the sciences, especially the social sciences. Such intrusion need not be supernaturalistic or irrational in character. For liberation theologians, scientific theories that mandate the inevitability of economic disparity are morally and theologically suspect, as are visions of the social order that suggest that coercion and hierarchy are unavoidable. Because such visions imply that a just, equitable, and free social ordering is impossible, they render liberation impossible, thus contradicting what the God of justice requires. Such *prima facie* contradictions can lead theologians to maintain that the science in question is pseudo-science or that unwarranted conclusions have been drawn from data capable of being otherwise interpreted.

The natural sciences are also suspect insofar as they suggest that human beings do not have the freedom or capacity to structure personal and social life in just and compassionate ways. Thus, if evolutionary biology or behavioral psychology is employed to undercut theological commitments to visions of full human flourishing, such scientific claims are subject to critical scrutiny and suspicion.

It is safe to assume that Christian theologians of liberation are in general more likely than Buddhists to question the putatively authoritative discoveries of natural or social science. This possibility suggests that such theologians allow for what Oliver would call a "conflict theory" model of the relationship between religion and science, rather than a compartment or complementarity model, because both modes of inquiry are making incompatible claims about the same domain of experience in the same respect.

These differing approaches to liberation seem to be intimately tied to each tradition's understanding of ultimate reality. Hindus can, in principle, maintain that the quest for liberation can be radically independent and non-intrusive about matters scientific. Christian claims about liberation, on the other hand, are not about a transcendent reality that is unrelated to conventional reality (as *brahman* is). The possibility of conflict between what is theologically required and what the sciences indicate cannot be overlooked.

For Buddhist thinkers, liberation is understood primarily as the transforming insight that enables one to recognize the radically relational character of reality, a recognition that generates compassion. While the emphasis on compassion is shared across traditions, Christian understandings of liberation are intimately connected to reordering contingent economic and sociopolitical structures so that communities can be freed from oppressive ideologies and structures. A wholly irenic relationship with the natural and social sciences seems unlikely when liberation is so understood. It would appear that Madhyamaka (the Middle School) Buddhists truly do hold the middle ground between Advaitins and Christian liberationists. Although M?dhyamika Buddhists can expect and commend discoveries that confirm their own relational intuitions, they are not compelled to critique the results of particular scientific ventures.

See also BUDDHISM; HINDUISM; KARMA; LIBERATION THEOLOGY; TRANSMIGRATION

Bibliography

Balasubramaniam, Arun. "Explaining Strange Parallels: The Case of Quantum Mechanics and Mādhyamika Buddhism." *International Philosophical Quarterly* 32, no. 2 (1992): 205-223.

Garfield, Jay L., trans. *The Fundamental Wisdom of the Middle Way: Nāgārjuna's Mūlamadhyamakakārikā.* New York: Oxford University Press, 1995.

Gutierrez, Gustavo. *A Theology of Liberation: History, Politics and Salvation.* Maryknoll, N.Y.: Orbis, 1988.

Mansfield, Victor. "Mādhyamika Buddhism and Quantum Mechanics: Beginning a Dialogue." *International Philosophical Quarterly* 29, no. 16 (1989): 371-391.

Mayeda, Sengaku, trans. *A Thousand Teachings: The Upadeśasāhasrī of Śaṇkara.* Albany: State University of New York Press, 1992.

Neville, Robert C., ed. *The Human Condition: A Volume in the Comparative Religious Ideas Project.* Albany: State University of New York Press, 2001.

Oliver, Harold H. "The Complementarity of Theology and Cosmology." In *Relatedness: Essays in Metaphysics and Cosmology.* Macon, Ga.: Mercer University Press, 1984.

Puligandla, Ramakrishna. "Science, Philosophy, and Religion: Quest for a Unitary Vision." In *Reality and Mysticism: Perspectives in the Upaniṣads.* New Delhi, India: D.K. Printworld, 1997.

Thatamanil, John. "Nonduality and Ecstasy: Śaṇkaraand Tillich on Theological Anthropology." Ph.D. diss., Boston University, 2000.

JOHN J. THATAMANIL

LIBERATION THEOLOGY

Liberation theology originated in Latin America during the 1960s in response to poverty, oppression, and failed development strategies. Methodologically it is described as theology "from below," beginning with social-historical reality and analysis and reflecting critically on it in the light of Christian tradition. Through a process of *conscientisation,* oppressed peoples are themselves involved in doing theology. The Exodus theme and the biblical motif of God's option for the poor are used as paradigms for reflection. Other theologies subsequently developed using the same methodology. These include black theology and feminist theology, which respond respectively to racism and sexism. All forms of liberation theology make use of social, economic, or political analysis in order to construct a stable interpretation of the conditions of life from which liberation is sought.

See also ECONOMICS; LIBERATION

JOHN W. DE GRUCHY

LIFE AFTER DEATH

Myths that explain the origin of death have been found among many cultures. Clearly, reflection on death and on life after death belongs to the oldest layers of religion. Yet because of the oral nature of these myths, their approach to the problem of death is relatively unsophisticated. A steady progress became possible only after the Greek invention of simplified writing. This process has continued through the twentieth century, and philosophy and theology, directly or indirectly, have exerted the most important influences on religious thinking about life after death.

The terms *soul* and *otherworld* have not always carried the same meanings during the course of history. "Primitive" conceptions of the soul were usually of two types: the so-called *free-soul,* which represents the individual personality but which becomes inactive when the body is active, and thus represents the person after death; and the *body-soul,* which endows the body with life and consciousness, and which perishes with the body. This dualistic conception of the soul changes when small "primitive" peoples become more differentiated. In these cases, the free-soul starts to acquire the qualities of the body-soul. The process is well documented in ancient Greece, where, after Homer, the free-soul (*psyche*), started to incorporate the *thymos,* the most important of these body-souls. As for the underworld, modern people are so used to thinking in terms of heaven and hell that they must be careful not to retroject them into earlier civilizations. Like ideas about the soul, conceptions of life after death have a history too.

Ancient Israel and ancient Greece

Even a cursory look at the Old Testament reveals that it has little to say about either soul or afterlife. In fact, ancient Hebrew does not even have a term equivalent to the modern English word *soul.* The closest equivalent is *nephesh,* which can be translated "life" or "life-force," but which can also signify the seat of emotions. Yet this term never refers to the "soul" of the dead, nor is it ever contrasted with the body. Israelite anthropology was strictly unitarian and remained so until influenced by the Greeks after Alexander the Great (356–323 B.C.E.). The grave must have played an important role in ancient Hebrew culture, since "to go down into the grave" (Gen. 37:35) is equivalent to "to go down into Sheol" (King James, Ps. 16:10). Sheol was a place located beneath the Earth, filled with worms and impossible to escape from, where the shadow-like deceased were supposed to continue their earthly existence. However, the scarcity of references to Sheol suggests that ideas about life after death were vague and played little role in the imagination of the early Israelites.

Ancient Greece presents a different situation. In Homer (c. 800 B.C.E.), who constitutes the earlist Greek source, the soul (*psyche*) does not yet have any connection with the emotions of living people. Yet in contrast with ancient Israel, the Greek notion of soul does represent people after their deaths. The soul goes straight to the underworld, Hades, an area located under the Earth, but also in the west; the soul can reach this "mirthless place" only by crossing the river Styx. The Greek picture of the underworld is bleak and sombre, causing the dead Achilles to remark: "do not try to make light of death to me; I would sooner be bound to the soil in the hire of another man, a man without lot and without much to live on, than be ruler over all the perished dead" (*Iliad* 11.489–491).

This traditional picture became radically nuanced in southern Italy during the fifth century B.C.E by Pythagoras (c. 570–495 B.C.E.) and the Orphics. The former is seen by many as the inventor of Western notions of reincarnation and celestial immortality. Unfortunately, information about the origin of ideas about reincarnation is scarce. It may well be that Pythagoras developed the idea in order to give his aristocratic followers new status in a time when the aristocracy was under stress. In any case, his new vision presupposed the idea of the immortality of the soul, an idea popularized by Plato (428–347 B.C.E.). Belief in celestial immortality became more evident around 432 B.C.E., when an official war monument pronounced the souls of fallen Athenians to have been received by the *aithêr* (upper air), but their bodies by the Earth. Shortly after Pythagoras, the Orphics, an intellectual movement named after the mythical poet Orpheus, introduced ideas about an attractive afterlife in the shape of a "symposium of the pure," where sinners had to wallow in the mud in a kind of hell. The contours of the Christian distinction between heaven and hell, then, first became visible in the fifth century B.C.E. This did not mean that the older

ideas disappeared. On the contrary, belief in a life after death remained limited to a small group of intellectuals; most ordinary Greeks did not seem to have expected much of an afterlife. "After death every man is earth and shadow: nothing goes to nothing," states a character in Euripides' play *Meleagros,* and it is this attitude that predominantly survived into the Roman and Byzantine periods, even among Christians.

A startling new conception of the afterlife developed after Alexander the Great spread Greek civilization into the Mediterranean world in the last decades of the fourth century B.C.E. Before this time, the Greeks had denied the possibility of resurrection, but the publication of the Aramaic fragments of Enoch in 1976 show that among an as yet unidentified group of Jews the belief in resurrection, which is absent in the Old Testament, had become apparent already in the early second century B.C.E., although it was not until the Maccabean revolt that it became widely popular. Moreover, the same book of Enoch mentions heaven and hell. It seems likely that intellectual Jews had made contact with Greeks, probably in Alexandria, and had received information about Orphic views of the afterlife.

Although several groups of Jewish intellectuals, such as the Sadducees, the Essenes, and the community of Qumran (that has given us the Dead Sea Scrolls) continued to reject resurrection, others like the Pharisees enthusiastically took up the idea. However, the resurrection was not exported outside the Jewish world until the appearance of Jesus of Nazareth, although Jesus himself did not believe in the restoration of the former body, since the resurrected would be "like angels" (Matt. 22:23–33). The caution of Jesus was soon abandoned by his followers. In fact, Christian apologists and theologians spent an enormous amount of energy explaining and defending the resurrection, beginning with Paul's words: "For if the dead rise not, then is Christ not raised. And if Christ be not raised, your faith is vain" (1 Cor. 15:16–17). Indeed, all four gospels reach their dramatic climax with reports of Jesus' resurrection. Paul seems also to have been the first to present Jesus' resurrection as the beginning of the collective eschatological resurrection, whereas in traditional Jewish thought individual resurrection, as in the case of Jesus, had been typical only of martyrs, such as the Maccabees. This intellectual Christian effort becomes more understandable against the backdrop of Greek skepticism regarding the afterlife, a skepticism that was shared by the Romans, who had virtually no idea of an afterlife and, correspondingly, lacked an idea of an immortal soul.

The early Christian era and the Middle Ages

Early Christian ideas regarding life after death received great stimulus through the Roman persecutions. Whereas the New Testament had been reticent about the actual nature of the afterlife, it now became necessary to develop a picture that would help martyrs persist in their faith. Reports of executions of Christians during this time show the gradual appearance of new views of the afterlife, not surprisingly beginning in North Africa where funerary attention was more prominent than elsewhere in the Roman empire. Inspired by the Jewish idea of paradise as the place for the deceased, as well as by the great parks of contemporary local grandees, there arises an idea of heaven as an attractive landscape with a mild climate and plenty of light, where the deceased walk around in the body. Their main activity consists in praising God. This theocentric view of heaven would dominate until the Enlightenment. Hell, on the other hand, is little mentioned in the Christian literature of the first centuries C.E. Early Christian theologians were primarily interested in salvation, not damnation.

At the same time, the Jewish heritage of Christianity meant that a marked body-soul opposition was introduced relatively late in the second century by Christian intellectuals, such as Justin (c. 100–165) and Tatian (late second century), who were heavily influenced by Greek philosophy. They tapped Greek concepts of the immortal soul in order to bolster their arguments for the resurrection, albeit with a number of modifications, such as different fates for sinners and saved. Speculation about the soul, fed by Stoic and Aristotelian views, occasionally appears in the writings of later Church fathers like Origen (c. 185–254) or Augustine of Hippo (354–430), but they did not much influence ideas about life after death.

It is only in the early Middle Ages that a major change in attitude towards the afterlife appears. Christianity's growth from a minority into a majority, coupled with Augustine's stress on sin, led to an emphasis on hell rather than heaven in medieval views of life after death. Whereas Origen had argued for the temporary nature of hell, theologians like Augustine and Gregory the Great (c. 540–604) started to paint the penalties of hell in the most shrill of colors. The latter was more concrete than the former and thought that the penalties of hell started immediately after death, unlike Augustine and the early Church Fathers, who most often let them begin after the Last Judgment.

In the twelfth century, ideas about life after death became more differentiated. The Church introduced Purgatory as a third place for the dead, where they could be purified from their sins before they go to heaven. Strangely enough, the intellectual milieu where Purgatory was invented is still uncertain, but there are indications of a Cistercian origin, fueled by the need to counter the eschatology of the Cathars who had made salvation much easier than normative Christianity. Although the tripartite division of life after death was never accepted by Greek-Orthodox Christianity, it was promoted by scholastic theologians like Thomas Aquinas (c. 1225–1274). They did not agreed on all details, and disagreed in particular on the moment when the elect would attain full beatitude and the precise relationship between body and soul. Nonetheless, this general picture of the afterlife did not change significantly until the Reformation.

The Reformation and the Enlightenment

With the arrival of Martin Luther (1483–1546) and John Calvin (1509–1564) on the theological scene in the sixteenth century, God returned to center stage. The Reformation rejected Purgatory and, like post-Tridentine Catholic theologians, concentrated on the encounter with God in the hereafter. Until the eighteenth century, Western Christianity was united in seeing heaven as the place for the elect, where life was perfected by existing with God, without decay, but also without everything that characterizes human life, such as sex, illness, and family. The idea of hell, on the other hand, was increasingly questioned, especially after the reprinting of Origen's works during the Renaissance and after a rise in sensitivity towards the suffering of others.

During the Enlightenment, both Christians and adherents of natural religion could still agree on the idea of the immortal soul, but for the first time in Western history materialists and atheists could publicly, if guardedly, pronounce their views. They went too far for the majority, but in varying ways philosophers like Thomas Hobbes (1588–1679), John Locke (1637–1704), Denis Diderot (1713–1787), and Voltaire (1694–1778) now openly brought belief in eternal punishment into discredit. David Hume (1711–1776) could even claim, not without exaggeration, that the damnation of one man was an infinitely greater evil than the subversion of millions of kingdoms. It seems safe to say that ever since this time the traditional picture of hell has remained unacceptable to enlightened classes.

The picture of a static, theocentric heaven could also no longer satisfy an age more interested in man than God. Starting with Gottfried Wilhelm Leibnitz (1646–1716), but especially in the work of Emanuel Swedenborg (1688–1772), ideas about life in heaven became adapted to the anthropocentric needs of the time. Swedenborg promoted a view of heaven that was not so different from life on Earth. According to Swedenborg, the souls of the deceased entered a spirit world where human frailties were clearly visible. Only after perfecting their spiritual outlook could souls move on to heaven, where they became angels. Here, life on Earth was continued but in a more attractive setting of parks and palaces. Eating, drinking, and sexuality remained vital needs, friends and family could be met, and progress meant that men and women became more and more like "noble savages." Condemnations to eternal torment or a Last Judgement had no place in this vision. Such a stress on heaven in the era of the Enlightenment may be surprising, but in fact in Germany in the 1750s alone more than fifty treatises appeared discussing the problem of immortality. Evidently, growing scepticism led to deepened interest in defending immortality.

The nineteenth and twentieth centuries

Swedenborg's view coincided, and was probably part of, the Romantic interest in love between man and wife, and this interest was shared by Protestants and Catholics alike. Although Swedenborg was viciously attacked, even by Immanual Kant (1724–1804), he was triumphant, especially in America. The Transcendentalists became much enamored of Swedenborg's thought, and their influence was felt in America and Europe. The Unitarians in England, in particular, embraced the new

insights against the more traditional views of the established churches. They began stressing that heaven consisted in "enjoying God through accordance with his attributes, multiplying its bounds and sympathies with excellent beings, putting forth noble powers and ministering, in union with the enlightened and holy, to the happiness and virtue of the universe" (Channing, pp. 225–226). Moreover, after Charles Darwin (1809–1882), this enjoyment was seen as the end of a long evolution. Immortality became a possibility rather than a reality. Similar conceptions of the afterlife were widely promoted in Germany as well. Naturally, even heaven could not escape the lure of Victorian "Muscular Christianity": "Want and pain, toil and trial, cannot be wholly banished out of *my* Heaven," wrote the brother of Cardinal Newman (Newman, p 34).

The heyday of Unitarian theology coexisted with the birth of spiritualism (1848). This movement would be the last attempt at proving scientifically the existence of the hereafter by means of controlled experiments. Yet the success of spiritualism would be short–lived; it was soon discredited by the frauds of its adherents and the trivialities of its results. Still, during its heyday, especially in America and England, its picture of heaven conformed closely to that developed by Swedenborg. Moreover, its rejection of hell, sin, and guilt was widely shared by liberal theologians everywhere.

By the end of the nineteenth century, the general picture of life after death had assumed the contours of what would be the rule for most of the twentieth century. Hell was no longer the subject of serious theological discussion and eventually disappeared even from folk belief, except perhaps for that of the most conservative Christians. In the wake of its demise and with the rise of a more materialistic view of the person, the idea of an immortal soul lost wide acceptance. Many people still believe in heaven, but it is no longer the subject of serious intellectual debate. Leading theologians, such as Reinhold Niebuhr (1892–1971) and Paul Tillich (1886–1965), even pronounced their hesitations about eternal life. Admittedly, systematic theologians have not given up presenting new eschatological designs, but none has found success in the last decades of the twentieth century. Not surprisingly, mainline churches have stopped worrying about the afterlife, since their members are too much concerned with this life. It seems that the world of theology, of rational reflection on life after death, is no longer influential among common believers.

Relection on life after death has not broken down completely, however. Among adherents of the so-called New Age there is a new interest in the soul, which is considered to be a part of the Higher Self, the New Age notion of an interface between the Universal Mind, or God, and the individual personality. It is the soul that continuously creates new lives and chooses its present incarnation. In other words, there no longer is a definite "Beyond" as the final resting point, but the soul is perpetually en route towards its spiritual perfection via reincarnation.

Finally, life after death has come once again to the fore in discussions of so-called near-death experiences, as first collected in the 1970s by Raymond Moody, an American philosopher turned psychiatrist. In these experiences, which relate a visit to the hereafter, the idea of a life after death seems to reflect widely ruling modern ideas: the dead go to heaven, but God is no longer there; the soul is not mentioned, and neither is hell or judgement. Scholarly discussions concentrate on the nature of these experiences, the age of those who have these visions, and the medical circumstances allowing such visions. Yet serious scholars no longer discuss these visions as testimonies of a postmortem existence. It seems that after a 2,500-year discussion, the problem of life after death has largely been abandoned.

See also DARWIN, CHARLES; HUME, DAVID; REINCARNATION; SOUL; THOMAS AQUINAS; TRANSMIGRATION

Bibliography

Almond, Philip C. *Heaven and Hell in Enlightenment England.* Cambridge, UK: Cambridge University Press, 1994.

Beck, Hans G. *Die Byzantiner und ihr Jenseits.* Munich, Germany: Verlag der Bayerischen Akademie der Wissenschaften,1979.

Bremmer, Jan N. *The Early Greek Concept of the Soul.* Princeton, N.J.: Princeton University Press, 1983.

Bremmer, Jan N. *The Rise and Fall of the Afterlife: The 1995 Read-Tuckwell Lectures at the University of Bristol.* London and New York: Routledge, 2002.

Channing, W. E. *Works,* 6 vols. Glasgow, UK: 1840.

Friedman, R. E., and Overton, S. D. "Death and Afterlife: the Biblical Silence." In *Judaism in Late Antiquity.* Vol. 4: *Death, Life-After-Death, Resurrection, and The World-to-Come in the Judaisms of Antiquity,* eds. Alan J. Avery-Peck and Jacob Neusner. Leiden, Netherlands, and New York: Brill, 2000.

Hällström, Gunnar af. *Carnis resurrectio: The Interpretation of a Credal Formula.* Helsinki, Finland: Societas Scientiarum Fennica, 1988..

Hanegraaff, Wouter J. *New Age Religion and Western Culture: Esotericism in the Mirror of Secular Thought.* Leiden, Netherlands, and New York: Brill, 1996.

Hick, John. *Death and Eternal Life.* New York: Harper, 1976.

Holleman, Joost. *Resurrection and Parousia: A Traditio-Historical Study of Paul's Eschatology in 1 Corinthians 15.* Leiden, Netherlands, and New York: Brill, 1997.

McDannell, Colleen, and Lang, Bernhard. *Heaven: A History,* 2nd edition. New Haven, Conn., and London: Yale Nota Bene, 2001.

McManners, John. *Death and the Enlightenment: Changing Attitudes to Death in Eighteenth-Century France.* New York and Oxford: Oxford University Press, 1981.

Moody, Raymond, A., Jr. *Life after Life: The Investigation of a Phenomenon—Survival of Bodily Death.* Atlanta, Ga.: Bantam, 1975.

Newman, Francis William. *Life after Death? Palinodia.* London: Trübner, 1886.

Nickelsburg, George. *Resurrection, Immortality, and Eternal Life in Intertestamental Judaism.* Cambridge, Mass.: Harvard University Press, 1972.

Nickelsburg, George. "Resurrection." In *Encyclopaedia of the Dead Sea Scrolls,* 2 vols., eds. Lawrence Schiffman and James C. VanderKam. New York: Oxford University Press, 2000.

Parker, R. "Early Orphism." In *The Greek World,* ed. Anton Powell. London and New York, Warwick Press, 1987.

Rowell, Geoffrey. *Hell and the Victorians: A Study of the Nineteenth-Century Theological Controversies Concerning Eternal Punishment and the Future Life.* Oxford: Clarendon Press, 1974.

Russell, Jeffrey Burton. *A History of Heaven: The Singing Silence.* Princeton, N.J.: Princeton University Press, 1997.

University of Virginia Department of Psychiatric Medicine, Division of Personality Studies: *Studying How Mind and Brain Relate and the Question of Postmortem Survival.* Available from: http://hsc.virginia.edu/personality-studies.

van Baaren. Th. P. "Death." In *Death, Afterlife, and the Soul,* ed. Lawrence E. Sullivan. New York and London: Macmillan, 1989.

van Uytfanghe, M. "Platonisme et eschatologie chrétienne: Leur symbiose graduelle dans les Passions et les panégyriques des martyrs et dans les biographies spirituelles (IIe–VIe s.)." In *Fructus centesimus: Mélanges offerts à Gerard J. M. Bertelink à l'occasion de son soixante-cinquième anniversaire,* eds. A. A. R. Bastiaensen, A. Hilhorst, and C. H. Kneepkens. Dordrecht, Netherlands: Kluwer, 1989.

van Uytfanghe, M. "Platonisme II." In *De Tertullien aux Mozarabes: Mélanges offerts à Jacques Fontaine, à l'ccasion de son 70e anniversaire,* 3 vols., eds. Louis Holtz and Jean-Claude Fredouille. Paris: Institut d'études augustiniennes, 1992.

Walker, Daniel Pickering. *The Decline of Hell: Seventeenth-Century Discussions of Eternal Torment.* Chicago: University of Chicago Press, 1964.

JAN BREMMER

LIFE, BIOLOGICAL ASPECTS

Biologically, life, as contrasted with death or with nonliving objects, is an evident fact but difficult to characterize precisely. Living organisms are self-maintaining systems; they grow and are irritable in response to stimuli. They resist dying. They reproduce. The developing embryo is especially impressive. Organisms post a defended, semipermeable boundary between themselves and the outside world; they assimilate environmental materials to their own needs. They can be healthy or diseased. Some accounts claim that the minimal form of autonomy necessary and sufficient for characterizing biological life is what is termed autopoiesis, literally self-making. Some defense of a "self" (a somatic self, having to do with the body, rather than a psychological self) is thus required.

Living organisms gain and maintain internal order against the disordering tendencies of external nature. They keep recomposing themselves, while inanimate things run down, erode, and decompose. Organisms pump out disorder. Life, as physicist Erwin Schrödinger notes in his 1945 work, *What is Life?,* is a local countercurrent to entropy, an energetic fight uphill in a world that overall moves thermodynamically downhill.

The organism as system

The constellation of these characteristics is nowhere found outside living organisms, although some of them can be mimicked or analogically extended to products designed by living systems, such as computers, and some are found in spontaneous abiotic nature. A crystal reproduces a pattern and may restore a damaged surface; a planetary system continues in an equilibrium; a volcano may grow in countercurrent to entropy. A lenticular altocumulus cloud, formed as a standing wave over a mountain range, is steadily recomposed by input and output of air flow. A target-seeking missile adjusts its course by environmental feedback. Computers are cognitive processors and can be running well or poorly.

The know-how for life is coded into genetic sets, which are missing in minerals, volcanoes, clouds, computers, and target-seeking missiles. An organism is thus a spontaneous cybernetic system, self-maintaining with a control center, sustaining and reproducing itself on the basis of information about how to make its way through the world. There is some internal representation that is symbolically mediated in the coded "program" and metabolism executing this goal, a checking against performance in the world, using some sentient, perceptive, or other responsive capacities by which to compare match and mismatch. On the basis of information received, the cybernetic system can reckon with vicissitudes, opportunities, and adversities that the world presents.

Organisms employ physical and chemical causes, but, distinctive to life, there is "information" superintending the causes. This information is a modern equivalent of what Aristotle (384–322 B.C.E.) called formal and final causes; it gives the organism a telos, or end, but not always a felt or conscious end-in-view. Formerly, biologists looked for entelechy, some distinctive component in organisms not found in merely physicochemical systems. Although entelechy was never found, the major discovery of biologists in the last half century has been massive amounts of information coded in DNA, a sort of linguistic molecule.

Living organisms impose a code on four nucleotide bases strung as cross links on a double helix. A triplet of bases stands for one of the twenty amino acids, and by a serial "reading" of the DNA, "translated" by messenger RNA, a long polypeptide chain is synthesized, such that its sequential structure predetermines the bioform into which it will fold. Ever-lengthening chains are organized into genes. Diverse proteins, lipids, carbohydrates, enzymes—all the life structures—are thus "written into" the genetic library.

The DNA representing life is thus, to continue analogies, a "cognitive set," not less than a biological set. Organisms use these molecular positions to code the information necessary for life. In this sense, the genome is a set of conservation molecules. The novel resourcefulness lies in the epistemic content conserved, developed, and thrown forward to make biological resources out of the physicochemical sources. The presence of this executive program is often said to be cybernetic, a word recalling a governor or helmsman. An open cybernetic system is partly a special kind of cause and effect system, partly a historical information system discovering and evaluating ends so as to map and make a way through the world, and partly a system of significances attached to operations, pursuits, resources.

Threshold of life

DNA codes a life that is carried on not merely at the level described above, but at the environmental, phenotypical level. What occurs at the level of molecular biology manifests itself, via a complicated translation and interaction from genotypic to phenotypic levels (i.e., from the microscopic level of the genes to the macro level of the whole organism). This translation occurs at the native ranges, where such life is selected for or against as it is defended in its environment. With this process in mind some analysts to define as alive whatever is subject to natural selection, thus presuming also mutation. These features typically do characterize life. Critics of this definition respond that some things (such as viruses or groups of organisms) are subject to natural selection but are not alive. Also, life sometimes continues with much reduced natural selection. This is seen in human in their cultural environment. This phenomenon is also witnessed in clonal organisms that are all genetically identical or in relatively constant environments where most genetic changes result from mutations that are categorized as drift (i.e., functional changes that neutral to survival, neither beneficial nor detrimental).

Various thresholds or borderlines of life are disputed. A person may be considered "brain

dead," although somatically the heart is still beating (often with a mechanical respirator). Many biologists hold that viruses are not (fully) alive, but are anomalous self-reproducing DNA fragments that parasitize living cells, largely borrowing most of their vital metabolisms from the host cell. Viruses are not self-contained, not cellular, but must be contained within other selves and cells. Computer advances have raised the possibility of "artificial life," with debates about what would count as a living computer, or perhaps as a living program, within a computer. Some organic molecules are known from space, but no extraterrestrial life is yet known. Scientists, philosophers, and theologians speculate, often intensely, about whether such life is likely to be present.

See also LIFE, RELIGIOUS AND PHILOSOPHICAL ASPECTS; LIFE SCIENCES

Bibliography

Kauffman, Stuart A. *The Origins of Order: Self-organization and Selection in Evolution.* Oxford: Oxford University Press, 1993.

Maturana, Humberto R., and Varela, Francisco J. *Autopoiesis and Cognition: The Realization of the Living.* Dordrecht, Netherlands, and Boston: D. Reidel, 1980.

Maynard Smith, John, and Szathmáry, Eörs. *The Origins of Life.* Oxford: Oxford University Press, 1999.

Rosen, Robert. *Life Itself: A Comprehensive Inquiry into the Nature, Origin, and Fabrication of Life.* New York: Columbia University Press, 1991.

Schrödinger, Erwin. *What Is Life?* Cambridge, UK: Cambridge University Press, 1945.

HOLMES ROLSTON, III

LIFE, ORIGINS OF

Fossilized microbes or their chemical traces have been found in the oldest rocks on Earth. These rocks, which are about 3.8 billion years old, draw a picture of the structurally complex and metabolically sophisticated microbiota that already existed at that time. This leaves for the emergence of living things on Earth only a relatively short period of less than three hundred million years. During that period, complicated metabolic pathways must have developed. How?

Many religious as well as philosophical ideas assume that the interference with matter by a creative force or a creator results in the appearance of self-replicating life. Often the teleological character of living things in combination with a lack of understanding of natural processes leads to the conclusion that life is, in principle, "not of this world." In contract, the materialistic philosophical tradition interprets life as the most refined form of self-organizing matter.

It is an enormous intellectual challenge to explain the transition from lifeless chemistry to biology. The possible scenarios for this transition push scientific theories, worldviews, and the imagination to their limits. The following questions need to be answered. How is it possible that the beautifully well-balanced and encapsulated web of interaction that constitutes a living cell arose unintended from abiotic building blocks? How did its metabolism evolve? How could it happen that all the information that a parent cell needs to reproduce itself in the form of progeny was written in the chemical letters of the DNA molecule? And what was the first step that linked information (DNA) to function (proteins)? None of these questions has yet been answered by experimental evidence, however, numerous theories propose plausible scenarios that could result in the appearance of all living things. In addition, chemists have recreated chemical reactions that result in the formation of numerous of the most essential organic building blocks, such as amino acids and nucleic acids. Chemists have so far failed, however, to reconstruct the abiological formation under prebiotic conditions of the molecule ribose, which is essential to life as the backbone of DNA and RNA molecules. It has also been shown that amphiphilic compounds, such as fatty acids, spontaneously self-assemble and form encapsulated spheres, which separate into an "inside" from an "outside," and thus represent the origin of *compartimentation.* The most prominent of theories about the origin of life will be presented in this entry, and some of the problems related to the models will be discussed.

The Oparin-Haldane model

The Oparin-Haldane model of prebiotic evolution and cell formation was developed independently during the 1920s by British biologist J. B. S. Haldane and Soviet biochemist Aleksandr Oparin. According to the Oparin-Haldane model, organic molecules were formed in the reducing atmosphere of the early Earth and then accumulated in the oceans, where a thin organic solution, the so-called primordial soup, formed. In addition to the atmospheric source of organics, the theory also considers input from comets and certain types of meteorites as an important source of organic building blocks.

In the primordial soup, amphiphilic molecules, such as fatty acids, continuously formed small fatty droplets called *coacervates.* During self-assembly these coacervates encapsulated a small amount of the soup, which supplied them with building blocks and energy sources. Further coacervates grew by incorporation of more amphiphilic compounds until they became large enough to be unstable, resulting in coacervate division. Even during the coacervate state, competition and selection among these structures were driving a progressive evolution. The Oparin-Haldane model assumed that the original way of feeding was *heterotrophic,* which means that the cellular structures grew by assimilation of prefabricated organic building blocks that also served as energy sources. Overall, the model supposes that cells came first, proteins second, and genes third.

The major contribution of the Oparin-Haldane model to the scientific origin of life debate was to link abiotic chemistry to the history of life. Haldane and Oparin broke with the powerful and experimentally supported paradigm of the French chemist Louis Pasteur that only life can be the source of new life and that life can not arise spontaneously from a nonliving material. Despite its narrative eloquence, the Oparin-Haldane model has serious scientific shortcomings: (1) The atmosphere of the early Earth was most likely different and less reduced than the Oparin-Haldane model requires for the synthesis of all the molecules necessary for prebiotic synthesis; (2) The intensity of ultraviolet radiation on the surface of the ocean would have constrained the accumulation of prebiotic molecules. In addition, complex molecules are less stable when dissolved in water, which seriously limits the formation of information and function-carrying macromolecules like RNA, DNA, and proteins; and (3) Prebiotic synthesis produces only small amounts of the desired organic compounds.

Template-based models

Clay-based template. Some scientists have proposed alternatives to the primeval soup model that can be summarized as *template-based* origin of life models. One of them, the *clay-based* origin of life theory, attributes to microcrystals of clay both an informational and a catalytic function. According to the theory, the matrix of clay contains a regular array of ionic sites, which are occupied by irregularly alternating patterns of metal ions such as magnesium or aluminum. The pattern of alternating metal ions contains information similar to the patterns of nucleic acids in DNA or RNA molecules. Organic molecules, which are present in the environment of clay crystals, may have been attracted by the electrostatic potential of the metal ions and positioned themselves in a way that facilitates a chemical reaction between the adsorbed molecules (i.e., those attached to the surface). In this scenario, clay surfaces have a catalytic function comparable to those of proteins. The information content of clay crystals was transferred to a new generation of crystals by accreting silicate and metals from the surrounding water and by reproducing the original pattern of metal ions associated with the new clay matrix. It may be that clay-based life existed for millions of years but was finally out-competed by RNA-based life, which had much better chemical properties, and all traces of these original clay-based life forms disappeared.

The clay model has two major strengths: (1) A variety of clays do in fact catalyze the polymerization of organic compounds under conditions that are realistic for the early Earth; (2) Stereospecific amino acid binding and polymerization have been demonstrated. Among several weaknesses of the clay model are: (1) a lack of environmental settings that support clay evolution and stability; (2) the late development of *cellularization*; and (3) the inability of the model to explain the relation between microorganisms and the presumed traits of early life.

Pyrite-based template. While the clay-model, like the Oparin-Haldane model, assumes that the organic molecules necessary for cell formation and polymerization were provided by a thin soup in the surroundings of the clay crystals, the *pyrite-based* template model rejects this concept and postulates the inorganic origin of life instead. In this scenario, organic molecules were synthesized in high temperature environments comparable to hydrothermal vents on the surface of growing pyrite crystals, which form from the reaction between ferrous sulfide and hydrogen sulfide. During the process of pyrite formation, electrons are released, which, due to the catalytic properties of the pyrite crystal, can be transferred directly to carbon dioxide. (In a later version of the theory based on experimental results, carbon monoxide replaced carbon dioxide.) In this process, simple reduced compounds like formic and acetic acid were formed. In addition to their catalytic properties, the positive charge of pyrite crystals allows them to retain the newly-synthesized negatively-charged organic molecules. Consequently, organic molecules accumulated on the pyrite surface, steadily coating it with an organic layer in a process of cellularization. It can thus also be attributed a selective property of the surface charge of the pyrite crystal: Molecules that do not stick to the crystal are lost by diffusion and do not participate in further processes. As simple molecules polymerized on the surface of the pyrite crystal, gradually more complex molecules were formed, including a membrane-like layer, which enclosed the pyrite crystal. In the pyrite model, metabolism came first. For a long time, competing cell-like structures resulted exclusively from the structuring properties of the pyrite crystal, which both served as the energy and electron source for carbon fixation, and as a cellularization nucleus without the involvement of information carriers such as RNA and DNA.

Unlike the other models, it is a major concern of the proponents of the pyrite model that all specific predictions, at least in principle, stand up to experimental investigation. Hitherto, several predictions deduced from the pyrite model have been verified experimentally. In addition, the presence of iron sulfur clusters in the catalytic centers of ancient enzymes has been interpreted as the remains of a pyrite past. Still the model is not without problems. Most of the criticism concerns the environmental sites where pyrite life potentially could have occurred. Hydrothermal vents are relatively short-lived structures, which limits the time available to pyrite-based life formation at a particular site. In addition, the high temperature, which may be required for some types of synthesis, may effect other processes negatively. Another serious concern addresses the phosphate necessary for the initial surface binding of organic compounds to pyrite. Because of precipitation, typical vent environments are strongly depleted in phosphate. If the same holds true for ancient vent systems, it is difficult to explain how life could have originated there.

RNA-world model. The most popular scenario of the origin of life is the so-called *RNA-world model,* which elaborates on the Haldane-Oparin theory. The RNA-world model proposes that RNA molecules were the precursors of proteins as catalysts and of DNA as information carriers. This concept gained support when the catalytic properties of modern RNA molecules were demonstrated. Proponents of this theory introduced the term *ribozyme,* which stresses the functional similarity of RNA molecules to protein molecules, in addition to their already established role as informational molecules. The following scenario has been outlined for the development of the RNA world: (1) Short RNA molecules formed from random combination of mononucleotides; (2) Some oligonucleotide structurally include the potential of catalyzing the synthesis of complementary copies of themselves, with the chemical energy for the process provided by reactive molecules combined with the mononucleotides; (3) RNA molecules developed that catalyzed their own synthesis, and as a consequence evolution by natural selection became possible.

Stage three in the RNA-world scenario can be summarized by the so-called hypercycle model, which links related RNA molecules in the form of a catalytic cycle. The interaction between RNA molecules was already characterized by a selection-constrained evolution potential. Steps one and two of the RNA-world model have some shortcomings which have yet to be overcome. These shortcomings include the synthesis of important components of the RNA molecule such as sugar ribose and reactive phosphate molecules. It has been proposed that not RNA itself but a simpler RNA-like molecule was at the origin of life.

Self-organizing models

As an alternative to the template-based scenarios described above, scientists have developed a theoretical framework that is based on the concept of *catalytic closure.* Here life started as *autocatalytic* sets of molecules, which means that all the molecules within the set catalyze their formation, and also catalyze the formation of their catalysts. A hypercycle is based on the interaction between RNA molecules. In principle, protein-based cycles or cycles which combine different types of macromolecules may also exist.

The scientific theories of the origin of life presented here are only preliminary and require numerous experiments and sophisticate modeling before they can gain general acceptance. At best, researchers will find answers to most of the open questions. At worst, they will end up producing more questions than they answer. The consequences of such scientific concepts for philosophical and religious traditions are likely to be marginal as the latter address mainly phenotypical expressions of living processes rather than "happenings" in the distant past.

See also AUTOPOEISIS; BIOLOGY; EMERGENCE; EVOLUTION, BIOLOGICAL; LIFE, RELIGIOUS AND PHILOSOPHICAL ASPECTS; LIFE SCIENCES

Bibliography

Brack, Andre, ed. *The Molecular Origins of Life, Assembling Pieces of the Puzzle.* Cambridge, UK: Cambridge University Press, 1998.

Crains-Smith, A. G. *Genetic Takeover and the Mineral Origins of Life.* New York: Cambridge University Press, 1982.

Davies, Paul. *The Fifth Miracle: The Search for the Origin and Meaning of Life.* London: Penguin Books, 1995.

Dyson, Freeman. *Origins of Life.* Cambridge, UK: Cambridge University Press, 1999.

Eigen, Manfred, and Peter, Schuster. *The Hypercycle: A Principle of Natural Self-Organization.* New York: Springer, 1979.

Kauffman, Stuart. *Investigations.* Oxford: Oxford University Press, 2000.

Oparin, Aleksandr. *The Origin of Life on the Earth,* 3rd edition, trans. Ann Synge. Edinburgh, UK: Oliver and Boyd, 1957.

Schrödinger, Erwin. *What is Life: The Physical Aspect of the Living Cell.* Cambridge, UK: Cambridge University Press, 1944.

Wächtershäuser, G. "Groundworks for an Evolutionary Biochemistry: The Iron-Sulfur World." *Progress in Biophysics and Molecular Biology* 58 (1992): 85–201.

KAI FINSTER

LIFE, RELIGIOUS AND PHILOSOPHICAL ASPECTS

Life is literally a biological term but extends by metaphor across a spectrum of key concerns in philosophy and religion. Life is a perennial experience, prescientific and universal in cultures ancient and contemporary, though recent advances in the biological sciences have recast classical ideas about life in new perspectives. By some accounts, molecular biologists decoding the human genome have discovered the "secret of life"; by other accounts evolutionary biologists have discovered the "secret of life" in natural selection. Philosophers, ethicists, and theologians reply with claims that, though science may teach much descriptively about life, it cannot teach how to value life and what one ought to do.

From the dawn of religious impulses, in the only animal capable of such reflection, this vitality has been experienced as sacred. Such experience has often been fragmentary and confused, as has every other form of knowledge that humans have struggled to gain, but at its core the insight developed that religion was about an abundant life, about life in its abundance. Classical monotheism—to take the Hebrew form of it—held that the divine Spirit or Wind (Greek: *pneuma*) breathes the breath of life into the dust of the earth and animates it to generate swarms of living beings (Genesis 2:7). Eastern religious forms can be significantly different: *Maya* spun over Brahman, or *samsara* over *sunyata*; but they too detect the sacred in, with, and under the profuse phenomena of life.

If anything is sacred, life is sacred. For theists, life, above all, is a gift from God. Elemental necessities, such as bread, water, blood, breath (*pneuma*), and birth are often taken up as symbols in religions. Native traditions may regard Earth, soil, waters, everything as alive. Scientists may now dismiss this as an innate tendency to be animistic, to ascribe living properties to inanimate forces. But quite sophisticated philosophical systems, such as panpsychism, pantheism, and forms of idealism, have held that ultimate reality is organic or spirit-like.

Organic life

Philosophical and religious concerns about life can be broadly divided into those involving life generically and those focusing on human life. One intense debate arising in the last half century has been over intrinsic value in life, whether organisms have value in themselves, and not simply instrumental value for humans. The background to this debate is an Enlightenment tradition of a value-free nature, seemingly plausible in the inanimate world of stars, asteroids, rocks, or dirt, an account continued by many biologists in a mechanistic biology, which views organisms as nothing but machines. However, contemporary biologists have not only described but come to celebrate the diverse array of forms of life (species, families, phyla), to systematize these, and then lament that humans are placing so many of them in jeopardy. Conservation biology today is as dominant and remarkable as is molecular or evolutionary biology.

The panorama of life on Earth, biologically described, raises issues of whether the species can also be ranked or graded for their worth. Levels of life move from microbes to multicellular plant and animals, with "higher" animals sentient, many of them capable of acquired learning during their lifetimes, and the "higher" of these enjoying psychological experiences, the "highest" of all human life with self-conscious experience, capable of generating meaningful communities gathering into cumulative transmissible cultures. Other thinkers, claiming a more egalitarian and less biased account, object to such hierarchy and anthropocentrism, advocating a biocentrism where all are valued with respect to their multiple and differing achievements and skills, including humans, but not preferential to humans. The capacity for photosynthesis is as valuable on Earth as is the capacity for ethics.

Darwinian natural history reveals an ambiguity in life, often taken to be problematic. Life is a ceaseless struggle; new life is generated by blasting the old. Darwinians may focus on the survival of the fittest, accentuating the competition in life, famously described by the nineteenth century English poet Alfred Lord Tennyson as "Nature, red in tooth and claw." Charles Darwin as well portrays connectedness in life, common ancestry, survival of the best adapted, life support in ecosystems, life persisting in the midst of its perpetual perishing, life generated and regenerated in spectacular biodiversity and complexity, with exuberance displayed over 3.5 billion years, an "abundance of life." Such a view of life echoes ancient religious motifs: Life is a table prepared in the midst of enemies, green pastures in the valley of the shadow of death.

Debate continues over whether the natural history of life on Earth is orderly, probable, inevitable, or contingent; over what mixture of law and openness characterizes it; and whether biological processes are adequate to account for life's origin and evolving diversity and complexity. Molecular biologists have discovered hitherto unsuspected intricacy and complexity at the molecular level, also endorsing life with its unity in diversity, and leaving as intense as ever the religious concerns about what to make of life, and what abundant life is possible and appropriate for humans.

The distinctiveness of human life

Turning to human life, a recurrent issue is whether and how human life is distinctive. The biological sciences evidently supply connections; humans differ in their protein molecules from chimpanzees by only a fraction of a percent. But the startling successes of humans doing biological sciences can as readily prove human distinctiveness: Chimpanzees have no capacities for cumulative transmissible cultures leading to a science by which they can decode their own genes, much less can they debate the ethics of cloning or have their religious convictions challenged by reading Darwin's *Origin of Species*.

Various human activities have their parallels and precursors in animal behaviors; animals get sleepy, angry, suffer pains, enjoy pleasures. Equally, myriads of human capacities are sui generis; animals do not pray, or seek forgiveness for sin, or worry whether the theory of relativity relativizes ethics. Humans are persons, made (as theologians like to say) "in the image of God." They have *Existenz* (as the Existentialists say). Humans anticipate death; they sense their finitude; they face limit questions. They know guilt, forgiveness, shame, remorse, glory, pride. They suffer angst and alienation. They build symbols with which they interpret their place and role in their world. They create ideologies, affirm creeds, and debate their rights and responsibilities. They are capable of religious faith and the worship of God. Many of them sense the sacred, worry about communion with the ultimate, or atonement of their sins. All of this can be summed up in the one word: spirit. In this life of the spirit, humans, latecoming on the planet, remain remarkably distinctive from the other millions of species, indeed the billions that have come and gone over evolutionary time.

One distinctive characteristic of human life is its brokenness, and here the religions classically offer salvation, or the good life. "I have set before you life and death, blessing and curse; therefore choose life" (Deuteronomy 30:19). Jesus says "I am the way, the truth, and the life" (John 14:6). The metaphor may be of new life; one is born again, or regenerated. This re-forming of life appears to many philosophers, ethicists, and theologians to be the area in which biology has so little purchase—the "ought to be"—however much biology has decoded what is describing the metabolisms and evolution of life, or perhaps found so-called *selfish genes* that dispose our behavior.

The relevance of religion to scientific explanations

Humanists may resist claims that biology explains religion, finding the secret of life in genes or in natural section, or finding that religion is (nothing but) a mythical belief system that favors survival. Theologians turn the tables, arguing that religion is needed to explain biology, that the prolific genesis of life on Earth, documented in natural history, generates religious responses. The prolific earthen fertility, or generative capacity, in which humans find themselves immersed, is what most needs to be explained. Humans alone confront the ethical duty of appropriate respect for such life, including their own human life. Nothing in biology settles questions about the meaning of life.

Advances in our biological understanding of life, as well as medical and technological capacities to intervene, have raised new issues that involve the beginning and ending of life (such as cloning, abortion, and euthanasia). Other advances make life more of a commodity (as with farm agriculture, genetically modified crops, stem cell lines, or patented genes).

Ethicists frequently claim that our concern ought to be for quality of life, not just life—and again religious convictions can seem as relevant as biological facts. Biology can set some standards for whether organisms are flourishing or diseased; quasi-evaluative terms such as "health" or "integrity" do have a foundation in biology. Beyond that, the quality of life demands evaluative judgments about right and wrong, censure and blame, good and evil. Life requires choosing a lifestyle. Life demands respect, and this respect passes over, often imperceptibly, to reverence. Though a secular science, biology invites an inquiry into the sacred.

Life has death as its opposite, or complement. Life survives death on Earth by reproducing biologically. Religions ask about the quality of life on Earth, but the inevitable earthen death of individuals raises the question of life after death, of eternal life, of what survives the bodily demise of an individual. Religions answer this question variously. Some, especially Eastern religions, suppose rebirth and reincarnation, a sequence of lives on Earth or in other worlds. Western monotheism, in Islam and Christianity, has favored life on Earth consummated in life in heaven, perhaps by a continuing immortal soul, or spirit, outliving the body, perhaps by a resurrection of the body. A perennial faith expects continued life in the spirit gathered into the Divine Spirit.

See also LIFE, BIOLOGICAL ASPECTS; LIFE SCIENCES

Bibliography

Barbour, Ian G. *Religion and Science: Historical and Contemporary Issues.* San Francisco: Harper, 1997.

Birch, Charles, and Cobb, John B. Jr. *The Liberation of Life: From the Cell to the Community.* Cambridge, UK: Cambridge University Press.

Darwin, Charles. *The Origin of Species* (1859). New York: Bantam Classic, 1999.

Hefner, Philip. *The Human Factor: Evolution, Culture, and Religion.* Minneapolis, Minn.: Fortress Press, 1985,

McCormick, Richard A. "The Quality of Life, the Sanctity of Life." *Hastings Center Report* 8, no. 1 (1978): 20–36.

Pannenberg, Wolfhart. *Anthropology in Theological Perspective.* Philadelphia, Pa.: Westminster Press, 1985.

Peacocke, Arthur R. *Creation and the World of Science.* Oxford: Clarendon Press, 1979.

Rolston, Holmes, III. *Genes, Genesis and God: Values and their Origins in Natural and Human History.* New York: Cambridge University Press, 1999.

Russell, Robert John; Stoeger, William R.; and Ayala, Francisco J. eds. *Evolutionary and Molecular Biology: Scientific Perspectives on Divine Action.* Vatican City: Vatican Observatory Publications, 1998.

Sterelny, Kim, and Griffiths, Paul E. *Sex and Death: An Introduction to Philosophy of Biology.* Chicago: University of Chicago Press, 1991.

HOLMES ROLSTON, III

LIFE SCIENCES

The life sciences, defined as biology and related subjects, encompass the detailed study of living organisms, which are broadly distinguished from inorganic matter through the capacity for growth, function, and change preceding death. Biology is not limited to physiology, the study of the growth and function of living organisms. It also includes the study of biochemical reactions taking place in particular cells of particular organs. At a physical level, biophysics considers, for example, electrical changes taking place across membranes. Even more specific is the field of molecular biology, which attempts to unravel the changes that occur in molecules during biochemical reactions. Genetic science is the study of molecules that act as templates of information for certain biochemical reactions and that are passed on to the next generation. Yet the life sciences include the study of more than just the interior of living organisms and the biological reactions in the cells of living organisms. The life sciences also include ecology, the study of the exterior context of particular environments and the interrelationships between species. More broadly, animal behaviorists examine the way animals react to environments, and psychologists explore the possible reasons for this behavior.

The different life sciences pose challenges to theological and religious interpretations of reality. Put simply, if the life sciences can offer explanations for the way life functions on Earth, there is no need to invoke a divine creator. Is it possible to recover the belief held in the seventeenth century that all aspects of creation are the works of a divine mind? Or, if one accepts that God creates the world through the processes of biology, how far might it be possible to take such knowledge into human hands? Do people have the right to become co-creators with God in shaping the course of their own evolution and that of other species? One's view of ethics will depend on the particular view of God that one presupposes. Another question often asked is how far the scientific understanding of life is equipped to answer the complex ethical questions that have emerged in contested areas such as genetics and environmentalism. In these scenarios it may be that theology has more to offer than simply a response to the problems that science poses to its own fundamental beliefs.

Exploring the science

Having given a rough sketch of the range of sciences included in the concept of the life sciences, it is necessary to explore the task and presuppositions of the different sciences in order to understand their theoretical interrelationships. Molecular biology, for example, made a dramatic contribution to the study of genetics by defining the double helical structure of deoxyribonucleic acid (DNA) found in chromosomes. This discovery, published in 1953, is attributed to James Watson and Francis Crick, although Rosalind Franklin and Maurice Wilkins also provided vital experimental data. DNA consists of two strands of sugars and phosphates that are joined together by pairing of particular bases attached to the sugars. The pairing of bases is always the same, adenine with thymine and cytosine with guanine. The DNA unravels once a gene becomes active so that a particular section of DNA codes for a particular carrier nucleic acid, and thence to a particular protein. Moreover, the DNA can replicate itself by unwinding, after which each single strand pairs with another.

Once scientists defined the structure of DNA, it became possible not only to understand the reasons for genetic diseases, but also to develop ways of changing DNA structure by cutting or adding particular sections of DNA to the existing template. The practical science to which genetics relates most naturally is medicine, though it also has implications for commercial use in biotechnology.

It is possible to think about the sciences as operative at different levels in the study of living organisms. At the most fundamental level, molecular biologists examine changes in molecules during particular reactions. However, some would argue that the physical changes taking place are even more primary than this, so that changes in physical fields are coincident with certain chemical and molecular changes. The movement of charged molecules or ions across membranes, for example, is accompanied by electrical changes in the membrane. Biophysicists are interested in unravelling the details of such changes. At the next highest level, cell biologists explore reactions taking place at a cellular level, for example, the biochemical interchange between different parts of the cell or organelles. Cells make up organs, and the deciphering of the function of different organs in relation to the overall health of the organism delineates the field of physiology. For example, the way organisms use nutrients is the concern of physiologists. The idea of nutrients is suggestive of the interaction between the organisms and their environment, and one of the concerns of ecologists is nutrient exchange between species.

Ecology is important as far as the human sciences are concerned because it bears on human interrelationships with other living creatures. At the broadest level, geophysiologists examine the relationship between living creatures and the planet as a whole. This science, provocatively named the *Gaia Hypothesis* by James Lovelock in 1969, suggests a different way of doing science, one that, like ecology, examines relationships, rather than biochemical or biophysical reactions. Lovelock's hypothesis is that the Earth's relatively stable temperature and the gaseous composition of its atmosphere are not accidental; rather the sum total of all living things, or *biota,* directly contribute to this stability. His hypothesis is difficult to prove, so it has been marginalized by the scientific establishment.

The history of the way life emerged on the planet looks to fundamental questions about the origins of life itself. Charles Darwin's theory of evolution explored the biological processes that underlie the diversity of life on this planet. His theory of natural selection states that the survival of individuals in a species depends on those characteristics that render them most fit for a particular environment, and therefore most able to have the most offspring. The scientific study of genetics has defined more precisely the mechanism through which these characteristics are inherited. Evolutionary ideas link genetic science with ecological science. On the one hand, the history of the evolution of species depends on genes passing from one generation to the next, the so-called selfish gene theory exemplified most famously by biologist Richard Dawkins. On the other hand, the ways genes are expressed depend on a particular environment, so that the combined effect of genetics and environment makes up the *phenotype* of the individual organism. Lovelock's hypothesis challenges the assumption that organisms are always adapted to their environment by suggesting that the activities of organisms in and of themselves not only influence but also regulate their environment. Most biologists, however, accept Darwin's basic theory of natural selection.

The life sciences are not only concerned with the history or origin of life on Earth—they also have their own story of development. Ecology, for example, in the early part of the twentieth century considered its task to be the examination of succession of plant communities that established particular habitats, niches, or homes for other species. After 1945 ecologists began to look at the relationships between species in terms of energy exchange, all contributing to a particular ecosystem. Ecosystems lend stability and equilibrium to communities of organisms, however, ecologists have become less convinced that ecosystems function as stable communities. Instead of balance there is disturbance; instead of equilibrium, there is a fluid landscape of different, loosely assembled, environments. In addition, the scale of measurements used is important; ecology could be studied at the level of the leaf, canopy, patch, or forest, moving up the scale of organization. Higher up the scale different emerging properties appear. Debates exist concerning the degree to which these properties are simply dependent on activities at the lower levels of organization (*bottom-up causation*), are unique to their own level, or perhaps even a result of activities further up the scale (*top-down causation*). Emergent properties are still open to scientific consideration. The philosophical idea that these properties consist of the addition of a unique substance known as *vitalism* is rejected by contemporary science. Some writers, by their suggestion that Gaia is a living organism, have interpreted Lovelock's ideas in such a way that it comes close to this view.

Exploring issues in science and religion.

Darwin's theory of evolution poses challenges to the Christian idea of divine creation and design. The way theologians respond to this challenge is likely to influence the way they approach the life sciences in general. For example, if Darwin's theory is rejected, then it is likely that a conservative approach to genetic science will ensue, and there

will be resistance to most, if not all, genetic engineering. According to this view, the diversity of species on the planet is the result of divine fiat associated with the story of Genesis.

Those in broad agreement with Darwinian science may either retain a classical model of God as creator of the world, with God creating through evolutionary processes, or they embed their view of God more specifically in biological processes themselves, so that God evolves with biological change. While both views can support technological change, the emphasis is different. For Celia Deane-Drummond, for example, God may be viewed as divine wisdom, which creates the world in love through wisdom. Hence the diversity of life is affirmed as the gift of God. Each species needs to be given respect on the basis that each is loved by God, even though God has allowed changes to evolve. Although the classical view of God is associated with an understanding of God as omnipotent and omnipresent, it is possible to affirm the transcendence of God without assuming a static and remote model of who God is. If changes are to be made in the genetic makeup of species, then these changes need to take into account the particular telos or purpose of each individual species as far as it is possible to understand it. Moreover, those who do attempt to re-order the natural world via biochemistry need to be aware that it requires a particular gift, namely the gift of wisdom and discernment, in order to assess the limits of such attempts.

The alternative view perceives God not so much as "other" to creation, but as one who allows creation to emerge and become itself through divine activity. Accordingly, for Philip Hefner, humans can become co-creators with God and look to their individual freedom and individuality as the basis for change. Just because humans have more freedom does not mean that God is in some way restricted in freedom. Genetic determinism is rejected by many authors, such as Ted Peters, who argue that human beings are more that just products of genetic activity. As co-creators humans have the authority to make changes to the genetics of human and other species. The suffering of those with genetic diseases engenders compassion that calls for action. The failure to contribute to such a change when the knowledge exists amounts to apathy, rather than arrogance. There are important issues in human genetics, but the issues depend more on analysis of the risks and benefits of particular actions, rather than on any fundamental resistance to change. Many see the responsible re-ordering of the world as a mandate for human beings; the gift from God is the gift of science and technology.

Both alternatives discussed above are in broad agreement about the limitations of extending biological understanding of reality to cultural experience. Stated simply, sociobiologists find in Darwin's theory of evolution reasons for the emergence not just of physical traits, but also of human character attributes. The philosopher Holmes Rolston III has argued convincingly that attempts to trace complex ethical characteristics to genetic changes are simplistic. He believes that although the tendency to socialize may have a genetic component, the content of moral laws cannot arise only from genes. However, while the first view would see the shape of such moral law as taking its orientation from the eternal law of God, the second view lays emphasis on the moral freedom of individuals to devise their own laws, where the will of God in this case is somewhat diffuse because God is part of the process of change. It is also not clear according to this view what contribution theology can make to debates over genetic change, other than showing that it is possible to affirm science and be Christian.

There are also wider environmental issues that impinge on genetic science when it is applied to biotechnology. Important questions include the effect of introducing new genetic varieties on human communities set in ecological communities. Plant and animal breeding has taken place for many millennia, but the tools now available in genetic science allow genes to be transferred across species in a way that is unique. What once took years can now be achieved in days. Many ecologists are concerned about the loss of diversity and other possible damaging influences on fragile ecological communities. Yet the understanding of ecology as inclusive of human activity and in flux, rather than equilibrium, needs to be taken into account. There is a clash between those in the biotechnological industry, keen to introduce change for the sake of individual benefits such as pest resistance, and those more inclined to consider the wider impact of such changes on natural habitats. Theologians are being forced to consider the complexity of these social issues in deliberations about genetics and environment. Some suggest that complexity itself challenges the merit of secular approaches to ethics that simply look to the consequences of actions in terms of risks and benefits. Might there, indeed, be a way of reshaping the direction of science so that it does not look at problems narrowly, but considers social issues and the wider context of public debate? Some suggest that the answer is a return to a more holistic view of science, one that seeks knowledge not just as information, but in the broader framework of a search for wisdom.

See also CREATED CO-CREATOR; DNA; ECOLOGY; EVOLUTION, BIOLOGICAL; GAIA HYPOTHESIS; LIFE; LIFE, ORIGINS OF; LIFE, RELIGIOUS AND PHILOSOPHICAL ASPECTS; SELFISH GENE; SOCIOBIOLOGY

Bibliography

Dawkins, Richard. *The Selfish Gene.* London: Paladin, 1978.

Deane-Drummond, Celia. *Creation Through Wisdom: Theology and the New Biology.* Edinburgh, UK: T&T Clark, 2000.

Deane-Drummond, Celia. *Biology and Theology Today: Exploring the Boundaries.* London: SCM Press, 2001.

Deane-Drummond, Celia, and Szerszynski, Bronislaw. *Re-Ordering Nature: Theology, Society and the New Genetics.* Edinburgh, UK: T&T Clark, 2002.

Hefner, Philip. *The Human Factor: Evolution, Culture, and Religion.* Minneapolis, Minn.: Fortress Press, 1993.

Lovelock, James. *Gaia: A New Look at Life on Earth.* Oxford: Oxford University Press, 1979.

Northcott, Michael. *The Environment and Christian Ethics.* Cambridge, UK: Cambridge University Press, 1996.

Peacocke, Arthur. *Theology for a Scientific Age.* Enlarged edition. London: SCM Press, 1993.

Peters, Ted. *Playing God? Genetic Determinism and Human Freedom.* London: Routledge, 1997.

Reiss, Michael, and Straughan, Roger. *Improving Nature? The Science and Ethics of Genetic Engineering.* Cambridge, UK: Cambridge University Press, 1996.

Rolston, Holmes III. *Genes, Genesis, and God: Values and Their Origins in Natural and Human History.* Cambridge, UK: Cambridge University Press, 1999.

Ruse, Michael. *Can a Darwinian Be a Christian? The Relationship Between Science and Religion.* Cambridge, UK: Cambridge University Press, 2001.

Worster, Donald. *Nature's Economy: A History of Ecological Ideas.* New York: Cambridge University Press, 1977.

CELIA DEANE-DRUMMOND

LINGUISTICS

See LANGUAGE

LOCALITY

Locality is a feature of the world that is suggested by the experience that local causes produce local effects. In quantum mechanics, however, the EPR Paradox conceived of widely separated situations entangled by virtue of their quantum histories, and it is possible for a quantum measurement to have a nonlocal effect. It has sometimes been suggested that nonlocality might form a basis for telepathy or some form of faster-than-light signaling or travel. However, it can be shown that within quantum mechanics it is not possible to transfer information faster than the speed of light by exploiting quantum nonlocality. No two quantum mechanical measurements can be connected to each other by a faster-than-light signal.

Albert Einstein's (1879–1955) General Theory of Relativity requires local behavior in ways that Newton's theory of gravity does not. In Isaac Newton's (1642–1727) theory there exist mysterious gravitational forces that act instantaneously over unlimited distances in space (for example, the gravitational force of the sun on the Earth). In Einstein's theory there are no instantaneous nonlocal gravitational forces. Everything acts locally. The presence of mass or energy in space makes space curved, and all bodies move in response to the local curvature of space that they encounter locally, not in response to long-range, nonlocal forces of attraction.

Locality played an important role in the development of Western science. Most early science in the West was nonholistic in the sense that it maintained that the world could be analyzed locally without having to understand the whole of the universe. By contrast, Eastern holistic philosophies were handicapped in the development of a successful working theory of nature because they held strongly to a holistic view of the world. There has been debate about the resonance between the holistic nature of some parts of modern physics, notably quantum mechanics, chaos, and complexity, and early Eastern holistic philosophies. It is clear that a local, nonholistic, largely reductionist outlook is advantageous in beginning a successful scientific enterprise. While there undoubtedly are holistic aspects of the world, they are most effectively understood after having understood the local aspects.

See also EPR PARADOX; PHYSICS, QUANTUM; RELATIVITY, GENERAL THEORY OF

Bibliography

Bell, John. "On the Einstein-Podolsky-Rosen Paradox." *Physics* 1, no. 3 (1964): 195-200.

D'Espagnat, Bernard. *In Search of Reality.* New York: Springer-Verlag, 1983.

Shimony, Abner. "Controllable and Uncontrallable Non-locality." In *Proceedings of an International Symposium on the Foundations of Quantum Mechanics,* eds. S. Kamefuchi, et al. Tokyo: Physical Society of Japan, 1984.

JOHN D. BARROW

MAIMONIDES

A twelfth-century rabbi and community leader, philosopher and physician, Maimonides was fascinated by the relation between science and religion from his earliest days. A polymath by inclination, he needed first to master the sciences then extant, including logic, mathematics and medicine, before being able to assess their relation to his Jewish faith. Indeed, he insisted on philosophy's mediating role in the mutual illumination of faith and reason, notably with regard to creation.

Early life and influences

Mosheh ben Maimon, called Maimonides by Latin authors and known to the Arabic-speaking world as Musa ben Maimun, Moses son of Maimon, was born on March 30, 1135 C.E., in the city of Córdoba, Spain, where eight generations of his ancestors had served as rabbis and rabbinical judges. Capital of the Umayyad emirs and caliphs in Spain since the eighth century, Córdoba had remained even in their political decline the center of a brilliant, prosperous civilization in which Jews and Christians, as well as Muslims, were active participants. Young Moses himself was not to enjoy this cosmopolitan milieu much past his bar mitzvah, as the family was forced to flee their home in the wake of the Almohads from North Africa, who forbade Jews or Christians to profess their religion openly. Yet in the relative calm prior to the shattering of their world, the Jews of Spain had built an intellectual capital from which Maimonides was to

profit immeasurably, even after the world that had produced it ceased to exist.

Poetry, astronomy, medicine, philosophy, scriptural exegesis, grammar, history, and mysticism were typically integrated into a comprehensive education. Moses's father, Maimon, led the family to Fez (in present-day Morocco), the very center of the Almohad movement, where they managed to survive for five years, only to move on to Palestine in 1165, where Maimonides journeyed to the site of the temple in Jerusalem to give thanks for the gift of this pilgrimage, and thence to Hebron, the traditional resting place of Abraham, who held a special place in Maimonides's vision of history, not only as the first spokesperson of a universal monotheism, but also as the first to base theological claims on arguments derived from reason. Since the rule of the Latin Kingdom of Jerusalem offered a less than favorable milieu for developing Jewish life and culture, the family proceeded to Egypt, where Maimon soon died, leaving his son to take up the roles in the community to which his learning entitled him.

Legal and philosophical writings

Remarkably, Maimonides continued his education under the stress of exile and travel, composing his commentary on the Jewish legal canon, the Mishnah, during the seven years of exile from his twenty-third to thirtieth years. Taking up residence in Fustat (Old Cairo), he was appointed judge of the rabbinical court and soon assumed leadership of the community. After the death of his brother and the loss of the family savings in a shipwreck,

Maimonides took up the responsibility of supporting the family as a physician, practicing medicine until his death. During this time he was court physician to Saladin (c. 1137–1193), the Sultan of Egypt and Syria, as well as the entire court, leaving him little time to study and write, yet he accomplished both, along with adjudicating disputes within the Jewish community. The completion of his groundbreaking codification of Jewish law, the *Mishneh Torah,* around 1178, brought him even greater fame that his earlier commentary, and he was beset with requests for legal opinions from communities throughout the Islamic world.

At this time, however, he also encountered Rabbi Joseph ibn Judah Aqnin, who insisted Maimonides guide him into the logic, cosmology, theology, and philosophy of the Greco-Arabic tradition, so as to be able to converse with other learned communities in the Islamicate. Following a course of study as old as Plato's Academy in the fourth century B.C.E., Maimonides initiated his student into astronomy and mathematics, and then logic, and finally metaphysics, by using its tools to explicate the conundra the revealed texts often left to readers of the Hebrew scriptures. This series of exercise in biblical interpretation and philosophical exegesis was published in 1190 as the *Guide to the Perplexed.* It was immediately translated from Arabic into Hebrew, and then into Latin, where it served as a model for Christian thinkers like Thomas Aquinas (c. 1225–1274) to integrate assertions of faith with explorations of reason.

Science and religion

The most vexing issue turned out to be the claim of Genesis that time itself began with creation, whereas the prevailing philosophical view had long been of a universe emanating necessarily and without beginning from a single unitary principle. Maimonides established the model for addressing this conflict between the divergent claims of reason and of faith by using his philosophical acumen to show that the authority whom philosophers had invoked—Aristotle—had neither intended nor achieved a demonstration of the universe coming forth from a single unitary principle without beginning. And having shown that, he proceeded to delineate the anomalies in the actual universe, notably the errant path of the planets (or "wandering stars"), to point out that no set of logical principles could account for the actual ordering of the heavens, despite the elegance of the necessary emanation scheme. So, he said, it makes more eminent sense to posit a free creator, whose intentional ordering could explain what logic cannot.

This central bit of reasoning displays how his scientific acumen could be put to use to make it possible for believers to accept the words of Genesis at face value, yet he was also quick to insist that neither view could be proven. Moreover, where scriptural texts did conflict with proven tenets of reason, then they would have to be interpreted figuratively; since the divine reality could not be bodily, texts referring to the "Lord's mighty arm" would have to be read metaphorically. He was even prepared to read Genesis that way, foregoing a first moment of time for creation, but the absence of a valid demonstration of the prevailing philosophical view reduced it to the level of mere opinion—however widely held it had been, and so opened the way to a belief in scripture that was straightforward yet sophisticated. Such is the legacy that all religious traditions received from Maimonides, whose strategies were transmitted to the Christian world by way of Aquinas and others after him. In short, what seem to be conflicts between faith and reason, religion and science, may often be defused by a proper understanding of each domain, yet doing so requires an education and a sensibility as astute as Moses Maimonides's. As the celebrated Hebrew saying has it: "from Moses to Moses, there arose none like Moses."

See also CREATION; GENESIS; HISTORICAL CRITICISM; JUDAISM; JUDAISM, CONTEMPORARY ISSUES IN SCIENCE AND RELIGION; JUDAISM, HISTORY OF SCIENCE AND RELIGION, MEDIEVAL PERIOD; THOMAS AQUINAS

Bibliography

Goodman, Lenn Evan. *Rambam: Readings in the Philosophy of Moses Maimonides.* New York: Viking, 1976.

Hartman, David. *Maimonides: Torah and Philosophic Quest.* Philadelphia: Jewish Publication Society of America, 1976.

Maimonides, Moses. *Guide for the Perplexed,* trans. Michael Friedlander (1904). New York: Dover, 1956.

Maimonides, Moses. *Guide of the Perplexed,* trans. Schlomo Pines. Chicago: University of Chicago Press, 1963.

Seeskin, Kenneth. *Maimonides: A Guide for Today's Perplexed.* West Orange, N.J.: Behrman House, 1991.

DAVID B. BURRELL

MANY-WORLDS HYPOTHESIS

One of the fundamental interpretive problems of quantum theory arises from the fact that from any two or more states for a system one can create another state, their *superposition* (mathematically, a linear combination). Let s and s' be possible states for a system, corresponding to two different values, k and k' respectively, for the observable, O. (That is, they are mutually orthogonal eigenstates of O.) Their superposition, which is another possible state for the system, is denoted by $s + s'$. According to the standard interpretation of quantum theory, a system in the state $s + s'$ does not have the value k for O, nor the value k' for O, nor neither, but if O is measured on the system, the system will be found to have either the value of k or the value of k' for O.

The standard interpretation works in practice, but many physicists and philosophers find it to be unsatisfactory for a variety of reasons, not least because it contains the unanalyzed notion of "measurement." With minimal experience, it is easy to judge when to say that a measure of O has occurred, but upon what principle can such a judgment be made? No satisfactory principle has been offered. The other problematic feature of the standard interpretation is that it countenances physical systems that are literally indeterminate with respect to their values for observables such as "position." In other words, a physical system (outside of a context in which its location is being measured) can literally have no location (though if its location is measured, it will be found to have a location). The Many-worlds Hypothesis, which originally arises from work by Hugh Everett (1930–1982), is an alternative approach to interpretation that purports to dispense with the notion of measurement and to resolve the problem of indeterminacy.

The central idea behind the Many-worlds Hypothesis is that a state such as $s + s'$ in fact describes a multiplicity of distinct, independent, worlds, some in which our system is in the state s and others in which our system is in the state s'. In most versions of the Many-worlds interpretation, there are, in all, an uncountable infinity of worlds, divided amongst the various states appearing in the superposition (in our case, s and s') according to the probabilities attached to the various states. So if, according to the standard interpretation, a measurement of O on our system would reveal the value k with probability $\frac{1}{3}$, and k' with the probability $\frac{2}{3}$, then according to the Many-worlds interpretations, in $\frac{1}{3}$ of the worlds our system is in the state s, and so has the value k for O, and in $\frac{2}{3}$ of the worlds our system is in the state s', and so has the value k' for O.

It is important to keep in mind that the "worlds" of the Many-worlds interpretation are not the same as the "possible worlds" of philosophy. This point is clear in light of the fact that the philosopher's possible worlds need not obey the laws of quantum theory, while the single "universe" of the Many-worlds interpretation does obey the laws of quantum theory. In the Many-worlds interpretation, therefore, there is a single "actual" world in the philosopher's sense, but it consists of many distinct independent "realms of reality." However, in standard usage, these realms of reality are called *worlds*.

A variant of the Many-worlds Hypothesis, called the *Many-minds Hypothesis,* asserts that the multiplicity in question is not a multiplicity of worlds, but a multiplicity of distinct, independent, minds. Each observer in fact has many minds (in most versions, an uncountable infinity of them), and when the observer observes a system in a superposition (for example, $s + s'$) some of the minds observe the system to be in the state s, while others observe it to be in the states s', the proportions again matching the quantum-mechanical probabilities. In the case of the Many-minds interpretations, rather than a single actual world with many realms of reality, there is a single "person" with many minds. Other than that, there are many similarities between the two interpretations.

The notion of a measurement is supposed to play no fundamental role in these interpretations. A measurement of an observable O on a system merely reveals the preexisting value in "your" world that the system had for O. That is, if you witness the result k, then you are in a world in which the system already had the value k for O. Similar remarks hold for the Many-minds theories, *mutatis mutandis.*

Many-worlds interpretations face a number of interpretive difficulties. One is that any quantum state can be written as a superposition in many ways. In the terms stated earlier, $s + s'$ is equivalent to an infinity of other superpositions, $t + t'$, where s and s' are different from $t + t'$. So given that the quantum state of the universe is $V = s + s' = t + t'$, are the realms of reality (the "worlds") defined by the states s and s' or t and t', or all of the above? If one of the former two, then the interpretation faces the obvious question why one (e.g., s and s') rather than the other (e.g., t and t'). If the latter, then the interpretation faces the problem of how to define a probability measure over all of the components that can appear in any decomposition of the quantum state. Indeed, if such a measure is supposed to represent "ignorance" about which world one occupies (or which mind is "one's own") then it is far from clear that a satisfactory measure can be defined.

This issue is related to another severe problem facing these interpretations, namely, how to justify, or even to understand, the probabilities of standard quantum theory. The most obvious way to conceive of probabilities in these interpretations is as a measure of ignorance either about which world one occupies or about which mind is one's own. The problem is that it is not at all clear why that ignorance should be measure by the quantum-theoretic measure (except by stipulation).

But perhaps the most significant obstacle facing the Many-worlds and Many-minds interpretations is the sheer implausibility of the hypotheses. The central issue facing these interpretations is whether the difficulties we have understanding quantum theory really force us to such extreme measures.

See also PHYSICS, QUANTUM

Bibliography

DeWitt, Bryce S., and Graham, R. Neill, eds. *The Many-Worlds Interpretation of Quantum Mechanics.* Princeton, N.J.: Princeton University Press, 1973.

Tipler, Frank J. "The Many-Worlds Interpretation of Quantum Mechanics in Quantum Cosmology." In *Quantum Concepts of Space and Time,* ed. Roger Penrose and Chris Isham. Oxford, UK: Oxford University Press, 1986.

W. MICHAEL DICKSON

MATERIALISM

The term *materialism,* derived from the Latin word *materia* (timber, matter), was coined about 1670 by the British physicist Robert Boyle (1627–1691). Its French equivalent, *materialisme,* was used probably for the first time by Pierre Bayle (1647–1706), although it was not yet listed in his famous *Dictionnaire historique et critique* (1697). The German term *Materialismus* seems to have been introduced around 1700 by Gottfried Wilhelm Leibniz (1646–1716). Since then it has been employed to denote any theory that considers all events in the universe to be sufficiently accounted for by the existence and nature of matter.

Historians of philosophy often distinguish between different versions of such theories: *theoretical materialism,* the philosophical doctrine according to which, in contrast to idealism, matter is the only substratum of all existence and all mental or spiritual phenomena are merely functions of it; *psychological materialism,* which claims that the soul or spirit of living organisms consists only of matter or is a function of physical processes; *physiological materialism,* according to which mental activities can be explained as biological processes; and *dialectical materialism,* or its variant *historical materialism,* which regards all important historical events as result of the economic developments of the human society. Finally, the term *materialism* is also used in the disapprobatory sense of denoting excessive desire for material goods and wealth.

Ancient Greek materialism

Following Friedrich Albert Lange's influential *History of Materialism* (1865), which opens with the statement that "materialism is as old as philosophy, but not older" (p. 7) many historians identify the beginning of materialism with the birth of Greek philosophy in the sixth century B.C.E. They regard Thales of Miletus, who is generally credited with having been the founder of Greek science, mathematics, and philosophy, as the first proponent of materialism. They claim that his well-known statement "all things are water" implies that water is the only and universal substratum of which all other bodies are merely modifications. Although Thales's specific choice of water as the fundamental matter did not satisfy his successors, his distinction between appearance and a reality that becomes comprehensible through the unifying function of reason was of lasting consequence for philosophical thought. His disciple, Anaximander of Miletus, replaced water by the more abstract *apeiron,* some kind of infinite and indistinct eternal matter to which everything that exists owes its being.

Anaximander's disciple, Anaximenes, in turn called the fundamental cosmic matter "air" or "breath" claiming that air, when cooled, becomes vapor or mist, when rarified fire, and when condensed wind, cloud, water, earth, or stone. It should be noted, however, that at those early times matter and mind, or body and soul, were not sharply distinguished from one another so that the apparently purely material substratum included a spiritual ingredient. Some historians of philosophy prefer therefore to call these Ionian philosophers not materialists but *hylozoist*. The term *hylozoism,* derived from the Greek words for wood and life, means that there exists only matter, but this matter is animated, matter and life being inseparable.

A more authentic materialism is the *atomism* developed by Leucippus and elaborated by his disciple Democritus of Abdera who flourished about 400 B.C.E. They taught that there exist only empty space and atoms, which are indivisible, indestructible, and imperceptibly small particles of matter, differing in size and shape and moving in space. About a century later, Epicurus (341–270 B.C.E.) adopted the Democritian theory of atoms as a mechanistic explanation of all phenomena and used it as the basis of his philosophical system, which became known as *Epicureanism*. The most influential expositor of Democritian materialism and Epicurianism was the Roman philosopher and poet Lucretius of the first century B.C.E. In the six books of his poem *De Rerum Natura* (On the nature of things), he presented a materialistic explanation of mind, of soul, and of sensation, as well as of the phenomena of life, and thus taught the groundlessness of the fear of death and divine punishment since the event of death is merely the dispersion of the atoms.

Modern materialism

Due to the facts that the Christian Fathers, like Tertullian (c. 160–c. 240 C.E.), Arnobius (253–c. 327 C.E.), or Lactantius (c. 250–c. 325 C.E.), rejected philosophy as a heathen product, and that since the thirteenth century Aristotelianism, which rejected atomism, dominated Western thought until the age of the Renaissance, materialistic theories were virtually anathematized prior to the seventeenth century. Their revival is attributed mainly to the empiricist Pierre Gassendi (1592–1655), a Catholic priest with orthodox views in theology, but never-theless a staunch opponent of Scholastic Aristotelianism, and to the political writer Thomas Hobbes (1588–1679), the son of a clergyman. Gassendi revived Epicurean atomism but made it compatible with Christian doctrine by asserting that atoms are not eternal but have been created by God. In his *Syntagma Philosophiae Epicuri,* published in 1658, Gassendi developed an atomistic theory that extends over physics and psychology without denying the existence of divine providence. Hobbes started with the notions of space and time, which he regarded as correlatives of the primary attributes of body, namely extension and motion. The resulting system turned out to be a rigorously deterministic materialism. Since all that really exists is, according to Hobbes, material and extended, the human soul cannot be immaterial; even thought must be some kind of an action of bodies. Furthermore, since human beings and the society of human beings are but groupings of bodies, the laws of human behavior and of human societies must obey the laws of motion as they are known in physics.

France. Gassendi's revival of Democritean atomism served as the foundation of what became known as the French materialism of the eighteenth century. Its main representatives are Julien Offray de la Mettrie (also called Lamettrie) (1709–1751), Claude-drien Helvétius (1715–1771), Denis Diderot (1713–1784), Paul Henri Thiry d'Holbach (1729–1789), and Pierre-Jean-Georges Cabanis (1757–1808).

Lamettrie came in contact with the Dutch philosopher and *iatromechanist* Hermann Boerhaave (1668–1738), who claimed that all organic processes can be explained by the laws of the physical sciences. Influenced by Boerhaave, Lamettrie published in 1745 his *Histoire Naturelle de l'Ame* (Natural History of the Soul), in which he presented his views concerning the nature of matter, its relation to form, and its capacity for motion and for sensation. Since matter becomes a definite substance through form, which it receives from another substance, form can only be known in its combination with matter. Matter itself is endowed not only with motion; it also possesses the capacity of sensation. In his *L'Homme machine* (1648), Lamettrie accepted René Descartes's (1596–1650) view that animals are merely machines and that all intellectual phenomena that they display must be mechanically explainable. But he went further than

Descartes when he argued that if an animal can feel and perceive without an immaterial soul due to its nervous and cerebral organization, there is no reason to assume that humans have spiritual souls. Since the laws of nature are the same for all that exists, plants, animals, and humans are subject to the same laws.

Lamettrie's books were publicly burned on account of their materialism and he had to flee to Berlin. Helvétius' work *De l'Esprite,* published in 1758, was also condemned by the Sorbonne as preaching a materialistic amorality and, like Lamettrie, Helvétius fled to Germany where he was received with high esteem. What Descartes was for Lamettrie, the French sensationalist Etienne Condillac (1715–1780) was for Helvétius. Following Condillac, according to whom all human faculties are reducible in essence to a sensory basis, Helvétius developed a materialistic philosophy on the fundamental assumption that all that people know they know only through the senses, and hence their ideas of deity, love, the soul, and so on, are merely modified forms of the objects that impress them in their daily material experience. Helvetius's materialism culminated with the conclusion that "enlightened self-interest is the criterion of morals."

Diderot, well known as the editor-in-chief of the French *Encyclopédie,* changed his views from an initial theism in which he was educated at a Jesuit school, through a period of deism, to an atheistic materialism. Diderot professed a biologically oriented materialism, since for him the entire universe is a perpetual circulation of life in which everything changes, evolution is a wholly mechanical process based on the laws of physics. In his *Pensées sur l'Interprétation de la Nature* (Thoughts on the Interpretation of Nature, 1754) he declared that the often pronounced view that body is in itself without action and without force is a monstrous error because "matter, but the nature of its essential qualities, whether it be considered in the smallest or largest quantities, is full of activity and force." The soul of the human being, who is part of nature, is not separate from body, and psychology is merely physiology of the nerves.

Holbach spent most of his life in Paris, where he wrote more than four hundred articles for the *Encyclopédie.* He is known chiefly as the author of the *Système de la Nature, ou des Lois du Monde Physique et du Monde Moral* (The System of nature, or the laws of the Moral and Physical world), published 1770. It has been called "the Bible of French materialism." It begins with the statement that although man imagines that there exists something beyond nature, all that exists is nature, and nature is nothing but matter and motion. Matter has always existed and has always been in motion. All particular things originate from matter by means of particular motions that are governed by unchangeable laws. Man, who is part of nature and as such a purely material being, only imagines that he has an immaterial soul. But all mental activity is in reality only some motion in the brain. Free activities or free will can not exist since all feelings, volitions, or thoughts are always subject to the eternal and unchanging laws of motion. Life is the sum of bodily motions and ceases when these come to an end. Holbach, more than any other materialist, stressed the point that materialism implies atheism. If there were a God, he argued, God would be located in nature, for there is nothing beyond nature; but if God were part of nature, God would be nothing but matter and motion. The idea of God, he concluded, is only a superstitious product of ignorance and desperation. Holbach even had no qualms to declare that the idea of God is the cause of all evil in society.

Cabanis, a friend of Holbach, was not always consistent in his philosophical writings, but judging from his principle work, *Rapports du Physique et du Moral de l'Homme* (On the Relation between the Physical and Moral aspects of man, 1802), he may be best characterized as having been a physiological, or even psychological, materialist. For, in his view, body and mind are not merely interacting with each other but are one and the same thing, and the human soul is matter endowed with feeling. The human being is simply a bundle of nerves, or as Cabanis phrased it, "Les nerfs—voilà tout l'homme!" (The nerves—that's all there is to man). Sensibility and thinking have their foundation in physical processes; when impressions reach the brain, they cause it to act and to "secrete" thoughts just like the liver secretes bile.

England. Cabanis and French materialism in general exerted a lasting influence on later philosophical movements, like that of the so-called *idealogues,* represented by Destutt de Tracy (1754–1836), or the *epiphenomenalists,* like Thomas Henry Huxley (1825–1895). On the other hand, retrospectively viewed, Cabanis's conceptions of materialism had much in common with the earlier formulation of materialism by Thomas Hobbes. Still, Hobbes was one of the earliest materialists in modern philosophy. As stated in his *De Corpore* (1655), philosophy means to think, and to think means to combine or separate thoughts; hence the objects of philosophy are composable and decomposable objects or bodies. Pure spirits or God cannot be thought. Since human beings and human society are but grouping of bodies it should be possible to deduce the laws of the behavior of human individuals and societies from the laws of bodies, that is, from the definitions of space, time, force, and power. Geometry describes the movements of bodies in space; physics the effects of bodies upon each other; ethics the movements of nervous systems; and politics the effects of nervous systems upon each other.

Hobbes, like most other English materialists, in contrast to their French counterparts, did not consider atheism to be a logical implication of materialism. In fact, most English materialists reconciled materialism with religious belief. John Toland (1670–1722), for example, professed in *Letters to Serena* (1704) and in *Pantheisticon* (1710) an extreme materialism that, in his view, does not conflict with deism. A typical example of an English materialist is also the physician David Hartley (1705–1757), the founder of the Associationalist School of psychologists. In *Observations on Man, his Frame, his Duty, and his Expectations* (1749) he reduced the whole of human thought and sensation to physical vibrations of the brain.

The most famous example of the compatibility of English materialism with religious faith is Joseph Priestley (1733–1804), known to chemists as the discoverer of oxygen. Although sympathizing with Hobbes and proclaiming the materiality of the soul, Priestley served as a Unitarian minister and believed in the existence of God and the immortality of the soul. As he emphasized in his *Disquisitions on Matter and Spirit* (1777), "there is nothing inconsistent with Christianity and the conception of the materiality of the human and divine soul."

Germany. In Germany a systematic philosophical materialism could gain ground only after the disintegration of the German idealism, which had culminated with Immanuel Kant (1724–1804) and collapsed with the death of George Wilhelm

Friedrich Hegel in 1831. Kant, in his influential *Critique of Pure Reason* (1781), condemned materialism, just like spiritualism, as utterly useless (*untauglich*) for any explanation of reality. So did Johann Gottlieb Fichte (1762–1814), the philosopher of romantic idealism, and his disciple Friedrich Wilhelm von Schelling, according to whom "God affirms himself in Nature." The rise of German materialism in the post-Kantian period received its chief motivation from the achievements of science. The synthesis of urea from cyanic acid and ammonia by Friedrich Wöhler (1880–1882) and of fructose and glucose from their chemical elements by Emil Fischer (1852–1919) shattered the traditional belief that organic matter could only be formed by vital processes. Hermann Helmholtz's (1821–1894) discovery of the conservation of energy in organic and inorganic systems, combined with the atomic theory and Charles Darwin's theory of evolution, contributed decisively to the conception that life, mind, and consciousness are properties of energized matter. Thus, Jacob Moleschott (1822–1893) denied in his *Der Kreislauf des Lebens* (The Circularity of life, 1852) the existence of dead matter or of a matter-free force of life.

An extremely antireligious version of materialism was published in 1855 by Karl Vogt (1817–1895) in his *Kohlerglaube und Wissenschaft* (Implicit faith and science) as a sequel to his famous Göttingen controversy (1852) with the physiologist Rudolph Wagner (1805–1864), the so-called *Materialismusstreit* (Controversy about materialism), which raised wide public attention. Of greater influence, however, was Ludwig Buchner's (1824–1899) materialistic and atheistic book *Kraft und Stoff* (Force and matter) which, first published in 1855, appeared in more than twenty German editions and was translated into fifteen languages. A noteworthy example of the enormous influence that this book exerted, especially in Germany, is the fact that it prompted Albert Einstein (1879–1955) in his adolescence to abandon completely his erstwhile youthful religious enthusiasm.

Hegel's death marked the rise not only of this "vulgar materialism," so called because of its propagandist appeal to the broad masses, but also of the politically oriented dialectical materialism. The "left Hegelians," among them Karl Marx (1818–1883), opposed Hegelian idealism and reduced all its standards to human needs and human existence. Marx and his collaborator Friedrich Engels

(1820–1895) rejected the idealistic philosophy, which regards matter as dependent on mind or spirit, and developed instead a materialistic philosophy called dialectical materialism, according to which a materialistic reality is the substructure to all human social manifestations and institutions. Marx, in *Das Kapital* (1867), argued on the basis of a historico-sociological analysis of economics that what he called the "bourgeoisie" is no longer capable of coping with the changed conditions of production and must give room to the proletariat. It was mainly Engels who blended Marx's economical doctrine with philosophical materialism. According to Engels the philosophy of materialism is based on the three laws of dialectic: the law of contradiction, the turning of quantity into quality, and the negation of negation to specific logical and methodological problems. Engels's conception of dialectical materialism lies at the foundation of Vladimir Ilyich Lenin's (1870–1924) *Materialism and Empiro-Criticism* (1919), which is his only work on philosophical principles and became the canon of the official philosophy of former Soviet Russia and modern China.

The challenge of physics

The conceptual foundations and scientific background of all materialistic systems of the eighteenth and nineteenth centuries was the notion of matter as conceived by classical physics, that is, as Isaac Newton (1642–1727) described it, "matter formed in solid, massy, hard, impenetrable, moveable particles" and "mass" being its numerical measure. These particles, whether of atomic or macroscopic size, move through space according to the strict laws of mechanics. The development of modern physics in the first quarter of the twentieth century led to a radical modification, if not complete disintegration, of this classical framework, a process often characterized as the "dematerialization of matter." The traditional representation of atoms, for example, as minute billiard balls complying with the classical laws of motion proved incompatible with the principles of modern physics, which is based on the theory of relativity and quantum mechanics. Einstein's famous mass-energy relation, for example, symbolized by $E = mc^2$, and a simple consequence of the special theory of relativity, is often interpreted as expressing the convertibility of mass or matter into energy or inversely of energy into matter. Werner Heisen-

berg's (1901–1976) Uncertainty Principle, one of the axioms of quantum mechanics, whether interpreted as expressing the essential property of material particles never to have simultaneously a definite position and a definite velocity, or whether regarded as reflecting only a limitation on the measurement, as well as Louis de Broglie's (1892–1987) related principle of wave-particle duality, showed that the ontology of classical physics, on which those materialistic doctrines were grounded, can no longer be maintained. Quantum field theories, which have become the most important tools in understanding the microscopic world, suggest that matter is merely some arrangement of properties of space-time itself, all elementary particles being described as manifestations of quantum mechanical fields.

Modern physics thus presents a serious challenge to conventional materialism. Perhaps the most acceptable answer to this challenge has been given by the philosopher Herbert Feigl in his response to Norwood Russell Hanson's paper "The Dematerialization of Matter," published in 1962 in the periodical *Philosophy of Science*. "I grant," says Feigl, "the abstract, unvisualizable character of most physical concepts, classical or modern. But I insist that physics deals with happenings in space-time, and that associated with those happenings there are aspects of mass, charge and motion which leave at least *some* characteristics of old-fashioned matter unaltered" (p. 569).

See also NATURALISM; SCIENTISM

Bibliography

Bloch, Ernst. *Das Materialismusproblem*. Frankfurt am Main, Germany: Suhrkamp, 1972.

Elliot, Hugh. *Modern Science and Materialism*. London: Longmann and Green, 1919.

Feibleman, James K. *The New Materialism*. The Hague, Netherlands: Nijhoff, 1970.

Feigl, Herbert. "Comment: Matter Still Largely Material." In *The Concept of Matter*, ed. Ernan McMullin. South Bend, Ind.: University of Notre Dame Press, 1969.

Gregory, Frederick G. *Scientific Materialism in Nineteenth Century Germany*. Dordrecht, Netherlands: Reidel, 1977.

Haldane, John Scott. *Materialism*. London: Hodder and Stoughton, 1932.

Hanson, Norwood Russell. "The Dematerilization of Matter." In *The Concept of Matter,* ed. Ernan McMullin. Nortre Dame, Ind.: University of Notre Dame Press, 1969.

Jammer, Max. *Concepts of Mass in Classical and Modern Physics.* Cambridge, Mass.: Harvard University Press, 1961; reprint New York: Dover, 1997.

Jammer, Max. *Concepts of Mass in Contemporary Physics and Philosophy.* Princeton, N.J.: Princeton University Press, 2000.

Lange, Frederick A. *The History of Materialism,* trans. Ernest Chester Thomas. New York: Humanities Press, 1950.

Mark, Siegfried. "Dialectical Materialism." In *A History of Philosophical Systems,* ed. Vergilius Ferm. New York: Philosophical Library, 1950.

O'Connor, John, ed. *Modern Materialism.* New York: Harcourt: 1969.

Parker, DeWitt H. *Experience and Substance.* Ann Arbor: University of Michigan Press, 1941.

Robinson, Harold. *Matter and Sense.* Cambridge, UK: Cambridge University Press, 1982.

Rosenthal, David M. *Materialism and the Mind-Body Problem.* Englewood Cliffs, N.J.: Prentice Hall, 1969.

Schofield, Robert E. *Mechanism and Materialism.* Princeton, N.J.: Princeton University Press, 1969.

Schwarz, Harmann. *Der moderne Materialismus.* Leipzig, Germany: T. Weicher, 1904.

Sellars, Roy Wood. *Philosophy for the Future: The Quest of Modern Materialism.* New York: Macmillan, 1949.

Wetter, Gustav A. *Dialectical Materialism.* New York: Praeger, 1959.

MAX JAMMER

MATHEMATICS

The ancient Greeks, building upon earlier work by the Egyptians and Babylonians, transformed mathematics into an integral part of liberal education during the fourth century B.C.E. The academic disciplines (*mathemata*) of arithmetic and geometry were then sharply distinguished from the menial rules of practical calculation (*logistica*) necessary for the everyday work of artisans, tradesmen, and money changers. Arithmetic studies the properties of whole numbers such as divisibility and factorization by primes, while geometry studies properties of magnitudes such as congruence, similarity, and proportion. Both are concerned with aspects of measurement, understood in a broad sense, but arithmetic deals with discrete quantities (multitudes of a unit) while geometry considers continuous magnitudes (line segments, planar areas, and solids).

The notion of a ratio (*logos*)—the size of one thing relative to another—plays a major unifying role, yet many advances in both classical and modern mathematics have sprung from the inherent tension between the continuous and the discrete. The tension we may sense today between our flowing, or continuous, temporal existence and the discrete digital world of the modern computer reveals the distinction between these cooperating opposites and suggests the possibility of a powerful interaction.

Pythagorean and Platonic connections

Measurement is made by expressing a ratio of the thing to be measured to a second thing, usually to a standard unit that is more familiar—nowadays taken to be a meter, second, liter, or the like. In the fifth century B.C.E. the Pythagoreans made much of the fact, said to have been well known already in China, that ratios of small whole numbers in arithmetic are related to harmonious musical intervals. Thus, to speak in modern terms, the easily recognizable octave is produced by two pitches in the ratio 2:1, while the ratio 3:2 yields a musical fifth, and 5:4 determines a third. Our ability to sense the ratios between pitches in music and their identification with ratios between numbers may have helped inspire the Pythagorean dictum, "All is number." By this is meant, presumably, that integers and their ratios (*logoi*) have the power to express underlying harmonies in nature that will be hidden from those ignorant of mathematics. Perhaps the most familiar modern (nineteenth-century) example of this power is the order induced in the periodic table by the assignment of an appropriate atomic number—an integer—to each basic chemical element.

Pythagoras (c. 560–c. 495 B.C.E.) is traditionally credited with putting together two Greek words to coin the word *philosophy* ("love of wisdom") and with objectifying the notion of order by taking the Greek word for it, *cosmos,* and giving this name to the universe. Despite his mystical leanings, Pythagoras is sometimes seen as the founder of Western science because his followers continually promoted mathematics as a means of finding order and harmony in the natural world. The Pythagoreans used the connection between arithmetic and the science of music to develop a musical scale based upon *just intonation* (and they appreciated the difficulties that were finally ameliorated in the eighteenth century by well-tempering). They also noted the more obvious connection between geometry and astronomy. Stars are like points and the constellations are formed by line segments joining pairs of stars—so that problems in navigation may become problems in geometry.

Aspects of astronomy are thus naturally modeled by geometry, just as some properties of music are modeled by arithmetic. But these sciences deal with things in motion—the rotating celestial sphere, the vibrating strings of a lyre—whereas the mathematics of arithmetic and geometry deal with idealized static objects such as whole numbers and stationary line segments. A striking analogy is due to Archytas (fifth century B.C.E.), a latter-day Pythagorean: Arithmetic is to Music as Geometry is to Astronomy. Almost a thousand years later these four mathemata became collectively known as the *quadrivium,* a name given them by the Roman philosopher Boethius (c. 480–c. 524), although his practical countrymen prized logistica more highly. Eventually, the quadrivium became an integral part of the classical liberal arts in medieval European universities.

The word *ratio* has long been associated with measured study and hence with reason itself, while *logos,* the Greek word for ratio, has taken on a wide-ranging religious significance as well. The unit generates all numbers, whose *logoi,* according to the Pythagorean faith, have the power to measure (know) everything in the cosmos. Thus, for the Pythagoreans, the logos is a mathematical means of expressing cosmic harmony. The variety of basic roles that the logos plays in mathematics, science, philosophy, liberal education, and religion is suggested by the wide usage of such cognate terms as *logic* and *analogy,* and the host of academic words with the suffix *-logy.* Pythagoras seems to have been drawn toward a holistic view encompassing all these spheres, but their explosive growth would make this view ever more difficult to sustain.

Plato (c. 427–347 B.C.E.) became familiar with Pythagorean doctrines through Archytas and endorsed their emphasis upon mathematics and their insistence upon the same basic education for men and women. Plato thought that our power of direct apprehension of idealized mathematical forms like the circle might be refined to help us apprehend such things as truth, beauty, and goodness—Platonic forms whose properties, moreover, might also be studied by deductive reason. If, as Plato insisted, mathematics helps train the mind to rise from the apparent and ephemeral to the true and permanent, then its study should promote both science and religion. Indeed, when Jewish and early Christian thinkers began to view Platonic forms as ideas in the mind of God, an important link was established between Platonism and Judeo-Christian thought.

Plato even suggested that the immortality of the soul is intimated by geometry, especially when learned by the Socratic method, where it may appear that we are remembering—rather than learning anew—connections between geometric forms that we had somehow forgotten. To Plato this implies the existence of some earlier state of fuller communion with the forms. We must therefore (re)search in order to remember where we came from. In the midst of this perhaps fanciful argument, however, is Plato's admonition with which all modern scientists would agree, that in research we must look beyond mere sensory impressions. The laws governing the stars are fairer than the stars.

Plato comes close to espousing a religious motivation for scientific inquiry by taking the position, ardently embraced much later by Johannes Kepler (1571–1630), that the universe is, in some sense, an expression of the nature of its creator. Many researchers in mathematics and science, including some to whom Plato's views might appear naïve, have occasionally expressed a belief that they are, so to speak, reading the mind of God. "We cannot read [the great book of Nature]," wrote Galileo Galilei (1564–1642), "unless we have first learned the language and the characters in which it is written .... It is written in mathematical language."

Mathematics as a human endeavor

A quick excursion sketching the rise of seventeenth-century calculus may help to put a human face upon the making of mathematics. In the early

Middle Ages a slowly growing quantitative sense began to evolve, later bolstered by the convenience of working with numerals developed in India that would eventually be used in Indo-Arabic decimal fractions. The preservation, refinement, and advancement of Greek and Indian ideas during the rising tide of the Islamic movement led to the development of algebra—the very word for which comes from Arabic (*al-jabr*) and has somewhat the sense of "rearrangement." Mohammed ibn Musa al-Khwarizmi (c. 780–c. 850 C.E.) began his influential algebra book of the ninth century by praising God for bestowing upon man the power to discover the significance of numbers. The word *algorism* (later, and more commonly, *algorithm*) derives from the author's patronymic.

Calculus may be seen as a post-Renaissance blending of these developments with a new propensity to think in terms of the intuitive notions of variable, function, and limit, coupled with the development of analytic geometry, which unites large parts of algebra and geometry through the use of Cartesian coordinates. The joining together of such diverse ideas gave mathematics (and physical science) an astounding vitality in the seventeenth century. Isaac Newton (1642–1727) and Gottfried Wilhelm Leibniz (1646–1716) were the first to see the calculus as a unified whole that studies the interplay between functions and derivatives. This interplay casts light upon previously perplexing philosophical and scientific problems concerning the notions of instantaneous velocity and acceleration, gives new and efficient ways to find optimal solutions to many types of problems, and provides natural and effective methods for solving equations and for finding lengths of curves and sizes of areas and volumes. Newton used the calculus, together with his physical laws (axioms) of motion, to show how Kepler's observations about planetary motion follow from the law of gravity.

The scientific successes of "reason" inspired attempts to extend its methods beyond science. The philosophy of René Descartes (1596–1650), who developed analytic geometry, drew a clear distinction between reason and ecclesiastical authority. Descartes—and, later, both Newton and Leibniz—made serious, rational contributions to theology.

The early reaction to such efforts by Blaise Pascal (1623–1662), who had helped develop several nascent branches of mathematics (probability, projective geometry, and calculus), would be telling.

Repelled by the idea of a god "of philosophers and scholars," Pascal abandoned everything for theology, returning to mathematics only once, in 1658, when he published some pretty results about the cycloid that calculus students still study. Pascal's writings exalting heart over mind ("Humble thyself, impotent reason!") would be seen to help inspire romanticism during a much later period, which left in its wake a great gap between the sciences and the humanities. Mathematics would find itself stretched ever more tenuously across this gap.

Ironically, the great mathematical advances of the so-called Age of Reason owe more to the imagination and intuition of mathematicians than to their logic and reason. The development of calculus was facilitated, as its developers were well aware, by a relaxation of the strictures of rigorous geometrical methods that proceed from precise definitions and clear first principles. Instead, mathematicians embraced loose numerical methods allowing unending decimal expansions and other *infinite sums*—thus going far beyond the finite arithmetic of the Greeks. This attitude led both to unprecedented progress in research and to occasional confusion and contradiction. The logical difficulties encountered were principally due to the suggestive, but slippery, notion of an *infinitesimal,* which was supposed to be a discrete entity that retained qualities of the continuous. Not until the precise formulation of the notion of a *limit* by Augustin-Louis Cauchy (1789–1857) and others were these difficulties decisively overcome.

In the meantime the shaky foundations of the calculus were exposed by the philosopher George Berkeley (1685–1753), an Anglican bishop, who published in 1734 a witty and acerbic essay called *The Analyst,* where he famously (and justly) ridiculed infinitesimals as "ghosts of departed quantities." His subtitle—*To an Infidel Mathematician*—reflects his purpose, to rebuke mathematicians of his day by showing that their discipline contains mysteries no less subtle than those of theology. Perhaps the best eighteenth-century advice to those who would learn the calculus was given by the French mathematician Jean le Rond d'Alembert (1717–1783): "Go forward, and faith will follow."

The search for coherence: Euclid's legacy

The *axiomatic method* consists in somehow intuiting basic accepted facts (axioms) about a discipline and logically deducing all else. Axiomatization of the real number system in order to derive rigorously the results of calculus—and thereby answer criticisms of Berkeley and others—did not occur until the late nineteenth century, when finally rational sense was made out of the huge mass of calculus-inspired research largely due to, but overly dependent upon, an unbridled trust in mathematical intuition. Pressure to provide such coherence to a discipline usually comes only when its elements have been basically established and it is time to synthesize a great web of connections into a consistent body of work.

The most celebrated example of such a synthesis is Euclid's *Elements,* which appeared in Alexandria around 300 B.C.E. Here, the towering edifice of geometry appears to be solidly built up by logic, unerringly applied to a small number of "self-evident" facts that we are willing to accept at the outset. The *Elements* is doubly valuable, however, because its study—with the help of a skilled tutor—will also impart the dual thinking techniques of analysis and synthesis that are indispensable in achieving rational coherence in any discipline. Analysis, as Plato used the term, refers to the testing of the truth of a proposition by deducing implications from it. If one of these implications is false, then the proposition must of course be false (*reductio ad absurdum*); otherwise, one hopes to deduce a consequence that is self-evidently true, and a synthetic proof is said to be obtained if the steps in this deduction can be reversed so as to obtain the given proposition as a logical consequence of self-evident truths.

The power of such analysis had been strikingly felt when the central tenet of the Pythagorean faith—the proposition that every ratio can be expressed as a ratio of whole numbers—was tested and proved false by *reductio ad absurdum*: If the proposition were true, then the ratio of the diagonal of a square to its side would be expressible as a ratio of integers. But this implies (to use modern terminology) that the square root of two is rational, which leads to contradiction, as first noted by the Pythagoreans about 430 B.C.E. Perhaps partly as a consequence of the limitations of arithmetic revealed by this shock, the Greeks came to look more favorably upon geometry, which Euclid attempted to put on a firm, rational foundation. It was not, however, until the nineteenth century that the foundations of mathematics were seen to require substantially more careful attention than Euclid had provided.

Archimedes (287–212 B.C.E.) effectively invented mathematical physics by giving an axiomatic development to hydrostatics, beginning by deriving from simple axioms the fundamental law of the lever. He then went on to discuss rigorously how to find centers of gravity of complicated solids, solving problems that are routinely handled today, but only by using calculus in a fairly sophisticated way. Mathematical physics came of age with Newton in the seventeenth century, and physicists today who seek an axiomatic basis for quantum mechanics follow in this tradition.

Western civilization has absorbed over a thousand editions of the *Elements,* whose influence is sometimes subtly felt. As noted by Bertrand Russell in *Wisdom of the West* (1959), a revealing moment in the Enlightenment occurred in 1776 when Benjamin Franklin spotted the phrase "sacred and undeniable" in the penultimate draft of the American Declaration of Independence and suggested that "self-evident" be substituted. A revolutionary list of moral and political rights of individuals was thus introduced to the world not with a religious invocation, but with an implicit salute to Euclid: "We hold these truths to be self-evident."

In contrast to Euclid, who presumably thought that his basic axioms about geometry were obviously true, both Nicolaus Copernicus (1473–1543) and Kepler on occasion spoke of an "axiom" of astronomy as a provisional truth that one might someday hope to establish. Axioms of empirical disciplines may alternatively be viewed simply as facts to be tested by analyzing their implications to see how well they model reality. The scope of axiomatics was decisively extended beyond the sciences when Baruch Spinoza (1632–1677) set down philosophical axioms and deduced the consequences in his *Ethics.* Systematic theology embraces a similar method of exposition when it exhibits the collective implications of basic religious tenets as a rationally coherent system.

In light of these modern points of view, the existence of non-Euclidean geometry—a startling development when Euclid was thought to represent "absolute truth"—is now seen as unsurprising. If "light rays" of physics are to be modeled by "lines" from geometry, why should the lines satisfy Euclid's axioms, now that we know of consistent mathematical structures developed by N.I. Lobachevsky (1792–1856) and G.F.B. Riemann (1826–1866) in which "points" and "lines" can be defined in such a way that Euclid's parallel postulate fails while the other axioms hold? Modern physicists routinely use non-Euclidean geometry to model the cosmos.

Faith in Euclid's absolute truth is thus clearly unfounded. In fact, modern mathematicians, when presented with axioms defining a vector space or some other mathematical structure, typically do not ask whether the axioms are "true," but instead set about deducing theorems that must hold for every structure satisfying the given axioms. The existence of foundational mathematical structures such as the real number system, out of which vastly complicated, useful, and interesting structures can be constructed, is generally regarded as unproblematic by working mathematicians. Mathematical logicians, on the other hand, study foundational questions intensely, usually basing their work upon the theory of sets. The surprising "incompleteness" theorem proved in 1931 by Kurt Gödel (1906–1978) demonstrated unforeseen limitations in the power of the axiomatic method and has sparked further study.

Conclusion

Modern mathcmatics has expanded far beyond the study of calculus and differential equations that has helped scientists to cope with continuous processes and, as well, beyond the developments in probability and statistics that have advanced the mathematical treatment of discrete processes. Carl Friedrich Gauss (1777–1855), perhaps the greatest modern mathematician, made deep contributions to almost all areas of the subject. By the early twentieth century, however, the scope of mathematics had grown so large that no single mathematician could claim to have mastered more than a small portion of the field.

The attraction of mathematics as a worthy human interest lies in discovering and establishing surprising and interesting connections between apparently disparate mathematical ideas that have not yet been fully comprehended. Mathematicians pursue useful goals, but while attaining them they often meet new ideas without immediate practical

value that are appealing in their own right. Sometimes, intriguingly, these ideas prove to be surprisingly useful, whereas their initial appeal is only aesthetic in the sense that they seem to call for an imaginative synthesis expressed with clarity and style. "The love of a subject in itself and for itself, where it is not the sleepy pleasure of pacing a mental quarter-deck, is the love of style as manifested in that study," said the mathematician and philosopher Alfred North Whitehead (1861-1947).

Whitehead contended that pure mathematics, in its modern developments, may claim to be the most original creation of the human spirit. A similar claim might be made in connection with an often overlooked feature of its ancient development. Howard deLong perceptively observes in *A Profile of Mathematical Logic* (1970) that early Greek interest in abstract thought owes much to the expansion, from the physical to the mental arena, of the familiar spirit of competition and play. The sportive aspect of the play of the mind, which animates mathematics in its purest form, is bound up with this remarkable growth of the human spirit so long ago.

In *A Mathematician's Apology* (1940), G. H. Hardy (1877-1947) bases his defense upon aesthetic grounds and confesses a genuine passion for his calling. Something akin to Hardy's passion is known to all who have experienced the revelation that follows a spell of total concentration and have found themselves echoing in their own tongue Archimedes's famous cry of eureka ("I have found it"). Mathematicians count heavily upon the spirit that compels such engagements and articulates such an involuntary cry of delight. What transpires under its spell may even seem like something done to—rather than by—a mathematician. No one seems ever to have argued, however, that a calling to an Archimedean engagement implies the existence of a "caller." Attitudes of mathematicians toward religion range from Whitehead's well-known sympathy for the religious experience to Hardy's strongly opposing view.

See also ALGORITHM; GALILEO GALILEI; PLATO

Bibliography

Bell, Eric Temple. *The Development of Mathematics*. New York: McGraw-Hill, 1945.

Berggren, J. L. *Episodes in the Mathematics of Medieval Islam*. New York: Springer-Verlag, 1986.

Burkert, Walter. *Lore and Science in Ancient Pythagoreanism,* trans. Edwin L. Minar Jr. Cambridge, Mass.: Harvard University Press, 1972.

Burtt, Edwin Arthur. *The Metaphysical Foundations of Modern Physical Science,* Rev. edition. New York: Harcourt, 1932.

Courant, Richard, and Robbins, Herbert. *What is Mathematics? An Elementary Approach to Ideas and Methods.* Ed. Ian Stewart. New York: Oxford University Press, 1996.

Crosby, Alfred W. *The Measure of Reality: Quantification and Western Society, 1250–1600.* Cambridge, UK: Cambridge University Press, 1997.

Davis, Philip J., and Hersh, Reuben. *The Mathematical Experience.* Boston: Birkhäuser, 1981.

DeLong, Howard. *A Profile of Mathematical Logic.* Reading, Mass.: Addison-Wesley, 1970.

Field, J. V. *Kepler's Geometrical Cosmology.* Chicago: University of Chicago Press, 1988.

Grant, Hardy. "Mathematics and the Liberal Arts." *College Mathematics Journal* 30 (1999): 96–105, 197–203.

Grattan-Guinness, Ivor. *The Fontana History of the Mathematical Sciences.* London: Fontana Press, 1997.

Hardy, G. H. *A Mathematician's Apology.* Cambridge, UK: Cambridge University Press, 1940.

Hersh, Reuben. *What is Mathematics, Really?* New York: Oxford University Press, 1997.

Kline, Morris. *Mathematics in Western Culture.* Oxford: Oxford University Press, 1953.

Lloyd, G.E.R. "Science and Mathematics." In *The Legacy of Greece,* ed. Moses I. Finley. Oxford: Clarendon Press, 1981.

Marrou, Henri Irénée. *A History of Education in Antiquity,* trans. George Lamb. New York: Sheed and Ward, 1956.

Priestley, William M. *Calculus: A Liberal Art.* New York: Springer-Verlag, 1998.

Russell, Bertrand. *Wisdom of the West: A Historical Survey of Western Philosophy in Its Social and Political Setting.* Garden City, N.Y.: Doubleday, 1959.

Stein, Sherman. *Archimedes: What Did He Do Besides Cry Eureka?* Washington, D.C.: Mathematical Association of America, 1999.

Westfall, Richard S. *Never at Rest: A Biography of Isaac Newton.* Cambridge, UK: Cambridge University Press, 1980.

Whitehead, Alfred North. "Mathematics as an Element in the History of Thought." In *Science and the Modern World.* New York: Macmillan, 1925.

Whitehead, Alfred North. "The Aims of Education." In *The Aims of Education and Other Essays.* New York: Macmillan, 1929.

W. M. PRIESTLEY

MEDICAL ETHICS

Moral concerns have always been implicit in medicine. Indeed, the division between science and values—the objectivity sought in the study of nature and the values governing human behavior—disappears at the bedside. The medical choices made by physicians and their patients must, by their very nature, reflect a complex array of values that determine how the findings of clinical science and the applications of their associated technologies are to be deployed in the care of the ill. Thus medicine necessarily obscures the line separating science and human values because of the intimate connection between clinical science and its object of study and intervention: the person—the nexus of politico-judicial action, moral agency, scientific scrutiny, and religious sanctification.

The origins of contemporary medical ethics may be traced to the Enlightenment, when the science of morals and the morals of science became the subject of intense deliberation, and from which medical ethics arose as a system of mutually related contracts between doctor and patient (Haakonssen 1997). But an even older religious tradition—Catholic (Kelly 1979), Protestant (Fletcher 1954), and Jewish (Jakobovits 1959)—has debated the moral implications of modern medicine generally, and in particular, since the mid-twentieth century, those matters arising in consequence of clinical interventions that challenged dogma about life and death, including abortion, terminal care, genetic counseling, and the like. But medical ethics in its present form—philosophical, secular, legalistic, and professionalized—has had a brief history.

During the late 1960s, medical ethics burst forth into the political arena. Rapid technological advances brought new challenges to the very definition of life and death. This in itself would have initiated speculations over how such new-found scientific power should be utilized. In addition, a massive social realignment was underway under the auspices of a renewed commitment to civil and human rights. Focused upon various forms of paternalism, particularly heated debates about informed consent for therapy, protection of subjects enrolled in human research, and recourse to medical malpractice, stimulated both a reexamination of the ethics underlying these issues as well as a more general discussion of medicine's moral philosophy and legal standing (Rothman 1991; Jonsen 1995). Soon, medical ethics became a formal discipline, replete with institutes, journals, books, conferences, and professionals devoted to what had heretofore been a subject reserved for religious contemplation.

Definitions and distinctions

Medical ethics may be defined as the discourse that seeks to define moral guidelines for the care of patients. Within this discipline, a distinction must be drawn between *judicial medical ethics* and *philosophical medical ethics*. In the former, medical ethics comprises rules or procedures established by governing agencies and the courts meant to guide decision-making in difficult areas like abortion, for example, or the involuntary commitment of a psychotic patient. In this context, medical ethics implicitly informs the legal directives, and "risk management," the distillation of this discourse, defines the procedures hospitals and health care professionals follow to minimize their legal liability. On the other hand, philosophical medical ethics has no proscribed rules, only a tradition of offering philosophical or theological perspectives to ethical dilemmas and proposing possible answers. Thus, diverse matters ranging from informed consent to end of life issues to new technological opportunities (e.g., artificial insemination) may be addressed at these two levels, the judicial and the philosophical: What, on the basis of the law, is the correct procedure for dealing with a clinical predicament? or, alternatively, What are the secular ethical or religious principles that offer ways of thinking about a morally ambiguous problem? Judicial medical ethics—practical instructions, rules, regulations, contracts, and ultimately the law—may be distilled from such philosophical deliberations, and these, together with judicial precedent and political considerations ultimately result in accepted practice. In short, although the law is the final arbiter of practice, philosophical ideas impact on the shape of social policy.

This entry will consider "medical ethics" solely in its philosophical mode. It is around this topic that one can most clearly discern how theologians, poised and ready to participate in a discourse they had already developed for their own purposes, offer insights (and ideologies) from their rich intellectual and religious heritage in order to influence the development of contemporary judicial and philosophical medical ethics (Lammers and Verhay 1987; Verhay and Lammers 1993; Camenisch 1994).

The competition of moral principles

Medicine reflects broad social values, and American multiculturalism has demanded a mixture of ethical precepts from diverse sources. In the end, citizens live together under a common law, one that seeks to satisfy the pluralistic demands of contemporary life and still remain faithful to the older core of foundational principles. Since at least World War II, America has developed a rights-based culture that endeavors to respect the autonomy of its citizens and thereby to enhance their ability to enjoy life's pursuits offered by the opportunities afforded by civil equality and respect for differences in religion, race, sexual orientation, and a whole host of differentiating characteristics (Sandel 1995). American medicine has been caught in this vast social experiment stimulated by cultural diversity and unified by constitutional law.

So when medical ethicists ponder, "Under what circumstances are particular ethical responses evoked?" or "What are the ethical implications of those ethical choices?" their answers draw upon a complex array of moral principles forged together from various religious traditions and secular moral philosophies. Given the current dominant legal and political culture based upon the protection of individual rights, autonomy as a governing philosophical principle has been prioritized in medical ethics. For, as noted above, in the process of deliberating medical ethics, philosophers consider the practical application of their studies, and these are, in a sense, over-determined by legal interpretation, one focused on rights. Thus, in the judicial context, medical ethics is like a lopsided table with five legs: Although autonomy, beneficence, justice, utilitarianism, and non-malfeasance each claim consideration, autonomy usually trumps other contenders (Beauchamp and Childress 2001). This dominance has been widely regarded as both a judicial and philosophical problem.

Autonomy draws on two understandings of freedom (Berlin 1969): One is negative, the freedom from oppression or interference by another, and the second is positive, the freedom to participate in the process by which one's life is controlled. In the research setting, autonomy in the form of informed consent is the governing principle that protects human research subjects from hidden manipulation (Belmont Report 1979). And while in the clinic and the hospital, similar rules of informed consent operate, a rights-based morality makes little attempt to articulate the ethics of other dimensions of the doctor-patient relationship. And here we discover an ambiguous moral construction lying at the foundation of medical care.

Indisputably, autonomy serves a vital judicial-legal function in our system of medical law, and this may well account for its continued importance, but it is more likely that the moral depth of our notions of respect for persons reflects a still deeper commitment to Western religious roots (Downie and Telfer 1969; Thomasma 1984; Engelhardt 1996). Our care of the ill is based on a deep metaphysical sense of response to the other, a reaction that generates *response-ibility* (Tauber 1999). This ethical metaphysics is essentially a theological assertion, not a philosophical one. This position was first espoused by the early founders of American medical ethics, Joseph Fletcher (1954) and Paul Ramsey (1970). They championed autonomy, because this principle reflected their basic humanitarianism as theologians (Jonsen 1998). But autonomy had little philosophical support in their writings, where it served as a placeholder for a humane medicine, one that held the sanctity of life paramount. Indeed, by not delineating how autonomy was in competition with other moral tenets, these early discussions inadvertently obfuscated the complexity of medicine's moral universe.

Physicians and nurses assume responsibility for the care of their patients, and the "moral space" in which patients reside is not necessarily coincident with that of autonomous citizens. Autonomy is inadequate, by itself, to account for medicine's moral calling because of two failings. First, from the patient's perspective, the notion of autonomy is frequently distorted in the clinical setting

(Schneider 1998; Tauber 2001). Patients necessarily relinquish their full autonomy to experts, and in this regard, they cannot make truly autonomous, self-reliant, fully informed decisions, and must instead ultimately rely on the competence and good will of their health-care providers to represent their best interests. Second, autonomy as a construct cannot account for the ethical responsibilities of the caregiver (Tauber 1999). The sense of responsibility exhibited by physicians and nurses arises from their sense of care for others, not primarily from a set of rules designed to protect patient autonomy. Respect for the person in this setting is implicit to their professional role, a role characterized by a profound sense of commitment to their charge. This ethic of compassion regards autonomy as only one of a number of moral principles governing the caring relationship, among which it finds in beneficence a more resonant expression of medicine's fundamental ethos. This is the moral principle that perhaps most obviously captures the Judeo-Christian religious ethos, the appreciation that God's work on Earth is articulated through the caring relationship between people and their respective responsibility for each other (Pelligrino and Thomasma 1988; Kultgen 1995). The foundations of social justice and much of the implicit understanding of our social mores are based on this deep moral maxim.

Thus "patients" and "citizens" are revealed as not necessarily occupying the same ethical domain. While their respective moral identities overlap, they nonetheless are distinct. The patient, at least in the autonomy model, receives medical attention only to the extent that his or her rights as an autonomous citizen are respected. This is essentially a defensive posture, one at potential odds with those moral (ultimately religious) concerns most prominent for the doctor or nurse, whose primary ethical affiliation is to beneficence (Pelligrino and Thomasma 1988) or, in another format, responsibility (Tauber 1999).

Seeking a synthesis

Much of philosophical medical ethics has been devoted to balancing the politico-legal view of individual autonomy with other moral principles that make strong claims in the medical culture. Although (secular) autonomy and (religious) beneficence has each followed a historical and philosophical trajectory of its own, they may be reduced to a more basic formulation, a moral foundation, which, for the sake of simplicity is, "Respect for the person" (Ramsey 1970). This idea of the inalienable sanctity and dignity of every human being derives most directly from ancient themes in the Western religious culture rather than from philosophy as such, and may account for the hold of "autonomy" on Western moral sensibilities. For theologians as well as nonbelievers, the sanctity of life—essentially a religious principle—remains paramount even as it was secularized into the political principle of autonomy (Callahan 1969; Jonsen 1998).

Autonomy, a relatively new moral tenet, claims a dual heritage: The first source derives from notions of Puritan personal religious responsibility and conscience, balanced against the obligations of persons to a community designed to serve God (Shain 1995); the second source, again religious in origin, arises from natural law's endowment of persons with natural rights, self-governance, and the freedom to pursue their own dictates (Schneewind 1998). This latter tributary, one we might call individualistic, grew at the expense of communal values in the development of American democracy, while European views of autonomy have more evenly balanced community interests and responsibilities (as evidenced by universal socialized health care) against autonomy-based rights in health care delivery. Consequently, in the United States, individual rights increasingly have been regarded as sacrosanct, and correspondingly the respect for persons has shifted from one centered on communal responsibility—both the citizen's identification with the state and the state's responsibility for the citizen—to one focused on autonomy in its more atomistic interpretation (Sandel 1996). And here we see how an ethos of responsibility for others ("caring") may be subordinated to a preoccupation with protecting the rights of the individual.

The seam that ties religious and secular philosophies together is not always evident, which is strong testament to the success of liberal society, but as this discussion has emphasized, conflicting moral orientations may still show signs of differing ethical perspectives straining against one another. While autonomy carries the ancient banner of life's sanctity, its contemporary secularized meaning and applications have shorn off its religious heritage,

leaving its more immediate allegiances plainly in view. So when this political and judicial principle is extended to medical ethics, the law accompanies the ill to the clinic and hospital to protect citizens. Due to this legal extrapolation, the more ancient basis of the doctor-patient relationship must accommodate a superimposed orientation different in kind and purpose to an older ethic of caring. And perhaps of more concern, telling lapses in judiciary medical ethics appear as the discourse stutters when addressing the legal basis of beneficent concerns: Physician fiduciary responsibility, those duties dictated by law that translate beneficence into standards of care, are restricted only to maintaining patient confidentiality, disclosing financial conflicts of interest, and prohibiting the abandonment of patients (Rodwin 1995); Good Samaritan laws protect doctors from suits arising from non-consented care only in the most dire of circumstances; empathy has no legal basis whatsoever.

In summary, the complexity of medical ethics begs for a full hearing, to reflect both the claims of individual rights as well as the demands of a morality that fosters responsibility. In that discussion, a combination of various moral principles allows for a philosophical discourse that attempts to represent fairly diverse interests and relationships, including the challenge of accommodating different belief systems. The product of that deliberation, which must draw upon the entire Western tradition of philosophy and its handmaiden, theology, frames a perspective on, and the terms of, the never-ending debate over the most crucial nexus of human endeavor, the life and death decisions so manifest within modern medicine's power to influence, if not control.

See also ABORTION; BIOTECHNOLOGY; MEDICINE; REPRODUCTIVE TECHNOLOGY

Bibliography

Beauchamp, Tom L., and Childress, James F. *Principles of Biomedical Ethics,* 5th edition. New York: Oxford University Press, 2001.

Berlin, Isaiah. "Two Concepts of Liberty." In *Four Essays on Liberty.* New York: Oxford University Press, 1969.

Callahan, Daniel. "The Sanctity of Life." In *Updating Life and Death: Essays in Ethics and Medicine,* ed. Donald R. Cutler. Boston: Beacon Press, 1969.

Camenisch, Paul E., ed. *Religious Methods and Resources in Bioethics*. Dordrecht, Netherlands: Kluwer Academic, 1994.

Engelhardt, H. Tristram. *The Foundations of Bioethics,* 2nd edition. New York: Oxford University Press, 1996.

Fletcher, Joseph. *Morals and Medicine. The Moral Problems of: The Patient's Right to Know the Truth, Contraception, Artificial Insemination, Sterilization, and Euthanasia*. Princeton, N.J.: Princeton University Press, 1954.

Haakonssen, Lisbeth. *Medicine and Morals in the Enlightenment: John Gregory, Thomas Percival, and Benjamin Rush*. Amsterdam and Atlanta, Ga.: Rodopi, 1997.

Jakobovits, Immanuel. *Jewish Medical Ethics: Comparative and Historical Study of the Jewish Religious Attitude to Medicine and Its Practice*. New York: Bloch, 1959.

Jonsen, Albert R. *The Birth of Bioethics*. New York: Oxford University Press, 1998.

Kelly, David F. *The Emergence of Roman Catholic Medical Ethics in North America: An Historical, Methodological, Bibliographical Study*. New York and Toronto: Edwin Mellen Press, 1979.

Kultgen, John. *Autonomy and Intervention: Parentalism in the Caring Life*. New York: Oxford University Press, 1995.

Lammers, Stephen E., and Verhey, Allen, eds. *On Moral Medicine: Theological Perspectives in Medical Ethics*. Grand Rapids, Mich.: Eerdmans, 1987.

National Commission for the Protection of Human Subjects of Biomedical and Behavioral Research. *Belmont Report: Ethical Principles and Guidelines for the Protection of Human Subjects of Research*. Washington, D.C.: Department of Health, Education, and Welfare, 1979. Distributed by the U.S. Government Printing Office.

Pelligrino, Edmund D., and Thomasma, David C. *For the Patient's Good: The Restoration of Beneficence in Health Care*. New York: Oxford University Press, 1988.

Ramsey, Paul. *The Patient as Person: Medical and Legal Intersections*. New Haven, Conn.: Yale University Press, 1970.

Rodwin, Mark A. "Strains in the Fiduciary Metaphor: Divided Physician Loyalties and the Obligations in a Changing Health Care System" *American Journal of Law and Medicine* 21 (1995): 241–257.

Rothman, David J. *Strangers at the Bedside: A History of How Law and Bioethics Transformed Medical Decision Making*. New York: Basic Books, 1991.

Sandel, Michael. *Democracy's Discontent: America in Search of a Public Philosophy*. Cambridge, Mass.: Harvard University Press, 1996.

Schneewind, J. B. *The Invention of Autonomy: A History of Modern Moral Philosophy*. New York: Cambridge University Press, 1998.

Schneider, Carl E. *The Practice of Autonomy: Patients, Doctors, and Medical Decisions*. New York: Oxford University Press, 1998.

Shain, Barry Alan. *The Myth of American Individualism: The Protestant Origins of American Political Thought*. Princeton, N.J.: Princeton University Press, 1994.

Tauber, Alfred I. *Confessions of a Medicine Man: An Essay in Popular Philosophy*. Cambridge, Mass.: MIT Press, 1999.

Tauber, Alfred I. "Historical and Philosophical Reflections on Patient Autonomy." *Health Care Analysis* 9, no. 3 (2001): 299–319.

Thomasma, David C. "The Basis of Medicine and Religion: Respect for Persons." *Linacre Quarterly* 47 (1984): 142–150.

Verhay, Allan, and Lammers, Stephen E. eds. *Theological Voices in Medical Ethics*. Grand Rapids, Mich.: Eerdmans, 1993.

ALFRED I. TAUBER

MEDICINE

Religion and medicine are twin traditions of healing. Although they have overlapped for most of their history, in the past three hundred years the two traditions have become separate and have often been in competition with one another. At the close of the twentieth century, serious consideration began to be given to reintegrating religion and medicine. In this discussion, a review of the historical connection between these two traditions will be offered. Research that has led to a possible rapprochement will be examined as will the implications for practicing clinicians.

Historical background

There is a long historical tradition that connects religion and medicine. The first hospitals in western civilization for care of the sick in the general population, particularly for those unable to pay for their own care, were built by religious groups. In the fourth century, Basil, the Bishop of Caesarea established one of the earliest hospitals based upon the good Samaritan story in the Bible. This building was resurrected in present-day Turkey among almshouses and leper colonies. For the next thousand years, the church would build and staff most hospitals throughout the western world. Many early physicians, especially those in Europe during the Middle Ages and in the New England colonies of the United States during the seventeenth and eighteenth centuries, were also members of the clergy. In Europe, licenses to practice medicine were in fact controlled by the church and church-sponsored universities.

Similarly, the profession of nursing was to emerge out of the Christian church in the 1600s and 1700s with the Daughters of Charity of St. Vincent de Paul, an order of Catholic sisters devoted to the care of the sick. The Daughters of Charity also established the first nursing profession in the United States in Emmitsville, Maryland, in the early 1800s, modeled after nursing in France. Florence Nightingale (1788–1849), after receiving a "calling" from God, would later receive nurses training from the Daughters of Charity and the Protestant deaconesses (started up by Lutherans in Germany). After the Crimean War, Nightingale applied what she learned to a secular setting. Interestingly, though, up until the early 1900s, most hospitals in Europe and the United States continued to be staffed by nurses who were primarily from religious orders.

Beginning in the fifteenth century, the profession of medicine began to split away from the church, and the state took over the role of administering licenses to practice medicine. That separation would continue to widen until the early 1800s when it was nearly complete. For the last two hundred years, religion and medicine have been divided into separate healing disciplines, with very little overlap and very little communication between the two. However, since about the mid-1990s, especially in the United States, there has been active dialogue about bringing religion and medicine together once again. This movement has been highly controversial and has met with considerable resistance. A growing volume of research showing a connection between religion and health, however, has been breaking down the resistance.

Although the history reviewed above applies primarily to the Christian church, there has been similar interest in health and healing running through nearly all the major world religious traditions, including Judaism, Hinduism, Buddhism, Islam, and Chinese religions. Space does not allow for an adequate discussion of historical connections with medicine for each of these traditions, although resources that do so include Lawrence Sullivan's *Healing and Restoring: Health and Medicine in the World's Religious Traditions* (1989) and *Caring and Curing: Health and Medicine in the Western Religious Traditions* (1998) by Ronald Numbers and Darrel Amundsen.

Research on religion and health

The recent trend towards integration of religion and medicine has been stirred primarily by medical research demonstrating intimate and often complex relationships between religion and health. First, many patients indicate that religious beliefs and practices help them to cope with the stress of medical illness. In some areas of the United States, nearly ninety percent of hospitalized patients report that they use religious beliefs to at least a moderate degree to help them to cope. Nearly fifty percent of this group indicate that religion is the most important factor that enables them to cope with medical conditions and the stress they cause. Over one hundred studies have now documented the high prevalence of religious coping among persons with a variety of diseases ranging from diabetes, kidney disease, heart disease, cancer, arthritis, and cystic fibrosis, to more general conditions such as chronic pain.

There is also research demonstrating that persons who are religious end up coping better with physical health problems and disabling conditions. Of nearly one hundred studies conducted during the twentieth century on the relationship between religion and emotional well-being (happiness, life satisfaction, optimism, and hope), nearly eighty percent find that the religious person experiences significantly greater well-being. This is particularly true when populations of medically ill subjects have been studied. The religious are less likely to become depressed or anxious, and if they do develop these mental conditions, they recover more quickly. Suicide is less common among the more religious, as is marital dissatisfaction and divorce, and alcohol and drug use. Nearly 850 studies have now examined these associations, with between two-thirds and three-quarters of these finding that the religious person tends to be healthier and better able to cope with illness.

Of course, a number of studies also report that religion can be associated with worse mental health, more depression, and greater anxiety. This is particularly true for practitioners of religions that are repressive, controlling, and do not emphasize caring for self and others in a responsible way. Religion can be used to justify hatred, aggression, prejudice, and social exclusion. It may induce excessive guilt in situations where guilt is not healthy. Religion may also be used to replace professional psychiatric care for serious mental or emotional problems that require medication and biological therapies. In all of these ways, religion may do a disservice to mental health. In most cases, however, the emotional benefits of religious faith tend to outweigh the negative effects.

There is also a growing volume of research suggesting that religious belief and practices are related to healthier lifestyles, better overall physical health, and longer survival. Studies demonstrate stronger immune functioning among religious persons who are older, who are HIV positive or have AIDS, or have breast cancer. Death rates from coronary artery disease are lower among the more religious, even when health behaviors, diet, and social factors are taken into account. The same applies to mortality from all causes. Since 1990, over a dozen careful studies have demonstrated that the religious person lives longer than the person who is less religiously involved. In these studies, religion is measured by frequency of church attendance, private prayer and scripture study, meditation, and religious coping. Studies have not demonstrated that the broader aspect of religion called *spirituality* is associated with greater longevity. Spirituality is a broad concept, making it difficult to measure, whereas religious beliefs, practices, and commitment can be more easily assessed and quantified.

Why does religious belief and practice correlate with and predict greater physical health? The answer may lie in the mind-body relationship. There is growing evidence suggesting that emotions influence physiological processes. Psychological stress, anxiety, and depression have been related to impairments in immune functioning, delayed wound healing, and increased risk for cardiovascular morbidity. If religious beliefs and practices reduce emotional stress, counter anxiety, and prevent or facilitate recovery from depression, then religion may help to neutralize the health-impairing effects that these negative emotions have on physical health, and do so through known biological pathways. Mainstream scientists in the field of psychoneuroimmunology are beginning to explore these connections more seriously.

Since about 1980, people have become increasingly disillusioned with medical care that relies solely on high technology and focuses on the biology of disease, while neglecting the care of the whole person. That disillusionment has caused many patients to express a desire to have their spiritual and emotional needs met, as well as their physical needs. Between one-third and two-thirds of patients consistently indicate that they wish their physicians to address religious or spiritual needs in addition to medical needs, particularly when they experience serious medical problems or terminal illness.

Furthermore, there is research indicating that religious and spiritual beliefs impact medical decision making and may even affect compliance with medical treatment, making it essential for physicians to know about these beliefs. Some patients may use religion instead of traditional medical care to treat their illnesses. For example, they may decide to pray for their illnesses and stop taking their medications. There is also research showing that certain types of negative religious beliefs may adversely affect physical health and recovery from medical illness. Patients who feel punished or deserted by God, who question God's power and love, or who feel abandoned by their spiritual community, experience greater mortality and worse mental health outcomes.

Application to medical practice

The growing body of research on religion and health suggests at least the following four applications to medical practice in the West. First, in light of this research, some have argued that physicians should consider taking a spiritual history on patients with serious, terminal, or chronic medical illness. In the United States, only about one in ten physicians consistently addresses spiritual issues by taking a religious history, despite suggestions by a consensus panel of the American College of Physicians and American Society of Internal Medicine that such a history can be obtained by asking a few simple questions. Such questions include the following:

(1) Are religious beliefs a sense of comfort or a source of stress for the patient?

(2) Is the patient a member of a spiritual community and is this a source of support for the patient?

(3) Does the patient have any religious belief that may influence medical decisions or conflict with medical care?

(4) There any religious or spiritual needs present that need addressing?

Taking a spiritual history should be done in addition to (not instead of) competently and completely addressing the medical issues for which the patient seeks help from the physician. Thus, a spiritual history is most appropriate when there is more time in the schedule, such as during a new patient evaluation or during a hospital admission workup.

Second, if spiritual needs are identified when the spiritual history is taken, then the research suggests that addressing those needs should improve the health and coping capacity of the patient. This can be done in a couple of ways. The patient can be referred to a trained clergyperson or chaplain. Chaplains in the United States are required to undergo extensive training that prepares them to address such issues in the medical setting. Before a chaplain is certified in the Association of Professional Chaplains, he or she must complete four years of college, three years of divinity school, one to four years of clinical pastoral education, and must take written and oral examinations. Thus, chaplains are skilled professionals with much to offer in this area. Sometimes, however, patients do not wish to speak with a chaplain or clergyperson. In that case, if the patient already has a trusting relationship with the physician, then the physician may need to be prepared to address such issues, even if this involves only listening and showing respect and concern. Nearly two-thirds of the medical schools in the United States have elective or required courses on religion, spirituality, and medicine. In these courses, medical students are trained to take a spiritual history and to address spiritual issues in a sensitive and appropriate manner.

Third, in addition to taking a spiritual history and, if necessary, addressing spiritual issues, the physician may choose to support healthy religious beliefs or practices that the patient finds helpful in coping with illness. Physicians should not prescribe religion for patients who are not interested in religion. There may be benefits, however, in physicians learning about the religious beliefs and practices of their patients and supporting those beliefs that the patient finds helpful and that do not conflict with medical care. Even when religious beliefs conflict with medical care, the patient is likely to profit when the physician tries to understand those beliefs and keep open lines of communication about religious issues with the patient. By way of supporting religious practice, some physicians have decided to pray with their patients. This activity is highly controversial in the medical setting. Conditions for its appropriateness include that:

(1) A spiritual history has been taken and the physician knows about the religious background of the patient.

(2) Religion is important to the patient and is used in coping.

(3) The religious background of the patient and the physician are similar.

(4) Either the patient asks the physician to pray (i.e., patient initiates the prayer) or, if the physician initiates it, the physician is certain that the patient would appreciate this activity.

(5) The situation calls for prayer (i.e., a difficult, uncontrollable, or stressful situation, severe medical condition, or terminal illness).

Under such circumstances, it may be helpful for a physician and patient to engage in prayer together, enhancing the doctor-patient relationship by increasing trust.

Finally, the research suggests that new social arrangements for medical care may prove beneficial. For example, physicians might develop a communication network with local clergy, both to facilitate a referral base and to allow physicians to assess the community resources that are available to the patient. Religious communities often already provide volunteers to assist with homemaker services, rides to the doctor, respite for exhausted family members caring for the patient, and emotional support to the patient and the patient's family. Religious communities may also monitor the patient to ensure that the medical regimen is being followed and that medical problems are detected early and treatment is obtained promptly. Such a system works especially well when volunteers are appropriately trained and coordinated by a parish or congregational nurse—a registered nurse who is a member of and works professionally as a nurse within the congregation. A parish nurse can coordinate health programs within the congregation that involve screening for high blood pressure, diabetes, depression, and other diseases. A parish nurse can also provide spiritual care, communicate with physicians and nurses within the formal healthcare setting about the health condition of members of the congregation, train and mobilize volunteers within the religious community to meet the needs of sick members, and provide health education to keep healthy members well.

Religion and Western medicine are indeed coming closer and closer together. The research suggests that this is a positive trend—good for the health of patients and for the maintenance of the health of the community. It is also arguably good for the profession of medicine in the West, which is truest to its most basic aims when its practices support the health of the patients in every dimension.

See also MIND-BODY THEORIES; PLACEBO EFFECT; SPIRITUALITY AND HEALTH; SPIRITUALITY AND FAITH HEALING

Bibliography

Carson, Verna Benner, and Koenig, Harold G. *Parish Nursing: Stories of Service and Care.* Radnor, Pa.: Templeton Foundation Press, 2002.

Koenig, Harold G. "Religion, Spirituality and Medicine: Application to Clinical Practice." *Journal of the American Medical Association* 284 (2000): 1708.

Koenig, Harold G; McCullough, Michael E.; and Larson, David B. *Handbook of Religion and Health.* New York: Oxford University Press, 2001.

Koenig, Harold G. *Spirituality in Patient Care: Why, How, When, and What.* Radnor, Pa.: Templeton Foundation Press, 2002.

Koenig, Harold G., and Cohen, Harvey J. *The Link Between Religion and Health: Psychoneuroimmunology and the Faith Factor.* New York: Oxford University Press, 2002.

Lo, Bernard; Quill, Timothy; and Tulsky, James. "Discussing Palliative Care with Patients." *Annals of Internal Medicine* 130 (1999): 744–749.

Mueller, Paul S.; Plevak, David J.; and Rummans, Teresa A. "Religious Involvement, Spirituality, and Medicine: Implications for Clinical Practice." *Mayo Clinic Proceedings* 76 (2001): 1225–1235.

Numbers, Ronald L., and Amundsen, Darrel W., eds. *Caring and Curing: Health and Medicine in the Western Religious Traditions.* Baltimore, Md.: Johns Hopkins University Press, 1998.

Sloan, Richrd P.; Bagiella, Emilia.; and Powell, T. "Religion, Spirituality, and Medicine." *The Lancet* 353 (1999): 664–667.

Sloan, Richard P.; Bagiella, Emilia; VandeCreek, Larry.; et al. "Should Physicians Prescribe Religious Activities?" *New England Journal of Medicine* 342 (2000): 1913–1916.

Sullivan, Lawrence E. *Healing and Restoring: Health and Medicine in the World's Religious Traditions.* New York: Macmillan, 1989.

HAROLD G. KOENIG

MEDITATION

Meditation, from the Latin word *meditari* (to meditate), means deep or continued reflection and is often seen as preparatory to contemplation, a state of direct spiritual or intuitive seeing. Meditation is found in all religious traditions but varies as to method, focus, and religious objectives. Practices range from the *apophatic,* an emptying procedure to clear consciousness (*via negativa*), to the *cataphatic,* where a specific image, idea, or deity is kept in mental focus (*via positiva*). Apophatic practices tend to be more cognitive and intellectual (mind), whereas cataphatic practices are more emotional and devotional (heart). Meditation is the focus of scientific research to determine the neurophysiological conditions productive of meditative awareness.

See also PRAYER AND MEDITATION; SPIRITUALITY

ERNEST SIMMONS

MEMES

The term *meme* was coined by British biologist Richard Dawkins in his 1976 book *The Selfish Gene* to describe a "unit of culture" (p. 203). Examples given are "tunes, ideas, catch-phrases and ... the idea of God." These entities might, he said, act independently as "replicators," like genes, thus determining the state of culture entirely by natural selection among themselves. Critics point out that, if taken seriously, this is a highly reductive and fatalistic doctrine, claiming that memes, rather than human beings, control cultural development. But the suggestion is obscure. Many would argue that elements of culture are not independent entities, nor are units the same as replicators.

See also GENETICS; SOCIOBIOLOGY

Bibliography

Dawkins, Richard. *The Selfish Gene.* Oxford: Oxford University Press, 1976.

MARY MIDGLEY

MENDEL, GREGOR

Although some leading scientists in the late nineteenth century considered religion to be an impediment to progress in science, the life of the monk Gregor Mendel serves as an important counter-example. The fact that a monk initiated one of the greatest advances in biology demonstrates the poverty of the notion of there being a perpetual war between science and religion. In Mendel's case, rather than hindering science, religious institutions promoted scientific knowledge, experimentation, and progress.

Early life and influences

On July 22, 1822, Mendel was born in the village of Heinzendorf (now Hyncice) in northern Moravia (in the present-day Czech Republic), a part of the Austrian Empire that was culturally German. Mendel was originally named Johann, but took the name Gregor in 1843 upon entering the Augustinian order of the Roman Catholic Church. His father was a peasant farmer with a keen interest in improving agriculture. A priest in his community, Father Schreiber, used his knowledge of fruit trees to help his parishioners practically. He studied the latest techniques for improving fruit yields, practiced artificial fertilization, and distributed grafts to community members, including the Mendel family.

Mendel's intellectual abilities were recognized early in his life, and his family sent him to school first in Leipnik (Lipnik) and then to Gymnasium in Troppau (Opava). After graduating from Gymnasium, he attended a two-year course of study at the Philosophical Institute in Olmütz (Olomouc), which was interrupted for a year due to illness. He graduated from the Philosophical Institute in 1843, having studied religion, philosophy, ethics, mathematics, and physics, in order to prepare for further studies in natural science at a university. While in Olmütz, Mendel had grave financial difficulties because his father was incapacitated from work as a result of an injury, and Mendel had difficulty finding tutoring jobs. His poverty probably brought on his illness and caused him continual travail.

Upon the recommendation of one of his teachers, Mendel entered the Augustinian monastery in Brno in 1843. He had begun contemplating entering the Catholic priesthood about three years earlier, but it is not known how seriously or deeply he felt a religious calling. Mendel's own account of entering the monastery emphasized his need to escape from poverty rather than an inner religious motivation. Mendel also knew that the monastery in Brno would be a hospitable environment for pursuing studies in the natural sciences.

Indeed, the Brno monastery, under the leadership of Abbott F. C. Napp, attracted a number of talented men interested in science. Napp himself studied horticulture and wrote a manual about improving plant varieties. He set up a nursery in the monastery where new plant varieties could be developed. Thus, the monastery provided a very propitious environment for the young Mendel, who was encouraged to teach science in nearby schools. The monastery also allowed him to attend the University of Vienna from 1851 to 1853 to study natural science so he could pass the exam to qualify him to teach in a Gymnasium. Mendel never passed this exam, however.

Although the monastery was a stimulating place for the study of natural science, the religious training and exercise in the Brno monastery seems to have been perfunctory. The bishop of Brno criticized Napp and the monastery for devoting so much attention to science, while neglecting the spiritual dimension of monastic life. Shortly after Mendel arrived, a monk there was stripped of his authority to teach because he was accused of introducing Hegelian and pantheistic doctrines into his scientific writings. Napp tried to defend this monk, but to no avail. Mendel never challenged the Catholic Church or its teachings, but his energies were clearly devoted more to scientific pursuits than to religious ones.

Experiments with peas

From 1854 to 1863 Mendel carried out his pea experiments, which later became famous for laying the groundwork for the modern science of genetics. Because Mendel relied on statistics to analyze the results of his work, his background in physics and mathematics provided him insight in developing these experiments. To perform his experiments, Mendel selected twenty-two varieties of pea plants that bred true (i.e., each was a pure variety that, when crossed with its own variety, always had offspring with the same traits as the parents). Each variety was crossed with another with which it differed in an obvious way, such as seed color, pod shape, position of flowers, or length of stem. For example, he crossed one pea variety that had round seeds with another variety that had angular seeds. In the first generation hybrids Mendel observed that all the offspring had the trait of only one of the parent varieties. The hybrid, between peas with round seeds and those with angular seeds produced all round seeds in the first generation. Mendel called the trait that appeared in the first generation the *dominant* trait. This demonstrated that hereditary characters did not blend, as many scientists of the time supposed they did, but rather they were discrete factors.

Mendel continued his experiment by self-fertilizing the first generation hybrids. He discovered that both original traits reemerged in a ratio approximating three (for the dominant trait) to one (for the recessive trait). In the case of the round and angular seeds, Mendel's actual data showed 5474 round seeds and 1850 angular seeds in the second generation. Mendel concluded from his experiments that each plant had two hereditary characters. Each parent would pass only one of its characters on to its offspring. These characters segregate randomly, leading to the ratios Mendel found. This explanation is known as *Mendel's Law of Independent Assortment*.

Mendel published the results of his pea experiments in 1866 in the *Proceedings of the Natural Science Society* of Brno, but even though some

botanists cited his work subsequently, none recognized the full significance of his experiments before 1900. Mendel even corresponded with Karl Nägeli (1817–1891), a prominent botanist, but despite his interest in Mendel's work, Nägeli never realized how important it was. When Mendel died on January 6, 1884, he was almost unknown, though he did express confidence late in his life that his work would be recognized in the future.

Historians still debate the significance of biological evolution for Mendel's work. Charles Darwin (1809–1882) had not yet published his theory of evolution when Mendel began his experiments, but Mendel was already conversant with Charles Lyell's (1797–1875) uniformitarian geology, which had been a formative influence on Darwin. Mendel also studied botany at the University of Vienna under Franz Unger (1800–1870), who embraced a pre-Darwinian evolutionary theory. Mendel was thus fully aware of debates about biological variation and speciation, and he may have hoped that his hybridization experiments would shed light on the evolutionary process.

The rediscovery of Mendel's work in 1900 by three different scientists—Hugo de Vries, Carl Correns, and Erich von Tschermak—occurred in the context of debates over evolution. Biological evolution was widely accepted by European scientists by 1900, but scientists did not have a satisfactory explanation as to how variation occurs or what the mechanisms of heredity are. Mendelian genetics provided new insights about heredity, but also posed new problems for evolutionary theory. De Vries argued that Mendelian genetics provided support for discontinuous variation rather than Darwinian gradualism. On the basis of his misinterpretation of primrose hybridization experiments he thought that mutations—the sudden emergence of new characters—drove the evolutionary process. These new characters were then passed on in Mendelian fashion. Other scientists opposed de Vries's mutation theory and continued arguing for gradual variations. The dispute over gradualism versus discontinuous variation was only settled in the 1930s and 1940s with the integration, known as the neo-Darwinian synthesis, of Darwinian natural selection theory with Mendelian genetics.

Implications for religion

The religious implications of Mendel's theory were minimal, so no significant religious opposition to

Mendelian genetics arose. However, in the early twentieth century, many eugenics proponents began using Mendelian genetics to promote various programs to control human heredity, including sterilization, birth control, incarceration, and regulation of marriage certificates. The Roman Catholic Church and some conservative Protestants opposed eugenics, but they did not criticize Mendelian genetics. Rather they rejected eugenics as a misuse of genetics.

Probably the most significant connection between Mendelian genetics and religion was the use of Mendelian genetics by creationists. Many creationists hailed Mendel's theory of heredity as a proof for biological stasis. The variations that Mendel (and de Vries) observed only involved the reshuffling of hereditary characters (genes) that were already present, not the introduction of new traits. They rejected the neo-Darwinian synthesis, which argued that micro-mutations could accumulate to produce speciation.

Mendel's life and the reception of his ideas demonstrates the way that religious communities and individuals in nineteenth and early twentieth-century Europe often nurtured scientific discovery. They were not only open to new scientific ideas, but in some cases actively cultivated them.

See also CREATION SCIENCE; EUGENICS; EVOLUTION; GENETICS

Bibliography

Bowler, Peter J. *The Mendelian Revolution: The Emergence of Hereditarian Concepts in Modern Science and Society.* Baltimore, Md.: Johns Hopkins University Press, 1989.

Callender, L. A. "Gregor Mendel: An Opponent of Descent with Modification." *History of Science* 26 (1988): 41–75.

Iltis, Hugo. *Life of Mendel.* New York: Hafner, 1966.

Olby, Robert. *Origins of Mendelism,* 2nd edition. Chicago: University of Chicago Press, 1985.

Orel, Vitezslav. *Gregor Mendel: The First Geneticist,* trans. Stephen Finn. Oxford: Oxford University Press, 1996.

Orel, Vitezslav. *Mendel,* trans. Stephen Finn. Oxford: Oxford University Press, 1984.

Stern, Curt, and, Sherwood, Eva R. *The Origin of Genetics: A Mendel Source Book.* San Francisco: W. H. Freeman, 1966.

Wallace, Bruce. *The Search for the Gene.* Ithaca, N.Y.: Cornell University Press, 1992.

RICHARD C. WEIKART

METAPHOR

The word *metaphor* (from the Greek *metaphor,* meaning "transfer") is an important language element in both science and religion. Since the time of the ancient Greek philosopher Aristotle, it has been understood that something strange happens in the process of creating a metaphor. Metaphors change the ways people understand things.

Common definitions of the terms *metaphor, simile,* and *analogy* are not discrete; they refer generally to the substitution of one thing for another. Authors sometimes use one term to refer to all three. For example, in his *Imagery in Scientific Thought* (1987), Arthur I. Miller makes heavy use of the concept of analogy but uses the terms *metaphor* and *metaphorical,* perhaps preferring the complexity, inscrutability, and sophistication of the term *metaphor* over the more mundane, even pedestrian, character of *analogy.* Among cognitive scientists, George Lakoff and Mark Johnson explore implied analogy as a window into the operations of thought calling it metaphor in *Metaphors We Live By* (1980).

Metaphors, however, are less widely found in science and religion, the composite interdisciplinary field of academic study. When metaphor is found in science and religion (the composite field of academic study), the relevant analysis is epistemological rather than aesthetic. That is not to say that the celebrated transfer of meaning, which metaphor is traditionally understood as effecting, is not of importance in the literature of science and religion. It is to observe merely that the linguistic object called a *metaphor* is of less importance than the cognitive process that brings about the transfer that creates new meaning. Accordingly, this entry will emphasize the process—metaphoric process—that brings about the changes in meanings that are found when science and religion are taken to be related and interacting cognitive fields of meaning.

Metaphor and analogy

An important first step is to distinguish metaphoric process from the making of analogies—the business of comparing two things that have similar characteristics. When one of two such things is understood and the other is not, one's overall understanding can be improved by making an analogy. One could say, for example, "Theology in religion is analogous to theoretical physics in natural science." Here one is making an analogy between a component of religious scholarship and a component of research in natural science. For those who know some of the theoretical laws of physics, the character and role of theology in its domain is clarified; the reverse occurs for those who read or write theology. We are here asserting an analogical relationship between a known and an unknown, in which the analogical statement advances understanding by comparing an unknown element with a element previously known. Analogical process dominates much of formal instruction. Metaphoric process is significantly different; it occurs infrequently in the field of science and religion taken together.

Metaphoric process presupposes two different phenomena (X and Y), each well understood within their respective field of meanings. A discovery then occurs, a gestalt-like realization that the different phenomena are the same. The effect of the discovery is to establish a host of new relationships between ancillary phenomena in the two fields, ancillary phenomena closely related with the original phenomena. Events (discoveries) of this kind serve to knit together the fabric of disparate disciplines, but not by making compromises in which one "side" must relinquish some point to gain some other. Rather, the disparate views are held together and resolved into a higher viewpoint, to use an expression of Bernard Lonergan's, much as binocular vision resolves two different flat images into a single three-dimensional view.

Many scholars, including Mary Hesse, Nelson Goodman, Paul Ricoeur, and Earl MacCormac, address the problem of understanding the metaphoric process in terms of an implied model of thought. For Hesse there is a "network of meanings"; Goodman spoke in terms of "worldmaking"; Ricoeur referred to "shift in the logical distance"; and MacCormac made use of what he called "a computational metaphor for cognition."

Metaphorical processes

Janet Martin Soskice has pointed out that religious metaphors retain their tension long after other kinds of metaphors have lost theirs. One of the most startling and perennially productive religious metaphors is the assertion in John's Epistle that "God is love" (1 John 4:8). The equation of God and love involves equating the field of traditional attributes associated with God, such as superlative potency and intelligence, with the field of meanings associated with love, here understood as human relationality at is best, including vulnerability.

In science, Isaac Newton (1642–1727) used metaphoric process by equating the mechanics of the heavens with the mechanics of earthly objects, thus generating a higher viewpoint that had a profound effect on people's lives. The "laws of the heavens" had been developed earlier by Johannes Kepler (1571–1630). These laws described, in quantitative terms, the motion of the planets (the "wandering" heavenly bodies) around the sun. Mechanical "laws of the of the world" (on the surface of Earth) were given by Galileo Galilei (1564–1642), who could, for example, calculate the motion of a projectile or the rate of fall of an object as it fell toward the ground. Subsequently Newton, in the famous falling apple allegory, realized that Galileo's laws of falling applied to the moon as well as to terrestrial objects, and, with that metaphoric act, caused the laws of Earth to become the laws of heaven—quite a reversal. The general laws of mechanics followed, and the resulting ability to analyze mechanisms and predict mechanical behavior reliably can be understood as having reshaped one world of meanings to create a new world of meanings, one that dominated science and technology for over two hundred years.

Other examples of metaphoric statements can be found. Examples in physics include: heat is motion (Benjamin Thompson, James Prescott Joule); light is particulate as well as undulatory (Albert Einstein); energy is particulate (Max Planck, Niels Bohr, Einstein); and mass is undulatory as well as particulate (Louis de Broglie). Examples in religion include: in the midst of life we are in death (Paul); an individual's ultimate concern is that person's god (Paul Tillich); the "natural" state of existence for human beings is to be graced (Karl Rahner); and Christ is *sophia* and logos (Elizabeth Johnson). Possible examples in science and religion include: evil is entropic degradation and personal relativistic time is the time of the second coming of Christ.

The discovery that two persons from different disciplines are talking about the same thing is not uncommon in closely related fields and can be highly profitable. The exchange interactions of quantum physics were found to correspond to the molecular bonds of chemistry, and chemical physics was born. It remains to be seen whether productive instances can be found in disciplines separated by as much cognitive space as natural science and religion. The hope for science and religion as a valuable academic discipline in its own right depends on such possibilities and on the metaphoric process that can knit them together.

See also MODELS

Bibliography

Gerhart, Mary, and, Russell, Allan M. *Metaphoric Process: The Creation of Scientific and Religious Understanding.* Fort Worth: Texas Christian University Press, 1984.

Goodman, Nelson. *Ways of Worldmaking.* Indianapolis, Ind.: Hackett, 1978.

Hesse, Mary. *Models and Analogies in Science.* Notre Dame, Ind.: Notre Dame Press, 1970.

Jones, Roger S. *Physics As Metaphor.* Minneapolis: University of Minnesota Press, 1982.

Lakoff, George, and Johnson, Mark. *Metaphors We Live By.* Chicago and London: University of Chicago Press, 1980.

Leatherdale, W. H. *The Role of Analogy: Model and Metaphor in Science.* New York: Elsevier, 1974.

MacCormac, Earl R. *Metaphor and Myth in Science and Religion.* Durham, N.C.: Duke University Press, 1976.

McFague, Sallie. *Metaphorical Theology: Models of God in Religious Language.* Philadelphia, Pa.: Fortress Press, 1982.

Miller, Arthur I. *Imagery in Scientific Thought: Creating Twentieth-Century Physics.* Boston: Birkhäuser, 1985.

Ricoeur, Paul. *The Rule of Metaphor: An Interdisciplinary Study.* Toronto, Ont.: University of Toronto Press, 1977.

Rogers, Robert. *Metaphor: A Psychoanalytic View.* Berkeley: University of California Press, 1978.

Schon, Donald Alan. *Displacement of Concepts.* London: Tavistock, 1963.

Soskice, Janet Martin. *Metaphor and Religious Language.* New York: Oxford University Press, 1985.

MARY GERHART
ALLAN M. RUSSELL

METAPHYSICAL NATURALISM

See NATURALISM

METAPHYSICS

The term *metaphysics* refers to the study of things that are removed from sense perception. Modern metaphysics studies the kind of things that exist and the way they exist.

In the dialogue of science and religion, *metaphysics, science,* and *religion* do not necessarily refer to separate endeavors that need relating. Religious faith, for example, can be pervasive so that nature is seen as divine creation and science as a form of worship. Neither do the terms refer to universal bodies of knowledge and belief independent of context. Metaphysics has affected the dialogue between science and religion. These effects have depended on the content of metaphysics and on whether it functioned as science or religion. Moreover, metaphysics and religion have shaped epistemology. Metaphysics has served as presupposition, sanction, motive, criterion for theory choice, criterion for the choice of kinds of explanation (regulative principle), and as part of explanations (constitutive principle). The focus in the dialogue between religion and science is on how God interacts with the world, and on the relation between knowledge of God (religious knowledge and the systematic reflection on it in theology) and knowledge of nature (views of nature, as well as the systematic development of empirical knowledge).

Ancient Greek metaphysics shaped the understanding of God's action in the world in each of the three Abrahamic religions. (Eastern Orthodoxy is an exception in this respect while Judaism can be said to have been only insignificantly influenced.) In Christianity and Islam, the possibility of dialogue between religion and science depended, among other considerations, on how the relationship between theory and observation was envisioned. For ancient Greek philosophers, reliable knowledge was knowledge of the ultimate. Different types of metaphysics had preferred ways of knowing ultimate reality. The Platonic ideas were best known by reason. For Democritus, the random movement of atoms was ultimate reality; their material combinations were best apprehended by sensation. Sensation was also the only source of knowledge of nature for the nominalists, who denied the existence of universal ideas. This reinforced the distinction between observation and reason in eleventh- and twelfth-century scholasticism. To protect divine intervention from naturalistic explanation, theologians distinguished between God's ordained power operating in regular natural phenomena and his absolute power manifested in miracles. In addition, reasoning in theology was limited to avoid conflict with divinely revealed knowledge. Thus the possibility and nature of dialogue between science and religion came to depend on how the relationship between nature and supernature was envisioned.

Metaphysics affected the dialogue between natural philosophy and religion via the content of both. While in Greek metaphysics the order of nature was autonomous and necessary, in the Abrahamic religions it depended totally upon the creator. These traditions were combined by medieval Christian theologians. They acknowledged both a relative autonomy of nature (God's ordinary power) and a divine sovereignty (God's absolute power). Yet theological responses also included the naturalism of William of Conches (c. 1080–c.1150). This set the stage for future discussions. One question was whether purpose in organisms reveals God's natural or supernatural action. Thomas Aquinas (c. 1225–1274) interpreted Aristotle's natural final cause as divine providence, thereby creating a link between natural philosophy and religion. When natural philosophers took purpose as a natural cause, theologians saw the power of God diminished. In response, different forms of voluntarism developed in both Muslim and Christian theology in which creatures were denied causal power because it detracted from God's power. When theologians insisted on God's purposive action in organisms, natural philosophers indicated that God could act through natural law. Responses to these questions regulated the content of both theology and natural philosophy. If animals generate their own purposes, Aquinas considered, inanimate things could prove God's existence more convincingly. Therefore, Aquinas excluded animals from his teleological proof for the existence of God. William Harvey (1578–1657) believed that everything has a God-given purpose. He reasoned that venous valves were created pointing in the same direction in order to prevent reverse flow and to assure the continuous circulation of blood.

In Western Christianity, the idea of absolute divine power did not discourage the exploration of nature's regularities because it was balanced by the idea of ordained power. No such balancing act occurred in the Ashirite school of Muslim theology even though it distinguished between Allah's absolute power and the derived power of humans. This distinction was not applied to natural phenomena. The Ashirites believed Allah creates a cause especially for the occasion of a phenomenon according to a regular pattern of cause and effect. This pattern, however, could be interrupted by prayer. Therefore, knowledge of this pattern remained unreliable even though it was believed to be implanted in the believer's mind by God. Western distinctions between sensation, reason, and faith as ways of knowing became separations. Thus raising the question of their relationship.

The answer further illustrates how metaphysics has affected the dialogue via epistemology. According to the German philosopher Immanuel Kant (1724–1804), scientific knowledge of phenomena arises when sensations are organized by the mind using concepts such as space, time, and cause. Beliefs about nature become scientific knowledge if they correspond to phenomena. Since beliefs about God do not result from sensations they can be accepted only on faith. This separated scientific and religious knowledge into different categories so that no dialogue was possible between them. This separation became an issue in the engagement between religion and biology. The German anthropologist Johann Friedrich Blumenbach (1752–1840) used purpose as a natural secondary cause in explanations of animal development and saw God as the primary cause. For Kant, however, this meant that supernatural causes had been included in explanations of nature. That is, the religious belief that God had created things for a purpose had constituted a scientific explanation. Kant was willing to accept only the regulative use of purpose as a guide to research.

The existence of purposive behavior in organisms is described by a concept of goal or function that excludes from scientific explanation both divine and animal intent. It is used both to guide research (what is the function of venous valves?) and to explain the observations (the function of venous valves is to block reverse flow). In twentieth-century positivism, metaphysics and religion were denied the status of knowledge and meaning because their concepts were believed not to refer to sensible realities. However, Kant's separation and its positivistic interpretation failed for a variety of reasons. As a result, there is renewed interest in metaphysics, which has revealed that it often mediates between science and religion.

See also DUALISM; EPISTEMOLOGY; KANT, IMMANUEL; MATERIALISM; NATURALISM; NATURE; ONTOLOGY

Bibliography

Brooke, John H. *Science and Religion: Some Historical Perspectives.* Cambridge, UK: Cambridge University Press, 1991.

Brooke, John H.; Osler, Margaret J.; and van der Meer, Jitse M. eds. *Science in Theistic Contexts: Cognitive Dimensions.* Chicago: University of Chicago Press, 2001.

Dhanani, Alnoor. "Islam." In *The History of Science and Religion in the Western Tradition: An Encyclopedia,* ed. Gary B. Ferngren; Edward J. Larson; Darrell W. Amundsen; and Anne-Marie E. Nakhla. New York: Garland, 2000.

Hull, David L., and Ruse, Michael, eds. *The Philosophy of Biology.* Oxford: Oxford University Press. 1998.

Kaiser, Christopher B. *Creational Theology and the History of Physical Science: The Creationist Tradition from Basil to Bohr.* Leiden, Netherlands: Brill, 1997.

Lindberg, David C., and Numbers, Ronald L. *God and Nature: Historical Essays on the Encounter between Christianity and Science.* Berkeley: University of California Press, 1986.

McMullen, Emerson T. "Anatomy and Physiology to 1700." In *The History of Science and Religion in the Western Tradition: An Encyclopedia,* eds. Gary B. Ferngren; Edward J. Larson; Darrell W. Amundsen; and Anne-Marie E. Nakhla. New York: Garland, 2000.

Midgley, Mary. *Science as Salvation: A Modern Myth and its Meaning.* London and New York: Routledge, 1992.

Nasr, Seyyed Hossein. *Religion and the Order of Nature.* New York and Oxford: Oxford University Press, 1996.

Qadir, C. A. *Philosophy and Science in the Islamic World.* London and New York: Routledge, 1988.

Richards, Robert J. "Kant and Blumenbach on the *Bildungstrieb*: A Historical Misunderstanding." *Studies in the History and Philosophy of Biology and Biomedical Sciences* 31 (2000): 11–32.

Southgate, Christopher; Deane-Drummond, Celia; Murray, Paul D.; Negus, Michael R.; Osborn, Lawrence; Poole, Michael; Stewart, Jacqui; and Watts, Fraser. *God, Humanity, and the Cosmos: A Textbook in Science and Religion.* Edinburgh, UK: T&T Clark, 1999.

Van Inwagen, Peter. *Metaphysics.* Boulder, Colo.: Westview, 1997.

JITSE M. VAN DER MEER

MILLENNIALISM

Millennialism constitutes the belief that at some point in the future the social world will be transformed into a utopian world of peace, justice, prosperity, and fellowship. The revolutionary quality of the idea derives from the focus on this "worldly" transformation (as opposed to the "other-worldly" promises of spiritual salvation after death) and its ultimately optimistic vision of a humanity that is redeemable "in the flesh." The vision takes both religious forms, such as Christianity's "thousand year reign of the saints," and secular forms, such as utopianism, communism, and Nazism. Both because it has always proved wrong (that millennium has still not arrived) and because of its radical and often violent forms, millennialism has provoked the hostility of many people, especially writers who view it retrospectively. As a result, millennialism has left only a vestigial trace in the documentary record, and it seems to have played a significantly larger role in the oral discourse and actions of the time, especially during periods before the expectations proved false. Historical writing was a hostile medium for the recording of millennial passions, and retrospective accounts often strip millennial commitments from major figures such as Charlemagne and Isaac Newton. Historians have just begun to reconsider this body of documentation and assess its larger role.

Millennialism is, at base, a profoundly optimistic view of a perfectible future. It takes a wide variety of forms, from a hierarchical vision of imperial perfection imposing order and harmony from above, to a demotic world of "holy anarchy" where there is no state and self-regulating saints live in perfect equality. Moreover, the anticipated apocalyptic transformation that moves humankind from its current "fallen" condition perfection can range from a cataclysmic one of immense destruction that leaves only a tiny remnant of saved "saints," to a vast, pacific, and voluntary transformational one that embraces "all the nations of the world" which no longer "lift up sword against [other] nation[s], nor study war any more" (Isa. 2:2–4; Mic. 4:1–4). Finally millennialism can endorse various combinations of a *passive* stance, in which, for example, God will act and humans should wait in penitence, or an *active* stance, in which chosen agents fulfill God's apocalyptic vision. Depending on how peaceful or violent the apocalyptic scenario, active behaviors can range from revivalism and proselytizing (e.g., Peace of God in France, 980s–1030s; Year of the Great Allelulia in Northern Italy, 1233; the Great Awakenings in America, 1730s–1740s and 1820s–1840s) to holy war and genocidal slaughters of the enemies of good (e.g., the Crusades of the eleventh to thirteenth centuries; the Jihads of the seventh century onward; totalitarian purges of the twentieth century).

Although in contemporary usage the term *millennialism* refers to any form of *this-worldly* collective salvation, its original meaning, from the Latin *mille* (one thousand) and *anni* (years), came from the marriage of messianic expectations and apocalyptic "world-ending" beliefs in the crucible of postexilic Judaism under the rule of first Persian, then Greek, then Roman imperial authorities. Here the Babylonian notion of a "great cycle" of seven (planetary) thousand-year ages joined with the biblical notion of a seven-day creation to produce a vision of the fate of the physical universe (creation) from genesis to consummation, passing through six thousand-year days/ages of travail, and climaxing at the completion of 6,000 years with the advent of the *sabbatical millennium,* the thousand years where the "saints" would reign.

Millennialism and chronology

This marriage of millennialism with chronology became especially strong in early Christian circles, and contributed significantly to the immense interest of Western Christian chronographers in precisely calculating both the history of the world and the patterns of yearly and liturgical cycles (*computus*), with which the larger cycles were expected to harmonize (which they do not). For the first thousand years of Christian history, the sabbatical millennium served primarily to delay apocalyptic expectations of an imminent end by using chronologies that pushed the apocalyptic year off by centuries.

Problems arose when the several-century long buffer of the anti-apocalyptic early adopters of the *era mundi* (the age of the world) approached its end, leaving those who inherited these increasingly apocalyptic chronographies in their sixtieth century. Although scholars have not yet been able to get a sense of the process in any detail, the long-term record over the course of the first Christian millennium (first to eleventh centuries) indicates clearly that at the approach of the millennial date, chronographers chose to "correct" their calculations, consistently adopting new systems that "put off" the end yet another several centuries. Thus, around 200 C.E., chronographers adopted an *era mundi* that located the present in 5,700 and the year-6,000 in 500 C.E. At the approach of that date in the fifth century, chronographers adopted a second *era mundi* that pushed the year-6,000 off until 801 C.E. At the approach of this second millennial date in the eighth century, chronographers adopted the *anno Domini* system, putting off the end the current millennium (and, by implication, the sixth and last "age") another two to three centuries to the year 1000 or 1033. These crises, inspired both by approaching apocalyptic dates and by the intractably asymmetric nature of planetary movement, had the unintended but significant consequence of intensifying Western European abilities to measure time, the only science to progress in the early middle ages.

Transformative apocalyptic beliefs and the "making" of the millennium

The apocalyptic scenarios accompanying the sabbatical millennium tended, as do most Christian and Jewish scenarios, to emphasize passive, cataclysmic apocalyptic expectation, since both the date and the actions were in God's hands. But already by the second year-6,000 (801 C.E., the year following Charlemagne's imperial coronation), there emerged a new and unusual form of active, transformational millennialism that channeled the disappointment of failed expectations into projects aimed at transforming the world. Some of the Carolingian theologians, normally known for their lack of originality, demonstrate an innovation that treats the "mechanical arts" as a form of redemptive knowledge and activity. This attitude reverses a classical disdain in Greco-Roman high culture for manual labor, and reflects a biblical respect for manual labor that was part monastic, part millennial ("swords into plowshares …").

At the turn of the millennium, demotic active millennialism had an extraordinary period of some fifty years (980s to 1030s) in France, during which large crowds gathered in open fields and the weapons-bearing elite took public oaths to exempt the unarmed (peasants and clerics) from their violence and rapine. This wave of popular millennialism, unusually affirmed and encouraged by the ecclesiastical and lay ruling groups (bishops, abbots, dukes, counts, kings), produced the largest active, transformational, demotic millennial movement in recorded history and seems to have aroused a great deal of energy among the commoner class, both in terms of their passion for Christianity and in their economic and social initiatives over the next three centuries.

The rise and spread of radically egalitarian (often heretical) apostolic movements that engaged in technology-based work (e.g., weaving) characterizes the centuries after 1000 C.E., a period of widespread and vigorous social, technological, and economic revolutions in Western Europe that transformed both urban and rural regions over the course of the next three centuries. In this period, especially with the "renaissance of the twelfth century," ecclesiastical writers invoked technology as a salvific and growing body of knowledge, and utopian fantasies appear in which automatons animated with magical arts play prominent roles.

By the late twelfth century, the visionary exegete Joachim of Fiore (d. 1202) had brought a revival of millennial thinking and action back to the most elite ecclesiastical circles with his notion of the dawning of the third age of "spiritual men." The power of this way of reading history as a process of (three) stages, with the present poised on the transition to the final, perfected age, to be brought about by active individuals (spiritual men), has proved one of the most potent in Western history (consider, for example, Karl Marx's historical dialectic). Such a system has remarkable resilience in dealing with disappointment: Every failure could take refuge in a renewal and reformulation of the preparatory project of spreading the working of the spirit. And in each new formulation, the role for human action increased and the role for a God, who did not deliver on the promises that prophets repeatedly made in his name, decreased. This drove European Christians on a steady path from a passive scenario, in which God created the millennium (*premillennialism*), toward an increasingly active, humanly driven one (*postmillennialism*).

And the most effective scenarios—effective not in actually bringing about the millennium, but, in their unintended and long-lasting consequences—involved technology. The millennial origins of the West's peculiar passion for technology seem to derive from a notion that if humankind could regain the knowledge it had before the Fall, it could recreate Eden. While there are multiple traces of this belief in the Middle Ages, its conflict with Augustine of Hippo's (354–430) doctrine of original sin kept it at the margins of official culture. But this desire to regain pre-lapsarian knowledge gained great force in the latter half of the fifteenth century with the translation of the *Corpus Hermeticum,* a Gnostic text from the first century C.E. attributed to Hermes Trismegistus. The self-styled magus, who turned to this text to gain the original knowledge (*prisca theologica*) of humankind, believed that at last the time had come to create and transform nature.

Francis Yates argues that these men, the hermetic *magi,* played a central role in the emergence of modern science, not so much by developing rational thought, but by "changing the will," unleashing the passion for the knowledge to transform and perfect nature. Even Francis Bacon (1561–1626), a vocal opponent of the magi, invoked hopes of pre-lapsarian knowledge through science in his call for the Royal Historical Society, as well as his utopian work *The New Atlantis* (1626). Utopian thought represented the first stirrings of secular millennialism, and, beginning with Bacon, they increasingly featured technology and scientific research. The rational, demythologized scientific tradition that is identified as beginning in the early modern period (sixteenth century to eighteenth century) appears to have arisen as an unintended consequence of this passion for esoteric knowledge. For almost a thousand years, Augustine had enforced on intellectuals the humility of original sin: "Fallen man" should not seek to change this world. That enforced humility ceded to a wave of active, transformational millennial enthusiasm that remains to the present.

The links between activist millennial hopes for creating a more perfect society on Earth and the advancement of science and technology from the fifteenth century onward are legion. The most striking link concerns Isaac Newton (1642–1727), a figure who, retrospectively, represents the giant of modern science and rationality. The millennial visionary poet and artist William Blake (1757–1827) heaped contempt on Newton, describing the constricted view of the world in Newton's cosmogony as "single vision and Newton's sleep." But a closer look at the vast and largely unpublished work into which Newton poured so much energy reveals a man at once *magus* (alchemical work) and classic biblical millennialist (ancient chronology designed to calculate the advent of the *Parousia* [the Second Coming of Jesus Christ]). Similar millennial dimensions can be found when one examines closely the careers of other great scientific figures, revealing the role of millennial hopes as a motivator for the scientist, as well as millennial rhetoric as a useful way to attract large sums of funding. Even Roger Bacon (1219–1294) linked the Antichrist to science as part of an appeal to the pope to fund his projects concerning teaching, learning, and disseminating scientific knowledge.

Modern millennialism and scientific megaprojects

Nor has this millennial dimension waned with time. On the contrary, one of the greatest and most portentous projects in history, the invention of atomic bombs, took place in the framework of a war of democratic Western culture against the aggression of technologically empowered Nazi millennialists (*tausendjähriger Reich* means "millennial kingdom"). The Manhattan Project, the United States initiative during the early 1940s to produce the first atomic bomb, has served as the standard for all subsequent grand scientific projects (e.g., space exploration) that raise enormous funds and create a cultural faith in the powers of science and technology, new stages in the "religion of technology." As an unintended consequence, the atomic bomb has revivified apocalyptic fears of the cataclysmic end of the world, just when conceptual scientific schemata had robbed earlier apocalyptic scenarios of any credibility.

Millennial dreams continue to breathe their inspirations into the great undertakings of modern humans, from the messianic belief in "modern civil society" spread the world over (the biblical quotation "nation shall not lift up sword against nation" is inscribed on a wall at United Nations Plaza in New York) to the fear of the apocalyptic annihilation of humankind, whether from environmental pollution and global warming, nuclear threats from the cold war, or terrorism. But this millennial thinking continues to inspire new directions in science as well. New fields of research, such as artificial intelligence and artificial life, have secured funding by appealing to the millennial dreams of both scientists and their backers. The pioneers of artificial intelligence speak about downloading the brain from the troublesome mortal coil and into nearly immortal silicon bodies, of launching an evolutionary step that would compare with the creation of the universe and the emergence of life, or more modestly, with the emergence of *homo sapiens*. Their visionary enthusiasm, simplistic dualism, and boundless megalomania are typical millennial characteristics and make clear how important it is for scientists to better understand their own millennial past. Then scientists and the broader culture might not make naïve and, in this age of immense technological potency, potentially dangerous choices.

But avoiding the dangers of millennial hubris should not lead, as many rationalists argue, to the jettisoning of the millennial vision. On the contrary, the millennial vision serves as one of the great inspirations for scientific and technological development. As Blake commented in *Marriage of Heaven and Hell* (1790), "what is now proved was once only imagined." Of course, not all that is now imagined will be proved, just as not every millennial idea leads to science. But the reverse—how, how much, and what kind of millennial imagination leads to science?—poses interesting questions, well worth trying to answer.

See also ARTIFICIAL INTELLIGENCE; END OF THE WORLD, RELIGIOUS AND PHILOSOPHICAL ASPECTS OF; ESCHATOLOGY

Bibliography

Benz, Ernst. *Evolution and Christian Hope: Man's Concept of the Future from the Early Fathers to Teilhard de Chardin,* trans. Heinz G. Frank. Garden City, N.Y.: Doubleday, 1966.

Fried, Johannes. *Aufsteig aus dem Untergang: Apokalyptisches Denken und die Entstehung der modernen Naturwissenschaft im Mittelalter.* Munich: C.H. Beck, 2001.

Head, Thomas, and Landes, Richard, eds. *The Peace of God: Social Violence and Religious Response around the Year 1000.* Ithaca, N.Y.: Cornell University Press, 1992.

Jacob, Margaret C. "Millenarianism and Science in the Late Seventeenth Century." *Journal of the History of Ideas* 37 (1976): 335–341.

Jacob, Margaret C. *The Cultural Meaning of the Scientific Revolution.* Philadelphia, Pa.: Temple University Press, 1988.

Landes, Richard. "Lest the Millennium Be Fulfilled: Apocalyptic Expectations and the Pattern of Western Chronography, 100–800 C.E." In *The Use and Abuse of Eschatology in the Middle Ages,* ed. Werner Verbeke, Daniel Verhelst, and Andries Welkenhysen. Leuven, Belgium: Leuven University Press, 1988.

Landes, Richard. "While God Tarried: Modernity as Frankenstein's Millennium." *Deolog* 4 (1997): 6–27.

Mannheim, Karl. *Ideology and Utopia.* London: Lund Humphries, 1936.

Manuel, Frank. *The Religion of Isaac Newton.* Oxford: Clarendon Press, 1974.

Maurer, Reinhart. "The Origins of Modern Technology in Millenarianism." In *Philosophy and Technology,* ed. Paul T. Durbin and Frederick Rapp. Dordrecht, Netherlands: Kluwer, 1983.

Mendel, Arthur. *Vision and Violence* (1992). Reprint, Ann Arbor: University of Michigan Press, 2000.

Noble, David. *The Religion of Technology: The Divinity of Man and the Spirit of Invention.* New York: Knopf, 1997.

Reeves, Marjorie. *Joachim of Fiore and the Prophetic Future.* New York: Harper, 1977.

Tuveson, Ernest Lee. *Millennium and Utopia: A Study in the Background of the Idea of Progress.* Berkeley: University of California Press, 1949.

Weber, Eugen. *Apocalypses: Prophecies, Cults, and Millennial Beliefs through the Ages.* Cambridge, Mass.: Harvard University Press, 1999.

Webster, Charles C. *Great Instauration: Science Medicine and Reform, 1626–1660.* New York: Holmes & Meier, 1976.

Yates, Frances Amelia. *Giordano Bruno and the Hermetic Tradition.* London: Routledge and Kegan Paul, 1964.

RICHARD LANDES

MIND-BODY DUALISM

See DUALISM; MIND-BODY THEORIES; SELF

MIND-BODY THEORIES

Mind-body theories are putative solutions to the mind-body problem. The mind-body problem is that of stating the exact relation between the mind and the body, or, more narrowly, between the mind and the brain. Most of the theories of the mind-body relation exist also as metaphysical theories of reality as a whole. While debates over the mind-body problem can seem intractable, science offers at least two promising lines of research. On the one hand, parts of the mind-body problem arise in research in artificial intelligence and might be solved by a better understanding of the relations between hardware and software. On the other hand, the study of emergence in biological systems may illuminate the mind-body relation.

Mind-body dualism

Dualism, or mind-body dualism, is the theory that both minds and brains exist, and no mind is a brain and no brain is a mind, nor is a mind any part of a brain or a brain any part of a mind. Hinduism and non-Advaitic Vedanta entail mind-body dualism because if the soul migrates through distinct incarnations then it is something that can exist independently of the body. If the fusion of *atman* with *Brahman* preserves *atman*'s individuality, then *atman* can exist without the existence of a human body.

The earliest Western philosopher to endorse dualism was the pre-Socratic Pythagoras (c. 569–475 B.C.E.). He inherited the ancient Egyptian religious doctrine that a nonphysical part of the person survives death, and he believed in the reincarnation of the soul. If Plato (c. 427–347 B.C.E.) is not correctly read as an idealist, then he was a mind-body dualist. In his dialogue *The Phaedo* especially, Socrates advanced arguments for the conclusion that the soul survives bodily death. Aristotle (384–322 B.C.E.) held that the soul is the "form" of the human body. He was nevertheless a mind-body dualist because he insisted that the intellectual part of the soul is immortal, even though he offered functionalist or materialist accounts of affective and sensory faculties.

Orthodox Christianity is not mind-body dualist in that human immortality consists in the hope of bodily resurrection, or the living again of the whole person by the grace of God, not in the immortality of a disembodied soul. Although the term *soul* is sometimes used in the Old and New Testaments it does not there explicitly denote an immaterial mental substance that could exist whether or not the body exists. The soul in this strong metaphysical sense was introduced into Christianity during the fourth and fifth centuries by Augustine of Hippo who, believing Platonism and Christianity mutually consistent and true, sought to fuse them into a single philosophical system. Augustine's synthesis accounts for the subsequent Christian belief in mind-body dualism even though a guarantee of the immortality of the soul would seem to make the hope of resurrection redundant. On the other hand, it might be that some resurrection can only be one's own resurrection if one is or one has a soul. If that is right, the immortality of the soul is a logical presupposition of the truth of Christianity.

The seventeenth-century French philosopher and mathematician René Descartes (1596–1650) argues in his *Meditations* (1641) that the only fact of which he can be certain is that he exists. The evidence of the senses, the truths of mathematics, and the whole physical world are ultimately dubitable, but his own existence cannot be doubted, because if he doubts, then he exists. On these premises Descartes concludes that he is a thing that thinks and that does not depend on the physical world, which includes his own body. Cartesian dualism is the view that each person is essentially a substantial soul that is distinct from the body.

Materialism

Materialism is the theory that the mind is the brain, or nothing over and above the brain. The ancient Greek atomist Democritus maintains that there exist only atoms and the void. Atoms are indivisible material particles and the void is the infinite empty space in which atoms are in motion. If atomism is true, then everything is either an atom or reducible to atoms. If there are minds or mental states then they are reducible to atoms and if atoms are physical then minds are physical.

Thomas Hobbes, the seventeenth-century English political theorist and philosopher, was a foundationalist about geometry: Unless the statements of geometry are true then no statement can be true. Geometry is the mathematics of space so it follows that everything is spatial. If everything spatial is physical then everything is physical, and so materialism is true. Hobbes has an account of how people come to be mislead into dualism or otherwise believing in nonphysical realities. Because a mind does not seem to be straightforwardly a physical object, people falsely assume it is a nonphysical object, but this is an abstraction caused by thinking away just some material properties, notably solidity. Hobbes thinks that if people think of anything they can only think of it as physical. One thinks of a ghost as having certain physical properties, perhaps extension and indeterminate shape. This sort of criticism of putative nonphysical realities was later adopted in the 1930s by the Vienna Circle, who sought to replace religion by natural science.

The mind-brain identity theory was influential from the mid-1950s into the 1980s. The main claim of the British philosopher U.T. Place's seminal 1956 paper "Is Consciousness a Brain Process?" is that consciousness is strictly or numerically identical with a physical process in the brain. The identity in question is a contingent and *a posteriori* one, not a necessary and *a priori* one. Place's claim is not to have proved that consciousness is a brain process, but to have removed *a priori* philosophical objections to it as a scientific hypothesis.

Idealism

Idealism is the theory that only minds exist and that physical objects, including the human body, are dependent on minds or consciousness for their existence. Although nondualistic, Vedanta entails the idealist doctrine that only subjective centers of experience exist and the empirical world is only an appearance. The first systematic thinker who could be construed as an idealist is the pre-Socratic monist Parmenides of Elea in the sixth and fifth centuries B.C.E. Parmenides believed that only what can be thought exists.

Plato insists that the Forms (*eidos*) are nonphysical types or essences that exist independently not only of space and time but the human mind. However, the Forms are in principle graspable by the human mind given appropriate training, and the soul "participates" in them before birth and after death. To the extent that the Forms are ideal, Plato is an idealist because he thinks the empirical world depends upon the Forms for its existence.

The third-century neo-Platonist philosopher Plotinus (205–270 C.E.) is plausibly construed as an idealist because he maintains that the empirical world is ultimately an emanation of the One, which is at least nonphysical and spiritual and possesses mental properties.

The eighteenth-century Anglo-Irish Bishop George Berkeley argues that it makes no sense to claim that physical objects exist independently of the possibility of thinking of them or perceiving them. He also argues that the concept of matter, or a physical substratum of which the properties of a physical object are properties, is incoherent.

The German philosopher Immanuel Kant (1724–1804) is usually read as an idealist because his own name for his philosophy was *transcendental idealism*. However, transcendental idealism is the epistemological doctrine that humans are cognitively constituted in such a way that people may only know things as they appear to them, not as they really are in themselves. People are psychologically equipped to formulate philosophical questions but not to answer them. There are no metaphysical propositions because putative claims about a reality beyond space and time are neither true nor false. So the word *idealism* in transcendental idealism is best read as *antirealism*. In so far as a solution to the mind-body problem may be extracted from Kant's *Critique of Pure Reason* (1781), it entails a repudiation of Cartesian mind-body dualism for misusing the category "substance" outside space and time, and an implicit endorsement of the construction of the mental-physical distinction out of a prior monism of phenomena.

It is in the writings of Kant's successors Johann Gottlieb Fichte (1762–1814) and Friedrich Wilhelm Joseph von Schelling (1775–1854) that transcendental idealism becomes a kind of idealism. Georg Wilhelm Friedrich Hegel's (1770–1831) Absolute Idealism is the doctrine that the multiplicity of kinds and degrees of consciousness are ultimately aspects or shapes (*Gestalten*) of the one ultimate cosmic consciousness called *Geist*. On this thesis, which is partly Brahmanist and partly neo-Platonist, the distinction between mental and physical ultimately depends on *Geist*.

Logical behaviorism

Logical (or analytical) behaviorism is the theory that minds can be reduced to publicly observable bodily behavior. According to this theory, any statement about minds or mental states may be translated into a claim or set of claims about actual or possible bodily behavior that is in principle observable. Logical behaviorism is a reduction of the inner to the outer, the subjective to the objective, the private to the public, the first person singular to the third person singular.

The German-born American positivist philosopher Carl Gustav Hempel (1905–1997) is a logical behaviorist in this defined sense. Austrian philosopher Ludwig Wittgenstein (1889–1951) and British philosopher Gilbert Ryle (1900–1976) offer subtle analyses of the uses of ordinary psychological language designed to show that seemingly Cartesian or introspective language in fact takes on its meaning from shared uses in a public world. In particular, Wittgenstein argues in his Private Language Argument in *Philosophical Investigations* (1953) that there have to be public third-person criteria for psychological ascriptions. Mental concepts cannot take on meaning by a kind of private ostensive definition, a sort of inner private labeling of one's own sensations. In that case, there would be no criterion for the correctness of a putative ascription: There would be nothing it would consist in for the ascription to be true or false. It follows that there are no logically private psychological ascriptions, and mental terms do not take on meaning only from one's own case.

Nevertheless, Wittgenstein would strongly resist being called a behaviorist. Ryle, who in *The Concept of Mind* (1949) argues that the myth of Cartesianism does not have to be true in order for people's psychological vocabulary to be meaningful, was not wholly uncomfortable with the label.

Functionalism

Functionalism is the theory that a mind is a set of states essentially causally related to sensory inputs, behavioral outputs, and one another. Functionalism may be partly understood as an attempt to overcome certain shortcomings of logical behaviorism. Behavior seems neither necessary nor sufficient for mentality. It is not sufficient because it does not follow from the fact that someone behaves in a particular way that they are in a particular mental state. Behavior is not necessary for mentality because from the fact that a person is in a particular mental state it does not follow that they behave in a particular way. Mind does not seem to be behavior. Mind seems to be the inner cause of behavior. The contemporary philosophers David Lewis and Hilary Putnam have argued that being in a mental state is being in a functional state, a state caused by sensory inputs and causing behavioral outputs. Functionalism does not entail a view about the intrinsic nature of a mental state, so in a sense avoids the mind-body problem. However, with the addition of just one extra premise—only physical events may be causes or effects—functionalism is a kind of materialism. Functionalism is consistent with the assumption of cognitive science that a person is best viewed as an information processing system.

Double aspect theories

According to double aspect theories, mind and body are two aspects of some jointly presupposed reality that is intrinsically neither mental nor physical. Dutch-Jewish philosopher Baruch Spinoza (1632–1677) argued that reality has two essential properties: thought and extension, or consciousness and physical size. The totality of what *is* could appropriately be called "God" or "Nature" (*deus sive natura*). As parts of the whole, human minds and bodies are two aspects of an underlying reality. Thought cannot exist without extension, nor extension without thought. As in many double aspect theories, this raises the question of what the underlying reality is if it is allegedly neither mental nor physical. Spinoza's answer is existence or being. However, the concept of existence or being has proved recalcitrant to analysis by philosophers from the ancient Greek Parmenides to Martin Heidegger in the twentieth century.

Bertrand Russell (1872–1970) endorsed two kinds of double aspect theories at different stages of his intellectual career. He endorsed the empiricist view that mind and matter are logical constructions of sense data: the contents of sensory experience as they are directly given. Intrinsically, mind and matter are neither mental nor physical. In *An Outline of Philosophy* (1927) Russell argues that there can be no distinction between mental and physical unless fundamentally there exist events that are not clearly mental or physical. In particular the smallest events postulated by science have no intrinsic mental properties and, on Russell's endorsement of the De Broglie/Shröedinger view of matter, are nonmaterial constituents of matter.

Peter Strawson argues in *Individuals* (1959) that the concept of a person is primitive with regard to the distinction between mind and body. Unless humans are already possessed of the concept of the person as a whole, they are not in a position to draw a mind-body distinction. There is a considerable class of predicates that are not clearly only mental or only physical, for example "is smiling," or "is running."

The philosopher and psychologist William James (1842–1910) invented the term *neutral monism* for the view that there are items neither mental nor physical that are ontologically or epistemologically prior to the distinction between mind and matter.

Phenomenology

Phenomenology offers ways of marking the distinction between mental and physical, and diagnoses of how the mind-body problem is thinkable. Phenomenology is the description of appearances just as they are given to consciousness. Assumptions about their objective reality or causal relations are suspended or bracketed by an *epoché* (Greek: suspension of judgement). The ambition of phenomenology is to show how knowledge, including all scientific, religious, and philosophical knowledge is possible. The philosopher Edmund Husserl (1859–1938) grounded knowledge in the transcendental ego, a subjective source of experience that one's own being ultimately consists in, even after ontological commitment to the empirical human being has been suspended by the *epoché*. The transcendental ego is purportedly neither mental nor physical, and phenomenology is purportedly prior to the drawing of that distinction. However, the construction of the world out of acts of consciousness on some interpretations entails idealism and Husserl sometimes called his own philosophy *transcendental idealism*. As is the case with Kant, however, the claim that consciousness of an object is necessary and sufficient for the objective giveness of that object does not appear to entail that the object is dependent on consciousness for its existence. Husserl's teacher and phenomenological predecessor, the Austrian philosopher and psychologist Franz Brentano (1838–1917), argued that the essence of consciousness is intentionality directedness towards an object.

Twentieth century phenomenologists Heidegger, Maurice Merleau-Ponty, and Jean Paul Sartre all reject the *epoche* and the transcendental ego and argue that the mental-physical distinction is dependent on the fundamental existential category *being-in-the-world*.

Conclusion

The mind-body problem cannot be solved scientifically. The brain is billions of atoms in motion in empty space. No amount of empirical observation and experimental testing will explain how awareness is generated by matter in motion. Although it is obvious that ordinary mental states depend empirically on the brain, their subjective interiority of those same states is scientifically inexplicable. The uniqueness of one's own mind is ultimately explicable only if we are souls.

See also ARTIFICIAL INTELLIGENCE; CONSCIOUSNESS STUDIES; DESCARTES, RENÉ; EMERGENCE; EXPERIENCE, RELIGIOUS: COGNITIVE AND NEUROPHYSIOLOGICAL ASPECTS; FUNCTIONALISM; IDEALISM; MATERIALISM; MIND-BODY THEORIES; MIND-BRAIN INTERACTION; NEUROSCIENCES; PLATO

Bibliography

Barnes, Jonathan, ed. *Early Greek Philosophy*. London: Penguin, 1987.

Berkeley, George. *The Principles of Human Knowledge with Other Writings*. London: Fontana Collins, 1977.

Borst, Clive V., ed. *The Mind-Brain Identity Theory*. London: Macmillan, 1970.

Davidson, Donald. *Essays on Actions and Events*. Oxford: Oxford University Press, 1980

Descartes, René. *Discourse on Method and The Meditations*, trans. F. E. Sutcliffe. Harmondsworth, UK: Penguin, 1974

Hegel, Georg Wilhelm Friedrich. *Phenomenology of Spirit* (1807), trans. A. V. Miller. Oxford: Oxford University Press, 1977.

Kant, Immanuel. *Critique of Pure Reason* (1781), trans. Norman Kemp Smith. London: Macmillan, 1978.

Lycan, William G. *Mind and Cognition: A Reader*. Oxford: Blackwell, 1990.

Place, U. T. "Is Consciousness a Brain Process?" *British Journal of Psychology* 47 (1956): 44–50.

Plato. *Phaedo*, trans. David Gallop. Oxford: Oxford University Press, 1975.

Priest, Stephen. *Theories of the Mind*. Boston: Houghton Mifflin, 1991.

Robinson, Howard, ed. *Objections to Physicalism*. Oxford: Oxford University Press, 1993

Russell, Bertrand. *An Outline of Philosophy* (1927). London and New York: Routledge, 1995.

Ryle, Gilbert. *The Concept of Mind*. London: Hutchinson, 1949.

Solomon, Robert C., ed. *Phenomenology and Existentialism*. Washington D.C: University Press of America, 1980.

Strawson, Peter. *Individuals: As Essay in Descriptive Metaphysics*. London: Methuen, 1959.

Wittgenstein, Ludwig. *Philosophical Investigations*. Oxford: Blackwell, 1952.

STEPHEN PRIEST

MIND-BRAIN INTERACTION

That psychophysical interaction occurs seems obvious. How it occurs seems inexplicable. It is a presupposition of common sense but prima facie inconsistent with science that mental events cause physical events and physical events cause mental events. If a commander's decision is a cause of an air strike, then a physical event has a mental cause. If eating overripe cheese causes vivid dreams, then a mental event has a physical cause. However, if the physical universe is a closed deterministic system, then any physical event is caused by distinct physical events sufficient for its occurrence. If physical causes are sufficient for physical effects, then nothing else is necessary, so no mental cause is necessary for any physical event to happen. It follows that mental causation is redundant in the physical universe.

The Third Law of Thermodynamics states that the quantity of energy in the universe is constant. If there were mental causation, extra energy would be introduced into the universe, so if the Third Law of Thermodynamics is true there is no mental causation.

It is just as scientifically inexplicable how mind, consciousness, or awareness could be produced by the brain. The brain is the most complex object known to exist. Nevertheless, for all its neurological complexity, the brain is only billions and billions of wholly physical atoms moving through empty space. It is hard to see how billions and billions of atoms could give rise to awareness: the reader's own awareness of this page, for example. Consciousness seems to be so radically qualitatively distinct from matter in motion it is unimaginable how it could arise out of it.

It is extremely difficult to specify exactly how it is possible for a neurological event to cause a mental event, or a mental event to cause a neurological event. If there exist both minds and bodies then the logically possible permutations of psychophysical interaction would seem to be these: Minds affect bodies but bodies do not affect minds; Bodies affect minds but minds do not affect bodies; Minds affect bodies and bodies affect minds; Minds do not affect bodies and bodies do not affect minds.

If the mental states of human beings bring about physical effects, then human beings are not wholly explicable in terms of scientific laws. One account of this inexplicability is that humans are spiritual beings. Humans as spiritual beings is explicable in turn if they are made in the image of God. It is then unsurprising if the finite mind-body relation is partly like the infinite God-world relation. If we could understand how the mental and the physical interact in causal relations, some insight might be gained regarding divine creation and divine intervention.

Cartesian problems

The pre-Socratic philosopher Anaxagoras (c. 500–c. 428 B.C.E.) famously claimed that "Mind … causes all things," but he neglected to explain how. Aristotle (384–322 B.C.E) claimed in the *Nicomachean Ethics* that choice is the efficient cause (sufficient condition) of action, so if choices are mental and actions are physical, there is mental causation. Nevertheless, Aristotle provided no account of how mental causation is possible. During the seventeenth century, the French philosopher and mathematician René Descartes argued for two-way psychophysical causal interaction between the immaterial soul and the human body, but he admitted to being incapable of explaining how this was possible.

One solution to the problem is to deny that there is causation in either direction, a view entailed by the psychophysical parallelism endorsed by Gottfried Wilhelm Leibniz (1646–1716), the German philosopher and mathematician, and his French partial contemporary Nicholas Malebranche. Leibniz argued that God has caused a "pre-established harmony" and thereby initiated the causal chain that results in mental events and the causal chain that results in physical events, which are correlated rather like the motions of two clocks, each of which tells the right time and therefore the same time. Malebranche agreed that God initiated both causal chains but claimed further that God intervened to determine the timing of each mental event and each physical event. Malebranche's version of psychophysical parallelism is sometimes called *occasionalism* for this reason. In the monist theory of Baruch Spinoza, the seventeenth-century Dutch-Jewish philosopher, thought and extension are two aspects of one substance and do not interact causally.

Much contemporary work on mental causation is also a reaction to Cartesianism. Descartes's mind-body dualism is rejected, but his recognition of psychophysical interaction is accepted. The attempt is then made to explain how mental causation is possible.

Anomalous monism

The most influential theory of mental causation of the last quarter of the twentieth century was anomalous monism, advocated by Donald Davidson (b. 1917), Professor of Philosophy at the University of California at Berkeley. Davidson argues in his 1970 paper "Mental Events" that mental events cause physical events because they are physical events. Davidson's motivation is to relieve the appearance of contradiction between three principles that he thinks are true: causal interaction, the nomological character of causality, and the anomalism of the mental.

According to the principle of causal interaction at least some mental events cause physical events and at least some physical events cause mental events. For example, if intentions, perceptions, and decisions are amongst the causes of the sinking of a battleship in a naval engagement then a physical event has at least some mental causes. If the perception of a physical object, say a battleship, causes beliefs then a mental state has at least some physical causes. On the principle of the nomological character of causality, if two events are causally related then they always fall under some strict deterministic law. On the principle of the anomalism of the mental there are no psychophysical laws, so there are no strictly deterministic laws relating mental events and physical events as causes and effects.

These three principles are prima facie mutually inconsistent. Seemingly, if mental events cause physical events or physical events cause mental events, then they are related by strict deterministic laws so it is then false that there are no psychophysical laws. On the other hand, it seems that if there are no psychophysical laws then either mental events do not cause physical events, and physical events do not cause mental events, or not every pair of events related as cause and effect falls under strict deterministic laws. Nevertheless, Davidson aims to reconcile the three principles by his anomalous monism.

Anomalous monism entails that mental events are identical with physical events. Every mental event is identical with some physical event, but not every physical event is identical with a mental event. Mental events are causes of physical events because they are physical events, and physical events cause physical events. Nevertheless, Davidson rejects the thesis that there exist psychophysical laws. According to nomological monism every mental event is a physical event, and there are psychophysical laws. Davidson accepts the first part of this statement but not the second. According to nomological dualism, no mental event is identical with any physical event, but there are nevertheless psychophysical laws because, for example, mental events are correlated with physical events in some close and invariable way that falls short of identity. Davidson rejects both parts of this. According to anomalous dualism (or Cartesian dualism) no mental event is identical with any physical event and there are no psychophysical laws. Davidson accepts the second part of this but not the first.

If there are no strictly deterministic psychophysical laws then there is no physical explanation of the mental. For example, it is not possible to predict someone's mental state given a complete knowledge of their physical state, or even a complete knowledge of their present and past physical states, or even a complete knowl-

edge of the prior state of the physical universe. If there are no psychophysical laws then no mental events may be subsumed under strictly deterministic scientific generalizations.

If the mental is anomalous then room seems to be left for human freedom. If there is no strict deterministic law relating one's choices or decisions to physical events then they are not necessitated by physical events. Indeed, if one's choices and decisions may cause physical events then one's mental states are at least amongst the causes of one's own actions and, arguably, this is part of what it means for a person to have free will, to be an autonomous agent.

Supervenience

Davidson holds that the dependence of the mental on the physical is very close. The mental is supervenient on the physical. This means that if two mental events differ in some mental respect then they cannot only differ in that mental respect but must differ in some physical respect. However, if they differ in some physical respect it does not follow that they differ in any mental respect.

The doctrine that some property F supervenes on some property G is expressed by a cluster of views, because the supervenience relation admits of variants and degrees. First, if being F supervenes on being G, then if two objects—a, b—are indiscernible with regard to being F, then they are indiscernible with regard to being G. So, if the mental supervenes on the physical then it is not possible for two persons to be indiscernible with regard to some mental property without being indiscernible with regard to some physical property.

Second, if being F supervenes on being G, then if a is F and b is exactly like a in being F, then b is G. So, if two people share a mental property then they share a physical property. Third, if being F supervenes on being G, then a cannot change with respect to being F without changing with respect to being G. So a person cannot change in any mental respect without changing in some physical respect. It is unclear how much is entailed by "without changing with respect to being G", but arguably if being F supervenes on being G, then a cannot cease to be F without ceasing to be G. In that case, a person cannot cease to posses a mental property without ceasing to possess a physical property. Also arguably if being *F* supervenes on being *G,* then *a* cannot begin to be *F* without beginning to be *G.* In that case a person cannot gain a mental property without gaining a physical property.

Weak supervenience is the doctrine that if in the actual world *a* is *F,* then in the actual world *a* is *G.* So if the mental is weakly supervenient on the physical, then if a person has a mental property in the actual world, then they have a physical property in the actual world. *Strong* supervenience is the doctrine that if in every possible world *a* is *F,* then in every possible world *a* is *G.* So if the mental is strongly supervenient on the physical, then if a person has a mental property in every possible world, then they have a physical property in every possible world.

Arguments for supervenience are harder to find than formulations. The supervenience of the mental on the physical is designed to capture the "intuition" that mental facts depend on physical facts but physical facts do not depend on mental facts. It also seems to promise dependence without reduction: Mental events are not nomologically reducible to physical events because there are no psychophysical laws. Mental events are not logically reducible to physical events because it is not true that any sentence or set of sentences about mental events can be translated into a sentence or set of sentences about physical events without loss of meaning.

Even though the mental supervenes on the physical there can be no hope of a reduction of psychology to neurology in the way in which, arguably, biology may be reduced to chemistry and chemistry reduced to physics.

Epiphenomenalism and psychophysical laws

It is objected to anomalous monism, notably by the Canadian philosopher Ted Honderich (b. 1933), that on this theory mental events do not cause physical events "in virtue of" being mental events but in virtue of being physical events. The mental properties of the mental events are not causally efficacious. Honderich points out that some pears on a weighing scale depress the scale in virtue of their physical property of being a certain weight, not in virtue of, say, being green. If

this sort of objection is right then in anomalous monism the mental properties of mental events do no causal work. Mental causation has not been explained because nothing mental qua mental is causing anything physical.

Anomolous monism arguably collapses into a kind of epiphenomenalism: the theory that mental events are caused by physical events but physical events are not caused by mental events. In reply it might be urged that the sentence "Mental events cause physical events" is true according to anomalous monism because mental events cause physical events because they are identical with physical events that cause physical events.

It has been argued, notably by Honderich in his *A Theory of Determinism* (1988), that the neurological is sufficient for the mental: The occurrence of some neurological event is a sufficient condition for the occurrence of some psychological event and, as is logically entailed by this, the occurrence of that psychological event is a necessary condition for the occurrence of that neurological event. On this view there seems to be no reason in principle why psychophysical laws should not be discovered because true sentences about neurology would entail true sentences about psychological events. It ought then to be possible to predict the occurrence of psychological events from knowledge of neurological events.

It is empirically uncontroversial in the case of human beings (if not souls, computers, and deities) that the neurological is necessary for the mental. Neurological impairment leads to psychological impairment. If the neurological is necessary for the mental, then the mental is sufficient for the neurological. Arguably the dependency of the mental on the neurological is ultimately an empirical and contingent one. If computers, souls, or God have mentality but no neurology, then it is not a necessary truth that the mental depends on the neurological.

Karl Popper (1902–1993) has argued that the self-conscious mind is an evolutionary product of the brain that nevertheless acts causally upon it. However, if mental events are sufficient for neurological events and if the physical universe is a closed deterministic system, then neurological events are overdetermined. Some event is overdetermined if at least two conditions sufficient for its occurrence obtain. This would seem to make either mental causes or neurological causes redundant. If a neurological event is sufficient for the occurrence of a neurological event then no mental event is necessary for it. If a mental event is sufficient for a neurological event then no neurological event is necessary for it.

One solution, adopted by the contemporary English philosophers Tim Crane and D. H. Mellor for example, is to give up the assumption that the universe is a closed deterministic system. Crane and Mellor see no reason in principle why there should not exist psychophysical laws as scientifically respectable as physical laws.

See also CONSCIOUSNESS STUDIES; DESCARTES, RENÉ; DETERMINISM; EXPERIENCE, RELIGIOUS: COGNITIVE AND NEUROPHYSIOLOGICAL ASPECTS; FUNCTIONALISM; MIND-BODY THEORIES; NEUROSCIENCES; SUPERVENIENCE

Bibliography

Block, Ned. "Can the Mind Change the World?" In Meaning and Method: Essays in Honor of Hilary Putnam, ed. G. Boolos. Cambridge, UK: Cambridge University Press, 1990.

Charles, David, and Lennon, Kathleen, eds. Reduction, Explanation and Realism. Oxford: Oxford University Press, 1992.

Crane, Tim, and Mellor, D. H. "There is No Question of Physicalism." Mind 99, no. 394 (1990): 185–206.

Davidson, Donald. Essays on Actions and Events. Oxford: Oxford University Press, 1980.

Haugeland, John. "Phenomenal Causes." Southern Journal of Philosophy 22, suppl. (1983): 63-70.

Heil, John, and Mele, Alfred. "Mental Causes." American Philosophical Quarterly 28 (1991): 61-71.

Heil, John, and Mele, Alfred, eds. Mental Causation. Oxford: Oxford University Press, 1993.

Honderich, Ted. "The Argument for Anomalous Monism." Analysis 42 (1982): 59–64.

Honderich, Ted. A Theory of Determinism: The Mind, Neuroscience, and Life-Hopes. Oxford: Oxford University Press, 1988.

Hornsby, Jennifer. "Which Mental Events are Physical Events?" Proceedings of the Aristotelian Society 81 (1981): 73-92.

Kim, Jaegwon. "Concepts of Supervenience." Philosophy and Phenomenological Research 65 (1984): 153-176.

Kim, Jaegwon. "Causality, Identity, and Supervenience in the Mind-body Problem." Midwest Studies in Philosophy 4 (1979): 31-49.

LePore, Ernest, and McLaughlin, Brian P., eds. Action and Events: Perspectives on the Philosophy of Donald Davidson. Oxford: Basil Blackwell, 1985.

Popper, Karl, and Eccles, John. The Self and Its Brain. Berlin: Springer-Verlag, 1977.

Priest, Stephen. Theories of the Mind. Boston: Houghton Mifflin, 1991.

Smith, Peter. "Anomalous Monism and Epiphenomenalism: A Reply to Honderich." Analysis 44 (1984): 83–86.

STEPHEN PRIEST

MIRACLE

In order to differentiate between the customary way in which God acts and his special miraculous action, theologians have traditionally distinguished his *providentia ordinaria* from the *providentia extraordinaria,* the latter being identified with miracles. Since the dawning of modernity, miracles have been widely understood to be "violations of the laws of nature." But so long as laws of nature are taken to be universal inductive generalizations, the notion of a violation of a law of nature is incoherent, since such statements must take account of everything that happens, so that exceptions to them are impossible. Although this fact led some Enlightenment philosophers to think that miracles can thus be defined out of existence, it ought rather to alert one to the defectiveness of the modern definition. Natural laws have implicit *ceteris paribus* conditions, so that a law states what is the case under the assumption of certain ideal conditions. If God brings about some event that a law of nature fails to predict or describe, such an event cannot be characterized as a violation of that law, since the law is valid only on the assumption that no supernatural factors come into play.

Miracles, then, are better defined as naturally impossible events, that is to say, events that cannot be produced by the natural causes (i.e., those described by physics) operative at a certain time and place. Whether an event is a miracle is thus relative to a time and place. Of course, some events may be absolutely miraculous in that they are at every time and place beyond the productive capacity of natural causes.

Possibility of miracles

What could conceivably transform an event that is naturally impossible into a real historical event? Clearly, the answer is the personal God of theism. For if a transcendent, personal creator exists, then this God could cause events in the universe that could not be produced by causes within the universe. Given a God who created the universe, who conserves the world in being, and who is capable of acting freely, miracles are evidently possible.

A widespread assumption persists that if historical inquiry is to be feasible, then one must adopt a sort of methodological naturalism as a fundamental historiographical principle. This viewpoint is a restatement of Ernst Troeltsch's principle of analogy, which states that the past does not differ essentially from the present. Though events of the past are, of course, not the same events as those of the present, they must be the same *in kind* if historical investigation is to be possible. Troeltsch realized that any history written on this principle will be skeptical with regard to the historicity of miracles.

Theologian Wolfhart Pannenberg, however, has persuasively argued that Troeltsch's principle of analogy cannot be legitimately employed to banish from the realm of history all non-analogous events. Properly defined, analogy means that in a situation that is unclear, the facts ought to be understood in terms of known experience; but Troeltsch has elevated the principle to constrict all past events to purely natural events. But that an event bursts all analogies cannot be used to dispute its historicity. Troeltsch's formulation of the principle of analogy destroys genuine historical reasoning, since the historian must be open to the uniqueness of the events of the past and cannot exclude events a priori simply because they do not conform to present experience. When myths, legends, illusions, and the like are dismissed as unhistorical, it is not because they are non-analogous, but because they *are* analogous to present forms of consciousness having no objective referent. When an event is said to have occurred for which no analogy exists, its reality cannot be automatically dismissed; to do this one would require an analogy to some known form of consciousness

lacking an objective referent that would suffice to explain the situation. Pannenberg has thus upended Troeltsch's principle of analogy such that it is not the *want* of an analogy that shows an event to be unhistorical, but the presence of a positive analogy to known thought forms that shows a purportedly miraculous event to be unhistorical. In this way, the lack of an analogy to present experience says nothing for or against the historicity of an event. Pannenberg's formulation of the principle preserves the analogous nature of the past to the present or to the known, thus making the investigation of history possible, without thereby sacrificing the integrity of the past or distorting it.

Identification of miracles

The question remains whether the identification of any event as a miracle is possible. On the one hand, it might be argued that a convincing demonstration that a purportedly miraculous event has occurred would only succeed in forcing the revision of natural law so as to accommodate the event in question. But a natural law is not abolished because of one exception; the anomaly must occur repeatedly whenever the conditions for it are present. If an event occurs that is anomalous and there are reasons to believe that this event would not occur again under similar circumstances, then the law in question will not be abandoned.

On the other hand, it might be urged that if a purportedly miraculous event were demonstrated to have occurred, one should conclude that the event occurred in accordance with unknown natural laws. What serves to distinguish a genuine miracle from a mere scientific anomaly? Here the religio-historical context of the event becomes crucial. A miracle without a context is inherently ambiguous. But if a purported miracle occurs in a significant religio-historical context, then the chances of its being a genuine miracle are increased. For example, if the miracles occur at a momentous time and do not recur regularly in history, and if the miracles are numerous and various, then the chances of their being the result of some unknown natural causes are reduced. Moreover, some miracles (e.g., the resurrection of Jesus) so exceed what is known of the productive capacity of natural causes that they could only be reasonably attributed to a supernatural cause. Thus, while it is difficult to know in many cases whether a genuine miracle has occurred, that does not imply pessimism with respect to all cases.

See also DIVINE ACTION; GOD; NATURALISM; LAWS OF NATURE; PROVIDENCE; SPECIAL DIVINE ACTION; SPECIAL PROVIDENCE; SPIRITUALITY AND FAITH HEALING;

Bibliography

Earman, John. "Bayes, Hume, and Miracles." *Faith and Philosophy* 10 (1993): 293–310.

Freddoso, Alfred J. "The Necessity of Nature." *Midwest Studies in Philosophy* 11 (1986): 215–242.

Geivett, R. Douglas, and, Habermas, Gary R. *In Defense of Miracles.* Downer's Grove, Ill.: InterVarsity Press, 1997.

Hume, David. "Of Miracles." In *Enquiries Concerning Human Understanding and Concerning the Principles of Morals* (1777), 3rd edition, ed. L. A. Selby-Bigge and P. H. Midditch. Oxford: Clarendon Press, 1975.

Pannenberg, Wolfhart. "Redemptive Event and History." In *Wolfhart Pannenberg, Basic Questions in Theology,* 2 vols., trans. G. H. Kehm. Philadelphia: Fortress, 1970.

Swinburne, Richard. *The Concept of Miracle.* New York: Macmillan, 1970.

Swinburne, Richard, ed. *Miracles: Philosophical Topics.* New York: Macmillan, 1989.

Troeltsch, Ernst. "Über historische und dogmatische Methode in der Theologie." In *Gesammelte Schriften.* Tübingen, Germany: J. C. B. Mohr, 1913.

WILLIAM LANE CRAIG

MISSING LINK

The term *missing link* refers to an idea derived in a fairly obvious manner from the "Great Chain of Being": a concept, much beloved of medieval scholars and theologians that traces its roots back to Aristotle. According to this notion of an inherent organismic *Scala Naturae,* all living creatures are ranked (or occupy positions) from "lower" to "higher," with humans, the crowning glory of creation, at the top (though between humans and God lie angels, archangels, and other spiritual beings). This archaic terminology still survives in some areas of science today, with vertebrates, for instance, continuing to be classified by many as "lower" (fish, amphibians, reptiles) versus "higher" (birds, mammals).

The metaphor of a chain of being, with its lowest members connected to the highest by an insensible gradation of intermediate forms, naturally adapts to the notion of a series of links. Thus in pre-Darwinian times it was widely held that every species must represent a link in this chain, just as it occupied its own preordained place in nature; some mid-nineteenth century naturalists, though, working in a world whose immensity and diversity were already becoming recognized, vaguely envisaged the eventual discovery of a complete set of living intermediates. With the advent of the notion of evolution by natural selection propounded by Charles Darwin (1809–1882) and his younger contemporary Alfred Russel Wallace (1823–1913) in 1858, and influentially enlarged upon by the former in *On the Origin of Species* in 1859, interpretation of the fossil record, already long known, assumed a new dimension. Earlier western scholars had tended to the view that the ancient fossil organisms, often very different from those familiar in the modern world, were best interpreted as victims of the Noachian flood—or, in view of the evidently complex stratigraphy involved, as witnesses to a series of "catastrophes" for which biblical authority was sought. With the introduction of the concept of evolution, an alternative explanation was at hand: that extinct organisms represent stages along the route through time from ancestral forms to the modern biota.

From this point it was but a short leap to the notion of ancient "missing links" in the chain. In popular lore the most famous of these lies between apes and humans, and many fossils have been acclaimed in this intermediate role. Darwin had emphasized in his *Descent of Man* (1871) that today's humans and apes are descended from nothing like an existing ape or monkey, but from a common ancestor (which, by definition, can be neither). Still, the half-human, half-ape image, of a form caught in the act of clawing its way up toward humanity, seized the public imagination, and even that of scientists. Among the latter the influential Ernst Haeckel (1834–1919) went so far as to name this hypothetical form *Pithecanthropus alalus* (the "ape-man lacking speech").

It is useless for paleoanthropologists to protest that if a form is missing, it cannot be a link, and that if it is to be a link, it cannot be missing. It is well known now that it is far more accurate to speak in terms of a ramifying bush of ancestors and descendants than of links in a chain. But it will be a long time before we are able to exorcise the evocative "missing link" from our vocabularies.

See also EVOLUTION, HUMAN

Bibliography

Darwin, Charles. *The Origin of Species* (1859). New York: Bantam Classic, 1999.

Darwin, Charles. *The Descent of Man* (1871). Amherst, N.Y.: Prometheus, 1997.

IAN TATTERSALL

MITOCHONDRIAL EVE

Mitochondrial Eve is the name given to the hypothesis proposed in 1987 by Rebecca Cann and others that all humans are descended from one female who lived around two hundred thousand years ago in Africa. The claim was based on study of mitochondria, parts of the cell (containing genes) that exist outside the central nucleus and that are passed on only by females. It should be noted what is not being claimed, namely that all humans beings are descended from just one woman. Humans could all be descended from many, or just a few, or some from one group and some from another. It is just that all humans share at least one female ancestor, who may or may not have had just one mate. The hypothesis is generally accepted as true although there are questions about the accuracy of the dating. In this respect, future research might demand substantial revision at some later point.

See also EVOLUTION, HUMAN

Bibliography

Loewe, L., and Scherer, S. "Mitochondrial Eve: The Plot Thickens." *Trends in Ecology and Evolution* 12, no. 11 (1997): 422–423.

MICHAEL RUSE

MODELS

Models are widely used in many disciplines to turn complex or abstract information or ideas into a form that is more easily understood and workable, basically as representations of the information or ideas. A scale model is an actual construction that resembles the original object. Models using analogy or mathematical logic display varying degrees of abstraction. Of the many types of models, several are commonly used in science and theology, though there are differences in their applications in each discipline.

In the natural sciences, the use of models generally implies the idea of interpretation of a deductive system, carried over from mathematical logic. Scale models and analogues are also commonly used, whether similar in substance to the thing modeled or similar in the relations between its parts. Formal analogies show analogy of structure between the model and the system modeled. Material analogies show material similarities between the original system and its model, such as in replicas. Mary Hesse notes that the relation of analogy—formal or material—implies differences, denoted as *negative analogy,* as well as similarities, called *positive analogy.* The billiard ball model of gases offers both positive and negative analogy. From the early part of the twentieth century on, there have been debates over whether models are essential to successful theorizing in the sciences or whether the use of such models is potentially misleading and dispensable.

In theology, models may be utilized in order to better understand doctrines such as the relation between God and the world, as well as doctrines of God or theological anthropology. In the history of theology, it has usually been the practice to speak in terms of analogy or metaphor, tropes of language that serve as a type of "momentary" model. By contrast, Sallie McFague defines models as metaphors with "staying power."

In discussions about the relation between religion and science over the last third of the twentieth century and into the early twenty-first, the use of models has played a highly significant role. Different epistemological models show how the modern period has described knowledge of the world and the status of models in scientific theorizing.

These include *naïve realism* (the model is a literal picture of reality), *logical positivism* (theories are directly deducible from data, dismissing models), *utilitarianism* (models are useful fictions), and *critical realism* (models are representations of reality in interaction with the observer). It is the last that has dominated discussions of the relation between religion and science. By the 1980s, other epistemological models began to be proposed. Challenges to standard interpretations of critical realism have been raised in the light of developments of the late twentieth and early twenty-first centuries. These challenges include postmodern critiques of foundationalism, "science and technology studies" that have expanded upon Thomas Kuhn's concept of paradigm *in The Structure of Scientific Revolutions* (1962) as well as feminist and postcolonial critiques and writings in the sociology of knowledge.

Models are also used in the science and religion dialogue and serve to show how relations between religion and science have been conceived. Most widely used of this kind of modeling is the four-fold typology of Ian Barbour: conflict, independence, dialogue, and integration. Models that include historical examples have come under criticism by historians, who point out that models give only a partial picture. Many argue that misunderstandings occur because models may oversimplify the historical situation. Many recent studies examine and elaborate upon the complexity of the social and political situations that bear upon the perception of a conflict between religion and science.

See also METAPHOR; PARADIGMS; SCIENCE AND RELIGION, METHODOLOGIES; SCIENCE AND RELIGION, MODELS AND RELATIONS

Bibliography

Barbour, Ian. *Myths, Models, and Paradigms: A Comparative Study in Science and Religion.* New York: Harper, 1974.

Gregersen, Niels Henrik, and Van Huyssteen, J. Wentzel, eds. *Rethinking Theology and Science: Six Models for the Current Dialogue.* Grand Rapids, Mich.: Eerdmans, 1998.

Ferré, Frederick. "Mapping the Logic of Models in Science and Theology." *Christian Scholar* 46, no. 1 (1963): 9–39.

Hesse, Mary B. *Models and Analogies in Science.* Notre Dame, Ind.: University of Notre Dame Press, 1966.

Kuhn, Thomas S. *The Structure of Scientific Revolutions* (1962), 3rd edition. Chicago: University of Chicago Press, 1996.

McFague, Sallie. *Metaphorical Theology: Models of God in Religious Language.* Philadelphia, Pa.: Fortress, 1982.

LOU ANN G. TROST

MODERNITY

The terms *modern* and *modernity* have been widely used in the expression of two contrasting perspectives. They either (1) suggest that certain new habits, practices, or worldviews are inferior to those of ancient, medieval, or classical times and origins; or (2) they claim the superiority of these habits, practices, or worldviews, ascribing a positive meaning to their being new, up to date, fashionable, progressive, or evolutionarily successful.

It is typical of the latter perspective that the emphasis has been on "current" developments and on "the present," and that contrasts such as primitive, old, antiquated, obsolete, as well as terms with the prefix *pre* (e.g., premodern, preindustrial), have been used. This perspective is applied to the most recent social, literary, and aesthetic developments, and it leads to an ideology of permanent qualitative progress.

A major shift between these two views of modernity is marked by the controversy called the *Querelle des Anciens et des Modernes* (Quarrel of the Ancients and the Moderns; a title derived from the writings of Charles Perrault), which began in England and France in 1687 and lasted for about a century. In this long debate several philosophers of the Enlightenment questioned the superiority of antiquity, its arts and values. They thus paved the way for the self-privileging of modernity over the other epochs of human history.

The term *modernity* also designates an epoch in human history that is characterized by the emergence of nation states that build on the political loyalty of their citizens, develop standardizations of the law, and establish legal institutions and bureaucratic forms of administration. Such nation states permit and even encourage public deliberation about the common social order, the common good, and the common goals. This development is connected to a consolidation of knowledge through institutionalized education and with strategies to acquire knowledge systematically by cultivating the "sciences." The political, educational, and scientific processes develop along with an industrial society that by the technological application of scientific knowledge generates a constant transformation of its natural and cultural environments.

Modernity as historical epoch

Since these developments have not occurred simultaneously across the globe, the localization of modernity in space and time is difficult to determine and remains open to debate. The Reformation is often designated, even in secular circles, as the breeding ground of typically modern mentalities. Modernity is also usually associated with the age of "enlightened thinking" that shaped Europe and North America from the second half of the eighteenth century on. During this period, the French revolution and the philosophy of Immanuel Kant (1724–1804) became the most important sources for political and intellectual ideas. During the last decades of the twentieth century, an ongoing international debate about the end of modernity set in, with Friedrich Nietzsche (1844–1900) acting as an early prophet of "postmodernism." The postmodern period is fuelled by the growing conviction that modernity's faith in the unity of reason and the rationality continuum was illusion, and by uncertainties about the future of nation states in the process of globalization.

The ambivalences of modernity

Whereas modernity can be regarded as an endeavor to escape religious and political tyranny and authoritarian traditionalism, it has itself become a metaphor for a deeply ambivalent global enterprise. The striving for liberation, the establishment of a public legal system, mandatory education for all people, and the development of welfare systems within the nation state were all aspects of the modern enterprise. The same modernity that fled the tyrannies of the past and strove for the unity of the state, the rule of law in political life, and political sovereignty based on the will of the people (democratization) also brought forth aggressive nation states characterized by

chauvinism, imperialism, colonialism, and ecological brutality. Similarly, the escape from prescientific and even mythical worldviews, the striving for a consolidation of knowledge through the sciences, the search for scientific truth, and the appeal to rationality and reason led to more than the triumph of public education and the flourishing of discovery and technological innovation. It also led to scientistic and naturalistic ideologies that promoted blindness to religious truths and cultural complexity.

Alfred North Whitehead (1861–1947) offered a subtle analysis of how the unfolding and the triumph of scientific thinking shaped the modern common sense, its modes of experience and expectation, and how it correlated with a relative deformation of aesthetic, ethical, and religious experience. According to Whitehead, "The modern world has lost God and is seeking him" (1960, p.72). The process of modernization finally led to the dominance of science-assisted technical reason (industrialization) and to the triumph of the powers of the market, the media, and technology—developments that have turned out to be culturally imperialistic and ecologically destructive.

Ambivalence over the blessings or curses of modernity is rooted in a structural conflict within modernity itself, which has lead to the deeply negative connotations associated with the term *modernity*. The conflict is usually spelled out by the dual of "modernity" and "postmodernity." It is also present in the ongoing discussion of whether postmodernity is merely an extension of modernity, a self-jeopardizing of the modern enterprise that would be better identified as *late modernity*.

On the one hand, modernity strives for the freedom of the person, the equality of all human beings, and for the universality of reason. Modernity's fight for justice and equality, and against tyranny, is connected with a passion for universal transparency and unity. For the modern mind, unity means consensus, mutual understanding, and harmony based on equality. On the other hand, modern societies have developed a multisystemic texture as modernity brought forth a differentiation of social institutions, sciences, and rationalities—differentiations that resist the plea for an overarching universal unity. Modernity thus created an ongoing conflict between unity and differentiation: a passion for unified reason, a universal rationality-continuum, and universal morality on the one hand, and a passion for differentiation of social systems, differentiation of the sciences, and a nonhierarchical differentiation of cultural spheres on the other hand.

Several social systems work for the sustenance and the wellbeing of the whole society. Such systems include, for example, politics, law, religion, education, the sciences, the market, the media, technology, the arts, and the family. In this multisystemic order each system performs a function that is essential and indispensable for the whole society. At the same time each system strives for autonomy and defends itself against interference from other systems. Each system optimizes its procedures, its rationalities, and its institutional forms. Along with the differentiation of the social systems, modern societies developed a rich texture of associations, such as political parties, ideological movements, and a variety of clubs and lobbies, all of which attempt to influence, strengthen, or question and reshape the "division of powers" within social systems. The universal and even grandiose claims of such associations grow out of the interests and goals of their members. Some associations perish quickly, while others have a long life. Some are normatively and institutionally stable, others are open to trends. These associations, which want to influence and actually do influence social systems, make up civil society. The complex, but by no means chaotic, interaction between social systems and civil associations constitutes so-called pluralistic society, which provides a structured and pluralistic setting for the sciences and other cultural formations, a setting that promises to cope with the inner conflicts of modernity.

Modernity and postmodernity

The structured pluralism of modern societies and cultures has brought a differentiation of rationalities: for example, those of the market, of the natural sciences, of historical investigation, of religion, and of common sense. This differentiation has challenged the modern ideal of the universal unity of knowledge and of mutual moral communication and understanding. Yet with its multisystemic setting it has also challenged the idea of an endless and relativistic differentiation and dissociation, an idea often connected with postmodernity. These multisystemic settings appear in many areas of life,

although the question of how many social systems there are and how they should be differentiated remains open to debate. But certainly their number is finite and small, and the evolution of a new system takes a long time, as evidenced, for example, by the development of the media during the nineteenth and twentieth centuries. The same holds true for differentiation in the sciences or for the family of confessions in Christianity, which constitute the pluralism of the academy and the pluralism of the ecumene. The world is much more complex than the typical modern mind is willing to admit, but it is much less chaotic than those who hope to exorcise the spirits of postmodernity would have it.

The one clear difference that divides modernity and postmodernity is reflected in many areas and on many different levels: This is the difference between the highest value and the interpretation of this value in both epochs. For modernity, the value of unity is paramount. For postmodernity, the value of difference is crucial. This, of course, includes different understandings and interpretations of *unity* and *difference* on both sides. For the typical modern mind, difference meant conflict, disagreement, inequality, or even oppression. For the postmodern mind, however, difference means freedom and creative engagement, while unity raises suspicions of adaptation, control, and even oppression. The postmodern mind would nevertheless acknowledge that not all forms of difference are creative and helpful. One must differentiate between the differences and recognize that some can be destructive. The postmodern mind would also welcome differentiated forms of unity. But all forms of unity have to allow for difference, have to appreciate and even treasure difference. Otherwise they breed oppressive ideologies.

The postmodern mindset is not simply based on some Nietzschean philosophical idea. Numerous cultural and scientific achievements, along with many experiences of oppression and pain, have led to the conviction and to the affirmation that the world is *poly-contextual*. Society must welcome multiperspectival approaches and should embrace and cultivate pluralistic settings if it wants to maintain the modern striving for truth, justice, and dignity. Different cultures, different traditions, and different rationalities have to be taken seriously.

Moreover, the human individual has to be taken much more seriously than modernity thought.

Modernity praised the value of the theoretical "human subject" and its autonomy, freedom, and rational self-control, but it failed to address the actual unique individual. Rather, modernity had in mind the idealized, standardized person of the bourgeois value system: the autonomous "subject," guided by reason and universal morals. But concrete human beings are much more subtle and complex. They are determined by unique personal histories, by complex biological endowments, by intricate passions and feelings, and by different forms of rationality. Some are more impressed by religion than others; some are devoted to the natural sciences, while others are skeptical of them. Some find their key values in family and friendship; others look for a more general orientation for the common good. The young Friedrich Schleiermacher (1768–1834) recognized the problems in the modern concept of the human person, and he accused Kant of having standardized modern subjectivity and of having attributed too much power to reason. Schleiermacher called for a new conception of individualism, one that takes each multifarious human person seriously—a sort of polyindividualism. In this respect, however, modernity itself provides possibilities for escape and for correcting its own reductionistic anthropological concepts. "All in all, resistance to rationalization has been as prominent a mark of modernity as has rationalization itself" (Bauman, p. 596).

See also POSTMODERNISM; POSTMODERN SCIENCE

Bibliography

Bauman, Zygmunt "Art, Modernity." In *The Oxford Companion to Politics of the World,* ed. Joel Krieger. Oxford and New York: Oxford University Press, 1993.

Berman, Marshall. *All that Is Solid Melts into Air: The Experience of Modernity.* London: Verso; New York: Simon and Schuster, 1982.

Black, Cyril Edwin. *The Dynamics of Modernization: A Study in Comparative History.* New York: Harper, 1966.

Giddens, Anthony. *Consequences of Modernity.* Stanford, Calif.: Stanford University Press, 1990.

Giddens, Anthony. *Modernity and Self-Identity: Self and Society in the Late Modern Age.* Stanford, Calif.: Stanford University Press, 1991.

Habermas, Jürgen. *The Philosophical Discourse of Modernity,* translated by Frederick Lawrence. Cambridge, UK: Cambridge University Press, 1987.

Habermas, Jürgen. *Between Facts and Norms,* trans. William Rehg. Cambridge, UK: Polity, 1996.

Heller, Agnes. *Can Modernity Survive?* Berkeley: University of California Press, 1990.

Köpping, Klaus-Peter; Wiehl, Reiner; Welker, Michael; eds. *Die Autonome Person—Eine Europäische Erfindung?* Munich, Germany: Fink, 2002.

Lash, Scott, and Friedman, Jonathan, eds. *Modernity and Identity.* Oxford: Blackwell, 1992.

Levy, Marion. *Modernization and the Structure of Societies.* Princeton, N.J.: Princeton University Press, 1966.

Luhmann, Niklas. *Die Gesellschaft der Gesellschaft,* 2 vols. Frankfurt am Main, Germany: Suhrkamp, 1997.

Riha, Karl. *Prämoderne, Moderne, Postmoderne.* Frankfurt am Main, Germany: Suhrkamp, 1995.

Waters, Malcolm, ed. *Modernity: Critical Concepts,* 4 vols. London and New York: Routledge, 1999.

Wehler, Hans Ulrich. *Modernisierungstheorie und Geschichte.* Göttingen, Germany: Vandenhoeck und Ruprecht, 1975.

Whitehead, Alfred North. *Science and the Modern World.* Cambridge, UK: University Press, 1925.

Whitehead, Alfred North. *Religion in the Making* (1926). New York: Meridian, 1960.

MICHAEL WELKER

MONISM

The term *monism* comes from the Greek word meaning *alone* or *single*. While the term was originally used by German mathematician and philosopher Christian Wolff (1679–1754) to refer to views asserting either that everything is mental (idealism) or everything is material (materialism), monism has wider applicability today, claiming that the various things or kinds of things encountered in the world are somehow reducible to, derivable from, or explicable in terms of one thing (substantival monism) or one kind of thing (attributive monism). The substantival and attributive views are logically independent—e.g., Baruch Spinoza (1632–1677) affirmed the first while holding a plurality of attributes; Gottfried Wilhelm Leibniz (1646–1716) held the second while countenancing a plurality of substances.

Monism must be distinguished from pluralism, which asserts that there are various things or kinds of things. Monism must also be distinguished from dualism, which claims that there are only two basic kinds of things. Often, however, the term monism is used imprecisely to refer to any fundamental dichotomy in a philosophical or religious system (e.g., good and evil, soul and body, male and female). Of particular interest in the science-theology conversation are the apparent dualisms of mind and body, and God and universe.

A primary motivation for monism is ontological simplicity—a world in which there is one basic thing or kind of thing makes fewer ontological claims than one asserting the existence of many things or kinds. Explanation for the monist is homogeneous and coherent; it makes no appeal to entities of a different ontological type when framing its causal stories. Moreover, the assumption of monism (particularly of physicalist variety) has been enormously fruitful. On the other hand, pluralism is motivated by the apparent multiplicity of things and kinds, and the desire to avoid purchasing simplicity at the expense of real complexity. A further advantage of monism is that, unlike pluralism, it does not need to offer an account of a relation that supposedly conjoins fundamentally disparate kinds.

In addition to materialist (physicalist) and idealist monisms, there is also neutral monism and anomalous monism. The first claims that both mental and physical phenomena are manifestations of an underlying neutral stuff. Spinoza and Bertrand Russell (1872–1970) are associated with this position. The second, advanced by twentieth century philosopher Donald Davidson, holds that while every mental event is token identical to some physical event, mental properties can nonetheless not be reductively identified with physical properties. Because mental properties are individuated holistically according to criteria of coherence, rationality, and consistency which, as Davidson notes, "have no echo in physical theory" (p. 231). Although all particulars are physical (physicalist monism), the incommensurability between mental and physical properties requires a property dualism.

Both substance and property dualism are of interest in the science-theology discussion. For example, most would claim that substantival and attributive monism are both incompatible with the substance dualism of divine and worldly stuff (or creator and created stuff) that theism presupposes. Others have suggested that since God can be understood immanently, a dualism of divine and worldly properties is compatible with a monistic ontological physicalism. The question for the science-theology conversation is whether God-universe or mind-body property dualism coupled with physicalist monism has the resources to avoid reductive explanation, and thus successfully to ground an ontology of the mental and the divine.

See also DUALISM; MATERIALISM; NATURALISM; PHYSICALISM, REDUCTIVE AND NONREDUCTIVE; PLURALISM

Bibliography

Davidson, Donald. "Mental Events." In *Essays on Actions & Events*. Oxford: Clarendon Press, 1980.

Drees, Willem B. *Religion, Science, and Naturalism*. Cambridge, UK: Cambridge University Press, 1996.

Spinoza, Baruch. *The Collected Works of Spinoza*. ed. and trans. Edwin M, Curley. Princeton, N.J.: Princeton University Press, 1984.

Van Inwagen, Peter. "Individuality." In *Metaphysics*. Boulder, Colo.: Westview Press, 1993.

DENNIS BIELFELDT

MONOTHEISM

Monotheism is the belief in a single personal God who is the creator of the cosmos and continues to exercise some influence on it. Monotheism is the core tenet of Judaism, Christianity, and Islam, as well as a basic belief about reality for many outside these traditions. God is often, but not always, held to be of unlimited power (omnipotence), unlimited knowledge (omniscience), unlimited extension (omnipresence), and unlimited goodness (omnibenevolence). Further beliefs—God is three persons in one, is self-revealing, is salvifically involved with human beings—are advanced by specific religious traditions; their beliefs about God share important commonalities and exhibit important contrasts.

See also GOD; PANENTHEISM; PANTHEISM; THEISM

PHILIP CLAYTON

MORALITY

Morality (Latin *mores,* from *mos,* implying custom, practice, or conduct) is a standard of character measured against established philosophical or other categories. Morality may be assessed by psychoanalytic and social theory as a degree of super-ego formation and socialization (Sigmund Freud). It can be seen as a mark of maturity in relation to stages of a cognitive-structural hierarchy (Lawrence Kohlberg). It is often viewed as a level of character formation and responsible self-appropriation (Erik Erikson). Moral self-consciousness is tangible in relation to the customs, manners, and character that constitute life within a shared space (Charles Taylor). The axes of moral reflection can generally be seen as constituted by deontological or teleological considerations, such as questions of obligation (actions, intentions, etc.) or value (respect, dignity, etc.).

See also FREUD, SIGMUND; VALUE

RODNEY L. PETERSEN

MORPHOGENESIS

See EVOLUTION

MUTATION

A mutation in a gene is a structural change in the sequence of nucleotide subunits in the chains that make up DNA. Changing the structure of a gene alters the design information contained in its nucleotide sequence, and generally affects the function of that gene's product. The design instructions for that gene product are spelled out in DNA as a particular sequence of the chemical subunits called *nucleotides,* each of which contains a nitrogenous base: *adenine* (A), *thymine* (T), *cytosine* (C), or *guanine* (G). Hundreds of nucleotides are linked in a DNA chain in the sequence that spells out instructions for a single gene. This is analogous to conveying instructions in printed books by particular arrangements of twenty-six kinds of alphabetical letters. In the case of genes, however, there are only four letters in the alphabet.

Gene products are usually proteins, and altering the design information in a particular gene will alter the structure and function of its corresponding protein. Since proteins do all the body's work, they account for all the biological characteristics (*phenotypes*) of any organism. Usually, a mutation in a gene produces a harmful effect, hindering the function of the protein designed by that gene, and sometimes the hindrance is lethal to the organism. Many cancers and inherited diseases are believed to be associated with mutations. In contrast, very occasionally a mutation may be beneficial. If a beneficial mutation is inherited it could cause progeny to adapt better to their environment than their parents could. Such mutations provide a substrate for natural selection in evolving new or better biological functions.

Mutations are produced from errors when cells copy DNA, or from damage caused by radiation or chemicals. Cells contain mechanisms for repairing DNA, but they are not perfect. Changes in the nucleotide sequence can include substitution of one nucleotide for another, insertion or deletion of one or more bases, or transposition of segments of the nucleotide chain.

Although some nucleotide sequences seem more prone to mutation than others, rules governing the specific location of mutations are not evident. The view that genetic variants are produced by chance, and that natural selection favors variants that best meet the necessities of survival, led to the claim that evolution is the product of mere chance and necessity. This claim was extended theologically to assert that there is no purpose in the universe, and therefore no designer, divine or otherwise. Some challenges to this claim are based on different concepts of chance.

There are reports of mutant genes that predispose their bearers to abnormal behaviors, such as violence or addiction. A complication in the interpretation of such reports is that a behavioral gene, like most genes, would be just one of many factors determining the behavior under consideration. In addition to environment, biological history, and cultural influences, those factors would include other genes having functions coordinated with those of the behavioral gene. Nevertheless claims for the existence of such mutant genes as the so-called violence gene have provoked theological discussion about personal culpability on sin.

See also BEHAVIORAL GENETICS; DESIGN; DNA; EVOLUTION; GENETIC DEFECT; GENETIC TESTING; GENETICS

Bibliography

Hefner, Philip. "Determinism, Freedom, and Moral Failure." In *Genetics: Issues of Social Justice,* ed. Ted Peters. Cleveland, Ohio: Pilgrim Press, 1998.

Kitcher, Philip. *The Lives to Come.* New York: Simon and Schuster, 1996.

Monod, Jacques. *Chance and Necessity.* London: Collins, 1972.

Peacocke, Arthur R. "Biological Evolution: A Positive Theological Appraisal." In *Evolutionary and Molecular Biology,* eds. Robert John Russell, William R. Stoeger, and Francisco J. Ayala. The Vatican and Notre Dame, Ind.: Vatican Observatory and Notre Dame University Press, 1998.

Peters, Ted. "Genes, Theology, and Social Ethics." In *Genetics: Issues of Social Justice,* ed. Ted Peters. Cleveland, Ohio: Pilgrim Press, 1998.

R. DAVID COLE

MYSTICAL EXPERIENCE

Defined in contradistinction to so-called ordinary or mundane experience, mystical experience conjures images of ecstatic rapture, overwhelming emotion, or profound quietude. An apparently universal aspect of human experience cross-culturally and interreligiously, subjective experiences of a mystical persuasion likely reflect universal but nonetheless unusual predispositions and propensities of the human mind. Continuing advances in cognitive science in general, and in the neurosciences in particular, promise to illuminate aspects of mystical experience previously hidden behind the mask of the phenomenological. At the same time, a historically more refined form of comparative phenomenology promises to coordinate the enormous variety of descriptions of mystical experiences. Research from both the sciences and the humanities will contribute to the development of a comprehensive, compelling interpretation of these experiences.

See also EXPERIENCE, RELIGIOUS: PHILOSOPHICAL ASPECTS; MYSTICISM

JENSINE ANDRESEN

MYSTICISM

Permeating each of the world's major religious traditions, mysticism may be described as the level of deep, experiential encounter with the divine, or ultimate, however that may be understood, that links religious and spiritual pursuits across cultures and across the centuries. Mysticism differs from more defined forms of religious experience, inasmuch as it frequently transports the individual beyond the confines of the religious tradition itself to a realm often described as lacking in any sense of differentiation, whether it be between aspirant and God, or between self and non-self.

The task of defining *mysticism* bears reevaluation, however. As Frits Staal has written, "If mysticism is to be studied seriously, it should not merely be studied indirectly and from without, but also directly and from within. Mysticism can at least in part be regarded as something affecting the *human* mind, and it is therefore quite unreasonable to expect that it could be fruitfully explored by confining oneself to literature about or contributed by mystics, or to the behavior and physiological characteristics of mystics and their bodies." (p. 123). That being said, according to a loose, phenomenological typology, one may consider mysticism to be that genre of subjectivity and behavior manifesting in an "altered," or nonconventional mode, framed in a religious or spiritual narrative, and experienced by those who are refered to, at least in English, as "mystics."

Mysticism in various religious traditions

The Christian tradition manifests varied branches of mysticism, including the Discalced Carmelites, a movement within the Carmelite order that espouses a form of mystical development still followed today in the Catholic Church. Founded by St. Teresa of Avila (1515–1582) and St. John of the Cross (1542–1591) in sixteenth-century Spain, the movement defended the practice of inner prayer against its persecution by King Philip II of Spain. Educated by Jesuits, John of the Cross began theological studies at the University of Salamanca in 1567 but left to help Teresa of Avila in her efforts to found the Discalced Carmelites. Imprisoned by the non-reformed Carmelites from 1575 to 1578, he used his imprisonment to his advantage, composed poetry, and, finally, escaped to face further suspicion regarding supposed connections to so-called illuministic books roundly condemned during the Inquisition. Only after the Apostolic See had examined his orthodoxy in the early seventeenth century were his books published openly.

St. John primarily articulates a systematic approach to mystical development appropriate to cloister spirituality, though he wrote his last book, *The Living Flame of Love*, for a laywoman, and used it as a vehicle of instructing both lay and monastic Christians in the methods for attaining mystical union. St. John may primarily be remembered for explicating a so-called via negativa mode of spiritual engagement in which one prays without focusing on imagery and without actively pursuing any specific intellectual content (Mallory, pp. 1–7). Some generations earlier, Dominican mystic Meister Eckhart (1260–1328) similarly utilized a kind of "negative theology" to point towards the inadequacy of human language and perception in capturing the fullness of mystical experience: "There is no knowing what God is" (Steere, pp. 143–144). And in the Indian Advaita tradition, as Mahadevan wrote in the preface to *The Wisdom of Unity*, one experiences transcendent unity as "the distinctions and differences that teem this world" fade away in the recognition of "the eternal non-duality of the Self."

The Sufi tradition exhibits the depth of Islamic spirituality and exemplifies the paradoxical quality of mysticism in general. According to Rumi (1207–1273), a Persian mystic and poet, "What is Sufism? He said: To find joy in the heart when grief comes." Rābi 'a (717–801), a Sufi mystic and an Islamic saint, "introduced the element of selfless love into the austere teachings of the early ascetics and gave Sufism the hue of true mysticism." Never marrying and not favoring the prophet Mohammad in any particular way, she loved God absolutely, and completely, losing herself in contemplation of him. Sufism also provides a good example of the nature of the path that carries mystics of all stripes, a series of steps towards a deep experience of God, toward the realization of emptiness, or towards whatever the goal may be. In Islam, Sufis follow the *ṭarīqa* (path), in which the mystic practices *īthār* (preferring others over oneself), a practice that later dissolves as the difference between oneself and the other is "subsumed in the divine unity" (Schimmel, p. 99).

The theme of total, devotional love also infuses Christian mysticism, as evidenced by the Franciscan movement of the *alumbrados,* those mystics "illuminated" by the Holy Spirit, some of whom practiced *dejamiento* (abandonment) of oneself to the love of God, with the result that the formal sacraments of the Church were seen to be superfluous (Hamilton, pp. 1–2). And according to the visions of the German mystic, Hildegard of Bingen (1098–1180), love appears as a beautiful apparition, such that "the fire of God's love runs through the world and its beauties, constantly re-enlivening the cosmos as a miracle of perfection" (Schipperges, pp. 68–69, citing Hildegard's *Book of Divine Works*).

The status of duality, or non-duality, occupies branches of mysticism otherwise separated by virtue of culture, time, or doctrine. This is unsurprising, particularly given the nature of mysticism itself in transcending boundaries, which are often perceived as limitation; for example, the dualisms of sense versus spirit, and attachment to creation versus attachment to God, pervade St. John's writings, as Marilyn Mallory posits in her 1977 book, *Christian Mysticism.* Interestingly, in attempting to express non-duality and paradox, mystics often choose poetry as a modality capable of pointing beyond the mundane levels of a world with defined, black and white borders, at the same time that it promises great aesthetic enjoyment to its listeners. And as Herbert Guenther indicates in *The Royal Song of Saraha* (1969), beginning with Mar pa (1012–1097), Tibetan teacher and translator, the Doha tradition in Tibet utilized melodious verses composed and sung by mystics to both express and indicate non-conventional modes of awareness and states of deep appreciation and joy.

Sometimes referred to as "states of infused contemplation" (Pike, p. ix), union exists as a central preoccupation of many mystics. In Christianity, for example, union covers experiences from prayers of silence, to prayers of union, to more intense experiences of rapture, so-called ecstasy states similar along certain dimensions to shamanic flights of the soul. As Nelson Pike puts it, "the paradigm union experience … unfolds through a dualistic stage into a state in which the distinction between subject and object is lost" (p. 59). Language fails at this important juncture, causing many mystics to resort to metaphor and poetry in describing their experiences. St. John of Ruysbroeck (1293–1381), for example, describes his experience of being permeated, stating, "the iron is within the fire and the fire is within the iron; and so also the air is in the sunshine and the sunshine in the air" (pp. 236–237).

Sociologically, mystical traditions in many religions rely upon a period of tutelage by a respected member of the community, and a period of discipleship on the part of the aspirant. As Frits Staal comments, "The need for a qualified teacher is stressed in almost all the traditions of mysticism …. In Islam it is the foundation of the *silsila* or 'spiritual lineage'" whereas in Indian religions, one refers to "the *guruparampara*, 'the direct lineage of teachers'" (p. 144). Tibet, for example, historically organized a good part of its country's social structure around this kind of hierarchical, lama-discipline relationship, and this tradition of devotion to idealized teachers in some cases stimulates the minds of Western academics who study Buddhism. One also may find the master-discipline lineage tradition in other religions, such as the Sufism of West Africa. 'Umar al-Shaykh (864–960) brought the Qādiriyyah order of Sufism to the western Sudan in West Africa, having been initiated into the order of the Qādiriyyah masters and *hajj,* as Ibrahim Doi posits in "Sufism in Africa" (1991).

In communities, and in some cases, entire societies, in which mystical achievement translates into positions of power and prestige, authenticity exerts itself as a powerful mediator of who will or will not be accepted by the group, which teachings will be honored, and whose interpretations will be valued. In the Islamic world, for example, Jami (1414–1492), a Persian poet and mystic, describes two types of mystics, those who are concerned with their own salvation and who practice in complete reclusion, "and those who return from their mystical experience in a higher, sanctified state of mind and are able to lead other people on the right path" (Schimmel, p. 7). Grace Jantzen also discusses the manner in a "gendered struggle for power and authority" permeates mysticism in early and medieval Christendom, though the same may easily be claimed for mystical traditions more generally (p. xv).

Members of mystical communities also distinguish between "the true Sufi, the *mutasawwif* who aspires at reaching a higher spiritual level, and the *mustawif,* the man who pretends to be a mystic but is a useless, even dangerous, intruder" (Schimmel, p. 20). In some cases, too, the mystic's life is seen to contradict that of the householder, and severe sanctions may ensue. For example, the father of Dnyaneshwar, a well-known fifteenth-century Indian saint, abandoned the world for the mystical path after leading a householder's life for many years. He later returned to family life, however, fathering Dnyaneshwar, who was condemned as an outcaste on the basis of his father's violation of the orthodox injunction that a *sanyasi* (renounced person) should never return to the life of the householder, according to Ian Ezekiel.

Throughout this brief account, the existential dimensions of mysticism should not be ignored. Mystics from all traditions often point towards aspects of reality beyond the conventional world of thoughts and forms. *Yesh,* a Hebrew term used by rabbis to indicate the treasure awaiting saints in the future life, roughly translates as *there is,* thereby signaling deeper existential dimensions than those normally encountered. As Abraham Isaac Kook (1865–1935), a Jewish mystic, writes, "So long as the world moves along accustomed paths, so long as there are no wild catastrophes, man can find sufficient substance for his life by contemplating surface events, theories, and movements of society." But "when life encounters fiery forces of evil and chaos," he continues, "the man who tries to sustain himself only from the surface aspects of existence will suffer terrible impoverishment, begin to stagger … then he will feel welling up within himself a burning thirst for that inner substance and vision which transcends the obvious surfaces of existence and remains unaffected by the world's catastrophes" (Weiner, pp. 3–4). In the Jewish mystical tradition of *Kabbala,* one searches for *yesh* in a kind of "subsurface reality," a dimension of existence in which "good and evil [lose] the distinction so apparent to surface vision" (Weiner, pp. 6–7).

Interpreting mysticism

Interpretative approaches to mysticism vary, from those influenced by traditional disciplines such as philology and the history of religions, to those that take their inspiration from contemporary Western sciences of the mind. Frits Staal, for example, canvasses dogmatic approaches, philological and historical approaches, phenomenological and sociological viewpoints, and physiological and psychological frameworks. In this last category, one moves from Freud's dislike for "dark" phenomena such as mysticism and Yoga, to Jung's archetypal metaphysics according to which a variety of mystical phenomena may be classified. Nevertheless, Staal himself claimed that he "would not be surprised if the study of mysticism would one day be regarded as a branch of psychology," by which he meant "that psychology would be deepened and widened so as to be in a position to take account of these particular aspects of the mind" (p. 116).

Psychology and cognitive science. Approaching mysticism from the interpretive lens of cognitive science, visions and locutions offer themselves as interesting candidates for investigation. Neurologist and author Oliver Sacks, for example, frames Hildegard of Bingen in terms of medical literature on migraine. He writes, "The religious literature of all ages is replete with descriptions of 'visions,' in which sublime and ineffable feelings have been accompanied by the experience of radiant luminosity." He continues, "It is impossible to ascertain, in the vast majority of cases, whether the experience represents a hysterical or psychotic ecstasy, the effects of intoxication, or an epileptic or migrainous manifestation" (p. 112). Somewhat similarly, mental health professionals also have investigated patterns of commonality between the reported mystical experiences of religious practitioners and psychotic inpatients, concluding, "Contemplatives and psychotics taken together could be separated from Normals, *but not from each other,* with the Hood Mysticism Scale. The Normals and Contemplatives taken together could be separated from the Pyschotics, *but not from each other,* with the EGO Scale (Knoblauch's Ego Grasping Orientation Inventory) and the NPI (Raskin and Hall's Narcissistic Personality Inventory)" (Stifler, p. 366).

Hindu and particularly Buddhist mysticism assumes "the perfectibility of man," as Herbert Guenther puts it (p. 42). This fact opens the way for some incredible claims concerning human capacities, such as the claims that enlightened humans may attain *ja 'lus,* or "rainbow body," at the time of death, such that their bodies dissolve into rainbow light and all manner of spectacular visions appear to the disciples left behind (Lhalungpa, pp. 82–97). Obviously, traditions postulating no ceiling on human accomplishments open the way for psychological grandiosity to manifest in the character structures of certain practitioners. Invoking a contemporary, psychiatric frame of interpretation, one

can recognize a pathological "mechanism of defense" in the "primitive fantasy" of omnipotence (Kernberg, pp. 2–21) and the signs of "narcissistic personality disorder" in fantasies of unlimited success (Beck, p. 234). Along somewhat similar lines, Schumaker argues that we should "understand religion and psychopathology (and, indirectly, hypnosis) as systems of artificial order that are dependent upon an active dissociation process" (p. 34). The fine line between insightful interpretation of one system of thought and practice in terms of the reality framework of another, and critical, almost condescending judgment, on the other hand, however, highlights the difficulties one encounters when employing one specific cultural lens to interpret behaviors arising in different segments of the same culture, or in different cultures altogether.

The status, experience, and understanding of consciousness, awareness, the mind, and the self, occupy tomes of mystical rumination. Indian philosophical systems of thought, and later Tibetan Buddhist writers, excel in this arena. For example, Prabhakara Mimamsaka philosophers occupy themselves with the question of whether or not the self is "self-luminous," concluding, "the self is not consciousness, and while consciousness *(samvit)* is self-luminous, the self is not" (Mahadevan, p. 11). Interestingly, this emphasis on consciousness and awareness makes mysticism a possible ally to contemporary brain science in the West. Mystical accounts from all of the world's major religious traditions, such as the *rnam thar* ("sacred biography") genre expressive of Tibetan Buddhist mysticism, frequently rely upon autobiography and sacred biography (hagiography) as narrative forms, further pointing to the centrality of the "self" and its transformations in the mystical journey. To oversimplify the situation, regular and frequently dramatic personal transformations wrought by the mystical path threaten to destabilize the self, a potentially dangerous, psychological situation mitigated by the creation of a "narrated self" (Wortham, p. 140), which can function as the hero or heroine in tales of miraculous accomplishment, thereby compensating for possible psychological fragmentation by means of a chronological narrative unfolding in which the mystic's own identity remains constant over the course of his or her lifespan.

The role of the body in providing a support for mystical experience constitutes another area in which mysticism and modern science, in this case, medicine, may complement one another. In the medieval Siddha traditions of Hindu alchemy and *hatha yoga,* for example, the body serves as the locus for complex worldly to transcendent transformations, as in when the practitioner utilizes *pranayama* (breath control) to transform mundane semen into the "divine nectar of immortality" and to transform mundane mind into "a state beyond mind" (White, p. 45). Because of its intricate involvement with body, speech, and mind, ritual plays an important role in catalyzing mystical states of awareness, as demonstrated, for example, by the tremendous emphasis placed on ritualized *mantra* repetition in both Hindu and Buddhist mystical traditions (Abe, pp. 138–149). Repetitive, ritualized *mandala* visualization provides a similar, corporeal engagement of the aesthetic sensitivities cultivated by mystical practitioners (Andresen 2000). Perversions of the relationship between self and body, as seen from the perspective of Western medicine's diagnostic recognition of eating disorders such as anorexia nervosa, also has plagued mystics of many traditions. Whitney Miller develops a methodology of "psychomysticism," a kind of "contemplative counseling" in which the counselor emphasizes awareness and sensitivity, "a willingness to pay attention," following Bernard Lonergan's transcendental precept "to 'be attentive'" (p. 1).

The importance of context. Scholars of mysticism continue to debate whether or not mystical experience itself is mediated by context. Constructivists have held the view that, "linguistic, social, historical, and conceptual contextuality" shape the mystic's experience. On the other side, essentialists articulate a position whereby a common, pure core to mystical experiences supposedly exists, not merely within a single tradition such as Christianity or Buddhism, but across cultures and traditions, too. It is possible, as argued by Jensine Andresen, that constructivist and essentialist ("perennialist") positions may be seen to be complementary, inasmuch as species-wide perceptual systems and consciousness, which mediate between the *qualia,* or felt experience of the subjective, and the hard and fast reality of what is conventionally perceived to be an external world, are shared between all members of the human family, mystics included.

See also EXPERIENCE, RELIGIOUS: COGNITIVE AND PHYSIOLOGICAL ASPECTS; EXPERIENCE, RELIGIOUS: PHILOSOPHICAL ASPECTS; MEDITATION; MONISM; MYSTICAL EXPERIENCE; MYSTICS; NEUROSCIENCES; PANTHEISM; PSYCHOLOGY; SPIRITUALITY; TRANSCENDENCE

Bibliography

Abe, Ryuichi. *The Weaving of Mantra: Kukai and the Construction of Esoteric Buddhist Discourse.* New York: Columbia University Press, 1999.

Andresen, Jensine. "Vajrayàna Art and Iconography." *Zygon: Journal of Religion and Science* 35(2) (2000): 357-370.

Andresen, Jensine. "Introduction: Towards a cognitive science of religion." In *Religion in Mind: Cognitive Perspectives on Religious Belief, Ritual, and Experience,* ed. Jensine Andresen. Cambridge, UK: Cambridge University Press, 2001.

Beck, Aaron T., and Freeman, Arthur. *Cognitive Therapy of Personality Disorders.* New York and London: Guilford Press, 1990.

Doi, Abdur-Rahman Ibrahim. "Sufism in Africa." In *Islamic Spirituality: Manifestations,* ed. Seyyed Hossein Nasr. New York: Crossroad, 1991.

Ezekiel, Ian A. *Sarmad.* Punjab, India: Radhasoami Satsang Beas, 1966.

Guenther, Herbert V. *The Royal Song of Saraha: A Study in the History of Buddhist Thought.* Seattle: University of Washington Press, 1969.

Hamilton, Alastair. *Heresy and Mysticism in Sixteenth-Century Spain: The Alumbrados.* Buffalo, NY, and Toronto: University of Toronto Press, 1992.

Jantzen, Grace M. *Power, Gender and Christian Mysticism.* Cambridge, UK: Cambridge University Press, 1995.

Kernberg, Otto F. "Omnipotence in the Transference and in the Countertransference." *The Scandinavian Psychoanalytic Review* 18 (1995): 2-21.

Lhalungpa, Lobsang. P. *The Life of Milarepa.* Boulder, CO: Prajna Press, 1982.

Mahadevan, T. M. P. *The Wisdom of Unity.* Madras, India: Ganesh, 1967.

Mallory, Marilyn May. *Christian Mysticism: Transcending Techniques.* Amsterdam: Van Gorcum Assen, 1977.

Miller, Whitney G. *Psychomysticism: Toward a Method of Contemplative Counseling.* Donaldson, Ind.: Graduate Theological Foundation, 1997.

Pike, Nelson. *Mystic Union: An Essay in the Phenomenology of Mysticism.* Ithaca, NY: Cornell University Press, 1992.

Ruysbroeck, Jan van. *John of Ruysbroeck.* London: John M. Watkins, 1951.

Sacks, Oliver W. *Migraine: The Evolution of a Common Disorder*. Berkeley and Los Angeles: University of California Press, 1970.

Schimmel, Aannemarie. *Mystical Dimensions of Islam*. Chapel Hill: University of North Carolina Press, 1975.

Schipperges, Heinrich. *The World of Hildegard of Bingen: Her Life, Times, and Visions*. Collegeville, Minn.: Liturgical Press, 1998.

Schumaker, John F. *The Corruption of Reality: A Unified Theory of Religion, Hypnosis, and Psychopathology*. New York: Prometheus Books, 1995.

Staal, Frits. *Exploring Mysticism: A Methodological Essay*. Berkeley: University of California Press, 1975.

Steere, Douglas V. *Together in Solitude*. New York: Crossroad, 1982.

Stifler, Kenneth; Greer, Joanne; Sneck, William; and Dovenmuehle, Robert. "An Empirical Investigation of the Discriminibility of Reported Mystical Experiences Among Religious Contemplatives, Psychotic Inpatients, and Normal Adults." *Journal for the Scientific Study of Religion* 32 (4) (1993): 366-372.

Weiner, Herbert. *$9\frac{1}{2}$ Mystics: The Kabbala Today*. New York: Macmillan, 1992.

White, David Gordon. *The Alchemical Body: Siddha Traditions in Medieval India*. Chicago and London: University of Chicago Press, 1996.

Wortham, Stanton. *Narratives in Action: A Strategy for Research and Analysis*. New York and London: Teachers College Press, 2001.

JENSINE ANDRESEN

MYSTICS

Mystics are individuals who follow a path towards a final goal or sustained state that is understood as somehow transcending, moving beyond, or more deeply perceiving or intuiting the conventional world of names and forms experienced by ordinary human beings. Prominent mystics, representing various religious traditions, include: eighth century Tibetan mystic Yeshe Tsogyal; Abhinavagupta (tenth century); Muhammed Ibn 'Ali Ibn 'Arabi (1165-1240); Julian of Norwich (1342-1416); St. Birgitta of Sweden (1471-1528); Rabbi Nachman of Brazlav (1772-1816); Ramakrishna (1836-1886); and Thomas Merton (1915-1968). Mystical experience resists easy generalization because of the great variety in personal practices of individual mystics and the marked differences in the broader contextual narratives of individual mystical experiences. Nevertheless, mystics commonly experience unusual states of awareness, utilize poetry and song as vehicles of self-expression, and remind members of societies in which they find themselves, through the attitude of eschewing limits, of the boundaries sometimes imposed by conventional living. At the same time, many mystics recognize their deepest experiences of transcendence within the conventional world, thereby pointing to paradoxes embedded within the mystical life itself.

See also MYSTICAL EXPERIENCE; MYSTICISM

JENSINE ANDRESEN

MYTH

Civilization cannot exist without stories. Every culture in recorded history has created its own narratives to cope with what was fearful, incomprehensible, or uncontrollable, from volcanic eruptions and comets to illnesses and death. These stories, called *myths*, are often, but not exclusively, deeply related to the religious beliefs of a given culture. Myths give order and meaning to the uncertainties of life, whether they are caused by physical or by emotional factors.

Humanity's first attempt to understand nature

Throughout history, different cultures have perceived nature as having a dual role: sometimes the giver of life, the provider of warmth and food, and sometimes the ruthless killer. This was as true to a hunter-gatherer tribe living ten thousand years ago as it is today. In order to appease the unpredictability of nature, it was necessary to somehow interact with it. This was originally achieved through the attribution of god-like status to nature and to the objects of the world that had some relevance to people's lives. In some cultures, Earth itself was a god, the mother goddess, and so were the sun and other celestial objects. Other cultures populated their forests, rivers, and mountains with gods and spirits. Through ritual and sacrifice it was possible to communicate with these gods, and, thus, to plead for their clemency and generosity.

The existence and actions of these many gods, and their interactions with human figures, were told through myths. Thus, mythical narratives translated what was feared and unknown into a language that was readily understandable by people, establishing a bridge between human existence and that which was perceived to be beyond its realm.

The power of a myth is not in its reality but in its persuasiveness. A tragic example is the myth of Aryan supremacy espoused by Nazism, which led to the murdering of Jews, Gypsies, and others during the Second World War. It is a common mistake to interpret a given myth in the light of one's culture and not within its own. The belief system of a Yanonami Indian from the Amazon Basin is quite different from that of a Dutch Calvinist or a Chinese Buddhist. Religious entrenchment, based on specific mythic narratives, often leads to disastrous social and political consequences.

Myths can be understood as humanity's first attempt to interpret and understand natural phenomena. As such, they can legitimately be considered as science's ancestors. In particular, there is an all-pervasive, cross-cultural need to understand the origin of human beings and of the world. These myths, called *creation myths,* are part of every culture, past and present. In the West, the most familiar is that narrated in the biblical book of Genesis, which attributes the origin of the world and of its beings to God. The vast majority of creation myths follow similar lines, in that they credit the existence of the world to the action of a god, goddess, or several gods. These myths fall in a category where time had a specific start in the past, the moment of creation. Still within this category, there are myths that claim the universe originated spontaneously out of chaos, without divine intervention, while others, such as the Maoris of New Zealand, claim it appeared out of nothing. Other creation myths, such as those from the Jains of India, say the universe has always existed and will always exist, while others, like the Hindus, believe the universe is created and destroyed in an eternal succession of cycles.

The transition from myth to science

The same basic concerns with nature and its impact on human existence that are addressed by mythic narratives play a crucial role in the development of science. Questions that were once the exclusive province of religion, such as the origin of the world, the origin of life, and the origin of mind, are now subjects of intensive scientific research. It is possible to trace a gradual, albeit not continuous, transition from the mythic to the scientific discourse. The first rupture with a purely religious description of nature is attributed to the pre-Socratic philosophers, who flourished in Greece during the sixth and fifth centuries B.C.E. For the first time, it is possible to identify an effort to answer questions about nature through natural causation mechanisms, as opposed to supernatural ones.

This tendency continued with Plato and Aristotle, although both included supernatural elements in their schemes of the world. The *Demiurge,* for Plato, was a cosmic intelligence, responsible for the rational design of the world; the *Unmoved Mover,* for Aristotle, was the first cause of motion, the world's primal dynamic impulse. As we move on to the Renaissance and the development of modern science, influences from Greek thought, combined with Christian theology, are clearly present in the works of several natural philosophers, including Johannes Kepler and Isaac Newton. Their task was to translate God's natural creations to humanity, using reason as the common language. The oral and verbal narratives of myths were increasingly substituted by mathematical descriptions of natural phenomena. The very success of the physical sciences served to distance the scientist from the theologian; as humanity learned more about nature through reason, a smaller role was attributed to God and the supernatural in the workings of the world.

Today, science is widely perceived as the antithesis of religion: In a world of reason, there is no place for God and the supernatural. This polarized view of science and religion leads to much confusion. Although it is often argued that there is no place for religion in the modern scientific discourse, it is also true that science cannot completely distance itself from its mythic roots. One of the strengths of science is its universality: A theory or explanation accepted by the scientific community will be correct for every scientist, irrespective of religious creed, nationality, or political stance. However, science comes from individuals who are often motivated by esthetic values. Concepts such as symmetry, harmony, simplicity, order, or mathematical elegance are a major driving force of the scientific creative process. Their origin can be traced back to the need to decode the workings of nature, as was first done through myths.

See also ARISTOTLE; CREATION; GOD OF THE GAPS; HINDUISM; NEWTON, ISAAC; PLATO; SUPERNATURALISM

Bibliography

Freund, Phillip. *Myths of Creation*. New York: Washington Square Press, 1996.

Gleiser, Marcelo. *The Dancing Universe: From Creation Myths to the Big Bang*. New York: Dutton, 1997.

Gleiser, Marcelo. *The Prophet and the Astronomer: A Scientific Journey to the End of Time*. New York: Norton, 2002.

Greene, Brian. *The Elegant Universe: Superstrings, Hidden Dimensions, and the Quest for the Ultimate Theory*. New York: Norton, 1999.

Munitz, Milton K., ed. *Theories of the Universe: From Babylonian Myth to Modern Science*. Glencoe, Ill.: Free Press, 1957.

Pagels, Heinz R. *Perfect Symmetry: The Search of the Beginning of Time*. New York: Bantam Books, 1986.

Sproul, Barbara C. *Primal Myths*. San Francisco: Harper, 1979.

Zee, Anthony. *Fearful Symmetry: The Search for Beauty in Modern Physics*. New York: Collier, 1986.

MARCELO GLEISER

NANOTECHNOLOGY

See BIOTECHNOLOGY

NATURALISM

Naturalism arouses strong emotions. Some see it as a banner to follow, some as the enemy to fight. Theological or religious naturalism is even more controversial: Is it truly religious? And if so, is it still naturalism? However, naturalism is a clear and unified category until one begins to think and read about it. The entry will consider four contexts in which the term arises. Thereafter, some issues in and varieties of theological or religious naturalism will be considered.

Four contexts and contrasts

P. F. Strawson distinguishes in his *Skepticism and Naturalism* (1985) between "soft" and "hard" naturalism. *Soft naturalism* refers to what human beings ordinarily do and believe about, for example, colors, feelings, and moral judgments. When a painting is "naturalist," it is so in a soft sense. *Hard naturalism* refers to attempts to view human behavior in an objective light as events in nature. Strawson argues that these two ways of viewing the world are compatible, but if he has to choose, he opts for soft naturalism. Critics, however, argue that soft naturalism plays down insights about the structures of reality "behind" experience, and thus avoids genuine engagement with the sciences and

secular thought. The remainder of this entry deals with forms of hard naturalism, as science not only extends but also corrects the soft natural understanding of reality.

Science is a human practice; its insights may be useful, but why might they be considered true? Cultures with particular social norms survived, but why would one call the intuitions and practices that have evolved good? Can one distinguish truth from mere beliefs, ethics from evolved morality? In this context naturalism stands in contrast to normative views of epistemic or moral values and procedures. Naturalists in this sense tend to deny that any demarcation between science and nonscientific activities, or between moral preferences and ethics, could be absolute. At the same time, however, such naturalists prefer science over pseudo-science and thus live by a distinction between what can be justified and what cannot. Naturalists who seek to ascribe normative standing to science and morality without introducing an absolute realm of values, truths, or procedures, may connect humble origins via a long trajectory across many thresholds to more lofty convictions that, in the end, need not be all too different from traditional ones on ethics and epistemology. For a naturalist, in the sense considered in this paragraph, the transition from description to prescription is never beyond modification, though hopefully approximating the true and good.

In anthropological reflections on the human person as one who acts, thinks, and experiences in this world, naturalism stands primarily in contrast to positions such as rationalism, which are not much interested in the way mental capacities are embodied. Naturalism invites the understanding of humans as materially constituted, owing their abilities to an evolutionary history of billions of years. Within the scientific community and within debates in the philosophy of mind, research projects such as embodied artificial intelligence and connectionism seem to indicate a shift away from the dualistic tendencies of rationalism. The challenge for the naturalist is similar to the one mentioned above: If human beings are nothing but messy natural processes, what can be said of the distinct character of consciousness, ideas, feelings, and the like?

A fourth context where naturalism arises is in contrast to supernaturalism, that is, in relation to theological and metaphysical reflections on transcendence and the ways in which transcendence might manifest itself in ordinary reality. In this context, some consider naturalism to be identical to atheism, but this need not be the case.

Naturalism and natural science

Naturalism often refers to a view of the world that follows the natural sciences as its main guide for understanding the world and human nature. Such a naturalism is not formally implied by the sciences because other logically coherent constructions may be possible, including less restrictive forms of naturalism, such as the one advocated by the Whiteheadian process philosopher David R. Griffin in his *Religion and Scientific Naturalism* (2000).

With respect to ontology, science-inspired naturalism holds that all objects, including human beings, consist of the stuff described by chemists in the periodic table of elements. This stuff is further understood to consist of elementary particles and forces, and beyond that is assumed to consist of quantum fields, superstrings, or whatever. Such a naturalist must grant that human knowledge has not reached rock bottom. Hence, naturalism cannot be articulated from a fundamental ontology upwards. Nor need it imply that all phenomena can be described in terms of physics and chemistry. A conceptual and explanatory nonreductionism may be possible, arguing that higher level properties and entities have their own causal efficacy, just as future entities will be real and causally efficacious even when they are produced by present ones.

With respect to history, naturalism understands living beings, including humans, as the current stage in a bundle of Darwinian evolutionary histories on the planet, which is itself a transient phenomenon in a universe that has been expanding for some fifteen billion years. These insights do not commit one to a particular view on processes near the "beginning of time," if there is one. It is with history as with ontology: Fundamental issues about the beginning of the universe and the nature of time, space, and substance need not be settled for the naturalist.

Naturalism sees social and mental life as one of the fruits of the long evolutionary process. The "understanding" of science and philosophy is one facet of this, even when it reflects upon its own emergence. Naturalism holds that this is not a vicious circularity. Rather, science and other intellectual enterprises can be seen as building upon human capacities for dealing with their environment, improved piecemeal over many generations. Science is seen as a social phenomenon that is cognitively reliable, and increasingly so. Philip Kitcher argues well in *The Advancement of Science* (1993) that the human, historical, and social character of science need not undermine scientific credibility.

The difference between integrity and self-sufficiency

Explanations of facts always assume an explanatory framework of laws and earlier conditions. Conditions and laws can be explained on the basis of other such assumptions. The various sequences of explanations, if pursued persistently, converge via biology and chemistry on the desks of physicists and cosmologists. Their disciplines form a boundary of the natural sciences, where speculative questions with respect to a naturalist view of the world come most explicitly to the forefront. The questions left at the metaphorical "last desk" are questions about the world as a whole, its existence and structure, and not only questions about its beginning. The development of science may change the actual ultimate questions considered at any time. However, naturalism need not imply the dismissal of such limit questions as answerable or meaningless, nor need it imply one particular answer to such limit questions.

Given the lawful integrity of the world as disclosed by the sciences, one may distinguish four views of God's relation to natural reality and its regularities, two of which might be considered naturalistic. These two views are often conflated, to the disadvantage of the religious one. First, a theist might hold that God may act against the laws of nature. Whereas on the basis of natural processes one would expect *a* to happen, God makes *b* occur. Such a view of God's relation to the world has adverse consequences for one's esteem for God's creation (which includes the laws), since created reality is apparently of such a kind that God has to interfere against God's own creation. Second, some authors in the religion and science field argue that there is enough looseness (contingency) in the web God created in the first place to allow for particular divine actions, without going against any laws of nature. This looseness might perhaps be located in complex and chaotic systems or at the quantum level. The natural order could result in a number of different outcomes, say *a, b, c,* and *d,* and God makes it that *c* happens rather than *a, b,* or *d*. This view depends on contingency of an ontological kind *in* nature, whether at the quantum level or elsewhere.

Naturalism need not deny the existence of such contingency in nature; perhaps natural reality is hazy and underdetermined. However, naturalists would in general abstain from supplementing natural reality with supranatural determining factors. Chance is taken as chance and not as divine determination. Naturalism accepts that nature is, when one considers the level of causal interactions, complete, without theologically relevant holes. As created reality, the natural world has an integrity that need not be supplemented within its web of interactions. However, this integrity is not to be confused with self-sufficiency; it does not imply that natural reality owes its existence to itself or is self-explanatory. Thus, it is important to distinguish between naturalism as emphasizing the integrity of the natural world (the third view), and naturalism as claiming also the self-sufficiency of the natural world (the fourth view).

Arguments about the self-sufficiency of reality need to be different from arguments about explanations within reality. This difference is often neglected in atheistic arguments that appeal to science, such as Peter Atkins in *The Creation* (1981), in which he claims that science is about to explain everything. He traces back everything to a beginning of utmost simplicity, but he cannot do so without assuming real existence and a framework wherein certain rules and mathematics apply. A naturalist need not assume the self-sufficiency of

the framework when seeing the framework itself as a whole that has integrity.

Transcendence: some naturalistic options

A naturalist who appreciates the integrity and lawfulness of reality can still conceive of a creator of this framework, the ground of its existence. This is best understood as a nontemporal notion. When God is not seen as one who interferes, the alternative is not to see God as the creator who started it all a long time ago but rather to think of God as the one who gives all moments and places of reality their existence and order. In such a way, one can combine a naturalist view of reality with theistic dualism, understanding the natural world as a whole as creation, dependent upon a transcendent creator. This might be articulated with the help of a distinction between primary and secondary causality, or between temporal processes in the world and timeless dependence of the temporally extended world on God. Such a view emphasizes, as do the monotheistic traditions, the distinction between God and everything that is not God.

The ontological dualism characteristic of such a naturalistic-theistic position is unattractive to many naturalists, who are concerned that any reference to a creator or ground introduces a supernaturalism that diminishes the integrity of the natural. Such naturalists might be attracted to a pantheist view, denying ontological duality of the natural and the divine; the natural is in some sense the divine. Traditional attributes of the divine, such as atemporality and omnipresence, can be associated with the laws of nature, which are upon this view not so much rooted in a transcendent source but immanent in natural reality. Reality may be *causa sui* in that quantum theories may allow a temporal universe to emerge, and at a smaller scale self-organization is characteristic of many processes. However, as in the preceding case, pantheistic answers are invoking further questions and objections, just as the theistic answer always allows for the further question about why such a god would exist.

A third option is an agnostic stance. Milton Munitz defends in his *Cosmic Understanding* (1986) that any actual theory of the universe is conceptually bounded; there might be a dimension of reality "beyond" any such account, but it could not be expressed adequately in language. "We shall be driven, consequently, and at the end, to silence, although the 'talk' on the way, if at all helpful, will have had its value in making the silence a pregnant one, and indeed an occasion for having an over-ridingly important type of human experience" (p. 231). Similarly, in his *In Face of Mystery* (1993), the theologian Gordon Kaufman points out various problems with the dualistic language of theism, as if we on this side of the great divide can know that which is on the other side; our knowledge of the world in which we live "always shades off into ultimate mystery, into an ultimate unknowing" (p. 326). Emphasizing "mystery," not-knowing is a safe strategy. However, it does not offer much guidance as to particular choices to be made in life; the notion of mystery is more epistemic than axiological or ontological.

These different theological views—the theist, the pantheist, and the mysterianist—are all generally compatible with a science-inspired naturalist understanding of reality. The way they are articulated and defended may be influenced by current scientific theories, but variants of these positions can be formulated again and again.

A different naturalistic challenge: religion as a phenomenon

Science-inspired naturalism is a challenge for religion since it presents a view of the world that differs from traditional religious images. This leads in religion and science to conflicts between science and religiously motivated beliefs, such as creationism. However, a naturalist view also considers religions as phenomena within reality. Thus, they can be studied just like other human practices. The neurosciences may inform us of aspects of our constitution that give rise to our "inner life." And in an evolutionary perspective most naturalists would explain the emergence of religions functionally along lines similar to explanations for political institutions, languages, and other social phenomena: Religions arose because they contributed to the inclusive fitness of individuals or communities in which they arose and which in turn were shaped by them. An alternative could be that religions arose as a side effect with the emergence of some other trait, such as the rise of consciousness. Thus, naturalists might see religions with their myths and rituals as valuable means of dealing with the challenges of life. However, a contested issue then becomes whether we should take the vehicles (the rituals, myths, narratives, conceptualities, etc) seriously as cognitive claims, or whether those who want to take the cognitive claims seriously should reject the functional naturalistic approach.

Religious naturalism as thick naturalism

Religious naturalism might be understood as a "thick" naturalism, with idiosyncratic elements that allow for a decent amount of coping with the vicissitudes of life, with stories that support values and motivate humans. The notion "thick" is appropriated here from a distinction made by the anthropologist Clifford Geertz between thin and thick descriptions of a culture. Whereas the one offers a fairly abstract and general (thin) description, the other concentrates on the multitude of habits, beliefs, skills, narratives, and the like, which make for a more tightly woven whole.

For the history of religious naturalism one might refer to philosophers, scientists, and theologians of various backgrounds, including Henry Nelson Wieman, George Santayana, John Dewey, Charles Sanders Peirce, Ralph Burhoe, Mordecai Kaplan, and Jack J. Cohen, and to some extent even Alfred North Whitehead and William James (there is a huge overlap between religious naturalism and American pragmatism). Beyond the last century and a half, one may go back further in time and claim to be heirs of Spinoza as well as of other pantheistic scientists. Claiming these as ancestors is to some extent appropriation out of context, but that is precisely the intellectually ambivalent practice that strengthens identity. These "ancestors" were all perceived as somewhat heretical in their times, while standing in close contact with, if not being part of, the scientific community—precisely the mix that may fit contemporary religious naturalism.

Like any subculture, religious naturalism is not uniform. To the contrary, as in any living community there have arisen dialects, with different speakers giving their own interpretations to the words. There are Christian and humanist dialects of religious naturalism, as well as biological, psychological, and physicalist ones, all of which reflect upbringing, training, and heritage, as well as needs and situations. Some dialects are dialects of another tradition as well, just as the local dialect near the border of the Netherlands is considered by some to be a dialect of Dutch, whereas others treat it as a dialect of German. Thus, liberal or revisionist forms of theology may be read as forms of Christianity, as well as of religious naturalism. There is a wide range of personal styles, from the sober, minimalist, and analytical (e.g., Jerome Stone, Charley Hardwick) to the evocative (e.g., Ursula Goodenough). Religious naturalism has become an umbrella that covers a variety of dialects, of which some are revisionary articulations of existing traditions, whereas others may be more purely naturalistic religions indebted almost exclusively to the sciences. There are family resemblances, with affinities and disagreements, but not unity.

See also SUPERNATURALISM

Bibliography

Almeder, Robert. *Harmless Naturalism: The Limits of Science and the Nature of Philosophy.* Chicago: Open Court, 1998.

Drees, Willem B. *Religion, Science, and Naturalism.* Cambridge, UK: Cambridge University Press, 1996.

Drees, Willem B. "Naturalisms and Religion." *Zygon* 32, no. 4 (1997): 525–541.

Drees, Willem B. "Thick Naturalism: Comments on *Zygon* 2000." *Zygon* 35, no. 4 (2000): 849–860.

Goodenough, Ursula. *The Sacred Depths of Nature.* New York: Oxford University Press, 1998.

Griffin, David Ray. *Religion and Scientific Naturalism: Overcoming the Conflicts.* Albany: State University of New York Press, 2000.

Griffin, David R. "Scientific Naturalism, The Mind-Body Relation, and Religious Experience." *Zygon* 37, no. 2 (2002): 361–380.

Hardwick, Charley D. *Events of Grace: Naturalism, Existentialism, and Theology.* Cambridge, UK: Cambridge University Press, 1996.

Kaufman, Gordon. *In Face of Mystery: A Constructive Theology.* Cambridge, Mass.: Harvard University Press, 1993.

Kitcher, Philip. *The Advancement of Science: Science Without Legend, Objectivity Without Illusions.* New York: Oxford University Press, 1993.

Moser, Paul K., and Trout, J. D. *Contemporary Materialism: A Reader.* London: Routledge, 1995.

Munitz, Milton. *Cosmic Understanding: Philosophy and Science of the Universe.* Princeton, N.J.: Princeton University Press, 1986.

Proudfoot, Wayne. *Religious Experience.* Berkeley and Los Angeles: University of California Press, 1985.

Schwartz, J. "Reduction, Elimination, and the Mental." *Philosophy of Science* 58 (1991): 203–220.

Stone, Jerome A. *The Minimalist Vision of Transcendence: A Naturalist Philosophy of Religion.* Albany: State University of New York Press, 1992.

Stone, Jerome A. "Religious Naturalism and the Religion-Science Dialogue: A Minimalist View." *Zygon* 37, no. 2 (2002): 381–394.

Strawson, P. F. *Skepticism and Naturalism: Some Varieties.* New York: Colombia University Press, 1985.

Wagner, Steven J., and Warner, Richard, eds. *Naturalism: A Critical Appraisal.* Notre Dame, Ind.: University of Notre Dame Press, 1993.

WILLEM B. DREES

NATURALISTIC FALLACY

The relation between is/ought, fact/value, objectivity/normativity, and science/ethics all touch on the notion of the naturalistic fallacy. In general terms, this notion is an expression of the philosophical argument that one cannot infer from the one to the other; one cannot infer from *is* to *ought,* nor can one make an inference from scientific observations to ethical arguments. Any such attempt means committing the naturalistic fallacy. Historically, David Hume (1711–1776) and G. E. Moore (1873–1958) were the primary advocates of the invalidity of a moral argument based on such an inference.

In *A Treatise of Human Nature* (1740) David Hume argued that morals cannot be derived from reason. Rather, feelings should be considered the proper basis of morals. Reason can not account for the passions and affections that arise in questions of morals, but only the questions of objectivity (i.e. truth and falsehood). What *is* cannot serve as a basis of what *ought* to be. One cannot derive the moral *ought* from the objective *is.*

The term *naturalistic fallacy* goes back to G. E. Moore, who in *Principia Ethica* (1903) argued that the notion of the good could not be based by reference to nonmoral entities. The good is a simple, indefinable concept, not composed by other nonmoral parts. This is precisely the problem of the naturalistic fallacy, which points to nature or to some other nonmoral entity and argues that this serves as the basis of moral normativity. Thereby the difference between these parts is ignored, as is the invalidity of inferring from one to the other. By committing the naturalistic fallacy, one would substitute "good" with a nonmoral property.

The ideas of Hume and Moore have had important consequences for the debate on the relation between science and ethics. If Hume and Moore are right, it is not possible to derive normative precepts from scientific observations. Objective findings have no bearing on the question of what one ought to do. The theory of evolution has no implication for ethics. The scientific understanding of human nature is not relevant to the normative understanding of human nature. *Is* and *ought* are two separate entities that are to be kept separate if one wants to establish a proper philosophical normative statement.

In a contemporary setting it is debatable whether the inference from *is* to *ought* is a fallacy. In various theories of environmental ethics, for example, it is stressed that one cannot isolate *ought* from *is*. Holmes Rolston argues that nature holds objective values, and it is necessary for ethical reflection not to ignore this fact. However, the human being's character as a valuer also implies the necessary reflection on these values. In this sense, there is a necessary inference from *is* to *ought*. J. Baird Callicott takes a similar stance, even if he does not stress the necessity of the reflective powers of the human being. Morality arises from the membership of human beings in the biotic community. Apart from these theories of environmental ethics, the necessary inference from *is* to *ought* is also found in most ethical theories based upon notions of evolution and the relation between the concept of nature and ethics. Therefore, the question of the justifiability of the critique of the naturalistic fallacy stands open.

See also NATURE

Bibliography

Callicott, J. Baird. *In Defense of the Land Ethic: Essays in Environmental Philosophy.* Albany: State University of New York Press, 1989.

Frankena, William K. "The Naturalistic Fallacy." *Mind* 48 (1939): 464–477.

Hume, David. *A Treatise of Human Nature* (1740). Oxford: Oxford University Press, 1983.

Moore, G. E. *Principia Ethica* (1903). Cambridge, UK: Cambridge University Press. 1965.

Rolston, Holmes III. *Environmental Ethics: Duties to and Values in the Natural World.* Philadelphia: Temple University Press, 1988.

Rolston, Holmes III. *Genes, Genesis and God: Values and Their Origins in Natural and Human History.* Cambridge, UK: Cambridge University Press, 1999.

ULRIK B. NISSEN

NATURALIZED EPISTEMOLOGY

Traditionally, epistemology was conceived as first philosophy, that is, as an autonomous and purely normative (*a priori*) discipline that lays down universal criteria of knowledge, truth, and justification. According to this influential tradition, knowledge is justified true belief, and a belief is justified if it is properly basic, that is, self-evident or evident to the senses, or if it is derived from such a belief, whether deductively, inductively, or abductively.

The rise of naturalized epistemology began in the 1950s and 1960s when logical positivists, such as Rudolf Carnap (1891–1970) and Hans Reichenbach (1891-1953), and critical rationalists, such as Karl Popper (1902–1994), still advocated the view that the theory of scientific knowledge should be purely normative, strictly confined to contexts of justification and to the logical aspects of scientific discovery. Referring to the work of Michael Polanyi (1891–1976), Norwood Russell Hanson (1924–1967), and Thomas Kuhn (1922–1996) in dislodging epistemology from its status as first philosophy, W. V. O. Quine (1908–2000) introduced the term *epistemology naturalized.* He suggested that the epistemological enterprise had better be conceived in terms of interplay between normative and empirical concerns. As the latter are relevant to the former this means that, on the one hand, epistemology now ought to make full use of the findings of biology, (cognitive) psychology, sociology, and linguistics when dealing with issues of perception, memory, reasoning, belief formation, knowledge acquisition, and the like. On the other hand, epistemology may go on dealing with the normative aspects of these issues whether in the guise of logical reconstruction or conceptual analysis, or both. Precisely how the balance between structure and genesis should be struck is a matter of ongoing dispute. All naturalizing epistemologists are empiricists, but some take epistemology as a branch of descriptive science (D. T. Campbell) while others uphold its normativity as part of a multidisciplinary endeavor (Alvin I. Goldman).

An early example of naturalized epistemology is the genetic epistemology of the French psychologist Jean Piaget (1896–1980), who in cooperation with logicians such as Evert Willem Beth (1908–1964) and Leo Apostel (1925–1995) did much to undermine the gap between structure and genesis of knowledge. Other examples are Polanyi's theory of tacit knowledge and Popper's evolutionary epistemology, though the latter's rationalist ideal of objective knowledge without a knowing subject appears to counter its naturalism. Further examples of sophisticated naturalist epistemologies are Goldman's epistemics, the Austrian biologist Franz M. Wuketits's evolutionary epistemology, and Alvin Plantinga's reformed epistemology.

In regard to science and religion, naturalizing religious epistemology would mean fully employing the resources of the natural sciences, including evolutionary biology, paleoanthropology, and sociobiology, in accounting for the experiential and cognitive aspects of religious life. This can be done in more or less radical ways—for example, as part of a radical naturalistic program in philosophy that has no place for transcendence, whether supernatural or not. Or, in an equally radical way it might be done as part of a theistic program with a naturalistic epistemology as a subsidiary. In a more modest way it might be done as part of an empirical theology that takes inner worldly experiences of transcendence seriously, whether in the life of modern human beings or in the traces left by the earliest human ancestors.

See also EPISTEMOLOGY; EVOLUTIONARY EPISTEMOLOGY

Bibliography

Campbell, D. T. "Evolutionary Epistemology." In *The Philosophy of Karl Popper,* ed. Paul Arthur Schilpp. La Salle, Ill.: Open Court, 1974.

Goldman, Alvin I. *Epistemology and Cognition.* Cambridge, Mass.: Harvard University Press, 1986

Kornblith, Hillary, ed. *Naturalizing Epistemology,* 2nd edition. Cambridge Mass.: MIT Press, 1994.

Piaget, Jean. *The Principles of Genetic Epistemology,* trans. Wolfe Mays. London: Routledge and Kegan Paul, 1972.

Popper, Karl. *Objective Knowledge. An Evolutionary Approach.* Oxford: Clarendon, 1972

Quine, W. V. O. "Epistemology Naturalized." In *Ontological Relativity and Other Essays.* New York and London: Columbia University Press, 1969.

Wuketits, Franz M. *Evolutionary Epistemology and Its Implications for Humankind.* Albany: State University of New York Press, 1990.

ANDY F. SANDERS

NATURAL LAW THEORY

Natural law is the understanding of a moral law that is either given with nature and known through reason or given with moral reason independently of nature. Natural law is universal and common to all humanity. It transcends differences in culture, religion, and various formulations of moral law. It is often understood as the fundamental source of normativity from which positively formulated moral norms must be derived if morally justifiable. As the counterpoint to positive laws, natural law is the criterion of justification for political and biblical law.

Historical overview

The notion of natural law can be traced to the stoic understanding of the common law (Greek: *nomos koinos*), which permeates being and constitutes a cosmopolis in which the human being as a rational being participates. On the basis of a monistic metaphysics, the Stoics argued that there was a similarity between the law of the universe and the law of reason. The right action is that which is in accordance with nature, the cosmic law of reason. The influence from the Stoics was quite clear in the works of early Christian leader Augustine of Hippo and especially the medieval philosopher Thomas Aquinas. Aquinas argued in *Summa Theologica* that "the participation of the eternal law by rational creatures is called the law of nature" (I, II, 91, 2). Natural law (lex naturalis) was understood as a reflection in reason of the eternal law (lex aeterna), which was the constitutive law of being. As an eternal law it was a metaphysical explanation of divine reason. Divine reason was the source of the perfect order of being. Due to the Aristotelian influence, Aquinas also argued that the natural world would strive for its perfection, which ultimately was defined according to the eternal law. In natural law this good was reflected as a natural good, the basic reason why natural beings would strive for perfection.

This close link between physical nature and natural law as a law of reason became increasingly problematic, even if one still finds many advocates of this view. For Protestant reformers natural law is often endorsed as a law of reason because the depravity of nature makes it impossible to let nature serve as the basis of moral normativity. Thomas Hobbes, the seventeenth-century English political theorist and philosopher, further lessened the link between nature and reason. Hobbes developed an understanding of natural law on the basis of a contractarian scheme of thought, where natural law was to be conceived of as articles of peace decided upon by the parties of the contract. The contractarian basis of natural law thought furthered the dissolution of the close link between nature and reason as the basis of natural law. By the time of the Enlightenment, natural law had become a law of reason. The German philosopher Immanuel Kant is the leading proponent of this understanding of natural law. In his major work, *The Metaphysics of Morals* (1797), Kant made extensive use of natural law thought, but natural law in a normative sense was now understood as a law of reason.

Contemporary reformulations

In a contemporary setting various attempts are made to reformulate the notion of natural law. If one could point to a common feature for most of these attempts, it would be a tendency to move beyond a metaphysical basis of natural law. Most can also be seen in the light of the impious hypothesis of seventeenth-century Dutch statesman Hugo Grotius: the endorsement that the normativity of natural law is valid, even if God does not exist. However, this does not necessitate a rejection of the existence of God. It merely stresses the independent normative basis of natural law.

The best known attempts at reformulation have their roots within a Thomistic tradition. The works of John Finnis and Germain Grisez during the 1980s have been the most influential from this train of thought. The common feature for Grisez and Finnis is an attempt to develop a normative moral theory based on a notion of basic human goods. Certain goods, such as life, knowledge,

play, aesthetic experience, and religion, are derived from human nature. Moral life is to further these goods. Jean Porter argues in *Natural and Divine Law* (1999) that the normativity of nature can be endorsed in a contemporary setting on the basis of an evolutionistic explanation of the genesis of morality. Furthermore, metaethical naturalism also supports such a reformulation. The normative concept of nature is, therefore, quite plausible in a contemporary setting. Apart from the Thomistic reformulations of natural law one also finds a few attempts of reformulation within a Protestant tradition by, for example Ian Ramsey and David Little.

In addition to these theories with a religious basis, one may also point to various theories of moral philosophy, which may be seen as contributing to the reformulation of natural law. If one is only concerned with explicit natural law thought, the philosophical attempts at reformulation are relatively few. However, if one takes more indirect uses of natural law thought into consideration, one can find various attempts to reformulate the idea of natural law in either a more rational or naturalistic sense. In the more rational sense, one can point to the political theory of John Rawls. Rawls's theory of political justice, which is based upon the contractual agreement of parties may be seen as a theory where the notion of reason holds a normative implication in the constructive sense. The Kantian influence in this theory is evident in the focus on reason as the source of normativity. More naturalistic reformulations include, for example, Holmes Rolston's theories of environmental ethics. Rolston argues that values are given in nature, moral values are independent of the moral valuer, and nature is the source of moral values. This applies to human as well as nonhuman nature. Every natural organism has a natural good that serves as the source of the moral good. The moral good is defined as being in accordance with nature. The theories of Rawls and Rolston are both examples of theories where the primary attempt is not to reformulate natural law theory. Both of these theories, however, demonstrate important similarities to this classical concept.

See also KANT, IMMANUEL; NATURAL THEOLOGY; THOMAS AQUINAS; VALUE, RELIGIOUS

Bibliography

Budziszewski, J. *Written on the Heart: The Case for Natural Law*. Downers Grove, Ill.: InterVarsity Press, 1997.

Cromartie, Michael, ed. *A Preserving Grace: Protestants, Catholics, and Natural Law*. Washington, D.C/Grand Rapids, Mich.: Ethics and Public Policy Center/Eerdmans, 1997.

Crowe, Michael Bertram. *The Changing Profile of the Natural Law*. The Hague, Netherlands: Martinus Nijhoff, 1977.

Finnis, John. *Natural Law and Natural Rights*. Oxford: Clarendon Press, 1980.

George, Robert P., ed. *Natural Law Theory: Contemporary Essays*. Oxford: Oxford University Press, 1992.

Kant, Immanuel. *The Metaphysics of Morals* (1797), trans. Mary Gregor. Cambridge, UK: Cambridge University Press, 1996.

Little, David. "Calvin and the Prospects for a Theory of Natural Law." In *Norm and Context in Christian Ethics*, ed. Gene Outka. London: SCM Press, 1969.

Porter, Jean. *Natural and Divine Law. Reclaiming the Tradition for Christian Ethics*. Grand Rapids, Mich.: Eerdmans, 1999.

Ramsey, Ian T. "Towards a Rehabilitation of Natural Law." In *Christian Ethics and Contemporary Philosophy*, ed. Ian T. Ramsey. London: SCM Press, 1966.

Rawls, John. *A Theory of Justice*, Rev. edition. Cambridge, Mass.: Belknap Press, 1999.

Rolston, Holmes III. *Environmental Ethics: Duties to and Values in the Natural World*. Philadelphia: Temple University Press, 1988.

ULRIK B. NISSEN

NATURAL SELECTION

See EVOLUTION, BIOLOGICAL; SELECTION.
LEVELS OF

NATURAL THEOLOGY

Natural theology is the part of theology that does not depend upon revelation. During the Middle Ages, natural theology included arguments for the existence and nature of God, for the immortality of the soul, and for the basic principles of morality insofar as they are founded on nature as created by God.

The first flourishing of natural theology was in ancient Greece. Plato's dialogue, the *Phaedo,* contains a number of weak arguments for the everlastingness of the soul, and Aristotle's *Metaphysics* contains arguments for a "Prime Mover," which is also the best of all possible beings. In the Christian tradition, medieval theologians, often appealing to Romans 1:18–20, developed the viewed that natural theology could establish the existence of God, which it is logically necessary to do before discussing the things that God had revealed. The first Vatican Council, held from 1869 to 1870, defined as a matter of faith that the existence of God could be demonstrated by reason. The best known arguments in this regard are those of medieval philosopher and theologian Thomas Aquinas, whose "Five Ways" for demonstrating God are drawn from Aristotle.

Aristotle's four causes

In Aristotle's (384–322 B.C.E.) work, there is no sharp distinction between physics and theology. The Prime Mover is part of a scientific explanation of the universe, which explains why and for what purpose the universe exists. Aristotle describes four basic types of causes, and a complete causal explanation would trace them to an ultimate self-evident origin. There must be an ultimate efficient cause of the universe, something that brings everything else into being without itself being capable of entering into being or of passing away (it will be eternal). It will cause changes without being capable of change (it will be immutable). It will generate all transient things without itself being affected by anything (it will be necessary). According to Aristotle, there must be an ultimate formal cause of the universe—something that includes the natures of all things in a higher and underived manner (it will contain all possible perfections). There must be an ultimate final cause of the universe—something to which all things strive, or for the sake of which they exist (a perfection that all things strive to imitate in their own way). And there must be an ultimate material cause of the universe—something out of which it is made, which is not itself made out of anything more basic.

For Aristotle, the eternal, immutable, necessary, perfect pattern of the universe is one and the same being, since an all-perfect being will be eternal, immutable, and necessary. Prime matter, however, the material cause, is in itself imperfect and formless, and is a basic brute fact alongside the perfect being. Aquinas (c. 1225–1274) adopted all these arguments, and agreed with Aristotle that the efficient, formal, and final cause of the universe is not its material cause. But he argued that matter is not an ultimate principle. It is brought into being "ex nihilo" by the cause of the universe which is wholly immaterial and which, he said, "all men call God" (*Summa Contra Gentiles* 1, 13).

These arguments for God are essentially arguments to an ultimate cause, which will provide an ultimate explanation for the universe. Perhaps the "first cause" simply exists, as the ultimate brute fact. But one might push the argument as far as it can go, and say that the first cause has to exist. It cannot fail to exist, since it is the very source of all possibilities, and without it nothing would be even possible. The twentieth-century philosopher Richard Swinburne calls this an "absolute explanation," since it arrives at a being that is self-explanatory, whereas an ultimate explanation simply arrives at a being that cannot be explained in simpler or more basic terms.

These arguments continue to be the basis for most arguments in natural theology, construed as an attempt to explain the universe, but they have ceased to be considered a part of science. This is largely because science has rejected Aristotelian forms of explanation as being both superfluous and vacuous. Aristotelian science looked for the "essences" or true natures of things, and assumed that the essences must be brought about by things which were like them and at least as "great" in reality, and that each thing must have a "final cause" or purpose for the sake of which it exists.

Since the sixteenth century, scientists have ceased to look for "real essences" or for "final causes," and have given up the causal principle that things must be brought into being by other things that are like but greater than themselves. Such investigations led to no practical results. Instead, the "new scientific method" consisted of close observation, repeated experiment, and the formulation of general precise laws that govern events. Using this new method, one discovers no real essences, final causes, or efficient causes in the sense of beings that "bring about" their effects by some inner propensity. What one finds are sets of general laws and regular principles that are effective in describing and predicting series of events.

"Explanation" becomes the formulation of such laws, and an ultimate explanation would consist in the formulation of a general law that cannot be subsumed under a higher, more general, or simpler law. The idea of a First Cause, in the sense of a perfect and causally efficacious being, has disappeared from science. Science still asks why the ultimate laws of nature exist, but a scientific answer is likely to lie in a demonstration that such laws exist by some sort of inherent necessity. The eternal and perfect originator of the universe of Aquinas has been transformed by science into the inherent necessity of an ultimate mathematical formula, which is not "what all men call God."

Experimental sciences and idealism

Natural theology thus lost its scientific credibility with the rise of the properly experimental sciences. For some, however, this merely indicated that the natural sciences had limited the range of their enquiries to phenomena that could be measured, repeatedly observed, and explained under general mathematical laws. Questions about the ultimate nature, origin, and destiny of the universe remain, and if science does not attempt to answer such questions, then metaphysics or "first philosophy" must try.

As a result, a second stage in the history of natural theology began in seventeenth-century Europe with the rise of philosophical Idealism—the view that the ultimate nature of the universe is spiritual, that physical phenomena are appearances of that spiritual realm, and that the intellect can uncover the structure of the spiritual world, with which the physical sciences cannot deal. It is characteristic of this approach that it seeks to take conscious experience as its fundamental clue to the nature of reality, and to explain physical phenomena as confused appearances of basically conscious entities, or perhaps of one supreme Spirit.

The Idealist approach raises in an acute way the question of the relationship between the sciences and the humanities, or between physical and mental states. It may be claimed that law-like explanation which is open to any detached observer is only appropriate to physical phenomena, whereas one must understand the phenomena of consciousness in terms of interpretation, empathetic understanding, and personal engagement. Whether such a broad difference between human and natural sciences exists and is irreducible, is strongly disputed.

Rationalist or Idealist philosophers seldom agree with one another, and there seems to be no way of objectively verifying their claims. However, this is to be expected from systems that claim to be based on personal engagement and interpretation. The difference between traditional natural theology and Idealist natural theology is clearly exemplified in the writings of German philosopher Immanuel Kant (1724–1804). Kant is best known for his destructive criticism of the traditional arguments for God, but he firmly believed that there is an underlying reality that is the cause of physical reality as it appears to our senses. According to Kant there can be no theoretical knowledge of such reality in-itself (what he termed "noumenal" reality), but the mind does provide a priori knowledge of the form and order of sensory appearances (so knowledge does not depend merely on empirical information). Knowledge depends on the inner structure of reason, and reason necessarily postulates God, freedom, and immortality as ideas in terms of which we must represent ultimate reality to ourselves.

Kant is also, as are most idealists, firmly committed to science understood as the investigation of the rational structure of phenomenal experience. The claim would be that idealism—i.e., the postulate that the universe must be thought of as basically mind-like—is the surest foundation of the natural sciences, which must presume there is a rational structure in the natural world. But Idealism also points out that there are limits to science, which are reached when it claims to disclose the ultimate structure of reality, or to extend its reach into the realm of the personal or spiritual. That is a realm into which philosophy can reach, with the aid of its principles of rational coherence, establishing a system within which consciousness, value, and purpose can have an intelligible place. The crucial question is whether the concepts of value and purpose have a place in explanations of the universe. If they do, then an Idealist approach offers a complement to science, which only comes into conflict with it if and insofar as value and purpose are denied.

Modern appropriations of the design argument

The failure to establish useful general laws in psychology and sociology, as well as the subjective nature of much of history and economics, suggests that these areas are not amenable to the scientific techniques that have been so useful in physics and chemistry. But the fields of neurophysiology and of evolutionary psychology contain promises (or threats) to explain consciousness itself in physical or evolutionary terms. Consciousness may be a by-product of past successful survival strategies, and its present functioning may be incidental to the adaptive functions (of discerning prey or avoiding predators) that it originally possessed. This sort of natural theology, which argues from consciousness to a supreme consciousness or Spirit, needs to argue that consciousness is an irreducible and distinctive phenomenon beyond the reach of experimental science. That remains a highly disputed issue.

A third, slightly different approach to natural theology reverts to the methodology of the sciences, not the Aristotelian method of searching for essential natures, but the experimental method of inferring hypotheses from observed evidence. The most famous example of this approach is found in the work of eighteenth-century English theologian William Paley, who inferred from evidences of design in nature the existence of a wise designer. This approach is unlike the Aristotelian approach, since it does not assume that all substances have final causes. Rather, Paley's approach looks at organisms, in particular, as highly organized and efficient systems for supporting animal and human life, and argues that it is much more probable that such systems are designed than that they originated by chance. If we found a watch, says Paley, we would surely infer that it had a designer, it is so intricately organized to a purpose, with all its parts finely balanced and tuned to one another. So we must infer that the world has a designer, for similar reasons.

This approach was dealt a severe blow by Charles Darwin's (1809–1882) theory of evolution and natural selection, which claims to show how well-designed organisms can evolve, if not by chance, than at least by random mutation and natural adaptation to the environment, in strongly competitive situations. Given the difficulty Paley has in accounting for why such strange organisms as giraffes and ichneuman flies (which lay their eggs in living caterpillars) exist, mutation and natural selection seem a better explanation than trying to figure out why God would design such odd or unpleasant creatures.

Nevertheless, design proponents argue that a wise creator may not have specifically designed every type of creature that exists. But such a creator might have designed the general laws of genetic mutation and environmental selection so that they would generate sentient rational organisms by a process that is partly random, yet directed to certain goals (the existence of rational agency). When one adds to this the extreme improbability of the laws of nature giving rise to a universe with life-forms in it at all, one has an argument to the general elegant design of the laws of nature and of evolution, if not to all their particular products. Many of the findings of physics, which disclose the elegance and integrated simplicity of the fundamental forces of the physical world, and those of biology, which reveal the amazingly complex structure of DNA and the adaptedness of living creatures to their environment, are strongly suggestive of design.

On the other hand, some argue that any universe with conscious beings in it would have to be complex and ordered in just such a way, so it is hardly surprising that we find such complex order. The structure is highly improbable, but so is the existence of any universe at all, so this universe is no more improbable than any other. In addition, it may be doubted whether it makes sense to speak of purpose or direction in evolution, and whether existence is worthwhile at all. So these probabilistic arguments of design-type natural theology are far from conclusive.

It seems that the universe, as science shows it to be, could be the work of an intelligent creator. But the universe may also just happen to exist as it does. The inference to a creator is not strictly required. The arguments of natural theology may seem to make a creator probable to many people. They do show the intelligibility and elegance of the universe, and thus enrich the idea of a creator that a theist might hold. But they are not overwhelming, and non-scientific factors concerning the value and possible purpose of creation will probably weigh the balance one way or another.

Contemporary assessment

Partly for this reason, many theologians deny that religious belief depends upon the success of natural theology. Some, like Swiss theologian Karl Barth (1886–1996), even argue that the program of natural theology is based on human arrogance, and flies in the face of revelation, which is to be accepted on faith, not because it seems on balance to be probable. Kant said, "I have had to deny

knowledge, in order to make room for faith" (p. 29). He meant that only when it could be shown that no speculative knowledge of transcendent reality is possible, so that one could neither affirm nor deny God by argument, was one free to adopt faith on practical or moral grounds.

It has come to be widely held in modern theology that faith results either from a commitment of the will (Søren Kierkegaard [1813–1855]), or from some basic and nonrational apprehension of the holy (Friedrich Schleiermacher [1768–1834] and Rudolf Otto [1869–1937]), or, as according to John Barth, simply from an act of divine grace, which has no rational grounds. The problem with such views is that they prevent anyone from giving a reason why they should adopt one faith (say the Christian) rather than another (Islam, perhaps). Such views are also in danger of isolating religious belief from scientific belief, so that religion and science have no relation to one another. Yet it seems odd to say that religious belief in a creator God is not affected by new discoveries about the nature of the created universe, or that religious beliefs (such as the belief that God is one rational purposive creator) have nothing to say about the nature of such a creation.

Natural theology is often no longer seen as the task of proving that God exists, or of showing to any independent observer that God is the most probable explanation of why the universe is the way it is. But, it might be said, one should be able to assemble the best human knowledge in all the diverse areas of human activity, and show how it can reasonably be construed, and even shaped into a more coherent form, by the insights of religion, which may themselves derive from some distinctive source in revelation or experience. Natural theology will then be the attempt to show how science, history, morality, and the arts are so related that a total integrating vision of the place of humanity in the universe may be formulated. Such a vision will be religious insofar as it includes reference to an encompassing reality that is transcendent in power and value, and that may disclose itself in distinctive ways. This will not be proof, or even probability, starting from some neutral, completely shared ground. It will be an integrating activity of reason, both provisional in its formulations and constructed from a standpoint of specific basic postulates and personal value commitments. Within such a perspective, science will be able to make a positive contribution to natural theology, and natural theology will develop ways of integrating scientific activity into a wider worldview. This will be more of an imaginative art than an inferential or deductive science. It will not be the intellectual foundation or prelude for faith, but will involve the construction of a general worldview within which faith can have an intelligible place. That is not too far from the aims of Aristotle, though the distinctions between natural science, philosophy, and religious belief are now clearer (but only in some ways) than they were for him. In this form, natural theology becomes the speculative and constructive part of the post-eighteenth-century discipline of the "philosophy of religion." As such, it is not confined to one particular religious tradition, and its exponents may hold any or no religious beliefs.

However, there are many philosophers of religion who would hold that systematic construction is not properly part of philosophy, the function of which should be primarily analytic and expository. Therefore, natural theology in all its form remains, like religion itself, a highly pluralistic and disputed discipline. It is clear, however, that this is an area in which science and religion fruitfully interact in examining the fundamental problem of the ultimate nature of existence.

See also ARISTOTLE; DARWIN, CHARLES; DESIGN ARGUMENT; EVOLUTIONARY PSYCHOLOGY; IDEALISM; KANT, IMMANUEL; RATIONALISM; THOMAS AQUINAS

Bibliography

Barrow, John D., and Tipler, Frank J. *The Anthropic Cosmological Principle.* New York: Oxford University Press, 1986.

Barth, Karl. *The Epistle to the Romans* (1921), trans. Edwyn Hoskyns. New York: Oxford University Press, 1933.

Davies, Paul. *The Mind of God; The Scientific Basis for a Rational World.* New York: Simon and Schuster, 1992.

Dennett, Daniel C. *Darwin's Dangerous Idea; Evolution and the Meanings of Life.* New York: Touchstone, 1995.

Hume, David. *Dialogues Concerning Natural Religion* (1779). Indianapolis, Ind.: Hackett, 1980.

Kant, Immanuel. *Critique of Pure Reason* (1781), trans. Norman Kemp Smith. London: Macmillan, 1933.

Kierkegaard, Soren. *Concluding Unscientific Postscript to the Philosophical Fragments* (1846), trans. Howard V. Hong and Edna H. Hong. Princeton, N.J.: Princeton University Press, 1992.

Otto, Rudolf. *The Idea of the Holy* (1917), trans. John W. Harvey. London: Oxford University Press, 1923.

Paley, William. *Natural Theology* (1802), eds. Henry Brougham and Charles Bell. London: C. Knight, 1836.

Schleiermacher, Friedrich. *On Religion: Speeches to its Cultured Despisers* (1799), trans. Richard Crouter. Cambridge, UK: Cambridge University Press, 1988.

Swinburne, Richard. *The Existence of God.* New York: Oxford University Press, 1979.

Ward, Keith. *God, Chance, and Necessity.* Oxford: Oneworld Press, 1996.

Ward, Keith. *Religion and Revelation.* Oxford: Clarendon Press, 1996.

Wilson, Edward O. *Consilience: The Unity of Knowledge.* New York: Knopf, 1998.

KEITH WARD

NATURE

Nature refers to the source out of which something has come into being. The word *nature* is derived from the Latin *natura* (birth) or *nasci* (to be born). A similar meaning is found in the Greek *physis,* which means growth. The concept of nature holds a variety of meanings, depending on the relation in which it is understood. In a political setting, nature is often seen in contrast to custom, culture, and law. In religious terms, nature is often opposed to grace and spirit. Viewed philosophically, nature can be understood in contrast to history and freedom. Nature can also be seen as: (1) the object of scientific observation and enquiry; (2) a normative notion, such as the question of "natural" behavior; (3) an essential notion, such as human "nature"; and (4) a notion concerning evidence, as in the exclamation "naturally!" These different meanings can be taken either as a sign of the philosophically problematic use of this notion or its need of specification.

Historical overview

Several of these concepts have their roots in ancient Greek philosophy. In pre-Socratic philosophy nature was seen in contrast to relativism. Cultures varied, but nature was considered constant and was therefore regarded as ethically normative. Aristotle, who understood nature in teleological terms, carried the notion of the normativity even further. The essence (form) of natural beings carried with it a certain purpose that determined the good life. The morally good life was believed to be in accordance with nature, an understanding further developed in Stoic philosophy, which argued for life in accordance with nature.

These concepts of nature had an enduring impact on theological and philosophical thought during the Middle Ages. During this period, however, a contrast between nature and the supernatural was increasingly endorsed. Nature was distinguished from the divine. For the Christian philosopher Thomas Aquinas (c. 1225–1274), however, nature was not opposed to the divine. Aquinas maintained an analogy of being (*analogia entis*) between eternal law (*lex aeterna*), the constitutive law of being that is identical to divine reason, and natural law (*lex naturalis*), which is understood as the participation of the rational being in eternal law.

During the sixteenth century, nature could also be set in contrast to divine will. Consequently, in the beginning of the seventeenth century, nature became increasingly understood as morally neutral. As physics became identified with mechanics during the scientific revolution, nature came to be understood in mechanistic terms, as something that could be described with physical laws. This change in the role of the sciences, and the corresponding change in the understanding of nature, implied a different relation to nature. Nature became understood as that which was different from human beings and that which humans, as rational beings, were to control. The natural sciences served this purpose as knowledge about nature was regarded as power over nature.

The philosopher Immanuel Kant (1724–1804) had an enduring impact on the scientific understanding of nature. According to Kant, the different objects of nature could not be known in themselves, but could only be known as appearances determined by the epistemological categories of space and time. Consequently, Kant's transcendental philosophy implied that in the apprehension of nature human beings were structuring the very same nature. Kant became influential for his emphasis on the interrelation between nature as an object and the formative impact of the human apprehension of nature.

Another fundamental turn in the scientific understanding of nature was the publication of Charles Darwin's *On the Origin of Species* (1859). According to Darwin's theory of evolution, new species originated from other species, and natural life was formed according to the principles of variation and natural selection. This view of nature has often been seen as opposed to a theological understanding of nature as designed by God. As a consequence, nature was no longer considered as good in itself, but as morally ambiguous.

Modern scientific concepts of nature

In a contemporary setting, the diversity of the notions of nature is as varied as in previous epochs, with a host of holistic, religious, and ecological understandings in play. Karen Gloy has demonstrated how an organicist notion of nature has been in use since the Renaissance. The ecological mode is present in environmental ethics. The philosopher J. Baird Callicott argues that nature is to be seen as a biotic community. Based on evolutionary theory, nature is regarded as an interrelated, interdependent, ecological web of life, which raises the ethical implication that the good is defined as that which furthers the stability of the biotic community. Jürgen Moltmann endorses a theological understanding of evolution in which evolutionary theory is not contrary to the doctrine of creation. Like Callicott, Moltmann argues that the ecological community of life serves as the basis of the moral demand to preserve nature. Furthermore, both Callicott and Moltmann endorse the connection between a holistic and normative notion of nature.

In other theories, nature is seen as self-organizing. Niels Henrik Gregersen views nature in the light of autopoietic systems theory. It is argued that the Christian theology of creation is not contrary to an understanding of nature as self-productive. God's self-consistency and self-relativization in exchange with nature is endorsed. God not only sustains nature but is also seen as a structuring cause. Michael Welker challenges the traditional concept of creation. Often creation is understood as a unique act of bringing into existence, but Welker argues that God is not simply active but also reactive in the creation of the world. The act of creation is an interaction between God and the activity and productivity of nature. Both Gregersen and Welker argue for the self-productivity of nature.

Nature continues to be a fundamental religious, philosophical, and scientific concept. The variety of meanings and aspects to this notion is perhaps one source of its continuing appeal to various discourses of enquiry.

See also AUTOPOIESIS; KANT, IMMANUEL

Bibliography

Callicott, J. Baird. *In Defense of the Land Ethic. Essays in Environmental Philosophy.* Albany: State University of New York Press, 1989.

Darwin, Charles. *On the Origin of Species* (1859). New York: Bantam, 1999.

Gloy, Karen. *Das Verständnis der Natur. I Die Geschichte des wissenschaftlichen Denkens.* Munich, Germany: Verlag C. H. Beck, 1995.

Gloy, Karen. *Das Verständnis der Natur. II Die Geschichte des ganzheitlichen Denkens.* Munich, Germany: Verlag C. H. Beck, 1996.

Gregersen, Niels Henrik. "The Idea of Creation and the Theory of Autopoietic Processes." *Zygon* 33, no. 3 (1998): 333–367.

Moltmann, Jürgen. *God in Creation: A New Theology of Creation and the Spirit of God,* trans. Margaret Kohl. San Francisco: Harper, 1985.

Soper, Kate. *What is Nature? Culture, Politics and the Non-Human.* Oxford: Blackwell, 1995.

Welker, Michael. "What is Creation?: Reading Genesis 1 and 2." *Theology Today* 48, no. 1 (1991): 56–71.

ULRIK B. NISSEN

NATURE VERSUS NURTURE

Nature and culture are classical opposites, or complements. By nature we are "born that way"; by nurture we learn to become civilized.

In one sense, "nature" refers to everything generated or produced. Etymologically, the Latin *natura* is the source from which all springs forth. For metaphysical naturalists, perhaps also for methodological scientists, nature is all that there is, without contrast class. Nothing non-natural or supernatural exists. Humans evolved within nature and break no natural laws. Another view holds that a straightforward contrast class for nature is culture, which nurtures humans into an inherited linguistic and symbolic system, a worldview, by which they communicate, perpetuate, and develop knowledge. This cultural genius makes possible the deliberate and cumulative, and therefore the extensive, rebuilding of nature. Humans reshape their environments, rather than being themselves morphologically and genetically reshaped to fit their changing environments. Humans come into the world by nature unfinished and become what they become by nurture.

Cultural education

Etymologically, "culture" is related to "cultivate," while "nurture" is related to "nurse" and "nourish," with overtones of rearing and training. Religious persons find their traditions vital in such nurture, and absent from nature. "Train up a child in the way in which he should go" (Prov. 22:6).

Such cultural education requires second-order intentionality. First-order intentionality is intent to change the behavior of another actor, and this is widespread in the animal world. Second-order intentionality is intent to change the mind (and usually also the behavior) of another animal; this seems absent among animals (or almost so). Although animals are variously socialized, they are not in this sense nurtured. Without some concept of teaching, of ideas moving from mind to mind, from parent to child, from teacher to pupil, a cumulative transmissible culture is impossible. Though language comes naturally to humans, what is learned has been culturally transmitted, using a specific language; the content learned during childhood education is that of an acquired, nongenetic culture.

Religious persons detect a supernature immanent in or transcendent to nature, perhaps even more in human culture. They find that neither nature nor culture is self-explanatory; both point to deeper forces, to a divine presence.

In contemporary biological and human sciences (anthropology, psychology, sociology), as well as in philosophy, there is much effort to naturalize culture, with equal amounts of resistance to such reduction (if that is what it is). Sociobiologists hold that genetic constraints are the principal determinants of culture; only those people and cultures survive that can place genes in the next generation. Evolutionary psychologists discover that humans have an "adapted mind," a modular mind with multiple survival subroutines more or less in-stinctive—in contrast to the highly rational *tabula rasa* (empty, pliable mind) once favored by hu-manist philosophers. Philosophical pragmatists may agree that the mind is mostly a survival tool, even in its cultural education.

Culture remains a major determinant, never-theless. Information in nature travels intergenera-tionally on genes; information in culture travels neurally as persons are educated into transmissible cultures. The determinants of animal and plant be-havior are never anthropological, political, eco-nomic, technological, scientific, philosophical, eth-ical, or religious. Animal imprinting and limited transmitting of acquired information notwithstand-ing, humans gain a deliberated modification of na-ture that separates humans in their cultures from nature, increasingly so in high-technology cultures. Since decoding the human genome, completed in 2001, people stand at the threshold of rebuilding even their own genetic nature.

Nature-culture dualism

Humans have a dual inheritance system, nature and nurture. The intellectual and social heritage of past generations, lived out in the present, re-formed and transmitted to the next generation, is regularly decisive. Cultures, especially modern ones, change rapidly in a few decades; the human genome hardly changes in thousands of years. Slow-paced genes are difficult to couple with fast-paced cultures.

A relatively pliable, educable mind is as great an adaptive advantage as is a mind with instinctive routines. The mind is so complex that the number of neurons and their possible connections (with resulting myriads of cultural options) far exceeds the number of genes coding the neural system; so it is impossible for the genes to specify all these connections. Human genes have generated an or-ganism whose behavior results from an education beyond direct genetic control. As more knowledge is loaded into the tradition (fire building, agricul-ture, writing, weaponry, industrial processes, ethi-cal codes, electronic technology, legal history) the genome selected will be one maximally instructible by the increasingly knowledgeable tradition. This will require a flexible intellect, able to accommo-date continual learning speedily, adopting behav-iors that are functional in whatever cultures hu-mans find themselves. This is consistent with the unusually long period of child rearing in nuclear families with unusually large-brained babies, found in human evolutionary history and uncharacteristic of any other species.

Critics complain that nature-culture dualism is an undesirable Cartesian legacy (perhaps also a Christian or Greek one). The "versus" in the title of this entry frames the connections wrongly. Nature is the milieu of culture, and supposing our cultures to be in exodus from nature is at the root of our environmental crisis. Culture remains tethered to the biosystem, and the options within built envi-ronments, however expanded, provide no release from nature. An ecology always lies in the back-ground of culture; no nurture is adequate that for-gets these connections.

Perhaps cultural nurturing reinforces natural genetic dispositions for some practices (such as in-cest avoidance), but not for others (learning nu-clear physics). Whether adults have enzymes for digesting fresh milk will determine their pastoral practices. But the differences between the Druids of ancient Britain and the Maoists in modern China are nongenetic and to be sought in the radically differentiating historical courses peculiar to these cultures—even though Druids and Chinese have a biological nature largely held in common and de-spite differences in skin color or in blood groups.

Humans are only part of the world in biologi-cal, evolutionary, and ecological senses—their na-ture; but *Homo sapiens* is the only part of the world free to orient itself with a view of the whole, to seek wisdom about who they are and where they are, and to develop their lives on Earth by means of culture. Such cumulative, ongoing nur-ture determines outcomes in the uniquely histori-cal behavior of humans, making the critical differ-ence, while human universals, biological, psychological, or social, which are a legacy of na-ture, have limited explanatory power.

See also DNA; GENETIC DETERMINISM; GENETICS

Bibliography

Barkow, Jerome H; Cosmides, Leda; and Tooby, John, eds. *The Adapted Mind: Evolutionary Psychology and the Generation of Culture*. New York: Oxford Univer-sity Press, 1992.

Bock, Kenneth. *Human Nature and History: A Response to Sociobiology*. New York: Columbia University Press, 1980.

Cavalli-Sforza, Luigi L., and Feldman, Marcus W. *Cultural Transmission and Evolution: A Quantitative Approach.* Princeton, N.J.: Princeton University Press, 1981.

Durham, William H. *Coevolution: Genes, Culture, and Human Diversity.* Stanford, Calif.: Stanford University Press, 1991.

Plumwood, Val. *Environmental Culture.* New York: Routledge, 2002.

Rolston, Holmes, III. "Culture: Genes and the Genesis of Human Culture." In *Genes, Genesis and God: Values and their Origins in Natural and Human History.* New York: Cambridge University Press, 1999.

Wilson, Edward O. *On Human Nature.* Cambridge, Mass.: Harvard University Press, 1988.

HOLMES ROLSTON, III

NEO-DARWINISM

Neo-Darwinism, the modern version of Charles Darwin's theory of evolution by natural selection, incorporates the laws of Mendelian genetics and emphasizes the role of natural selection as the main force of evolutionary change. The term *neo-Darwinism* was first used in the 1880s by August Weismann, a German naturalist, who incorporated his theory of the germ plasm into Darwin's theory of evolution by natural selection. Weismann advocated the theory that the body is divided into germ cells, which can transmit hereditary information, and somatic cells, which cannot. Weismann thereby added a mechanism of heredity different from Jean Baptiste de Lamarck's inheritance of acquired characteristics, which prepared the ground for the rediscovery of Gregor Mendel's laws of inheritance by Erich von Tschermak, Hugo deVries, Carl Correns, and William Bateson around 1900.

The rediscovery of Mendel's work led first to a critique of Darwin's theory of evolution, as the new school of *Mendelians* (Bateson, deVries, and others) believed that differences in discrete traits among individuals were too big to fit into Darwin's theory of gradual change of phenotypes. Another school of thought that developed during the first two decades of the twentieth century involved the *biometricians* (Karl Pearson, Francis Galton, and others), who opposed the view of the Mendelians and studied small differences in so-called quantitative traits (e.g., body size), using statistical methods and assuming that most genes had only minor effects on traits. The controversy between Mendelians and biometricians was resolved by R. A. Fisher in 1918 when he showed that Mendelian inheritance and gradual changes in phenotypes were not incompatible. In the following two decades Fisher, J. S. B. Haldane, and Sewall Wright used mathematical tools to elaborate on this combination of the laws of genetics and Darwin's theory of evolution, thereby developing the *modern synthesis* and the new field of population genetics.

Modern synthesis, which has since been called the "neo-Darwinian theory of evolution," was soon accepted and integrated into different biological disciplines, including population genetics, comparative anatomy, zoology, biogeography, palaeontology, and systematics. Influential books, such as *Genetics and the Origin of Species* (1937) by Russian-born American experimental biologist Theodosius Dobzhansky, *The Modern Synthesis* (1942) by British biologist Julian S. Huxley, *Systematics and the Origin of Species* (1942) by German-born American zoologist Ernst Mayr, and *Tempo and Mode of Evolution* (1944) by American palaeontologist George Gaylord Simpson are examples of this development and of the neo-Darwinian theory of evolution as having become broadly accepted among contemporary biologists.

Evolution from a neo-Darwinian viewpoint is defined as genetic change in populations through time (descent with change), with modern organisms being descendents of earlier, different organisms. In addition to natural selection, mutation, random genetic drift (i.e., random fluctuations in gene frequencies due to chance), and gene flow are considered important factors of evolutionary change with mutation being the ultimate source of genetic variation.

See also DARWIN, CHARLES; EVOLUTION; GENETICS; LAMARCKISM; MENDEL, GREGOR

Bibliography

Dobzhansky, Theodosius. *Genetics and the Origin of Species.* New York: Columbia University Press, 1937.

Huxley, Julian S. *Evolution: The Modern Synthesis.* London: G. Allen and Unwin, 1942.

Mayr, Ernst. *Systematics and the Origin of Species.* New York: Columbia University Press, 1942.

Simpson, George Gaylor. *Tempo and Mode of Evolution.* New York: Columbia University Press, 1944.

VOLKER LOESCHCKE

NEO-ORTHODOX THEOLOGY

See CHRISTIANITY, REFORMED, ISSUES IN SCIENCE AND RELIGION

NEURAL DARWINISM

Neural Darwinism is a theory of brain development laid out in 1987 by neurobiologist Gerald Edelman (b. 1929). According to this theory, selective forces, both of development and experience, operate on neuronal groups rather than on single neurons. Movement-sensation categories are continually re-categorized, producing maps that interact in ensemble, and establish the coherent temporal patterns of a unified notion of brain. This is an empirically viable neurobiological theory of individuality, about how a person's unique memories, perspectives, and autonomous mental life evolves. The role it may play in a wider theory of consciousness as a kind of "remembered present" is as yet unclear, despite its advantages over other connectionist or neural network models.

See also NEUROPHYSIOLOGY; NEUROPSYCHOLOGY; NEUROSCIENCES

Bibliography

Edelman, Gerald M. *Bright Air, Brilliant Fire: On the Matter of the Mind.* New York: Basic Books, 1992.

JOHN A. TESKE

NEUROPHYSIOLOGY

Neurophysiology is the area of neuroscience that studies the functioning of nerve cells, with a primary focus on their information coding, transmission, and storage capacities. Neurophysiology includes study of the electrical properties of the nerve cell membrane, the generation of *action potentials* that carry information, and the communication of this information between cells over the synaptic space. One important question occupying a great deal of time and effort is the nature of changes in synaptic efficiency that occur with learning. The functioning of groups of neurons, including reflex loops and assemblages of neurons into neural networks, is also widely studied.

See also MIND-BODY INTERACTION; NEUROSCIENCES

WARREN S. BROWN

NEUROPSYCHOLOGY

Neuropsychology is the area of neuroscience that studies relationships between brain function and behavior, with a central focus on human brain-behavior relationships. Neuropsychological research attempts to map the brain structures and functions that are critical for particular mental/cognitive, emotional, and behavioral capacities. Clinical neuropsychology involves assessment of persons with diseased or damaged brains to evaluate whether the patient's cognitive, behavioral, or emotional functioning has been compromised. Developmental neuropsychology is the study of the relationship between the development of brain structure and function, and the emergence of cognitive abilities. Finally, neuropsychological rehabilitation attempts to ameliorate the negative impact of brain damage.

See also MIND-BRAIN INTERACTION; NEUROSCIENCES

WARREN S. BROWN

NEUROSCIENCES

Neuroscience is the scientific study of the nervous system and its function. Since the nervous system can be studied at many levels—from the molecular structure of nerve cell membranes to the whole-brain functions involved in the highest of human mental activity—neuroscience is a multidisciplinary field. Neuroscientists might study the nervous systems of simple creatures (e.g., sea slugs), more complex animals (e.g., rats, cats, and monkeys), or human beings. At meetings of the Society for Neuroscience one finds over ten thousand scientists representing a wide variety of fields such as microbiology, histology, neuroanatomy, neurophysiology, physiological psychology, developmental psychology, neuropsychology, neuroradiology, neurology, psychiatry, and cognitive science.

The various domains of research in neuroscience might be grouped into the following topic areas:

- Cellular and molecular neurophysiology;
- Developmental neuroscience;
- Sensory and motor neuroscience;
- Regulatory neuroscience;
- Behavioral and cognitive neuroscience; and
- Clinical neuroscience.

After a brief review of the history of neuroscience, each of these areas will be described. This will be followed by a summary of current research on religious experience and brain function. Finally, the philosophical presuppositions of neuroscience will be briefly summarized.

The history of neuroscience

The ancient-to-modern history of neuroscience involved resolution of four major issues. The first issue was whether mental activity and control of behavior emanated from the brain or the heart. Next, there was the issue of whether the critical parts were the ventricles and cerebral fluids (the pneumatic theory) or the brain tissue itself. When it became clear that the various structures of the brain were the organs of thought and behavior, there was a controversy over localization of these functions in specific brain areas versus a holistic view of brain function. Finally, with respect to neural tissue, research in the late nineteenth and early twentieth centuries established that independent neural cells (neurons) are the basic functional units of the nervous system.

The work of the ancient Greek physician Hippocrates (460–375 B.C.E.) on epilepsy is among the most important ancient contributions to neuroscience. Hippocrates denied that epilepsy was a divine or sacred manifestation, arguing instead that it was a disease of the brain. He considered the brain to be the seat of all mental experience. The alternative view was advanced by Aristotle (384–322 B.C.E.), who is considered by many to be the greatest biologist of antiquity. Aristotle taught that the heart was the center of sensation, movement, and intelligence. Around the same time, important contributions were also being made in Alexandria. Herophilos and Erasistratos (third century B.C.E.) distinguished various brain structures, provided the first description of the ventricles, and associated intelligence with the greater number of convolutions in the cortex of the brain.

The progress of these ancient neuroscientists was extended in the work of Galen (129–199 C.E.) in Rome. Galen contributed important studies of the cranial nerves and the spinal cord. Using transsections of the spinal cord, he determined that the spinal cord was an extension of the brain and the conduit of sensory and motor information. However, Galen's theory of brain function was pneumatic, focusing on the ventricles rather than brain tissue. During the medieval period, the theories of Galen became dogma and were transmitted without much modification into the Renaissance.

New advances in neuroscience during the Renaissance were triggered by a rediscovery of the work of the ancients, including descriptions of the original work of Galen. Progress during the Renaissance was made by Andreas Vesalius (1514–1564), who discredited the ventricular theory; René Descartes (1596–1650), who had the idea of the body as a machine and developed the concept of a reflex; and Thomas Willis (1612–1675), an anatomist who provided the most complete description to that date of the anatomy of the brain (and whose book was famously illustrated by Christopher Wren).

The progress in neuroscience achieved in the Renaissance was accelerated during the Enlightenment. Important progress during this period was made by Franz Joseph Gall (1758–1828) and Johann Casper Spurzheim (1776–1832). These investigators proposed that the gyri of the cortex were composed of cells that connected to the brain stem and spinal cord, and, therefore, the cortex could control movement via its connections to the spinal cord. The most famous aspect of the work of Gall and Spurzheim was phrenology, the study of the relationship between skull surface features and mental faculties. What is important about this work is that skull features were thought to reveal the size of underlying cortical gyri, thus phrenology was the first extensive theory of the cortical localization of cognitive functions.

Pierre Flourens (1794–1867) is credited with demolishing phrenology, while advocating the idea that all intellectual functions are coextensive within the cortex (a holist view). Flourens developed the research strategy of removing or lesioning parts of the brains of animals and observing consequent changes in their behavior. However, the localizationist view was kept alive by the work of Paul Broca (1796–1881) and Carl Wernicke (1848–1904), who identified the expressive and receptive language areas of the left cerebral hemisphere (respectively). Based on the discovery of the bioelectric nature of the function of muscles by Luigi Galvani (1737–1798), Gustav Theodor Fritsch (1838–1929) and Eduard Hitzig (1838–1907) demonstrated that the brain was electrically excitable, and that electrically stimulating different cortical locations produced different behavioral effects.

During the nineteenth and early twentieth centuries advances were also being made in understanding the microstructure and microfunction of the nervous system. Due to the availability of improved microscopes, Theodore Schwann (1810–1882) was able to discover and describe the fact that the organs and tissues of animals, including the brain, were made up of many individual cells. However, Schwann believed that the brain, unlike other organs, was made up of cells that were not separated by membranes, but rather were a continuously interconnected network. It took a lifetime of painstaking work by the Spanish neuroanatomist Santiago Ramón y Cajal (1852–1934) to demonstrate that each neuron is an independent and discontinuous cell. Charles Scott Sherrington (1857–1952) was the first to describe the *synapse*, the point of communication between neurons. The microstructure of the nervous system became dynamic with the description of the action potential by A.L. Hodgkin (1914–1998) and A. F. Huxley (1917–). Finally, the hypothesis (since substantiated) that the site of learning within the nervous system is the synapse was advanced in 1949 by Donald O. Hebb (1904–1985).

Cellular and molecular neurophysiology

Cellular and molecular neurophysiology is the study of the molecular structure and physiological functioning of nerve cells. The critical property of a neuron is that it has a membrane that is an electrochemical battery. There is a difference in electrical charge between the inside and outside of the cell created by an uneven distribution of sodium and potassium ions. Also critical to neural function are the processes by which this electrochemical potential can be disturbed so as to trigger an action potential that can be transmitted from one end of an axon to the other. Research has demonstrated that the electrical properties of neurons are based on voltage controlled ion channels within the nerve cell membrane. These channels open or close depending on surrounding voltage levels. Voltage controlled ion channels are the subject of intense study in molecular neuroscience since they are the basis of the resting potential, the excitability threshold of the membrane, the phenomena of the action potential and its transmission, and most of the critical events at the synapse, where information is transmitted from one neuron to another.

Much work in cellular neurophysiology is focused on events occurring at the synapse. In simple outline, it has been demonstrated that the arrival of the action potential at the end of the axon (the terminal button) causes calcium ions to enter the cell. This causes packets of a transmitter substance to release their contents into the extremely small space between neurons. The transmitter substance attaches to receptors on the post-synaptic neuron, causing ion gates to open, resulting in a slight electrical perturbation in this post-synaptic cell. Various other mechanisms have been found that clear activated receptors, take back excess transmitter substance, and recreate the transmitter substance packets.

Another active area of work in neurophysiology is the investigation of the ways that synaptic functions are modified by learning. Using the nervous system of a sea slug, it was demonstrated that learning involved changes in the conductive properties of synapses. Where in the human nervous system such synaptic changes can occur, and how they occur, are important issues in the study of human learning and memory. An important recent advance was the identification of the NMDA receptor that appears to be important in triggering the synaptic changes involved in learning. NMDA receptors are present on neurons within the hippocampus, a brain structure that is known to be important for some forms of memory.

Transmitter substances, and their respective types of post-synaptic receptors, come in a wide variety. Among the major transmitter substances identified are acetylcholine, dopamine, norepinephrine, serotonin, GABA, and glycine, but there are many more than this. There are, for example, at least four variants of dopamine. The field of neuropharmacology attempts to exploit this variety by finding drugs that act in a specific manner on synapses that use a particular neurotransmitter so that specific functions of the brain can be modulated. The drug Prozac, for example, inhibits the reuptake of transmitter substance within synapses that utilize serotonin, causing these particular synapses to be active for a longer period of time.

Developmental neuroscience

Developmental neuroscience studies the fetal and childhood development of the nervous system. There are stages in development of the brain and nervous system: development of cell identity, cell migration, axon growth and guidance, growth of dendrities and synaptic formation, differentiation of connections based on early experiences, and myelinization of axons.

Nerve cells differentiate from undifferentiated stem cells. Stem cells become precursor neuroblasts that eventually produce neurons, glial cells, or other cells within the nervous system. This differentiation process is based primarily upon interactions with neighboring cells. Because of the potency of the influences of neighboring cells in causing undifferentiated stem cells to become neurons, a great deal of research is being done in an attempt to introduce undifferentiated stem cells into the adult brain as a means of reinstituting developmental processes within areas of damaged neural tissue (e.g., stem cells into the spinal cord in individuals who are paralyzed from spinal cord injury).

Cells differentiate into neurons in the middle of the brain surrounding the neural tube and ventricles. However, these cells must migrate outward to form various brain structures. Once cells have migrated to their appropriate place in the nervous system, axons form and begin to grow toward distant targets. For example, neurons in the motor cortex may send axons all the way down into the spinal cord to synapse on motor neurons there. Mechanisms for stimulating and guiding cell migration and axonal growth are topics of intensive

study. An example of a congenital brain abnormality related to a failure of appropriate axonal growth is agenesis of the corpus callosum, a condition in which the axons that are supposed to cross between the two cerebral hemispheres do not find their way and, instead, end up traveling toward the back of the brain.

Another important developmental process is the growth of dendrites and the formation of synapses. An interesting aspect of this process is the overexuberance of dendrite and synapse formation in the first two years of life, and the subsequent loss of dendrites and synapses. It is thought that this loss of dendrites and synapses represents brain differentiation based on experience, such that connections that get incorporated into information processing and memory circuits survive, and the others do not survive.

A final developmental process is the progressive increase in myelinization of axons that, in some systems (e.g., the interhemispheric axons of the corpus callosum), are still increasing in myelinization well into the second decade of life. The myelin sheath allows a neuron to transmit actions potentials more rapidly and efficiently. Thus, myelinization of axons contributes to increased cognitive processing speed and power.

Sensory and motor neuroscience

This domain of neuroscience studies the way sensory information (vision, hearing, etc.) is received, coded, and recognized by the nervous system, and the means by which the nervous system controls motor activity in service of both reflexive and purposive movement.

The largest volume of work in sensory neuroscience has involved vision. What is becoming clear from this research is that different properties of the visual signal are processed by separate brain areas. In the cortical area that first receives visual signals, there are different cellular systems for detecting light-dark boundaries and for coding color. As information is further processed, there are separate cortical areas for processing complex visual properties: the parietal lobe for visual guidance of movement, the inferior temporal lobe for object recognition, and a superior temporal area for spatial analysis. Similar processes occur in the processing of sound, touch, and pain. The existence of multiple visual processing areas raises an interesting question regarding how these various sensory properties are reconnected to create a unified percept. This problem is known as the binding problem, a problem that has yet to be solved.

Motor systems are studied by neuroscientists all the way from simple reflexes controlled by the spinal cord, to the voluntary control of skilled movement initiated and regulated by the motor cortex and various subcortical structures. One of the knotty issues in the study of motor activity is determining the modes by which spinal cord reflexes, more complex innate motor responses (such as eating, drinking, sleeping, fear, aggression, etc.), learned habitual behaviors, and conscious voluntary activity are all coordinated with each other and with important vestibular, propriocpetive, and visual sensory information.

Regulatory neuroscience

Regulatory neuroscience studies widely distributed neural and hormonal systems by which the brain influences bodily systems both to insure homeostasis and to prepare the body for particular forms of response to the environment. These neural systems provide regulatory control of breathing, cardiac function, food intake and metabolism, water intake and retention, stress responses, reactions to pain, and sexual development and activity. Regulatory neuroscience overlaps with research in developmental neuroscience with respect to hormonal influences on growth, sexual differentiation, and brain development. The class of regulatory substances called neuromodulators lies somewhere between the direct neural control of bodily systems carried out by the autonomic nervous system, and the release of hormones into the blood stream by the brain's pituitary gland. Neuromodulators are substances that act like synaptic transmitters, but which are released into extracellular space bathing large areas of the brain in order to regulate the general level of activity in specific brain systems.

Another important phenomenon studied within regulatory neuroscience is the interactions between psychological states, brain function, and the activity of the immune system (called psychoneuroimmunology). This research focuses on a number of recently discovered ways by which the neural activity that constitutes certain psychological and affective states (such as responses to stress, general levels of depression or distress, or a sense of well-being) can affect the activity level of the immune system. This area of research is beginning to explain why the belief that one is receiving a beneficial treatment has such a ubiquitous and powerful positive effect on health and recovery from illness (i.e., the placebo effect).

Behavioral and cognitive neuroscience

One of the most significant scientific trends of the latter half of the twentieth century has been the joining of cognitive science and neuroscience into a field called cognitive neuroscience. This field studies the role of various neural systems in complex forms of thought and behavior such as attention, object recognition, spatial orientation, skilled motor activity, language production and comprehension, arithmetic, music, historical (episodic) memory, and the affective-cognitive aspects of social perception.

Methodological developments were an important catalyst for this merger. During the first two-thirds of the twentieth century, methods for studying brain processes contributing to more complex cognition was limited to studies of changes in the behavior of animals created by lesions made in different areas of the brain, or elicited by electrical stimulation of various brain structures. It was also possible to record electrical activity from the depths of the brain of behaving animals. Investigation of human cognition was generally limited to study of individuals with various forms of brain damage, or to brain wave recordings from the scalp.

Technical advances in the methodologies available to neuroscience have remarkably enhanced the ability of investigators to study complex human cognition. Most notable has been the development of the various forms of neuroimaging: computer assisted tomography (CAT), magnetic resonance imaging (MRI), functional MRI (fMRI), positron emission tomography (PET), and single photon emission computed tomography (SPECT). These methods provide the cognitive neuroscientist with noninvasive ways of viewing the structure of the nervous system (CAT and MRI), or the relative level of functional activity of various brain areas (fMRI, PET, and SPECT) in an alive, awake, and mentally active human being.

One example of the kinds of studies that can be done with neuroimaging methods is a 1999 study that compared PET scans taken while Italian-,

French-, and English-speaking dyslexic individuals were attempting to read. This research demonstrated that, despite the fact that reading disability took somewhat different forms in the different languages, there was nevertheless a consistent area of diminished brain activity during reading (in the left temporal lobe). This study illustrates the capacity of neuroimaging to reveal, non-invasively, characteristics of human brain processing that occur during a complex cognitive task, such as reading, in normal and cognitively impaired individuals.

Clinical neuroscience

Much of the early history of the field of neuroscience involved the study of individuals with brain damage or brain disease. Studies of patients with epilepsy, brain tumors, traumatic brain damage, or brain diseases (e.g., multiple sclerosis, Parkinson's disease, and Alzheimer's disease) have contributed much to new ideas and theories about how the brain works.

A few individual cases in clinical neurology have been particularly influential. For example, in 1861 Paul Broca (1824–1880) described a patient who had suddenly lost his speech, but was otherwise cognitively normal. The patient has been called "Tan" in the literature, since "tan" was the only word the patient could utter. Autopsy of the brain of this patient showed a lesion of the left frontal lobe, suggesting that this frontal area, subsequently called Broca's area, was important for expressive language. Similarly, a single case referred to in the literature by the initials "H. M." made a substantial contribution to the understanding of explicit, episodic memory. In 1953, H.M. underwent neurosurgical removal of the medial temporal lobes of both hemispheres to control seizures. The result was a profound amnesia in which old memories were preserved, but the ability to form new conscious, explicit memories was permanently lost. This case focused intensive neuroscientific study on the role of the hippocampus (a structure of the medial temporal lobe) in memory formation—research that is still ongoing.

The contribution of new ideas about brain function goes not only from clinical cases to basic neuroscience, but also from neuroscience to clinical medicine. All of the areas of neuroscience described above feed critical information into areas of investigation concerned with those human diseases and disorders of the nervous system that are

diagnosed and treated by neurologists, neurosurgeons, psychiatrists, neuroendocrinologists, and neuropsychologists. An example of the impact of basic neuroscience on clinical medicine is the contribution made by studies of the synapse and synaptic transmitters to the development of new drugs that affect the nervous system (neuropharmacology) and behavior (psychopharmacology).

Neuroscientific study of religious experience and moral agency

Most persons identify as most uniquely spiritual their experiences of religious ecstasy and awe—those moments when one feels most transcendent or overwhelmed by the feeling of divine presence. However, the fact that such religious experiences can accompany epileptic seizures (or drug intoxication) has been recognized since ancient times. This observation caused many ancient cultures to associate epilepsy with possession by gods or demons.

There is a significant literature in modern neurology that suggests that in some cases of temporal lobe epileptic seizures, religious experiences result from the abnormal neural activity in the temporal lobes and limbic system. Consistent with the clinical data from temporal lobe epilepsy, investigators have shown that electromagnetic stimulation of the temporal lobes increases the likelihood of experiencing a "sense of presence," leading some investigators to speculate that abnormal temporal lobe activity is the neural basis of all religious experiences.

Other investigators studying the activity of the brain during religious experiences have suggested the importance of other brain areas. Andrew Newburg and Eugene d'Aquili have argued that the sense of diminishment of self and an awareness of oneness with god or the universe that is experienced by some during transcendental meditation or some forms of prayer is associated with diminished activity in the parietal lobes, rather than increased activity in the temporal lobes. These investigators interpret these results as indicating a neural correlate of an absence of the sense of self and the achievement of a sense of "absolute unitary consciousness."

These studies of brain activity during religious experiences at least make it clear that religious experiences (whether feelings of ecstasy, awe, or oneness) have correlates in brain functional states. What is as yet unclear is whether these functional brain states are unique to religious experiences or also occur in similar situations that the person would not report as religious. Is the religious attribution to the experience being studied a matter of the context in which the state occurs, or rather a matter of the particular brain state? Nevertheless, over the last two decades of the twentieth century, there has been increasing interest in the neuroscientific study of religious experiences, such that a new field has taken shape that is being called *neurotheology*.

There has also been considerable neuroscientific study of the processes involved in moral decision-making and moral behavior. A long history of cases from clinical neurology has pointed to the important role of the medial frontal cortex in interpersonally responsible action and moral behavior. Important work by Antonio Damasio has strongly suggested that deficits in these areas involve absence of the unconscious elicitation of negative and positive emotions in relationship to contemplated behaviors, and that the medial frontal cortex is important in triggering emotional reactions to contemplated actions. In a similar vein, fMRI studies of persons attempting to solve moral dilemmas have suggested that areas of the brain involved in emotion are activated to the degree that the particular moral dilemma would demand direct action toward another person.

Philosophy of neuroscience

As is evident in what is described above, neuroscience as a field is committed, to a greater or lesser degree, to four basic philosophical positions: empiricism, physicalism, reductionism, and determinism. Like all science, neuroscience is empiricist in attempting to learn what is true through systematic observations and experimentation. However, neuroscientists might differ regarding whether empiricism is the only contributor to knowledge of truth. Physicalism maintains that human (or animal) mind and behavior are the product of the physical activity of the nervous system. While some neuroscientists might have an extra-scientific commitment to body-soul or mind-body dualism, neuroscientific theory and research would not admit the concept of any nonmaterial entity. Reductionism refers to at least two different positions. Methodological reductionism is merely the idea of breaking more complex things into parts and studying the parts, such as studying changes in synaptic efficiency as a part of what happens in the brain during learning.

Causal (or explanatory) reductionism presumes that the causes of any particular mental or behavioral event can be found in more and more elementary mechanisms, such that eventually all mental activity is explainable in a bottom-up manner by chemistry and physics. Some neuroscientists have begun to adopt the concept of non-reductive (or top-down) causal principles emerging within complex systems such as the brain, thus loosening the grip of causal reductionism on neuroscience. However, methodological reductionism is still a predominant principle within the field. Finally, determinism suggests that the physical state of the brain at one point in time is entirely determinative of the immediate future activity of the brain. Certainly, much research in the neurosciences proceeds as if current brain activity is predictive of future brain (mental) activity. However, neuroscientists differ with respect to the question of existence of conscious agency or free will. There is, as yet, no generally accepted theory as to how conscious agency might emerge from brain activity, or how such agency would create a nonreducible causal influence on the processes studied by molecular neuroscience.

See also ARISTOTLE; CONSCIOUSNESS STUDIES; DETERMINISM; EXPERIENCE, RELIGIOUS: COGNITIVE AND NEUROPHYSIOLOGICAL ASPECTS; EXPERIENCE, RELIGIOUS: PHILOSOPHICAL ASPECTS; MIND-BODY THEORIES; MIND-BRAIN INTERACTION; NEURAL DARWINISM; NEUROPHYSIOLOGY; NEUROPSYCHOLOGY; NEUROTHEOLOGY; PHYSICALISM, REDUCTIVE AND NONREDUCTIVE; PLACEBO EFFECT; PSYCHOLOGY

Bibliography

Adelman, George, ed. *Encyclopedia of Neuroscience.* Boston and Stuttgart, Germany: Birhäuser, 1987.

Bechtel, William; Mandik, Peter; Mundale, Jennifer; et al. eds. *Philosophy and the Neurosciences: A Reader.* Malden, Mass.: Blackwell, 2001.

Brown, Warren S., Murphy, Nancey; and Malony, H. Newton. *Whatever Happened to the Soul? Scientific and Theological Portraits of Human Nature.* Minneapolis, Minn.: Augsburg Press, 1998.

Damasio, Antonio. *Descartes' Error: Emotion, Reason, and the Human Brain.* New York: Putman, 1994.

Damasio, Antonio. *The Feeling of What Happens: Body and Emotion in the Making of Consciousness.* New York: Harcourt, 1999.

D'Aquili, Eugene, and Newburg, Andrew B. *The Mystical Mind: Probing the Biology of Religious Experience.* Minneapolis, Minn.: Fortress Press, 1999.

LeDoux, Joseph. *The Emotional Brain: The Mysterious Underpinnings of Emotional Life.* New York: Touchstone, 1996.

Libet, Benjamin; Freeman, Anthony; and Sutherland, Keith, eds. *The Volitional Brain: Toward a Neuroscience of Free Will.* Thorverton, UK: Impact Academic, 1999.

Greene, Joshua D.; Sommerville, R. Brian; Nystrom, Leigh E.; et al. "An fMRI Investigation of Emotional Engagement in Moral Judgement." *Science.* 293, no. 5537 (2001): 2105–2108.

Kandel, Eric R.; Schwartz, James H.; and Jessell, Thomas M., eds. *Principles of Neural Science,* 3rd edition. Norwalk, Conn.: Appleton & Lange, 1991.

Kolb, Bryan, and Whishaw, Ian Q. *Fundamentals of Human Neuropsychology.* New York: W.H. Freeman, 1996.

MacKay, Donald M. *Behind the Eye.* Oxford: Basil Blackwell, 1991.

Pansky, Ben, and Allen, Delmas J. *Review of Neuroscience.* New York: Macmillan, 1980.

Paulesu, Eraldo; Démonet, Jean-François; Fazio, F.; et al. "Dyslexia: Cultural Diversity and Biological Unity." *Science* 291, no. 5511 (2001): 2165–2168.

Russell, Robert J; Murphy, Nancey; Meyering, Theo; and Arbib, Michael A., eds. *Neuroscience and the Person: Scientific Perspectives on Divine Action.* Vatican City: Vatican Observatory Publications, 1999.

Saver, Jeffery L., and, Rabin, John. "The Neural Substrates of Religious Experience." *Journal of Neuropsychiatry* 9 (1997): 498–510.

Zigmond, Michael J; Bloom, Floyd E.; Landis, Story C.; et al., eds. *Fundamental Neuroscience.* New York: Academic Press, 1998.

WARREN S. BROWN

NEUROTHEOLOGY

The term *neurotheology* refers to the attempt to integrate neuroscience and theology. Depending on whether its subject matter is defined in terms of religiosity or human personhood, neurotheology may be divided in two main lines of research.

The first line of research was dominant during the 1970s and 1980s when Eugene d'Aquili, Charles Laughlin, and others attempted to relate neuropsychology to religious phenomena, for example, by looking for the neuropsychological determinants of ritual behavior. Researchers also studied the psychological characteristics linked to dominance of the left or right hemisphere of the brain in relation to various patterns of belief and images of the divine. John Ashbrook suggested the term *neurotheology* for this type of inquiry.

Since the 1980s, the search for specifiable brain structures and brain functioning in correlation to religious or mystical experiences has come to the foreground. Along this line, Michael Persinger as well as Vilayanur Ramachandran have claimed a direct relation between religious experience and temporal lobe activity. Persinger interprets this relationship atheistically, but others point out that it validates neither an atheistic nor a theistic conclusion.

D'Aquili and Andrew Newberg have gone considerably beyond the temporal lobe hypothesis by developing a model for religious experiences that involves the entire brain. This model is based in part on non-invasive neuroimaging of the working brain during ritual behavior and meditation. It is especially this kind of work that is commonly labelled *neurotheology*. Its aim is to explore the question of how religion and God are perceived and experienced by the human brain and mind. This research has revealed that during meditation and worship, the level of activity in those parts of the brain that distinguish between the self and the outside world is diminished. D'Aquili and Newberg regard their research not only as neuroscience but also as a contribution to theology because they feel that it will bring all the elements of religion under one rational explanatory scheme, namely that of neuroscience.

The second line of research concerns a portrayal of human personhood, which is both neuroscientifically and theologically accurate. The neuroscientific discourse on the human person, increasingly vocal since "the decade of the brain" (1990–2000), seems to be at variance with theological discourse on that subject. In the latter, mind and soul, free will, consciousness, responsibility, and the human being's contact with God are thought to be fundamental characteristics of the human person. In neuroscience, all of these are either seriously doubted or reduced to their underlying material relationships.

This second type of neurotheology aims at improving the compatibility of theology and neuroscience with regard to the concepts of human personhood. Here, conceptual analyses, such as the analysis of free will, and concepts from the philosophy of mind, such as supervenience, play an important role. The work of the international research group co-sponsored by the Vatican Observatory and the Center for Theology and the Natural Sciences in Berkeley, California, represents this type of inquiry. Beyond compatibility, this "neurotheology of the person" also aims at the mutual enrichment of theology and neuroscience. Whereas the latter may help theology incorporate materiality in its conceptions of human personhood, theology may stimulate neuroscience to be mindful of the more holistic or synthetic characteristics of being human.

See also COGNITIVE SCIENCE; CONSCIOUSNESS STUDIES; EXPERIENCE, RELIGIOUS: COGNITIVE AND NEUROPHYSIOLOGICAL ASPECTS; EXPERIENCE, RELIGIOUS: PHILOSOPHICAL ASPECTS; FREEDOM; NEUROSCIENCES; PRAYER AND MEDITATION; SOUL

Bibliography

Ashbrook, James B. "Neurotheology: The Working Brain and the Work of Theology." *Zygon* 19 (1984): 331–350.

D' Aquili, Eugene G., and Newberg, Andrew B. *The Mystical Mind: Probing the Biology of Religious Experience.* Minneapolis, Minn.: Fortress Press, 1999.

Persinger, Michael A. "Religious and Mystical Experiences as Artifacts of Temporal Lobe Function: A General Hypothesis." *Perceptual and Motor Skills* 57 (1983):1255–1262.

Russell, Robert John; Murphy, Nancey; Meyering, Theo C.; and Arbib, Michael A.; eds. *Neuroscience and the Person: Scientific Perspectives on Divine Action.* Vatican City State: Vatican Observatory; Berkeley, Calif: Center for Theology and the Natural Sciences, 1999.

PALMYRE OOMEN

NEW PHYSICS

The term *new physics* refers to a range of fundamental developments and paradigm shifts that occurred in the physical sciences during the last half of the twentieth century. These include the theory of quarks, which is essential to the standard model of fundamental particle physics; the study and application of macroscopic manifestations of quantum phenomena such as superconductivity, superfluidity, lasing, and other types of spontaneous quantum self-organization; the realization of electroweak unification and the quests for grand and total unification of the four fundamental interactions; the burgeoning successes in gravitational physics, including gravitational wave and black hole physics; and inflationary, fundamental-particle, and quantum cosmology, which ultimately rely on total unification and quantum gravity schemes.

Another component of the new physics is the study of chaos and complexity, which involves modeling complex physical processes using nonlinear, often dissipative, deterministic mathematical systems in which there is extreme sensitivity to initial conditions, leading to loss of predictability, the importance of top-down causality together with a lack of reducibility to more fundamental systems and processes, and the emergence of higher-level self-organization out of lower-level erratic behavior. Some of the key features of the new physics are the fundamental indeterminism at the basis of all quantum phenomena due to the Uncertainty Principle, and the appearance of one of more levels of global chaotic or self-organizing behavior accompanied by radical unpredictability and irreducibility in complex systems, such as fluid turbulence, weather systems, and the dynamics of insect populations.

See also COSMOLOGY, PHYSICAL; GRAND UNIFIED THEORY; PHYSICS; PHYSICS, QUANTUM

Bibliography

Davies, Paul. "The New Physics: A Synthesis." In *The New Physics,* ed. Paul Davies. Cambridge, UK: Cambridge University Press, 1989.

WILLIAM R. STOEGER

NEWTON, ISAAC

When a tiny and frail boy was born in the obscure Lincolnshire hamlet of Woolsthorpe on Christmas Day 1642, the attendant maids did not believe he would survive the hour, let alone eighty-four years. As it was, Isaac Newton went on to become a Fellow of Trinity College and the Royal Society, Cambridge's second Lucasian Professor of Mathematics, the author of the *Principia mathematica* (1687) and the *Opticks* (1704), a member of Parliament, Master of the Royal Mint, a knight and President of the Royal Society. When he died in 1727, he was given a state funeral and buried in a place of honour at Westminster Abbey. His work in physics gave us universal gravitation, a mathematical explanation for the elliptical orbit of planets, and a precise celestial mechanics that still serves the world in the space age. His optical experiments confirmed the heterogeneous nature of white light, and he constructed the first practical reflecting telescope. He discovered calculus and showed more than any other thinker before him how well mathematics could explain the workings of the universe. Hagiographic celebrations of Newton in the years and decades after his death ensured his fame as an enduring icon of science and as having produced one of the greatest revolutions ever in the study of nature. But the range of his intellectual endeavour was even broader than this. What is less well known is that for more than half a century Newton was carrying out a private revolution in theology.

Newton's science and his religion

When the young Cambridge-educated clergyman Richard Bentley was called upon in 1692 to deliver the first Boyle Lectures for the defence of Christianity against infidelity, he buttressed his natural theological arguments for the existence of God with support from Newton's *Principia*. While revising his lectures for the press, he wrote the author of the *Principia* to determine if his deployment of its physics would meet the approval of the great man himself. In his first reply to Bentley Newton confirmed: "When I wrote my treatise about our Systeme I had an eye upon such Principles as might work wth considering men for the beleife of a Deity & nothing can rejoyce me more then to find it usefull for that purpose." Newton went on and asserted that "ye diurnal rotations of ye Sun & Planets as they could hardly arise from any cause purely mechanical ... they seem to make up that harmony in ye systeme wch ... was the effect of choice rather than of chance."

Even though Newton's letters to Bentley were published in 1754 and thus became part of the public record, the *Principia*'s original theological backdrop receded in the wake of the profoundly successful Enlightenment portrayal of Newton,

which made him the patron saint of the Age of Reason. It was in the eighteenth century that the still-common association between Newton and the secular clockwork universe emerged. Yet the notion of a self-sustaining clockwork universe, originally wound up at the beginning by a remote deity, is precisely the sort of view of creation and providence that Newton himself opposed in the General Scholium, which portrays the biblical "Lord of Lords" as a personal God with an ongoing, interventionist relationship with creation. Enlightenment apologists and later positivist scientists also developed the two variations of the "Two-Newton" thesis: first, that Newton only turned to theology with old age and dotage (and thus after the "first Newton" had produced his great works of science) and, second, that Newton kept his science separate from his religion in a kind of early modern anticipation of methodological naturalism. Although the vestiges of the second variant of the Two-Newton thesis can still be found in current literature, the recent availability of Newton's long-inaccessible manuscripts for study has made such claims untenable. A steadily increasing body of scholarly literature is both explicating Newton's theological views (the main contours of which were mainly in place *prior* to or around the time of the appearance of his *Principia*) and revealing ways in which his theology interacted with his natural philosophy. Although some of the conclusions will remain tentative until the manuscript corpus has been thoroughly analyzed, the view of Newton now emerging is that of a natural philosopher who was both profoundly religious and who saw no firm cognitive barrier between theology and the disciplines now called scientific. Isaac Newton the natural philosopher cannot be understood apart from his religion.

Newton's theology and prophetic studies

In addition to being the preeminent natural philosopher in the West in the late seventeenth and early eighteenth centuries, Newton was a theologian and prophetic exegete in his own right. It is also now known that he left behind one of the largest corpora of theological writings in the early modern period (totaling as much as four million words). In his zeal to plumb the depths of biblical theology and comb the records of the early church, Newton far out-stripped all but a few of his contemporaries, including those known as divines or religious figures in the first instance. Newton himself was to remain a lay member of the Church. When Newton became a Fellow of Trinity College, Cambridge, he was obligated to become ordained as a priest in the Anglican Church by 1675. The impending deadline was likely one motivation for the initiation of a comprehensive study of Christian theology and ecclesiastical history that began by the early 1670s. But as the deadline neared, Newton sought ways to avoid taking holy orders. An eleventh-hour exemption from ordination (granted by no less a personage than King Charles II) allowed him to avoid the resignation of his fellowship, which he had been prepared to do. Whatever academic reasons Newton may have had for avoiding ordination, theological discoveries that he made by the early 1670s made ordination (and subscription to the Anglican Thirty-nine Articles) impossible. Among the results of Newton's early theological studies was the conclusion that Christianity's chief doctrine, the Trinity, was a corruption deviously imposed on the Church in the fourth century by Athanasius.

Newton gravitated toward the position of the fourth-century Arians who, according to Trinitarian historiography, were the doctrinal losers in the Christological controversies of that era. As in Arianism, Newton viewed the Father as the only true God, while Christ was of a lesser status and nature, albeit pre-existent before his appearance on Earth. But Newton's Christology was not precisely isomorphic with Arianism, and his discomfort over the Athanasian injection of the Greek notions of essence and substance into Christian theology extended to the Arians, who conceived of Christ as being of similar substance (*homoiousios*) to the Father, while the Athanasian Trinitarians saw Christ and the Father as of the same substance (*homoousios*). In his stress on the moral rather than the essential relationship between the Father and Son Newton's theology shows affinities with that of the seventeenth-century Socinians and English Unitarians, some of whose works were in his library. It is also evident that Newton's powerfully monotheistic conception of a unipersonal "God of dominion" owes something to Hebraic and Judaic thought.

Nor did Newton's heresy stop here. By the early 1690s his study of key biblical texts led him to reject the orthodox doctrine of the soul's natural immortality in favour of a mortalist viewpoint. For Newton such texts as Psalms 6:5 and Ecclesiastes 9:5 and 9:10 demonstrate that there is no intermediate conscious state between death and resurrection. Around the same time Newton concluded that demons (thought by many in his day to be departed spirits) in the Bible were not literal evil spirits, but rather delusions or distempers of the mind. Similarly, Newton rejected the belief that Satan is a fallen angel, asserting instead that the devil is a symbol of human lust and ambition. His final position on the devil is almost identical to the Jewish teaching of *yetzer ha-ra* ("the evil inclination"), in which sinful desires are personified as Satan. Newton's conception of human temptation thus shifted from a focus on external and ontologically real evil spirits to a psychology of the inner demons of the mind.

Denial of the Trinity was illegal in Newton's day and for many years afterward. The rejection of the soul's immortality was viewed as scandalous and the denial of evil spirits was seen, ironically, as tantamount to atheism. Until his dying day Newton hid these maligned heresies from the notice of all but a few trusted confidants. Although kept secret, Newton's heterodox theology was at the core of his existence and helped to shape many aspects of his thought, including his natural philosophy. While heretical from the perspective of traditional Christianity, these departures from orthodoxy do not make Newton into some sort of protodeist. On the contrary, Newton was a fervent biblicist who always cast his theological language in scriptural terms and supported his views amply with biblical texts. Newton's friend the philosopher John Locke, who was also a lay student of the Bible, once referred to Newton as "a very valuable man not onely for his wonderful skill in Mathematicks but in divinity too and his great knowledg in the Scriptures where in I know few his equals." Newton knew his Bible; he believed it too.

No true deist adheres to the literal fulfilment of biblical prophecy, and Newton was nothing if not passionate about just that. Newton wrote his first monumental treatise on the Apocalypse in the 1670s and continued to study prophecy until his death. He was fascinated by the symbols of biblical prophecy and methodically developed a lexicon of prophetic emblems. He also produced studies of the architectural structure of the Jerusalem Temple. Following Cambridge's Joseph Mede, Newton's eschatology was premillenarian. Newton believed that the Jews would be restored to Israel, the Temple rebuilt in Jerusalem, and that Christ would return to the earth in the future to set up a terrestrial Kingdom of God (which he put off to no sooner than the twentieth century). As with his theology, Newton's prophetic views were virulently anti-Catholic. Newton departed from most of his contemporary Protestant prophetic exegetes, however, in placing the doctrine of the Trinity at the center of the great apostasy.

The fulfilment of prophecy also provided Newton with one of the best lines of evidence for the existence of God. In his posthumously published *Observations* (1733), he wrote that "the event of things predicted many ages before, will … be a convincing argument that the world is governed by providence." At the same time, he looked askance at exegetes who overconfidently set dates, believing that such enthusiasm inevitably brought discredit on Christianity when the predicted dates failed. When speaking about a particular prophecy in his *Observations,* he wrote: "The manner I know not. Let time be the interpreter."

Religious motivations for Newton's natural philosophy

Newton's theology related to his natural philosophy at two levels. First, in a general way Newton's piety and religious beliefs acted as a stimulus to the study of nature (the weak relationship between science and religion). Second, in some cases the particulars of Newton's theology helped shape the cognitive content of his physics and mathematics (the strong relationship between science and religion). Beginning with examples of the first type, Newton had imbibed the seventeenth-century Protestant culture of natural theology and, like the chemist Robert Boyle, saw himself as a priest of nature. Manuscripts dating from around the time of the *Principia* indicate that Newton believed the priests of the Ur-religion (for Newton a prescriptive ideal) were also adept natural philosophers. The study of nature, then, was intrinsically related to piety and could itself be a form of worship and devotion. Religion and piety served as a stimulus to unravel the secrets of nature. Newton's adherence to the Renaissance notion of the *prisca sapientia* (lost ancient wisdom) served as one common motivator of both his natural philosophy and his religion, with Newton striving to recover the original, pure manifestations of both. Like other natural philosophers of his age, Newton believed that natural philosophy had as one

of its chief ends the understanding of God and his attributes. Thus, he held that one aim of experiment, which he promoted assiduously as President of the Royal Society, was to discover God's attributes. Moreover, because he also was committed to the *topos* of the Two Books—that God has revealed Himself in both the Book of Scripture and the Book of Nature—Newton employed similar methods of analysis in his natural philosophy and his theology. Analogies between Newton's prophetic hermeneutics and his natural philosophical methodology may also be explained by his commitment to the Two Books. Newton used the distinction between the absolute and relative in both his science (to distinguish absolute and relative time and space) and his theology (e.g., to distinguish between the absolute and relative use of the term *God*). In his theology Newton adhered to an epistemological dualism in which he divided knowledge into open and closed levels. This esoteric-exoteric divide, which may owe something to Newton's involvement in alchemical networks, was also operative in his natural philosophy. Other examples of the weak relationship could be cited. For example, Newton's animosity toward Jesuit critics of his optics can be illuminated by an understanding of his theologically inspired animus against Catholicism.

Newton's aforementioned letters to Bentley confirm his adherence to natural theology. Newton's belief in the argument from design was given public acknowledgement when he added his General Scholium to the conclusion of the second edition of the *Principia* in 1713. In this new appendix Newton states confidently that "This most elegant system of the sun, planets, and comets could not have arisen without the design and dominion of an intelligent and powerful being." The theological part of the General Scholium concludes with the claim that discoursing of God "from phenomena is certainly a part of experimental philosophy" ("natural philosophy" in the third edition of 1726). This was not Newton's only public articulation of the design argument; the later editions of his *Opticks* also conclude with powerful expressions of natural theology. In one of his unpublished papers he wrote that "God is known from his works," thus confirming a natural theological empiricism that he shared with such contemporaries as Boyle. In a document dating from the early 1690s, Newton stated: "there is no way (without revelation) to come to the knowledge of a Deity but by the frame of nature." There was also an apologetic edge to Newton's use of the design argument, and in one place he wrote that "Atheism is so senseless & odious to mankind that it never had many professors," and then went on to speak about symmetry and unity in nature, citing the fact that animals share homologies in their physiological structures.

Newton's adherence to the Two Books tradition is made plain in his early treatise on the Apocalypse, where he argues that the same "God of order" who embedded simplicity in creation also ensured that the fundamental meaning of biblical prophecy would be simple. This analogy between parsimony in Scripture and nature helps explain why Newton believed that similar inductive methods could be utilized in the interpretation of both Books:

> It is the perfection of God's works that they are all done with the greatest simplicity. He is the God of order not confusion. And therefore as they that would understand the frame of the world must indeavour to reduce their knowledg to all possible simplicity, so it must be in seeking to understand these visions.

For Newton all truth (God's Word and God's Works) is a unity because all Truth comes from the same, powerful Deity.

Newton's theology and the content of his natural philosophy

Examples of the weak relationship between theology and natural philosophy in Newton's career serve as the substratum for cases of the strong relationship, which has only recently begun to be presented by scholars with force. It goes without saying that interaction between matters of faith and facts of nature should be entirely plausible for a scholar who was committed to the Two Books tradition and for whom there were no rigid methodological or conceptual barriers between theology and natural philosophy. Nevertheless, the strong relationship is more difficult to convey and, while certain examples (such as Newton's conception of space as the divine *sensorium*) are transparent, some case studies used to confirm it still require further investigation and refinement.

First, it is evident that some examples of the weak relationship or analogies, on closer inspection, lead into strong ones. This is the case with the symmetry between Newton's prophetic hermeneutics and his natural philosophical methods, for Newton's rules of reasoning in the final edition of the *Principia* appear to have been related to or even based in part on his rules of prophetic interpretation, which were written decades earlier. And the analogy between the methods of interpretation in both these disciplines is itself based on Newton's conception of God. Just as René Descartes used God to guarantee deductive logic, so Newton employed the guaranteeing God to support his use of induction. For Newton natural philosophers can use inference in experimental philosophy precisely because the faithful God of order allows one to expect parsimony in nature and since the unity of creation ensures that specifically observed principles and structures point to universals.

Newton's conception of space and time is thoroughly imbued with a profound sense of God's omnipresence and omnitemporality. For Newton absolute space is rigid and immovable, thus providing a stable frame of reference within which relative motion occurs. All of this is possible because absolute space is coextensive with God's omnipresence, a belief Newton came to in part from his exposure to the Rabbinical notion of God as *māqôm* ("place"). As J. E. McGuire put it, space for Newton was God's "sacred field." Similarly, Newton conceived of absolute time as flowing evenly and uniformly largely because it is coterminus with God's eternal duration. Newton's calculus also depended on his conception of absolute time, which for Newton rested on a belief in God's eternal, evenly flowing duration. God's omnipresence further provided an explanation for the phenomenon of gravity, and in private Newton speculated that God was the upholder of universal gravitation. His notion of attraction may have also owed something to his engagement with alchemical doctrines. Newton saw the deity as a God of dominion who ruled creation directly and continuously, intervening with particular providence when necessary to keep history or nature on track. Here Newton's view of the providence of nature stands in stark contrast to that of Gottfried Leibniz, whose *Supramundana* used his supreme intelligence and perfect foreknowledge to set the world in motion at creation, obviating the need for intervention. The differences between these two views are articulated eloquently in the famous debate between Leibniz and Newton's disciple Samuel Clarke.

Newton's distinction between absolute and relative space and time has a heretical corollary, since in his theology God is equated with immovability and the absolute, and Christ with motion and the relative. It is also likely that Newton's antitrinitarian view of a unipersonal God supported his understanding of the unity of nature. That even the heretical elements of Newton's theology permeated his natural philosophical program is made plain by his General Scholium, which, although an appendix to an ostensibly purely natural philosophical work, is embedded with antitrinitarian biblical hermeneutics, in addition to its more overt anti-Cartesian stance. For Newton, the feigned natural philosophical hypotheses of Descartes are no different than the vain doctrinal hypotheses of Trinitarianism. Corrupt interpretative practices in natural philosophy and theology are linked, just as the correct methods of arriving at Truth are unified. Newton's General Scholium epitomizes his dual reformation, a grand program that sought to restore the original, pure forms of both natural philosophy and religion.

Newton's integrated program for science and religion

The foregoing must not be taken as evidence that it was only the case that Newton's theology informed his natural philosophy, but not the other way around. The same considerations that explain the first dynamic also make the reverse perfectly reasonable. Thus, Newton's methodological approach to the interpretation of prophecy may owe something to his satisfaction with the results of mathematics, although Whiston records that when pressed Newton eschewed the notion that prophecy could be demonstrated. It is also clear that Newton's conception of God was in part based on a possibly unconscious desire to create God in his own image: in his letters to Bentley Newton spoke of the "cause" of the solar system as not "blind & fortuitous, but very well skilled in Mechanicks & Geometry"—a characterization of God in keeping with the views of Galileo and Johannes Kepler before him, and one in which a vestige of Platonism is in evidence.

Newton's published and unpublished writings demonstrate that his religion interacted with his natural philosophy at a high level. Newtonian physics cannot be disentangled from Newtonian theology. Although it is clear that Newton recognized disciplinary and methodological distinctions, the lack of firm barriers within Newton's intellectual life suggests that it is problematic to speak in terms of "influence" of one sphere on another. Instead, Newton's lifework evinces one grand project of uncovering God's truth. Science and religion for Newton were not two completely distinct programs, but two aspects of an integrated whole. For Newton, the unity of truth meant that there was ultimately one culture, not two.

See also CLOCKWORK UNIVERSE; GOD; GRAVITATION; NATURAL THEOLOGY; REVELATION; TWO BOOKS

Bibliography

Dobbs, Betty Jo Tetter. *The Janus Faces of Genius: The Role of Alchemy in Newton's Thought.* Cambridge, UK: Cambridge University Press, 1991.

Force, James E. and Popkin, Richard H. *Essays on the Context, Nature, and Influence of Isaac Newton's Theology.* Dordrecht, Netherlands: Kluwer, 1990.

Force, James E., and Popkin, Richard H., eds. *The Books of Nature and Scripture: Recent Essays on Natural Philosophy, Theology, and Biblical Criticism in the Netherlands of Spinoza's Time and the British Isles of Newton's Time.* Dordrecht, Netherlands: Kluwer, 1994.

Force, James E., and Popkin, Richard H., eds. *Newton and Religion: Context, Nature, and Influence.* Dordrecht, Netherlands: Kluwer, 1999.

Manuel, Frank. *The Religion of Isaac Newton.* Oxford: Clarendon, 1974.

McGuire, J. E. *Tradition and Innovation: Newton's Metaphysics of Nature.* Dordrecht, Netherlands: Kluwer, 1996.

Newton, Isaac. *Observations upon the Prophecies of Daniel, and the Apocalypse of St. John.* London: Darby and Browne, 1733.

Newton, Isaac. *Newton: Texts, Backgrounds, Commentaries,* ed. I. Bernard Cohen and Richard S. Westfall. New York: Norton, 1995.

Newton, Isaac. *The Principia: Mathematical Principles of Natural Philosophy,* trans. I. Bernard Cohen and Anne Whitman, assist. Julia Budenz. Berkeley: University of California Press, 1999.

Osler, Margaret J., ed. *Rethinking the Scientific Revolution.* Cambridge, UK: Cambridge University Press, 2000.

Snobelen, Stephen D. "'God of Gods, and Lord of Lords': The Theology of Isaac Newton's General Scholium to the *Principia.*" *Osiris* 16 (2001): 169–208.

Stewart, Larry. "Seeing Through the Scholium: Religion and Reading Newton in the Eighteenth Century." *History of Science* 34 (1996):123–65.

Turnbull, H. W.; Scott, J. F.; Hall, A. Rupert; and Tilling, Laura, eds. *The Correspondence of Sir Isaac Newton,* 7 vols. Cambridge, UK: The Royal Society at the University Press, 1959–1977.

Westfall, Richard H. *Never at Rest: A Biography of Isaac Newton.* Cambridge, UK: Cambridge University Press, 1980.

STEPHEN D. SNOBELEN

NONFOUNDATIONALISM

Nonfoundationalism (or anti-foundationalism) is a philosophical view that is dialectically defined by its negation of *foundationalism.* Rejecting the asymmetric image of basic (immediately justified, foundational) beliefs that support nonbasic beliefs, nonfoundationalists prefer the image of a web of mutually supporting beliefs, which are mediated through a particular community. Nonfoundationalists in theology have drawn attention to the way in which doctrine operates as an intrasystematic grammar that regulates the form of life of a believing community. Insofar as they reduce doctrinal beliefs to this function, they are susceptible to the same objections that are generally raised against relativistic forms of coherentism and pragmatism.

See also FOUNDATIONALISM; POSTFOUNDATIONALISM

F. LERON SHULTS

NONLOCALITY

See LOCALITY; PHYSICS, QUANTUM

NONREDUCTIVE PHYSICALISM

See PHYSICALISM, REDUCTIVE AND NONREDUCTIVE

NUCLEAR ENERGY

Nuclear energy, strictly conceived, has received rather scant attention within the literature of science and religion. However, if the focus is broadened to include nuclear technology—that is, nuclear energy and nuclear weapons considered together—then there is a modest increase in its treatment.

Benefits and risks

Nuclear energy has long been viewed as an alternative energy source to coal and petroleum, which are currently the principal sources of energy. Coal and petroleum provide efficient sources of energy, but their combustion also generates considerable carbon dioxide that escapes into the atmosphere. Although a few dissenters remain, the vast majority of climatologists hold that the build up of carbon dioxide in the atmosphere creates a greenhouse effect. This greenhouse effect dramatically warms the planet, which leads, in turn, to global climate change, resulting in different impacts on different regions of the planet.

Nuclear energy provides an especially attractive alternative to coal and petroleum because it does not contribute to the concentration of carbon dioxide in the atmosphere. Shifting to nuclear energy could potentially lead to a cleaner, healthier environment without a reduction in the human consumption of energy. However, the benefits of nuclear energy must be weighed against its substantial costs and risks. The principal cost of nuclear energy occurs with the safe disposal of radioactive wastes. In addition to the costs of disposal, there is the risk that nuclear radiation could be released into the environment, either at the nuclear power plant or at the site of waste disposal. Such a release could be accidental, the result of equipment malfunction or human error. There is also the risk of an intentional release of nuclear radiation as an act of terrorism. Whether accidental or intentional, such a release could potentially destroy all biotic life in the affected area and make the area sterile for life for the foreseeable future.

Although as of 2002 there have been no intentional releases of nuclear radiation into the environment, there have been two serious accidents at nuclear power plants. In 1979, there was an accident at the Three Mile Island nuclear power plant in Pennsylvania. There was another accident in 1986 at the Chernobyl nuclear power plant in Ukraine. Although very little nuclear radiation escaped from the Three Mile Island accident, nuclear radiation did escape from the Chernobyl accident, causing substantial ecological damage and the deaths of a number of people.

Theological perspectives

Within the science and religion literature, Ian Barbour provides one of the few focused treatments of nuclear energy in his book *Ethics in an Age of Technology* (1993). Barbour begins his examination with a discussion of risk. If risk is defined as the probability of an accident multiplied by the magnitude of its consequences, then the risk posed by nuclear energy is low, compared to other daily activities, such as driving a car. However, Barbour argues that evaluations of such technological risks must also be influenced by assumptions about human nature and social institutions. Taking a Christian religious perspective, Barbour argues that the individual and social sin inherent in the human condition calls for extreme caution in the development of nuclear energy because the risks and consequences are so high.

Shifting his focus to the safe disposal of radioactive wastes, Barbour identifies three ethical issues. First, Barbour notes that an issue of regional justice arises because radioactive waste disposal imposes extreme risks for a local population in order to provide a national benefit for everyone. Intergenerational justice raises a second ethical issue. The present generation would enjoy the benefits of nuclear energy, but passes on some of the burdens and risks of waste disposal to future generations. Finally, Barbour identifies the loss of public confidence in governments and the energy industry as a third ethical issue. His point here is that historically government and industry have been secretive and have failed to protect the public, rather than being transparent and promoting public discourse concerning the benefits, costs, and risks of nuclear energy. Barbour believes that more promising energy alternatives lie in energy conservation and in the use of other renewal energy sources, such as solar power.

In the 1980s, several religious writers warned that nuclear weapons and nuclear war threatened not only human life but the ecological viability of the planet. Two Christian theologians, Gordon

Kaufman and Sallie McFague, argued further that these interconnected challenges were rooted in what has become a flawed understanding of God's power. In *Theology for a Nuclear Age* (1985), Kaufman argues that the threat of nuclear war and annihilation elicits two contrasting responses from traditional Christian conceptions of God. On the one hand, nuclear annihilation is interpreted in eschatological terms as God's action to bring the present age to an end. On the other hand, the threat of nuclear war is discounted because of the view that an almighty creator God, who loves humans and the rest of creation, would not allow such a disaster to occur. Kaufman notes that both responses have the effect of obscuring and undermining the responsibility that humans have for their actions. While the traditional understanding of God as omnipotent may have been appropriate for earlier times, Kaufman argues that this understanding is no longer appropriate in a nuclear age. In light of the threat of nuclear weapons, Kaufman proposes that Christian theologians need to reconceive of God's power, moving from a dualistic to an interdependent understanding. This would require theologians to rethink their formulation of the symbols "God" and "Christ." McFague concurs with Kaufman's analysis in her book *Models of God: Theology for an Ecological, Nuclear Age* (1987). As alternative models for thinking about God, McFague proposes mother, lover, and friend.

While both Kaufman and McFague were thinking initially of the threat of nuclear annihilation, they both extend their analyses to include ecological concerns. Thus, whether conceived broadly as nuclear technology, or more narrowly as nuclear energy, the literature of science and religion has consistently seen critical ecological implications for the planet.

See also ECOLOGY; ECOLOGY, ETHICS OF; ECOLOGY, RELIGIOUS AND PHILOSOPHICAL ASPECTS; ECOLOGY, SCIENCE OF; GREENHOUSE EFFECT

Bibliography

Barbour, Ian. *Ethics in an Age of Technology.* San Francisco: Harper, 1993.

Kaufman, Gordon D. *Theology for a Nuclear Age.* Manchester, UK: Manchester University Press, 1985.

McFague, Sallie. *Models of God: Theology for an Ecological, Nuclear Age.* Philadelphia: Fortress Press, 1987.

RICHARD O. RANDOLPH

OMEGA POINT THEORY

The concept of the Omega Point in science and religion discussions was introduced by Jesuit paleontologist Pierre Teilhard de Chardin (1881–1955) as a reference to Christ as the final goal of the evolutionary process. The Omega Point Theory, inspired by the language of Teilhard, is quite distinct from Teilhard's original idea. This theory was put forward by physicist and mathematician Frank Tipler in a series of articles in the late 1980s and popularized in his 1994 book *The Physics of Immortality*. Tipler theorizes that all matter will converge to an infinite all-knowing point at the end of a closed universe and that this point to which the universe is moving is the Omega Point. This Omega Point is the "god" that necessarily exists but is not the personal God of traditional theism.

See also CLOSED UNIVERSE; COSMOLOGY; TEILHARD DE
  CHARDIN, PIERRE

Bibliography

Tipler, Frank J. *The Physics of Immortality: Modern Cosmology, God, and the Resurrection of the Dead.* New York: Doubleday, 1994.

MARK WORTHING

OMNIPOTENCE

Divine omnipotence means that God possesses all power and potency without any external limitation. The notion of omnipotence indicates a basic principle for the description of divine agency within monotheistic thought. However, in a monistic and emanative conception of God (e.g., as the perfect One in the philosophy of Plato and Plotinus, or Baruch Spinoza's idea of the intrinsic unity of perfection, necessity, and reality), there is no need of divine action. Within theism, divine omnipotence means the power to do all possible things that are not contrary to God's will and knowledge. The concept of God is often characterized by omnipotence in the description that God is the all-determining reality (Wolfhart Pannenberg), although others regard omnipotence as a projection of human desires onto an illusory, usually male, godhead (Sigmund Freud).

The idea of omnipotence comprises not only the actual reign over all human history as *Pantokrator* (the Septuagint translation of the Hebrew *YHWH Sebaoth* [Psalms 24:10], meaning "the almighty" and "the ruler of all things"), but also God's unlimited potential for agency (Augustine of Hippo), and for that reason it is religiously an argument for trusting God's guidance of salvation history. Therefore, it relates the concepts of creation and providence; the omnipotent God sustains the created reality. Since medieval theology, a distinction is made between the *potentia absoluta* (by which God can effectuate all non-self-contradictory possibilities) and the *potentia ordinata* (power limited by God's decision to create and maintain the orders of nature and of grace). God's creative power is neither exhausted by creating the natural order nor determined by it but makes room for the miraculous. The notion of ordained power signifies the complete absence of arbitrariness in God's agency. Sometimes theologians and philosophers neglected the religious meaning of omnipotence by speculating on the boundaries of God's absolute power, whether, for example, laws of logic or mathematical principles were created and maintained by divine power like the laws of nature (René Descartes). Although the notorious paradox of the stone (can an omnipotent being make a stone that it cannot lift?) seems to contradict the possibility of divine omnipotence, it is more a curious puzzle that has, however, a theologically more important equivalent. That is: Can the omnipotent God create people who are agents with a free will without simultaneously losing the control of the course of human history?

This question relates to the problem of evil: Can one believe in God almighty who is simultaneously omniscient and perfectly good, and who creates human agents with moral freedom and responsibility, and who permits suffering in the world? Is such a concept of divine omnipotence consistent? Process theologians, like Charles Hartshorne, try to avoid this dilemma by claiming that God's power is finite and limited by the freedom and power of human creatures. This kind of balance, however, presupposes a quantitative distribution of power at the same level, whereas providence entails divine omnipotence sustaining the created power at a different level. The so-called "free will defense" argues that the possibility of evil is given with the human reality of moral responsibility (Alvin Plantinga). This concept is compatible with God providing room for human freedom by limiting divine omnipotence (i.e., by not permanently actualizing it in all its respects). But it does not touch the problem of natural evil (diseases, floods, etc.). In light of this, the question can be raised whether we may refer to God as *perfectly* good when this same God created a universe in which moral and natural evil are possibilities. Moreover, when we consider the possibility that this may be a universe over which God, after the act of creation, has no further control, and thus cannot influence the outcome of events, we might consider such a God morally blameworthy for taking the initiative of creation.

See also AUGUSTINE; CREATION; DESCARTES, RENÉ; DIVINE ACTION; EVIL AND SUFFERING; FREEDOM; FREE WILL DEFENSE; FREUD, SIGMUND; GOD; MIRACLE; OMNISCIENCE; PLATO; PROCESS THOUGHT; PROVIDENCE; THEODICY

Bibliography

Case-Winters, Anna. *God's Power: Traditional Understandings and Contemporary Challenges.* Louisville, Ky.: Westminster Press, 1990.

Freddoso, Alfred J., ed. *The Existence and Nature of God.* Notre Dame, Ind.: University of Notre Dame Press, 1983.

Hartshorne, Charles. *Omnipotence and Other Theological Mistakes.* Albany: State University of New York Press, 1984.

Van den Brink, Gijsbert. *Almighty God: A Study of the Doctrine of Divine Omnipotence.* Kampen, Netherlands: Kok Pharos, 1993.

LUCO J. VAN DEN BROM

OMNIPRESENCE

The divine attribute of omnipresence is the theological interpretation of God's hiddenness, whose presence in history is unlimited and transcends local space. Concepts like transcendence, immanence, agency, knowledge, indwelling, place, and spiritual substance are basic to omnipresence. God's omnipresence is an active presence, which means that creation and providence find their place within God's creative presence. Classical theology distinguishes omnipresence by virtue of power, knowledge, and being. Divine power fills everything and God's being is by nature wholly present in all things, therefore God's place is where the divine power and activity manifests itself as dynamic omnipresence. Divine presence by virtue of knowledge means that every entity is created in accordance with divine ideas and is thus mentally present to God.

After the demythologization of "heaven above," the question is how to imagine the relation between the divine sphere and the world of human experience. Is God's presence spatial or nonspatial? An answer to this question depends on the theory of space people handle. One can distinguish idealistic, realistic, and relational theories. An idealistic theory of space denies the independent existence of space, but holds that one's observing capacity arranges objects spatially. A realistic theory holds that space exists independently of the objects therein or of any observer. A relational theory claims that space is given with objects in their mutual relations, as the order of coexistent things.

Three theories interpret God's omnipresence by means of a realistic theory of space. *Absolute monism* imagines that God and created reality coincide (Baruch Spinoza: *Deus sive natura*). *Organic monism* interprets the relation between God and the world as a psychosomatic unity, thus the world is God's body. God is both present in and all over the world and transcends the world at the same time (Grace Jantzen; process theology). *Spatial dualism* conceives God's omnipresence as extended in absolute space without coinciding with the created world. God is thought of as active everywhere and therefore God is also substantially present everywhere as an omnipresent non-material substance (*no actio in distans,* Isaac Newton).

Traditionally theologians have thought of God's active presence as the universal, nonspatial, sustaining principle that prevents disintegration (Anselm of Canterbury), or as the nonspatial, spiritual cause of the hierarchy of created causes (Thomas Aquinas). Because God is "simple" or nondivisible, God is, as a whole, in every place (Augustine). Although these theologians presuppose a realistic theory of space, their view appears to be compatible only with idealistic theory.

Given the scientific picture of the world, God's omnipresence is imagined as God's own space (Karl Barth). With reference to mathematical conceptuality in natural science one can picture three-dimensional space as a subspace of an infinitely higher dimensional space in which God exists (Karl Heim). Now omnipresence means that within God's own space of an infinite number of dimensions, God is present in every position in three-dimensional space. Thus, God is simultaneous with all objects in three-dimensional space, without being contained by this three-dimensional space or four-dimensional space-time (Luco van den Brom).

See also AUGUSTINE; GOD; MONISM; NEWTON, ISAAC; THOMAS AQUINAS

Bibliography

Alexander, H. G., ed. *The Leibniz-Clarke-Correspondence.* Manchester, UK: Manchester University Press, 1956.

Barth, Karl. *Church Dogmatics* (II. 1, Section 31). Edinburgh, UK: T&T Clark, 1957.

Fuerst, Adrian. *A Historical Study of the Doctrine of the Omnipresence of God in Selected Writings between 1220–1270.* Washington D.C.: Catholic University of America Press, 1951.

Jantzen, Grace M. *God's World, God's Body.* London: Darton, Longman, and Todd, 1984.

Taliaferro, Charles. *Consciousness and the Mind of God.* Cambridge, UK: Cambridge University Press, 1994.

Thomas Aquinas. *Summa contra Gentiles* (III. 68), trans. Anton C. Pegis; J. F. Anderson; V. J. Bourke; and C. J. O'Neil et al. Notre Dame, Ind.: Notre Dame University Press, 1975.

Thomas Aquinas. *Summa Theologiae* (Ia. 8), ed. Timothy McDermott. London: Blackfriars, 1970.

van den Brom, Luco J. *Divine Presence in the World: A Critical Analysis of the Notion of Divine Omnipresence.* Kampen, Netherlands: Kok Pharos; Louvain, Belgium: Peeters, 1993.

van den Brom, Luco J. "As Thy New Horizons Beckon: God's Presence in the World." In *Understanding the Attributes of God,* eds. Gijsbert van den Brink and Marcel Sarot. Frankfurt am Main, Germany: Peter Lang, 1999.

LUCO J. VAN DEN BROM

OMNISCIENCE

Omniscience concerns God's (a priori) knowledge about the course of people's lives. More generally, it concerns God's knowledge about the whole course of history, including the future. This appears in that aspect of prophetical literature that expresses itself in a forecasting style, which, in turn, rests upon divine foreknowledge.

In the biblical literature, knowledge of the future is a distinctive characteristic of God over against pseudo-gods. In Christian theology, the notion of omniscience refers to the property by which God knows all past, present, and future things and all events, including all their circumstances and boundary conditions. Omniscience encompasses both the actual and possible things and events in past and present, but it includes knowledge of the possibilities that will be actualized as well as those that will not be actualized. Divine knowledge is therefore perfect as absolutely true. But characteristic of divine omniscience is also its immediate (intuitive) nature: It will never be discursive by means of any mediating epistemological process of experience and deduction.

The classical notion of divine omniscience states that God knows all events in past, present, and future simultaneously—in one perspective, from the eternal (timeless) stance outside of time. Therefore, God knows all things "from eternity" at once because this knowledge transcends every temporal order, including that of its epistemological object, for example, the temporal course of the historical process, as discussed by the Roman philosopher Boethius (c. 480–524) and the Christian theologians Augustine of Hippo (354–430) and Thomas Aquinas (c. 1225–1274). Boethius's metaphor describes the all-knowing God outside time like a person who stands on the top of a mountain and sees what happens along the road in the valley. That person sees, as it were, simultaneously the past, the present, and the future of people walking along the road. A similar type of simultaneity was also defended by Wolfhart Pannenberg (1928–). Within omniscience one distinguishes a *scientia necessaria* (knowledge about God and about all possibilities) and a *scientia libera sive visionis* (complete knowledge or vision of actual reality in past, present, and future).

One conceptual difficulty of this interpretation of divine omniscience concerns its epistemological range: Is experiential or existential knowing possible for an intuitively knowing God? Another difficulty: Is knowledge of a nonexistent future real knowledge? Knowledge of the future is conceivable in an atemporal ontology, but that makes time-experiences illusionary. Apart from that, such a reality seems to be determined because of the co-existence of past, present, and future. How is human freedom related to God's eternal knowledge of it? Is human moral responsibility in such a reality a real option? So-called incompatibilists will answer in the negative: Absolute timeless divine foreknowledge is incompatible with human freedom. Therefore, some of them argue against absolute foreknowledge whereas others use it against human freedom. Compatibilists will answer in the affirmative: Human freedom and absolute foreknowledge are compatible. Some of them will argue that there are alternative interpretations of a *scientia media* (middle or consequent knowledge about what each creature would freely do in any possible situation) that might solve the problem of compatibility.

See also GOD

Bibliography

Craig, William Lane. *The Only Wise God: The Compatibility of Divine Foreknowledge and Human Freedom.* Grand Rapids, Mich.: Baker Book House, 1987.

Fischer, John Martin, ed. *God, Foreknowledge, and Freedom.* Stanford, Calif.: Stanford University Press, 1989.

Kvanvig, Jonathan L. *The Possibility of an All-Knowing God.* Houndmills, UK: Macmillan, 1986.

Pike, Nelson. "A Latter-day Look at the Foreknowledge Problem." *International Journal for Philosophy of Religion* 33 (1993): 129–164.

Swinburne, Richard. (1993). *The Coherence of Theism.* Oxford: Oxford University Press, 1993.

Zagzebski, Linda Trinkaus. *The Dilemma of Freedom and Foreknowledge.* New York: Oxford University Press, 1991.

LUCO J. VAN DEN BROM

ONTOLOGICAL ARGUMENT

Ontological arguments attempt to establish the existence of God by relying on one's concept of God, or the definition of the word *God,* without involving truths known through experience. Such arguments have had many proponents in the history of philosophy, notably Anselm of Canterbury (1033/34–1109) and René Descartes (1596–1650), as well as many detractors, including Thomas Aquinas (c. 1225–1274) and Immanuel Kant (1724–1804). Today ontological arguments are widely considered flawed, but exactly what is wrong with them remains a matter of controversy.

The *locus classicus* is chapter two of Anselm's *Proslogion,* where he calls attention to the idea of a being greater (more excellent) than any other conceivable being, that is, the idea of a maximally great being. Anselm maintains that even those who reject the existence of a maximally great being still possess the concept of one. Now—and this is the key premise—if there were no maximally great being, one could conceive of something even greater than it by conceiving of a maximally great being *that exists.* But it involves a contradiction to say that one can conceive of a being greater than a maximally great being. Hence, absurdity results from the supposition that God does not exist.

A common response focuses on an assumption behind the key premise, namely that something can be greater than another thing simply by virtue of existence. What is one to make of this thesis? It appears to be false for the simple reason that a comparison of greatness requires (at least) two *existing* things to compare. But the proponent of the argument might reply that one can compare things without assuming their existence—for example, the strength of Achilles and Hector. It is therefore important how this is done. Perhaps it simply involves a comparison of the relevant concepts. Then the key premise means, "If nothing in existence corresponded to one's concept of God, one could generate a superior concept by representing God as existing." But this seems false; one's initial concept, which failed to correspond to anything, might well have been the concept of God-as-existing.

More plausibly, to compare the greatness of two things without assuming that they exist is to ask which of them would be greater if both were to exist. But if to compare the greatness of two things they must both be thought of as existing, existence itself cannot be considered a respect in which they differ in greatness. Thus, as Immanuel Kant argued, existence is not a "perfection"; it is not a property that can contribute to something's greatness.

There are at least two ways to avoid this objection: (1) one could claim that some objects of thought possess a mode of being distinct from existence; or (2) one could alter the argument to build on the claim that *necessary* existence (rather than *mere* existence) is a perfection.

According to the first approach, there are such things as, for example, unicorns; they just do not exist. They are abstract objects of thought that lack spatiotemporal location and causal powers. Thus, one could really consider the "greater than" relation to involve two entities even if one or both of those entities do not exist. And one can treat existence as a property that enhances the greatness of something after all.

Another general objection to the ontological argument, however, causes problems for this approach. Could one not use reasoning similar to Anselm's in order to establish the existence of all kinds of things? Consider the idea of an island greater than any other island that can be conceived. Since such an island can be the object of one's thoughts, it must (on this view) be an abstract entity, even if it lacks existence. If it does lack existence, however, one could think of a greater island, namely an island that also exists. So a maximally great island must exist. But (unfortunately) the greatest conceivable island does not exist, so the argument form cannot be sound. This parody was conceived by the monk Gaunilo, a contemporary of Anselm's.

Replying to Gaunilo's parody, Anselm insisted that the argument form can only establish the existence of that which is greatest or most perfect *simpliciter,* and not the most perfect island or bluebird. The argument form, he suggests, will only work if the concept one begins with is that of a being that could not have failed to exist. But all islands and other material objects are the sorts of things that could be destroyed. A rejoinder might alter the parody to involve the idea of a spiritual entity with almost every perfection (e.g., a godlike being lacking only a certain amount of knowledge but nevertheless a necessary being).

Inspired by passages in Anselm that suggest a different kind of ontological argument, some proponents avoid the above dispute by focusing on God's necessary existence rather than on God's existence. This is the approach of Charles Hartshorne, Norman Malcolm, and Alvin Plantinga. For anything to count as God, they argue, it would have to be absolutely perfect. But anything that exists and yet might not have existed is thereby deficient in some way. So if God exists, God exists necessarily; it could never be that God just happens to exist. Now, one can think of a necessary being as something that exists according to all the ways the world might have been, or "possible worlds." So either God exists in every possible world or in none. But this means that, so long as it is possible that God exists, God actually exists; after all, the way things actually are is one of the ways things can be. Thus, the argument forces a dilemma between the necessity of God's existence and its impossibility.

The key question, then, is whether the existence of God (conceived of as a necessary being) is even possible. Certain philosophers have held that possibility is something conceptual, and that unless the concept of God is somehow incoherent, the existence of God is possible. Thus Charles

Hartshorne has argued that either God exists or else the term *God* is meaningless or self-contradictory. And on the face of it, the existence of God certainly does not appear to be incoherent, like the existence of a round square. It seems perfectly conceivable.

The trouble is that the nonexistence of God also seems conceivable. And if it were even possible—assuming that God is by definition a necessary being—it would follow that God does not exist. So it would appear that the link between conceivability and possibility in this case is tenuous. And philosophers today are widely in agreement that states of affairs may be metaphysically impossible without involving any absurdity that is accessible to a priori reflection. So it is hard to see how one can assess the possibility of God's existence unless one has reason to affirm or deny God's actual existence, which is the point at issue.

See also COSMOLOGICAL ARGUMENT; GOD, EXISTENCE OF

Bibliography

Adams, Robert Merrihew. "The Logical Structure of Anselm's Arguments." *The Philosophical Review* 80 (1971): 28–54.

Hartshorne, Charles. *Man's Vision of God and the Logic of Theism*. New York: Harper, 1941.

Kane, Robert. "The Modal Ontological Argument." *Mind* 93 (1984): 336–350.

Lewis, David K. "Anselm and Actuality." *Noûs* 4 (1970): 175–188.

Oppy, Graham. *Ontological Arguments and Belief in God*. Cambridge, UK: Cambridge University Press, 1995.

Plantinga, Alvin. *The Ontological Argument from St. Anselm to Contemporary Philosophers*. New York: Doubleday, 1965.

van Inwagen, Peter. "Necessary Being: The Ontological Argument." In *Philosophy of Religion: The Big Questions,* eds. Eleonore Stump and Michael J. Murray. Oxford and Malden, Mass.: Blackwell, 1999.

DAVID MANLEY

ONTOLOGY

Ontology is the study of being, insofar as being is possessed by any kind of entity. Although the term *ontologia* derives from the early seventeenth century, ontology is as old as philosophy itself. While German mathematician and philosopher Christian Wolff (1679-1754) identified ontology with *metaphysica generalis* (inquiry into the general categories of being), the relationship between ontology and metaphysics has become less precise. Some believe the two synonymous; others hold that while metaphysics deals with the nature and structure of all *possible* being, ontology only concerns actually *existing* beings. Ontological questions permeate the science-religion conversation; for example, what is the ontological status of the divine, and of putative emergent properties (e.g., the mental)?

See also METAPHYSICS

DENNIS BIELFELDT

OPEN UNIVERSE

Within standard Big Bang cosmology the universe is considered to be "open" if it contains insufficient matter to produce enough gravitational pull to stop its present expansion. In so-called Friedmann type universes (from mathematician Alexander Friedmann's [1888–1925] calculations based on Einstein's theory of relativity) only three universes are possible: the closed, in which the universe has sufficient matter to cause its recollapse; the flat, in which the universe will only just avoid recollapse; and the open. For the purposes of scientific eschatology, flat and open universe models lead to similar ends, namely, an eternally expanding universe that finally ends in heat death when all energy sources are exhausted. While most cosmologists are pessimistic about the long-term prospects for life and intelligence in such a universe, some hope has been offered. The problem and possibility of life in the remote future within an open universe was treated by Freeman Dyson (b. 1923) in 1989. For life to exist indefinitely in such a universe, however, Dyson suggests that it must either hibernate for very long periods or evolve into large clouds of dust carrying positive and negative charges that enable it to organize and communicate via electromagnetic forces. This vision is far removed from the heavenly existence postulated by many traditional religions.

See also CLOSED UNIVERSE; COSMOLOGY, PHYSICAL ASPECTS

Bibliography

Dyson, Freeman. "Time without End: Physics and Biology in an Open Universe." *Review of Modern Physics* 51, no. 3 (1989): 447–460.

Milne, E. A. *Modern Cosmology and the Christian Idea of God.* Oxford: Clarendon Press, 1952.

MARK WORTHING

ORDER

In most religions the world is believed to be an embodiment of divine wisdom. Paradoxically, the divine is both present (immanent) and absent (transcendent). This paradox is expressed in a hierarchy of degrees of manifestation of divine wisdom, each representing a kind of order. Further, both the natural and the moral order are seen as normative. In the Abrahamic religions order is created and, therefore, dependent on the creator. Since order is a manifestation of divine wisdom, it reveals knowledge about God. Accordingly, the created order has been seen as a unity in diversity, a machine, a work of art, or an embodiment of reason, beauty, and goodness. Disorder invaded the natural and the moral order, which require re-creation. In the Gnostic religions, however, disorder originates from an evil creator who battles a good redeemer. In response, the early Christian theologian Irenaeus (c. 130–200) emphasized that the creator and redeemer are one God who controls disorder and restores order. John Calvin (1509–1564) added that the created order required constant divine support to protect it from collapse into disorder: It could not exist independently. In contrast, for the theologian John Haught (1942–), disorder is the price God paid to grant freedom and independence to the created order.

Kinds and hierarchy of order

Science, philosophy, and theology recognize different kinds of order, as well as an order for the different kinds of order:

(1) One kind of inanimate order concerns energy. It refers to interactions with irreversible cause and effect relationships (heat melts ice).

(2) The order of life involves complexity. A complex sequence of molecules (DNA) carries information, which is transmitted from parent to offspring in a causal genetic relation. Mutations are not directed by the environment or the needs of the organism. This random order of mutation and the nonrandom order of natural selection produces organisms that are adapted to their environment.

(3) The order of reasoning involves the self-reflective awareness of norms for making distinctions, such as the principle of identity and the principle of the excluded third, as well as norms for correct arguments.

(4) The spiritual order concerns one's relationship with the divine. It is often characterized as a form of love, as it is, for example, in Hinduism and in the Abrahamic religions. These kinds of order represent ways in which entities exist, as well as ways in which people experience them.

The kinds of order are integrated in a hierarchy of order. In living things, the order of complexity, such as that of DNA, requires the order of energy with its chemical interactions, but chemical interactions do not require the complexity of living things. In a scientific explanation, the order of reasoning requires the order of sensation, but sensation does not require knowledge. In religious faith, the spiritual order of love requires the order of reasoning with its distinctions, but not vice versa. Thus, any kind of order is a necessary but insufficient condition for a higher kind of order. The complete hierarchy of kinds of order is found in persons and includes number, space, motion, interaction, life, sensation, perception, reasoning, human relations, lingual expression, legality, morality, and spirituality. Further, the order of life is not reducible to the order of energy. Nor can reasoning be reduced to sensation, or love to reasoning.

Entities can be ranked according to their highest kind of order, producing a hierarchy of entities. Chemical reactions exchange energy, but they do not transmit information to offspring. Plants transmit information to offspring, but they do not have knowledge. Animals have knowledge, but no spirituality as people do. Thus, the highest order in which entities function is the order of energy for chemical reactions, the order of life for plants, the order of knowledge for animals, and the order of love for people.

Order in the science-religion dialogue

One necessary condition for a mutual relevance of scientific and religious perspectives on order is that it is interpreted as divine action in the world. This, however, is not sufficient because a religiously interpreted order can be explored in science apart from its religious meaning (methodological atheism). Or the creator may be seen as utterly other than the created order so that what is known about nature is irrelevant for what could be known about God and vice versa (Eastern Orthodoxy, voluntarism in Western Christianity and Islam).

One sufficient condition for mutual relevance is that religious views of natural order serve in science as presupposition, sanction, motive, criterion for theory choice, criterion for the choice of kinds of explanation (regulative principle), or as part of explanations (constitutive principle), and vice versa. The rejection by Albert Einstein (1879–1955) of the probabilistic view of quantum physics was regulated by his belief that "God does not play dice." In reverse, the switch from a fixed to an evolving order of nature has motivated the development of evolutionary theologies and has constituted new conceptions of God, creation, divine grace, divine power, and redemption. For instance, instead of conceiving of divine power as a coercive force it is seen as persuasive love because divine love implies giving the universe the freedom to produce itself. Here, the biological idea of random mutation has been translated into the religious idea of a nature free from divine coercion.

A different type of sufficient condition is met in reductionism. In it a scientific definition of order is generalized into a metaphysical ideal of order. For instance, the empiricists as well as the neo-positivists reduced the cognitive order to the order of sensation. Since God cannot be known by sensation, knowledge of God is not possible and religion is reduced to belief without grounds in knowledge. This places knowledge and belief in different categories preventing a cognitive relationship between them. Similarly, biologist Edward O. Wilson (1929–) replaced a spiritual description of God as a being independent of matter with a naturalistic description: God is nothing but an objectification of the imagination. This was his way of including God in a kind of order that science can deal with by gathering empirical evidence. By re-describing God, sociobiology changed the content of religious belief and theology.

A third kind of sufficient condition is satisfied when a reduced view of order functions as religion (scientism). Biology functioned as (anti-)religion when biologists Jacques Monod (1910–1976) and Richard Dawkins (1941–) interpreted the randomness of mutations to mean that there is neither God nor purpose or when Wilson wrote that scientific materialism and evolutionism are his substitute religion in which the purpose of life is to promote evolutionary progress. This substitute religion motivated his re-description of God and, thereby, constituted the content of sociobiological explanations of religion. Here, science as a substitute religion influences religion.

See also HIERARCHY; NATURE

Bibliography.

Clouser, Roy A. "A Sketch of Dooyeweerd's Philosophy of Science." In *Facets of Faith and Science*, Vol. 2: *The Role of Beliefs in Mathematics and the Natural Sciences: An Augustinian Perspective,* ed. Jitse van der Meer. Lanham, Md. The Pascal Centre and University Press of America, 1996.

Haught, John F. *God after Darwin: A Theology of Evolution.* Boulder. Colo.: Westview Press, 2000.

Lovejoy, Arthur O. *The Great Chain of Being: A Study of the History of an Idea.* New York. Harper, 1936.

McGrath, Alister E. *The Foundations of Dialogue in Science and Religion.* Malden, Mass., and Oxford: Blackwell, 1998.

Midgley, Mary. *Science as Salvation: A Modern Myth and Its Meaning.* London and New York: Routledge, 1992.

Nasr, Seyyed Hossein. *Religion and the Order of Nature.* New York and Oxford: Oxford University Press, 1996.

Peacocke, Arthur. *Theology for a Scientific Age: Being and Becoming—Natural, Divine and Human.* Enlarged edition. London: SCM Press. 1993.

Stenmark, Mikael. *Scientism: Science, Ethics, and Religion.* Aldershot, UK, and Burlington, Vt.: Ashgate, 2001.

Torrance, Thomas F. *Divine and Contingent Order.* Oxford: Oxford University Press. 1981.

Torrance, Thomas F. *The Christian Frame of Mind: Reason, Order, and Openness in Theology and Natural Science.* Colorado Springs, Colo.: Helmers and Howard, 1989.

van der Meer, Jitse M. "The Engagement of Religion and Biology: A Case Study in the Mediating Role of Metaphor in the Sociobiology of Lumsden and Wilson." *Biology and Philosophy* 15 (2000): 669–698.

JITSE M. VAN DER MEER

ORIGINAL SIN

See EVIL AND SUFFERING; FALL; SIN

ORIGIN OF LIFE

See LIFE, ORIGINS OF

ORIGIN OF UNIVERSE

See BIG BANG THEORY; COSMOLOGY; COSMOLOGY, PHYSICAL ASPECTS; T = 0

ORTHODOXY, EASTERN

See CHRISTIANITY, ORTHODOX, ISSUES IN SCIENCE AND RELIGION

P

PAIN

See EVIL AND SUFFERING; THEODICY

PALEOANTHROPOLOGY

Paleoanthropology is an umbrella term for the diverse group of sciences contributing to the knowledge of human evolution, generally interpreted to include not only studies of extinct (and, in evolutionary contexts, living) humans and their exclusive ancestors and relatives, but also of the wider biological framework within which the hominid family exists. At the core of paleoanthropology are the paleontologists who study human fossils, and the archaeologists who investigate the behavioral record of ancient humans. They are complemented by paleoenvironmentalists, taphonomists, dating specialists, functional anatomists, paleodemographers, molecular geneticists, and a host of others who contribute to producing as well-rounded a picture as possible of the background from which humans emerged.

See also EVOLUTION, HUMAN; PALEONTOLOGY

IAN TATTERSALL

PALEONTOLOGY

Paleontology is the branch of science devoted to the understanding of past life as revealed by the fossil record. Normally, when an organism dies, its physical remains are scattered and destroyed by the elements in a short span of time. Such elements include not only wind, weather, and decay, but also water and the activities of carnivores and scavengers of many kinds. Occasionally, however, bony remains (and, very exceptionally, some soft tissues) lying on the surface or in superficial cavities may be covered by accumulating sediments (most often river or lake muds in the case of terrestrial organisms, and sea-bottom particulates in that of marine forms) before they are totally destroyed. Among the remains that escape destruction, complete articulated skeletons are extremely rare; more commonly preserved are individual bones and teeth, often broken. Unless the enclosing sediments are chemically hostile, or become melted by heat from the Earth's interior or pressure from above, bones thus incorporated into the accumulating sediment pile can survive more or less indefinitely, though their distortion due to local Earth movements is not uncommon. As water carries minerals in solution through both the sediments and the contained animal or plant remains, the organic constituents of those remnants become replaced by minerals, in a process most often known as mineralization. If erosion of the enclosing sediment pile subsequently sets in, the now-fossilized remains may become exposed once more at the Earth's surface, where they are yet again subject to the forces of natural destruction. However, for a brief period they are also available to be collected by human beings, who have been picking up unusual re-exposed objects for the last few hundred thousand years, at least.

Fossils are found all over the world, and are a vast storehouse of information about past life.

Those who professionally find fossils and extract such information from them are known as *paleontologists.* From the very beginning, paleontology has been integral to the study of Earth history, which began with attempts to order the sedimentary rocks, laid down by water and wind, which contain fossils. The other grand categories of rocks exposed on the Earth's surface include igneous rocks (extruded from Earth's molten core by volcanoes and by the physical rising through the solid crust of lighter rocks such as granite), and metamorphic rocks, which are sedimentary rocks that have been recrystallized by pressure and heat. Volcanic rocks are particularly helpful in dating the ages of various events in Earth history because reliable techniques exist by which to measure the time that has elapsed since they last cooled. These techniques depend on the phenomenon of radioactivity, by which unstable forms of certain elements "decay" to stable states at known rates. Volcanic rocks do not contain fossils themselves (unless you count as fossils such things as the vacuities in the shape of human bodies found at Pompeii, or the ancient hominid footprints at Laetoli), but they represent single points in time and are often interleaved among sedimentary fossil-bearing layers, which can be dated by reference to them.

Early history

The basic principles of the study of sedimentary rocks were established by the Danish-born naturalist and physician Nicolaus Steno (1638–1686) in the mid seventeenth century. These principles state that all stratified sedimentary rocks—however distorted they may subsequently have become—started life as horizontal bands of sediments and that they were laid down in sequence, with the oldest layers at the bottom and the youngest at the top. Such layering is usually readily visible in local sedimentary basins, but there is a problem in correlating the strata that are exposed in different basins and geographical areas. This is the context within which fossils entered the picture. The fossil record clearly shows that past time has been characterized by a long succession of distinctive *biotas,* or communities of organisms; it was the resulting diagnostic assemblages of fossils that were seized upon by early stratigraphers as the key to ordering regionally exposed rocks into their temporal sequences.

During the early years of the nineteenth century, the engineer and geologist William Smith (1769–1839) demonstrated in England that sedimentary units could be identified by their distinctive fossil content. At about the same time in France, naturalist Georges Cuvier (1769–1832) worked out the sequence of sedimentary units in the Paris Basin using fossil terrestrial vertebrates as markers, and showed that many large animals had no living counterparts. In doing the latter, Cuvier made extinction a reality to be contended with. And he went farther, showing that as the rocks became younger they contained faunas steadily more similar to those of today. He concluded that this pattern revealed an advancing complexity of life, but he was unable to find gradations among the various faunas preserved in the Paris Basin (where stratigraphic discontinuities are in fact rife, as they are in most terrestrial situations). Instead, he found that distinctive faunas were replaced by other distinctive fossil associations. This suggested to Cuvier that a series of catastrophes had wiped out successive faunas, which were re-created anew after each extinction event. Popular opinion rapidly adopted the last such event as evidence of the Biblical deluge, and conveniently equated the earlier faunas with the biblical "days" of creation.

Thus, improbably, was paleontology born as a science. For several decades following the pioneering work of Cuvier and Smith, paleontologists labored within the confines of biblical constructs even as they gradually built up a robust picture of the Earth's sedimentary history based on an expanding fossil record. During this period the beginnings of specialization within paleontology began to appear, with today's division of the science into *vertebrate* and *invertebrate* branches emerging. The distinction is important, not simply because of the distinctiveness and the rapid swelling of the database in each branch, but because invertebrate paleontology came to be dominated by the study of marine organisms, just as vertebrate paleontology was dominated by terrestrial forms. Neither branch was (or is) exclusively focused on one side or the other of the marine-terrestrial dichotomy, but a subtle difference in outlook was almost inevitably introduced because the marine sedimentary record is much more continuous than its terrestrial equivalent, which is repeatedly interrupted by erosional cycles.

Paleontology and evolutionary ideas

By the time that Charles Darwin (1809–1882) published his epochal *On the Origin of Species* in 1859, the outline shape of the fossil record was fairly well established. Inconveniently well-established, in fact, as far as Darwin was concerned. For while Darwin favored an elegantly simple model of evolution as a more or less straight-line process involving gradual change in living populations from generation to generation under the guiding hand of natural selection, the fossil record itself showed a pattern of discontinuities among *taxa* (a generalized term given to taxonomic units at any rank: species, genera, and more inclusive groupings such as families and orders). There was much early debate over the application of Darwinian ideas to the fossil record. Some scientists, such as the eminent Victorian comparative anatomist Richard Owen (1804–1892), who appropriated the study of the remarkable fossil reptile bones discovered by Gideon Mantell (1790–1852) in the 1820s (and who coined the term *dinosaur*), reacted negatively to Darwin's publication. Owen preferred to see the fossil record as evidence of the unfolding of a divine plan, and clung throughout his life to an essentialist view of species as fixed and unchanging. Others, such as the brash Thomas Henry Huxley (1825–1895), took up the cudgels on Darwin's side, most famously in his debate with Bishop Samuel Wilberforce (1805–1873) in Oxford on June 30, 1860. Huxley supported Darwin's view of fossils as witnesses to a process of gradual transformation of organisms over time—although, significantly, he never managed to place the newly-discovered Neanderthal fossil into this perspective, preferring to interpret it as a lowly form of modern human.

Interestingly, following a scandalized initial reaction to his evolutionary ideas, Darwin's central tenet of "descent with modification," whereby all life forms are related by descent from a common ancestor, became quite rapidly accepted by scientists and public alike. What was not so readily accepted was the mechanism of *natural selection,* which involves the gradual modification of population gene frequencies over long periods of time due to the greater reproductive success of *fitter* individuals, those best adapted to prevailing environments. Indeed, natural selection did not assume its current central place in paleontology and other branches of evolutionary biology until the second quarter of the twentieth century, when the *Evolutionary Synthesis* took biology by storm. The product of agreement among influential geneticists, paleontologists, and systematists, the Synthesis eventually succeeded in reducing virtually all evolutionary phenomena to generation-by-generation changes in gene frequencies. This notion emphasized the linear, transformational, dimension of evolution at the expense of the histories of taxa, and it encouraged paleontologists to ignore the discontinuities in the fossil record that Darwin had been aware of, but had ascribed to the record's incompleteness.

It was not until the 1970s that paleontologists started to realize that perhaps the gaps in the fossil record were actually revealing something after all. Thus was born the notion of *punctuated equilibria* (long periods of stasis interrupted by brief bursts of change), which was presented as an alternative to the *phyletic gradualism* preached by the Synthesis. Paleontologists in general began to realize that the Synthesis, elegant though its simplicities might have been, was incomplete as an explanatory framework for all of the evolutionary phenomena evoked by the fossil record. It turned out, indeed, that although natural selection undoubtedly plays a role in the differentiation of species and in their accommodation to local environments, many other influences enter the evolutionary equation. These include *speciation,* the set of mechanisms by which new species come about, and *competition* among closely and more distantly related species, which involves *extinction* as a regular event. All of this occurs, moreover, within a context of constantly fluctuating environmental conditions. Modern paleontologists are hence much more acutely aware than their predecessors were of the complexities of the evolutionary process and of the roles played in it by competing taxa, as well as by competing individuals.

Hypothesis formation in paleontology

For many years paleontologists pursued their work—of sorting out the relationships among the myriad life forms represented in the fossil record—largely by intuition and the assessment of overall resemblance. Admittedly, this process got them a long way in sketching the outlines of the tree of life, but it did lead to some anomalies. Thus while it may appear counterintuitive to claim that lungfishes are more closely related to cows than to salmon, in terms of ancestry and descent this claim is demonstrably true. Paleontology was thus revolutionized during the 1970s by the widespread introduction of *cladistics,* an approach to comparative biology that provided an explicit recipe for recognizing relationships among taxa. In a nutshell, cladistics argues that only the common possession of derived characters, those inherited from an immediate ancestral taxon, is useful in deducing relationships among taxa. The common possession of primitive attributes, those inherited from more remote common ancestors, shows only that two taxa belong to the wider group descended from that ancestor. Thus having a spine shows simply that you belong to the large taxon of vertebrates, while having three bones in the middle ear indicates that you are a mammal, a member of a taxon that is nested inside that group. The distribution of derived characters within a group is summarized in a branching diagram known as a *cladogram,* which in its simplest form states nothing more than that "taxon *A* and taxon *B* are more closely related by common ancestry than either is to related taxon *C.*" Cladograms are the only statements in systematics that are truly testable.

More elaborate is the *evolutionary tree,* which adds ancestry and descent as well as time to the mix. Trees are more interesting than cladograms, but cannot be tested since the age of fossils has no direct connection to their relationships, and because in theory an ancestor has to be primitive in all respects relative to its descendant, in which case there is nothing to link them. Yet more complex (and more interesting) is the *evolutionary scenario,* in which paleontologists add everything they know about function, environment, adaptation, and so forth to the information present in the tree. Competing scenarios are comparable only on the basis of their plausibility, which makes them inherently unscientific; yet their plausibility can be reasonably objectively judged if they are based on specifically stated cladograms and trees. Scenarios are constructed using a bewildering variety of types of information derived from many different sciences. Paleontologists take into account information derived from *paleoclimatology* (the study of past climates), *taphonomy* (the science of what happens to organic remains after death), *sedimentology* (environments in which fossils were deposited), *stratigraphy* (in the broadest sense, the sequence and relationships of rock strata, and their dating by a host of means), and *functional anatomy* (the study of the morphology of fossil forms, and how they may have functioned in life), to name but a few of the areas that contribute to the most complete understanding possible of the lives,

environments, and relationships of fossil species. *Molecular genetics* has also begun to contribute to our knowledge of affinities among extinct species, and even newer technologies are on the way.

Paleontology in a wider context

Since about 1970, then, paleontology has vastly refined its abilities to teach us about our past and about the broader biological context from which our remarkable species has emerged. Literally, paleontology has played and continues to play a central role in establishing our own place in nature. And the lesson is a humbling one. The living world of today is mind-bogglingly diverse and marvelous indeed, heedless though so many of us are of its welfare. But looking around ourselves today we see only a single slice of time; and when we add the paleontological dimension we can at last begin to glimpse the truly extraordinary richness and majesty of the organic context—creation, if you will—of which we form part.

This recognition of the vastness of nature in time as well as in space has had a profound impact. Since medieval times and probably long before, people in the Western tradition had viewed *Homo sapiens* as the center of earthly creation, around which all else revolved. But paleontology, especially in concert with the more recent revelations of cosmology, has demonstrated that our species is in fact an infinitesimal part of an enormous and still-enlarging universe. Among many members of our egotistical species, the tendency has been to ignore this uncomfortable fact. But it is nonetheless a fact to be faced, and some theologians have sought to reconcile the findings of paleontology with the traditions of Christian theology. The best-known of these was the Jesuit Pierre Teilhard de Chardin (1881–1955), a practicing geologist and paleontologist, whose posthumously published *The Phenomenon of Man* had a particularly broad impact. Teilhard viewed the process through which humanity emerged in teleological terms, envisioning the appearance of human consciousness as the outcome of directed change from a more generalized state, in pursuit of an ultimate union with the "Omega." This latter was taken by many to represent a "cosmic Christ," as the biologist Julian Huxley (1887–1975) put it. Teilhard's arguments are often obscure, but his wide following bears witness to the profound urge that exists among so many to incorporate the perspectives of paleontology into a wider worldview.

See also DARWIN, CHARLES; EVOLUTION, HUMAN; GRADUALISM; LIFE, ORIGINS OF; PALEOANTHROPOLOGY; PUNCTUATED EQUILIBRIUM; TEILHARD DE CHARDIN, PIERRE

Bibliography

Darwin, Charles. *The Origin of Species By Means of Natural Selection* (1859). New York: Bantam Classic, 1999.

Darwin, Charles. *The Descent of Man, and Selections in Relation to Sex* (1871).

Eldredge, Niles. "Testing Evolutionary Hypotheses in Paleontology: A Comment on Makurath and Anderson." *Evolution* 28 (1974): 479–481.

Eldredge, Niles. "Rates of Evolution Revisted." *Paleobiology* 2 (1976): 174–177.

Gould, Stephen J., and Eldredge, Niles. "Punctuated Equilibria Comes of Age." *Nature* 366 (1993): 223–227.

Schwartz, Jeffrey H. *Sudden Origins: Fossils, Genes, and the Emergence of Species.* Chichester, UK: Wiley, 1999.

Schwartz, Jeffrey H. "Homeobox Genes, Fossils, and the Origin of Species." *Anatomical Record* 257 (1999): 15–31.

Tattersall, Ian. *The Fossil Trail: How We Know What We Think We Know About Human Evolution.* New York: Oxford University Press, 1995.

Tattersall, Ian. *Becoming Human: Evolution and Human Uniqueness.* New York: Harcourt, 1998.

Tattersall, Ian. "Paleoanthropology: The Last Half-century." *Evolutionary Anthropology* 9 (2000): 2–16.

Teilhard de Chardin, Pierre. *The Phenomenon of Man.* New York: Harper, 1976.

IAN TATTERSALL
KENNETH MOWBRAY

PANENTHEISM

The term *panentheism* (from the Greek) literally means "all (is) in God." As a concept of God, panentheism attempts to do justice both to divine transcendence (God is beyond or more than the world) and divine immanence (God is in the world). Panentheism maintains that the world is in God, included in the divine life, but that God's reality is not reducible to nor exhausted by the reality of the individuals or the structures of the universe or of the universe as a whole. Thus God is all-inclusive or all-encompassing with respect to being.

Strictly construed this entails that all divine relations are internal relations, that is, relations between God as integrated whole and the creatures as included parts. For panentheism then, while the universe is part of God, God and the universe do not form an undifferentiated whole. Panentheism draws definite distinctions between God as the including whole and the nondivine parts of the universe considered in themselves. Certain properties of divinity, such as *aseity* (self-existence) or necessary existence and the all-encompassing attributes of omnipresence (everywhere present), omniscience (all-knowing), and omnipotence (all power or all-powerful) apply to God but definitely not to individual creatures or to the universe itself. (Note though that process forms of panentheism find the notion of divine omnipotence problematic.)

Another important distinction drawn between God and creatures concerns mutual freedom. Panentheism upholds indeterminism: Spontaneity and free will in the universe mean that antecedent causes do not fully determine present events and actions, so the future is not fully predictable or foreknown, even by God; creatures have real choices. In summary, while God is not an individual simply distinct from the nondivine individuals, in the way, for example, that one human being is distinct from another, neither is God to be equated with the universe or its constituents.

Panentheism as alternative

In construing divine transcendence and immanence as above, panentheism mediates between deism and certain forms of traditional theism on the one hand and pantheism on the other hand, attempting to avoid pitfalls of both. Deism, as developed in the European Enlightenment of the seventeenth and eighteenth centuries, holds that God created the world to operate according to natural laws but is uninvolved in its destiny. The God posited by traditional theism is not as separate from the universe as is in deism; however, panentheists judge what they call *classical theism* to be equally inadequate. Classical theism, in affirming certain divine attributes stemming from ancient Greek philosophy—immutability (unchangeability), impassibility (to be unaffected by another), and eternity (in the sense of strict timelessness)—does not permit God to be in genuine relation to the world.

The term *pantheism* literally means "all (is) God." That is, everything at least in its true essence is divine. Clearly panentheism has affinities with pantheism. American Charles Hartshorne (1897–2000), the principle theological interpreter and developer of process philosophy, at first labeled his concept of God "The New Pantheism." The trajectory of German idealism produced both pantheists and panentheists. One could say that panentheism attempts to get as close to pantheism as possible in stressing the intimate relationship between God and nature, while still maintaining clear distinctions between them. A key difference is that pantheism tends to a (quasi) materialistic or (quasi) substantialistic understanding of God: Entities in the world share the divine essence or substance to a greater or lesser degree. Therefore, any distinction between God as a whole and the constituents of the universe is a matter of degree rather than of kind. In addition, since everything is a mode or attribute of God, pantheism typically denies indeterminate freedom.

The metaphor or analogy of the world as the body of God is popular among panentheists. Hartshorne compares the God-world relationship to that between a person's mind and the cells of its body. Arthur Peacocke (1924–), a key figure in the science and religion dialogue, speaks approvingly of the feminine, womb imagery that panentheism encourages: As with a fetus in its mother, creation is within God. American Christian theologian Sallie McFague (1933–) has been the principal developer of the metaphor of world as body of God. British philosophical theologian Grace Jantzen (1948–), in drawing the connection between God and world so tightly as to jettison indeterminate freedom, offers a pantheistic version of the metaphor.

Some connections with science

Panentheism offers diverse advantages for those interested in the intersection of science and religion. Alfred North Whitehead (1861–1947), in his role as a philosopher of science, and others have observed that the dominant model for the natural world moved from mechanism to organism during the nineteenth century. Panentheism offers an organistic understanding of the God-world relation in contrast to deism's mechanistic understanding. Like deism, panentheism offers a concept of God where natural laws or processes are respected, where God refrains from interventions that overturn nature. The crucial difference is that panentheism posits a God intimately involved, continuously interacting, with the world.

Panentheism's intimate connection of God with a world in time entails a God who in some sense or dimension is also temporal. As the trajectory of modern science—from the Newtonian mechanics of the Enlightenment to evolution to Albert Einstein's theory of relativity—has put an exclamation point on the temporal nature of reality, panentheism offers a consonant concept of the divine.

As indicated above, creaturely spontaneity and indeterminate freedom are crucial for panentheism in its distinction of God from creation. Both quantum mechanics, in stating that the motions of subatomic particles are probabilistic rather than determinable from known antecedent conditions, and chaos theory, in demonstrating the unpredictability of future events, provide openings for panentheists and other supporters of indeterminacy. In particular, Peacocke, a British physical chemist, Anglican priest, and panentheistic theologian, applauds panentheism's picture of a God who is continuously creative in relation to an open universe. It must be noted, though, that no consensus exists among scientists that quantum indeterminacy or, even less, chaos theory unpredictability entail any ultimate indeterminacy in the universe.

Avoiding violation of natural processes is not only a concern of panentheists but of other theologians involved in the science and religion dialogue, including Americans Thomas F. Tracy and Nancey Murphy. It may seem that such thinkers must renounce any traditional Christian notion of special providence, namely, that God causes particular events in natural or human history (in contrast to general providence, that God determines the general laws or processes of the universe), however, this is not uniformly the case.

For example, in his later writings, Peacocke develops his notion of top-down causation, maintaining that divine action with respect to the universe not only upholds general laws or patterns but causes specific events. Whether such divine predetermination is compatible with indeterminate creaturely decisions and their chance interactions is a major difficulty for this viewpoint.

Murphy and Tracy purchase special providence by positing that God determines the probabilistic quantum movements of subatomic particles and that these in turn produce macro-effects that result in specific events. The virtue of this notion is that it contravenes no natural laws or regularities: The quantum events that God determines are within the scientifically permissible ranges of motion, and apparently no conceivable method exists for discerning God's causation on the quantum level. At the same time, this "invisibility" is problematic: That God ultimately causes a valued event (as opposed to, say, an event issuing in tremendous evil) appears to be a matter of blind faith, at least as far as physics is concerned. Other problems for this viewpoint are the speculative nature of the connection between quantum events and macro-effects and, for advocates of indeterminacy and openness, the denial that quantum events are ultimately indeterminate. More broadly, critics of the above approaches might judge them to be backdoor attempts to reintroduce too much transcendent or interventionist causation by God.

Panentheism's history

The term *panentheism* was coined by German idealist philosopher Carl Christian Friedrich Krause (1781–1832). As mentioned above, German idealism, with strong ties to nature romanticism, produced various panentheistic and pantheistic thinkers. The clearest and most fully developed panentheistic model was that of physicist, experimental psychologist, and philosopher Gustav Theodor Fechner (1801–1887). Earlier examples of panentheism or panentheistic tendencies include Western mysticism and Hindu *bhakti* (referring to devotion to a personal god) and its principal theologian Ramanuja (traditional dates, 1017–1137). These examples are not surprising, as mysticism generally softens the creator-creature distinction, while in India that distinction is not drawn as sharply as is typical in Western religions.

Various philosophers and theologians of the twentieth century have been labeled panentheists, including Nicolai Berdyaev, William Pepperell Montague, Paul Weiss, Karl Rahner, and John Mac-Quarrie. While the panentheistic affinities of these thinkers are undeniable, some failed to develop a clear panentheistic model, others promoted ideas contrary to basic premises of panentheism, while still others explicitly refused the label *panentheism* for their thought. Coming out of German idealism, American Paul Tillich (1886–1965), an exile from the Nazis, is regarded as one of the premier theologians of the twentieth century. Tillichians widely acknowledge his panentheism. His famous phrase, "God is not a being, but being-itself," has obvious panentheistic implications. Tillich, who claimed the phrase "eschatological pan-en-theism," was accused by some critics of pantheism, to which he would jokingly respond, "This pantheist is going to take a walk in his garden." Tillich's reluctance to disavow the attributes of divine immutability, impassibility, and eternity compromise his manifest panentheistic intentions, according to American theologian David Nikkel (1952–).

The fullest explicit development of panentheism in the twentieth century came from process thought. Whitehead, a British mathematical physicist and philosopher, originated process philosophy, its theism developed and to some extent modified by Hartshorne. For process thought, reality at its depth is not static being but rather a process of becoming. God is not an exception to, but the highest exemplar of, this ultimate or metaphysical principle. As did Fechner, process thought advocates *panpsychism,* that all integrated entities of the universe possess some degree of sentience or feeling. The fundamental unit of reality for process philosophy is an occasion of experience. God, in the consequent nature for Whitehead or the concrete pole of divinity for Hartshorne, includes all past occasions of experience. Process panentheism emphasizes omniscience and, to coin a word, *omnipathy* (all-feeling). God intimately knows all experience, is affected by, sympathizes with, all feelings. As Whitehead puts it, "God is the fellow sufferer who understands" (1928, p. 351). Whitehead purchases divine transcendence through the primordial nature, which is the reservoir of all possibility. Hartshorne purchases the same through the abstract pole of divinity, which refers to the changeless character of God, namely, that God will always lovingly know and integrate whatever experiences occur in the universe. If the world influences God as object of divine knowledge, God likewise influences the nondivine individuals as object of their awareness, as a lure providing preferences for their actions. To what extent the divine lure only persuades versus constrains decisions as the unavoidable object of awareness is debated by process theologians. What is beyond dispute is the rejection of omnipotence, if interpreted to mean God is all-powerful, which would overthrow indeterminate freedom.

Contemporary issues

McFague, mentioned earlier in relation to feminist divine imagery, has presented one of the most well-known models of panentheism in the late twentieth and early twenty-first centuries. Her development of metaphors for a God in intimate relation with the world enflesh and enhance the sense of the concept of panentheism. On the other hand, her doubts concerning what we can actually know about God pose a potential problem for her panentheism. McFague's minimal Christian theistic claim is that there is a power in the universe on the side of life that is, metaphorically speaking, personal. When McFague adds that this power is many rather than one, critics may question whether God in her concept or metaphor is sufficiently integrated to panentheistically include the universe; critics may question whether there is a difference of substance between her view and American Christian theologian Gordon Kaufman's serendipitous creativity, that *God* should refer to the cosmic and evolutionary forces that have resulted in life and human life rather than to any personal or agential reality. Contrast McFague's outlook to that of Tillich and Hartshorne, who maintained that God is "not less than conscious" or superconscious (while recognizing the anthropomorphic dangers of attributing conscious personhood to God).

Many theologians in the science and religion dialogue affirm some notion of God's sustaining creativity common to the Western religious traditions: Every aspect of every particular constituent of the universe is radically contingent, dependent upon divine power for its continued existence moment by moment. Process theism rejects such an understanding of divine power. Whitehead is clear that both divine and finite occasions of experience are manifestations of the ultimate metaphysical principle of creative synthesis, each such occasion possessing ultimate independence of being. Whitehead reasons that if God were upholding the very existence of occasions, then indeterminate freedom would be overridden and his panentheism would transmute into a pantheism. Christian process theologians, while often neglecting to acknowledge this Whiteheadian perspective on divine power, have not challenged it either. The question for panentheists who wish to retain a notion of divine sustaining activity is this: Can *omnipotence* be defined as "all power" rather than "all-powerful"? Can God panentheistically encompass all power by sustaining and thus empowering the existence of each creature, as an existence with indeterminate freedom? If such a concept is not self-contradictory, then one can avoid pantheism and affirm a notion of divine power more consonant with the all-inclusive logic of panentheism.

See also CHAOS THEORY; DEISM; DOWNWARD CAUSATION; EINSTEIN, ALBERT; GOD; NEWTON, ISAAC; PHYSICS, QUANTUM; PROCESS THOUGHT; PROVIDENCE; THEISM; WHITEHEAD, ALFRED NORTH

Bibliography

Fechner, Gustav Theodor. *Zend-Avesta: Oder ueber die Dinge des Himmels und des Jenseits, Vom Standpunkt der Naturbeschreibung,* 5th edition. Leipzig, Germany: Leopold Voss, 1922. Translated excerpts appear in *Philosophers Speak to God,* ed. Charles Hartshorne and William L. Reese. Chicago: University of Chicago Press, 1953.

Hartshorne, Charles. *Man's Vision of God and the Logic of Theism* (1941). Hamden, Conn.: Archon Books, 1964.

Hartshorne, Charles. *The Divine Relativity: A Social Conception of God.* New Haven, Conn.: Yale University Press, 1948.

Jantzen, Grace M. *God's World, God's Body.* Philadelphia, Pa.: Westminster Press, 1984.

McFague, Sallie. *Models of God: Theology for an Ecological, Nuclear Age.* Philadelphia, Pa.: Fortress Press, 1987.

McFague, Sallie. *The Body of God: An Ecological Theology.* Minneapolis, Minn.: Fortress Press, 1993.

Nikkel, David H. *Panentheism in Hartshorne and Tillich: A Creative Synthesis.* New York: Peter Lang, 1995.

Peacocke, Arthur R. *Intimations of Reality: Critical Realism in Science and Religion.* South Bend, Ind.: University of Notre Dame Press, 1984.

Peacocke, Arthur R. *Theology for a Scientific Age: Being and Becoming—Natural, Divine, and Human,* 2nd edition. Minneapolis, Minn.: Fortress Press, 1993.

Russell, Robert John; Murphey, Nancey; and Peacocke, Arthur R., eds. *Chaos and Complexity: Scientific Perspectives on Divine Action*. Berkeley, Calif.: Center for Theology and the Natural Sciences, 1995.

Tillich, Paul. *The Courage to Be*. New Haven, Conn.: Yale University Press, 1952.

Tillich, Paul. *Systematic Theology*, 3 Vols. Chicago: University of Chicago Press, 1951–1963.

Whitehead, Alfred North. *Science and the Modern World*. New York: Macmillan, 1925.

Whitehead, Alfred North. *Process and Reality: An Essay in Cosmology* (1929), corrected edition, ed. David Ray Griffin and Donald W. Sherburne. New York: Macmillan, 1978.

Whitehead, Alfred North. *Adventures of Ideas*. New York: Macmillan, 1933.

DAVID H. NIKKEL

PANTHEISM

Derived from the Greek words *pan* (all) and *theos* (God), thus meaning "all is God," pantheism is the view that the universe or nature as a whole is divine. In relation to rival views, pantheism is defined as the doctrine that God is neither externally transcendent to the world, as in classical theism, nor immanently present within the world, as in panentheism, but rather is identical with the world.

As a religious position, pantheism holds that nature is imbued with value and worthy of respect, reverence, and awe. As a philosophical position, pantheism is the belief in an all-inclusive unity, variously formulated. Historically, the nature of the unity has been defined quite differently in Plotinus's "One," Baruch Spinoza's "Substance," Georg Wilhelm Friedrich Hegel's "Geist," and Charles Hartshorne's "All-Inclusive Totality." Due to ambiguities in the chief analogies used by philosophers (whole-part; mind-body) the line between pantheistic and panentheistic positions is often difficult to draw. In general, pantheism represents an alternative to the classical theistic notion of God in Western philosophy and theology, and has close counterparts in Taoism, Advaita Vedanta, and certain schools of Buddhism. It is also the *ism* closest in spirit to Native American religions.

Types of pantheism

Two broad types of pantheism may be distinguished: monistic pantheism and pluralistic pantheism. Examples of monistic pantheism are classical Spinozistic pantheism, which devalued the importance of dynamic and pluralistic categories, and Hindu forms of pantheism, which have relegated change and pluralism to the realm of the illusory and phenomenal. In addition, the romantic and idealistic types of pantheism that flourished in nineteenth-century England and America were generally monistic.

The pluralistic type of pantheism is found in William James's *A Pluralistic Universe* (1908) as a hypothesis that supersedes his earlier "piecemeal supernaturalism" in *The Varieties of Religious Experience* (1902). James's conception emphasizes the full reality of insistent particulars, embedded in a complex web of conjunctive and disjunctive relations in which manyness is as real as oneness. Religiously, pluralistic pantheism affirms that evil is genuine, the divine is finite, and salvation, in any sense, is an open question. Further exemplifications of pluralistic pantheism are found in a series of late twentieth-century movements, including James Lovelock's Gaia hypothesis that the earth behaves like a single entity, the deep ecology movement, the feminist spirituality movement, and the New Age movement. In 1990 American historian Catherine Albanese, canvassing diverse forms of pantheistic piety since the early republic, considered nature religion in America "alive and well, growing daily, and probably a strong suit for the century to come" (p. 198).

Challenges to pantheism

The chief challenge to pantheism, according to critics, is the difficulty of deriving a warrant for the criteria of human good. How is one to establish any priority in the ordering of values and commitments if nature as a whole is considered divine and known to contain evil as well as good, destruction as much as creation? In light of this concern, John Cobb and other process theologians recommend a fundamental distinction between creativity as the ultimate reality and God as the ultimate actuality. In this way, the divine character is identified only with the good. Other theologians, like David Tracy, view such a metaphysical distinction as dubious and point out that the denial of any identity between ultimate reality and the divine may foster the view that ultimate reality is not finally to be trusted as radically relational and self-manifesting (Tracy, p. 139). The pantheistic model is capable of countering both of these concerns. On the first point, pantheism underscores the blunt fact that the rain falls on the just and the unjust alike, whatever model of the divine one holds. Critics of pantheism observe that human efforts toward compassion and justice are frequently not reinforced by ultimate reality. Nature is often indifferent to human desires and deaf to moral urgencies. Pantheists say this is indicative of the remorselessness of things, not of the superiority of either the theistic or the panentheistic model. In the second place, by collapsing the distinction between creativity and the divine, pluralistic pantheism does identify the religious ultimate with the metaphysical ultimate, but this identification may or may not entail the further (Christian) specification of ultimate reality as radically relational and self-manifesting. Due to its extreme generality, the pantheistic model is susceptible to multiple specifications of various kinds, on lesser levels of generality as found within the more concrete symbols and images of the world's religious traditions.

For secularist critics, the most significant objection to pluralistic pantheism is the semantic question. Why call it "God" or divine? According to nineteenth-century German philosopher Arthur Schopenhauer, calling nature or the universe God does not explain anything, but only serves "to enrich our language with a superfluous synonym for the word 'world'" (p. 40). Pantheists are apt to concede this point but to urge attentiveness to nature's terrible beauty all the same. In the words of the early twentieth-century American poet Harriet Monroe, "Call the Force God and worship it at a million shrines, and it is no less sublime; call it Nature, and worship it in scientific gropings and discoveries, and it is no less divine. It goes its own way, asking no homage, answering no questions" (p. 454). Recoiling from anthropomorphic mythmaking, modern pantheists like Monroe express astonishment over the way religious creeds impose a name and person-like traits upon the creative force animating the universe. Avoidance of personalistic imagery and preference for vague talk of a "force" in nature is characteristic of contemporary pantheism.

Science and religion

Without using the term pantheism, many people who are not traditionally religious acknowledge the feeling that nature is sacred. While panentheism is a theological construction, pantheism probably has more grass roots appeal among ordinary people, artists, and scientists. As the most important challenge that the sciences pose to traditional religion is their skepticism about the existence of "another world" not of human making or open to human inquiry, supernaturalism is less and less an option among scientifically educated populations. In the engagement of science and religion issues, the relevant religious alternatives tend to reduce either to pantheism or to panentheism. Astrophysicist Carl Sagan spoke for those who prefer a straightforward pantheistic orientation over what they regard as the equivocations of panentheism: "A religion, old or new, that stressed the magnificence of the universe as revealed by modern science, might be able to draw forth reserves of reverence and awe untapped by the conventional faiths. Sooner or later, such a religion will emerge" (p. 52).

See also CREATION; DEEP ECOLOGY; FEMINIST COSMOLOGY; GAIA HYPOTHESIS; GOD; NATURE; SUPERNATURALISM; THEODICY

Bibliography

Albanese, Catherine. *Nature Religion in America: From the Algonkian Indians to the New Age.* Chicago: University of Chicago Press, 1990.

Cosby, Donald. *Wings of the Morning: A Religion of Nature.* Albany: State University of New York Press, 2002.

James William. *The Varieties of Religious Experience* (1902). New York: Scribner, 1997.

James, William. *A Pluralistic Universe* (1908). Lincoln: University of Nebraska Press, 1996.

Levine, Michael P. *Pantheism: A Non-Theistic Concept of Deity.* London and New York: Routledge, 1994.

Monroe, Harriet. *A Poet's Life: Seventy Years in a Changing World.* New York: Macmillan, 1938.

Sagan, Carl. *Pale Blue Dot: A Vision of the Human Future in Space.* New York: Random House, 1994.

Schopenhauer, Arthur. "A Few Words On Pantheism." In *Essays from the Parerga and Paralipomena,* trans. T. Bailey Saunders. London: George Allen and Unwin, 1951.

Tracy, David. "Kenosis, Sunyata, and Trinity: A Dialogue with Masao Abe." In *The Emptying God: A Buddhist-Jewish-Christian Conversation*, eds. John B. Cobb Jr., and Christopher Ives. Maryknoll, N.Y.: Orbis, 1990.

NANCY FRANKENBERRY

PARADIGMS

The word *paradigm* comes from the Greek *paradeigma*: evidence, example, pattern, model, archetype. In linguistics, a paradigm provides an example of a conjugation or a declension. In philosophy, its meanings include an archetype, a standard of measurement, a typical case or suggestive example, and a dominating scientific orientation. The term *paradigm* is frequently used in the social sciences. In popular understanding, *paradigm* often simply means a collection of ideas, a cluster of theories, models or actions representing a guiding idea, or a conceptual framework.

The concept of paradigm since
Thomas S. Kuhn

Thomas S. Kuhn's seminal work *The Structure of Scientific Revolutions* (1962) initiated intense discussions on the concept of paradigm, making the word *paradigm* part of the general intellectual discourse, though not always in the sense intended by Kuhn. According to one of the definitions given by Kuhn, paradigms are "universally recognized scientific achievements that for a time provide model problems and solutions to a community of practitioners" (p. x). A paradigm consists of a group of fundamental assumptions forming a shared framework that provides the scholar with instruction on what to view as issues of inquiry and how to deal with these issues. Hence, a paradigm works as a criterion for choosing problems that, as long as the paradigm is taken for granted, can be assumed to have a solution. Paradigms structure observation and define reality. Kuhn's perspective is historical: Preparadigmatic periods in science are followed by a time where a valid paradigm allows "normal science" (to use Kuhn's terminology) to take place. Under the conditions of normal science and its "strong network of commitments—conceptual, theoretical, instrumental and methodological" (p. 42), the community of researchers concentrates on the routine activity of "puzzle-solving" without testing the paradigm itself. However, an increasing number of observed anomalies leads to a crisis and eventually to a revolution and to the establishment of a new paradigm that is incommensurable with the old one. A paradigm shift has traits of a conversion. New candidates for paradigms are often presented by young scientists or scholars who are new to the field.

Kuhn's book created enough interest to make it a classic. Criticisms targeted the vagueness of his concept of paradigm both in definition and in use, the alleged incommensurability of the old and the new paradigm, and the notion of revolution as a description of development in science. Kuhn was charged with subjectivity, irrationality and relativism. The change of paradigm, which Kuhn described as "the selection by conflict within the scientific community of the fittest way to practice future science" resulting in "an increase in articulation and specialization" (p. 172), was said to belong to the realm of the social psychology of discovery rather than to the philosophy of science because the change follows values rather than formal rules. Kuhn's overstatement of revolution at the expense of the cumulative aspects of development in science and his emphasis on the consecutive at the expense of the simultaneous were modified to allow for the coexistence and even the interaction of different paradigms. Kuhn himself specified his notion of paradigm in two ways: a broad sense, also called a disciplinary matrix, which includes all the components of scientific consensus; and a narrow sense, which denotes exemplary solutions to problems. A paradigm has both descriptive and prescriptive functions, and it implies commitment by those who work in and under it.

Kuhn's concept of paradigm both in its initial and its modified shape has contributed to a number of achievements. The concept highlighted the historical situatedness of scientific research and the role of consensus in rationality. It lifted up the interplay of scientific and nonscientific components in the development of science. It focused on the ambiguity of commitment as that which can both undercut rationality and make scientific work successful. It acknowledged the circularity of abstracting data into a paradigm that informs the selection and interpretation of new data. Thus it contributed to fostering an interest in the sociology of scientific knowledge and in the hermeneutics of holistic nonuniversalist rationality. In the philosophy of science, the concept of paradigm has been followed by alternative concepts, such as *competing research programs* (Imre Lakatos) and *research traditions* (Larry Laudan).

The concept of paradigm in science and religion

The exploration of the concept of paradigm has had an impact on the relation between science and religion. The study has broadened the concept of rationality and affirmed its complexity and contextuality. It has nourished the discussion of the translatability of various discourses. It has also inspired a process of paradigm critique that questions the self-assuring power of paradigms and calls for an examination of the role of race, gender, culture, and political and economic power in the process of forming guiding ideas. In *Myths, Models, and Paradigms* (1974) and *Religion and Science* (1997), Ian G. Barbour uses the central features of the Kuhnian paradigm to argue that some of the same spirit of inquiry found in science also applies to religion: Religious experiences depend on a paradigmatic interpretive framework, religious paradigms are highly resistant to falsification, and no univocal rules exist for the choice between religious paradigms. These analogies presuppose a flexible definition of paradigm communities and of continuities versus discontinuities in paradigm shifts. Referring to paradigms as universal phenomena that provide comprehensive contexts for interpretation, Sallie McFague demonstrated in *Metaphorical Theology* (1982) that metaphorical thinking is basic to human understanding of the world. In *Christianity* (1995) Hans Küng used the concept of macro-, meso-, and microparadigms to structure the history of Christian theology around five major paradigms—Jewish Apocalyptic, Ecumenical Hellenistic, Mediaeval Roman Catholic, Protestant Evangelical, and Modern. Nancey Murphy used the Lakatosian concept in *Theology in the Age of Scientific Reasoning* (1990) in her contribution to the dialogue between science and religion.

In numerous areas of academic and nonacademic research, *paradigm* is used in a variety of ways. It is frequently spoken of in terms of new, emerging, or shifting paradigms. In the wake of a more pluralistic approach, an increasingly metaphorical use of the concept can be noted. The word *paradigm* has come to describe more or less well-defined bodies of knowledge or beliefs, world views, and guiding or dominant standards that are apt to change over time and that need not always be explicit. Nuances of *paradigm* are often value-laden: Paradigms are described both as enhancing creativity and as restricting creative thought and action.

See also WORLDVIEW

Bibliography

Barbour, Ian G. *Myths, Models, and Paradigms: A Comparative Study in Science and Religion.* New York: Harper and Row, 1974.

Gutting, Gary, ed. *Paradigms and Revolutions: Appraisals and Applications of Thomas Kuhn's Philosophy of Science.* South Bend, Ind.: University of Notre Dame Press, 1980.

Kuhn, Thomas S. "Second Thoughts on Paradigms." In *The Structure of Scientific Theories,* 2nd edition, ed. Frederick Suppe. Urbana: University of Illinois Press, 1977.

Kuhn, Thomas S. *The Structure of Scientific Revolutions,* 3rd edition. Chicago: University of Chicago Press, 1996.

Küng, Hans. *Christianity: Its Essence and History.* London: SCM Press, 1995.

Lakatos, Imre, and Musgrave, Alan, eds. *Criticism and the Growth of Knowledge.* Cambridge, UK: Cambridge University Press, 1970.

McFague, Sallie. *Metaphorical Theology: Models of God in Religious Language.* Philadelphia: Fortress Press, 1982.

Murphy, Nancey. *Theology in the Age of Scientific Reasoning.* London and Ithaca, N.Y.: Cornell University Press, 1990.

van Huyssteen, J. Wentzel. *The Shaping of Rationality: Toward Interdisciplinarity in Theology and Science.* Grand Rapids, Mich.: Eerdmans, 1999.

ANTJE JACKELÉN

PARADOX

Paradox appears in any context of explanation where two fundamental but contradictory (or contrary) propositions, both well-attested to be true, must be claimed simultaneously to provide a full and adequate account of the phenomenon in question. The nature of light as fully wave and fully particle according to the Copenhagen epistemology of complementarity, or the nature of the person of Jesus Christ as fully God and fully human according to Nicene theology, are both examples of irreducible paradox designed to explain the nature of a given phenomenon.

See also CHRISTOLOGY; COPENHAGEN INTERPRETATION; SELF-REFERENCE; WAVE-PARTICLE DUALITY

Bibliography

Loder, James E. and Neidhardt, W. Jim. *The Knight's Move: The Relational Logic of the Spirit in Theology and Science.* Colorado Springs, CO: Helmers and Howard, 1992.

JAMES E. LODER

PARALLEL DISTRIBUTED PROCESSING

See ARTIFICIAL INTELLIGENCE; INFORMATION TECHNOLOGY

PARTICLE PHYSICS

See PHYSICS, PARTICLE

PHASE SPACE

In classical mechanics, the complete state of a particle is given by three components of momentum and three components of position. The *phase space* of a particle is a six-dimensional space, three axes for momentum and three for position, so that each point of a particle's phase space represents a complete state of the particle, and the entire phase space represents all possible states of the particle. For an N-particle system, the phase space has $6N$ dimensions, 6 for each particle, and a single point

in the phase space represents the simultaneous complete states for each of the N particles.

See also PHYSICS, QUANTUM

W. MICHAEL DICKSON

PHILOSOPHY OF RELIGION

Philosophy of religion can be broadly described as an inquiry into problems involved in religion or originated by religion from a philosophical point of view. Since, however, there are various understandings of religion and of philosophy and of the relation between them the field of philosophy of religion has become vast and varying. As a separate subject it originates from the European enlightenment, but its content can be traced back to the early stages of European philosophy, and there are rich traditions related to Hinduism, Buddhism, and Chinese religions. Islamic philosophers have also played an important role in the development of the subject. The focus of this entry lies on the Western philosophical tradition and its interplay with the Jewish and Christian religions.

The competence of reason. There is a widespread view according to which human reason lacks all ability to form any adequate idea of God. In the twentieth century the incompetence of reason in religious questions was clearly stated by the Swiss Protestant theologian Karl Barth (1886–1968) and his followers. The existence and actions of God can only be adequately dealt with in answer to the revealed word of God. Accordingly, religion and science belong to quite different sections of human activity, and ordinary philosophy is of minor importance compared to true religion. The bankruptcy of reason can hardly be defended by reasonable arguments, but it has an anchorage in feelings and experiences from various periods of the Christian tradition. The dominant view in Christian and Jewish traditions is that human reason is important for clarification of religious questions and that philosophy of religion provides a meeting ground for religion and science. A string of mysticism, however, often accompanies the religious thinking among those who defend the competence of human reason in the realm of religion.

Analysis of religious language. The use of symbols, metaphors, and analogies in religious language has attracted much philosophical interest, Thomas Aquinas's (c. 1225–1274) doctrine of analogy being an example. Analysis of language has been a main theme in modern philosophy of religion. Similarities to, and differences from, scientific language have been discussed. An analytic philosopher like Alfred J. Ayer denied the theoretical meaningfulness of religious language, but this was defended by John Hick, for example. A noncognitive view was developed by Richard B. Braithwaite, seeing God-talk as a commitment to an agapeistic form of life. Similar theories, as represented by D. Z. Phillips, have been developed on the basis of Ludwig Wittgenstein's later philosophy.

God in philosophical systems. The idea of God provides a cornerstone in the philosophical construction of the world by Plato and Aristotle. The influence from Plato and Aristotle in Western religious traditions can hardly be underestimated. Aristotle especially has often been a common point of reference both for scientists and theologians. Muslim philosophers, such as Averroës (1126–1198), brought the Aristotelian heritage to Christian scholasticism. Many arguments frequently used in later philosophy and relevant to the religion-science discussion are presented in the dialogue *De Natura Deorum* of Cicero (106–43 B.C.E.). In the further development of European philosophy, different concepts of God have played a decisive role, and the western philosophical tradition is hardly understandable without noticing the influence of Jewish and Christian theology. To the classical heritage from philosophy of religion belong Aquinas's philosophical arguments for the existence of God, the so-called Five Ways, the most influential being the cosmological and the teleological arguments.

René Descartes (1596–1650), who had great influence on the rise of modern science, offered many arguments for the existence of God, including the ontological one. An interesting pantheistic concept of God is important in Baruch Spinoza's (1632–1677) philosophy. He equates God and nature. A philosophical discussion that is especially fruitful for elucidating the relationship between religion and science followed the rise of so-called physico-theology and deism in the seventeenth

and eighteenth centuries, its peak being Bishop George Berkeley's *Alciphron* (1732), Bishop Butler's *Analogy* (1736), and David Hume's *Dialogues Concerning Natural Religion* (1779). An idea of God separated from the theoretical and scientific realm is found in the philosophy of Immanuel Kant (1724–1804). God is a practical postulate, necessary for the development of morals. In twentieth-century philosophy, God as a principle involved in the development of nature can be encountered in Alfred North Whitehead's (1861–1947) complicated system.

Some modern philosophers of religion, including Frederick Copleston, Bernard Lonergan, and Richard Swinburne, argue that the traditional arguments for the existence of God can give a higher probability to the God hypothesis. Other modern philosophers, following Søren Kierkegaard (1813–1855), see the parallel between belief in God and a scientific hypothesis as completely misleading. According to Gordon Kaufman, the religious belief in God proceeds from an encounter with the holy, or, as William Alston argues, it can be founded on direct god-experiences. Inspired by the later Wittgenstein many philosophers have argued against all attempts to see doctrines of God as analogous to scientific theories.

Philosophical criticism of religion. The tradition of philosophical criticism of religion is often related to scientific development. It has been argued by Karl Marx (1818–1883), Sigmund Freud (1856–1939), and Emile Durkheim (1858–1917), among others, that the world can be understood without religious suppositions and the existence of religious ideas is explained by scientific arguments that contain no religious suppositions. A considerable part of the critical philosophy of religion, as represented by Hume, Kant, and Bertrand Russell (1872–1970), consists of criticism of the positive arguments indicated above. There are also classical debates focusing on contradictions in religious systems of doctrines; the best known is the relation between belief in a good God and the apparent evils of the world, as discussed by Gottfried Wilhelm Leibniz (1646–1716) and Voltaire (1694–1778). Since the 1970s, the religious consequences of the new evolutionary biology have been seriously debated, with some, like biologist Richard Dawkins, stating their atheistic implications, while others, including theologian Keith Ward, argue their compatibility.

Philosophical tools in religious thinking. The development of religious doctrines from the church fathers and onward is highly dependent on philosophical concepts. The tools from different branches of analytical philosophy have been used by Basil Mitchell and Antony Flew to clarify religious reasoning in the twentieth century. The same holds true for existentialism and other branches of contemporary philosophy, including postmodernism.

Many key questions in debates about the relation between religion and science emerge from the various fields of philosophy of religion presented above. Is it reasonable, for example, to seek a coherent model of the world, or is it impossible to advance further than developing good linguistic tools for different activities in life, such as prayer or physics? Can one base a worldview solely on scientific reasoning, and does it then contain or exclude the idea of a creator? Are there points of access to the real world other than purely empirical observation—religious and moral experiences for example? What happens when coherence is used as a criterion of truth in the totality of scientific, religious, moral, and aesthetic ideas?

See also ARISTOTLE; AVERROËS; COSMOLOGICAL ARGUMENT; DESCARTES, RENÉ; LANGUAGE; ONTOLOGICAL ARGUMENT; PANTHEISM; PLATO; TELEOLOGICAL ARGUMENT; THEODICY; THOMAS AQUINAS

Bibliography

Flew, Antony, and MacIntyre, Alasdair, eds. *New Essays in Philosophical Theology*. New York: Macmillan, 1955.

Hick, John. *Philosophy of Religion*. Englewood Cliffs, N.J.: Prentice Hall, 1973.

Phillips, D. Z. *Faith after Foundationalism*. New York: Routledge, 1988.

Smart, Ninian. *Historical Selections in the Philosophy of Religion*. New York: Harper, 1962.

Swinburne, Richard. *Is there a God?* London: Oxford University Press, 1996.

Tracy, David. *The Analogical Imagination: Christian Theology and the Culture of Pluralism*. New York: Crossroad, 1981.

ANDERS JEFFNER

PHILOSOPHY OF SCIENCE

The phrase "philosophy of science" can be used most broadly to describe two different, though related, sorts of inquiry. On the one hand it can be used to describe the philosophy of particular sciences, such as the philosophy of physics, biology, or economics. On the other hand, it can be used to describe the study of epistemological issues in science more generally. Although an increasing majority of work in the philosophy of science is being done in the philosophy of particular sciences, it is this latter construal of the philosophy of science that remains the heart of the field and is the focus of this entry.

Scientific methodology

In a tradition that can be traced back to John Stuart Mill (1806–1873) and Francis Bacon (1561–1626), many have taken the scientific method to be inductive. An inductive inference is *ampliative* (i.e., the content of the conclusion goes beyond the content of the premises) and *nondemonstrative* (i.e., all true premises do not guarantee a true conclusion; at best they render the conclusion more probable). For example, suppose that one has observed a large number of mammals and every kind of mammal that one has observed has teeth; from this evidence one might make the inductive generalization that all mammals have teeth. It is possible, however, that the next mammal one observes (say, an anteater) might turn out not to have teeth. The fallibility of inductive inferences is often referred to as Hume's problem of induction, after the philosopher David Hume (1711–1776).

Carl Hempel (1905–1997) argues that the scientific method begins not with observations but with hypotheses. According to this hypothetico-deductive method one deduces certain observational predictions from the hypothesis and then rigorously tests them through further observation and experimentation. If the predictions are borne out, then the hypothesis is confirmed. Thus Hempel's method is still broadly inductive. Although the conclusion of an inductive argument is not certain, one would like to determine quantitatively how probable the conclusion is, given its premises (the evidence). The logical positivist Rudolf Carnap (1891–1970) sought to develop such a logic of confirmation. Other models of confirmation, such as Bayesian and bootstrapping models, are reviewed in John Earman's *Testing Scientific Theories* (1983).

Karl Popper (1902–1994) insists that the scientific method is deductive, not inductive. Observation always requires a prior point of view or problem. Like Hempel, Popper believes science begins with a bold hypothesis or conjecture. The way in which the scientist comes to the hypothesis (context of discovery) is irrelevant (e.g., it could come to the scientist in a dream); all that matters is the way in which it is tested (context of justification). Unlike Hempel, Popper does not think that hypotheses can be confirmed. If the observational prediction is borne out, deductively the scientist is unable to conclude anything (to conclude that the hypothesis is confirmed is to commit the deductive fallacy of affirming the consequent). If, however, the predictions are falsified, then, by the valid deductive inference *modus tollens* (if *p* then *q*, not *q*, therefore not *p*) one can conclude that the hypothesis is falsified. Hence, Popper's method is known as *falsificationism*. According to Popper, the scientist should not seek to confirm theories but rather, refute them. A theory that has survived repeated attempts of falsification—especially in those cases where it has made risky predictions—has been corroborated, though not confirmed. On this view, a theory is demarcated as scientific if there are observational conditions under which one would be willing to reject the theory as falsified.

As a matter of historical fact, however, scientists typically do not abandon their theories in the face of falsifying evidence. Furthermore, in many cases it turns out to be sound scientific judgment to continue developing and modifying a theory in the face of recalcitrant evidence. In response to these sorts of difficulties, Popper's student, Imre Lakatos (1922–1974), developed a sophisticated falsificationism known as the "methodology of scientific research programs." For Lakatos, instead of evaluating an individual theory or modification of a theory as scientific or ad hoc, one should evaluate a whole series of theories developed over time. This series, called a *research program*, consists of a *hard core*, which defines the research program and is taken to be irrefutable, and a *protective belt*, which consists of auxiliary hypotheses and background assumptions to be modified in the face of falsifying data, thereby protecting the hard core.

According to Lakatos, a research program is demarcated as scientific if it is progressive—that is, it continues to make new predictions that become corroborated. Once a research program ceases to make new corroborated predictions it becomes degenerative and its hard core should be abandoned.

Paul Feyerabend (1924–1994) was a close friend of Lakatos and also a student of Popper's. In his book *Against Method* (1978) he denies that there is such thing as the scientific method. He writes, "the idea of a fixed method, or a fixed theory of rationality, rests on too naïve a view . . . there is only *one* principle that can be defended under *all* circumstances. . . . It is the principle: *anything goes*" (pp. 27–28). Feyerabend's view is known as *epistemological anarchism*.

Scientific rationality and theory change

Beginning in the early 1960s there was a shift away from concerns about scientific methodology towards concerns about scientific change. This shift was in large part due to the publication in 1962 of Thomas Kuhn's (1922–1996) *The Structure of Scientific Revolutions*. Kuhn argues that the philosophy of science ought to be the product of a careful examination of the history of science. This involves recognizing the integrity of the science within its own time and not simply viewing it in relation to one's contemporary perspective. This new historiographical approach leads Kuhn to reject much of traditional philosophy of science: the confirmationist and falsificationist accounts of theory evaluation, the view that science is cumulative, the distinction between context of discovery and context of justification, and the idea of a crucial experiment.

Kuhn argues that science is characterized by three sorts of phases: pre-paradigm science, normal science, and revolutionary science. Central to understanding these phases is his notion of a *paradigm,* which he uses in two primary ways. First, he means an exemplar, a concrete problem solution or scientific achievement that serves as a model for solving other scientific problems (e.g., the planetary dynamics laid out in Isaac Newton's *Principia*). Second, and more broadly, he means by paradigm a disciplinary matrix, which includes not only exemplars, but laws, definitions, metaphysical assumptions, and values (e.g., Newton's dynamical laws, the definitions of mass and space, and the mechanical philosophy). The paradigm determines what is to count as an acceptable scientific problem and an acceptable scientific solution. In the process of normal science, anomalies emerge that resist solution within the framework of the paradigm; if these anomalies persist and proliferate, they can lead to a state of crisis. Revolutionary science is described as "those noncumulative developmental episodes in which an older paradigm is replaced in whole or part by an incompatible new one" (p. 92). Kuhn refers to the pre- and post-revolutionary periods of normal science as incommensurable, and says that there is a sense in which scientists from different paradigms work in different worlds. Kuhn polemically refers to the conversion from the old to the new paradigm as being analogous to a Gestalt switch or religious conversion. Ian Barbour draws analogies between Kuhnian paradigms and religious paradigms in *Religion and Science* (1997).

In the 1969 postscript to *The Structure of Scientific Revolutions* and in the article "Objectivity, Value Judgment, and Theory Choice" (1977) Kuhn responds to charges that his account of science makes science irrational and leads to relativism. Against the charge of irrationality, Kuhn notes that values (such as predictive accuracy, simplicity, internal consistency, and coherence with neighboring theories) provide scientists with a shared basis for theory choice. Against the charge of relativism, Kuhn notes that ultimately paradigms are to be evaluated by their ability to set up and solve "puzzles." In this sense Kuhn does believe that there is objective progress in science: Newton solves more puzzles than Aristotle, and Albert Einstein more puzzles than Newton. What Kuhn rejects is realism, which claims that there is a coherent direction of ontological development and that science is getting closer to the truth.

Subsequent philosophers of science influenced by Kuhn developed different strands of his thought in different directions. Feyerabend, who developed an incommensurability thesis around the same time as Kuhn, came to later embrace the label of relativist. Others, such as Larry Laudan, sought to preserve the rationality of science against the threat perceived in Kuhn's holist picture of scientific change. According to Laudan, a closer look at the history of science shows not a wholesale exchange of one paradigm for another, but rather the components of the disciplinary matrix (e.g., methods,

values, and ontology) being negotiated individually. Regarding theory choice he writes, "there is enough common ground between the rivals to engender hope of finding an 'Archimedean standpoint' which can rationally mediate the choice" (1984, p. 75). He calls this alternative view the reticulated model of scientific change.

Scientific realism versus antirealism

The labels *realism* and *antirealism* are each used to cover a wide spectrum of views. The main positions can be roughly distinguished by their answers to three questions: (1) Is there a mind-independent world? (2) What is our epistemic access to that world? (3) What is the aim of science? Realists (along with many antirealists) accept the existence of a mind-independent world. Those antirealists who deny this advocate some form of idealism. While realists tend to be optimistic about epistemic access to the world, antirealists argue in various ways that this optimism is unwarranted. Realists typically see the aim of science being truth, whereas antirealists argue the aim is something less.

At one end of the realist spectrum is naïve realism—the view that science is a perfect, undistorted mirror of the mind-independent world and that scientific theories are literally true. More sophisticated versions of realism, such as the view of Ernan McMullin, hold that realism means the long-term success of a scientific theory gives reason to believe that something like the entities and structures postulated by the theory actually exist (p. 26). According to McMullin, an important part of the aim of science is the development of fruitful metaphors. Many have argued for realism on the grounds that it provides the best explanation for the success of science; the widespread success of science would be "miracle" if scientific theories were not at least approximately true (Boyd 1984, Putnam 1975). Others argue that the proper question for realism is not whether some theory is true or approximately true, but whether some entity exists. According to Ian Hacking's entity realism, one can conclude, for example, that electrons exist because researchers experimentally build devices that use electrons to investigate other parts of nature. Between theory realism and entity realism is another view known as *structural realism*. This view, which John Worrall attributes to Henri Poincaré

(1854–1912), affirms a mind-independent world but takes epistemic access to that world to be limited to its structural features. Thus, there is a continuity of structure across theory change despite radical changes in ontology. Although what is meant by *structure* is not entirely clear, in the physical sciences it is typically taken to be the structures expressed in the mathematical formalism of the theory.

Challenges to realism come from many sources and have led to a variety of antirealist views. Both Kuhn (1962) and Laudan (1981) argue that the history of science undermines realism. Kuhn's view can be classified as a form of instrumentalism, according to which scientific theories are merely useful instruments for making predictions and solving problems. Other antirealist views, such as Bas van Fraassen's constructive empiricism, come out of the empiricist tradition. According to van Fraassen (1980), science only aims to give theories that are empirically adequate and a theory is empirically adequate if what it says about observable things is true, that is, if it saves the phenomena (p. 12). On this view, one is not compelled to accept the existence of unobservable entities, such as electrons.

A third strand of antirealism, known as *social constructivism,* comes from sociology. The social constructivist seeks to understand scientific practice in the laboratory in a manner similar to an anthropologist seeking to understand a foreign culture. Social constructivists, such as David Bloor of the Edinburgh School, reject the philosophical understanding of knowledge as justified true belief, and instead take knowledge to be whatever is collectively endorsed by a particular group of people at a particular time (p. 5). This makes social constructivism a form of relativism. It is called *constructivism* because it takes scientific knowledge and facts to be constructed rather than discovered. Stronger and weaker versions of this view are obtained depending on whether this process of constructing scientific knowledge is, or is not, taken to be purely social. Arthur Fine, who argues that social constructivism has important methodological lessons for the philosophy of science (1996), himself rejects both realism and antirealism. Instead Fine advocates a minimalist position he calls the *natural ontological attitude,* which prescribes accepting the claims of science in the same way that

one accepts the evidence from one's senses, without adding any additional claims such as "and it is really true" or "and it is only a useful fiction" (1986, p. 127).

Feminist philosophies of science

Since the 1970s, many feminist philosophers, historians, and scientists have been asking why there have traditionally been so few women in science and whether certain sexist, racist, or nationalist biases have shaped the practice and content of science. Detailed case studies, a representative sample of which can be found in Janet Kourany's *The Gender of Science* (2001), reveal many ways in which such biases have affected science. In response to these findings, many feminists sought to develop a new epistemology or philosophy of science. Following Sandra Harding (1986), feminist philosophies of science can be roughly divided into three traditions: feminist empiricism, feminist standpoint theory, and feminist postmodernism.

Helen Longino, whose work falls largely within the feminist empiricist tradition, introduces a view known as *contextual empiricism.* Longino sees empirical data as constraining, but nonetheless underdetermining, theory choice. This gap between theory and evidence is bridged by value-laden background assumptions belonging to a particular context. These contextual assumptions are one way biases can enter science. Longino criticizes traditional portrayals of the scientific method as individualistic. Instead she sees the objectivity of science being secured by its social character (e.g., peer review, replication of experiments, and an openness and responsiveness to criticism). She argues that diversity in science is important for making these often invisible assumptions explicit and open to criticism.

Harding takes this point about diversity in science a step further in her feminist *standpoint theory.* In contrast to empiricism, standpoint theory argues that the legitimacy of the knowledge claim depends on the social identity of the knower. Harding writes, "women's subjugated position provides the possibility of more complete and less perverse understandings. Feminism . . . can transform the perspective of women into a 'standpoint'—a morally and scientifically preferable grounding for our interpretations and explanations of nature" (p. 26). One standard criticism that Harding considers is whether there is such a thing as a "feminist standpoint" that cuts across all classes, races, and cultures.

Donna Haraway's work *Simians, Cyborgs, and Women* (1991) exemplifies the feminist postmodernism tradition. Haraway rejects the idea of single feminist standpoint and instead argues that all knowledge is locally situated. Like Longino, Haraway offers an alternative account of objectivity. She writes, "Feminist objectivity is about limited location and situated knowledge, not about transcendence and splitting of subject and object. In this way we might become answerable for what we learn how to see" (p. 190). Although Haraway's view shares some affinities with social constructivism, she explicitly rejects the label "relativist." She explains, "the alternative to relativism is not totalization and single vision. . . . [Rather, it is] partial, locatable, critical knowledges. . . . Relativism is a way of being nowhere while claiming to be everywhere equally. The 'equality' of positioning is a denial of responsibility and critical enquiry" (p. 191). Underlying many of these feminist philosophies is a central concern for the social and ethical implications of science.

Scientific explanations and laws

The most influential account of scientific explanation is Hempel's *covering law model*. On this model, explanations are understood as arguments in which the explanandum (the event, feature, or law to be explained) appears as the conclusion of an argument. The premises of the argument must contain at least one universal or statistical law used essentially in the derivation, and empirically verifiable statements describing particular facts or initial conditions. If the argument is deductive and involves a universal law, it is called a *deductive-nomological explanation*; if the argument is inductive and involves a statistical law, then it is called an *inductive-statistical explanation*. For example, suppose one wants to understand why an ice skater's angular velocity increases as she draws her arms in during a spin. The explanation would show that this event can be logically deduced from premises involving the law of conservation of angular momentum and statements such as her initial angular momentum was nonzero and her moment of inertia was reduced by drawing her arms in.

Several philosophers and historians have objected that Hempel's conditions are neither necessary nor sufficient for a scientific explanation. The most famous counterexamples fall into the categories of either irrelevance (although the event follows from the premises, as a matter of fact those premises are irrelevant to the explanation of the event) or symmetry (if the law involves a biconditional or equation then one can switch one of the premises with the conclusion and "explain" things such as why a flagpole is a certain height in terms of the length of its shadow). These sorts of problems have led philosophers largely to abandon Hempel's model and propose new alternatives. To handle the problems of irrelevance and symmetry, Wesley Salmon (1925–2001) introduces a causal model explanation, whereby to explain an event is to identify the causes of that event. Alternatively, van Fraassen in his pragmatic account of explanation embraces the possibility that the length of a shadow may explain the height of a pole. For van Fraassen (1980), an explanation is always relative to a particular context. Yet another model of explanation is provided by Philip Kitcher (1981), who understands explanation to be a unification of diverse phenomena by means of a common underlying structure or small number of processes. He sees Charles Darwin's theory of evolution as illustrating this model of explanation. The link between explanation and unification is challenged by Margaret Morrison in her book *Unifying Scientific Theories* (2000).

From reductionism to theoretical pluralism

Reductionism can be construed as a thesis about ontologies, laws, theories, linguistic expressions, or some combination of these. Considered as a relationship between scientific theories, it can be taken as a synchronic relation between two concurrent theories belonging to different levels of description or a diachronic relation between a historical predecessor theory and its successor. The classic formulation of theory reduction is due to the logical empiricist Ernest Nagel (1901–1985), who takes it to involve the logical derivation of one theory from another. More specifically, "a reduction is effected when the experimental laws of the secondary science . . . are shown to be the logical consequences of the theoretical assumptions . . . of the primary science" (p. 352). The standard example is the reduction of thermodynamics (secondary science) to statistical mechanics (primary science). In the physical sciences, reductionism is more often taken to be a correspondence between two theories under certain conditions, typically characterized by the limit of some quantity. As Thomas Nickles notes, this view is "best described by 'inverting' the usual concept of reduction, so that successors are said to reduce to their predecessors . . . under limiting operations" (p. 181). For example, special relativity is said to reduce to Newtonian mechanics in the limit of small velocities.

Challenges to reductionism have come from detailed case studies of the relations between particular scientific theories. One recurring challenge is known as the problem of *multiple realizability*. For example, in reducing Mendelian genetics to molecular biology, as Alexander Rosenberg points out in his 1989 "From Reductionism to Instrumentalism?",one discovers that a single Mendelian trait can be realized by a variety of molecular mechanisms, and furthermore, the same molecular mechanism can produce different Mendelian characteristics. Another set of challenges arises when the reducing theory is statistical (such as statistical mechanics or quantum mechanics) and the reduced theory is not as Lawrence Sklar indicates in this 1999 essay, "The Reduction (?) of Thermal Dynamics to Statistical Mechanics." These sorts of difficulties have led many to reject reductionism and instead argue for theoretical pluralism, or the so-called disunity of science. According to pluralism, each scientific theory has its own proper domain of applicability. In her book, *The Dappled World* (1999), Nancy Cartwright raises the possibility that "nature is governed in different domains by different systems of laws not necessarily related to each other in any systematic or uniform way" (p. 31). This view has been criticized on the grounds that it forfeits the benefits that come from examining inter-theoretic relations. The question of the unity or disunity of science remains a controversial topic.

See also EXPLANATION; PHILOSOPHY OF SCIENCE, HISTORY OF; POSITIVISM, LOGICAL

Bibliography

Barbour, Ian. *Religion and Science: Historical and Contemporary Issues.* New York: HarperCollins, 1997.

Bloor, David. *Knowledge and Social Imagery,* 2nd edition. Chicago: University of Chicago Press, 1991.

Boyd, Richard. "The Current Status of Scientific Realism." In *Scientific Realism,* ed. Jarrett Leplin. Berkeley: University of California Press, 1984.

Carnap, Rudolf. "On Inductive Logic." *Philosophy of Science* 12, no. 2 (1945): 72–97.

Cartwright, Nancy. *The Dappled World: A Study of the Boundaries of Science.* Cambridge: Cambridge University Press, 1999.

Earman, John, ed. *Testing Scientific Theories.* Minneapolis: University of Minnesota Press, 1983.

Feyerabend, Paul. *Against Method: Outline of an Anarchistic Theory of Knowledge.* London: Verso, 1978.

Fine, Arthur. *The Shaky Game: Einstein, Realism, and the Quantum Theory.* Chicago: University of Chicago Press, 1986.

Fine, Arthur. "Science Made Up: Constructivist Sociology of Scientific Knowledge." In *The Disunity of Science: Boundaries, Contexts, and Power,* ed. Peter Galison and David Stump. Stanford, Calif.: Stanford University Press, 1996.

Hacking, Ian. *Representing and Intervening: Introductory Topics in the Philosophy of Natural Science.* Cambridge, UK: Cambridge University Press, 1983.

Haraway, Donna. *Simians, Cyborgs, and Women: The Reinvention of Nature.* New York: Routledge, 1991.

Harding, Sandra. *The Science Question in Feminism.* Ithaca, N.Y.: Cornell University Press, 1986.

Hempel, Carl. *Aspects of Scientific Explanation and Other Essays in the Philosophy of Science.* New York: Free Press, 1965.

Hempel, Carl. *Philosophy of Natural Science.* Upper Saddle River, N.J.: Prentice-Hall, 1966.

Hume, David. *An Enquiry Concerning Human Understanding* (1748). *A Critical Edition,* ed. Tom L. Beauchamp. New York: Oxford University Press, 2001.

Kitcher, Philip. "Explanatory Unification." *Philosophy of Science* 48 (1981): 507–531.

Kourany, Janet. *The Gender of Science.* Upper Saddle River, N.J.: Prentice Hall, 2001.

Kuhn, Thomas S. "Objectivity, Value Judgment, and Theory Choice." In *The Essential Tension: Selected Studies in Scientific Tradition and Change.* Chicago: University of Chicago Press, 1977.

Kuhn, Thomas S. *The Structure of Scientific Revolutions,* 3rd edition. Chicago: University of Chicago Press, 1996.

Lakatos, Imre. "Falsification and the Methodology of Scientific Research Programmes." In *Criticism and the*

Growth of Knowledge, ed. Imre Lakatos and Alan Musgrave. Cambridge, UK: Cambridge University Press, 1970.

Laudan, Larry. "A Confutation of Convergent Realism." *Philosophy of Science* 48 (1981): 19–49.

Laudan, Larry. *Science and Values: The Aims of Science and Their Role in Scientific Debate.* Berkeley: University of California Press, 1984.

Longino, Helen. *Science as Social Knowledge: Values and Objectivity in Scientific Inquiry.* Princeton, N.J.: Princeton University Press, 1990.

McMullin, Ernan. "A Case for Scientific Realism." In *Scientific Realism,* ed. Jarrett Leplin. Berkeley: University of California Press, 1984.

Morrison, Margaret. *Unifying Scientific Theories: Physical Concepts and Mathematical Structures.* Cambridge, UK: Cambridge University Press, 2000.

Nagel, Ernest. *The Structure of Science: Problems in the Logic of Scientific Explanation* (1961). Indianapolis, Ind.: Hackett, 1979.

Nickles, Thomas. "Two Concepts of Intertheoretic Reduction." *The Journal of Philosophy* 70, no. 7 (1973): 181–201.

Popper, Karl. *The Logic of Scientific Discovery.* London: Routledge, 1959.

Popper, Karl. *Conjectures and Refutations: The Growth of Scientific Knowledge.* London: Routledge, 1963.

Putnam, Hillary. *Mathematics, Matter, and Method,* Vol. 1. Cambridge, UK: Cambridge University Press, 1975.

Rosenberg, Alexander. "From Reductionism to Instrumentalism?" In *What the Philosophy of Biology Is: Essays Dedicated to David Hull,* ed. Michael Ruse. Dordrecht, Netherlands: Kluwer Academic, 1989.

Salmon, Wesley. *The Foundations of Scientific Inference.* Pittsburgh, Pa.: University of Pittsburgh Press, 1967.

Salmon, Wesley. *Scientific Explanation and the Causal Structure of the World.* Princeton, N.J.: Princeton University Press, 1984.

Sklar, Lawrence. "The Reduction (?) of Thermodynamics to Statistical Mechanics." *Philosophical Studies* 95 (1999): 187–202.

van Fraassen, Bas. *The Scientific Image.* Oxford: Clarendon Press, 1980.

Worrall, John. "Structural Realism: The Best of Both Worlds?" *Dialectica* 43, nos. 1–2 (1989): 99–124.

ALISA BOKULICH

PHILOSOPHY OF SCIENCE, HISTORY OF

In tracing the history of the philosophy of science, it should be noted that philosophy and science were not clearly distinguished from each other until the early eighteenth century; furthermore, the philosophy of science, as a distinct subdiscipline, did not emerge until the nineteenth century. Nonetheless, almost from the beginning of philosophy, there were thinkers who reflected on the methods, aims, and epistemological status of inquiry into nature. In this respect, Aristotle (384–322 B.C.E.) is generally regarded as the first philosopher of science.

Ancient and medieval periods

Aristotle's views on the philosophy of science are primarily found in his *Posterior Analytics.* For Aristotle, genuine scientific knowledge has the status of necessary truth. This necessity comes from the fact that scientific explanations are to be demonstrations—that is, logical deductions from premises that are necessarily true. He argued that these premises must function as "first principles," which are primitive (they cannot themselves be demonstrated), known immediately, and known better than the conclusions. Each science, whether it be zoology or physics, has its own first principles. Aristotle thought that we come to know these first principles inductively through experience; that is, we can intuit or perceive the essences of things in our observations of nature.

In the Middle Ages, reflections on the scientific method were primarily focused on elaborations and criticisms of the views laid out in Aristotle's *Posterior Analytics* (which was reintroduced to Western scholars in the twelfth century). In the thirteenth and fourteenth centuries many scholars began to call into question Aristotle's assertion that scientific knowledge is demonstrative—that it, has the status of necessary truth. For many theologians, this assertion seemed to be in conflict with the doctrine of God's omnipotence and with revelation as the preeminent source of knowledge. The growing tension between Aristotelian natural philosophy and church doctrine led the Bishop of Paris, Etienne Tempier, in 1277 to issue a condemnation of 219 propositions. Among these were propositions relating to Aristotle's views that the world is eternal and that a vacuum is impossible. Both Pierre Duhem and the contemporary historian of science Edward Grant has argued that the condemnation of 1277 was an important stone in paving the way, not only for the scientific revolution, but for new philosophical views about the methods and epistemological status of science.

Early modern period

In 1620 Francis Bacon (1561–1626) published his *Novum Organum,* or *New Organon,* in which he laid out a new philosophy and methodology of science that he hoped would replace Aristotle's *Organon* (the name given to the collection of Aristotle's six books on logic and scientific method: *Categories, De Interpretatione, Prior Analytics, Posterior Analytics, Topics,* and *Sophistical Refutations*). Whereas Aristotle emphasizes deductions from necessary first principles, Bacon emphasizes induction as the central scientific method. Bacon was not, however, a naïve inductivist: He notes that impressions from the senses can be deceptive and that it is a bad induction to infer the principles of science through simple enumeration (*Novum Organum,* Book I, Aphorism 69). Bacon famously compares the proper scientist to a bee:

> Those who have handled the sciences have been either Empiricists or Rationalists. Empiricists, like ants, merely collect things and use them. The Rationalists, like spiders, spin webs out of themselves. The middle way is that of the bee, which gathers its materials from the flowers . . . but then transforms and digests it by a power of its own. (*Novum Organum,* Book I, Aphorism 95)

Bacon is often referred to as the father of experimental science. Instead of simply observing nature, Bacon advocates the use of experiments, which are skillfully thought out and framed for the purpose of inquiry. An important and controversial legacy of Bacon's philosophy of science is his notion of a crucial experiment or "instance of the fingerpost" (described in Aphorism 36 of Book II), which is designed to unambiguously decide in favor of one hypothesis or theory and refute another.

Although René Descartes (1596–1650), like Bacon, saw himself as providing a new epistemological foundation for science, in many respects his views on science were a return to the Aristotelian ideal of science as a set of deductions from necessary first principles. According to Descartes, these first principles are known not through observations, but by the "light of nature" that is given to us by God. Towards the end of his life, however, Descartes seemed to concede that this deductive ideal is unattainable.

Descartes's contemporary, Galileo Galilei (1564–1642), blended a Baconian emphasis on experimentation with a Cartesian emphasis on the importance of geometry for physics. In *The Assayer* he famously claims:

> Philosophy is written in this grand book, the universe, which stands continually open to our gaze. But the book cannot be understood unless one first learns to comprehend the language and read the letters in which it is composed. It is written in the language of mathematics, and its characters are triangles, circles, and other geometrical figures. (p. 238)

One of Galileo's most important contributions to the methodology of science is his use of idealization. As Ernan McMullin (1985) notes, Galileo uses not only mathematical idealization, but also a sort of causal idealization, whereby one considers nature not in its full causal complexity but in an idealized situation in which all but the causal line of interest have been eliminated. Whether the conclusions drawn from these "artificial" scenarios apply to nature in its full complexity as well was an issue of debate between Galileo and the Aristotelian natural philosophers.

Scientific Revolution

In the generation following Descartes, Christian Huygens (1629–1695) argues that the method of science differs distinctly from that of geometry and that the conclusions of science are, at best, highly probable. In the preface to his *Treatise on Light,* he argues for the hypothetico-deductive method in science. According to this method one first puts forward a hypothesis and then deduces from it certain observational predictions. If those predictions are born out then the hypothesis is rendered more probable.

Isaac Newton (1642–1727), by contrast, famously declared that hypotheses have no proper place in science—a declaration that was not entirely consistent with his practice. In the General Scholium to his *Principia* he writes, "I frame no hypotheses; . . . and hypotheses, whether metaphysical or physical, whether of occult qualities or mechanical, have no place in experimental philosophy" (p. 443). Instead, Newton advocates the method of analysis and synthesis, which he describes in Query 31 at the end of his *Opticks.* According to this method one begins with "analysis," which consists of making observations and experiments and then inductively drawing conclusions from them. Once one has these inductive generalizations in hand, the method of "synthesis" consists in using them in turn to explain the phenomena. Although Newton's name is often associated with the godless mechanistic worldview, Newton himself believed that blind necessity could not account for the diversity in the world (General Scholium). He furthermore believed that the uniform motions of the planets required the intervening maintenance of God. In Query 31 of the *Opticks* he writes:

> For it became him who created them [all material things] to set them in order. And if he did so, it is unphilosophical to seek for any other Origin of the World, or to pretend that it might arise out of Chaos by the mere Laws of nature. . . . [B]lind Fate could never make all the Planets move one and the same way in Orbs concentrick [sic]. (p. 402)

By the end of the eighteenth century an important shift had taken place, namely figures such as Huygens and Newton realized that the empirical sciences could at best yield probable knowledge; the ideal of scientific knowledge as certain knowledge came to be largely abandoned.

Early nineteenth century

In the early nineteenth century three important books were published on the philosophy of science: John Herschel's *A Preliminary Discourse on the Study of Natural Philosophy* (1830), William Whewell's *The Philosophy of the Inductive Sciences, Founded Upon Their History* (1840), and John Stuart Mill's *System of Logic* (1841). In Part I of his *Discourse* Herschel defends the study of natural philosophy (science) against the charge that it leads one to "doubt the immortality of the soul, and to scoff at revealed religion," arguing instead that it

leads to the betterment of one's moral character and undermines atheism (section 5). In Part II of the *Discourse* he lays out three methods by which one can come to discover scientific laws: first, by inductive reasoning; second, "by forming at once a bold hypothesis . . . and trying the truth of it by following out its consequences and comparing them with facts" (section 210); and third, by a process that combines both. With regard to the second (hypothetico-deductive) method, Herschel notes "when a theory will bear the test of such extensive comparison, it matters little how it has been original framed" (section 220). Passages such as this have led the contemporary philosopher of science John Losee to attribute to Herschel the invention of the distinction between what Hans Reichenbach (1891–1953) would later call the "context of discovery" and the "context of justification."

Whewell (1794–1866) was the first philosopher of science to take the historical turn, arguing that the philosophy of science ought to reflect—and be a product of—a close historical examination of the practice of science. Despite this important insight, Whewell's own philosophy of science was probably to a greater extent shaped by the philosophies of Bacon and Immanuel Kant (1724–1804), than the history of science. Like Herschel, Whewell recognizes the important role that hypotheses play in science, though he thinks that these hypotheses are to be grounded inductively. Whewell sees his work as a renovation of the inductive method laid out in Bacon's *Novum Organum.* The most striking renovation was Whewell's (Kantian) claim that the mind supplies from within itself certain "fundamental ideas" that shape, and are a necessary precondition for, experience and the empirical knowledge on which the sciences are based. Whewell represents a surprising return to the claim that science aims for, and can obtain, the status of necessary truth. The contemporary philosopher of science, Laura Snyder, has cogently argued that these two aspects of Whewell's philosophy of science (fundamental ideas and empirical science as necessary truths) can be properly understood only in the context of his natural theology. Snyder explains:

> we are able to have knowledge of the world because the Fundamental Ideas which are used to organize our sciences resemble the Ideas used by God in his

creation of the physical world. . . . [T]he Divine origin of both our Ideas and our world is what enables Whewell to claim that axioms knowable a priori from the meanings of our Ideas are informative about the empirical world, and necessarily true of it. (p. 796)

In 1833 Whewell contributed his "Astronomy and General Physics Considered with Reference to Natural Theology" to the well-known Bridgewater Treatises.

John Stuart Mill (1806–1873) debated Whewell on the nature of induction in science. In Book II, chapter 5 of his *System of Logic* Mill rejects Whewell's claim that science can obtain the status of necessary truths. Mill writes:

I may have seen snow a hundred times and may have seen that it was white, but this cannot give me entire assurance even that all snow is white, much less that snow *must* be white. However many instances we may have observed of the truth of a proposition, there is nothing to assure us that the next case shall not be an exception to the rule . . . experience cannot offer the smallest ground for the necessity of a proposition. (pp. 155–156)

Here it is clear that Mill is squarely in the empiricist tradition of David Hume (1711–1776) and is construing induction narrowly as induction by simple enumeration. Mill's best known contribution to the philosophy of science is his four methods of experimental inquiry (typically referred to as "Mill's Methods" though, as Losee and others have noted, they can be found in the works of earlier medieval natural philosophers) described in chapter 8 of Book III of *System of Logic*. They can be summarized as follows:

- Method of Agreement: If two or more instances of the phenomenon have only one circumstance in common, the circumstance in which the instances agree is the cause of the phenomenon.

- Method of Difference: If an instance when the phenomenon under investigation occurs and an instance in which it does not occur have every circumstance in common save one, then that circumstance by which they

differ is the cause (or an indispensable part of the cause) of the phenomenon.

- Method of Residues: Subtract from any phenomenon those parts that are known to be the effect of certain antecedent causes; the remaining part of the phenomenon (the residue) is the result of the remaining antecedents.

- Method of Concomitant Variations: Whatever phenomenon varies when another phenomenon varies is either a cause, or an effect of that phenomenon or is causally related to it some way (e.g., both the product of a common cause).

Late nineteenth and early twentieth centuries

New challenges to the English inductivist tradition came from the French physicist and historian of science Pierre Duhem (1861–1916). Duhem argues that physics is subject to certain methodological limitations that do not affect other sciences. In his book *The Aim and Structure of Physical Theory* (1914) Duhem provides a devastating critique of Baconian crucial experiments. According to Duhem, an experiment in physics is not simply an observation, but rather, is an interpretation involving a theoretical framework. Furthermore, no matter how well one constructs one's experiment, it is never a single hypothesis that faces an experimental test. Instead, it is a whole interlocking group of hypotheses, background assumptions, and theories. This thesis has come to be known as *holism*. According to Duhem, it is this holism that renders crucial experiments impossible. More generally, Duhem is critical of Newton's description of the method of physics as a firm and straight forward "deduction" from facts and observations.

In the appendix to *The Aim and Structure*, entitled "Physics of a Believer," Duhem draws out the implications that he sees his philosophy of science as having for those who argue that there is a conflict between physics and religion. He writes, "metaphysical and religious doctrines are judgments touching on objective reality, whereas the principles of physical theory are propositions relative to certain mathematical signs stripped of all objective existence. Since they do not have any common term, these two sorts of judgments can neither contradict nor agree with each other" (p.

285). Nonetheless, Duhem argues that it is important for the theologian or "metaphysician" to have detailed knowledge of physical theory in order not to make illegitimate use of it in speculations.

This separation of physics from metaphysics that Duhem describes is characteristic of the positivist movement founded by Auguste Comte (1798–1857) and developed by the Austrian physicist and philosopher Ernst Mach (1838–1916). Mach's philosophy can be characterized as a form of sensationalism, according to which the world consists not of things, but sensations. In other words, an object, such as an apple, is nothing but a composite of various elements of sensations: red, round, crunchy, and sweet; and talk about apples is really just an economical way of talking about collections of sensations. Indeed, all scientific theories, for Mach, are just economical ways of talking about sensations. Mach's elements of sensation are neither subjective, nor purely mental: Sensations can also be considered physical in so far as they depend in various ways on each other. Although this view may be reminiscent of Bishop George Berkeley's (1685–1753) idealism (the view that there are no material substances—only ideas and the minds that contain them), Mach explicitly distinguishes his view from both Berkeley and Kant: "Berkeley regards the 'elements' [of sensation] as conditioned by an unknown cause external to them (God); accordingly Kant, in order to appear as a sober realist, invents the 'thing-in-itself'; whereas, on the view which I advocate, a dependence of the 'elements' on one another is theoretically and practically all that is required" (pp. 361–362). Mach sees sensationalism as providing a framework in which to unify the newly emerging psychological sciences with the physical sciences. Both progress and unification require eliminating all concepts in physics that do not correspond directly to sensations (i.e., eliminating all metaphysical concepts). On these grounds, Mach famously denied atomism, which he took to be an unnecessary metaphysical assumption. Mach's philosophy—in particular, his rejection of metaphysics and concern for the unity of science—greatly influenced the founders of the Vienna Circle.

Henri Poincaré (1854–1912) was a French physicist, mathematician, and philosopher. In the preface to his *Science and Hypothesis* (1902) he distinguishes three kinds of hypotheses in science: "some are verifiable, and when once confirmed by experiment become truths of great fertility; . . . others may be useful to us in fixing our ideas; and finally, . . . others are hypotheses only in appearance, and reduce to definitions or to conventions in disguise" (p. xxii). It is his defense of this third kind of "hypothesis" that makes Poincaré's philosophy of science a form of conventionalism. While he does not think that all of science is a matter of convention, he does take the geometry of space and certain principles of mechanics to be simply stipulated, rather than discovered. By saying that something is conventional, Poincaré does not mean that it is arbitrary—there are certain constraints and consequences that come with fixing a convention. For example, although neither logic nor experience forces us to accept Euclidean geometry, rather than non-Euclidean geometry, as the correct description of our space (i.e., it is a free choice), choosing to adopt one geometry rather than another will require us to adjust our physical theories in certain ways (e.g., will require introducing new forces). Despite his conventionalism, Poincaré adopts a realist stance toward science. He writes, "we daily see what science is doing for us. This could not be unless it taught us something about reality; the aim of science is not things themselves . . . but the relations between things" (p. xxiv). This has led some contemporary philosophers to attribute to Poincaré the first expression of a view known as structural realism. Poincaré concludes the preface to his book by noting, "No doubt at the outset theories seem unsound, and the history of science shows us how ephemeral they are; but they do not entirely perish, and of each of them some traces still remain. It is these traces which we must try to discover, because in them and in them alone is the true reality" (p. xxvi). While Poincaré's remarks may or may not be true of the history of science, they do seem to be true of the history of philosophy of science.

See also PHILOSOPHY OF SCIENCE; SCIENCE AND
   RELIGION, HISTORY OF FIELD

Bibliography

Aristotle. *The Complete Works of Aristotle*, Vol. 1, ed. Jonathan Barnes. Princeton N.J.: Princeton University Press, 1984.

Bacon, Francis. *Novum Organum, With Other Parts of The Great Instauration*, ed. and trans. Peter Urbach and John Gibson. Chicago: Open Court, 1994.

Descartes, René. *The Philosophical Writings of Descartes,* Vol. 1, trans. John Cottingham, Robert Stoothoff, and Dugald Murdoch. Cambridge, UK: Cambridge University Press, 1985.

Duhem, Pierre. *The Aim and Structure of Physical Theory,* 91914) trans. Philip Wiener. Princeton N.J.: Princeton University Press, 1954.

Galileo Galilei. *The Assayer,* trans. Stillman Drake. In *Discoveries and Opinions of Galileo,* ed. Stillman Drake. New York: Anchor, 1957.

Grant, Edward. *The Foundations of Modern Science in the Middle Ages: Their Religious, Institutional, and Intellectual Contexts.* Cambridge, UK: Cambridge University Press, 1996.

Herschel, John. *A Preliminary Discourse on the Study of Natural Philosophy* (1830). Chicago: University of Chicago Press, 1987.

Huygens, Christiaan. *Treatise on Light,* trans. Silvanus Thompson. Chicago: University of Chicago Press, 1945.

Laudan, Larry. "Theories of Scientific Method From Plato to Mach: A Bibliographical Review." *History of Science* 7 (1968): 1–63.

Losee, John. *A Historical Introduction to the Philosophy of Science.* Oxford: Oxford University Press, 1972.

Mach, Ernst. *The Analysis of Sensations and the Relation of the Physical to the Psychical* (1897), trans. C. Williams. New York: Dover, 1959.

McMullin, Ernan. "Galilean Idealization." *Studies in the History and Philosophy of Science* 16, no. 3 (1985): 247–273.

McMullin, Ernan. "The Development of Philosophy of Science, 1600–1900." In *Companion to the History of Modern Science,* ed. Robert Olby, G. Cantor, J. Christie, and M. Hodge. London: Routledge, 1990.

Mill, John Stuart. *System of Logic Ratiocinative and Inductive: Being a Connected View of The Principles of Evidence and the Methods of Scientific Investigation,* (1841). New York: Harper, 1846.

Newton, Issac. *The Principia* (1687), trans. Andrew Motte. Amherst, N.Y.: Prometheus, 1995.

Newton, Issac. *Opticks: or A Treatise of the Reflections, Refractions, Inflections and Colours of Light* (1704). New York: Dover, 1952.

Poincaré, Henri. *Science and Hypothesis* (1902). New York: Dover, 1952.

Reichenbach, Hans. *Experience and Prediction: An Analysis of the Foundations and Structure of Knowledge.* Chicago: University of Chicago Press, 1938.

Snyder, Laura. "It's *All* Necessarily So: William Whewell on Scientific Truth." *Studies in History and Philosophy of Science* 25, no. 5 (1994): 785–807.

Whewell, William. *The Philosophy of the Inductive Sciences, Founded Upon Their History.* London: J. Parker, 1840.

ALISA BOKULICH

PHYSICALISM, REDUCTIVE AND NONREDUCTIVE

Physicalism is a doctrine that asserts that ultimately only physical particulars exist. While physicalism and materialism are sometimes considered equivalent, the former is more ontologically open, for while materialism claims that everything is composed of matter, physicalism holds that everything is comprised ultimately of those entities assumed in the basic statements of fundamental physical theory (fields, particles, strings, or whatever). The thesis that only these physical entities exist is often termed *ontological physicalism.*

While ontological physicalism is often presupposed in the philosophical discussion, controversy arises about the properties possessed by these physical particulars. For example, what is the ontological status of putative mental properties? Are they reducible to underlying physical properties, or do they have a kind of being of their own? The reductive physicalist affirms, while the nonreductive physicalist denies, that mental properties are "nothing but" the physical. Broadly conceived, reductive physicalism asserts that all nonphysical properties are coextensive with particular physical properties. Nonreductive physicalism, on the other hand, conjoins the irreducibility of nonphysical properties (property dualism) to ontological physicalism.

Since the 1960s considerable doubt has been cast on the reductive physicalist project. In Ernest Nagel's (1901–1985) classic account, physicalist reduction occurs when nonphysical predicates are biconditionally connected to particular physical predicates such that the nonphysical property is instantiated when and only when a particular physical property is instantiated, (e.g., the mental property of a particular headache pain is instantiated when and only when a particular neuro-property is). However, one can imagine a silicon-based Martian having the same headache pain as an earthling, but because of the Martian's different neurophysiology, different physical properties will be instantiated. Because the same mental state seems to be realizable in different physical systems, reductive physicalism is called into question. Consequently, nonreductive physicalism has generally replaced reductive physicalism in the philosophy of mind. Accordingly, while the instantiation of an upper-level mental property is not reducible to the instantiation of a lower-level one, it is nonetheless realized by some lower-level property. Thus, instead of a *type* identity between property kinds, (every time mental property *m* is instantiated, physical property *p* is instantiated), there is a *token* identity between an instantiation of *m* and the instantiation of some physical property or other.

Issues of reductive and nonreductive physicalism are important in the science/theology discussion. If, as the natural sciences methodologically assume, only physical entities have causal powers and hence ultimately exist, then what kind of sense can be made of religion and its talk of God? In responding to this problem, nonreductive physicalism seems initially promising, for it holds with the natural sciences that only physical entities exist, and yet agrees with religion in claiming that there are irreducible nonphysical properties. If it can be shown that our mental life is irreducible to neuroscience, then insofar as religion concerns our mental life, it too is irreducible to the physical.

But large questions loom. Can upper-level properties be something more than mere epiphenomena, if they are token identical to physical properties that do all the causal work? Alternately, if physical properties do not do all the causal work, can dualism be avoided? Finally, if the irreducible mental is nonetheless completely realized by the physical, then in charting this physical realization, is one not offering a reductive explanation of the mental, and its religious experience, after all?

See also MATERIALISM; MIND-BRAIN INTERACTION; NATURALISM; REDUCTIONISM; SUPERVENIENCE

Bibliography

Beckermann, Ansgar. "Introduction—Reduction and Nonreductive Physicalism." In *Emergence or Reduction? Essays on the Prospects of Nonreductive Physicalism,* eds. Ansgar Beckermann, Hans Flohr, and Jaegwon Kim. Berlin and New York: Walter de Gruyter, 1992.

Davidson, Donald. "Mental Events." In *Essays on Actions & Events*. Oxford: Clarendon Press, 1980.

Kim, Jaegwon. *Mind in a Physical World: An Essay on the Mind-Body Problem and Mental Causation*. Cambridge, Mass.: MIT Press, 1999.

Murphy, Nancey. "Physicalism without Reduction: Toward a Scientifically, Philosophically, and Theologically Sound Portrait of Human Nature." *Zygon* 34 (1999): 551-572.

Nagel, Ernest. *The Structure of Science: Problems in the Logic of Scientific Explanation*. New York: Harcourt, Brace, and World, 1961.

DENNIS BIELFELDT

PHYSICS

Physics is the branch of scientific investigation that focuses its attention on fundamental concepts, patterns, and relationships involving matter, energy, space, and time. Other natural sciences, such as chemistry, biology, geology, and astronomy, also deal with these categories in their investigation of material systems like atoms, molecules, life processes, organisms, planets, stars, and galaxies, but physics is concerned with the most basic and universal principles that apply to all of these diverse systems.

It is sometimes convenient to divide physics into several different arenas of concern, such as mechanics (the study of motion), electromagnetism and optics, thermodynamics, quantum physics, atomic physics, nuclear physics, particle physics, and relativity (the study of space, time, and gravity).

Classical mechanics is the study of motion in the manner established by Isaac Newton in the seventeenth century. Among its major contributions is a fruitful method for describing the cause-effect relationship for motion in a quantifiable manner. A force, like the familiar push or pull, functions as the cause of acceleration (any change in the speed or direction of motion), which is its effect. Another major contribution of Newton was his concept and description of the force of gravity that is experienced and exerted by every object possessing the quality of mass. The gravitational force that causes apples to fall earthward is also the kind of kind of force that steers the moon in its orbit around the Earth and the planets in their orbits around the sun.

Electromagnetism encompasses all phenomena in which electric and magnetic fields play a role. In classical physics, fields may be thought of as qualities of space that lead objects with certain properties to experience a force. Any object possessing the property of electric charge, for example, will experience a force in the presence of an electric field. Electromagnetic radiation (light, X-rays, radio waves) may be understood as variations in electric and magnetic fields that travel at the characteristic speed of three hundred thousand meters per second through space.

Thermodynamics is concerned with the manner in which energy, especially heat energy, affects the state of a system and its interaction with its environment. Energy, often characterized as the capacity to do work, appears in a diversity of forms and may be changed in either form or location as a consequence of some physical process. In all processes, however, the sum of the energy possessed by a system and its environment remains constant. This principle, called the First Law of Thermodynamics, or the conservation of energy, is thought to apply without exception to all physical phenomena.

Quantum theory describes the structure and behavior of systems like atoms, atomic nuclei, and molecules. Extremely small structures behave in a manner different from the predictions of classical mechanics. The quantities of energy possessed by a system or exchanged between systems, for instance, is restricted to certain values only. Furthermore, the outcome of many processes is open to diverse options, each outcome having a calculable probability of occurrence.

Relativity theory provides a framework for speaking of the interactive relationships among space, time, mass, and gravity. Special Relativity describes the way in which the experience of time and space are interrelated, while General Relativity focuses its attention on the interrelationships among mass, space, gravity, and motion.

See also COSMOLOGY, PHYSICAL ASPECTS

Bibliography

Asimov, Isaac. *Understanding Physics*. New York: Barnes and Noble Books, 1988.

Kuhn, Karl. *Basic Physics: A Self-teaching Guide*, 2nd edition. New York: Wiley, 1996.

Halliday, David; Resnick, Robert; and Walker, Jearl. *Fundamentals of Physics*, 6th edition. New York: Wiley, 2000.

Feynman, Richard P.; Leighton, Robert B.; and Sands, Matthew L. *The Feynman Lectures on Physics*. Boston: Addison-Wesley, 1994.

HOWARD J. VAN TILL

PHYSICS, CLASSICAL

Classical physics is the science of physics as it was conceptualized and practiced in the three centuries prior to the advent of either quantum physics or relativity early in the twentieth century. The character of classical physics is well-represented by Isaac Newton's (1642–1727) formulation of the study of motion and James Clerk Maxwell's (1831–1879) approach to the study of electromagnetism.

Classical mechanics

Classical mechanics, the scientific study of motion in the style developed in the seventeenth century by Newton, is often taken as the foundational branch of classical physics. General physics courses commonly begin with the study of motion and use Newtonian mechanics as the setting in which numerous basic concepts, such as energy, force, and momentum, are first introduced.

Physics has long been concerned with understanding the nature and causes of motion. In the tradition of ancient Greek philosophy, the cosmos was thought to be divided into two distinctly differing realms—the terrestrial (near Earth) realm and the celestial realm (the region of the moon and beyond). As conceived in Greek thought, these two realms were not only spatially distinct, but they differed in character from one another in substantial ways. For one thing, the "natural" motions of things (motions that needed no further causation) in these two realms were presumed to be radically different.

According to Aristotle (384–322 B.C.E.), who was for nearly two millennia taken to be the authority on these matters, motion in the terrestrial realm required the continuous application of a cause. Remove the cause, and motion would cease. When a horse ceases to pull a cart, for instance, the cart comes to a halt. In Newton's formulation, however, what requires an active cause is not motion itself, but acceleration—any change in the speed or direction of motion. In effect, Newton's First Law of Motion asserts that the natural motion of things is uniform motion, straight-line motion at constant speed. Any deviation from this—any acceleration, that is—would require a cause. The name for this cause is force—specifically, the force exerted on one object by interaction with another. Expressed more traditionally, Newton's First Law states that unless acted upon by an applied force, an object will continue in a state of rest or uniform motion.

What happens when a force is applied to an object? The answer to that question is the subject of Newton's Second Law of Motion: When acted upon by an applied force, an object will accelerate; the resultant acceleration will be in the same direction as the applied force, and its magnitude will be directly proportional to the magnitude of the applied force and inversely proportional to the object's mass. Stated more succinctly, acceleration is proportional to force divided by mass. This statement, more than any other, functions as the core of Newtonian dynamics, Newton's formulation of the fundamental cause-effect relationship for motion. Force is the cause; acceleration is the effect. For a substantial class of motions, with exceptions to be noted later, this formulation continues to provide a fruitful way to predict or account for acceleration in response to applied forces.

Newton's Third Law of Motion is a statement about the character of the applied forces mentioned in the first two laws. All such forces occur in pairs and are the result of two bodies interacting with one another. When two bodies interact, says Newton, each exerts a force on the other. When bodies A and B interact, the force exerted on A by B is equal in magnitude and opposite in direction to the force exerted on B by A. This is sometimes abbreviated to read, "action equals reaction," but the meanings of *action* and *reaction* must be very carefully specified.

Among the various types of forces that contribute to the acceleration of terrestrial objects is the force of gravity—the force that causes apples, for example, to fall to the ground, or to "accelerate earthward." It was the genius of Newton that allowed him to consider the possibility that the orbital motion of the moon, which entails an acceleration toward the Earth, might also be a consequence of the Earth's gravitational attraction.

This suggestion required a remarkable break with Aristotelian tradition. According to Aristotle, the natural motion of the moon, of the planets, or of any other member of the celestial realm was entirely different from the terrestrial motions considered so far. The natural motion of celestial bodies was neither rest nor uniform straight-line motion. Rather, the motion of celestial bodies would necessarily be based on uniform circular motion, motion at constant speed on a circular path. In the spirit of this assumption, Claudius Ptolemy in the second century crafted a remarkably clever combination of uniform circular motions with which to describe the motions of the sun, moon, and planets relative to the central Earth.

However, building on the fruitful contributions of astronomers Nicolaus Copernicus (1473–1543), Galileo Galilei (1564–1642), and Johannes Kepler (1571–1630), Newton was able to demonstrate that Kepler's sun-centered model for planetary motions could be seen as but one more illustration of Newton's theory regarding the cause-effect relationship for motion. The moon was steered in its orbit around the Earth in response to a force exerted by the Earth on the moon. The Earth and the other planets orbited the sun in response to a force exerted on them by the sun. What was the force operating in these celestial motions? The same kind of force that caused apples to accelerate earthward—the universal gravitational force.

It was helpful to recognize gravity as a force exerted by one object on another. It was exceptionally insightful for Newton to propose that every pair of objects everywhere in the universe exerted gravitational forces on one another. Gone was the confusion of two kinds of natural motions. Gone was the even greater distinction between terrestrial and celestial realms—one characterized by imperfection and change, the other characterized by perfection and constancy. The cosmos is one system, not two. The world is a universe made of one set of substances and behaving according to one set of patterns. Classical mechanics provided the means to study all motions, both terrestrial and celestial, with one and the same methodology.

Classical electromagnetism

Classical electromagnetism provided a systematic account of numerous phenomena involving the interaction of electric charges and currents. Electric charges at rest were considered to be the source of electric fields—modifications in the nature of space that cause other charges to experience a force. Electric charges in motion, giving rise to an electric current, were considered to be the source of magnetic fields, modifications in the nature of space that could be detected by a magnetic compass and caused other electric currents to experience a force. Given any static distribution of electric charge, the configuration of the resultant electric field could be computed. Given any distribution of electric currents, the configuration of the resultant magnetic field could be computed. Given these electric and magnetic field configurations, the forces on all electric charges and currents could be predicted.

In addition to phenomena involving static charge distributions and steady electric currents, another important category of phenomena arises from dynamically changing configurations of charge or current. When charge or current configurations change, the resultant electric and magnetic fields will also change. However, changes in these field configurations must propagate at a finite speed—now called the speed of light, approximately 300,000 kilometers per second. Electromagnetic radiation is the phenomenon of traveling variations, or waves, in electric and magnetic field strength caused by accelerated electric charges. The electromagnetic spectrum spans the full range of wavelength values from very short to very long—from gamma rays, X-rays, and ultraviolet to visible light, infrared, microwaves and radio waves. Maxwell's equations—four mathematical statements that systematically integrated the work of predecessors like Charles-Augustin de Coulomb (1736–1806), Hans Christian Oersted (1777–1851), Michael Faraday (1791–1867), and André-Marie Ampère (1775–1836)—were taken to be the complete specification of all electromagnetic phenomena, including electromagnetic radiation.

Limitations of classical physics

Until the early twentieth century, classical physics appeared to be adequate to account for all observed phenomena. But new discoveries soon demonstrated that, although classical physics would continue to provide a convenient and powerful means of dealing with many phenomena, it needed to be supplemented with other theoretical strategies based on differing sets of assumptions regarding the fundamental character of the physical universe. In the arena of electromagnetism, for instance, classical physics assumed that electromagnetic energy could be continuously varied in value and that its transmission could be fully described in terms of traveling electromagnetic waves. However, in order to account for such phenomena as blackbody radiation (electromagnetic energy radiated by any warm object) and the photoelectric effect (electrons ejected from the surface of a metal illuminated by light), physicists had to propose and accept the idea that electromagnetic energy was transmitted in particle-like quanta of energy, now called *photons*. Phenomena in which the photon character of electromagnetic radiation plays a central role requires the employment of quantum physics in place of classical physics.

Quantum physics is also needed to account for the behavior of extremely small systems like atoms and molecules. The motion of electrons relative to atomic nuclei cannot be adequately described in the language of classical mechanics. Contrary to Newtonian expectations, the energy of atoms and molecules is not continuously variable, but is quantized—restricted to certain specific values. And, contrary to the expectations of classical electromagnetism, electrons in motion relative to atomic nuclei do not radiate energy continuously, but only when making a transition from one stable energy state to another of lower energy value. Consistent with the Principle of Conservation of Energy, the amount of energy lost by the atom is exactly equal to the energy carried away by the emitted photon.

A second shortcoming of classical physics becomes evident when Newtonian mechanics attempts to deal with things that are moving at very high speed relative to an observer. When this speed becomes a substantial fraction of the speed of light, several Newtonian expectations require modification. Many of these modifications are accounted for by the Special Theory of Relativity proposed by Albert Einstein (1879–1955) in 1905. The relationship between kinetic energy (energy associated with motion) and speed must be modified. Distance and time intervals once thought to be invariant become dependent on relative motion. Even the mass of an object is measured differently by different observers. Other modifications are accounted for by Einstein's General Theory of Relativity, published in 1916, which deals with the interaction of mass and the geometry of space. The General Theory describes the force of gravity in a manner very different from Newton's and is able to account for several discrepancies between observation and Newtonian predictions.

Religious concerns and classical physics

Classical physics gave support to the idea that the world was fundamentally deterministic. Given full information about the configuration and motion of some system today, its entire future could, in principle, be computed. Its future was considered to be fully determined by its present. But is there room in such a universe for contingency or choice? The apparent absence of choice presents difficulties for religious concepts like human responsibility and human accountability to God for obedience to revealed standards for moral action.

Another religious concern arises when one inquires about the character and role of divine action in the universe. When Newton considered the future motions of the planets in the solar system, for instance, he judged that this set of orbital motions was inherently unstable and would, from time to time, need to be adjusted by God to restore the desired array of orbits. This introduction of occasional supernatural interventions may be considered a form of the *God of the gaps* approach to divine action: the universe is presumed to lack some quality or capability that must be compensated for by direct divine action. In the case of planetary motions, for example, Newton considered the universe to lack the capability of maintaining a stable set of orbits. This "capability gap" could, however, be bridged with occasional acts of supernatural intervention. Eventually, however, it was demonstrated that the system of planetary orbits was, in fact, stable, thereby removing the need for occasional gap-bridging interventions. When a "gap" of this sort becomes filled, the God of the gaps becomes superfluous. For this reason, many

contemporary theologians are inclined to see divine action, not as a supernatural compensation for capability gaps in the universe, but as an essential aspect of an enriched concept of what takes place naturally.

See also ARISTOTLE; DETERMINISM; DIVINE ACTION; GOD OF THE GAPS; GRAVITATION; NEWTON, ISAAC; PHYSICS, QUANTUM; RELATIVITY, GENERAL THEORY OF; RELATIVITY, SPECIAL THEORY OF; WAVE-PARTICLE DUALITY

Bibliography

Bernal, J. D. *History of Classical Physics.* New York: Barnes and Noble, 1997.

Pullman, Bernard. *The Atom in the History of Human Thought,* trans. Axel R. Reisinger. Oxford: Oxford University Press, 1998.

Feynman, Richard P.; Leighton, Robert B.; and Sands, Matthew L. *The Feynman Lectures on Physics.* Boston: Addison-Wesley, 1994.

Goldstein, Herbert; Poole, Charles; and Safko, John L. *Classical Mechanics,* 3rd edition. Upper Saddle River, N.J.: Prentice Hall, 2002.

Griffiths, David J. *Introduction to Electrodynamics,* 3rd edition. Upper Saddle River, N.J.: Prentice Hall, 1998.

Halliday, David; Resnick, Robert; and Walker, Jearl. *Fundamentals of Physics,* 6th edition. New York: Wiley, 2000.

Jackson, John David. *Classical Electrodynamics,* 3rd edition. New York: Wiley, 1998.

Symon, Keith R. *Mechanics,* 3rd edition. Boston: Addison-Wesley, 1971.

HOWARD J. VAN TILL

PHYSICS, PARTICLE

The thought that the bewildering variety of the world might be the result of many different arrangements of certain simple kinds of basic stuff is a very old one. In the sixth century B.C.E., various pre-Socratic philosophers explored such ideas. Thales thought that the fundamental entity might be water, while Anaximenes favored air. Such attempts were both insightful and hopelessly premature. A more sophisticated notion was the atomism introduced by Democritus a century later and promoted with considerable literary skill by the Latin poet Lucretius in the first century B.C.E.

Progress of a recognizably modern kind began with chemist John Dalton's (1766–1844) atomic theory, which introduced in 1803 the notion of atomic weights, derived principally from the properties of gases. Chemist and physician William Prout's (1785–1850) observation in 1815 that most of these weights were near integer multiples of the atomic weight of hydrogen led to what one might call the first true theory of elementary particles, with hydrogen as the conjectured fundamental building block.

Twentieth-century developments

In 1897, physicist Joseph Thomson (1856–1940) convincingly demonstrated that there are light, electrically negative particles (subsequently called *electrons*) that are constituents of what, until then, had been considered to be the indivisible atom. In 1911, physicist Ernest Rutherford (1871–1937) successfully interpreted experiments in which projectiles called *alpha particles* were significantly deflected by a thin gold foil as showing that the positive charge in the atom was concentrated at its center. Rutherford had discovered the nucleus.

In the rest of the twentieth century there followed a series of discoveries, each of which led in turn to a yet deeper conception of the structure of matter, expressed in terms of still smaller constituents playing the role of "elementary" particles. Each phase of these investigations, often pictured metaphorically as peeling another layer off the nuclear "onion," had a sequential form. The process of discovery took place in two parts. The first half consisted in the revelation of an increasing proliferation of putative elementary entities. An example would be the varieties of different nuclei generating the chemical properties of the ninety-two elements of the periodic table. There is a strong conviction in the human mind (exemplified as much by the pre-Socratic philosophers as by twentieth-century physicists) that the fundamental structure of matter should take a simple form, elegant and economical in its character. Proliferation threatens this conviction, but rescue comes in the second half of the process of discovery. Patterns are discerned linking together the proliferating elements, and these patterns are interpreted as reflecting the ways in which a small number of yet more fundamental constituents can be combined. In this way the next level of structure is revealed. It seems fun-

damental enough until, in turn, it too begins to proliferate, and the cycle begins again.

Thus, nuclei were first recognized as being made up of two kinds of nuclear particles, protons and neutrons. Then experimentalists began to discover many short-lived cousins of these nuclear particles and a proliferation began to threaten. However, the association of these different forms of nuclear matter into certain patterns (called *the eight-fold way* by its most insightful investigator, Murray Gell-Mann [b. 1929]) eventually led to the identification of the quark level in the structure of matter.

Consideration of symmetry provides an important mathematical tool for the understanding of pattern formation. For example, the beautiful pattern of a snowflake is due to the sixfold symmetry that leaves it unchanged under a rotation of sixty degrees. It turned out that the patterns of nuclear matter were also generated by symmetry principles, though principles of a more abstract kind than those given by simple rotations in space. Gell-Mann identified the relevant symmetry as being associated with what mathematicians call the group $SU(3)$. The $SU(3)$ structure involves certain kinds of transformation applied to a set of three basic objects. Such a mathematical fact did not necessarily imply a physical counterpart but, if it did, the corresponding physical entities would generate the next layer in the nuclear onion. Gell-Mann named these entities *quarks*.

There was initially doubt about the physical reality of quarks. The theory requires them to have fractional electric charge ($\frac{2}{3}$; $-\frac{1}{3}$), and no such particles have ever been observed in nature. However, when indirect evidence of their existence came to light, it proved to be very convincing. The experiments involved what is called *deep inelastic scattering*. This is the analogue of the experiments that enabled Rutherford to discover the nucleus, but conducted at much higher energy. Projectiles, such as electrons, when scattered off protons and neutrons, were discovered sometimes to "bounce back" in just the way that they would if they were hitting pointlike quarks lying within these nuclear particles. Physicists could eventually understand why projectiles behaved this way, but in the case of quarks there was a new feature without any precedent in physical experience. However strong the impact of the projectiles, it never proved powerful enough to actually eject a single quark. Eventually, physicists were forced to conclude that quarks were "confined," that is to say, the forces that bound them inside protons and neutrons were always strong enough to overcome the effect of the impact, however great that might be. No one has ever seen an individual quark.

The forces that produce quark confinement are generated by the exchange of further particles that, in the relentlessly jokey terminology endemic in particle physics, are called *gluons*. Further discoveries of exotic kinds of nuclear matter increased the number of types of quark from three to six. These ideas, together with others of a more technical character, constitute what has come to be called the *Standard Model*.

Only one piece in the jigsaw that defines the standard model is still missing. This is the particle proposed by Peter Higgs as the source of mass within the theory. Particle accelerators can yield energies that are just on the border of where this Higgs particle (as it is called) may be expected to show up. Establishing its existence would be extremely satisfying.

The Standard Model describes very well the properties of subnuclear matter but, with its six varieties of quark and with other somewhat inelegant elaborations, there is an air of proliferation about it. Most physicists, therefore, do not feel a final satisfaction with the Standard Model. There are two ways in which one might hope eventually to go beyond it. One is the discovery of a *Grand Unified Theory* (GUT).

In terms of directly observed phenomena there seem to be four basic forces of nature: strong nuclear forces (holding nuclei together); electromagnetic forces (holding atoms and bulk matter together); weak nuclear forces (causing matter to decay); and gravity. One of the triumphs of the Standard Model was to show that two of these forces, electromagnetic and weak, are in reality aspects of a single phenomenon, a fact that becomes clear experimentally at very high energies. Physicists believe that at even higher energies (such as would be present in the very early universe) these two forces would unite with the strong nuclear force to give a GUT. The detailed form this theory might be expected to take has not been established.

At higher energies still, there is the possibility that gravity and the GUT unite. For technical reasons, however, a theory of this super-unified kind is even harder to formulate than a GUT. The best

speculative prospect appears to be superstring theory (or its generalizations), in which quarks and electrons are pictured as modes of vibration of extremely tiny strings oscillating in many dimensions, all but four of which (space and time) are "rolled up" out of empirical sight.

Lessons for theology

Particle physics is methodologically the most reductionist form of physics. It encourages the thought of constituent reductionism, implying that were a human being to be decomposed into bits and pieces, the ultimate result would be an immense collection of quarks, gluons, and electrons. This observation, however, by no means proves that human beings are nothing but collections of elementary particles, since such a decomposition would kill the person. In fact, quantum physics encourages an antireductionist stance, because it has been shown that there is a counterintuitive mutual entanglement of quantum entities, even when they are spatially separated (the EPR effect). It does not seem that even the subatomic world can be treated purely atomistically.

An important technique of discovery in fundamental physics has proved to be the search for equations endowed with the unmistakable quality of mathematical beauty. Paul Dirac (1902–1984), one of the founding figures of quantum mechanics, once expressed the opinion that it was more important to have mathematical beauty in one's equations than to have them fit experiment. Of course, he did not mean that empirical adequacy is irrelevant to physics, but apparent failure to fit experiment might be due to a number of reasons, such as making an incorrect approximation in solving the equations, or even to the experimental results themselves being wrong. But if the equations were ugly, there was really no hope, for ugliness ran counter to everything that experience of fundamental physical theory had led one to expect. Dirac made his own significant discoveries through just such a quest for mathematical beauty, and the same principle is the guiding strategy followed by the bold proponents of superstring theory. It seems that the physical world is not only rationally transparent to our enquiry, it is also rationally beautiful. Beneath the vast variety of everyday objects, at the subatomic level there is a fundamental structure that is intellectually exciting in its simplicity and profoundly satisfying in the elegance and economy of its order. The reward for doing particle physics is the sense of wonder at its discoveries. The theistic religious believer will readily see the mind of the Creator behind the rationally beautiful order of the physical world.

Another lesson one may learn from particle physics is that human powers of rational prevision are severely limited. Time and again, nature has proved surprising as it resists our prior expectations. In the 1950s, particle physicists who were attempting to make sense of certain weak decays faced profound difficulties. After much fruitless struggle, the situation was transformed and made intelligible when in 1956 two physicists, Tsung Dao Lee and Chen Ning Yang, proposed the abandonment of what had been a cherished belief of particle physicists. Until then, it had been an article of faith that there could be no intrinsic handedness in nature, meaning that fundamental processes should show no preference for right-handed versions over left-handed versions or—putting it another way—that the laws of physics seen in a mirror should look exactly the same as the laws of physics observed directly. This supposed property was called the *conservation of parity,* and it was believed to be a self-evident truth about nature. Lee and Yang showed that this was not so, a discovery for which they rightly and promptly received the Nobel Prize.

Particle physics teaches us that the physical world is extremely surprising. It would be strange if that were not also true of human encounter with the much deeper mystery of divine reality. Physicists do not favor the question "Is it reasonable?" with its tacit presumption that one knows beforehand what form rationality should take. Rather, they ask the more open question "What makes you think this might be the case?" Theology too can benefit from seeking belief motivated by experience rather than by a priori expectation.

Finally, particle physicists believe in unseen realities (quarks) because such a belief makes sense of great swathes of physical experience. For them, it is intelligibility that affords the clue to existence. This does not seem altogether different from the reasons for theology's belief in the unseen reality of God.

See also FORCES OF NATURE; GRAND UNIFIED THEORY; STRING THEORY; SUPERSTRINGS; SYMMETRY

Bibliography

Greene, Bryan. *The Elegant Universe: Superstrings, Hidden Dimensions, and the Quest for an Ultimate Theory.* London: Jonathan Cape, 1999.

Pagels, Heinz R. *The Cosmic Code: Quantum Physics and the Language of Nature.* London: Michael Joseph, 1982.

Pais, Abraham. *Inward Bound: Of Matter and Forces in the Physical World.* Oxford: Oxford University Press, 1986.

Polkinghorne, John. *The Particle Play: An Account of the Ultimate Constituents of Matter.* Oxford: W. H. Freeman, 1979.

Polkinghorne, John. *Rochester Roundabout: The Story of High Energy Physics.* Harlow, UK: Longman; New York: W. H. Freeman, 1989.

Weinberg, Steven. *Dreams of a Final Theory: The Search for the Fundamental Laws of Nature.* London: Hutchinson, 1993.

JOHN POLKINGHORNE

PHYSICS, QUANTUM

Quantum theory is one of the most successful theories in the history of physics. The accuracy of its predictions is astounding. The breath of its application is impressive. Quantum theory is used to explain how atoms behave, how elements can combine to form molecules, how light behaves, and even how black holes behave. There can be no doubt that there is something very right about quantum theory.

But at the same time, it is difficult to understand what quantum theory is really saying about the world. In fact, it is not clear that quantum theory gives any consistent picture of what the physical world is like. Quantum theory seems to say that light is both wavelike and particlelike. It seems to say that objects can be in two places at once, or even that cats can be both alive and dead, or neither alive nor dead, or—what? There can be no doubt that there is something troubling about quantum theory.

Early research

Quantum theory, more or less as it is known at the beginning of the twenty-first century, was developed during the first quarter of the twentieth century in response to several problems that had arisen with classical mechanics. The first is the problem of blackbody radiation. A *blackbody* is any physical body that absorbs all incident radiation. As the blackbody continues to absorb radiation, its internal energy increases until, like a bucket full of water, it can hold no more and must re-emit radiation equal in energy to any additional incident radiation. The problem is, most simply, that the classical prediction for the energy of the emitted radiation as a function of its frequency is wrong. The problem was well known but unsolved until the German physicist Max Planck (1858–1947) proposed in 1900 the hypothesis that the energy absorbed and emitted by the blackbody could come only in discrete amounts, multiples of some constant, finite, amount of energy. While Planck himself never felt satisfied with this hypothesis as more than a localized, phenomenological description of the behavior of blackbodies, others eventually accepted Planck's hypothesis as a revolution, a claim that energy itself can come in only discrete amounts, the *quanta* of quantum theory.

A second problem with classical mechanics was the challenge of describing the spectrum of hydrogen, and eventually, other elements. Atomic spectra are most easily understood in light of a fundamental formula linking the energy of light with its frequency: $E = h\nu$, where E is the energy of light, h is a constant (Planck's constant, as it turns out), and ν is the frequency of the light (which determines the color of the visible light).

Suppose, now, that the energy of some atom (for example, an atom of hydrogen) is increased. If the atom is subsequently allowed to relax, it releases the added energy in the form of (electromagnetic) radiation. The relationship $E = h\nu$ reveals that the frequency of the light depends on the amount of energy that the atom emits as it relaxes. Prior to the development of quantum theory, the best classical theory of the atom was Ernest Rutherford's (1871–1937), according to which negatively charged electrons orbit a central positively charged nucleus. The energy of a hydrogen atom (which has only one electron) corresponds to the distance of the electron from the nucleus. (The further the electron is, the higher its energy is.) Rutherford's model predicts that the radiation emitted by a hydrogen atom could have any of a continuous set of possible energies, depending on the distance of its electron from the nucleus. Hence a large number of hydrogen atoms with energies randomly distributed among them will emit light of many frequencies. However, in the nineteenth century it was well known that hydrogen emits only a few frequencies of visible light.

In 1913, Niels Bohr (1885–1962) introduced the hypothesis that the electrons in an atom can be only certain distances from the nucleus; that is, they can exist in only certain "orbits" around the nucleus. The differences in the energies of these orbits correspond to the possible energies of the radiation emitted by the atom. When an electron with high energy "falls" to a lower orbit, it releases just the amount of energy that is the difference between the energies of the higher and lower orbits. Because only certain orbits are possible, the atom can emit only certain frequencies of light.

The crucial part of Bohr's proposal is that electrons cannot occupy the space between the orbits, so that when the electron passes from one orbit to another, it "jumps" between them without passing through the space in between. Thus, Bohr's model violates the principle of classical mechanics that particles always follow continuous trajectories. In other words, Bohr's model left little doubt that classical mechanics had to be abandoned.

Over the next twelve years, the search was on for a replacement. By 1926, as the result of considerable experimental and theoretical work on the part of numerous physicists, two theories—experimentally equivalent—were introduced, namely, Werner Heisenberg's (1901–1976) *matrix mechanics* and Erwin Schrödinger's (1887–1961) *wave mechanics.*

Matrix mechanics. Heisenberg's matrix mechanics arose out of a general approach to quantum theory advocated already by Bohr and Wolfgang Pauli (1900–1958), among others. In Heisenberg's hands, this approach became a commitment to remove from the theory any quantities that cannot be observed. Heisenberg took as his "observable" such things as the transition probabilities of the hydrogen atom (the probability that an electron would make a transition from a higher to a lower orbit). Heisenberg introduced operators that, in essence, represented such observable quantities mathematically. Soon thereafter, Max Born (1882–1970) recognized Heisenberg's operators as matrices, which were already well understood mathematically.

Heisenberg's operators can be used in place of the continuous variables of Newtonian physics. Indeed, one can replace Newtonian position and momentum with their matrix "equivalents" and obtain the equations of motion of quantum theory, commonly called (in this form) *Heisenberg's equations*. The procedure of replacing classical (Newtonian) quantities with the analogous operators is known as *quantization*. A complete understanding of quantization remains elusive, due primarily to the fact that quantum-mechanical operators can be incompatible, which means in particular that they cannot be comeasured.

Wave mechanics. Schrödinger's wave mechanics arose from a different line of reasoning, primarily due to Louis de Broglie (1892–1987) and Albert Einstein (1879–1955). Einstein had for some time expressed a commitment to a physical world that can be adequately described causally, which meant that it could be described in terms of quantities that evolve continuously in time. Einstein, who was primarily responsible for showing that light has both particlelike and wavelike properties, hoped early on for a theory that somehow "fused" these two aspects of light into a single consistent theory.

In 1923, de Broglie instituted the program of wave mechanics. He was impressed by the Hamilton-Jacobi approach to classical physics, in which the fundamental equations are wave equations, but the fundamental objects of the theory are still particles, whose trajectories are determined by the waves. Recalling this formalism, de Broglie suggested that the particlelike and wavelike properties of light might be reconcilable in similar fashion. Einstein's enthusiasm for de Broglie's ideas—both because de Broglie's waves evolved continuously and because the theory fused the wavelike and particlelike properties of light and matter—stimulated Schrödinger to work on the problem from that point of view, and in 1926 Schrödinger published his wave mechanics.

It was quickly realized that matrix mechanics and wave mechanics are experimentally equivalent. Shortly thereafter, in 1932, John von Neumann (1903–1957) showed their equivalence rigorously by introducing the Hilbert space formalism of quantum theory. The Uncertainty Principle serves to illustrate the equivalence. The Uncertainty Principle follows immediately from Heisenberg's matrix mechanics. Indeed, in only a few lines of argument, one can arrive at the mathematical statement of the Uncertainty Principle for any operators (physical quantities) A and B: $\Delta A \Delta B \geq Kh$, where K is a constant that depends on A and B, and h is Planck's constant. The symbol ΔA means "root mean square deviation of A" and is a measure of the statistical dispersion (uncertainty) in a set of values of A. So the Uncertainty Principle says that the statistical dispersion in values of A times the statistical dispersion in values of B are always greater than or equal to some constant. If (and only if) A and B are incompatible (see above) then this constant is greater than zero, so that it is impossible to measure a both A and B on an ensemble of physical systems in such a way as to have no dispersion in the results.

Schrödinger's wave mechanics gives rise to the same result. It is easiest to see how it does so in the context of the classic example involving position and momentum, which are incompatible quantities. In the context of Schrödinger's wave mechanics, the probability of finding a particle at a given location is determined by the amplitude (height) of the wave at that location. Hence, a particle with a definite position is represented by a "wave" that is zero everywhere except at the location of the particle. On the other hand, a particle with definite momentum is represented by a wave that is flat (i.e., has the same amplitude at all points), and, conversely to position, momentum becomes more and more "spread" as the wave becomes more sharply peaked. Hence the more precisely one can predict the location of a particle, the less precisely one can predict its momentum. A more quantitative version of these considerations leads, again, to the Uncertainty Principle.

Quantum field theory. Perhaps the major development after the original formulation of quantum theory by Heisenberg and Schrödinger (with further articulation by many others) was the extension of quantum mechanics to fields, resulting in quantum field theory. Paul Dirac (1902–1984) and others extended the work to relativistic field theories. The central idea is the same: The quantities of classical field theory are quanticized in an appropriate way. Work on quantum field theory is ongoing, a central unresolved issue being how one can incorporate the force of gravity, and specifically Einstein's relativistic field theory of gravity, into the framework of relativistic quantum field theory. A related, though even more speculative, area of research is quantum cosmology, which is, more or less, the attempt to discern how Big Bang theory (itself derived from Einstein's Theory of Gravity) will have to be modified in the light of quantum gravity.

Contemporary research

Contemporary research in the interpretation of quantum theory focuses on two key issues: the "measurement problem" and locality (Bell's Theorem).

Schrödinger's cat. Although the essence of the measurement problem was clear to several researchers even before 1925, it was perhaps first clearly stated in 1935 by Schrödinger. In his famous example, Schrödinger imagines a cat in the following unfortunate situation. A box, containing the cat, also contains a sample of some radioactive substance that has a probability of 1/2 to decay within one hour. Any decay is detected by a Geiger counter, which releases poison into the box if it detects a decay. At the end of an hour, the state of the cat is indeterminate between "alive" and "dead," in much the same way that a state of definite position is indeterminate with regard to momentum.

The cat is said to be in a *superposition* of the alive state and the dead state. In standard quantum theory, such a superposition is interpreted to mean that the cat is neither determinately alive, nor determinately dead. But, says Schrödinger, while one might be able to accept that particles such as electrons are somehow indeterminate with respect to position or momentum, one can hardly accept indeterminacy in the state of a cat.

More generally, Schrödinger's point is that indeterminacy at the level of the usual objects of quantum theory (electrons, protons, and so on) can easily be transformed into indeterminacy at the level of everyday objects (such as cats, pointers on measuring apparatuses, and so on) simply by coupling the state of the everyday object to the state of the quantum object. Such couplings are exactly the source of our ability to measure the quantum objects in the first place. Hence, the problem that Schrödinger originally raised with respect to the cat is now called the *measurement problem*: Everyday objects such as cats and pointers can, according to standard quantum theory, be indeterminate in state. For example, a cat might be indeterminate with respect to whether it is alive. A pointer might be indeterminate with respect to its location (i.e., it is pointing in no particular direction).

Approaches to the measurement problem. Thus, the interpretation of quantum theory faces a serious problem, the measurement problem, to which there have been many approaches. One approach, apparently advocated by Einstein, is to search for a *hidden-variables* theory to underwrite the probabilities of standard quantum theory. The central idea here is that the indeterminate description of physical systems provided by quantum theory is incomplete. Hidden variables (so-called because they are "hidden" from standard quantum theory) complete the quantum-mechanical description in a way that renders the state of the system determinate in the relevant sense. The most famous example of a successful hidden-variables theory is the 1952 theory of David Bohm (1917–1992), itself an extension of a theory proposed by Louis de Broglie in the 1920s. In the Broglie-Bohm theory, particles always have determinate positions, and those positions evolve deterministically as a function of their own initial position and the initial positions of all the other particles in the universe. The probabilities of standard quantum theory are obtained by averaging over the possible initial positions of the particles, so that the probabilities of standard quantum theory are due to ignorance of the initial conditions, just as in classical mechanics. According to some, the problematic feature of this theory is its *nonlocality*—the velocity of a given particle can depend instantaneously on the positions of particles arbitrarily far away.

Other hidden-variables theories exist, both deterministic and indeterministic. They have some basic features in common with the de Broglie-Bohm theory, although they do not all take position to be "preferred"—some choose other preferred quantities. In the de Broglie-Bohm theory, position is said to be "preferred" because all particles always have a definite position, by stipulation.

There are other approaches to solving the measurement problem. One set of approaches involves so-called *Many-worlds* interpretations, according to which each of the possibilities inherent in a superposition is in fact actual, though each in its own distinct and independent "world." There is a variant, the *Many-minds* theory, according to which each observer observes each possibility, though with distinct and independent "minds."

These interpretations have a notoriously difficult time reproducing the probabilities of quantum theory in a convincing way. A slightly more technical, but perhaps even more troubling, issue arises from the fact that any superposition can be "decomposed" into possibilities in an infinity of ways. So, for example, a superposition of "alive" and "dead" can also be decomposed into other pairs of possibilities. It is unclear how Many-worlds interpretations determine which decomposition is used to define the "worlds," though there are various proposals.

Yet another set of approaches to the measurement problem is loosely connected to the Copenhagen Interpretation of quantum theory. According to these approaches, physical quantities have meaning only in the context of an experimental arrangement designed to measure them. These approaches insist that the standard quantum-mechanical state is considered to describe our ignorance about which properties a system has in cases where the possible properties are determined by the experimental context. Only those properties that could be revealed in this experimental context are considered "possible." In this way, these interpretations sidestep the issue of which decomposition of a superposition one should take to describe the possibilities over which the probabilities are defined. Once a measurement is made, the superposition is "collapsed" to the possibility that was in fact realized by the measurement. In this context, the collapse is a natural thing to do, because the quantum mechanical state represents our ignorance about which experimental possibility would turn up. The major problem facing these approaches is to define *measurement* and *experimental context* in a sufficiently rigorous way.

Another set of approaches are the *realistic collapse* proposals. Like the Copenhagen approaches, they take the quantum-mechanical state of a system to be its complete description, but unlike them, these approaches allow the meaningfulness of physical properties even outside of the appropriate experimental contexts. The issue of how to specify when collapse will occur is thus somewhat more pressing for these approaches because the collapse represents not a change in our knowledge, but a physical change in the world. There are several attempts to provide an account of when collapse will occur, perhaps the two most famous being *observer-induced* collapse and *spontaneous*

localization theories. According to the former, notably advocated by Eugene Wigner (1902–1995), the act of observation by a conscious being has a real effect on the physical state of the world, causing it to change from a superposition to a state representing the world as perceived by the conscious observer. This approach faces the very significant problem of explaining why there should be any connection between the act of conscious observation and the state of, for example, some electron in a hydrogen atom.

The spontaneous-localization theories define an observer-independent mechanism for collapse that depends, for example, on the number of particles in a physical system. For low numbers of particles the rate of collapse is very slow, whereas for higher values, the rate of collapse is very high. The collapse itself occurs continuously, by means of a randomly distributed infinitesimal deformation of the quantum state. The dynamics of the collapse are designed to reproduce the probabilities of quantum theory to a very high degree of accuracy.

The problem of nonlocality. The other major issue facing the interpretation of quantum theory is *nonlocality*. In 1964, John Bell (1928–1990) proved that, under natural conditions, any interpretation of quantum theory must be nonlocal. More precisely, in certain experimental situations, the states of well-separated pairs of particles are correlated in a way that cannot be explained in terms of a common cause. One can think, here, of everyday cases to illustrate the point. Suppose you write the same word on two pieces of paper and send them to two people, who open the envelopes simultaneously and discover the word. There is a correlation between these two events (they both see the same word), but the correlation is easily explained in terms of a common cause, you.

Under certain experimental circumstances, particles exhibit similar correlations in their states, and yet those correlations cannot be explained in terms of a common cause. It seems, instead, that one must invoke nonlocal explanations, explanations that resort to the idea that something in the vicinity of one of the particles instantaneously influences the state of the other particle, even though the particles are far apart.

On the face of it, nonlocality contradicts special relativity. According to standard interpretations of the theory of relativity, causal influences cannot travel faster than light, and in particular, events in one region of space cannot influence events in other regions of space if the influence would have to travel faster than light to get from one region to the other in time to influence the event.

However, the matter is not so simple as a direct contradiction between quantum theory and relativity. The best arguments for the absence of faster-than-light influences in relativity are based on the fact that faster-than-light communication—more specifically, transfer of information—can lead to causal paradoxes. But in the situations to which Bell's theorem applies, the purported faster-than-light influences cannot be exploited to enable faster-than-light communication. This result is attributable to the indeterministic nature of standard quantum theory. In de Broglie and Bohm's deterministic hidden-variable theory, one could exploit knowledge of the values of the hidden variables to send faster-than-light signals; however, such knowledge is, in Bohm's theory, physically impossible in principle.

Other areas of research. There are of course many other areas of research in the interpretation of quantum theory. These include traditional areas of concern, such as the classical limit of quantum theory. How do the nonclassical predictions of quantum theory become (roughly) equivalent to the (roughly accurate) predictions of classical mechanics in some appropriate limit? How is this limit defined? In general, what is the relationship between classical and quantum theory? Other areas of research arise from work in quantum theory itself, perhaps the most notable being the work in quantum computation. It appears that a quantum computer could perform computations in qualitatively faster time than a classical computer. Apart from obvious practical considerations, the possibility of quantum computers raises questions about traditional conceptions of computation, and possibly, thereby, about traditional philosophical uses of those conceptions, especially concerning the analogies often drawn between human thought and computation.

Applications to religious thought

Quantum theory was the concern of numerous religious thinkers during the twentieth century. Given the obviously provisional status of the theory, not to mention the extremely uncertain state of its interpretation, one must proceed with great caution here, but we can at least note some areas of religious thought to which quantum theory, or its interpretation, has often been taken to be relevant.

Perhaps the most obvious is the issue of whether the world is ultimately deterministic or not. Several thinkers, including such scientists as Isaac Newton (1642–1727) and Pierre-Simon Laplace (1749–1827), have seen important ties to religious thought. In the case of classical mechanics, Newton had good reason to believe that his theory did not completely determine the phenomena, whereas Laplace (who played a key role in patching up the areas where Newton saw the theory to fail) had good reason to think that the theory did completely and deterministically describe the world. Newton thus saw room for God's action in the world; Laplace did not.

In the case of quantum theory the situation is considerably more difficult because there exist both indeterministic and deterministic interpretations of the theory, each of which is empirically adequate. Indeed, they are empirically equivalent. Those who, for various reasons, have adopted one or the other interpretation, though, have gone on to investigate the consequences for religious thought. Some, for example, see in quantum indeterminism an explanation of the possibility of human free will. Others have suggested that quantum indeterminism leaves an important role for God in the universe, namely, as the source of the agreement between actual relative frequencies and the probabilistic predictions of quantum theory.

Other thinkers have seen similarities between aspects of quantum theory and Eastern religions, notably various strains of Buddhism and Daoism. Fritjof Capra (1939–), who is perhaps most famous in this regard, has drawn analogies between issues that arise from the measurement problem and quantum nonlocality and what he takes to be Eastern commitments to the "connectedness" of all things. Other thinkers have seen in the interpretive problems of quantum theory evidence of a limitation in science's ability to provide a comprehensive understanding of the world, thus making room for other, perhaps religious, modes of understanding. Still others, drawing on views such as Wigner's (according to which conscious observation plays a crucial role in making the world determinate), see in quantum theory a justification of what they take to be traditional religious views about the role of conscious beings in the world. Others, including Capra, see affinities between wave-particle duality, or more generally, the duality implicit in the Uncertainty Principle, and various purportedly Eastern views about duality (for example, the Taoist doctrine of yin and yang, or the Buddhist use of koans).

Finally, quantum cosmology has provided some with material for speculation. One must be extraordinarily careful here because there is, at present, no satisfactory theory of quantum gravity, much less of quantum cosmology. Nonetheless, a couple of (largely negative) points can be made. First, it is clear that the standard Big Bang theory will have to be modified, somehow or other, in light of quantum theory. Hence, the considerable discussion to date of the religious consequences of the Big Bang theory will also need to be reevaluated. Second, due to considerations that arise from the time-energy Uncertainty Principle, even a satisfactory quantum cosmology is unlikely to address what happened in the early universe prior to the Planck time (approximately 10^{-43} seconds) because quantum theory itself holds that units of time less than the Planck time are (perhaps) meaningless. Some have seen here a fundamental limit in scientific analysis, a limit that is implied by the science itself. Of course, others see an opportunity for a successor theory.

This situation is, in fact, indicative of the state of quantum theory as a whole. While it is an empirically successful theory, its interpretations, and hence any consequences it might have for religious thought, remain matters of speculation.

See also COPENHAGEN INTERPRETATION; EPR PARADOX; HEISENBERG'S UNCERTAINTY PRINCIPLE; INDETERMINISM; LOCALITY; MANY-WORLDS HYPOTHESIS; PHASE SPACE; PLANCK TIME; QUANTUM COSMOLOGIES; QUANTUM FIELD THEORY; SCHRÖDINGER'S CAT; WAVE-PARTICLE DUALITY

Bibliography

Bohm, David. *Quantum Theory.* New York: Dover, 1989.

Gribbin, John. *In Search of Schrödinger's Cat: Quantum Physics and Reality.* New York: Bantam, 1984.

Heisenberg, Werner. *Physical Principles of the Quantum Theory.* New York: Dover, 1930.

Shankar, Ramamurti. *Principles of Quantum Mechanics.* New York: Plenum, 1994.

W. MICHAEL DICKSON

PLACEBO EFFECT

Although the term *placebo effect* might appear logically to refer to "the effect produced by a placebo," that definition is not in fact the one most commonly used. It would be more accurate to define the *placebo effect* as "the mind-body interaction triggered by medical treatment, historically discovered as a result of placebo use." That is, medical science may first have learned about the potential impact of the patient's mental state on healing by observing the effects of *placebos* ("dummy" or "sham" therapies thought to be lacking in any ingredients capable of producing bodily changes by chemical or physical means). If patients' bodies and symptoms were altered in impressive ways after the administration of placebos, the absence of any chemical explanation for the change suggested that it could only be by means of the patients' minds that such changes occurred. Once this basic observation is made, one may go on to divorce the patients' mental state from the use of dummy or sham remedies. Virtually any aspect of the encounter with a physician or other health worker could stimulate the requisite mental state, whether that state is one of expecting that one will get better, feeling trust in the caregiver, or whatever the precise psychological mechanism may be. It is in keeping with most modern usage to define *placebo effect* as "a change in a person's health status attributable to the symbolic or emotional impact of a healing intervention."

History

Ancient Greek medicine and the humoral medicine of the Middle Ages and Renaissance simply took for granted that words had the power to both cause or cure disease and that the mind and the body were constantly interacting to determine the individual's state of health. The earliest known reference to deliberate use of a placebo appears in a 1580 essay by Montaigne (1533–1592) describing a hypochondriac who was cured by an enema administered with great fanfare but without any substance actually being injected into the body. It is almost certain, however, that the use of placebos in medicine antedates this essay, probably by many centuries.

Medical science underwent a more materialistic turn and began to ignore the mind during the nineteenth century, but even then, citations appeared in the medical literature testifying to the power of placebos, and to the imagination generally, to alter disease. Placebos were frequently administered in the nineteenth century, in part because the profession lacked more effective medicines for most diseases.

Benjamin Franklin (1706–1790) was one of the first to use a *single-blind* technique in experiments on the power of mesmerism (hypnosis) conducted in 1785. Franklin was able to show by concealing the hypnotist behind a curtain that subjects' reactions were based on what they thought was happening and not on what was actually happening. Medicine increasingly demanded a blind technique when investigating "unconventional" or "quack" remedies in the nineteenth century but resisted the idea that conventional medical drugs and other remedies ought to be subjected to the same methods. After World War II, medical scientists became more aware of the potential for bias to skew research results if either the subject of the experiment, or the physician observing the experiment, knew who was receiving the "true" medicine, so the *double-blind* design, with neither party knowing which subject got the study medication and which got the placebo, gradually was adopted as the standard of valid research. Thus, precisely when placebos were less often used in medical practice (because so many powerful new drugs were available), placebos began to be used much more often as a research tool.

Modern medical ethics demands frank disclosure to the patient of the nature of any treatment administered. This, in most cases, rules out the deceptive use of placebos in therapy. But ethics does not rule out the attempt to elicit a placebo effect by creating a positive emotional environment during interaction with the patient. After largely dismissing the mind for many decades as largely unimportant and resistant to scientific study, modern medical science has developed a renewed interest in understanding the mechanisms by which the placebo effect might work. In 2001, the U.S. National Institutes of Health announced a new research program specifically aimed at understanding the mechanisms of the placebo effect and helping practicing physicians to enhance the effect.

Scientific understanding

Two psychological mechanisms appear to contribute to the placebo effect: *expectancy* (believing that a positive bodily change will occur) and *conditioning* (being in circumstances that, in the past, produced a positive bodily change). Evidence is accumulating that expectancy of pain relief can produce the release of endorphins, naturally occurring morphine-like chemicals in the brain that produce analgesia. In one study, when patients in pain following surgery were given a visible injection of a narcotic painkiller into their intravenous tubing, they experienced twice as much pain relief as when the same drug was given by hidden injection and the patient was unaware of receiving the drug. When naloxone, a drug that antagonizes the effects of endorphins, is administered to patients in the same manner, the placebo effect can be reversed.

Modern brain imaging techniques promise to expand the understanding of the mechanisms of the placebo effect. Using positron emission tomography (PET) scanning, for instance, patients experiencing a placebo effect in Parkinson's disease were shown to be manufacturing more dopamine in their brains, indicating that the placebo effect in Parkinson's may work by the same biochemical mechanism as the standard drug therapy.

Amidst new findings on how the placebo effect works, some skeptics continue to question whether the effect even exists. A systematic review of 114 randomized double-blind clinical trials (Hróbjartsson and Gøtzsche, 2001) concluded that there is no good evidence that administering placebos in the context of scientific trials produces any significant change in the subjects. (The authors did not intend their findings to address whether the placebo effect might exist in actual medical practice.) The methods used in this review have been challenged by placebo-effect advocates. Regardless, an important lesson from skeptical research such as this is that there are many mimics whose effects must be carefully separated from true placebo effects. Perhaps the most common mimic is the natural history of the illness, or the body's inherent healing powers. Many older studies that are quoted as confirming a powerful placebo effect in fact failed to distinguish between the patient's getting better because the illness was self-limited and the body's defenses were capable of eliminating it (as is the case with most common viral illnesses) and improvement that truly depended on the patient's mental or emotional state.

Implications for religion

Placebo effects may be of greatest interest in one category of so-called complementary and alternative medicine (CAM): methods of healing that rely particularly on religious faith or religious practices.

Religiously-based healing might be thought, by believers, to occur in one of two ways. In what one might call the *natural* route, faith, prayer, or other religious practices may be seen as stimulating the same chemical and physical processes in the human body as would be produced by any other system of medicine or healing. In what one might term the *supernatural* route, faith or prayer comes directly from a divine source and does not depend solely upon processes that science can measure or understand.

In religious healing by the natural route, the placebo effect could account for some and perhaps all of the healing observed. Faith and prayer may produce positive expectancies, and religious ritual may be a powerful source of psychological conditioning. So long as one believes that the human mind is part of the natural world, molded by the same creator who is responsible for any other healing modality, it seems logical that one would seek to harness the powers of the mind as part of whatever healing occurs. On this understanding the placebo effect becomes simply one means by which faith can heal.

In religious healing by the supernatural route, it might appear by contrast that if one could show that a placebo effect were occurring, that would exclude the possibility of the postulated healing effect. This seems particularly true for studies of intercessory prayer, in which believers claim that patients can be healed when people pray for them unbeknownst to the patients themselves. By definition, no emotional or mental effect can be generated if the subjects are completely unaware of

the intervention. Therefore, to claim that the results of intercessory prayer are a placebo effect would be the same as denying that intercessory prayer works.

Another important implication of the placebo effect for religious healing is shared with other types of CAM: the design of appropriate comparison groups to conduct reliable research. What counts as adequate evidence that any form of CAM, including religious or faith healing, works? Some scientists reject all CAM out of hand as based on superstition and quackery, but more careful scientists are willing to accept CAM insofar as it can be shown to be effective in rigorous scientific studies. The question then arises as to what counts as adequate scientific "rigor" given the subject matter under study.

One way to approach this concern is to view science as a highly systematic way to show with a high level of probability that one explanation is the correct explanation for the phenomenon in which we are interested. Showing this requires that we consider all other plausible explanations and find ways to exclude them, so that we are left with only one explanation that appears to be correct. This is what it means in general terms to have a controlled study. It follows from this analysis that having a placebo or sham-treatment control group is one good way to eliminate several plausible explanations for healing. A placebo control group can eliminate the placebo effect, the natural course of illness, and a number of chance statistical associations as reasons why the subjects receiving the healing intervention got better. Because the placebo control is useful for many study purposes, it is tempting to assume that the only valid scientific study is one with a placebo control, but this would be mistaken. Depending on the question being investigated and which alternative explanations are most plausible, there may be other scientific methods to exclude the alternative explanations with a high degree of reliability. In many possible studies of religious healing, the usual methods to assure scientific rigor will simply not be possible. It is hard, for example, to imagine a population of both believers and nonbelievers agreeing to be assigned randomly to receive real or sham faith-healing.

See also MEDICINE; MIND-BODY THEORIES; SPIRITUALITY AND HEALTH

Bibliography

Amanzio, Martina; Pollo, A.; Maggi, G.; and Benedetti, Fabrizio. "Response Variability to Analgesics: A Role for Non-specific Activation of Endogenous Opioids." *Pain* 90 (2001): 205–215.

Brody, Howard, with Brody, Daralyn. *The Placebo Response: How You Can Release the Body's Inner Pharmacy for Better Health.* New York: HarperCollins, 2000.

Brody, Howard. "The Placebo Effect: Implications for the Study and Practice of Complementary and Alternative Medicine." In *The Role of Complementary and Alternative Medicine: Accommodating Pluralism,* ed. Daniel Callahan. Washington, D.C.: Georgetown University Press, 2002.

De la Fuente-Fernandez, Raúl; Ruth, Thomas J.; Sosi, Vesna; et al. "Expectation and Dopamine Release: Mechanism of the Placebo Effect in Parkinson's Disease." *Science* 293 (2001): 1164–1166.

Guess, Harry A.; Kleinman, Arthur; Kusek, John W.; and Engel, Linda W., eds. *The Science of the Placebo: Toward an Interdisciplinary Research Agenda.* London: BMJ Books, 2002.

Hróbjartsson, Asbjørn, and Gøtzsche, Peter. "Is the Placebo Powerless? An Analysis of Clinical Trials Comparing Placebo with No Treatment." *New England Journal of Medicine* 344 (2001): 1594–1602.

HOWARD BRODY

PLANCK TIME

The Planck time is a unit of time that is defined by three of the fundamental constants of nature: Isaac Newton's constant of gravitation, G; the velocity of light in vacuum, c; and Max Planck's constant, h. These constants may be combined in one and only one way to give a quantity that has the dimensions of a time:

$$t_{\text{PLANCK}} = (Gh/c^5)^{1/2} = 1.3 \times 10^{-43}\ s$$

This unit of time exists independently of all human standards of time measurement. It is defined by the gravitational, relativistic, and quantum aspects of the universe. The universe can be said to be "old" in the well defined sense that it is about 10^{60} Planck times in age (about thirteen billion years). The Planck time has cosmological significance. It marks the time before which the entire universe displays wave-particle duality. In order to understand events earlier than the Planck time, quantum cosmology is required. The Planck time was first identified by German theoretical physicist Max Planck (1858–1947) in 1899, although the idea of a natural unit of time based on the fundamental constants G, c, and e (the charge on the electron) was first presented by Irish physicist George Johnstone Stoney (1826–1911) in 1881.

See also AGE OF THE UNIVERSE; COSMOLOGY, PHYSICAL ASPECTS; PHYSICS, QUANTUM

Bibliography

Barrow, John. *The Constants of Nature.* London: Jonathan Cape, 2002.

JOHN D. BARROW

PLATO

In his written dialogues, Plato developed accounts of knowledge, reality, humanity, society, goodness, God, and beauty. Usually, when people speak of Platonism, they are referring to his theory of Forms, accompanied by a doctrine of the immortality of the soul and values that transcend power, prestige, and pleasure. Western thought has developed either by following and adapting his accounts or by reacting to them, either directly or indirectly through, most notably, Aristotle, Plotinus, Philo, and Augustine. The theory of Forms established the most basic concept of science as it came to be practiced in Europe, namely, that science aims to discover objective principles, in other words, "Forms." Plato's doctrine of the immortality of the soul and values that transcend the material world have reinforced and shaped systematic thinking within Judaism, Christianity, and Islam.

Life and times

Plato (428–347 B.C.E.) was born in Athens to a rich and politically powerful family. Instead of taking his place in the ruling class, he became a philosopher. He founded the Academy and invented a new form of literature, the dramatic dialogue. His dialogues, featuring the philosopher Socrates (469–399 B.C.E.), have profoundly shaped history, in a way comparable to the writings of Paul about Jesus.

Plato chose philosophy because he fell under the spell of Socrates as a young man while witnessing the horrors of political life in his time and city. At the time of Plato's birth, Athens, a city-state in Greece, was the world's first democracy, inventing such wonders as trial by jury, as well as some of the greatest sculpture, architecture, and drama of any age. But during this time of extraordinary human achievement, the wisest man of all, as confirmed by a religious oracle, was one who professed to have no wisdom at all: Socrates. Socrates would closely question people who professed to know politics, religion, or any deep wisdom about life, and he would show that their pretenses to wisdom were false. Socrates would also use his chains of questions to lead anyone who would speak with him to agree human excellence was exclusively a matter of wisdom, and that the search for wisdom was the best way to spend one's life.

Plato was fascinated by Socrates and joined other young men in spending time in his company. At the same time Plato observed how demagogues led Athens to prolong its Peloponnesian War (431–404 B.C.E.) against Sparta, a war that ended in utter defeat for Athens. The Spartans installed an antidemocratic government that included members of Plato's family. This government ruled murderously, but briefly, until a citizens' armed rebellion restored the democracy, although Athens's empire and military preeminence were gone forever. Under this same democracy, just a couple of years later (399 B.C.E.), a religiously conservative prosecutor brought Socrates to trial on charges of atheism, heresy, and corrupting the young. The jury found Socrates guilty and sentenced him to death. It is no wonder that Plato became disillusioned with a life aimed at political rule, and decided instead to devote his life to developing Socrates's ideas.

Plato spent his time in private conversations with friends about Socrates' ideas, honoring his memory by continuing to seek wisdom. Some of these friends were Pythagoreans. Pythagoras lived about a hundred years before Plato in Greek colonies in the south of Italy. According to reports, Pythagoras had supernatural powers and formed a religious school of followers. He believed that human souls are reincarnated in animal and human bodies. Pythagoras also was aware of the mathematical structure of musical harmony and believed that numbers provide the explanation of all the order in the universe. Plato traveled to southern Italy a couple of times in his life, at least in part because of his interest in Pythagoras. In his written dialogues, Plato developed Pythagorean as well as Socratic ideas. Plato also followed Pythagoras in forming a school, which became known as the Academy.

Work

Next to nothing is known of the way the Academy was run, but a great deal is known about Plato's writings, since all of his dialogues have survived. The dialogues present at least three different theoretical systems, probably from Plato's early, middle, and late periods, though any such dating is speculative and controversial. The early dialogues focus on ethical issues, and usually end with the speakers admitting their ignorance. For example, in the *Laches* the question is "What is courage?" in the *Euthyphro* "What is reverence?" in the *Charmides* "What is moderation?" in the *Lysis* "What is a friend?" and in the *Protagoras* "How are the virtues alike?" Though the arguments are inconclusive, they give an account of virtue as purely a matter of intellect, which is contrary to the widespread belief, then and now, that virtue requires proper desires or a good will in addition to technical know-how.

The middle and late dialogues end with the speakers reaching positive conclusions that are not limited to ethics. In the middle dialogues, such as the *Phaedo, Symposium, Phaedrus,* and *Republic,* Plato uses arguments to prove, as well as myths and metaphors to embellish, an account of the soul as having three parts: reason, which aims at truth; emotion, which seeks social values such as prestige; and desire, which aims at material satisfaction. This soul is immortal and destined to enjoy the beauty of divine objects that are not seen with the senses but understood, in much the way one understands mathematics with the intellect. It is the nature of these souls to be constantly reincarnated into various human and animal bodies. The process of reincarnation disorients the soul and makes it believe that sense objects are the only realities. Proper reflection on human crafts and sciences, as reflected in the use of language, enables human souls to recognize ultimate reality. The crucial turning point comes when one realizes that all well-made or beautiful or good objects share the same qualities or structure or *Form.* For example, it is not by sensory perception of particular beds that an expert carpenter or engineer designs and builds a bed, but by an intellectual recognition of what function beds are meant to perform. When the soul recognizes the reality of the Forms, and turns away from the senses towards such intellectual, math-like reasoning, it begins its path towards salvation. The soul achieves salvation by recognizing that the realm of Forms, not the material world, is true reality, so that one's desires for bodily and social goods cease to attach the soul to the material world, with the result that, at death, the soul is not drawn back into another body but ascends to the realm of the gods, if only for a limited time.

In the *Timaeus,* perhaps his most influential contribution to the dialogue between science and religion, Plato extends this account to general cosmology, explaining the design in the visible world by referring to a divine craftworker who fashioned the whole (by referring to Formal reality, of course) and insured its proper function by making it a living thing with a soul. Plato begins the tradition of *perfect-being theology,* which argues that God must be perfect, hence good, unchanging, eternal, and so on. In the later dialogues, beginning with the *Parmenides,* Plato raises problems with his theory of Forms, leading him not to abandon it but to abandon his middle period confidence that the Forms are simple enough that human minds can unmistakably know them without possibility of error.

Influence

Plato's influence on science and religion is probably greater than any other single person's. He lived at a time when there was no sharp distinction between the methods of religion and of science, and he was early enough in the history of western civilization to cast his shadow over the development of western science and religion. His influence on science is largely through Aristotle, who accepted with modifications Plato's view that the world can be explained in terms of form and matter and teleology, that is, the function objects are designed to perform. These categories dominated, and perhaps stifled, scientific thinking until the scientific revolution of the 1600s, when mathematical advances allowed scientists to try to explain the laws of nature in purely mechanistic terms (of particles pushing and pulling particles). Even in that revolution, Plato's influence continued. For instance, Galileo

Galilei (1564–1642) used Plato's method of writing dialogues in the great debate between Ptolemaic and Copernican world systems to challenge the weight of religious authority by appeal to the light of reason.

Plato's influence on religion is even more profound. Philo (c. 20 B.C.E.–c. 50 C.E.) attempted to explain Jewish religion in Platonist terms and set a model that would be followed by Christians. In the three centuries after the death of Jesus, Christians had to choose between different interpretations of their faith as found in their sacred writings. As they worked to establish a biblical canon and creeds, they found themselves engaging in discussions shaped by Plato's and Aristotle's metaphysical and theological ideas. Some of these early writers, such as Tertullian (c. 160–c. 225), deplored any attempt to produce a platonic Christianity. Others, such as Origen (c. 185–c. 254), used platonic reasoning to defend the faith in a manner that would be followed by Augustine of Hippo (354–430), who in turn influenced all later Christian theology. Christian apologists appealed to platonic arguments to show that God exists and is perfectly good, that God designed the world, and that human beings have immortal souls. Then they supplemented these arguments with revelations from scripture. While critics of Christianity's Hellenization continue to this day, orthodox Christianity remains in the mold of perfect-being theology, and apologists continue to use platonic arguments.

See also ARISTOTLE; AUGUSTINE; CHRISTIANITY; GALILEO GALILEI; IDEALISM; JUDAISM; SOUL; TELEOLOGY

Bibliography

Burtt, Edwin A. *The Metaphysical Foundations of Modern Physical Science.* London: Routledge and Kegan Paul, 1932.

Cantor, Norman F. *The Civilization of the Middle Ages.* New York: HarperCollins, 1993.

Cooper, John M. *Plato: Complete Works.* Indianapolis, Ind.: Hackett, 1997.

Copleston, Frederick. *A History of Philosophy,* Vol. 1. New York: Doubleday, 1962.

De Santillana, Giorgio. *The Origins of Scientific Thought.* Chicago: University of Chicago Press, 1961.

Guthrie, W. K. C. *A History of Greek Philosophy,* Vol. 5. Cambridge, UK: Cambridge University Press, 1975.

Hare, R. M. *Plato.* Oxford and New York: Oxford University Press, 1982.

Irwin, Terrence. *Classical Thought*. Oxford and New York: Oxford University Press, 1989.

Kenny, Anthony, ed. *The Oxford History of Western Philosophy*. Oxford and New York: Oxford University Press, 1994.

Livingstone, R. W. *The Legacy of Greece*. Oxford: Clarendon Press, 1921.

Lovejoy, Arthur O. *The Great Chain of Being*. Cambridge, Mass.: Harvard University Press, 1933.

Nietmann, William F. *The Unmaking of God*. Lanham, Md.: University Press of America, 1994.

Russell, Bertrand. *Wisdom of the West*. New York: Crescent Books, 1959.

Tarnas, Richard. *The Passion of the Western Mind*. New York: Harmony Books, 1991.

GEORGE H. RUDEBUSCH

PLAYING GOD

The phrase "playing God" is not a theological term; rather, it derives from secular culture and functions as a naturalistic proscription against scientific or technological interventions into nature. It functions as a warning that manipulation of natural processes may precipitate a disaster, one ironically triggered by human action but uncontrollable by human remedy. The commandment against playing God appears most frequently at the intersection where new developments in genetic research meet public policy.

The phrase "playing God" carries at least three overlapping meanings. The first refers to the sense of awe rising from new discoveries into the depths of life. Natural mysteries are being revealed, and scientists, who are the revealers, sense that humans are on the threshold of acquiring God-like powers, especially in matters of life and death.

The second meaning of "playing God" supposes that scientists are substituting themselves for God. Like Prometheus, scientists are said to be overstepping finite limits; out of pride or hubris they are risking a backlash from nature. This leads critics to prescribe a new commandment: Thou shalt not play God. This commandment relies on the Bible: "pride goes before destruction" (Prov.

16:18). "Playing God" means confusing knowledge with the wisdom one needs to decide how to use knowledge. In the battle between science and society, critics point to the deterioration of the ecosphere as an example of the consequences of unwise employment of science and technology.

In the field of genetics, the phrase "playing God" refers to the sacralization of DNA, manifest in moral injunctions against altering human DNA, especially altering the germline that could influence future generations. The sacralization of what evolution has created appears also in the opposition to genetically modified foods (GMFs), wherein what is natural is presumed to better for health than what is technologically modified.

Even though it is a secular phrase, the three meanings of "playing God" prompt theologians to ask questions about the relationship between the divine creator and the human creature. Unlike a naturalism that treats nature itself as sacred and inviolable, Christian, Jewish, and Muslim theists hold that God as creator and lover of all things is alone sacred. Natural life, important as it is, is not ultimate. The creator, not the creation, is sacred.

See also GENE THERAPY; GENETIC DETERMINISM; GENETIC ENGINEERING; GENETICS; HUMAN GENOME PROJECT

Bibliography

Dutney, Andrew. *Playing God: Ethics and Faith*. San Francisco: HarperCollins, 2001.

Peters, Ted. *Playing God? Genetic Determinism and Human Freedom*. London and New York: Routledge, 1997.

Rifkin, Jeremy, and Howard, Ted. *Who Should Play God? The Artificial Creation of Life and What It Means for the Future of the Human Race*. New York: Dell, 1977.

TED PETERS

PLURALISM

The term *pluralism* is applied to philosophical positions emphasizing diversity and multiplicity over homogeneity and unity. The word first appeared in the work of Christian Wolff (1679–1754) and was later popularized by William James (1842–1910).

Ontological pluralism

Just as one can distinguish substantival monism (everything is explicable in terms of one thing) from attributive monism (everything is explicable in terms of one kind of thing), so can one discriminate *substantival pluralism* (everything is explicable in terms of a multiplicity of substances) from *attributive pluralism* (everything is explicable in terms of a multiplicity of kinds). Sometimes substantival pluralism is called *weak pluralism,* and attributive pluralism is called *strong pluralism.*

Opposing the monistic metaphysics of Parmenides' Eleatic School, ancient proponents of pluralism include Empedocles (495–435 B.C.E.), who held that everything is comprised of four elements (earth, air, fire, and water); Anaxagoras (500–428 B.C.E.), who asserted that all things are made of up of bits of every thing; and the atomists Leucippus (fl. 450–420 B.C.E.) and Democritus (460–370 B.C.E.), who asserted that all things are constituted by indivisible particles configured in different ways. Aristotle (384–322 B.C.E.) and Gottfried Wilhelm Leibniz (1646–1716 C.E.) can also be considered pluralists, the first because of his claim that reality is ultimately comprised of individual substances, the second because of his view that reality is made up of an infinite number of elemental monads having the fundamental attribute of perception.

Like substantival and attributive monism, substantival and attributive pluralism are logically independent. Because Baruch Spinoza (1632–1677) held that there is one substance with an infinity of attributes, he is a substantival monist and an attributive pluralist. Alternately, because Leibniz claimed that all monads have the same attributes, he is an attributive monist and a substantival pluralist.

In *A Pluralistic Universe* (1909), William James links pluralism and monism to the acceptance or rejection of the doctrine of internal relations. Accordingly, pluralism "means . . . that the sundry parts of reality *may be externally related*" (p. 274). While the pluralist believes that things are what they are apart from their relationship with other things, the monist claims that each thing is what it is only because of its relationship with other things—and ultimately with the whole containing them.

Cognitive pluralism

While the Western philosophical and theological tradition has generally sought fundamental unity in ontology, truth, and meaning, recent thinking has soundly criticized this project. Among the complex reasons for this is the contemporary rejection of the correspondence theory of truth. If one cannot justifiably speak of a determinate contour of the world apart from human awareness, conception, and language about that world, then it seems there can be no "mirroring" of the world in representation and language, no ultimate criteria by which to adjudicate conflicting interpretations of reality. Accordingly, all that remains are perspectival interpretations based upon discipline-specific assumptions about rationality and truth. Thus *cognitive pluralism* arises, a situation owing much of its popular development to the later Ludwig Wittgenstein, Thomas Kuhn, Paul Feyerabend, Richard Rorty, and the French postmodernists.

Jean-Francois Lyotard describes such a pluralism in his work, *The Postmodern Condition* (1984). Over and against modernity's universalizing reason and discourse, he points to the existence of various epistemic social practices and to the multiplicity of linguistic signifiers, discourse genres, and narratives. Because the assumptions underlying scientific activity are not self-evident, scientific discourse is controlled by various meta-prescriptive rules. Since such rules are locally assumed, there can be no universally applicable, rational discourse. Accordingly, postmodernism privileges antirealism over realism, perspectival epistemology over neutral epistemic and transcendental standpoints, pragmatic truth over the correspondence theory, and local narratives over overarching metanarratives. Cognitive pluralism rejects any foundationalist claim that knowledge is ultimately derivable from indubitable propositions or experiences; it recognizes a diversity of cognitive styles, patterns of rationality, and sensibilities, and it assumes that different sets of justified beliefs can exist alongside each other.

Other pluralisms

One can also identify *ethical pluralism, discourse pluralism,* and *explanatory pluralism.* Ethical pluralism claims that there are a number of incommensurable perspectives on the good or just society. (It can also mean the existence of a plurality of self-justifying, fundamental moral principles.) Discourse pluralism affirms the legitimacy of various kinds of discourse in speaking about a region of being. It holds that there can be irreducible levels of description, yet denies that each description refers to entities having metaphysical existence (e.g., possible worlds, numbers, mental states, etc.). Finally, explanatory pluralism asserts that explanations at different levels of description (e.g., psychology and neuroscience) can profitably be offered in the absence of reduction and without claiming the mutual metaphysical existence of the events and entities referred to in each (e.g., Cartesian dualism).

Pluralism, science, and theology

Is genuine dialogue between postmodern science and theology possible, or does the pluralism and localization of postmodern discourse produce epistemological incommensurability? Are there only isolated local narratives whose "truths" cannot be interrelated? Many in the theology-science discussion deny this radical claim. Wentzel van Huyssteen suggests that evolutionary epistemology reveals the biological roots of all rationality and thus provides a suitable basis for postfoundationalist rationality. Niels Gregersen attempts to fit cognitive pluralism into a common framework of rationality by using Nicholas Rescher's pragmatist coherence theory. Gregersen claims that coherence is the critical norm for all types of knowledge and that it provides a middle way between modernity's critical realism and the radical pluralism espoused by many postmodernists.

Explanatory pluralism is also important in the science-theology discussion. Accordingly, events within a common domain having both a physical and theological description can have both a physical and theological explanation. One can, however, question the coherence of explanatory pluralism, citing what Jaegwon Kim has called the "Principle of Explanatory Exclusion": There cannot be two complete and independent explanations of the same event.

Finally, one might ask if and how *ontological pluralism,* either in its substantival or attributive forms, is more conducive than monism for conceiving how God might act within the universe.

See also EXPLANATION; ONTOLOGY; POST-
FOUNDATIONALISM; POSTMODERNISM; PRAGMATISM

Bibliography

Gregersen, Niels Henrik. "A Contextual Coherence Theory for the Science-Theology Dialogue." In *Rethinking Theology and Science: Six Models for the Current Dialogue,* eds. Niels Henrik Gregersen and J. Wentzel van Huyssteen. Grand Rapids, Mich.: Eerdmans, 1998.

James, William. "A Pluralistic Universe." In *Essays in Radical Empiricism and A Pluralistic Universe,* ed. Ralph Barton Perry. New York: Dutton, 1971.

Kim, Jaegwon. "Mechanism, Purpose and Explanatory Exclusion." In *Supervenience and Mind: Selected Philosophical Essays,* ed. Jaegwon Kim. Cambridge, UK: Cambridge University Press, 1993.

Lyotard, Jean-Francois. *The Postmodern Condition: A Report on Knowledge,* trans. Geoff Bennington and Brian Massumi. Minneapolis: University of Minnesota Press, 1984.

van Huyssteen, J. Wentzel. *Duet or Dual: Theology and Science in a Postmodern World.* Harrisburg, Pa.: Trinity Press International, 1998.

DENNIS BIELFELDT

PNEUMATOLOGY

Pneumatology refers to either the Christian doctrine of the nature and work of the Holy Spirit, or the study of human beliefs in spiritual beings. The term *pneumatology* also refers to the scientific study of air or gases. The Greek word *pneuma* suggests both wind and smell, as well as divine or human breath. Whereas notions of *pneuma* and spirit in ancient and medieval times referred to an earthly or bodily quality, since the sixteenth century the dichotomy of spirit and body emerged, modifying the conception of *pneuma* in time with the modern split of man and nature. The question of whether and how nature and human beings are empowered by spiritual energies and a divine spirit ought to be at the core of a dialogue between religion and sciences that claim to investigate nature in regard to invisible dialectics behind visible phenomena. The Judeo-Christian tradition offers a manifold of concepts for pneumatology, even if these have not yet been adequately tapped in a larger-scale dialogue with modern science.

See also HOLY SPIRIT

SIGURD BERGMANN

POSITIVISM, LOGICAL

The term *logical positivism* is particularly associated with the so-called Vienna Circle, a group of leading philosophers, mathematicians, and scientists that met in Vienna, Austria, in the late 1920s and early 1930s, with German philosopher Moritz Schlick (1882–1936) as chairman. They put forward what they regarded as a "scientific world-conception," which was both anticlerical and opposed to metaphysics. It was, they believed, characterized by two main features. The first was a general empiricism, and the second a devotion to a certain rigorous way of thinking that they called *logical analysis*. This relied particularly on the techniques of modern formal logic.

Empiricism, in the tradition of such philosophers as David Hume (1711–1776), holds that knowledge can only be obtained from direct experience. Although explicitly a science-based philosophy, it always causes problems for science because science always wishes to generalize from present experience through induction. A strict empiricism will, however, wish to deduce all claims to knowledge from the direct experience of which we are infallibly aware. Knowledge is the product of our pooled, intersubjective experience. What is beyond the reach of human perception and observation cannot be judged to be real. In its effects, the view becomes centered on human judgment and dependent on human capabilities. It is anthropocentric in that it will only deal with what exists in so far as it is accessible to human experience. The latter is defined in terms of what is "immediately given." In other words, what is in principle beyond the reach of the human senses cannot be meaningfully discussed. Science defines what it is possible to know, and a strict empiricism sets the limits, as the manifesto for the Vienna Circle puts it, "for the content of legitimate knowledge" (p. 309).

The Circle held that "the meaning of every statement of science must be statable by reduction to a statement about the given" (p. 309). This puts the whole of science (and hence, they believed, of knowledge) on a firm empirical footing. It is, however, worth noting that, even at the time, it was questionable whether this gave an adequate account of physics. Modern quantum mechanics has been plagued by disputes about the status of subatomic particles. These disputes often themselves stem from positivist views about the dependence of knowledge on sense experience. The difficulty is how far we can posit entities that by definition we cannot observe. Can they be thought really to exist even though they cannot be directly observed? That these kinds of questions were major stumbling blocks can be illustrated by considering that for logical positivists even the issue of the other side of the moon was a problem before humans had actually observed it. They could only say that it could be observed "in principle," and indeed it was eventually observed by humans. There are, however, many items to which modern physics wishes to refer that cannot be observed even in principle, unless those words are stretched beyond any recognizable use. What of the other side of the universe, or the interior of a black hole, not to mention quarks and other subatomic particles?

The influence of the Vienna Circle

The fame and influence of the Vienna Circle began to be felt in the 1930's. Such eminent figures as philosophers Rudolf Carnap (1891–1970), Herbert Feigl (1902–1988), and Friedrich Waismann (1896–1959), mathematician Kurt Gödel (1906–1978), and sociologist and economist Otto Neurath (1882–1945) were members, and their own individual influence was spread as they were all scattered across the globe as a result of the political upheavals of the 1930's in Central Europe, leading up to the Second World War. Other well-known figures were associated in some ways with the Circle. They tended to see Ludwig Wittgenstein (1889–1951) as one of their own, although, particularly in his later philosophy, he reacted very much against the idea that only science could set the standard for knowledge. Philosopher Karl Popper (1902–1993) also betrays some of the influence of the Circle, not least by arguing that the test for science was its ability to test empirically its theories by seeing if they could be falsified. This was a variation on the Circle's insistence of being able to test scientific theories through empirical verification. His argument was that conclusive verification was impossible to achieve. One can never know that all members of a class have been seen. For example, it is better policy to try to refute the theory that all swans are white than to seek to confirm it. A single black swan will be enough to falsify the theory. Popper's philosophy of science is therefore geared to making conjectures and attempting to refute them, rather than trying to confirm them. The result inevitably implies a certain agnosticism about scientific truth. Theories always have to be tested for possible falsehood. Yet we cannot know that they are true but only that they have so far survived scrutiny.

W. V. O. Quine. Two other philosophers attended the meetings of the Circle and were influenced by its outlook. W. V. O. Quine (1908–2000) was one of the leading American philosophers of the twentieth century and put forward a science-based philosophy. He was, however, also influenced by American pragmatism and criticised some of the Vienna Circle's basic tenets. In particular, it was held that all statements were either *synthetic* (subject to empirical checking and verification) or *analytic* (true by definition or by virtue of the meanings of the words used). An example of a synthetic statement would be, "All swans are white." One can discover there are black swans. Analytic statements would include, "All bachelors are unmarried" and "Two and two are four." One could not discover either statement to be false by looking at the world. Quine, however, challenged the whole analytic-synthetic distinction, and in so doing, undermined much of its empiricism. He also made space for theoretical entities, such as electrons, which might not be cashed out wholly in empirical terms. He did, however, continue in the belief, strongly held by the Circle, that philosophy was to be subordinated to science, and that there was no room for metaphysics, which could justify the practice of science in the first place.

A. J. Ayer. The other major philosopher who attended meetings of the Circle was A. J. Ayer (1910–1989). He became the voice of logical positivism in the English-speaking world through the publication of his influential *Language, Truth and Logic*. First published in 1936 as the first book of a young man, it argued that meaningful statements were to be divided into the two categories of the analytic and synthetic. Any other category of statement had to be dismissed as meaningless. He thus dismissed all metaphysics, and that explicitly included religious statements about God. Genuine statements of fact had to be empirically verifiable. Nothing could be factually significant to people unless they knew how to verify the proposition it purports to express. This was the *criterion of verifiablity* or the *verification principle*.

Since the existence of God is not a mere tautology (true by definition), according to Ayer, it could only be a factual statement with empirical consequences. His argument can be illustrated by the way he deals with the suggestion that the occurrence of regularities in nature could be evidence for the existence of God. Yet, according to Ayer, if the claim that there is a god amounts empirically to no more than the claim that certain types of phenomena occur in certain sequences, then talking of God is equivalent to talking of those regularities. Ayer could not allow reference to anything beyond our experience. Speaking of the transcendent, like the metaphysical, was just so much hot air, not a genuine assertion of anything. A parallel might be the claim that there is a *heffalump* in the garden. If a person said there was a heffalump, but did not know what a heffalump looked like, or indeed how to ever recognise a heffalump, it becomes difficult to know what one is saying. Talking of something that is in principle unverifiable becomes perilously like not saying anything at all.

What went for religion also applied to other wide categories of apparent statements, such as those of ethics and aesthetics. They are not scientifically verifiable and therefore cannot be regarded as saying anything that could be true or false. It has already been remarked that even contemporary physics may want to refer to what lies beyond possible human observation, so the verification principle is a blunt instrument even in science. It was commonly seen, though, to get into most trouble when people questioned the status of the verification principle itself. If one states that the only meaningful statements are those that can be empirically verified, or that all metaphysical claims are literally nonsense, how can one empirically verify those assertions? Is not the basic claim itself meaningless because it is beyond the scope of empirical observation? Ayer's later claim was that the verifiability criterion was "an axiom," but particular axioms do not have to be chosen. If someone sees that the adoption of such a rule, or starting point, involved the jettisoning of much that is deemed important in human life, that might seem a good reason for not having the axiom in the first place.

Positivism and the status of science

Despite its shortcomings, Ayer's verification principle, and the veneration for science expressed by the repudiation of metaphysics, had a profound affect on theology and the philosophy of religion for many years in the middle of the twentieth century. In many ways, logical positivism still casts its shadow. The idea that religion is not entitled to talk of realities beyond human experience is a seductive one. Yet it strikes at the root of any belief that the physical world is not all that there is, but that there is another nonmaterial realm. Even within theology, there is a constant temptation to reduce talk of a nonmaterial, transcendent realm, such as the Kingdom of Heaven, to matters of everyday experience. It is still often thought that what cannot ultimately be cashed out in empirical terms cannot refer to anything real. This involves changing our concentration from, say, the reality of God, to issues concerning human reactions, attitudes, and practices. Yet in the end, this is an old-fashioned materialism in a sophisticated guise. It is no different from Thomas Hobbes (1588–1679), the seventeenth-century philosopher, saying that there is no difference between God speaking to someone in a dream and dreaming that God spoke.

In the debate about the relations between science and religion, the legacy of logical positivism is to accord science a philosophical status that is denied metaphysics in general and theology in particular. The tendency will be to assume that the assertions of science have an epistemological priority that theology must always respect. In any dispute science must always be given priority. Yet, logical positivism was an anthropocentric view. It related everything to actual and possible sense experience, which had to be human sense experience. We could not understand claims of radically different kinds of experience. By definition, therefore, it was related to human understanding, and the possibilities of human knowledge. This, though, is different from issues concerning the nature of reality. Science is always human science, but it purports to be about a reality that goes beyond, or transcends, our limited and provisional understanding. Philosophy, and metaphysics in particular, has to recognise these limitations. We have to accept that what exists and how we can know it, are radically different kinds of question. This is the difference between ontology and epistemology. The mistake of the Vienna Circle and those it has influenced is to reduce references to what exists to talk of how we can find it out, when who "we" are is not always clearly defined. Any exaggerated respect for science never

makes it clear whether it is upholding present science, or science as it one day could be. Yet the latter idea itself begins to seem highly metaphysical in the sense that it outstrips any possible method of verification at present available to us.

Logical positivism represents the extreme version of the respect for science that permeates contemporary thinking. Yet the status of science is itself an issue of major philosophical concern that cannot be taken for granted. Not least is the fact that science has to assume the existence of an ordered and regular world. This is a resupposition of science. We may as a matter of fact experience nature as uniform, but why is this? Why do humans have the ability, through reason, to understand the innermost workings of the physical world? Why is mathematics somehow applicable to the workings of nature? For logical positivism, questions like these were insoluble, and therefore meaningless in the first place. Yet the worst way of dealing with awkward questions is to pretend that they do not exist on the grounds that they are meaningless.

See also CRITICAL REALISM; EMPIRICISM; PHILOSOPHY OF SCIENCE

Bibliography

Ayer, A J. *Language, Truth and Logic,* 2nd edition. London: Gollancz, 1946.

Feigl, Herbert. *Inquiries and Provocations: Selected Writings, 1929-1975.* Dordrecht, Netherlands: D. Reidel, 1981.

Gödel, Kurt. *Collected Works,* vols. 1 and 2, ed. Solomon Feferman. Oxford and New York: Oxford University Press, 1986 and 1990.

Karnap, Rudolph. *The Unity of Science.* London: Kegan Paul, 1934.

Popper, Karl. *Logic of Scientific Discovery.* London: Hutchinson, 1959.

Popper, Karl. *Conjectures and Refutations: The Growth of Scientific Knowledge.* London: Routledge and Kegan Paul, 1963.

Quine W. V. O. *Word and Object.* Cambridge, Mass.: MIT Press, 1960.

Quine, W. V. O. *From a Logical Point of View.* Cambridge, Mass.: Harvard University Press, 1963.

Trigg, Roger. *Rationality and Science: Can Science Explain Everything?* Oxford, UK, and Cambridge, Mass.: Blackwell Publishers, 1993.

Vienna Circle. "The Scientific Conception of the World: The Vienna Circle" (1929). Reprinted in Otto Neurath. *Empiricism and Sociology*, eds. Marie Neurath and Robert S. Cohen; trans. Marie Neurath and Paul Foulkes. Dordrecht, Netherlands: D. Reidel, 1973.

Waismann, Friedrich. *Ludwig Wittgenstein and the Vienna Circle*. Oxford: Basil Blackwell, 1979.

Wittgenstein, Ludwig. *Tractatus Logico-Philosophicus*(1922), trans. David Pears and Brian McGuinness. New York: Routledge, 2001.

ROGER TRIGG

POSTFOUNDATIONALISM

One of the central methodological issues in the dialogue between theology and science is the nature of rationality. The way one imagines the operation of reason within and between these disciplines will shape the way one works to bring them into dialogue. The postfoundationalist model of rationality has emerged out of this ongoing discussion as an explicit attempt to move beyond the impasse between foundationalist and nonfoundationalist models. Unlike the foundationalist, the postfoundationalist acknowledges that rational reflection (and more broadly, experience itself) is always and already conditioned by communal and historical contexts. Unlike the nonfoundationalist, the postfoundationalist does not believe that this contextuality makes it impossible to reach beyond the confines of particular communities or to strive for interdisciplinary and transcommunal conversation. The *post* is not merely *after,* nor simply *against* foundationalism (as in nonfoundationalism), although it is both of these. Postfoundationalism is the search for a middle way between the objectivism of foundationalism and the relativism of many forms of nonfoundationalism.

The philosophical theologian most closely associated with this view is J. Wentzel van Huyssteen. His book *Essays in Postfoundationalist Theology* (1997) outlines the contours of this model of rationality, and he fills out the details in *The Shaping of Rationality: Toward Interdisciplinarity in Theology and Science* (1999). Philip Clayton also illustrates this model of rationality in several of his works, including *The Problem of God in Modern Thought* (2000). In his earlier methodological contribution to the dialogue, *Explanation from Physics to Theology* (1989), Clayton argued that rejecting foundationalism does not mean that one automatically falls into the waiting arms of the nonfoundationalists. Several other scholars share the family resemblance of postfoundationalism (for examples, see F. LeRon Shults *The Postfoundationalist Task of Theology,* 1999). Both van Huyssteen and Clayton suggest that the entire debate between foundationalism and nonfoundationalism is based on an outdated epistemological dilemma. Several dichotomies are at play here, but they are all embedded in a deeper assumption that separates epistemology from hermeneutics.

Epistemology and hermeneutics

In the search for apodictic knowledge (*episteme*), classical foundationalists privileged epistemology as the primary enterprise of philosophy, and eschewed the subjective factors that lead to mere opinion (*doxa*). Nonfoundationalists valorize the play of hermeneutics as philosophy's task; since all we have is opinionated interpretation, the ancient (and "modern") goal of objective knowledge must be given up. Postfoundationalism aims to accommodate the postmodern critique of neutral *episteme* without collapsing into relativist hermeneutics. Conversely, it affirms the modernist interest in general patterns of rationality, but rejects foundationalist absolutism. Postfoundationalism insists on a constitutive reciprocal relation between epistemology and hermeneutics, avoiding a collapse into the former (with its "meta-narrative") or the latter (with its isolated narratives). The goal is to maintain the search for truth as an ideal that drives inquiry, without asserting that any particular claim to knowledge provides a totalizing and final metanarrative. For van Huyssteen the search for "intelligibility" is upheld as a common link between theology, philosophy, and the sciences. Accepting the ideal of intersubjective intelligibility, however, does not entail objectivism. An awareness of the "fallibility" of all human knowledge, argues van Huyssteen, protects against the absolutism and hegemony that worry the nonfoundationalist. Further, to avoid fideism, which sometimes haunts nonfoundationalist appeals to the faith of a particular community, the postfoundationalist holds onto the ideals of truth, objectivity, and rationality, while at the same time acknowledging the provisional, contextual, and fallible nature of human reason.

Experience and belief

As a theory of belief-justification, foundationalism distinguishes between "basic" beliefs, which are justified without reference to other beliefs, and "nonbasic" beliefs, which are justified by their inferential relation to basic beliefs. In this view, basic beliefs emerge out of and are immediately justified by experience (whether rational or empirical); inferential justification then flows in one direction—from basic to nonbasic beliefs. One can imagine a "pyramid" of knowledge secured by its firm foundation. Nonfoundationalists typically hold to a form of coherentism, which is the main competitor of foundationalism vis-à-vis the debate over the justification of belief. The favorite images here are a "web" of interconnected beliefs or a "raft" that must be repaired while afloat. Foundationalism has difficulty defending its criteria for the basicality of a belief and accounting for the interdependence of all human beliefs; nonfoundationalism, insofar as it maintains strict adherence to coherent relations among beliefs as the only criterion of justification, has difficulty indicating the truth of its beliefs outside the system. If these are the only options, then philosophers of science and theologians must choose between the alleged security of the foundationalist pyramid and the turbulence of the coherentist raft.

In *The Shaping of Rationality,* van Huyssteen suggests a balance that affirms the broader networks of belief in which rationally compelling experiences are already embedded and recognizes the way in which beliefs are anchored in interpreted experience. Against the foundationalist idea that some beliefs enter the web neutrally (without being interpreted), van Huyssteen insists that all experience is interpreted. Rather than leading to nonfoundationalist relativism, however, he argues that one can critically explore the experiential roots of beliefs without feeling compelled to throw out one's commitment to the explanatory power of those beliefs. In her *Evidence and Inquiry* (1993) Susan Haack asserts that foundationalism and coherentism do not exhaust the options. Against coherentism, foundationalism requires that justification occurs in one direction; against foundationalism, coherentism insists that justification is exclusively accomplished in terms of the relations among

beliefs. Haack argues for a middle way that she calls *foundherentism*—the justification of beliefs is not unidirectional *and* a coherent relation among beliefs is not sufficient for their justification.

Individual and community

The debate over belief-justification is closely linked to the question about the way in which individual and communal factors shape the formation of beliefs. The Enlightenment ideal was the "man of reason" who stands alone and objectively measures the world. All rational individuals can and ought to come to the same conclusion, irrespective of their subjective interests or communal background. Nonfoundationalists build upon the historicist critique of this model of rationality, and emphasize the contextual factors that influence an individual's acceptance of criteria for what is reasonable. Pointing out the linguistic and communal mediation of an individual's web of beliefs, nonfoundationalists argue not only that the modernist ideal is impossible but also that it is undesirable because it so easily leads to the domination of one narrative rationality over another. In its extreme relativist forms, this leads to the conclusion that local theologies and local sciences have their own incommensurable rationalities and are not accountable to other communities of inquiry.

The postfoundationalist agrees that we must move beyond foundationalist theories of rationality that aim for universality and certainty, but finds the nonfoundationalist price for the immunization of theological rationality from critique from other sciences too much to pay. Postfoundationalism accepts the nonfoundationalist sensitivity to the hermeneutical conditioning effected by being situated in a community of inquirers, but refuses to give up the intuition that it is the individual who actually makes rational judgments. This model of rationality recognizes that an individual is always a participant within a particular community of inquiry and so works out of the standards of its tradition, but also acknowledges that the personal voice of a rational agent may also critique those standards through distanciation from the tradition.

Explanation and understanding

The dialogue between science and theology has been shaped by the separation in western culture between the natural and the human sciences. This modern dichotomy was made explicit by Wilhelm Dilthey in the nineteenth century, but was grounded in the metaphysical dualisms of early modern thought (extended vs. thinking substance, nature vs. mind). On this model, the natural scientist objectively observes and measures the material world, offering an *explanation* of the facts in terms of universal laws. The human (or social) scientist examines the behavior of human beings over time, presenting an *understanding* of the value of a particular event in the pattern of a broader context. With these as the available options, some theologians tried to model the study of the Christian religion after the natural sciences; this typically took a foundationalist form in which basic data is posited (e.g., in Scripture or religious experience) and propositions are objectively inferred. Nonfoundationalists, on the other hand, are often satisfied with categorizing theology as a "human" science, involving the depth description of particular linguistic communities.

For the postfoundationalist, all human knowing and so all of the sciences are characterized by both hermeneutical understanding and the drive toward experientially adequate and intersubjective explanation. In *Explanation from Physics to Theology* Philip Clayton proposes a mediating position that recognizes the shaping influence of contexts of meaning, but simultaneously allows for general standards or criteria for explanation in the sciences. He defines *understanding* broadly as an intuitive grasping of patterns of meaning, and *explanation* as a rational reconstruction of these interrelated structures in a primarily theoretical context. Although the values, interests and goals that guide their operation will differ, explanation and understanding are interdependent and operative in both theology and science. By exploring the dynamics of rationality that lay across these fields, postfoundationalism aims to contribute to a safe interdisciplinary space for the dialogue between science and theology.

See also COHERENTISM; FALLIBILISM; FOUNDATIONALISM; NONFOUNDATIONALISM; POSTMODERNISM

Bibliography

Clayton, Philip. *Explanation from Physics to Theology: An Essay in Rationality and Religion.* New Haven, Conn.: Yale University Press, 1989.

Clayton, Philip. *The Problem of God in Modern Thought.* Grand Rapids, Mich.: Eerdmans, 2000.

Gregersen, Niels Henrik, and van Huyssteen, J. Wentzel, eds. *Rethinking Theology and Science: Six Models for the Current Dialogue.* Grand Rapids, Mich.: Eerdmans, 1998.

Haack, Susan. *Evidence and Inquiry: Towards Reconstruction in Epistemology.* Oxford: Blackwell, 1993.

Murphy, Nancey. *Beyond Liberalism and Fundamentalism: How Modern and Postmodern Philosophy Set the Theological Agenda.* Valley Forge, Pa.: Trinity Press International, 1996.

Schrag, Calvin O. *The Resources of Rationality: A Response to the Postmodern Challenge.* Bloomington: Indiana University Press, 1992.

Shults, F. LeRon. *The Postfoundationalist Task of Theology: Wolfhart Pannenberg and the New Theological Rationality.* Grand Rapids, Mich.: Eerdmans, 1999.

Stenmark, Mikael. *Rationality in Science, Religion, and Everyday Life: A Critical Evaluation of Four Models of Rationality.* South Bend, Ind.: University of Notre Dame Press, 1995.

van Huyssteen, J. Wentzel. *Essays in Postfoundationalist Theology.* Grand Rapids, Mich.: Eerdmans, 1997.

van Huyssteen, J. Wentzel. *The Shaping of Rationality: Toward Interdisciplinarity in Theology and Science.* Grand Rapids, Mich.: Eerdmans, 1999.

F. LERON SHULTS

POSTMODERNISM

Postmodernism is an abstract, theoretical term and should be distinguished from *postmodernity,* which describes a sociological or cultural climate. The term *postmodernism* was coined in the late 1940s by British historian Arnold Toynbee, but used in the mid-1970s by the American art critic and theorist Charles Jencks to describe contemporary antimodernist movements like Pop art, Concept Art, and Postminimalism. Jean-François Lyotard, in his book *The Postmodern Condition: A Report on Knowledge* (1979), was one of the first thinkers to write extensively about postmodernism as a wider cultural phenomenon. He viewed it as coming both before and after modernism, the reverse side of it. As such, postmodern moments have subsequently been discerned in thinkers as various as the eighteenth-century Scottish philosopher David Hume, the nineteenth-century Danish philosopher, Søren Kierkegaard, and the German philosopher Friedrich Nietzsche.

Characteristics of the postmodern

For Lyotard, the postmodern is characterized by an incredulity towards metanarratives. By *metanarratives* he means the appeal to explanatory principles that presume to tell the story of the ways things are. Metanarratives are accounts of the origin, foundations, and formations of the various forms of human knowledge: for example, motion (Isaac Newton), the mind (René Descartes and Immanuel Kant), history (George Wilhelm Friedrich Hegel), the economy (Karl Marx), psychology (Sigmund Freud), and society (Emile Durkheim). Metanarratives assume the world and human activity within it can be known as a whole because it is rational and organized according to certain universal and verifiable laws or principles. Postmodernism announces a radical scepticism towards such universalism and the objectivity or view from no where that is presupposed in investigations into and accounts of these foundational laws or principles. Postmodernity, then, would describe a cultural situation in which such scepticism was culturally dominant. In such a time, the postmodern would not just be a theoretical critique of modernity's rational understanding of the world and the universalism of that reasoning. The postmodern would be an attempt to rethink and experience the world according to that antifoundationalism and the turn towards local knowledges or views from a specific standpoints: gendered knowledges, ethnic knowledges, religious knowledges, for example.

The postmodern world is composed of little other than grand narratives, accounts of knowledge that are aware they are partial in nature, refracted through a certain cultural perspective and constructed. Their constructedness is important, specifically when attempting to assess the impact of postmodernism on religion, science, and the debates between them. The constructedness of knowledge challenges the foundational realism of the empirical sciences in which language is simply viewed as transparently communicating the world as it is, mediating between mind and matter. When knowledge of "what is" is understood as constructed, then reality is soft, pliable, and ultimately open to endless interpretation and reinterpretation. Language no longer simply mediates or acts like a clear window on the world. Language creates,

fashions what people see and what they understand by what they see. The universal concepts governing thinking in both the human and natural sciences in modernity—truth, nature, reality, history—are viewed as unstable. The instrumental thinking that accumulated "neutral" data, measured it, calculated the options, and arrived at general statements through an inductive reasoning is seen, at best, as just one form of rationality. Explanation becomes a mode of interpretation. Time (as a sequence of present moments), space (as that which either contains or is the extension of things), matter (as composed of atomized particles) all are refigured by the nonrealism and antifoundationalism of the postmodern. Attention to the constructed nature of representing the world leads to an emphasis upon the metaphoric, the symbolic, the allegorical, the theatrical, and the rhetorical. Rather than a world of inert entities, passive before objective enquiry, in the postmodern all things signify, entities are expressive. The real is an aesthetic effect so that belief in the literal is exactly that, *a belief*. The literal, the transparency of modernity's understanding of the meaning *behind* language, becomes an ideology.

Postmodern science and religion

While Silicon Valley scientists were establishing both themselves and cyberspace, the postmodern condition was producing its own understanding of virtual reality. And while astrophysicists were exploring the collapse of stars and the creation of black holes, the postmodern condition was producing its own understanding of the implosion of secular modernity and the sacredness of the void. The parallelisms between what the empirical sciences term "discoveries" and the cultural sciences in postmodernity would call "inventions" are not felicitous but inevitable. If knowledge is produced rather than found within a particular cultural milieu, then such parallelism will necessarily occur. Mary Hesse had already demonstrated this in her book *Revolution and Reconstructions in the Philosophy of Science* (1980). Paul Feyerabend had taken cultural pluralism right into the heart of the empirical sciences with his *Against Method* (1975).

At the same time, the French philosopher and historian Michel Foucault was developing his genealogies and "archaeologies" of clinics, economics, madness, punishment, and sexuality, and extending the thesis that the way the world is understood and organized is governed by discursive acts of power and practical disciplines in which the body becomes the prisoner of the soul (or the way mind conceives the world to be). A sociology of knowledge led to a sociology of scientific knowledge. New histories were written that countered modernity's "progress" model of scientific discovery. New epistemologies and methodologies were sought, like the feminist standpoint work of Sandra Harding and Helen Longino, which examined *abduction*—or the choices made in scientific research prior to and governing inductive reasoning.

At the same time, a new marriage was emerging between the mythological and the technological. In modernity, as the sociologist Max Weber's "disenchantment thesis" taught, the job of science was to demystify the world, and the various technological revolutions were the practical outworking of this rigorous demythologizing. The success of science was measured by progress in terms of human control over the world. Everything could be explained; science would provide the answers, and technology would harness the answers in order to liberate human beings from the drudgery of labor for the pursuit of civilized living. The supernatural was for the superstitious and the ignorant; religion was for those needing private consolation. Stripped of its liturgies, stories, and priestcraft, religion expressed human ideals of the good life. The priest at the altar was replaced by the scientist in the laboratory as religion, among the enlightened, was viewed as mythological clothing for human aspirations, fears, and projections. As such, modernity's dreams were often secularized religious ones: a new Jerusalem of technological efficiency as intellectually hygienic as it was biologically controlled. The "disenchantment" of the world, cultivated by technological progress, was a fundamental tool in the secularization of the sacred. All values were to be found in this world, not beyond it, and human beings were capable of realizing the very highest of these values themselves, through rationalization and forward planning.

The emergence of the postmodern condition, in critiquing the grand narratives of explanation and pointing up the ideologies of control, appealed to what lay outside of the secular worldview. From the mid-1970s there has been revival of romantic thinking. The gothic imagination flourishes again in popular culture, not only in terms of vampires, warlocks, angels, dungeons, dragons, and fascination with the psychotic, but in terms also of a renewed interest in all things medieval. The mythopoetic was revived, and the character of that revival can be estimated by comparing the Narnia Chronicles of C. S. Lewis to Philip Pullman's *Dark Materials* trilogy or J. K. Rowling's Harry Potter series. For Lewis, Narnia was a separate realm reached only through the wardrobe in a professor's rambling Oxfordshire home. But in *Dark Materials,* the supernatural world is not distinct from the natural world, there is neither one nor the other.

Popular science (promoted in part by various governments wanting to interest the young in the technological and nurture a new generation of scientists and technicians) and science fiction assist now in the re-enchantment of the world. With the spread of home computers, the developments in telecommunications, digital graphics, and cinematic special effects, science promotes the bending of modernity's understanding of the real. Virtual reality is now not standing alongside some naturalistic prototype, virtual realities (plural) confuse any boundary between the natural and the supernatural. Science now promotes the transcendence of the human.

Two important thinkers have helped us to understand this postmodern science: Bruno Latour and Michel Serres. Latour's best known book, *We Have Never Been Modern* (1993), points out how modernity aspired to a transparency that separated one thing clearly from another. Modernity was committed to distillation. What it feared and policed was *hybridities.* As such, modernity produced and fostered a series of dualisms: the objective and the subjective; the body and the mind; the public and the private; the organic and the mechanical; the natural and the cultural. But the production and fostering of such dualisms required mediating agencies. The postmodern world is witnessing the return of the hybrid, as the mediating agencies can no longer cope with the infiltration of one category into another. The vampire, the cyborg, and the angel all figure this transcendence of the human, the instrumental, the calculated, and the rational in contemporary culture. The priest and the scientist are, as they often were in the mediaeval world, the same person.

Michel Serres book *Angels: A Modern Myth* (1993) expounds this new world-view in which postmodern science and religion fuse. Sketching a profound interrelatedness of all things, Serres denies material things are inert. All things communicate—the waves of the sea, weather systems, rock formations, human beings. The world is caught up in endless relays and interchanges of messages. As angels have traditionally been conceived as the purest of messengers, so the world can be viewed as participating in an angelic intercommunication that transcends this particular person or that particular object. Global telecommunications become an expression and development of this participation in a complex, discursive interconnectedness which, ultimately, for Serres, sings a doxology to the Most High. Serres practices the hybridity Latour informs us is the state of things, relating it specifically to a theological (in fact specifically Christian and sacramental) worldview.

Conclusion

The postmodern condition announces the collapse of secularism, but it also announces a new dialogue between religion and science. In premodernity, scientific enquiry submitted itself to religious judgement. In modernity, religion was deemed outdated, if not pathological, by the rise of the new sciences. In postmodernity, neither the oppositions nor the hierarchies pertain. And so the character of the debates between religion and science will change also. The earlier debates concerned themselves with attempting to show that there was no incompatibility between scientific discoveries and the religious perspective. They were conducted frequently by scientists with religious commitments, in an attempt to integrate two divergent views of the world. They constituted a form of liberal apologetics in which science offered the vision of what was, and religionists showed how that did not conflict with a theological worldview. The metaphysics of empiricism and positivism remained firmly in place, dictating the terms of the struggle and the attempts at *détente*. Postmodernism, having challenged those empiricisms and positivisms, having announced a contemporary incredulity in such foundationalism, will usher in a round of new debates between religion and science that will demonstrate a shift in cultural power, a reciprocal learning, a new respect. Serres's work shows the way, but religionists have recently appealed also to the work of the Oxford mathematician Roger Penrose who, in a different way, endorses an indeterminacy between the brain and

the world such that both the material and the immaterial are caught up in complex informational processes. The various alliances between new age religions and concerns with ecology are also significant indicators of cultural change. The basis for the new discussions is an emphasis upon interconnectedness and attention to participating within open-ended informational systems in which the psychic and the material are not distinct but inseparable, mutually informing dimensions.

See also NONFOUNDATIONALISM; POST-FOUNDATIONALISM; POSTMODERN SCIENCE

Bibliography

Harding, Sandra. "Rethinking Standpoint Epistemology 'What is Strong Objectivity?'" In *Feminist Epistemologies,* eds. Linda Alcoff and Elizabeth Potter. London: Routledge, 1993.

Latour, Bruno. *We Have Never Been Modern,* trans. Catherine Porter. Cambridge, Mass.: Harvard University Press, 1993.

Latour, Bruno, with Michel Serres. *Conversations on Science, Culture and Time,* trans. Roxanne Lapidus. Ann Arbor: University of Michigan Press, 1995.

Longino, Helen. "Subjects, Power and Knowledge." In *Feminist Epistemologies,* eds. Linda Alcoff and Elizabeth Potter. London: Routledge, 1993.

Lyotard, Jean-François. *The Postmodern Condition: A Report on Knowledge* (1979), trans. Geoff Bennington and Brian Massumi. Manchester, UK: Manchester University Press, 1984.

Poovey, Mary. *The History of the Modern Fact: Problems of Knowledge in the Sciences of Wealth and Society.* Chicago: University of Chicago Press, 1998.

Serres, Michel. *Angels: A Modern Myth,* trans. Francis Cowper. Paris: Flammarion, 1993.

Shapin, Steven. *A Social History of Truth: Civility and Science in Seventeenth Century England.* Chicago: University of Chicago Press, 1994.

Shapin, Steven, and Schaff, Simon. *Leviathan and the Air-Pump.* Princeton, N.J.: Princeton University Press, 1985.

Taylor, Mark C. *About Religion: Economies of Faith in Virtual Culture.* Chicago: University of Chicago Press, 1999.

Ward, Graham. *Cities of God.* London: Routledge, 2000.

GRAHAM WARD

POSTMODERN SCIENCE

Postmodern science challenges the modern ideal of the neutral scientist who applies formal rules of deduction to develop theories that objectively explain empirical data. Alongside feminist (and other) critiques of metanarratives, it emphasizes the local contextual factors (i.e., language, culture, gender) that shape the theory-formation and practices of scientists. Modern (and especially positivist) science was characterized by a strong distinction between the objective (hard) sciences and the subjective (soft) sciences. Insofar as postmodern science blurs these boundaries and recognizes the overlap between explanation and understanding in divergent forms of human rationality, it helps to foster the dialogue between science and religion.

See also POSTMODERNISM

Bibliography

Toulmin, Stephen. *The Return to Cosmology: Postmodern Science and the Theology of Nature*. Berkeley: University of California Press, 1982.

F. LERON SHULTS

PRAGMATISM

Is pragmatism the optimistic expression of the industrial era, deemed to be vanishing in the postindustrial society, or is it a serious philosophical alternative to traditional rationalism and empiricism, idealism and realism? What is labeled *pragmatism* ranges from the philosophy of nineteenth-century American scholar Charles Sanders Peirce (1839–1914), who claimed inquiry for truth's sake, to Richard Rorty's (b. 1931) twentieth-century neopragmatism, which claims, in an antirealist spirit, that criteria of evidence are not objective but only conversational constraints. Most pragmatists, however, try to find a middle way between metaphysical realism and relativism, between dogmatism and skepticism, by using the pragmatic maxim. This maxim holds that in order to ascertain the meaning of an idea one should consider the practical consequences that might conceivably result from it.

Belief is considered to be guiding people's actions in that it is a habit, a disposition to behave. Its opposite is doubt, which, unlike René Descartes's methodological doubt, is involuntary and unpleasant, usually caused by some surprising phenomenon that is inconsistent with one's previously accepted beliefs. Inquiry starts when humans, like other organisms, strive to obtain an equilibrium with their environment, the inquiry manifesting itself in new habits and revised beliefs. Successful inquiry results in a stable viewpoint, but only temporarily stable, seen in the long run. Sophisticated inquirers will therefore always be motivated to further inquiry, transforming the primitive homeostatic process into scientific inquiry.

Universalizing pragmatism: John Dewey

American philosopher John Dewey (1859–1952) was deeply influenced by Peirce's idea of scientific method and inquiry, but Dewey broadens it to take on universal scope. He conceives of the scientific method simply as the way people actually think, or ought to think. Unlike Peirce, Dewey also emphasizes the immediacy of experience, generally characterized in terms of its aesthetic quality, as felt immediacy and, as such, basic and irreducible. Cognitive experience is the result of inquiry. The process starts when a person encounters some difficulty, proceeds through the stage of conceptual elaboration of possible resolutions, and results in a final reconstruction of the experience into a new unified whole. With this idea, Dewey and other pragmatists question what are labeled "spectator theories of knowledge," according to which knowledge is a kind of passive recording of antecedent facts. Instead, knowing is seen as a constructive conceptual activity, anticipating and guiding our adjustment to future experiential interactions with our environment. The classical ontological distinctions in philosophy between mind and body, between means and end, and especially between fact and value, therefore cannot be ascribed an absolute status but should rather be functionally and contextually understood. Consequently, Dewey rejects the idea of truth as correspondence of thought to unknowable things-in-themselves. Instead, it is a matter of successful adjustment of ideas to problematic situations. For that reason, Dewey prefers to talk about warranted assertability.

Pragmatism in science: W. V. O. Quine

Like all pragmatists, the neo-pragmatist W. V. O. Quine (1908–2000), one of the leading American philosophers of the twentieth century, also rejects the idea of reaching the balance between language, truth, and reality once and for all as an unusable fiction. He develops the idea of the interactivity between conceptual invention and discovery of content in the sense that the conceptual system as a whole has to pass the test against experience. There is no guarantee that any kind of truth could be excepted from a future process of revision. Since there is no unique method of finding truth, nor any universal language for finding the final conceptualization of the world, there is no way of talking about reality as such. Nevertheless, for Quine, the danger of relativism is illusionary. What has been obtained in scientific research through epistemological and ontological decisions is absolutely binding, although in the future it will probably have to be modified or even given up. In what way there will be a change, however, lies beyond present cognitive abilities.

Pragmatism in religion: William James

The objection of subjectivism and relativism is also directed against nineteenth-century American philosopher William James's (1842–1910) conception of truth. Unlike Peirce (and to some extent Dewey), James does not focus only on the empirically testable consequences of a belief. He rather shifts the emphasis to what the consequences of a person having a belief are. True beliefs work. Not surprisingly, this conception of truth has been taken as a straight identification of truth with utility. James, however, distinguishes between the different ways that different beliefs work. Concerning empirical judgments, "true" means "verified through observation and experiment." Thus, the accusation of identifying truth with utility cannot be applied to empirical judgments. Neither does it affect a priori truths since they are truths that one is prepared to accept in the sense of conceptual presuppositions by means of which one talks about reality. Only concerning a third kind of truths—moral, aesthetic, and religious ones—is the pragmatic identification of truth and usefulness valid. The kind of judgment involved here cannot be empirically verified. The truth-value of such judgments is given by their practical working in life. If religions shall be more than idle talk, they have to have practical consequences for the people who choose them; they have to work psychologically satisfactorily in their lives. James defends people's right to have religious beliefs if the choice between believing them and disbelieving them is unavoidable, and if they offer a real option, even though religious beliefs cannot be decided on the basis of empirical evidence.

Pragmatism in science and religion

In one specific sense there is, according to pragmatism, no difference between science and religion. Both activities have to be understood in relation to the kind of beings human are. Neither science nor religion can address reality as independent of human experience. However, whereas science deals with experimental, observational experience, religion concerns existential experience. A theory is empirically adequate if it enables people to generate testable hypotheses and thereby maintain what is true in the observable world. Religions and their secular counterparts are existentially adequate if they provide people with conceptions of life at its best so that, in the tension between how life is and how it could be, they can attain a feeling for good and evil, right and wrong, and thus generate values and meaning, and express what is true in their lives.

See also CONSTRUCTIVISM; CONTEXTUALISM; IDEALISM; REALISM

Bibliography

Dewey, John. *Logic: The Theory of Inquiry* (1938). In *John Dewey: The Later Works, 1925–1953*, Vol. 4, ed. Jo Ann Boydston. Carbondale: Southern Illinois University Press, 1986.

Herrmann, Eberhard. "A Pragmatic Approach to Religion and Science." In *Rethinking Theology and Science: Six Models for the Current Dialogue*, eds. Niels Henrik Gregersen and J. Wentzel van Huyssteen. Grand Rapids, Mich.: Eerdmans, 1998.

Hookway, Christopher. *Peirce*. London: Routledge and Kegan Paul, 1985.

James, William. *Pragmatism: A New Name for Some Old Ways of Thinking* (1907). In *The Works of William James*, ed. Frederick H. Burkhardt. Cambridge, Mass.: Harvard University Press, 1975.

Murphy, John. *Pragmatism: From Peirce to Davidson.* Boulder, Colo., and San Francisco: Westview Press, 1990.

Pihlström, Sami. *Pragmatism and Philosophical Anthropology: Understanding Our Human Life in a Human World.* New York: Peter Lang, 1998.

Putnam, Hilary. *Pragmatism: An Open Question.* Oxford: Blackwell, 1995.

Putnam, Ruth Anna, ed. *The Cambridge Companion to William James.* Cambridge, UK: Cambridge University Press, 1997.

Quine, W. V. O. *Ontological Relativity and Other Essays.* New York: Columbia University Press, 1969.

Rorty, Richard. *Consequences of Pragmatism.* Minneapolis: University of Minnesota Press, 1982.

EBERHARD HERRMANN

PRAYER AND MEDITATION

Prayer is the practice of communion with God and traditionally involves components such as confession, thanksgiving, and intercession (praying for the needs of others). Meditation is a form of spiritual practice based on focused attention that is restrained in its use of words or images. Whereas prayer is conceptualized in terms of a relationship with God, meditation does not necessarily make theistic assumptions. Prayer and meditation raise several issues for the science-religion discussion, including the effects of intercessory prayer for those prayed for and the more general benefits of prayer and meditation for those who practice them. There are both outcome questions about the extent of the benefits, and process questions about how benefits are mediated.

Intercessory prayer

The efficacy of intercessory prayer is not easy to investigate scientifically. To do so would obviously require a control group of people who are not prayed for. It would also be necessary to ensure that those being prayed for do not know that they are being prayed for; otherwise any benefits might be considered a kind of placebo effect. Indeed, it is often considered desirable during such a study that the people who pray do not know the full identities of those for whom they are praying. In a hospital setting, the medical staff also should not know the identifies of those being prayed for to ensure that they do not influence clinical outcomes by treating the prayed-for people differently.

Meeting all these methodological requirements involves creating highly artificial conditions. For example, it is questionable whether it is possible to pray effectively for people whose identities have been concealed. Even if such prayer is possible, it may be less powerful than heartfelt prayer for a known person. It is also arguable that knowing that the prayer is being undertaken for the sake of a scientific experiment undermines its effectiveness; perhaps prayer ought only to be undertaken out of concern for the person prayed for. There is also the theological question of how God might respond to testing the effectiveness of prayer scientifically. Prayer is primarily a matter of a person's relationship with God, not of control of the world.

Despite these problems, a number of scientific investigations of the efficacy of prayer have, in fact, been undertaken. The results are mixed and inconclusive, with some studies finding an effect, others not. However, there is certainly more evidence for the effectiveness of prayer than would be expected by chance. In the 1980s, Randolph Byrd carried out a study of nearly four hundred coronary care patients. A control group was prayed for, while an experimental group was not; other patients and medical staff were kept blind about who was in which group. When this experiment was concluded, the patients who had been prayed for had a better outcome. A number of well-designed studies have been conducted since then and have found significant effects from intercessory prayer, though some experts remain unconvinced by these studies.

Is there a way of explaining the efficacy of prayer that is consistent with the scientific worldview? In general, explanations are divided between those who invoke God and those who do not. Those who do not invoke God see the efficacy of intercessory prayer as a form of psychokinesis or remote mental influence. Those who invoke God see it as a special case of divine action.

A series of well-designed experiments have been conducted on "bio-psychokinesis" that indicate that it is possible to influence a range of specific biological functions in others without any immediate contact. Several of these effects have been well-replicated. It is possible that intercessory prayer, such as prayer for physical healing, is a specific example of bio-psychokinesis. Of course, that does not completely explain the phenomenon because researchers do not understand how bio-psychokinesis itself works. It may be preferable to look first for some not-yet-understood naturalistic explanation of bio-psychokinesis, rather than assume that a wholly non-naturalistic explanation is required.

Alternatively, the effect of prayer can be seen as a special case of divine action, but one in which divine action is triggered or facilitated by prayer. This raises the theological conundrum of why God should act in response to prayer rather than acting on God's own initiative. It is theologically objectionable to suppose that God is unaware of human needs or not motivated to respond unless prayer occurs. It is also objectionable to suppose that God is powerless to act without human prayer, though it is perfectly acceptable to suggest that, out of voluntary self-restraint, God might prefer to act in conjunction with the prayerful initiatives of human beings. If so, prayer could be seen as establishing a union of wills between human beings and God. Science provides a source of analogies for how that could come about. For example, it may be analogous to a nuclear resonance, or some kind of attunement.

A divine action model would probably predict that the prayer of people who have strong faith and lead good lives would be the most effective. A psychokinesis model of prayer would probably predict that prayer would be most powerful if carried out by people with psychic powers (which would, of course, have to be assessed in some independent way, to avoid circularity). There is thus some prospect of testing the different predictions of the two kinds of theories empirically.

Benefits to the person who prays

Next, there is the question of whether prayer benefits the person who prays. Here we are concerned not just with intercessory prayer but with the full range of prayer, including thanksgiving, adoration, confession, and petition. It is almost certain that prayer makes a valuable contribution to personal coping. However, actual evidence for this is not easy to collect. It would be hard to conduct a controlled study in which an experimental group prayed regularly over a sustained period, and a control group never prayed. Most people would not be willing to allow whether or not they prayed to be dictated by the requirements of an experimental design, certainly not for long enough to show a broad range of effects.

That means that the evidence will only be correlational in nature. There is indeed a good range of studies showing that people who pray tend to be better adjusted. One of the most sophisticated of such studies is that of G. Parker and L. B. Brown (1982), who found that prayer was one of the coping strategies that apparently helped to protect against depression. However, the problem with all such studies is that they are correlational, which interferes with firm conclusions about causal effects, particularly when so little is known about the causation of the phenomenon under investigation. There is also the problem that prayer is closely related to other aspects of religion, such as religious beliefs, experience, and public rituals. It is hard to be sure that it is prayer that helps, rather than those other aspects of religion.

It is nevertheless highly plausible that prayer is helpful, and it is not difficult to suggest how it might be so. It seems to serve as a cognitive method of coping with stress in which events are conceptualized in a broad framework of meaning. The religious frame of reference does not look at events primarily in terms of whether they are enjoyable, but in terms of how they relate to the purposes of God. It is a basic belief of many faith traditions that God can bring blessing out of adversity, and prayer facilities the application of that belief to particular events.

Attributional processes are important in coping generally, and the beneficial aspects of prayer are probably mediated in part by the attributional aspects of prayer. Prayer invites attributions to God, whereas otherwise there may be little alternative to attributions to one's own strengths or weaknesses, or to seeing events as the result of mere chance processes. Thanksgiving is an aspect of prayer that plays a particularly important role in the reformulation of attributions.

Meditation

Meditation has been widely studied scientifically, especially transcendental meditation. There is clear evidence that transcendental meditation produces a distinctive arousal pattern of relaxed alertness, and there is evidence also of its therapeutic value, not only on subjective measures such as anxiety, but on more objective measures such as use of drugs and alcohol. However, none of that may have much to do with religion; it may be that transcendental meditation is little more than a technique for deep relaxation.

The cognitive aspects of meditation are more interesting from a theological point of view. A pointer to the distinctive mode of cognition induced by meditation comes from the classic laboratory studies of Arthur Deikman during the 1960s in which college students gazed at a blue vase while refraining from thinking discursively about the vase in any way. The unusual sensations of vividness experienced were interpreted as arising from a suspension of the normal "automatization" of perception.

Though some meditation moves beyond words and images, much of it still uses them, albeit in an unusual way. Words and images are characteristically used sparingly, but each is allowed to resonate with maximum depth of meaning. Layers of meaning may be uncovered that are felt to be "ineffable." That sense of ineffability may arise from making use of a meaning system of the cognitive architecture that is distinct from, and to an unusual extent decoupled from, propositions that lend themselves to articulation.

See also SPIRITUALITY

Bibliography

Braud, William. "Empirical Explorations of Prayer, Distant Healing, and Remote Mental Influence." *Journal of Religion and Psychical Research* 17 (1994): 62–73.

Brown, Laurence B. *The Human Side of Prayer: The Psychology of Praying.* Birmingham, Ala.: Religious Education Press, 1993.

Byrd, Randolph "Positive Effects of Intercessory Prayer in a Coronary Care Unit Population." *Southern Medical Journal* 81 (1988): 826–829.

Chibnall, John T.; Jeral, Joseph M.; and Cerullo, Michael A. "Experiments on Distant Intercessory Prayer: God, Science, and the Lesson of Massah." *Archives of Internal Medicine* 161, no. 21 (2001): 2529–2536.

Deikman, Arthur. "Deautomisation and the Mystic Experience." *Psychiatry* 29 (1966): 324–338.

Eysenck, Hans J., and Sargent, Carl. *Explaining the Unexplained: Mysteries of the Paranormal.* London: Prion, 1993.

Francis, L. J., and Astley, J., eds. *Psychological Perspectives on Prayer.* Leominster, Mass.: Gracewing, 2001.

Hood, Ralph W., Jr.; Spilka, Bernard; Hunsberger, Bruce; and Gorsuch, Richard. *The Psychology of Religion: An Empirical Approach,* 2nd edition. New York: Guilford Press, 1996.

Parker, G., and Brown, L. B. "Coping Behaviours that Mediate Between Life Events and Depression." *Archives of General Psychiatry* 39 (1982): 1386–1391.

Stannard, Russell. *The God Experiment: Can Science Prove the Existence of God?* London: Faber and Faber, 1999.

Watts, Fraser. "Prayer and Psychology." In *Perspectives on Prayer,* ed. Fraser Watts. London: SPCK, 2001.

Watts, Fraser. *Theology and Psychology.* Aldershot, UK: Ashgate, 2002.

West, Michael A., ed. *The Psychology of Meditation.* Oxford: Clarendon, 2002.

FRASER WATTS

PRIMATOLOGY

Primatology is the study of primates, an order that includes prosimians, monkeys, apes, and humans. Similarities between humans and monkeys were noted already by Aristotle in the fourth century B.C.E., and the Greek physician Galen even dissected a monkey for comparison. In the eighteenth century, Swedish botanist and taxonomist Carl Linnaeus created the order of primates to include monkeys, apes, and humans. The similarity between apes and humans was also noted by Charles Darwin, who argued in *The Descent of Man* (1871) that human beings evolved from an ape-like ancestor.

Even so, relatively little was known about primates until the twentieth century. In 1917, psychologist Wolfgang Kohler published work demonstrating chimpanzees' ability to learn and perform problem solving. In the 1920s, Robert Yerkes established a center for studying primates that was eventually located at Emory University in Atlanta, Georgia. After World War II, significant fieldwork was spearheaded by paleontologist Louis Leakey, who supported research by Jane Goodall with chimpanzees, Diane Fossey with gorillas, and Biruté Galdikas with orangutans. Of the three, Goodall's work has been the most significant, providing remarkable evidence of tool use, social complexity, coordinated hunting, and meat-eating. Modern primatology is a diverse field, involving biologists, anthropologists, and psychologists. Primate species continue to be discovered, and knowledge of many species is comparatively scant.

The question of human uniqueness

While there are many motivations for studying primates, the similarity between humans and other primates has been a key factor in funding and theorizing. Among primates, the great apes (including chimpanzees, bonobos, gorillas, and orangutans) are most similar to humans on anatomical, evolutionary, and genetic grounds. Studies of genetic relatedness indicate that humans and chimpanzees have 98.4 percent of their genes in common, making chimpanzees more closely related to human beings than to gorillas or orangutans. Partly because of this, chimpanzees have attracted far more attention by researchers. Bonobos, a species rediscovered in the 1970s, have also attracted considerable interest in recent years because of their intelligence and unique social behaviors. In virtually all cases, however, the question of the similarity of the great apes to humans has explicitly or implicitly informed research agendas and directions.

The most obvious question of philosophical and theological import raised by primatology is the question of human uniqueness. Since Aristotle (384–322 B.C.E.), philosophers and theologians have frequently claimed that human beings are unique by virtue of their cognitive abilities, especially their abilities for reason, language, and self-consciousness. Work with the great apes, however, has consistently shown that the gap is not as absolute as has been traditionally claimed. Claims of uniqueness based on tool use were the first criterion to go, as fieldwork by Goodall demonstrated that chimpanzees fashioned tools out of blades of grass, which they used to extract termites from termite mounds. Later research has also indicated that chimpanzees in Côte d'Ivoire carefully select appropriate rocks to crack different kinds of nuts.

In the 1970s, extensive efforts were made to teach the great apes versions of sign language and symbolic communication. B. T. and R. A. Gardner's early work with a chimp named Washoe and Francine Patterson with a gorilla named Koko provided mixed results and generated intense controversy as to whether or not apes were capable of producing or merely mimicking language. E. Sue Savage-Rumbaugh used improved methods in the 1980s and 1990s with chimps and bonobos, and her work is seen by many to have established that these apes are indeed capable of true symbolic communication, even though their abilities seem to stop short of full-fledged language.

Other research has focused on the abilities of apes for self and other representation. Experiments by Gordon Gallup indicated that both chimpanzees and orangutans (but not gorillas) are capable of recognizing their images in a mirror. Observations of chimpanzees and other primates in the wild and in zoo settings indicate the ability to deceive, which implies an awareness of one's actions and the effect that they have on others. Efforts to establish by experiment that apes develop models of the thoughts of others (what is called by researchers a "theory of mind") are more controversial and the question remains unsettled.

While research on cognitive abilities is often understood to challenge traditional claims of human uniqueness, research on the social behavior of primates is frequently understood to reveal the evolutionary roots of human nature, altruism, and morality. Expectations that primate sociality was primarily peaceful were shattered by observations made by Goodall that male chimpanzees formed raiding parties and could engage in brutal attacks. Since then, it has come to be recognized that primate societies in general and ape societies in particular are highly complex and stratified. Chimpanzee dominance hierarchies are maintained by group support and mutual aid, but may be usurped by shifting alliances. While some emphasize the negative aspects of this sociality, described by Andrew Whiten and Richard Byrne as "Machiavellian intelligence," primatologist Frans de Waal has emphasized that positive social behavior and altruism are essential to primate societies and, therefore, to human societies as well. In this regard, bonobos in particular have been noted for peaceful coexistence and conflict resolution. At the same time, feminist primatologists and scholars have been concerned to correct sexist bias in the study of primate behavior. Work by Barbara Smuts with baboons revised understandings of sex and courtship in primates. Historian of science Donna Haraway wrote *Primate Visions* (1989) in an effort to deconstruct the ideological bias that has been part of the history of primatology.

Implications for theology

Despite a vigorous science-religion dialogue in the 1980s and 1990s, primatology as a field has been almost completely ignored by theologians. A number of works, however, do cover some of the issues that primatology raises, even if only indirectly. Theologians such as Jay McDaniel and Andrew Linzey have addressed issues of animal rights. Broader themes of evolution and their implication for human nature have also been addressed by a number of theologians, including Philip Hefner, Arthur Peacocke, and John Haught. Works by these authors, however, only partially address the questions that primatology raises, and more theological reflection and analysis remains to be done.

See also ALTRUISM; ANIMAL RIGHTS; ANTHROPOLOGY; EVOLUTION; LANGUAGE; EXPERIENCE, RELIGIOUS: COGNITIVE AND NEUROPHYSIOLOGICAL ASPECTS

Bibliography

Byrne, Richard, and Whiten, Andrew, eds. *Machiavellian Intelligence: Social Expertise and the Evolution of Intellect in Monkeys, Apes, and Humans*. Oxford and New York: Oxford University Press, 1988.

Cheney, Dorothy L., and Seyfarth, Robert M. *How Monkeys See the World: Inside the Mind of Another Species*. Chicago: University of Chicago Press, 1990.

Darwin, Charles. *The Descent of Man* (1871). Amherst, N.Y.: Prometheus, 1997.

De Waal, Frans. *Good Natured: The Origins of Right and Wrong in Humans and Other Animals*. Cambridge, Mass.: Harvard University Press, 1996.

Haraway, Donna. *Primate Visions: Gender, Race, and Nature in the World of Modern Science*. New York: Routledge, 1989.

Hefner, Philip. *The Human Factor: Evolution, Culture, and Religion*. Minneapolis, Minn.: Fortress Press, 1993.

Linzey, Andrew. *Animal Theology*. Champaign: University of Illinois Press, 1995.

Savage-Rumbaugh, Sue, and Lewin, Roger. *Kanzi: The Ape at the Brink of the Human Mind*. New York: Wiley, 1994.

GREGORY R. PETERSON

PROCESS THOUGHT

Process thought emphasizes the ultimate significance of time's forward flow and the change of those things that exist in time. The accent upon time as integral to existence means that process thought considers life to be comprised of events or, as the philosopher William James (1842–1910) would say, "drops" of experience whose character is established by how each becomes. What might appear to be solid matter is really a dance of energy events and interconnections.

Alfred North Whitehead (1861–1947), considered by many to be process thought's chief philosopher, argued that the elucidation of meaning involved in the phrase "all things flow" is one chief task of philosophy. All actually existing "things" change due to their temporality, but the metaphysical principles, mathematic and definitional abstractions, and the essence of God do not change.

Process cosmology

The world is not made up of vacuous substances or wholly self-contained atoms whose relationship to others is entirely external. Rather, argue process thinkers, all actually existing things (events) are internally related to other things. Life itself evolves through mutual influence. Reality is social, but individual events construct the particular factual character of social existence through moment by moment decisions in relationship with others. The process philosophical notion that all existence is interrelated corresponds well with quantum and relativity theories in physics. The interconnectedness of existence is supported by the observation made by physicists that observers of a particular phenomenon produce changes by merely observing the phenomenon.

Comprehending what process thinkers reject may also be helpful when identifying this movement. Process thought rejects the notion that existence is fundamentally comprised of mechanistic, lifeless matter. Instead, process thinkers affirm that existence is organismic, enchanted, and interrelated. The organismic nature of process thought fits well with general evolutionary hypotheses pertaining to the gradual emergence of new and complex species through natural selection, randomness, and adaptation. Process thought affirms that the emergence of highly developed life forms typically entails genealogical connection and descent with modification.

Process thought rejects the claim that creatures are entirely determined or predestined either by the laws of nature, their genes, the environment, or God. Instead, freedom, creativity, novelty, and individual purpose are affirmed because each event is partly self-creative as it responds to the influence of others. Process categories affirm both that individuals are partly self-organized and partly fashioned by others.

Process thinkers typically reject mind-body dualism whereby one's mind or soul is entirely mental and one's bodily members are entirely physical. Process thinkers also typically reject materialistic physicalism, which ultimately denies that mentality and mind exist at all. Instead, many process thinkers speak of mind in nature when adhering to the panexperientialist (or panpsychist) hypothesis proposed by Whitehead and others. The panexperientialist solution to the mind-body problem entails the nondualist hypothesis that all events, including mind events and those events that comprise one's body, have both mental and physical aspects. Events of the same kind can be mutually influencing.

Process views of God

Although most process thinkers are theists, they typically reject theistic doctrines influenced by traditional metaphysical philosophies. The process theologies emerging from the thought of Whitehead and Charles Hartshorne (1897–2000) exert the greatest influence. These two process scholars call God *dipolar* to signify two different dualities: God is influenced by others and influences others, and God is changing and unchanging.

The first dipolarity, God's influence upon the world and the world's influence back on God, is more pronounced in Whitehead's thought. Whitehead speculates that God adds Godself to that from which every creative act emerges. Creatures respond to this divine action, and their response subsequently exerts influence back upon God.

The second dipolarity, God as both unchanging and changing, is more pronounced in Hartshorne's thought. By this dipolarity, Hartshorne means that God's abstract essence is absolute, necessary, and eternal, while God's concrete actuality is everlastingly relative or contingent. The unchanging pole of the divine essence includes attributes that classical philosophical theologies often ascribe to divinity (e.g., necessity, impassibility, infallibility, eternality, and immutability). The changing aspect of God is expressed in God's experience (e.g., suffering, rejoicing, sympathy, and contingency) as deity interacts, moment-by-moment, with creation.

Process thinkers often speculate that God relates essentially with the world, and Hartshorne calls this God-world model *panentheism* (all things are in God). Panentheism is illustrated by the relationship the members of one's body have with one's soul (or mind) because this relationship is analogous to the way the world is in God. Just as the mind naturally interacts with the brain and other members of the body without being ontologically different, so God naturally interacts with the world without being ontologically different. Just as the mind is an actuality distinct from other actualities in the body, so God is an actuality distinct from other actualities in the world.

Process panentheism agrees with classical pantheism by affirming that God is essentially related to the finite order, without agreeing that God's essence requires this particular finite order. It agrees with traditional theism by affirming that God is distinct from and not fully governed by finite relations, without agreeing that God could have chosen not to be in relation with the world. God is essentially immanent in the world because God necessarily influences all. God is essentially transcendent because God's decision about how to react to such influences is not fully determined by them. This divine decision becomes God's influence upon subsequent individuals.

It should also be noted that process thought escapes the "God of the gaps" charge because theistic process thinkers deny that the causal processes of the universe are occasionally filled by divine acts. Instead, process theism supposes that God is always active in the causal processes, although deity never unilaterally determines any particular causal process or the causal processes of the whole. Whitehead expresses these concepts when he claims that God is not an exception to the metaphysical principles designed to save the scheme from theoretical collapse.

See also *See also* GOD OF THE GAPS; MIND-BODY THEORIES; PANENTHEISM; PANTHEISM; THEISM; WHITEHEAD, ALFRED NORTH

Bibliography

Barbour, Ian G. *Religion in an Age of Science: The Gifford Lectures 1989-91,* Vol. 1. San Francisco: Harper, 1990.

Browning, Douglas, and, Myers, William T. *Philosophers of Process.* New York: Fordham University Press, 1998.

Cobb, John B. Jr., and, Griffin, David Ray. *Process Theology: An Introductory Exposition.* Philadelphia: Westminster Press, 1976.

Griffin, David Ray, ed. *The Reenchantment of Science: Postmodern Proposals.* Albany: State University of New York Press, 1988.

Griffin, David Ray. *Founders of Constructive Postmodern Philosophy: Peirce, James, Bergson, Whitehead, and Hartshorne.* Albany: State University of New York Press, 1993.

Griffin, David Ray. *Religion and Scientific Naturalism: Overcoming the Conflicts.* Albany: State University Press of New York, 2000.

Hartshorne, Charles, and, Reese, William L. *Philosophers Speak of God* (1953). Amherst, N.Y.: Humanity Books, 2000.

Haught, John F. *God After Darwin: A Theology of Evolution.* Boulder, Colo.: Westview, 2000.

Jungerman, John A. *World in Process: Creativity and Interconnection in the New Physics.* Albany: State University of New York Press, 2000.

Teilhard de Chardin, Pierre. *The Phenomenon of Man* (1955), trans. Bernard Wall. New York: Harper, 1976.

Whitehead, Alfred North. *Science and the Modern World.* New York: Macmillan, 1925.

Whitehead, Alfred North. *Process and Reality: An Essay in Cosmology* (1929), corrected edition, ed. David Ray Griffin and Donald W. Sherburne. New York: Free Press, 1978.

THOMAS JAY OORD

PROGRESS

The idea of progress is an invention of the eighteenth century, fueled by discoveries in science and technology. Although it took different forms in different countries, the underlying theme was that, through human effort, it is possible to improve human understanding of the nature of reality. This in turn leads to improvement in the standard of living and of education and health and general wellbeing. More a metaphysical aspiration than a matter of empirical fact, progress was seen as (and intended to be) a secular alternative to traditional religious views, especially inasmuch as it challenged the notion of a providential God, one who controls completely the future fate of humans according to God's desires and unmerited grace.

Many early progressionists were deists rather than theists, believing in an unmoved mover, who lets the universe run according to unbroken law, rather than subjecting it to God's extra-natural intervention. It was almost to be expected, therefore, that many progressionists were favorable to some form of biological developmentalism, or evolution. Notable were Erasmus Darwin (1731–1802, the grandfather of Charles) and Jean Baptiste de Lamarck (1744–1829). They took the idea of progress in the social and cultural world, read it into the biological world, seeing life's history as an upward movement from the simple (the monad) to the complex (the human being), and then in circular fashion read evolution back into the cultural world as confirmation of their social beliefs about the possibility of intellectual and cultural improvement. It is not surprising that many of the early critics of evolution, notably the French comparative anatomist Georges Cuvier (1769–1832), were as critical of the philosophy of progress as they were of the lack of evidential support for transmutation. Although Cuvier was a Protestant, he was more disturbed by the denial of providence than he was by the challenge to literal interpretation of Genesis.

Charles Darwin (1809–1882), the author of *On the Origin of Species* (1859), in which he put forward his theory of evolution by natural selection, had a somewhat complex relationship with the idea of progress. Socially and intellectually he believed in it absolutely. It is also to be found in his biology, for he clearly regarded humans as the outcome and triumph of evolution. But he realized that his mechanism for change was relativistic. Natural selection means that some will survive and reproduce and others will not, and those that are successful in one situation will not necessarily be successful in other circumstances. Darwin had to invoke the idea of what today's evolutionists call an *arms race,* where there is competition between lines and eventual change and progress—the predator gets faster, and then the prey gets faster. Overall, Darwin thought that this would lead to intelligence and ultimately to humans.

After Darwin, socially and biologically, progress reigned supreme. It was the philosophy of the industrialist and educator alike. In biology, the leading spokesman for evolution was Herbert Spencer (1820–1903), who argued that it is a general law of nature that homogeneity tends towards heterogeneity, and this means that humans are superior to animals, and the English to all other peoples. Many Christian thinkers also started to suggest that perhaps progress and religion are not as opposed as traditionally supposed. If God creates through developmental law, who is to say that God is against the worth and success of human effort? Such particularly were the themes of liberal American protestant preachers like Henry Ward Beecher (1813–1887), as well as of the future Archbishop of Canterbury, Frederick Temple (1821–1902).

The twentieth century saw a major decline in support for cultural and social notions of progress. How could one think in terms of improvement in the face of two world wars, the horrors of Stalinist Russia, Auschwitz, the atomic bomb, global warming, and more? Religious thinkers again increasingly invoked the distinction between progress and providence, arguing that the latter is incompatible with the former. In the between-war years, the Anglican poet T. S. Eliot (1888–1965) explored this theme in depth, and the Jewish philosopher Emil Fackenheim (1916–) made this point repeatedly after World War II. To believe in progress was not simply wrong but immoral.

In biology also the notion of progress became much less prominent. After the coming of Mendelian genetics (which emphasizes the randomness of variation), and the development of what was known as neo-Darwinism or the synthetic theory of evolution, there were far fewer scenarios painting a general sweep upward from the blob to humankind. But one might query whether this decline in visible claims of progress was more a function of a general lack of enthusiasm for the overall idea, or more a realization that the intrusion of social ideas into supposedly straight science is not acceptable. Certainly, the most prominent Christian believer who was also a practicing evolutionist, the French Jesuit paleontologist Pierre Teilhard de Chardin (1881–1955),

was an ardent progressionist, following the philosopher Henri Bergson (1859–1941). Among those adopting and endorsing Teilhard's progressivist ideas were such prominent neo-Darwinians as the Englishman Julian Huxley (1887–1975) and the Russian-born American Theodosius Dobzhansky (1900–1975).

The Harvard entomologist and sociobiologist Edward O Wilson (1929–) also endorses biological progressionism. Standing in a tradition that goes back to Spencer, Wilson argues that the evolutionary process gives human beings a backbone on which to build a fully secular substitute for traditional religions like Christianity. For Wilson, progress tells humans where they came from, what status they have in the overall scheme of things (namely the place at the top), and what moral injunctions are laid upon them—to strive to prevent decline and to preserve the human species and, if possible, to send it on to still higher regions of evolution. There have been many critics of this kind of thinking—notably, in biology, Julian Huxley's grandfather Thomas Henry Huxley (1825–1895) and, in philosophy, the early twentieth-century philosopher G. E. Moore (1873–1958)—but in biological circles, if not in general society, belief in progress seems set for the time being. And this probably means that even though such practices may not be in general favor among theologians and Christian believers, there will continue to be those with religious sympathies who attempt to blend progress into their overall world picture.

See also COMPLEXITY; EVOLUTION

Bibliography

Richards, Robert J. *The Meaning of Evolution: The Morphological Construction and Ideological Reconstruction of Darwin's Theory.* Chicago, Ill.: University of Chicago Press, 1992.

Ruse, Michael. "Evolution and Progress." *Trends in Ecology and Evolution* 8, no. 2 (1993): 55-59.

Ruse, Michael. *Monad to Man: The Concept of Progress in Evolutionary Biology.* Cambridge, Mass.: Harvard University Press, 1996.

Wagar, W. Warren. *Good Tidings: The Belief in Progress from Darwin to Marcuse.* Bloomington, Ind.: Indiana University Press, 1972.

Wilson, Edward O. *The Diversity of Life,* Cambridge, Mass.: Harvard University Press, 1992.

MICHAEL RUSE

PROVIDENCE

The concept of providence expresses the idea that divine knowledge, will, and goodness are at work in the design and governance of the world. Adherents of the Abrahamic traditions, (i.e., Judaism, Christianity, and Islam), characteristically affirm not only that God creates and sustains the world but also that God guides its history toward the fulfillment of divine purposes. The idea of providence, therefore, is closely related to ideas of creation, redemption, and eschatological consummation, as these topics are developed within particular religious traditions.

A distinction has often been made between general and particular (or special) providence. *General providence* refers to God's governance of the universe through the design of creation and the conservation, or sustenance, of all finite things. In establishing the fundamental structures of the created world, God sets the parameters of its history, building in various possibilities and ruling out others. In the modern era, this has often been interpreted in terms of God's role as the creator of the structures of natural law that the sciences seek to disclose. By establishing these causal laws and setting the conditions under which they operate, God directs the developing history of the universe. A theological interpretation of nature, quite without any commitment to the design argument in natural theology, can understand the so-called fine-tuning of the universe as an expression of God's general providence, which orders the world in such a way that life can emerge in the course of cosmic evolution.

Particular providence refers to God's actions within the world's history to advance the divine purposes in specific ways. Each of the monotheistic traditions, for example, includes some form of the story in which God calls Abraham and his descendants into a special covenant relationship that unfolds in an historical drama continuing to this day. The faithful in these traditions typically construe both their individual lives and the history of their communities to be caught up in this ongoing relationship to the providence of God, though it may be difficult to discern God's plan in the apparently chaotic course of history. On some modern interpretations, such as that given by the German theologian Friedrich Schleiermacher (1768–1834), particular providence is understood entirely as the outworking of God's general providence in specific instances. God's purposes for human history are built into the design of creation, and God does not so much act within the stream of historical events as enact history as a whole. This avoids a battery of modern objections to certain sorts of special divine actions (e.g., miraculous intervention). There are theological costs to this interpretation, however, and a number of contemporary theologians have sought ways to conceive of God acting responsively to shape the course of events without intervening in or disrupting the natural order.

Traditional theological accounts of providence agree in affirming the perfection of God's knowledge, power, and goodness in governing the world, but they differ in their accounts of what these attributes entail about God's relation to the course of events. Some doctrines of providence assert that God specifically wills and controls everything that happens; God's sovereign and unconditioned intention for the world embraces all the details of cosmic and human history. Reformation theologian John Calvin (1509–1564), for example, contended that God does not just foreknow but rather foreordains all things, including the destiny of the saved and the damned. This appears to constitute a universal divine determinism, and it triggers the objections, first, that it truncates or eliminates human freedom and, second, that it makes God the cause of human sin, thus compounding the problem of evil. Defenders of positions of this type have usually argued that divine governance of human action, unlike determination by finite causes within the world, does not negate human freedom. Some Thomists argue that because God acts in the utterly unique mode of creator, giving being to creatures and not merely acting as a cause of changes in already existing things, God can bring about a finite event *as* a contingent occurrence or as a free human choice. God wills the human agent's act, but this divine willing does not displace the human agent's freedom, rather it posits the agent and the free act in existence.

Other theologians contend that while all finite things are created and sustained by God and all events are accommodated within God's plan for creation, some events are contrary to God's purposes. On this account, God allows a limited freedom to some creatures, who may act against God's will, but whose misuse of their powers nonetheless falls within the range of possibilities provided for in God's creative purposes. There are various accounts of how this creaturely freedom to act against God's will is nonetheless embraced within God's will, so that God's good purposes remain sovereign in fixing the destiny of creation. In the sixteenth century, Luis de Molina (1535–1600) and his followers developed the view that God's omniscience includes knowledge of what every possible free creature would choose to do under every conceivable circumstance. On this account, God is able to take the free actions of creatures into account in the plan of creation, building in responses that assure the final achievement of the good that God intends. Even if divine omniscience does not include this peculiar type of foreknowledge, some modern thinkers have suggested that God, like a master chess player, is always in a position to incorporate the finite agent's actions into the process of realizing God's purposes. If God's providential governance of history involves this type of responsive action, however, then theologians must grapple with questions about how God's special acts engage and affect the ongoing course of events in the world.

See also DETERMINISM; DIVINE ACTION; OMNISCIENCE; SPECIAL DIVINE ACTION; SPECIAL PROVIDENCE

Bibliography

Aquinas, Thomas. *Summa Theologiae* (1266–1273), Ia, QQ. 22–23, 103–105, ed. Timothy McDermott. London: Blackfriars, 1964.

Augustine. *The City of God Against the Pagans,* trans. R. W. Dyson. Cambridge, UK: Cambridge University Press, 1998.

Burrell, David. *Freedom and Creation in Three Traditions.* South Bend, Ind.: University of Notre Dame Press, 1993.

Calvin, John. *Institutes of the Christian Religion* (1535–1559), ed. John T. McNeill. Louisville, Ky.: Westminster John Knox Press, 1960.

Barth, Karl. *Church Dogmatics* (1935), Vol. 3, Pt. 3: *Doctrine of Creation, the Creator, His Creature,* eds. G. W. Bromiley and T. F. Torrence. Edinburgh, UK: T&T Clark, 1977.

Flint, Thomas. *Divine Providence: The Molinist Account.* Ithaca, N.Y.: Cornell University Press, 1998.

Schleiermacher, Friedrich. *The Christian Faith* (1830–1831), Vols. 1 and 2, trans. H. R. Mackintosh. Edinburgh, UK: T&T Clark, 2001.

Tanner, Kathryn. *God and Creation in Christian Theology.* London: Blackwell, 1988.

THOMAS F. TRACY

PSYCHOLOGY

Psychology is a broad-ranging discipline concerned with human mind and emotion, experience and behavior, and personality development and disorder. It goes back at least to the pre-Socratics of ancient Greece, and has always been a central topic in philosophy. It has also been a concern of many religious thinkers, perhaps especially in the Christian and Buddhist traditions. However, psychology as a distinct autonomous discipline only goes back to the nineteenth century.

After considering the implications for theology of the emergence of psychology as a distinct discipline, three different strands in the relationship between psychology and religion will be examined. First there are theological issues raised by the approach to human nature found within general psychology. Second, there is the investigation of religion using the methods and theories of psychology. Finally, there is the possibility of a psychological contribution to a broad range of topics in theology.

Psychology as science

Modern psychology is self-consciously scientific. It accepted the natural sciences as representing the paradigm of rational inquiry and has sought to mould itself in their image. That has often led to giving priority to mechanistic and materialistic approaches, and to experimental method and repeatable observations.

One key problem for psychology has been deciding what to use as its data. Much psychology is based on self-report data, which includes people reporting their own thought processes and experiences, describing their attitudes or behavior, or completing questionnaires about themselves. Questionnaire research has become the stock methodology of much psychology; it is an easy method to use and has probably been overused.

Other self-report data, such as the clinical data collected by Sigmund Freud (1856–1958), may be rich, but there are serious questions about its dependability. One problem with self-report data is that many people are not reliable observers of themselves; the other is that people may not choose to report accurately what they know.

Psychology has also made much use of observable behavior and performance, including observations of how people perform cognitive tasks and how they interact with other people. There was a period in the early twentieth century when psychology imagined that it could base itself entirely on the observation of behavior, and abandon any attempt to study the human mind. However, *behaviorism*, in its strict form, did not last, and mind was readmitted under the heading of *cognition*. It proved impossible to study even conditioning in rats without inferring mental processes such as expectations. Also, psychologists became increasingly sophisticated in the use of task performance to infer cognitive processes. In this more emancipated climate, self-report data was re-admitted, but used cautiously.

The scientific movement out of which modern psychology arose was explicitly secular in that it deliberately avoided making any religious assumptions. The relation of modern secular psychology to the more explicitly religious psychological reflection that preceded it is a complex matter. Some would emphasize the parallelism between the two. Even though psychology appears to be secular, it can be argued that it is much indebted to its religious past and has often recycled theological ideas in apparently secular form. For example, it has been argued that the concept of original sin lies just below the surface of Freud's avowedly secular psychology.

In contrast, John Milbank has robustly argued that modern social theory, because it is avowedly secular and has no place for God, should be regarded as antitheological and inconsistent with Christian thought. The same might also be said about modern psychology. Against that, however, it could be argued that psychology has become religiously neutral and atheological, capable of being combined either with religious or secular worldviews. The model of science that guided modern psychology in the nineteenth century would now be widely regarded as over-restrictive. However,

psychology has gradually become broader, more pluralistic, and more flexible ideologically (i.e., more postmodern).

Psychological approaches to human nature

Psychology contains general assumptions about human nature, and a key issue that arises at the interface of psychology and theology is how compatible are their respective views of human nature. Given the breadth of psychology as a discipline, it is not surprising that it contains a variety of such models, ranging from the biological to the social. Psychology makes use of the radically different methodologies of the social and biological sciences within the same discipline. Not surprisingly, that means that psychology tends to fragment, but it is important that there should be a discipline that tries to hold together these different approaches to the human person. People are both biological and social creatures, and no discipline that ignored one or the other could hope to understand human nature adequately.

There is a tendency for psychology to emphasize the biological aspects of human nature and for theology to emphasize the social and relational aspects. However, a polarized debate should be avoided. An adequate psychology needs to be social as well as biological. Equally, there is no reason why theology should be reticent about the biological aspects of human nature. It is part of the Judeo-Christian tradition, especially in the Old Testament, that human beings come from the "dust" and have much in common with the "beasts." There has been a growing recognition that both theology and psychology in their different ways emphasize the psychosomatic unity of human nature. Theology and psychology both need to hold together the biological and the social aspects of human nature, and could learn from each other's attempts to do so.

One strand of biological psychology seeks to understand human characteristics in terms of their evolutionary origins. There were precursors of this in the sociobiology of Edward O. Wilson (b. 1929), Richard Dawkins (b. 1941), and others; their approach has now been extended into *evolutionary psychology*. A key issue for theology is how strongly reductionist a form evolutionary psychology takes. There is no theological objection to exploring the evolutionary origins of particular human abilities and characteristics, and this has been fruitful in many areas, such as linguistic ability. Problems only arise when it is suggested that the evolutionary approach can explain everything, or that human characteristics are nothing more than the products of their evolutionary origins. Fortunately, cautious research-based approaches to evolutionary psychology are available.

The other important strand of biological psychology is concerned with the brain. Research in neuropsychology has been especially fruitful and has demonstrated close links between cognitive functions and brain activity. The key issue for theology is how this information should be interpreted, which is essentially a philosophical problem. There have been suggestions that the mind and brain are identical, or that mind is an epiphenomenon of the physical brain of no real significance. However, there is no need for psychology to take the kind of strong reductionist approach represented by the biologist Francis Crick (b. 1916), who in 1994 described people as "nothing but a pack of neurons" (p. 3).

Strong forms of social constructionism can be equally reductionist. Human concepts are, of course, the product of particular cultures, and in some respects they are contingent and could be conceptualized otherwise. Further, concepts are psychologically influential, and human experience and behavior is much influenced by how people conceptualize their world. However, there is no need for this to be linked to a nonrealist claim that there is no reality to what concepts represent beyond cultural conventions, or that social constructs completely determine social behavior.

A final area of psychology that carries strong assumptions about human nature is the computer modeling of human intelligence. The analogy between computers and the human mind has been fruitful scientifically and has given cognitive psychology much of its current rigor. However, the indications are that human beings and computers function in such different ways that the analogy between them should not be pressed too far. There is no warrant for asserting that all human functions can be captured in computer form, or that the human mind is nothing but a computer program.

Psychology of religion

The psychology of religion was an active area of psychology in the early days of the discipline and, after a period of decline, has regained some of its former vigor. To realize its potential, it needs to maintain close links with general psychology and apply the most promising advances; generate a broad theoretical approach to religion and relate data to clear research hypotheses; use a range of different methodologies and not rely too much on questionnaire data; and explore the practical applications of psychology for religious life.

The issues about reductionism that arise in general psychology recur in the psychology of religion and can be illustrated in connection with religious experience. There is growing interest in the brain processes involved in religious experience. An example is the research of Eugene d'Aquili and Andrew Newberg, who have analyzed the holistic and causal elements of some types of religious experience and tried to identify their neural substrates. However, whatever progress is made in discovering how the brain is involved in religious experience, there is no reason to conclude that because the brain is involved religious experience has nothing to do with God.

There has also been much interest in the social constructionist approach to religious experience. How people conceptualize experience in religious terms is clearly influenced by the various faith traditions, and may explain the different emphases in religious experiences within different faith traditions, despite the common elements that can also be found. Some have suggested that reports of religious experience are entirely the product of such cultural learning, but there is no basis for asserting that religious experience is nothing more than learning to use a particular set of constructs. Broad-brush social constructionism is being replaced by sophisticated theory and research on the specific cognitive processes involved in religious modes of understanding.

When particular examples of religious experiences are studied, it becomes particularly clear that it is valuable to combine a variety of psychological approaches. This can be illustrated in relation to glossolalia (speaking in tongues), the best investigated of the charismatic phenomena. There is evidence for an element of social learning, in that people benefit from seeing other people speak in tongues, and get better at it with practice. However, the dissociation of semantics from speech production that occurs in glossolalia suggests an unusual mode of cognitive functioning for which there must be a neurological substrate. There is no incompatibility between approaches from social psychology and from cognitive neuroscience, nor is either of them incompatible with a religious account of the role of the Holy Spirit in glossolalia.

There is currently a growing interest in the evolutionary approach to religion, though as yet it is largely speculative. The capacity for religious experience may well be related to the distinctive capacity for self-consciousness of human beings. It can also be seen as having advantages in natural selection terms through the promotion of social cohesion, moral behavior, mental health, and so on. This is supported by the fact that there is growing evidence that religion is positively associated with good personal adjustment.

The link between religion and personal adjustment becomes clearer if religious people are subdivided, for example into those for whom religion is intrinsic or central to their lives (who have good mental health) and those for whom it is extrinsic or serves other goals (who have poor mental health). Though it is always difficult to move with confidence from correlations to casual conclusions, the mechanisms by which religion might promote good adjustment are becoming clear and include the therapeutic value of religious practices and the support provided by the religious community.

Though religious experience illustrates the breadth of the psychological approach needed in studying religion, it is important to remember the multifaceted nature of religion. There is an equally fruitful psychology of religious beliefs and observances. Psychology has often found it fruitful to study how people differ from one another, and how they develop and change. Both have been central to the psychology of religion.

Psychology and theology

Finally, there can be psychological contributions to theology, although these have not been very fully explored as of 2002. For example, the story of the "fall" in Genesis and the doctrine of original sin invite psychological elucidation. Though the story of the "fall" is widely taken by theologians as making an ontological point about human sinfulness, it can equally well be taken as indicating, in narrative form, the gradual evolutionary development of self-conscious cognitive discrimination, represented by the "knowledge of good and evil." This would be,

in a sense, a fall upwards, but it would imply a new capacity to do wrong deliberately, that is, to sin. In addition, emerging self-consciousness would lead to a new awareness of human limitations and fallibility, which would permit human awareness of sinfulness and of separation from God.

Eschatology invites elucidation in terms of the psychology of hope. Though there has been much interest in the relation between cosmological predictions and theological eschatology, it would be a misreading of eschatology to see it as solely concerned with such objective predictions. Eschatology is concerned with a good future that is a gift of God, not just with survival of the universe, and also with an attitude of hope in the present, not just with predictions about the future. Psychology can help to elucidate the nature of eschatological hope. It seems to be not just a matter of optimism (making positive predictions about the future), but a hopeful attitude that can be sustained even when there is little basis for optimism.

There are many theological topics that can be complemented by a psychological approach that does not compete with or displace the theological one. For example, a theology of grace can be complemented by a psychological account of how the benefits of grace work themselves out at a human level. Similarly, a theology of prayer can be complemented by a psychological account of how the activity of prayer helps to transform those who participate in it. The act of thanksgiving, for example, involves a reappraisal, both of the evaluation of experiences as positive or negative, and of the role of God in causal attributions.

See also ARTIFICIAL INTELLIGENCE; BEHAVIORISM; EVOLUTIONARY PSYCHOLOGY; EXPERIENCE, RELIGIOUS: COGNITIVE AND NEUROPHYSIOLOGICAL ASPECTS; FREUD, SIGMUND; MIND-BRAIN INTERACTION; NEUROPHYSIOLOGY; NEUROSCIENCES; PSYCHOLOGY OF RELIGION; SELF

Bibliography

Brown, Warren S.; Murphy, Nancey; and Malony, H. Newton, eds. *Whatever Happened to the Soul? Scientific and Theological Portraits of Human Nature.* Minneapolis, Minn.: Fortress Press, 1998.

Crick, Francis H. *The Astonishing Hypothesis: The Scientific Search for the Soul.* London: Simon and Schuster, 1994.

D'Aquili, Eugene, and Newberg, Andrew B. *The Mystical Mind: Probing the Biology of Religious Experience*. Minneapolis, Minn.: Fortress Press, 1999.

Hefner, Philip. *The Human Factor: Evolution, Culture, and Religion*. Minneapolis, Minn.: Fortress Press, 1993.

Hood, Ralph W.; Spilka, Bernard; Hunsberger, Bruce; and Gorsuch, Richard. *The Psychology of Religion: An Empirical Approach*. 2nd edition. New York: Guilford Press, 1996.

Jeeves, Malcolm A. *Human Nature at the Millennium: Reflections on the Integration of Psychology and Christianity*. Grand Rapids, Mich.: Baker Books, 1997.

Meissner, William W. *Life and Faith: Psychological Perspectives on Religious Experience*. Washington, D.C.: Georgetown University Press, 1987.

Milbank, John. *Theology and Social Theory: Beyond Secular Reason*. Oxford: Blackwell, 1990.

Spilka, Bernard, and McIntosh, Daniel N., eds. *The Psychology of Religion: Theoretical Approaches*. Boulder, Colo.: Westview Press, 1997.

Watts, Fraser; Nye, Rebecca; and Savage, Sara. *Psychology for Christian Ministry*. London: Routledge, 2001.

Watts, Fraser. *Theology and Psychology*. Aldershot, UK: Ashgate, 2002.

FRASER WATTS

aims primarily to demonstrate the illusion of a perceived transcendent and the regressive and oppressive effects of being religious.

See also FREUD, SIGMUND; PSYCHOLOGY; SELF

Bibliography

Hood, Ralph W., Jr.; Spilka, Bernard; Hunsberger, Bruce; and Gorsuch, Richard L., eds. *The Psychology of Religion. An Empirical Approach*. New York: Guilford, 1996.

Koteskey, Ronald L. *Psychology from a Christian Perspective*. Lanham, Md.: University Press of America, 2002.

Kurtz, Paul. *The Transcendental Temptation: A Critique of Religion and the Paranormal*. Buffalo, N.Y.: Prometheus Books, 1991.

Reich, K. Helmut. "Scientist vs. Believer?: On Navigating Between the Scilla of Scientific Norms and the Charybdis of Personal Experience." *Journal of Psychology and Theology* 28, no. 3 (200): 190-200.

Vetter, George B. *Magic and Religion: Their Psychological Nature, Origin, and Function*. New York: Philosophical Library, 1958.

Wulff, David M. *Psychology of Religion: Classic and Contemporary*. New York: Wiley, 1997.

K. HELMUT REICH

PSYCHOLOGY OF RELIGION

From the perspective of science and religion, there exist three kinds of psychology of religion. *"Secular" empirical psychology* (e.g., Hood) – the most widely practiced – excludes the question of the transcendent and researches religious experiences and behavior in terms of meaningful psychological concepts such as cognition, emotion, motivation, attribution, social interaction, and development. The two other kinds are more mission-oriented. *"Theistic" religious psychology* (e.g., Koteskey; cf. Reich) includes the transcendent and aims to understand God's creation and make people more God-like by improving their mental functioning, their moral judgment, their empathy and so forth. *"Atheistic" psychology of religion* (e.g. Kurtz; Vetter)

PUNCTUATED EQUILIBRIUM

An addition to the neo-Darwinian theory of evolution proposed by paleontologists Stephen Jay Gould and Niles Eldredge in 1972, punctuated equilibrium is intended to explain the lack of intermediate steps in fossil records. Gould and Eldredge propose that biological species do not evolve gradually (as in gradualism) but exist in a state of stable equilibrium (stasis) with no or very slow evolution followed by a burst of fast evolution that quickly, by geological timescale, results in the formation of new species. Gould and Eldredge also suggest that not all evolutionary changes are adapted (as in adaptationism) and that some evolution occurs at the level of species. Punctuated equilibrium is sometimes confused with saltationism, evolution by sudden large changes due to macromutations.

See also CATASTROPHISM; EVOLUTION; GRADUALISM

ARN O. GYLDENHOLM

QUANTUM COSMOLOGIES

Quantum cosmological theories attempt to extend Albert Einstein's theory of gravitation to include quantum theory. There have been many attempts to carry out this extension of Einstein's work and as yet there is no single satisfactory theory. A quantum cosmology is needed in order to draw conclusions about the nature of the initial state of the universe and to interpret the meaning of the idea that it might have quantum-mechanically tunneled out of "nothing," or some version of the quantum vacuum. A quantum cosmological theory is expected to be a particular application of a full theory of quantum gravity (sometimes referred to as a "theory of everything") that would unite and extend all existing theories of the forces of nature. The favored candidate for such a theory at present is *M-theory,* a version of the theory formally known as superstring theory. Theories of this sort are highly constrained by mathematical requirements of symmetry and finiteness, as well as by the requirement of explaining all known elementary particle physics. Quantum cosmologies lead naturally to the Many-Worlds Interpretation of quantum mechanics.

See also COSMOLOGY, PHYSICAL ASPECTS; GRAND UNIFIED THEORY; SUPERSTRINGS

Bibliography

Smolin, Lee. *Three Roads to Quantum Gravity.* London: Weidenfeld, 2001.

JOHN D. BARROW

QUANTUM FIELD THEORY

Quantum field theory is obtained by combining special relativity and quantum mechanics. Until 1981 this was the primary tool for the understanding of elementary particles of matter and the nongravitational forces of matter. However, such theories were known to possess deficiencies and many calculations of observable quantities led, formally, to infinite answers. Yet, by the application of well defined rules these infinities could be removed to leave finite answers that agree with observation to as many as fourteen decimal places of precision. It was then discovered that these deficiencies could be avoided by replacing their theories of pointlike particles by string theories that treated the most fundamental entities in nature as lines or loops of energy (*strings*) possessing a certain symmetry (*supersymmetry*).

String theories avoid the infinities and paradoxes of quantum field theories and are a promising candidate for a complete theory of all elementary particles and forces of nature. The stringlike loops of energy in these theories possess a tension that increases as the temperature of the environment falls. Thus at very high temperatures, for example in the first moments of the expansion of the universe, they would have behaved in an intrinsically stringy manner. As the universe expanded and cooled, the string tensions would increase and the loops of string would behave more and more like single points of mass and energy. As a result, in the low temperature world all the predictions of the earlier quantum field theories are expected to be obtained, in agreement with experiment.

See also PHYSICS, QUANTUM; FIELD THEORIES; STRING THEORY

Bibliography

Barrow, John. *Theories of Everything*. London: Vintage, 1992.

Greene, Brian. *The Elegant Universe*. New York: Norton, 1999.

JOHN D. BARROW

QUANTUM MECHANICS

See PHYSICS, QUANTUM

QUANTUM PHYSICS

See PHYSICS, QUANTUM

QUANTUM THEORY

See PHYSICS, QUANTUM

QUANTUM VACUUM STATE

The Heisenberg Uncertainty Principle allows for the rapid creation and annihilation of particles even in a vacuum, which is by definition the state of lowest possible energy. Careful experimentation has confirmed that this picture of the vacuum as a sea of virtual particles is accurate. For example, it explains the so-called Casimir force between two metal or dialectric plates and the so-called Van de Waal's force in chemistry. This conception of the vacuum is significant for philosophical and religious cosmologies in at least three ways. First, the concept of the quantum vacuum suggests a picture of a primeval chaos of virtual particles being tamed and ordered by conservation laws—the opposite of the classical picture in which a quiescent, perfectly well-ordered state lies beneath the chaos of matter and energy, with implications for the idea of creation in western religious traditions. Second, Daoist interpretations of reality as emergent from an inexpressible state of highly structured dynamism seem resonant with the idea of the quantum vacuum. Third, Buddhist ideas of dependent coarising from emptiness seem amenable to interpretation in terms of the quantum vacuum state. Each of these possibilities, and others besides, needs thorough study.

See also HEISENBERG'S UNCERTAINTY PRINCIPLE

NIU SHI-WEI

REALISM

Realism is the doctrine that existence is separate from conceptions of it. People may think and talk of different entities, but the entities themselves have a reality that is logically independent of thought and language. This may seem a matter of common sense; surely chairs and tables do not exist only in so far as one thinks of them, or perhaps perceives them. People do not conjure things into existence through their minds, in the way that dreams create a world that vanishes when one wakes up. Yet to appeal to common sense is to appeal to the philosophical views of previous generations that have gained common currency. The position itself needs some philosophical justification. Dr. Samuel Johnson is supposed to have dealt with Bishop George Berkeley's idealism by simply kicking a stone and exclaiming "I refute it thus!": This is hardly an argument.

Contention with idealism

Realism is in fact most often opposed to idealism. The latter claims that all reality is a construction out of mental processes. As Berkeley (1685–1753) said in his *Treatise Concerning the Principles of Human Knowledge,* "To be is to be perceived." In other words, what exists does so because it is perceived, and is not perceived because it exists. The latter would be the realist position. Yet Berkeley's position not only makes all reality mental, it also restricts what can exist to what is within the range of someone perceiving it. Berkeley met this by appealing to the omniscience of God, so that everything is perceived by God, and therefore exists. The danger is that God is removed from the picture; this is a move empiricism tends to encourage. The view then becomes one that ties reality to actual or possible human experience. This, in turn, makes reality anthropocentric. What humans cannot perceive cannot exist. Since contemporary physics wishes to deal with subatomic particles and other unobservable entities, such as, say, the interior of a black hole, this does not seem to give an adequate account of the assumptions of present-day science.

Although realism may be classically opposed to idealist tying of existence to mind, realism comes in many shapes and sizes. It can be a global, metaphysical doctrine, or it can be limited to particular areas of human activity. One could be a realist about the objects of scientific investigation, but not about the concerns of morality. The main point of realism, though, is always to pull apart the fact of existence from issues concerning how anyone can know what exists. Ontology and epistemology should not be confused. (So-called critical realism tends to link the two). The metaphysical realist will stress the objectivity of the "world" or whatever exists. It cannot depend in any way on the way people think about it or discover it. Even scientific realism may seem realist in its insistence on the independent reality of the objects of science. It can, however, become antirealist when it asserts that only the objects of science can exist. In other words, existence is then restricted to what lies within the scope of actual or conceivable science. Because that must be human science, reality is being artificially restricted to what is within the scope of human capabilities to discover.

Ontological bases of science and religion

The focus of realism must always be reality, and not issues of how one can come to know reality. Otherwise questions about existence become changed into questions about human abilities. What lies beyond human abilities cannot even be conceived to exist. A major motive for scientific research is the knowledge of human ignorance. The world is not limited to present knowledge, nor to what people are able to discover. This becomes of crucial importance in the field of religion, which is normally understood as attempting to talk of what is transcendent, or ontologically separate, from the world with which people are normally familiar. Empiricist philosophy from the time of David Hume (1711–1776) has attempted to restrict language to what is within human experience. This is always to change the subject from reality to human knowledge. Yet realism cannot rest content with metaphysical assertions about the status of reality. A reality to which people are oblivious is no better than nothing at all. Ontology needs epistemology: It is just not identical to it.

Both science and religion need a strong realist underpinning. They must be about something. Science has to assume that it is investigating a world that has an independent existence. Otherwise it is a mere social construction reflecting the conditions of particular societies at a particular time. Similarly, any religion must assume that it is concerned with a reality that is not the creation of human imagination. Theism must have a realist outlook. It is making claims about an objective reality that are contradicted by atheism, itself also a realist view. Indeed, if God or other spiritual realities are mere projections of human thought or language, religion is guilty of a massive bout of wishful thinking. If the realities described do not actually exist, there is no ground for any cosmic optimism. The antirealist may complain that this is already assuming a realist interpretation of religion. Yet, the idea that neither religion nor science engage with anything beyond themselves seems to negate their most important function of claiming truth. If they are conceived of as conceptual schemes, practices, or forms of life, with no external justification, there seems no point in taking part in them. There can

be no justification or reason for being religious, or doing science.

According to realist understanding, however, there is an independent world for both science and religion to relate to. Moreover, each purports in various ways to describe parts of the same objective world. This in itself provides sufficient ground for trying to show connections between the two. Whatever their distinctive methods, one can not rule out either the possibility of conflict or of mutual support. For example, if this is God's world, this might give an explanation for the inherent order and regularity, which science needs to assume, in order to generalise from particular findings.

See also CRITICAL REALISM

Altson, Walter. "Realism and the Christian Faith." *International Journal for Philosophy of Religion* 38 (1995): 1-3, 37-60.

Hick, John. *An Interpretation of Religion.* London: Macmillan, 1989.

Phillips, D.Z. "On Really Believing." In *Wittgenstein and Religion.* London: Macmillan, 1993.

Phillips, D. Z. "Philosophy, Theology, and the Reality of God." In *Wittgenstein and Religion,* London: Macmillan, 1993.

Polkinghorne, John C. *Beyond Science.* Cambridge, UK: Cambridge University Press, 1996.

Runzo, Joseph, ed. *Is God Real?* New York: St. Martin's Press, 1993.

Trigg, Roger. *Reality at Risk: A Defence of Realism in Philosophy and the Sciences,* 2nd edition. Hemel Hempstead, UK: Harvester Wheatsheaf, 1989.

Trigg, Roger. *Rationality and Religion: Does Faith Need Reason?* Oxford and Malden, Mass.: Blackwell Publishers, 1998.

ROGER TRIGG

REDUCTIONISM

When theoretical statements use terms that refer to objects and properties whose existence seems awkward, puzzling, redundant, or ontologically problematic, there is motivation to analyze or *reduce* such statements to others that employ better understood terms. Reductionism must be distinguished both from *eliminativism* and *supervenience*. Consider two domains of properties M and P (e.g., the mental and the physical). Eliminativism claims that since only P exists, M can be eliminated (e.g., there is no such thing as demonic possession, but only a biochemical problem in the brain). Supervenience asserts that both M and P are real and distinct, though M is determined by P (e.g., headache pain is real, and while not identical to neurophysiological processes, is nonetheless realized by such processes). Reduction, however, asserts that there is but one thing that is both M and P, with P having explanatory priority (e.g., Mary's particular headache pain is just a particular complex neurological event).

Semantic and theoretic reduction

Examples of reductions in philosophy include *logicism* (reducing statements about numbers into statements of logic and set theory), *phenomenalism* (reducing statements about external macro-objects into statements of actual and possible experience), *logical behaviorism* (reducing statements about mental states into stimulus-response conditionals), *logical positivism* (reducing statements employing theoretical entities to ones referring only to observed objects), and *naturalism* (reducing normative ethical statements to ones whose terms refer to natural properties only). All these philosophical reductions are semantic, for all use definitional equivalences linking terms of the reduced to those of the reducing statements, (i.e., statements in the reduced theory just mean equivalent statements in the reducing theory). Broadly speaking, semantic reductions have been out of favor in philosophy since the 1950s. This is due in part to four developments: the heightened sensitivity to the "paradox of analysis" (i.e., if a semantic reduction is successful it is not informative and if it is informative it cannot be successful); the realization of the enormous practical difficulties of actually carrying out the proposed reductions; an increasing recognition of the holistic nature of sentence meaning; and the growing doubt about the very possibility of foundational discoveries.

Of more interest to the science-religion conversation is the status of scientific reductions. Consider physics, chemistry, biochemistry, biology, physiology, neuroscience, psychology and sociology. How are these various disciplines related? How does one

connect hadrons, atoms, chemical compounds, amino acids, cells, synapses, thoughts, and cultural tendencies? If physicalism is true in asserting that all that ultimately exists are those entities referred to in the most basic physical theory, then in what sense can thoughts and cultural tendencies exist? Should talk of such things be eliminated, or should we understand theories making reference to them to be reducible to more basic theories, and ultimately to theories referring to fundamental physical entities? Theoretic reduction in the philosophy of science attempts to show how entire theories, and the entities and properties specified by them, are reducible to more basic theories.

Unlike semantic reduction, theoretic reduction understands the biconditionals connecting theoretical terms in the reducing and reduced theories to be empirically discoverable bridge laws specifying coextensive property instantiations. While statements in the reduced theory mean something different from statements in the reducing theory, it is nonetheless true that the reduced theory statements are true if and only if their reducing statements are true. Examples of theoretical reduction within science include the reduction of chemistry to physics, the reduction of thermodynamics to statistical physics, the reduction of Mendelian genetics to molecular genetics, and the partial reduction of psychiatry to neurophysiology.

Reductions can also be found in theology and religion, though they are not often presented as such. For example, Immanuel Kant (1724–1804) semantically reduced talk of God to discourse about morality, while Friedrich Ernst Schleiermacher (1768–1834) reduced it to modifications of the feeling of absolute dependence. Karl Marx (1818–1883), Sigmund Freud (1856–1958), and Emile Durkeim (1858–1917) attempted theoretically to reduce religion to economics, psychology, and sociology respectively.

Varieties of reduction

There are different types of reduction, and also different typologies of these reduction types. One might distinguish methodological, epistemological, and ontological reduction. Accordingly, the first is a research strategy in which the behavior of complex wholes is analyzed into their component parts; the second an explanatory strategy claiming that theories and laws at the higher levels are analyzable or otherwise explainable in terms of the theories and laws of the lower levels; and the third an ontological strategy holding that reality is ultimately comprised of nothing but simple components (e.g., quarks, strings) organized in particular ways.

This "nothing but" relation can be understood as reduction's defining characteristic: *M* reduces to *P* if and only if *M* is nothing but *P*. Accordingly, one can distinguish ontological, property, semantic, theoretical, and causal reduction. Ontological reduction claims that upper-level entities and events are nothing but complex configurations of lower-level entities and events; property reduction asserts that the instantiation of every upper-level property is nothing but the instantiation of a particular lower-level property; semantic reduction declares that the meaning of statements in the reduced theory is nothing but the meaning of statements in the reducing theory; theoretic reduction claims that laws of the reduced theory are nothing but the laws of the reducing theory; and causal reduction asserts that the causal powers of upper-level entities are nothing but the causal powers exhibited by their lower-level physical realizers.

Property reduction and causal reduction are of particular interest in the science-theology discussion. One can hold that while only physical particulars exist, property dualism nonetheless obtains because higher-level properties are not reducible to, and thus not coextensive with, any specific lower-level properties. Some in the science-theology discussion believe such a nonreductive physicalism of emergent mental properties can protect religious discourse and experience from reduction or elimination.

Causal reduction is extremely important for the question of the ontological status of putative emergent entities and properties. If entities at the upper-levels wholly inherit their causal powers from the lower-levels, and if ontological status only pertains to causally efficacious entities, then it seems that emergent phenomena are not fully real. The question of the causal status of emergent properties is at the heart of the controversy about downward causality. Some in the science-theology discussion suggest that the emergent itself can effect the causal distribution at the lower-levels, not just the lower-level realizers of that emergent, (e.g., consciousness itself is causally efficacious.) But if particular lower-level actualizations are sufficient for the instantiation of an emergent property, then it seems that these actualizations are also sufficient for the effects this emergent property is said to cause.

Conclusion

Many in the science-theology discussion wish to provide an account of emergent phenomenon that does not presuppose reductive explanation. Unfortunately, even in the absence of the straightforward reduction of the emergent, the admission of its physical realization seems to accomplish much of what reduction initially sought, for the causal loop still gets closed at the lowest physical levels. It seems that the "something more" of the emergent may be "nothing more" when it comes to the issue of causal reduction. This is not a result that would cheer many in the science-theology conversation.

See also BEHAVIORISM; CAUSALITY, PRIMARY AND SECONDARY; CAUSATION; DOWNWARD CAUSATION; MATERIALISM; NATURALISM; PHYSICALISM, REDUCTIVE AND NONREDUCTIVE; SUPERVIENIENCE

Bibliography

Beckermann, Ansgar; Flohr, Hans; and Kim, Jaegwon, eds. *Emergence or Reduction? Essays on the Prospects of Nonreductive Physicalism.* Berlin and New York: Walter de Gruyter, 1992.

Bielfeldt, Dennis. "How Does the Mental Matter?" *Center for Theology and Natural Science Bulletin* 19, no. 4 (2000): 11-21.

Charles, David, and Lennon, Kathleen, eds. *Reduction, Explanation, and Realism.* Oxford: Oxford University Press, 1993.

Kim Jaegwon. *Supervenience and Mind: Selected Philosophical Essays.* Cambridge, UK: Cambridge University Press, 1993.

Kim, Jaegwon. *Mind in a Physical World: An Essay on the Mind-Body Problem and Mental Causation.* Cambridge, Mass.: MIT Press, 1999.

Murphy, Nancey. "Supervenience and the Nonreducibility of Ethics to Biology." In *Evolutionary and Molecular Biology: Scientific Perspectives on Divine Action.* eds. Robert John Russell, William Stoeger, and Francisco Ayala. Vatican City and Berkeley, Calif.: Vatican Observatory Publications and the Center for Theology and the Natural Sciences, 1998.

Murphy Nancey. "Physicalism Without Reduction: Toward a Scientifically, Philosophically, and Theologically

Sound Portrait of Human Nature." *Zygon* 34 (1999): 551-572.

Nagel, Ernest. *The Structure of Science: Problems in the Logic of Scientific Explanation.* New York: Harcourt, 1961.

Peacocke, Arthur. "Reductionism: A Review of the Epistemological Issues and Their Relevance to Biology and the Problem of Consciousness." *Zygon* 11, no. 4 (1976): 307–334.

DENNIS BIELFELDT

REDUCTIVE PHYSICALISM

See PHYSICALISM, REDUCTIVE AND NONREDUCTIVE

REINCARNATION

Reincarnation or *samsara* is the beginningless cycle of birth, death, and rebirth. The rebirth idea follows from the traditional Yoga psychology concept of *karma,* the memory trace or "seed" laid down in the unconscious by each freely chosen action or thought, which is stored until the opportunity arises for it to sprout forth as an impulse to do a similar action or thought again. The unconscious contains all the karmic seeds laid down during this life and from all previous lives. The presence of such *karmas* and their impulse to sprout is the cause of one's rebirth. Removal of *karma* from one's unconscious by spiritual discipline (*Yoga*) results in release (*moksa*) from rebirth. Originating from Hinduism, this idea was adopted by Jainism and Buddhism in India, and is also found in Platonic thought.

See also HINDUISM; KARMA; LIFE AFTER DEATH

HAROLD COWARD

RELATIVITY

See GRAVITATION; RELATIVITY, GENERAL THEORY OF; RELATIVITY, SPECIAL THEORY OF

RELATIVITY, GENERAL THEORY OF

Albert Einstein radically reshaped the understanding of gravity through his proposal of the General Theory of Relativity in 1916. The problem he tackled was to create a theory of gravity that was consistent with his Special Relativity Theory, including its radical transformation of the understanding of space and time measurements through the introduction of a unified concept of space-time. Special relativity is based on the invariance of the laws of physics under any constant change of velocity, and hence the equivalence from a physical viewpoint of all uniformly moving (non-accelerating) observers. General relativity extended these ideas to a special class of accelerating observers.

Einstein's insights

Einstein's first brilliant insight was that, in consequence of Galileo Galilei's (1564–1642) discovery in the seventeenth century that all falling bodies near the Earth accelerate at the same rate, any uniform gravitational field can be transformed away (i.e. made to vanish) by changing to a suitably accelerating reference frame; indeed for any observer in free fall, gravity effectively ceases to exist. We have seen this in films of astronauts in free fall, where gravity does not seem to act (objects float freely in the air), even though they are in spacecraft that are relatively close to the surface of the Earth, where the gravitational field is strong enough to make the spacecraft move in a circular orbit.

Thus, from a physical viewpoint, inertial and gravitational effects are indistinguishable; this is Einstein's Principle of Equivalence. There is no invariant gravitational force, in analogy to the electromagnetic force, but rather effective gravitational forces are felt by observers in consequence of their choice of reference frame. One consequence is the prediction of the phenomenon of gravitational *redshift* (a shifting of light toward the red end of the spectrum as a result of a gravitational field rather than a relative velocity). This has been verified by high accuracy measurements on Earth.

Einstein's second major insight (building on previous work by others, particularly German mathematician Georg Friedrich Riemann [1826–1866]) was that the principle of equivalence could be made compatible both with experimental evidence concerning gravity and with the special theory of relativity by embracing the idea that space-time is curved. Freely falling objects and light rays move on geodesics in curved space-time, that is, curves whose space-time direction is unchanging (these curves are the closest that one can get to a straight line in a curved space-time). When projected into surfaces of constant time, these paths can appear highly curved; indeed, the nearly circular motion of the Earth around the sun is the result of the Earth moving in an undeviating direction in the curved space-time around the sun. A consequence is the prediction of the bending of light by a gravitational field, which was verified in a famous experiment in 1917, when bending of light by the sun was measured during a solar eclipse. This bending leads to gravitational lensing of distant objects (quasi-stellar objects and galaxies) by nearer galaxies and cluster of galaxies, resulting in distorted images and multiple images.

Einstein's third major insight was that the space-time curvature is determined by the matter in it. This is a major revolution in our understanding of the nature of geometry. Previously, the geometry of space (and space-time) had been assumed to be fixed and invariant, a purely mathematical construct. Einstein's proposal meant that space-time geometry varies according to the matter present; consequently geometry became a branch of physics. Einstein spent many years pondering the nature of this relation, and eventually completed his theory by proposing his gravitational field equations, which relate the stress-energy *tensor* of the matter present to space-time curvature. (A tensor is a physical quantity that has many components that, taken together, characterize its nature. The physical energy tensor combines in one quantity the energy density, quantum density, isotropic pressure, and anisotropic pressures characterizing a fluid. These quantities combine in different ways when different reference frames are used.) This theory can predict the motion of planets around the sun more accurately than Newtonian theory can, explaining in particular the anomalous precession of the perihelion of the planet Mercury. Indeed Einstein's theory has been tested with high precision in the solar system and has passed all observational tests with flying colors.

Predictions of the theory

The General Theory of Relativity also predicts radically new phenomena. Firstly, black holes are predicted to result at the end-point of the lives of massive stars when they have burnt all their nuclear fuel. Black holes are objects where the gravitational field is so strong that light cannot escape; a radially outgoing light ray will be halted and will fall back in to the center. Consequently an outside observer receives no light or radiation from the interior and cannot observe what is going on there. The gravitational field at the center will become so strong that a space-time singularity occurs. It is believed that black holes have been detected through the X-ray emissions associated with hot dust falling in across the event horizon, which is the surface bounding the black hole region. Any object crossing the event horizon to the interior cannot then escape; it is doomed to fall into the singularity. It is now believed that black holes exist at the center of many galaxies, including our own, and provide the power sources for incredibly luminous quasi-stellar objects. Secondly, gravitational waves will be generated by the motion of astronomical objects such as binary pulsars. It is difficult to detect them directly because they are extremely weak, but they have been indirectly detected because of their effect on the orbits of a binary pulsar (Russell Hulse and Joseph Taylor were awarded the 1993 Nobel Prize in physics for this observation). A new generation of gravitational wave observatories are being constructed, and it is hoped they will detect gravitational waves within the next ten years.

A problem with the theory is that it predicts that under many conditions (e.g., at the start of the universe, and at the end of gravitational collapse to form a black hole), space-time singularities will occur. Scientists still do not properly understand this phenomenon, but presumably it means that they will have to take the effect of quantum theory on gravity into account in some suitable generalization of general relativity, which is a purely classical theory. Additionally, general relativity in principle allows a variety of causal violations to occur (e.g., you can travel through space-time in such a way as to talk to your grandfather when he was ten years old). There is considerable debate on how to regard this feature.

The Einstein equations are extraordinarily unique, but they do allow the possibility of a cosmological constant (effectively, a very weak long-range repulsive force). This has been the subject of dispute ever since Einstein included it in his equations in 1917 in order to allow a static universe solution. He abandoned it when the expansion of the universe became generally accepted, but it keeps recurring in various forms, for example in the inflationary universe idea. There is good observational evidence that the recent expansion of the universe is dominated by a cosmological constant, however the physical origin of this universal repulsive force is unexplained. From the viewpoint of quantum field theory, its existence is highly problematic.

See also BLACK HOLE; COSMOLOGY; EINSTEIN, ALBERT; GRAVITATION; INFLATIONARY UNIVERSE THEORY; RELATIVITY, SPECIAL THEORY OF; SPACE AND TIME

Bibliography

Begelman, Mitchell C., and Rees, Martin J. *Gravity's Fatal Attraction*. San Francisco: W. H. Freeman, 1996.

D'Inverno, Ray. *Introducing Einstein's Relativity*. Oxford: Oxford University Press, 1996.

Ellis, George F. R., and Williams, Ruth M. *Flat and Curved Space-times*. Oxford: Oxford University Press, 2000.

Hawking, Stephen W., and Ellis, George F. R. *The Large-scale Structure of Spacetime*. Cambridge, UK: Cambridge University Press, 1973.

Misner, Charles W.; Thorne, Kip S.; and Wheeler, John A. *Gravitation*. San Francisco: W. H. Freeman, 1973.

Thorne, Kip S. *Black Holes and Time Warps: Einstein's Outrageous Legacy*. New York: Norton, 1994.

Wald, Robert M. *General Relativity*. Chicago: University of Chicago Press, 1984.

GEORGE F. R. ELLIS

RELATIVITY, SPECIAL THEORY OF

The Special Theory of Relativity describes the way in which an observer's experience of time and space is interrelated, while the General Theory of Relativity addresses the interrelationships among mass, space, gravity, and motion. Motivated by his concerns about problematic features of electromagnetism—especially the relationship between electric and magnetic fields—Albert Einstein (1879–1955) proposed the Special Theory of Relativity in 1905. However, since most of the character and consequences of Special Relativity can be more easily developed in the arena of kinematics

(the description of motion), this entry will focus on the ways in which motion influences the outcome of measurements regarding space and time.

Inertial reference frames

The term *reference frame* ordinarily refers to a *coordinate system* (like the Cartesian system with three mutually perpendicular axes labeled *x, y,* and *z*) in which the location and motion of an object can be conveniently described, along with a set of synchronized clocks with which to determine the time at any location in that coordinate system. Given such a reference frame, one can specify the coordinates of any event *E* by stating its location (*x, y, z*) and the time (*t*) of its occurrence in the notation: *E* (*x, y, z, t*).

Of all possible reference frames, Special Relativity is concerned only with *inertial reference frames*—reference frames in which Newton's First Law (sometimes alled the Law of Inertia) holds. It can be shown that any reference frame that moves with constant velocity (constant speed and direction) relative to an inertial frame is also an inertial reference frame.

Postulates

Einstein's Special Theory of Relativity proceeds from two fundamental postulates regarding the results of comparing the observations of physical phenomena (sets of events) by observers in two or more inertial reference frames. These two postulates may be stated as follows: (1) The speed of light is the same in all inertial reference frames, independent of the motion of the source; and (2) The form of all physical laws (not only those pertaining to mechanics) is the same in all inertial reference frames. The first postulate represents a break from the common expectation that the speed of light relative to its source would be fixed, as would be the case for a bullet fired from a gun. The second postulate represents a significant extension of the classical principle of relativity that applied only to the laws of mechanics.

Predictions

From these two postulates a number of fascinating predictions can be deduced.

The relativity of simultaneity. The *Lorentz transformation,* named after Dutch physicist

Hendrik Anton Lorentz (1853–1928), is a set of equations that allows the calculation of event coordinates in one reference frame from the coordinates of the same event in another frame. Suppose that in reference frame S an observer notes two events that occur at different locations, but at the same time. The S observer says that these two events occurred simultaneously. Then consider another reference frame S' that is moving at a constant velocity relative to S. Applying the Lorentz transformation to the event coordinates in S to obtain the coordinates for the same two events in S' leads to a remarkable result. Observers in S' would say that these two events occurred at different times. That is, events that appear simultaneous in one inertial reference frame would not be observed as simultaneous in any other inertial frame. The amount of time separation would depend on the relative speed of the two frames. Simultaneity is not absolute, but is dependent on the observer's reference frame. In other words, there is no universal time on which all observers can agree.

Length contraction. Consider a meter stick oriented parallel to the x axis of a references frame S that is moving at speed v along that same x axis. Let S' now be a reference frame attached to the meter stick. An observer in S' affirms that the length of this stick, at rest in S', is one meter. Now suppose that an observer in S wishes to measure the length of the stick that he observes to be moving at speed v. This must be done by noting the locations of the two ends of the stick simultaneously in S and calculating the distance between these two locations. Doing so, however, would lead to the interesting result that, as measured in S, the length of the meter stick is less than one meter. This is the phenomenon called *length contraction*. The measured length of a moving object is contracted in the direction of its motion. Dimensions perpendicular to the direction of motion are not affected.

Time dilation. Using the same notation for reference frames S and S', consider a clock that is at rest in S'. Relative to any observer at rest in S, that S' clock is moving at speed v. As it moves, it passes numerous S clocks that are distributed throughout reference frame S. Suppose that the S' clock was synchronized to display exactly the same time as one particular S clock at the instant the S' clock passed it. Now suppose that at some later time, the display of the S' clock is compared with a second S clock as it passes it. Once again, applying the

Lorentz transformation to predict the coordinates of this second clock-passing event leads to a surprising result: The S' clock will lag behind the second S clock. A moving clock (the S' clock is moving relative to reference frame S) records less elapsed time than do stationary S clocks. This is the phenomenon called *time dilation*. Numerous empirical tests have affirmed this peculiar effect.

There is a symmetry that must be acknowledged in regard to the time dilation phenomenon. Comparing equivalent observations by observers in two different reference frames, each would say (with justification) that the clocks of the other were running slowly. That symmetry has led some persons to question the idea of twins with differing motion histories actually achieving different ages. The standard scenario for the so-called twin paradox posits a pair of twins with a keen interest in testing relativity theory. While one of the twins stays at home, the other takes off in a rocket and travels at a substantial fraction of the speed of light for a few years, as measured on his own calendar watch, and then turns around to reverse the trip. Upon reunion with his twin, how will the age of the traveler compare with the stay-at-home sibling? From the viewpoint of the homebody, the traveler's clocks have been running slowly for most of the trip, both outbound and inbound (the direction of travel is irrelevant). So, it would seem that at the reunion, the traveler would be younger than his homebound twin. However, what about looking at things from the standpoint of the traveler? Would it not be the case that the homebody's clocks were running slowly so that the homebody would be the younger sibling at reunion? That's the usual presentation of the twin paradox—conflicting conclusions flowing from the symmetry of the time dilation phenomenon.

It turns out, however, that there is no actual paradox, no conflicting predictions. The traveler really is the younger at reunion. There was no effective symmetry in the motion histories of the twins. One stayed in a single reference frame the entire time; the other accelerated from one frame to another several times. The amount of time elapsed between the twins' separation and reunion events will be different for each as a consequence of differing histories of motion. Strange, perhaps, but apparently true.

The mass-energy relationship. If there is one mathematical relationship that best characterizes the popular conception of special relativity it would have to be the equation $E = mc^2$, where E represents energy, m represents mass, and c is the speed of light. But what does this familiar equation actually signify? In very general terms it signifies that mass is one particular form of energy and that it could, given suitable circumstances, be transformed into other forms of energy. Nuclear reactors, for example, provide the circumstances for a controlled transformation of some of the mass-energy of selected radioactive nuclei into heat, which is then used to drive conventional electrical energy generators. In a similar way, a coal-fired power plant accomplishes the same transformation of mass-energy into heat by means of chemical rather than nuclear reactions.

There is more, however, in the familiar $E = mc^2$. The mass, m, that appears in this equation is the *relativistic mass,* whose value depends on the speed of the object under consideration. In fact, as an object's speed, v, approaches the speed of light, the value of its relativistic mass approaches infinity. In effect, that means that it would require an infinite amount of energy to accelerate an object to the speed of light. With only finite amounts of energy available, the speed of small objects (such as atomic constituents) can be increased (in a particle accelerator device) to a value approaching the speed of light, but never equaling or exceeding it. Nothing having mass can be given a speed relative to a local observer that is equal to or greater than the speed of light. This is a speed limit that is enforced not by legal decree, but by the very nature of the universe itself—specifically the relationships among space, time, motion, and energy.

This speed limit applies only in a localized region of space. If one is considering the motion of extremely distant objects, say billions of light-years away, another factor must be included—the expansion of space itself. In the language of General Relativity, space is not merely a nothing in which things may be placed, but a specific something that has properties and is able to act and be acted upon. One of the things that cosmic space is doing, apparently, is expanding. Distant galaxies are observed to be receding from the Earth because the space between them and the Earth is expanding. The motion of distant galaxies that can be attributed to this spatial expansion phenomenon is not restricted by the speed of light limitation just discussed.

Implications for religious thought

The theory of relativity must be clearly distinguished from what is ordinarily denoted by the word *relativism.* Moral relativism, for instance, presumes that there are no universal standards of right and wrong behavior. Likewise, epistemic relativism presumes that there are no observer-independent standards for objective knowledge. As noted above, however, the special theory of relativity entails no denial of standards for comparing the observations of various observers. On the contrary, relativity theory specifies those standards with great clarity. Relativistic mechanics differs from classical mechanics not by abandoning standards, but by offering a specific and new set of standards that bring predictions and observations into agreement.

Another feature of Special Relativity theory that suggests an application to religious thought is its demonstration of the fact that common sense sometimes needs to be corrected. Most people have common sense notions of space and time that function perfectly well as they go about their daily routines of life. People use these notions as they plan their travels from place to place and as they proceed throughout the course of a day. These common sense notions include the following:

(1) All impartial observers should agree on the time interval between two events.

(2) All impartial observers should agree on the distance between two points.

(3) Things can always be made to go faster.

(4) Twins remain equal in age no matter what they do.

However, each of these expectations turns out to be incorrect, and concepts of space and time must be modified in order to comprehend what careful observations and measurements have revealed.

The origin of such shortcomings in common sense notions of space and time is easy to identify: These notions are based on limited experience. Until physicists performed observations and measurements on particles moving at speeds approaching the speed of light, the shortcomings of human concepts of space and time could not be detected. Extending human experience with space, time, and motion into new speed regimes revealed those shortcomings and inspired modifications of the sort proposed by Lorentz and Einstein. The lesson is evident: Epistemic dogmatism (I have the complete and final understanding of *X*) must often be replaced with epistemic humility (what I now think I know may someday need to be modified in response to an expansion of experience). This is not to despair and claim no knowledge whatsoever. This is rather to remain open to correction, even while celebrating the knowledge of the day. On these matters theology and science enjoy full agreement.

See also EINSTEIN, ALBERT; RELATIVITY, GENERAL THEORY OF; SPACE AND TIME

Bibliography

Adams, Steve. Relativity: *An Introduction to Space-time Physics.* London: Taylor and Francis, 1997.

Eisntein, Albert. *The Meaning of Relativity* (1921). Princeton, N.J.: Princeton University Press, 1966.

Harrison, Edward R. *Cosmology: The Science of the Universe,* 2nd edition. New York: Cambridge University Press, 2000.

McFarland, Ernie. *Einstein's Special Relativity: Discover It for Yourself.* Toronto: Trifolium, 1998.

Mermin, N. David. *Space and Time in Special Relativity.* Prospect Heights, Ill.: Waveland Press, 1989.

Moore, Thomas A. *A Traveler's Guide to Spacetime.* New York: McGraw Hill, 1995.

Rindler, Wolfgang. *Introduction to Special Relativity,* 2nd edition. Oxford: Clarendon Press, 1991.

Taylor, Edwin F., and Wheeler, John A. *Spacetime Physics: Introduction to Special Relativity,* 2nd edition. San Francisco: W. H. Freeman, 1992.

HOWARD J. VAN TILL

RELIGION AND VALUES, ORIGINS OF

The word *value* expresses worth in a broad generic sense, but this usage only dates to about from the mid-nineteenth century. The classical meaning of *value* was more limited, referring to goods, excellence, riches, benefits, utilities. The word *value* occurs in the Bible almost always translating Hebrew and Greek economic terms referring to price. The word *religion* includes the Latin root *liga* (also in *ligament* and *obligation*),

which means *binding,* here intensified by the prefix *re-*. Hence, religion is that to which one is most deeply bound. "The essence of religion," claims Harald Höffding, "consists in the conviction that value will be preserved" (p. 14). If one finds a world in which value is given and persists over time, one has a religious assignment. A central function of religion is the conservation of fundamental values. Frederick Ferré defines religion: "One's religion . . . is one's way of valuing most intensively and most comprehensively" (p. 11).

Genesis of value in natural history

A frequent claim is that science deals with causes, religion with values. That is an overstatement: Scientists evaluate better and worse science; theologians ask whether divine agency can be detected in natural history. Nevertheless, natural science is a systematic study of causes in nature; religion is a life-orienting inquiry into meanings of life in the world. But these crisscross.

In the course of natural history, "mere" causes (operating in rocks, winds, waters) generate life, events of deepening significance (DNA molecules coding for adapted fit). Where once there was matter, energy, and where these remain, there appears information, symbolically encoded, and life. Signals emerge. A rock conserves no identity. An oak tree, by contrast, conserves a metabolism and an anatomy over time. Organisms are self-maintaining systems. There is a new state of matter, neither liquid nor gaseous nor solid, but vital.

Speciation generates biodiversity; some species become increasingly animated with neural evolution, evolving felt experience. *Homo sapiens* develops capacities for religious experience. Out of physical precedents there appear biological, then psychological, then spiritual consequences. Matter gives birth to spirit.

Religion valuing abundant life

Religions arise to rejoice in, wonder over, protect, reform, and regenerate, that is, to save this gift of life, to which humans are intensely bound. The life "information," in contrast to matter and energy, is not inevitably conserved, but rather is inevitably lost in death, unless life is regenerated. If anything is of abiding value on Earth, surely it is the life incarnate in human beings. From the dawn of religious impulses in the only animal capable of such reflection, this vitality has been experienced as sacred. Such experience has often been fragmentary and confused, as has every other form of knowledge that humans have struggled to gain, but at its core the insight developed that religion was about life in its abundance.

Classical monotheism claims—to take the Hebrew form of it—that the divine Spirit or Wind (Greek: *pneuma*) breathes the breath of life into earth and animates it to generate swarms of living beings (Gen. 2.7). Eastern forms can be significantly different: *maya* spun over Brahman, or *samsara* over *sunyata,* but they too detect the sacred in, with, and under the profuse phenomena. Some have opposed as seemingly too self-centered the idea that religions are about fertility. But the fertility hypothesis is quite right in this respect: Humans reside on a fertile Earth.

In that sense, the fact that religious conviction cherishes and conserves this fertility is no reason to think religion suspect; to the contrary, it is reason to think it profound. Perhaps the animal in which such faith emerges, *Homo sapiens,* is coping now because it is detecting that there is a divine will for life to continue. At this point, we pass from supposing that biology can explain religion (as a survival myth) to needing religion to explain biology (how to evaluate this genesis in natural history). Earthen fecundity is hard fact and difficult to explain without some sort of generative principles before which many persons incline to become religious.

Biological value and a value-free nature?

The question of value in biology is paradoxical, both in biological science and in biological phenomena in nature. On the one hand, science thinks of itself as being value-free and as describing a natural world that also is value-free. There is no value without an experiencing valuer, just as there are no thoughts without a thinker, no targets without an aimer. Valuing is "felt preferring" by human choosers. Values can be instrumental or intrinsic; domains of value are economic, moral, legal, aesthetic (including etiquette), cognitive (including science), and religious. Human kinship with the higher animals does extend some of these values to those sentient enough to suffer pains and pleasures. But an event that involves no felt preferences cannot be an event of value or disvalue. Such nature just *is,* devoid of dimensions of value.

Values are, in the usual psychological account, deeply felt and considered, bringing humans back into the main focus. Milton Rokeach defines value: "I consider a value to be a type of belief, centrally located within one's belief system, about how one ought or ought not to behave, or about some end-state of existence worth or not worth obtaining" (p. 124). Values have to be thought about, chosen from among options, persistently held, and they have to satisfy felt preferences. Such values are at the roots of religion.

But this is not adequate biologically. Indeed, by this account, there are no values present in any plants, nor in most animals, which are incapable of such capacities. The paradox arises now, however, because value of another sort is perfused through biology: survival value. An organism lives successfully on the basis of adaptive traits, even if the organism is not a sentient valuer.

So it seems biology is not value-free at all for it is difficult to dissociate the idea of value from natural selection. Every organism has a good-of-its-kind; it defends its own kind as a good kind. A genome encodes what has been discovered to be of value to that form of life. Despite value-free science, value generated and conserved is the first fact of natural history.

Turning to more systematic trends in evolutionary history, biologists are often divided over whether this generation of diversity and complexity is inevitable, probable, contingent, or mixedly all three. Biologists since Charles Darwin (1809–1882) generally dislike the idea of progress or teleology in evolutionary history, though most biologists acknowledge that the evolving Earth did result in increases of both diversity and complexity. Many hold that some systemic tendencies best explain this, even if Darwinism is uncertain about such directions of development.

Within this perspective, humans are not so much lighting up value in an otherwise valueless world as they are psychologically joining an ongoing natural history in which there is value wherever there is positive creativity.

Religions and survival value

Humans evolve with unique traits, especially their dispositions to behave ethically and to be religious. Continuing with Darwinian biology, the only readily available explanation is that these traits convey greater survival value. Most biologists favor the idea of selection at the individual level; if they are right, both ethical action and religious practice must increase the reproductive fitness of individuals who embody these values. But individuals live in communities—intimately in family, where reproductive success is critical, locally in tribes, and regionally in states. Those tribes whose people share religious values usually out-compete other tribes. Religion is reciprocating self-interest, enlarged and enlightened into communities as more fundamental survival units. This account has precedents in the thought of sociologist Émile Durkheim (1858–1917).

Advocates of religion will welcome the survival value of religious beliefs and ethical practices. Abraham was promised numerous descendants, and they became a great nation; the commandments were given to keep Israel, through love and justice, inhabiting the promised land for many generations. But advocates of religion will also resist the idea that religion is nothing but a coping myth, discounting any truth value. Rather, as noted above, the Earth has been perennially prolific. Religion repeatedly arises to encounter this heritage and to insure life's regeneration. Such regeneration includes not only biological survival but requires redemption, the repair of a brokenness in human life. Such salvation is of everlasting value.

This has involved families, tribes, peoples, and nations. The major world faiths, however, have also become universal, evangelizing unrelated others. This proves difficult to explain under the biological account, since such missionary concern conveys no preferential survival advantage on the proselytizers. Rather others are more altruistically valued, a conviction also recently enshrined in universal human rights.

At the metaphysical level, it will be claimed, science neither describes nor evaluates the full genesis of value adequately. Religion is about the finding, creating, saving, and redeeming of such persisting sacred value in the world. In this sense, whatever the quarrels between religion and biology, there is nothing ungodly about a world in which values persist in the midst of their perpetual perishing, or one in which such values, through religious activity, become widely shared. That is as

near as earthlings can come to an ultimate concern; that is where, on Earth, the ultimate might be incarnate.

See also BIOLOGICAL DIVERSITY

Bibliography

Ferré, Frederick. "The Definition of Religion." *Journal of the American Academy of Religion* 38 (1970): 3–16.

Höffding, Harald. *The Philosophy of Religion.* London: Macmillan, 1906.

Pugh, George E. *The Biological Origin of Human Values.* New York: Basic Books, 1977.

Reynolds, Vernon, and, Tanner, Ralph. *The Biology of Religion.* New York: Longman, 1983.

Reynolds, Vernon, and, Tanner, Ralph. *The Social Ecology of Religion.* New York: Oxford University Press, 1995.

Rokeach, Milton. *Beliefs, Attitudes, and Values: A Theory of Organization and Change.* San Francisco: Jossey-Bass, 1968.

Rolston, Holmes, III. *Genes, Genesis, and God: Values and their Origins in Natural and Human History.* New York: Cambridge University Press, 1999.

Wilson, Edward O. *On Human Nature.* Cambridge, Mass.: Harvard University Press, 1978.

HOLMES ROLSTON, III

RELIGION, THEORIES OF

The theoretical study of religion emerged in the eighteenth century. Like the concept of religion itself, it is the product of, among other influences, the Age of Exploration and Empire (fifteenth and sixteenth centuries), the Protestant Reformation (sixteenth century), and the Augustan Age (eighteenth century). In *The Meaning and End of Religion* (1962), Wilfred Cantwell Smith documents how the premodern etymological antecedents of the modern word *religion* (e.g., Latin *religio*) generally mean something like "the pious Christian rites of worship," not what the modern word means. The practice of translating the premodern terms as *religion,* therefore, often misleads. Non-Western cultures, furthermore, did not have terms with anything like the same connotations or semantic scope.

In premodern Europe, the known religious horizon consisted of (1) the mythology of ancient

Greek and Roman pagans, (2) Jews, (3) Muslims, and (4) Christians. These four could be arranged in a unified narrative by any of the three latter groups. Christians, for instance, could view Jews as stiff-necked people who refused to accept the gospel, and Muslims as schismatics who split Christ's Church. In his poem *The Inferno* (c. 1308), Dante Alighieri consigns Mohammed to the circle of hell reserved for "sowers of scandal and schism" (p. 326). Finally, Christians assimilated Greek mythology to biblical history by arguing that the Greek gods were actually demons, that the Greek myths were actually biblical stories about biblical characters but were corrupted through transmission, or that the Greek myths were allegories representing biblical or Christian virtues. Jews and Muslims had their own unifying narratives. Indeed, the Qur'an itself carefully positions Jews and Christians in relation to Islam. It claims to confirm, continue, correct, and complete earlier revelation.

This comparatively coherent religious horizon eventually collapsed under the growing pressure exerted by European expansion. The Age of Exploration and Empire increased European contact with non-European cultures and non-Western religions. The reports of seafarers about exotic beliefs and practices introduced ethnographic data that could not easily be incorporated into the narratives of premodern Europe. This new cosmopolitanism eroded some of the inevitability clothing Western forms of theism. Renewed attention to, and esteem for, ancient authors (e.g., Lucretius and Cicero) during the Augustan Age, moreover, supplied sources for naturalistic explanations of religion, critique of ritual, and materialistic cosmologies.

Most importantly, perhaps, the Protestant Reformation shattered the relative uniformity of religious thought and culture in Christian Europe. It produced different and warring "religions" (i.e., conceptions of piety and worship), justified by competing criteria of religious authority. This impasse made necessary a neutral stance for assessing religious claims. Only a standpoint that abstracts from contested religious criteria could resolve such a dispute. In the service of religious polemic, early modern thinkers devised canons of inquiry and argument that were independent of religious presuppositions. In order better to conduct religious debate, early modern thinkers secularized inquiry.

Conceived by Jansenists to defend their theology against papal condemnation, modern probability theory, for example, both rendered religious presuppositions optional, and facilitated modern science (Stout, 1981). The social discord in which the Reformation culminated made it necessary, furthermore, to privatize religion, to push it out of public affairs for the sake of peace. Religion came to be viewed as a discreet domain of culture, distinct from morality, and ranged alongside law, science, politics, and art. The general term *religion* reflects this differentiation. The Reformation made possible a nonreligious position from which to reflect critically on religion, conceived as a general category identifying one aspect of human intellectual, emotional, and social life.

The emergent theoretical study of religion had its inception in apologetics and polemics. Religionists of one persuasion or another sought out the origin of religion to defend their view from competing religious accounts or irreligious explanations. The bloodshed caused by religious violence and the growing explanatory power of science led others to adopt a nonreligious stance to try to explain religion in nonreligious terms, often with the intention of hastening its supposed demise. Though the polemical inspiration for theories of religion has receded in many quarters, one can nevertheless profitably make a heuristic distinction between humanistic theories of religion and religious theories of religion. Humanistic theories explain religion in terms of the humans who create or subscribe to them. Religious theories explain religion in terms of a religious object, entity, force, or ultimate reality.

This distinction provides only a provisional orientation because humanistic theories can be given religious significance. Ludwig Feuerbach, for instance, argued in *The Essence of Christianity* (1841) that humans unconsciously project the essential characteristics of the human species outside themselves and reify them in the form of a divine being. He insisted that humanity must overcome its self-induced self-alienation by self-consciously restoring its nature to itself. To this extent, Feuerbach's theory is humanistic. Feuerbach complicates matters, however, by insisting that theological statements predicating attributes of God must be inverted. If God is conceived as love, for example, humanity must come to see that love, as an essential component of human nature, is divine. Some read *The Essence of Christianity* as a theological text because they view Feuerbach as collapsing the distinction between a humanistic theory and a religious theory. They see him both explaining religion in terms of the humans who create it, and treating humanity as a religious entity. On this interpretation, Feuerbach's humanistic theory has religious inspiration; it articulates a religious naturalism. Eugene d'Aquili and Andrew Newberg present another case where the distinction between humanistic and religious theories breaks down. In *The Mystical Mind* (1999) they provide models of brain function to explain mystical experience, myth, and ritual. They explicitly aver that their models explain the origin of religion. Yet, they believe this humanistic theory culminates in what they call *neurotheology,* a "megatheology" whose content could be adopted by most of the world's major religions.

Early humanism

David Hume's *The Natural History of Religion* (1757) is the most influential eighteenth-century humanistic theory of religion. In composing a "natural history" of religion, Hume brings religious phenomena within the purview of science. As part of his larger project to create a science of human nature, Hume seeks both to isolate the causes of religion in human nature and to identify the consequences of religion in light of human nature. Not only does Hume consider religion a fit object for scientific investigation, he also theorizes that religion arises in the absence of science. In his pithy phrase, "Ignorance is the mother of devotion" (p. 75). Religion, Hume believes, fills the void when humans lack the aptitude for better founded explanatory principles.

Hume rejects the theological anthropology of his forebears' Calvinism wherein God endows humans with an innate religious sense. In Hume's naturalistic anthropology, religious principles are derivative. They are not an "original instinct or primary impression of nature," like self-love, sexual drive, or love of progeny (p. 21). These latter are all universal, he claims, and have a "precise determinate object," whereas religion is not universal and is not uniform in its "ideas." In this last judgment Hume attends to the extraordinary diversity of religious beliefs. Despite this diversity, he claims, all particular religious phenomena coincide in "the belief of invisible, intelligent power" (p. 21).

If religion itself is not universal, it is, nevertheless, a response to universal feelings. Concern about the "various and contrary events of human life" elicits hopes and fears whose object are the unknown causes of those events (p. 28). Because they need "to form some particular and distinct idea" of the causes and because science "exceeds" their comprehension, "the ignorant multitude" allow the imagination to clothe the unknown causes with human features (p. 29). Hume posits a natural propensity in humans to "conceive all beings like themselves, and to transfer to every object, those qualities, with which they are familiarly acquainted, and of which they are intimately conscious" (p. 29). A French admirer of Hume's theory, Baron d'Holbach, coined the term *anthropomorphism* to capture the tendency Hume describes. Humans, Hume argues, anthropomorphize the unknown causes behind significant events and, thereby, create gods. Anthropomorphizing the unknown causes not only renders them more familiar and comprehensible, but also furnishes the possibility of gaining their favor "by gifts and entreaties, by prayers and sacrifices" to control future events (p. 47).

Hume believed that these two facets of anthropomorphism, that it provides both familiarity (explanation) and the possibility of gaining favor (control), result in opposed tendencies in religion. The need for familiarity and concrete, even sensible, representations of unknown causes explains idols, polytheism, and mythology. The need to gain favor, on the other hand, leads to the obsequious pursuit of ever more exalted terms of praise (and abject means of self-abasement), culminating in iconoclasm, monotheism, and an insistence on mystery. Blatant contradictions in theologies of all types manifest the tension between these needs. The two tendencies produce contrary movements, furthermore, and initiate a continuous "flux and reflux" between polytheism and monotheism. Although Hume believes that both polytheism and monotheism compromise and distort natural human virtue, he believes that monotheism engenders intolerance and exhibits a greater proneness to enormities.

Religious feelings

Hume's theory explains religion in intellectual terms: as an account of the unknown causes at work in the natural and social worlds. An enterprise fundamentally concerned with explanation, prediction, and control, religion, on Hume's view, directly competes with science. Later, Victorian anthropologists like Edward Tyler, James Frazer, and Herbert Spencer likewise adopt a fundamentally intellectualist explanation of religion. They too see religion in conflict with science. As early as 1799, however, an alternative explanation of religion emerges. Unwilling to declare religion obsolete, Friedrich Schleiermacher argues that it constitutes an autonomous domain distinct from science. Religion, he claims in *On Religion: Speeches to its Cultured Despisers* (1799), consists in "the sensibility and taste for the infinite" within finite experience (p. 103). This religious feeling is independent of, and prior to, all thought or belief, though it naturally finds expression in language. The growth of science need not, therefore, conflict with religion because beliefs and judgments are essentially foreign to religion.

Schleiermacher's religious approach to religion influenced later theory as much as Hume's humanistic one. The nineteenth-century German scholar, Max Muller, for instance, theorizes that religion begins in perceptions of the infinite glimpsed in awesome natural phenomena like the sun. Through a "disease of language," the names for the powerful natural phenomena became misconstrued and taken to be the names of superhuman beings. Myths nevertheless metaphorically express the experience of the infinite. In the mid-twentieth century Mircea Eliade interpreted religious symbolism in light of what he called *hierophanies,* the religious experiences wherein one perceives a mode of the transcendent, wholly other "sacred" in a mundane object. In various ways *"homo religiosus"* builds different myths, rites, and beliefs out from the universal symbols.

William James also holds that religious feelings are primary and the explanation of religion. In *The Varieties of Religious Experience* (1902), he argues that various inarticulate feelings of the presence or reality of an unseen something more that is congruent with human interests explain religion. Unlike Schleiermacher, James admits that religious beliefs can conflict with science, but religious beliefs are merely secondary interpretations of religious feeling. Ultimately, he ventures the humanistic hypothesis that the subconscious explains the experiences he describes, but he countenances religious

theory by allowing that a religious reality could work through the subconscious. The attempt to safeguard religion from science by maintaining the primacy of feeling—the approach shared by Schleiermacher, Muller, Eliade, and James—runs aground on the fact that religious feelings are not in truth independent of, and prior to, religious beliefs. As Wayne Proudfoot makes evident in *Religious Experience* (1985), religious feelings are constituted by the subject's implicit commitment to a religious explanation of their cause and a religious description of their object. This commitment belies the alleged priority of religious feeling to religious belief.

Society and symbolism

Emile Durkheim conceives his humanistic theory of religion in self-conscious opposition to intellectualist theories of religion. In *The Elementary Forms of Religious Life* (1912) he insists that the generative source of religion cannot simply be ignorance. Otherwise, religion would have disappeared long ago under the pressure of massive disconfirmation because religious beliefs are "barely more than a fabric of errors" (p. 227). Durkheim proposes to explain the persistence of religion (its "ever-present causes") despite the errors it contains (p. 7).

An explanation of religion must, Durkheim argues, recognize that religion is a social fact. Previous theorists grounded their explanations in anthropology, or a theory of the person. One cannot explain social facts in this way, he claims, because societies, though composed of individuals, exhibit laws and properties of their own. Social facts place constraints on individuals and can contribute to explanations of individual psychology. Individual psychology, however, cannot explain a social fact. One should ground explanations of social facts in sociology, or a theory of society. To try to explain religion through a theory of the person entirely misses the social dynamics creating this social fact.

Durkheim grossly overstates the gulf between the social and individual levels of explanation, and even violates his own methodological prescriptions when he appeals to individual psychology in his theory of religion. Nevertheless, he offers a salutary corrective. Hume exemplifies the sort of theory about which Durkheim complained. Despite Hume's interest in the social consequences of religion, his theory of the origin of religion completely neglects social considerations. It almost seems, on Hume's view, as if each individual concocts religion independently. Schleiermacher and James also flout the proper order of explanation. Religion, as a social fact, can help explain the individual's religious feelings better than the individual's religious feelings can explain religion.

Whereas Hume deems belief in invisible, human-like beings to be the hallmark of religion, Durkheim argues that the category of religion includes systems without spiritual beings (or, at least, systems like Buddhism, where spiritual beings possess, he claims, only minor importance). To characterize religion most generally, he introduces a notion that influenced Eliade and his followers, and that eventually succumbed to ethnographic counterexamples. Religion, Durkheim claims, universally entails an absolute distinction between the sacred, "things set apart and forbidden," and the profane (pp. 44). A religion is a shared system of beliefs and practices concerning sacred things that unites a community. For Durkheim community is intrinsic to the idea of religion. This definition, based on the "readily visible outward features" of religion, bears a symmetrical relation to Durkheim's hypothesis concerning its "deep and truly explanatory elements" (p. 21). Inverting his definition of religion, Durkheim ultimately claims that the uniting of the community explains the beliefs and practices about sacred things.

Durkheim believes that the key to explaining religion is a consideration of the individual's relationship to society. The individual depends on society for his or her well-being, yet society demands service from the individual and frequently requires that the individual set aside his or her own interests and inclinations. Society subjects individuals to restraints and privations, but social interaction also fosters courage and confidence. Durkheim argues that the members of a society objectify and project outside their minds the feelings that the social collectivity inspires in them. They feel acted on by a mighty moral force to which they are subject, and, not surprisingly, they imagine it external to them. They fix the feelings on some object, which thereby becomes sacred. Moments of what Durkheim calls "collective effervescence," when the social group physically gathers and the individual feels uplifted and fortified by the crowd, are especially powerful, Durkheim claims, in creating religious ideas and the sacred. Although Durkheim relies on irremediably faulty ethnography and untenable assumptions

about the simplicity of "primitive" societies, his interpretation of Australian religion well illustrates his general theory. The Australian totem, he reports, stands both as the emblem of the clan (i.e., the society) and the emblem of sacred power. The sacred power, he concludes, derives from the clan itself.

Two features of Durkheim's theory influenced later twentieth-century theories profoundly. First, Durkheim argues that religious beliefs and rites, the beliefs and practices related to sacred things, symbolize society and social relations. He claims that "religion is first and foremost a system of ideas by means of which individuals imagine the society of which they are members and the obscure yet intimate relations they have with it" (p. 227). Although the believer understands them literally, religious beliefs and practices are fundamentally not attempts at explanation, prediction, and control. Rather, they are metaphorical expressions of social realities. Taking inspiration from Durkheim's injunction that "we must know how to reach beneath the symbol to grasp the reality it represents and that gives the symbol its true meaning" because the "most bizarre or barbarous rites and the strangest myths translate some human need and some aspect of life, whether social or individual," many twentieth-century scholars interpret religious beliefs primarily as symbolic expressions of existential concerns (p. 2). Others, like Mary Douglas and Edmund Leach, who follow even more closely in Durkheim's footsteps, have documented rich correlations between social arrangements and religious representations.

Second, Durkheim supplements his explanation of the origin of religion with a functional explanation of its persistence. Prevalent in biology, functional explanations explain something by its function, or what it does. In the social sciences they explain an institution or behavior in terms of its unintended, beneficial effects. Durkheim argues that religion persists because it satisfies social needs. Society requires a periodic strengthening of the social bond through communal activity that reinforces collective feelings and ideas. Worship, undertaken to maintain the relationship between the individual and the sacred, actually maintains the relationship between the individual and the reality behind the sacred—society. Rituals, meant to strengthen society's relationship to the sacred, strengthen society. That religion fulfils this social function explains, for Durkheim, how it persists despite its errors. Many twentieth-century anthropologists and sociologists adopt functionalism as an explanatory paradigm, but employ it uncritically. Sometimes they naïvely assume that extant religious beliefs or practices must serve some beneficial purpose. Sometimes they heedlessly suppose that the (putative) benefits maintain the beliefs or practices. Not everything that exists, of course, serves a beneficial purpose (some things work to the detriment of individuals and societies) and not everything that has beneficial effects exists for the sake of its effects.

In *Ulysses and the Sirens* (1984) Jon Elster provides the most penetrating analysis of the logic and the pitfalls of functional explanation. He argues that simply demonstrating that unintended, beneficial effects result from the presence of an institution or behavior in a society does not suffice to explain the presence of the institution or the behavior. To explain an institution or behavior's presence by its effects, one must also identify a feedback loop "whereby the effect maintains its cause" (p. 32). In biology, natural selection provides the feedback loop whereby the effect of an adaptation explains its presence in a population. Elster remarks that virtually all social scientists who invoke functional explanations fail to specify a comparable feedback loop. Durkheim's functional explanation of religion arguably does include a feedback loop: The effects of religious rites (strengthened social bonds) maintain their cause (religion) precisely because social bonds produce religion. Elster, nevertheless, rightly criticizes the all too frequent assumption in social scientific theory that unintended beneficial effects provide sufficient explanation for their cause.

Hume *redivivus*

Despite Durkheim's enormous influence over subsequent social scientific theory of religion, some late twentieth-century theory sustains themes advanced by Hume in the eighteenth century. Robin Horton, for example, in a series of essays spanning thirty years (and collected in 1993) argues for an intellectualist explanation of religion. While allowing that religious beliefs can reflect social preoccupations, he rejects symbolic understandings of religion because the subjects of his fieldwork in Africa construe their religious beliefs literally. The motivation to interpret religious beliefs symbolically derives, he argues, from liberal scruples about attributing massive error to so-called primitives.

Horton finds this liberal attitude patronizing. Taken literally, religion, like science, represents an attempt to explain, predict, and control the environment. Unlike science, however, which employs impersonal processes and entities as its explanatory idiom, religion employs personal forces and entities. It represents "an extension of the field of people's social relationships beyond the confines of purely human society," an extension "in which the human beings involved see themselves in a dependent position *vis-à-vis* their non-human alters" (pp. 31–32).

Though Horton revives both intellectualism and a variation of Hume's definition of religion, he repudiates the sort of distasteful elitism Hume epitomizes and remedies Hume's neglect of the social factors causing religion. He argues that societies with relatively stable patterns of social organization and relatively poor means of technological control draw on social analogies in constructing their theories because for them the social world represents predictability. Rapidly changing societies with good technological control, on the other hand, draw their analogies from the natural and artificial realms, which to them seem most predictable. Horton maintains that in addition to the use of a "personal idiom" to explain, predict, and control events, humans enter into "communion" relationships—personal relationships viewed as ends in themselves—with the personal entities postulated by religion. Religion-as-theory and religion-as-communion represent two poles or aspects of religion with varying relative salience depending on circumstance. In the modern West science has largely replaced the theoretical role for religion, granting communion greater prominence. This fact, he argues, helps explain the tendency of Western scholars to dismiss intellectualist explanations of religion.

In offering a sociological explanation of the personal beings that define religion, Horton departs from Hume. Stewart Guthrie, on the contrary, adheres to Hume's anthropological approach. In *Faces in the Clouds* (1993) Guthrie adduces copious evidence to suggest a propensity in human nature to anthropomorphize the world. Humans must constantly draw implicit or explicit explanatory conclusions about their surroundings. Guthrie claims that over the course of human evolution, the importance of other humans to human existence selected for traits that facilitate the detection of human agency in ambiguous or uncertain circumstances. A well-developed cognitive predisposition to perceive agents will inevitably produce erroneous results. Religion, Guthrie argues, represents one such result. He characterizes religion as a system of partial anthropomorphism (i.e., gods are only human-like, they are not human *simpliciter*) centered on communication with human-like beings through symbolic action. Science as an institution, by contrast, has historically resisted the tendency to anthropomorphize.

In *Religion Explained* (2001), Pascal Boyer supplies a complementary cognitive theory that likewise characterizes religion as essentially concerned with person-like beings and explains it as a by-product of evolved mental dispositions. From cognitive psychology Boyer adopts the conclusion that humans display cognitive biases that predispose the mind to attend to certain kinds of information, to classify it in specific ways, and to draw certain sorts of conclusions about it. The mind has biases toward a few "ontological categories" (e.g., inanimate objects, animate objects, and agents) that activate specialized "inference systems" (e.g., intuitive physics, intuitive biology, and intuitive psychology). These mental subsystems produce a set of intuitive default expectations concerning members of the category. Boyer contends that supernatural concepts preserve most intuitive expectations, but conspicuously violate a few (e.g., invulnerable organisms or percipient artifacts). These cognitively interesting concepts gain salience from their relative counterintuitiveness, and Boyer provides experimental evidence to show that they are more memorable than intuitive ones.

Specifically religious concepts (as opposed to folklore, myths, etc.) are those supernatural concepts that are "serious" and arouse strong emotions. They gain this additional salience from their "aggregate relevance" to important social and moral processes. Religious concepts concern agents who counterintuitively have full access to information pertinent to social interaction. Concepts involving "full-access strategic agents" gain plausibility and significance from the role they can play in moral reasoning, their congruity with human intuitions about the causes of misfortune, and their capacity to explain the social effects created in ritual. Religion does not produce morality, intuitions about misfortune, or ritual. Rather, the latter simply make some supernatural concepts—the one's concerning full access strategic agents—more relevant.

Though Boyer is critical of intellectualist explanations, both Guthrie and Boyer share Hume's view that religion does not represent "an original instinct or primary impression" in human nature. Like Hume, they believe that religion derives from more fundamental human propensities and predispositions. Religion, they contend, is a by-product of evolved cognitive biases. This approach enjoys considerable advantages. They do not need to show that religion itself confers an evolutionary advantage, nor to delineate a feedback loop independent of natural selection.

Marx and Freud

Sigmund Freud (1856–1939) and Karl Marx (1818–1883) both authored prominent humanistic theories of religion with scientific or quasi-scientific pretensions. Marx endorses Feuerbach's view of religion as alienation and projection, but argues that religion, or alienated consciousness, is only an epiphenomenal reflection of a more basic dehumanizing alienation at the level of social and economic organization. Religion reinforces prevailing social and economic arrangements by both consoling the oppressed and justifying their oppression. Freud's "psychoanalytic" theory explains religion as both the delusional fulfillment of powerful wishes for a protector, and as a symbolic enactment of ambivalence about the father. He describes a primal crime in which jealous sons kill and devour their father. Religions are attempts to allay guilt by deferred obedience to the father. Freud equivocates about the historicity of this oedipal conflict. Sometimes he portrays the primal crime as an historical phylogenetic truth. Sometimes he treats it purely as an illustration of a universal psychological conflict.

Detractors have labeled both Marx and Freud pseudo-scientific. The extraordinary plasticity of their interpretive principles renders their systems virtually invulnerable to counter-evidence. Sometimes they both also explain away and stigmatize objections, rather than meeting them. These features, together with the all-encompassing nature of their theories and the reverence accorded to the founders and the founding texts, leads some critics to liken Marxism and psychoanalysis to religions.

See also FREUD, SIGMUND; HUME, DAVID; MYSTICISM; NEUROTHEOLOGY; SOCIOLOGY

Bibliography

Alighieri, Dante. *The Divine Comedy,* Vol. 1: *The Inferno,* trans. Mark Musa. New York: Penguin, 1984.

Andresen, Jensine. *Religion in Mind: Cognitive Perspectives on Religious Belief, Ritual, and Experience.* Cambridge, UK: Cambridge University Press, 2001.

Boyer, Pascal. *The Naturalness of Religious Ideas: A Cognitive Theory of Religion.* Berkeley: University of California Press, 1994.

Boyer, Pascal. *Religion Explained: The Evolutionary Origins of Religious Thought.* New York: Basic Books, 2001.

D'Aquili, Eugene, and Newberg, Andrew. *The Mystical Mind: Probing the Biology of Religious Experience.* Minneapolis, Minn.: Fortress Press, 1999.

Douglas, Mary. *Purity and Danger.* London: Routledge and Kegan Paul, 1966.

Douglas, Mary. "Self-evidence." In *Implicit Meanings.* London: Routledge and Kegan Paul, 1975.

Durkheim, Emile. *The Elementary Forms of Religious Life* (1912), trans. Karen Fields. New York: Free Press, 1995.

Eliade, Mircea. *The Sacred and the Profane: The Nature of Religion,* trans. Willard Trask. New York: Harcourt, 1959.

Elster, Jon. *Ulysses and the Sirens: Studies in Rationality and Irrationality,* Rev. edition. Cambridge, UK: Cambridge University Press, 1984.

Feuerbach, Ludwig. *The Essence of Christianity* (1841), trans. George Eliot. New York: Harper, 1957.

Fraser, James. *The Golden Bough* (1922). London: Macmillan, 1976.

Freud, Sigmund. *Totem and Taboo: Some Points of Agreement Between the Mental Lives of Savages and Neurotics* (1913), trans. James Strachey. New York: Norton, 1950.

Freud, Sigmund. *The Future of an Illusion* (1928), trans. James Strachey. New York: Norton, 1975.

Geertz, Clifford. "Religion as a Cultural System." In *The Interpretation of Cultures.* New York: Basic Books, 1973.

Guthrie, Stewart. *Faces in the Clouds: A New Theory of Religion.* Oxford: Oxford University Press, 1993.

Horton, Robin. *Patterns of Thought in Africa and the West: Essays on Magic, Religion, and Science.* Cambridge, UK: Cambridge University Press, 1993.

Hume, David. *The Natural History of Religion* (1757). Stanford, Calif.: Stanford University Press, 1956.

James, William. *The Varieties of Religious Experience* (1902). New York: Mentor, 1958.

Lawson, Thomas, and McCauley, Robert. *Rethinking Religion: Connecting Cognition and Culture.* Cambridge, UK: Cambridge University Press, 1990.

Leach, Edmund. *Political System of Highland Burma.* London: Athlone, 1954.

Leach, Edmund. "Magical Hair." *Journal of the Royal Anthropological Institute* 88 (1958): 147–164.

Manuel, Frank. *The Eighteenth Century Confronts the Gods.* Cambridge, Mass.: Harvard University Press, 1959.

Marx, Karl, and Engels, Frederick. *On Religion.* Moscow: Progress, 1957.

Muller, F. Max. *Introduction to the Science of Religion* (1873). New York: Arno Press, 1978.

Penner, Hans. *Impasse and Resolution: A Critique of the Study of Religion.* New York: Peter Lang, 1989.

Preuss, J. Samuel. *Explaining Religion: Criticism and Theory from Bodin to Freud.* New Haven, Conn.: Yale University Press, 1987.

Proudfoot, Wayne. *Religious Experience.* Berkeley: University of California Press, 1985.

Schleiermacher, Friedrich. *On Religion: Speeches to its Cultured Despisers* (1799), trans. Richard Crouter. Cambridge, UK: Cambridge University Press, 1996.

Smith, Wilfred Cantwell. *The Meaning and End of Religion* (1962). Minneapolis, Minn.: Fortress Press, 1991.

Spencer, Herbert. *First Principles.* New York: D. Appleton, 1862.

Stout, Jeffrey. *The Flight From Authority: Religion, Morality, and the Quest for Autonomy.* Notre Dame, Ind.: University of Notre Dame Press, 1981.

Tylor, Edward. *Primitive Culture.* London: Murray, 1871.

MATTHEW C. BAGGER

RELIGIOUS EXPERIENCE

See EXPERIENCE, RELIGIOUS: COGNITIVE AND NEUROPHYSIOLOGICAL APSECTS; EXPERIENCE, RELIGIOUS: PHILOSOPHICAL ASPECTS

REPRODUCTIVE TECHNOLOGY

The field of assisted reproduction, or reproductive technology (often called ART), dates to the birth of the first "test tube baby," Louise Brown, in England in 1978. The term *assisted reproduction* is used to indicate the conception of children by means of technology designed to assist the fertility efforts of couples or individuals who might not be able to conceive children without technological assistance.

In vitro fertilization

In vitro fertilization (IVF) is the process by which a woman's ovaries are artificially stimulated with fertility drugs. The drugs are injected into the woman, whose eggs, released from the ovaries, will be stimulated to develop, grow, and mature with the aid of the administered medications. This process, also known as *hyperstimulation,* is physically demanding and carries some risks for the woman whose eggs will be retrieved. The mature eggs are retrieved using a needle inserted intravaginally and guided by ultrasound technology, requiring only a local anesthetic. The older technique of administering general anesthesia and aspirating the woman's eggs through laparoscopy is used less often.

After retrieval, each egg is cultured in a separate laboratory dish and combined with sperm from the woman's partner or from a donor; when the sperm penetrate the egg, fertilization results and IVF has occurred. This happens in an incubator under highly controlled laboratory conditions that mimic the internal body environment. As the fertilized eggs grow and divide, early embryos develop. Technological advances have made it possible to allow the embryos to grow in culture for up to six days, at which point the blastocyst is formed. A blastocyst is often referred to as a *pre-embryo* because it has yet to implant itself in the uterine wall; after implantation it will become a developing embryo. Allowing pre-embryos to develop to the blastocyst stage, in vitro, enables scientists to select those embryos for implantation that are deemed to have the highest chance for a resulting pregnancy, which is the goal of the process.

In order to enhance the chances of pregnancy, it is standard procedure to transfer several embryos back into the uterus (bypassing the fallopian tubes). Consequently, although birth rates are relatively low (ten to thirty percent by most estimates), in the early years of IVF the rate of multiple births was often comparatively high. Over the last decade, in part due to the freezing of embryos (cryopreservation), scientists are able to select fewer embryos for transfer at one time, based on the health and quality of the early embryos in culture. Thus the odds of a woman having a multiple pregnancy are reduced. IVF was performed successfully for the first time in the United States at the Jones Institute for Reproductive Medicine in Norfolk, Virginia.

Blastocyst transfer

Blastocyst transfer, or embryo transfer, is the process by which the pre-embryo is transferred from the laboratory culture dish to the woman's uterus via a tiny hollow needle. Since a fertilized egg subdivides into cells over time (fertilization is a process that takes between twenty-four and forty-eight hours after the sperm penetrates egg), it has been proven to be useful to maintain the process in culture until the fertilized egg has reached cell division of between four and sixteen cells (five to six days is optimal). The transfer of the blastocyst or pre-embryo at this stage then increases the chances of survival in utero and decreases the chances of abnormal or defective embryos being implanted. Developing embryos that do not survive through the blastocyst stage have been found to have chromosomal deficiencies that are not optimal for healthy pregnancies.

Other technologies

Other reproductive technologies related to IVF include *intracytoplasmic sperm injection, preimplantation genetic diagnosis, gamete intrafallopian transfer,* and *zygote intrafallopian transfer. Somatic cell nuclear transfer,* a developing and controversial technology, is associated with human cloning. Each of these techniques makes use of the basic process of IVF but refines the process in ways that are specific to one or more obstacles to fertility.

Intracytoplasmic sperm injection. (ICSI) is a technique developed in 1992 that is used primarily to assist in male factor infertility cases where sperm count is low or nonexistent. In this procedure, sperm are individually isolated by means of micromanipulation and are then individually inserted into the cytoplasm of the retrieved egg in a culture dish. It is possible to combine ICSI with Microsurgical Epididymal Sperm Aspiration (MESA) and Testicular Sperm Extraction (TESE). In MESA, sperm are retrieved from the part of the testes where they mature and are stored; then ICSI is used for the fertilization process. In TESE, the testes are biopsied so that sperm can be obtained from the testicular tissue directly; then ICSI is used to fertilize the sperm.

Pre-implantation genetic diagnosis. (PGD) allows scientists to screen embryos prior to implantation to check for genetic diseases and defects. The technique combines ICSI with IVF and blastocyst transfer. The developing pre-embryos are allowed to grow in culture to the six-to-eight cell stage, at which point one or two cells are removed and biopsied to check for chromosomal abnormalities or single gene defects by analyzing the DNA. Those embryos found to contain chromosomal abnormalities or gene defects are not transferred to the uterus, and scientists are able to select "normal" embryos for transfer with the goal of a pregnancy and birth free from disease. Specifically, fertility clinics using PGD are able to test for single gene defects such as, for example, cystic fibrosis, Tay-Sachs disease, thalassemia, sickle cell anemia, x-linked diseases such as hemophilia and muscular dystrophy, and spinal muscular atrophy. PGD can also test for abnormal numbers of specific chromosomes and associated diseases such as Trisomy 21/Down syndrome, Turner's syndrome, and other such conditions.

PGD, combined with IVF, has been used successfully in several cases, some of which are ethically controversial. On August 29, 2000, Adam Nash was born as a result of this procedure. Adam's parents chose to use PGD to make sure that, in vitro, only embryos found not to contain Fanconi's anemia disease would be transferred to the uterus of Adam's mother. Adam's older sister, Molly, had Fanconi's anemia, a rare bone marrow disease, and her only hope of a cure was a bone marrow transfer from an exact donor match. After Adam was born, cells were collected from his umbilical cord and transplanted into Molly's circulatory system.

The ethical controversy surrounding the Nash case centered on two issues: (1) whether it is permissible to create a child as a means for assisting someone else (in this case, his sister); and (2) whether it is ethical to allow screening and selection of traits and conditions prenatally. The second issue raises the specter of what has colloquially been referred to as *designer babies*. Ethicists tend to be wary of the move to use technology prenatally to select out various traits, although the use of

this technology to avoid conceiving a child with a destructive disease such as Tay-Sachs is, for many ethicists, less morally problematic than selecting out, for example, children with Down syndrome. The technique of PGD, combined with continuing advances from the Human Genome Project, raises the theoretical possibility of selecting out embryos for implantation based on traits connected with certain genes. For example, should the genes for homosexuality, intelligence, obesity, or a host of other conditions be clearly identified, it would be possible to select for or against those embryos by means of IVF and PGD.

Gamete intrafallopian transfer. (GIFT) and its related technology, zygote intrafallopian transfer (ZIFT), are technologies that use donor gametes (sperm or egg) combined with IVF to transfer the resulting embryo to the fallopian tubes of the woman who wishes to conceive. Specifically, in GIFT, fertilization occurs in vivo, in the body. ZIFT places already developed zygotes into the fallopian tubes.

When donated gametes are used for this process, donors are usually paid, raising issues about the commodification of reproduction (Holland). Such procedures make it possible for single persons and gay and lesbian couples to have children using assisted reproduction. Selection of donor gametes also raises the issue of eugenics (selective breeding) because it is now widely possible to "shop" for gametes by making up a list of desirable factors and finding them with the help of egg and sperm brokers.

Somatic cell nuclear transfer. (SCNT) is another form of assisted reproduction. This process, famously pioneered on Dolly the sheep and announced in 1997 by Ian Wilmut and his colleagues, has been experimented with in human fertility clinics. In its simplest sense, somatic cell nuclear transfer involves taking an adult somatic cell (not a reproductive cell), removing its nucleus, and transferring the DNA into an enucleated (containing no nucleus) donor egg. The donated egg is then "tricked" into the fertilization process by an electrical (or chemical) stimulation and begins cell division. Theoretically, the cloned embryo would then be implanted in the uterus using IVF techniques. Although several kinds of animals have been cloned, primates have not, and as of mid-2002, there is no public evidence that human cloning has been attempted, though there have been reports that Antinori Severino, an Italian fertility doctor, is engaged in this work.

The American public has been overwhelmingly opposed to the use of SCNT because it raises fears of madmen such as Adolf Hitler cloning armies of an Aryan master race, and other such scenarios. The technology is so difficult that these fears have no grounding in fact; however, it will certainly be possible one day to "clone" a human being via the process described. This type of cloning may be accurately thought of as "delayed twinning," for the cloned child would in fact be the genetic twin of the original donor. It raises some of the same ethical concerns as those raised under PGD, although at this point PGD technology has proven to be safe, while SCNT is not at all safe for use in human reproduction. As such, several ethics advisory boards, including the National Bioethics Advisory Commission (1997) and the California Advisory Committee on Human Cloning (2002), have recommended a moratorium on the use of this technology in humans until such time as it is proven to be safe.

Fertility specialists are also working on nuclear transfer techniques that would make it possible for a woman who wishes to conceive to have the nucleus from one of her unfertilized eggs removed and inserted into an enucleated egg donated by another woman. This is nuclear transfer, but not with a somatic cell. The goal of this procedure, when perfected, will be to assist older woman whose eggs are not ideal become pregnant using the eggs from a younger woman while retaining the DNA from the mother-to-be. One pioneer of this technique is Jamie Grifo at New York University Medical Center (Holt).

Religious responses

Assisted reproduction is now widely used around the world, and especially in the United States, although specific techniques continue to be of concern to ethicists, and religious communities have a variety of perspectives on the matter. The religious institution most clearly opposed to assisted reproduction is the Roman Catholic Church. In its 1987 instruction *Donum Vitae* (Gift of Life), the Catholic Church clearly states: "Through in vitro fertilization and embryo transfer and heterologous artificial insemination, human conception is achieved through the fusion of gametes of at least one donor other than the spouses who are united in marriage. Heterologous artificial fertilization is contrary to the unity of marriage, to the dignity of the spouses, to the vocation proper to parents, and to the child's right to be conceived and brought into the world in marriage and from marriage" (O'Rourke and Boyle, p. 63). Thus the Roman Catholic Church's objection to assisted reproduction is grounded in classical natural law theology that opposes the separation of procreation from the conjugal act of love in marriage. Nevertheless, many Catholics in the United States deviate in practice from their church's official teachings on contraception, abortion, and assisted reproduction.

Moderate and liberal Protestant denominations in the United States, often referred to as *mainline Protestant,* include the American Baptist Church, the Episcopal Church, the Presbyterian Church USA, the United Church of Christ, the United Methodist Church, and the Evangelical Lutheran Church. In general, these denominations emphasize fidelity to Scripture in formulating one's moral response to a situation, as distinct from the emphasis on church doctrine or tradition that one finds in Roman Catholicism. Thus, as Christian Green and Paul Numrich point out in their 2002 book, *Religious Perspectives on Sexuality,* these mainline Protestant denominations, while they have a variety of official responses to reproductive issues, tend to affirm the right of individuals to discern for themselves how to make use of reproductive technologies.

Conservative Protestantism includes the Southern Baptist Convention, the Assemblies of God, the Association of Vineyard Churches, and a variety of independent, evangelical fundamentalist churches. They have in common with mainline Protestants an emphasis on the primary authority of the Bible, but these churches are generally distinguished by an insistence on a literal interpretive framework. Their positions on reproductive matters tend to include an active opposition to abortion, but assisted reproduction has not been much considered in formal church statements. In general, "They tend to approve of methods intended to correct physical problems that cause couples to be infertile, but they disapprove of methods that would violate the sanctity of the marriage bond by using donated sperm and eggs, as well as any method that would tamper with or discard a fertilized embryo" (Green and Numrich, p. 11).

The three branches of Judaism—Orthodox, Conservative, Reform—each have a variety of responses to assisted reproduction and their concerns are relative to the importance each branch places on upholding Jewish law or *halachah*. Assisted reproduction tends to be permitted in most branches of Judaism, although there are more and less problematic forms of reproductive technologies. Those forms of assisted reproduction that make use of the eggs and sperm of the couple trying to conceive are less problematic than those that make use of donor gametes; indeed, in Orthodox Judaism, donor gametes raise concerns of adultery. Surrogacy, too, is permissible for Jews, and there is ancient Biblical precedent for it. Since conception and the raising of children are cornerstones of Judaism, assisted reproduction tends to be viewed as permissible and even a good thing if it results in childbearing. Moreover, since, for example, Tay-Sachs disease is a devastating disease for Ashkenazi Jews, the use of PGD and other forms of assisted reproduction that prevent the birth of Tay-Sachs children has been widely embraced by Judaism. Moreover, therapeutic cloning (using SCNT for obtaining stem cells) has been approved by the Union of Orthodox Jewish Congregations of America and the Rabbinical Council of America, the two largest Orthodox Jewish organizations. It is widely expected that the other branches of Judaism will follow suit (Cooperman, Dorff).

Islam is also characterized by many schools of thought and practice: Sunni Muslims consider themselves followers of Muhammad's tradition; Shiite Muslims, the second-largest branch of Islam, adhere to the authority of the supporters of Ali, Muhammad's son-in-law; Sufi Muslims, the smallest branch, stress mysticism and personal worship. In the United States, many African-Americans have joined the Nation of Islam, which is based on the teaching of Elijah Muhammad. So although there is a wide variety of Islamic expression and values, in general the views of Islam on assisted reproduction are similar to those of Judaism in that most forms of assisted reproduction are permitted, with the caveat that only the eggs and sperm of the married couple are used. Surrogacy, however, is generally not permitted.

See also CHRISTIANITY; CHRISTIANITY, ROMAN CATHOLIC, ISSUES IN SCIENCE AND RELIGION; CLONING; ISLAM; JUDAISM; REPRODUCTIVE TECHNOLOGY

Bibliography

American Society of Reproductive Medicine (ASRM). Available from http://www.asrm.org.

Report of the California Advisory Committee on Human Cloning. *Cloning Californians?* July 11, 2002. Available from http://lawschool.stanford.edu/library/special/cloning.californians.pdf.

Congregation for the Doctrine of the Faith. "Donum Vitae (Gift of Life): Instruction on Respect for Human Life in Its Origins and on the Dignity of Procreation, Replies to Certain Questions of the Day." Washington, D.C.: United States Catholic Conference, 1987.

Cooperman, Alan. "Two Jewish Groups Back Therapeutic Cloning." *The Washington Post,* Wednesday, March 13, 2002: A04.

Dorff, Elliott. N. *Matters of Life and Death: A Jewish Approach to Modern Medical Ethics.* Philadelphia, Pa.: Jewish Publication Society of America, 1998.

Foubister, Vida. "Ethicists Debate New Use of Genetic Testing." *American Medical News* (amednews.com), January 15, 2001. Available from http://www.ama-assn.org/sci-pubs/amnews/pick_01/prse0115.htm.

Green, Christian M., and Numrich, Paul D. *Religious Perspectives on Sexuality: A Resource Guide.* Chicago, Ill.: Park Ridge Center, 2002.

Holland, Suzanne. "Contested Commodities at Both Ends of Life: Buying and Selling Gametes, Embryos, and Body Tissues." *Kennedy Institute of Ethics Journal* 11, no. 3 (2001): 263–284.

Holt, Sarah. "The 18 Ways (and Then Some)." Boston: WGBH and Nova, 2001. Available from http://www.pbs.org/wgbh/nova/baby/18ways.html.

Jones Institute for Reproductive Medicine. Available from http://www.jonesinstitute.org.

Mead, Rebecca. "Annals of Reproduction: Eggs for Sale." *New Yorker* 75, no. 22 (August 1999): 56–65.

National Bioethics Advisory Commission. *Cloning Human Beings.* Available from: http://bioethics.georgetown.edu/nbac/pubs.html.

O'Rourke, Kevin D., and Boyle, Philip. *Medical Ethics: Sources of Catholic Teachings,* 3rd edition. Washington, D.C.: Georgetown University Press, 1999.

Presiding Bishop's Consultation on Bioethics. *Anglican Theological Review* 81, no. 4 (1999): 559–682.

Ryan, Maura A. *The Ethics and Economics of Assisted Reproduction: The Cost of Longing.* Washington, D.C.: Georgetown University Press, 2001.

Wilmut, Ian; Schneike, A. E.; McWhir, J.; Kind, A. J.; and
Campbell, K. H. S. "Viable Offspring Derived from
Fetal and Adult Mammalian Cells." *Nature* 385
(1997): 810–813.

Worldwide Fertility Network (Ferti.net). "Treatment of Infertility." Available from http://www.ferti.net/i_and_t/
treatment/treatment.asp.

SUZANNE HOLLAND

REVELATION

Prior to the twentieth century, it was usually assumed that revelation was received in two modes.
"Special" revelation represented communication
of knowledge about God through supernatural
agency. "General" revelation consisted of what
could be known of God through either abstract philosophy or reflection on the nature of the universe.

Twentieth-century challenges

In the twentieth century, however, there were
strong challenges both to the concept of revelation
as disclosure of propositional knowledge and to
the validity of a "natural theology" based on general revelation. The work of the Swiss Protestant
theologian Karl Barth (1886–1968), in particular,
had led, by the middle of the century, to both a
new emphasis on the centrality of special revelation for theological thinking and a perspective in
which theological propositions represented no
more than human reflection on God's historical
acts. This emphasis on "revelation in history" had a
major influence in making propositional understandings of revelation unfashionable.

This tendency was subsequently reinforced,
for some, by instrumentalist understandings of religious language, such as those associated with existentialism, with "linguistic" understandings, and
with more specifically postmodernist approaches.
As a result, except in neo-orthodox circles, which
still looked to Barth for inspiration, the focus for
many shifted from historical revelation towards existential criteria and existing religious communities.
Despite the ways in which this gap was bridged by
the work of people like Yves Congar, on revelation, and of Janet Soskice, on religious language,
these perspectives resulted in a widespread belief
that theological reflection was essentially unaffected by scientific understanding.

Perspectives from science and religion

The dialogue of science and theology during the
second half of the twentieth century was based, in
large part, on a reaction to this "independence"
thesis, as Ian Barbour called it. The simplistic separation of science and religion that had arisen from
seeing the one as based purely on empirical problems, and the other as based purely on special revelation, was strongly challenged. Beginning with
the work of Barbour himself, it was increasingly
stressed that science itself was more complex in its
rationality than was commonly understood, and
that there were important parallels between the
ways in which religious and scientific languages
were employed.

Two factors were characteristic of this phase of
the dialogue of science and theology. One was that
the dialogue was often seen in apologetic terms, its
goal being to vindicate the consonance of scientific
and theological worldviews. This consonance was
interpreted, however, largely in terms of the way in
which both disciplines could be seen as using revisable models of reality. This owed much to Karl
Popper's (1902–1994) analysis of the sciences, and
manifested little recognition of broader, postfoundationalist perspectives. The other, and related,
factor was that theological language was often approached from a perspective that stressed the more
conservative aspects of the sort of "critical realism"
that had become, among philosophers of science,
the dominant understanding of scientific language.

Modifications that might have been made to
this position, through an awareness of recent
thinking about revelation, were conspicuous by
their absence. At the level of epistemology, dissenting voices—such as that of Thomas Torrance—
tended to look back to Barthian viewpoints. Only
in the last decade of the century were there significant challenges based on new perspectives, which
attempted either to modify the realist position in a
major way (Christopher Knight), to dispute realism
in favor of an emphasis on methodological parallels (Nancey Murphy), or to emphasize the importance of postfoundationalist insights (J. Wentzel
van Huyssteen). Despite these challenges, however, the older, quasi-propositional approach remained influential.

One of the more fruitful aspects of this approach was, even for some who were otherwise critical, the attempt to challenge the Barthian rejection of the concept of "natural theology." Few attempted to defend its historical forms—recognizing, for example, that neo-Darwinian understandings had rendered design arguments such as William Paley's (1743–1805) redundant. Nevertheless, although it was acknowledged that no "proof" of God's reality could now be provided, people like John Polkinghorne advocated a "revived and revised natural theology"—persuasive but not logically coercive—based on issues such as the anthropic cosmological principle. Similarly, people like Arthur Peacocke urged the relevance of the concept of inference to the best explanation.

The propositional understandings of revelation implicit in these approaches were, however, further undermined by another issue that took on new importance towards the end of the twentieth century. It was the question of whether, and how, religious faiths other than one's own can be seen as having arisen from God's revelation of himself within different cultures. Keith Ward, in particular, attempted to develop an understanding of revelation that took up the pluralist insights of earlier investigators into the relationship between different faiths.

One of the most comprehensive responses to this issue from within the science and religion debate was that of Christopher Knight, who advocated a pluralist understanding of revelation based on an essentially naturalist understanding of divine action. Using the experiences of the risen Christ as his prime example, Knight explored the psychological basis of revelatory experience to affirm what he called a psychological-referential model of revelatory experience. As Ward's own position indicated, however, Knight's type of naturalism was not the only approach through which a pluralist understanding could be affirmed. A more conservative understanding of divine action can also give rise to a pluralistic position.

It is perhaps in the context of postfoundationalist understandings of rationality that the concept of revelation will most markedly affect the dialogue of science and theology in the near future. J. Wentzel van Huyssteen's approach, for example, is one that assumes, in the views of some, too great a distinction between theological and scientific rationality. Nevertheless, his way of acknowledging

crucial areas of overlap provides a challenge to the simplistic distinction between empirical problems and God's revelation, which is often still held to separate science and theology. This acknowledgement is likely to be of considerable influence in an era profoundly influenced by postmodernist perspectives. A more subtle understanding of revelation than is yet common can, arguably, allow the implications of his insights to be fully explored.

See also ANTHROPIC PRINCIPLE; CRITICAL REALISM; DIVINE ACTION; EPISTEMOLOGY; LANGUAGE; NATURAL THEOLOGY; POSTFOUNDATIONALISM; POSTMODERNISM

Bibliography

Barr, James. *Biblical Faith and Natural Theology: The Gifford Lectures for 1991.* Oxford: Clarendon Press, 1993.

Brook, John Hedley. *Science and Religion: Some Historical Perspectives.* Cambridge, UK: Cambridge University Press, 1991.

Congar, Yves. *The Revelation of God,* trans. A. Manson and L. C. Sheppard. New York: Herder and Herder, 1968.

Henn, William. *The Hierarchy of Truths According to Yves Congar, O.P.* Analecta Gregoriana 246. Rome: Editrice Pontificia Università Gregoriana, 1987.

Knight, Christopher C. *Wrestling With the Divine: Religion, Science and Revelation.* Minneapolis, Minn.: Fortress Press, 2001.

Peacocke, Arthur R. *Intimations of Reality: Critical Realism in Science and Religion.* Notre Dame, Ind.: University of Notre Dame Press, 1984.

Polkinghorne, John. *Faith, Science and Understanding.* London: SPCK, 2000.

Soskice, Janet Martin. *Metaphor and Religious Language.* Oxford: Clarendon Press, 1985.

Torrance, Thomas F. *Reality and Scientific Theology.* Edinburgh, UK: Scottish Academic Press, 1985.

van Huyssteen, J.Wentzel. "Postfoundationalism in Theology and Science." In *Rethinking Theology and Science: Six Models for the Current Dialogue,* eds. Niels H. Gregersen and J. Wentzel van Huyssteen. Grand Rapids, Mich.: Eerdmans, 1998.

Ward, Keith. *Religion and Revelation: A Theology of Revelation in the World's Religions.* Oxford: Clarendon Press, 1994.

CHRISTOPHER C. KNIGHT

RITUAL

Ritual is normally defined as gestures and, often, linguistic actions that follow a preestablished schedule and have a communicative purpose. Anthropologist Roy Rappaport (1926–1997) defined *ritual* as "the performance of more or less invariant sequences of formal acts and utterances not entirely encoded by the performers" (p. 24). According to this minimal definition, rituals occur among animals and human beings. Religious rituals are a subgroup of human rituals. A more specific definition depends on the definition of religion, which normally refers to ultimate values or transempirical beings.

Ritual is related to phenomena such as rite, cult, service, liturgy, ceremony, and feast. *Rite* often designates a single ritual act, *ritual* a series of rites. Quasi-synonyms such as *cult* and *service* designate a subclass of religious rituals. *Liturgy* normally means the spoken part of a service. *Ceremony* designates religious and nonreligious rituals, often with a connotation of something superficial, formal, less important. *Feast* can designate a class of rituals with a connotation of the uncontrolled, chaotic, and a violation of norms.

Ritual is normally understood as being a collective phenomenon. The Scottish scholar W. Robertson Smith (1846–1894) regarded religious rituals as more basic than doctrines or individual convictions, rituals being common for a group and relatively durable, while doctrines and convictions may vary individually and are more vulnerable to changes over time. French philosopher and sociologist Émile Durkheim (1858–1917) regarded rituals as the occasions where the holy is articulated and preserved. Religion, the rational core of which is a society's morals, ideals, and principles, is mediated to the individual participants when they gather together to form a community. The assembly also signifies a rupture with the routines of daily life. Therefore, a certain effervescence, conditioned by group psychological mechanisms, often arises, where the individual participants experience a moment of self-forgetfulness and of collective identity. Hereby the individual's obligation toward common ideals is strengthened; new ideals may also develop more or less spontaneously in such gatherings. All religion, and in fact all social fabric, from the most archaic to the most modern forms, presupposes gatherings with at least a touch of effervescence.

Henri Hubert (1872–1927), Marcel Mauss (1872–1950), and Arnold Van Gennep (1873–1957) described a basic syntagm in three parts for all rituals: first, the participants are drawn out of the profane, daily world; second, the central acts are performed; finally, the participants are reconnected with the profane. Van Gennep pointed out the universal occurrence and significance of rituals of transition and initiation

The effervescence of ritual and its partial violation of norms was elaborated by Roger Caillois (1913–1978) and Georges Bataille (1897–1962), who emphasized the extravagant consumption of values in feasts and offerings. Mircea Eliade (1907–1986) saw ritual as an occasion for the abolition of historical and linear time and for contact with archaic notions of the origin of the world and the regeneration of life. Victor Turner (1920-1983) analyzed the central part of initiation, the phase of *liminality,* as a state where the structures of normal life are suspended, the normal differences between the participants are replaced with a temporary community and brotherhood or sisterhood (a *communitas*), and often the initiates are under strict surveillance of ritual leaders with extensive authority. Typically, the initiates are instructed in the mythic and normative foundation of their society, but alternative understandings of life and norms may also be articulated. Turner has seen tendencies to formations of permanent forms of communitas in, for example, monastic movements and pilgrimages. According to Turner, the fertile chaos of liminality has been the origin of theater and performance.

Walter Burkert (1931–) and René Girard (1923–) both emphasized bloody sacrifice as a central ritual; here a group of human beings mitigates internal aggression by directing it toward a designated animal, which is slaughtered and sometimes eaten. Inspired by ethological studies, Burkert stressed the origin of rituals in the life of animals; rituals are sequences of actions, where an original pragmatic purpose has been replaced by a communicative content. To Burkert, different rituals can have different origins. Girard assumed that rituals of all types have been "generated" by a common original form, which is the spontaneous expulsion of a common adversary, a scapegoat.

The structure "all-against-one," common in many rituals, is such a remnant of the primeval scene.

To Rappaport, who combines a Durkheimian inspiration with phenomenology of religion, semiotics, theory of speech acts, and evolutionary theory, the ritual is the place where linguistically formulated norms and conventions are made obligatory for a group of human beings; ritual is "the basic human act." Purely linguistic meaning is conventional and open for misuse (lies) and misunderstanding (Babel). In order to withstand disintegrating tendencies from without or within, every group of human beings must commit its members to a certain amount of consensus and predictability. By their mere participation in a ritual—that is, by their self-submission under its preestablished rules for acts and linguistic utterances—the participants signal that they give up a part of their subjectivity and commit themselves to a common universe of norms and significations, in spite of their own "inner" thoughts and feelings. Therefore ritual typically includes performative, self-committing speech acts. The relative "weight" of ritually mediated meaning is reflected in the fact that ritual demands not only the thoughts and feelings of the participants, but also the presence of their bodies.

At least in Protestant-Christian theology, rituals have been problematic since the age of Enlightenment. Already in the early Reformation, the sacraments, which are key examples of rituals, were interpreted as preaching in other forms. Often rituals have been considered external, figurative, affective, and possibly infantile or archaic, and in any case secondary in relationship to rational theology, which necessarily is formulated in symbolic language, spoken and written. Normally the marginalizing of ritual does not assume the shape of a polemic, which aims at abolishing ritual altogether, but rather a disinclination for a proper reflection on it. On the other hand, rituals are often appreciated by those who want to keep a strong emotional dimension in church services.

See also SEMIOTICS

Bibliography

Burkert, Walter. *Homo necans: The Anthropology of Ancient Greek Sacrificial Ritual and Myth,* trans. Peter Bing. Berkeley: University of California Press, 1983.

Caillois, Roger. *Man and the Sacred,* trans. Meyer Barash. Champaign: University of Illinois Press, 2001.

Durkheim, Émile. *The Elementary Forms of Religious Life,* trans. Karen E. Fields. New York: Free Press, 1995.

Eliade, Mircea. *The Sacred and the Profane: The Nature of Religion,* trans. Willard Trask. San Diego, Calif.: Harvest Books, 1968.

Gennep, Arnold Van. *The Rites of Passage,* trans. Monika B. Vizedom and Gabrielle L. Cafee. Chicago: University of Chicago Press, 1960.

Girard, René. *Violence and the Sacred,* trans. Patrick Gregory. Baltimore, Md., and London: John Hopkins University Press, 1979.

Hollier, Denis, ed. *The College of Sociology (1937–39).* Minneapolis, Minn.: University of Minnesota Press, 1988.

Hubert, Henri, and Mauss, Marcel. *Sacrifice: Its Nature and Function,* trans. W. D. Halls. London: Cohen West, 1964.

Rappaport, Roy A. *Ritual and Religion in the Making of Humanity.* Cambridge, UK: Cambridge University Press, 1999.

Smith, W. Robertson. *Lectures on the Religion of the Semites.* London: A&C Black, 1889.

Turner, Victor Witter. *The Ritual Process: Structure and Anti-Structure.* Ithaca, N.Y.: Cornell University Press, 1969.

HANS J. L. JENSEN

ROBOTICS

The term *robot* derives from the Czech word *robota,* which means slavery, drudgery, or compulsory labor. In 1920, the Czech author Karel Čapek (1890-1938) wrote a play entitled *R.U.R.: Rossum's Universal Robots,* where he used *robota* for machine-humans, giving rise to the English word *robot.* The science fiction writer Isaac Asimov coined the term *robotics* as the field of academic study of the construction of robots. This connection to fiction points already to the utopian and eschatological elements in the science of robotics.

Kinds of robots

Basically, one can distinguish between industrial robots and artificial intelligence (AI) robots. Industrial robots are either remote controlled devices or machines that repeat constantly a series of movements, as in a factory. AI robots have some level of intelligence that enables them to react more flexibly and autonomously in their environment. The two kinds of AI robots mirror the two camps within AI. *Classical* AI robots are controlled by a central processor running a specific program. Such robots are used in highly restricted static environments. *Embodied* robots on the other hand are distributed systems interacting with natural worlds. Both technologies have a wide array of applications ranging from household robots, nurses, search and rescue robots, robots used as social agents for global communications, and robots used in ubiquitous computing (intelligent agents hidden in everyday tools such as stereos and coffeemakers).

The understanding of human intelligence in AI robotics mirrors specific theories about humans and their intelligence. In Classical AI, intelligence is understood as information processing. The most important elements of intelligence are learning, knowledge representation, searching, language, and mathematical theorem proving. One of the most well-known applications for this type of intelligence is chess. When applied to robots, this concept makes for very good and reliable machines that act in clear defined, restricted, and unchangeable environments. In natural worlds, however, these robots can navigate only very slowly and cannot deal with rapidly changing surroundings.

Embodied AI understands intelligence as a result of the evolutionary process and thus as the capability to survive. Abstract features such as logic and chess are seen as by-products of the human capability to survive in many different environments. Robots built according to this understanding of intelligence are increasingly autonomous. During the late 1990s, researchers started to build autonomous robots with social features for natural human-robot interfaces, which enlarges the field of possible applications.

Ethical and religious perspectives

Several theological and ethical problems arise in robotics. One argument for the use of robotics in industry and manufacturing is that it liberates humans from tedious work. But robotics also threatens to make many humans superfluous and to eliminate jobs. However, this issue is not specific for robotics but relates to the whole area of technology and will not be explored in this entry. The following ethical and theological problems refer to AI robots only.

Playing God. Often people think that AI researchers do their work out of hubris. AI roboticists who build autonomous creatures are sometimes accused of "playing God." The dangers of such actions are described in myths, including the myth of Prometheus, and the story of Frankenstein in Western culture. The Jewish Kabbalah provides an alternative view in the construction of *golems* (artificial humans made from clay), which is seen as a form of prayer. The *imago dei* (the Biblical statement that God has created humans in God's image) symbolizes the divine creativity in human beings so that whenever people are creative they praise God. In "rebuilding" themselves, people create the most complex being God created, thus praising and celebrating God to the utmost. Many of the founders of AI come from this Jewish tradition and understand their work in that sense.

Anthropomorphization and human uniqueness. If it were possible for researchers to build robots that work like humans, does that mean humans are also some kind of machine? Many people feel threatened by AI products because they seem to undermine human uniqueness. Because most people react more strongly to physical entities, the threat is perceived to be even greater with robots. Instead of just being connected to a computerized entity via a keyboard and screen, people connect with robots in a physical, sensual way, and they have to deal with creatures that share their physical space.

Experiments by Byron Reeves and Cliff Nass have demonstrated the degree to which humans anthropomorphize gadgets that are in some way responsive. Their experiments reveal that anthropomorphization of stereos, cars, or computers is a natural reaction in humans, and it takes a conscious effort for people to *not* react that way to the technical tools with which they interact in daily life. That is, people tend to react to robots as if they were partners, yet this reaction, stemming from innate social mechanisms, triggers fears not just that humans will loose their uniqueness but also that robots may surpass humans and make humans superfluous.

In most cultures, the human understanding of self contains an element of specialness; humans are distinct and cannot be compared with other species. In the Jewish and Christian tradition this sense of specialness has often been based on the *imago dei*. For millennia, people have attempted to identify with empirical human features, such as the humanoid body, human intelligence, or humor. A *relational* interpretation of the *imago dei* seems to have become prevalent. Based on *a relational ontology,* the *imago dei* is a promise of God to start and maintain a relationship with humans. Human uniqueness is then based not on special human capabilities but only on the faith-based statement that God has chosen humans as partners with whom God can interact and who will answer (sometimes).

The fear of losing human uniqueness when researchers are capable of building machines that are as smart as people is thus based on a traditional interpretation of the *imago dei* and can be overcome by this relational understanding of the concept. With this concept in mind, the idea of humans constructing robots as a spiritual enterprise, as depicted in the golem tradition, gains a stronger foundation. Christians may add that just as God is relational in the trinity and in the relation with humans, humans are relational. In building robots, humans create creatures with whom they can interact and who will answer. What is amazing is that even the simplest insect is much more complex and more interactive than any robot the most brilliant engineers have been able to build as of the beginning of the twenty-first century. Building autonomous robots in the image of God's creatures does not therefore make humans arrogant, but rather increasingly modest and admiring of the complexity of God's creation.

See also ARTIFICIAL INTELLIGENCE; CYBERNETICS; CYBORG

Bibliography

Asimov, Isaac. *The Robot Collection.* New York: Doubleday, 1983.

Brooks, Rodney Allen. *Cambrian Intelligence: The Early History of the New AI.* Cambridge, Mass.: MIT Press, 1999.

Čapek, Karel. *R.U.R.* In *Čapek: Four Plays,* trans Peter Majer and Cathy Porter. New York: Methuen, 2000.

Minsky, Marvin. *The Society of Mind.* Cambridge, Mass.: MIT Press, 1985.

Reeves, Byron, and Nass, Clifford. *The Media Equation: How People Treat Computers, Television, and New Media Like Real People and Places.* Cambridge, UK: Cambridge University Press, 1999.

Wiener, Norbert. *God and Golem, Inc.: A Comment on Certain Points Where Cybernetics Impinges on Religion.* Cambridge, Mass.: MIT Press, 1964.

ANNE FOERST

ROMAN CATHOLICISM

See CHRISTIANITY, ROMAN CATHOLIC, ISSUES IN SCIENCE AND RELIGION

S

SACRAMENTAL UNIVERSE

Sacramental universe (SU) is a conception of the universe as sacred, a holy temple wherein divinity and creatures play, co-create, and bestow grace. According to the medieval Christian philosopher Thomas Aquinas, "God has produced a work in which the divine likeness is clearly reflected—the universe itself." All beings possess intrinsic worth, participating in divine beauty; each being is a "Cosmic Christ" or "Buddha nature," reflecting divine radiance. German physicist Fritz-Albert Popp's finding that every atom contains photons underscores this teaching that microcosm as well as macrocosm share in the radiance of SU. Destruction of the ecosystem is a sacrilege against SU. A "universe as machine" ideology denies SU and replaces holy sacrament with blind materialism.

Bibliography

Fox, Matthew. *The Coming of the Cosmic Christ*. San Francisco: Harper, 1988.

MATTHEW FOX

SACRAMENTS

From the Latin word *sacramentum,* meaning oath, a sacrament is an outward sign or ritual (*signum*) connected to an invisible reality (*res*). In Christian context, it bears a promise from God for the comfort and encouragement in faith of the believer.

Augustine of Hippo (354–430) was among the first of Christian theologians to propose a theory of sacraments, and his proposal has been most influential: "The word [of God] comes to the element and it becomes a sacrament." Peter Lombard (c.1100–1160) then added the idea of causation to sacramental actions; thus the popular definition in virtually all Christian traditions: A sacrament is a visible sign of an invisible grace of God and causes what it signifies (*efficit quod figurat*).

Whereas Eastern Christianity understands sacraments as primary media for God's continuing creation of authentic humanity (*theosis,* or divinization, often misunderstood as a qualitative changing process of natural humanity into nonhuman divinity), Western Christianity, because of its understanding of sin as a rupture in the relation between God and humanity, would come to emphasize the assurance of forgiveness through the sacraments. Protestantism would add to this perspective the criterion that a sacrament be clearly mandated by God through Holy Scripture, thus always tying sacraments to God's word. This definition led to a Protestant narrowing of the number of acts identified as sacraments to two or possibly three (baptism, Eucharist, and penance), though the Council of Florence (1438–1445) fixed the number for Roman Catholicism at seven (baptism, confirmation, Eucharist, penance, extreme unction, ordination, and marriage). Some Protestant perspectives, especially within Radical Protestantism movements, hold that sacraments are more symbolic than actually bearing and effective of divine presence.

Cross-cultural perspectives

Judaism does not have sacraments per se, but the philosophy of time involved in such celebrations as the Passover meal enables the Jewish believer to claim participation in holy historical events, like the deliverance from captivity (Exodus). Islam is deeply suspicious of anything that could be interpreted as an image and therefore idolatrous. Even so, the practice of *salat*, disciplined prayer five times a day, is deeply sacramental. *Salat* is said to mimic the Prophet's mystical experience of receiving prayerfulness as a gift and then with prayer ascending through the heavens to the divine throne. Turning to the East, though Buddhism generally insists on the ephemeral and transitory character of nature, the practice of Tantric *pancamakarapuja* in both Buddhism and Hinduism, as well as in Jainism, places the goddess directly or symbolically (depending upon the sect) within forms of nature. These love feasts, guarded carefully against purely sensualist interpretations, display a deeply embodied sensibility about divine presence, and are echoed in the better known phenomena of ritual river washings. Daoism's belief that all nature is united in the Dao, with concern that the forces of nature be properly directed within one's own body, also suggests a profoundly personalized as well as embodied concept of divine presence. Nevertheless, a formally sacramental character about these examples cannot be claimed, though their consonance is noteworthy.

Sacraments in the science-religion dialogue

The use and theology of sacraments (sacramentology) begs the question of the relation between nature and grace, also known as the question of the relation between nature and supernature or between matter and spirit. Where theologians and scientists may agree that their disciplines are neither merely opposed nor in mutual avoidance, use of sacraments may be the most palpable example of how theology and science might converge, particularly as new theology informed by science proposes integrated or complementary descriptions of *what* happens and *how* in sacramental practice. Christian tradition often has invoked imagery from the natural world metaphorically to commend the value and meaning of sacraments. Still, religion and science are careful not to overemphasize their common grounds. Theologians and scientists are usually wary of conflating their disciplines with

one another, and such wariness is hardly more evident than with sacramentology. Thus, Christian theology normally would not advert to the ultimate authority of a scientific explanation, nor would such explanation presume to "prove" the Christian claim.

But religion could and increasingly does explore how the meaning of its dogmatic claims—as with what happens in the Christian Eucharist— might be more illumined in engagement with scientific observation. For example, the quantum physical phenomenon of particle entanglement— wherein the actions of one particle in relation to another have ineluctable influences on all other particles both have encountered—suggests a physical image of the depth and breadth of relationship between all believers initiated in Baptism, which the Eucharist (Holy Communion) is believed to sustain and deepen.

Contemporary sacramentology also, with much help from the sciences, prefers to speak of the sacramental phenomenon in more holistic terms, rather than speaking in a reductionistic way of only the elements and words themselves. Even the most solitary act, like extreme unction, is to be seen, like Baptism and Eucharist, as one around which the whole community of believers is marshaled. Borrowing from evolutionary biology and contemporary sociology, one might say that a sacramental action is an emergent event, irreducible to its parts, that is a unique collective of worshipers and their gifts gathered in dedicated spaces around central rites and forms. As a collective representation in a gathered community of diversity, a sacrament represents something of divine activity, and even of divine character (e.g., God as a community of diversity, as Trinitarian theology suggests).

The collective representation thus both creates and extends the reality it expresses, though it does not understand the creation to be *de novo* as much as it is an incarnation. Sacramental change, then, is not so much a matter of what happens to the material foci of the sacramental act, as it is especially a matter of what happens in the relations to and of all the people gathered into and around the act, and so also to the world brought with them. The language of relations softens categorical distinctions. Perhaps more than analogously, the terminology of phase transitions in scientific description suggests the same point. Indeed, such is the conclusion of much ecumenical conversation, which advances Christian theology well beyond the medieval doctrines of substances and accidents that dominated sacramentology until the mid-twentieth century.

Sacraments are not concerned only with human relations, however. Nor are they conceived to be mere bridges between the evidently natural and the divine. They are believed indeed to be those occasions most expressly where the divine and human intimately relate and wherein the distinction between divine and natural can be ambiguous. Sacraments express a primary conviction that nothing human or natural is alien to God. In no way, however, do sacraments allow simple identification of divinity with the natural, otherwise known as pantheism. They are, according to their traditions, promises of tangible times and places where the divine may be encountered and mediated. Thereby sacraments suggest how God intends divine and natural relation in the rest of the world.

Personal sacramental understanding is a matter of faith's being informed by experience, and perhaps theory, but finally resting in the mystery of God. Science may illuminate for religion something of sacramental meaning, and even suggest modes thereby of God's action in the world. But neither science nor religion could reasonably or dogmatically claim absolute comprehension of the topic of sacraments, related as they are to God, who is by definition ultimately transcendent as well as immanent. There also remains for the believer nurtured by sacraments the significant ethical charge to carry forward and enact the divine will in the natural world. This charge includes the creation and care of a materially and spiritually just and peaceful world. Sacraments, so it would appear with Christianity and analogous activities in most other religions, intend the re-constitution and nurturing of divine/human community.

See also SACRAMENTAL UNIVERSE

Bibliography

Gunton, Colin. "Relation and Relativity: The Trinity and the Created World." In *Trinitarian Theology Today, Essays on Divine Being and Act,* ed. Christoph Schwöbel. Edinburgh, UK: T&T Clark, 1995.

Jenson, Robert. "Sacraments." In *Christian Dogmatics,* vol. 2, Carl Braaten and Robert Jenson, eds. Philadelphia: Fortress Press, 1984.

Lindberg, David C., and Numbers, Ronald L, eds. *God and Nature: Historical Essays on the Encounter Between Christianity and Science.* Berkeley: University of California Press, 1986.

McMullen, Clarence O. *Rituals and Sacraments in Indian Religions.* Delhi: Indian Society for the Publication of Christian Knowledge, 1979.

DUANE H. LARSON

SAMSARA

See TRANSMIGRATION; LIBERATION

SCHRÖDINGER'S CAT

Schrödinger's Cat is a famous thought experiment conceived by Austrian physicist Erwin Schrödinger (1887–1961) in 1935 to highlight some of the paradoxes of the quantum picture of the subatomic world if applied to everyday experience. Schrödinger was motivated by a paper on the EPR paradox by Albert Einstein, Boris Podolsky, and Nathan Rosen that had appeared earlier that year. Schrödinger opposed the Copenhagen Interpretation of quantum mechanics developed by physicist Niels Bohr (1885–1951) and others, and Schrödinger regarded his thought experiment as a "ridiculous case" that challenged its rationality.

Quantum theory allows only probabilistic statements to be made about the expected outcome of a measurement or observation. We can predict only the probability of finding an electron in a particular state in the future even if we are in possession of all possible information about its present state. Schrödinger imagined observing a cat in a sealed room along with a Geiger counter sitting beside an occasional source of radioactivity. If the Geiger counter records one of these random radioactive decays then it triggers the release of poisonous gas, which kills the cat. If no radioactive decay occurs, the cat survives. The experiment ends after one hour, when we look in the room to see if the cat is dead or alive. According to the Copenhagen Interpretation of quantum mechanics, Schrödinger claims, before we look into the room the cat is described by a wave function that is some mixture of "dead cat" and "live cat." When and where does the half-dead-half-alive mixed cat state turn into the definite dead cat or live cat state that we discover on looking in the room? Who is the observer who produces the definite state? Is it the cat, the Geiger counter, or the person who looks in the room? How do we interpret the state of cat that is half-dead and half-alive before an observation takes place?

See also COPENHAGEN INTERPRETATION; EPR PARADOX; PARADOX; PHYSICS, QUANTUM

Bibliography

Herbert, Nick. *Quantum Reality Beyond the New Physics.* London: Rider, 1985.

Mermin, David. "Is the Moon There When Nobody Looks? Reality and the Quantum Theory." *Physics Today* 38, no. 4 (1985): 38–47.

JOHN D. BARROW

SCIENCE AND RELIGION

The immediate historical roots of the academic field of "science and religion" lie in the 1960s when major developments in the philosophy of science and the philosophy of religion, new theories and discoveries in the natural sciences, as well as complex shifts in the theological landscape, made possible constructive interaction between often separate or even hostile intellectual communities. Most of the discussion has focused on interaction among the sciences and the diversity of Christian theologies, but this is changing as more and more voices from other religions enter the conversation.

Methods for relating science and religion

Scholars first set out in the 1960s to develop more constructive ways of relating the two areas. Scientist-turned-theologian Ian Barbour provided the initial "bridge" between science and religion in his *Issues in Science and Religion* (1971), drawing on the work of Thomas Kuhn, Michael Polanyi, Stephen Toulmin, Mary Hesse, Frederick Ferré, Norwood Hanson, and others in both the philosophy of science and the philosophy of religion. Barbour's crucial insight was to recognize the similarity between the methodological, linguistic, and epistemological structures of science and theology:

Both make cognitive claims about the world expressed through metaphors and models, and both employ a hypothetico-deductive method within a revisionist, contextualist, and historicist framework. This approach, which Barbour called "critical realism," was later pursued in Europe by such scholars as Arthur Peacocke and John Polkinghorne. Theologian Wolfhart Pannenberg introduced to the discussion Karl Popper's understanding of theories as revisable hypotheses in his *Theology and the Philosophy of Science* (1976). Philosopher of religion Nancey Murphy developed a related approach in her *Theology in an Age of Scientific Reasoning* (1990), deploying Imre Lakatos's notion of a "scientific research program," which includes a central commitment or "hard core," a surrounding protective belt of auxiliary hypotheses, and criteria for choosing between competing programs. Additional important contributions came from scholars such as Philip Clayton, Niels Gregersen, Thomas Torrance, and Wentzel van Huyssteen.

The chief concern of these scholars was to create a framework for dialogue that allows for methodological reductionism (studying wholes in terms of their parts and applying successful strategies in one area to others) as a legitimate scheme for scientific research but respects the irreducibility of processes and properties referred to by theology and other higher-level disciplines to those of lower levels (epistemic antireductionism or holism). Some antirealists and postmodernists criticize this broad approach by pointing to difficulties that confront realist interpretations of scientific theories and theological concepts (e.g., quantum mechanics and the idea of "God") and by questioning the "metanarrative" role of science. On balance, though, this methodological bridge remains an enduringly important contribution to the field, both for its crucial historical role and as a point of departure for current research.

Key areas of engagement

In numerous and subtle ways, the contemporary sciences challenge and reshape the God-nature problematic for theological perspectives as diverse as panentheism, process theology, feminist theology, trinitarian theology, neo-Thomism, and evangelical theology. This section briefly reviews several key topics of discussion.

In physics, Albert Einstein's theory of special relativity challenges our ordinary sense of time's flow and the assumption of a universal present moment, problematizing the idea that God experiences and acts in the world in the flowing "now." Equally challenging is the relation between divine action and natural causality. Because Newtonian mechanism depicted nature as a closed causal system, special divine action was subsequently either understood in terms of interventionism or reduced to human subjectivity. Developments in the philosophical interpretation of quantum mechanics, chaos theory, and cosmology (and the neurosciences as well) may provide the basis for a new theory of noninterventionist, objective, special providence. With regard to cosmology, scholars such as Willem B. Drees, George Ellis, Ted Peters, Robert John Russell, William Stoeger, Mark Worthing, and Joseph Zycinski discuss the consonance and dissonance between the theological notion of the universe as "creation" and features of the standard Big Bang scenario including the apparent beginning of the universe ($t = 0$) and the curious fact that physical constants have precisely the values needed for life's emergence (the Anthropic Principle).

In response to biological evolution, theologians such as Barbour and Peacocke champion "theistic evolution," the view that what science describes in terms of evolutionary biology can be seen, from a religious perspective, as God's action in the world. However, billions of years of natural disaster, suffering, death, and extinction of species, not to mention the lack of overall directedness to evolutionary change, present this view with serious challenges. Barbour and Peacocke, along with Holmes Rolston and Thomas Tracy, provide careful assessments of suffering and evil in light of evolutionary theory, and Rolston offers a helpful analysis of the complex role of "values" in nature. Evolutionary and ecological thought also play an important role in Sallie McFague's model of the world as God's body and Rosemary Radford Ruether's discussion of Gaia and God.

How will genetics, sociobiology, the neurosciences, and the computer sciences affect the way we understand the human person? Can we relate knowledge gained from these disciplines to the biblical view of the person as a "psychosomatic unity"? Fruitful insights into these issues come from such scholars as Francisco Ayala, Lindon Eaves, Denis Edwards, Anne Foerst, Philip Hefner, Noreen Herzfeld, and Murphy. Ted Peters and Ronald Cole-Turner also draw together scientific and religious perspectives on important social issues such as genetic discrimination, gene patenting and cloning, stem cell research, genetic determinism and human freedom, and somatic versus germ-line intervention.

Several of the sciences challenge the theological notion of redemption, which in Christianity draws together the doctrines of incarnation, christology, resurrection, and eschatology. The vast size and complexity of the cosmos force us, whether scientists, persons of faith, or both at once, to look beyond our concern for humanity, or even the Earth, to the destiny of the universe as a whole. Can religious belief countenance the prediction that the universe's far future will be "freeze or fry," either endless universal expansion or violent recollapse? This scientific forecast presents one of the most serious challenges to any belief in human salvation, the meaning and future of life in the universe, or the eschatological consummation of the cosmos as new creation.

Methodological frontiers

Several important concerns are emerging at the frontier of the science and religion discussion. Science itself is increasingly recognized as a thoroughly human endeavor open to the critical insights of, for example, gender analysis. The work of Evelyn Fox Keller and Helen Longino on this topic provides a helpful starting point for gender analysis of the science and religion field itself. Additional voices from the world's religious and indigenous cultures need to be brought into the science and religion discussion to shed new light on the complex relations among science, religion, and culture in an interreligious context. Other important areas include the history of science and religion, the theological critique of scientism, the relation of science to nature and spirituality, the creative roles of philosophy and theology in scientific research, and the possibility of these diverse fields entering into a mutually constructive dialogue where each partner receives something of intellectual value from the other.

See also SCIENCE AND RELIGION, HISTORY OF FIELD; SCIENCE AND RELIGION IN PUBLIC COMMUNICATION; SCIENCE AND RELIGION, METHODOLOGIES; SCIENCE AND RELIGION, MODELS AND RELATIONS; SCIENCE AND RELIGION, PERIODICAL LITERATURE; SCIENCE AND RELIGION, RESEARCH IN

Bibliography

Ayala, Francisco, ed. *Studies in the Philosophy of Biology: Reduction and Related Problems*. Berkeley: University of California Press, 1974.

Barbour, Ian G. *Issues in Science and Religion* (1966). New York: Harper, 1971.

Barbour, Ian G. *Religion and Science: Historical and Contemporary Issues*. San Francisco: Harper, 1997.

Cajete, Gregory. *Native Science: Natural Laws of Independence*. Santa Fe, N.M.: Clear Light, 2000.

Clayton, Philip. *Explanation from Physics to Theology: An Essay in Rationality and Religion*. New Haven, Conn.: Yale University Press, 1989.

Cole-Turner, Ronald. *The New Genesis: Theology and the Genetic Revolution*. Louisville, Ky.: Westminster/John Knox Press, 1993.

Drees, Willem B. *Beyond the Big Bang: Quantum Cosmologies and God*. La Salle, Ill.: Open Court, 1990.

Eaves, Lindon J. *Genes, Culture, and Personality: An Empirical Approach*. San Diego, Calif.: Academic Press, 1989.

Edwards, Denis. *The God of Evolution: A Trinitarian Theology*. New York: Paulist Press, 1999.

Ellis, George F. R. *Before the Beginning: Cosmology Explained*. New York: Boyars and Bowerdean, 1993.

Foerst, Anne. "Cog, a Humanoid Robot, and the Question of the Image of God." *Zygon* 33 (1998): 91–111.

Gregersen, Niels H. "A Contextual Coherence Theory for the Science-Theology Dialogue." In *Rethinking Theology and Science: Six Models for the Current Dialogue,* ed. Niels H. Gregersen and J. Wentzel Van Huyssteen. Grand Rapids, Mich.: Eerdmans, 1998.

Hefner, Philip J. *The Human Factor: Evolution, Culture, and Religion*. Minneapolis, Minn.: Fortress Press, 1993.

Herzfeld, Noreen. *In Our Image: Artificial Intelligence and the Human Spirit*. Minneapolis, Minn.: Fortress Press, 2002.

Keller, Evelyn Fox, and Longino, Helen E., eds. *Feminism and Science*. Oxford: Oxford University Press, 1996.

McFague, Sallie. *The Body of God: An Ecological Theology*. Minneapolis, Minn.: Fortress Press, 1993.

Murphy, Nancey C. *Theology in the Age of Scientific Reasoning*. Ithaca, N.Y.: Cornell University Press, 1990.

Murphy, Nancey C., and Ellis, George F. R. *On the Moral Nature of the Universe: Theology, Cosmology, and Ethics*. Minneapolis, Minn.: Fortress Press, 1996.

Pannenberg, Wolfhart. *Theology and the Philosophy of Science,* trans. Francis McDonagh. Philadelphia, Pa.: Westminster Press, 1976.

Peacocke, Arthur. *Theology for a Scientific Age: Being and Becoming—Natural, Divine and Human,* enlarged edition. Minneapolis, Minn.: Fortress Press, 1993.

Peters, Ted, ed. *Cosmos as Creation: Theology and Science in Consonance*. Nashville, Tenn.: Abingdon Press, 1989.

Peters, Ted. *Playing God?: Genetic Determinism and Human Freedom*. New York: Routledge, 1996.

Polkinghorne, John C. *Faith, Science, and Understanding*. New Haven, Conn.: Yale University Press, 2000.

Rolston, Holmes, III. *Genes, Genesis and God: Values and Their Origins in Natural and Human History*. Cambridge, UK: Cambridge University Press, 1999.

Ruether, Rosemary Radford. *Gaia and God: An Ecofeminist Theology of Earth Healing*. San Francisco: Harper, 1992.

Stoeger, William. "Contemporary Physics and the Ontological Status of the Laws of Nature." In *Quantum Cosmology and the Laws of Nature: Scientific Perspectives on Divine Action,* ed. Robert J. Russell, Nancey C. Murphy, and Chris J. Isham, 2nd edition. Vatican City: Vatican Observatory; Berkeley, Calif.: Center for Theology and the Natural Sciences, 1996.

Torrance, Thomas. *Theological Science*. Oxford: Oxford University Press, 1969.

Tracy, Thomas F., ed. *The God Who Acts: Philosophical and Theological Explorations*. University Park: Pennsylvania State University Press, 1994.

van Huyssteen, J. Wentzel. *Theology and the Justification of Faith: Constructing Theories in Systematic Theology*. Grand Rapids, Mich.: Eerdmans, 1989.

Worthing, Mark W. *God, Creation, and Contemporary Physics*. Minneapolis, Minn.: Fortress Press, 1996.

Zycinski, Joseph M. "Metaphysics and Epistemology in Stephen Hawking's Theory of the Creation of the Universe." *Zygon* 31, no. 2 (1996): 269–284.

ROBERT JOHN RUSSELL
KIRK WEGTER-MCNELLY

SCIENCE AND RELIGION, HISTORY OF FIELD

Among many celebrations coinciding with a new millennium was one that had much to do with the subject of science and religion. According to a report by Thomas J. Oord in the January 2002 issue of *Research News and Opportunities in Science and Theology,* at the November 2001 meeting of the

American Academy of Religion (AAR) in Denver, Colorado, "hundreds gathered in the Grand Ballroom to . . . celebrate the remarkable advance of this interdisciplinary field" (p.34). From an earlier obscurity within the AAR, science and religion was now attracting a large audience, boasting a burgeoning literature, and, in some quarters, even claiming to be a new discipline. In the closing years of the twentieth century, a heightened awareness of ethical issues raised by biotechnology, exciting advances in the neurosciences, a greater sensitivity to environmental concerns, and a reconsideration of relations between physical and spiritual health were creating new spaces for dialogue within and between scientific and faith communities. With strong support from philanthropic organizations, particularly the John Templeton Foundation, new research and teaching initiatives were launched, designed to explore the many contexts in which scientific and religious interests might intersect.

Claims for a new field can easily be exaggerated. As James Gilbert observed in *Redeeming Culture* (1997), during the last century a science-religion dichotomy was often used by individuals and organizations in the United States to construct distinctive identities. Without an understanding of the many meanings with which the words *science* and *religion* have been invested, attempts to establish definitive relations between them can easily be naïve. Conversely, definitions proposed for both *science* and *religion* sometimes reflect decisions already taken on the relations between them and how they are to be presented for polemical purposes. Many of the issues currently discussed under the banner of "science and religion" have been recognized from antiquity and have repeatedly been subject to searching analysis. It has even been suggested that the periods during which it has been unfashionable to discuss the mutual bearings of scientific and religious beliefs have been the exception, not the rule. When Alfred North Whitehead (1861–1947) wrote his *Science and the Modern World* (1925), he considered it a matter of urgency that the relations between scientific and religious views of the world should be clarified. And it was already possible for him to argue that, far from a perennial hostility, modern science had been a derivative of medieval theology, and one that could help to purge traditional religions of their superstitious elements. Much earlier still, again with an eye to history, Isaac Newton

(1642–1727) had suggested that the sciences had only prospered in monotheistic cultures.

From antiquity to the Middle Ages

Among recurrent issues discussed in antiquity were the nature of causality, the role of a deity or deities in the making of the world, the ultimate nature of matter, the nature of body and soul, and the place of humans in the cosmos. In the works of the Greek atomists, and later Lucretius during the first century B.C.E., a case was made for a naturalistic philosophy in which worlds came into being and passed out of existence as a result of the chance collision of atoms. There might be life on other worlds, and nature could run by itself without the aid of gods. Other ancient thinkers, such as the second-century physician Galen, were more responsive to the appearance of design, especially in anatomical structures. An Epicurean rejoinder was, however, always possible—that the appearance of design was illusory, simply reflecting the fact that nature had experimented with every possible combination of organs and limbs, the nonviable combinations having long since perished.

The relationship between sacred and secular knowledge and the degree to which the physical world could be considered autonomous were issues faced by the early Church fathers, among whom a diversity of views existed. Augustine of Hippo (354–430) addressed the question of whether the exegesis of Scripture should reflect current secular knowledge, observing that too tight a dependency could prove embarrassing when the state of knowledge changed. In both Christian and Islamic cultures the problem of assimilation was thrown into relief by divergent reactions to Aristotle's conception of a world that had existed from eternity. Thomas Aquinas (c. 1225–1274) was to take the sophisticated view that the Christian doctrine of creation, affirming the continual dependence of all that exists on a transcendent being, was compatible with either the eternalist position or with the conception of a definite beginning. Reason alone could not decide the issue. Aquinas also illustrates the practice, many times repeated, of appropriating and modifying certain aspects of the latest science for theological purposes. Aristotle's emphasis on the primacy of final causes (of "goals" inherent in nature) in governing physical processes was attractive because one could ask deeper questions about the coordination of physical processes which, in remarkable combination, constituted a viable world. For Aquinas the natural philosophy of Aristotle was incomplete without the postulation of the "Being" ultimately responsible for the coordination.

Seventeenth- and eighteenth-century discussions

Even such fragmentary examples from the past confirm that what are perceived today as major issues in the field of science and religion have a long history. In seventeenth-century Europe, as today, scientific innovations prompted new forms of theological reflection. Robert Boyle (1627–1691), for example, found evidence of divine craftsmanship in the exquisite structures of minuscule creatures revealed by the microscope. In response to the overly mechanized universe of René Descartes (1596–1650), Newton saw in the gravitational force a source of activity in the natural world that could not be explained by reference to innate properties of matter. In a celebrated controversy that took place in the second decade of the eighteenth century, Newton's defender Samuel Clarke (1675–1729) and the German philosopher Gottfried Wilhelm Leibniz (1646–1716) debated the fundamental question of how a divine being might act in the world. If, as Clarke argued, the laws of nature simply defined the way God *normally* chooses to act, there was nothing in the laws themselves to prevent other divine initiatives. Using an analogy that still has currency, Newton argued that it was easier for God to move and control the matter in the world than it is for people to move and control their limbs. Leibniz, by contrast, insisted that the best of all possible worlds, the world made by God, had to be one that needed no maintenance, and emphatically not the "reformations" of the solar system that Newton required for its continuing stability.

Some three hundred years later, comparable metaphysical positions are being staked out in debates over the sufficiency of evolutionary theory to explain the appearance of design in organic systems. Those who argue for a divinely bestowed functional integrity in nature often resemble Leibniz, while advocates of more interventionist models of divine creativity bear some resemblance to Newton. In the original Newtonian debates, positions of subtlety and sophistication were achieved, Newton arguing that the deity would use

secondary causes as instruments of the divine "Will" where they were available. Then, as now, such debates were often infused with political significance, Leibniz seeking to score points against Newton when they were at loggerheads over priority for the calculus and when, with the prospect of the Hanoverian succession to the English throne, Leibniz saw opportunities for advancement in the country of his foe.

From the seventeenth century onwards a discourse involving theological elements has featured in the promotion of the applied sciences and technology. Francis Bacon (1561–1626) argued that empirically based knowledge when applied for altruistic purposes must have a religious sanction and could even restore human dominion over nature which had been lost at the Fall. In one of the manuscripts (Add. 4003) of the Portsmouth collection held in Cambridge University Library, Newton argued that it was not sacrilegious for a chemical initiate to imitate the creative work of the deity because a creator who could produce a cocreator displayed the greater power:

> If any think it possible that God may produce some intellectual creature so perfect that he could, by divine accord, in turn produce creatures of a lower order, this so far from detracting from the divine power enhances it; for that power which can bring forth creatures not only directly but through the mediation of other creatures is exceedingly, not to say infinitely greater.

There is a metaphysical position here, reinforceable through the religious claim that humans are to be collaborators with the deity, which finds expression in current debates in biotechnology. There have long been theological resources for both countenancing and criticizing attempts to improve upon nature. Particularly in dissenting religious traditions, concepts of improvement and concepts of providence have been indissolubly linked, as they were for the eighteenth-century minister and chemist Joseph Priestley. Science was prized by Priestley because, together with a rational religion, it helped to eliminate superstition, to promote human welfare and to explode the "arbitrary power" of an established Church. In his *Disquisitions Relating to Matter and Spirit* (1777), Priestley also reconsidered the relationship between body and mind, preferring a monistic view to the matter/spirit dualism prevalent in Christian tradition.

Such examples indicate that the intellectual preconditions of the "field" of study that is called "science and religion" have long existed and that core issues have been repeatedly discussed as constituents of other fields: philosophy, natural philosophy, and metaphysics. Newton could say that it was part of the business of natural philosophy to discuss the question of God's attributes and relation to the world. But precisely because elements of theology might still be incorporated within natural philosophy, precisely because in the Anglophone world the word *science* did not take on its modern specialized meaning until the nineteenth century, it would be anachronistic to ask how a field of "science and religion" might have been constituted in earlier periods.

In specific European contexts there were also political pressures that could undo attempts at what today might be described as dialogue. In eighteenth-century France, Voltaire popularized Newton's natural philosophy as part of his attack on the power of the Catholic Church, whose intolerance toward other religious persuasions he deplored. In eighteenth-century Germany, Immanuel Kant exposed the logical weakness of attempts to argue for a deity on the basis of what was known of nature. The practice of natural science had to proceed on the supposition that nature behaved *as if* it were orderly and designed, but the "as if" introduced an element of agnosticism. In eighteenth-century Edinburgh, David Hume did construct a dialogue—his scintillating *Dialogues Concerning Natural Religion* (1779). These were designed, however, to expose the fragility of the analogies on which the design argument rested. Even if the natural world did resemble a human artifact, such as a clock or a ship, it did not follow that it was made by only one artificer, and certainly not one whose attributes necessarily coincided with those assumed in the main religions. Behind Hume's critique was an ethic of civic virtue, a commitment to the material improvement of his society and at odds with what he despised as the "whole train of monkish virtues."

Nineteenth- and twentieth-century research

During the nineteenth and twentieth centuries there were innumerable critiques of religious discourse, contributing to forms of skepticism that would militate against sympathetic attempts at dialogue. In the positivism of Auguste Comte (1798–1857), human culture, through the facts and laws established by the sciences, was emancipating itself from the theological and metaphysical stages of its development. In England the scientific naturalism of Thomas Henry Huxley (1825–1895) was an ideological as well as a methodological tool in the promulgation of professional standards that would exclude the clerical amateur. Battling to gain greater cultural authority for the sciences, Huxley found in Darwinian evolution welcome support for the continuity and sufficiency of natural causes in accounting for human origins. In the early twentieth century the austere logical positivism of the Vienna Circle precluded meaningful dialogue between science and religion because only scientific propositions had the essential virtue of verifiability. Pretensions to reinterpret religious beliefs in the light of modern science have not surprisingly encountered resistance from theologians themselves, especially those who have shared Karl Barth's (1886–1968) perception that natural theologies (with their tendency to naturalize prevailing but sometimes insidious social and political orders) embody the presumption of human reason rather than the gift of grace in calls to a spiritual life.

Such deterrents have left their mark, but so too have the pressures that have encouraged assertions of complementarity and efforts at integration. Of these pressures two have been paramount: the desire of scientists with religious convictions to harmonize their loyalties; and the desire of religious institutions to deflect anticlerical hostility. Galileo Galilei (1564–1642) provides an excellent example of the former, since he wished to show that a loyal Catholic could be at the frontier of physical science. The Vatican itself, so often vilified for having condemned him, provides an example of the latter in its reestablishment of an observatory to demonstrate that it was not opposed to the exploration of God's creation. In his announcement in 1891, Pope Leo XIII said that the plan was that everyone might see that the Church and its pastors were not opposed to true and solid science but that they embraced it, encouraged it, and promoted it with the fullest possible dedication. An opportunity to do so arose when the Vatican Observatory contributed to a major international collaboration, involving a total of eighteen observatories, in which the entire sky was to be mapped and photographed.

Other pressures, too, have sustained a discourse of science and religion. For much of the nineteenth century new scientific theories were examined for their religious implications and often viewed with suspicion if they appeared subversive. Theories of evolution would be a prime example, Darwin smarting from the fact that his contribution was often judged more by its supposed religious ramifications than for its scientific merits. The popularization of science was a task in which it was always tempting to invoke a supposed relevance to religion as a way of winning attention, a practice still visible today as science writers reserve a place for God in their titles if not in their universe. It has been observed of the mid-Victorian period that many members of the public were more interested in science versus religion than in science. In some parts of the world this may still be true, with the caveat, now as then, that much of the conflict has been between competing methods of harmonization.

Until the third quarter of the nineteenth century there would have been little evidence from the titles of books that a separate *field* of study bearing the description "science and religion" might be constituted. Polemical works could, however, set an agenda and two were to prove extremely influential: John Draper's *History of the Conflict between Religion and Science* (1875) and Andrew White's *A History of the Warfare of Science with Theology in Christendom* (1895). Strong personal motives were at work in each. Draper's *History* was a Protestant tirade against the Catholic Church, energized by his reaction to the encyclical *Quanta cura* (1864) and to the assertion of papal infallibility (1870), which he saw as epitomizing illegitimate constraint on the freedom of scientific enquiry. White's *History* reflected animosity toward the dogmatism he had encountered when, as a consequence of advocating a nonsectarian charter for Cornell University in Ithaca, New York, of which he was the first President, he had incited stormy reactions from clerics wishing to preserve their hold over education. Because of the historical orientation of these works, and their more tendentious claims, an important precursor of the modern field took shape in a body of historical literature of increasing sophistication in which the inadequacies of the conflict metaphor were exposed. For example, James Simpson's *Landmarks in the Struggle between Science and Religion* (1925) was

deeply critical of Draper and White for their unsympathetic treatment of the early Church Fathers, notably Augustine, a historiographical correction that continues today. Revisionist literature has recognized a tension among the Church fathers between approving the study of nature and warning that it must not displace the higher priorities of the spiritual life. Classic texts in the history of science, such as E. A Burtt's *The Metaphysical Foundations of Modern Physical Science* (1949), E. J. Dijksterhuis's *The Mechanization of the World Picture* (1961), Robert Merton's *Science, Technology, and Society in Seventeenth-Century England* (1938 and 1970), Charles Webster's *The Great Instauration* (1975), and many more, identified respects in which religious values and beliefs had provided stimulus and not merely obstruction to scientific activity. Historians of science with Catholic, Protestant, and Marxist sensibilities, such as Stanley Jaki, Reijer Hooykaas, and Joseph Needham, respectively, helped to create a literature in which religious variables were germane to any discussion as to why the scientific movements of the sixteenth and seventeenth centuries had proved more enduring in Europe than elsewhere.

In 1962 the work of another historian of science, Thomas Kuhn's *The Structure of Scientific Revolutions,* with its telling critique of linear models of scientific progress, contributed to an emerging disenchantment with positivist accounts of scientific rationality. By focusing on the shared beliefs of scientific communities and the clash of incommensurable paradigms at times of revolution, Kuhn among others emphasized a social dimension to scientific practice that was subsequently explored in depth. As historians and sociologists became increasingly sensitive to the ways in which social, economic, and political forces had shaped the sciences in local contexts, so the relevance of religious variables had also to be taken seriously.

A field of study is one that can be mapped, and during the 1960s such a map appeared in the shape of Ian Barbour's *Issues in Science and Religion* (1966). Significantly, this work also began with a historical overview, but took within its purview the methods of science; the question of objectivity and personal involvement in both the natural and social sciences; the methods of religion; the languages of science and religion; the implications of the indeterminacy arising from quantum physics; the physical basis of life; and the many issues that could be subsumed under "Evolution and Creation." The existence of such a comprehensive text helped to make possible the teaching of courses on science and religion in the late 1960s. Such courses were increasingly visible during the 1970s in both Great Britain and North America. In Britain, for example, several thousand Open University students took a course entitled "Science and Belief from Copernicus to Darwin" that was launched in 1974, and later "Science and Belief from Darwin to Einstein." As a consequence, good quality teaching materials, complemented by radio and television programs, were produced that allowed students to assess their own understanding and progress.

References to teaching remind us that the cultivation of a field assumes not only a map but also an institutional base. In the United States, associations dedicated explicitly to "science and religion" began to appear in the middle years of the twentieth century. They multiplied as a need was felt to address the adversarial positions that manifested themselves in public on such matters as the status of scientific expertise, the moral implications of nuclear weapons, the wisdom of genetic engineering, and the seriousness of environmental degeneration. An early association was the Institute on Religion in an Age of Science (IRAS) founded in 1954 by Ralph Burhoe and Harlow Shapley. Enjoying support from Unitarian constituencies, it sought a new religiousness derivable from science. For Burhoe this required a detailed evolutionary cosmology with science as its base. For Shapley too it meant the proclamation of scientific primacy in religious contexts, which could however attract pessimistic responses even from sympathetic scientists. The neurophysiologist R. W. Gerard could not think that the great bulk of people would accept the austerity of a rational religion any more than they accepted the austerity of science. His question would still be salient in many contexts: How can publicly misunderstood science and publicly dogmatic religion ever illuminate each other? In 1966, Burhoe, with Shapley's aid, established the journal *Zygon,* diverse in the essays it has published, but retaining a vision of unity between science and religion, achievable through the scientizing of theology. Twenty-five years earlier, another enduring organization, with quite different objectives, had taken shape—the American Scientific Affiliation (ASA). Having evangelical roots, the ASA wished to promote a unity between the sciences and the fundaments of a biblical theology. One of its immediate postwar tasks was to produce a science handbook for college students, reflecting the concern of its leaders that the nation's universities had ceased to be Christian.

Most of the earliest organizations dedicated to an underlying unity of science and religion had their distinctive religious agendas, which could make cooperation difficult. An attempt in 1958 to establish a formal link between the ASA and the Society for the Scientific Study of Religion (SSSR), which had been founded in 1949 to explore the relations between religion and the social sciences, ended in failure. The very meaning of the word *religion* was often a bone of contention. In Europe as well as North America, societies for the study of science and religion increased in number during the latter part of the twentieth century. A moving spirit in England was Arthur Peacocke who founded a Science and Religion Forum and a Society of Ordained Scientists. Out of the Research Scientists Christian Fellowship, a branch of the evangelical Inter-Varsity Fellowship, a Christians in Science association was formed, publishing the journal *Science and Christian Belief.* A step toward a more international association was taken with the inauguration in 1986 of the European Society for the Study of Science and Theology (ESSSAT), which continues to hold biennial conferences and to award prizes for promising work by young scholars.

The expansion of a field, especially one seeking greater academic recognition, can be difficult when academic and apologetic goals are not clearly distinguished. Even if the majority of scientists do not share the strident antireligious rhetoric of well-known science writers, it has long been part of scientific culture that scientific academies are not the place for religious debate. The common conviction that a person's religion is a private matter adds to the reticence and the resistance. Issues discussed at conferences on science and religion can sometimes seem naïve to historians and philosophers who may observe the reinvention of wheels that turn on axioms long since discredited. A constraint of a different kind concerns the dearth of career opportunities, particularly within academe, for those whose research has been in such an interdisciplinary and multidisciplinary arena.

At the beginning of the twenty-first century, it is, however, possible to discern signs and advances that may presage a shift into a less transitional state. Those scientific societies concerned with the public image of science, such as the British and American Associations for the Advancement of Science, have opened their doors wider for sessions on science and religion. The European Science Foundation has sponsored workshops on the theme of science and human values. During the 1990s, there was a quantum leap in the number of courses on science and religion taught in universities and colleges of higher education. This was in large measure due to incentives provided by the John Templeton Foundation, which defines its mission as the pursuit of "new insights at the boundary between theology and science through a rigorous, open-minded and empirically focused methodology," privileging the "methods and resources of scientific inquiry having spiritual and theological significance." Independently of such support, academic posts were created during the 1990s at Britain's oldest universities with science and religion as their specified field—the Starbridge Lectureship in Cambridge and the Andreas Idreos Chair in Oxford. Though few in number, chairs in science and religion have also been established elsewhere. The first of these, the James I. McCord Chair in Theology and Science, was established at the Princeton Theological Seminary in New Jersey. Other American centers have been particularly active in cultivating the field, especially the Center for Theology and Natural Sciences (founded by Robert J. Russell in 1981) in Berkeley, California, and the Chicago Center for Science and Religion (founded in 1988). New encyclopedic works of reference have begun to appear (of which this is an example), including *The History of Science and Religion in the Western Tradition* (2000) published by Garland. The year 2002 saw in Granada, Spain, the first meeting of a new *International Society for Science and Religion,* part of whose mission was to embrace and encourage the discussion of science and religion in religious traditions other than Christianity. In a world where partisan and warring identities are still so strongly reinforced by religious beliefs, few would deny that such interfaith dialogue has become as great a priority as a disembodied dialogue between science and religion.

See also BUDDHISM, HISTORY OF SCIENCE AND RELIGION; CHINESE RELIGIONS, HISTORY OF SCIENCE AND RELIGION IN CHINA; CHRISTIANITY, HISTORY OF SCIENCE AND RELIGION; HINDUISM, HISTORY OF SCIENCE AND RELIGION; ISLAM, HISTORY OF SCIENCE AND RELIGION; JUDAISM, HISTORY OF SCIENCE AND RELIGION, MEDIEVAL PERIOD; JUDAISM, HISTORY OF SCIENCE AND RELIGION, MODERN PERIOD

Bibliography

Barbour, Ian G. *Issues in Science and Religion.* London: SCM Press, 1996.

Bowler, Peter J. *Reconciling Science and Religion.* Chicago: University of Chicago Press, 2001.

Brooke, John H. *Science and Religion: Some Historical Perspectives.* Cambridge, UK: Cambridge University Press. 1991.

Brooke, John H., and Cantor, Geoffrey. *Reconstructing Nature: The Engagement of Science and Religion.* Edinburgh, UK: T&T Clark; New York: Oxford University Press, 1998.

Brooke, John H.; Osler, Margaret J; and Van Der Meer, Jitse, eds. *Osiris,* Vol. 16: *Science in Theistic Contexts: Cognitive Dimensions.* Chicago: University of Chicago Press, 2001.

Ferngren, Gary, ed. *The History of Science and Religion in the Western Tradition.* New York: Garland, 2000.

Gilbert, James. *Redeeming Culture: American Religion in an Age of Science.* Chicago: University of Chicago Press, 1997.

Kuhn, Thomas S. *The Structure of Scientific Revolutions.* Chicago: University of Chicago Press, 1962.

Lindberg, David C., and Numbers, Ronald L., eds. *God and Nature: Historical Essays on the Encounter between Christianity and Science.* Berkeley and Los Angeles: University of California Press, 1986.

Merton, Robert K. *Science, Technology, and Society in Seventeenth-Century England* (1938). New York: H. Fertig, 1970.

Moore, James R. "Speaking of 'Science and Religion:' Then and Now." *History of Science* 30 (1992): 311–323.

Nesteruk, Alexei V. "Patristic Theology and the Natural Sciences," Parts 1 and 2. *Sourozh: A Journal of Orthodox Life and Thought* 84 (2001): 14–35; 85 (2001): 22–38.

Numbers, Ronald L. *The Creationists: The Evolution of Scientific Creationism.* New York: Knopf, 1992.

Oord, Thomas J. "From Obscurity to the Grand Ballroom." *Research News and Opportunities in Science and Technology* 2, no. 5 (2002): 34–35.

Russell, Colin A.; Hooykaas Reijer; and Goodman, David. *The Conflict Thesis and Cosmology*. Milton Keynes, UK: Open University Press, 1974.

Sardar, Ziauddin, ed. *The Touch of Midas: Science, Values, and Environment in Islam and the West*. Manchester, UK: Manchester University Press, 1984.

Wertheim, Margaret. "The John Templeton Foundation Model Courses in Science and Religion." *Zygon* 30 (1995): 491–500.

JOHN HEDLEY BROOKE

SCIENCE AND RELIGION IN PUBLIC COMMUNICATION

After World War II, the United States faced a considerable challenge: How would communications continue in the aftermath of a nuclear war? The solution proposed was a network of computers that had no central authority and were capable of almost infinite message rerouting. This system, known as ARPANET (Advanced Research Projects Agency Network), debuted in 1969. Telenet, the first commercial version of the ARPANET, appeared in 1974. In 1979 the first network-wide discussions groups were up and running as USENET. But before cyberspace could become readily navigable, hypertext, the World Wide Web, and search engines had to be developed. The first point-and-click way of navigating Internet files, known as *gopher,* was released in 1991, and the same year the first computer code of the World Wide Web debuted in the relatively innocuous newsgroup alt.hypertext. Thus, the rich global communications medium called the Internet was born.

By the mid-1990s several science and religion organizations had a basic presence on the World Wide Web. Typically this consisted of information about the organization and its upcoming events and programs. One of the first sites of this kind was a web site for the Institute on Religion in an Age of Science (www.iras.org). Online discussion on science and religion topics was initially confined to private email distribution lists and various USENET newsgroups such as *The Talk.Origins Archive* (www.talkorigins.org), which covers the creation/evolution controversy.

The need to handle an ever increasing number of discussion participants led to the employment of listservs (managed email discussion lists), such as the *Meta-lists,* now *Metanexus,* which began operating in 1997. An "edited, moderated, and public listserv dedicated to promoting the constructive engagement of science and religion and to sharing information and perspectives among the diverse organizations and individuals involved in this interdisciplinary field," by 2002, *Metanexus* had over six thousand subscribers in approximately sixty countries.

By their second generation, many web sites had incorporated some basic science and religion content in addition to the organizational information. Initially the content was preexisting text made available in plain electronic form, but there has been a constant evolution in the sophistication with which the web has been used to present science and religion content.

In 1998, the Counterbalance Foundation based in Seattle, Washington, in conjunction with the Center for Theology and the Natural Sciences (CTNS) in Berkeley, California, developed a suite of interactive topics specifically for the web. Initially available at the web site for the PBS/New River Media documentary television program *Faith and Reason,* (www.pbs.org/faithandreason) the content was also accessible from www.ctns.org and www.counterbalance.org. This suite was tailored to the web in three ways: It included extensive use of hypertext linking, a writing style that allowed the reader to visit topics in any particular order, and use of streaming audio. These features allowed readers from diverse backgrounds to approach the same content and follow different paths through it. The availability of streaming audio opened up the appeal of science and religion topics to a still broader audience.

In 2000, Counterbalance combined the CTNS content with new material, including the textbook *God, Humanity, and the Cosmos* (1999) edited by Christopher Southgate, to create the *Meta-Library.* The *Meta-Library* is a single shared location that provides content to several science and religion sites, most notably www.metanexus.net. As of 2002, the *Meta-Library* had over one hundred hours of interactive video material and thirty thousand links in the text material.

By mid-2002, the web was home to a variety of sites on science and religion that were diverse both in terms of approach and services offered; the Yahoo! directory contained links to dozens of web sites on evolution and creation alone. Some science and religion sites were still primarily informational, such as those of the American Scientific Affiliation (www.asa3.org), the American Association for the Advancement of Science site for DoSER (Dialogue on Science, Ethics, and Religion; www.aaas.org/spp/dser), and the National Academy of Science's site on science and creationism (www7.nationalacademies.org/evolution). Others web sites offered both information and discussion. Exemplars are the *Access Research Network* (www.arn.org), which discusses Intelligent Design theory, and *Metanexus*. Furthermore, such undertakings as *Project Gutenberg* (www.gutenberg.net) and the *Internet Public Library* (www.ipl.org) guaranteed that the classic texts of luminaries such as Charles Darwin, Thomas Henry Huxley, and Alfred Russel Wallace were available to the global public. In summary, persons all over the planet had access a vast repertoire of information on science and religion.

The future holds several possibilities. The web will continue to be an effective medium through which science and religion organizations can reach out to both the academic and broader community. Increase in fast "broadband" access to the web will allow sites to become progressively richer and more interactive, and will provide more video, including interviews and conference presentations (available both live and archived for later access), real-time chat rooms, tutorials, and so on. The content will no doubt broaden in scope, reaching beyond the core sciences and core religions, and become available in languages other than English. The conversation will also become more "world-wide" as the cost of computer equipment and web access allows smaller institutions and local societies to make use of the medium. In addition, an increasing number of distance education courses in science and religion will likely become available. However, the so-called digital divide must also be considered. While the dialogue between science and religion is certain to have a bright future on the Internet, participation in this part of the conversation will remain restricted to that small fraction of the global community with access to the necessary technology. This is likely to remain a real issue into the far future.

See also INFORMATION TECHNOLOGY; SCIENCE AND RELIGION, PERIODICAL LITERATURE

Bibliography

L-Soft (Listserv software). Available from http://www.lsoft.com.

PBS. "Life on the Internet: Net Timeline." Available from http://www.pbs.org/internet/timeline/#62.

Sterling, Bruce. "Short History of the Internet." Available from http://www.forthnet.gr/forthnet/isoc/short.history.of.internet.

VRX. "Some History [of USENET]." Available from http://www.vrx.net/usenet/history.

STACEY AKE
ADRIAN M. WYARD

SCIENCE AND RELIGION, METHODOLOGIES

A primary concern of contemporary scholarship on science and religion is the question of precisely how the two areas should be related. Historically, there has been a wide range of such theories. While the situation is in many ways similar today, the growth of a specific field of religion and science has provided some increased sophistication. Modern methodologies of science and religion generally seek to do two things. First, any methodology of science and religion almost inevitably has to give an account of the nature of both science and religion. That is, it must give an account of the realities that science and religion each describe, as well as how knowledge in each field is acquired. Second, any methodology must then account for how the truths in the respective fields can be related to one another. Most current methodologies of science and religion attempt both these tasks to varying degrees. In much of the current literature on science and religion methodology, the sciences in question are usually the physical and biological sciences, while the aspects of religion of most concern are the theological and metaphysical claims that undergird religious life and practice.

Independence models

For much of the twentieth century, many (if not most) philosophers and theologians conceived of religion and science as two completely separate disciplines that were each legitimate in their own right but which explained or described completely different realms of experience. Of these, the earliest was the theological movement of neo-orthodoxy, championed in particular by Swiss theologian Karl Barth (1886–1968), but widely represented in both Europe and the United States. Neo-orthodox theologians emphasized revelation as the primary means of knowing God, and they emphasized the separateness of this revelation from all other spheres of knowledge. This emphasis on the uniqueness of theology with respect to the sciences tended to also be supported by existentialist theologians such as Paul Tillich (1886–1965) and Rudolf Bultmann (1813–1855).

Independence models of religion and science received a further boost from the mid twentieth-century development of linguistic philosophy, deriving primarily from the later works of Ludwig Wittgenstein (1889–1951), who argued that human discourse and knowledge could best be understood as separate and incommensurable language games that each possess a unique vocabulary and logic. In some versions of this, science could be said to be about facts, religion about values. Both areas of practice and experience are equally legitimate, but cover completely separate spheres of life. In some later writings, this mode of independence received metaphorical support from the idea of complementarity derived from the Copenhagen interpretation of quantum physics championed by Niels Bohr (1885–1962). Just as modern physics was forced to alternatively describe subatomic particles as either waves or particles, but not both simultaneously, so too could religion and science be understood as giving complementary but distinct accounts of reality. Once again, both religion and science are legitimate areas of inquiry and practice, but are pursued and understood separately.

Forms of these independence models remain championed today. Neo-orthodoxy's emphasis on the separate character of religion strongly influenced British theologian Thomas Torrance and, more recently, Alistair McGrath. Paleontologist and science writer Stephen Jay Gould (1941–2002) also attempted to revive the linguistic philosophy version of independence. Despite this, these are now minority views for a number of reasons. Independence views presume that a clear distinction can be made between the provinces of science and religion, with an implication either that religion does not rely on facts about the world or that the facts of religion and the facts of science are completely different. Historically, however, this has not been the case, and most modern theologians believe that there are at least important border areas where science and religion overlap. Moreover, the more general theological and philosophical frameworks (particularly neo-orthodoxy and linguistic philosophy) are no longer seen to be nearly as persuasive as they once were, with the result that their more specific claims about the relationship of science and religion are found wanting.

Critical realism as a default view

Among current views of the relationship of religion and science, the most prominent has been that of critical realism. This prominence is due in no small part to its advocacy by three of the most important contributors to the field of science and religion: Ian Barbour, Arthur Peacocke, and John Polkinghorne, all three originally practicing scientists who later wrote on issues of religion and science. On the critical realist view, both religion and science describe the world as it is, and so there is some correspondence between the statements of religion and science and the real world that such statements describe. Critical realism differs from a naïve realism, however, in its recognition of the role of the possibility of error, bias, and partiality in all descriptions.

The most elaborate defense of critical realism within the field of science and religion has been given by Ian Barbour. Drawing on the philosophy of science of Thomas Kuhn (1922–1996) and others, Barbour argues that both science and religion have elements of subjectivity in their models of the world. While theories are based on evidence, they consistently overdetermine it. Consequently, theory choice is never simply a matter of verification or falsification, but includes criteria of coherence, scope, and even beauty. The way that a theory speaks of the world may thus be rather indirect, depending on data but not determined by it.

For critical realists, science and religion both provide partial views of the world that may overlap on a range of issues. Arthur Peacocke has argued that theology can be placed along a hierarchy of knowledge, with physics providing the most basic facts at the lowest level and theology providing the most general at the highest level. Because there can be significant overlap between science and religion on particular issues such as cosmic origins and human nature, critical realism is committed to providing theological perspectives that are capable of harmonizing with modern science.

While critical realism has been highly influential within the field of science and religion, it has also been the subject of significant criticism. The issue of how exactly scientific and especially religious models can be said to correspond to reality has been especially problematic. The more one acknowledges the critical element in any theory or model, the less realist it seems to be, a problem that is well recognized more broadly in the philosophy of science. Despite much early work in promoting critical realism, its advocates have yet to provide a sophisticated response to its critics, and for this reason its appeal has languished some since the 1990s.

Alternative methodologies from the philosophy of science

Despite the perceived shortcomings of the critical realist movement, it has been highly influential in its view that science and religion (and, more specifically, theology) can be said to employ similar methods of exploring reality, thus providing a basis for dialogue and engagement between the two areas of experience. Reasons for this view stem not only from critical realism, but also from more general developments in the philosophy of science, from which critical realism also drew. Consequently, there has been widespread support for employment of insights from the philosophy of science for explaining the nature and relationship of religion and science, even though significant disagreement remains as to whose philosophy of science should be employed and to what extent. While critical realists such as Ian Barbour were influenced by the work of Thomas Kuhn, German theologian Wolfhart Pannenberg utilized the earlier philosophy of science of Karl Popper (1902–1994), arguing that theological claims should be capable of being falsifiable, just as Popper argued that scientific claims should be. A number of theologians and philosophers of religion, including Philip Hefner, Nancey Murphy, and Philip Clayton, have preferred to build on the thought of Hungarian philosopher of science Imre Lakatos (1922–1974).

Influenced by both Popper and Kuhn, Lakatos argued that science should be understood in terms of competing research programs, each with an unfalsifiable core, which nevertheless must prove to be progressive over time.

Notable in these approaches is an abandonment of a strong commitment to a metaphysical realism for explaining the nature of both science and religion. Murphy has been the most vocal in rejecting realism as an explanatory category, and has argued, following philosopher W. V. O. Quine (1908–2000), that foundationalism, the view that knowledge claims can be deductively built one on another, must be abandoned. Rather, human beings build webs of belief that are complexly interconnected, but with only a weak sense (if that) of some beliefs being more primary than others. Nevertheless, there remain clear criteria for preferring some beliefs and theories over others.

Philosophy of science and post-modernism

The abandonment of both foundationalism and realism are important elements of the broad set of movements characterized as postmodern. A general feature of post-modern movements have been an increased skepticism towards certainty of knowledge, especially with regard to the sciences, combined with a deep awareness of hidden ideologies in apparently objective knowledge claims that influence power relations of race, class, and sex. Feminist philosophers of science such as Sandra Harding and Evelyn Fox Keller have noted how sexual bias can pervade scientific theory and practice. Advocates of the strong program of sociology of science such as Steve Fuller have argued that science, in essence, has no objective basis and is simply one discourse among others. Taken to extremes, such views are debilitating to a science and religion dialogue, as they destroy any possible ground of knowledge. There are, however, profound insights to be derived from these postmodern approaches, and these have been, to varying degrees, employed by some science and religion scholars. Theologian J. Wentzel van Huyssteen has attempted to carefully incorporate a postmodern, postfoundationalist critique while still maintaining the legitimacy of both science and religion as intellectual endeavors. Distinctly feminist perspectives have had a harder time entering into the mainstream of religion and science scholarship, although a number of elements of feminist thought (e.g., an abandonment of dualism, rejection of foundationalism, and an acknowledgement of ideological bias) are now widely acknowledged.

An alternative approach to a number of characteristically postmodern perspectives has been provided by process theology, which received initial inspiration from the philosophy of Alfred North Whitehead (1861–1947). Rather than drawing on the philosophy of science, process theology is based on a broader metaphysical perspective that encompasses both science and religion. Theologian David Ray Griffin has argued at length for a new understanding of naturalism that is based on process theology and does not exclude God. Because of its metaphysical commitment, process theology does not share the skepticism of other forms of postmodernism, and claims some confidence about providing a robust understanding of the world and, consequently, of religion and science.

Prospects

The 1980s and 1990s saw a particularly rich discussion of religion and science methodological issues. Despite this, there remains a considerable array of opinions about the proper relationship of religion and science, both within the field of religion and science proper as well as outside of it. It should be expected that the philosophy of science will continue to play an important role in methodological research, particularly since most of the philosophy of science research currently cited in the field of religion and science dates before 1980. Among perspectives from philosophy of science that may play an increasing role are characterizations of the practice of science as a process of inference to the best explanation (employed by some) and characterizations based on information and probability theory.

A number of methodological perspectives remain under-represented in the field of religion and science. Most notable of these may be the philosophical movement of pragmatism, founded by Charles Sanders Peirce (1839–1914) and William James (1842–1910) and now widely represented in the United States and abroad. Likewise, more radical forms of postmodernism need to be engaged at a more serious level than has been the case to date. A further complicating factor is the growing engagement of a number of the world religious traditions, whose different presuppositions will likely alter perceptions of how religion and science should, in the end, be related.

See also SCIENCE AND RELIGION; SCIENCE AND RELIGION, HISTORY OF FIELD; SCIENCE AND RELIGION IN PUBLIC COMMUNICATION; SCIENCE AND RELIGION, MODELS AND RELATIONS; SCIENCE AND RELIGION, PERIODICAL LITERATURE; SCIENCE AND RELIGION, RESEARCH IN

Bibliography

Barbour, Ian. *Myths, Models, and Paradigms: A Comparative Study in Science and Religion.* San Francisco: Harper, 1974.

Barbour, Ian. *Religion and Science: Historical and Contemporary Issues.* San Francisco: Harper, 1997.

Clayton, Philip. *Explanation from Physics to Theology.* New Haven, Conn.: Yale University Press, 1989.

Fuller, Steve. *Social Epistemology,* 2nd edition. Indianapolis: Indiana University Press, 2002.

Gould, Stephen Jay. *Rocks of Ages: Science and Religion in the Fullness of Life.* New York: Ballentine, 1999.

Griffin, David Ray. *Religion and Scientific Naturalism: Overcoming the Conflicts.* Albany: State University of New York Press, 2000.

Harding, Sandra. *Whose Science? Whose Knowledge? Thinking from Women's Lives.* Ithaca N.Y.: Cornell University Press, 1991.

Kuhn, Thomas. *The Structure of Scientific Revolutions.* Chicago: University of Chicago Press, 1962.

Lakatos, Imre. "Falsification and the Methodology of Scientific Research Programmes." In *Criticism and the Growth of Knowledge,* eds. Imre Lakatos and Alan Musgrave. Cambridge, UK: Cambridge University Press, 1970.

Murphy, Nancey. *Theology in the Age of Scientific Reasoning.* Ithaca, N.Y.: Cornell University Press, 1990.

Pannenberg, Wolfhart. *Theology and the Philosophy of Science.* Philadelphia, Pa.: Westminster Press, 1976.

Popper, Karl. *The Logic of Scientific Discovery.* New York: Basic Books, 1959.

Torrance, Thomas. *Theological Science.* Oxford: Oxford University Press, 1969.

van Huyssteen, J. Wentzel. *The Shaping of Rationality: Toward Interdisciplinarity in Theology and Science.* Grand Rapids, Mich.: Eerdmanns, 1999.

GREGORY R. PETERSON

SCIENCE AND RELIGION, MODELS AND RELATIONS

A number of categories have been proposed for classifying diverse views of how science and religion can be related to each other. John Haught has suggested the categories of Conflict, Contrast, Contact, and Confirmation. A more detailed eightfold classification has been offered by Ted Peters. This article uses a fourfold typology proposed by Ian Barbour: Conflict, Independence, Dialogue, and Integration.

Conflict

The trial of the Italian astronomer Galileo Galilei in 1633 is often cited as the first prominent example of the conflict of religion with modern science. However, several factors in this trial were not typical of conflicts in subsequent centuries. Galileo challenged the respected authority of Aristotle who had held that the sun and planets revolve in orbits around the earth. Galileo also challenged the authority of the Catholic church at a time when it felt threatened by the Protestant Reformation. He did indeed challenge the literal interpretation of scripture, but this was not crucial in his day because metaphorical and allegorical interpretations of scriptural passages had been widely accepted since the writings of Augustine of Hippo in the 5th century.

Responses to Charles Darwin's *On the Origin of Species* (1859) provide examples of Conflict, but also examples of alternative responses. A long, gradual process of evolution clearly conflicts with the seven days of creation in Genesis, which some theologians interpreted literally. Some religious conservatives accepted a long evolutionary history, but insisted on the special creation of the human soul, whereas liberals were soon speaking of evolution as God's way of creating. The evolutionary origins of humanity seemed a threat to human dignity, especially when "the survival of the fittest" was used by several social philosophers to justify ruthless economic competition and colonialism. After all, the idea of an impersonal process of variation and natural selection challenged the traditional idea of purposeful design. Darwin himself did not believe that every species had been specifically designed by God, but he did believe that God had designed the whole process through which differing species had evolved.

The Conflict thesis is represented today by two views at opposite ends of the theological spectrum: creation science and scientific materialism. Each gains a following partly by its opposition to the other. The popular image of "the warfare of science and religion" is perpetuated by the media, for whom controversies provide dramatic stories.

Creation Science. Fundamentalism, started as a movement in the United States since early in the twentieth century that took a strong stand defending biblical inerrancy. In the Scopes trial in Dayton, Tennessee, in 1925, fundamentalists argued that the teaching of evolution in the schools should be forbidden because it is contrary to scripture. Beginning in the 1960s, proponents of creation science have claimed that there is scientific evidence against evolutionary theory and evidence for the sudden appearance of creatures in their present forms. Several state legislatures passed laws requiring that creationist theory be given equal time with evolutionary theory in public high school biology classes. But in 1987, the U.S. Supreme Court ruled that creation science does not constitute legitimate science and that it has been promoted in order to support a particular religious viewpoint, which is prohibited by the separation of church and state in the U.S. Constitution.

More sophisticated critiques of Darwinism have appeared in recent years, focusing on the rarity of transitional forms between species in the fossil record, and pointing to the sudden burst of new species in the early Cambrian period. According to the biochemist Michael Behe, the complex sequences of molecular reactions in organisms today could not have arisen gradually because if even one step were missing the sequence would not fulfill an adaptive function. Proponents of *intelligent design,* such as William Dembski, assert that such complexity could only be the product of purposeful intelligence. A number of biologists have replied that there are plausible Darwinian explanations for many of these phenomena, and that where such explanations are lacking one should seek more adequate testable hypotheses rather than positing supernatural intervention, which would inhibit rather than encourage further research.

Scientific materialism. Materialism is the assertion that matter is the fundamental reality in the universe. Materialism is a form of *metaphysics* (a claim concerning the most general characteristics and constituents of reality). Scientific materialism makes a second assertion: The scientific method is the only reliable path to knowledge. This is a form of *epistemology* (a claim concerning inquiry and the acquisition of knowledge). The two assertions are linked; if the only real entities are those with which science deals, then science is the only valid path to knowledge.

In addition, many forms of materialism express *reductionism*. Epistemological reductionism claims that the laws and theories of all the sciences are in principle reducible to the laws of physics and chemistry. Metaphysical reductionism claims that the behavior of any system is determined by its component parts, which alone are causally effective.

Two well-known sociobiologists have explicitly defended scientific materialism. Richard Dawkins argues that evolution provides proof that there is no purpose in the universe. He holds that our actions are determined by our genes, which are the product of deterministic laws and chance events. He asserts that religion has always been harmful to human welfare. Edward O. Wilson believes that all human behavior can be explained by biological origins and genetic inheritance. He acknowledges that religious traditions served a useful function in the past by uniting groups around common loyalties, but he argues that this function can be better served today by loyalty to science. Critics suggest that scientific materialism is an interpretive philosophical position that conflicts only with other philosophical and religious positions, not a scientific theory that is part of science itself.

Independence

Conflicts between science and religion can be avoided if they are taken to be inquiries in separate domains. They employ differing languages fulfilling contrasting functions in human life. Science asks about lawful regularities among events in nature, whereas religion asks about ultimate meaning and purpose in a wider interpretive framework. If both science and religion are selective, neither can say that its account of reality is complete.

Separate domains. Starting in the nineteenth century, biblical scholars used historical methods to study the cultural context in which various parts of the Bible were written. They noted that the creation stories of the Bible made significant affirmations that the world is good, orderly, and dependent on a purposeful God. These convictions were conveyed through a symbolic and poetic story that assumed the prescientific cosmology of its day, which included a seven-day creation, an earth-centered astronomy, and a three-part universe with heaven above and hell below the world. But the central message of Genesis can be accepted today because it is not dependent on its ancient cosmology, and it is also quite independent of modern scientific cosmology. Its message is not actually about events in the past, but about the fundamental relation of God to the world and to persons in every moment, which is not a scientific question. Cultural anthropologist point out that creation stories around the world provide models for human behavior. Communities participate in such stories by enacting them in rituals. The role of creation stories is primarily to provide patterns for human life in the present rather than to provide explanatory accounts of events in the past.

The idea of separate domains has also been defended by some natural scientists. The biologist Stephen Jay Gould uses the Latin word *magisterium* to refer to a domain of teaching authority. "The magisterium of science covers the empirical realms, what is the universe made of (fact) and why does it work this way (theory). The magisterium of religion extends over question of ultimate meaning and moral value" (p. 6). Each domain has its own distinctive questions, rules, and criteria of judgment. Gould is critical of scientists who try to derive philosophical, theological, or ethical conclusions from science. He points out that Darwin's idea of natural selection has been misused to defend war, colonialism, ruthless economic competition, and eugenics.

Differing languages. Among philosophers in the 1950s, the logical positivists took scientific statements as the norm for all cognitive assertions and claimed that any statement not subject to empirical verification is either meaningless or purely emotive. In response, the analytic philosophers insisted that differing types of languages serve differing but equally legitimate functions in human life, and each has its distinctive rules. Science and religion do different jobs and neither should be judged by the standards of the order. Science asks strictly delimited questions in the interest of prediction and control. Religious language expresses a way of life through the rituals, stories, and practices of a religious community. The analytic philosophers have usually accepted an instrumentalist account of both science and religion. Both forms of language serve useful practical functions and neither of them need to make truth claims that might lead to conflict.

Critics reply that religious language presupposes distinctive religious beliefs. Classical realism had taken both scientific theories and religious beliefs to be descriptions of reality in itself. At the opposite extreme, instrumentalism took theories and beliefs to be useful fictions serving pragmatic human purposes. Critical realism has defended a middle ground in which conceptual models in both fields make tentative cognitive claims as imaginative representations of aspects of reality in its interaction with human observers.

Science and religion are sometimes said to offer complementary perspectives on the world that supplement rather than compete with each other. Some authors draw a more specific analogy to the Complementary Principle in physics. Physicist Niels Bohr noted that a subatomic entity such as an electron or a photon of light sometimes behaves like a wave and sometimes like a particle; it cannot be represented by a single model. Some authors have extended the principle to characterize the relation between science and religion. The idea of complementarity is a reminder that no set of concepts provides an exhaustive description of reality.

Dialogue

Dialogue portrays more constructive relationships between science and religion than does either the Conflict or the Independence view, but it does not offer the degree of conceptual unity claimed by advocates of Integration. Independence emphasizes differences between science and religion, whereas Dialogue emphasizes several kinds of similarity including the *presuppositions* and *boundary questions* of the scientific enterprise and *methodological* and *conceptual parallels* between the two fields.

Presuppositions and boundary questions. Historians have wondered why modern science arose in the Judeo-Christian West among all world cultures. Some suggest that the doctrine of creation helped to set the stage for scientific activity. Both

Greek and biblical thought asserted that the world is orderly and intelligible. But the Greeks held that this order is necessary and therefore one can deduce its structure from first principles. Only biblical thought held that God created both form and matter, so the world did not have to be as it is, and the contingent details of its order can be discovered only by observation. Historians say that many factors contributed to the rise of modern science, including the humanistic interests of the Renaissance and the growth of commerce and trade, but they point out that the idea of creation gave religious legitimacy to scientific inquiry. Many of the founders of modern science believed that they were studying the handiwork of the Creator.

Boundary questions are raised but not answered by science. Why is the universe intelligible? Why is there a universe at all? The cosmologist Stephen Hawking writes: "What is it that breathes fire into the equations and makes a universe for them to describe? The usual approach of science of constructing a mathematical model cannot answer the questions of why there should be a universe for the model to describe" (p. 174).

The cultural contexts of both science and religion have been explored by feminist authors. They have pointed to correlations among the polarities that have been pervasive in Western thought: mind/body, reason/emotion, objectivity/subjectivity, domination/submission, power/love. In each case, the first term of each pair (mind, reason, objectivity, domination, power) is identified in our culture as male, the second term (body, emotion, subjectivity, submission, love) as female. A historically patriarchal culture in which men have held most of the positions of power perpetuated a predominantly male image of God. Moreover the first term of each pair has been prominent in science, especially in its attempt to dominate and control nature. Feminist sensibilities, it is said, might lead to new topics for scientific research, more holistic theoretical concepts, and more ecological technologies. On the religious side, radical feminists turn to indigenous cultures for feminine symbols of the divine and for recovery of the sacred in nature. Reformist feminists, on the other hand, believe that the patriarchal features of historic Christianity can be rejected without rejecting the whole tradition, and they seek to relate this understanding to new possibilities in science.

Methodological and conceptual parallels. It has often been assumed that science is strictly objective. It is said that theories are validated by their agreement with indisputable theory-free data that are unaffected by individual preference or cultural influences. By contrast, religion seems to be highly subjective and strongly influenced by individual and cultural assumptions. But historians and philosophers have called into question this sharp contrast, arguing that science is not as objective nor religion as subjective as had been assumed. There are indeed differences of emphasis between the fields, but the distinctions are not absolute.

Philosophers of science have maintained that all data are theory-laden, not theory-free. Theoretical assumptions enter the selection, reporting, and interpretation of what are taken to be data. Moreover, theories do not arise from logical analysis of data but from acts of creative imagination in which metaphors and analogies often play a role. Models help one imagine what is not directly observable, especially in the realm of the very large (astronomy) and the very small (quantum physics). In the case of religion such data as religious experience, rituals, and scriptural texts are even more heavily laden with human interpretation. In religious language, metaphors and models are even more prominent.

The term *paradigm* was used by Thomas Kuhn to refer to a cluster of conceptual, metaphysical, and methodological presuppositions embodied in a tradition of scientific work. With a new paradigm the old data are reinterpreted and seen in new ways, and new kinds of data are sought. An established paradigm is resistant to falsification, since discrepancies between theory and data can be set aside as anomalies or reconciled by introducing ad hoc hypotheses. Religious traditions can also be regarded as communities that share a common paradigm. Their interpretation of data (such as religious experience and historical events) is even more paradigm-dependent and resistant to falsification, but it is not totally immune to challenge.

Many authors have also explored conceptual parallels between particular scientific and religious ideas. Recent discussion of human nature has drawn from both theology and science. The dualism of body and soul in classical Christianity has been questioned by theologians who find in the Bible itself a more integral view of the person as an embodied unity of thinking, feeling, and acting. Some scientists, on the other hand, have challenged reductionism and look on the person as a multileveled psychosomatic unity. Neuroscientists studying the brain have found that emotional as well as rational capacities are important in human life, as the biblical tradition has long maintained. The social character of selfhood is a theme common to biblical thought and research in cognitive psychology and anthropology.

Parallels between the holism of quantum physics and the holism of Eastern mysticism have often been noted. The quantum description of an atomic system must be given for the whole system, which cannot be analyzed as the sum of its separate parts. Nonlocal connections are evident in experiments in which two particles originating in a single event continue to be entangled with each other when they reach widely separated detectors. The physicist David Bohm and in a more popular vein, Fritof Capra, have seen a striking similarity between quantum holism and the experience of undifferentiated oneness encountered in the depth of meditation. In quantum physics the observer and the observed are inseparable; so, too, the mystic tradition speaks of the union of subject and object. Because these writings stress personal experience and the limitations of human knowledge, they can be considered as forms of Dialogue, but in their more systematic and metaphysical elaboration they might be considered as examples of Integration.

Integration

Advocates of Integration call for reformulations of traditional theological ideas that are more extensive and systematic than those envisaged by advocates of Dialogue. In natural theology it is claimed that the existence of God can be inferred from (or is supported by) the evidence of design in nature. In a theology of nature, the main sources of theology lie outside science, but scientific theories strongly affect the reformulation of certain doctrines. In a systematic synthesis, both science and religion contribute to the development of an inclusive metaphysics, such as that of process philosophy.

Natural theology. The medieval theologian Thomas Aquinas held that some of God's characteristics can be known only from revelation in scripture, but the existence of God can be known by reason alone. His teleological argument (from *telos,* Greek for purpose or goal) starts from orderliness and intelligibility as general characteristics of nature, but he goes on to cite specific evidence of design in nature. Scientists in the seventeenth century, including Isaac Newton and Robert Boyle, saw God's hand in the details of natural systems from the structures of animals to the solar system. In the early nineteenth century, an Anglican priest, William Paley, said that if one finds a watch on a heath one is justified in concluding that it was designed by an intelligent being; if in the eye many complex parts function together to achieve a single end, it, too must have had a designer. Darwin dealt a serious blow to the traditional design argument, for he showed that adaptation can be explained by random variation and natural selection. But Darwin himself accepted a revised version of the argument; he said that God did not design the particular details of individual species, but designed the laws of evolutionary processes through which the species were formed, leaving the details to chance.

Traditionally, design referred to the execution of a detailed preexisting plan. But chance seems to have played a large role in evolutionary history. Mutations are random and the overwhelming majority are harmful. Some changes were the product of contingent circumstances, such as the comet that was probably responsible for the extinction of the dinosaurs. Yet evolutionary history dos show an overall trend toward greater responsiveness and awareness. The capacity to gather, store, and process information has steadily increased. Design can now be identified with an open-ended direction of change rather than with an exactly specified end product.

The Anthropic Principle in writing by contemporary cosmologists can be interpreted as a new form of design argument. The fundamental parameters of the early universe seem to be fine-tuned for the conditions needed for the emergence of life and intelligence. If the expansion rate one second after the Big Bang had been smaller by even one part in a hundred thousand million million, the universe would have recollapsed before evolution could have occurred. If the expansion had been even a tiny fraction faster it would have dispersed too rapidly for galaxies and planets to have formed. The universe seems to be balanced on a knife-edge, too improbable to be a fortunate chance occurrence.

Most defenders of natural theology, such as Paul Davies, do not claim to offer proofs for the existence of God, but argue that a cosmic designer who does not intervene is a more plausible ultimate explanation than naturalistic alternatives. Some proponents of a modest natural theology combine it with adherence to a theistic religious tradition. But critics point out that in itself natural theology leads only to the God of deism who started the universe and was inactive thereafter, not to the God of theism who is actively involved in the world.

Theology of nature. A theology of nature does not start from science, as natural theology usually does. Instead, it starts from a religious tradition based on religious experience and historical revelation. But it holds that some traditional doctrines need to be reformulated in the light of current science. Here science and religion are considered to be relatively independent sources of ideas, but with some areas of overlap in their claims. An extensive literature has addressed the question: How could God act in the world described by the laws of science without intervening supernaturally and discontinuously?

Our understanding of the general characteristics of nature will affect our models of God's relation to nature. In contemporary views, nature is understood to be a dynamic evolutionary process with a long history of emergent novelty, characterized throughout by both law and chance. The natural order is ecological, interdependent, and multileveled. These characteristics will modify our representation of the relation of both God and humanity to nonhuman nature. This will, in turn, affect our attitudes toward nature and will have practical implications for environmental ethics. The problem of evil will also be viewed differently in an evolutionary rather than a static world.

For the biochemist and theologian Arthur Peacocke the starting point of theological reflection is past and present religious experience in an ongoing religious community. But Peacocke is willing to reformulate traditional beliefs in response to current science. He discusses at length how chance and law work together in cosmology, quantum physics, nonequilibrium thermodynamics, and biological evolution. He gives chance a positive role in the exploration of potentialities at all levels. Peacocke describes the emergence of distinctive forms of activity at higher levels of complexity in the multilayered hierarchy of organic life and mind.

God creates through the whole process, not by intervening in gaps in the process. Peacocke defends the idea of top-down causality within organisms and goes on to speak of God as a top-down cause.

Another proposal starts from the indeterminacy of quantum theory. In contrast to the determinism of classical physics, quantum physics gives only a range of probabilities rather than exact values in predicting individual events in subatomic systems. Some physicists think this unpredictability is attributable to the limitations of current quantum theory. But most physicists hold that indeterminacy is a property of the atomic world itself. Physicist and theologian Robert John Russell has argued that if quantum events are not completely determined by the laws of physics, the final determination could be made by God. God would not have to intervene to alter a determinate state, but would actualize one of the multiple potentialities present, all of which have identical energy, so that no input of energy would be required. In many situations indeterminacies at the atomic level average out to give predictable behavior for larger groups of atoms. But in some cases very small differences can be greatly amplified. A genetic mutation could change the course of evolutionary history. Where science finds only chance, the theist can see providential guidance. Traditionalist critics of such views hold that by representing God's action as a subtle influence that is not scientifically detectable, rather than as a more dramatic supernatural intervention, these authors have accommodated too much to science.

Systematic synthesis. A more systematic integration can occur if both science and religion contribute to a coherent world view elaborated in a comprehensive metaphysics. Metaphysics is the province of the philosopher rather than of the scientist or the theologian, but it can serve as an arena of common reflection. In the thirteenth century, Thomas Aquinas articulated an impressive metaphysics that has remained influential in Catholic thought. His voluminous writings systematically integrated ideas from earlier Christian authors with the best philosophy and science of his day, derived largely from the works of Aristotle.

The process philosophy of Alfred North Whitehead and his followers is a promising candidate for a mediating role today. Whitehead was familiar with quantum physics and its portrayal of reality as a series of momentary events and interpenetrating fields rather than separate particles. For him, as for evolutionary thinkers, nature is a dynamic web of interconnected events, characterized by novelty as well as order. Process thought holds that the basic constituents of reality are not two kinds of enduring entity (mind/matter dualism) or one kind of enduring entity (materialism), but one kind of event with two aspects or phases. All integrated events have an inner and an outer reality, but these take very different forms at different levels. Viewed from within, interiority can be construed as a moment of experience, though conscious experience occurs only at high levels of organization.

According to process philosophy, God elicits the self-creation of individual entities, thereby allowing for freedom and novelty as well as order and structure. Process thinkers reject the idea of divine omnipotence; they portray a God of persuasion rather than coercion, and they have provided distinctive analyses of the place of chance, human freedom, evil, and suffering in the world. Christian process theologians such as John Haught point out that the power of love, as exemplified in the cross, is precisely its ability to evoke a response while respecting the integrity of other beings. The thought of Jesuit paleontologist Pierre Teilhard de Chardin shows some similarities with process theology, including affirmation of an evolutionary cosmos and postulation of interiority in all beings, though his approach is less philosophical and more poetic—and sometimes more mystical—than that of authors indebted to Whitehead.

Process theology has been criticized for departing too far from classical Christianity. It does emphasize divine immanence (without excluding transcendence), whereas classical Christianity emphasized transcendence. More philosophers have abandoned the search for a unifying metaphysics, though there has been some revival of interest in questions once dismissed as metaphysical. The majority of authors who want to move beyond Conflict and Independence hold that we will have to be content with Dialogue or with less philosophical forms of Integration.

See also CHRISTIANITY; INTELLIGENT DESIGN; SCIENCE AND RELIGION, HISTORY OF THE FIELD

Bibliography

Barbour, Ian G. *Religion and Science: Historical and Contemporary Issues.* San Francisco: Harper, 1997.

Barbour, Ian G. *When Science Meets Religion*. San Francisco: Harper, 2000.

Behe, Michal. *Darwin's Black Box*. New York: Free Press, 1998.

Bohm, David. *Wholeness and the Implicate Order*. Boston: Routledge and Kegan Paul, 1980.

Capra, Frijof. *The Tao of Physics*. New York: Bantam Books, 1977.

Cobb, John B., and Griffin, David Ray. *Process Theology: An Introduction*. Philadelphia, Pa.: Westminster Press, 1976.

Darwin, Charles. *The Origin of Species* (1859). New York: Bantam Classic, 1999.

Davies, Paul. *The Mind of God: The Scientific Basis for a Rational World*. New York: Simon and Schuster, 1992.

Dawkins, Richard. *The Blind Watchmaker*. New York: Norton, 1987.

Dembski, William A., and Kushiner, James M., eds. *Signs of Intelligence: Understanding Intelligent Design*. Grand Rapids, Mich.: Brazos Press, 2001.

Gould, Stephen Jay. *Rocks of Ages: Science and Religion in the Fullness of Life*. New York: Ballantine, 1988.

Haught, John F. *Science and Religion: From Conflict to Conversation*. Mahwah, N.J.: Paulist Press, 1995.

Haught, John F. *God After Darwin: A Theology of Evolution*. Boulder, Colo.: Westview Press, 2000.

Hawking, Stephen. *A Brief History of Time*. New York: Bantam Books, 1998.

Kuhn, Thomas. *The Structure of Scientific Revolutions,* 2nd edition. Chicago: University of Chicago Press, 1970.

Peacocke, Arthur. *Theology for a Scientific Age,* enlarged edition. Minneapolis, Minn.: Fortress Press, 1993.

Peters, Ted. "Science and Theology: Toward Consonance." In *Science and Theology: The New Consonance,* ed. Ted Peters. Boulder, Colo.: Westview Press, 1997.

Polkinghorne, John. *The Faith of a Physicist*. Princeton, N.J.: Princeton University Press, 1994.

Russell, Robert John. "Special Providence and Genetic Mutation: A New Defense of Theistic Evolution." In *Evolutionary Biology and Molecular Biology: Scientific Perspectives on Divine Action,* eds. Robert John Russell, William R. Stoeger, and Francisco J. Ayala. Berkeley, Calif.: Center for Theology and the Natural Sciences; Vatican City: Vatican Observatory, 1998.

Southgate, Christopher, et al. *God, Humanity, and the Cosmos*. Harrisburg, Pa.: Trinity Press International, 1999.

Teilhard de Chardin, Pierre. *The Phenomenon of Man,* trans. Bernard Wall. New York: Harper and Row, 1959.

Wilson, Edward O. *Consilience: The Unity of Knowledge*. New York: Knopf, 1998.

IAN BARBOUR

SCIENCE AND RELIGION, PERIODICAL LITERATURE

Every major field of human discourse spawns a literature proportional to the intensity of the conversation. Science and religion is no exception. Fascinating topics, historic and contemporary, have arisen at the intersection of these two very different fields, and a periodical literature has emerged, both to facilitate communication among scholars who have entered into this conversation, and to report the conversation to a larger audience.

Given the diversity within science and among religions, it is no surprise that the field's periodicals address the disciplines differently. In some journals *religion* means *theology,* and the editorial approach is primarily theoretical. Some periodicals intend *religion* to include all world religions, whereas others intend it as a synonym for a particular brand of faith. Still other publications address issues of applied religion, meaning spirituality or public morality, and applied science, such as medicine, politics, or economics.

The field's most scholarly journal is the quarterly *Zygon: Journal of Religion and Science,* founded in 1965. *Zygon* has three sponsors: the Institute for Religion in an Age of Science (IRAS), the Center for Advanced Study in Religion and Science (CASIRAS), and Rollins College in Winter Park, Florida. *Zygon* construes religion broadly as anything that relates to the human quest for purpose and the journal has an exceptionally broad base of scholarly contributions.

The Center for Theology and the Natural Sciences (CTNS) in Berkeley, California, launched a new journal, *Theology and Science,* in 2003, with an intellectual focus on Christian theology. This journal is the continuation of the quarterly *CTNS Bulletin,* founded in 1982. Animated and enduring conversations have arisen within the Christian evangelical camp, which continues to debate vigorously the truth and significance of Darwinism. The most substantial journal in this category is the quarterly *Perspectives on Science and Christian*

Faith, the official journal of the American Scientific Affiliation (ASA), which serves about 2,500 readers. Founded in 1941, the ASA and its journal promote the idea that both the Bible and science are revelations from God. Most of the articles relate to the creation-evolution controversy, and the journal has become a primary vehicle for the critical discussion of theistic evolution and Intelligent Design. A more conservative journal, *Origins and Design,* founded in 1980 and published by the Access Research Network, is devoted almost exclusively to the promotion of Intelligent Design. The quarterly glossy magazine, *Facts and Faith,* founded in 1987 (now discontinued), had almost seven thousand paid subscribers, and was published by the apologetics organization Reasons to Believe. It used design arguments to bolster faith in the Bible.

A number of fundamentalist publications promote a more conservative, biblically literalist view of science and religion. Two of the most influential are *Acts and Facts,* founded in 1971, a free monthly newsletter sponsored by the Institute for Creation Research in Santee, California, and *Creation Magazine,* founded in 1978, a more populist and politically oriented publication published by the Back to Genesis group.

Reports of the National Center for Science Education is a bimonthly newsletter founded in 1980 that reaches more than four thousand readers with articles and resources to refute creationism. These journals reflect America's ongoing struggle with Darwinism.

Outside of the United States, the science and religion conversation is much less intense but no less diverse. The ambitious semiannual journal *Science and Christian Belief* is the product of two organizations based in Britain. The Victoria Institute, founded in 1865 as the first anti-evolution group, merged its journal in 1989 with that of Christians in Science. The resulting journal, launched in 1988, resembles ASA's *Perspectives,* though it has a more scholarly and theologically eclectic approach. Given the journal's British roots, the editorial bent leans less toward the creation-evolution controversy, which is primarily an American phenomenon.

Other European science and religion publications include the twice-yearly book review compendium *Reviews,* founded in 1983 and published by the British Science and Religion Forum. The European Society for the Study of Science and Theology (ESSSAT) publishes two biennial texts: *Issues in Science and Theology* (2000) and *Studies in Science and Theology* (1987), which are basically book series.

In India, the Muslim Association for the Advancement of Science publishes the *Journal of Islamic Science,* founded in 1984, which looks at the historical and philosophical questions raised by science from an Islamic perspective. The *South African Science and Religion Forum,* founded in 1993, is a newsletter that reaches about five hundred readers, published by the Research Institute for Theology and Religion at the University of South Africa.

Two web sites, *Metanexus* and *Counterbalance,* span the geographic borders of science and religion and provide timely, comprehensive internet resources. *Metanexus* was launched in 1998 and by 2002 had thousands of subscribers in nearly sixty countries. It operates several electronic list servers that disseminate news updates daily and it publishes a monthly email newsletter. Since 1996, *Counterbalance* has provided a tightly woven web of materials that encapsulate the discussions taking place in the science and religion field, including such resources as video clips of lectures.

There are also two popular publications that support the field of science and religion: *Science and Spirit* is a bimonthly glossy magazine, and *Research News and Opportunities in Science and Theology* is a monthly newspaper. *Science and Spirit,* launched in 1989 and repositioned in 2001 for a general audience, explores the religious dimensions of scientific discoveries and technological advances. Brief, timely, articles by well-known thinkers illuminate the nexus of science and spirituality, while incorporating the wisdom of a world of faiths. Paid subscribers exceeded nine thousand in 2002. *Research News and Opportunities in Science and Theology* was launched in 2000 as a general clearinghouse of information for the field of science and religion. This monthly paper reports on the science and religion community's activities, organizations, and opinion leaders, and it publishes book reviews and interviews that address emerging and established topics of scientific and religious inquiry. *Research News* also serves the former readership of *Bridgebuilding* and *Progress in Theology,* two small specialized publications disbanded in 2000. *Research News, in 2002,* had a paid circulation over five thousand and readership of about thirty thousand.

Beyond the established scholarly periodicals and the emerging popular ones are a number of newsletters that, while connected to specific science and religion centers, often contain articles and reviews of general interest. Some of the more significant are *The Pascal Centre Notebook* from the Pascal Centre for Advanced Studies in Science and Faith at Redeemer College in Ancaster, Ontario; *Science and Religion Forum* from the Institute on Religion in an Age of Science (IRAS); and the *Journal of the Faith and Science Exchange,* published by the Boston Theological Institute.

See also SCIENCE AND RELIGION IN PUBLIC COMMUNICATION

KARL GIBERSON

SCIENCE AND RELIGION, RESEARCH IN

It is essential to begin by noting that research in science and religion covers a wide range of exploration. The frequent use of the terms "science-and-religion field" and "science-religion debate" tends to obscure not only the range of relationships between different sciences and different religions, but also different approaches to researching these relationships. There is a diverse matrix of relationships between the cognitive claims of different sciences and different religions. As argued by Willem B. Drees in *Religion, Science, and Naturalism* (1996), religions have different aspects, which have different relations to the science under consideration, and the phenomenon of religion is itself a proper object of scientific study. But the matrix is yet broader and more intricate than that—sciences do not consist only of propositional claims being tested by experiment, but of communities of individual scholars whose work is informed both by their individual spiritual attitudes and by the ethos of their community. That ethos is in turn informed by social, cultural, and political factors.

Some historical considerations

That the matrix of relationships mentioned above has been in constant shift throughout the last few hundred years has been an emphasis in the work of historians such as John Hedley Brooke. Brooke's determined insistence that, viewed historically, the unfolding of these relationships is often more surprising and paradoxical than might have been supposed has been a significant counter to the devising of overly simplistic grand narratives of *the* relationship between science and religion. In Brooke's book with Geoffrey Cantor, *Reconstructing Nature* (1998), he explores the range of approaches by which history can enrich and subvert trite preconceptions, and includes a fascinating chapter on chemistry, a subject too often omitted from historical surveys of the science-religion matrix.

A problem that will continue to beset historical research in science and religion is: What was it about European Renaissance Christendom that particularly predisposed it to give rise to modern Western science? Important markers in this debate have been Reijer Hooykaas's stress on the importance of Protestantism, Stanley Jaki's emphasis on the contribution of Catholic thinking, and Amos Funkenstein's important *Theology and the Scientific Imagination from the Middle Ages to the Seventeenth Century* (1986). The question can be put another way: How can we account for the "failure of early science," as Philip Luscombe puts it in *Groundwork of Science and Religion* (2000)? Neither Ancient Greek culture, nor the "Golden Age of Islam" in the tenth and eleventh centuries, nor indeed Chinese or Indian civilization, gave rise to any expansion of experimental enquiry and technological development that remotely parallels that of the modern West. This question will need particularly sensitive handling in the twenty-first century, when religious conviction and political and economic aspiration have become so evidently intertangled with the question of what is a truth to be lived by.

The character of the science-religion debate

The apparent unity of the science-religion debate in the Western world has had much to do with two particular dynamics. First, certain prominent scientists continue to make assertions about the reach of science, claiming that in some way it falsifies the truth-claims of religion. Names that come to mind include Stephen Hawking and Peter Atkins (in their different ways) in respect of physics, and Edward O. Wilson and Richard Dawkins (again in their different ways) in respect of biology. These assertions tap into a perception in the public mind that indeed religion is in headlong retreat before science. People therefore seek overviews of how this supposed battle is going, overviews which have been provided with consistent distinction over many years by the Minnesota-based philosopher and theologian Ian Barbour, whose typologies of possible relationships between the disciplines—in terms of conflict, independence, dialogue, and integration—have done so much to put the "conflict" hypothesis in perspective.

The second ingredient tending to promote a sense of the unity of the field is the eloquent and sustained contribution made since the 1970s by four scholars in particular. Barbour has already been mentioned. His name is often linked with those of the British scientist-theologians Arthur Peacocke and John Polkinghorne, but the contribution of the American philosopher Holmes Rolston III has been of comparable stature. All emerged from a background in hard sciences—Peacocke in physical biochemistry, the other three in physics itself. All have surveyed the relationship between sciences and religions as being a unity; all have explicitly taken issue with the "falsifiers" mentioned above. Though they differ in the degree of their debt to process philosophy, and in their theological inclinations, all remain deeply committed to a critical-realist view of human enquiry. Science finds things out; over time, it tells us more and more about the world. Science is therefore an ally in enquiring more faithfully into the creativity of God. Theology too is a realist discipline; over time, it can expect to rid itself of formulations that are not coherent with other robust understandings of the world and of ourselves. For all four, in their different ways, Christian monotheism is at the cutting-edge of this exploration.

The relationship of ecological theology to science-religion research

For far too long ecological theology has lived in a separate ghetto from what is usually thought of as research into science-and-religion. It is interesting to consider why this might have been so. "Scientist-theologians" (as Barbour, Peacocke, and Polkinghorne were dubbed in Polkinghorne's comparative study *Scientists as Theologians* [1996]) all take an essentially positive view of science and seek to learn how theology in the Christian tradition might resemble it. Much ecological thinking, however, has reflected on how the discoveries of science have been used to develop technologies that oppress and destroy nature—also on how patriarchal monotheism has seemed to be an ally of that oppression, and in parallel also of the oppression of women. Ecological theology, then, has been the home not, typically, of the celebration of science but of suspicious readings of the texts of power—scientific as well as scriptural. It has also been a domain of remythologizations: for example, the universe as the body of God as in Sallie McFague's *The Body of God* (1993); the planet Earth (Gaia) as the sacred space on which human beings depend as in Anne Primavesi's *Sacred Gaia* (2000).

Barbour has written extensively on the ethics of technology, but it is Rolston who has been a key figure in this uneasy relationship, since he has made significant contributions both on science-and-religion and in environmental ethics. He has carefully analyzed how value is intrinsic to all living things and the systems within which they function, but he has also insisted that a practical approach to environmentalism must insist on an element of philosophical realism. Science is not only a vital diagnostic aid as to the extent of the environmental crisis because it does tell us things about the way the world is; it is also a source of potential solutions. There is much work to do to widen the bridge Rolston has begun to build.

The divine action debate

Central in the divine action debate has been the contribution made by six Vatican Conferences on science and theology held between 1987 and 2000, the first subtitled "A Common Quest for Understanding" and the last five "Scientific Perspectives on Divine Action." All the proceedings have been edited by Robert John Russell and colleagues (1988, 1993, 1995, 1998, 1999, 2001). The debate about God's providential activity and how it might be related to the story of the universe has been the biggest single engine driving research in science and theology in this period. At two poles of the debate have been (1) the Thomist understanding of "double agency," according to which God's primary agency lies behind each and every event, but God's providence operates through secondary causes, such as human activity, the stress being on the ultimate sovereignty of God; and (2) the process-theological view that divine persuasion is an ingredient of every event, luring entities toward harmony and creativity, but never determining outcomes. Here the stress is on God the fellow-suffering persuader. Neither of these positions in itself makes for easy conversation with the sciences.

Important markers in the effort to understand divine action within a scientifically described universe include (1) the proposal, going back to William Pollard in the 1950s, but further developed in particular by Russell and the South African physicist George F. R. Ellis, that quantum indeterminacy provides the "gap" in which God can act undetectably on the physical universe; (2) Polkinghorne's provocative assertion in his *Science and Providence* (1989) that we should look for the locus of God's action in the openness and indeterminacy of the universe at the macroscopic level, as illustrated by the equations of chaos theory; (3) Peacocke's insistence on the importance of "top-down causation," later "whole-part influence"; and (4) Nancey Murphy's masterly assessment of these views, which can be found in the Vatican Conference proceedings published as *Chaos and Complexity* (1995). The divine action conferences have covered physics and cosmology, chaos theory, evolutionary and molecular biology, and neuroscience. These subjects will be touched on further below. The current state of the argument on quantum indeterminacy is summarized in the Vatican Conference proceedings entitled *Quantum Mechanics* (2001).

The Vatican Conferences have been invaluable conversations among eminent thinkers, and essential resources for research students. However, the overall conclusion from the debate must be that efforts to press too closely the question of God's action, to allow the relevant science to frame too closely how that action might be formulated, have consistently failed. Polkinghorne, the most ambitious thinker in this area, retreated in books such as *Belief in God in an Age of Science* (1998) into much more theological and less physical formulations.

One of the key theological issues underlying the debate is that of God's relation to time. Again this sharply divides the classical Thomist approach, which places God beyond time, from process-influenced schemes. The relation of this debate to understanding of time in physics is much debated. Polkinghorne has insisted that an omnipresent God can be in time but equally present to every point in space. Drees has objected that relativistic understandings of space-time permit no such vantage point.

Another key issue is that of divine kenosis—self-emptying. Two meetings of senior scholars on this topic in 1998 and 1999 led to an important series of essays, *The Work of Love (2001)*, edited by Polkinghorne. Does God's creative activity involve an element of self-limitation, reaching a climax (for Christians) at the Incarnation and Passion of Christ? A particular importance of these meetings was that they not only brought together the four senior figures in the debate—Barbour, Peacocke, Polkinghorne, and Rolston—but also a major philosopher of religion, Keith Ward, and eminent figures from the rest of the theological world, including Jürgen Moltmann, Paul Fiddes, and Sarah Coakley. It is vital to the future of explorations in this interdisciplinary area that research does not remain confined within its own little interest group, but hears from and responds to other branches of theology.

The contribution of philosophy of science

Research in science and religion necessarily involves asking what sort of enterprise is the science in question? Reference to the philosophy of science, however, is complicated by the fact that most practicing scientists would not recognize the descriptions of their activity offered by most contemporary philosophy. Philosophers, working in the context of postmodern critiques of foundationalism, and with a profound awareness of the cultural embeddedness of all descriptions, tend to stress the practice of science as the activity of a particular community, a particular type of rational enterprise. Most scientists simply think of themselves as finding out more about the way things really are. This is no doubt why the thinkers who have done most to develop theological conversation with working scientists have tended to espouse a fairly strong form of critical realism. Significant support for critical realism, particularly with respect to science, has come from Ernan McMullin; an even more robust insistence on realism can be found in Roger Trigg's *Rationality and Religion* (1998).

Among the philosophers who have most engaged with the challenge of postmodernism, it is important to mention the work of Murphy and of J. Wentzel van Huyssteen. Murphy made a bold bridge from the methodology of science into theology in her *Theology in the Age of Scientific Reasoning* (1990), using the model of core and auxiliary hypotheses developed by Imre Lakatos. In the process, she rejected critical realism in theology on the grounds that it makes too great a claim as to our knowledge of elements of reality beyond our ordinary human ways of knowing. Since then, Murphy has worked with Ellis to develop a model in which cosmology might inform ethics, as in their *On the Moral Nature of the Universe* (1996).

In contrast to Murphy, van Huyssteen wants to defend "a weak form of critical realism," essentially as an inference from the evolved capacity of human beings to make sense of the cosmos. He has made a telling diagnosis of the predicament of contemporary theology as being, in a sense, between a rock and a soft place, between the strong progressivist truth-claims of science and post-modernity's relativizing suspicion of all grand narratives. Yet van Huyssteen asserts that this makes the conversation between science and theology a particularly important one. As he claims in *The Shaping of Rationality* (1999), if any rational communities are to be in conversation, it should be these two.

The conversation with the physicists

This conversation is best known through the works of the Australia-based British physicist Paul Davies, in particular *God and the New Physics* (1983) and *The Mind of God* (1992). Davies is a fascinating example of a physicist of no particular religious affiliation whose explorations of the lawfulness and fruitfulness of the cosmos draw him to God-language. It led him in his early days to postulate that there are senses in which science may teach us more about God than religion can; later he was disposed to remark not only on the astonishing intelligibility of the universe but also on the limits of human understanding—the laws of nature will not of themselves answer every question about existence. Interestingly, Davies has also explored the theologically intriguing question as to whether life on Earth may have extraterrestrial origins.

Two arguments at the boundary of physics and metaphysics currently generate a lot of energy and lead to a great deal of God-talk, if not always of the most informed or nuanced kind. The first concerns the so-called anthropic coincidences. If certain fundamental constants were even minutely different, or if the early history of the universe had unfolded even slightly differently, this universe could not be fruitful of life. So, did God fine-tune the cosmos? This is a discussion dogged by imprecision of terms and by the temptation to try and resolve a metaphysical issue by argument in physics (a mistake against which Polkinghorne has consistently argued). The main alternative to divine fine-tuning is the many-universes theory, and neither alternative is subject to physical test. However, it must be admitted that developments in theoretical physics, in particular those concerning the possibility of universes giving rise to other universes (see for example Lee Smolin's *The Life of the Cosmos* [1997], for a different approach see Hawking's *The Universe in a Nutshell* [2001]) could influence the balance of the argument, though they could not settle it. A change in the balance would be a change in the apparent consonance between the picture physical science offers and the notion of a God designing the universe. If the universe as described by science looks unique and precisely fine-tuned for life, the consonance is high. If this looks like one of many trillion universes constantly budding off from one another, the anthropic coincidences look less suggestive, and consonance is lower. *Consonance* is a felicitous term, first developed by McMullin and further explored by Ted Peters, for describing the way scientific and theological formulations seem sometimes to come into harmony. But apparent consonances come and go; mature interdisciplinary research in this area requires that they not be too much relied upon.

This is nowhere more important than in the other major area of debate between physics and philosophical theism—the question of the origin and cause of the universe. The enthusiasm of Pope Pius XII for the apparent consonance between early Big Bang cosmology and Genesis 1 has long been subverted by a series of alternative proposals in physics. The Big Bang model continues as a description of the development of the universe, including its apparent rapid early inflation. However, various models of the origin of the universe and its very early growth, in a context in which quantum effects may have dominated, now suggest that the arising of this fourteen-billion-year-old universe, containing a hundred billion galaxies, may have been some form of chance fluctuation in a pre-existing state of zero net energy. This has been taken by some to challenge both the Christian doctrine of creation-out-of-nothing (*creatio ex nihilo*) and the notion of "God's moment" before the laws of physics took effect. However, more rigorous thinking shows that the "nothing" of the quantum vacuum is a highly structured state, hardly *nihil* in theological terms. Robert John Russell's analysis, published in *Religion and Science: History, Method, Dialogue* (edited by W. Mark Richardson and Wesley J. Wildman, 1996), shows that a discrete temporal moment of becoming would be an interesting consonance with Genesis but is not necessary to a Christian theology of creation.

Russell has also remarked that accounts of the end of the universe will necessarily exhibit a dissonance between scientific prediction and Christian formulation. All the different scientific accounts suggest that this universe will have a finite lifespan, and even if new universes bud off from it or are born out of it, there seems little likelihood that structure or information, let alone living things, could survive such a transition. The Christian hope, however, anticipates a new creation and a continued bodily existence of persons. Perhaps because of this dissonance there has been surprisingly little work in this area of the science-religion debate. Some interesting new science continues to emerge (for a summary see Martin Rees' *Our Cosmic Habitat* [2002]), but few theologians have explored the territory, honorable exceptions being Polkinghorne and Welker's edited work *The Ends of the World and the Ends of God* (2000) and Arnold Benz's *The Future of the Universe* (2000).

Theology and biology

In 1996, Holmes Rolston contributed an interesting essay entitled "Science, Religion and the Future" to Richardson and Wildman's *Religion and Science*. In it he remarks that "Outspokenly monotheistic biologists are as rare as those who think physics is compatible with monotheisms are common" (p. 65). There is a contrast between the tone of mutual curiosity in much of the conversation between philosophical theism and physics and the often acrimonious conversation between theologians and certain biologists, particularly Dawkins, Wilson, and Lewis Wolpert. It may be argued that Dawkins has had his uses in stirring up the debate, as Jacques Monod did before him. Strongly reductionist denials of the significance of human existence and humans' search for God did much to provoke Peacocke's long engagement with theology's relation to evolutionary biology, as summarized in his *Paths from Science towards God* (2001). The British philosopher Mary Midgley has also

been important for her rejection of trite reductionism, and her insistence that there can be many "maps" of the character of existence and that these maps are not mutually exclusive, that mortgages are in a sense as real as membranes or muons.

However, too much adversarial writing sometimes distracts theologians from their central task. The long battle, especially in the United States, over creationism has distracted attention from the fascinating questions that arise if a generally Darwinian picture is accepted. Two questions particularly come to mind.

First, when and how did evolving hominids develop the status Christian theology accords humans as being in the image and likeness of God? When did they develop the capacity for worship, and what view of the world did this early religious practice reflect? Beyond the oft-repeated statement, much insisted on by Peacocke, that theology must discard a picture of a historical fall from a preparadisal state, little progress has been made in this area. Perhaps theologians are right to be cautious, since the paleontological evidence changes continually and seems to push the development of artistic and symbolic skills further and further back in time.

Many of the details of the second question were already known to Charles Darwin by the mid-1800s. It concerns the theodicy problem raised by evolution through natural selection. How could a loving God use a process so replete in casualties—individual organisms that never grow to their potential or die in horrible pain, species that go extinct—to realize other ends, such as the evolution of humans? Again, scientist-theologians need to learn from ecotheologians and move beyond the very anthropocentric ambit of theodicy as it has tended to be done. Some early evolutionary theodicies can be seen in Ruth Page's *God and the Web of Creation* (1996), John Haught's *God After Darwin* (2000), and Christopher Southgate's "God and Evolutionary Evil" (2002).

One of the most intense areas of ethical debate in the early twenty-first century is the area of genetic manipulation and cloning. This focuses questions as to the role and status of the human person. Are we "plain citizens of the biotic community" as Aldo Leopold stated, or the "created co-creators" (suggested by Philip Hefner in *The Human Factor* (1993)? Issues of genetic reductionism also stalk the debate—to what extent do we understand an organism by understanding the location and function of its genes? Ted Peters has made an interesting move here, arguing in *Playing God?* (1997) that much of the opposition to genetic technologies is itself reductionist. Celia Deane-Drummond in her survey *Biology and Theology Today* (2001) insists that the missing ingredient in the debate is an appeal to wisdom, a promising route by which Christian theology might inform this branch of ethics.

A further question, still embryonic, is to what extent work on chaos and complexity theory, the self-organizing behavior of systems such as those that gave rise to and nurtured life on Earth, may alter our perspective on the evolutionary history of the biosphere. The Danish scholar Niels Gregersen has been at work on the significance of autopoiesis in ways which may bear rich fruit in addressing questions of the "designedness" of the biosphere and the theology of God's interaction with evolving life.

Theology and psychology

This conversation between theology and psychology promises to be a great growth area in the first half of the twenty-first century. As Philip Clayton has noted in his *God and Contemporary Science* (1997), human agency is the best analogy, however weak it may be, to the agency of a personal God. It is therefore of the first importance that theologians track research into the psychology of agency. Secondly, religious experience (a particular research interest of Fraser Watts, the Starbridge Lecturer at Cambridge) is properly the subject of both theological and scientific investigation. Thirdly, our view of the attributes of human personhood has historically been profoundly influenced by theological formulations. In Christian societies this has often been expressed in terms of "soul" language. Yet in contemporary Western society it is science that principally informs ethical and legal judgments as to when personhood begins and ends. Hence the special significance of the project involving Warren Brown, Nancey Murphy, and H. Newton Maloney, helped by (among others) a distinguished evolutionary biologist in Francisco Ayala and an eminent neuroscientist in Malcolm Jeeves. This led to the book *Whatever Happened to the Soul?* (1999), in which the authors explore a nonreductive physicalist model of the mind-brain relation. On this model, soul language becomes adjectival, not in any way an assertion that some sort of

separate entity exists within each human which carries the spiritual life of the person. The ethical implications of such a model are still to be worked out, though John Habgood's gradualist model of the beginning and end of personhood in his *Being a Person* (1998) is a challenging starting point, particularly in relation to terminal illness, dementia, and persistent vegetative state.

Religions other than Christianity

There are good, if hotly debated, reasons why Christian theologians have led the debate on the relationship of theology to Western sciences. However, the science-religion debate must not consist solely of a retelling of some Christian story that Christendom fostered modern science, made a brief mistake with Galileo, survived the assaults of atheism and Darwinism, and now flourishes as a trendy partner to contemporary cosmology. It is self-evident that science's relationships with religions and theologies other than the Christian are not only important in themselves but may supply wholly new perspectives from which to understand interdisciplinary conversation of this type.

The Christian theologian must not seek to mold other traditions into the particular thought-patterns that happen to have informed the debate between sciences and textual, critically aware Christian theology. However, long established questions are bound to occur to that theologian such as (1) does the radical monotheism of Islam, with its great emphasis on the authority of the literal text of the Qur'an, provide a climate for conversation with the forms of knowledge offered by various sciences; and (2) can the apparently non-realist attitude to matter in much Eastern thought be reconciled with a realist cosmology?

The answer to these questions needs much further exploration. Recent accounts by practicing Muslims who are scientists, such as Mehdi Golshani and Bruno Guiderdoni in Richardson and Slack's *Faith in Science* (2001), suggest that science can be regarded as worship, as responding to the Qur'anic command to see Allah's signs in the universe, yet there is no question that for many Islamic thinkers a theory such as Darwinian evolution is profoundly unpalatable. As Michael Robert Negus relates in the textbook *God, Humanity, and the Cosmos* (1999, edited by Southgate), two of the approaches in K. A. Wood's classification of ways to account for the sciences as compatible with

Islam—compartmentalism and a phenomenological approach to scriptural texts—would seem to show promise in encouraging distinguished Muslim scientists and theologians in the integration of contemporary science with an Islamic metaphysics. The third approach, scientific exegesis, seeking to infer scientific truths from the scriptural texts themselves, seems fraught with problems.

As for Eastern thought, it does seem that its apparently nonrealist attitude toward matter can be, up to a point, reconciled with a realist cosmology. An article by Vaharaja V. Raman on Hinduism in *When Worlds Converge* (2002, edited by Matthews, Tucker, and Hefner) suggests that indeed the material world, and scientific conclusions about it, can be taken seriously in Hindu thought, provided there is no suggestion that the descriptions arrived at have objective reference or that they are of parallel importance to the discoveries of the spiritual masters. Points of contact can be noted here with the debate within Christian theology. Likewise an article on Buddhism by Pinit Ratanakul (in the same volume) indicates an openness to the findings of science, as long as the central moral insights of the faith remain preeminent. The Buddhist concepts of nonharming and interdependence remain important resources for developing ecological ethics.

Resources, sponsors, and key organizations

It is enormously challenging to engage with the complex matrix that is the science-religion debate, and books that can function as textbooks for the student remain few. Rolston's *Science and Religion* (1987) was an early example, and Barbour has produced a series of overviews, of which *Religion and Science* (1997) is perhaps the most useful. The first comprehensive, purpose-designed textbook to appear was *God, Humanity, and the Cosmos* (1999), edited by Southgate.

The extraordinary patronage of conversations between science and religion by Sir John Templeton, far and away the biggest single sponsor of this type of research, has done much to build a single community of enquirers. Extensive funding has been made available for the Templeton Foundation's Science and Religion Course Program, which has supported courses in several hundred colleges throughout the world, and other types of workshops and symposia on the classic issues discussed above. An important element in this has been the exploration of the spiritualities of practicing scientists and the effect faith, or lack of it, has on their work.

A couple of centers of excellence in the current debate also deserve mention. Long-term research into profoundly difficult problems—cosmological, theological, and ethical—is conducted with rigor and passion at the Center for Theology and the Natural Sciences in Berkeley, California, under the direction of Robert John Russell. Also important is the Zygon Center for Religion and Science in Chicago, from which Philip Hefner edits *Zygon,* the premier journal in the field. The two most prominent chairs in the field are the James I. McCord Chair in Theology and Science at Princeton Theological Seminary in New Jersey, occupied by J. Wentzel van Huyssteen, and the Andreas Idreos Chair at Oxford University, occupied by John Brooke. The novelist Susan Howatch has endowed another important post at Cambridge University, the Starbridge Lectureship. Europe has the most vigorous society: the European Society of the Study of Science and Theology (ESSAT), whose biennial meetings are not only a major encouragement to scholars from poorly resourced institutions in Eastern Europe, but profoundly generative in themselves. Extensive information can be found at www.metanexus.net and www.counterbalance.org, which have done much to make current research available online.

Concluding thoughts

The conversations between scientists and theologians that have been discussed above have had a wider impact than might be thought simply by noting the main developments. It is slowly coming to be recognized that it is respectable for those trained in the humanities to know about science. Novels and poems based on scientific ideas and images are now proliferating. Well-known theologians who have specialized in other areas in the past are being drawn into the debate, including, strikingly, the British evangelical scholar Alister McGrath, who published two books on science and religion in 1998. Likewise, eminent scientists are now entering the conversation not, as in the past, to dismiss theology, nor yet to defend it, but to remark on the relationship between disciplines, as in Stephen Jay Gould's model of "nonoverlapping magisteria" in his *Rocks of Ages* (1999). If van Huyssteen is indeed right that the science-theology debate is the paradigmatic case of the possibilities of conversation between two rational communities, these "cross-over" works are of particular significance for the unfolding of human rationality and creativity.

See also SCIENCE AND RELIGION; SCIENCE AND RELIGION, HISTORY OF FIELD; SCIENCE AND RELIGION IN PUBLIC COMMUNICATION; SCIENCE AND RELIGION, METHODOLOGIES; SCIENCE AND RELIGION, MODELS AND RELATIONS; SCIENCE AND RELIGION, PERIODICAL LITERATURE

Bibliography

Barbour, Ian G. *Religion and Science: Historical and Contemporary Issues.* San Francisco: Harper, 1997.

Barbour, Ian G. *When Science Meets Religion: Enemies, Strangers or Partners?* San Francisco: Harper, 2000.

Benz, Arnold. *The Future of the Universe: Chance, Chaos, God?* New York and London: Continuum, 2000.

Brooke, John Hedley, and Cantor, Geoffrey. *Reconstructing Nature: The Engagement of Science and Religion.* Edinburgh, UK: T&T Clark, 1998.

Brown, Warren; Murphy, Nancey; and Maloney, Newton H. *Whatever Happened to the Soul? Scientific and Theological Portraits of Human Nature.* Minneapolis, Minn.: Fortress Press, 1998.

Clayton, Philip. *God and Contemporary Science.* Edinburgh, UK: Edinburgh University Press, 1997.

Davies, Paul. *God and the New Physics.* Harmondsworth, UK: Penguin, 1983.

Davies, Paul. *The Mind of God: Science and the Search for Ultimate Meaning.* Harmondsworth, UK: Penguin, 1992.

Davies, Paul. *The Fifth Miracle: The Search for the Origin of Life.* Harmondsworth, UK: Penguin, 1998.

Deane-Drummond, Celia. *Biology and Theology Today: Exploring the Boundaries.* London: SCM Press, 2000.

Drees, Willem B. *Religion, Science, and Naturalism.* Cambridge, UK: Cambridge University Press, 1996.

Funkenstein, Amos. *Theology and the Scientific Imagination from the Middle Ages to the Seventeenth Century.* Princeton, N.J.: Princeton University Press, 1986.

Gould, Stephen Jay. *Rocks of Ages: Science and Religion in the Fullness of Life.* London: Jonathan Cape; New York: Ballantine, 1999.

Gregersen, Niels H. "Autopoiesis: Less than Self-Constitution, More than Self-organization." *Zygon* 34, no. 1 (1999):117–138.

Habgood, John. *Being A Person: Where Faith and Science Meet.* London: Hodder and Stoughton, 1998.

Haught, John F. *God After Darwin: A Theology of Evolution.* Oxford and Boulder, Colo.: Westview Press, 2000.

Hawking, Stephen. *The Universe in a Nutshell.* London: Bantam, 2001.

Hefner, Philip. *The Human Factor: Evolution, Culture, and Religion.* Minneapolis, Minn.: Fortress Press, 1993.

Luscombe, Philip. *Groundwork of Science and Religion.* London: Epworth Press, 2000.

McFague, Sallie. *The Body of God: An Ecological Theology.* London: SCM Press, 1993.

McGrath, Alister. *The Foundations of Dialogue in Science and Religion.* Oxford: Blackwell, 1998.

McMullin, Ernan. "The Case for Scientific Realism." In *Scientific Realism,* ed. Jarrett Leplin. Berkeley and Los Angeles: University of California Press, 1984.

Matthews, Clifford N.; Tucker, Mary Evelyn; and Hefner, Philip, eds. *When Worlds Converge: What Science and Religion Tell Us About the Story of the Universe and Our Place in It.* La Salle, Ill.: Open Court, 2002.

Midgley, Mary. *Science and Poetry.* New York and London: Routledge, 2001.

Murphy, Nancey. *Theology in the Age of Scientific Reasoning.* Ithaca, N.Y.: Cornell University Press, 1990.

Murphy, Nancey, and Ellis, George F. R. *On the Moral Nature of the Universe: Theology, Cosmology, and Ethics.* Minneapolis, Minn.: Fortress Press, 1996.

Page, Ruth. *God and the Web of Creation.* London: SCM Press, 1996.

Peacocke, Arthur. *Theology for a Scientific Age: Being and Becoming—Natural, Divine, and Human,* Rev. edition. London: SCM Press, 1993.

Peacocke, Arthur. *Paths from Science Towards God: The End of all our Exploring.* Oxford: Oneworld, 2001.

Peters, Ted. *Playing God? Genetic Determinism and Human Freedom.* New York and London: Routledge, 1997.

Peters, Ted, ed. *Science and Theology: The New Consonance.* Oxford and Boulder, Colo.: Westview Press, 1998.

Polkinghorne, John. *Science and Providence: God's Interaction With the World.* London: SPCK, 1989.

Polkinghorne, John. *Scientists as Theologians.* London: SPCK, 1996.

Polkinghorne, John. *Belief in God in an Age of Science.* New Haven, Conn.: Yale University Press, 1998.

Polkinghorne, John, ed. *The Work of Love: Creation as Kenosis*. London: SPCK; Grand Rapids, Mich.: Eerdmans, 2001.

Polkinghorne, John, and Welker, Michael, eds. *The Ends of the World and the Ends of God: Science and Theology on Eschatology*. Harrisburg, Pa.: Trinity Press International, 2000.

Primavesi, Anne. *Sacred Gaia: Holistic Theology and Earth Science*. London and New York: Routledge, 2000.

Rees, Martin. *Our Cosmic Habitat*. London: Weidenfeld and Nicolson, 2002.

Richardson, W. Mark, and Slack, Gordy. *Faith in Science: Scientists Search for Truth*. New York and London: Routledge, 2001.

Richardson, W. Mark, and Wildman, Wesley J. *Religion and Science: History, Method, Dialogue*. New York and London: Routledge, 1996.

Rolston, Holmes, III. *Science and Religion: A Critical Survey*. New York: Random House, 1987.

Rolston, Holmes, III. *Environmental Ethics: Duties to and Values in the Natural World*. Philadelphia, Pa.: Temple University Press, 1988.

Rolston, Holmes, III. *Genes, Genesis, and God: Values and their Origins in Natural and Human History*. Cambridge, UK: Cambridge University Press, 1998.

Russell, Robert J.; Clayton, Philip; Wegter-McNelly, Kirk; and Polkinghorne, John, eds. *Quantum Mechanics: Scientific Perspectives on Divine Action*. Vatican City: Vatican Observatory; Berkeley, Calif.: Center for Theology and the Natural Sciences, 2001.

Russell, Robert J.; Murphy, Nancey; and Isham, C. J., eds. *Quantum Cosmology and the Laws of Nature: Scientific Perspectives on Divine Action*. Vatican City: Vatican Observatory; Berkeley, Calif.: Center for Theology and the Natural Sciences, 1993.

Russell, Robert J.; Murphy, Nancey; Meyering, Theo C.; and Arbib, Michael A., eds. *Neuroscience and the Person: Scientific Perspectives on Divine Action*. Vatican City: Vatican Observatory; Berkeley, Calif.: Center for Theology and the Natural Sciences, 1999.

Russell, Robert J.; Murphy, Nancey; and Peacocke, Arthur, eds. *Chaos and Complexity: Scientific Perspectives on Divine Action*. Vatican City: Vatican Observatory; Berkeley, Calif.: Center for Theology and the Natural Sciences, 1995.

Russell, Robert J.; Stoeger, William R.; and Coyne, George V., eds. *Physics, Philosophy, and Theology: A Common Quest for Understanding*. Vatican City: Vatican City Publications, 1988.

Russell, Robert J.; Stoeger, William R.; and Ayala, Francisco, eds. *Evolutionary and Molecular Biology: Scientific Perspectives on Divine Action*. Vatican City: Vatican Observatory; Berkeley, Calif.: Center for Theology and the Natural Sciences, 1998.

Smolin, Lee. *The Life of the Cosmos*. London: Weidenfeld and Nicolson; New York: Oxford University Press, 1997.

Southgate, Christopher, ed. *God, Humanity, and the Cosmos: A Textbook in Science and Religion*. Edinburgh, UK: T&T Clark; Harrisburg, Pa.: Trinity Press International, 1999.

Southgate, Christopher. "God and Evolutionary Evil: Theodicy in the Light of Darwinism." *Zygon* 37, no.4 (2002): 803–824.

Trigg, Roger. *Rationality and Religion*. Oxford: Blackwell, 1998.

van Huyssteen, J. Wentzel. *Duet or Duel? Theology and Science in a Postmodern World*. London: SCM Press, 1998.

van Huyssteen, J. Wentzel. *The Shaping of Rationality: Toward Interdisciplinarity in Theology and Science*. Grand Rapids, Mich.: Eerdmans, 1999.

Ward, Keith. *God, Chance, and Necessity*. Oxford: Oneworld, 1996.

Wilson, Edward O. *Consilience: The Unity of Knowledge*. New York: Knopf, 1998.

Wood, K. A. "The Scientific Exegesis of the Qur'an." *Perspectives on Science and Christian Faith* (*Journal of the American Scientific Affiliation*) 45, no. 2 (1993): 90–94.

CHRISTOPHER SOUTHGATE

SCIENCE FICTION

Science fiction is the genre of stories and film in which a significant element of the plot depends on the laws of mathematics and the physical sciences, or on the use of technology as currently known or as developed in a credible way. Stories in which natural laws are suspended or violated fall into the realm of fantasy rather than science fiction. Most science fiction plots take place in the future, on a fictional planet, or posit the use of a new technology. They explore the best and worst case scenarios that could result from the application of technology or from a variation in the natural world, though remain based on scientific laws as we know them. Though it seems that science fiction is based on science and the material world, most modern works are character based; science fiction explores human life and action within the context of a fictional but possible world. This fictional world allows the author clearly to explore issues in a context that is contrived, thus without the myriad mitigating or confounding factors the real world might present.

The genre of science fiction can be traced back to nineteenth-century novels such as Mary Shelley's *Frankenstein* (1818) and Jules Verne's novels of the 1860s and 1870s (*Journey to the Center of the Earth* and *Twenty Thousand Leagues Under the Sea*). However, the term *science fiction* was not widely used until the 1930s, when a group of pulp fiction magazines featuring stories based on the premises of modern science was established. Beginning with Hugo Gernsback's *Amazing Stories* (after whom the Hugo award in science fiction writing is named), the format was soon copied by several other American and British publications (John Campbell's *Astounding Science Fiction, Science Wonder Stories*). Among writers in Britain, a genre called *scientific romance* grew in the years following World War I with such writers as Olaf Stapledon, J. D. Beresford, H. G. Wells, and Aldous Huxley. In the United States, science fiction remained primarily magazine based until the rapid rise in the production of paperback books in the 1960s, which moved the genre from a predominance of short stories to novels. The science fiction novel emerged as a distinct literary genre in the second half of the century, exemplified in the works of writers such as Isaac Asimov, Ray Bradbury, Arthur C. Clarke, Robert Heinlein, and Kurt Vonnegut.

As the public became sensitized to the effects of science through the dropping of the atomic bomb in 1945, the development of the digital computer, and new advances in biotechnology, science fiction also became a staple for radio (Orson Welles's 1938 radio production of H. G. Wells's *War of the Worlds*), television (*The Jetsons, The Twighlight Zone, Star Trek, The X-Files*), and film plots (Fritz Lang's *Metropolis* [1927], Stanley Kubrick's *Dr. Strangelove* [1964] and *2001: A Space Odyssey* [1968], Ridley Scott's *Blade Runner* [1982] and *Alien* [1979], Steven Spielberg's *E.T.* [1982], and George Lucas's *Star Wars* [1977]). Although science

fiction novels continue to be popular and widely published, a larger contemporary audience is reached through film and television, mediums that make it easy for audiences to suspend disbelief and that appeal to our highly visual culture. The plots of science fiction films tend to be more adventure- and special-effects-based and less introspective than the written literature, though there are notable exceptions, such as Kubrick's *2001: A Space Odyssey*.

Popular themes in today's science fiction, regardless of the medium, include intelligent computers or robots, alternative worlds, travel to other planets, encounters with other life forms, the future evolution of the human race, and the ravages of atomic destruction or biochemical warfare. Science fiction has also spawned several subgenres in the late twentieth century, including *cyberpunk,* stories that take place in a virtual world sustained by computers and dominated by multinational corporations (William Gibson's *Neuromancer* [1984] and Scott's film *Blade Runner,* based on Philip K. Dick's *Do Androids Dream of Electric Sheep?* [1968]); *ecoscience fiction,* stories set in either an ecological utopia or distopia (Vonnegut's *Galapagos* [1985], Spielberg's *Jurassic Park* [1993], John Brunner's *The Sheep Look Up* [1972]); and *feminist science fiction* (Ursula K. LeGuin's *Left Hand of Darkness* [1969], James Tiptree's "The Women Men Don't See" [1973] and "The Screwfly Solution" [1977]).

Themes related to religion

The early science fiction pulp magazines were devoted primarily to adventure stories in which the exploration of religious themes or any explicit reference to religion was taboo. However, as science fiction moved into the mediums of novel and film, these strictures fell away. Modern science fiction deals extensively with religion, at times explicitly, at other times through the exploration of metaphysical systems, the nature of humanity or of social structures, the question of mystical powers, or the nature of moral decision making.

A number of science fiction novels have dealt directly with the nature of God. In *A Romance of Two Worlds* (1886), Marie Corelli explores the idea of God as an electrical force. H. G. Wells explores the nature of a finite or an unknowable God in *God the Invisible King* (1917) and *The Undying Fire* (1919). Mary Shelley in *Frankenstein* (1818), one of the earliest books in the science fiction genre, takes as her premise the question of human usurpation of the prerogatives of God. Stories that examine what it feels like to be God or to have godlike powers of omniscience, omnipotence, or the ability to create life forms range from short stories such as Edmond Hamilton's "Fessenden's Worlds" (1937) and Frank Russell's "Hobbyist" (1947), to novels such as Frank Herbert's *The God Makers* (1972) and Stanislav Lem's *Solaris* (1961). The idea of humans who create a god or computers that develop godlike powers is raised in Frederic Brown's "Answer" (1954), Isaac Asimov's "The Last Question" (1956), and Martin Caidin's *The God Machine* (1989). Many stories raise the possibility that a more advanced civilization would seem godlike to human beings. Philip K. Dick explores the question of beings with godlike powers in *Our Friends from Frolix 8* (1970) and the *Three Stigmata of Palmer Eldritch* (1964). Stories that posit an evil or incompetent god include Lester Del Ray's "Evensong" (1967), James Tiptree's *Up the Walls of the World* (1978), and Philip K. Dick's "Faith of Our Fathers" (1980). John Varley questions the basic requirements for being a god in his *Titan* series (1980).

The nature of humankind is so common a theme in science fiction that it has been used as a definition of the genre. Brian Aldiss writes in *Trillion Year Spree: The History of Science Fiction* (1986): "Science fiction is the search for definition of man and his status in the universe which will stand in our advanced but confused state of knowledge (science)" (p. 25). Almost all science fiction works deal implicitly, if not explicitly with the question of what it means to be human. Common plot vehicles include confrontation by an alien race or by intelligent computers, the challenges of disaster or of a dystopian world, and ethical decision making under limited conditions.

The question of not only what human beings are but what we might ultimately become is explicitly dealt with in Olaf Stapledon's *Last and First Men* (1930) and *Star Maker* (1937). Human transformation into a mystical or spiritual form is also examined in Arthur C. Clarke's *Childhood's End* (1953) and *2001: A Space Odyssey* (1968) and Philip Farmer's *To Your Scattered Bodies Go* (1955). The evolutionary ideas of Pierre Teilhard de Chardin are explicitly foundational to George

Zebrowski's *The Omega Point* (1972) and appear implicitly in Clarke's *Childhood's End*. Clarke also examines what it means to be human from the perspective of Buddhism in *The Fountains of Paradise* (1979).

A few novels and short stories deal with explicitly Christian themes. The star followed by the magi forms the basis for Arthur C. Clarke's "The Star" (1955). Richard Matheson's "The Traveler" (1952) and Michael Moorcock's *Behold the Man!* (1966) use time travel to examine the crucifixion of Jesus. While these are among the few stories that mention Jesus specifically, a figure whose advent and saving of a culture are messianic in nature is common and can be found in J. D. Beresford's *What Dreams May Come* (1941), L. Ron Hubbard's *Final Blackout* (1940), and Frank Herbert's *Dune* series (1965). The Apocalypse and the second coming of Christ have also formed a backdrop for much science fiction. C. S. Lewis wrote a trilogy in the form of science fiction that moves from a retelling of the story of the garden of Eden to the days before the second coming of Christ in which Merlin plays the role of messiah (*Out of the Silent Planet* [1938], *Perelandra* [1943], and *That Hideous Strength* [1946]). Walter Miller's, *A Canticle for Leibowitz* [1959] and Vonnegut's *Cat's Cradle* [1963] continue the apocalyptic theme, examining human behavior and the role of the church in worlds that have been or are being largely destroyed.

A number of science fiction novels posit a future theocracy, generally in a negative light. This is a particularly strong theme in feminist science fiction, and societies based on a version of Christian or Islamic fundamentalism are found in Margaret Atwood's *The Handmaid's Tale* (1986), Marion Zimmer Bradley's *The Shattered Chain* (1983), Sylvia Engdahl's *This Star Shall Abide* (1972) and Sheri Tepper's *Grass* (1990), *The Fresco* (2000), and *The Visitor* (2002). Feminist science fiction has also explored societies that follow a goddess based religion, a theme in Elizabeth Hand's *Walking the Moon* (1996), Starhawk's *The Fifth Sacred Thing* (1993), Marie Jakober's *The Black Chalice* (2000) and Suzette Elgin's *The Judas Rose* (1994). The effects of a theocracy are also explored outside of a feminist context, as in Lester Del Rey's *The Eleventh Commandment* (1962), John Brunner's *The Stone that Never Came Down* (1973), and Keith Robert's *Kiteworld* (1985).

With or without a theocracy, the priest or cleric is a fairly common protagonist. The strong religious grounding of such a character allows the author to examine human behavior in the light of challenges to one's religious or moral ground. Examples of clerical protagonists are found in James Blish's *A Case of Conscience* (1963), Marion Zimmer Bradley's *Darkover Landfall* (1972), Gordon Harris's *Apostle From Space* (1978), and Lester Del Ray's "For I am a Jealous God" (1973).

Science fiction is also an excellent vehicle for the consideration of moral questions. In *Science Fiction: The Future* (1971), Dick Allen describes the genre as "a form of literature that argues through its intuitive force that the individual can shape and change and influence and triumph; that [human beings] can eliminate both war and poverty; that miracles *are* possible; that love, if given a chance, can become the main driving force of human relationships" (p. 3). Ethical issues that are explored in science fiction include the appropriate use of technology, human relationships in the face of hardship, human responsibility in the face of new technologies, and the conflicts between disparate social groups or species. Many science fiction novels explore the conflicts that result when two societies with disparate ethical systems come in contact with one another. Examples include Isaac Asimov's *The Caves of Steel* (1954), Spider Robinson's *Night of Power* (1985), and Ken MacLeod's *The Cassini Division* (2000).

Bibliography

Aldiss, Brian W., with Wingrove, David. *Trillion Year Spree: The History of Science Fiction*. New York: Atheneum, 1986. Originally published as *Billion Year Spree*. London: Weidenfeld and Nicolson, 1973.

Allen, Dick, ed. *Science Fiction: The Future*. New York: Harcourt, 1971.

Cassutt, Michael, and Greeley, Andrew M., eds. *Sacred Visions*. New York: St. Martin's, 1991.

Greenberg, Martin H., and Warrick, Patricia S., eds. *The New Awareness: Religion through Science Fiction*. New York: Delacorte, 1975.

Reilly, Robert, ed. *The Transcendent Adventure: Studies of Religion in Science Fiction*. Westport, Conn.: Greenwood, 1985.

Ryan, Alan, ed. *Perpetual Light*. New York: Warner, 1982.

NOREEN L. HERZFELD

SCIENCE, METHODOLOGICAL ISSUES

See PHILOSOPHY OF SCIENCE

SCIENCE, ORIGINS OF

An enquiry into the origins of science is immediately faced with fundamental questions about the nature of science itself. Is science a discrete activity that endures over time? Can it adequately be distinguished from related human activities such as magic and religion? Is it a peculiarly Western phenomenon? Traditional histories of science have tended to answer each of these questions in the affirmative. Science is customarily defined as the systematic description or explanation of natural phenomena along with the habits of mind that make that possible—typically logic and mathematics. Working with this understanding of science, historians have traced the origins of Western science to Greek thinkers living on the west coast of Asia Minor in the sixth century B.C.E.

Science in antiquity

The speculations of these ancient Greek philosophers—principally Thales (c. 625–546 B.C.E.), Anaximander (c. 611–547 B.C.E.), and Anaximenes (500s B.C.E.), all from Miletus—are regarded as distinctive for three reasons. First, they offered naturalistic accounts of various phenomena that differed significantly from earlier mythological explanations that invoked arbitrary or supernatural causes. Second, they attempted to deal with the universal rather than the accidental and particular, and they sought unitary, underlying principles that could account for the diverse phenomena of nature. Third, they engaged in rational criticism of alternative explanations. On the first count, while the Greek poets Homer and Hesiod had tended to attribute lightning or earthquakes to the anger of Zeus or Poseidon, the Milesian natural philosophers explained these phenomena in terms of the forces of nature. Thales, for example, believed that Earth was supported by water, and that earthquakes were caused by disturbances in the water in which the Earth floats. Anaximander suggested that thunder is caused by the wind. It should be noted that the Milesian philosophers were not, on this account, atheists—Thales had once observed that "all things are full of gods"—it was just that they excluded the gods from their explanations. These thinkers also endeavored to isolate a single material principle that could account for the varied forms found in nature. For Thales, this was water; for Anaximander, "the boundless"; for Anaximenes, air. Anaximenes also provided an explanation of the transformations that air would undergo in order to give rise to the diverse phenomena of nature. Finally, the Milesians engaged in the critical appraisal of rival theories, providing reasons why one hypothesis should be preferred to another. Again, this is quite distinctive, for the purveyors of myth found it unnecessary to defend their accounts in the face of alternatives, and seemed untroubled by inconsistencies between different mythological accounts.

These features of early Ionian science found their way into later schools of Greek thought. The sixth- and fifth-century Pythagoreans, for example, located the principles of all things in numbers, and demonstrated how numerical ratios were manifested in nature. They were the first to attempt to provide knowledge of nature with a mathematical foundation. The fifth-century atomists, by way of contrast, proposed that all physical objects were composed of different arrangements of atoms. These schools thus anticipated what were much later to become central features of modern science—the mathematization of nature and atomic theory.

Greek science culminated in the thought of Aristotle (384–322 B.C.E.), who was to provide such a comprehensive and compelling account of natural phenomena that it dominated much of Western thought up until the seventeenth century. Aristotle wrote on virtually every contemporary discipline—physics, logic, biology, psychology, along with metaphysics, poetry, ethics, and politics. His biological works were informed by impressively accurate observations of animals, and provide descriptions of their anatomy, reproduction, and behaviors. He also made enduring contributions to taxonomy. Most important of all, Aristotle developed a metaphysical framework that set out the conditions required for a complete explanation. These were Aristotle's four causes, which sought answers to fundamental questions of the "what," the "how," and the "why" of natural phenomena.

The scientific revolution

When Aristotle's writings were rediscovered in twelfth-century Europe, having been preserved in the interim by Islamic scholars, they became the cornerstone of the university curriculum, and were dislodged from this privileged position only after considerable controversy in the early modern period. Over the course of the seventeenth century the preeminence of Aristotle was successfully challenged by such figures as Galileo Galilei (1564–1642), Francis Bacon (1561–1626), René Descartes (1596–1650), Robert Boyle (1627–1691), and Isaac Newton (1642–1727). So great was the intellectual upheaval effected by these individuals that later historians were to describe their achievements as a "scientific revolution." This period witnessed the birth of experimental methods, the mathematization of nature, and the introduction of new taxonomic principles. It might thus be said that if science, broadly conceived, had its origins in the thought of the ancient Greeks, modern science, with its distinctive use of mathematics and experimentation, began in the seventeenth century.

Non-Western science?

This standard account of the origins of science is susceptible to a number of criticisms. These concern both Western claims to a monopoly on scientific thinking, and the idea that science has some identifiable essence or method that endures over time. One line of criticism points to archaeological evidence of remarkable technological achievements in China and the ancient civilizations of the near East, which preceded the speculations of the early Greek natural philosophers. However, it makes sense in this context to distinguish technology from science. The former could well be based on trial and error combined with accumulated experience. The practical ability to produce useful artifacts, however impressive, is something quite different from the systematic attempt to arrive at an understanding of the operations of nature as a whole or to provide a theoretical account of laws of nature.

It has also been suggested that the definition of *science* that operates in the standard account is too restrictive. *Science* might be defined more broadly as a set of behaviors geared towards mastery of the natural environment. On this more inclusive definition, *science* can be said to have originated in a number of different cultures at different times. There is a wealth of anthropological evidence that points to the fact that many traditional societies developed remarkably sophisticated and complex understanding of natural phenomena. Whether such indigenous knowledge counts as science will, of course, ultimately depend on how the term is defined. It must be said, however, and without wishing to devalue such traditional knowledge, that its inclusion in the category "science" tends to make that designation rather vague.

The nineteenth-century alliance

Perhaps the most telling criticism is the opposite contention, that the definition of science that informs the standard account of the origins of science is too broad. "Science," it can be objected, is a modern category, and not an ancient or even an early-modern one, and its application to those periods is anachronistic. The ancient Greeks did not have a word for *science* as we understand it, and thinkers from Thales to Aristotle regarded themselves as pursuing "philosophy." Something similar is true for other ancient cultures. A comparable situation also existed in the seventeenth century, when the disciplines "natural history" and "natural philosophy" were the closest analogues to modern science. Isaac Newton thus explicitly identified himself as being engaged in the pursuit of natural philosophy. Individuals like Newton did not think in terms of science and nonscience, and the now-familiar distinctions between chemistry and alchemy, astronomy and astrology, even science and religion, were at this time at best fluid, at worst meaningless. For much of the seventeenth and eighteenth centuries natural history and natural philosophy were intimately linked with religious concerns and included theological explanations. For this reason alone they are to be carefully distinguished from science as we understand it. The term *scientist* was not invented until the nineteenth century, and a good case can be made that it was only at this time that modern science came into being. During this period a new alliance of disciplines was formed, linked together by the professional designation "scientist." Natural history was superseded by a laboratory-based biology, and for the first time the sciences began to occupy a central place in the university curriculum. Crucially, just as the new professional category of scientist now excluded the clergy, who had hitherto played a central role in natural history and natural philosophy, the sciences eschewed religious explanations. Charles Darwin's (1809–1882) naturalistic account of the origins of life helped make this transition possible. The contemporary idea of science as a professional, secular activity that is conducted primarily in a laboratory setting dates from this period.

In sum, it is possible to answer the question of the origins of science in four ways:

(1) Science originated amongst Greek natural philosophers in the sixth century B.C.E.

(2) Science originates whenever and wherever human beings attempt mastery of their natural environment.

(3) The origins of science can be traced to the "scientific revolution" of the seventeenth century.

(4) Science began only with the professionalization of various scientific disciplines in the nineteenth century.

While there is something to be said for each of these alternatives, the last is perhaps the least anachronistic and most historically respectable.

See also ARISTOTLE

Bibliography

Cunningham, Andrew. "Getting the Game Right: Some Plain Words on the Identity and Invention of Science." *Studies in History and Philosophy of Science* 19 (1988): 365–389.

Cunningham, Andrew, and French, Roger. *Before Science: The Invention of the Friars' Natural Philosophy.* Aldershot, UK: Scolar Press, 1996.

Huff, Toby. *The Rise of Early Modern Science: Islam, China, and the West.* Cambridge, UK: Cambridge University Press, 1993.

Lindberg, David C. *The Beginnings of Western Science: The European Scientific Tradition in Philosophical, Religious, and Institutional Context, 600 B.C. to A.D. 1450.* Chicago: University of Chicago Press, 1992.

Lloyd, G. E. R. *Early Greek Science: Thales to Aristotle.* London: Norton, 1970.

Needham, Joseph. *Science and Civilization in China,* 7 Vols. Cambridge, UK: Cambridge University Press, 1954–1987.

Ross, Sydney. "'Scientist': The Story of a Word." *Annals of Science* 18 (1962): 65–86.

Sarton, George. *A History of Science.* Vol. 1: *Ancient Science through the Golden Age of Greece.* Cambridge, Mass.: Harvard University Press, 1952.

Shapin, Steven. *The Scientific Revolution.* Chicago: University of Chicago Press, 1996.

Turner, Frank. "The Victorian Conflict between Science and Religion: A Professional Dimension." *Isis* 49 (1978): 356–376.

PETER HARRISON

SCIENCE WARS

The term *science wars* refers to a complex of discussions about the way the sciences are related to or incarnated in culture, history, and practice. These discussions came to be called a "war" in the mid 1990s because of a strong polarization over questions of legitimacy and authority. One side of the controversies is concerned with defending the authority of science as rooted in objective evidence and rational procedures. The other side argues that it is legitimate and fruitful to study the sciences as institutions and social-technical networks whose development is influenced by linguistics, economics, politics, and other factors surrounding formally rational procedures and isolated established facts.

The science wars began when a group of scientists and philosophers of science launched fierce attacks on a cluster of schools of social, historical, philosophical, anthropological, and multidisciplinary science studies. Such programs are variously called *social studies of science*; *science, technology, and society studies* (often abbreviated STS); and *sociology of scientific knowledge studies* (SSK). The attack saw itself and presented itself as a counterattack necessitated by what the attackers felt was a growing destructive criticism of science and rationality. The assault was aimed not just at science studies but also at a general leftist/critical academic trend of disrespect of tradition, so that the science wars were, in effect, a front in the greater "culture war." In fact, several expressions of the attack have claimed to defend just such human and cultural values (e.g., socialism, feminism, critique of ideologies) that traditionally are the domain of the left, but were allegedly betrayed by the left's attempt to undermine traditional standards.

It may be argued that there need not be a conflict between the acknowledgement of the social and historical contextuality of science and its legitmacy and status as a resource for solving human problems. Indeed, much work in the philosophy of science after Thomas Kuhn's *Structure of Scientific Revolutions* (1962) has been devoted to the development of the affirmative understanding of scientific rationality and progress under the constraints of historicity and contextuality. But as schools of science studies began to develop more radical accounts, explicitly stating that no core of rationality is independent of history and context, with some of them making such statements as a direct provocative challenge to traditional understandings of science, the discussions turned into a bitter conflict, particularly in the United States, although a few fierce attacks have also been seen in Europe. The metaphor of a war tends to blur the great range of views within the schools of science studies, as well as the fact that the fierce counterattacks only represent a relatively small group of scientists.

The literature on science studies and their critical discussion is vast and only a fraction is mainly concerned with the issue of strong scientific realism versus radical social constructivism. The famous culmination of the science wars was physicist Alan Sokal's exposure of the lack of standards in his article "Transgressing the Boundaries: Toward a Transformative Hermeneutics of Quantum Gravity," published in 1996 in the leftist academic journal *Social Text*. A more complete expression of the science war argument was made by Paul Gross and Norman Levitt in the 1994 book *Higher Superstition*. Classical expressions of radical science studies are found in works by Barry Barnes and David Bloor, as well as Bruno Latour and Steve Woolgar. Less aggressive and more reflective discussions of the issues involved can be found in Andrew Pickering's 1992 book *Science as Practice and Culture*.

The science wars debate has obvious interest in the context of the science-religion relationship because it exposes the institutions of science and shows them reacting to a form of critical pressure with obvious parallels to the situation facing religion during the first centuries of modernity.

See also POSTMODERN SCIENCE

Bibliography

Barnes, Barry, and Bloor, David. "Relativism, Rationalism and the Sociology of Knowledge." In *Rationality and Relativism,* eds. Martin Hollis and Steven Lukes. Oxford: Blackwell, 1981.

Gross, Paul R., and Levitt, Norman. *Higher Superstition: The Academic Left and its Quarrels with Science.* Baltimore, Md.: Johns Hopkins University Press, 1994.

Latour, Bruno, and Woolgar, Steve, ed. *Laboratory Life: The Social Construction of Scientific Facts.* London: Sage, 1979.

Pickering Andrew, ed. *Science as Practice and Culture.* London and Chicago: University of Chicago Press, 1992.

Sokal Alan. D. "Transgressing the Boundaries: Toward a Transformative Hermeneutics of Quantum Gravity." *Social Text* 14, no. 46/47 (1996): 217–252.

Sokal Alan D. "A Physicist Experiments with Cultural Studies." *Lingua Franca* 6, no. 4 (1996): 62–64.

NIELS VIGGO HANSEN

SCIENTIFIC MATERIALISM

See MATERIALISM; SCIENTISM

SCIENTIFIC METHOD

See MODELS; SCIENCE AND RELIGION, MODELS AND RELATIONS; SCIENCE AND RELIGION, METHODOLOGIES; SCIENCE AND RELIGION, RESEARCH IN; SCIENTISM

SCIENTIFIC REALISM

See CRITICAL REALISM

SCIENTISM

Advocates of the doctrine of scientism believe that the boundaries of science (that is, typically the natural sciences) could and should be expanded in such a way that something that has not previously been understood as science can now become a part of science. Thus a possible synonym to scientism is *scientific expansionism.* How exactly the boundaries of science should be expanded and what more precisely is to be included within science are issues on which there is disagreement.

Scientism in one version or another has probably been around as long as science has existed. From about 1970 to 2000, however, a number of distinguished natural scientists, including Francis Crick (b. 1916), Richard Dawkins (b. 1941), and Edward O. Wilson (b. 1929), have advocated scientism in one form or another. Some promoters of scientism are more ambitious in their extension of the boundaries of science than others. In its most ambitious form, scientism states that science has no boundaries: eventually science will answer all human problems. All the tasks human beings face will eventually be solved by science alone.

Epistemic and ontological scientism

The most common way of defining scientism is to say that it is the view that science reveals everything there is to know about reality. Scientism is an attempt to expand the boundaries of science in such a way that all genuine (in contrast to apparent) knowledge must either be scientific or at least be reducible to scientific knowledge. This epistemological form of scientism must be distinguished from its ontological form: The view that the only reality that exists is the one science has access to. One common way of stating ontological scientism is to maintain that nothing is real but material particles and their interaction. Ontological scientism entails epistemic scientism, but epistemic scientism does not entail ontological scientism. This is because one can affirm the view that knowledge obtainable by scientific method exhausts all knowledge and yet deny that whatever is not mentioned in the theories of science does not exist. One can do this because epistemic scientism does not preclude the existence of things that cannot be discovered by scientific investigation or experimentation. If there are such things, all it says is that one cannot obtain knowledge about them. Epistemic scientism sets the limits of human knowledge but not, like ontological scientism, the limits of reality.

It is often taken for granted that scientism and traditional religions such as Christianity and Islam are incompatible. But this is not necessarily the case. If, for instance, religion is taken to deal essentially with value questions, religion can be compatible with the epistemic and ontological forms of scientism. Of course, many believers are not satisfied with such a conception of religion. They claim that God really exists, that one can know that God is love, and so on. Are not such religious beliefs then incompatible with scientism? After all, scientism denies that it is possible to obtain knowledge of God or of a divine reality (epistemic scientism) and that there exists a transcendent or nonphysical reality beyond the physical universe (ontological scientism). But to the contrary, scientism does not necessarily deny these things. While Dawkins, Crick, Wilson, and others think along these lines, they could be wrong on scientific grounds. This is possible because all that scientism claims is that religious beliefs must satisfy the same conditions as scientific hypotheses to be knowable, rationally believable, or about something real. Scientists like Dawkins, Crick, and Wilson take for granted that religious beliefs cannot meet these requirements, which could of course be questioned. The British philosopher Richard Swinburne (b. 1934), among others, argues that theism can be confirmed by evidence in much the same way that evidence supports scientific hypotheses. Therefore, scientism cannot be equated with scientific naturalism or scientific materialism.

Value scientism and existential scientism

Another way of expanding the boundaries of science is to maintain that not only can science fully explain morality, but it can also replace traditional ethics and tell people how they morally ought to behave. Ethics can be reduced to or translated into science. However, for a claim to be *scientistic* in this sense, it must maintain more than that science is relevant to ethics. Nobody would deny that. It must rather state that science is the sole, or at least the most important, source for developing a moral theory and explaining moral behavior. There are advocates of this axiological form of scientism (called *value scientism*) within the ranks of evolutionary biology. Part of the idea is that evolutionary theory is rich enough to fully explain morality. The explanation is, roughly, that morality exists and continues to exist because it emerged and continues to function as a strategy adapted to secure the fitness of the individuals or of their genes. Some,

like Wilson, even think that evolutionary biologists will be able to discover a genetically accurate and completely fair code of ethics and thus provide people with scientific, moral knowledge.

Defenders of scientism can also go beyond morality and expand the boundaries of science so that religion or existential questions fall within its scope. Existential scientism is the view that science alone can explain and replace traditional religion. Dawkins, for instance, maintains that since the advent of modern science, people no longer have to resort to superstition when faced with deep problems such as "Is there a meaning to life?" and "What are we for?" because science is capable of dealing with all these questions and constitutes in addition the only alternative to superstition. Wilson claims that science can explain religion as a whole material phenomenon and suggests that scientific naturalism or materialism should replace religion.

Some advocates of scientism endorse both value scientism and existential scientism. However, it is important to distinguish these two forms. It is possible to affirm that evolutionary theory is the sole, or at least the most important, source for developing a moral theory and explaining moral behavior, while at the same time to deny that biology or any other science can explain the meaning of human life or fulfill the role of religion in peoples' lives. One could maintain that evolutionary theory can show which ethical principles should be used when trying to solve moral problems concerning (e.g., abortion, population growth, conflicts between people of different classes, genders, or races) and stop there, thereby accepting that the choice of religion or worldview is beyond the scope of science.

Thus value scientism does not entail existential scientism. But does existential scientism entails value scientism? This is less clear. Religions and worldviews generally include some ideas about how people should live and what a good life is. If this is correct then the acceptance of existential scientism implies also an acceptance of value scientism. But, on the other hand, it is perhaps possible to say that science alone can answer some existential questions and thus that science can partially replace religion. In other words, one doubts or denies that science can, so to speak, deliver the whole package in the shape of a complete worldview. If this is so, one could maintain, like

Dawkins, that every organism's sole reason for living is that of being a machine for propagating DNA, but still deny that science can offer ethical guidelines for how people should conduct their lives. Science can answer, at least, some existential questions, but it can not solve moral problems.

The relation between different forms of scientism

What then is the relation of value scientism and existential scientism to the first two forms of scientism? Neither value scientism nor existential scientism entails epistemic scientism or ontological scientism. It is coherent to claim that science can answer moral questions and replace traditional ethics or that science can answer existential questions and replace traditional religion, without maintaining that the only knowable reality or the only reality that exists is the one science has access to. Although there is no logically necessary connection between the two later forms of scientism, on the one hand, and the two earlier forms of scientism, on the other, these are, nevertheless, often combined.

This variety of forms of scientism shows that one should not equate scientism with scientific naturalism or materialism because there are possible forms of scientism that do not entail an acceptance of scientific materialism or naturalism. This variety also demonstrates that the relation between scientism and traditional religions is not a given. Only between existential scientism and traditional religions is there a direct conflict. Other forms of scientism may be compatible with traditional religions.

The main criticism directed against scientism is that its advocates, in their attempt to expand the boundaries of science, rely in their argument not merely on scientific but also on philosophical premises and that scientism therefore is not science proper.

See also MATERIALISM; NATURALISM; PHYSICALISM, REDUCTIVE AND NONREDUCTIVE; VALUE; WORLDVIEW

Bibliography

Almeder, Robert. *Harmless Naturalism: The Limits of Science and the Nature of Philosophy.* Chicago: Open Court, 1998.

Crick, Francis. *The Astonishing Hypothesis: The Scientific Search for the Soul.* New York: Scribners, 1994.

Dawkins, Richard. *The Selfish Gene,* 2nd edition. Oxford and New York: Oxford University Press, 1989.

Midgley, Mary. *Science as Salvation: A Modern Myth and Its Meaning.* London: Routledge, 1992.

Olafson, Frederick A. *Naturalism and the Human Condition: Against Scientism.* London: Routledge, 2001.

Smith, Huston. *Why Religion Matters: The Fate of the Human Spirit in an Age of Disbelief.* San Francisco: Harper, 2001.

Sorell, Tom. *Scientism: Philosophy and the Infatuation with Science.* London: Routledge, 1991.

Stenmark, Mikael. *Scientism: Science, Ethics and Religion.* Aldershot, UK: Ashgate, 2001.

Swinburne, Richard. *Is There a God?* Oxford: Oxford University Press, 1996.

Wilson, Edward O. *On Human Nature.* Cambridge, Mass.: Harvard University Press, 1978.

MIKAEL STENMARK

SCOPES TRIAL

Perhaps the most famous symbol of the science-religion clash, the Scopes Trial took place during July 1925 in the small town of Dayton, Tennessee. On trial for teaching evolution was high school teacher John Thomas Scopes, who agreed to serve as defendant in a case to challenge Tennessee's recently-passed *Butler Act* (Public Acts of the State of Tennessee, 1925, Chapter 27). This statute was the first effective legislation that emerged from the anti-evolution crusade, the most dramatic manifestation of the religious movement known as Protestant Fundamentalism. The *Butler Act* prohibited the teaching in public schools of "any theory that denies the story of Divine Creation of man as taught in the Bible, and to teach instead that man has descended from a lower order of animals." The Scopes Trial was precipitated by citizens of Dayton, who hoped to use the resulting publicity to boost their community, and by the American Civil Liberties Union (ACLU), which hoped to secure a judicial ruling that such anti-evolution laws were unconstitutional. The trial attracted worldwide attention, in part because noted attorney Clarence Darrow (1857–1938) was a member of the defense team, while famous politician and anti-evolutionist William Jennings Bryan (1860–1925) assisted the prosecution.

The Scopes Trial generated significant media comment, virtually all of it negative. Writers such as H. L. Mencken portrayed Bryan and his supporters as buffoons and dismissed the rural South as a backward region. Although the trial produced a few dramatic moments, such as Darrow's examination of Bryan as a Biblical expert, the courtroom activity proved relatively inconsequential. The ACLU was unable to use the trial as a forum to discuss evolutionary concepts because the judge had prohibited expert testimony as irrelevant. Assuming that Scopes would be convicted, the defense planned an extensive appeal leading to the U. S. Supreme Court and thus took the Dayton proceedings somewhat casually. The local jury had little trouble finding Scopes guilty, after which the defense appealed to the Tennessee Supreme Court. Although this court affirmed that the *Butler Act* was legitimate, it overturned Scopes's conviction on a technicality and urged the state to drop the matter. This decision ended all appeals and left the constitutional status of the *Butler Act* undecided.

Although the Scopes Trial is often seen as a defeat for the anti-evolution forces, it actually served to stimulate the movement. Mississippi and Arkansas joined Tennessee in adopting anti-evolution statutes, all of which remained in place until the late 1960s. After the Scopes Trial, evolutionary concepts largely disappeared from the nation's public school science curriculum, as textbook publishers ignored the topic to maintain sales. During the final third of the twentieth century, new anti-evolution campaigns emerged in the form of "creation-science" and "intelligent design" arguments, which sought to convince the public that evolution was bad science and that there existed scientific evidence for the literal interpretation of the Genesis account of creation. Among the states that attempted to compromise the teaching of evolution in this fashion were Arkansas, Arizona, California, Indiana, Kansas, Louisiana, New Mexico, and Tennessee. Although efforts to enact state legislation to mandate the inclusion of these concepts in the science curriculum failed to survive constitutional analysis, the place of evolution in American public schools remained nebulous in the early years of the twenty-first century.

See also CREATION; CREATION SCIENCE; CREATIONISM; DARWIN, CHARLES; DESIGN; EVOLUTION; FUNDAMENTALISM; INTELLIGENT DESIGN

Bibliography

Larson, Edward J. *Summer for the Gods: The Scopes Trial and America's Continuing Debate Over Science and Religion*. New York: Basic Books, 1997.

Numbers, Ronald L. *The Creationists*. New York: Knopf, 1992.

Webb, George E. *The Evolution Controversy in America*. Lexington: University Press of Kentucky, 1994.

GEORGE E. WEBB

SCRIPTURAL INTERPRETATION

The history of the relationship between scriptural interpretation and the rise of modern science is complex and convoluted. Within the so-called Abrahamic religions of Judaism, Christianity, and Islam, the relationship was intimately close from the Middle Ages to early modern era but became distant during the final decades of the twentieth century.

Key texts

When scholars in the Abrahamic traditions have addressed the relationship of science and religion, they have emphasized scriptural texts that assert God's role and activity as creator, sustainer, and governor of the universe. Key texts from the scriptures of Judaism and Christianity include the following:

- Genesis 1:1–28 31; 2:1–25; 5:1–2; 9:6
- Exodus 20:11
- 1 Samuel 2:8
- 2 Kings 19:15
- 1 Chronicles 16:26
- Nehemiah 9:6
- Job 9:8–9; 10:3, 8; 12:7–9; 26:7–13; 28:23–26; 37:16, 18; 38:4–38
- Psalms 8:3; 19:1, 4; 24:1–2; 33:6–9; 65:6; 74:16–17; 78:69; 89:11–12, 47; 90:2; 95:4–5; 96:5; 102:25; 103:22; 104:2–3, 5–6, 24, 30–31; 119:90–91; 121:2; 124:8; 136:5–9; 146:5–6; 148:5–6
- Proverbs 3:19; 8:26–29; 16:4; 22:2; 26:10; 30:4
- Ecclesiastes 3:11; 7:29; 11:5

- Isaiah 17:7; 37:16; 40:12, 26, 28; 42:5; 44:24; 45:7, 12, 18; 48:13; 51:13, 16; 66:2

- Jeremiah 5:22; 10:12–13, 16; 27:5; 31:35; 32:17; 33:2; 51:15–16, 19

- Amos 4:13; 5:8; 9:6

- Jonah 1:9

- Zechariah 12:1

- Mark 10:6; 13:19

- Acts 4:24; 7:50; 14:15; 17:24–26

- Romans 1:20; 11:36

- 1 Corinthians 8:6; 11:12

- 2 Corinthians 4:6; 5:5, 18

- Ephesians 3:9

- 1 Timothy 6:13

- Hebrews 1:1–2; 2:10; 3:4; 11:3

- Revelation 4:11; 10:6; 14:7

Key Islamic texts from the Qur'an include the following: 2:23–30, 3:190, 4:1, 6:38, 6:98, 7:189, 10:90–92, 11:7–13, 15:26, 15:28, 15:33, 16:66, 17:88, 21:30, 22:61, 25:59, 36:36, 39:6, 41:53, 42:47, 43:12, 50:38, 51:47, 54:49, 55:33, 57:6, 71:14, 76:1, 79:30, 91:7–8, 96:2.

These texts are referenced with great frequency in scriptural commentaries of the Abrahamic religions. They are characterized by their description of a single deity, who creates and maintains the universe and guides human beings in their relations with this deity and their world.

Premodern period

In many respects, the first-century Jewish theologian Philo was the first to draw a connection between the natural philosophy of the ancient world and scripture. In his *On the Creation,* Philo reflects upon God as creator of the universe, draws comparisons with Greek philosophy, and offers correctives based upon scripture. The great early Christian scriptural scholar and theologian Origen (182–251) builds on Philo in his commentary on Genesis and the first of his Christian theologies, *On First Principles.* In these works, Origen establishes the basic tendency of Christian theology to

appropriate natural philosophy while following scripture. Early in the history of Christian theology, scripture is not regarded as in conflict with scientific knowledge of the world, although some early interpreters of scripture sought to correct ancient science by rejecting the notion of the eternity of the universe.

The millennium that spanned the fourth to the fourteenth centuries brought forth an abundance of Jewish, Christian, and Muslim reflection on scripture and science. Jewish scriptural interpretation during the early part of this period was largely devoted to the refinement of its religious traditions in an effort to sustain Jewish diaspora communities. Scientific reflection was not entirely absent in Jewish theology of the period, but it does not become extensive until the appearance of Maimonides (1135–1204). In Maimonides's writings, scripture is regarded as not at odds with knowledge of the natural world, although Maimonides did believe that scripture could provide a corrective to that knowledge at crucial points. He asserts that the universe was created *ex nihilo* (from nothing); that is, the story of God's creation excludes the possibility that the universe was made of eternal or pre-existing matter. Indeed, divine action includes a relation to every individual entity rather than either detachment or panentheism. Maimonides is also remarkable for his early rejection of astrology in favor of an "astronomical" approach to the study of the universe.

The Christian theologians Athanasius (c. 290–373) in the East and Augustine (354–430) in the West offered arguments from scripture that God was the creator of all things and that therefore the universe could not be identified with God because it had a beginning. Maximus Confessor (580–662) further asserted that scripture teaches the freedom of God in creation, a view that countered the ancient metaphysical notion of the inferiority of physical matter. Instead, the dictum that God created everything by free initiative and with good intentions suggested a moral harmony between matter and spirit. The *Summa Theologica* of Thomas Aquinas (1225/26–1274) represents the pinnacle of medieval Christian reflection on the relation between scripture and science. Aquinas's major contribution to the discussion was his argument for the design of the universe. Indeed, it is his reading of God as the designer of all things, as opposed to the classical universe of eternal forms and temporal objects, that formed the basis of Aquinas's five "proofs" for God's existence.

Islam reached the height of its scientific attainments during the medieval period when enormous resources were brought to bear in support of Islamic science. During this time, the scripture was not considered incompatible with knowledge of nature, and astronomical science was considered necessary because every Muslim throughout the world was required by the Qur'an to turn toward Mecca to pray. The early development of astronomical science was necessary in order to plot a point on any horizon toward which the devoted would bow. As a result, Arabic mathematics and astronomy flourished with the likes of Abu Isa al-Mahani (c. 860–874/84); Hamid ibn Ali, the inventor of the astrolabe; and Jabir ibn Sinan al-Battani (c. 858–929). These men, probably the greatest of the Muslim astronomers, developed numerous standard astronomical formulas.

Islamic science is characterized by close attention to the Qur'an and its stress upon the correspondence between the one deity, Allah, and the uniform lawfulness of the universe. The Muslim anatomist and philosopher Averroës (also known as Ibn Rushd, 1126–1198) expressed a typical opinion when he said that the study of the natural world strengthened belief in the Qur'an. Averroës's rejection of absolute determinism and absolute free will is largely the result of his avoidance of any particular philosophical conclusion and his reliance on the religious narratives of the Qur'an. Western scholars depended on Arabic copies of ancient texts, and Averroës's commentaries on Aristotle, which interpret Aristotle according to a monotheistic scripture, greatly influenced Thomas Aquinas. Muslim science continued to advance until the fourteenth century, after which it suffered setbacks that persist into the twenty-first century. Many interpreters of culture regard this reality as rooted in the struggle of religion to come to grips with the successes of modern science.

Modern period

Christianity, Judaism, and Islam experienced different fates from the sixteenth to the final decades of the twentieth century. As the natural sciences began to receive widespread patronage from the noble and mercantile classes in the West, religious and political realities prohibited Jewish and Muslim involvement.

One of the events that marks the beginning of the modern period in science is the astronomical labors of Nicolaus Copernicus (1473–1543). His great work, *On the Revolutions of the Celestial Spheres,* published shortly before his death, established the heliocentric model of the solar system. This system was defended by Johannes Kepler (1571–1630) and Galileo Galilei (1564–1642), but was condemned by the Vatican. Galileo's motto concerning scripture has become something of a byword for how persons of faith reconcile their study of the natural world with their readings of scripture: "The intention of the Holy Spirit is to teach us how one goes to heaven, not how heaven goes." In attempting to substantiate the Copernican rejection of an Earth at rest in its celestial position, Galileo cited Proverbs 8:26, which speaks of the "hinges" of the Earth, and therefore its motion. Kepler's view regarding scripture was different and represented an early strategy of coping with the moments in interpretation when science and scripture appear to be at odds. This strategy was to define scripture as governing religious experience and moral development; as such, it was proposed that religion should simply rule its own domain and avoid the domain of science.

The Reformation of the sixteenth century, spawned by the religious writings of Martin Luther (1483–1546), Huldreich Zwingli (1484–1531), John Calvin (1509–1564), and others, established an important epistemological principle that aided the advancement of scientific method, namely the investigation of sources over against traditional authorities and practices. To the extent that scripture was regarded as the source of true religion, the Reformation encouraged a kind of experimental attitude in which it was assumed that traditions and schools of interpretation could be subjected to critical methods in the interest of advancing truth. Experimental science, which had to contend with traditional assumptions about the world within the wider culture, won a measure of courage from the developments within religion itself. Protestantism tended to be much more open to scientific advancement; in many ways it adapted to what it regarded as the necessary implications of such advancement. Examples of this would include the compatibility of the scriptural notions of creation, prophecy, miracles, and religious experience with various scientific understandings of the universe and of human nature.

In many respects, the role of scripture as primarily the source of religious experience and moral formation emerges as an ongoing resource for science, since scientists themselves are cultural beings. Indeed, this view was one of the characteristics of the transition to postmodernism in science and religion. The English philosopher of science Francis Bacon (1561–1626) in his great work *Novum Organum: Indications Respecting the Interpretation of Nature* (1620) was enamored with an analogy of two sources or "books" of human knowledge: scripture and nature. Both, according to Bacon, came from God, but they had separate, albeit related, functions in human life. Bacon believed that it was necessary for a scientist to follow Jesus' teaching to "become like a little child" before the natural world in order to be freed from the arrogant prejudices that blocked experimental thinking. A kind of humility, a first admission of ignorance, was required before observation and the recording of empirical data could serve as an authority for scientific inquiry. For Bacon, even earlier successes in science must not hold captive any future practice of science. Much of what allowed this development was the Protestant capacity for self-critique and an allowance for the separation of the domain of science from that of religion and scripture.

But these early modern attempts at reconciling science and scriptural interpretation did not produce all of the cultural changes needed for the advancement of science. Extreme skepticism was engendered by a penchant on the side of religion for "scientific proofs" for divine existence and presence in the world. From Gottfried Wilhelm Leibniz (1646–1716) to William Paley (1743–1805), numerous arguments to "prove" the existence of God were advanced on commonly accepted philosophical grounds. Unfortunately, these arguments are fraught with problems because scriptural traditions do not claim that the natural knowledge of God's existence can be cognitively derived from such "proofs." The upshot was a bifurcation of faith and science, with the latter assuming a kind of ideological status sometimes called *scientism*. Scientism during the nineteenth century tended to be positivistic and to rule out the possibility of sensible claims for the knowledge of God and, therefore, any truthfulness to religious scriptures. Fortunately, during this century, restrictions in the West toward the presence of Jews in the universities began to disappear and Jewish science achieved a great revival. Islamic scientists also made their way into major research centers during the latter part of the century.

Late modern era

The modern distancing between religion and science has meant for some a kind of fundamentalist abandonment of science for a supposedly scripture-based view of the world. So-called creationists claim that certain literal interpretations of scripture are the only permissible ones. For others, however, the preferred approach is the recognition of the respective domains of religion's interpretation of scripture and science's interpretation of nature. Since the time of Charles Darwin (1809–1882), natural science has been understood by many interpreters as compatible with the narratives of their religion's scriptures. Such approaches transcend the politically charged labels of "liberal" and "conservative" and more often reflect the kind of cultural space where scriptural interpretation is accomplished. Science does not require scripture, let alone metaphysics, to perform its work, but its work is often performed by persons religiously committed to classic religious texts and metaphysical systems. Throughout the twentieth century, proponents of scientism have had to acknowledge the limits of science and, with this acknowledgement, the persistence of religious interpretation of scripture as a guide to the lives of many scientists and a scientifically shaped world.

In many respects, the transition from modern to late modern is marked by the use of criticism as an intellectual enterprise. The modern tendency of maintaining a "critical distance" between science and religion (and its scriptures) is paralleled by the late modern tendency to maintain a "critical distance" between culture and science, whereby science is not considered to be the sole source of knowledge of the world. Although this situation could be regarded as a fragmenting of culture, it also represents attempts to resolve what the philosopher Immanuel Kant (1724–1804) called "the conflict of the faculties." The many disciplines of human inquiry possess a mutual compatibility because they are all part of the cultural project of understanding the world. Each make their own contribution and, not surprisingly, scriptural interpretation as a religious practice continues to contribute to that project.

See also AUGUSTINE; AVERROËS; CHRISTIANITY; CREATIONISM; DARWIN, CHARLES; FUNDAMENTALISM; ISLAM; JUDAISM; SCIENTISM; THOMAS AQUINAS

Bibliography

Aviezer, Nathan. *In the Beginning: Biblical Creation and Science.* Hoboken, N.J.: Ktav, 1990.

Barr, James. *Biblical Faith and Natural Theology.* Oxford and New York: Oxford University Press, 1994.

Brooke, John Hedley. *Science and Religion: Some Historical Perspectives.* Cambridge, UK: Cambridge University Press, 1991.

Brooke, John Hedley, and Cantor, Geoffrey. *Reconstructing Nature: The Engagement of Science and Religion.* Edinburgh, UK: T&T Clark, 1998.

Herzfeld, Noreen L. *In Our Image: Artificial Intelligence and the Human Spirit.* Minneapolis, Minn.: Fortress, 2002.

Helm, Jürgen, and Winkelmann, Annette, eds. *Religious Confessions and the Sciences in the Sixteenth Century.* Boston and Leiden, Netherlands: Brill, 2001.

Hooykaas, R. *Religion and the Rise of Modern Science.* Edinburgh, UK: Scottish Academic Press, 1973.

Linzey, Andrew, and Cohn-Sherbok, Dan. *After Noah: Animals and the Liberation of Theology.* London and Herndon, Va.: Mowbray, 1997.

Noll, Mark A., ed. *Princeton Theology 1812–1921: Scripture, Science, and Theological Method from Archibald Alexander to Benjamin Breckenridge Warfield.* Grand Rapids, Mich.: Baker, 2001.

Schacht, Joseph, and Bosworth, C. E., eds. *The Legacy of Islam,* 2nd edition. Oxford and New York: Oxford University Press, 1974.

KURT ANDERS RICHARDSON

SECOND LAW OF THERMODYNAMICS

See ENTROPY; THERMODYNAMICS, SECOND LAW OF

SELECTION, LEVELS OF

In the *Origin of Species* (1859), Charles Darwin introduced his theory of *natural selection,* the generally accepted mechanism for evolutionary change. More organisms are born than can survive and reproduce; there will consequently be a struggle for existence. Given naturally occurring variation, the struggle will bring on a process equivalent to a breeder's artificial selection: a *differential reproduction* leading to evolutionary change of a kind that centers on adaptation, producing contrivances like the hand and the eye. A matter of immediate interest was the level at which natural selection was supposed to operate. Does the struggle occur between individuals or between groups like species? If the latter, can adaptations benefit the group at the expense of the individual? Could one have "altruistic" adaptations where, instead of an organism selfishly serving its own ends, it sacrifices its well-being and possibilities for reproduction to the common good? Darwin himself was inclined to think not, although he did equivocate with regard to human beings. A contrary tradition was initiated by the co-discoverer of natural selection, Alfred Russel Wallace, who, as a good socialist, was convinced that selection can work for the good of the group, even if the individual suffers thereby.

Matters went essentially unresolved until the 1960s. Although some (notably R. A. Fisher) stuck to the Darwinian line, a position like Wallace's, endorsing what came to be known as *group selection,* was assumed implicitly by most evolutionists. Then a strong reaction set in, and thinking swung to a Darwinian mode. Biologists realized that the trouble with group-directed altruistic adaptations is that they are open to cheating. While the altruist is working for the good of the group at its own expense, the selfish individual is benefiting thereby, and at the same time serving itself by refusing to direct any effort to others. Selfishness will therefore win out in the struggle for existence and altruism will go extinct.

At about the same time, a number of new models based on selection for self (*individual selection*) were devised. Notable was the idea of *kin selection,* introduced by British evolutionist William Hamilton, which showed how close relatives help each other for shared biological ends.

Particularly impressive was the way in which Hamilton demonstrated how his new mechanism could account for the sterility of worker ants, bees, and wasps. These groups are exceptional in that only females have both mothers and fathers, males being born of unfertilized eggs. This leads to nonstandard genetic relationships where females are more closely related to sisters than they are to daughters. Hence, selection favors adaptations (including sterility) that motivate females to raise fertile sisters rather than fertile daughters. In so doing, one is accomplishing more to increase one's genetic representation in future generations than one would if one followed more traditional patterns of reproduction.

The Hamiltonian-type approach is often referred to as *genic selection* because ultimately it sees evolution as a matter of the sorting of the genes, the units of inheritance, and evolutionary change as a simple function of change of gene ratios. While this is true, it does not mean that the individual organism drops out of sight, for it is organisms that package genes and it is organisms that compete in the struggle for existence. For this reason, it is helpful to distinguish between genes as *replicators,* the markers of evolutionary change, and organisms as *vehicles* or *interactors,* the carriers of genes and the units that struggle for supremacy. At both levels and in both appropriate senses, one has units of evolution.

Other models similar to kin selection were devised showing how "selfish genes" can nevertheless lead to cooperative behavior between organisms. The best known is perhaps *reciprocal altruism* (something of which Darwin had an inkling) where organisms cooperate because benefits given are linked to the expectation of benefits to be received. At the same time, students of the evolution of social behavior turned to game theory to work out how organisms, mainly animals but some plants, adopt different strategies to maximize their evolutionary success. This activity is all a thriving part of the evolutionary enterprise, both theoretically and empirically. It is true that in the past a number of evolutionists have produced theories and experiments showing that, under certain circumstances, group effects within a species can swamp individual interests, but this is in no sense a return to old-fashioned group selection. It is also true that some paleontologists think that in the course of history one sees some species succeeding in systematic ways, while others do not. But such *species selection* is compatible with an individualist approach at the level of the organism. There is a richness to the evolutionary process, something that can work in many ways and at many levels.

See also ADAPTATION; ALTRUISM; EVOLUTION; FITNESS; SELFISH GENE

Bibliography

Ruse, Michael. *Darwin and Design: Science, Philosophy, and Religion.* Cambridge, Mass.: Harvard University Press, 2003.

Sober, Elliot, and Wilson, David Sloan. *Unto Others: The Evolution and Psychology of Unselfish Behavior.* Cambridge, Mass.: Harvard University Press, 1998.

Sterelny, Kim, and, Griffiths, Paul E. *Sex and Death: An Introduction to Philosophy of Biology.* Chicago: University of Chicago Press. 1999.

MICHAEL RUSE

SELF

Although it has been a subject of fascination for thousands of years, *self* is an ill-defined concept in philosophy and psychology, generally taken to refer vaguely to the "inner" being of the individual that is, at times, both the subject and object of experience. It should be seen as distinct from both *person* (the totality of an individual being) and *identity* (an individual's sense of who they are in relation to a social and physical world). When people refer to the "problem" of the self, they are, in fact, referring to a great many problems. Is there really a self at all? What sort of methodology should be used to investigate it? Does a person have one self or many selves? Where is the self located? How does the self develop? How does one self interact with another? What is broadly agreed is that the experience of self is somewhat paradoxical since the self can appear to be simultaneously unified yet fragmented, continuous yet disparate, immanent yet transcendent, apparent yet elusive, private and personal yet social. These problems, as they arise in the behavioral sciences, share a history with the world's religions. Theologians and philosophers alike have attempted to address them.

The self in psychology

In the 1890's psychologist and philosopher William James (1842–1910) proposed that the self-as-subject, the *I-self,* be differentiated from the self-as-object, the *me-self.* His model contended that the me-self, which is created from an individual's subjective interpretation of experience, could be subdivided into three components: the bodily, material self at the bottom; the social self in the middle; and the spiritual self, the extremely precious enduring dispositions and moral constitution of a person, at the top. The elusive I-self, he proposed, is an active agent that is able to shape its own destiny and is responsible for perceived continuity and the construction of the me-self.

James's differentiation of "me" and "I" remains intrinsically attractive to many theorists, but although an abundance of complex structural and systemic models of the self have been proposed, the very existence of the I-self is still frequently questioned. Empirical and theoretical psychology, however, has generally taken each individual's development of a sense of an inner self for granted.

One way of categorising models of the self is through their division into *global unidimensional models,* which emphasize a single factor such as the importance of self-esteem for the maintenance of the self, and *multidimensional models,* which implicate a network of hierarchically organized cognitive structures that collectively constitute the self. Though these two types are not strictly antithetical, there has been a dramatic shift towards hierarchical models in recent years and the self is more often discussed as a complex system rather than a unitary entity.

On these lines, the psychologist George Kelly argued that the self-system should be likened to a theory constructed by the individual, which serves to organize their relationship to the world. Some information processing models suppose that the individual's cognitive experiential organization results in the formation of *self-schemata,* which are constructs that serve both to give a sense of self and to guide and govern future behavior. Others

argue that the components of what is generally known as the self are interconnected so as to form a loosely integrated whole giving the illusion of continuity but continuing to exist as a multiplicity, each retaining the capacity for a degree of autonomous functioning—in the cognitive scientist Marvin Minsky's terms, a "society of mind." A common way of accounting for the apparent sense of an inner self, whilst remaining ambivalent about its literal existence, is to appeal to the idea of nar-ratisation—the notion that what is called a self is actually just a dynamic process of integrating a personal experiential history into a coherent unified life story. The autobiographical narrative so constructed effectively amounts to a person's unique identity, but this does not equate to some mysterious transcendent inner entity. Many have argued, however, that the demands of living in postmodern society raise certain difficulties for an individual's construction of a singular coherent identity; the essential fragmentation of the self is a common theme in postmodern thought.

Social psychology is concerned not so much with the individual representation and functioning of the self but with its genesis and development in a social context. In William James's opinion, there was not one single "social self" but, rather, a multiplicity, each of which could find expression at any one time. This idea of multiple selves that are essentially relational, situation-specific constructs arising from social encounters, is a central feature of social psychological models. In 1902 sociologist Charles Horton Cooley (1864–1929) and, subsequently in the 1920s, philosopher and social psychologist George Herbert Mead (1863–1931), developed perspectives in which an individual's social interactions in the form of linguistic exchanges (symbolic interactions) were deemed to be central to the construction of self. Indeed the theory of the social construction of the self finds its most straightforward expression in Cooley's famous concept of the "looking-glass self," the idea that an individual comes to know themselves only by assimilating the reactions of others towards oneself into a self-image. Here, the "me" and "I" components of the self are deemed to be interdependent, each continuously redefining the other. Modern empirical social psychology has identified a variety of different socially determined factors that come to bear on the development of the self, even to the extent that an individual's perceptions of especially close others may come to be integrated into their concept of themselves.

Other, psychoanalytic theories, most notably object relations theory, also emphasize the importance of the role played by an individual's relationships in the healthy development as well as the psychopathology of the self. According to object relations theorists, who rejected the Freudian psychosexual developmental model of the individual as narcissistic and pleasure seeking, the self develops as a complex matrix of representations acquired through emotionally laden experiences of oneself in relation to others.

So, different theories have collectively enhanced the knowledge of the self, but none could individually lay claim to offer a complete account. Psychoanalytic psychology, for example, has the benefit of a holistic approach to the self and the personality, but not the (alleged) fine grained, empirically verifiable explanatory power of information processing approaches. Information processing accounts, by contrast, often fail to pay adequate heed to the roles of affective psychological processes when modelling the self. Despite considerable differences of opinion over its contributory structures and processes, competing theories of the self do generally converge on a number of basic principles, such as its essential dynamism and the notion that much of the self remains unconscious, invisible to introspection. Some recent work has been directed towards further uniting apparently disparate theories of the self that have arisen in distinct psychological schools.

Non-western concepts of the self are often difficult to translate into western psychological terminology. Although the sense of self has frequently been supposed to be an innate, pan-cultural feature of the human psyche, ethnographers are agreed that what amounts to the sense of self arises from a vast array of interconnected individual-cognitive and sociocultural influences. The innateness controversy rages on, but it appears unlikely that anything as complex as the self could be determined by the genes of an individual. All this is not to say, however, that evolutionary theories of the phylogeny of the self should be discounted; the "modern" self, in as much as it is partly determined by evolved mental and physiological processes, must surely have been influenced by the pressures of natural selection.

The self in religion

Several theorists have observed that Christian theological notions of the soul are the immediate ancestors of Western philosophical and psychological notions of the self, and there is a very strong tradition of positioning knowledge of self in conversation with Christian doctrine and the knowledge of God. Contemporary analyses of this tradition such as Charles Taylor's *The Sources of the Self* (1989), which charts the genesis and phylogeny of the modern identity in Western philosophy and social thought, traces the origin of introspection back to Augustine of Hippo (354–430 C.E.), although the writings of mathematician and philosopher René Descartes (1596–1650) effectively inaugurated the form of critical self-reflection that characterises the "modern" period. Often, the theological influence on the development of thinking about self in non-Christian cultures is also readily apparent. Personal senses of self, as well as concepts of the nature and function of the self in a religious context, differ markedly between cultures. These range from those of the modern western Christian world, with their overt emphasis on individualism and personal autonomy, to those of certain cultures and other religious traditions where concepts of person and self are less explicit or even absent.

In the western world, then, the origin of the "inner self" as an inwardly focused and centered entity that is distinct from the physical body lies in the works of Augustine, who emphasized the importance of adopting a first person standpoint in the understanding of oneself, and in doing so, fundamentally changed the way that people conceived of the soul and subsequently the self. For Augustine, appreciation of the meaningful order of the world, grounded in the goodness of God, was possible only through introspection of the soul. God, as an inner light—the light of the soul—was conceived by Augustine to be the underlying principle of knowing itself.

A major strand of Christian theological thought concerning the origin and nature of the inner self can be identified in discussions that are centred upon the *imago dei,* the triune God in whose image, Christianity teaches, human beings are created. Augustine's discernment of the triadic structures of human thought, which he grounds in the being of God is a celebrated example of this type of theory, but this theme has been revived and elaborated upon many times.

Conceiving the nature of God as Trinity, some (such as Alisdair McFadyen) argue that a theory of human nature might be analogously informed. They argue that the model of the Trinity as a unique community of persons does not entail the autonomous individuality of each person nor an understanding of each person as a specific mode of relation to the other persons of the Trinity. Echoing of the *dialogical personalism* developed by the Jewish thinker Martin Buber, this understanding of the Trinity is reflected in the understanding of human persons as acquiring identity only through their relations with others, including their relationships with God. At all times an individual self is engaged in a threefold living relation with human others, with his or her environment and, through faith, with God.

In Islam, where the word *Nafs* may be equally well translated as soul or self, it is generally discussed in the context of *Hudan* (the right guidance), and the appropriate path to virtue as taught in the Qur'an. Although the Islamic concept of the soul is affected by both inner and cultural factors the notion of an essential self is less explicit than in the West, being more of a social construct made manifest through the taking of roles. In submission to Allah the self is both controlled and cultivated as part of a hierarchical cultural and religious order.

The various collections of teachings subsumed under the generic name Buddhism, by contrast, teach that the sense of an inner self (which is really not-self), as expressed in words such as "I" and "me," is a source of suffering and that only through surrendering this sense can a state of bliss really be found. All sentient beings are deemed by Buddhists to be part of a continuous cycle of birth, death, and rebirth. Nirvana, effectively the escape from this cycle, can only be achieved by a successive rooting out of all greed, hatred, confusion, and delusion from what passes as one's self. In Buddhist thought, it is by ceasing to grasp after the perceived continuity of self, and thereby accepting the present as an opportunity to develop th░ ░░░░░░ ░░rt░░s of wisdom and mindfulness that completely transcend the pro░

The self at the interface o
religion

Some psychologists and philosophers of religion have succeeded in coordinating certain aspects of their respective theories and models of the self and in many cases these theories are mutually informative. Francisco Varela, in *The Embodied Mind* (1991), for example, draws his primary inspiration for his theory of the self from *Mahayana* Buddhist teachings. However, although empirical social and cognitive psychology has attempted to quantify the impact of various religious influences on self-development, the emphasis on explanation in these models seems very different to the more interpretative, discursive theories that have arisen in theological discourse. Although not all psychological theories of the self are as antitheological as those of Sigmund Freud or some evolutionary psychologists, even those psychological models of mental health and development that accentuate the importance of an individual's perceived relationship to God portray the self in a fundamentally different light to that of explicitly religious theories. It tends to be seen as a product of innate and acquired individual and social influences rather than, as in Christian thought for example, an entity created and sustained by God, which stands in perpetual relation to God. It seems, then, that although the relationship between religious and psychological theories of the self has great historical significance, and there may be dialogue between them, their objectives, their identities and, ultimately, their raisons d'être remain distinct.

See also BUDDHISM; DESCARTES, RENÉ; EVOLUTIONARY PSYCHOLOGY; EXPERIENCE, RELIGIOUS: COGNITIVE AND NEUROPHYSIOLOGICAL ASPECTS; FREUD, SIGMUND; GOD; IMAGO DEI; ISLAM; PSYCHOLOGY; SELF-TRANSCENDENCE; SOUL

Bibliography

Ashmore, Richard D., and Jussim, Lee, eds. *Self and Identity: Fundamental Issues*. New York: Oxford University Press, 1997.

Bracken, Bruce A., ed. *Handbook of the Self-Concept*. New York: Wiley 1996.

Harré, Rom. *The Singular Self: An Introduction to the Psychology of Personhood*. London: Sage, 1998.

Kippenberg, Hans G.; Kuiper, Yme B.; and Sanders, Andy F., eds. *Concepts of Person in Religion and Thought*. Berlin and New York: Mouton de Gruyter, 1990.

Levin, Jerome D. *Theories of the Self*. London: Taylor and Francis, 1992.

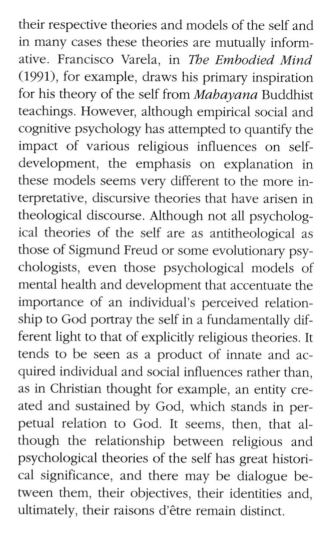

McFadyen, Alistair I. *The Call to Personhood: A Christian Theory of the Individual in Social Relationships.* Cambridge, UK: Cambridge University Press, 1990.

Miller, David L., ed. *The Individual and the Social Self: Unpublished Work of George Herbert Mead.* Chicago and London: University of Chicago Press, 1982.

Pannenberg, Wolfhart. *Anthropology in Theological Perspective,* trans. Matthew J. O'Connell. Edinburgh, UK: T&T Clark, 1985.

Proudfoot, Wayne. *God and the Self: Three Types of Philosophy of Religion.* London: Associated University Presses, 1976.

Schwöbel, Christoph, and Gunton, Colin E., eds. *Persons, Divine and Human: King's College Essays in Theological Anthropology.* Edinburgh, UK: T&T Clark, 1991.

Suls, Jerry M., ed. *Psychological Perspectives on the Self,* Vol. 4. Hillsdale, N.J.: Erlbaum, 1993.

Taylor, Charles. *Sources of the Self: The Making of the Modern Identity.* Cambridge, UK: Cambridge University Press, 1989.

Varela, Francisco J.; Thompson Evan; and Rosch, Eleanor. *The Embodied Mind: Cognitive Science and Human Experience.* Cambridge, Mass.: MIT Press, 1991.

White, Vernon. *Paying Attention to People: An Essay on Individualism and Christian Belief.* London: SPCK, 1997.

Yu, Carver T. *Being and Relation: A Theological Critique of Western Dualism and Individualism.* Edinburgh, UK: Scottish Academic Press, 1987.

LÉON TURNER
FRASER WATTS

SELFISH GENE

The term *selfish gene* was coined by Richard Dawkins (b. 1941) in his 1976 book of that name to convey the central sociobiological idea that it is reproductive success, rather than individual excellence, that determines the course of evolution. Thus "the survival of the fittest" does not really mean the survival of outstanding individuals themselves. It means the prevalence of their type in later generations through increasing numbers of descendants.

Biologists such as J. B. S. Haldane (1892–1964) had suggested this understanding of evolution as a solution to the "problem of altruism"—that is, the question how it was possible for animals often to act in ways that sacrificed their own individual interests to those of others around them. This undoubtedly happens, not only in the care of the young but in many other social activities. How had the trait developed? The answer lay in reproduction. Tendencies to act altruistically can survive and spread through a species, even if they shorten the life of their first owners, provided that those owners have first transmitted them to a sufficient number of descendants. Thus it is the genetically-determined trait rather than the individual that, in some sense, is selected and survives.

Dawkins's contribution to this approach was to dramatize it by depicting the gene involved as a kind of counter-individual—a hidden agent exploiting the organism it rides in:

> We are survival machines—robot vehicles blindly programmed to preserve the selfish molecules known as genes. . . . We are machines created by our genes. Like successful Chicago gangsters, our genes have survived, in some cases for millions of years, in a highly competitive world. This entitles us to expect certain qualities in our genes. I shall argue that a predominant quality to be expected in a gene is ruthless selfishness. . . . A gene leaps from body to body down the generations, manipulating body after body in its own way and for its own ends, abandoning a succession of bodies before they sink in senility and death. The genes are the immortals. (pp. x, 2, and 36)

This powerful image certainly conveyed the point about the importance of reproduction. But the cost in clarity has been heavy.

The dramatic picture of genes as freeloading individualists is not actually compatible with serious genetics. Genes are not fixed units at all. They are varying lengths of DNA, and they cannot take effect without cooperating in highly complex groupings. Nor, of course, are they immortal, since each gene dies with the cell that it belongs to. It is only their type that survives—just as a species survives the death of its individual members. This may not be a very interesting kind of immortality

However, the most substantial scientific question that does arise here concerns the level at which natural selection takes place. Sociobiologists resisted earlier suggestions that new developments were directly determined by the interest of the group or of the species. They rightly pointed out that, in order for inherited traits to change, there must be changes at the genetic level. Gene-selection must therefore indeed operate.

It is not, however, obvious that gene-selection excludes selection at other levels also. At the individual level, organisms are not powerless vehicles. An individual animal can influence the evolution of its species by, for example, exploring a new habitat or finding a new source of food. At the level of selection between groups, social tendencies can have considerable effect on species-survival, though in less direct ways than earlier theorists had supposed.

These scientific issues are still being discussed, although they may not have much direct relevance to the relation between science and religion. What does make the topic relevant here is Dawkins's rhetoric: His personification of genes as forces ruling helpless humans seems to involve a sort of fatalism, and his choice of the word *selfish,* instead of some neutral term such as *selectable,* to describe the part that genes play in evolution gives this fatalism a personal twist by appearing to credit these forces with a motive. This is recognizable religious imagery.

What is the point of the colorful metaphor? Readers often see in it the familiar doctrine of psychological egoism—the view that selfishness, in the literal, everyday sense of self-interest, is the sole motive determining the behavior of all organisms, including humans. This, however, cannot be right, and it is not what Dawkins is technically saying. He, like other sociobiologists, is trying to solve the problem of altruism—that is, to explain why animals often act against their own interest. Dawkins's explanation is that they are pawns, being manipulated in the interests of the genes. Yet he often writes as if he did attribute the selfishness to the organisms themselves:

> Be warned that if you wish, as I do, to build a society in which individuals cooperate generously and unselfishly towards a common good, you can expect little help from biological nature. Let us try to teach generosity and altruism, because we are born selfish. Let us understand what our own selfish genes are up to, because we may then at least have the chance to upset

their designs, something which no other species has ever aspired to. (p.3)

In this and similar passages there is a radical confusion between attributing selfishness to genes in a technical sense, as a causal property in population genetics, and using the word with its normal meaning to describe a motive attributed to individual organisms. Other sociobiologists such as Edward O. Wilson (b. 1929) also constantly slide into this ambiguity between the technical and the everyday sense of the word, though most of them use it only for organisms, not, like Dawkins, for genes.

The confusion is perhaps a natural consequence of choosing to use such a highly emotive everyday word as *selfishness* as a technical term. In any case, it seems plain that the official, scientific message of sociobiology does not actually give any kind of support to psychological egoism. As for Dawkins's alarming suggestions of fatalism, the last sentence of the passage just quoted implies that they are meant rather as melodrama than as serious determinist metaphysics.

See also ALTRUISM; DNA; EVOLUTION, BIOLOGICAL; GENETICS; NATURAL SELECTION; NATURE VERSUS NURTURE; SOCIOBIOLOGY

Bibliography

Dawkins, Richard. *The Selfish Gene*. Oxford: Oxford University Press, 1976.

Goodwin, Brian. *How the Leopard Changed His Spots: The Evolution of Complexity*. London: Weidenfeld and Nicolson, 1994.

Haldane, J.B.S. *The Causes of Evolution*. London: Harper and Brothers, 1932.

Midgley, Mary. *Evolution as a Religion: Strange Hopes and Stranger Fears*. London: Methuen, 1985.

Midgley, Mary. *Beast and Man*. Ithaca, N.Y.: Cornell University Press, 1978.

Rose, Steven. *Lifelines: Biology, Freedom, and Determinism*. London: Penguin, 1997.

Trigg, Roger. *The Shaping of Man: Philosophical Aspects of Sociobiology*. Oxford: Blackwell, 1982.

Wilson, Edward O. *Sociobiology: The New Synthesis*. Cambridge, Mass.: Harvard University Press, 1975.

Wilson, Edward O. *On Human Nature*. Cambridge, Mass.: Harvard University Press, 1978.

MARY MIDGLEY

SELF-ORGANIZATION

The term *self-organization* refers to a spontaneous emergence of order in complex processes. The idea of an emergence of order has very old roots, but its importance as a scientific concept, and concomitantly its relevance for the ongoing science and religion debate, have only recently been recognized.

History of the idea

Though the idea of self-organization is often presented as a twentieth-century revolution in science, some of its basic notions are as old as human reflection on the origin of the world's orderliness. Many cosmogonic myths narrate the struggle between chaos and cosmos, and the emergence of order out of chaos.

In ancient philosophy, Heraclitus (c. 540–480 B.C.E.), Aristotle (384–322 B.C.E.), and Lucretius (c. 96–55 B.C.E.) attempt to rationally cope with nature's self-organization. In modern times, germs of the contemporary theory of self-organization are to be found in René Descartes (1596–1650), Gottfried Wilhelm Leibniz (1646–1716), and Immanuel Kant (1724–1804), who in his *Kritik der Urteilskraft* (*Critique of Judgment,* 1787) introduced the term *self-organization.* After Kant the idea of self-organization was a focal point in the philosophy of nature of Friedrich Schelling (1775–1854) and in the metaphysics of Alfred North Whitehead (1861–1947).

In scientific discourse, the concept of self-organization was introduced in 1947 by W. Ross Ashby, who elaborated on it in the context of cybernetics and systems theory. From the 1950s on, the scientific idea of self-organization was further developed by Heinz von Foerster (order from noise); Ilya Prigogine (dissipative structures); Hermann Haken (synergetics); Humberto Maturana and Francisco Varela (autopoiesis); Manfred Eigen (hypercycles); Norman Packard, Chris Langton, and Stuart Kauffman (the edge of chaos); Per Bak (self-organized criticality); and many others.

The scientific concept

Self-organization is the process of the spontaneous emergence and maintenance of order in a complex dynamic system. The capacity for self-organization enables the system to develop or change its internal structure spontaneously and adaptively in relation to its environment. The term *spontaneous* is meant to refer to the absence of control by an external or central agent. The global ordering results from interactions between the initially independent components of the system, all of which follow their own local laws. Thus, the development of the ordered structure takes place primarily in and through the system itself.

One of the fundamental traits that distinguish self-organizing systems from systems studied in more traditional cybernetics is the absence of centralized control. The "control" of the organization is typically distributed over the entire system. Because of this distributed character, such organization tends to be robust and to resist perturbations.

The internal and distributed "control" is often effected by circular or network relations between the components. Though the laws governing the global behavior are still imperfectly understood, the complex process is known to generally involve positive feedback loops alongside the "normal" negative feedback loops (known from standard cybernetic control systems). Negative feedback works to stabilize by reducing variations; positive feedback on the other hand amplifies the variations (e.g., autocatalytic processes). The interaction between these two forms of feedback may create a nonlinear dynamics, intricately developing itself until it reaches a stable situation, an *attractor.*

An attractor is a state, or set of states, toward which the system tends to evolve, and in which, when reached, it tends to stay. If the attractor contains an infinite number of states so that the system oscillates in an a-periodic way between them, the system is said to be chaotic An isolated system usually has a single, trivial, attractor: the equilibrium state with maximum entropy ("disorder"). A self-organizing system, conversely, evolves toward an ordered state. This may be an ordered equilibrium state (e.g., in crystallization), but in typical complex self-organizing systems (such as living organisms), it will be an ordered nonequilibrium (in those systems equilibrium means "death"). Such ordering processes may seem to contradict the entropy law of thermodynamics. This, however, is not the case, either because the systems involved are not at all thermodynamical (e.g., economies), or—if thermodynamic considerations do apply—because these systems are thermodynamically open: Many of them import "order" from their environment (e.g., sunlight or food), and all of them export entropy to their environment (e.g., heat or waste).

Though self-organization eminently applies to living organisms, it is also seen in nonbiotic systems. Examples include crystallization, gravitational coalescence of cosmic dust to planets, the forming of galaxies, patterns in heated liquids, chemical compounds, living cells and organisms, the flocking of birds, evolution of life, ecosystems, brains and cognitive functions, artificial intelligence, and economies.

Relevance for religion and theology

In respect of religion, the idea of self-organization primarily presents a challenge because it suggests, as some physicists have been tempted to conclude, that the ability of cosmological, physical, chemical, and biological systems to organize themselves makes God as creator and director of the universe superfluous. Such conclusions may be premature, because many aspects of the theories about the origins of the universe and the origins of life are still highly hypothetical and uncertain; but, pointing to still existing gaps in those theories is not without danger for theology: Doing so may easily lead to a reintroduction of God as the filler of gaps. So, the real challenge for theology is to explore how the idea of God's agency with respect to the world, which is at the heart of the three monotheistic religions, can be related to the idea of nature's self-organization.

On the other hand, the idea of self-organization might give theology a chance to overcome its neglect—ever since theology's anthropological turn—of nature as a theological issue. According to modern theological insights, God is involved in human actions, mentality, morality, freedom, and finality, all of which the dominant mechanistic worldview regards as typically uncharacteristic of nature. A nearly total gap in theology between nature and God is the result. However, a number of scientists who describe certain natural processes as self-organizing, claim that the introduction of the concept of self-organization signifies a shift with respect to the accepted mechanistic paradigm, in the sense that to some extent these nonhuman processes might also be characterized in terms of finality and freedom. This new, nonmechanistic, view of nature might help theology to explore new conceptualizations of God's relationship to nature.

Apart from the question whether or not self-organization implies a paradigm shift, it is relevant to theology in another way. Studies of complex, dynamic, self-organizing systems involve themes such as order, chaos, waste and conservation, temporality, equilibrium, teleology, life and death, and consciousness, all of which also figure prominently in theological anthropology and in the religious interpretation of the world. It is therefore conceivable that the new insights arising from the study of complex, self-organizing systems may intensify and enrich the theological reflection on religiosity and religious interpretation.

See also AUTOPOIESIS; CHAOS THEORY; COMPLEXITY; EMERGENCE; ENTROPY

Bibliography

Ashby, W. Ross. "Principles of the Self-Organizing System." In *Principles of Self-Organization: Transactions of the University of Illinois Symposium on Self-Organization, June 8–9, 1961,* ed. Heinz von Foerster and George W. Zopf. Oxford: Pergamon Press, 1962.

Camazine, Scott; Deneubourg, Jean-Louis; Franks, Nigel R.; Sneyd, James; Theraulaz, Guy; and Bonabeau, Eric. *Self-Organization in Biological Systems.* Princeton, N.J., and Oxford, UK: Princeton University Press, 2001.

Capra, Fritjof. *The Web of Life: A New Scientific Understanding of Living Systems.* New York: Anchor, 1996.

Gregersen, Niels Henrik. "The Idea of Creation and the Theory of Autopoietic Processes." *Zygon* 33 (1998): 333–367.

Kauffman, Stuart A. *At Home in the Universe: The Search for Laws of Self-Organization and Complexity.* London: Penguin, 1995.

Oomen, Palmyre M. F. "Divine 'Second Order' Design and Natural Self-Organization." *Studies in Science and Theology: Yearbook of the European Society for the Study of Science and Theology* 8 (2002): 3–16.

Paslack, Rainer. *Urgeschichte der Selbstorganisation: Zur Archäologie eines wissenschaftlichen Paradigmas.* Braunschweig, Germany: Vieweg, 1991.

Schrödinger, Erwin. *What is Life?: The Physical Aspect of the Living Cell.* Cambridge, UK: Cambridge University Press, 1944.

Weber, Bruce H.; Depew, David J.; and Smith, James D., eds. *Entropy, Information, and Evolution: New Perspectives on Physical and Biological Evolution.* Cambridge, Mass.: MIT Press, 1990.

PALMYRE OOMEN

SELF-REFERENCE

The concept of *self* is ambiguous; this discussion will limit *self* to its reflexive use. This reflexive usage appears when the knower is a premise of any explanation and an active part of whatever is to be known. Such a use of *self* is epitomized in the Copenhagen epistemology of complementary or exemplified in Heisenberg's Uncertainty Principle. This argues that at a subatomic level of investigation there cannot be any objectively neutral data to be considered. All data are observer conditioned.

More generally, self-reference is the nemesis of all rationally continuous statements. Cambridge thermodynamicist A.B. Pippard spoke of this as the "invincible ignorance of science." According to him self-awareness of any mechanical system is intrinsically impossible. In *The Emperor's New Mind* (1989), physicist and mathematician Roger Penrose argues that a computer can not answer self-reflexive questions such as "What does it feel like to be a computer?"

More abstractly, consider the analysis of adjectival phrases under the rubrics of autological and heterological as to whether they do or do not have the property they denote. *Short* is autological and *abbreviated* is heterological. In this self-referential exercise a paradox arises when one asks whether heterological is itself autological or heterological. Self-referential statements raise similar paradoxical issues. Willard V. O. Quine argues that statements such as "This statement is false" are not admissible as rational propositions since it can not be determined whether they are true or false. Science accordingly tries to avoid such self-referential statements, but such avoidance can eliminate the human factor all together. Self-referential statements are at the very heart of what it means to be human, which theologians as diverse as Søren Kierkegaard and Wolfhart Pannenberg make plain. Therefore self-referential statements are central to the theology-science dialogue.

See also COPENHAGEN INTERPRETATION; HEISENBERG'S UNCERTAINTY PRINCIPLE; PARADOX; PHYSICS, QUANTUM

Bibliography

Loder, James E., and Neidhardt, W. Jim. *The Knight's Move: The Relational Logic of the Spirit in Theology and Science.* Colorado Springs, Colo.: Helmers and Howard, 1992.

Penrose, Roger. *The Emperor's New Mind: Concerning Computers, Minds, and the Laws of Physics.* New York: Oxford University Press, 1989.

JAMES E. LODER

SELF-TRANSCENDENCE

Self-transcendence is a determining feature of all mystical experience. In the context of theistic mysticism, the self is to be transcended since it is considered to block the mystic from the divine influx, and to be a barrier to the goal of union with the divine. "No-one hears [God's] word and doctrine unless he has abandoned self," wrote the medieval Christian mystic Meister Eckhart (Kelly p. 220). And, according to the Hasidic master Dov Baer of Mezritch, "One must think of oneself as nothing and forget oneself totally. . . . If one thinks of oneself as something, . . . then God cannot clothe Himself in him, for God is infinite" (Matt p. 86). In the nontheistic teaching of Buddhism, belief in the substantiality and permanence of self is considered the root of delusion and the primary obstacle to achieving Nirvana. In Buddhagosa's poetic formulation:

> For there is ill but none to feel it;
> For there is action but no doer;
> And there is peace, but no-one to enjoy it;
> A way there is, but no-one goes it.
> *(Pérez-Ramon p. 11)*

In Vedanta, similar principles apply, although the terminology can be confusing. The everyday sense of self, the personal self or *I,* is regarded as illusory. The individual mind is merely an appearance, a portal to the true self, *atman,* the ultimate source and divine essence. The spiritual goal is achieved by transcending I and recognizing the self as the true witnesses—that which eternally observes and knows via the individual human senses and mind.

Scientific approaches

The experience of losing the individual bounds of self is also a hallmark of altered states outside the religious context, for example, in cases of neuropathology, drug-induced states, and trance. Scientific approaches have frequently assumed that a common explanatory cause may bridge differences of context. Thus, for example, the loosening of self-experience observed in some cases of temporal lobe epilepsy has led to the view that self-transcendence in religious contexts may be attributable to similar disturbances in these regions of the brain. In his 1987 book *Neuropsychological Bases of God Beliefs,* neuropsychologist Michael Persinger argues that micro-seizures in the right temporal lobe trigger "God experiences," as he calls them; Persinger has demonstrated that similar experiences may be induced by artificially stimulating these brain regions. Eugene D'Aquili and Andrew Newberg propose that the experience of self-transcendence follows a loss of input to the left parietal lobe, which, they argue, normally maintains the self-other divide.

These neurological views have been complemented by biological theories based on the evolutionary value of experiences of self-transcendence. It has been repeatedly observed that such experiences have a profoundly uplifting effect on mood. As the Psalmist writes, "From the straits I called to the Lord; the Lord answered me and set me in an expansive place" (Ps. 118:5). The biological argument holds that such positive shifts in mood aid survival value. Accordingly, self-transcendent experiences have adaptive value and the genes responsible for brain systems likely to engender them have been selected into the gene pool.

These biological and neurological approaches may be criticized for their reductionist slant, which fails to credit the claims of mystics and others that self-transcendence brings about a "higher" state. "Higher" in this context implies, first, access to a richer source of knowledge and, second, contact—or even union—with a realm distinct in metaphysical terms from the worldly reality.

The approach of cognitive psychology offers an understanding of the gnostic element here, for the self-system may be seen to limit the mental representation of knowledge. Thoughts and perceptions that enter consciousness are predicated on extensive preconscious processing of information, which is characterized by the absence of any reference to self. This preconscious processing includes a considerably wider breadth of information than that which finally enters consciousness. Becoming conscious is effectively a process of limiting the possibilities of meaning that were opened up preconsciously. The passage of information from preconscious to conscious is characterized both by this limitation of diverse meanings and by the integration of content with the cognitive representation of self. In this sense, the self can be understood as a limiting factor in the organization of the mind. The relevance of this to issues of self-transcendence lies in the suggestion that mystical practices curtailing the sense of self effectively prolong the preconscious stage. The mystic becomes aware of preconscious information processing, which appears "richer" than normal consciousness on account of the wider realm of meaning it supports.

This cognitive view of self as a kind of master referencing system for the mental representation of information accords with the mystics' own testimony. "On the knowing and feeling of self hangs the knowing and feeling of all creatures," states the *Cloud of Unknowing,* a sixth-century Christian contemplative text (Underhill p. 179). It is, of course, the "knowing and feeling of self" that the text urges the contemplative to transcend.

Conclusion

Cognitive science, as we have seen, can suggest a basis for the "higher" knowledge claimed via self-transcendence: The mental representation of self habitually locks the person into conventional ways of perceiving and thinking, and its dissolution opens the way to fresh and creative contact with ideas and objects. What, however, of the second meaning of "higher" noted earlier, namely contact with a metaphysically separate realm? This aspect of self-transcendence stretches the bounds of science since science is classically tied to our spatiotemporal realm. Nevertheless, an increasing number of psychologists argue that a broader view of science that will incorporate subjective experience within its remit is needed, especially because no current scientific procedures are able to disclose the ontology of consciousness. Along such lines, the reality of higher realms may be demonstrable through the kind of hypothesis-testing that is central to all science. Are there any real effects reported by those who follow practices promoting self-transcendence, as taught in the major mystical traditions? If, as most studies suggest, the answer is "yes," then serious consideration needs to be given to the higher sphere that practitioners claim to experience. As William James famously noted, "that which produces effects within another reality must be termed a reality itself" (p. 491).

See also EXPERIENCE, RELIGIOUS: COGNITIVE AND
NEUROPHYSIOLOGICAL ASPECTS; MYSTICISM;
NEUROSCIENCES; PSYCHOLOGY; PSYCHOLOGY OF
RELIGION; SELF; SOUL

Bibliography

Andresen, Jensine, and Forman, Robert K. C., eds. *Cognitive Models and Spiritual Maps: Interdisciplinary Explorations of Religious Experience*. Thorverten, UK: Imprint Academic, 2000.

D'Aquili, Eugene G., and Newberg, Andrew B. *The Mystical Mind: Probing the Biology of Religious Experience*. Minneapolis, Minn.: Fortress Press, 1999.

Harman, Willis, and Clark, Jane. *New Metaphysical Foundations of Modern Science*. Sausalito, Calif.: Institute of Noetic Sciences, 1994.

Hick, John. "Mystical Experience as Cognition." In *Understanding Mysticism,* ed. Richard Woods. New York: Image Books, 1980.

Hunt, Harry T. "A Cognitive Psychology of Mystical and Altered-State Experience." *Perceptual and Motor Skills* 58 (1984): 467–513.

James, William. *The Varieties of Religious Experience: A Study in Human Nature* (1902). London: Collins, 1960.

Kelley, Carl F. *Meister Ekhardt on Divine Knowledge*. New Haven, Conn.: Yale University Press, 1977.

Matt, Daniel C. "*Ayin*: The Concept of Nothingness in Jewish Mysticism." In *Essential Papers on Kabbalah,* ed. Lawrence Fine. New York: New York University Press, 1995.

Pérez-Ramon, Joaquín. *Self and Non-self in Early Buddhism*. The Hague, Paris, and New York: Mouton, 1980.

Persinger, Michael. *Neuropsychological Bases of God Beliefs*. New York: Praeger, 1987.

Torrance, Robert M. *The Spiritual Quest: Transcendence in Myth, Religion, and Science*. Berkeley: University of California Press, 1994.

Underhill, Evelyn, ed. *The Cloud of Unknowing*, 5th edition. London: John M. Watkins, 1950.

Wilber, Ken. *Integral Psychology: Consciousness, Spirit, Psychology, Therapy*. Boston: Shambhala, 2000.

BRIAN L. LANCASTER

SEMIOTICS

Semiotics is the study of signs and signification. Its subject matter includes the processes involved in both the production and interpretation of signs, as well as the classification of signs into various types and categories. The term itself has Greek roots (*semeiotike*) and a complex history of usage. Although it has become the word most commonly used to designate this area of study, ironically, it was employed by neither of the two great theorists who most decisively shaped modern semiotics. The American philosopher Charles S. Peirce (1839–1914) preferred *semiotic* (parallel to terms like logic and rhetoric) as a label for the study of the doctrine of signs, or frequently *semeiotic* to indicate its derivation from the Greek. And the French structuralist Ferdinand de Saussure (1857–1913) conceived of language as a particular system of signs, linguistics itself as being one part of the comprehensive science of signs that he called *semiology*.

Semiotics has sometimes been understood as a specific discipline, with its own method and determinate subject matter. In this case, the semiotician will attend most directly to the basic structure of the sign relation, the conditions of possibility for anything functioning as a sign of anything else. Here semiotics is closely related to philosophy (especially to inquiries in formal logic) and to theoretical linguistics. More typically, however, semiotics has been portrayed as a complex, interdisciplinary field of study, drawing not only upon philosophy and linguistics, but also with vital links to literary and communication studies, hermeneutics, the history and theory of art, anthropology, sociology, psychology, and even biology and the natural sciences.

In the earliest usage of the term, *semiotics* referred to a branch of ancient Greek medicine, the identification of physical symptoms for the purpose of making diagnostic inferences. During the same period, Greek philosophers were laying some of the theoretical foundations for the development of western semiotics with their analyses of the nature of signs, language, and meaning; especially important in this regard were the logical investigations of Aristotle (384–322 B.C.E.) and of the Stoics. In late antiquity, Augustine of Hippo (354–430 C.E.) developed what some scholars regard as the first systematic theory of semiotics in his treatises *De magistro* (The Teacher) and *De doctrina christiana* (On Christine doctrine). Augustine drew upon earlier Stoic deliberations, but generated new insight in an account that treated both nonverbal and verbal signs. His theory was essentially communicative, addressing not only the relation between signs and what they signify, but also exploring how signified meanings are conceived or brought to awareness in an interpreter's mind.

Medieval semiotics was heavily indebted to both the Aristotelian and Augustinian legacies. As it had with Augustine, semiotics took on a theological significance for the scholastics. A coherent doctrine of signs was essential for understanding the nature and efficacy of those special symbols of divine grace known as sacraments. At the same time, it was characteristic of the medieval outlook that the entire universe was perceived as signifying the divine will, just as any created effect is an index of its cause. The "book of nature" as well as the book of Scripture was a potentially fertile source of divine revelation, a general perspective that would serve as a stimulus to inquiry in the natural sciences as well as in theology.

Even while scholastic philosophy was on the decline elsewhere in Europe, in Spain and Portugal there were important advances in semiotics late in the medieval period and beyond. Here the writings of Peter Fonseca (1528–99) and John Poinsot (1589–1664) are particularly notable for their anticipation of modern developments. It was the British philosopher, John Locke (1632–1704), however, who first utilized the Greek term *semeiotike* to refer to that part of philosophy that deals with the "doctrine of signs." Its purpose is to explore questions about the nature of signs, their role in human understanding and in the communication of knowledge to others.

It was probably from Locke that Peirce borrowed the term when he reintroduced it into philosophical discourse late in the nineteenth century. But Peirce's pioneering work in semiotics was most clearly indebted to Aristotle and the scholastics, as well as to certain discoveries in modern logical theory. Peirce conceived of all of logic as semiotics. As such, it is a formal rather than an empirical science, concerned with what must be or would be true about signs in any and all cases. He developed a complex system and terminology for the classification of signs. The trichotomy of *icon* (a sign that signifies its object by resemblance), *index* (by a causal relation) and *symbol* (by virtue of some habit or rule) is the most well known, widely adopted component of that elaborate

scheme. For Peirce, the proper object of study in semiotics was not the sign but rather *semiosis,* the entire process by means of which a sign stands for something to someone, a process schematized as the relationship among *sign-object-interpretant.* The realm of possible semiosis is unlimited. Peirce argued that there is no separate class of things that can be called "signs" since potentially anything can function as a sign. All thinking is in signs. Persons are themselves complex symbols. The universe, he claimed, is "perfused with signs," the rationale for his description of it as "God's great poem."

Independently but almost simultaneously with Peirce, Saussure was conducting his own semiotic inquiries. Saussure conceived of meaning not as the property of signs viewed as isolated units, but as something that they possess by virtue of their relationship to other signs in a complex system. Meaning is always contrast of meaning, the value of a sign being determined by comparison with other signs in the system. Each sign represents an indissoluble unity of perceived *signifier* and meaning *signified,* so that Saussure's dyadic model of semiosis differs from Peirce's essentially triadic account.

These two dominant strands of thought in modern semiotic began to intersect late in the twentieth century as poststructuralist thinkers, steeped in the Saussurean tradition, began increasingly to drawn upon Peircean concepts and arguments. At the same time, the potentially enormous significance of semiotic theory for theology and religious studies still remains to be assessed. Peirce's contemporary, Josiah Royce (1855–1916) had begun to adapt some of Peirce's ideas for the purpose of developing his own theosemiotic perspective, in his late work, *The Problem of Christianity* (1913). Peirce remains a rich source of inspiration for any future work in theosemiotic, as do the medieval philosophers whom he studied so carefully, thinkers for whom the religious importance of semiotic theory was paramount. While semiotic historiographers have focused their attention on a narrative that links ancient Greek with modern western thought, future inquiry will require a broadened purview. The resonance of certain Buddhist ideas, for example, with aspects both of poststructuralist thought and of Peirce's philosophy, has been observed by some scholars. This suggests that a Buddhist contribution to semiotics (typically neglected, perhaps, because of a perceived Buddhist suspicion of the religious efficacy of words and images) still needs to be evaluated.

See also AUGUSTINE; BIOSEMIOTICS; LANGUAGE

Bibliography

Aristotle. *The Complete Works of Aristotle: The Revised Oxford Translation,* ed. Jonathan Barnes. Princeton, N.J.: Princeton University Press, 1997.

Augustine, Aurelieus. *Augustine de Doctrina Christiana,* ed. R. P. H. Green. Oxford: Oxford University Press, 1996.

Deely, John. *Introducing Semiotic: Its History and Doctrine.* Bloomington: Indiana University Press, 1982.

Eco, Umberto. *A Theory of Semiotics.* Bloomington: Indiana University Press, 1979.

Peirce, Charles S. *Collected Papers of Charles Sanders Peirce,* eds. Charles Hartshorne, Paul Weiss, and Arthur Burks. Cambridge, Mass.: Harvard University Press, 1935–1958.

Peirce, Charles S. *Semiotic and Significs: The Correspondence Between Charles S. Peirce and Victoria Lady Welby,* ed. Charles Hardwick. Bloomington: Indiana University Press, 1977.

Poinsot, John. *Tractatus de Signis: The Semiotic of John Poinsot,* ed. John Deely. Berkeley: University of California Press, 1985.

Royce, Josiah. *The Problem of Christianity* (1913). Chicago: University of Chicago Press, 1968.

Saussure, Ferdinand de. *Course in General Linguistics,* trans. Wade Baskin. New York: McGraw-Hill, 1966.

MICHAEL L. RAPOSA

SHINTO

Shinto is a practice of religious rites based on the Japanese polytheistic idea of *kami* (deity). The word *Shintō* literally means "Way of Kami." Scholars of Shinto often maintain that it is the indigenous religion of Japan. Certainly Shinto has no obvious foreign origin, although there have been Korean and Chinese influences in the development of Shinto.

Institutional Shinto

Jinja Shinto (Shrine Shinto) is the institutional form of Shinto. *Jinja Honchō* (the Association of Shinto Shrines) in Tokyo is the administrating office for about eighty-thousand Shinto shrines in Japan. *Ise Jingū* (the Grand Shrine of Ise) in Ise, Mie Prefecture, which enshrines *Amaterasu Ōmikami* (the Sun Goddess), is considered to be the most sacred Shinto shrine. The emperor of Japan is considered to be the divine descendant of *Amaterasu Ōmikami* and the highest Shinto priest. The emperor's most important religious duty is to pray to the *kami* for the prosperity of Japan, the happiness of the Japanese people, and peace in the world.

Shinto has no holy scriptures in the strict sense, but the mythologies collected in Japanese classics such as *Kojiki* (the *Record of Ancient Matters*), compiled in 712, and *Nihonshoki* (also known as *Nihongi,* the *Chronicles of Japan*), compiled in 720, are regarded as important texts. In many cases, the mythologies have political implications to justify the rule of the emperor, but they also have cosmological implications.

General phenomenology of Shinto

Shinto is one of the most widely practiced religions in Japan; for centuries the Japanese people have been practicing Shinto alongside Buddhism. Although there are some cases of syncretism, mostly a clear distinction is made between Shinto and Buddhism. Generally, Shinto concerns happiness and prosperity in this world, whereas Buddhism, for the Japanese, relates to the peace of deceased souls.

The grounds of a Shinto shrine are usually marked by a grove of tall evergreen trees surrounding a gateway called a *torii.* In the main building of the shrine, a *shintai* (divine object), which is supposed to bear the spirit of a particular *kami,* is enshrined. Typically, a *shintai* is an ancient-style mirror, which is contained in a special case. No one is allowed to view the *shintai* directly. With few exception, there are no images or statues of *kami.*

Most Japanese go to a Shinto shrine on certain occasions, often on New Year's Day, to pray for the *kami*'s blessings. According to tradition, the prayer first washes his or her hands and mouth at a fountain located near the gateway. Then the prayer proceeds to the front of the main building, casts a few coins into an offertory box, rings the bells, bows twice, claps his or her hands twice, and bows one more time. The whole procedure takes only a few minutes.

A number of rites and one major festival are held annually at each Shinto shrine. In a Shinto festival, priests first solemnly offer prayers and foods such as rice and *sake* (rice wine) to the *kami,* thanking the *kami* and asking for the *kami*'s blessings. Dances and music are then performed for the *kami* and the people to enjoy together. The highlight of the festival is when portable shrines or floats are energetically paraded through the parish, usually carried by male parishioners. Many stalls that sell snacks or goods may be set up on or near the shrine grounds on the day of the festival.

A special ritual called *jichinsai* (Earth-pacifying ritual) is almost always performed by Shinto priests when construction begins on a new building or facility. It is believed that, without such a ritual, accidents may happen because the deities or spirits that dwell on the construction site become angry.

Characteristics of Shinto

Scholars of Shinto often point out that Shinto has no dogma, although some characteristics of Shinto have continued relatively unchanged during its long history. Muraoka Tsunetsugu (1884–1946) was one of the first scholars to outline the characteristics of Shinto thought. Stimulated and informed by Muraoka's studies, historian Delmer Brown reconsidered and reformulated the Japanese cultural paradigms. The following characteristics of Shinto are largely based on Brown, with a few revisions.

Vitalism. The scholar Motoori Norinaga (1730–1801) once defined *kami* as whatever seems strikingly impressive, possesses the quality of excellence, or inspires a feeling of awe. Certainly Shinto includes an animistic view of nature, but Shinto has a more distinctive characteristic. The *kami* enshrined in a Shinto shrine varies from a deity that appears in the mythologies in *Kojiki* or *Nihonshoki* to the spirit of a historical figure such as an outstanding emperor, feudal lord, or scholar. However, the *kami* is always believed to have mysterious power to create, enrich, prolong, or renew any form of life.

In other words, what the *kami* symbolizes is vitality, productivity, or fertility in this world. Shinto vitalism has roots in agricultural rites that may date back to the third or fourth centuries B.C.E. Even in modern times, people pray to *kami*

for worldly happiness, prosperity, success, safety, or health.

Ritualism. In Shinto tradition, performing and participating in rituals has been given greater emphasis than believing and confessing a certain creed. Although theological treatises of Shinto were written as early as the thirteenth century, no established creed or orthodox dogma ever developed. It is more likely that the articulation of principles was intentionally eschewed than that Shinto failed to establish creed or dogma. Some rituals, such as the *Niinamesai* (Feast of New Rice Crops), which is performed by the emperor himself, are considered to be so sacred that the entire procedure and even the name of the *kami* involved are kept secret.

According to surveys, only a small percentage of Japanese confess that they believe in Shinto, but the majority of them visit a Shinto shrine on New Year's Day. Such data provoke some scholars to maintain that Shinto is a cultural custom rather than a religion.

However, State Shinto is an exceptional case. From 1871 to 1945, Shinto was the Rite of State, also called State Shinto. Toward the end of World War II, the sacredness and invincibility of Japan as the nation of *kami,* was so strongly believed that State Shinto became fanatical, leading many Japanese soldiers to suicidal attacks. Yasukuni Shrine in Tokyo enshrines the spirits of the soldiers who died for Japan and the emperor, not as souls of the dead but as *kami* (i.e., deities that have power to give vitality).

Particularism. Shinto is a national religion practiced only by the Japanese, including Japanese immigrants in other countries. With few exceptions, Shinto has had no interest in overseas missions or in universal principles or values that are considered valid for all human beings. Scholars of Shinto tend to emphasize the "uniqueness" of Shinto rather than its universality. Each *kami* enshrined in a local shrine is supposed to concern only the people in the local community. This particularism also originates in Shinto's development from agricultural rites focusing on the sacredness of the particular water source of each local community. Nonetheless, when Japan annexed Korea in the early twentieth century, the Japanese government built Shinto shrines in Korea and forced Korean people to worship Shinto *kami.*

Shinto and science

From ancient times, arts, sciences, and technologies, including philosophy, mathematics, astronomy, astrology, medicine, and alchemy, were continuously imported into Japan from China and Korea, and studied and developed in Japan in various ways. However, neither Shinto nor Japan gave birth to anything similar to modern science. In fact, the characteristics of Shinto discussed above, especially the animistic view of nature and the avoidance of establishing universal principles, may have stood in the way of the development of a modern scientific methodology or view of nature.

On the other hand, the Japanese studied and learned modern science earnestly and quickly once it was introduced. Some Japanese scholars started to study modern science when Shogun Tokugawa Yoshimune permitted the importation of nonreligious Western books in 1720. After the Meiji Restoration of 1868, the study of science was accelerated. Kōgakuryō (College of Science and Technology) was established in Tokyo in 1873 and was merged with Tokyo University in 1886. By the end of the twentieth century, Japan had become a world leader in science and technology. In that process, Shinto did not serve as an obstacle. Once science became associated with success and prosperity in this world, its study and application could be encouraged. Neither Copernican heliocentrism nor the Darwinian theory of evolution raised significant controversy in Japan, probably because the human being has no special status as the crown of creation in Shinto or Buddhism. In Shinto the human being is simply a harmonious part of nature.

The animistic element of Shinto that respects the vitality immanent in nature should certainly have the potential to make a positive contribution to human efforts to preserve the natural environment. Interdisciplinary conferences involving scholars of Shinto are occasionally held, although some feel that the politically conservative tendency of Shinto may work contrary to the efforts of environmentalism.

Bibliography

Asquith, Pamela J., and Kalland, Arne, eds. *Japanese Images of Nature: Cultural Perspectives*. Richmond, Va.: Curzon, 1997.

Aston, William George, tr. *Nihongi, Chronicles of Japan from the Earliest Times to A. D. 697*. Rutland, Vt. and Tokyo: C. E. Tuttle, 1972.

Brown, Delmer M., ed. *The Cambridge History of Japan, Volume I: Ancient Japan*. Cambridge, U.K.: Cambridge University Press, 1993.

Hardacre, Helen. *Shinto and the State, 1868-1988*. Princeton, N. J.: Princeton University Press, 1989.

Kitagawa, Joseph M. *Religion in Japanese History*. New York: Columbia University Press, 1966.

Nakayama, Shigeru; Swain, David L.; Yagi, Eri, eds. *Science and Society in Modern Japan: Selected Historical Sources*. Tokyo: University of Tokyo Press, 1974.

Nelson, John K. *A Year in the Life of a Shinto Shrine*. Seattle and London: University of Washington Press, 1996.

Ono, Sokyo. *Shinto: The Kami Way*. Rutland, Vt. and Tokyo: C. E. Tuttle, 1962.

Philippi, Donald L., tr. *Kojiki*. Princeton, N. J.: Princeton University Press, 1969.

Philippi, Donald L., tr. *Norito: A Translation of the Ancient Japanese Ritual Prayers*. Princeton, N. J.: Princeton University Press, 1990.

MASAKAZU HARA

SIN

Sin is the condition or act by which a human person produces evil. Evil is suffering produced by either sin, disease, or accident. Suffering that leads to death and loss of relationship to God is the ultimate evil. The classic Christian list of seven deadly sins includes pride, covetousness, lust, envy, gluttony, anger, and sloth. Islam, led by the Qur'an, sees sin in terms of pride and opposition to God. Iblis or Satan provided the model for human sinning when he refused to obey God's command to prostrate himself before Adam. In an ancient Hindu-Buddhist myth of the fall a primordial disembodied mind living in the golden age descends into a physical body where desire, lust, passion, and covetousness prevail. Others follow, souls taking on flesh. Greed leads to stealing and violence, and the human soul becomes trapped in a physical world of temporal temptation from which it longs to escape to eternity.

Phenomenologically, evil is first experienced biologically as suffering. The most primitive awareness of sin takes the form of defilement, of external contamination deriving from physical contact with what is profane. Rituals of cleansing, usually with water, become the liturgical means for ridding the sinner of defilement. When this becomes internalized, defilement is associated with physical passions welling up from within, with carnal desires that tempt by threatening to overwhelm the rational mind by chaotic passion. Fleshly desires become identified with the lower nature, while mind or soul or spirit becomes identified with the higher nature. The higher nature is where the human will is lodged, and the highest form of sin is a freely willed act of evil.

The Hebrew and Christian scriptures advance no theory of sin, yet examples of sinning abound. Sins corrupt a person's whole heart, and total corruption requires total transformation or renewal by an act of divine grace. Sin applies to the individual heart as well as to a people or nation, warranting transformation of all things into a new creation.

Twentieth-century theologians and psychologists tended to associate the origin of sin with anxiety, anxiety understood existentially as feeling threatened by loss, threatened by dissolution into nonbeing. Death is nonbeing to a human, and the threat of death triggers in the human psyche a panic impulse to steal what it can from the imagined life force. In the moral sphere the pursuit of virtue becomes sinful, as those fleeing anxiety engage in self-justification and scapegoating. To define oneself as virtuous simultaneously requires assigning responsibility for the evil in the world to someone else, usually an enemy; this provides justification for decimating the enemy through gossip, lawsuits, war, or genocide.

Some religious theories associated with sin have been challenged during the era of modern science. The biblical story of Adam and Eve in paradise falling into sin, for example, has long been considered a historical event in Judaism, Christianity, and Islam, though interpreted quite differently. With the rise of evolutionary theory and deep time, the idea of a single pair of human progenitors has lost scientific credibility. No sinless paradise would be possible according to evolutionary theory because natural selection and survival of the fittest would necessarily apply at the point of origin. This

dilemma has left theologians with two options. One is to deny acceptance to evolutionary theory, the path taken by scientific creationists in American Christianity and fundamentalist Muslims in Turkey. The other is to admit evolutionary theory and deny historicity to the Garden of Eden, the path followed by liberal Protestant Christian and Jewish commentators who see the Adam and Eve story as a myth describing everyday human activity.

A second challenge is indirect, the challenge to human free will from biological reductionism in genetics. During the era of the Human Genome Project, public belief in the determining power of DNA grew, and molecular biologists began to assign genes for not only physical traits but also predispositions to behavior. Antisocial behavior such as a propensity toward alcoholism, aggression, and violence were postulated as genetic in origin, as was homosexuality. Sociobiologists added the idea of the *selfish gene*, the principle that genes employ human bodies and human culture to insure their own replication through reproduction— their version of survival of the fittest. The fittest are those genes that bring their hosts to reproductive age. This idea allegedly explains why families and clans protect their own kin and are willing to prosecute war or even genocide against others. Moral behavior and religious practices became explainable as the result of genetic expression. Some scientists began to claim they had produced a biological explanation for original sin in the sense of an inherited propensity to survive to reproductive age even if it means perpetrating violence against genetic competitors.

The naturalistic question arises here for theologians. If theological interpretations of sin are compossible with genetic or other forms of biological determinism, one needs to ask: If something is natural is it good? If a doctrine of creation asserts that what exists presently in nature is due to God's will, then biological impulses even toward aggressive behavior must become normative. This is a theological version of what philosophers call the naturalistic fallacy: *What is is what ought to be.* However, much of traditional spirituality in Asia as well as the West has regarded human biological makeup as the source of misleading desire and dangerous passion; biological determinism would only increase religious resolve to pit the power of the spirit over the power of the flesh.

See also EVIL AND SUFFERING; FALL; GENETIC DETERMINISM; SELFISH GENE; SOCIOBIOLOGY

Bibliography

Medina, John. *The Genetic Inferno: Inside the Seven Deadly Sins*. New York: Cambridge University Press, 2000.

O'Flaherty, Wendy Doniger. *The Origins of Evil in Hindu Mythology*. Berkeley and Los Angeles: University of California Press, 1976.

Peters, Ted. *Sin: Radical Evil in Soul and Society*. Grand Rapids, Mich.: Eerdmans, 1994.

Ricoeur, Paul. *Symbolism of Evil*, trans. Emerson Buchanan. Boston, Mass.: Beacon, 1967.

Suchocki, Marjorie Hewitt. *The Fall to Violence: Original Sin in Relational Theology*. New York: Continuum, 1994.

Tillich, Paul. *Systematic Theology*. Chicago: University of Chicago Press, 1951–1963.

Wright, Robert. *The Moral Animal*. New York: Pantheon, 1994.

TED PETERS

SINGULARITY

Singularities occur at the center of black holes. Because the General Theory of Relativity is a theory of space-time as well as of gravity, the consequences of the unbounded energy densities predicted by that theory at the end of gravitational collapse and at the start of the universe are catastrophic, for they imply an end to space-time itself. The possible history of an observer or particle simply comes to an end; physics breaks down, and space-time ceases to exist. It is difficult even to begin talking about this situation, for even the word *exist* ceases to have meaning. It is unclear if quantum gravity theories will avoid this implication.

An unresolved problem pertaining to singularities is whether gravitational collapse can lead to a *naked singularity,* that is, one that will be visible from far away and so can influence events in the outside world. The contrary of this possibility is that a naked singularity can only lead to a black hole, where a singularity occurs but is hidden from the outside world by an event horizon.

See also BLACK HOLE; COSMOLOGY, PHYSICAL ASPECTS; GRAVITATION; RELATIVITY, GENERAL THEORY OF; SPACE AND TIME

GEORGE F. R. ELLIS

SKYHOOKS

The metaphor of skyhooks, typically used pejoratively, is a label for explanations that appeal to powers transcending nature, a supernatural beyond the secular order. The idea is similar to *deus ex machina* interventions in ancient Greek plays, where a god was brought in from above by stage machinery to resolve a complicated plot, often unconvincingly. In his 1995 book, *Darwin's Dangerous Idea,* Daniel C. Dennett argues that Darwin replaced "skyhooks" with "cranes," mechanistic forces building up over evolutionary history, not mind-like designing, which is only a resulting appearance. However, with genetics, a cybernetic model of DNA that encodes an evolutionary increase of information suggests a more cognitive account, indifferent to whether the novel information appears from above or below. The fundamental issue is whether naturalistic explanations are complete. This especially the case for those explanations featuring the emergence or superposition of genetic complexity with escalating cognitive powers, eventuating in human minds.

See also EVOLUTION; GENETIC DETERMINISM

Bibliography

Dennett, Daniel C. "The Tools for R and D: Skyhooks or Cranes?" In *Darwin's Dangerous Idea: Evolution and the Meanings of Life.* New York: Touchstone, 1995.

HOLMES ROLSTON, III

SOCIOBIOLOGY

In the *Origin of Species* (1859), Charles Darwin argued that the main mechanism of evolutionary change is a process he called *natural selection.* More organisms are born than can survive and reproduce, bringing on a struggle for existence. Given naturally occurring variation, there will be a differential reproduction—some reproduce, some do not—akin to the artificial selection practiced by animal and plant breeders, with the end result of permanent change. In a drought, animals able to do with less water are "fitter" than those that need to drink more. Moreover, organisms will be adapted: they will show the organic contrivances highlighted by those natural theologians intent on showing that there is a designing God. Examples include the hand and the eye and such like. Darwin applied this mechanism to many different fields of biology, including paleontology, embryology, systematics, and biogeography. Behavior was included in Darwin's theory, for he saw that what an organism *does* is as crucial in the struggle for existence as what an organism *is*. There is little point in having the physique of Tarzan if you have the mind of a monk.

The evolution of sociobiology

Darwin was particularly fascinated by certain social behavior, especially that of ants, bees, and wasps (hymenoptera), where an organism sacrifices itself for the good of the group. It seems prima facie that such behavior is at odds with the kinds of self-centered acts that would lead to individual success in the struggle for existence. Darwin understood how the sterility of a worker ant, for example, might be transmitted through fertile nest members—the domestic world had shown how one can select vicariously, as it were, for characteristics in animals that will not themselves breed—but he could not see how sterility itself would come into being. Darwin was convinced that all selection must be for the individual, not the group; sociality—worker sterility, in particular—was a major challenge. Although Darwin concluded that one can regard the colony (of ants and so forth) as a kind of superorganism on which selection can operate as a whole, he never really resolved the problem of sociality.

For a number of reasons, the study of the evolution of social behavior lagged after Darwin. First, the rise of the social sciences with their interests in behavior discouraged biologists from addressing the subject. Social scientists tended to experiment on rats and mice, to generalize, and then to conclude that transpecific differences were irrelevant. Social scientists also tended to work in artificial situations and so were generally not interested in natural behavior, and unable to recognize it when it appeared. Second, in the first half of the twentieth century, the racial doctrines of the Third Reich convinced many that the study of social behavior from a biological perspective would lead to claims about the innate behaviors of humans, with consequent belittling of the worth of those not in one's own group. Although some protested that such fears should not tar all biological studies on behavior, the damage was done and remained for many years after the Second World War. Most importantly, no one really knew how to move theoretically beyond Darwin so that social scientists could study social behavior while staying true to the principles of natural selection. The social sciences needed new approaches that eschewed group selection, allowing evolutionists to dissect nature and drag forth its secrets.

Kin selection. Breakthroughs came in the 1960s. A number of models were devised that allowed scientists to study social behavior in animals, while staying true to the individualist or "selfish" nature of selection. Notable was the theory of *kin selection,* devised by the English biologist William Hamilton, who showed that close relatives have a biological interest in helping each other because by doing so they indirectly support the success of their own units of heredity, their own genes. Hamilton applied this thinking to the ants, bees, and wasps, pointing out that these animals have a peculiar breeding system, where only females have fathers (males being born from unfertilized eggs). This means that sisters are more closely related to each other than normal. In the usual case (e.g., humans), mothers and daughters are 50 percent related, as are sisters. In the hymenopteran case, a female gets the same genetic input as her sister from their shared father and then 50 percent input from their shared mother. Thus sisters are 50 percent and one-half 50 percent (75%) related, whereas mothers and daughters are just 50 percent related. It is in a worker's reproductive interests to raise fertile sisters rather than fertile daughters—an activity that is aided rather than hindered by the worker's own sterility. There is no need to treat the colony as but one unit for one can see individual interests being played out in this, the most integrated and harmonious of social situation.

Reciprocal altruism. Other models were devised, including one that Darwin himself sensed, even if he did not fully articulate it. *Reciprocal altruism* works on the principle that when an organism gives help, it is entitled to receive help when needed. Reciprocal altruism can work even among non-relatives, or—at the extreme—across species. Certain fish are major predators, but they tolerate other types of fish that swim directly into their mouths and pick out harmful bacteria and fungi on their gums. The predators practice dental hygiene and the cleaners get a good meal because the larger fish does not swallow the smaller fish in its mouth. Everyone benefits.

Evolutionary equilibrium. Evolutionists turned to game theory in cases where participants adopt various strategies to succeed in the light of the fact that other players (in biological terms, other members of the species) are also trying to succeed. In *The Selfish Gene* (1976), a provocative popularization of this theory, British biologist Richard Dawkins showed how certain evolutionary situations achieve equilibrium, or reveal what he called "Evolutionary Stable Strategies," when no one member of the group can achieve more than limited benefits, given the conflicting interests of the group. To take one of Dawkins's examples, consider a group with two kinds of members. Some members of the group are "hawks," who in any potential conflict situation are aggressive and will fight if need be. Others in the group are "doves," who always run if a fight looms. One might assume that the hawks would dominate and that selection would produce a population without any doves. But this is not so. A hawk's encounter with another hawk always leads to a fight, which may end with one hawk injured or, dead. Doves, however, never get beaten up because they run. So, on average, there is a cost to being a hawk. But doves cannot dominate either, because, on average, there is a cost to being a dove. Hawks always win confrontations between a hawk and a dove. The birds of the group therefore end up in a balanced if uncomfortable midpoint, with neither hawks nor doves able to increase their representation at the expense of the other.

Armed with these theories, naturalists and experimentalists turned to the larger world to determine if they could understand the social behavior not just of insects and fish, but of more complex animals like birds and mammals. The widest range of topics was covered. Notable was a study (led by Cambridge biologist Tim Clutton Brock) of red deer on an island off the coast of Scotland that showed how male deers strive to capture harems and will compete (or not) as it proves to be in their interest, and how female deers, which seem to be controlled by males, will in turn employ tricks and strategies to improve their reproductive options and results. A female wants her offspring, particularly her sons, sired by a male who will pas on his superior breeding qualities. Another study (conducted by Cambridge biologist Nicholas Davies) looked at the dunnocks (hedge sparrows), a bird that has the widest of breeding patterns—*monogamy, polygyny* (one male, several females), *polyandry* (one female, several males), and something primly referred to as *polyandryny* (group sex, with several males and several females). By doing DNA fingerprinting on the birds and their offspring, researchers could trace relationships, demonstrating just how much behavior was controlled by reproductive interests. This study revealed that dunnocks do not raise chicks with whom they have little reason to think they have real blood ties. Moreover, a dominant male (an "alpha") will tend to spend more time chick rearing and to have more offspring than a lesser male (a "beta"). Another study in Holland (reported by ethologist Franz de Waal) looked at relationships within a troop of chimpanzees—how males needed female help to dominate a situation, and how different alliances would be formed according to different interests. Two weaker males might prefer to gang up to defeat a stronger male, rather than simply acting individually.

Edward O. Wilson. Research went ahead with speed and enthusiasm, and before long, the science of the evolution of social behavior—now called *sociobiology*—was ready to take its proper place in the Darwinian family, along with paleontology and the other subjects. But controversy loomed. Darwin had wanted to apply his ideas to humans, and in the *The Descent of Man* (1874) he did just that, as did Darwinian scientists who came later, in particular, Harvard entomologist Edward O. Wilson. In a major overview of the field, *Sociobiology: The New Synthesis (1975),* and later in a work addressing the human species, *On Human Nature (1978),* Wilson argued that nearly every aspect of human life and nature is a function of biology, or, more accurately, the genes as fashioned by natural selection. Sexual differences, family structures, religion, warfare, language, and much more, are the end result of natural selection working on the units of heredity. Even homosexuality could be biologically caused, as gay and lesbian members of the family aid close relatives, like sterile mammalian workers at the nest. Moreover, argued Wilson, while humans may be able to change some things, biology will be resistant and, in many respects, people are locked into being what they are. Utopian plans for change would be counterproductive.

Early objections to sociobiology

As expected, there were many objections to the new field of sociobiology. Social scientists became tense because they felt that biologists were poaching on their domain. Rather than accepting biology as a complement or an aid to social science, they saw it as a threat and feared sociology would vanish and sociobiology (social-group division) would take its place. Feminists abhorred what they considered a direct attack on their ideology, which held sexual differences and family structures to be purely cultural rather than biological constructions. Darwin was painted as the archetypical Victorian male chauvinist, and sociobiology was seen as an excuse for the status quo that oppresses women and children. Marxists, and this included some eminent biologists, felt that a biological approach was a travesty of the truth, because it pretended that evolution and natural selection had accomplished what was truly a function and result of economic deprivation. Their ideological ancestor, Friedrich Engels, had inveighed against a reductionist approach to understanding, and human sociobiology was the worst of all possible offenders.

Interestingly, the one group that might have been expected to explode—those members of the Christian community interested seriously in science—was far more receptive. Creationists, of course, would have nothing to do with any evolutionary science, and they fully enjoyed the controversy that pitted evolutionist against evolutionist. More moderate Christian thinkers reacted in a different way. Although they hardly welcomed human sociobiology with unalloyed joy, they could see that the new science was a serious approach to serious problems, and responded in this spirit. Even Christians drawn to feminism and Marxism realized that there was more to life than simple matters of culture, tradition, and economics. God, they argued, is not a social constructivist.

Later interpretations

By the dawn of the twenty-first century, much of the dust had settled. There is certainly no question that some of the early enthusiasts for sociobiology let their imaginations outstrip the evidence, filling in gaps with creative intelligence. But some of the most interesting work has come from evolutionists who have actually turned biology on its head. Sarah Hardy, for instance, has argued that female humans conceal ovulation, thereby ensuring that males have to stay around and participate in child rearing—if they do not, they cannot be sure of paternity. In other words, in good feminist fashion, she argues that the evolutionary scales are balanced, and may, if anything, be tipped in favor of women. Others have argued that sociobiology underlies the unity of the human community, thus belying fears of racism. People can, of course, interpret biology and form prejudices as they will, but there is no reason for thinking that biology supports or contains such prejudices.

In many other ways, human sociobiology transcends the parody portrayed by the critics. Typical of modern sociobiological research (often now hidden under less flamboyant and provocative names like *human behavioral ecology* or *evolutionary psychology*) is a careful study of homicide by the Canadian researchers Martin Daly and Margo Wilson. They have shown that murder falls into stable patterns, which lend themselves to a sociobiological interpretation. For example, the killing of children by parents (other than infanticide, which follows its own rules) is almost always perpetrated by step-fathers rather than biological fathers. This is a pattern very much in line with the rest of the animal world, where it is well-documented that males moving in on a new female will attack her already-existing young, so that their own new offspring get more attention. Paradoxically, when Daly and Wilson began their study, they could find no firm evidence against which to test their hypotheses. Authorities thought it prejudicial to reconstituted families to collect statistics on whether or not family violence involved step-parents or biological parents. It was only when Daly and Wilson insisted on the collection of the data, that the patterns emerged.

Implications for religion and philosophy

Sociobiology suggests much to the philosopher or the theologian interested in the deeper questions about human nature. Traditional approaches to evolution and ethics—so-called social Darwinism—argue that moral codes follow from the need to cherish and promote the evolutionary process. Thus, British philosopher Herbert Spencer endorsed laissez-faire economics in the name of evolution, seeing it as part of the struggle for existence in the human world. Just as in nature the weak fall because they are inadequate, so in society the weak fall because they are inadequate; this, argued Spencer and his fellows, is nature's way and to try to prevent it is to lead to decay and degeneration. Most sociobiologists avoid arguments of this type. Following more sensitive thinkers, like Darwin's "bulldog" Thomas Henry Huxley, sociobiologists refuse to identify the "evolved" with the "good." They see that although evolution can produce the worthwhile, evolution can also produce the absolutely horrible. Although Daly and Wilson think that child killing may be biologically motivated, they stress that it is not moral in any sense. Their work indeed is intended to throw light on the problem, so that people might change or control such behavior. Male lions and lemmings may kill the young of other males, but this is no reason for humans to do likewise.

There are, however, other ways to tackle issues of morality, while still bringing sociobiology to bear. First, one might argue, as many do, that humans are social animals in the extreme, and as such need mechanisms to get on with other humans. If humans did not have adaptations to protect against disease—as native Tasmanians did not—the human species would soon die out. The same is true of behavioral and motivational adaptations. By nature people are selfish—that is a direct consequence of the struggle for existence— but this selfishness, untamed and unmodified, would lead to disaster in social situations. People would quarrel and fight nonstop and be unable to work together. So they need special adaptations to overcome this counterproductive consequence of natural selection. But what could these adaptations be? Humans are too complex simply to have social sentiments hardwired in, like ants. Apart from anything else, simple hardwiring gives no room for reflection and regrouping when things go wrong or when facing new or unexpected situations. Humans need something more subtle than the simple rules of social behavior followed by the hymenoptera. Here, argue sociobiologists, is the place for a moral sense, something that humans have innately (that is, put in place by selection and backed by the genes) that allows them to meet social demands and to work together with other humans. People have a sense of moral obligation that they *ought* to help others (and equally a sense of moral obligation that when they are in need, others *ought* to help them). It is something that aids people in social situations, and at the same time is obviously an instrument with sufficient subtlety and flexibility to allow people to adapt as situations and environments change. In other words, biologists of human social behavior argue that ethics has been put in place by human biology to make people good cooperators. Ethics is an adaptation.

The atheistic interpretation. What implications does this discussion have for the foundations of ethics (what philosophers call *metaethics*)? If ethics, the human sense of right and wrong, is an adaptation, is it thereby no more than a subjective sentiment, on a par with a liking for certain foods? The answer depends on one's theological commitments. Atheists and skeptics will probably conclude that there are no foundations, that ethics is simply an epiphenomenon of the genes, with no more ultimate meaning than any other adaptation like eyes or teeth. However, the tendency toward ethical behavior is not simply a subjective sentiment like a fondness for ice-cream. For a start, it has to be universally shared by other humans (except perhaps psychopaths), otherwise it would not function. Moreover, subjective emotion or not, it has to have an illusion of objectivity—of a foundation—otherwise it would simply collapse, as people decided to cheat and look after themselves alone. A conscience is essentially a part of the moral sense, even if (especially if) it is just an adaptation like everything else. But ultimately, the nonbeliever thinks that there is nothing to ethics but a naturalistic explanation of where it came from and why it has the hold on people that it does.

The Christian interpretation. What if one is a Christian or a member of any other theistic religion, however? Can this rather bleak philosophy take on a different, more hopeful and fulfilling hue? If one is a believer, one can (and must) surely interpret the situation as God's way of instilling an ethical sense in humankind. After all, the believer has to agree that God has instilled an ethical sense, and if one is an evolutionist then surely the sociobiological scenario is as plausible a scenario as any other. In fact, the Christian—certainly the Christian who takes seriously the teaching of Thomas Aquinas—knows this already. Natural law is something imposed upon us by the way that God has created humans. Human sexuality is intimately bound up with the fact that (in the first place) there are two sexes, and that to fulfill this sexuality people have the various emotions and organs that they do. Moral dictates follow from the nature of this creation. Promiscuity, for instance, is immoral because it is a violation of the natural—that is, God-made and God-ordained—bonds of erotic love that can and should exist between two people exclusively. For the theist who accepts sociobiology, ethics is part of creation, and the emotions and reasons that constitute it are very much part of the God-made natural order. Hence, inasmuch as one's moral sense (and the awareness to which it leads) is something natural, it is something to be cherished and obeyed and respected by God's creatures.

Sociobiology and original sin. But what about original sin? No one who has lived through even part of the past century can be insensitive to this issue, and those who were wont to downplay its significance in theology are now surely in the minority. How else does one—how else does the Christian—explain the evils of national socialism and all of the other vile movements of the past hundred years? The idea that humans are in some sense tainted—not wholly bad but with a dark side to their natures—is pressing on the nonbeliever and obligatory for those who think that Jesus was the Christ, the Son of God who died on the Cross for the sins of humans. The traditional position, that of Augustine of Hippo, is that the sins of Adam and Eve are transmitted to us all through sexual intercourse—people inherit their faults. No evolutionist can take this literally—indeed, it is unlikely that Augustine, who was sensitive to the development of knowledge and who had full awareness of the need to interpret the Bible allegorically, would now interpret the Adam and Eve story literally. He too would feel a need for revision.

A sociobiological approach shows a way of updating the belief in original sin—a way that takes modern science seriously and yet in no sense

denies or belittles the significance of such sin. Sociobiology starts with the fact that humans are destined to be selfish animals—that is the way of natural selection. Group selection is no longer a viable mechanism, and all must be interpreted in the light of advantage to the individual. If people were not selfish—if they did not take for ourselves—then they would have become extinct long ago. But at the same time, sociobiology stresses that humans are social animals that need to get on together. So humans evolved ethics. But humans are not locked in blindly, like ants. They have moral sentiments, and though they may not have much choice about the moral sentiments—a fact that no one, other than existentialists at their most extreme, has ever denied—they can decide whether or not to obey the sentiments, as it pleases them. And sometimes it does please people, and sometimes it does not. Sometimes people continue in their selfish ways even though others would suffer, and sometimes they listen to conscience and do the right thing—sometimes indeed they do not even have to listen to conscience before doing the right thing. In other words, humans are an ambivalent mixture of good and ill—sometimes doing the kind and charitable thing, and sometimes failing in their obligations and duties. And humans are this way in their deepest nature, something they inherit rather than create anew. And that surely is precisely the Christian position on original sin. People are tainted. They cannot escape this. It is inherited as part of human nature. But humans have the abilities to do the right thing, to act against this side to their nature. Sometimes they do, and sometimes—all too often—they do not.

Freedom and determinism. Finally, one must address the question of freedom and determinism. It is an absolutely crucial part of Christian, as well as Jewish and Muslim, belief that people are made in the image of God, and therefore have the freedom to choose between good and ill. God may know what people will do, but God does not constrain them in what they will do. Each person's faults are his or her own responsibility. Can such a conception of freedom be reconciled with human sociobiology, a discipline that some critics complain is committed to genetic determinism? Those who dislike human sociobiology argue that sociobiologists portray humans as marionettes on the strings of the genes, with no more power of choosing right or wrong than the puppets Punch and

Judy have of living in domestic harmony. People are as clockwork, set up and simply set to run. The wife beater resorts to violence because he is male and that is the way of men. The child whines because it is a child and that is the way of children. The racist has genes for xenophobia and is no more at fault that the person with Down syndrome who cannot pass an intelligence test. Biology is destiny, and that is the end to freedom.

A more thoughtful approach, however, shows that Christian conceptions of freedom and sociobiological conceptions of determinism are not necessarily contradictory and can indeed be complementary. On the one hand, the Christian recognizes that freedom does not mean stepping outside of the laws of nature, for in that direction lies randomness or madness. Augustine, again, saw that true freedom means working according to human nature. God is free and yet cannot do ill. It is against God's nature to do ill. Likewise, people are free, but what they do is part of their nature. That is why God knows what will happen even though God does not control or will it. People are free to kill their children and yet most could no more do so than they could jump over the Atlantic Ocean. They are free to refrain from boasting, and yet could no more do so than they could climb Mount Everest. Conversely, for all the talk about determinism, the sociobiologist recognizes, in fact insists on, a dimension of human freedom. Ants are hardwired to do what they do. They have no choice. But humans are not hardwired to do what they do. They do have a choice; they must have a choice if they are to function as the complex social animals they have evolved into. Humans may be part of the causal nexus, but they have a dimension of freedom denied to rocks or lower animals and plants. If ants are like cheap rockets shot off and then, once fired, beyond further control, humans are like expensive rockets with feed-back mechanisms enabling them to respond to changes in the target. In short, the Christian recognizes that human freedom takes place within rules and restraints, and the sociobiologist recognizes that human determinism is open to dimensions of choice and alternative action. Why then should not the Christian and the sociobiologist work together to find a meeting point on these issues, harmony rather than conflict? Far greater gaps exist between Christians and their critics than between sociobiologists and their critics.

Conclusion

Other issues could be raised, and some are still far from resolution. If evolutionary theory is true, then presumably human minds—in line with everything else biological—are part of gradual development in time. Yet Christians have tended to see minds (and souls) as a sharply demarcated phenomenon—either humans have them or they do not. Animals do not have souls; humans, all humans, do. There is a brittle break in nature at this point. This is certainly a place where some compromise is necessary if consistency is to be achieved. There is surely much work and serious rethinking still needed on the connection (if there is one) between the human mind, either the Christian human mind or the sociobiological human mind, and the teachings about the nature and existence of the immortal soul. But these and other problems are challenges, not road blocks. Certainly the larger Christian community was correct in its intuitions when, on the arrival of human sociobiology, it took a position of welcome, albeit guarded welcome, rather than of hostility and rejection. All human understanding is grist for the theological mill, and sociobiology is no exception.

See also BEHAVIORAL GENETICS; DARWIN, CHARLES; DETERMINISM; DNA; EUGENICS; EVOLUTION, BIOCULTURAL; EVOLUTION, BIOLOGICAL; FREEDOM; GENETIC DETERMINISM; GENETICS; MEMES; MUTATION; NATURE VERSUS NURTURE; SELFISH GENE; SIN

Bibliography

Caplan, Arthur L., ed. *The Sociobiology Debate: Readings on Ethical and Scientific Issues.* New York: Harper and Row, 1978.

Clutton-Brock, Timothy H.; Guiness, Fiona E.; and Albon, Steve D. *Red Deer: Behaviour and Ecology of the Two Sexes.* Chicago: University of Chicago Press, 1982.

Daly, Martin, and Wilson, Margo. *Homicide.* New York: De Gruyter, 1988.

Darwin, Charles. *The Origin of Species* (1859). New York: Bantam Classic, 1999.

Darwin, Charles. *The Descent of Man* (1871). Amherst, N.Y.: Prometheus, 1997.

Davies, Nicholas B. *Dunnock Behaviour and Social Evolution.* Oxford: Oxford University Press, 1992.

Dawkins, Richard. *The Selfish Gene.* Oxford: Oxford University Press, 1976.

Degler, Carl N. *In Search of Human Nature: The Decline and Revival of Darwinism in American Social Thought.* New York: Oxford University Press, 1991.

DeWaal, Franz. *Chimpanzee Politics: Power and Sex Among Apes.* London: Cape, 1982.

Hrdy, Sarah Blaffer. *The Woman That Never Evolved.* Cambridge, Mass.: Harvard University Press, 1981.

Kitcher, Philip. *Vaulting Ambition: Sociobiology and the Quest for Human Nature.* Cambridge, Mass.: MIT Press, 1985.

Ruse, Michael. *Sociobiology: Sense or Nonsense?* 2nd edition. Dordrecht, Netherlands: Reidel, 1985.

Ruse, Michael. *Taking Darwin Seriously: A Naturalistic Approach to Philosophy.* 2nd edition. Amherst, NY: Prometheus, 1988.

Ruse, Michael. *Can a Darwinian be a Christian? The Relationship between Science and Religion.* Cambridge, UK: Cambridge University Press, 2001.

Ruse, Michael. *The Evolution Wars: A Guide to the Controversies.* Santa Barbara, Calif.: ABC-CLIO, 2001.

Wilson, Edward O. *On Human Nature.* Cambridge, Mass.: Harvard University Press, 1978.

Wilson, Edward O. *Sociobiology: The New Synthesis.* Cambridge, Mass.: Harvard University Press, 1975.

MICHAEL RUSE

SOCIOLOGY

Although it may be argued that all the sciences can trace their roots in some measure or other to religion inasmuch as religion dominated institutional scholarship well into the nineteenth century, sociology is unique in that its formal origin was actually cast in the context of a new putatively religious movement. The term *sociology* was coined by Auguste Comte in his *Cours de philosophie positive* (1830–1842); for Comte *la sociologie* was nothing less than the capstone of the new religion of positivism, replacing older theological or philosophical principles for social organization with those of science. Sociologists were to be nothing less than the "high priests" of this new moral order. The coining of a term does not a science make, however, and the fact that "sociology" received relatively quick and widespread acceptance among diverse constituencies suggests that Comte created an acceptable label for an intellectual movement that was

already in process in the nineteenth century—namely, the two-fold premise that human social behavior could be studied with the same investigative canons that are applied to other "natural" phenomena and that human social behavior was irreducible to psychological or biophysical explanations.

Although the explicitly religious expression given to sociology went with Comte to his grave, virtually all of the leading lights of early sociology devoted considerable attention to aspects of religious life—what religion is, how it works, how it came into being, why it persists or recedes. These questions were among the most burning that early sociologists confronted. Karl Marx, Émile Durkheim, Max Weber, Georg Simmel, Herbert Spencer, and others whose work spanned the transition from the nineteenth to the early twentieth centuries tried to comprehend the role of religion within the larger sociocultural setting that makes human existence possible. Each realized that religion was a uniquely human experience, without any analog in the animal world, that, in the past at least, seemed to have had a controlling effect on the way people lived.

These early sociologists provided different images of religion, raising different kinds of questions. Through these images, however, runs a single theme—religion and social change. Marx throughout his work saw religion as a significant part of structural systems of oppression. Durkheim in his crucial work *The Elementary Forms of the Religious Life,* published in 1912 at the culmination of his career, saw religion maintaining social order or equilibrium. Weber, in a brilliant series of essays known as *The Protestant Ethic and the Spirit of Capitalism* (originally published serially in German from 1904 to 1905, and issued in English as a single volume in 1930), saw religion as a vehicle for enabling social change.

Sociology in America: the early years

Although the roots of sociology are certainly European, the discipline came to fullest flower in the United States. Its course was by no means singular. The first book to use the word in its title was the *Treatise on Sociology* (1854) by the apologist for slavery Henry Hughes, who with George Fitzhugh and Stephen Pearl Andrews attempted to formulate an American sociology according to a peculiar reading of Comte that would hardly be recognizable by anyone in the field today. The Confederate loss of the American Civil War and Hughes's death in it largely ended this line of development. Of much more sustained influence were the writings of Herbert Spencer, and it was William Graham Sumner, a Spencerian, who taught the first course in sociology ever offered in the United States at Yale in 1876. Sumner, who was ordained within the Episcopal Church (though he apparently did not officiate once at Yale), was an enormously popular professor: "no one was supposed to have 'done' Yale as a gentleman should," Albion Small recorded in 1916, "without having taken at least one course with 'Billy' Sumner" (p. 732).

A further influence was that of Christian sociology, an American variant of British Christian socialism. Explicitly introduced by J. H. W. Stuckenberg's *Christian Sociology* (1880), the Christian sociology movement experienced a groundswell of interest in the last two decades of the nineteenth century, particularly through the Chautauqua movement and "summer schools" at Oberlin College in Ohio and Hartford Seminary in Connecticut. Christian sociology might well have become the dominant mode in America society had it not been for a series of circumstances, ironically arising out of this very movement, that led to Albion Small establishing the first free-standing department of sociology in the United States at the University of Chicago in 1893.

Brought to Chicago by Chautauqua-inspired, Rockefeller-funded William Rainey Harper, Small walked a series of tightropes to shape a distinctive American sociology. First, he courted Lester Frank Ward, termed by Samuel Chugerman in his 1939 biography "the American Aristotle," in many ways the first American sociologist in his own right, who only late in his life received a university connection (at Brown University in Rhode Island). Ward was important to Small because Ward offered a Comtean alternative to the proslavery apologists that at the same time moved away from Sumner's exposition of Spencer's evolutionism—although there were, in fact, connections between Ward and Spencer through the Unitarian theologian M. J. Savage. Second, in what may well have been his most important single institutional step, Small founded the *American Journal of Sociology* in 1895, which became his personal implement for the operational definition of sociology in America and the invention of its history. Third, Small simultaneously courted and distanced himself from Christian sociology by enlisting the liberal University of Chicago theologian Shailer Matthews to write a series of articles in the first issues of this new journal, which effectively redefined Christian sociology to exclude the positions of the most ardent advocates of Christian sociology. Fourth, he built an empirical sociological style that came to define American sociology for the first half of the twentieth century: sociology of the Chicago School.

In addition to a large collection of volumes dealing with a variety of issues generated by the burgeoning urban life of Chicago, the Chicago School also initiated a distinct American theoretical approach, most generally known as *symbolic interactionism,* through the work particularly of George Herbert Mead, William Isaac Thomas, and Charles Horton Cooley. Although symbolic interactionism has become a diversified cluster of approaches, associated with universities where its different proponents have settled, the perspective continues to find its roots in the work of these scholars and has been revivified in social constructionist or situationalist theories among contemporary sociologists.

American sociology: tradition and transitions

By the end of World War II, American sociology dominated the profession throughout the world. In many respects, American sociology *was* sociology. World War I wreaked havoc among European sociologists. A number of the most promising young French sociologists were killed in the war, and Durkheim, Simmel, and Weber died of natural causes within three years of each other at the end of the war. The Great Depression, followed by the next war and the Nazi pogroms of the Jews, largely devastated the European intellectual currents most sympathetic to sociological scholarship. Some of those scholars managed to escape to the United States from the ravages of fascism and became part of the movement toward American dominance of the field.

During this period, American sociology sought to distance itself further not merely from religion, but from applied concerns in general. The social conditions of the depression followed by the exigencies of war made glib social pronouncements vacuous, while increasing the demand for "hard data" upon which to devise and implement programs for change. The depression and World War II served to underwrite empiricism, as various funding agencies poured money into research.

Though not necessarily in agreement themselves, figures such as Harry Elmer Barnes, Luther L. Bernard, F. Stuart Chapin, William Fielding Ogburn, and especially George Lundberg, who answered his rhetorical soteriological query *Can Science Save Us?* (1947) with unfettered assurance, nevertheless produced a more rigorously empirical discipline, with little use for higher-order analyses. Under Samuel Stouffer, a multivolume *American Soldier* series beginning in 1949 was produced, innovations were made in content analysis through captured enemy documents, and Paul Lazarsfeld led studies at Columbia, a historic center of sociological empiricism, on the effects on public opinion of radio propaganda.

Small died in 1926, and his mantle at Chicago fell to Robert E. Park. Although Park is arguably more distinguished than Small in his lasting intellectual contributions, times had changed sufficiently—in part a testimony to the success of Small's enterprise—so that a single institution could not expect to exercise the kind of disciplinary hegemony that Small had managed to effect at the turn of the century. The final sign of the dehegemonization of the Chicago School was the establishment of the *American Sociological Review* as the "official journal" of the American Sociological Society (now the American Sociological Association, hence ASA) in 1935. The *American Journal of Sociology* continues to be published, and vies with the *American Sociological Review* in various ranking systems for the "most important" in the profession.

The Chicago School was by no means out of touch with the profession, however, and in the 1930s brought a young, European-educated Harvard professor named Talcott Parsons to discuss the role of theory in research. Later, Chicago would bring Parsons's sometime coauthor Edward Shils to its faculty. Revisioning the field and in so doing founding Harvard's Department of Social Relations, Parsons's functionalism, a unique attempt to merge Durkheim and Weber, came to dominate American sociology for the larger part of two decades, reaching its quintessence in Kingsley Davis's triumphalist presidential address to the ASA in 1959: "The Myth of Functional Analysis as a Special Method in Sociology and Anthropology." Moreover, a friendship that grew between Parsons's former student Robert K. Merton and Paul Lazarsfeld as they both served on the Columbia faculty (1954) did much to heal the rift between empirical and theoretical sociological styles.

In that process, Talcott Parsons—particularly, but certainly not only, as the translator of the Protestant ethic essays—also "brought religion back in" as a field for sociological inquiry. But because he did it in the context of an attempt to synthesize Durkheim and Weber, who had far more differences than commonalities, he created an odd construction of religion that focused on a particular historical mode of religious organization that delegitimated religion as an independent variable. The outcome came to be articulated under the rubric of *secularization theory,* though as this ideology was recrafted it turned from something largely positive in Parsons's specific use to something negative, particularly at the hands of popular essayist Will Herberg.

Contemporary theory

Although Parsonian functionalism remained the primary mode of sociological analysis into the early 1960s, it was increasingly challenged by neo-Marxist sociologies. Columbia sociologist C. Wright Mills—who, ironically, was the other major American importer of Weber—and German sociologist Ralf Dahrendorf became two exemplars of the new styles of analysis. Mills was strident and politically active; Dahrendorf was a more dispassionate exemplar of leftist theory. The succeeding decades brought diverse elaborations of alternative themes in the work of such figures as Pierre Bourdieu, Anthony Giddens, and Immanuel Wallerstein. Because the reaction against Parsons's functionalism had Marxist leanings, sociology again distanced itself from religion. This breach was to some extent restored by the emergence of Latin American liberation theologies, which used Marxist categories for Christian ends.

Far more significant to the field as a whole, however, was the collapse of the Soviet system beginning in 1989 and the role of religious actors on the global sociopolitical scene as early as 1979. It could be argued that sociology at the beginning of the twenty-first century is in a state of theoretical fragmentation and fermentation, as no single paradigm exercises disciplinary hegemony, and critiques of "grand narratives" based on postmodernist understandings make disciplinary consensus difficult to achieve. As an alternative to postmodernist nihilism, however, globalization theory, as evidenced, for example, in the work of Roland Robertson, offers itself as a viable construct for integrating diverse social phenomena and expressions. Considering the world (or globe) as the unit of analysis, globalization theory takes some of its cues from Parsons in its differentiation between the universal and the particular as a major axis for understanding social action, but it draws toward conflict theory inasmuch as it recognizes the importance of particularistic universalisms and universalistic particularities as dynamics of destabilization and reintegration of social systems. By recognizing that in the high-technology multinational capitalism that characterizes late-modern society all social and cultural forms are potentially interrelated to all others, globalization theory allows for the full interplay of all institutional sectors, including religion, within the explanatory structure of social action. Reaching back, then, into the early American sociology of W. I. Thomas, which Parsons himself intimated in an essay in his 1977 *Social Systems and the Evolution of Action Theory* (p. 48), is the basis of Parson's own "pattern variables" approach within social theory; globalization reinvigorates the study of religion as a category of human action precisely because of its effects within the global system—religion is real because it is real in its effects. As a macro form of Thomas's situationalism, globalization theory achieves what Durkheim attempted to do in removing truth questions from the study of social phenomena (including religion), but could not accomplish using a functionalist definition of social institutions.

Sociology of religion

Because of the intimate relationship between the founding of sociology and its concern with investigating questions of religion, the sociology of religion was among the earliest of the field's subdisciplines, yet, in the United States especially, was among the last to be institutionalized formally in the sectional substructure of the ASA—though it is now among the largest. In most respects, the course of development of the sociology of religion reflects issues and strategies of the larger discipline on the one hand, and general social issues on the other. Especially after the 1950s, leadership from general sociology permeated the sociology of religion and vice versa. For example, J. Milton Yinger wrote crucial texts for the field in the 1960s and 1970s, and was subsequently elected president of

the ASA. Similarly, Talcott Parsons was among the founders and one of the first presidents of the Society for the Scientific Study of Religion (as well as a president of the ASA). In other cases, sociologists of religion were among the first to challenge the diffident scientism of the late 1930s and 1940s. Catholic sociologist Paul Hanly Furfey's critique of Lundberg's *Can Science Save Us?* remains a classic in general theory. And it is in the Catholic sociology movement of the late 1930s that the Association for the Sociology of Religion finds its roots.

The 1980s began to see an important shift in sociology of religion approaches in the United States, characterized by what R. Stephen Warner has termed a "new paradigm." The new paradigm particularly shifted away from the secularization model that had dominated sociology from its earliest days and came to emphasize religion as more than either epiphenomenon or residue. In his presidential address to the Southern Sociological Society in 1987, Jeffrey K. Hadden led a direct assault on the core principles of the secularization model. Currently, the new paradigm is most actively pursued through the "supply side" or "rational choice" modeling of a group of scholars whose perspective and conclusions are most fully articulated in Rodney Stark and Roger Finke's *Acts of Faith* (2001), but that rest upon the premise that religious decisions and action patterns are undertaken by people using the same kinds of processes, social or psychological, as characterize all other forms of decision making and action pattern formation—a view that draws heavily upon the work of contemporary Chicago economics professor Gary Becker.

Sociology of knowledge

The sociology of science has usually been treated as a major theme within the sociology of knowledge, which has had close ties with the sociology of religion. Max Weber, for example, tends to use the terms *secularization* and *intellectualization* interchangeably. Secularization refers primarily to a change in epistemological frames; in other words, theological or religious categories no longer provide the major frame of analysis through which everyday life experiences are understood. To the larger debate on the nature of science, Weber also contributed the widely cited essay "Science as a Vocation" ("*Wissenschaft als Beruf*," perhaps more accurately translated "Scholarship as a Calling," delivered in 1917, published in 1919, and translated into English in 1946). This essay specifically identified detached academic investigation with the Lutheran concept of vocation or calling, ending (as does the Protestant ethic series) with a biblical quote and a prophetic call.

Weber also indirectly influenced the sociology of science through the work of Robert K. Merton, whose Ph.D. thesis, published as *Science, Technology, and Society in Seventeenth-Century England* (1938) used the style of Weber's Protestant ethic thesis to argue for a relationship between Protestantism and the rise of modern science (now known as the *Merton thesis*). Other major contributions within the sociology of knowledge include Karl Mannheim's *Ideology and Utopia* (1936) and Antonio Gramsci's *Prison Notebooks* (written between 1926 and 1937), which is particularly important for Gramsci's treatment of hegemony. Although not strictly sociology, Thomas Kuhn's *Structure of Scientific Revolutions* (1962) must be considered a crucial work for any subsequent sociology of knowledge. In addition to these theoretical contributions, there has also been an enormous volume of empirical work on the demographic, educational, sociocultural, and other background characteristics of people who become scientists, and to a lesser extent to the processes by which scientific communication takes place.

See also LIBERATION THEOLOGY

Bibliography

Bannister, Robert C. *Sociology and Scientism: The American Quest for Objectivity, 1880-1940*. Chapel Hill: University of North Carolina Press, 1987.

Lazarsfeld, Paul F., and Merton, Robert K. "Friendship as a Social Process: A Substantive and Methodological Analysis." In *Freedom and Control in Modern Society*, ed. Monroe Berger, Theodore Abel, and Charles Hunt Page. New York: Van Nostrand, 1954.

Martindale, Don. *The Nature and Types of Sociological Theory*. Boston: Houghton Mifflin, 1960.

Parsons, Talcott. *Social Systems and the Evolution of Action Theory*. New York: Free Press, 1977.

Small, Albion W. "Fifty Years of Sociology in the United States." *American Journal of Sociology* 21 (1916): 721–864.

Swatos, William H., Jr. *Faith of the Fathers: Science, Religion, and Reform in the Development of Early American Sociology*. Bristol, Ind.: Wyndham Hall Press, 1984.

Vidich, Arthur J., and Lyman, Stanford M. *American Sociology: Worldly Rejections of Religion and their Directions*. New Haven, Conn.: Yale University Press, 1985.

WILLIAM H. SWATOS, JR.

SOCIOLOGY OF KNOWLEDGE

See SOCIOLOGY

SOCIOLOGY OF RELIGION

See SOCIOLOGY

SOUL

In English, the term *soul* can refer to a metaphysical entity or to the state of one's character. A philosopher may disdain the first and applaud the second. This entry focuses on the soul as an entity but concludes with noting why work on the soul is often centered on values.

Evolution of the idea

In ancient Greek philosophy the soul was thought of as a principle of life; the soul is what gives a person life as a human being. For Aristotle (384–322 B.C.E.) the soul (Greek, *psyche*) was identified as the form of the body. Aristotle delimited a host of different kinds of souls befitting nonhuman animal and plant life. In plants, for example, the soul was thought to be comprised of the plant's nutritive and reproductive powers. The human soul shares many of the powers of other living things but has distinctive intellectual powers as well. Aristotle's teacher, Plato (428–348 B.C.E.) thought of the human soul as an immaterial concrete subject capable of preexisting the body and living on after the body's destruction. In the important work *De Anima* (On the soul), Aristotle hints at an incorporeal, immaterial aspect to the human soul, but falls short of Plato's more enthusiastic delineation of the soul as independent of the body.

The medieval period favored Plato over Aristotle on the soul, until the Italian philosopher and theologian Thomas Aquinas (1225–1274) appropriated and rethought Aristotle's philosophy of nature in a Christian context. While Aquinas more firmly identified the embodiment of the soul in concrete, material terms, he retained belief in an individual's afterlife and did not embrace a thorough materialism.

The early modern era was profoundly ambivalent about the soul. Modern science was deeply suspicious of Aristotle, and the success of mechanical explanations of the material world were not especially hospitable to the soul and its principles of life. The French philosopher and mathematician René Descartes (1596–1650) demarcated the mind as distinct from the body, but increasingly a form of materialism or naturalism gained ground. Unease about the soul as a distinguishable entity was also fueled by some theologians during the Reformation. Some reformers did not believe the Hebrew Bible welcomed Platonism. In the creation story God makes human beings out of the dust of the ground, into which God breathes the breath of life (Gen. 2:7).

Challenges

The wholesale identification of the soul and the body met with obstacles, however. From the vantage point of modern science, matter (and eventually matter and energy) is not intentional; fundamental physical causal processes do not involve beliefs and desires. If complete and adequate explanations of the cosmos do not involve beliefs and desires, how is one to account for, let alone describe, everyday human activities? Very basic reasoning ($1 + 1 = 2$) seems to be based on beliefs and reasons (because I grasp $1 + 1$, and I grasp that 2 is $1 + 1$, I see that the mathematical relationship is necessary). Mechanistic science seems to write off such psychological accounts of our reasoning. This causes an especially difficult challenge with a mechanistic philosophy, for such a philosophy is customarily introduced as a theory that ought to be accepted based on some plausible beliefs about the evidence. But if the theory is correct, then beliefs play no essential role in explaining states of the world. In other words, mechanical, reductive materialism faces the danger of undermining the common sense understanding of humans as rational agents.

Materialists have developed different replies. The most dramatic, as represented by contemporary cognitive scientists and philosophers Stephen Stich, Paul Churchland, and Patricia Churchland, has been to deny that there are any such things as beliefs and desires. Other materialists have denied that psychological explanations are truly explanations in the same category as a scientific explanations. Some consider these two options desperate, for the first risks self-refutation (Stich *believes* that there are no beliefs) or refutation from common sense, while the second recommends a radical dualism more severe than Descartes's. The alternative, deemed by many to be more promising, is to develop some kind of nonreductive materialism, a theory that recognizes the beliefs, desires, and other powers that used to be associated with the soul, and yet views these beliefs as either identical to, constituted by, or emergent upon physical processes. As of the early 2000s, there is no universally accepted version of nonreductive materialism. Perhaps largely because of this lack of consensus on a problem-free form of materialism, there are some prominent philosophers who defend a form of dualism in which the soul is a distinctive, nonphysical entity.

Arguments over the metaphysics of the soul and arguments over values are closely related. If the whole scope of powers associated with the soul (beliefs, desires) does not exist or has no role to play in a mature explanation of the cosmos, then the values that appear to permeate and define human lives seem to be in jeopardy. It was his perception of this plight that led Stich to revise his radical skepticism about beliefs and desires. The moral implications of eliminating beliefs also led Paul Churchland to try to secure morality within his reductive science; he took on this project under a book title that explicitly refers to the soul: *The Engine of Reason, the Seat of the Soul* (1995).

Some contemporary theologians are highly motivated to see the soul in material terms. Your soul is your material body, functioning physically, psychologically, and spiritually. A dualist view of the soul is sometimes described as more Platonic than Christian. The effort to see human embodiment in integrated terms is easily appreciated, but it is difficult to avoid the dualist implications of the Bible and Christian tradition. If the soul can survive the death of the body (perhaps to be reembodied at the Resurrection), then it appears that the soul and body are not identical.

As in the Christian tradition, Jewish and Islamic philosophers have shifted between material accounts of the soul in the spirit of Aristotlean and Platonic mind-body dualism. Hinduism, Buddhism, and other religions that allow for reincarnation (a rebirth of the soul in distinct material embodiments) explicitly teach or implicitly assume a distinction between body and soul.

While Judaism, Christianity, and Islam have traditionally seen the soul as a substantive individual, enduring over time, Hindu and Buddhist literature have cast the individuality of the soul in more conditional terms. In Advaita Hinduism, different human souls are identical with the singular Divine Being. In the Buddhist tradition, the soul is a composite of perception, intelligence, form, feeling, and volition.

Popular culture in North America since the mid-1980s has seen a great revival of talk about the soul. Popularized forms of Renaissance Platonism have become fashionable. There is also some effort by philosophers to rekindle language about the soul in which having a soul is understood to involve depth of character or a meaningful presence or availability. People may be said to have a soul when they have deep convictions and integrity. The result is that there is more than one way to lose one's soul, either through a radical form of materialism, or through ethical failure, or a break down of integrity, or the refusal to lead an examined life.

See also ARISTOTLE; CONSCIOUSNESS STUDIES; DESCARTES, RENÉ; DUALISM; HUMAN NATURE, RELIGIOUS AND PHILOSOPHICAL ASPECTS; IMAGO DEI; MATERIALISM, PLATO; SPIRIT; THOMAS AQUINAS; VALUE

Bibliography

Churchland, Paul. *The Engine of Reason, The Seat of the Soul.* Cambridge, Mass.: MIT Press, 1995.

Corcoran, Kevin, ed. *Soul, Body, and Survival.* Ithaca, N.Y.: Cornell University Press, 2001.

Rorty, Amélie. *Mind in Action: Essays in the Philosophy of Mind.* Boston: Beacon Press, 1988.

Stich, Stephen. *From Folk Psychology to Cognitive Science.* Cambridge, Mass.: MIT Press, 1983.

Swinburne, Richard. *The Evolution of the Soul.* Oxford: Oxford University Press, 1986.

Taliaferro, Charles. *Consciousness and the Mind of God.* Cambridge, UK: Cambridge University Press, 1994.

Taylor, Charles. *Sources of the Self.* Cambridge, UK: Cambridge University Press, 1989.

CHARLES TALIAFERRO

SPACE

See SPACE AND TIME

SPACE AND TIME

Archeological excavations of ancient temples and tombs have shown that solar seasonal movements were known in neolithic times. Such knowledge depends on a recognition of former events as being in the past and an expectation of events to come as being in the future and, therefore, presupposes awareness of time. Prehistoric peoples must also have appreciated time sequence in the rhythm of the seasons, in plant growth and decay, and in the cycle of birth, life, and death. These cycles of heavenly and earthly events would have suggested that time itself perpetually recurred; to prehistoric peoples, a sense of temporal rhythm was more important than temporal sequence.

Time and religions

It has been suggested that religion originated from human awareness of the inevitable cycle of events. Rites and sacrifices were performed on specific occasions and these were often associated with particular phases of the moon or solar solstices. Other heavenly bodies, as well as the sun and moon, were often regarded as gods. The gods had superhuman powers, but they were thought to have desires and emotions analogous to those of humans, so that they were amenable to entreaty and flattery through propitiation ceremonies. Those who conducted these ceremonies were accorded high status in society: They were priests and often priest-kings. Priests observed the rhythms and movements of heavenly bodies and could predict their positions in the heavens. Babylonian priests, who could predict eclipses of both the sun and the moon, kept continuous records by the first millennium B.C.E.

A theory of time. For ancient civilizations, astronomical knowledge was practical rather than theoretical. The ancient Greeks were the first to develop a more abstract concept of time and its relation to space. Plato (c. 427–347 B.C.E.) and Aristotle (348–322 B.C.E.) had the most profound influence on later Western religious thought. Plato held that the creation of the cosmos was the work of a divine craftsman, the demiurge. The demiurge was not to be conceived as a god in the sense of a powerful spirit, but to be regarded as a principle of reason, who imposed order on the formless and chaotic raw materials of the world. Plato's ideal cosmos was a nonmaterial mathematical model that was immobile, immaterial, eternal, and timeless. But the created material universe was subject to change, a change manifested in the revolutions of the heavenly bodies that Plato identified as time. Therefore, at the creation, the demiurge had produced time as well as space.

Both Plato and Aristotle were influenced by cyclical theories and thought that the circle was a perfect figure because it had no end; it was a symbol of eternity and of a changeless immutable reality. Circular motion, apparent in the revolutions of the heavenly bodies, also displayed this perfection and need have no end. By contrast, motion in a straight line could not continue indefinitely unless the line were of infinite length, and Aristotle did not believe that there could be such a line. Whereas the cyclical theory of events in time ended with Christianity, the almost mystical view of the circle and of perfect, potentially eternal, circular motion permeated and strongly influenced philosophical and religious thought until the seventeenth century.

The Christian concept of time. Plato's postulate of an original chaos from which the demiurge created space and time is unique because he took the material universe to be but a pale reflection of an immaterial, eternal, and changeless reality. The idea of a universe formed from chaos, however, is a feature of many creation myths. It is echoed in Genesis: "In the beginning God created the heaven

and the Earth. And the Earth was without form, and void" (Gen. 1:1–2).

The early Christian saint Augustine of Hippo (354–430 C.E.) agreed with Plato that there could be no time without a created universe and that people were aware of time as the sequence of events in the created world. "I know that if nothing passed, there would be no past time; if nothing were going to happen there would be no future time; and if nothing were, there would be no present time" (p. 261). God was the creator of time, though God was outside time. Addressing God, Augustine wrote "although you are before time, it is not in time that you precede it. If this were so you would not be before all time. It is in eternity, which is supreme over time because it is a never-ending present, that you are at once before all past time and after all future time. For what is now the future, once it comes will become the past, whereas you are unchanging, your years can never fail" (p. 263). But Augustine disagreed with Plato's identification of time with the motions of the heavenly bodies. He argued, as had Aristotle, that time measures motion and therefore had to be distinguished from motion. Other Christian philosophers also disagreed with earlier views about the cyclical nature of time. For Christians the crucifixion was a unique event, and time had to be thought of as a unidirectional linear progression from the past, through the present, and on to the future. Though God was aware of past, present, and future in eternity, humans could only proceed forward in time.

Aristotle and the Christian cosmology. After the rediscovery of Aristotle's writings and their evaluation by the Christian saint Thomas Aquinas (1224–1274), Aristotle's cosmology became part of Christian doctrine and also played a major part in philosophical and scientific thought. Aristotle's cosmos was a closed and complicated system of transparent crystalline spheres revolving round the central immobile Earth. In all there were fifty-five such spheres. The moon, the sun, and each of the five planets were embedded in a separate sphere and each was carried round the Earth as its particular sphere rotated in its circular orbit. The fixed stars were all embedded, rather like lights in a ceiling, in an eighth sphere beyond these and beyond that penultimate sphere was the outermost sphere, the sphere of the unmoved mover. Circular motion was perfect and eternal and, for Aristotle, it was the natural motion of the heavens. Aristotle's account was developed further by Claudius Ptolemy (90–168 C.E.), who constructed a table, the *Almagest,* which provided a basis for predicting the positions of the planets in the sky. It was used in navigation, to foretell eclipses, and to calculate the dates of the equinoxes and the date of Easter.

For medieval Christians, Aristotle's cosmology had a religious significance that went far beyond its role in calculating the date of Easter. They regarded the system of spheres as a heavenly hierarchy. Aristotle's ninth sphere, the sphere of the unmoved mover was, for them, the sphere of God in glory. As well as being incorporated into Christian doctrine, the Aristotelian cosmos played an important role in medieval and renaissance literature. In the Paradise of his *Divine Comedy,* the Italian poet Dante (1265–1321) described his ascension outward to higher and higher spheres. For though they were all heavenly, the higher (outer) spheres were considered nearer perfection and the abode of God. This cosmos was closed and finite; there might be disturbances and disarray on Earth but above the sphere of the moon the heavens were an ordered hierarchy showing eternal, regular unchanging circular motion, and creating heavenly harmony: the music of the spheres. More than two centuries after Dante, William Shakespeare described this music in *The Merchant of Venice:*

> Look how the floor of heaven
> Is thick inlaid with patines of bright gold;
> There's not the smallest orb which thou
>   behold'st
> But in his motion like an angel sings,
> Still quiring to the young-eyed cherubims;
> Such harmony is in immortal souls;
> But whilst this muddy vesture of decay
> Doth grossly close it in, we cannot hear it.
> (5.1)

A new cosmology

By the early sixteenth century, navigators voyaging to America and around Southern Africa to India and the Spice Islands found the *Almagest* inadequate; it was also proving unsatisfactory in fixing the date of Easter. Nicolaus Copernicus (1473–1543) was one of several distinguished mathematician astronomers asked to revise and improve on Ptolemy's work. In 1543, the year of his death, Copernicus published his new cosmology placing an immobile sun at the center of the universe and displacing the Earth, which now orbited the sun along with the planets. Copernicus did not think his theory was revolutionary. He regarded it as a modification of the Aristotelian and Ptolemaic cosmos. Copernicus's universe still consisted of concentric crystalline spheres and was closed and finite. However, as a physical account it was incompatible with contemporary (Aristotelian) physics, and it also seemed to flout common sense. In addition there were grave theological objections. Aristotle's cosmology had become part of religious dogma and could not be rejected without firm evidence. Moreover in the early seventeenth century there was an alternative cosmology, that of the Danish astronomer Tycho Brahe (1546–1601), that retained a central immobile Earth and accounted for new observations equally well.

The cosmos of classical physics. In 1543, the crystalline spheres had seemed essential in order to carry the heavenly bodies and to keep them in their orbits. In proposing a Copernican-type cosmos (with a central sun but with no spheres) Galileo Galilei (1564–1642) had to explain how those spheres could be dispensed with. He asserted that all bodies had a natural (inertial) circular motion bestowed by God that would continue indefinitely. This was in accord with the universal belief in the perfection of the circle and of circular motion, a belief that had to be abandoned after Johannes Kepler (1571–1630) showed that the planets revolved in elliptical orbits. But the important change in the cosmology was that the universe, and therefore space, was no longer closed and finite. Copernicus himself had postulated a much larger universe but, for him, it was still closed. After Galileo the universe was seen as potentially infinite. Moreover, since there was no sphere of the moon separating the Earth from the heavenly bodies, the same physical laws that were beginning to be established on Earth also ruled in the heavens. The French philosopher and mathematician René Descartes (1596–1650) was the first to call them the laws of nature. Later he formulated the principle of inertial motion in a straight line. Descartes justified the principle partly by appeal to direct human experience of motion but also by appeal to religious belief. He affirmed that God must be the ultimate cause of all motion and that the amount of motion in the universe must remain constant, an implicit reference to God's perfection and consequent immutability.

Absolute space. Isaac Newton (1642–1737), who developed what is known as classical physics, took the principle of inertial motion in a straight line and, using his laws of force and of gravitational attraction, he was able to confirm Kepler's theory of elliptical orbits. More importantly, Newton established the classical concepts of absolute space and time and distinguished these from relative space and relative time.

If one assumes a homogeneous space extending indefinitely in all directions, then the position of a lone object can not be specified because position has to be related to something, for example another object. Likewise the concept of change of position can have no significance for a lone object. If one assumes just two objects, then if their relative positions change can it be said that only one object moves? If so, which one? Or do both of them move? The answer depends entirely on what one decides to adopt as a point of reference. In everyday experience there are an indefinitely large number of objects in space, and people take reference points that suit their purposes. But is there an absolute reference point? Can space itself provide a reference so that in principle even the position of a lone object could be established? Newton conceived of space itself as having an absolute position, so that any portion of space (as opposed to any body in space) was fixed. For him, space was *sensorium-Dei* (a sense organ of God) and was a manifestation of God. Thus space was eternal and changeless and, therefore, there were absolute, as opposed to relative, positions in space. But only God could know these; Newton appreciated that human beings could not distinguish the parts of space and so had to be content with the relative positions of objects in space.

Absolute time. There is an analogous problem in relation to the measure of time. If nothing whatever were to change, not only would one be unable to measure time, one would not be aware of time passing; time would stand still. Galileo is said, wrongly as it happens, to have used his pulse to time the swings of the pendulum in the cathedral at Pisa. This would not have been an accurate measure because pulses are not completely regular. But how is this known? By comparing pulse rates with a more regular sequence. The most regular sequence is shown to be the most regular because it consistently correlates all other time intervals: This is the only way regularity can be tested.

Like Augustine's concept, the mathematical/scientific concept of time in classical physics was that of a steady stream in which "the present," the flow of events, moved forward at a constant rate. Without events and therefore without any change, people could not be aware of time, it would have no empirical significance.

Is it then legitimate to assume an absolute and perfectly regular flow of time? Newton took the existence of absolute time as a fundamental metaphysical postulate: "Absolute time and mathematical time, of itself and from its own nature, flows equably without relation to anything external" (Koyré, p. 7). Newton appreciated that absolute time had to be distinguished from the time that could be measured; he called the latter "relative time," "apparent time" or "common time," and he realized that there was no way to know how close "sensible measures" were to measuring the absolute flow of time. He based his metaphysical assumption on appeal to God. Like absolute space, absolute time was a manifestation of God.

Relativity and the geometry of space

During the fourth century B.C.E., the Greek mathematician Euclid elucidated the nature of space. His geometry consisted of a system of theorems logically deduced from five axioms. The axioms were held to be self-evident and so constituted a set of indubitable premises. Euclidean geometry specified the properties of Euclidean space and these properties were assumed to be logically certain. This was the space of the Greeks, medieval space, and the space of classical physics. During the nineteenth century two mathematicians, Georg Friedrich Bernhard Riemann (1826–1866) and Hermann Minkowski (1864–1909), suggested two different geometries for two theoretical spaces that could be devised by changing Euclid's fifth axiom. That axiom is: Through a point not on a given line there can be only one line that will not cross the given line. Riemann, and later Minkowski, offered alternatives: There is no line that will not cross the given line, or there are an indefinitely large number of lines that will not cross the given line. The changed axioms defined two different non-Euclidean spaces, but when first formulated they were regarded as nothing more than mathematical speculations that did not apply to the real world.

In the nineteenth century no one questioned the assumption that space was Euclidean space and that measurements of space and measurements of time were independent of the motion of the observer. Parallel lines did not meet, distances remained constant, and clocks ran at a constant rate. It was these assumptions that were to be undermined by Albert Einstein (1879–1955). Einstein's new physics arose from his study of problems relating to the transmission of light and other electromagnetic vibrations. To solve the problems, Einstein had to postulate that the velocity of light was constant in all so-called inertial frames of reference so that it would remain the same for two or more observers moving at different velocities relative to each other. Such a postulate would have been nonsensical in classical physics and entailed a fundamental reassessment of assumptions about time, space, and motion.

In his reassessment. Einstein did not jettison common sense; rather he invited his colleagues to consider fundamental concepts on the basis of a common-sense analysis of the significance of familiar and ordinary terms. Einstein argued that the crucial element in a person's notion of time was that of simultaneity because any judgment made of time and the time of an event must be a judgment of the simultaneity of that event with another event. For example, to say that a train arrives at seven o'clock is equivalent to saying that it arrives when the small clock hand points to seven; the two events are claimed to be simultaneous. Einstein was the first to point out that there had to be a finite time for the light conveying the information about the position of the clock hand to reach a site a finite distance from the clock, and that clocks must be calibrated to allow for this. Calibration is possible if the clock and the observer are in the same frame of reference. But because light travels at the same velocity for observers in different frames of reference (e.g., traveling in cars toward the station) calibration is not possible. It follows that there can be no agreement about simultaneity and therefore no agreement about the time of the train. Of course because light travels millions of times faster than any car, the disagreement would not be noticed, but a discrepancy can be detected in careful experiments. Einstein was able to show that as the velocity of a frame of reference increased relative to an observer outside the frame, the bodies within the moving frame would appear

to contract. Observers in the moving system would see no change and to them the objects in the "stationary" frame of reference would seem to shrivel. Thus time and space could not be regarded as absolutes: They were observation-frame-dependent. A further consequence of Einstein's new physics was that space and time themselves were distorted by mass and were to be described by the geometry of Riemann or Minkowski rather than that of Euclid.

Minkowski had been Einstein's teacher and he proposed a way to establish independence of the frame of reference. In a lecture "Space and Time," given in 1908, Minkowski suggested that events should be identified and described by their positions in space-time. This would allow objective measurements but it would entail making space and time interdependent because the "time axis" would be as necessary for a description as the three space axes. Unfortunately, people find it very difficult to envisage events in four (as opposed to three) dimensions, and Minkowski's suggestion removes physical accounts of objects and events from common-sense intuitions. Space-time is a concept that can be regarded as providing a different metaphysical framework that could replace the two Newtonian concepts of absolute space and absolute time. However, within any given frame of reference, one can use classical physics and it can apply in a different frame with velocities that are small compared to the velocity of light. This is the case in most situations, and why classical physical laws still hold. But these laws are approximation, and one must concede that classical (and indeed intuitive) concepts of time and space are flawed.

Metaphysics and religious belief

Although this account has been primarily concerned with Christianity, the nature of the religious beliefs of Copernicus, Galileo, Kepler, Descartes, Newton, and many others was grounded in a mystical acceptance of a higher power rather than in Christian doctrine. Underlying their heterodox and even heretical opinions was the faith that human reason was a gift of God and it was adequate to the task of explaining events in the world.

By the end of the twentieth century, science rarely made direct appeal to religious faith. The theoretical physicist Stephen Hawking (b. 1942) allows for the need to appeal to some power transcending human capacities to account for creation. In a chapter significantly called "The Origin and Fate of the Universe," in his popular book *A Brief History of Time* (1988), Hawking reveals a Cartesian concept of laws of nature, and though, unlike Descartes, he does not postulate that they are divine decrees, he does entertain the notion. Hawking argues that events cannot be random and, whether they be divine or no, there must be laws of nature. He appears reasonably confident that human beings will arrive at a complete explanation (a unified theory) "within the lifetime of some of us" (p. 156). But his confidence may be misplaced, not only because evidence from the past gives greater grounds for pessimism than Hawking is prepared to acknowledge, but because it remains an open question as to whether the laws of nature are not *human* constructions. What Hawking does clearly reveal is the necessity for metaphysical and possibly religious beliefs. His expositions show that the basic metaphysical assumptions of Aristotle, the medieval scholars, the founders of classical physics, and the founders of modern physics are still in play. The assumption is that there is an objective order and that humanity is capable of discovering that order.

See also ARISTOTLE; AUGUSTINE; EINSTEIN, ALBERT; GALILEO GALILEI; GEOMETRY: PHILOSOPHICAL ASPECTS; GEOMETRY, MODERN: THEOLOGICAL ASPECTS; NEWTON, ISAAC; PLATO; RELATIVITY, GENERAL THEORY OF; THOMAS AQUINAS

Bibliography

Aristotle. *On the Heavens,* trans. W. K. C. Guthrie. Cambridge, Mass.: Harvard University Press, 1945.

Augustine. *Confessions,* trans. R.S. Pine-Coffin. New York: Penguin, 1976.

Hawking, Stephen W. *A Brief History of Time: From the Big Bang to Black Holes.* New York: Bantam, 1988.

Koyré, Alexander. *Newtonian Studies.* London: Chapman and Hall, 1965.

Plato. *Timaeus and Critias,* trans. Desmond Lee. New York: Penguin, 1983.

Whitrow, G. J. *The Natural Philosophy of Time.* Oxford: Clarendon Press, 1980.

JENNIFER L. TRUSTED

SPACE-TIME

See SPACE AND TIME

SPECIAL DIVINE ACTION

Special, or particular, divine action stands in contrast to ordinary, or general, divine action. God can be said to act generally through the regular structures of the world, which God creates and sustains. In addition, God may perform particular actions to achieve specific divine purposes in history, as in the self-revealing and redemptive acts depicted in biblical narratives. Modern theologians have found that the idea of special divine action presents difficult interpretive challenges, especially in light of scientific descriptions of the world as an integral structure of natural causes, and they have sought ways to identify what makes such events special other than miraculous divine intervention in the world.

See also DIVINE ACTION; PROVIDENCE; SPECIAL PROVIDENCE

THOMAS F. TRACY

SPECIAL PROVIDENCE

Classical forms of Judaism, Christianity, and Islam claim that God guides or intervenes in human history. God's intentions are thereby manifest not just in the general laws of nature but in specific events like Abraham's call to worship God, Christ's life, and the revelation of God's word to Muhammad. Theologians in monotheistic traditions have generally understood God's specific will for empires or individuals as governed by God's will for the good of all creation. From this point of view, God's having a "chosen people" is for the benefit of all. God's special provident action is at the heart of the prophetic tradition in monotheism. It also plays a role in the ancient and contemporary practice of prayer in which one petitions God for some good. Ancient polytheistic religions in Greece and Rome were largely built around divinization (determining the disposition of the gods toward one's petition) and supplications backed by bargains, whereas monotheistic spirituality over the centuries has tended to shun the practice of trying to control God's will out of self-interest.

Three lively philosophical issues arise over special providence: the scope of providence (Is the future predetermined or predestined? Is freedom compatible with providence?); the relation between God's general and special intentions (Can God suspend certain general ethical prohibitions?); and the existence and nature of miracles. Some specific provident acts may be in keeping with, and thus allowed by, the laws of nature, whereas others seem to involve going beyond or against the natural course of events (e.g., a dead man being resurrected).

See also DIVINE ACTION; FREEDOM; MIRACLE; PROVIDENCE; SKYHOOKS; SPECIAL DIVINE ACTION

Bibliography

Flint, Thomas P. *Divine Providence: The Molinist Account.* Ithaca, N.Y.: Cornell University Press, 1998.

Hasker, William. *God, Time, and Knowledge.* Ithaca, N.Y.: Cornell University Press, 1989.

Helm, Paul. *The Providence of God.* Downers Grove, Ill.: InterVarsity, 1994.

CHARLES TALIAFERRO

SPECIAL THEORY OF RELATIVITY

See RELATIVITY, SPECIAL THEORY OF

SPIRIT

Spirit is a complicated, nebulous term extending from the sacred and holy to the depths of the human. It captures human consciousness of meanings and purposes extending beyond individual lives, and directs people to the boundaries of self. Spirit may also refer to the supernatural or immaterial, the divine or sacred, an animating principle, a property of the person, mind or consciousness, the process of emergence or coming into being, an orientation to ultimate mystery, and the ethical or transformative. There is a Christian tradition, from Irenaeus in the second century to Erasmus in the sixteenth, that views the human person as a tripartite complex of spirit, soul, and body, but there is an alternative sense in which these are varying orientations of a unitary person. With reference to the individual, spirit and soul are used almost interchangeably, although spirit tends to be less individuated, and the soul more tied to the religious.

Theological development

Theological developments begin with the ancient understanding of spirit as life. The Hebrews used the word *ruach* to refer to divine breath, and the word *nephesh* to refer to a product of the spirit, translated as "person" or "soul." The Greek term *pneuma,* meaning "breath of life," is translated as "spirit" of life and breath and is distinguishable from the images and ideas of the *psyche,* translated as "soul" or "mind.". This sense of spirit may also include the "new life" of prophetic inspiration, art, poetry, and courage.

The ancient Hebrews understood humans to be unitary persons, which is also consistent with the early Epistles of the New Testament. The medieval Christian philosopher Thomas Aquinas (c. 1225–1274) drew on Aristotle's understanding of form as inseparable from substance, seeing the human spirit inseparable from its corporeality. A disembodied soul may be theologically problematic, both in failing to fulfill the total life of a person and in negating of the body. A deeply immanent view of the relation between spirit and life is also found in modern theologies like that of Pierre Teilhard de Chardin (1881–1955), Karl Rahner (1904–1984), and Wolfhart Pannenberg (b. 1928). On this view, evolution itself is the continuous development of matter towards spirit, nature becoming conscious of itself in human beings, systems open to the future.

The idea of spirit is restricted to *mind* in early Christian syntheses, equivalent to the Latin word *mens* for Augustine of Hippo (354–430 C.E.). He sees the self as transcendent in all of its functions, including memory and understanding, and his emphasis on private experience contributed to the inwardness institutionalized by Christianity. During the seventeenth century, René Descartes argued that mental faculties are largely explainable as bodily activities, except for conscious thought. To account for consciousness, Descartes posits a nonmaterial dual substance, causally interacting with the brain, knowable only through privileged and incorrigible introspection. Contemporary solutions to the mind-body problem recognize an inescapable dependence on mind upon brain, but have not yet explained subjective experience.

A tension remains between a view of spirit as internal or as external to the human mind. Pannenberg warns that while the identification of spirit with mind may be a human projection, its Christian opposition often results in irrational subjectivism (p. 127). Spirit as the principle of life may be generative of mind, more than an individual's brain function, but a set of interiorized relationships. Even a scientific understanding of mind may require more than individual neurobiology, but it is not clear whether spirit requires a further step, since human invention and divine inspiration are not mutually exclusive.

Human spirit has also been equated with self-transcendence, intimately tied to human freedom and development. The theologies of Teilhard de Chardin and Paul Tillich (1886–1905) treat spirit as a dimension of life that takes one's biological, individual self-awareness into the personal and communal, with ecstatic acts of self-transcendence overcoming existential anxiety. According to Rahner, human minds enable the abstraction by which people move beyond themselves to a horizon of meaning. If spirit is about the meanings that transcend human finitude, it can encourage an obliteration of a bounded and autonomous self. The theological idea of *kenosis* captures this idea of emptying the self into a larger vessel. The spirit is then constituted by stepping beyond the boundaries of self, in relating to others and, as Rahner writes, to the "unutterable mystery of life we call God" (Grenz and Olson, p. 240).

Science and religion

In the dialogue between science and religion, spirit is a bridging concept between the ultimate metaphysical concerns of religion and their embodiment within human experience. The sense of spirit as an immanent creative force finds expression in process theology's use of developments in physics to understand even matter as including an experiential interior. This sense is also seen in the use of chaos theory, complexity theory, and autopoesis to understand the work of spirit. Ian Barbour sees spirit in the emergent novelties of evolution, including unique activities at higher levels of organic complexity.

Most uses of spirit in the science-religion dialogue have been in making sense of the evolutionary biology of human mental and moral lives, including both an opposition to theological dualism and an understanding that a reductive materialism would explain away much of what is important about human life. The beacon for theological anthropology is the view that spirit, soul, person, and mind are emergent properties of evolved human biology. Under this view, persons are psychosomatically unitary organisms, characterized by an inner life of extreme complexity, unpredictability, and novelty in which the evolution and development of complex nervous systems bring autonomy, identity, and will into being. The human spirit is a contingent product of a hierarchy of biological functions on which personal existence depends, and which gives rise to capacities like morality and religious experience. In theologies of nature like those of Ian Barbour, Arthur Peacocke, and Philip Hefner, human personal and social lives are intimately related to the rest of natural creation by virtue of evolutionary emergence and novelty, mind and spirit. Religious neuroscientists, such as Donald Mackay, Malcolm Jeeves, and Fraser Watts, also emphasize a complementarity or compatibilism between neuroscience and theology. While higher-order properties physically depend on their components, relationships between the emergent unit and its elements is neither identical with nor derivable from them. Philosophically oriented thinkers, such as Nancey Murphy and Philip Clayton, describe spiritual and mental events as "supervenient" over neurophysiological ones, and as both multiply realizable and multiply constitutable. Warren Brown and John Teske suggest further that human spirituality is neuropsychologically constituted only in the context of personal relationships, and in the shaping of human brains by cultural forces.

A range of naturalistic theories of religious experiences ties them to patterns of emotional attachment and to neural structures as in Eugene d'Aquili's life-long program, synthesized in *The Mystical Mind* (1999). Disciplines like prayer and meditation have documentable physical effects, and a whole literature exists on the psychological benefits of spirituality. A tradition of research in the psychology of spiritual development, of which James Fowler's *Stages of Faith* (1981) is the best known, also connects the interdependent self of mature ego-development to the breakdown of self/other boundaries sought by spiritual and ethical traditions. At higher levels of development, spirit is really not about the individual, nor is it otherworldly, but still strongly opposes a materialistic ethic.

See also ARISTOTLE; AUGUSTINE; DESCARTES, RENÉ; DUALISM; FREEDOM; HOLY SPIRIT; HUMAN NATURE, RELIGIOUS AND PHILOSOPHICAL ASPECTS; KENOSIS; MATERIALISM; NEUROSCIENCES; PHYSICALISM, REDUCTIVE AND NONREDUCTIVE; PNEUMATOLOGY; PROCESS THOUGHT; SELF; SELF-TRANSCENDENCE; SOUL; SPIRITUALITY; SUPERNATURALISM; TEILHARD DE CHARDIN, PIERRE; THOMAS AQUINAS; WHITEHEAD, ALFRED NORTH

Bibliography

Barbour, Ian G. *Religion and Science: Historical and Contemporary Issues.* New York: Harper, 1997.

Brown, Warren S.; Murphy, Nancey C.; and Malony, H. Newton, eds. *Whatever Happened to the Soul? Scientific and Theological Portraits of Human Nature.* Minneapolis, Minn.: Fortress Press, 1998.

D'Aquili, Eugene, and, Newberg, Andrew B. *The Mystical Mind: Probing the Biology of Religious Experience.* Minneapolis, Minn.: Fortress Press, 1999.

Drees, Willem B. *Religion, Science, and Naturalism.* New York: Cambridge University Press, 1996.

Flanagan, Owen. *The Science of the Mind,* 2nd edition. Cambridge, Mass.: MIT Press, 1991.

Gregersen, Neils; Drees, Willem; and Gorman, Ulf, eds. *The Human Person in Science and Theology.* Grand Rapids, Mich.: Eerdmans, 2000.

Grenz, Stanley J., and Olson, Roger E. *Twentieth Century Theology.* Downers Grove, Ill.: InterVarsity Press, 1992.

Hefner, Philip. *The Human Factor: Evolution, Culture, and Religion.* Minneapolis, Minn.: Fortress Press, 1993.

Pannenberg, Wolfhart. *Toward a Theology of Nature: Essays on Science and Faith,* ed. Ted Peters. Louisville, Ky.: Westminster John Knox Press, 1993.

Peacocke, Arthur. *Theology for a Scientific Age: Being and Becoming—Natural Divine, and Human,* 2nd edition. Minneapolis, Minn: Fortress Press, 1993.

Rahner, Karl. *Foundations of Christian Faith.* New York: Seabury, 1978.

Sacks, Oliver. "Neurology and the Soul." *New York Review of Books,* November 20 (1990): 44–50.

Spong, John Shelby. *Why Christianity Must Change or Die: A Bishop Speaks to Believers in Exile.* San Francisco: Harper, 1998.

Teske, John A. "The Genesis of Mind and Spirit." *Zygon* 36, no. 1 (2001): 93–104.

JOHN A. TESKE

SPIRITUALITY

In the contemporary context, the term *spirituality* has a vast spectrum of meanings. It can refer to an interior journey, to the practice of prayer and meditation, to faithful and righteous living, or to a general commitment to authenticity and self-awareness. The term originated in the Roman Catholic tradition, but has been embraced by many Protestants as well as Jews, Buddhists, Muslims, Hindus, Taoists, Confucianists and even secular persons. Indeed, many today claim spirituality while renouncing institutional religion.

Spiritual practice

Prayer, ritual, and meditation remain central spiritual practices across religious traditions. Yet, the notion of what constitutes a spiritual practice also is expanding. Spirituality does not mean simply the interior life or religious discipline. Rather, spirituality relates also to social action, ethical choice, family commitments, friendship, work, and politics. Thus, both private and public practices form the human being and can be spaces for spiritual expression and growth. Indeed, some are defining spirituality so broadly as to include a wide range of contemporary secular practices. One may point, for example, to the 1996 book *Spirituality and the Secular Quest* edited by Peter Van Ness, which includes chapters on scientific inquiry, sports, psychotherapy, the arts, ecological activism, and holistic health practices. These expansive understandings of spirituality rightly avoid a narrow focus on interiority and counter an otherworldly or individualistic notion of the spiritual life. Yet, as the words *spiritual* and *spirituality* are applied to a wider range of beliefs and practices, their meanings can become diffuse and vague. This situation calls for careful theological and philosophical exploration of the wide-ranging meanings of the terms in specific cultural and religious contexts.

Contemporary persons embrace spirituality because they seek to live more deeply, to connect with the ultimate, to find meaning in ordinary activities and the experiences of fragmentation, moral challenge, grief, illness, and death. Spirituality can be understood as the universal human desire for self-transcendence, as Christian theologian Sandra Schneiders writes in her 1986 article "Theology and Spirituality: Strangers, Rivals, or Partners?" (p. 266). Such a broad, anthropological perspective attempts to provide a general, inclusive understanding of spirituality that can speak to the wide range of practices and worldviews that fall under the heading of *spirituality.* Such definitions of spirituality enable dialogue and even shared practice in pluralistic settings. Thus, for example, the editors of Crossroad Publishing's World Spirituality series arrived at a shared definition applicable to studies in everything from Native American to Jewish to Buddhist to Confucian spirituality. As stated in Ewert Cousins's preface to each volume, authors would focus on the discovery of "the deepest center of the person . . . [where] the person is open to the transcendent dimension; it is here that the person experiences ultimate reality."

Yet, every definition of spirituality reflects a theological perspective and an historical and cultural context. Thus, more theologically explicit and context specific definitions of spirituality are important. Christian spirituality, for example, could be understood as life in the Spirit of God, a path in which one walks as a disciple of Jesus Christ—revealed by the Creator in history—within the community of the church. Buddhist spirituality has been defined in terms of "cultivation" that leads, according to the Buddhist monk Rahula Walpola, to "the attainment of the highest wisdom which sees the nature of things as they are, and realizes the Ultimate Truth, Nirvana" (Yoshinori, p. xiii). One then would explore how the particular contours of these paths take shape differently in diverse cultures and historical periods. For indeed, history and culture shape how humans understands themselves, the nature of the ultimate, and the relationship between the two. For example, medieval notions of a hierarchy of spiritual paths—with the celibate path being higher and more perfect than the lay path—reflected a hierarchical social order as well as a specific theological tradition. Scientific discoveries challenge traditional understandings of prayer and divine agency. Contemporary spirituality strongly reflects the "turn to the subject" and the powerful influence of therapeutic perspectives.

Spirituality and the practice of science. As understandings of spirituality widen, science can be understood as a spiritual practice—an attentive search for understanding of the intricate and extraordinarily complex world around us (or within us). The practice of science merges the power of reason with the humility and curiosity needed to see beyond the self. Whether tracing the working of the neuron or investigating the organization of the universe, scientific inquiry requires discipline, awareness, and creativity.

Spirituality and health. While Western medicine has become highly secularized, there remains a strong academic and popular interest in exploring connections between spirituality and health. This interest takes two forms. One is the general insistence on the relatedness of body, mind, and spirit. For example, Robert C. Fuller notes that the holistic healing movement seeks a natural renewal of physical well-being through an individual's own psychological and spiritual energies (Van Ness, pp. 227-250). These practices need not claim a metaphysical reality responsible for healing. The second kind of interest presupposes a higher being— a life-giving Creator—that sustains or restores bodily health. Studies have found a correlation between prayer and religious beliefs and effective coping, resilience, and healing (e.g., Oxnam et al.; Levin and Schiller). The question is whether spiritual practices simply benefit one's mental outlook and physical condition or whether they effectively draw supernatural power upon the body.

Spirituality and faith healing. Diverse religious traditions long have believed that a divine being can cure illness. Faith in God enables human beings to convey God's healing touch or combat evil forces. Many Christians, for example, believe that spiritual practices such as prayer, exorcism, and anointing can restore health as Christ is chronicled as doing in the Gospels (e.g., Mark 6:13).

Christian Scientists make faith healing the center of their belief system and maintain as a principal tenet that true understanding alleviates disease. Adherents to Buddhism, Shintoism, and Daoism often wear amulets to ward off illness. In different ways, various spiritual practices orient one toward the divine healing power.

Study of spirituality

The study of spirituality must be an interdisciplinary enterprise. It draws on multiple fields in order to understand the human quest for the ultimate and the practices that open one to truth and wisdom. The study of spirituality incorporates theology, history, anthropology, psychology, neurophysiology, medicine, literary studies, and the arts. In the early centuries of Christianity, spirituality and theology were integrated and inseparable. One could not seek knowledge of God without praying and meditating on the scriptures. With the rise of scholasticism in the Middle Ages, theology in Western Christianity gradually became understood as a conceptual science distinct from ascetical or mystical life. This was an unfortunate separation of science and spirituality, a separation resisted in Eastern Orthodoxy and one that some contemporary scholars, such as Philip Sheldrake and Mark A. McIntosh, are reconsidering.

Spirituality has also suffered from misunderstandings about the relationship between the spiritual and the material. Within Christianity, for example, the spiritual too often is seen as that which is beyond or even opposed to the physical, the body, and the material world. It is worth reviewing the meanings of the term *spirit* in the Jewish and Christian traditions—a complicated subject, for this term has multiple meanings in different texts. With this caution in mind, one may note that in the Hebrew Bible the term *ruah* refers to the breath or spirit of God, a life-giving force. In the New Testament, *pneuma* (Greek) or *spiritus* (Latin translation) refers often to the Holy Spirit or the animating principle of the human being. To be a spiritual person, then, is to be infused with the life, the breath, of the divine. The Letters of Paul contrast *pneuma* to *sarx* (Greek: flesh). This distinction has been interpreted as pitting the spirit against the flesh. In reality, the texts contrast those things that are "of the Spirit" to those things that are counter to God. To live "in the Spirit" is not necessarily to reject the physical, but to live according to the will of God as revealed in Jesus Christ. Certainly, Christian theology has perpetuated deep ambiguity about the value of the physical. While a dichotomy between the physical and the spiritual persists in numerous religious traditions, contemporary writers in spirituality also promote more holistic notions of spirituality. Widespread interest in such practices as yoga and Tai Chi demonstrate a hunger to integrate spirituality and physicality. Spirituality refers to an authentic and holy life in all its aspects. Thus, spirituality incorporates holy treatment of, or relationship to, the body and the physical world. It also includes a lively curiosity about the material world.

See also MYSTICISM; PRAYER AND MEDITATION

Bibliography

Bass, Dorothy, ed. *Practicing Our Faith: A Way of Life for a Searching People.* San Francisco: Jossey-Bass, 1997.

Green, Arthur, ed. *Jewish Spirituality: From the Sixteenth Century Revival to the Present.* New York: Crossroad, 1987.

Hanson, Bradley, ed. *Modern Christian Spirituality: Methodological and Historical Essays.* Atlanta, Ga.: Scholars Press, 1990.

Levin, Jeffrey S., and Schiller, Preston L. "Is There a Religious Factor in Health?" *Journal of Religion and Health* 26 (1987): 9-36.

McIntosh, Mark A. *Mystical Theology: The Integration of Spirituality and Theology.* Oxford: Blackwell, 1998.

Oxnam, Thomas E.; Freeman, Daniel H. Jr.; Manheimer, Eric D. "Lack of Social Participation or Religious Strength and Comfort as Risk Factors for Death After Cardiac Surgery in the Elderly." *Psychosomatic Medicine* 57, no. 1 (1995): 5-15.

Schneiders, Sandra. "Theology and Spirituality: Strangers, Rivals, or Partners?" *Horizons* 13 (1986): 253-274.

Sheldrake, Philip. *Spirituality & Theology: Christian Living and the Doctrine of God.* Maryknoll, N.Y.: Orbis Press, 1998.

Van Ness, Peter, ed. *Spirituality and the Secular Quest.* New York: Crossroad, 1996.

Wolfteich, Claire E. *American Catholics Through the Twentieth Century: Spirituality, Lay Experience, and Public Life.* New York: Crossroad, 2001.

Yoshinori, Takeuchi et al., eds. *Buddhist Spirituality: Indian, Southeast Asian, Tibetan, and Early Chinese.* New York: Crossroad, 1993.

CLAIRE E. WOLFTEICH

SPIRITUALITY AND FAITH HEALING

Seen from a cross-cultural perspective, diverse traditions of healing, which respond to different conceptions of illness itself, fall under the heading of what may be called faith healing. This entry surveys faith healing activity according to seven categories: (1) intercessory prayer; (2) mind-body research; (3) laying on of hands; (4) complementary and alternative medicine; (5) Asian healing practices; (6) shamanistic practices; and (7) African and other tribal practices. Although these categories by no means represent the entire range of practices that could be construed as faith healing, they do epitomize a spiritual approach to healing. They are also areas in which important scientific and other scholarly research has been conducted.

Western approaches

Evidencing increasing respect for spirituality within the healthcare community, scientific research in the domain of modern Western medicine has examined the impact of spirituality on healing in the areas of intercessory prayer, mind-body connectivity, laying on of hands, and complementary and alternative medicine.

Intercessory prayer. In attempting to determine the impact of faith on health, some researchers have looked to prayer to determine its impact on the health and well being of patients. For example, in 2000, D. A. Matthews and colleagues published a study on the impact of intercessory prayer on patients suffering from rheumatoid arthritis. The study showed that patients receiving in-person prayer "showed significant overall improvement during 1-year follow-up," causing the study's authors to conclude that "in-person intercessory prayer may be a useful adjunct to standard medical care for certain patients with rheumatoid arthritis." In 2001, W. J. Matthews and colleagues published a discussion of the impact of intercessory prayer and other behavioral interventions for kidney dialysis patients.

In another example, noting, "intercessory prayer (praying for others) has been a common response to sickness for millennia," W. S. Harris and colleagues examine whether or not remote (as opposed to nonremote) intercessory prayer reduces "overall adverse events and length of stay" for hospitalized cardiac patients. Employing a controlled,

double-blind, parallel-group trial in a private university-associated hospital, Harris and colleagues examined 990 consecutive patients admitted for coronary care. Researchers randomized patients, who received either remote intercessory prayer (the "prayer group") or no prayer (the "usual care group"). Outside intercessors, who did not know and did not meet the patients, prayed for patients in the prayer group daily for four weeks. The patients themselves did not know that people were praying for them. At the conclusion of the study, the researchers reported that, although the two groups did not evidence any differences in the lengths of their coronary care unit and hospital stays, the group that was prayed for displayed lower coronary care unit scores, suggesting "that prayer may be an effective adjunct to standard medical care." Despite this optimistic conclusion, peers have questioned the potential increase in clinical outcome of patients receiving intercessory prayer. For example, R. M. Hamm's article "No Effect of Intercessory Prayer Has Been Proven" (2000) claims that the study described above may have attributed too much importance to results of minimal statistical significance, while another 2000 article by D. R. Hoover and J. B. Margolick in the Archives of Internal Medicine questions the appropriateness of the study's statistical methods in relationship to the type of data collected.

In "The Healing Power of Intercessory Prayer" (2001), O. G. Harding provides an interesting treatment of the more metaphysical implications of efficacious, remote, intercessory prayer. Harding states that "arising from an emerging world view in philosophy, it is argued that the mind can function beyond the individual and is not constrained by time and distance; it is in fact non-local. Prayer is cited as an example of non-local manifestation of consciousness." Harding presents two case studies providing evidence for non-local healing and asks "whether there is no place in medicine for a multiple approach to healing," and, further, if "reported studies of [efficacious] prayer therapies are meaningful, are physicians not using these additional treatments withholding something curative from their patients?" In general, if, despite methodological criticisms of existing research, one emerges convinced that prayer successfully improves health outcomes in some circumstances, one still must answer the question of what mechanisms support healing, both in cases when patients are aware they are being prayed for, but also when they are unaware that others engage in prayers on their behalf. While some may adopt a theological interpretation of such results by claiming that God answers prayers on behalf of the sick and dying, others may prefer to believe that either the patient's own response to the knowledge that they are being prayed for (in the case of nonremote intercessory prayer) or the force of positive, non-localized human intentionality (in the case of remote intercessory prayer) may exert some influence on actual events, such as whether or not a patient recovers from an illness.

Mind/body research. In addition to researching the impact of intercessory prayer, the Western medical community has also examined the impact of spirituality on health in the context of research on the connection between mind and body. Initiatives emanating out of the Mind/Body Medical Institute at Harvard Medical School in Cambridge, Massachusetts, lead research in this area and focus primarily on the positive therapeutic effects of quieting, meditative practice (called "the relaxation response" by Dr. Herbert Benson and his colleagues) on general health outcomes in a range of areas. Benson and his colleagues define the relaxation response "as a series of coordinated physiologic changes elicited when a person engages in a repetitive word, sound or phrase or prayer, and passively disregards intrusive thoughts. Relaxation response practice results in decreased metabolism, heart rate, rate of breathing, and distinctive slower brain waves. These changes are the exact opposite of those induced by the fight or flight response" (Mind/body, 2002). Benson and his colleagues claim that, when combined with exercise, stress management, and proper nutrition, the relaxation response functions as an effective therapeutic intervention for "cardiac disease, many forms of chronic pain, infertility, insomnia, premenstrual syndrome, the symptoms of cancer and HIV/AIDS, anxiety, and mild and moderate depression" -i.e., any condition "caused or made worse by stress" (Mind/body, 2002). By far the most high-profile provider of spirituality and health research and treatment, the Mind/Body Medical Clinic and Beth Israel Deaconess Medical Center in Massachusetts and affiliate sites throughout the United States enjoy over nine thousand patient visits per year. The Mind/Body Medical Institute offers training in the relaxation response to teachers and students, business people, health care professionals, and members of the public.

Laying on of hands. Western medical attention has also focused on the "laying on of hands," which although viewed by some as more of a supplemental, palliative nursing treatment, also serves as a topic for rigorous research. In one interesting study, researchers examined physician attitudes toward the laying on of hands in the context of the AIDS epidemic and concern about HIV infection. The researchers concluded that physicians believed touch facilitated healing and strengthened rapport, though younger physicians, those working in primary care, and those who did not prefer to wear gloves were more likely to express such attitudes.

Complementary and alternative medicine. Although scientific investigation in faith-based healing has increased significantly, M. R. Tonelli and T. C. Callahan ask in their article "Why Alternative Medicine Cannot Be Evidence-Based" (2001) whether the scientific method adequately assesses many "alternative" approaches to healing. They note that "the concept of evidence-based medicine (EBM) has been widely adopted by orthodox Western medicine. Proponents of EBM have argued that complementary and alternative medicine (CAM) modalities ought to be subjected to rigorous, controlled clinical trials in order to assess their efficacy. However, this does not represent a scientific necessity, but rather is a philosophical demand: promoters of EBM seek to establish their particular epistemology as the primary arbiter of all medical knowledge." Tonelli and Callahan believe instead that "methods for obtaining knowledge in a healing art must be coherent with that art's underlying understanding and theory of illness. Thus, the method of EBM and the knowledge gained from population-based studies may not be the best way to assess certain CAM practices, which view illness and healing within the context of a particular individual only." Since many alternative approaches to healing admit the existence of "non-measurable but perceptible aspects of illness and health (e.g., Qi)," controlled clinical trials may not offer appropriate methods of assessment. The authors conclude that "orthodox medicine should consider abandoning demands that CAM become evidence-based, at least as 'evidence' is currently narrowly defined, but insist instead upon a more complete and coherent description and defense of the alternative epistemic methods and tools of these disciplines."

Some studies (e.g., Eisenberg et al, 2001; Parkman, 2002) demonstrate that a growing number of people consider the combination of orthodox treatments and complementary and alternative therapies to be more effective than either kind of treatment alone. Patients with higher anxiety approach faith healers more often, though not to reject more conventional scientific approaches, but as a continuation of them (Conroy et al, 2000). In his article "'Physician, Heal Thyself': How Teaching Holistic Medicine Differs from Teaching CAM" (2001), J. Graham-Pole differentiates CAM ("a system of health care not generally recognized as part of mainstream medical practice") and holistic medicine ("the art and science of healing the whole person-body, mind, and spirit-in relation to that person's community and environment"). Although at least two-thirds of medical schools in the United States offer coursework in CAM, and while an increasing number of courses in the medical humanities focus on spirituality and health, courses on holistic medicine remain rare. According to Graham-Pole, "offering physicians-to-be more coursework in holistic medicine could lay the groundwork for future physicians' adopting and modeling healthy lifestyles."

Non-Western approaches

Moving from Western approaches to non-Western ones, studies on Asian, shamanistic, and African tribal healing practices have contributed to the overall discussion of faith healing. Cross-cultural forms of faith-related healing have also achieved prominent medical investigation, both by Western researchers and by professionals from within particular cultural contexts. For example, V. Griffiths in "Eastern and Western Paradigms" (1999) comments on the holistic nature of Chinese medicine and its attention to observation, subjectivity, and feeling. Chinese medicine revolves around the notion of qi, "an alleged vital force that underlies functioning of body, mind, and spirit" (Raso, 2000) According to a 2002 article by W. Yao and colleagues, "cardiac deficiency of qi (vital energy)" is "one of the main syndromes in terms of TCM (Traditional Chinese Medicine)." Furthermore, based upon a study of forty-four Wistar female rats, B. W. Fang and colleagues contend that "the mixture of reinforcing qi

and promoting blood circulation has the function of alleviating pathological changes of liver, reducing the content of liver collagen, improving erythrocytic function of clearing away immune complexes and regulating humoral immune response."

Specialists in Chinese medicine channel qi as part of qigong therapy, which aims "to 'stimulate' and 'balance' the flow of qi . . . through meridians ('energy pathways')." Qigong is a Chinese form of self-healing somewhat similar to some forms of meditative or prayer-based healing. "It involves contemplation, visualization (imagery), assumption of postures, and stylized breathing and body movements" (Raso, 2000). Somewhat similar to qigong, a Japanese form of healing, shinkiko, also relies on interaction with a spiritual realm of energy for healing. Although researchers have not yet studied this form of healing extensively, its popularity is growing in the West in conjunction with the increasingly high profile enjoyed by energy-based healing arts.

Some aspects of faith healing in cross-cultural perspective, such as shamanism and tribal practices, involve belief in spiritual realms accessible by healers on behalf of their patients. Shamanic healing practices often include "sensing and removing 'localized spiritual illness and pain'" in addition to techniques such as soul retrieval and the integration of parts of the soul (Raso, 2000). In the article "Clown Doctors: Shaman Healers of Western Medicine" (1995), L. M. van Blerkom observes similarities between shamanic healing and various palliative treatments in the West, specifically the Big Apple Circus Clown Care Unit, which works with children in New York City hospitals. According to van Blerkom, "there is not only superficial resemblance-weird costumes, music, sleight of hand, puppet/spirit helpers, and ventriloquism-but also similarity in the meanings and functions of their performances. Both clown and shaman violate natural and cultural rules in their performances. Both help patient and family deal with illness. Both use suggestion and manipulation of medical symbols in attempting to alleviate their patients' distress."

As Western medicine continues to gain acceptance in other parts of the world, it increasingly will face the task of integrating itself gracefully with traditional healing systems such that the different traditions can work together in a complementary fashion. For example, in Israel, Bedouin-Arabs (especially women) approach traditional healers before they seek biomedical health care. "The traditional system struck a stronger therapeutic alliance, tended to diagnose more comprehensibly, and was perceived by many patients as being more clinically beneficial." Furthermore, traditional healers can help biomedical practitioners "incorporate the family/community in treatment, and communicate in the patient's cultural idiom" (Al-Krenawi and Graham).

In the context of Africa, traditional tribal healing practices can work together with Western methods effectively, as, for example, in the case of treatment and education for diabetes in South Africa (Peltzer et al). Additionally, V. G. Chipfakacha argues in "STD/HIV/AIDS Knowledge, Beliefs, and Practices of Traditional Healers in Botswana" (1997) that "rapport between traditional healers and scientific medical personnel is essential for an effective and successful HIV/AIDS prevention and control programme" in the context of Africa because approximately seventy percent of African patients see traditional healers. Traditional healers experience increasing risk of contact with HIV/AIDS, which makes it imperative that they receive correct information about the virus and the disease.

See also PRAYER AND MEDITATION; SPIRITUALITY AND HEALTH

Bibliography

Al-Krenawi, A., and Graham, J. R. "Gender and Biomedical/Traditional Mental Health Utilization Among the Bedouin-Arabs of the Negev." *Culture, Medicine, and Psychiatry* 23, no. 2 (1999): 219-243.

Andresen, Jensine. "Meditation Meets Behavioral Medicine." *Journal of Consciousness Studies* 7, nos. 11-12 (2000): 17-73.

Chipfakacha, V. G. "STD/HIV/AIDS Knowledge, Beliefs, and Practices of Traditional Healers in Botswana." *AIDS Care* 9, no. 4 (1997): 417-425.

Conroy, R. M.; Siriwardena, R.; Smyth, O.; and Fernandes, P. "The Relation of Health Anxiety and Attitudes to Doctors and Medicine to Use of Alternative and Complementary Treatments in General Practice Patients." *Psychology, Health, and Medicine* 5, no. 2 (2000): 203-212.

Eisenberg, D. M.; Kessler, R. C.; van Rompay, M. I.; Kaptchuk, T. J.; Wilkey, S. A.; Appel, S.; and Davis, R. B. "Perceptions About Complementary Therapies Relative to Conventional Therapies Among Adults Who Use Both: Results from a National Survey." *Annals of Internal Medicine* 135, no. 4 (2001): 344-351.

Fang, B. W.; Zu, Q. G.; and Zhu, J. N. "Reinforcing Qi and Promoting Blood Circulation to Prevent Hepatic Fibrosis Due to Bovine Serum Albumin Immunologic Injury." *Zhongguo Zhong Xi Yi Jie He Za Zhi* 12, no. 12 (1992): 710, 738-740.

Fischer, J. E. "Laying On of the Hands." *Bulletin of the American College of Surgeons* 86, no. 1 (2001): 24-28.

Graham-Pole, J. "'Physician, Heal Thyself': How Teaching Holistic Medicine Differs from Teaching CAM." *Academic Medicine* 76, no. 6 (2001): 662-664.

Griffiths, V. "Eastern and Western Paradigms: The Holistic Nature of Traditional Chinese Medicine." *Australian Journal of Holistic Nursing* 6, no. 2 (1999): 35-38.

Hamm, R. M. "No Effect of Intercessory Prayer Has Been Proven." *Archives of Internal Medicine* 160, no. 12 (2000): 1872-1873.

Harding, O. G. "The Healing Power of Intercessory Prayer." *West Indian Medical Journal* 50, no. 4 (2001): 269-272.

Harris, W. S.; Gowda, M.; Kolb, J. W.; Strychacz, C. P.; Vacek, J. L.; Jones, P. G.; Forker, A.; and McCallister, B. D. "A Randomized, Controlled Trial of the Effects of Remote, Intercessory Prayer on Outcomes in Patients Admitted to the Coronary Care Unit." *Archives of Internal Medicine* 159, no. 19 (1999): 2273-2278.

Hoover, D. R., and Margolick, J. B. "Questions on the Design and Findings of a Randomized, Controlled Trial of the Effects of Remote, Intercessory Prayer on Outcomes in Patients Admitted to the Coronary Unit." *Archives of Internal Medicine* 160, no. 12 (2000): 1875-1876.

Linn, L. S., and Kahn, K. L. "Physician Attitudes Toward the 'Laying on of Hands' During the AIDS Epidemic." *Acad Med* 64, no. 7 (1989): 408-409.

Matthews, Dale. *The Faith Factor: Proof of the Healing Power of Prayer.* New York: Viking, 1998.

Matthews, D. A.; Marlowe, S. M.; and MacNutt, F. S. "Effects of Intercessory Prayer on Patients with Rheumatoid Arthritis." *Southern Medical Journal* 93, no. 12 (2000): 1117-1186.

Matthews, W. J.; Conti, J. M.; and Sireci, S. G. "The Effects of Intercessory Prayer, Positive Visualization, and Expectancy on the Well-Being of Kidney Dialysis Patients." *Alternative Therapeutic Health Medicine* 7, no. 5 (2001): 42-52.

Mind/body Medical Institute. Available from http://www.mbmi.org/pages/about5.asp.

Parkman, C. A. "CAM Therapies and Nursing Competency." *Journal of Nurses Staff Development* 18, no. 2 (2002): 61-65.

Peltzer, K.; Khoza, L. B.; Lekhuleni, M. E.; Madu, S. N.; Cherian, V. I.; and Cherian, L. "Concepts and Treatment for Diabetes Among Traditional and Faith Healers in the Northern Province, South Africa." *Curationis* 24, no. 2 (2001): 42-47.

Raso, Jack. *Dictionary of Alternative-Medicine Methods* (2000). Available from http://www.canoe.ca/AltmedDictionary.

Tonelli, M. R., and Callahan, T. C. "Why Alternative Medicine Cannot be Evidence-Based." *Academic Medicine* 76, no. 12 (2001): 1213-1220.

van Blerkom, L. M. "Clown Doctors: Shaman Healers of Western Medicine." *Medical Anthropology Quarterly* 9, no. 4 (1995): 462-475.

Yao, W.; Ding, G.; Shen, X.; Yang, J.; Chen, E.; Dang, R.; Chen, H.; Gu, Q.; Wang, S.; and Wei, H. "A hemodynamics model describing cardiac deficiency of qi." In *Sheng Wu Yi Xue Gong Cheng Xue Za Zhi* 19, no. 1 (2002): 53-56.

JENSINE ANDRESEN

SPIRITUALITY AND HEALTH

The topic of spirituality and health concerns the ways in which spirituality broadly understood is intertwined with concrete health status, both positive and negative. For example, in both indigenous and world religions, beliefs that demons or other malevolent spirits inhabit one's body may be taken as an explanation for mental or physical illness. Native healers and priests appropriately prescribe exorcisms in such cases, with "appropriateness" determined by the mythopoetic and narrative frameworks of the cultural context. Similarly, some religious communities (Benedictines, for example) view spirituality itself as an indicator of good health, understood as one's degree of meaningful integration with the fabric of the cosmos.

Since about 1980, such traditional portrayals of the relationship between spirituality and health have given way to a burgeoning literature bridging empirical and impressionistic domains that seeks to demonstrate linkages between one's type and level of spiritual and religious involvement on the one hand, and one's health status on the other. A comprehensive survey of this literature reveals many articles on the relationship between spirituality and coping that examine, for example, how spirituality assists in coping with major health challenges (Koenig, et al. 2001), such as cancer (Acklin, Borman), AIDS (Somlai et al.), stress (Joseph), and abuse (Ryan); how spirituality assists in coping with mortality and death (Rutledge et al., Atkinson); and how spirituality and aging relate to one another (Markides et al.). Another interesting category of research focuses on the long-term and therapeutic dimensions of religiosity and spirituality as they relate to mental health and therapy (Fukuyama and Sevig).

One prominent researcher in the field of spirituality and health, Harold G. Koenig, has worked with colleagues to examine religion as a coping strategy (Harold G. Koenig et al 1998) and how cultural diversity impacts care at the end of life (Barbara Koenig 1998). Harold Koenig also explores the relationship between spirituality, health, and aging (Koenig et al 1988), specifically focusing on mental health (Koenig 1994).

Additionally, in conjunction with the twelve-step movement, some researchers have posited that spirituality helps alleviate tendencies toward substance abuse (Pardini et al., Peetet). This last category of research raises interesting possibilities concerning a potential underside to the relationship between spirituality and health, since literature on religious addiction (Arterburn and Felton) may imply that spiritual practices themselves have the potential to activate the same neurocognitive pathways that support addictive behaviors in general.

Investigators also have examined the role of forgiveness, empathy, and altruism in contributing to positive health outcomes (Aderman and Berkowitz). Future research in this area, which will continue to be complemented by research in evolutionary biology on altruism among nonhuman primates and on the evolution of altruism itself, promises to expand the picture of what "health" itself may mean for human beings, for other sentient creatures, for ecosystems, and for the Earth's biosphere as a whole.

Because health and its maintenance necessarily employ the services of caregivers, another strand of research in the area of spirituality and health focuses on caregivers' own spiritual resources (Wright et al.) as they experience the ongoing, potentially exhausting exigencies of caring for others. Research on spirituality and ethics focuses on patients' rights when they receive care (Muldoon), particularly on patients' spiritual needs, and on arguments calling upon health care workers to provide spiritual resources to their patients. Researchers have also addressed the cultural dimensions of spirituality and healthcare, including immigrants' and minorities' experiences in the U.S. healthcare system (Andresen, Ahia). Finally, not all studies support the conclusion that spirituality functions favorably in supporting positive health outcomes. For example, a study published in 2001 by Kenneth Pargament, Harold Koenig, Nalini Tarakeshwar, and June Hahn demonstrates that patients who experience "religious struggle" (e.g., feelings that God has abandoned or punished them) experience a higher mortality rate than other patients.

As research at the interface of spirituality and health continues to gain acceptance within the medical community, patients' experience in the healthcare system may reflect improved sensitivity regarding their spiritual needs and concerns. Particularly at the end of life, or when confronted with traumatic or chronic conditions, patients may be expected to feel the need to understand their own experiences in the context of their religious or spiritual worldviews. Indeed, doing so may prove crucial to patients' recovery or their experience of peace at the time of death. Patients' families, too, may experience increased comfort when health care providers and medical institutions permit the incorporation of culturally appropriate religious or spiritual practices and explanations alongside the delivery of medical care in an effort to address their loved ones' suffering and existential questioning in an integrated and holistic manner. At the same time, religious worldviews that blame the sick for their own conditions are best avoided, not only because they have been demonstrated to increase mortality (as reported above), but also because justifying such interpretations theologically presents itself as a dubious endeavor, at best.

See also ALTRUISM; MEDICINE

Bibliography

Acklin, Marvin E. "The Role of Religious Values in Coping with Cancer." *Journal of Religion and Health* 22 (1983): 322–333.

Aderman, D., and Berkowitz, L. "Empathy, Outcome, and Altruism." *Proceedings of the Annual Convention of the American Psychological Association* 4 (1969): 379–380.

Ahia, C. E. "A Cultural Framework for Counseling African Americans." In *Multicultural Issues in Counseling: New Approaches to Diversity,* 2nd edition, ed. Courtland C. Lee. Alexandria, Va.: American Counseling Association, 1997.

Arterburn, Stephen, and Felton, Jack. *Toxic Faith: Understanding and Overcoming Religious Addiction.* Nashville, Tenn.: Oliver-Nelson, 1991.

Atkinson, M.E. "The Relationship of Coping Behaviors, Resurrection Beliefs, and Hopelessness Scores Among Bereaved Spouses of Hospice Patients." Ph.D. diss., George Fox College, 1995.

Borman, P. D. "Spirituality and Religiosity and Their Relationship to the Quality of Life in Oncology Patients." Dissertation Abstracts International: 2000.

Fukuyama, Mary. A., and Sevig, Todd D. *Integrating Spirituality into Multicultural Counseling.* Thousand Oaks, Calif.: Sage, 1999.

Hill, P. C.; Pargament, K. I.; Hood, R. W., Jr.; McCullough, M. E.; Sayers, J. P.; Larson, D. B.; and Zinnbauer, B. J. "Conceptualizing Religion and Spirituality: Points of Commonality, Points of Departure." *Journal of the Theory of Social Behavior* 30 (2000): 51-77.

Joseph, Mary. "The Effect of Strong Religious Beliefs on Coping with Stress." *Stress Medicine* 14, no. 4 (1998): 219–224.

Koenig, Barbara. "Cultural Diversity in Decision Making About Care At the End of Life." In *Approaching Death: Improving Care at the End of Life,* ed. Marilyn J. Field and Christine K. Cassel. Washington, D.C.: National Academy Press, 1998.

Koenig, Harold G.; Kvale, J. N.; and Ferrel, C. "Religion and Well-Being in Later Life." *The Gerontologist* 28, no. 1 (1988): 18–28.

Koenig, Harold G. "Religion and Prevention of Emotional Disorder in Later Life." Abstract published as part of the Symposium on Spirituality and Aging, 47th Gerontological Society of America Annual Scientific Meeting (Atlanta, Ga.; November 20–21, 1994). Published in *The Gerontologist* 34 (1994; special issue).

Koenig, Harold G.; Pargament, K. I.; and Nielsen, J. "Religious Coping and Health Status in Medically Ill Hospitalized Older Adults." *The Journal of Nervous and Mental Disease* 186, no. 9 (1998): 513–521.

Koenig, Harold G.; Larson, David B.; and Larson, Susan S. "Religion and Coping with Serious Medical Illness." *Annals of Pharmacotherapy* 35, no. 3 (2001): 352–359.

Markides, Kyriakos. S.; Levin, J. S.; and Ray, L. A. "Religion, Aging, and Life Satisfaction: An Eight-Year, Three-Wave Longitudinal Study." *The Gerontologist* 27 (1987): 660–665.

McCullough, M.; Pargament, K.; and Thorenson, C., eds. *Forgiveness: Theory, Research, Practice*. New York: Guilford Press, 2000.

Muldoon, M. H. "Spirituality, Health Care, and Bioethics." *Journal of Religion and Health* 34 (1995): 329–349.

Pardini, D. A.; Plante, T. G.; Sherman, A.; and Stumpe, J. E. "Religious Faith and Spirituality in Substance Abuse Recovery: Determining the Mental Health Benefits." *Journal of Substance Abuse Treatment* 19, no. 4 (2000): 347–354.

Pargament, Kenneth I.; Koenig, Harold G.; Tarakeswar, Nalini; and Hahn, June. "Religious Struggle as a Predictor of Mortality Among Medically Ill Elderly Patients: A Two Year Longitudinal Study." *Archives of Internal Medicine* 161 (2001): 1881–1885.

Pargament, Kenneth, and Maton, K. "Religion in American Life: A Community Psychology Perspective." In *Handbook of Community Psychology*, ed. J. Rappaport and E. Seidman. New York: Kluwer-Plenum, 2000.

Pargament, Kenneth I.; Poloma, M.; and Tara Keshwar, N. "Spiritual Healing, Karma, and the Bar Mitzvah: Methods of Coping from the Religions of the World." In *Coping and Copers: Adaptive Process and People*, ed. C. R. Snyder. New York: Oxford University Press, 2001.

Peteet, J. R. "A Closer Look at the Role of a Spiritual Approach in Addictions Treatment." *Journal of Substance Abuse Treatment* 10, no. 3 (1993): 263–267.

Rutledge, C. M.; Levin J. S.; Larson D. B.; and Lyons J. S. "The Importance of Religion for Parents Coping with a Chronically Ill Child." *Journal of Psychology and Christianity* 14, no. 1 (1995): 50–57.

Ryan, Patricia L. "Spirituality Among Adult Survivors of Childhood Violence: A Literature Review." *Journal of Transpersonal Psychology* 30, no. 1 (1998): 39–51.

Somlai, A. M.; Kelly, J. A.; Kalichman, S. C.; Mulry, G. W.; Sikkema, K. J.; McAuliffe, T.; Multhauf, K. E.; and Davantes, B. R. "An Empirical Investigation of the Relationship Between Spirituality, Coping, and Emotional Distress in People Living with HIV Infection and AIDS." *Journal of Pastoral Care* 50, no. 2 (1996): 181–191.

Wright, S.; Pratt, C.; and Schmall, V. "Spiritual Support for Caregivers of Dementia Patients." *Journal of Religion and Health* 24 (1985): 31–38.

JENSINE ANDRESEN

SPIRITUALITY AND THE PRACTICE OF SCIENCE

The notion of spirituality pertains to the practice of science in two ways. First, the spiritual character of scientists sometimes informs the ways in which they conduct scientific research. Indeed, some scientists like the astronomer Johannes Kepler (1571–1630) regarded their scientific research as a type of spiritual discipline. Second, for practitioners of the human sciences the recognition of a spiritual dimension in the people they study can have implications for how they work. It is also plausible to posit a relationship between these two points. Scientists who acknowledge a spiritual dimension in their own experience are probably more inclined to regard spirituality as a relevant feature of the people they study. Likewise, scientists with no spiritual inclinations are probably less attentive to what others call the spiritual aspects of life.

The psychologists William James (1842–1910) and Sigmund Freud (1856–1958) respectively illustrate these tendencies. Religious experience figured prominently in James's corpus of psychological writings as it did in his own personal life. Freud professed no religious commitments himself and sought to explain religion in others with reductive appeals to ideas such as wish fulfillment and obsessional neurosis. The Augustinian monk Gregor Mendel (1822–1884) is an exception to the pattern of religious scientists attending to spiritual aspects of their subject matter because he formulated general principles of inheritance without speculation about applications to spiritual traits in human beings. Charles Darwin (1809–1882) is a partial exception to the pattern of nonreligious scientists having little sense for the spiritual dimensions of what they study. Even though he eventually lost his religious faith, he retained until his death a sense of wonder at the complexity and beauty of nature's ways, including evolution by natural selection.

In contemporary Western culture spirituality is an ambiguous and vague notion. Part of its ambiguity arises because many people using the term insist upon defining it in their own way for their own purposes. Part of its vagueness occurs because it is often defined by what it is not (e.g., religion) and in relation to terms in well-known dichotomies (e.g., spirit versus matter). Given the focus here on the practice of science, spirituality will be identified with reference not to the ontological dualism of classical Greek philosophy (e.g., spirit versus matter), but to the phenomenological differentiation of whole and part. Most scientists think that spirituality loses relevance to the practice of science insofar as it presupposes aspects of archaic worldviews.

The spirituality of human experience is conceived as having outer and inner aspects. Facing outward, human existence is spiritual insofar as one engages reality as a maximally inclusive whole and makes the cosmos an intentional object of thought and feeling. Facing inward, life has a spiritual dimension to the extent that it is apprehended as a project of a person's most enduring and vital self and is structured by experiences of sudden self-transformation and subsequent gradual development. These two formulations need not be rigidly separated. Their integration is well expressed in first-century C.E. Roman writer Seneca's dramatic ideal: *Toti se inserens mundo* ("Plunging oneself into the whole world"; *Epistulae ad Lucilius,* 66.6). Considered as a whole, the spiritual dimension of human life is the embodied task of realizing one's truest self in the context of reality apprehended as a cosmic whole, of attaining an optimal relationship between what one truly is and everything that is.

The human relationship to the whole of reality has been variously expressed. In *The Republic* (532b) Plato (c. 427–347 B.C.E.) attributed to philosophers a supramental apprehension (*dialektos* or dialectic) of goodness itself. In 1984, the biologist Edward O. Wilson coined the word *biophilia* to mean "an innate tendency to focus on life and lifelike processes" (p. 1). In mystic and naturalistic idioms respectively these phrases identify a relationship with the world that is facilitated by scientific knowledge but that is rife with wider meanings. These two thinkers hold that whether people attain this relationship has momentous consequences: Wise government is at stake for Plato and biological diversity for Wilson.

The Spirituality of scientists

The practical implications of the spirituality of scientists are consequent to characteristic metaphysical and methodological principles. Three are of special importance: holism, realism, and determinism. The Greek notion of *kosmos* (cosmos) as a limited, ordered whole provides the basic concept that Pythagorean and Platonic philosophy elaborated

into a doctrine of metaphysical holism. Noting that diverse phenomena such as the movements of heavenly bodies, the harmonies of musical octaves, and the shapes of physical objects can be described with mathematical concepts, the Pythagoreans posited an underlying unitary numerical principal (*arithmos* or number). According to Aristotle (384–322 B.C.E.), some Pythagoreans gave such great priority to one numerical archetype—the *decad*—that they posited the "counter-earth" in order to instantiate it (*Metaphysics* 985b 22). When added to sun, moon, and the seven planets observable to the naked eye, the counter-earth became the tenth heavenly body. Practices like this have discredited naïvely metaphysical versions of holism, but the viewpoint survives in more modest methodological forms such as an aversion to descriptive forms of reductionism. Freud's reduction of religious phenomena to psychological factors is a prominent form of such reductionism.

Isaac Newton's *Philosophiae Naturalis Principia Mathematic* (Mathematical principles of natural philosophy) of 1687 proposed mathematical principles that govern "the system of the world." In a famous scholium in this work Newton set forth the absolute framework of space and time that is the precondition for the system. Although renowned for his aversion to speculative hypotheses (*hypotheses non fingo*) Newton offered no inductive argument for this absolute framework but, as in the case of the universal law of gravitation, he appealed informally to the will of God as an ultimate cause. Newton is typical of seventeenth-century scientists whose dual inheritance of Greek rationalism and biblical theism combined to give them great confidence that the world is real and orderly and that its order is knowable by human beings. Scientists whose spirituality posits reality as God's creation tend to find social constructionism uncongenial. For instance, ways of understanding religion similar to Peter Berger's and Thomas Luckmann's *The Social Construction of Reality* (1966) allow religion parity with other socially constructed phenomena but diminish its capacity to evoke awe and devotion. Sociological studies report higher levels of communal worship and private prayer among persons who identify themselves as traditionally religious than among more liberal religious persons and more diffusely spiritual respondents.

Many Western scientists have seen God's presence in providential care as well as in aboriginal creativity. Albert Einstein (1879–1955) is preeminent among such scientists in the twentieth century. Physicist Niels Bohr (1885–1951) said that Einstein once expressed reservations about a probabilistic interpretation of quantum mechanics by declining to consider "whether God plays dice with the universe." Einstein's commitment to deterministic explanations motivated him to seek an interpretation of quantum mechanics more compatible with his way of thinking than Bohr's idea of complementarity and Heisenberg's Uncertainty Principle. In a like fashion Einstein's good friend Kurt Gödel (1906–1978)—a mathematical Platonist—was not ready to allow his own limitative theorems to be the final word in mathematical logic; he preferred to think that more powerful axioms would one day be forthcoming. Spirituality sometimes motivates scientists to seek systems of thought more synthetic than those with which their colleagues are satisfied.

As the spirituality of contemporary scientists becomes less closely tied to classical philosophy and biblical theism, the commitment to traditional varieties of realism and determinism has waned. Fritjof Capra's *The Tao of Physics* (1975) is an example of this new sensibility and is notable for its embrace of both a metaphysical and methodological holism. Capra finds resources in Asian mystical traditions for a nonmaterialistic sort of realism and a nondeterministic conception of causality. Feminist thinkers have also offered alternatives to scientific worldviews emphasizing the domination and control of nature and the divorce of intellect from emotion and other noncognitive traits. Some feminist reinterpretations of scientific practice draw upon the experience of women scientists. For instance, Evelyn Fox Keller has clearly been influenced by the mystical elements in the character and practice of the biologist Barbara McClintock. Many contemporary ecofeminists are inspired by the spiritual approach to nature evident in the life and work of Rachel Carson (1907–1964).

The practice of science in understanding spirituality

Efforts of social scientists to attain scientific standing for their disciplines have proceeded along two different trajectories. The French positivist tradition of Auguste Comte (1798–1857) and Emile Durkheim (1858–1917) de-emphasized individual experience in favor of scientifically accessible features of human groups, and Durkheim pioneered the development of quantitative techniques for identifying regularities in social phenomena. In this context religion and spirituality are treated as epiphenomena that can be accounted for by more readily observable social, economic, and psychological factors. The German hermeneutic tradition of Max Weber (1864—1920) and Wilhelm Dilthey (1833–1911) gave more prominence to the scientist's intuitive understanding (*Verstehen*) of subjects who presumably share basic attributes and habits of valuations with their interpreters. For Weber a sociological law is "a statistical regularity that corresponds to an intelligible intended meaning" (quoted in Winch, p. 113). Efforts to understand religion and spirituality are paradigmatic of the challenge facing the social sciences (*Geistwissenschaften*) as Weber and Dilthey understand them. Religious phenomena such as God and salvation are not publicly observable and so must be apprehended by intuitive understanding.

The hermeneutic principle stating that any cultural artifact, such as a literary text or an architectural structure, should be interpreted in the context of the whole to which it belongs invokes the whole/part differentiation constitutive of the idea of spirituality described above. The most inclusive whole in which such understanding takes is often given spiritual meaning. The American philosopher Charles Sanders Peirce (1839–1914) did this with his novel ideas of *abduction* and *musement*. Abduction is a variety of inference (complementing induction and deduction) that consists of engendering and adopting a good explanatory hypothesis for a given phenomenon. It involves discovery more than justification. Musement occurs when people allow the powers of observation and reflection the liberty of "pure play." Peirce claimed that when musement is genuinely experienced it spontaneously gives rise to the "God-hypothesis" as the most basic hypothesis of human thought and the widest horizon in which human understanding occurs. Peirce was also a logician who advocated the view that scientific laws in both the natural and social sciences are ineluctably social and probabilistic. As with Capra's appeal to Asian mysticism, Peirce illustrates a spiritual sensibility that is scientific in a way that departs from classical realism and determinism.

Spirituality plays a role in the practice of science not only with regard to how statistical regularities are interpreted, but also with regard to how and why data is collected and analyzed. Efforts of epidemiologists, sociologists, and psychologists to understand the impact of various aspects of religiousness and spirituality on health outcomes illustrate the way in which studying spiritual subject matter influences scientific practice. For most of the twentieth century, epidemiologists were so disinclined to study the relationship between religion and health that one researcher, David Larson, described religion as the "forgotten variable." This same epidemiologist documented the high frequency with which religious phenomena illustrated psychopathologies in a recent version of the *Diagnostic and Statistical Manual of Mental Disorders* (*DSM*). Through the efforts of epidemiologists like Larson who acknowledge a spiritual dimension in both themselves and the people they study, epidemiological research into the relationships between religiousness and health is now funded and reviewed by agencies of the National Institutes of Health. Newer editions of the *DSM* have sought to provide a more empirical treatment of religion as factor related to mental health. In these specific ways the practice of epidemiology as a research activity has changed.

The results reported by epidemiologists about relationships between religion and health have also begun to inform clinical medicine and public health. Efforts toward "holistic medicine" predate the research of epidemiologists. For instance, the introduction of chiropractic techniques by Daniel David Palmer in the late nineteenth century were motivated by a conviction that health was dependent upon a free flow of "an intelligent force . . . usually known as spirit." Misplaced vertebrae impede the flow of spirit and so should be realigned. Chiropractic techniques are exemplary of spiritually motivated but demonstrably effective practices that have gradually been acknowledged by medical professionals, even when they reject the causal explanations underlying them. Meditation practices—often described more neutrally as relaxation or biofeedback techniques—have gained similar acceptance and for them epidemiological studies have provided empirical evaluations.

Public health practitioners have found that interventions addressed to communities, such as regular cancer screening and increased physical activity, are sometimes more effective at promoting healthy lifestyles than similar ones addressed to individuals. Results from epidemiological studies also show that religious people tend to have healthier lifestyles, with, for example, less use of tobacco and alcohol and more social support. Noting these points public health practitioners have started to work with religious communities, and especially with urban African-American churches, in order to implement disease prevention programs of various sorts. Seeing religious communities as potential partners rather than as ideological opponents is a major shift in public health policy and portends a productive change in public health practice.

Conclusion

In an influential 1948 World Health Organization document, health was defined as "a state of complete physical, mental, and social well-being and not merely as the absence of disease or infirmity." Some epidemiologists now advocate that spiritual well-being should be included in such comprehensive definitions. People, they contend, are never entirely free of disease or infirmity and so part of good health is the ability to cope with adversity. Religiousness has been shown to be associated with quicker recoveries from conditions like acute cardiovascular disease. It has also been shown to be associated with higher levels of life satisfaction and lower levels of pain in conditions like cancer, for which religion and psychosocial factors generally are less associated with quicker recoveries or longer survival. In conclusion, the impact of spirituality on the practice of science is most positive when it helps scientists be agents for achieving and understanding human well-being in its fullest sense and amidst the widest range of circumstances.

See also ARISTOTLE; DARWIN, CHARLES; ECOFEMINISM; EINSTEIN, ALBERT; FEMINISMS AND SCIENCE; NEWTON, ISAAC

Bibliography

Berger, Peter L., and Luckmann, Thomas. *The Social Construction of Reality: A Treatise in the Sociology of Knowledge.* New York: Doubleday, 1966.

Capra, Fritjof. *The Tao of Physics: An Exploration of the Parallels Between Modern Physics and Eastern Mysticism.* New York: Random House, 1975.

Darwin, Charles. *The Autobiography of Charles Darwin: 1809–1882.* New York: Norton, 1958.

Einstein, Albert. *Ideas and Opinions.* New York: Bonanza Books, 1954.

Keller, Evelyn Fox. *A Feeling for the Organism: The Life and Work of Barbara McClintock*. New York: W.H. Freeman, 1983.

Koenig, Harold G.; McCullough, Michael E.; and Larson, David B. *Handbook of Religion and Health*. New York: Oxford University Press, 2001.

Peirce, Charles Sanders. "A Neglected Argument for the Reality of God." In *The Collected Papers of Charles Sanders Peirce*, eds. Charles Hartshorne and Paul Weiss. Cambridge, Mass.: Harvard University Press, 1960.

Van Ness, Peter H. ed. *Spirituality and the Secular Quest*, Vol. 22: *World Spirituality: An Encyclopedic History of the Religious Quest*. New York: Crossroad, 1996.

Weber, Max. *Economy and Society: An Outline of Interpretative Sociology* (1922), trans. Ephraim Fischoff. Berkeley: University of California Press, 1978.

Wilson, Edward O. *Biophilia*. Cambridge, Mass.: Harvard University Press, 1984.

Winch, Peter. *The Idea of a Social Science and Its Relation to Philosophy*. London: Routledge and Kegan Paul, 1958.

PETER VAN NESS

STEADY STATE THEORY

The Steady State Theory of the universe was put forward in 1948 by cosmologists Hermann Bondi (b. 1919) and Thomas Gold (b. 1920), who were later joined by Fred Hoyle (1915–2001). The theory was an alternative to the standard Big Bang cosmology of the day, which suggested that the universe has a finite age. Motivated openly by philosophical implications of a non-eternal universe, Bondi, Gold, and Hoyle sought to discover whether an alternate explanation for the astronomical observations that produced the Big Bang theory was possible. The theory proposed the continuous creation of new matter in the empty spaces of expanding space-time. The idea of continuous creation was argued to be less problematic than the dramatic singularity of the Big Bang, which the Steady State Theory could avoid.

The theory was largely abandoned after the discovery by Arno Penzias (b. 1933) and Robert Wilson (b. 1936) in 1965 of the microwave background radiation in the universe, which showed that the universe was much denser in the distant past, contrary to the predictions of the Steady State Theory. While the theory never gained widespread support it played an important role in the history of modern science. It helped to tentatively confirm the status of standard Big Bang cosmology, it showed the importance and necessity of seeking alternate theories, and it demonstrated that philosophical and even theological views can be significant sources of inspiration for scientific theories.

See also BIG BANG THEORY; CREATIO CONTINUA

MARK WORTHING

STEM CELL RESEARCH

Few topics in science and religion have been as hotly contested in recent years as stem cell research, largely because it involves the fate of, disposition of, and research on the human embryo. There are two basic types of stem cell research—that involving adult cells (AS cells) and that involving human embryonic cells (ESCs or hES cells); only the latter is a source of controversy. In both cases, research is still at the early stages regarding the programming and uses of these cells, and there is comparatively little data about the efficacy of AS and hES cells for human therapies. That is why most scientists agree that, in the United States, government funding should be widely available for research on both types of stem cells, an issue that has been contested in the U.S. Congress.

Stem cells are unspecialized and so are able to renew indefinitely; they also have the capacity to differentiate into specialized cells. In humans, these cells are found in some adult organs, in blood, and in bone marrow (Mezey et al. 2000; Bjornson et al.1999); in the inner cell mass of the human embryo at the blastocyst stage (five to six days after fertilization) (Thomson et al. 1998); on the gonadal ridge of aborted or miscarried fetuses (Shamblott et al. 1998); and in the placenta and umbilical cord (hematopoetic stem cells).

Because stem cells have the capacity to regenerate, particularly ESCs, they have ushered in the era of "regenerative medicine," signaling that, in theory, these cells can be used to regenerate human tissues and cells, and ultimately increase quality of life and the human life span. Embryonic stem cells are the progenitor cells for the human body and at their earliest stage (the blastocyst stage) they are completely undifferentiated and can give rise to any cell type in the human body (totipotent, pluripotent, and multipotent are all terms that have been used to describe this phenomenon). At this stage the cells have not yet received their "marching orders" for what they will become; therefore, scientists have been experimenting with controlling the programming of ESCs in culture in order to direct their ends (controlled differentiation) to specialized cells such as blood, skin, and nerve cells.

In order to extract these embryonic stem cells, scientists must collapse the trophectoderm that surrounds the blastocyst in order to get the stem cells from the inner cell mass (ICM) where they reside within the blastocyst or pre-embryo. Such a technique destroys the pre-embryo and renders it incapable of implantation in the uteran wall. This is the crux of the ethical problem for those who oppose embryonic stem cell research.

Studies in 2001 and 2002 indicate the potential for primate parthenotes to form embryonic stem cells and to develop a variety of differentiated cell types in culture (Cibelli et al. 2001; Holden 2002). Parthenotes are embryos that grow from unfertilized eggs (chemically tricked into fertilizing and retaining the full choromosomal complement) that are, so far as is known, incapable of becoming viable fetuses in primates and humans. Thus, scientists hope that this may prove to be an ethically uncontroversial way to obtain stem cells, allowing researchers to avoid therapeutic cloning as means to this end.

The ethical and religious issues surrounding stem cell research concern not so much the therapeutic ends of the research (cures for Parkinson's disease, juvenile diabetes, Alzheimer's disease, heart disease, and a host of other degenerative diseases); rather, the controversy surrounds the status of the human embryo and points to larger issues about what it means to be human and when life begins.

The Roman Catholic Church and conservative Protestant churches have made the strongest opposition to embryonic stem cell research of all religious traditions in the United States. The Catholic position is that life begins at conception; thus the human embryo is accorded the full rights and dignity of a human person from the very moment that the sperm penetrates the egg. Therefore, it is a grave sin to destroy any human embryo since the act constitutes destruction of life itself, a responsibility belonging only to God. Moreover, the Catholic Church has opposed the creation of human embryos for research purposes (therapeutic cloning, for example) for two reasons: To do so would be to treat human life as a mere means to an end, which is a violation of human dignity and the sanctity of life; and embryos ought only to be created in conjunction with the conjugal act of love within the context of marriage (natural law). (Donum Vitae 1987). It is important to note, however, that there are a variety of dissenting Catholic positions on this issue.

Conservative Protestant churches such as the Southern Baptist Convention and fundamentalist independent Christian churches have tended to join the Catholic protest against ESC research and have emphasized prioritizing AS research as an acceptable means to the end of regenerative therapies. The rationale for such opposition does not emphasize a natural law approach to ethics and emphasizes instead a biblical approach. An argument that the Christian tradition has a mandate to protect the weakest and most vulnerable members of society (the embryo in this case) is advanced by Lutheran theologian Gilbert Meilaender in his essay "Some Protestant Reflections" (2001).

On the other hand, mainline Protestant denominations (United Church of Christ, Episcopal, Presbyterian, Methodist) tend to be supportive of all stem cell research so long as the human embryo is treated with respect. In 2001, the General Convention of the Presbyterian Church voted to endorse embryonic stem cell research. Mainline Protestantism has focused on the great amount of good that can come of this research and on concerns of distributive justice to ensure that the poor will receive the benefits of stem cell research equally with the rich. Moreover, most mainline Protestants (and many Catholics) support using excess embryos for stem cell research. These embryos have been frozen in fertility clinics and would be thawed and discarded eventually if they were not put to what many believe is a good end—human healing. One Lutheran theologian who supports ESC research, in contrast to Meilaender's argument, is Ted Peters (Peters 2001).

Although there are three main branches of Judaism (Orthodox, Conservative, and Reform), and it is sometimes difficult to find agreement on bioethical issues, in this case most Jewish scholars are supportive of all stem cell research. This is due, primarily, to the fact that Judaism professes a strong mandate from God to heal and to reduce human suffering. Moreover, in Jewish law the embryo has no moral standing outside the womb; a developing embryo in laboratory culture is morally neutral until implantation. Therefore, the ends of all stem cell research appear to be morally coherent with Jewish ethics (Dorff).

Islam is also a diverse religious tradition. However, in general, Islam would be in favor of all forms of stem cell research since there appear to be no "recent rulings in Islamic bioethics regarding the moral status of the blastocyst from which the stem cells are isolated" (Sachedina). Islamic scholars have found that the Qur'an's focus is primarily on the developing fetus in the womb. Islam shares with Judaism a concern with human healing; thus, if ESCs hold real (not just speculative) potential for therapeutic healing, there would be no objection to proceeding with such research.

See also BIOTECHNOLOGY; CHRISTIANITY, ROMAN CATHOLIC, ISSUES IN SCIENCE AND RELIGION; CLONING; DNA; GENE PATENTING; GENE THERAPY; GENETIC ENGINEERING; GENETICS; JUDAISM; ISLAM

Bibliography

Bjornson, Christopher R. R., et al. "Turning Brain into Blood: a Hematopoietic Fate Adopted by Adult Neural Stem Cells In Vivo." *Science* 283 (1999): 534–7.

Cibelli, Jose B., et al. "Parthenogenetic Stem Cells in Nonhuman Primates." *Science* 295 (2002): 819.

Chapman, Audrey R.; Frankel, Mark S.; and Garfinkel, Michele S. "Stem Cell Research and Applications: Monitoring the Frontiers of Biomedical Research." In *AAAS Science and Technology Policy Yearbook,* eds. Albert H. Teich, Stephen D. Nelson, Ceilia McEnaney, and Stephen J. Lita. Washington, D.C.: American Association for the Advancement of Science, 2000. Available from http://www.aaas.org/spp/yearbook/2000.

Doerflinger, Richard. "Destructive Stem-Cell Research on Human Embryos." *Origins* 28 (1999): 769–773.

Congregation for the Doctrine of the Faith. "Donum Vitae (Gift of Life): Instruction on Respect for Human Life in Its Origins and on the Dignity of Procreation, Replies to Certain Questions of the Day." Washington, D.C.: United States Catholic Conference, 1987.

Dorff, Elliot N. "Stem Cell Research: A Jewish Perspective." In *The Human Embryonic Stem Cell Debate: Science, Ethics and Public Policy,* ed. Suzanne Holland, Karen Lebacqz, and Laurie Zoloth. Cambridge, Mass.: The MIT Press, 2001.

Farley, Margaret A. "Roman Catholic Views on research Involving Human Embryonic Stem Cells." In *The Human Embryonic Stem Cell Debate: Science, Ethics and Public Policy,* ed. Suzanne Holland, Karen Lebacqz, and Laurie Zoloth. Cambridge, Mass.: The MIT Press, 2001.

Green, Ronald M. "The Stem Cell Conundrum." *Religion in the News* 4 (2001): 18–20, 25.

Holland, Suzanne; Lebacqz, Karen; and Zoloth, Laurie, eds. *The Human Embryonic Stem Cell Debate: Science, Ethics, and Public Policy.* Cambridge, Mass.: MIT Press, 2001.

Meilaender, Gilbert. "Some Protestant Reflections." In *The Human Embryonic Stem Cell Debate: Science, Ethics, and Public Policy,* eds. Suzanne Holland, Karen Lebacqz, and Laurie Zoloth. Cambridge, Mass.: MIT Press, 2001.

Mezey, Éva, et al. "Turning Blood into Brain: Cells Bearing Neuronal Antigens Generated In Vivo from Bone Marrow." *Science* 290 (2000): 1779–82.

National Bioethics Advisory Commission. *Ethical Issues in Human Stem Cell Research,* 3 vols. Rockville, Md.: NBAC, 1999–2000.

National Research Council Committee on Biological and Biomedical Applications of Stem Cell Research; United States Institute of Medicine Board on Neuroscience and Behavioral Health; and National Research Council Board on Biology. *Stem Cells and the Future of Regenerative Medicine.* Washington, D.C.: National Academy Press, 2002.

Peters, Ted. "Embryonic Stem Cells and the Theology of Dignity." In *The Human Embryonic Stem Cell Debate: Science, Ethics and Public Policy,* eds. Suzanne Holland, Karen Lebacqz, and Laurie Zoloth. Cambridge, Mass.: MIT Press, 2001.

Sachedina, Abdulaziz. "Islamic Perspectives on Research with Human Embryonic Stem Cells." In *Ethical Issues in Human Stem Cell Research,* Vol. 3. Rockville, Md.: National Bioethics Advisory Commission, 2000.

Shamblott, Michael J., et al. "Derivation of Pluripotent Stem Cells from Cultured Human Primordial Germ

Cells." *Proceedings of the National Academy of Sciences* (USA) 95 (1998): 13726–31.

Thomson, James A., et al. "Embryonic Stem Cell Lines Derived from Human Blastocysts." *Science* 282 (1998): 1145–7.

SUZANNE HOLLAND

STRING THEORY

String theory, also called *superstring theory,* is, generally speaking, any physico-mathematical framework that describes fundamental physical reality in terms of superstrings *Strings* in this context should not be confused with *cosmic strings,* which are one-dimensional (string-like) regions of cosmic extent containing vacuum energy different from that of the true vacuum. The superstrings of string theory, in contrast, are extremely tiny loops, or possibly segments, that have been suggested as the most fundamental of all physical entities, and as the source of all other fields and particles.

Before the 1980s, the most fundamental entities were most often considered to be *particles,* which are zero-dimensional objects, but it has become clear that particle models do not provide a rich and flexible enough basis for fundamental quantum field theories; strings are much more suitable. More specifically, string theory provides promising candidates for an adequate quantum theory of gravity and, at the same time, for theories of the total unification of all four fundamental physical interactions (gravity, electromagnetism, and the strong and weak nuclear forces. Grand Unified Theory (GUT) will provide unification of the three nongravitational interactions.

Quantum mechanics (along with its extension to quantum field theory) and Albert Einstein's (1879–1955) theory of gravitation are two important pillars of contemporary physics. And yet, as they are presently formulated, they are deeply incompatible with one another. As of 2002, constructing a complete and adequate quantum theory of gravity has evaded the best efforts of theoreticians. Exciting and surprising work on superstrings since about 1984, however, has moved science much closer to achieving quantization of the gravitational field, thus resolving and healing this incompatibility. It is already clear that the leading string theory candidates yield general relativity as their low-energy limit. Essentially, this means that string theory, if successful, will become not only the quantum theory of gravity, but also the quantum theory of space and time, with crucial applications to early-universe cosmology.

It also appears likely that some version of string theory will at the same time unify all four fundamental physical interactions, including gravity, thus bringing to successful completion the much heralded quest for unification that motivated the physicist James Clark Maxwell (1831–1879), Einstein, and so many others. In order to accomplish this unification, the strings must manifest *supersymmetry*—they must be *superstrings.* Consider that all fundamental particles have either half-integral spin ($\frac{1}{2}$, $\frac{3}{2}$, . . .) or integral spin (0, 1, 2, . . .). The half-integral spin particles are called *fermions,* and constitute the building blocks of matter; protons, neutrons, electrons, and quarks are all fermions. The integral spin particles are called *bosons,* and are the force-carriers between the fermions, mediating the electromagnetic, gravitational, and strong and weak interactions. *Photons, W massive bosons, Z massive bosons, gluons,* and *gravitons* are the bosons that mediate the electromagnetic, weak, strong, and gravitational interactions, respectively.

Fermions and bosons satisfy different statistics and symmetries, and have to be treated differently in standard quantum field theory. The first seriously considered string theories—studied for purposes other than those for which newer superstring theories are studied—were bosonic strings, which only incorporated the symmetries and statistics of bosons. Obviously, if a theory is going to unify all particles and fields, it will have to incorporate the symmetries of both fermions and bosons within the same framework; it will have be *supersymmetric,* and the strings will therefore have be superstrings.

Where would the superstring description of reality be needed? Certainly, it would provide a detailed and physically complete explanation of all the characteristics and parameters of material reality, including their deep interconnections and their origins in the vibrations and interactions of the fundamental superstrings. It would, at the same time, provide an adequate description of material reality at temperatures higher than 10^{32} K, where the general relativistic description of space, time, and mass-energy breaks down. There was a time in the very early universe, immediately after the Big Bang, when those temperatures obtained and during which the physics of the universe was that of a single unified fully quantitized superforce. This era is referred to as the *Planck era,* after the German theoretical physicist Max Planck (1858–1947). In fact, it is only in such terms that the Big Bang itself, as well as the emergence or origin of space, time, and matter, can really be characterized.

Superstring theories resolve a number of difficult anomalies and divergences in quantum theory. But they also lead to some features that are, at first sight, puzzling. One of these is that they almost always require higher dimensions—for example ten or twenty-six—rather than the three spatial dimensions and one time dimension that characterize the low-energy world. How then can these superstring theories be reconciled with reality as we know it? The answer is straightforward but surprising. At very high energies or temperatures, such as immediately after the Big Bang, reality will be ten dimensional or twenty-six dimensional, as described by superstring theory. But, as the universe exits the Planck era, and enters the classical domain where gravity is adequately described by Einstein's general relativity and is no longer unified with the other interactions, the extra dimensions compactify (curl up into infinitesimal knots) leaving only the four-dimensional spacetime with which we are familiar. Of course, if this is true, scientists should find some evidence of these extra curled-up dimensions. Such relics of the supersymmetric past would constitute powerful confirmation of superstring theories. This is an active area of research.

Relevance to theology

The relevance of string theory for the relationship between science and theology is clear, particularly in light of its applications to very early universe cosmology. First, a fully adequate string theory would give a complete unification and explanation of the laws of nature at the level of physics. In so doing, it would fill out the description of one of the most fundamental and pervasive sets of relationships through which God creatively acts in the universe. Secondly, it would give a much better description of the physics of the earliest phase of the universe's evolution, doing away with the initial singularity and helping scientists to speak more precisely about the origin of space and time, of all the laws of physics, and possibly of mass-energy. This would certainly help to delineate the limits of scientific explanation more compellingly. It is extremely unlikely, for instance, that the ultimately successful string theory will entail the existence of a unique universe or that it will explain why there is something rather than absolutely nothing, or that it will account for why there is this type of order, as specified by the string theory, rather than some other order. A clear appreciation of such limitations would enhance the understanding of the interactions, possible and desirable, between religion and science.

See also COSMOLOGY; GRAND UNIFIED THEORY; GRAVITATION; PHYSICS, QUANTUM; SUPERSTRINGS

Bibliography

Davies, Paul. "The New Physics: A Synthesis." In *The New Physics,* ed. Paul Davies. Cambridge, UK: Cambridge University Press, 1989.

Green, Michael B; Schwarz, John H.; and Witten, Edward. *Superstring Theory,* Vol. 1. Cambridge, UK, and New York: Cambridge University Press, 1987.

Greene, Brian. *The Elegant Universe: Superstrings, Hidden Dimensions, and the Quest for the Ultimate Theory.* New York and London: Norton, 1999.

Kaku, Michio. *Introduction to Superstrings and M-Theory,* 2nd edition. New York, Berlin, and Heidelberg, Germany: Springer-Verlag, 1998.

Polchinski, Joseph. *String Theory,* volume 1. Cambridge, UK: Cambridge University Press, 1998.

Salam, Abdus. "Overview of Particle Physics." In *The New Physics,* ed. Paul Davies. Cambridge, UK: Cambridge University Press, 1989.

WILLIAM R. STOEGER

SUBJECTIVITY

See CONSCIOUSNESS STUDIES; EPISTEMOLOGY

SUFFERING

See EVIL AND SUFFERING

SUPERNATURALISM

The meaning and the history of the word *supernatural* depends entirely upon the order that it seems to supersede: the natural. The French Jesuit theologian Henri de Lubac (1896–1991), in his erudite and controversial book *Surnatural* (1946), provides a significant history of the transmission of the word. He informs us that it was only in the ninth century, with Carolingian translations of Pseudo-Dionysius (c. fifth century C.E.) and John Scotus Eriugena (c. 810–877), that the Latin word *supernaturalis* entered theology. Even then its usage was rare until the middle of the thirteenth century, and it did not come into standard use until after the Council of Trent in the middle of the sixteenth century.

History of the word and the concept in the West

The reason for the hesitancy of its use prior to the dawning years of modernity, before the rise of the secular as a domain distinct from the sacred and the physical as distinct from the metaphysical, was an older semantic resonance associated with the word *natural*. The early Christian fathers, in speaking of the difference between Adam's fallen state of sin and carnality and the salvation wrought in Christ, interpreted Adam and Eve's previous nakedness as the "natural" state. The "natural" was the human condition without sin; the pristine state in which was manifested the untarnished image of God. Such a natural condition was to be redeemed, not superseded. Even in the late sixteenth century, when the English poet and courtier Sir Philip Sidney (1554–1586), came to write his famous *Defence of Poesie,* the point could be made that poetry's efficacy lay in being able to transmute this corruptible world back into its pristine and idealized naturalness. The "supernatural" then arrives late in the cultural history of the West.

Early cosmology certainly conceived of realms, powers, and principalities beyond the mundane. The ancient Greeks had their notion of the heavens (*ouranios*) and even of a place above the heavens (*uperouranios*) from which the gods descended. Derived in part from Plato's *Timaeus* and Aristotle's *Physics,* the ultraheaven, and its synonym the hypercelestial (*uperkosmios*), announced a cosmological, epistemological, ethical, aesthetic,

and ontological hierarchy. Everyday experience was mythologized as one traversed the lines between the visible and the invisible, the sensuous and the intelligible, the body and the soul. Such was the veneration for the ancients and for ancient knowledge (which was believed to be closer to the truth because nearer in time to Adam and Eve's experience in Eden), that this cosmology remained in place throughout Christendom until the maps of the universe were redrawn in the seventeenth century.

In the New Testament, the writer of the Gospel of John has Jesus speaking of the need to be born from above (*anothen*). In his first Letter to the Corinthian, in a series of distinctions between the body, soul, and spirit, Paul (himself experiencing a translation to the third heaven) writes of the celestial man (*anthropos ex ouranou*) whose image humans bear. This usage seemed to have sanctioned the adoption of the term, and its cosmological associations, by the early Greek fathers (particularly Clement of Alexandria (c. 150–215) and Origen (c. 185–254)). The celestial and hypercosmic as realms of the spiritual and divine became spheres occupied by Christ, the Spirit, and God himself. The term was translated directly into Latin, for we find Tertullian (c. 155–220) writing about Christ as supercelestial in *De carnis resurrectione.* Other Latin writers used *supermundialis* or *supermundanus* similarly. As with the ancient Greeks, the orders of existence differed in the celestial realms, and so Origen, and later Augustine of Hippo (354–430), described angels as having a supercelestial nature (*phusis*). Gradually, discussions begin to appear of the celestial essence (*uperousios, uperousiotes*) and descriptions of the Trinity as the super-essential. These words are translated in Latin as *supersubstantialis* and *superessentialis.* But it still remains significant that *supernaturalis* arrives much later, only to become the most common word of all.

What is different about *supernaturalis* is that it more explicitly defines a nature, powers, and dominions that are unearthly. There had, of course, been the dualistic myths of the Zoroastrians and, later, Gnostics, that had separated the forces in the world above from those operating in the sublunar realm. But despite the dualistic cosmology, the transit between the above and the below constituted a continuum. With *supernaturalis* a distinction was being made such that, by the seventeenth century, any incursions from the supernatural realm were understood as ruptures of the natural order. As such, *supernaturalis* could only gain currency as that which was *naturalis* came to be understood as the order of things in the postlapsarian, rather than the prelapsarian, world. This distinction arose in mediaeval theology.

For the medieval Christian philosopher Thomas Aquinas (c. 1225–1274) God is the supernatural truth contemplated by the fathers, the supernatural cause of all things, a supernatural principle whose effects are registered throughout the created world. These were not entirely separate, or even antithetical, orders of being as the latter participated in the former by being the effects of the God who maintained and sustained them. The participation of creation in the operations of the divine constituted the *sacramentum mundi*. Nevertheless, for Aquinas, theological knowledge as a divine science rested upon understanding the effects of God within creation as revealed in Christ, the operation and pedagogy of salvation. He distinguished such knowledge from the knowledge of created things in themselves, which was a natural science.

This distinction between knowledge on the basis of revelation and knowledge on the basis of observation led increasingly to a division of intellectual labor, and the examination of things created took on an independence that, ultimately, led to the establishing of "Nature." The Reformation emphasis upon faith as distinct from human reasoning, revelation opposed to fallen creation, called into question the older construals of the *sacramentum mundi*. So by the time of the Council of Trent (and the Catholic counterreformation), "Nature" was becoming an autonomous, rule-governed realm open for systematic enquiry, manipulation, and improvement. When the older Platonic and Ptolemaic cosmologies were being superseded, then the supercelestial lost its valance. The "supernatural" arrives as that which transcends the natural and is superior to the natural insofar as it is more powerful (for both good and evil) in being more spiritual.

Secularization and disenchantment

According to M. H. Abrahams, the contemporary understanding of the supernatural is a cultural product of early romanticism and the processes of secularization. With modernity and the authority given to human reasoning, the increasing exploration and cataloguing of the natural world, and with the continuing Protestant attacks upon superstition, the world became secularized.

Secularization brought about a demythologisation of human experience, just as the technological calculation and manipulation of the world brought about what the sociologist and economist Max Weber (1864-1920) termed its "disenchantment." The process of disenchantment took place through the systemic rationalization of observable (and therefore verifiable) phenomena. The early romantics were themselves reacting against the stripping of the world of its mysteries and mythologies—the world according to the mathematics and mechanics as Isaac Newton (1642–1727) conceived it and the industrial revolution constructed it.

In an early essay titled "Language and Human Nature," the philosopher Charles Taylor wrote of a distinction between two views of the world, the objectivist and the expressivist. In premodern cosmologies what was real was expressive of creation's divine and spiritual origins. But from René Descartes (1596–1650) onwards the world was not viewed in terms of its theological provenance, but in terms of what the human subject observed. Objectivism conceived the world as a realm of contingent, neutral facts that could be gathered encyclopedically. Materiality lost its translucence and became opaque. Objects lay passive beneath the scrutinizing gaze of a subject who calibrated and catalogued them. This objectivist realm, from the seventeenth century onwards, became nature and all its values, laws, and dynamics were immanent and self-manifesting. The natural was that which presented itself to the senses and could therefore be examined by empirical science. It was a state that lent itself to systematic explanation. Nature could be made to deliver up whatever secrets it contained so that people might learn how the use them to their own advantage.

A new functionalist, instrumentalist, pragmatic, and utilitarian approach to the world cut creation free from a dependency upon a creator. In doing this a series of further divisions followed: subject and object, the cultural and the natural, the private and the public, the freedom of enlightenment and the dangerous darkness of ignorance. The supernatural was born of these new binaries. It was conceived as the opposite of the natural, that which stood outside of the rational and integrated orders of nature. The supernatural was then irrational, disordered, a realm of darkness, ignorance, and superstition. Religion—a conceptual category also coined during this time—was to be purged of these cruder, mythological elements and refigured, as the philosopher Immanuel Kant (1724–1804) termed it, within the limits of reason alone. As such, religion—a private devotion that no longer trespassed on public truth—was clawed back from the supernatural. Catholicism, with its liturgical and doctrinal commitment to the sacramental world view, was repeatedly condemned by both deists and Protestants for its supernaturalism and its promotion of superstition.

Re-enchantment

The supernatural as it emerged from the gothic imagination came to be defined as a realm of forces and dominions beyond the human. These forces and dominions are either mythically organized in some cosmic battle between good and evil (angels, demons, wizards, and vampires) or make manifest another dimension following death (ghosts, hauntings, and intimations of heaven). Both of these forms of the supernatural have a history within the Western tradition, but, as Mark Edmundson has noted, what is striking in contemporary Western and Eastern cultures is the resurgence of that gothic imagination.

There has been a cultural shift with respect not only to the credibility of the supernatural but also to its interface with the everyday. Postmodernity, as the sociologist Zygmunt Bauman observes, has re-enchanted the world. The everyday is again being mythologized, such that where once C. S. Lewis placed his supernatural world of Narnia on the far side of the wardrobe, the writers Philip Pullman and J. K. Rowling have their supernatural worlds investing the ordinary. Furthermore, the scientific reasoning that Weber saw as fundamental to the process of disenchantment plays an important role in the re-enchantment of the world. In the popular imagination the cyborg, the clone, the alien, and the android have all joined the traditional array of supernatural figures. Science has absorbed the supernatural, as more and more cyberspace games trade in gothic fantasies, and the exhilaration of surfing the net is being described in terms once reserved for mystical experiences of self-transcendence.

See also NATURALISM; NATURE; THOMAS AQUINAS

Bibliography

Abrams, Meyer Howard. *Natural Supernaturalism: Tradition and Revolution in Romantic Literature.* New York: Norton, 1971.

Bauman, Zygmunt. "Introduction." In *Intimations of Postmodernity.* London: Routledge, 1992.

Edmundson, Mark. *Nightmare on Main Street: Angels, Sadomasochism, and the Culture of the Gothic*: Cambridge, Mass.: Harvard University Press, 1997.

Heim, Michael. *The Metaphysics of Virtual Reality.* Oxford: Oxford University Press, 1993.

Lubac, Henri de. *Surnaturel: Etudes Historiques.* Paris: Aubier, 1946.

Lubac, Henri de. *Le Mystère du Surnaturel.* Paris: Editions Montaigne, 1965. Available in English as *The Mystery of the Supernatural,* trans. Rosemary Sheed. New York: Crossroad, 1998.

Taylor, Charles. "Language and Human Nature." *In Human Agency and Language: Philosophical Papers 1.* Cambridge, UK: Cambridge University Press, 1985.

Ward, Graham. *Cities of God.* London: Routledge, 2000.

GRAHAM WARD

SUPERSTRINGS

Superstrings are extremely tiny, theoretically postulated, one-dimensional loops or segments that are conceived as being the most fundamental physical entities, superseding point particles in that role. All other particles and fields, both bosonic (integer spin, interaction carrying) and fermionic (half-integer spin, matter constituting), are then considered to be the result of the vibrations and interactions of these superstrings. Superstring theories hold the best hope for unifying quantum theory with Albert Einstein's General Relativity. They should at the same time effect the total unification of the four fundamental physical forces: electromagnetism, the weak and strong nuclear interactions, and gravity. These fundamental objects are called *superstrings* instead of just *strings* because they manifest *supersymmetry,* which means that both bosons and fermions are treated within the same mathematical framework, or symmetry group.

See also STRING THEORY

WILLIAM R. STOEGER

SUPERVENIENCE

Ever since Donald Davidson introduced the notion of supervenience within the philosophy of mind in 1970, it has come to play a key role in philosophical discussions regarding reducibility and the ontological structure of the world in general. With its help, philosophers of mind, in particular, hoped to solve the question of whether a nonreductive kind of materialism could be upheld that would avoid the pitfalls of traditional dualism on the one hand and of traditional materialism on the other. The key attraction of supervenience was that it seemed to deliver dependence without reduction. Events at higher levels of reality could thus be seen as totally determined by lower-level events without higher-level laws of the so-called special sciences being reducible to physics.

Definition and types

In a loose sense, the core idea is as follows: B-properties (e.g., mental properties) supervene on A-properties (e.g., physical properties) if any two possible situations identical in their A-properties are identical in their B-properties. In other words, the B-facts "come along with" the A-facts, hence supervenience. The term is derived from the Latin words *venire* (to come) and *super* (on top of). Thus, if B-properties supervene on A-properties, then once the A-facts are fixed, the B-facts are fixed. They are automatically put in place as soon as the lower-level properties are put in their place. This is because, where supervenience reigns, there is no room for variation of the higher-level properties independently of the lower-level (e.g., physical) properties. In this way supervenience yields ontological dependency relations. At the same time supervenience has also been supposed to bar reducibility, thus freeing the way for a novel nonreductive brand of materialism in the philosophy of mind and, more generally,

allowing special sciences to be autonomous without abandoning, as in traditional dualism, a unified materialist picture of the world.

The dependency relations enabled by supervenience may in fact vary in strength depending on the specific kind of supervenience relation involved. The above definition of supervenience, in effect, generates in its turn four different kinds of supervenience relations. First, the word *situation* as used in that definition may refer either to individuals or to entire worlds. Accordingly, local and global supervenience must be distinguished. Secondly, the word *possible* may refer to either logical or nomological possibility, giving rise to logical versus natural supervenience.

For the former distinction between local and global supervenience, consider an animal and its molecular "twin" (a molecule-by-molecule replica of the given animal). Although they must share the same shape, they do not necessarily share the same degree of fitness, since they do not necessarily share type-identical environments. Hence, shape, but not fitness, supervenes locally on physical properties. However, fitness does supervene globally on physical properties. When all the physical facts of this world are duplicated so that molecular twins will also be located in type-identical habitats, then physical duplicates must share exactly the same degree of fitness.

Clearly, local supervenience is the stronger of the two supervenience relations. Properties that are locally supervenient must also be globally supervenient, but not vice versa. Conversely, many more properties turn out to be dependent on lower-level properties when considered under broad conditions of global supervenience than when they are considered in local isolation, so to speak, regardless of context. Thus it can easily be seen that if we duplicate all the physical facts of the entire universe down to the minutest details of the distribution of microphysical properties in space and time (and we do nothing else), then all the biological facts of our world will be duplicated as well. Since the physical "recipe" of our world fixes all its objects, including the way they move and function and the way they physically interact, it, in effect, also fixes the biological facts. Even God could not have created a world that was physically identical to ours but biologically distinct. There simply is no logical space for the biological facts to vary independently of the physical facts of our world when considered in *toto*. Furthermore, since this holds for any logically possible physical duplicate of our world, it follows that biological properties logically (globally) supervene on physical properties.

This is a remarkable result. One may well wonder whether under such broad conditions of global supervenience there can be any property at all that could fail to supervene on the (micro-) physical facts of an entire world. If not, physicalist materialism would carry the day. This brings us to the second distinction mentioned above, the distinction between logical and natural supervenience. This is the more interesting distinction because it leads straight into highly controversial territory. Generally speaking, B-properties naturally supervene on A-properties if any two naturally possible situations with the same A-properties also have the same B-properties. In other words, in the case of natural supervenience, the B-facts are nomologically, though not logically, implied by the A-facts. That is to say, in possible worlds that are governed by the same natural laws as the actual world, the A-facts naturally necessitate the B-facts (assuming natural supervenience). Clearly, natural possibility is much stricter than logical possibility. For example, a (stable) cubic kilometer of uranium-235 is logically, but not naturally, possible. The critical question then is: Are there any (higher-level) properties that accompany the physical facts in all naturally possible worlds without being fixed by the physical facts in all logically possible worlds? And the controversial answer given by some philosophers is: Consciousness is such a property. On the one hand, they argue, consciousness at least naturally supervenes on the physical facts because any two physically identical creatures in the natural world will presumably have qualitatively identical phenomenal experiences. Nevertheless, these philosophers go on to argue, consciousness fails to supervene logically on the physical facts of our world. Here they appeal to two famous thought experiments. It seems entirely conceivable that a creature physically identical to a conscious creature might lack consciousness altogether (like a zombie), or might have experiences qualitatively very different from ours (they might have so-called inverted qualia, so that, for example, they might have our sensation of phenomenal red when looking at the sky). Therefore, if these two intuitions hold, materialism is false. A full account of the physical facts of our world, including a specification of the minutest details of the distribution of its microphysical properties over space and time, would yet leave entirely undetermined the quality, even the existence, of the phenomenal properties of our world.

Principle of multiple realizability

As discussed above, supervenience may yield ontological dependency relations of varying degrees. But how do things stand with respect to the other philosophical benefit reputedly reaped from this recently developed notion of supervenience, that of barring reducibility? This becomes apparent when one focuses on the converse relation implied in the definition of supervenience. Assuming supervenience, while two situations cannot differ in their B-properties without a corresponding difference in their A-properties, the converse does not hold. That is to say, type-identical B-situations may be realized by an indefinite variety of type-different A-situations. In other words, the notion of supervenience brings in its wake an important corollary notion, that of multiple realizability. And again, this feature holds special interest for the philosophy of mind because multiple realizability is just what we expect in the mental realm. Pain in humans may be realized by C-fibers firing, while in dolphins it may be realized by D-fibers firing without ceasing to be just another simple instance of pain. Indeed, the situation may be vastly more diverse and confusing at the physical level than this example suggests: Your headache may be physically realized differently from mine, as, for that matter, may my headache today versus my headache tomorrow. Similarly, the property of being a monetary transaction, which is a unitary concept at the level of economics, may be physically realized by a wide variety of physical events lacking any perspicuity or explanatory integrity at the level of physics. Accordingly, the predicates of a given special science will only map onto predicates of physics that are at best wildly disjunctive. Thus, inasmuch as supervenience entails multiple realizability, higher-level supervening properties turn out to be irreducible. In psychology, in particular, it has been argued, there cannot be any type-type identities between mental properties and the physical properties realizing them. Nor, consequently, is there any room for strict psychophysical laws so as to reduce psychology to neurophysiology and ultimately to physics. In general, supervenient properties, in spite of being ontologically dependent upon their subvenient base properties, retain their ontological and explanatory autonomy.

Principle of multiple supervenience

The above argument for irreducibility appealed to supervenience in connection with the corollary notion of multiple realizability. More recently, however, supervenience has also been invoked in an antireductionist line of argument deemed to be more effective, in which the crucial corollary notion was not multiple realizability but rather multiple supervenience. An analogy with dispositional properties may clarify the point. Usually one and the same categorical base may "realize" more than one disposition. Even so, only one of those will be causally relevant for a given event. Thus, Sally's death is related to the electrical conductivity of her aluminum ladder. But the categorical base thereof (the cloud of free electrons permeating the metal) also "realizes" such diverse dispositions as the thermal conductivity or the opacity of the metal. Clearly, the correct explanation for the tragic accident would be the one that cited the relevant disposition, not just the categorical base property. Thus explanations couched in terms of supervenient properties (dispositional or otherwise) cannot be reduced to explanations citing no more than the corresponding base properties. But the important point in this context is that the irreducibility in question clearly does not consist in the fact that these higher-level properties may be multiply realizable, but precisely in the opposite fact that a given categorical base property does not identify which of the higher-level properties realized is explanatorily relevant in a given case. In other words, it is not multiple realizability but rather multiple supervenience of macroproperties onto one and the same subvenient categorical base that necessitates citing that supervenient property, which is responsible for the given effect. Similarly, if the aluminum ladder had been exposed to the heat of the sun for a while, it would have been the thermal conductivity, not the electrical conductivity, that would have been causally responsible for Sally's burning her feet, as the case might have been, even though either disposition is realized in the very same categorical base. Thus the special character of higher levels of organization in nature can be vindicated in principle, and perhaps even more effectively, by invoking multiple supervenience in addition to the more conventional appeal to multiple realizability. Such hierarchical levels necessitate the need for macroexplanations with the causal depth and the theoretical appropriateness corresponding to the grain of the explanatory level in question.

In sum, supervenience affords the insight that macrocausation is a real force in nature at multiple levels of existence. Consequently, downward causation may be assigned a stable place in our picture of how the world is organized without upsetting our conception of the various domains of physics as constituting a closed and complete system of physical events at the physical level of description.

See also CONSCIOUSNESS STUDIES; DOWNWARD CAUSATION; MIND-BODY THEORIES; MIND-BRAIN INTERACTION; NEUROSCIENCES

Bibliography

Chalmers, David. *The Conscious Mind: In Search of a Fundamental Theory.* New York: Oxford University Press, 1996.

Davidson, Donald. "Mental Events." In *Experience and Theory,* eds. L. Foster and J. W. Swanson. Amherst, Mass.: 1970.

Fodor, Jerry A. "Special Sciences." *Synthese* 28 (1974): 77–115.

Kim, Jaegwon. "Supervenience." In *A Companion to the Philosophy of Mind,* ed. Samuel Guttenplan. Cambridge, Mass.: Blackwell, 1994.

Meyering, Theo C. "Mind Matters: Physicalism and the Autonomy of the Person." In *Neuroscience and the Person: Scientific Perspectives on Divine Action,* eds. Robert Russell; Nancy Murphy; Theo C. Meyering; and Michael Arbib. Berkeley: Vatican Observatory and Center for Theology and the Natural Sciences, 1999.

Savellos, Elias E., and Yalcin, Ümit D., eds. *Supervenience: New Essays.* Cambridge, UK: Cambridge University Press, 1995.

THEO C. MEYERING

SYMBIOSIS

The term *symbiosis,* from the Greek words *syn* (together with) and *bios* (life), refers to different kinds of organisms living together in ongoing physical association. Although symbiosis is a fundamental biological relationship, it was a disputed concept until the late 1800s, and the term was only first used in 1878. Its role in ecology and evolutionary theory is still developing.

Biologists recognize several variations of symbiotic association. *Obligate symbiosis,* such as the tropical reef relationship between Zooxanthellae algae and the coral they inhabit, is necessary for the survival of one or more partners. *Facultative symbionts* are optional; in tidepools, some sea anemones have green flecks of algae growing inside them, while neighboring anemones do not. *Endosymbiosis* occurs when one species lives inside another, as cellulose-digesting bacteria inhabit the gut of herbivores. *Ectosymbiosis,* which does not involve internalization, occurs when, for example, birds or fish clean larger species. Finally, there is a range of interactive impacts. In *mutualism,* both species benefit; all the above and what is perhaps the first-described case, the algae-fungus association that forms lichens, are examples of mutualism. *Commensalism* involves advantage to one species and neutral impact on another. *Parasitic symbiosis* benefits one species at a cost to another. Some biologists use the term symbiosis only for mutualistic associations, although scholarly literature and popular textbooks are ambiguous on this point.

Symbiosis was catapulted to prominence in evolutionary theory by the notion that mitochondria and chloroplasts (internal organelles within cells) originated through the endosymbiotic internalization of simpler prokaryotic cells. This theory has been championed by Lynn Margulis, who developed the *serial endosymbiosis theory,* which attempts to account for the successive development of all eukaryotic cells (cells with nuclei), through a sequence of unions between various prokaryotic bacteria (non-nucleated cells). While some details of serial endosymbiosis theory are still debated, the endosymbiotic origin of eukaryotes is found in virtually all textbooks.

Symbiosis theory has been extended in several profound but controversial ways. The notion of *symbiogenesis* suggests that symbiosis contributes significantly to the origin of novel traits and new species. Traditional Darwinian theory argues that speciation occurs by natural selection operating on random genetic mutations. Symbiogenesis posits that the symbiotic union of diverse genetic information is a source of creative novelty on which selection acts. Some symbioses, such as lichens, result in an altogether different kind of organism. Moreover, instead of the win-lose scenarios of competitive individual selection, symbiogenesis may more readily create win-win cooperative scenarios that entail new capabilities and resources. Symbiosis as a major evolutionary mechanism has significant though still debated implications, especially for notions of cooperation and complexity in evolutionary history.

Another provocative extension of symbiosis theory entails the scale at which symbiotic associations are conceived to exist. Traditional examples of symbiosis involve individual organisms in physical association with other individuals: for example, a plant and the nitrogen-fixing fungi in its roots. However, one could think of symbioses as involving groups of organisms, such as oxygen-breathing animals and oxygen-generating plants in a pond community. In principle, this could be extended to communities interacting in an ecosystem, or global ecosystems interacting with each other on a planetary scale. James Lovelock's notion of Gaia holds that the entire living world, or biosphere, interacts to regulate water, atmospheric gasses, pH, and temperature. Margulis and others suggest that this reflects the symbiotic integration of life into a global superorganism.

See also COMPETITION; EVOLUTION, BIOLOGICAL

Bibliography

Margulis, Lynn. *Symbiotic Planet: A New Look at Evolution.* New York: Basic Books, 1998.

Paracer, Surindar, and Ahmadjian, Vernon. *Symbiosis: An Introduction to Biological Associations.* New York: Oxford University Press, 2000.

Sapp, Jan. *Evolution by Association: A History of Symbiosis.* New York: Oxford University Press, 1994.

Seckbach, Joseph, ed. *Symbiosis: Mechanisms and Model Systems.* Dordrecht, Netherlands: Kluwer, 2002.

JEFFREY P. SCHLOSS

SYMMETRY

In the most general sense, *symmetry* can be defined as a property that an entity has whereby it preserves some of its aspects under certain actual or possible transformations. A sphere is symmetrical because a rotation about its axis preserves its shape. A crystal structure is symmetrical with respect to certain translations in space. The existence of symmetries in natural phenomena and in human artifacts is pervasive. However, nature also displays important violations of symmetry: Some organic molecules come only or predominantly in left-handed varieties; the bilateral symmetry of most organisms is at best only approximate.

The general concept of symmetry applies not only to objects and their collections, but also to properties of objects, to processes they may undergo, as well as to more abstract entities such as mathematical structures, scientific laws, and symbolic and conceptual systems, including mythology and religion. Symmetry symbols pervade ancient cosmologies. Thus the concept of *axis mundi* (the world axis) is a famous mytho-poetic archetype expressing the idea of centrality in the arrangement of the Cosmos. Whether *axis mundi* is represented as a sacred mountain, tree, or ladder, it invariably signifies a possibility for humans to connect with heaven. The central image of Christianity, the cross, belongs in the same broad category, as far as its symbolic connotations are concerned. The concept of *triadicity* so essential to many religions is closely linked to symmetry considerations.

The abstract notion of symmetry also lies at the very foundation of natural science. The fundamental significance of symmetries for physics came to the fore early in the twentieth century. Prior developments in mathematics contributed to this. Thus, in his Erlangen Program (1872), the German mathematician Felix Klein (1849–1925) proposed interpreting geometry as the study of spatial properties that are invariant under certain groups of transformations (translations, rigid rotations, reflections, scaling, etc.). Emmy Noether (1882–1935) applied Klein's approach to theoretical physics to establish in 1915 a famous theorem relating physical conservation laws (of energy, momentum, and angular momentum) to symmetries of space and time (homogeneity and isotropy). By that time, Albert Einstein's (1879–1955) Theory of Relativity had engendered the notion of *relativistic invariance,* the kind of symmetry all genuine physical laws were expected to possess with respect to a group of coordinate transformations known as the *Lorentz-Poincaré group.* With this came the realization that symmetry (invariance) is a clue to reality: Only

those physical properties that "survive" unchanged under appropriate transformations are real; those that do not are merely *perspectival* manifestations of the underlying reality.

With the development of particle physics the concept of symmetry was extended to internal degrees of freedom (quantum numbers), such as C (charge conjugation, the replacement of a particle by its antiparticle) and isospin (initially the quantum number distinguishing the proton from the neutron). Along with P (parity, roughly a mirror reflection of particle processes) and T (time-reversal operation), these were long believed to be exact symmetries, until the discovery in 1956 of C- and P-symmetry violations in certain weak interactions, and the discovery in 1964 of the violation of the combined CP-symmetry. However, theoretical considerations preclude violation of the more complex CPT-symmetry.

The emergence of quantum electrodynamics (QED), the first successful quantum relativistic theory describing the interaction of electrically charged spin-1/2 particles with the electromagnetic field, made the notion of gauge symmetry central to particle physics. The exact form of interaction turns out to be a consequence of imposing a local gauge invariance on a free-particle Lagrangian with respect to a particular group (U(1) in the case of QED) of transformations of its quantum state. Extending this principle to other interactions led to the unification of electromagnetic and weak forces in the Weinberg-Salam-Glashow theory on the basis of the symmetry group SU(2) × U(1) and to quantum chromodynamics (a theory of strong quark interactions based on the group SU(3)), and eventually paved the way for the ongoing search for a theory unifying all physical forces.

See also LAWS OF NATURE

Bibliography

Mainzer, Klaus. *Symmetries of Nature: A Handbook for Philosophy of Nature and Science.* Berlin and New York: Walter de Gruyter, 1996.

Rosen, Joe. *Symmetry in Science. An Introduction to the General Theory.* New York: Springer-Verlag, 1995.

YURI V. BALASHOV

SYSTEMS THEORY

Systems science emerged as a response to the need for finding ways of understanding and dealing with complexity. The expanding orientation of systems thinking enables a quest for connections and meaning that can expand the boundaries of what traditionally has been considered science. Systems thinking has been compared to Buddhism, and evolutionary systems thinking can be appreciated as the integration of the sciences with the works of mystical and transpersonal thinkers such as Sri Aurobindo (1872–1950) in the East and Carl G. Jung (1875–1961) and Pierre Teilhard de Chardin (1881–1955) in the West. This convergence of science, philosophy, and religion is manifested in the systemic inquiry on conscious evolution and its underlying ethic.

This entry reviews the core ideas within systems science, and in particular the development of General Systems Theory (GST) as a cornerstone of the systems movement. General Evolution Theory (GET) is introduced as the natural unfolding of GST in the study of complex dynamic systems. The emergent view of evolution has implications for the understanding and guidance of human systems and can become the basis for the integration of critical insights for science, philosophy, and religion to surface a new global ethic. Having become conscious of the evolutionary processes of which human beings are a part, and with a sense of awe and responsibility, the challenge is to learn to "dance to the rhythms of evolution" for the purposeful creation of a sustainable and evolutionary future.

The emergence of systems science

In the 1920s, a handful of scientists from different fields became aware of the potential to develop a general theory of organized complexity. The biologist Ludwig von Bertalanffy (1901–1972) formulated the fullest expression of the emerging systems field in his General System Theory (GST). According to Fritjof Capra, Bertalanffy's work "established systems thinking as a major scientific movement (p. 46)" that responded to the limitations of modern analytical science and enabled a broader conception of science.

Analytical (as opposed to holistic) *reductionism* prevailed as the most central principle of scientific inquiry during the eighteenth and nineteenth centuries. Reductionism involves analysis of the isolated elements of the phenomena under study and seeks objectivity, repeatability of results, and refutation of hypotheses in order "to provide explanations for the new unknown, in terms of the known" (Checkland, p. 64). However, "the emergence of new phenomena at higher levels of complexity is itself a major problem for the method of science, and one which reductionist thinking has not been able to solve" (p. 65).

Systems science emerged from interdisciplinary studies and is characterized by a diversity of perspectives, foci, and approaches. Systems science is not a discipline, per se, but a meta-discipline or field whose subject matter—organized complexity—can be applied within virtually any particular discipline. Systems science has become the broader scientific area that embodies all the thinking and practices derived from, and related to, advances in systems theory, methodology, and philosophy. The main professional association dedicated to the study and the advancement of this area is the International Society for the Systems Sciences (ISSS). When established in 1954 by von Bertalanffy, Ralph Gerard, Anatol Rapoport, James G. Miller, and Kenneth Boulding, it was originally called the Society for the Advancement of General Systems Theory.

General system theory

A *system* is a set of interconnected components that form a whole and show properties that are properties of the whole rather than of the individual components. This definition is valid for a cell, an organism, a society, or a galaxy. Therefore, as Joanna Macy expressed it, a *system* is less a thing than a pattern. Systems thinking uses the concept of *system* to apprehend the world. It "is a framework of thought that helps us to deal with complex things in a holistic way" (Flood and Carson, p. 4). When formalized in explicit, conventional and definite form, it can be termed *systems theory*.

Systems theory provides a knowledge base that goes beyond disciplinary boundaries; it seeks isomorphism between and among concepts, principles, laws, and models in various realms of experience; it provides a framework for the transfer and integration of insights relevant to particular domains of research; and it promotes the unity of science through improving communication among disciplines. Bertalanffy's General System Theory (GST) is "a theory, not of systems of a more or less special kind, but of universal principles applying to systems in general" (Bertalanffy, p. 32). GST "aims to provide a framework or structure of systems on which to hang the flesh and blood of particular disciplines and particular subject matters in an orderly and coherent corpus of knowledge" (Boulding, p. 248).

General systems theorists acknowledge that specialized knowledge is as important as a general and integrative framework. Specific systems theories have emerged and include cybernetics, autopoietic systems theory, dynamical systems theory, chaos theory, organizational systems theory, and living systems theory, among others. Considered together, these specific systems theories comprise the systems sciences, many of which have become known as the so called new sciences or sciences of complexity.

General evolution theory

Following the systems tradition, General Evolution Theory (GET) looks for isomorphisms in the patterns of irreversible change over time at different systems levels. GET postulates that the evolutionary trend in the universe constitutes a "cosmic process" specified by a fundamental universal flow toward ever increasing complexity.

Evolution manifests itself through particular events and sequences of events that are not limited to the domain of biological phenomena but extend to include all aspects of change in open dynamic systems with a throughput of information and energy. In other words, evolution relates to the formation of stars from atoms, of Homo sapiens from the anthropoid apes, as much as to the formation of complex societies from rudimentary social systems. The process involves periods of dynamic stability (homeostasis), and when this stability can no longer be maintained, the system enters a period of turbulence—or bifurcation—when it self-organizes into a higher level of organization, structural complexity, dynamism and autonomy—or else, it devolves. In this way, complex open systems become more dynamic, more in control of themselves and of their environment, moving further and further away from the inert state of equilibrium.

The understanding of dynamic complexity, emergence, and self-organization manifested in general evolutionary processes has important implications for human activity systems. Ilya Prigogine and Isabelle Stengers reflect on the social threats and possibilities implied by an understanding of nonlinearity by recognizing that in "our universe the security of stable, permanent rules are gone forever. We are living in a dangerous and uncertain world that inspires no blind confidence. Our hope arises from the knowledge that even small fluctuations may grow and change the overall structure. As a result, individual activity is not doomed to insignificance" (Prigogine and Stengers, p. 313).

Human science and conscious evolution

Human science makes reference to an inclusive approach to the study of human phenomena that uses multiple systems of inquiry, including descriptive studies and prospective interventions. According to Marcia Salner, discussion about human science "was once conducted on the grounds of philosophy, professional researchers who must face up to practical problems of social survival are pragmatically moving toward what will work to provide answers where no reliable guides exist. . . . How we understand our world, how we learn about it, how we teach the young about their place in it, have consequences for our survival in it" (p. 8). Only a science that is both humanistic and systemic can deal effectively with complex human challenges and create evolutionary opportunities for human development in partnership with Earth.

Human science involves both systems (within the systems field) and systemic (outside the systems field) approaches. On the one hand, it involves the application of systems theories and methodologies in order to understand, ameliorate, and transform social systems. On the other hand, human science also incorporates systemic and holistic approaches, beyond the systems field, that challenge traditional assumptions about knowledge and science. For instance, critical theory seeks to combine philosophy and science, idealism and realism, and concepts and experiences to confront social injustice. Feminism seeks the emancipation of women for the betterment of humanity as a whole through the promotion of issues such as sexual equality, development, and peace. Scholars interested in qualitative research are articulating a comprehensive epistemology for a participatory paradigm that involves different ways of knowing.

What is common to all these alternative approaches is their holistic character and their commitment to bridge theory and practice for understanding and transforming social realities.

Following the trend in systems science of looking for theoretical and methodological complementarity, there are approaches that seek to integrate the knowledge base of systems thinking, general evolutionary processes, and human science. Evolution, both as a scientific theory and as a universal myth, is a powerful story for the transformation of consciousness and society. The implications of this knowledge base provide rich opportunities for manifold inferences for social action and research. First, humans do not need to be the victims of change— change can happen *through* humans, not *to* humans. Second, the future is not probabilistic, but rather, possibilistic: Humans can influence the direction of change through their intentions and actions. Third, for the first time in human history, human beings can experience joy "while working for the most ambitious goal available to the human imagination: To blend our individual voice in the cosmic harmony, to join our unique consciousness with the emerging consciousness of the universe, to fold our momentary center of psychic energy into the current that tends toward increasing complexity and order" (Csikszentmihalyi, p. 293). Indeed, science and spirituality are coming together in the ultimate exploration of the meaning and purpose of human existence: Conscious evolution—the evolutionary phase in which a developing being becomes conscious of itself, aware of the processes of which it is a participant, and begins voluntarily to co-create with evolution.

A new global ethic

"If our society is not working well," Lester Milbrath reflects, "we get the message that we need to rethink our value structure" (Milbrath, p. 67). Scientists and religious leaders agree: A new global ethic is required if human misery and irreversible damage to the planet is to be avoided.

Regardless of postmodernist or relativist positions, Mihalyi Csikszentmihalyi reflects on how similar are the world's major moral systems. He believes that "we have to find an appropriate moral code to guide our choices. It should be a code that takes into account the wisdom of tradition, yet is inspired by the future rather than the past; it should specify right as being the unfolding of the maximum individual potential joined with the achievement of the greatest social and environmental harmony" (Csikszentmihalyi, p. 162). From a systemic and evolutionary perspective, a multilevel ethic would promote:

(1) Human actions that benefit (or at least not harm) the individual—it must promote personal freedom;

(2) Human actions that benefit (or at least not harm) society—it must promote social justice;

(3) Human actions that benefit (or at least not harm) the planet—it must promote ecological harmony.

To focus exclusively on one level corresponds to what Carolyn Merchant has called egocentric, homocentric, or ecocentric ethics, respectively. The challenge is to strive for the ideal of a multilevel ethical approach that promotes what is good for the whole of individual humans, societies, ecosystems, and future generations at the same time, in order to promote sustainability in an evolutionary sense. In other words, as Evrin Laszlo proposes, to live simply and meaningfully allowing other people and other species to live with dignity as well, so that a favorable dynamic equilibrium in the evolution of the biosphere can be reached and sustained.

An important aspect of this new emerging ethic is its process orientation. Rather than considering morality as a set of static norms and rules, it should be embraced as an ongoing inquiring process, a conversation as suggested by West C. Churchman, in which human values are neither relative nor absolute. In the past, philosophy and moral inquiry have been restricted to a privileged minority of mainly white men. An ethical society requires that every member of society become a lifelong learner engaged in the ongoing ethical conversation that purposefully informs the actions and decisions that shape the present and the future.

Science is evolving. The convergence between systems views and mystical views allow a more comprehensive and meaningful articulation of the human-as-part-and-process-of-cosmos story. This "New Story," as theologian Thomas Berry calls it, can guide people in the adventure of ethically evolving human systems.

See also COMPLEXITY; EVOLUTION; VALUE, VALUE THEORY

Bibliography

Banathy, Bela H. *Guided Evolution of Society: A Systems View*. New York: Kluwer Academic, 2000.

Berry, Thomas. *The Great Work: Our Way Into the Future*. New York: Crown, 2000.

Bertalanffy, Ludwig von. *General System Theory: Foundations, Developments, Applications*. New York: George Braziller, 1968.

Bohm, David. *Wholeness and the Implicate Order*. London: Routledge, 1980.

Boulding, Kenneth E. "General Systems Theory—The skeleton of science." In *Facets of Systems Science,* ed. George J. Klir. New York: Plenum Press, 1991.

Briggs, John P., and Peat, F. David. *Looking Glass Universe: The Emerging Science of Wholeness*. New York: Touchstone, 1984.

Capra, Fritjof. *The Web of Life: A New Scientific Understanding of Living Systems*. New York: Anchor, 1996.

Chaisson, Erich. *The Life Era: Cosmic Selection and Conscious Svolution*. New York: Norton, 1987.

Checkland, Peter. *Systems Thinking, Systems Practice*. New York: Wiley, 1981.

Churchman, C. West. *The Systems Approach*. New York: Laurel, 1968.

Csikszentmihalyi, Mihalyi. *The Evolving Self: A Psychology for the Third Millennium*. New York: Harper Collins, 1993.

Eisler, Riane Tennenhaus. *The Chalice and the Blade: Our History, Our Future*. Cambridge, Mass.: Harper, 1987.

Elgin, Duane. *Awakening Earth: Exploring the Evolution of Human Culture and Consciousness*. New York: William Morrow, 1993.

Feinstein, David, and Krippner, Stanley. *Personal Mythology: The Psychology of Your Evolving Self*. New York: Jeremy Tarcher, 1988.

Flood, Robert L., and Carson, Edwart R. *Dealing with Complexity: An Introduction to the Theory and Application of Systems Science*. New York: Plenum Press, 1990.

Gleick, James. *Chaos: Making a New Science*. New York: Viking, 1987.

Goerner, Sally. *Chaos and the Evolving Ecological Universe*. Langhorne, Pa.: Gordon and Breach, 1994.

Heron, John, and Reason, Peter. "A Participatory Inquiry Paradigm." *Qualitative Inquiry* 3, no. 3 (1997): 274–294.

Hubbard, Barbara Marx. *Conscious Evolution: Awakening the Power of our Social Potential*. Novato, Calif.: New World Library, 1998.

Huxley, Aldous. *The Perennial Philosophy*. New York: Harper, 1944.

James, William. *The Varieties of Religious Experience: A Study in Human Nature*. New York: Modern Library, 1929.

Jantsch, Eric. *Design for Evolution: Self-Organization and Planning in the Life of Human Systems*. New York: George Braziller, 1975.

Laszlo, Alexander. "The Epistemological Foundations of Evolutionary Systems Design." *Systems Research and Behavioral Science* 18, no. 4 (2001): 307–321.

Laszlo, Alexander, and Krippner, Stanley. "Systems Theories: Their Origins, Foundations, and Development." In *Systems Theories and A Priori Aspects of Perception,* ed. J. Scott Jordan. Amsterdam: Elsevier, 1998.

Laszlo, Alexander, and Laszlo, Ervin. "The Contribution of the Systems Sciences to the Humanities." *Systems Research and Behavioral Science* 14, no. 1 (1997): 5–19.

Laszlo, Ervin. *Introduction to Systems Philosophy: Toward a New Paradigm of Contemporary Thought*. New York: Gordon and Breach, 1972.

Laszlo, Ervin. "The Meaning and Significance of General System Theory." *Behavioral Science* 20, no. 1 (1975): 9–24.

Laszlo, Ervin. *The Age of Bifurcation: Understanding the Changing World*. Philadelphia, Pa.: Gordon and Breach, 1991.

Laszlo, Ervin. *The Choice: Evolution or Extinction?* New York: Tarcher/Putman, 1994.

Laszlo, Ervin. *Evolution: The General Theory*. Cresskill, N.J.: Hampton Press, 1996.

Laszlo, Ervin. *The Whispering Pond: A Personal Guide to the Emerging Vision of Science*. Boston, Mass.: Element, 1996.

Laszlo, Ervin. *Macroshift 2001–2010: Creating the Future in the Early 21st Century*. New York: toExcel, 2001.

Laszlo, Kathia Castro. "Global Challenges and Human Opportunities: The Path of Evolutionary Systems Design." *Advances in Systems Science and Applications* 1, no. 1 (2001): 100–105.

Lowenthal, David. "Lost in the Cosmos? Mind and Purpose in a World of Chance." *Perspectives on Political Science* 30, no. 2 (2001): 95–101.

Loye, David, and Eisler, Riane. "Chaos and Transformation: Implications of Nonequilibrium Theory for Social Science and Society." *Behavioral Science* 32 (1987): 53–65.

Loye, David. "Scientific Foundations for a Global Ethic at a Time of Evolutionary Crisis." *World Futures* 49, nos. 1–2 (1997).

Macy, Joanna. *Mutual Causality in Buddhism and General System Theory*. Albany: State University of New York Press, 1991.

McWaters, Barry. *Conscious Evolution: Personal and Planetary Transformation*. Los Angeles: New Age Press, 1981.

Merchant, Carolyn. "Environmental Ethics and Political Conflict: A View from California." In *Contemporary Moral Issues: Diversity and Consensus,* ed. Lawrence Hinman. Upper Saddle River, N.J.: Prentice Hall, 1996.

Merry, Uri. *Coping With Uncertainty: Insights from the New Sciences of Chaos, Self-Organization, and Complexity*. Westport, Conn.: Praeger, 1995.

Milbrath, Lester W. *Envisioning a Sustainable Society: Learning Our Way Out*. Albany: State University of New York Press, 1989.

Morin, Edgar. "From the Concept of System to the Paradigm of Complexity." *Journal of Social and Evolutionary Systems* 15, no. 4 (1992): 371–385.

Ornstein, Robert, and Ehrlich, Paul. *New World, New Mind: Moving Toward Conscious Evolution*. New York: Touchstone, 1989.

Prigogine, Ilya, and Stengers, Isabelle. *Order Out of Chaos*. New York: Bantam, 1984.

Richards, Ruth. "Seeing Beyond: Issues of Creative Awareness and Social Responsibility." *Creativity Research Journal* 6, nos. 1–2 (1993): 165–183.

Salk, Jonas. *The Survival of the Wisest*. New York: Harper, 1973.

Salner, Marcia. "A New Framework for Human Science." *Saybrook Perspectives* (San Francisco, Calif.) Spring Issue (1996): 6-8.

Teilhard de Chardin, Pierre. *The Phenomenon of Man*. New York: Harper, 1959.

KATHIA CASTRO LASZLO

T

T = 0

The common notation *t* = 0 simply means "time equals zero." It expresses the radical and fundamental conclusion of standard Big Bang cosmology. It recognizes the connection between space and time by implying that the Big Bang did not occur *in* time but that time began with the Big Bang singularity. For many theological thinkers, the scientific articulation of *t* = 0 has significant implications for understanding creation, particularly the idea of a creation out of nothing (*creatio ex nihilo*).

See also BIG BANG THEORY; COSMOLOGY, PHYSICAL ASPECTS; CREATIO EX NIHILO

MARK WORTHING

TACIT KNOWLEDGE

Though it is a psychological fact that human beings acquire, retain, and employ tacit knowledge, accounts of its nature and function in perception, memory, cognition, language, and learning vary across disciplines. In epistemology, the concept of tacit knowledge was pioneered by the scientist and philosopher Michael Polanyi (1891–1976) in his *Personal Knowledge* (1956) and *The Tacit Dimension* (1966). Drawing on Gestalt psychology, Polanyi developed a theory of tacit knowledge by extending the perceptual model of attending *from* subsidiary clues or particulars (bodily processes, sensory experiences, memory, intimations) *to* a focal whole (pattern, object, entity) to a general model that holds cognitive processes ranging form identifying objects, performing skills, solving (scientific) problems to understanding texts or persons. Tacit knowing is seen to consist in relying on integrated and interiorized particulars for attending to the comprehensive entity on which these particulars bear, and in terms of which they are (tacitly) known. Accordingly, a formal definition of tacit knowledge and its structure may read thus: a person *A* has tacit knowledge of a collection of subsidiary clues *S* if (1) *S* is integrated by *A*, (2) *A* is not directly aware of *S*, and (3) *A* has integrated *S* such that (4) *S* bears on a focal whole, *F*.

On this construal, all knowledge is more or less embodied and either tacit or rooted in tacit knowledge. Moreover, tacit knowledge can be seen as the model of all skillful problem solving, of which scientific discovery is the paradigm case. Inquirers follow rules they can hardly specify and are seldom aware of. In this respect, tacit knowledge is more like knowing how to do things or what things are for than propositional knowledge that something is the case. Near parallels here are Gilbert Ryle's distinction between "knowing how" and "knowing that," and Bertrand Russell's between "knowledge by acquaintance—knowledge by description." Finally, the personal character of tacit knowledge does not make it subjective or irrational. Acquired in the context of social practices of learning and inquiry, it is both personal and social.

The implications of this theory for the dialogue between science and theology are at least the following. First, by emphasizing that contexts of "coming to know" cannot be governed wholly by general rules, the theory would support historical, evolutionary, and cognitive approaches to science and religion, rather than rationalist, metaphysical, and logical ones. Next, by presenting an alternative to impersonal and reductionist accounts of science that focus exclusively on questions of justification or methodology, the theory influenced many theologians, including Thomas F. Torrance, Ian Barbour, Arthur Peacocke, and Lesslie Newbigin. It advocates the personal and fiduciary nature of scientific knowing in practice that is not at odds but consonant with religious understanding. Finally, tacit knowledge as embodied, personal, and social points to a common ground for science and religion, not of a methodological or metaphysical nature, but of an evolutionary, cognitive, and anthropological nature. Permeating all human inquiry—scientific as well as scholarly, aesthetic, moral, and religious—tacit knowledge shows that all claims to know and understand are voiced from within traditions and shaped by values that can only be upheld within a free society that allows people to adhere to them.

See also EPISTEMOLOGY

Bibliography

Gill, Jerry H. *The Tacit Mode: Michael Polanyi's Postmodern Philosophy*. Albany: State University of New York Press, 2000.

Polanyi, Michael. *Knowing and Being: Essays,* ed. Marjorie Grene. London: Routledge and Kegan Paul, 1969.

Polanyi, Michael. *Scientific Thought and Social Reality: Essays,* ed. Fred Schwartz. New York: International Universities Press, 1974.

Sanders, Andy F. *Michael Polanyi's Post-Critical Epistemology: A Reconstruction of Some Aspects of Tacit Knowing*. Amsterdam: Rodopi, 1988.

ANDY F. SANDERS

TAOISM

See CHINESE RELIGIONS, DAOISM AND SCIENCE IN CHINA

TECHNOLOGY

The definition of *technology* is a much controverted topic. At one extreme, the word is used for an intellectual discipline, analogous to *biology* or *psychology*. This is a refined use, emphasizing the Greek root *logos* (word or meaning) combined with *techne* (artifice), to focus on the study or science of arts and artifices. Thus, distinguished institutions that offer sustained investigation of practical arts are often called institutes of technology. But at the other extreme, the word *technology* is often used to refer to concrete objects, tools, and implements themselves, or their workings. When archaeologists speak of digging up samples of a culture's technology, they are not referring to learned studies but to pots, tools, or weapons. Historians and anthropologists refer to the technologies of a society as the practical arts and implements themselves, not studies about them. And ordinary usage tends also toward the concrete. When one is baffled by the technology in a new car, it is the knobs and switches that are at issue, recalcitrant things.

Another polarity is found regarding the involvement of science in technology. Is technology (whether a study or a set of artifacts) simply applied science? If so, then science must have come first, to be applied, and there could be no prescientific technologies. The distinguished institutes of engineering tend to lean toward this understanding, but historians of human craftsmanship tend to see important continuities between pre- and post-scientific arts, and emphasize vital technological achievements (such as the telescope and microscope) that made science possible, thus predating and empowering the rise of modern science, not shrinking to its mere application.

There are other significant disputes over the essential nature of technology: for example, whether it must be embodied, somehow, perhaps in metal or plastic, or whether it can be entirely conceptual, as in the important Arabic invention of the number zero, which greatly advanced the calculational power of mathematics. Another example is the question whether technology can be said to exist outside the human context, as in the sometimes elaborate constructions of animals like beavers and many birds, or must it by definition be the product of human making? This raises the broader issue whether technology is ever a natural phenomenon or is necessarily artificial. Unfortunately, the relatively new field of philosophy of technology has yet to come to consensus on these definitional issues.

Technology and language

In the absence of consensus, the process of constructing and evaluating a definition is actually clarified. One cannot pretend that a proposed definition is inevitable, or is the only one that stands to reason. It becomes more obvious that language is conventional, that a definition is a rule for linking concepts together in ways that are clarifying or helpful. Since what is clarifying or helpful is always relative to some context-giving purpose, there may be as many differently helpful resolutions for using words as there are purposes for doing so. Deans of distinguished institutions for the systematic study of industrial arts may find it helpful to use words in one way; aircraft maintenance personnel may find it more helpful to use them in another.

Since the purpose in this entry is philosophical, its aim will be for as much comprehensiveness as reasonably possible, combined with as much critical coherence as can be achieved in light of the variety of data in hand. The norm of adequate comprehensiveness will warn against premature exclusions of whole domains from the extension of the term under discussion, and the norm of critical coherence will warn against such excesses of inclusion as might make the term vacuous by referring uncritically to everything. For example, if we are to understand technology from the broad philosophical perspective, it will probably be more useful to include prescientific craft traditions within the concept of technology, to see the internal similarities and differences brought by modern science, than to exclude the earlier practical arts from notice by definition. But, contrariwise, since understanding a subject must allow for contrast with what is not that subject, it will probably not be useful to accede to such all-inclusive definitions as would identify the mind-activated body as the primary all-purpose tool. This would imply that a conscious human being is never without tools, is never in a nontechnological condition. With an over-broad definition it is harder to express the significant difference that the introduction of a tool makes to the naked hand; with an over-narrow definition it is harder to notice significant similarities between tools of different types.

Venturing our own definition, in this context, must be an exercise in balance. We must be conscious of what we will include and what exclude by our proposed linguistic rule, and must be ready to stand by these consequences as long as we support the rule. For example, the concept of the *practical* has been central in all the discussion thus far. If we make this concept essential, then we exclude from the concept of technology what is purely theoretical or aesthetic or otherwise done for its own sake, without practical motives. If this seems appropriate, we are entitled to make this decision. Again, the concept of the *purposive* runs throughout, implying *intelligent goals* as essential to the idea of technology. If this cluster of concepts is taken as essential, then we shall be excluding the purely instinctive from our definition. This need not eliminate a priori all animal constructive activities from the domain of the technological, but it draws the line at a new place: To what extent are the apparent artifacts of animals actually the result of art, or intelligence? If the human species is not alone intelligent, then the concept of technology will apply quite naturally to flexible, environmentally responsive implementations of animal aims, but will not apply to behaviors that are hard-wired, immune to modification in changing conditions. Is this an appropriate distinction? If so, we may legitimately adopt it. Finally, the concept of *physical embodiment* remains to be resolved, whether technology must necessarily be *implemented* in material things. If we so decide, then purely conceptual discoveries or inventions, like the Arabic zero, will be excluded from the technological, while the abacus, another great aid to calculation, implemented variously by pebbles in sand or beads on wires, will be included. Like all the other decisions, this is a judgment call. Will it be more helpful for understanding technology to require that it be *implemented*, especially if that requirement can be understood to include not just metal or plastic but also social and biological implementations, as in the invention of armies and corporations or in the selective breeding of new strains of grain or livestock? If the answer is positive, then this resolution may reasonably be made.

Thus, once we are alert to the conceptual consequences, and accept them, a possible definition of technology, one that could reconcile a number of clashing linguistic intuitions and lay a foundation for further clarifications in this important domain, could be: Technology is the practical implementation of intelligence.

Technology and science

Approaching technology as implemented intelligence aimed at practical goals helps to resolve the contentious question of its relationship to science. There is no doubt that the character of technologies changed radically after the emergence of modern science. There is also no doubt that prescientific technologies, such as the art of lens making and glass-blowing, were indispensable to that emergence, since without them there would have been no telescopes, microscopes, thermometers, or barometers to serve the new goals of precise theoretical intelligence represented by the scientific revolution.

But the differences between the type of intelligence embodied in ancient craft technologies and in modern high technologies are not in kind but in goals and norms. Practical intelligence, as old as our species, is interested in getting jobs done and clinging to techniques that have been found (usually by luck, or trial and error) to work. The norm for such intelligence is practical success, with deep reluctance to fix what is not broken. Simplicity is preferred over complication, the how is elevated over the why, and close enough is favored over abstract precision. In contrast, theoretical intelligence (rooted in the same ancient quest that sometimes leads to myth-making and sometimes, as in classical Greece, is disciplined by logic) thirsts for understanding why, is not satisfied by successful results alone but wants to know in addition what makes things happen so, and is willing to take great pains to achieve precision despite whatever complexity is required. These two contrasting expressions of intelligence, usually isolated by socioeconomic class, made an improbable marriage in seventeenth century Europe, through which the demand for theoretical precision could be served by instruments provided by ancient craft traditions, and the quest for why could be disciplined by attention to the how.

For the first time, practical wants could be suggested by theoretical understanding of the hidden workings of things. The radio could not even be desired without first conceiving abstractly of radio waves. Atomic energy could not be a goal without the modern theory of the atom. After the emergence of modern science, so-called high technologies could be led by theoretical intelligence powerfully outfitted by practical intelligence.

Technology and culture.   Technology is the implementation not only of intelligence in various interacting modes but also equally of values, goals, wants, and fears. Without motivating values, intelligence would not be moved to make or do anything. But in culture, values often clash. Early biblical pessimism about technological hubris is shown in the story of the Tower of Babel (Gen. 11: 1–9), foreshadowing modern negative theological and philosophical attitudes such as those expressed by Jacques Ellul and Martin Heidegger. Science-led high technologies stimulate even stronger condemnation from those suspicious of the practical implementations of human intelligence, but the involvement of modern science is not essential to setting off warnings. Agricultural technology, and urban living itself, is seen as corrupting by the nomadic and sheepherding author, called J, in early biblical thought.

More positive theological assessments, ranging from Harvey Cox's early enthusiastic embrace of the liberating technologies of the secular city to W. Norris Clarke's more measured approval of human co-creation through selective technology, also abound in the literature. Philosophers and social commentators like Herbert Marcuse, Erich Fromm, and Bernard Gendron defend in different ways the technological impulse and its impacts on culture.

The technological impulse, to intervene intelligently in nature by implementing means for achieving valued ends, is extremely general, however, and open to indefinitely many expressions. The qualities of the intelligence being implemented, as well as the values being embodied, are worthy of analysis and assessment epistemologically no less than ethically and theologically. Though the activities of intelligence may bind all sorts of technologies into a single wide domain, its implemented expressions through modern science are strikingly different in standards and consequences from its prescientific embodiments. Artificiality comes in many degrees, depending on the extent to which the artificial object is dependent on the intervention of intelligence for its production. A neatly planted orchard, for example, is more artificial than a primal forest, but less artificial than the shopping mall that may replace it. On such a scale, modern high technology is artificial to the highest degree because it is completely dependent on the intervention of theoretical intelligence for its existence. Some of the felt discomfort directed toward such technologies may be rooted in the cognitive gap between ordinary experience of the world, familiar to our species from earliest times, and the theoretical structures inhabited by scientific intelligence and materialized in scientific engineering.

Importantly, too, the internal goals of scientific intelligence tend to favor quantification. Much science-led technology may not surprisingly, then, embody the tendency to favor quantity over more ineffable qualities, such as the aesthetic or traditional. Further, scientific values, though powerful in advancing knowledge, are conspicuously lacking in compassion for its subjects of investigation. The typical technological implementations of scientific thought, with some exceptions (e.g., anesthesia) have not been especially kind or gentle. We may speculate that if we are to hope for a kinder, gentler postmodern variety of high technology, sensitive to qualitative concerns in culture, there may need to rise a new, postmodern variety of scientific thinking as well.

See also BIOTECHNOLOGY; INFORMATION TECHNOLOGY; REPRODUCTIVE TECHNOLOGY; TECHNOLOGY AND ETHICS; TECHNOLOGY AND RELIGION; VALUE, SCIENTIFIC

Bibliography

Drengson, Alan. *The Practice of Technology: Exploring Technology, Ecophilosophy, and Spiritual Disciplines for Vital Links*. Albany: State University of New York Press, 1995.

Ellul, Jacques. *The Technological Society,* trans. John Wilkinson. New York: Vintage, 1964.

Feenberg, Andrew. *Critical Theory of Technology*. New York: Oxford University Press, 1991.

Ferkiss, Victor. *Technological Man: The Myth and the Reality*. New York: New American Library, 1969.

Ferré, Frederick. *Philosophy of Technology*. Athens: University of Georgia Press, 1995.

Fromm, Erich. *The Revolution of Hope: Toward a Humanized Technology*. New York: Harper, 1968.

Gendron, Bernard. *Technology and the Human Condition*. New York: St. Martin's Press, 1977.

Heidegger, Martin. *The Question Concerning Technology and Other Essays,* trans. William Lovitt. New York: Harper, 1977.

Ihde, Don. *Existential Technics*. Albany: State University of New York Press, 1983.

Illich, Ivan. *Tools for Conviviality*. New York: Harper, 1973.

Leiss, William. *Under Technology's Thumb*. Montreal, Quebec, and Kingston, Ont.: McGill-Queens University Press, 1990.

Marcuse, Herbert. *One-Dimensional Man: Studies in the Ideology of Advanced Industrial Society*. Boston: Beacon Press, 1964.

Mitcham, Carl, and Mackey, Robert, eds. *Philosophy and Technology: Readings in the Philosophical Problems of Technology*. New York: Free Press, 1972.

Pacey, Arnold. *The Culture of Technology*. Cambridge, Mass.: MIT Press, 1983.

Schuurman, Egbert. *Technology and the Future: A Philosophical Challenge,* trans. Herbert Donald Morton. Toronto, Ont.: Wedge Publishing Foundation, 1980.

Winner, Langdon. *Autonomous Technology: Technics-out-of-Control as a Theme in Political Thought*. Cambridge, Mass.: MIT Press, 1977.

FREDERICK FERRÉ

TECHNOLOGY AND ETHICS

If the concept of *technology* includes human arts and crafts, generally, not simply the science-led *high technology* of modern times, then the influence of technology precedes the dawn of history itself. This entry assumes the more inclusive sense, taking *implemented intelligent practical purpose* as key to the subject, thus binding both traditional and high technologies into a common domain for ethical assessment.

Ethical assessment itself tends to divide into two great approaches. One tradition looks primarily to the consequences of what is being evaluated. Is an action or policy (or habit or trait of character, etc.) likely to produce good results? If so, on this tradition, the action is ethically right, morally to be approved, because of its consequences. The other tradition focuses primarily on the type of action or policy under consideration, whether it conforms to a rule that defines what is right. If so, the action reflects what is morally to be approved, regardless of its consequences.

It is clear that these approaches to ethical assessment can and often do argue past one another. The first position, here called *outcome-ethics* (also often called *teleological* or *consequentialist* ethics), may declare that policy P does no good, while the second position, here called *rule-ethics* (also often called *deontological* ethics), may insist that policy P flows inescapably from accepted rule R. Both may be correct in what they hold. But if they come to opposing views on the ethical wrongness or rightness of P, they have missed each other's point. Rule-ethics is not interested in outcomes but in the principle of the thing; outcome-ethics is impatient with abstract principles, when concrete helps and harms are at stake.

Reconciling ethical methods

Ethical assessment of technology is made still more difficult because of tensions within the approaches themselves. Outcome-ethics is based on maximizing *good,* but differences abound on defining this key term. Pleasure, honor, well-functioning, and so on, are all possible candidates, but different definitions would call for different policies and would cast different ethical light on the technological means for achieving them. Defining the good in terms of honor, for example, might give a positive ethical assessment to the erection of catapults and the casting of cannon, while defining it in terms of pleasure might call for a more negative stance toward the implements of war.

Another difficulty for outcome-ethics, however the good is defined, is in determining when the ethically relevant outcome has come out. Events roll on, and a positive situation (e.g., avoiding the pains of battle) may be supplanted by a negative one (e.g., falling under an oppressive conqueror), which in turn leads endlessly to others. The openness of the future seems to make an ethical verdict on any outcome only provisional.

If the future is a problem for outcome-ethics, so also is the past. Taken literally, the measuring of ethical worth by future outcomes alone seems to leave the past without ethical significance. A promise once made would need continual reevaluation by changing future probabilities. Destructive acts in the past should be punished, if at all, only by reference to future good to be achieved; good

deeds, once done, should be rewarded, if at all, only by looking toward future results.

These counterintuitive consequences are escaped by rule-ethics, which does not need a prior concept of good for its concept of right, does not make its ethical judgments hostage to a receding future, and is not required to ignore ethical obligations from the past. But there are analogous equally deep problems for rule-ethics, if taken alone. First, there are many disagreements within this approach as to which rules should rule. Even excluding, in this entry, many conflicting claims of divine commands, profound disagreements may be expected on the source and authority of proffered ethical principles. Do they rise from an innate intuition? From societal enculturation? From a rational imperative? How much weight should these principles, given their sources, command? How general or specific should ethical rules be? The more they are detailed and specific, the more particular circumstances—even outcomes—dominate the rules; the more they are general and abstract, the more ethics loses touch with the concrete particularities of life. Rule-ethics gains much of its power from its principled distance from particular circumstances, but such distance makes it vulnerable to the temptations of fanaticism.

Somehow the clashing approaches to ethical assessment need to be reconciled if past technological decisions are to be adequately evaluated and future policies properly assessed. Technological implements are means to practical purposes. Since means are always aimed at ends, consequences must count in technological ethics. But also, since purposes can be formulated in terms of general motives, norms must also be applicable to technology.

A balance might be struck by acknowledging that concrete outcomes are the matter of ethical concern, while general rules constitute its form. Outcome-ethics could recognize that among alternative outcomes, some might be deeply unfair in their distribution of the good, and these would be worse outcomes than more equitable ones. But fairness is not simply one more addition to the good; it is a principle or rule on how the good should be spread. Cost-benefit analyses of technological outcomes are weak if they ignore the question of who bears the costs and who enjoys the benefits, and whether these are justly proportioned. Further, outcome-ethics needs to consider rights and wrongs of past technological decisions, even if nothing can be done about them any longer. Recognizing mistakes in the past and formulating guidelines to help avoid similar mistakes in the future, is an important ethical activity utilizing norms and principles, not just predictions. In these ways outcome-ethics (in order to do its own chosen job well) needs to learn from rule-ethics.

Reciprocally, rule-ethics needs to learn from outcome-ethics if it is to remain relevant to the fears and hopes that drive technological activity. Consequences do matter ethically to real people. Rules must not be allowed to blind moral concern from seeing concrete pains. Rules need to be responsive. This is especially obvious in the context of high technology, where possibilities of doing things become practical for the first time. When entirely new types of doing are contemplated, existing rule-books may not be adequate for guidance. This does not mean that rules are not relevant. But rules need to be extended, amended, and reviewed in light of novel facts and unprecedented possibilities. Modern technology, with its radical novelties, makes this extension of traditional ethics (both outcome- and rule-ethics) vital.

Examining historical cases

Over the course of human history, the outcomes sought by technological implements reflect every kind of practical good (real, imagined, or perverse) that human beings are capable of craving. Food, shelter, the death of enemies, the docility of slaves, accurate records—a list without end—have been sufficiently valued so that intelligence has been put to work creating artifacts to secure them. For one grisly example, some medieval cities in Europe maintain so-called police museums displaying the technologies of punishments once meted out to malefactors. Cleverly devised implements of torture, including metal seats for roasting, iron claws for tearing, racks for dislocating, were the embodiment of purposeful design in quest of something taken by many in that society as a public good. We may shudder today at these artifacts, and question whether those goals of inflicting extreme pain were really good, or whether the larger good of public order really required such measures, just as it is possible to shudder and ask the same questions about the practical intelligence and values embodied in our publicly approved electric chairs, gas chambers, and paraphernalia of lethal injection. Here we encounter the appropriate critical

task of technological ethics. Using the methods of outcome-ethics, one needs to examine whether the consequences sought can really be approved as good over the longest anticipated time horizon, and if so, whether in fact the means proposed are the best ones for achieving these critically examined results. At the same time, using the methods of rule-ethics, one must ask whether the principle of fairness is being served in distributing the various goods and ills concerned, whether the type of action contemplated falls under clearly stated and approved principles, whether these specific principles can be further justified by a hierarchical order of still more general norms, and whether this more comprehensive set of interlocking norms itself is clear, consistent, adequate to the larger circumstances, and coherently defensible to a thoughtful, unbiased judge.

A famous rejection of industrial technology occurred in the early nineteenth century in northern England, when the Luddites, followers of a (possibly mythical) Ned Ludd—purportedly a home weaver displaced by new factory-based machines—smashed the power looms that threatened their ways of life. It is likely that this direct action was motivated more by economic than ethical values, and it was put down by gunfire and hangings, but many ethical issues are raised. What were the ethically relevant consequences of the shift from home industry to the factory system? One consequence was greatly increased volume of production, a prima facie good. Another was the replacement of a society of small producers, owners of their own looms, with a laboring class, required to sell their services to others who owned the means of production. This outcome is prima facie negative, involving a decrease of dignity, loss of cohesion in family life, and a corresponding increase in alienation and insecurity. The factory system, and eventually the assembly line, produce mixed consequences. Ethical examination needs to sort these out, and weigh them. In terms of principle, as well, there are profound issues of involuntary social change forced by technological efficiencies. To what extent should the autonomy of persons to choose their basic conditions of life be honored above the promise of greater economic productivity? On whom will the burdens fall when technology uproots life? Will those who bear these burdens receive a fair share of the new rewards, or will these flow disproportionately to others?

Should society provide institutional opportunities for all the people involved to discuss and decide these ethically vital questions? Can any society that fails to do so consider itself genuinely democratic?

These questions reveal a serious general problem in technological ethics: the arrival of many revolutionary changes as faits accompli. Well before the appearance of high technologies, simple trial-and-error discoveries deeply altered valued conditions of life before they could be prevented or even discussed. Alfred Nobel (1833–1896) was keenly aware of how much his invention of dynamite would shake the world. The invention itself, in 1867, was wholly in the craft-tradition, a chance discovery that nitroglycerine could be absorbed by a certain porous siliceous earth and thus be made much safer to use. Various types of dynamite were used in blasting tunnels and mines, as well as in cutting canals, and building railbeds and roads. The consequences of these applications deserve analysis as ethically quite mixed, socially and environmentally, but of course the most spectacular use of the high explosives stemming from Nobel's invention was in war. Nobel himself established his prizes, including the Peace Prize, to coax the world toward better outcomes. He even dared to hope that the power of dynamite would make future wars unthinkable. In this he was sadly mistaken.

Assessing contemporary challenges

The leap from chemical high explosives to high nuclear technology may on the surface seem short, but in fact it represents a qualitative change. The high explosives of the nineteenth century were grounded in the same tradition of craft advancement that had characterized human technique from prehistoric times. A lucky empirical discovery was noted, remembered, repeated, applied, extended, and exploited—a paradigm instance of excellent practical reasoning. The atom bomb, in contrast, had to await a spectacular achievement in theoretical reasoning about nature even to be conceived. Specifically, a revolutionary change in understanding the relationship between matter and energy, wrought in the mathematical imagination of Albert Einstein (1879–1955), and stated in his famous energy-mass equation, $E = mc^2$, was a necessary condition for even recognizing the phenomenon of nuclear fission energy release when it occurred in German laboratories in 1938, and certainly also for seeking fission energy as a practical goal. Einstein

himself was skeptical of this practical possibility, when first alerted to it in 1939 by Niels Bohr (1885–1962), but he was soon convinced by further experiments conducted immediately for him at Columbia University. Later in the same year, Einstein signed a letter to President Franklin D. Roosevelt alerting him to the danger of allowing German scientists to be first in unlocking the huge energies predicted by his theory. From this warning sprang the Manhattan Project, at that date the largest science-led technological project ever launched. The ethical ambiguities of the atom bomb, its use in the war against Japan and its role in deterring a third world war in the twentieth century, have been much discussed. Conflicting estimates of the consequences for good or ill, conflicting identification of the relevant ethical principles involved, are well known. Although of a new type, as offspring of theoretical intelligence, and of new scales in magnitude and urgency, nuclear bomb-making is subject to all the old ethical concerns.

What adds a special challenge for ethical assessment after the rise of theory-led technology is a new responsibility of assessing major technological innovations after they are conceived in principle but before they are born in practice. Technology policy can be ethically deliberated. Two examples will serve to illustrate.

Shifting from nuclear fission to fusion, we may assess the still-unrealized technology of electrical energy production by controlled thermonuclear reaction. In 1939, the hitherto mysterious source of the sun's prodigious energy output began to be understood theoretically as coming from energy released in a process by which four hydrogen nuclei are joined, when enormously high pressures and temperatures overcome electrical charge repulsion, thus forming one helium nucleus. This source is quite different in principle from the nuclear energies released when a heavy nucleus, such as the isotope uranium-235, splits into lighter nuclei. The two distinct processes are spectacularly combined in thermonuclear (so-called hydrogen) bombs, when the enormous but uncontrolled heat and pressure of a fission reaction forms the momentary star-like environment in which heavy hydrogen isotopes deuterium and tritium are forced to fuse into helium.

The theoretical lure to create useful electrical energy from a controlled fusion process is strong. The fuel, primarily deuterium, is plentiful, widely distributed, and relatively cheap. Every eight gallons of ordinary water contains about one gram of deuterium, which in principle could provide as much energy as 2,500 gallons of gasoline. There is no radioactive waste to guard or dispose. The practical difficulties, however, are extreme. The main technical problem is containing the unimaginably hot plasma of nuclei so tightly that a sustained reaction can occur. No material container could be used without instant vaporization. Strong magnets need to hold the writhing plasma away from all objects while a net surplus of energy is somehow extracted. Intense efforts have been under way for decades; perhaps someday the theoretical possibilities will be actualized.

But should fusion energy be practically realized? Ethical questions remain open for debate. Many positive outcomes are promised. Human society might be freed from dependence on oil, natural gas, and coal, with positive economic and environmental consequences. The rule of fairness in distribution of the fuel itself is better met, since water is a more widely available resource than oil or coal. Distribution of devices for deuterium extraction and of expensive fusion reactors would of course need scrutiny for fairness. One seldom considered question is whether human beings, in principle, should be freed of all need to deliberate and choose between energy expenditures. Has our species earned the right to be trusted with the capacity to pave over the world? This worrisome question forces attention again to the complexity of the long-term consequences that could reasonably be expected. The ethical debates have hardly begun.

The ethical debates over our second example, the technology of cloning, exploded into public consciousness with the appearance of Dolly, a cloned sheep, in 1997. Significantly, this is a technology led by theoretical biology, not to be confused with the techniques of selective breeding, which are as old as agriculture itself. Cloning technology is made possible by the revolution in understanding organic life brought about by the science of molecular biology, and especially by DNA analysis in genetics. Dolly's type of cloning, long believed to be impossible, depends on replacing the nuclear DNA in an egg cell with the nuclear DNA from an adult somatic cell of another organism. The donor cells are made quiescent by starvation, after which the donated DNA from those cells

is fused into the host egg cells by electrical pulses, and the activated eggs, after a short period of in vitro development, are implanted into a womb.

Ethical assessment of various types of cloning in agricultural application, where the production of sheep, cattle, and pigs is concerned, is likely to dwell on outcomes more than rules, though there are significant voices calling for a moratorium or prohibition, in principle, against so-called Frankenfoods, because of their unnatural origin, or perhaps because of offense taken by the possibility of transgenic manipulation of genetic characteristics. Ethical consideration of consequences will point to the increased good of more and better quality food in a hungry world, while opponents will urge the possible dangers to health, both of consumers and of over-manipulated organisms designed too narrowly by genetic engineers focused exclusively on the dinner table. A great deal more information is needed on these hopes and fears. Meanwhile, the principle of informed consent may be important in the marketing of artificial life-forms, so that consumers are given full information about what they buy and eat.

Still more intense passions rise in ethical debates on the possible cloning of human beings. Here appeals to rules tend to come first, though ethical concerns about consequences are also important. Aside from religious objections, ethical principles concerned with the uniqueness and dignity of human individuals may be invoked. Certainly, in principle, no human person should be cloned merely to serve as an organ bank, to provide rejection-free transplants for an ailing heart, for example. But might cloning be allowed from a dying child's tissues to alleviate an aching heart, if this could provide a DNA-identical replacement to nurture and love? Although all might agree with the rule that no person (including clones) should be treated as nothing but a means, might there be legitimate mixed situations, where a clone could be valued primarily as an end but also to some degree as a means?

Factual outcomes need close attention here, as well. If the motive is to produce mere replicas of specific persons (musicians, athletes, soldiers, scientists, perished loved ones, etc.), this may be both objectionable in principle and also unachievable as an outcome. Cloning will never be able to replicate persons exactly. Persons, within general genetic limits, are partially self-creating beings. Monozygotic twins (or triplets, etc.) are not really identical persons, despite shared DNA and largely similar in utero and childhood conditions. Much greater differences of environmental conditions, in the womb and throughout life, will assure that even the identical DNA shared by donor and clone will not violate the latter's uniqueness of personhood. Ethical evaluation of this luring and horrifying possible technology, like many other technologies still aborning, needs to become more subtle in analyzing principles and anticipating outcomes.

See also CLONING; INFORMATION TECHNOLOGY; BIOTECHNOLOGY; REPRODUCTIVE TECHNOLOGY; TECHNOLOGY; TECHNOLOGY AND RELIGION

Bibliography

Alcorn, Paul A. *Social Issues in Technology: A Format for Investigation,* 2nd edition. Upper Saddle River, N.J.: Prentice Hall, 1997.

Barash, David P. *The Arms Race and Nuclear War.* Belmont, Calif.: Wadsworth, 1987.

Barbour, Ian G. *Ethics in an Age of Technology: The Gifford Lectures 1989–1991,* Vol. 2. San Francisco: Harper Collins, 1993.

Beckman, Peter R.; Campbell, Larry; Crumlish, Paul W.; Dobkowski, Michael N.; and Lee, Steven P. *The Nuclear Predicament: An Introduction.* Englewood Cliffs, N.J.: Prentice Hall. 1989.

Bray, Francesca. *Technology and Gender: Fabrics of Power in Late Imperial China.* Berkeley: University of California Press, 1997.

Bromberg, Joan Lisa. *Fusion: Science, Politics, and the Invention of a New Energy Source.* Cambridge, Mass.: MIT Press, 1982.

Ellul, Jacques. *The Technological Society,* trans. John Wilkinson. New York: Vintage. 1964.

Ferré, Frederick. *Living and Value: Toward a Constructive Postmodern Ethics.* Albany: State University of New York Press, 2001.

Forester, Tom, ed. *The Information Technology Revolution.* Cambridge, Mass.: MIT Press, 1985.

Germain, Gilbert G. *A Discourse on Disenchantment: Reflections on Politics and Technology.* Albany: State University of New York Press. 1993.

Higgs, Eric; Light, Andrew; and Strong, David; eds. *Technology and the Good Life?* Chicago: University of Chicago Press, 2000.

Holdredge, Craig. *Genetics and the Manipulation of Life: The Forgotten Factor of Context.* Hudson, N.Y.: Lindisfarne Press, 1996.

Ihde, Don. *Technology and the Lifeworld: From Garden to Earth.* Bloomington: Indiana University Press, 1990.

Iannone, A. Pablo, ed. *Contemporary Moral Controversies in Technology.* New York: Oxford University Press, 1987.

Johnson, Deborah G., and Nissenbaum, Helen, eds. *Computers, Ethics, and Social Values.* Englewood Cliffs, N.J.: Prentice Hall, 1995.

Sassower, Raphael. *Cultural Collisions: Postmodern Technoscience.* New York: Routledge, 1995.

Tobey, Ronald C. *Technology as Freedom: The New Deal and the Electrical Modernization of the American Home.* Berkeley: University of California Press, 1996.

Winner, Langdon. *The Whale and the Reactor: A Search for Limits in an Age of High Technology.* Chicago: University of Chicago Press, 1986.

FREDERICK FERRÉ

TECHNOLOGY AND RELIGION

Technology, understood as *practical implementation of intelligence,* is a matter of know-how expressing values. Thus technology must somehow relate to religion, positively, negatively, or neutrally, since religion is also supremely a matter of values and ideas. Values come first for both, though ideas—strongly valued ones—will always be importantly present in both domains as long as *Homo sapiens* is a thinking species.

Religions are differentiated by a conflicting plethora of symbols and beliefs, but are alike functionally in expressing worship. *Worship* is here understood as directed to what is taken to be of first importance (last to be sacrificed) and of widest relevance (impossible to be marginalized). Thus *religion,* in principle, is our most intense and comprehensive way of valuing. This is a highly abstract characterization of religion. Actual people, on this understanding, are more or less concretely religious; some, who are casual about their values and see nothing as of comprehensive importance, may hardly be religious at all. Religious institutions, made up of actual people, are also more or less religious, since admixtures of economics, politics, cultural tradition, and the like, may be expected in every major human context.

Asian religions and technology

Divergent intuitions divide the primary world religions over what is ultimately worthy of worship, and thereby influence attitudes toward technology. Hinduism, in its Vedic and Brahmanistic forms, focuses its ultimate valuations on *brahman,* the transcendent, impersonal principle of universal order, paradoxically identified with *atman,* the individual soul. Although intermediate castes include warriors, producers, and servers, all of whom might take an interest in worldly technology, the most intense and comprehensive valuations of this many-stranded religious tradition focus on the priestly caste's ultimate goal of renunciation—the termination of an otherwise endless round of birth, death, and rebirth. Implements expressing practical intelligence for uses in this world, therefore, are of little religious significance. The predominant stance of Hinduism toward technology is neutrality, bordering on indifference.

Buddhism, Hinduism's offspring religion, takes a similar posture, though with a more pronounced negative tilt. Buddhism, because of its enormous variety and complexity, as cultural form and philosophy as well as religion, resists most generalizations. But the Four Noble Truths, traditionally traced to the Buddha's first sermon following his enlightenment, are as fundamental to all versions as can be found. The First Noble Truth diagnoses the basic human condition as suffering (*duhkha*), while the Second identifies craving or desire (*tanha*) as the cause of this suffering. The Third Noble Truth affirms that suffering can cease with the cessation of craving, for which the Fourth prescribes an Eightfold Path (right view, right thought, right speech, etc.) as the cure. But since technology, as intelligence seeking practical goals, is fundamentally powered by a desire or craving for something either to be achieved or prevented, it is hard to imagine an honored place for it if craving itself is the primary enemy. True, Buddhism steers for a middle way between the extremes of asceticism and hedonism, and would not advocate a brutish life, devoid of tools. But since Buddhism's oldest, highest value is the state of nothingness, transcending desire as

such (that is, the state of *nirvana,* where all craving and all suffering have completely vanished), we would look in vain to Buddhism for religious guidance on technology policy.

Confucian thought is far more practical. Its emphasis on the sage of virtue, properly hierarchical society, and correct ceremonial practices, in order to retain both balance and the blessings of heaven, is emphatically this-worldly. However, its strong emphasis on the rectitude of the ruler and on virtues proper to the sage tended to deflect concern from the humbler manual arts. Chinese technology, for all its ingenuity, developed in relative isolation from religious attention—assuming, as we do, that Confucianism qualifies as a religious phenomenon, despite its secular and humanistic spirit. This spirit expressed for its adherents what, in the widest possible context, is most to be valued.

Daoism represents another religious tradition, but one with which Confucianism was able to co-exist for millennia. It is said that in the late sixth century B.C.E., Confucius visited Laozi, the Daoist philosopher, to consult him on ceremonies, adopting the role of disciple. At any rate, the cosmic balance sought in Daoism is compatible in many ways with Confucian ideals. The metaphysical scale, however, is much grander in early Daoism, formulated in the *Dao de jing* (or *Tao-te ching;* attributed to Laozi), in which the Dao (or Way) is identified as a featureless, eternal, primordial reality, the mother of the world, giving birth to all things. Unity, above all, is to be sought, with the masculine principle (*yang*) requiring completion and balance with the feminine principle (*yin*). Everything, metals, geographical directions, seasons, colors, and so on, could be classified in terms of these oppositions in need of harmonization, calling for a yin-yang way of life beginning with attention to one's own bodily health. To Daoism's metaphysical enlargement is added a mystical spirit strongly contrasting with Confucian worldliness. Unity is so important that it drives out the possibility of discursive thought, which inevitably breaks up into multiplicity of ideas. Similarly, the Daoist sage, unlike the Confucian, is warned against intervening in the course of events. This policy, called *wu-wei,* is not one of absolute inactivity, but stresses the importance of respect for the autonomy of other happenings, both in their independence from the self but also in their complete relatedness to the network of things and processes as a whole.

Through disciplined nonaction the Daoist relates to the eternal Dao, finding increased personal longevity and mystic ecstasy as reward. Technology, as we know it, however, has no place within the spirituality of *wu-wei*. Indeed, in our short survey of the primary religious traditions of Asia, we have found none with a positive place for the technological in general.

Biblical religions and technology

The three great religions of the Book, Judaism, Christianity, and Islam, all have mixed records regarding technology. There are characteristic differences between them, but even greater differences between strands internal to each faith.

Judaism, as the oldest, contains within its early scriptures the fundamental tensions felt within all three of the religions rooted in the Hebrew Bible. At the outset, the created world is pronounced good (*Gen.* 1:31). The sun, the moon, the stars, the birds and beasts, the trees and Earth, are all realities, neither indifferent illusion nor tricky *Maya,* and they are of genuine importance. They are not as important as the creator, of course, but they are divinely approved. They are given their names by the first man, and they are handed into permanent human care. Adam and Eve, as exemplary humanity, are from the start commanded to till and keep the garden entrusted to them (*Gen.* 2:15). Even after expulsion from the initial paradise, humanity must continue to till the ground, though in consequence of the great disobedience that led to this expulsion, tilling would henceforth involve toil and sweat (*Gen.* 3: 17–19).

In the ensuing world of mixed morality, God not only commissioned and approved the first recorded technological project (*Gen.* 6: 14–16) but also provided the design (three hundred cubits long, three internal decks, etc.) and the specifications (gopher wood and pitch). This was for the great ark that Noah was commanded to build in order to preserve a basic breeding stock to repopulate the world after God's impending flood. There is no hint of disapproval here of tools or the practical arts in general. On the contrary, human construction is a pious act and is rewarded with survival. But immediately following the story of Noah, after the human race has had a chance to replenish itself and spread once more, the descendants of

Noah are depicted as offending God by their technological hubris (*Gen.* 11: 1–9). Having only one language, they are capable of unlimited engineering ambitions and decide to construct an enormous tower, reaching all the way to heaven. Before they can succeed in such blasphemy, God says: "Behold, they are one people, and they have all one language; and this is only the beginning of what they will do; and nothing that they propose to do will now be impossible for them. Come, let us go down, and there confuse their language, that they may not understand one another's speech" (*Gen.* 11: 6–7, RSV). In the ensuing linguistic confusion, attempts to complete the tower of Babel are aborted. God clearly disapproves when technological pride oversteps its limits.

This duality in attitude continues to express itself in different strands of Christianity. The mystical, otherworldly side, often (but not exclusively) associated with the Eastern Church, centered in Constantinople, noteworthy for its iconography and other sacred arts, has characteristically distanced itself from the secular crafts. In contrast, the Western, European, side of Christian faith, initially centered in Rome, contains (though itself internally mixed) craft-affirming strands that have blessed technological dynamism in principle and eventually encouraged the emergence of the world of science and high technology. Those monasteries following the Rule of Saint Benedict (c. 480–547) were particularly significant for maintaining a sanctified balance between prayer, reading (or copying) scripture, and practical work, including labor in the gardens and fields and devoted craftsmanship of many kinds.

Islamic religion inherited what Christians call both the Old and the New Testaments, in addition to its own Qur'an and prophetic writings. Not surprisingly, the relationship between Muslim faith and technological prowess shows the same ambivalence we have noted in the other two Biblical religions. One of the technological domains enthusiastically entered by early Islamic culture was architecture. Islam requires frequent centralized meetings of the faithful, but existing structures were seldom adequate. The earliest practice of meeting in private houses was quickly outgrown, as Arab conquest spread Islam during the seventh and eighth centuries. Existing synagogues and churches were also usually unsuitable for mosques, which were used not simply as places of worship but also as community centers. In response, the hypostyle mosque, a rectangular building of many columns supporting a roof, was invented, allowing easy expansion by the addition of columns in the event of community growth. Minarets, initially built only in non-Muslim cities as prominent vantages for calls to prayer, were also created. But, simultaneously, decoration of Muslim artifacts was tightly restricted. Fierce rejection of even a hint of idolatry in this ardently theocentric religion strongly opposes the representation of living forms, lest human creativity usurp the exclusive prerogatives of the sole Creator. Iconoclasm, familiar in Jewish prohibitions on graven imagery and appearing at least sporadically among Christians, is a powerful governor in Muslim attitudes toward arts and crafts.

Historical development

Not surprisingly, the religious background of a culture makes a large difference in its characteristic readiness to respond to or incorporate technologies, as such possibilities present themselves. In Tibet, deeply steeped in classical Buddhist thought and perception, for example, the *Manichos khor,* or prayer wheel, a mechanical device consisting of a hollow metal cylinder containing a written mantra, has been in use for centuries. Each revolution of the cylinder is thought equal to one oral recitation of the mantra. From ancient times, these prayer wheels have been attached to windmill or waterwheel devices that have served to multiply prayers without human attention or effort. But, significantly, the harnessing of wind or water power did not extend to grinding grain or sawing lumber.

Western European attitudes, set in a branch of Christianity generally favoring the biblical affirmation of the importance of creation under human dominion, were far more ready to accept technological innovation. Monks, squinting over their copy work, were quick to accept the benefits of eyeglasses, when glassblowing crafts made lenses possible. The Christian peasants of northern Europe, perhaps as early as the seventh century, invented the moldboard plow to cut deeply into and turn the soil, rather than settle for Near Eastern and southern Mediterranean plows—suited to lighter soils—that merely scratched the surface and required cross plowing. The historian, Lynn White, Jr., comments in "The Historical Roots of Our Ecologic Crisis" (1967): "Formerly, man had been part of nature; now he was the exploiter of nature. Nowhere else in the world did farmers develop any analogous agricultural implement. Is it coincidence that modern technology, with its ruthlessness toward nature, has so largely been produced by descendants of these peasants of Northern Europe?" (p. 1205).

Countless other technologies were grasped and put to practical work by the Western Europeans, with encouragement from its dominant religion. The magnetic compass freed seamen from hugging the coasts, making European exploration (and ultimately domination) of the rest of the world practical. The voyages of Christopher Columbus and other explorers were enthusiastically supported by Church interests, and it is no coincidence that missionary priests accompanied him and other openers of the New World.

In the twentieth century, the technologies of urbanization and modernization were subjects of theological celebration by at least some Christians. In *The Secular City* (1966), Harvey Cox praised what he called the disenchantment of nature, the elimination of its ghostly terrors, at first permitted in biblical religions by the concentration of all sacredness in the creator, excluding everything created, and then at last achieved by the antiseptic powers of modern science. He also welcomed the desacralization of politics and the freedoms of anonymity provided by technological society.

In sharp contrast, reminding us of the deep ambivalence of the biblical religions toward technology, particularly technologies suggesting hubris or idolatry, many theological voices were raised in opposition to the atomic bomb during the twentieth century. A particularly forceful voice was that of Jacques Ellul, whose indictment of nuclear energy included not only the bomb, but also the megalomania of atomic power generation in general, and of the heedless science that makes it all possible. In a 1974 essay called *"Le Rapport de l'Homme à la Création Selon la Bible"* ("The Relationship between Man and Creation in the Bible"), Ellul summarizes: "The effort to affirm science by itself, without limit, as judge of everything and carrying its own legitimization *inevitably* involved, as the other side of the coin, the devastation of the world, the squandering of possibilities, the frenzy of destruction" (p. 153).

Contemporary challenges

Most great religions have traditional ways of dealing with such apocalyptic anticipations, and even short of apocalypse, religions have (alas) had much experience with mayhem and devastation. Standard theological responses, even when the scale of devastation is very great, may be expected. A great fire is a great fire whether caused by burning pitch, chemical explosives, or nuclear fission. What is radically new, however, is the empowerment provided by science-led (or *high*) technologies to accomplish hitherto inconceivable ends.

For one major example, theoretical biology has inspired mapping the molecular basis for the complete array of genes in the cells of a human person. This could never have been so much as an objective, apart from the theoretical work leading to the understanding of the double helix of DNA codons that constitute the alphabet spelling out all living organisms. Now that the Human Genome Project has succeeded, and genetic engineering is an established technology, unprecedented practical possibilities are opened for exploitation. New powers of diagnosis of such feared diseases as Tay-Sachs, Huntington's, cystic fibrosis, and muscular dystrophy, are in human hands. Diagnosis is not cure, but genetic engineering promises the synthesis of new medical helps, such as interferon, to increase resistance to viruses. Direct somatic gene therapy is another entirely new possibility, stirring the hopes of sufferers from otherwise incurable conditions such as Huntington's disease. And, beyond curing individuals, the way is opening to modification of the their offspring, and their offspring's offspring, by engineering the germline itself to eliminate unwanted genetic conditions, either in sperm or egg, and either before conception or in the fertilized egg.

Finding adequate religious responses to these, and vastly many other, completely new human powers is the primary challenge for the future. For religions depending upon ancient scriptures to provide divine commands, there is the challenge to avoid objectionable eisegesis and special pleading when clear textual guidance is simply lacking. There is a similar challenge to avoid the common fallacy of begging the question against a technological novelty by (correctly) identifying the new as *artificial,* therefore (correctly) as *unnatural,* and therefore (fallaciously) as *wrong.* Simply to be artificial, the partial product of art or intelligence (and to that extent unnatural), is not necessarily to

be illicit. All major religions have come to terms with the interventions of human intelligence and practical purpose in ways that alter nature. Some, like agriculture, are universally recognized as licit. Eyeglasses and hearing aids are also in this inoffensive sense unnatural. The challenge for religious thinking in radically novel cases is to wrestle with what, specifically, it is about practical interventions led by theoretical intelligence—from in vitro fertilization to germ line therapy or even cloning—that makes them unnatural in a bad sense.

Such careful thinking, in order to be relevant and responsible, will need to become well informed about the sciences that lead new high technologies to conceive their novel technological possibilities. In this lies still another challenge for the future relations of technology and religion, since the values and belief-systems of the great religions have not hitherto been forced to take serious account of the values and belief-system of the modern sciences. Modern science has made thinkable, and modern technology has made practical, many gadgets that have been used for religious purposes inimical to the values and beliefs of science. A prime example is the use of electronic tape recorders by the Ayatolla Ruhollah Khomeini (1900–1989) in sending his fiery sermons of Islamic fundamentalism from his home in Paris, rousing the Iranian populace to overthrow Mohammad Reza Shah Pahlavi in 1979. Neither the scientific understanding of the electromagnetic universe, nor the scientific methods and values that made this technology possible, is compatible with the content of those sermons or with the methods and values they espoused. But it is likely that using technologies without appreciating their intellectual and valuational foundations (especially if high technologies are to be manufactured worldwide) will become increasingly difficult. Perhaps gradually, over the current millennium, if religious leaders are forced increasingly to think deeply about the unprecedented technological possibilities being opened to their followers by the practical embodiments of scientific theory, there may be an increased coming to terms with the beliefs and values of science itself.

Such a global coming to terms would require wrenching reforms but not necessarily the abandonment of essential symbols in the great religions of the world. Though it has not been easy, many Christians since Galileo have found ways of accommodating their defining beliefs to established science, and it is not impossible to conceive a similar process globally, spurred by the spread of high technology with its implicit scientific content. If this should occur, a new basis for interfaith ecumenical dialogue might gradually emerge, as well. Such a dialogue could be accelerated by common concerns shared by the great religions for global justice among persons and for the protection of our vulnerable planet against technological hubris.

See also BIOTECHNOLOGY; BUDDHISM; CHINESE RELIGIONS, CONFUCIANISM AND SCIENCE IN CHINA; CHINESE RELIGIONS, DAOISM AND SCIENCE IN CHINA; EINSTEIN, ALBERT; HINDUISM; HUMAN GENOME PROJECT; INFORMATION TECHNOLOGY; ISLAM; JUDAISM; REPRODUCTIVE TECHNOLOGY; TECHNOLOGY; TECHNOLOGY AND ETHICS; VALUE, SCIENTIFIC

Bibliography

Barbour, Ian G. *Science and Secularity: The Ethics of Technology*. New York: Harper, 1970.

Barbour, Ian G., ed. *Earth Might Be Fair: Reflections on Ethics, Religion, and Ecology*. Englewood Cliffs, N.J.: Prentice-Hall, 1972.

Callahan, Daniel, ed. *The Secular City Debate*. New York: Macmillan, 1966.

Cobb, John B., Jr. *Sustainability: Economics, Ecology, and Justice*. Maryknoll, N.Y.: Orbis Books, 1992.

Cox, Harvey. *The Secular City: Secularization and Urbanization in Theological Perspective*, Rev. edition. New York: Macmillan, 1966.

Daly, Herman E., and Cobb, John B., Jr. *For the Common Good: Redirecting the Economy toward Community, the Environment, and a Sustainable Future*. Boston: Beacon Press, 1989.

Ellul, Jacques. "The Relationship Between Man and Creation in the Bible" (1974), trans. W. Deller and Katharine Temple. In *Theology and Technology: Essays in Christian Analysis and Exegesis*, eds. Carl Mitcham and Jim Grote. Lanham, Md.: University Press of America, 1984.

Ferré, Frederick. *Shaping the Future: Resources for the Post-Modern World*. New York: Harper, 1976.

Ferré, Frederick, ed. *Technology and Religion*, Vol. 10: Research in Philosophy and Technology. London and Greenwich, Conn.: JAI Press 1990.

Ferré, Frederick. *Hellfire and Lightning Rods: Liberating Science, Technology, and Religion*. Maryknoll, N.Y.: Orbis Books, 1993.

Haigerty, Leo J., ed. *Pius XII and Technology*. Milwaukee, Wisc.: Bruce, 1962.

Hargrove, Eugene C., ed. *Religion and Environmental Crisis*. Athens: University of Georgia Press, 1986.

Kohák, Erazim. *The Embers and the Stars: A Philosophical Inquiry into the Moral Sense of Nature*. Chicago: University of Chicago Press, 1984.

Marx, Leo. *The Machine in the Garden: Technology and the Pastoral Ideal in America*. New York: Oxford University Press, 1964.

McDaniel, Jay B. *Of God and Pelicans: A Theology of Reverence for Life*. Louisville, Ky.: Westminster Press, 1989.

Mitcham, Carl, and Grote, Jim, eds. *Technology and Theology: Essays in Christian Analysis and Exegesis*. Lanham, Md.: University Press of America, 1984.

Murphy, Nancey, and Ellis, George F. R. *On the Moral Nature of the Universe: Theology, Cosmology, and Ethics*. Minneapolis, Minn.: Fortress Press, 1996.

Oelschlager, Max. *Caring For Creation: An Ecumenical Approach to the Environmental Crisis*. New Haven, Conn.: Yale University Press, 1994.

Rasmussen, Larry L. *Earth Community Earth Ethics*. Maryknoll, N.Y.: Orbis Books, 1996.

Schumacher, E. F. *Small Is Beautiful: Economics as if People Mattered*. New York: Harper, 1973.

Schuurman, Egbert. *Technology and the Future: A Philosophical Challenge*, trans. Herbert Donald Morton. Toronto, Ont.: Wedge Publishing Foundation, 1980.

Shinn, Roger Lincoln. *The New Genetics: Challenges for Science, Faith, and Politics*. Wakefield, R.I.: Moyer Bell, 1996.

Tatum, Jesse S. *Energy Possibilities: Rethinking Alternatives and the Choice-Making Process*. Albany: State University of New York, 1995.

United Methodist Council of Bishops. *In Defense of Creation: The Nuclear Crisis and a Just Peace*. Nashville, Tenn.: Graded Press, 1986.

White, Lynn, Jr. "The Historical Roots of our Ecologic Crisis." *Science* 155, no. 3767 (1967): 1203–1207.

FREDERICK FERRÉ

TEILHARD DE CHARDIN, PIERRE

The thought and works of Pierre Teilhard de Chardin represent the widest and deepest attempt to reconcile Christian theology and the scientific worldview of biological evolution. Teilhard de Chardin noted the peculiar contributions of modern science to the vision of creation. Arguing that evolution moves toward complexity and consciousness, he noted that the order implied by creation is in the future and is achieved as a result of both the mechanisms of evolution and the action of humankind. The theological vision of the movement of creation toward unity, redemption, and salvation is now referred to as the evolutionary universe.

Early life and influences

Pierre Teilhard de Chardin was born in Sacernat in the French region of Auvergne in 1881, a year before the death of Charles Darwin. Teilhard died in New York in 1955. He entered the Society of Jesus in 1899 and was ordained a Roman Catholic priest in 1911. A year later he started his scientific training in natural science with a special interest in paleontology at the Institute of Human Paleontology in Paris, under the direction of Marcellin Boule, one of the most eminent human paleontologists of that time. There Teilhard completed all his scientific training until the doctoral thesis.

Teilhard de Chardin's vocation became clear to him during the first world war; he wrote in his diary: "I would like to reconcile with God what is good in the modern world—its scientific intuitions, its social desires, it proper criticisms" (*Journal*, pp. 90–91). For Teilhard, one of the great novelties of the modern world was evolution: the theory that life, Earth, and the whole universe are subject to a nonreversible change over time. From his point of view, evolution was not only a theory to be investigated, but also the scientific description of a peculiar way of creation, which required new approaches from theologians and philosophers "The adoption of the evolutionary mode for the formation of the world implies a particular mode of appareance 'ex nihilo subjecti' and suggests that this world has a deep *ontological reason*" (*Journal*, p. 264).

After completing his doctoral degree, Teilhard became chair of geology at the Catholic Institute of Paris. There, together with the French philosopher Edouard LeRoy and the Soviet geochemist Vladimir Vernadskij, he coined the word *Noosphere*, which he defined as the totality of all thinking creatures, "the psychically reflexive human surface." According to Karl and Nicole Schmitz Moormann in *Pierre Teilhard de Chardin, L'oeuvre Scientifique,* Teilhard also started to envision a new global approach to evolution as a matter concerning the whole biosphere.

Darwin and evolution

In the meantime, he wrote a private note on original sin, in which he suggested that, in an evolving universe, order is not to be found at the beginning, only to be ruined by human sin, but order will come in the future and has to be constructed by human action. According to Teilhard, there is no gap in the history of life, no nature uncorrupted before sin and corrupted after sin. The mechanism of biological evolution, which involves the undeterministic and dramatic events first elucidated by Darwin, are present from the very beginning of life and are a general characteristic of the evolution of the universe.

Teilhard's unconventional views resulted in his removal from his academic chair and his invitation to stay in China. Yet his theological revolution was only beginning. Because the promise of order resides in the future, he speculated, Christians are not only asked to reach their own eschatological salvation in paradise, but also to construct the Earth and a new type of human on Earth. At the end of the process of evolution humankind will reach a single point of convergence, the Omega Point, where there will be the second and final coming of Christ. A new ontological value is suggested in this scientific description of nature: evolution as movement toward an endpoint, a goal. The deep meanings of the universe, from both the theological and philosophical points of view, are related to this idea of movement toward something: of matter toward life, of life toward consciousness, of consciousness toward the thinking creature and the Noosphere, the Noosphere toward the Omega Point. Teilhard considered this movement the result of the *complexity-consciousness* law and he argued that it recovers the theological necessity for the emergence of humankind.

Teilhard was well aware of new research and discoveries in evolutionary biology. He was most interested in the aspect of Darwinism in which chance plays a central role, but he thought that a correct scientific analysis would be able to demonstrate the presence of *canalisation* (the determination of a direction to evolution in a particular phyletic branch) and *parallelisms* (phyletic branches that separate off a common branch evolve in parallel and develop similar characteristics). In fact, Teilhard discussed the parallelisms of primates toward increasing brain size in his first scientific papers as a trained palaeontologist. For Teilhard, if there is a general movement that characterizes evolution, this movement has to be evidenced from an experimental point of view. He grappled with the question of how to reconcile this vision with the revision of Darwinism called *modern synthesis,* which was in vogue at the time Teilhard was working in palaeontology and which seemed to deny any epistemological meaning to evolutionary direction.

Teilhard de Chardin believed that only a global experimental approach could demonstrate the directional movement of evolution. Most palaeontologists relied on fossil records, and the lack of a broader global approach by the proponents of the *modern synthesis,* who used a reductionistic approach based on genes and populations, was the epistemological reason for their rejection of the idea of evolution as moving toward a goal. Some of the innovations of biology, for example, the global approach and the definition of biology as the science of complexity, were developed by Teilhard in an attempt to answer questions posed by theology.

Global approach

Central to the evolution of Teilhard's thought was his move to China in 1923, where he worked on the geology, palaeontology, and paleoanthropology of the Asiatic continent. Here, he was able to study evolution on a large scale, both in time and space, and the possibility of a global approach to evolutionary biology became more possible. He intended such a global approach to be part of his program of studying the biosphere, and the continental evolution that he had in mind at the time was an epistemological tool, by which he could study the evolution of the biosphere on a reduced scale but without distortions.

A new model of the interaction of science and theology became apparent: Some of the characteristics of theology, such as the eschatological movement toward an endpoint, and some level of necessity of the thinking creature, are recovered as the metaphysical frame of a true scientific research program. In addition, research that describes the evolution of the universe and its mechanisms can

form a starting point for a new theological program. The epistemological model of Teilhard, presented in the introduction of *The Human Phenomenon* (1955), is that there are points where science, philosophy, and theology converge, and these points must be handled in the correct way. The main philosophic frame is that of totality because it is the concept of totality that requires general connections, but totality is also the way to propose the global view in construction of evolutionary theories concerning the biosphere. The peculiarities of the whole can be lost in a reductionistic approach. Teilhard wrote these ideas in letters from China just after an expedition in the Gobi desert, where he envisioned the mystical experience of totality and where he was inspired to write the "Mass on the World." There is the possibility that mystical knowledge, or at least mystical experience, was at the very basis of his research program.

Geobiology

From these connections, Teilhard de Chardin developed the notion of "complexity" and proposed a new science called *geobiology,* the science of continental evolution, which he intended as part of his global program to study evolution. He was able to develop an experimental approach to fossil evolution that showed that evolution is characterised by canalisation and parallelisms. The main parallelism, at least in animals, was the moving of different evolutionary branches toward increasing cerebralization, which Teilhard saw as experimental proof of the directional movement of evolution. The present day discussion about the increasing in complexity of life evolution has in Teilhard one of its forerunners.

Finally, developing Teilhard's vision, evolution is moving toward complexity and consciousness with mechanisms not strictly deterministic: There is room for chance and blind movements. Teilhard looked for philosophical and theological meanings of these mechanisms, and found them in the idea of freedom. He believed that freedom is the third ontological characteristic of the universe suggested by modern science.

These mechanisms are not proof of the lack of purpose or design, but they are compatible with the idea that design implies freedom and that the nondeterministic structure of the universe is the only way to allow room for the free action of the thinking creature. The lack of order at the beginning of the universe gives the thinking creature room for free action in order to conduct general movement toward the Omega Point. The creation and evolution of the Earth is owed to (or thanks to) the freely accepted alliance of creator and the created. The synthesis of interaction of science and faith finds here its climax.

See also CHANCE; CHRISTIANITY, ROMAN CATHOLIC, ISSUES IN SCIENCE AND RELIGION; COMPLEXITY; CONVERGENCE; DARWIN, CHARLES; EMERGENCE; EVOLUTION; FREEDOM; INCARNATION; MYSTICISM; PALEONTOLOGY

Bibliography

Arnould, Jacques. *Darwin, Teilhard de Chardin, et Cie.* Paris: Desclée de Brouwer, 1996.

Galleni, Lodovico. "Relationships between Scientific Analysis and the World View of Pierre Teilhard de Chardin." *Zygon* 27 (1992): 153–166.

Galleni, Lodovico. "How Does the Teilhardian Vision of Evolution Compare with Contemporary Theories?" *Zygon* 30 (1995): 25–45.

Galleni, Lodovico. "Teilhard de Chardin, le message." *Concilium* 284 (2000): 137–148.

Galleni, Lodovico, and Groessens-Van Dyck, Marie Claire. "Lettres d' un paléontologue. Neuf lettres inédites de Pierre Teilhard de Chardin à Marcellin Boule." *Revue des questions scientifiques* 172, no. 1 (2001): 5–104

Piveteau, Jean. *Le Père Teilhard de Chardin savant.* Paris: Fayard, 1964.

Heller, Michael. "Teilhard's Vision of the World and Modern Cosmology." *Zygon* 30 (1995): 11–23.

Schmitz Moormann, Karl, and Salmon, James F. *Theology of Creation in an Evolutionary World.* Cleveland, Ohio: Pilgrim Press, 1997.

Schmitz Moormann, Nicole, and Schmitz Moormann, Karl. *Pierre Teilhard de Chardin, L'oeuvre scientifique,* Freiburg, Germany: Walter-Verlag, 1971.

Teilhard de Chardin, Pierre. *The Divine Milieu,* trans. Bernad Walls. New York: Harper, 1960.

Teilhard de Chardin, Pierre. *Les Oeuvres Complètes.* Paris: Seuil, 1955–1970.

Teilhard de Chardin, Pierre. *L'oeuvre Scientifique,* eds. Nicle Schmitz-Moormann and Karl Schmitz-Moormann. Freiburg, German: Walter Verlag, 1971.

Teilhard de Chardin, Pierre. *The Phenomenon of Man* (1959), trans. Sarah Appleton-Weber. Brighton, UK: Sussex Academic Press, 1999.

Teilhard de Chardin, Pierre. "Mass of the World." In *Hymn of the Universe,* trans. Simon Bartholomew. New York: Harper, 1965.

LUDOVICO GALLENI

TELEOLOGICAL ARGUMENT

According to the teleological argument, the order and complexity exhibited by the world are properly attributed to a purposive cause rather than a blind, undirected process. Historically, in looking for evidence of purpose, the argument has focused on the world as a whole, its laws, and structures within the world (notably life). The teleological argument has two recent incarnations. One employs the Anthropic Principle and focuses on the fine-tuning or "just-so" aspects of the physical universe required for human observers. The other constitutes a revival of design-theoretic reasoning in biology and is known under the rubric "intelligent design."

See also DESIGN

WILLIAM A. DEMBSKI

TELEOLOGY

Teleology, from the Greek *telos* (purpose), is a term generally thought to have been coined by the German philosopher Christian Wolff in 1728. *Teleology* refers to the science of final causes. In Aristotle's philosophy, there were four sorts of causes, or principles for explaining the nature of things. One of these is the *final cause,* for the sake of which an object exists. Aristotle held that virtually all objects, especially organic objects, have a final cause. It is a principle inherent in them, which disposes them to realize a particular state, which can be seen as the purpose for their existence. It is closely related to the *formal cause,* which is the essential nature (the *form*) of an object. For many objects, the final cause simply is the fullest realization of the formal cause. Aristotle saw organisms as striving to realize their true natures as they grew and developed.

The final cause of an acorn, for example, is a fully grown oak tree. The acorn is naturally disposed to become an oak tree. That is the proper realization of its nature, the reason it exists. The idea of final causality applies most obviously to organisms. It has two forms. One might be called *part-whole teleology*—the parts of an organism exist for the sake of the whole (the heart exists in order to pump blood around the body). The other might be called *goal-oriented teleology*—the purpose of a seed or embryo is to grow into a particular organic form. Aristotle implied that all objects act for a purpose or end, so that even rocks have an inherent purpose for existence, even if it just to be a good solid rock. Aristotle did not appeal to a God for this idea, but saw final causality and formal causality as a principle inherent in all existent objects.

When medieval philosophers in Judaism, Christianity, and Islam took over Aristotelian categories, they explicitly introduced a creator God as a being who gives all things their final causes, and that is itself the final cause of the entire universe, for the sake of which it exists. Thus, one of Thomas Aquinas's (c. 1225–1274) arguments for God is that, since all bodies tend to a goal, they must be directed to it by some being with awareness and intelligence, "and this we call God" (*Summa Theologiae* 1a, 2, 3). Aquinas includes the fact that bodies obey natural laws as a form of final causality. They do not act by accident, but obey the laws as if intended to do so, and this points to the fact that they are so intended.

A marked feature of post-sixteenth century science was its rejection of, or at least indifference to, any doctrine of final causes in nature. Laws of nature were seen as general principles of interaction between objects (perhaps ultimately between atoms), which have no purpose; they just happen to be (perhaps by some unknown mathematical necessity) the way they are. The last remnant of Aristotelian teleology was *vitalism,* the belief that at least organisms are actuated by some immaterial *vital principle* that explains their structure and development. Most biologists reject this notion as unnecessary mystification, and look for purely physical causes of organic structure and development.

The Design argument

In eighteenth-century Europe, a new form of design argument took shape that did not appeal to inherent final causes in things. Instead, it pointed to the way in which the parts of nature cooperate to produce apparently well-designed wholes. A general mechanism of nature is accepted, but that mechanism is seen as producing elegant and de-

sirable states, conducive to the survival and flourishing of organisms, particularly human beings. Nature is a well-designed machine, and its ultimate purpose is the pleasure of conscious human beings. William Paley wrote *A View of the Evidences of Christianity* in 1794, and it became for many years the standard exposition of the design argument. It adduced a host of biological and natural facts to show that nature is an efficient process that realizes highly desirable ends, which shows that nature is designed and that a designer is therefore needed. This could be called the *universal design argument,* since it refers to the general structure of the universe and its laws. Paley also argued that there are many evidences of particular design in nature, from the fact that the eye is perfectly designed for vision to the fact that camels are specially constructed to store water in the desert.

David Hume's *Dialogues Concerning Natural Religion,* published posthumously in 1779, was a devastating critique of such design arguments, and he is generally felt to have refuted Paley's views fifteen years before they appeared. Immanuel Kant, in his *Critique of Pure Reason* (1781), wrote that the design argument was naturally convincing to all, but it was not logically compelling. In particular, it does not show the necessity for an all-perfect creator. According to Kant, there is a definite appearance of design in nature, but there could be another explanation for it.

That other explanation was provided by Charles Darwin's theory of *descent with modification,* or *natural selection,* in the *Origin of Species* (1859). This theory, later broadened into *universal Darwinism* by a number of philosophers, posits that multiple replication and random mutation of organisms, together with ruthless selection by environment, naturally leads over many generations to just the sort of improvements or adaptations that look as if they have been designed, though in fact the mechanism of repeated mutation and natural selection is sufficient to produce that appearance.

Teleology and evolution

To many it seems that teleology has at last been extruded from natural science, and from any reasonable account of the general structure of the universe. Others, however, think this is not the case. In 1928, the Cambridge philosopher F. R. Tennant published his *Philosophical Theology,* in which he gave an extended argument for a teleological view of evolution. In opposition to the Darwinian, or neo-Darwinian, view that mutation is random and undirected, he argued that one can discern a direction in the evolutionary process towards an increase of consciousness, intelligence, and intentional action. Individual mutations are random, in the sense that they are not all directed toward the improvement of the species. But they have an overall propensity, in conjunction with the supportive nature of the environment, to lead to the development of intelligent organisms like human beings. That the environment supports such developments is not an accident, but suggests that the whole cosmic system, in its general evolutionary structure, is well adapted to the production of conscious life forms.

There is, according to Tennant, probably not a particular teleology whereby camels are specially designed to live in deserts. But there is a general teleology whereby organisms that live in deserts continue to produce genetic mutations, some of which will eventually lead to the existence of water-storing organisms like camels. Tennant admits that all this could logically happen by chance, given the existence of laws governing genetic mutation and environmental change. But is it not a puzzle that these laws are just what they need to be to produce organisms like camels and human beings? Darwin himself apparently felt there was a puzzle, but he never solved it.

There would be no puzzle if humans were considered to have no greater value than specks of dust. But if humans are seen as immensely complex integrated structures (and the brain is the most complex structure known in the universe) that value their own existences and may even be of unique intrinsic dignity and value, then there is a puzzle. An evolutionary teleological argument will only work on two conditions—if the evolutionary process is an efficient way of producing its putative goal, and if that goal is indeed of great desirability, perhaps just what an intelligent designer would want to produce.

Darwinians may argue that the process is inefficient or cruel—there are too many mistakes and blind alleys. And they may argue that humans are not of unique value, except, naturally enough, to themselves. Tennant responds that the "mistakes" are necessary parts of a process in which freedom, and therefore some degree of indeterminacy, is an

essential part. And the value of human persons lies in their possession of moral responsibility and the ability to relate to one another and to the creator in love.

Is this a scientific argument? It seems not, for the biological facts are not in dispute. It is an argument about how one evaluates organic existence and human personhood. One's attitude toward teleology depends upon evaluative judgments about whether the evolutionary process is "worth it," and about whether humans have a special dignity and moral status.

Belief in God is not necessary to a teleological view—that is, a view that there is a direction in the evolutionary process towards states of unique and unexpected value. One could be a humanist or a Marxist and hold such a teleological view. Many Marxists, for instance, and probably Karl Marx (1818–1883) himself, saw nature as progressively realizing its own inherent drive towards a free and creative society of persons, without the existence of any "external" or omniscient intelligence. If there were to be such an intelligence, it would be the final consequence of the cosmic process, not its precondition.

Among Christian thinkers, the paleontologist Pierre Teilhard de Chardin (1881–1955) has restated a Christian teleological view that owes much to both Darwin and Marx. According to Teilhard, the universe as a whole moves towards greater complexity and higher levels of consciousness. The emergence of human consciousness was a saltation in the process, by which the universe (or parts of it) became capable of conscious self-direction for the first time, so far as we know. The process will continue in the development on Earth of a *noosphere*, in which all individual consciousnesses become progressively unified. The final culmination will be the Omega Point, when the whole material universe will be unified in the life of one omniscient and wholly self-directing spirit. However, Teilhard posits that this Omega Point, being beyond historical time, has in fact always existed as the causal basis of the whole historical process. It is, in fact, God, which, though timelessly complete, realizes itself progressively in cosmic time.

This grand cosmic vision takes evolutionary theory back to its philosophical origins in the work of George Wilhelm Friedrich Hegel (1770–1831), for whom evolution was a gradual self-realization of absolute spirit. This form of evolutionary theory is cosmically optimistic, and committed to a teleological view of the universe as directed towards its final consummation, and perhaps transformation, in the spiritual reality of God. For many, however, this is both too optimistic and too grandiose a vision for the available evidence, which seems to them much more ambiguous in its indications of continued improvement towards a final goal. Just as the dinosaurs were wiped out, so too all life on Earth could be wiped out by some catastrophe, which would eliminate any possibility of purpose in evolution.

Teilhard considered, however, that the cosmic purpose could be completed beyond this physical space-time, in a new environment created by God. So one can hold that there is a purpose in evolution—to produce conscious beings capable of relating to God. But the real final goal is eschatological; it lies in the fulfillment of persons in God beyond the present space-time. This view is clearly not open to empirical testing, though questions of whether persons can survive the death of their physical bodies are relevant to its plausibility.

Teleology in modern thought

Within modern science, there are those, like Michael Behe and William Dembski, who argue that there is still a need to appeal to teleology. They hold that small incremental mutations cannot account for the existence of organs like the eye, which need to exist as a whole in order to function at all. The so-called Intelligent Design argument is about the adequacy of Darwinian explanations to account for all features of organic life.

More widespread, however, are arguments of cosmologists like Paul Davies that the amount of "fine-tuning" of physical constants and laws that is required to produce conscious life in a physical universe is much too great to be due to chance. Some physicists are so impressed by the complex interrelation of physical laws needed to produce life that they think some sort of intelligence must underlie the universe. For most, this intelligence is not a God like that of orthodox religion. It is more like a vast intelligence that is not morally concerned with the lives and happiness of organisms.

Other physicists, like Steven Weinberg, think the hypothesis of an intelligence is superfluous. They would like to see the derivation of the laws of this universe as necessarily following from some impersonal and invariant superset of laws. The supposition that such a superset is necessarily there, however, seems to posit a sort of necessity that science cannot establish. To the religious believer, that necessity might well lie in the intentions of a creator God, who has an ultimate purpose in creating it.

On a less speculative level, there remains the important question, harking back to Aristotle, of whether some sort of teleological, purposive explanation is needed for a complete account of observed reality. In modern science, nomological explanation (in terms of general laws, without reference to purpose) is firmly established as a fruitful explanatory principle. But it is not at all clear whether it is adequate for explaining the facts of human consciousness and social life. Many would argue that explanation in terms of purpose or intention is needed to explain why humans act as they do. After all, they often do things because they intend to. They do seem to have purposes. Others, however, hope to discover nomological forms of explanation that will cover all these factors—probably by investigating sorts of brain activity. The question remains: Is there a teleology, at least in human affairs, that does not reduce to nomological explanation?

Again, this question does not necessarily involve questions of religious belief. But if teleological explanation were found to be necessary for parts of the universe, this might keep open the genuine question of whether the universe has a purpose or goal. In that case, it will be a compelling thought to many that there must be a God, something like a cosmic mind by which such a purpose could be formulated and implemented.

The question of whether teleology is a basic feature of the universe is unresolved. It looks as if such ultimate "scientific" questions go beyond the realms of verifiable fact to questions of the ultimate nature of reality, questions traditionally regarded as philosophical in nature. Consideration of scientific facts is relevant to such questions, but in the end the interpretation of the facts seems to depend on evaluations and on basic attitudes to a materialistic philosophy, both of which go beyond the scientific evidence.

See also ARISTOTLE; CAUSATION; CHRISTIANITY,
  HISTORY OF SCIENCE AND RELIGION; DARWIN,

CHARLES; DESIGN ARGUMENT; ESCHATOLOGY; FREEDOM; GOD; HUME, DAVID; INTELLIGENT DESIGN; ISLAM, CONTEMPORARY ISSUES IN SCIENCE AND RELIGION; JUDAISM, CONTEMPORARY ISSUES IN SCIENCE AND RELIGION; KANT, IMMANUEL; TEILHARD DE CHARDIN, PIERRE; THOMAS AQUINAS

Bibliography

Davies, Paul. *The Mind of God.* New York: Simon and Schuster, 1992.

Hume, David. *Dialogues Concerning Natural Religion* (1799). In *Dialogues Concerning Natural Religion and the Natural History of Religion,* ed. J. C. A. Gaskin. Oxford: Oxford University Press, 1998.

Kant, Immanuel. *Critique of Pure Reason* (1781), trans. Norman Kemp Smith. London: Macmillan, 1978.

Paley, William. *A View of the Evidences of Christianity* (1794).

Polkinghorne, John. *Science and Creation: The Search for Understanding.* London: SPCK, 1988.

Taylor, Richard. *Action and Purpose.* Englewood Cliffs, N.J.: Prentice-Hall, 1966.

Teilhard de Chardin, Pierre. *The Phenomenon of Man,* trans. Bernard Wall. New York: Harper, 1959.

Tennant, F. R. *Philosophical Theology.* Cambridge, UK: Cambridge University Press, 1928.

Ward, Keith. *God, Chance, and Necessity.* Oxford: Oneworld Press, 1996.

Ward, Keith. *God, Faith and the New Millennium.* Oxford: Oneworld Press, 1998.

KEITH WARD

THEISM

Theism is the belief in the existence of a supernatural force or forces, understood to have a personal nature. The term is often used synonymously with *monotheism*. Taken generically, however, theism should include a broad variety of metaphysical positions that are opposed to atheism: polytheism (the belief in many gods), monotheism (the belief in a single God), deism (the belief in a creator God who does not have any subsequent influence upon the world), and panentheism (the belief that the world is within God, although God is also more than the world). Theism contrasts with nonpersonal understandings of ultimate reality, such as the law of karma or the principle of emptiness in Buddhism. Theistic beliefs can set the stage for the science-religion dialogue because these beliefs are not contained within contemporary scientific theories and may stand in *prima facie* tension with them.

See also DEISM; GOD; MONOTHEISM; PANENTHEISM

PHILIP CLAYTON

THEODICY

A theodicy is an argument for the justice of God in the face of evil and suffering in the world. The word *theodicy* is derived from the Greek words *theos* (god) and *dike* (justice). It was first used by the philosopher Gottfried Wilhelm Leibniz (1646-1716) in the early eighteenth century. It is common to talk about the theodicy problem, or the problem of evil, as created by the tension, found mainly in monotheistic religions, between the belief that the world is created by a God who is omnipotent, omniscient, and wholly good, and the observation that there exists immense evil and suffering in the world. Critics argue that such a religious belief is either contradictory or morally unacceptable, and, consequently, can not be true.

Theodicy in world religions

The actuality of evil is a concern in many religions. In Buddhism and Hinduism it is a principal goal to be released from the suffering in the world. In these religions, however, the question of divine justice and its possible conflict with suffering has not been a main concern. For Buddhists and Hindus, individual suffering is the result of each individual's karma; suffering can not be blamed on the gods, for even the gods are submitted to karma.

The problem of evil has mainly challenged Christianity, Judaism, and Islam. In Judaism, the incomprehensibleness of God and of God's justice is stressed. The rabbinical discussion contains several approaches to the theodicy problem. According to a frequent interpretation, suffering is the consequence of human disobedience to God. Jewish teaching also stresses the educational and disciplinary value of suffering. This interpretation is often based on the Old Testament book of Job, in which a righteous man endures immense suffering. In Islamic tradition there is a strong emphasis on the omnipotence of God. This applies not only to the strong tradition of divine predestination, but also to the belief that human beings must obey and surrender to the will of God and that God is not accountable to human moral judgement.

A solution to the theodicy problem presented in classic Christian theology is the idea that evil is a kind of nonexistence or a lack of completeness. Another classic effort is the idea presented by Leibniz that evil is bad only from a limited perspective, and may be necessary for the goodness of reality as a whole. Leibniz used an aesthetic metaphor to illustrate this view: The dark parts in a painting are necessary for the beauty of the whole.

Varieties of theodicy

The nature of God's omnipotence is widely discussed within Christianity. One influential theodicy is to deny that God has the capacity to carry out anything God wants to do. According to this view, the Christian understanding of God as almighty is not identical to the philosophical idea of a capacity to predetermine everything that happens. A modern version of this interpretation can be found in process theology. However, in other Christian traditions, predestination is seen as an important capacity of God.

Another form of theodicy is the claim that suffering is an unavoidable means to a greater end. God's main goal is not to create a paradise on earth, but rather this world is a kind of school to prepare for heaven. Christian teaching often goes beyond the harmonious vision of Leibniz. Not only is suffering seen as an integral part of life, but God is also described as engaging in human misery by taking suffering upon himself through Jesus Christ. Within Christianity there are divergent interpretations of why Christ assumes this vicarious suffering and what function it has.

A frequent argument is the idea that evil is a consequence of human free will. What is commonly called the *free will defense* is the contention that evil in the world can be explained and justified by the free will of human beings. The main idea is that God has granted human beings a kind of independence. The goal of this freedom is to give humans the possibility to become like God and thereby achieve a communion with God, which would be impossible without such freedom. As a consequence, humans may not always act in accordance with the will of God, and they may cause evil and suffering in the world. The free will defense, if accepted, seems to explain only evil caused by humans, but it does not explain natural evil, not caused by humans.

All these efforts to defend the goodness of God in the face of the evil continue to be widely debated, but many give only partial explanations of evil. However, a theodicy must not only provide an intellectually satisfying explanation for evil, the explanation must be morally convincing.

Scientific perspectives on theodicy

Developments in science have interesting consequences for the traditional discussion on the theodicy problem. One important development in biology is the understanding of the role of the nervous system and the possibility of pain in living beings. Physical pain is part of a complex and life-sustaining system for organisms that helps them avoid dangerous situations in which they may be hurt. Pain helps living beings survive by warning them to avoid what causes pain. Individuals whose pain signal system does not work properly have difficulty orienting themselves in the world and avoiding dangers. Similarly, anxiety can be regarded as a by-product or as an integral part of consciousness and imagination, which is highly developed in humans. Consciousness helps people foresee and calculate the future, but it also leads to anxiety.

Another aspect of current biology is the understanding of death as a prerequisite for evolution. From the perspective of evolutionary biology, reproduction of the individual is an instrument for evolution because it facilitates recombination of genes. Thus, the death of the individual is a necessary aspect of life. An individual life is only a link in a series of generations, where the reproduction and extinction of individuals and generations are necessary for evolution.

These scientific insights have inspired new approaches to the theodicy problem because they encourage an understanding of suffering and death as integral parts of reality, hardly to be explained by human disobedience or freedom.

See also EVIL AND SUFFERING; FREE PROCESS DEFENSE; FREE WILL DEFENSE

Bibliography

Adams, Marilyn McCord, and Adams, Robert Merrihew, eds. *The Problem of Evil.* Oxford: Oxford University Press, 1990.

Bowker, John. *Problems of Suffering in Religions of the World.* Cambridge, UK: Cambridge University Press, 1970.

Hick, John. *Evil and the God of Love,* 2nd edition. New York: Harper, 1977.

Görman, Ulf. *A Good God? A Logical and Semantical Analysis of the Problem of Evil.* Stockholm, Sweden: Verbum, 1977.

Gregersen, Niels Henrik. "The Cross of Christ in an Evolutionary World." *Dialog: A Journal of Theology* 40, no. 3 (2001): 192–207.

Ormsby, Eric L. *Theodicy in Islamic Thought: The Dispute Over al-Ghazali's "Best of All Possible Worlds".* Princeton, N.J.: Princeton University Press, 1984.

Whitney, Barry L. *Theodicy. An Annotated Bibliography on the Problem of Evil 1960–1990.* New York and London: Garland, 1993.

ULF GÖRMAN

THEOLOGICAL ANTHROPOLOGY

Theological anthropology concerns humans beings and their relationship with God. It addresses humans as created in the image of God, with a special qualitative relation to God compared to other species. Sin is the corruption of the relation, indicating that humans are constitutionally opposed to God. Theological anthropology also deals with the restoration of the human relationship with God through the life, death, and resurrection of Jesus Christ. Theological anthropology can, but need not, be carried out in dialogue with other disciplines studying different aspects of humanity, and it can offer a theological framework for the interpretation of these. Scientific contributions claiming to have positive bearings on a religious understanding of humanity usually relate to the doctrinal content of theological anthropology.

See also IMAGO DEI; SIN

JAN-OLAV HENRIKSEN

THEOLOGY

Theology is the cognate of the ancient Greek word *theologia,* meaning discourse or study of the gods or divine things, as in Plato's *Republic.* The term was retained when monotheistic conceptions of God became much more abstract than references to an individual god, as in neo-Platonic conceptions of the One, the Thomistic act of *Esse* (being), and twentieth-century theologian Paul Tillich's Ground of Being. In contemporary usage, the term refers to the comparative discourse among religions, some of which, such as Buddhism and Confucianism, do not have serious conceptions of gods but rather alternatives to monotheistic notions.

See also THEOLOGY, THEORIES OF; THOMAS AQUINAS

ROBERT CUMMINGS NEVILLE

THEOLOGY, THEORIES OF

The term *theology,* in its Greek cognate roots, means discourse about or study of gods or divine things. It was not originally distinguished from philosophy about gods and divine matters, and for some contemporary thinkers, such as process theologians, theology retains that connection with philosophy. These kinds of issues raised regarding the relationship of science and religion depend in many respects on one's conception of theology as it pertains to rationality, authority, and the communities and sources of theology.

Early Christian thinkers used the term *theology* (or its cognates) to describe their expressions of the Christian faith to other Christians and to non-Christians. In this context, theology had an apologetic function, that is, explaining and justifying religious beliefs and practices to people for whom explanation and justification is needed, including Christians themselves. In late Christian antiquity, as represented, for example, by Augustine of Hippo (354–430 C.E.), theology as reflection on religious beliefs and practices embraced philosophy, history, interpretation of scripture, appeal to the scientific understanding of the day, rhetoric, and other modes of discourse as they might bear upon the divine, as found in Augustine's *The City of God.* Although the ancients were self-conscious about these modes of thought, they did not focus on theology as a special mode of thought.

By the Christian middle ages, however, theology was understood theoretically in a three-fold way. A distinction was drawn, for instance by Thomas Aquinas (c. 1225–1274), between natural theology and revealed theology. Natural theology consisted in what could be known by reason without the aid of revelation, and revealed theology was based on revelatory sources. Although there were many sources for this distinction, comprehensively explored in Etienne Gilson's classic *Reason and Revelation in the Middle Ages* (1938), a primary source was the extraordinarily fruitful dialogue between Christians and Muslims. They shared a common reason that was exercised in rational argument and in the interpretation and criticism of Aristotle. They disagreed about revelatory sources and hence about some doctrines that were particular to those sources. Aquinas himself believed that truth is one and consistent, and that natural and revealed theology must therefore be complementary. Some (e.g., Roger Bacon, c.1212–c.1292) said that revelatory claims that disagree with reason must be superstitions whereas others (e.g., William of Ockham, c.1290–1349) said that revelation trumps reason and takes the form of paradox when it does so. Although the distinction between reason and revelation was not sharp until the European medieval period, antecedents of these emphases are ancient; Origen (c.185–c.254), for instance, interpreted revelatory sources so that they conformed to reason, and Tertullian (c. 160–c.225) delighted in paradoxical irrationality of scriptural theology.

In addition to the theory that theology is either natural or revealed, the medieval period saw the development of theology in a rhetorical mode, as in Bernard of Clairvaux (1090–1153). In this mode, theology arises from the interpretation of scriptures in sermons and inspirational writings, often taking the form of allegories. Rhetorical theology to this day is often suspicious of natural and revealed theology for attempting to make theology a science or explanatory description of divine matters, preferring instead that theology move the soul to greater spiritual competence.

Whereas the term *theology,* by the medieval period, was used mainly within Christian circles, the discourse itself was shared with Muslims and Jews. Islam and Judaism developed rational modes of theology something like Thomistic natural theology, and also revelational modes of theology, sometimes in complementary and sometimes in competing forms relative to natural theology.

From the vantage point of the twenty-first century, the term *theology* has expanded its scope of subject matter. Ancients such as Plato could use the term *theology* to refer to the study of gods while at the same time believing that there are higher principles than gods, the Form of the Good in Plato's case. Under the impact of the great monotheistic religions of West Asia, however, theology came to interpret only the highest principles as divine and hence the object of theology. By the end of the twentieth century, the term *theology* had been generalized to mean discourse about ultimate matters regardless of whether ultimacy is interpreted in a theistic way, as discussed, for instance, by the Comparative Religious Ideas Project in *Ultimate Realities (2001).* Some forms of Hinduism are plainly theistic, and these contest with others that are nontheistic, all as theology. Various kinds of Buddhism, like many kinds of Hinduism, represent the existence of hundreds or thousands of gods without treating them as ultimate. Buddhist theology uses concepts such as emptiness, suffering, attachment, Buddha-mind, and enlightenment, to treat ultimate matters. Daoism also represents many non-ultimate gods but discusses the ultimate in terms of the Dao. Confucianism regards most beliefs in gods as superstitions and interprets the ultimate in terms of Heaven and Earth, or Principle and Material Force.

Theories of theological publics

Contemporary theories of the nature of theology can be understood in terms of the publics they address, the sources and justifications to which they appeal, and their mode of logical presentation.

Acknowledging that there are different types of theology, some theorists distinguish them by the publics to which they are addressed. One of the most influential recent typologies was developed by David Tracy in his *The Analogical Imagination* (1981). Admitting that the boundaries are not fixed, his typology says that systematic theology takes the Church (or a religious community, Christian in Tracy's case) for its public, fundamental theology takes the academy for its public, and practical theology takes society, usually addressed by a social movement, as its public. Systematic theology thus is thinking in, by, and for a religious community, framed in the language of its historical symbols, and aimed to give a coherent and clarifying account of the community's beliefs. Fundamental theology, as Tracy explained it, is open to philosophical considerations that might undermine a religious community's assumptions and at any rate has to employ rational discourse to engage members of the intellectual community (the academy and its neighbors) who might not be members of the religious community. Practical theology, for Tracy, aims to understand the religious implications of social conditions and perhaps to change them.

One problem with Tracy's typology is that much theology that takes place within the exclusive public of a religious community is not systematic. In *On Christian Theology* (2000), Rowan Williams provides an alternative typology of celebratory, communicative, and critical styles. Celebratory theology arises from the scriptural symbols, liturgies, and hymnody of a religious community and weaves these together so as to exercise the symbolic and affirmative thinking of the living community, a kind of theology in direct lineage from rhetorical theology of Bernard of Clairvaux's sort. Williams points out that this is unstable when the community exists within a larger environment and that communicative theology arises as church theologians interact with the languages and concerns of others. The use of Greek theology by the early Christian apologists, the engagement of Islamic theology in the medieval period, and the use of Marxism in recent Christian theology are examples of this.

Celebratory theology is primarily focused on the public of the religious community whose symbols it exercises. Communicative theology has the public of some elements of the larger environment as engaged by the religious community. Sometimes those engagements go so far as to call into question the continuities of the community's faith with its participation in larger discourses, and sometimes the very meaningfulness of the celebratory concepts and symbols. Then theology becomes critical in the sense of objectifying and questioning the very meaning and truth of original affirmations celebrated by the religious community. The result can be a conservative reaffirmation of them, as in the theology of the Yale School as represented by George Lindbeck in his *The Nature of Doctrine*

(1984), or a radical break from traditional notions, as represented by Mark C. Taylor in *Erring: A Postmodern A/Theology* (1984). Williams cites classical apophatic (that is, negative) theology as preeminently critical. The public for critical theology is anyone with a relevant critical argument.

Both Tracy's and Williams's theories of types of theology assume that theology begins from and is rooted in a religious community (Christian in both cases). Their distinctions of publics have to do with how far theology ventures from the symbolic language and doctrines of the community itself, and in both cases they would call all their types "Christian" theology. Sometimes this community-based theology is called "confessional," in reference to the traditional confessions that constitute the identity boundaries of some, though not all, religious, even Christian, communities. Tracy's fundamental and Williams's critical types of theology call the confessional identity into question, but themselves are defined by reference to the confession in so doing.

The confessional publics, including the outreach in fundamental and critical theologies, can be contrasted with scientific publics. Some theologies, for instance those of the Yale school, would treat the religious and scientific publics as defined by separate communities, each with its own cultural-linguistic system (Lindbeck's category), such that the membership of a person in both communities would be adventitious. Much of the late twentieth–century religion and science discussion, however, had to do with whether the beliefs from the different religion and science publics could be made compatible, as in the work of Nancey Murphy in *Theology in the Age of Scientific Reasoning* (1990) and John Polkinghorne in *Science and Christian Belief* (1994). Such discussion does not question extensively the results of the confessional theologies or sciences in their respective publics, or cause them to learn from one another so as to change; rather it attempts reconciliation of the publics left as they are.

Yet another kind of public for theology is simply the global array of perspectives that might have something to contribute to inquiry about divine matters (broadly understood). Although individual theologians aiming at this global public might come from a specific religious tradition, the orienting base is, at first, comparative religions. The language of theology for a global public includes extremely vague theological categories that might be specified in different and perhaps incompatible ways by different religions. Ultimacy, as discussed above, is a vague category specified differently by God, the Dao, and so forth. Debates in global theology both adjudicate these differences and aim to develop claims more adequate than any tradition's symbols by themselves. Moreover, not only religions, but also imaginative literature, the arts, and indeed the sciences have contributions to make to inquiry about theology's topics. All these disciplines have articulate bearings on ultimate matters. So the orienting base of theology with a global public is not only comparative religions but all the disciplines that might bear upon the topic. In this case, scientific publics do not stand in contrast to theological ones but are components of the discipline of theology insofar as they have relevance to ultimate matters. For theology in a global public, no particular issues of reconciling religion and science are fundamental but only questions of what can be learned from each for understanding theological matters. The language of global theology draws on many religious, imaginative, artistic, and scientific sources, as well as practical politics and ethics. Twenty-first-century theology aiming at a global public is stimulated by global problems such as in ecology and distributive justice, and aided by the rapid communication of thinkers in many fields and cultures about these global problems.

Sources for theology

Theories of theology are sometimes distinguished by what they take to be the most important sources for theology and the roles those sources play. The commonly cited sources are scriptures, such as the Vedas, the Hebrew and Christian Bibles, and the Qur'an; historical traditions as expressed in creeds, commentarial texts, and special teachings; experience, usually contextualized, as in mysticism, popular piety, and liberation movements for the poor or marginalized; and reason, as in philosophy, the arts, imaginative literature, sciences, common sense, and practical endeavors such as politics and law.

Most religious traditions have employed all these sources in their theologies, but different theories of theology have emphasized one or several over the others. A fundamental distinction between theories of theology is whether the theory takes one or several of these sources to be absolutely authoritative in the sense of trumping claims arising

from the other sources. The alternative theory is that theology respects all or some of these sources as important authorities but considers all to be liable to reinterpretation by some or all of the others. The theories claiming that some one or several sources must be absolutely authoritative include biblical fundamentalisms in Islam and Christian Protestantism, deference to infallible elements of tradition in Roman Catholicism, insistence that a theology is valid only if it supports women's experience in some forms of feminism, and rationalisms such as Charles Hartshorne's process theology. Hans W. Frei's *Types of Christian Theology (1992),* a classic of the Yale School, classifies theologies according to whether their sources are primarily biblical, philosophical, or social scientific in various combinations, while holding that the public for theology is the Christian community.

Because of the rise of modern science in connection with the Enlightenment, the Protestant Reformation, and the Roman Catholic Counter-Reformation in Europe, a special story needs to be told about the modern connection of theological sources with science. Martin Luther and other reformers attacked the authority of tradition and traditional church institutions to assert the primary and almost exclusive authority of the Christian Bible—the doctrine of *sola scriptura.* This had the force within much subsequent reformed Protestant theology of subordinating, marginalizing, or even dismissing the rich philosophical, literary, and scientific language of medieval Christian theology. Protestant theology found itself constrained to use the language of the Bible with its serious personifications of God and highly political imagery of the divine kingdom. Conceptions of God as the transcendent One in Christian neo-Platonism, or as pure Act of Esse in Thomism, found little place in Protestant theology, which developed increasing suspicion of metaphysics. The reformers' emphasis on *sola scriptura* had the opposite impact on the Roman Catholic Counter-Reformation, namely the fixing upon a scholastic form of theology as a near unalterable and absolute authority.

Both Protestant biblical theology and Roman Catholic scholastic theology were seriously ill-equipped to respond to the burgeoning findings of modern science that might have been a delight and inspiration to a continuing imaginative and creative development of the medieval synthesis of philosophy, scripture, and politics. As a result, a tradition of philosophical theology developed parallel to and often in hostile relation to both Protestant and Roman Catholic church theologies, with thinkers who themselves were often also scientists. The greats include René Descartes, Thomas Hobbes, John Locke, Gottfried Wilhelm Leibniz, Benedict de Spinoza, George Berkeley, David Hume, Immanuel Kant, Georg Hegel, Søren Kierkegaard, and Alfred North Whitehead. That list includes Roman Catholics, Protestants, Anglicans, and a Jew (Spinoza); Berkeley was an Anglican bishop. Yet their theologies all were outside the mainstream of their church communities, however influential they might have become later. All those thinkers understood theology to require a reconception of God and creation in relation to the findings of modern science. Neither the biblical representations of God nor the Roman Catholic scholastic conceptions, which had become fairly authoritative for their religious traditions, were adequate in the scientific world.

At the end of the twentieth century, discussions of theology and science were torn between two sets of assumptions. One is that religion or theology is to be represented by a defense of what some Protestants call the "classical" conception of God: a personal being with conscious subjectivity and infinite power, knowledge, and goodness who can interact with the world in ways at least analogous to the ways described in the biblical narratives. Keith Ward's *Religion and Creation* (1996) contains an elegant defense of an Anglo-Catholic version of this view. The question science raises for religion under this set of assumptions is whether the conception of God as a personal being with agency in the world can be made compatible with science. The other set of assumptions is that the conception of God needs to be rethought as science causes us to reconceive other foundational aspects of reality. Process theologians following from Alfred North Whitehead in *Process and Reality* (1929) and Charles Hartshorne in *The Divine Relativity* (1948) claim there is a need for a "neo-classical" conception to replace the "classical" conception of God. By "classical" the process theologians mean the Thomistic idea, not the biblical idea of God as a personal being that the other set of assumptions calls "classical," though Whitehead found both problematic. Many philosophical approaches other than those of process theology contend within the second set of assumptions.

Some have great potential for relating to religions other than Christianity, as in existential theologies such as Paul Tillich's in *Systematic Theology* (1951–1963), Heideggerian theologies such as John Macquarrie's in *Principles of Christian Theology* (1966), Karl Rahner's in *Foundations of Christian Faith*(1989), and pragmatic theologies such as Charles Sanders Peirce's in his 1908 essay "A Neglected Argument for the Reality of God."

All the world's theological traditions are affected by modern science in that they have to re-examine the relation of contemporary practice to ancient texts and symbols. The dialectical relation between Reform, Orthodox, Conservative, and Reconstructionist Judaism developing over the last two centuries is a case in point. The introduction of Western science into China in the nineteenth century caused both a revolution within Confucianism as it westernized and revolutions against Confucianism, most notably the Marxist. The theological traditions of South Asia were greatly dislocated by European imperialism from the seventeenth through the nineteenth centuries, and were recovered in the nineteenth and twentieth centuries in forms usually positively related to science. Some of these forms enjoy the positive relation by distancing religion as spiritual from science as material; others claim scientific standing for ancient techniques and ideas. Relating to "Eastern Mysticisms" generally, Fritjof Capra's popular *The Tao of Physics* (1975) reconciles science to mystical ultimates by modifying both beyond what the home communities recognize easily.

How theology related to science at the end of the twentieth century depended very much on the kind of authority different conceptions of theology gave to scripture and scholasticism, on the one hand, and to philosophical reason and the sciences as sources for theology on the other. For many of the philosophical traditions of theology, science has been a more important source for conceptions of God than scriptural symbols, with scriptural symbols being given interpretations based on the scientifically shaped philosophical conceptions.

Modes of theology

Few, if any, pure modes of theological argument exist, although in theory four have been defended as particularly important: expository, hypothetico-deductive, practical, and dialectical inquiry.

The expository mode takes as given, although not necessarily infallible, some core set of texts or claims, and seeks to unfold, elaborate, interpret, and bring them to relevance. Williams's celebratory and communicative theologies, Tracy's systematic theology, classical biblical theologies, and commentarial theologies in all religions have this mode.

The hypothetico-deductive mode, as illustrated for instance in Peirce's "A Neglected Argument for the Reality of God" and Whitehead's cosmological scheme in *Process and Reality,* elaborates an abstract scheme of conceptions that is then treated as an hypothesis to explain the world and God or ultimate matters. This mode is explicitly derived from a conception of how science works, and emphasizes that the conceptions are hypotheses whose plausibility consists in their capacity to interpret reality as well as in their consistency and coherence. Theology in this mode is heavily empirical. Wolfhart Pannenberg's proleptic theology, which says that his particular conception of Christian theology will be proved right in the End Time, and John Hick's conception of eschatological verification, are empirical in a different sense.

The practical mode of theology combines both expository and perhaps hypothetico-deductive philosophy as well as other forms of analysis to interpret the religious situation and to develop strategies for religious response. The situation might call for reform of social circumstances as in liberation theologies, the production of art and culture, the care of a religious congregation or community, or service to people in times of disaster. Science relates to practical theology both as offering important means of analysis of the situation to be addressed and in some instances as providing instruments of action.

Theology in the mode of dialectical inquiry focuses on the topics of theology—God or ultimacy and the bearing of this on human life—and looks to all possible sources and to all the modes of argumentation for learning from these sources. The word *dialectic* has been used to mean some kind of unfolding of reason from within, as in the theories of Hegel or Thomas J. J. Altizer, but that is not the meaning here. Dialectical inquiry means combining as many different modes of thinking as exist in religions, the arts, sciences, and practical domains of experience so as to learn what they might teach about ultimacy. The combinations and the

limitations of the various modes of thinking can only be adjudicated in particular arguments. Dialectical inquiry is simply making the best case in the sense articulated by the contemporary historical theologian Van Harvey in *The Historian and the Believer* (1966), and is the mode most appropriate for theology in a global public.

See also THOMAS AQUINAS; NATURAL THEOLOGY; PROCESS THOUGHT; REVELATION

Bibliography

Capra, Fritjof. *The Tao of Physics: An Exploration of the Parallels Between Modern Physics and Eastern Mysticism.* Berkeley, Calif.: Shambhala, 1975.

Frei, Hans W. *Types of Christian Theology,* eds. George Hunsinger and William C. Placher. New Haven, Conn.: Yale University Press, 1992.

Gilson, Etienne. *Reason and Revelation in the Middle Ages.* New York: Scribners, 1938.

Hartshorne, Charles. *The Divine Relativity: A Social Conception of God.* New Haven, Conn.: Yale University Press, 1948.

Harvey, Van A. *The Historian and the Believer: The Morality of Historical Knowledge and Christian Belief.* New York: Macmillan, 1966.

Hick, John. *Faith and Knowledge: A Modern Introduction to the Problem of Religious Knowledge.* Ithaca, N.Y.: Cornell University Press, 1957.

Lindbeck, George A. *The Nature of Doctrine: Religion and Theology in a Post-liberal Age.* Philadelphia, Pa.: Westminster Press, 1984.

Macquarrie, John. *Principles of Christian Theology.* New York: Macmillan, 1966.

Murphy, Nancey. *Theology in the Age of Scientific Reasoning.* Ithaca, N.Y.: Cornell University Press, 1990.

Neville, Robert Cummings, ed. *Ultimate Realities.* A volume in the *Comparative Religious Ideas Project.* Albany: State University of New York Press, 2001.

Pannenberg, Wolfhart. *Systematic Theology,* trans. Geoffrey W. Bromily. Grand Rapids. Mich.: Eerdmans, 1988–1993.

Peirce, Charles Sanders. "A Neglected Argument for the Reality of God." *The Hibbert Journal* 7 (1908): 90–112. Also in *The Collected Papers of Charles Sanders Peirce,* Vol. 6, eds. Charles Hartshorne and Paul Weiss. Cambridge, Mass.: Harvard University Press, 1935.

Polkinghorne, John. *Science and Christian Belief: Theological Reflections of a Bottom-Up Thinker.* London: SPCK, 1994.

Rahner, Karl. *Foundations of Christian Faith: An Introduction to the Idea of Christianity.* New York: Crossroad, 1989.

Taylor, Mark C. *Erring: A Postmodern A/Theology.* Chicago: University of Chicago Press, 1984.

Tillich, Paul. *Systematic Theology.* Chicago: University of Chicago Press, 1951–1963.

Tracy, David. *The Analogical Imagination: Christian Theology and the Culture of Modernity.* New York: Crossroad, 1981.

Ward, Keith. *Religion and Creation.* Oxford: Clarendon Press, 1996.

Whitehead, Alfred North. *Process and Reality: An Essay in Cosmology* (1929), eds. Donald W. Sherburne and David Ray Griffin. New York: Free Press, 1978.

Williams, Rowan. *On Christian Theology.* Oxford: Blackwell, 2000.

ROBERT CUMMINGS NEVILLE

THERMODYNAMICS, SECOND LAW OF

The Second Law of Thermodynamics expresses a fundamental and limiting characteristic of all physical systems: In any closed system, the measure of disorder, or entropy, of that system must either remain the same or increase. Equivalently, in any isolated system, the amount of energy available for work—the free energy—must either remain the same or decrease. Processes in which the entropy remains the same are reversible; those in which the entropy increases are irreversible, that is, there is no realistic possibility of recovering the initial state of the system. It is principally because of the Second Law of Thermodynamics that all physical and biological systems are destined for eventual dissolution or death, even the universe itself. Without the continual input of work, energy, or material (food), every system (not necessarily closed) moves towards equilibrium, which is characterized by maximum entropy. Organization, order, and life require that the system in question be maintained far from equilibrium, and this requires input of energy from outside—from its environment.

Formulations

Long before the Second Law was expressed in terms of the change in entropy of a closed system, Sadi Carnot (1796–1832) formulated it in terms of heat and work: It is impossible to convert heat back into work at a given temperature. Although work can be converted into heat at a given temperature, the reverse cannot be effected without other changes. Heat will never travel up a temperature gradient on its own. It is only with further work that heat can be transferred from a body or a system at a given temperature to one that is either at the same temperature or at a higher temperature. Of course, heat can indeed flow from a hotter system to colder system without any work being necessary. Thus, another formulation of the Second Law is that heat cannot flow from a given system to a hotter one without work being done. A refrigerator must use energy in order to function. Other expressions of the Second Law are: A perfect heat engine is impossible to construct (Lord Kelvin's formulation), and similarly, it is impossible to construct a perfect refrigerator (Rudolf Clausius's formulation).

The clearest and most applicable formulation of the Second Law of Thermodynamics, however, is: During any process the entropy of any isolated system must either remain the same or increase. But what is entropy? It is sometimes defined as the measure of the unavailability of the energy of a system for work. An isolated system in perfect equilibrium has maximum entropy and thus has no energy available for work. It is now more usual, however, to define entropy by employing the statistical mechanical underpinnings of thermodynamics in terms of the number of microstates available to the system at a given energy. Any given macroscopic state of a system (given, for instance, by its temperature, pressure, and volume) corresponds to many different possible microscopic states of that system (arrangements and velocities of the molecules constituting it). The larger the number of possible microstates corresponding to a given macrostate, the larger the entropy of the system, and the larger the disorder of the system. The maximum entropy—and therefore the maximum disorder—is given by the situation in which the actual macrostate of the system possesses the maximum number of accessible microstates for the energy it contains. This is the state of equilibrium. Thus, what is really significant is not the absolute value of the entropy for an isolated system, but rather how far its entropy is from the maximum—how far away the system is from equilibrium. As already mentioned, this also indicates how much free energy (for work) is available in it.

The determination of the entropy and the maximum entropy, and therefore the application of the Second Law of Thermodynamics to gravitating systems, such as a cluster of stars, the galaxy, or the universe, is somewhat more complex than it is for non-gravitating systems. This is because the total entropy of such systems must include gravitational entropy as well as thermodynamic entropy, and the lowest gravitational entropy state of a system is realized when it is perfectly homogeneous—no clustering or clumping. A homogeneous self-gravitating system is obviously far from equilibrium. As the matter gradually coalesces and clumps, the gravitational entropy increases, releasing free energy through heat and radiation, which is now capable of being harnessed for work. Eventually the cores of some of these mass concentrations become hot enough for the initiation of nucleosynthesis, and even more free energy is released. Maximum gravitational entropy is achieved when the whole system becomes a single black hole. For that to happen all the free energy of the system has to be exhausted.

What was the origin of the initial extreme gravitational disequilibrium? Possibly it was an inflationary phase of the universe almost immediately after the Big Bang, during which the universe expanded incredibly fast (exponentially) in a very short time; perhaps it was certain quantum-gravity effects even earlier during the Planck era that rendered the initial state of our part of the universe very smooth. How will the universe as we know it end? In entropic death or heat death. This will occur when either the universe evolves to become something like a single black hole, or when it expands so much and so rapidly that gravity is no longer effective in drawing together whatever relic mass concentrations remain (particles or black holes). In either case, a state of equilibrium has been reached; the entropy of the universe is a maximum, and no useful energy for work or for nourishment can be found.

Sometimes people mention that life-generating or life-maintaining systems do not obey the Second Law of Thermodynamics, because in generating order they are lowering the entropy. But, in fact, they are perfect examples of the application of the Second Law. The system one must consider in this case is not just the living organism itself, nor just the community of living organisms in question, which are *not* isolated systems (they are in crucial and continual interaction with their environment), but rather the entire ecological system itself as isolated from what occurs outside it. Yes, the entropy of each organism and community of living organisms is kept relatively low, but only at the expense of increasing the entropy of their surroundings. The entropy of the whole isolated ecological system is increasing. If one isolates organisms in a box with a certain limited amount of food and available energy and no interactions with the world outside the box, the organisms will live and reproduce for a certain length of time. But eventually the available energy will be depleted and the food supply (both the food they started with and the food they subsequently produced) will run out, and everything in the box will reach the equilibrium that is death.

Implications for religion

The inescapable limits placed on physical and biological reality by the Second Law of Thermodynamics confront theology and religion with a serious challenge. If all is finite, transient, and destined for death and dissolution, what meaning and hope can theology and religion legitimately assert? How is the eternal destiny proclaimed by religions to be understood, and how is this seemingly insuperable limit to be transcended? These are eschatological questions. There are also questions relating to natural evil. Assuming that God works through all the laws of nature, including the Second Law, to create and maintain the world, how can one conceive God as the creator of a world in which death, disease, suffering, and the exploitation of resources is not only pervasive but essential? Finally, according to religious perspectives, the Second Law of Thermodynamics cannot have the last word. The "new heavens and the new earth," though in continuity with this world, are promised to be devoid of the transience, suffering, death, and natural evil that accompany human existence.

See also BIG BANG THEORY; DEATH; ENTROPY; ESCHATOLOGY

Bibliography

Feynman, Richard P.; Leighton, Robert B.; and Sands, Matthew. *The Feynman Lectures on Physics,* Vol. 1. Reading, Mass.: Addison Wesley, 1963.

Frautschi, Steven. "Entropy in an Expanding Universe." In *Entropy, Information and Evolution: New Perspectives on Physical and Biological Evolution,* eds. Bruce H. Weber, David J. Depew, and James D. Smith. Cambridge, Mass.: MIT Press, 1990.

Layzer, David. "Growth of Order in the Universe." In *Entropy, Information, and Evolution: New Perspectives on Physical and Biological Evolution,* eds. Bruce H. Weber, David J. Depew, and James D. Smith. Cambridge, Mass.: MIT Press, 1990.

Puddefoot, John C. "Information Theory, Biology and Christology." In *Religion and Science: History, Method, Dialogue,* eds. W. Mark Richardson and Wesley J. Wildman. New York and London: Routledge, 1996.

Reif, F. *Fundamentals of Statistical and Thermal Physics.* New York: McGraw-Hill, 1965.

Russell, Robert John. "Entropy and Evil." *Zygon: Journal of Science and Religion* 19 (1984): 449–468.

WILLIAM R. STOEGER

THINKING MACHINES

The term *thinking machine* (or intelligent machine) refers to a computer or a robot that has human intelligence. No such machine exists as of 2002, and whether it can be built in principle and how many years of research this would take is a matter of much dispute. The feasibility of thinking machines has been promoted by representatives of strong artificial intelligence (AI), such as John McCarthy, Marvin Minsky, and Doug Lenat. A principle formal argument against conscious and thus intelligent machines has been posed by mathematician and physicist Roger Penrose. To testify that a computer agent is a thinking machine it would have to pass the Turing Test.

See also ARTIFICIAL INTELLIGENCE; ROBOTICS; TURING TEST

THIEMO KRINK

THOMAS AQUINAS

Thomas Aquinas held that revelation was essential for grasping truth of faith but he relied on reason to understand the world that God created. Mindful of this division, Thomas warned against dogmatic interpretations in areas of faith that might have to be abandoned if subsequent natural evidence falsified them. Convinced that Aristotle's (384–322 B.C.E.) natural philosophy provided the most accurate interpretation of cosmic operations, Thomas refused to Christianize natural philosophy and, to the greatest extent possible, he applied reason to both science and theology.

Life and works

Thomas Aquinas was born near Monte Cassino, Italy, around 1225. He was the youngest of nine children. After elementary education in the abbey of Monte Cassino, Thomas was sent to Naples in 1239, where he studied at the University of Naples. In 1244, while still at Naples, Thomas entered the Dominican order, contrary to the wishes of his family. From 1245 to 1252, Thomas studied at Paris and then Cologne. At Cologne, and perhaps at Paris, Thomas's teacher was Albert the Great (Albertus Magnus) (c. 1206–1280), one of the great scientists and natural philosophers of the Middle Ages and a thorough student of Aristotle's writings. After training as a theologian, Thomas became a professor of theology at the University of Paris (1256–1259). He spent the years between 1259 and 1268 in Italy serving different popes at their papal courts. During 1269 to 1272, Thomas returned to another professorship at the University of Paris, after which he returned to Naples, where his health began to fail. Thomas died in 1274 while on his way to the second Council of Lyons.

Thomas was a prolific author who left approximately fifty works that have been thus far identified. He wrote on numerous topics, the most significant of which are his theological treatises, especially his famous *Summa of Theology* (Summa theologiae), commentaries on books of the Bible, and commentaries on various works of Aristotle, especially those on natural philosophy, which include Aristotle's *Physics, On the Heavens, On Generation and Corruption, Meteorology,* and *On the Soul.* In addition, Thomas composed sermons, letters, and replies to queries.

Thomas on the relationship of faith and reason

Issues of science and religion in the Middle Ages involve the relationship between natural philosophy and religion. By the time Thomas began writing, Aristotle's works on logic and natural philosophy had been adopted as the basic curriculum in faculties of arts of medieval universities. Because Aristotle's natural philosophy raised issues that were directly relevant to theology and the Catholic faith, it was inevitable that Thomas, who was both a theologian and a natural philosopher, would have to confront those issues in his works on theology and natural philosophy.

When Thomas dealt with issues of science and religion, he was guided by his overall view of the relationship between faith and reason. Thomas emphasized the importance and power of reason, but insisted that it was inadequate to gain knowledge of unseen things, such as God, for which faith and divine revelation are essential. For knowledge of the physical cosmos and its regular operations, however, reason—embodied in the works of Aristotle—was Thomas's instrument for understanding those operations. But reason was also an instrument for the study of theology. In the very first question of his *Summa of Theology,* Thomas asked whether theology is a science and replied affirmatively. He is usually regarded as the scholar who gave credence to the claim that theology is a science, a claim that was widely assumed in the late Middle Ages.

Two principles derived from the early Christian leader Augustine of Hippo (354–430 C.E.) and expressed in the *Summa of Theology,* guided Thomas in his explanations of natural phenomena. He insisted: (1) that the truths of Scripture must be held inviolate, but that (2) no passage in Scripture should be interpreted rigidly and dogmatically because it might later be proved false by convincing arguments, thus leading to a loss of credibility that would inhibit nonbelievers from adopting the faith.

Thomas and Aristotle

Although Aristotle's natural philosophy formed the basic curriculum in the arts faculties of medieval universities, those aspects of his work that conflicted with basic Christian beliefs evoked opposition through most of the thirteenth century. In the 1260s, and 1270s, when Thomas was writing, the opposition was led by the Franciscan theologian Bonaventure (1221–1271), whose neoconservative Augustinian colleagues eventually prevailed upon the bishop of Paris to condemn certain of Aristotle's articles deemed offensive to the faith; thirteen articles were condemned in 1270 and 219 articles were condemned in 1277, three years after the death of Thomas. Since Thomas was a supporter of Aristotle's philosophy, as were many Dominicans, some of the hostility was plainly directed against him and his colleagues. It was not until 1325, two years after the canonization of Thomas Aquinas, that the bishop of Paris, Stephen Bourret, revoked the condemnation of all articles condemned in 1277 that were directed against the teachings of Thomas.

The most significant idea condemned in 1277 was Aristotle's claim for the eternity of the world, which was denounced at least twenty-seven times in a variety of contexts. In a treatise he titled *On the Eternity of the World,* Thomas neither rejected nor accepted the eternity of the world. By absolute power, God could have created a world that was coeternal with God. For as Thomas argued, "The statement that something was made by God and nevertheless was never without existence . . . does not involve any logical contradiction." If God wishes, God can choose not to precede any effect God decides to produce, and thus God can make the world eternal. Although God could make the world coeternal with God, an eternal world would still be a created effect, because it is wholly dependent on an immutable God, thus guaranteeing that the world cannot be coequal with God. Of the articles condemned in 1277, Article 99 was probably directed against Thomas's interpretation of the eternity of the world. Thomas's approach to the question of the world's duration proved popular and found supporters up through the Renaissance. Bonaventure and others were convinced that Aristotle had denied the personal immortality of the soul, but Thomas thought Aristotle had believed it.

Since Aristotle firmly believed that every material thing is derived from previous matter, he would have been opposed to the Christian doctrine of creation from nothing. Article 185 condemned the view that something could not be made from nothing. Indeed, the Fourth Lateran Council of 1215 had declared belief in creation from nothing to be an article of faith. On this issue,

Thomas, and all Christians, were compelled to reject Aristotle's interpretation.

Thomas's conception of the physical world and its operations was basically the same as that held by Aristotle, from whom he derived it. In his commentaries on Aristotle's natural philosophy, Thomas considered the numerous problems Aristotle presented, accepting most of Aristotle's solutions, but disagreeing on some important issues. Although Thomas believed with Aristotle that the existence of void spaces was impossible, he disagreed with the absurd consequence Aristotle deduced from the assumption of motion in a vacuum, namely that because of an absence of material resistance, a body would move instantaneously in a vacuum and, as a consequence, no ratio could obtain between motions in a hypothetical void and motions in a space filled with matter. Thomas rejected these conclusions. A body falling or moving in a void space would have a definite speed and take a definite time to move successively between two distant points. This is so, argued Thomas, because any distance in a three-dimensional void has prior and posterior parts that a body must traverse to get from one point to another, which requires time. Hence there could indeed be a ratio between motions in a vacuum and motions in a plenum.

In a letter to a soldier, Thomas explained how bodies could perform actions that do not follow from the nature of their constituent elements, as, for example, the attraction of a magnet for iron. Thomas regarded such actions as occult, explaining the causes of such phenomena by the behavior of two kinds of superior agents: (1) celestial bodies, or (2) separate spiritual substances, which included celestial intelligences, angels, and even demons. A superior agent can either communicate the power to perform the action directly to an inferior body, as is the case with the magnet; or the superior agent can, by its own motion, cause the body in question to move, as, for example, the moon causes the ebb and flow of the tides.

Whatever disagreements Thomas had with Aristotle, whether doctrinal or otherwise, it is obvious that Thomas was an Aristotelian in natural philosophy. As an Aristotelian natural philosopher and a professional theologian, one may appropriately inquire how Thomas related natural philosophy and theology, the medieval equivalent of the relations between science and religion. Thomas followed in the path of his teacher, Albert the Great, and generally refrained from introducing theological ideas into his treatises on natural philosophy, whereas he did not hesitate to introduce natural philosophy to elucidate his theological discussions. As a theologian doing natural philosophy, Thomas could easily have resorted to theological appeals and arguments in his natural philosophy, but he did not think it appropriate to do so. As he explained in a reply to one of forty-three questions sent to him by the master general of the Dominican order, "I don't see what one's interpretation of the text of Aristotle has to do with the teaching of the faith." Thomas refused to Christianize Aristotle's natural philosophy and to confuse natural philosophy with theology. In this, Thomas followed the practice of most medieval theologians and natural philosophers.

See also ARISTOTLE; AUGUSTINE; CHRISTIANITY, ROMAN CATHOLIC, ISSUES IN SCIENCE AND RELIGION; CREATIO EX NIHILO; CREATION; GOD

Bibliography

Copleston, Frederick C. *Aquinas*. Harmondsworth, UK: Penguin Books, 1955.

Thomas Aquinas. *Summa Theologiae*, Vol. 10: *Cosmogony*, trans. and ed. William A. Wallace. London: Blackfriars, 1967.

Dijksterhuis, E. J. *The Mechanization of the World Picture*, trans. C. Dikshoorn. Oxford: Clarendon Press, 1961.

Gilson, Etienne. *History of Christian Philosophy in the Middle Ages*. London: Sheed and Ward, 1955.

Pegis, Anton C., ed. *Introduction to Saint Thomas Aquinas*. New York: Modern Library, 1948.

Wallace, William A. "Aquinas on Creation: Science, Theology, and Matters of Fact." *Thomist* 38 (1974): 485-523.

Wallace, William A. "Aquinas, Saint Thomas." In *Dictionary of Scientific Biography*, Vol. 1, ed. Charles C. Gillispie. New York: Scribner, 1970.

Weisheipl, James A. *Friar Thomas d'Aquino: His Life, Thought, and Work*. Garden City, N.Y.: Doubleday, 1974.

Weisheipl, James A. "Motion in a Void: Aquinas and Averroes." In *St. Thomas Aquinas 1274-1974, Commemorative Studies*, ed. A. A. Mauer. Toronto: Pontifical Institute of Medieval Studies, 1974.

EDWARD GRANT

TIME

See SPACE AND TIME

TIME: PHYSICAL AND BIOLOGICAL ASPECTS

Insofar as science aims at reconstructing the laws of nature, which describe the temporal development of nature's physical constituents and allow for predicting future events out of data derived from past events, time is a fundamental and crucial notion of empirical sciences. Science, however, does not deal with time itself, but with changes and events in time. Consequently, what really matters in science "is not how we define time, but how we measure it" (Feynman, p. 5-1). As such, time constitutes the realm, rather than the object, of scientific investigation. The nature and character of time must be derived from interpretation of the basic structure of science and its method. And because time does not refer to external objects of investigation, but to the presupposed internal order of physical phenomena, it is closely related to human experience and the human perception of time, which is the sequential, nonspatial order of events, structured by the relation of cause and effect. Unlike space, time as sequential order shows a fundamental asymmetry between the past (fixed in documents, which can be investigated) and the future (still to come and not totally fixed—it can only be predicted). People can remember the past but not the future; people can alter the future, but not the past. The astronomer Arthur S. Eddington (1882–1944) was the first to speak of the "arrow of time," which points from the past to the future, to symbolize this fundamental asymmetry.

The physics of time

The crucial question of the interpretation of time in physics and biology is whether this asymmetry is due to physical laws, or whether it is a subjective illusion due to the human experience of time. The laws of both classical and relativistic physics, as well as the basic equations of quantum physics, are time reversal invariant and provide no scientific ground for an arrow of time. On the other hand,

an irreversible directedness of time does turn up in empirical sciences related to different phenomena:

(1) According to the Second Law of Thermodynamics, disorder (entropy) increases in a closed system from past to future.

(2) The measurement of quantum events constitutes an irreversible difference between past and future.

(3) Biological systems and their evolution constitute a historical development from past to future.

(4) The universe is expanding in time.

Because time and irreversibility seem to have different meanings in different physical theories, and because the notions of causality involved are a matter of dispute as well, a comprehensive and commonly accepted interpretation of time in natural sciences is neither at hand nor in sight. This entry will refer to some aspects of an ongoing discussion.

Newtonian time of classical physics. In his *Mathematical Principles of Natural Philosophy*, Isaac Newton (1642–1727) distinguishes between *absolute* and *relative* time: "Absolute, true, and mathematical time . . . flows equably without relation to anything external, and by another name is called duration: relative, apparent, and common time, is some sensible and external (whether accurate or unequable) measure of duration by the means of motion, which is commonly used instead of true time; such as an hour, a day, a month, a year" (p. 6). The notion of absolute time is crucial for Newtonian physics because its First Law of Motion implies that a body on which no forces act moves uniformly in a straight line at constant speed, or it is at rest. Only against the background of absolute time and space can rest and equable translation as free from external influence stand out against those deformations of motion that indicate external forces. Thus, absolute time in Newtonian physics is an a priori presupposition, and it is essential for the frame of reference, against which all forces are determined. Newton himself considered that in reality there might exist no absolutely equable form of motion representing this absolute time: It might not be the time of a particular clock. But still, the assumed flowing of absolute time should not be liable to any change.

However, the laws of classical mechanics, which describe the motions of massive bodies, do not distinguish a direction of absolute time: No feature of the mechanical world would change, if time were reversed. Because the basic differential equations of classical mechanics are time reversal invariant, the future development of any mechanical system is in principle derivable from its past state, and vice versa. Thus, development from past to future and from future to past are physically equivalent.

The arrow of time in thermodynamics. But what people experience in reality are often processes, which appear to be irreversibly "directed," such as the cooling of hot water or the erosion of a rock. Especially inanimate natural systems show a tendency to spontaneously evolve to equilibrium of order, energy, or temperature, where these macroscopic parameters remain approximately stable, and they never leave this state, provided no external intervention takes place. The physics to describe such processes is called *thermodynamics*. Elaborated in the mid-nineteenth century, classical thermodynamics is based on two laws, the second of which expresses the temporally asymmetric behavior of all isolated (adiabatic) systems, with the universe as the biggest of them, to approach equilibrium in due course of time. The universe thus faces *heat death,* the equilibrium state in which no energy differences remain and all physical processes come to an end, as its final fate. In order to express this fundamental law, Rudolf Clausius (1822–1888) coined the term *entropy* (from Greek *entrope,* turning toward) as a measure of dispersed and irretrievable energy that becomes unavailable for producing work. Clausius further stated that the entropy of the universe strives toward a maximum. Because entropy is at a maximum when the molecules of a system are at the same energy level, entropy can be understood as a measure of disorder. Thus, the Second Law of Thermodynamics implies the increase of disorder in due course of time, ruling out all reverse processes that could create order spontaneously within a closed system.

When James Maxwell (1831–1879) and others developed the kinetic theory of heat and gases, Ludwig Boltzmann (1844–1906) tried to reduce thermodynamics to mechanical laws and interpret the Second Law as only statistical: Systems generally develop toward states of higher entropy because such states are more probable than others.

But the discussion about the statistical interpretation of thermodynamics revealed that the time reversal invariance of the mechanical laws cannot model the irreversible phenomena of macroscopic systems striving toward equilibrium. In the light of classical mechanism, the irreversible direction of time from past to future, the arrow of time as indicated by the Second Law of Thermodynamics, seems to rest on no physical ground.

Time in Special and General Theory of Relativity. The direction of time from past to future seemed to become even more illusionary when Albert Einstein's (1879–1955) Theory of Relativity succeeded in overcoming the Newtonian notion of absolute time. In his 1905 Special Theory of Relativity, Einstein stated that the time interval (and the distance) between two events depends on the observer's velocity relative to the events, while the velocity cannot exceed the speed of light.

In Einstein's theory, space and time together constitute the four-dimensional space-time, while each reference frame of an observer divides space-time differently into a temporal and a spatial component relative to its state of velocity. There is no simultaneity of events and absolute duration of time for every observer, as well as no absolute spatial distance. Still, there is an objective causal connection between events, because one event cannot interact with another instantaneously, but only mediated by forces, whose propagation speed is final and equals or is less than the speed of light. Thus temporal as well as spatial intervals between causally related events cannot become zero, and their causal relation cannot be reversed. Relativistic time still represents the order of causal chains.

Shortly after Einstein's discovery, the Russian mathematician and physicist Hermann Minkowski (1864–1909) united space and time into one four-dimensional continuum, the space-time of the so-called Minkowksi-world: "Henceforth space by itself, and time by itself, are doomed to fade away into mere shadows, and only a kind of union of the two will preserve an independent reality" (*Space and Time,* p. 75). This view of the physical world, in which no independent time exists, suggests that the world is to be envisioned as a four-dimensional *being,* rather than a *becoming* within three-dimensional space. Then, as Einstein himself stated, for a physicist "the distinction between past, present and future is only an illusion, however persistent" (quoted in Davies, 1983, p.128).

Time in quantum theory. In the Schrödinger-equation, which is the basic formula of quantum mechanics, time is not an observable, but just a parameter. Although it is time reversal invariant, in its common interpretation, the equation refers to probabilities and only allows for the determination of probabilities for certain states. When a state is measured, the Schrödinger wave-function of an object, which is derived from the Schrödinger-equation, "collapses," and a certain value for an observable is provided. Some physicists interpret this as a new notion of irreversible physical time: "The concept of becoming acquires a meaning in physics: The present, which separates the future from the past, is the moment when that which was undetermined becomes determined, and 'becoming' means the same as 'becoming determined'" (Reichenbach, p. 269).

Thus, quantum theory seems to include two concepts of time: time in the form of a classical, reversible parameter of continuous time, in which the realm of probabilities unfolds; and time in the form of the discontinuous interaction between objects, which reduces knowledge of possible states into factual, documented knowledge. Because of fundamental theoretical reasons and because of the very precise empirical data available, a dynamical description of the transition from the probability description to the factual description cannot be modeled within the theory. Thus quantum-measurement seems to establish a fundamental distinction between past and future within physics, with past and future being closely related, but without the possibility of completely deriving the factual future out of the factual past, and vice versa.

Time and biological systems

According to the Second Law of Thermodynamics, flows of energy arise far from equilibrium in order to compensate energy differences and to increase entropy. The Earth, for example, receives a constant flow of energy from the sun and dissipates energy into its cold surroundings. This energy flow establishes a direction of time, which can be identified as the source of the temporality of complex systems, biological systems in particular. Such systems are able to exploit energy flows to locally inverse the increase of entropy and to maintain themselves in a steady state far from equilibrium by functional closure against their environment. They may even develop toward states of increased

order and organization, as the contingent and irreversible evolution of life on the planet shows. Biological systems can differentiate, interact, and organize themselves; they can form populations, families, and ecosystems; and, in the case of human beings, they can begin to establish history as the temporal unfolding of rational, self-conscious, and moral social agency.

The cosmological foundation of time

All manifestations of irreversible time can be seen as a consequence of the fact that the universe started off with the Big Bang in a smooth and organized state of low entropy. The interplay of its expansion with the contracting force of gravitation, which agglomerates matter into bodies of high density that start to radiate and disperse their energy into the expanding void, is responsible for the cosmos still being far away from equilibrium. It remains a matter of dispute whether cosmic time will end in a final collapse of the universe, when gravitation will have superseded expansion and reversed it into contraction, or whether expansion will go on forever, until all order and structure of the universe has been dissolved into an ever dispersing radiation field with decaying minimal fluctuations. But the expansion of the universe establishes a cosmic time, which is the origin of the large-scale arrow of time, in whose due course, in a favored niche far away from equilibrium, biological systems could evolve and develop into conscious beings, who start wondering what time is all about.

See also ENTROPY; PHYSICS, QUANTUM; RELATIVITY, GENERAL THEORY OF; RELATIVITY, SPECIAL THEORY OF; SPACE AND TIME; THERMODYNAMICS, SECOND LAW OF; TIME: RELIGIOUS AND PHILOSOPHICAL ASPECTS

Bibliography

Albert, David Z. *Time and Chance.* Cambridge, Mass.: Harvard University Press, 2000.

Callender, Craig, and Edney, Ralph. *Introducing Time.* Cambridge, UK: Icon, 2001.

Davies, Paul C. *God and the New Physics.* New York: Simon & Schuster, 1983.

Davies, Paul C. *About Time: Einstein's Unfinished Revolution.* London: Viking, 1995.

Denbigh, Kenneth G. *Three Concepts of Time.* Berlin and New York: Springer-Verlag, 1981.

Eddington, Arthur S. *The Nature of the Physical World.* Cambridge, UK: Cambridge University Press, 1928.

Feynman, Richard. *The Feynman Lectures on Physics,* Vol. 1. Reading, Mass.: Addison-Wesley, 1963.

Friedman, Michael. *Foundations of Space-Time Theories: Relativistic Physics and Philosophy of Science.* Princeton, N.J.: Princeton University Press, 1983.

Hawking, Stephen, and Penrose, Roger. *The Nature of Space and Time.* Princeton, N.J.: Princeton University Press, 1996.

Macey, Samuel L. *Time: A Bibliographic Guide.* New York: Garland, 1991.

Minkowski, Hermann. *Space and Time* (1908). In *The Principle of Relativity,* ed. Albert Einstein, et al. New York: Dover, 1952.

Newton, Isaac. *The Mathematical Principles of Natural Philosophy* (1729), trans. Andrew Motte. Facsimile Reprint. London: Dawson, 1968.

Reichenbach, Hans. *The Direction of Time.* Berkeley and Los Angeles: University of California Press, 1956.

Turetzky, Philip. *Time.* London: Routledge, 1998.

DIRK EVERS

TIME: RELIGIOUS AND PHILOSOPHICAL ASPECTS

According to Augustine of Hippo (354–430) time cannot be satisfactorily described using one single definition. In his words: "What, then, is time? If no one asks me, I know: if I wish to explain it to one that asketh, I know not" (*Confessions* 11, c. 14). The attempt to establish a conclusive definition of time ultimately leads to confusion. Time is not definable by any other concepts. Time, in its fullness, is unique and *sui generis*. This view is now generally accepted among philosophers of time. No attempt to clarify the concept of time is claimed to be more than an accentuation of some aspects of time at the expense of others. The statement of Plato (428–347 B.C.E.) that time is the "moving image of eternity" and Aristotle's (384–322 B.C.E.) suggestion that "time is the number of motion with respect to earlier and later" are no exceptions.

Time and eternity

Many philosophical and religious schools have assumed that no beginning or end can be attributed to time. For instance, in Indian thought the universe is largely conceived as undergoing repeated creation and dissolution. According to this cosmological model, each world-cycle has to be measured in terms of billions of humans years (Balslev, p. 140 ff.). Ancient Greek thought includes the even stronger idea of cyclic time according to which not only the cosmological processes but all individual destinies are repeated in every detail in time (Whitrow, p. 14 ff.). Jewish, Christian, and Muslim philosophers have had to reject this idea of cyclic time because it leaves no room for genuine progress or final salvation. Augustine, in particular, was very clear about this: "Heaven forbid, I repeat, that we should believe that. For Christ died once for our sins, but rising from the dead he dies no more, and death shall no longer have domain over him" (*De Civitate Dei* 12; vol. 4, p. 63)

Some Muslim thinkers such as al-Farabi (873–950) and Avicenna (980–1037) held that the act of creation should be conceived as atemporal and purely logical. In Judaism and Christianity, however, most philosophers have rejected this view maintaining that God's creation of the world was in fact its temporal beginning. In Judaic thought some have argued that time existed and the Torah was created before the creation of the world. This view of time would allow the notion of the universe being created *in time.* However, according to the most common view in traditional medieval philosophy, time is considered to be relational; that is, there can only be time in relation to a world of events. With this view of time, *creatio ex nihilo* means that the universe does not owe its existence to anything in the physical world, and it can only be explained by reference to something that is not a part of this temporal world. The idea of the absolute beginning of the universe does not imply any change from one state to another.

Medieval writers typically held that time itself began with creation. Thomas Aquinas (c. 1225–1274) stated this view in the following way: "The phrase about things being created in the beginning of time, means that the heavens and earth were created together with time" (*Summa Theologica* 1a, 46, 3). A similar view had been expressed earlier by the great Jewish scholar Moses Maimonides (1135–1204), according to whom the biblical statement of God's existence before the creation of the world has to be interpreted in terms of a "supposition or imagination of time" (Sorabji, p. 237). In the same vein, Aquinas stated:

> God is before the world by duration. The term 'duration' here means the priority of eternity, not of time. Or you might say that it betokens an imaginary time, not time as really existing, rather as when we speak of nothing being beyond the heavens, the term 'beyond' betokens merely an imaginary place in a picture we can form of other dimensions stretching beyond those of the body of heavens. (*Summa Theologica* 1a, 46, 1)

This means that God's eternity should not be understood as some sort of everlasting existence of the same kind as human existence. God's eternity is a dimension other than that of human time. For this reason the biblical statement that God is before creation should not be understood in a temporal way. It must be admitted, however, that it seems almost impossible to clarify this nontemporal use of *before,* although "logically before" must be a part of the meaning. But if the reality of a spiritual world is accepted, it is certainly likely there are relations that cannot be fully explained or understood by human beings.

Aquinas compared this view with the relation between the center and the circumference of a circle. The relation between the center and the circumference is the same all the way round; in a similar manner, God relates in the same way to all times.

> Furthermore, since the being of what is eternal does not pass away, eternity is present in its presentiality to any time or instant of time. We may see an example of sorts in the case of a circle. Although it is indivisible, it does not co-exist simultaneously with any other point as to position, since it is the order of position that produces the continuity of the circumference. On the other hand, the center of the circle, which is no part of the circumference, is directly opposed to any given determinate point on the circumference. Hence, whatever is found in any part of time coexists with what is eternal as being present to it, although with respect to some other time it be past or future. (*Summa contra gentiles* 1, c. 66)

The reality of the tenses

Since antiquity two images of time have been discussed: the line made up of stationary points and the flow of a river. Philosophically speaking, these images correspond to two positions: "being as timeless" and "being as temporal." The two positions can be found in early Indian thought, for instance, as held in Brahmanism and Buddhism, respectively. The different schools in the Brahmanical tradition have maintained that the ultimate being is timeless (i.e., uncaused, indestructible, beginningless, and endless). Buddhists, on the other hand, have claimed that being is instantaneous and that duration is a fiction since according to their view a thing cannot remain identical at two different instants (Balslev, p. 69 ff.).

In classical Greek thought the tension between the dynamic and the static view of time has been expressed, for example, by the Aristotelian idea of time as the number of motion with respect to earlier and later—an idea that comprises both pictures. On the one hand time is linked to motion (i.e., changes in the world), and on the other hand time can be conceived as a stationary order of events represented by numbers. This discussion is also reflected in Isaac Newton's (1642–1727) ideas of time, according to which absolute time "flows equably without relation to anything external" (*Principia,* 1687).

The basic set of concepts for the dynamic understanding of time are *past, present,* and *future.* After J. M. E. McTaggart's analysis of time in "The Unreality of Time" (1908), these concepts (i.e., the tenses) are called the *A-concepts.* They are well suited for describing the flow of time, since the present time will become past (i.e., flow into past). The basic set of concepts for the stationary understanding of time are *before, simultaneously,* and *after.* Following McTaggart, these are called the *B-concepts,* and they seem especially apt for describing the permanent and temporal order of events.

Philosophers discuss intensively which of the two conceptions is the more fundamental for the philosophical description of time. The situation can be characterized as a debate between two Kuhnian paradigms: the ideas embodied by the well-established B-theory, which were for centuries predominant in philosophical and scientific theories of time, and the rising A-theory, which in the 1950s received a fresh impetus due to the advent of the tense logic formulated by Arthur N. Prior (1914–1969). Still, many researchers do not want to embrace the A-conception. According to A-theorists, the tenses are real, whereas B-theorists consider tenses to be secondary and unreal. According to the A-theory the "Now" is real and objective, whereas the B-theories consider the "Now" to be purely subjective.

Following the ideas of Aquinas, some argue that time from God's perspective should be understood in terms of B-concepts because time is given to God in a timeless way. But it should be mentioned that Aquinas also maintained that divine knowledge can be transformed into the temporal dimension by means of prophecies. It seems that Aquinas was suggesting a distinction between time as it is for temporal beings such as humans and time as it is for God, who is eternal. However, this does not answer the important question: Are the tenses real? Is the "Now" real?

Most writers in Christian philosophy defend the view that "my Now," "my present choice," or "my present awareness" actually represents something real. This will lead most writers in Christian philosophy to the A-theory. They normally find it obvious that the concept of time has to be related to the human mind. Therefore it becomes more natural to describe time by means of tenses (past, present, and future) than by means of instants (dates, clock-time, etc.). With tenses, one can express that the past is forever lost and the future is not yet here. Without these ideas one cannot hope to grasp the idea of the passing of time. Phenomena such as memory, experience, observation, anticipation, and hope are all essential for the way time is understood. Notions of past and future time, the interpretation of the past, and expectations of the future are all interwoven in the human mind. Nevertheless, A-theorists claim that the distinction between past and future is objective, or at least intersubjective.

Human freedom and divine foreknowledge

During the Middle Ages logicians felt that they had something important to offer with regard to solving fundamental questions in theology. The most important question of that kind was the problem of the contingent future. The intellectuals of the Middle Ages saw the problem as intimately connected with the relation between two fundamental Christian dogmas: human freedom and God's omniscience. God's omniscience is assumed to comprise knowledge of future choices to be made by human beings but apparently gives rise to a straightforward argument from divine foreknowledge to necessity of the future: If God already knows the decision one will make tomorrow, then there is already now an inevitable truth about one's choice tomorrow. Hence, there seems to be no basis for the claim that one has a free choice, a conclusion that violates the dogma of human freedom. The argument proceeds in two phases: first from divine foreknowledge to necessity of the future, and from that argument to the subsequent conclusion that there can be no real human freedom of choice. The problem obviously bears on the theological task of clarifying questions such as "In which way can God know the future?" or "What is to be understood by *free will* and *freedom of choice*?" In his treatise *De eventu futurorum*, Richard of Lavenham (c. 1380) suggested a systematical overview of basic approaches to the problem: If two dogmas are seemingly contradictory, then one can solve the problem by denying one of the dogmas or by showing that the apparent contradiction is not real (Øhrstrøm and Hasle, p. 87 ff.).

Denial of the dogma of human freedom leads to fatalism (first solution). Denial of the dogma of God's foreknowledge can either be based on the claim that God does not know the truth about the future (second solution) or the assumption that there is no truth about the contingent future since nothing has yet been decided (third solution). One can alternatively demonstrate that the two dogmas, rightly understood, can be united in a consistent way (fourth solution). The first two solutions were seen as contrary to Christian belief, according to which humans are free at least to a certain degree, and according to which God knows all truth. Peter Aureole (c.1280–1322) is notable among the defenders of the third solution. He claimed that neither the statement "the Antichrist will come" nor the statement "the Antichrist will not come" is true, whereas the disjunction of the two statements is actually true. From that point of view, one can naturally claim that the dogma of God's omniscience is still tenable, even if God does not know if the Antichrist will come or not. God knows all the truths given and cannot know if the Antichrist will come due to the simple reason that no truth about the Antichrist's future decisions yet exists. In modern philosophy, this third solution has been defended by Prior and by Charles Sanders Peirce (1839–1914). This idea of a totally open future is often illustrated using a branching time model:

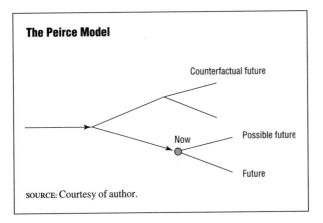

SOURCE: Courtesy of author.

The Peirce Model

The central feature of the fourth solution is its use of the notion of a "true future" among a number of possible futures. This solution was originally formulated by William of Ockham (c. 1284–1347). He discussed the problem of divine foreknowledge and human freedom in his work *Tractatus de praedestinatione et de futuris contingentibus*. He asserted that God knows all future contingents, but he also maintained that human beings can choose between alternative possibilities. Ockham was aware that considerations on the communication from God to human beings are essential. God can communicate the truth about the future to human beings. Nevertheless, according to Ockham, divine knowledge regarding future contingents does not imply that they are necessary. As an example, Ockham considered the prophecy of Jonah: "Yet forty days, and Nineveh shall be overthrown" (Jonah 3:4). This prophecy is a communication from God regarding the future. Therefore, it might seem to follow that when this prophecy has been proclaimed, then the future destruction of Nineveh is necessary. But Ockham did not accept that. Instead, he made room for human freedom in the face of true prophecies by assuming that "all prophecies about future contingents were conditionals" (Ockham, p. 44). So, according to Ockham, the prophecy of Jonah must be understood as presupposing the condition "unless the citizens of Nineveh repent." Obviously, this is exactly how the citizens of Nineveh understood the statement of Jonah.

Ockham realized that the revelation of the future by means of an unconditional statement, communicated from God to the prophet, is incompatible with the contingency of the prophecy. If God reveals the future by means of unconditional statements, then the future is inevitable, since the divine revelation must be true. The concept of divine communication (revelation) must be taken into consideration, if the belief in divine foreknowledge is to be compatible with the belief in the freedom of human actions. However, Ockham had to admit that it is impossible to express clearly the way in which God knows future contingents. He also had to conclude that, in general, divine knowledge about the contingent future is inaccessible. God is able to communicate the truth about the future to human beings, but if God reveals the truth about the future by means of unconditional statements, the future statements cannot be contingent anymore. Hence, God's unconditional foreknowledge regarding future contingents is in principle not revealed, whereas conditionals can be communicated to the prophets. Even so, that part of divine foreknowledge about future contingents, which is not revealed, must also be considered as true according to Ockham.

It can be argued that Anselm (1033/34–1109) had suggested long before Ockham a similar solution to the problem of divine foreknowledge and human freedom. Much later, Gottfried Wilhelm Leibniz (1646–1716) worked out a metaphysics of time, which from a systematical point of view is similar to the thoughts of Anselm and Ockham. The Ockhamistic solution can be illustrated using the modern notion of "branching time":

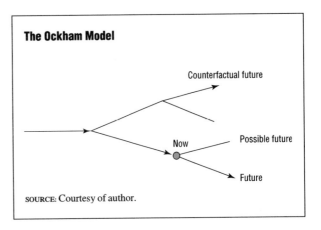

SOURCE: Courtesy of author.

The Ockham Model

From a theological point of view this model presupposes what has been called *middle knowledge,* which is God's knowledge of what every possible free creature would do under any possible set of circumstances (Craig, p. 127 ff.).

Toward a common language for the study of time

In order to gain more knowledge about the temporal aspects of reality, time has to be studied within many different strands of science. If such studies are to lead to a deeper understanding of time itself, various disciplines have to be brought together in the hope that their findings may form a new synthesis, even though one should not expect any ultimate answer regarding the question of the nature of time. If a synthesis is to succeed, a common language for the discussion of time has to be established.

The twentieth century has seen a most striking rediscovery of the importance of time and tense. This is first and foremost due to the work of Arthur Prior, who was deeply inspired by his studies in ancient and medieval logic. During the 1950s and 1960s Prior laid out the foundation of tense logic and showed that this important discipline was intimately connected with modal logic. He revived the medieval attempt at formulating a temporal logic corresponding to natural language. In doing so, he also used his symbolic formalism for investigating the ideas put forward by these logicians. Prior argued that temporal logic is fundamental for understanding and describing the world in which human beings live. He regarded tense and modal logic as particularly relevant to a number of important theological as well as philosophical problems. The main parts of temporal logic have been developed using mathematical symbolism and calculus, but nevertheless it has first and foremost been a philosophical enterprise.

According to Augustine, all humans have a tacit knowledge of what time is, even though they cannot define time. In a sense, the endeavor of temporal logic is to study some manifestations of this tacit knowledge. The concept of time can in fact be studied using temporal logic. It seems likely that Prior's tense logic may become a crucial part of a common language for the discussion of time.

In his temporal logic Prior, among many other things, took the uncertainty of the future into account. This means that it is assumed that no description of the future can be complete because it must be discussed in terms of open statements and ambiguous expressions. The reason is that some future events cannot be specified fully and satisfactorily in terms of the present vocabulary. In his temporal logic Prior suggested a notion of *unstability.* According to this idea, the language needed for a proper description of the temporal world is growing, and present events can be described more fully than was possible earlier when the events were still part of the future.

See also T = 0; TIME: PHYSICAL AND BIOLOGICAL ASPECTS

Bibliography

Ariotti, P. E. "The Concept of Time in Western Antiquity." In *The Study of Time: Proceedings of the Conference of the International Society for the Study of Time,* Vol. 2, ed. J. T. Fraser and N. Lawrence. Berlin and New York: Springer-Verlag, 1975.

Augustine. *The City of God Against the Pagans (De Civitate Dei),* 7 vols. Vol. 4 (Books 12–15), trans. Philip Levine. Cambridge, Mass.: Harvard University Press, 1957–1972.

Balslev, Anindita Niyogi. *A Study of Time in Indian Philosophy.* Wiesbaden, Germany: Harrassowitz, 1983.

Craig, William Lane. *The Only Wise God: The Compatibility of Divine Foreknowledge and Human Freedom.* Grand Rapids, Mich.: Baker Book House, 1987.

Gale, Richard M. *The Philosophy of Time: A Collection of Essays.* Atlantic Highlands, N.J.: Humanities Press, 1968.

Goldman, S. L. "On Beginnings and Endings in Medieval Judaism and Islam." In *The Study of Time IV,* ed. J. T. Fraser. Berlin and New York: Springer-Verlag, 1981.

McTaggart, J. M. E. "The Unreality of Time." *Mind* 17 (1908): 457–474.

Øhrstrøm, Peter, and Per, Hasle. *Temporal Logic: From Ancient Ideas to Artificial Intelligence.* Boston and Dordrecht, Netherlands: Kluwer, 1995.

Prior, Arthur N. *Past, Present, and Future.* Oxford: Clarendon Press, 1967.

Prior, Arthur N. *Papers on Time and Tense.* Oxford: Clarendon Press, 1968.

Thomas Aquinas. *Summa theologiae,* ed. Timothy McDermott. London: Blackfriars, 1970.

Thomas Aquinas. *Summa contra gentiles,* trans. Anton C. Pegis; J. F. Anderson; V. J. Bourke; and C. J. O'Neil. Notre Dame, Ind.: Notre Dame University Press, 1975.

Whitrow, G. J. *What is Time?* London: Thames and Hudson, 1972.

William of Ockham. *Predestination, God's Foreknowledge, and Future Contingents,* trans. Marilyn McCord Adams and Norman Kretzmann, New York: Appleton, 1969.

PETER ØHRSTRØM

TOP-DOWN CAUSATION

See DOWNWARD CAUSATION

TRANSCENDENCE

The term *transcendence,* from the Latin *transcendere* (to climb up), means to go beyond, surpass, or rise above, particularly what is given in personal experience. In theology, transcendence is associated with the beyondness and holiness of God, in the sense of the existence of God being prior to the physical cosmos and exhalted above it. Referring to divine ascent beyond the world, transcendence is frequently contrasted with immanence, the presence of God in the world. Historically, deism emphasized total transcendence of the world while pantheism stressed the total immanence of God in the world. Most theistic traditions seek a balance between the two.

See also DEISM; GOD; HUMAN NATURE, RELIGIOUS AND PHILOSOPHICAL ASPECTS; IMMANENCE; PANTHEISM

ERNEST SIMMONS

TRANSMIGRATION

The term *transmigration,* from the Latin *transmigrare* (to migrate across or over), means to pass from one condition, place, or body to another. Transmigration is usually identified with the Greek word *metempsychosis* (change of soul), the "transmigration of souls" drawing on the Greek Orphic

mysteries. In South Asian religions, transmigration is related to the karmic cycle where one's moral action determines the condition of the soul and the quality of its rebirth. In Hinduism, the cycle of rebirth is eternal unless the soul is liberated (*moksha*) by knowledge or arduous effort (Yoga). In Buddhism the soul and transmigration are ultimately illusory (*maya*), being passing emergents from *samsara,* the eternal, undifferentiated stream of being.

See also KARMA; LIFE AFTER DEATH

ERNEST SIMMONS

TRUTH, THEORIES OF

The question of truth is inherent in human rationality. A core feature of rationality is self-reflection in the sense that we can critically reflect upon how we see the world. In the question of truth our relation to reality is called into question, and the pursuit of truth is therefore pivotal to both science and religion.

When we are asking for a theory of truth, we take a step back and focus on our conception of truth. The first thing to be noted is that we use the word *true* as an adjective for various things: A statement can be true, but so can a friend or an act of friendship, or a democracy. In the latter cases we may substitute *real* for *true*: A true friend is a real friend whom we can count on. But if the sentence "She is a true friend" is true, it is so in a sense where we cannot substitute *real* for *true*. This indicates that a theory of truth deals with mental acts (e.g., beliefs) or statements (judgments, propositions) as truth bearers. Mental acts or statements are about something. A theory of truth thus operates at the level where we relate to something, and relate in such way that we make truth claims about what we relate to (i.e., claims as to what it is and how it is). The key issue for a theory of truth is the relation between beliefs or statements that can be true or false, and that which these beliefs or statements are about. We can then distinguish between the following types of truth theories: the correspondence theory, the coherence theory, and pragmatic theories.

Correspondence theory of truth

According to a correspondence theory of truth, the truth relation is a correspondence between a statement and a fact. A theory of this kind reflects a commonsense idea of truth to the effect that a statement is true if it corresponds to how things actually are. This is captured in the classic formulation of the correspondence theory in Aristotle (384–322 B.C.E.): "To say of what is that it is not, or of what is not that it is, is false, while to say of what is that it is, and of what is not that it is not, is true" (Aristotle, 1011b26f). Thus, *truth* means agreement with reality. However, a statement cannot correspond to a thing or an event. In order to ascertain whether a statement is true or false we need to know what it is about, that is, what the thing or the event in question is. What makes a statement *p* (e.g., "He was late") true is the *fact* of *p* (i.e., that he actually was late). Correspondence is thus correlation between statements and facts. It need not be congruence, however, in the sense that the structure of the statement somehow reflects the structure of the fact.

But this does not solve the problem of explicating what it is that statements correspond to. We do not have two separate entities, statements, and facts. It might be argued that facts are what true statements state, not what they are about. And if we are going to determine what the fact is to which the statement corresponds—in order to compare statement and fact—then we must make another statement. Thus, the relation between statements and reality can only be determined by other statements.

Coherence theory of truth

A coherence theory of truth seeks to meet this problem by transforming correspondence between statement and fact into coherence between statements. A statement or belief is true to the degree it coheres with other accepted statements or beliefs related to it, or to be more precise, if it fits into the most coherent set or system of statements or beliefs. What is required for a set of statements or beliefs to be coherent is internal consistency, or even mutual entailment between the statements or beliefs in question. To this can be added the further requirement that the system not only is coherent, but also gives the most complete picture of the world. Thus, the argument for a coherence theory

not only is that a statement can only be compared to other statements, but also that a statement or a belief never is without context: It presupposes other statements in order to be true, and it does so because a thing is what it is due to its relations to other things. Consequently, a coherence theory of truth often is linked to a metaphysics according to which reality basically is a coherent system. But the context can also be construed as a system of interpretations that we presuppose when making a statement. We can only compare interpretations with other interpretations. A coherence theory thus favors an antirealist ontology to the effect that there is no mind-independent or extralinguistic reality.

The coherence solution however engenders problems of its own. First, standard versions of the coherence theory confuse the meaning of truth (the definition) with the criterion of truth (the test). Second, it seems possible to have two internally coherent, but mutually inconsistent sets of beliefs concerning the same reality. The further requirement that a coherent system must also give the most complete picture of the world implies that we should be able to compare competing sets of beliefs as interpretations of the same world. Third, if a statement is true when it coheres with what we already accept to be true, how do we decide the truth of these other statements or beliefs, upon which the first statement depends? And how is our view of reality changed?

Pragmatic theories of truth

A pragmatic theory of truth takes a step further by focusing on the social context of understanding. One version is a consensus theory that translates the meaning of truth into the context of argumentation. It is not sufficient to say that a statement is true if it coheres with our accepted views. A stronger condition is that a statement is true if it is accepted by the most informed participants or by everyone with sufficient relevant experiences to judge it. But if truth amounts to what the most informed participants or everyone sufficiently experienced agree upon, the question is how to decide who are the most informed participants or when we are sufficiently experienced. In order to avoid this problem, the criterion of consensus can be made both stronger and more open-ended: If truth is what everybody will ultimately agree upon, a theory of consensus can place some stronger conditions on what is meant by *ultimately*.

Jürgen Habermas (1929–) reformulates the consensus theory as a discourse theory: The meaning of truth is "warranted assertibility." Statements are true if their truth claims are warranted in a discourse in which we only enter by presupposing an ideal situation of communication where no participant is in a privileged position. Truth is thus defined in the context of argumentation in which we meet various or even conflicting truth claims that are open to discussion in a discourse. But if the meaning of truth is defined by the procedure of argumentation, this procedure cannot recur to the concept of truth. If truth is translated into the consensus to be reached, this consensus cannot in turn be measured by truth. The argumentation in a discourse about truth claims, however, is not about consensus but about truth. If it aims at consensus, it is a consensus concerning what the truth is. Consequently, there remains a normative dimension of truth, which in Habermas is translated into the ideal situation of communication.

A second version of a pragmatic theory of truth is an instrumentalist theory that measures the truth of beliefs or statements by their consequences: "That which guides us truly is true—demonstrated capacity for such guidance is precisely what is meant by truth. . . . The hypothesis that works is the true one; and truth is an abstract noun applied to the collection of cases, actual, foreseen and desired, that receive confirmation in their works and consequences" (Dewey, p. 156–157). The problem here is how to decide what *truly* means. The reference to consequences is in need of qualification as to which consequences would meet the requirement of guiding us truly. In fact, an instrumentalist theory substitutes utility for truth.

As an alternative to an instrumentalist theory ("The truth is what works"), the central pragmatist idea can be reformulated in a performative theory of truth that focuses on what we are doing when we take something to be true. This is outlined by Robert B. Brandom (1950–) in a model that emphasizes the act of calling something true rather than the descriptive content of truth statements. It further gives an account of that act in terms of a normative attitude: Taking some claim to be true is committing oneself to it. Endorsing a truth claim is understood as adopting it as a guide to action, and the correctness of adopting it can be measured by the success of the actions it guides (involving here what Brandom calls "stereotypical" pragmatism).

Once we have understood acts of "taking-true" according to this model, we have "understood all there is to understand about truth." This means that truth "is treated, not as a property independent of our attitudes, to which they must eventually answer, but rather as a creature of taking-true or treating-as-true" (Brandom, p. 287). This performative analysis of truth talk in terms of a theory of "taking-true" can be combined with a redundancy theory of truth: When we state "It is true that *p*," we only make explicit the claim implicit in stating *p*. In calling the statement *p* true, we are not describing a property of that statement. We are doing something—we are committing ourselves.

A pragmatic theory of truth takes as its point of departure that there is no absolute or universal truth at our disposal. Still, as we have seen, a pragmatic theory can maintain and seek to account for the normative dimension of truth. It here differs from a radical instrumentalist theory according to which truth is a fiction in the sense of human construction. According to Friedrich Nietzsche (1844–1900), truth is not something to be found but something to be created. Although, in Nietzsche, truth is itself illusion, fiction, or construction, there still seems to be a normative dimension unaccounted for in his unmasking of illusions.

Truth in religion

Coherence and pragmatic theories of truth derive much of their plausibility from the ambition to avoid the problems facing a correspondence theory. However, the question is whether we can do without a strong normative concept of truth that reflects the experience of a reality not corresponding to our beliefs or interpretations. Truth as an open question implies a strong concept of truth in the sense that we ourselves have to experience whether our beliefs are true or not. The key issue in theories of truth can be reformulated as the relation between our cognitive attitudes and reality. The challenge facing us is to account both for the fact that we do not have access to a reality outside of our attitudes or our interpretations of reality, and for the normative dimension of truth. The line of argument has led from descriptive attitudes that consider the world from outside to cognitive attitudes embedded in social practices in which we partake in the reality we are talking about. Truth claims can be implicit in nondescriptive attitudes.

When we are talking about the world we are not only describing how things are, but we are relating to the world in various ways.

That truth is a question of how we relate to the world is brought out in what can be called an existential conception of truth, which should not be confused with an existentialist or subjectivist reduction of truth. According to Søren Kierkegaard (1813–1855), "the truth is only for the individual in that he produces it in action," but in the same vein it is stated that "the truth makes a human being free" (1980, p. 138). The dictum that "subjectivity is truth" (Kierkegaard, 1992, p. 240) does not mean that each of us freely chooses what should count as the truth. The point is conversely that subjectivity itself is to be determined by the truth. Taking something to be true implies that it should determine the way we relate to ourselves and to others.

This leads to the issue of truth in religion. The truth question is basic not only to the rational inquiry into nature, but also to the understanding of religion. Indeed, the issue of rationality and religion turns on the question of truth. What happens when the question of truth is seen within the context of religion? First, the tension between uncertainty (implicit in asking the question) and certainty (in answering it) is intensified: What is meant by the truth in view of conflicting truth claims? Second, religion represents a double possibility. It can suspend the truth question by giving an answer to it that is not open for discussion, but it can also reopen the truth question by calling our attitudes and self-understanding into question. Third, in religion, the relation between cognitive attitudes, on the one hand, and volitional and affective attitudes on the other, and between attitudes and action, is complicated. To believe in the truth implies that we understand ourselves in the light of the truth, which means that it should form our life. Fourth, what religion can do is reverse the perspective: The truth question is not only a question for us to decide, but also calls into question how we relate to the world. When religion speaks of the truth, it is also implied that truth is not at our disposal, but conversely questions us: What is the truth about us? The truth question is also disturbing when it calls into question who we, the subjects of the question, are.

See also IDEALISM; PLATO; PRAGMATISM; REALISM

Bibliography

Aristotle. *Metaphysics.* In *The Works of Aristotle,* Vol. 8, trans. W. D. Ross. Oxford: Oxford University Press, 1972.

Blanshard, Brand. *The Nature of Thought.* New York: Macmillan, 1941.

Brandom, Robert B. *Making It Explicit: Reasoning, Representing and Discursive Commitment.* Cambridge, Mass.: Harvard University Press, 1994.

Dewey, John. *Reconstruction in Philosophy* Boston: Beacon Press, 1985.

Habermas, Jürgen. "Wahrheitstheorien." In *Vorstudien und Ergänzungen zur Theorie des kommunikativen Handelns.* Frankfurt am Main, Germany: Suhrkamp, 1984.

Kierkegaard, Søren. *The Concept of Anxiety: A Simple Psychologically Orienting Deliberation on the Dogmatic Issue of Hereditary Sin.* In *Kierkegaard's Writings,* Vol. 8, trans. and ed. Howard V. Hong and Edna H. Hong. Princeton, N.J.: Princeton University Press, 1980.

Kierkegaard, Søren. *Concluding Unscientific Postscript.* In *Kierkegaard's Writings,* Vol. 7.1, trans. and ed. Howard V. Hong, and Edna H. Hong. Princeton, N.J.: Princeton University Press, 1992.

Kirkham, Richard L. *Theories of Truth: A Critical Introduction.* Cambridge, Mass.: MIT Press, 1992.

Peirce, Charles S. *Collected Papers of Charles Sanders Peirce,* ed. Charles Hartshorne and Paul Weiss. Cambridge, Mass.: Harvard University Press, 1931–1958.

Skirbekk, Gunnar. *Wahrheitstheorien.* Frankfurt am Main, Germany: Suhrkamp, 1977.

ARNE GRØN

TURING TEST

The Turing Test was proposed by computer pioneer Alan M. Turing (1912–1954) to determine whether a computer program is intelligent. This modern interpretation of the so-called imitation game is based on a setup where a person, a computer, and an interrogator are in three separate rooms and connected via computer terminals. The task of the interrogator is to figure out by asking questions which of the two connected terminals is operated by the human and which is the test computer. The computer is considered to be intelligent if the interrogator fails to determine its identity.

The Turing Test is recognized as a critical test for computer intelligence and, as of 2002, had not been passed by any computer.

See also ARTIFICIAL INTELLIGENCE; THINKING MACHINES

THIEMO KRINK

TWO BOOKS

Permeating the Western Christian tradition of natural theology is a metaphor expressing the belief that God is revealed in a complementary pair of sources: the book of scripture and the book of nature. The idea of nature as a book was used by early modern writers as shorthand for the design argument for God's existence. Thomas Browne (1605–1682), for example, wrote, "There are two books from whence I collect my divinity: besides that written one of God, another of his servant, nature, that universal and public manuscript that lies expansed unto the eyes of all" (*Religio Medici* I.16).

Origins of the metaphor

The metaphor was born at the confluence of a number of streams: the common human experience of the transcendent, the conviction of the reality of divine-human communication, and the Western fascination for books as repositories of knowledge. The conviction that God is made known through divine works is celebrated in *Psalm* 19, and *Wisdom* 11: 6–9 articulates the idea that even gentiles who have not enjoyed the benefit of revelation are without excuse for their unbelief, a tradition persisting at least until the time of John Calvin (1509–1564). The New Testament *locus classicus* for the natural knowledge of God is the Pauline declaration, "For what can be known about God is plain to them, because God has shown it to them. Ever since the creation of the world his invisible nature, namely, his eternal power and deity, has been clearly perceived in the things that have been made" (*Romans* 1:19–20).

The elements of what would become the "book of nature" metaphor are scattered throughout Patristic literature. Justin Martyr (c. 100–165) built his second-century apologetic upon the Stoic idea of the *logos spermatikos*, arguing that the world is permeated by seeds of the divine word (*Second Apology* VIII), and Irenaeus (c. 130–200) provided the two essential ingredients of the theme in the works and the word of God (*Adversus haereses*, Book I, ch. 20). Tertullian (c. 160–225) regarded the works of God as an important revelatory counterpart to the Bible (*Adversus Marcionem*, Book II, ch. 3). For Augustine of Hippo (354–430) the book of the heavens provided milk for the spiritually immature (*Confessions*, Book XIII, ch. 18.23, 26). The closest thing to a formal Patristic statement of the metaphor of "the book of nature" may be found in John Chrysostom's (c. 347–407) *Homilies to the people of Antioch*, in which he declared that nature serves the function of a book of revelation: "Upon this volume the unlearned, as well as the wise man, shall be able to look, and wherever any one may chance to come, there looking upwards towards the heavens, he will receive a sufficient lesson from the view of them. . . ." (*Homily* IX. 5).

The metaphor became firmly established in the Middle Ages, expressing a mature binary epistemology of revelation. Alain of Lille (c. 1128–1203) held every created thing to be like a book; Hugh of Saint Victor (1096–1142) regarded both the creation and the incarnation as "books" of God, comparing Christ—as primary revelation—to a book. Bonaventure (c. 1217–1274) suggested that there are three volumes: sensible creatures are "a book with writing front and back," spiritual creatures are "a scroll written from within," and scripture is "a scroll written within and without" (*Collations on the Hexaemeron* 12.14–17). For Thomas Aquinas (c. 1225–1274) the first element of the threefold knowledge of divine things is "an ascent through creatures to the knowledge of God by the natural light of reason" (*Summa Contra Gentiles*, IV.1.3). For the poet Dante Alighieri (1265–1321), the godhead is the book in which all the loose pages scattered throughout the universe will eschatologically be bound in one volume (*Paradiso* XXXIII). Raymond of Sabunde (d. 1436) gave the metaphor its fullest medieval articulation in his *Theologia Naturalis sive Liber Creaturarum*. He regarded every created thing as a letter written by the finger of God, and human beings as the first letters of this book. His work attracted the attention of the censors, however, because of his incautious opinion that the book of nature is more accurate than the Bible, and his assertion of the preeminent importance of natural knowledge; it was placed on the Index (the official list of books prohibited by the Roman Catholic church) in 1595.

Early modern variations on the theme

The "book of nature" enjoyed its greatest currency in the early modern period. The emphasis of the Reformers on the literal sense of scripture cut through the profusion of "meanings" and "signatures" found by medieval scholars in nature and reinforced the idea of there being two books. However, the book of nature was clearly subordinate to biblical revelation in Calvin's theology, which held scripture to be a necessary corrective to the deficiencies of nature (*Institutes* I.6.1). The Reformed tradition retained this Calvinist interpretation of the two books in the *Belgic Confession* adopted by the Dutch Reformed Church. In contrast, Paracelsus (1493–1541) suggested an empirical approach: Whereas scripture was to be explored through its letters, the book of nature had to be read by going from land to land, since every country was a different page.

The metaphor was affected in the seventeenth century by both the elaboration of natural theology and the development of the sciences in novel empirical and theoretical directions. Pierre Gassendi (1592–1655) saw purpose in all of nature and suggested that if René Descartes (1596–1650) wanted to prove the existence of God, he ought to abandon reason and look around him, and that the two books were not to be kept on separate shelves. Although Francis Bacon (1561–1626) seems in practice to have kept the two books distinct, he articulated their essential complementarity:

> The scriptures reveal to us the will of God; and the book of the creatures expresses the divine power; whereof the latter is a key unto the former: not only opening our understanding to conceive the true sense of the scriptures, by the general notions of reason and rules of speech; but chiefly opening our belief, in drawing us into a due meditation of the omnipotency of God, which is chiefly signed and engraven upon his works. (*The Advancement of Learning* VI, 16)

Bacon set the tone for the seventeenth-century scientific enterprise in his redirection of the "two books" metaphor toward the improvement of the human estate.

Galileo Galilei (1564–1642) argued that the book of nature is written in the language of mathematics, not only implying that mathematics is the sublimest expression of the divine word, but *de facto* restricting its full comprehension to those who are appropriately educated:

> And to prohibit the whole science [of astronomy] would be but to censure a hundred passages of holy Scripture which teach us that the glory and greatness of Almighty God are marvelously discerned in all his works and divinely read in the open book of heaven. . . . Within its pages are couched mysteries so profound and concepts so sublime that the vigils, labors, and studies of hundreds upon hundreds of the most acute minds have still not pierced them, even after continual investigations for thousands of years. (*Letter to Grand Duchess Christina*)

Galileo's famous dictum that scripture teaches "how one goes to heaven, not how heaven goes" should be interpreted in light of his conviction of the complementarity of the two books.

The metaphor flourished in the natural theological climate of seventeenth-century England, particularly in the "physico-theology" of the Boyle Lectures. But its two terms were not always held in comfortable balance. The dissenting theologian Richard Baxter (1615–1691), for example, argued that "nature was a 'hard book' which few could understand, and that it was therefore safer to rely more heavily on Scripture" (*The Reasons for the Christian Religion,* 1667). In contrast, Isaac Newton (1642–1727) saw nature as perhaps more truly the source of divine revelation than the Bible, although he spent decades of his life investigating the prophetic books. Frank Manuel, in *The Religion of Isaac Newton* (1974), argues that in virtually abolishing the distinction between the two books, which Newton revered as separate expressions of the same divine meaning, Newton was attempting to keep science sacred and to reveal scientific rationality in what was once a purely sacral realm, namely, biblical prophecy. By the early eighteenth century there was a significant faction within the Royal Society opposed to any mention of scripture in a scientific context.

Decline and survival

Although the metaphor of the book of nature persisted vigorously into the nineteenth century, various movements began to undermine its cogency. The Enlightenment critiques of David Hume (1711–1776) and Immanuel Kant (1724–1804) undermined the project of natural theology in broad strokes, and the Deist movement challenged the uniqueness of the Christian revelation. Thomas Paine (1737–1809) asked defiantly, "Do we want to know what God is? Search not the book called the Scripture, which any human hand might make, but the Scripture, called the creation" (*The Age of Reason,* 1794).

Other trends exercised equally damaging effects. The revolutions in geology and biology eroded longstanding traditions of a young Earth and an immutable creation, and wore away the bedrock beneath a coherent "book of nature" temporally coextensive with the "book of scripture." Charles Babbage (1791–1871) advanced a view in his *Ninth Bridgewater Treatise* (1838) that seems to verge almost on asserting the superfluity of scriptural revelation in light of the book of nature. Parallel to the "historicization" of geology and biology, the development of an historical critical approach to study of the scripture affected the "two books" theme no less, challenging profoundly rooted tradition about the Bible constituting an integral and timeless record of the Word of God.

Despite the developments outlined above, the metaphor continued to thrive during the nineteenth century among both conservative anti-Darwinians and more liberal thinkers who enthusiastically adopted the principles and discoveries of contemporary science. A decade after the publication of Darwin's *Origin of Species* in 1859, Herbert Morris (1818–1897) argued that scripture and nature represent respectively the verbal and the pictorial aspects of divine wisdom, correlating the "inspired record of creation" with contemporary science (*Science and the Bible,* 1871). Paul Chadbourne (1823–1883) regarded nature as an unchangeable record, written in the language of the sciences of which geology comprised the most clearly comprehended volume (*Nature and the Bible from the Same Author,* 1870). Geologist Joseph Le Conte (1823–1901) declared that "the whole object of science is to construct the theology of the divine revelation in nature." Although quite clear about the limits of science as a commentary on the book of scripture, he held that "of these two books, nature is the elder born, and in some sense, at least, may be considered the more comprehensive and perfect" (*Religion and Science,* 1902).

The innovations in hermeneutics and science pushed the more religiously conservative wings of society in a precritical direction of maintaining verbal inerrancy and defending the ancient understanding of Earth history. The metaphor of the "book of nature" would gain weight as one of the cornerstones of their position, thriving in evangelical and fundamentalist-creationist circles right through the end of the twentieth century.

However, in both liberal and neo-orthodox theology the metaphor of "God's two books" entered into steady decline after 1900. Parallel to the development of historical geology and biblical criticism was the erosion of confidence that one can easily interpret natural processes teleologically, as William Paley (1743–1805) had once argued. The discovery of extinction in the fossil record challenged the ancient assumption of the immutability of species, rendering it increasingly difficult to read the "book of nature" as self-evidently revealing the divine plan, or at least a plan worthy of admiration. Additionally, the metamorphosis of "natural philosophy" and "natural history" into the variety of sciences as they are known today undercut both terms in the metaphor of "God's two books." As each new scientific discipline developed its own sphere of study, the "nature" underlying the "book of nature" lost its metaphorical coherence, and the replacement of science as commentary on authoritative texts by the empirical investigation of the natural world essentially removed the "book" from the "book of nature." Finally, the gradual recognition over the last two centuries that the human community embraces a plurality of religious faiths has had the effect of relativizing the Bible as a source of revelation. The "two books" metaphor truly functions only if the claim can be defended that the Bible is *the* book of scripture.

The complex theme of the "book of nature" has enjoyed a long and convoluted history. For nearly two millennia the metaphor variously framed, constituted, negated, or otherwise reflected the relationship between the two human institutions now referred to as science and religion. If it appears to be a less convincing rhetorical device in postmodernity, understanding the lifecycle of the metaphor can reveal a great deal about the conversation between religion and science.

Bibliography

Blumenberg, Hans. *Die Lesbarkeit der Welt*. Frankfurt am Main, Germany: Suhrkamp, 1981.

Bono, James J. *The Word of God and the Languages of Man: Interpreting Nature in Early Modern Science and Medicine*. Madison: University of Wisconsin Press, 1995.

Curtius, Ernst Robert. *European Literature and the Latin Middle Ages,* trans. Willard R. Trask. New York: Pantheon, 1953.

Harrison, Peter. *The Bible, Protestantism, and the Rise of Modern Science*. Cambridge, UK: Cambridge University Press, 1998.

Howell, Kenneth. *God's Two Books: Copernican Cosmology and Biblical Interpretation in Early Modern Science*. Notre Dame, Ind.: University of Notre Dame Press, 2002.

Manuel, Frank E. *The Religion of Isaac Newton*. Oxford: Clarendon Press, 1974.

Pedersen, Olaf. *The Book of Nature*. Vatican City: Vatican Observatory Press, 1992.

Sabundus, Raimudus. *Theologia Naturalis Seu Liber Creaturarum* (1852). Stuttgart, Germany: Bad Cannstatt, 1966.

PETER M. J. HESS

UFO

The modern UFO phenomenon began in 1947 with the eyewitness account of pilot Kenneth Arnold of nine flying disks near Mount Rainier in Washington. The newspapers called them *flying saucers*. UFO is the more technical term, standing for *unidentified flying object*. A sighting acquires this designation only after scientific attempts to identify it as a star, meteor, balloon, aircraft, or hallucination have failed. UFO refers to what is unidentified after attempts to identify it.

Types of sightings

As a phenomenon of perception, scholars study both the perceiver and the perceived, both the UFO and its witness. Sightings are classified as: (1) daylight disks; (2) nocturnal lights; (3) radar sightings or combinations of radar and visual sightings; (4) close encounters of the first kind, when the witness is within 500 feet of the object or craft; (5) close encounters of the second kind, when physical traces of the object or craft are left for investigation; and (6) close encounters of the third kind, when witnesses claim to encounter beings connected to a flying craft. Investigators give higher credibility to multiple witness sightings, especially when witnesses are independent of one another. Such categorizing is itself part of the UFO phenomenon, reflecting the scientific attitude investigators take to their work.

Government evaluations of UFOs

Seldom has the academic community taken up the subject of UFOs for research and analysis. The U.S. government sponsored various investigative programs from 1947 through 1969 such as Project Sign and Project Bluebook; but the government's interest was primarily national defense. Convinced that UFOs provided no threat to national security, these efforts deliberately sought to debunk public claims to UFO sightings in an attempt to reduce the quantity of reports various governmental agencies would need to process.

From 1967 to 1969, Edward U. Condon at the University of Colorado conducted a federally funded study, *Final Report of the Scientific Study of Unidentified Flying Objects*. What became known as the Condon Report concluded that "nothing has come from the study of UFOs" that would warrant "further extensive study." On this basis, the U.S. Air Force dropped Project Bluebook and ceased collecting data. J. Allen Hynek, the principal astronomer and scientific debunker for Project Bluebook, converted, so to speak, and began his own private research organization, the Center for UFO Studies at Northwestern University.

Social and cultural aspects

As a social phenomenon, since their first appearance following the Second World War, two elements have been present in public perception: an association of UFOs with the possibility of extraterrestrial intelligent life, and vociferous criticism of the U.S. government for allegedly withholding vital secrets from its citizens and the world. In addition, UFO research organizations, such as the Mutual UFO Network (MUFON), have been established, and new religious movements such as Heaven's

Gate, the UNARIUS Society, the Aetherius Society, and the Raelians see great significance in UFOs.

The UFO phenomenon is frequently confused with science fiction, although no relationship exists between the two, which followed separate paths in the first decades after the Second World War. Science fiction literature and films generally depicted extraterrestrials as enemies, invaders threatening earth and against whom earthlings would have to unite in self-defense. In contrast, within the UFO community extraterrestrials were viewed as either benign or, in many cases, as benevolent, as celestial saviors coming to Earth to rescue humanity from self-destruction. Two notable Hollywood films portrayed the UFO experience as UFO believers interpret it: Robert Wise's *The Day the Earth Stood Still* (1951) and Steven Spielberg's *Close Encounters of the Third Kind* (1977).

For the first forty years of the phenomenon the space visitors were pictured as benign or benevolent. Then in the late 1980s reports were published of abductions in which the UFO abductors behaved much like abusers. Attributed to them were plots to impregnate earth women with extraterrestrial sperm to raise a hybrid race that unites heaven and Earth. After a decade of such reports, subsequent interviews of alleged abductees revealed a shift in interpretation. Abductees who originally reported a sense of violation by their space captors began to interpret extraterrestrial motives as spiritually beneficial and healing.

As a cultural phenomenon, UFOs have picked up surface and subtle sublimated meanings. On the surface, they are strange objects seen in the sky. Below the surface, UFOs function symbolically to bear religious meaning in a secular culture imbued by natural science and secular self-understanding. Sublimated religious meaning expresses itself in at least four forms: *transcendence, omniscience, perfection,* and *redemption.*

Transcendence. In many archaic religions the sky was a natural symbol of transcendence, and in the modern world outer space has replaced the sky in this role. Sky gods were powerful gods, wielding thunderbolts and scorching the earth with a blazing hot sun. With airplanes and weather reports mastering the sky, modern people have lost the sense of celestial transcendence. The apparent infinity of outer space, however, revives this lost spiritual sensibility. Because UFOs are seen in the

sky and associated with outer space, they allegedly have mastered travel over unfathomable distances. They come from beyond, a physical beyond that easily slips over to become a spiritual beyond.

Omniscience. The worldview of modern society includes evolutionary theory in its self-understanding, and when the question of extraterrestrial life is raised, evolution is exported to outer space. Although biologists see no scientific basis for progress in biological evolution on earth, the popular mind identifies evolution with technological advance. When projected onto possible beings in space, they are thought to be more "advanced" than earthlings. Their technological knowledge is superior. In UFO religious groups, extraterrestrials are said to have gained telepathic powers so they can read earthlings' minds, a quality previously attributed to angels.

Perfection. Again, projecting evolution understood as progress infers that the extraterrestrials who have evolved for a very long time not only have perfected technology but have also perfected bodily health and social morality. They have conquered disease, live for extraordinarily long periods, and, most importantly, they are pictured as living in peace, especially peace with nuclear power and without ecological deterioration.

Redemption. Having achieved transcendent travel, ultimate technological knowledge, and social perfection, the space travelers are in a position to save the earth from the threat of nuclear war and ecological disaster. The extraterrestrials are Gnostic redeemers because, as new religious groups forming around UFO belief testify, their mission is to teach citizens of Earth to pull together into a single planetary society that lives in peace, prosperity, and harmony with nature. This entire belief structure is a modern myth—what Carl Jung called a "myth of things seen in the sky."

The UFO phenomenon, which includes both believers and what is believed, provides a gate into understanding the dynamics of a culture totally imbued with natural science, so much so that religious sensibilities must make their appearance in sublimated form.

See also EXOBIOLOGY; EXTRATERRESTRIAL LIFE

Bibliography

Condon, Edward U. *Final Report of the Scientific Study of Unidentified Flying Objects*. New York: Dutton, 1969.

Hynek, J. Allen. *The UFO Experience*. New York: Ballantine, 1972.

Jung, Carl. *Flying Saucers: A Myth of Things Seen in the Sky*. New York: Bantam, 1959.

Klass, Philip. *UFOs Explained*. New York: Random House, 1974.

Lewis, James R. *The Gods Have Landed: New Religions from Other Worlds*. Albany: State University of New York Press, 1995.

Peters, Ted. *UFOs—God's Chariots: Flying Saucers in Politics, Science, and Religion*. Louisville, Ky.: Westminster John Knox, 1976.

Peters, Ted. "Heaven's Gate and the Theology of Suicide." *Dialog, A Journal of Theology* 37, no.1 (Winter 1998): 57–66.

TED PETERS

UNPREDICTABILITY

The term *unpredictability* refers to the failure of predicting future events out of a given state of affairs with the help of scientific laws, which relate effects to causes. By establishing fundamental unpredictability within the basis of scientific description itself, quantum theory and the theory of complex systems have undermined a central conviction of classical physics namely, that precise predictability is in principle achievable. While quantum theory seems to point to a fundamental ontological indeterminism, unpredictability entailed by the theory of complex systems can be reduced to deterministic laws and is routed in the sensitivity of complex systems to minimal deviations of their initial conditions.

See also CHAOS, QUANTUM; CHAOS THEORY; PHYSICS, QUANTUM

DIRK EVERS

UPWARD CAUSATION

When the direction of causal influence extends from 'higher' levels of reality (say, those above the level of physics) down to 'lower' levels of reality, we speak of *downward causation*. The various sciences are commonly, though not uncontroversially, assumed to stand in some hierarchical relationship to each other. Physics is considered the basic science, with the other sciences (chemistry, biology, psychology, and the social sciences) stacked on top, each dealing with mereologically more complicated fusions of physical events than its predecessor. This assumption is often complemented with the principle of the *causal closure* of the physical realm. This principle states, in effect, that physical events (even huge conglomerates of physical events possibly constituting such macroevents as earthquakes, mental states, or a crash in the stock market) are causally produced by antecedent physical events alone (though these latter events may in their turn be more illuminatingly describable in the jargon of relevant nonphysical sciences). That is to say, fundamentally there is only one kind of "real" causation, namely, causation at the level of microphysical events. Thus, causation extends upward all the way from the physical domain to the higher-level domains supposedly stacked up on top.

Consequently, according to this view, causation at these higher levels of existence, in particular mental causation, is always in some sense derivative or epiphenomenal. Jaegwon Kim's doctrine of *supervenient causation,* for example, holds that there exists a macro-causal relation between two events just in case there is a micro-causal relation between the two events upon which they supervene. Clearly such a definition of supervenient causation renders all macro-causation epiphenomenal. In particular, since mental causation is a species of macro-causation, the way the mind matters in this world is, on this view, epiphenomenal as well. It has been observed, however, that Kim's doctrine presupposes an unnecessarily restricted notion of event-supervenience known as *local supervenience*.

See also CAUSATION; DOWNWARD CAUSATION; SUPERVENIENCE

Bibliography

Kim, Jaegwon. "Epiphenomenal and Supervenient Causation." *Midwest Studies in Philosophy* 9 (1984): 257–270.

THEO C. MEYERING

VALUE

The word *value* commonly refers to the worth of something: an object or event, a person or action, an idea or institution. Its value can be understood as objective, a quality or feature it possesses independently of one's experiencing it. The sunset is beautiful whether it is observed or not; honesty is the best policy even if people do not think so. A thing's value can also be understood as subjective, a positive feeling or idea that it arouses or that is imputed to it. Good art is whatever one happens to like; moral codes are social constructs. In economics, the (subjective) market value of a commodity or service is the price someone is willing to pay for it at a given time; its (objective) normal value is the price it would command in a perfectly functioning open market. By metaphorical extension, the value of a variable in mathematics is its assignable numeric worth: The value of x in $2 \times x = 6$ is 3.

Value is also a verb. To value something is to esteem it, to take it into account in making a choice, to assert its objective or subjective worth. The American philosopher and educator John Dewey distinguishes between prizing and apprizing: To prize something is to like it, to appreciate it, to enjoy the experience of it. There is no explanation required: People simply like what they like. Dewey calls these *de facto* values, which he contrasts with *de jure* values, values that have been judged, with respect to their causes and consequences and by comparison to other alternatives, to be genuinely worthwhile, not only desired but desirable. Just as science has an experimental method for discriminating warranted from unwarranted hypotheses, Dewey argues, so a method of criticism is needed for discriminating among values, helping people select those values most conducive to their self-realization and to the attaining of a common good.

A thing's value can be either intrinsic, itself the source of its value, or extrinsic, the source of its value lying elsewhere: in God's will, a subjective judgment, or another value upon which it is dependent. In a context of means and ends, a thing has *final* value (sometimes, confusingly, called its intrinsic value) if it is the goal of a purposive effort; it has *instrumental* value if valued as a means for achieving that goal. Dewey argued that all values are both final and instrumental: Any end one seeks is also a means toward further ends. In the eighteenth century, the philosopher Immanuel Kant argued that rational beings are ends in themselves: They have infinite worth because there is no other value for which their value could legitimately be sacrificed, made merely a means. Note that all instrumental values are extrinsic, but some extrinsic values are not instrumental: Theistic religions claim that persons are valuable not intrinsically but because they are created by God.

Value theory, or *axiology,* an approach in which value as a general category is made the primary object of philosophical analysis, is a nineteenth and twentieth century development in Western thought. Among the leading value theorists are Bernard Bosanquet, J. N. Findlay, Alexius Meinong, and Max Scheler in Europe; Alejandro Korn in Latin

America; and C. I. Lewis, Ralph Barton Perry, John Dewey, and Stephen Pepper in the United States. Their strategy is usually to provide a generic analysis of the nature and conditions of value, then to apply these concepts to the various realms of value their theory either predicts or interprets.

Traditionally, however, thinkers have concerned themselves not with value in general but with specific values: aesthetic (beauty), ethical or religious (goodness), and scientific or philosophical (truth). Sometimes these kinds of value are thought to be distinct, for instance, claiming that the criteria for a thing's being true have nothing to do with its desirability. Others argue for a hierarchy among the kinds, usually in terms of some version of Plato's divided line, beginning with the transient values of immediate perception and imagination, rising through practical and then theoretical concerns, and arriving finally at something ultimate, the source of all lesser values: a contemplation of the Form of the Good or of Beauty, or communion with God or the Absolute. In the early nineteenth century, the philosopher Georg Wilhelm Friedrich Hegel temporalized this hierarchy, so that the ultimate became not an eternal governing ideal but a historical culmination, not a governing rule but an achievable goal.

The notion of a "final value" for individuals to achieve is usually given an ethical slant. Aristotle, for instance, finds this achievement to be the happiness that comes from a life of appropriate actions accomplished with excellence. Confucius recommends combining principled action with energetic striving, melding Heaven and Earth into a moderate way of living. For the Stoic, one's culminating humanity is to be found in tranquility of mind; for the Christian, in selfless love; for Friedrich Nietzsche, in the effective exercise of one's will to power; for Josiah Royce, in loyalty to a cause; for Jean-Paul Sartre, in authenticity.

This notion of a value as an achievement, as a quality of something made, has been explored metaphysically by pragmatists and process philosophers. For instance, Robert Cummings Neville, influenced by Charles Sanders Pierce and Alfred North Whitehead, argues that all values are achievements of harmony. A value is an integration of diverse elements. The more they are diverse, the more complex the attained harmony; the more

complete or intense their integration, the more simple the harmony. Complexity and simplicity are opposites, however. The challenge is to increase both in a harmonic contrast, making the most value possible in a given circumstance. Neville then works out the implications of this theory for the traditional realms of value, defining truth, beauty, and goodness as kinds of harmonic contrast.

One's personal values are evidenced by the things one finds valuable. Insofar as they are compatible and consistently held, they comprise one's personal value system. Emile Durkheim argues that for people to be organized into communities it is necessary that individual value systems be subordinated to a shared social value system. God, says Durkheim, is that historically fashioned cultural value system projected as an ultimate reality independent of those who hold it. Hence should the societal order break down, its members will feel alienated from God, stripped of their sense of worth: They will suffer a condition of valuelessness, the despair of anomie.

See also AESTHETICS; AXIOLOGY; BEAUTY; VALUE; VALUE THEORY; VALUE, RELIGIOUS; VALUE, SCIENTIFIC

Bibliography

Aristotle. *Nicomachean Ethics,* trans. Martin Ostwald. Englewood Cliffs, N.J.: Library of Liberal Arts, 1962.

Confucius. *The Analects,* trans. Raymond Dawson. New York: Oxford University Press, 1993.

Dewey, John. *Experience and Nature* (1929). New York: Dover Publications. 1958.

Durkheim, Emile. *Suicide: A Study in Sociology,* trans. John A. Spaulding and George Simpson. New York: Free Press, 1966.

Kant, Immanuel. *Grounding for the Metaphysics of Morals* (1785), trans. James W. Ellington. Indianapolis, Ind.: Hackett, 1981.

Neville, Robert Cummings. *Recovery of the Measure: Interpretation and Nature.* Albany: State University of New York Press, 1989.

Perry, Ralph Barton. *Realms of Value: A Critique of Human Civilization.* Cambridge, Mass.: Harvard University Press, 1954.

Scheler, Max. *Formalism in Ethics and Non-formal Ethics of Values: A New Attempt Toward the Foundation of an Ethical Personalism,* trans. Manfred S. Frings and

Roger L. Funk. Evanston, Ill.: Northwestern University Press, 1973.

GEORGE ALLAN

VALUE, RELIGIOUS

Value functions in religion in at least three ways: as the ground of obligation, as the framing values orienting culture and thinking, and as specific moral traditions.

Value as the ground of obligation

One of the chief functions of religion is to explain why people should be moral or spiritual at all, and to cultivate a fundamental human constitution of living under obligation. Religions define people as responsible. Even in vaguely antireligious secular societies such as those of the North Atlantic nations at the beginning of the twenty-first century, this obligation-making function is recognized as "civil religion." When religions fail to function even as civil religions, serious relativism gains currency, as has been analyzed by Robert Bellah (b. 1927) and his collaborators.

Religions represent fundamental human obligatoriness to rest on what they take to be ultimate, as examined by the Comparative Religious Ideas Project in *The Human Condition* and *Ultimate Realities,* as well as by Ninian Smart (1927–2001). Roughly speaking, the religions of East Asia, Confucianism and Daoism, take the ultimate or Dao to be intrinsically good with powers by which human beings can become great. Obligation in the East Asian context has connotations of attunement and participation in cosmic and social orders, and as such is friendly to science in the form of practical technology, ranging from ancient practices of medicine and dietary regulation to modern scientific technology. The main religions of South Asia, including the many forms of Hinduism and Buddhism, consider the ultimate to involve some version of a contrast between what is apparently real in daily life and what is really real. The notion of living under obligation in these religions has connotations of coming to enlightenment about this distinction, observing culture-building obligations regarding daily life on the one hand and religious

fulfillment or actualization obligations regarding what is really real on the other. Because science is regarded as studying the daily world of appearances, South Asian religions can encourage both theoretical and practical science with great enthusiasm: Science is detached from concerns for what is really real, and can stand in little conflict with theological interests.

The West Asian monotheistic religions of Judaism, Christianity, and Islam symbolize the ultimate as a God who creates the world and to whom people are responsible in freedom. In the ancient metaphors, God is like a king who issues decrees that obligate people; to be a person is to stand before God as before a judge. Science often is prized in West Asian religions as a way of understanding God, creation, and the divine norms. This was particularly so in medieval Islam and in European science in the modern world. Nevertheless, the imperatives associated with the moral traditions of these religions can be in conflict with those that seem to arise from scientific understanding. West Asian religions engender conflicts between "conservative" religious values and "modern" scientific ones, conflicts that are more difficult to engender in some other Asian religious traditions.

The common distinction in modern European science between facts and values is of utmost importance regarding the religious function of defining obligation. Early modern science modeled itself on mathematical systems and sought to characterize the world as a set of explainable facts and value-neutral laws. By implication, value was supposed to be derived from human interest or projection, not from the nature of things. Although there have been attempts to define human obligation within a scientific system, as for instance in the modern social contract theories of Thomas Hobbes (1588–1679) or John Locke (1632–1704), the cultural upshot of the modern scientific distinction between fact and value is to say that the ground of obligation cannot be known and is a matter of personal or subjective preference. Hence the existential cultural importance of the question, Why be moral? If a person can choose not to be moral, there seems to be nothing in the nature of things to indicate that this would be a mistake. So long as modern science has a "factual, non-value" philosophy of nature, it tends to undermine the religious grounding of obligation, regardless of which religious conception of ultimacy is operative.

Value as cultural orientation

The function of religions to provide framing or orienting values for cultures has already been mentioned. The East Asian orientation to the ultimate as attunement and participation is associated with positive assessments of the value of life, nature, and human social affiliations. Disease, moral failings, and spiritual perversity are interpreted as mis-attunements, not invincible ignorance or sin. Whereas Confucianism emphasizes positive cultural work to attain attunement, Daoism emphasizes co-ordination with nature. The South Asian emphasis on a contrast between the world of appearances and the really real produces a divided and balanced kind of orientation: attention to the everyday and a search for release from ignorance (at least on the part of those ready for it). The common belief in the West that South Asian religions do not have strong ethical or scientific traditions is false; those religions just do not associate ethics or science with the religious quest except as preliminaries or supports. The West Asian religions, by contrast, strongly prize freedom and responsibility, and take the issues of justice and righteousness to have an ultimate, divine dimension; human moral failure is a religious offence against God. These religions orient people to the world as a positive expression of divine creation, but also sometimes treat nature as providing temptations to sin because people have a direct relation to God (namely, obligation) setting them apart from nature.

The great religious traditions have evolved through centuries, and the shape of their framing value orientations has shifted accordingly. The East Asian religions were deeply impacted for centuries by Buddhism from India. The South Asian religions have interacted with Islam and Christianity. The West Asian religions have exhibited both world-denying forms (as in early Christian asceticism) and world-celebrating forms. The contemporary interactions of the great world religious traditions reflect both their long histories and the fact that each has become a global religion, with cultural embodiments in each of the world's cultures.

Precisely because religions are culturally embodied, the values otherwise resident in their various cultures are powerful within the thinking of the religions themselves. National interests, for instance, can define different expressions of a religion against one another. The wars between Iran and Iraq in the twentieth century, or between the Christian nations of Europe, have involved calling upon the same religious tradition to justify each side against the other, reinforcing different interpretations of what the religion means.

As orientations to science, the framing values of the different religions have the effects already suggested. East Asian religions value science for its practical benefits. South Asian religions promote an objective detachment about science because it is not concerned with ultimate matters in the form of the really real or ultimate religious quests. West Asian religions can promote science as a kind of piety inquiring into the mind and work of God, on the one hand, and fear it as the source of norms different from those of the tradition, especially the norm of objectivity that treats the world as a mere fact without value.

Value as traditions of morality

The great religions have long traditions of moral interpretation reflecting their historical and cultural locations and changes. Within each tradition are often to be found arguments representing many sides of basic issues treating war and peace, patterns of family and social life, proper respect for people in conditions of birth and death, life transitions, and suffering. For instance, most religions have both pacifist and just-war moral traditions.

The development of modern science has affected religious moral traditions in many ways, two of which are the following. Most moral problems are framed by conceptions of natural conditions. For instance, the ancient Greek belief that the homunculus or complete human being is contained in the male sperm made it plausible to condemn as murder any male sexual activity, including masturbation, not reasonably intended for impregnation. This argument, though perhaps not the sentiment, falls away completely when it is realized that a human being requires genes from the mother's egg as well as from the father's sperm. Or to mention an example from the social sciences, distributive justice could not be taken to have a global scope so long as international economics was not understood in systematic ways. For example, during the

Middle Ages, the Christian thinker Thomas Aquinas (c. 1225–1274) could consider distributive justice as limited to a king's domain. But with the advent of empirical global economic theory, the problem of developing theories of global distributive justice is suddenly a forced option for religious moral thinkers.

In addition to the impact of science on moral theory, the development of scientific technologies has led to moral problems that did not exist before. The invention of large bombs makes the old just-war theories, which are based on restraint, obsolete. Biological technologies of cloning, organ transplantation, and genetic manipulation lead to dilemmas that were not previously imagined. Insofar as moral responses to new problems raised by technological advances are to come from developments of the religious moral traditions, the religious values themselves are in process of evolution.

See also NATURAL LAW THEORY

Bibliography

Bellah, Robert. *The Broken Covenant: American Civil Religion in Time of Trial*. New York: Seabury/Crossroad, 1925.

Bellah, Robert; Madsen, Richard; Sullivan, William M.; Swidler, Ann; and Tipton, Steven M. *Habits of the Heart: Individualism and Commitment in American Life*. Berkeley: University of California Press, 1985.

Bellah, Robert; Madsen, Richard; Sullivan, William M.; et al. *The Good Society*. New York: Knopf, 1991.

Neville, Robert Cummings, ed. *Ultimate Realities*. A volume in the *Comparative Religious Ideas Project*. Albany: State University of New York Press, 2001.

Neville, Robert Cummings, ed. *The Human Condition*. A volume in the Comparative Religious Ideas Project. Albany: State University of New York Press, 2001.

Richardson, W. Mark, and Wildman, Wesley J., eds. *Religion and Science: History, Method, Dialogue*. New York: Routledge, 1996.

Smart, Ninian. *Dimensions of the Sacred: An Anatomy of the World's Beliefs*. Berkeley: University of California Press, 1996.

Whitehead, Alfred North. *Science and the Modern World*. New York: Macmillan, 1925.

ROBERT CUMMINGS NEVILLE

VALUE, SCIENTIFIC

Few terms are as subject to confusion as the word *value*. Used as a noun, it denotes objective things, states, processes, or qualities that are approved, desired, or found worthy by at least one valuer (e.g., "At first, money was Scrooge's only value."). Used as a transitive verb, however, it denotes the subjective condition of appreciating, approving, or desiring something (e.g., "I value your smile."). It may refer to what is positively appreciated by a single subject, but also to what is found worthy by groups, who may share purposes, preferences, and norms (e.g., "Middle class values are in flux."). Since different individuals or groups may approve different things, values between valuers may clash, and debates may rage over whether someone else's value is really a value at all. Further, since many different, and sometimes incompatible, types of things may be found worthy even within the same group or by the same individual, there may be internal clashes. Wealth, practical skills, social graces, moral virtue, artistic beauty, intellectual insight, spiritual fulfillment—all may be found worthy in principle, but perhaps not equally worthy in all circumstances. When values conflict, were some not really values after all? The response of this entry will be pluralistic, recognizing many different species of value as entirely genuine, firmly grounded in human goals and purposes, and therefore inescapably interconnected, though often in tension.

The purposes of science, a human activity involving economic consequences, technical skills, social mores, ethical concerns, aesthetic judgments, intellectual thirsts, metaphysical preferences, and religious implications weave themselves into a skein of reinforcements and conflicts within at least three distinguishable domains: the needs of scientific practices, the goals of scientific theorizing, and the norms of culture generally.

Values and scientific practices

Sometimes overlooked are the values that initially draw people into engaging in scientific practices. Today going into science is a way of earning a living. This has not always been so. Before the professionalization of the modern sciences, scientific work required private means or wealthy sponsors. Private economic values, though real, can hardly be basic. Sheer delight in acquiring and using skills for manipulating the natural order would doubtless be more fundamental historically and psychologically. Even deeper would be a lively curiosity about the way things work that leads some people to probe and tinker. And behind the enterprise as a whole loom human needs that might be met if only answers could be found and events controlled. Social goals, such as fame and prestige, or the hope to be first at solving a problem or developing a technique, also figure into the rich mixture of motivating values.

Techniques carry with them their own set of values. A *technique* is a generalized way of doing something. It presents a norm for approximation. A *skill* is the disciplined capacity to carry out a technique, requiring attentiveness and muscular control coordinated to deal with particular circumstances. At a minimum, scientific practices inherently call for the technical values of accuracy and precision, and of approximating, as well as possible, the norm represented by the technique. They demand that the practitioner acquire and maintain personal skills capable of providing regular, repeatable outcomes. Replicability, therefore, emerges from practice as a primary scientific value. And with replication comes counting. Quantifiability, to whatever extent circumstances allow, is a value rooted in the practice even of a lone scientific investigator.

The social character of modern scientific practice underscores and amplifies the importance of these values of accuracy, replicability, and quantification. Others who have acquired the necessary skills must to be able to achieve similar results. They must come up with similar numbers. Further, the practice of scientific publication reinforces the built-in need for such values as precise experimentation and record-keeping, accurate reporting, accountability to colleagues, readiness to submit to community standards, and (in principle at least) even the willingness to welcome the possibility of falsification in the larger interests of scientific reliability.

Where truth-telling, cooperation, and community responsibility are involved, technical values implicit in scientific practices lead inexorably to ethical ones. But not all ethical values relevant to scientific practices are internal to the requirements of technique alone. Scientific values do not generate compassion. Independently acquired moral standards of scientists are needed to forbid some kinds of practices—where humans might be subjected to torture or vivisection, for example—despite the possibility of making interesting discoveries. Such external restraints involve still larger normative conceptions. What is it to be a human person? What sorts of practices are compatible with a person's moral status? Different ages and cultures give different answers, which may ultimately root in religious commitments or metaphysical convictions. The science of anatomy was dependent at one time on systematic grave robbery, since autopsy was forbidden on theological grounds. The practice of vivisection on dogs and cats was supported by the followers of René Descartes (1596–1650), who held that animals, lacking speech and rationality, had no souls and therefore were incapable of feeling pain.

Values and scientific theories

Values motivating the construction of scientific theories certainly include the same curiosity noted in connection with scientific practices, but now the quest is not simply for how things work, but why. What is going on behind the scenes? What makes things happen as they do? Part of what is valued here is enhanced ability to control outcomes by grasping hidden processes. But for many there is also a deep thirst for understanding simply for its own sake.

If understanding offers intrinsic as well as instrumental value, there are other important values prerequisite to achieving this end. These are the intellectual values that make intelligible theory possible, beginning with logical consistency (since inconsistency cancels meaning and makes any account of things impossible), including systematic coherence (since the elements of an account need to hang together if they are to tell a unified story), and—in the case of all empirical sciences—resting on evidential adequacy and comprehensiveness (since if a theory is to be about something, it must take account of as much data about that something as possible). There are potential conflicts among these values, since coherence is more easily achieved if evidence can be limited to exclude inconvenient facts; contrarily, adequacy can have freer run if it ignores norms of consistency and coherence. Still, the job of theorizing must operate within these tensions.

Working within such human limitations, additional values are often important to the construction and later acceptability of theories. Theorists may be inspired in their constructive quests by the aesthetic values, for example, of simplicity and symmetry. Community acceptance may be influenced, as well, since an elegant theory is more to be admired, and may be easier for minds to grasp, than a ramshackle construction. However, since there are many different ways of approaching simplicity and other aesthetic values, as well as multiple interpretations of coherence, and arguably clashing estimates of relevance, it is clear that human judgments of better or worse continue to be indispensable and pervasive in the theoretical sciences.

Undergirding all such judgments are fundamental ethical and religious values. Moral integrity is required in acknowledging available evidence, perhaps despite personal preferences, and following the logic of argument where it leads. Further, acceptance of the value of knowledge as a fundamental good, commitment to the norms of honesty, and reverence for the pursuit of truth, even in limited domains, may lead to (or flow from) unlimited, or ultimate, expressions of value so intense and comprehensive as to be functionally religious.

Values and scientific culture

Cultures shaped by scientific practices and theories reap huge economic values, as technologies developed by unprecedented understanding of how things work provide unprecedented means of control and exploitation of the Earth's wealth. Unfortunately, equally huge economic and environmental disvalues, too, haunt scientific cultures whose grasp of physics and chemistry outstrips understanding in ecology, sociology, and the humanities.

Intellectually, scientific theories offer scientific cultures unprecedentedly adequate and coherent accounts of how things are, as well as how they work. In particular, the grand narrative woven from scientific cosmology, physics, astronomy, geology, evolutionary biology, paleontology, and archaeology provides a new framework for interpreting the universe. Since the powerful hunger for such frameworks has long been fed by older, nonscientific narratives, there is inevitable conflict with comprehensive prescientific alternatives in which maximally intense values have long been invested. Efforts to oppose or nullify evolutionary theory, for example, can be seen as counter-attacks against scientific thinking by disaffected members of scientific culture whose primary religious values are threatened.

The primary scientific values, in contrast, are found in loyalty to a public method—in experimental practices as in theorizing—in which all evidence is honored in principle and conclusions are proportioned to fact and norms of logic. Such values advocate a rational culture, in which all disputes are resolved by dialogue. As noted above, however, unsupplemented scientific values emphasize quantitative over qualitative considerations and are notably lacking in compassion. In the much needed dialogue between science and its culture, scientists are not the only ones who deserve a hearing.

See also VALUE, VALUE THEORY

Bibliography

Barbour, Ian G. *Myths, Models and Paradigms: A Comparative Study in Science and Religion*. New York: Harper, 1974.

Bronowski, Jacob. *Science and Human Values,* Rev. edition. New York: Harper, 1965.

Burtt, Edwin Arthur. *The Metaphysical Foundations of Modern Physical Science,* Rev. edition, Garden City, N.Y.: Doubleday, 1954.

Eisley, Loren. *Darwin's Century: Evolution and the Men Who Discovered It*. Garden City, N.Y.: Doubleday, 1958.

Ferré, Frederick. *Knowing and Value: Toward A Constructive Postmodern Epistemology*. Albany: State University of New York Press, 1998.

Kaplan, Abraham. *The Conduct of Inquiry: Methodology for Behavioral Science*. San Francisco: Chandler, 1964.

Kuhn, Thomas S. *The Structure of Scientific Revolutions,* 2nd edition. Chicago: University of Chicago Press, 1970.

Medawar, Peter. *The Limits of Science*. New York: Oxford University Press, 1988.

Monod, Jacques. *Chance and Necessity: An Essay on the Natural Philosophy of Modern Biology,* trans. Austryn Wainhouse. New York: Vintage, 1972.

Scheffler, Israel. *Science and Subjectivity*. Indianapolis, Ind.: Bobbs-Merrill, 1967.

Toulmin, Stephen. *Foresight and Understanding: An Enquiry into the Aims of Science.* Bloomington: Indiana University Press, 1961.

Whitehead, Alfred North. *Science and the Modern World.* New York: Free Press, 1925.

FREDERICK FERRÉ

VALUES, ORIGINS OF

See RELIGION AND VALUES, ORIGINS OF

VALUE, VALUE THEORY

A value theory indicates the characteristics common to values of all kinds, classifies them, and clarifies the meaning of value-propositions. The kinds or "realms" of value are always said to include moral and aesthetic values, but other kinds are usually mentioned also. For instance, Paul Taylor (1925–) lists six others: intellectual, religious, economic, political, legal, and customary realms of value. All value theorists claim that even though there are striking or important differences among kinds of value, their similarities are more fundamental. As Ralph Barton Perry (1876–1957) puts it, value theory pulls concerns "dispersed among the several philosophical and social sciences" into a single "comprehensive inquiry" in which these various pursuits are "unified and distinguished," so as "to bring to light the underlying principles common to these sciences, and then to employ this principle for the purpose of arbitrating between them" (p. 9).

Value theory is a nineteenth-century development in Western philosophy. Its initiator is usually said to be the German philosopher Rudolf Hermann Lotze (1817–1881) who sharply distinguished *fact* and *value,* arguing that fact was the province of the natural sciences, whereas the humanities concerned themselves with value. Value theorists after Lotze can be grouped into two strands: those who claim that values are discovered or created solely by minds, and those who claim that values are empirical features of things or actions. Contemporary analytic philosophers belong to both strands, differing from their predecessors by limiting their investigations to the language used in asserting or recommending a value. Some metaphysicians reject this limitation and offer grounds for thinking that values are ontologically fundamental.

Strand one: conceptual

Franz Brentano (1838–1917) argues that values are rooted in human emotions, in the contrast between favorable (love) and unfavorable (hate) intentional attitudes toward objects and events. His student Alexius Meinong (1853–1920) elaborates this notion by identifying four aspects of any value experience: a *value subject* who experiences, a *value feeling* or emotion, a *value object* toward which this feeling is directed, and an *existence judgment* that ascribes the feeling's cause to the object. For example, a person watching a sunset has a positive emotional feeling, which the person claims is because of the sunset. Meinong argues that a value emotion is neither independent of publicly verifiable (scientific) fact, as Lotze claims, nor reducible to fact: It is a subjective feeling that can be judged to be reasonable or not by reference to the relevant facts.

J. N. Findlay (1903–1987) offers a mid-twentieth century version of the Brentano-Meinong view. Consciousness, he argues, has an "intentional" structure: It is always of an object. Belief is unconditional assent to the reality of the object of an intention; action is an endeavor to bring an intended object into existence. For an action to be sustained over the time needed to achieve this goal, the feelings of assent and endeavor that accompany it need to persist. A person's values are those feelings that function as "the relatively fixed points of the compass" by means of which one's "choices are guided" (p. 204). The "firmament" of the values by which a person is guided is "rationalized" by abstracting from the particularities of the several values and framing general integrative guiding principles that are detached from the urgency of particular pragmatic interests. The apotheosis of this generalization process is the formulation of "absolute values," norms governing both individual and collective endeavors.

Religious values, Findlay argues, are absolute values extended beyond those associated with human beliefs and efforts, having to do with intentional structures that are holy—in the sense of strange and numinous—because radically inclusive. They are radically impersonal, however, expressing "the pattern of a detached, suprapersonal, norm-setting *mind*" (p. 399). The genius of Judaism, Christianity, and Islam is that they recognize the need people have for this impersonal absolute to be embodied in a supreme religious object that has some direct connection with common everyday realities; the absolute value must be incarnate in history, in specific acts or persons.

Strand two: empirical

Feelings or intentions are unobservable mental states. Those who want value theory to be a scientific enterprise therefore turn from feelings to "interests," from intentions to "behaviors," from introspection to "motor-affective responses." C. I. Lewis (1883–1964), for instance, insists that evaluations are a form of empirical knowledge. Their truth or falsity, is determined in exactly the same way as the truth or falsity of nay other kind of empirical knowledge is justified. Directly experienced satisfactions have "intrinsic" value, but no object can have intrinsic value because its value consists not in what it is in itself but rather in the possibility of its leading to some realization of directly experienced value. The object need not in fact lead to such experiences, but only have the potentiality for doing so: A Paleozoic sunset had objective value even if no human being was actually there to enjoy it. Where an intrinsic value experience is afforded by the presentation of an object, that object has inherent extrinsic value. Where one object is a means by which to come into the presence of another object that has inherent value, the first object has "instrumental" and possibly "contributory" extrinsic value.

Ralph Barton Perry makes this notion of intrinsic value central. Any object acquires value by becoming the target of some interest: "that which is an object of an interest is *eo ipso* invested with value" (p. 115)—"x is valuable = interest is taken in x" (p. 116). Perry distinguishes between a "value preference" (a subject has more interest in x than in y) from a "judgment of comparative value" (a subject asserts that x is better than y). The latter involves standards of measurement and so, unlike a value preference, is open to correction. Love is a favorable interest in the satisfaction of a second interest, that of another person. So the highest possible value is that of an all-loving will. Such love

could not be the interest of a single person, however. Perry's alternative to Lewis's religious absolute is a "federation," a multiplicity of independent equally valued persons, united by their devotion to the same value ideal, expressed through reciprocal acts of love.

John Dewey (1859–1952) rejects the distinction between value judgments and factual judgments. Valuation takes place whenever a problematic situation exists, whenever an expected enjoyment is blocked. Some inquiry needs to be undertaken in order to resolve the problem, to reshape things in the light of an ideal about how things might be such that the desired enjoyment might be experienced. A value is not an enjoyment but an interest in attaining one, and hence involves a proposal for how to do so. Values can therefore be appraised—critiqued, ranked, and revised—with respect both to how effective they are as guides for attaining the enjoyment sought and to how satisfying that result is. Values are an important aspect of the natural sciences, since hypothesis formation in scientific inquiry is an instance of valuation and its critique. Dewey argues that progress in the improvement of the human condition is impeded by the traditional insistence that actions guided by aesthetic, moral, political, and religious values are timeless absolutes grasped emotionally, matters of tradition or feeling or faith—values isolated from scientific values, and hence from "intelligent" meliorative rational control.

The language of valuation

Twentieth-century Western philosophy has been dominated by linguistic concerns, and so value theory for many thinkers has been limited to a consideration of value-propositions: What the nature of assertions of value is and whether or how values are justified. These approaches can be grouped into the same two strands as earlier value theories: those primarily conceptual and those primarily empirical.

One kind of mind-centered approach claims that value-propositions make no reference to facts and so are neither true nor false. Charles Stevenson (1908–1979) calls such propositions "emotive." A person who asserts that "this is a beautiful sculpture" says nothing about the sculpture. He only expresses his positive feelings toward it: "this sculpture, wow!"

A quite different approach, with G. H. von Wright (1916–) as a key figure, is to explicate a "logic of preference," to assess value-assertions in terms of a logical system governed by syntactic and semantic rules. For instance, "possible worlds" might be ranked by means of an "index of merit." Next a proposition could be assigned a "generic value," understood as the average of the merit rankings of the worlds in which its value is meaningful. Then proposition x would be "rationally preferable" to proposition y if its generic value is higher than y's. Game theory and decision theory are two related developments of this logico-mathematical approach to valuation.

Those analysts of the language of values who stand in an empiricist tradition draw from informal rather than formal logic, with the later writings of Ludwig Wittgenstein (1889–1951) often key. Paul Taylor's work is illustrative. He distinguishes normative discourse from scientific discourse, arguing that they are governed by differing "canons of reasoning." Taylor is particularly concerned with the way in which value judgments, the "first-order" content of normative discourse, can be justified. To "verify" a value judgment is to appeal to established standards or rules of evaluation. If these are questioned, one must "validate" them by appealing to higher-order standards or rules, and ultimately by appealing to those principles that determine a "value system." To take a "point of view" is to commit oneself to following a certain set of rules of relevance in deciding which value system to accept as governing one's value judgments. There are as many points of view as there are kinds of value systems: for instance, a moral point of view and an aesthetic point of view. A "way of life" is the set of value systems expressing all one's points of view, arranged in some integrative hierarchical manner. If a person's value system is questioned, it is "vindicated" by appeal to one's way of life. When a way of life is questioned, the only justifying appeal is to "rational choice": showing that one's value commitment has been arrived at by a deliberative process that is free, enlightened, and impartial.

Metaphysical value theories

Dewey argues that value theory is a response to the expulsion of teleology from nature: the claim of modern science that facts are adequately explicated in terms of efficient causes, without recourse to final causes or purposes. Value theories of almost any sort can be challenged by attacking the metaphysical presuppositions of modern science, arguing that the natural order is in some sense purposive, that ends and ideals are features of all natural processes, and that to exist is to have and to be making value.

A contemporary example of such a value-based metaphysics is found is the work of Frederick Ferré (1933–). He argues that "the process of an entity's coming to be something definite" involves "the generation of intrinsic value for the entity concerned" (1996, p. 357). The basic factual entities of the universe are self-fashioning processes involving the integration of diverse elements into a definite unity, a harmony. To achieve any sort of harmony is to generate beauty, so for Ferré a cosmos composed of beauty-fashioning entities is "inherently kalogenic." Given such a universe, an ethic obviously follows in which not only persons but other organisms, indeed entities of every sort, should be treasured for the value achieved in their existing and for their relevance to possibilities for future value realization.

William Desmond (1951–) takes a different approach, recognizing the diversity of value-creators but insisting that their power to create value and their aspiration to do so depends on recognizing the origin of what-is in a transcendent power. Humans live in the *metaxu,* between Being and nothing at all—astonished that they exist, affirming that it is good they and others exist, dwelling together. Insofar as humans are "mindful" of these wondrous facts, they will be aware that there is an origin of their existing, that their lives are a gift, a good that need not have been but nonetheless has been freely given them. Desmond calls this overflowing good of the originative power "agapeic"— a good given for the other's good, a freedom that frees others rather than subordinating them, a power that empowers others to express their powers in a giving such that the good of others and the common good are enhanced. Desmond therefore argues that the ideal of human moral development is "agapeic service"—practicing a self-surpassing ethics of generosity in response to God's freely given infinitely valuable gift of life.

See also AESTHETICS; BEAUTY; VALUE; VALUE, RELIGIOUS; VALUE, SCIENTIFIC

Bibliography

Brentano, Franz. *The Origin of Our Knowledge of Right and Wrong* (1889), trans. Roderick M. Chisholm and Elizabeth H. Schneewind. London: Routledge and Kegan Paul, 1968.

Desmond, William. *Being and the Between*. Albany: State University of New York Press, 1995.

Desmond, William. *Ethics and the Between*. Albany: State University of New York Press, 2001.

Dewey, John. *Theory of Valuation: International Encyclopedia of Unified Sciences*. Chicago: University of Chicago Press, 1939. Reprinted in *John Dewey: The Later Works, 1925–1953*, Vol. 16: *John Dewey: The Later Works: 1934–1952*, ed. Jo Ann Boydston. Carbondale and Edwardsville: Southern Illinois University Press, 1988.

Ferré, Frederick. *Being and Value: Toward a Constructive Postmodern Metaphysics*. Albany: State University of New York Press, 1996.

Ferré, Frederick. *Knowing and Value: Toward a Constructive Postmodern Epistemology*. Albany: State University of New York Press, 1998.

Ferré, Frederick. *Living and Value: Toward a Constructive Postmodern Ethics*. Albany: State University of New York Press, 2001.

Findlay, J. N. *Values and Intentions: A Study in Value-Theory and Philosophy of Mind*. New York: Macmillan, 1961.

Lewis, Clarence Irving. *An Analysis of Knowledge and Valuation*. La Salle, Ill.: Open Court, 1946.

Lotze, Hermann. *Microcosmus: An Essay Concerning Man and His Relation to the World* (1857–1864), trans. Elizabeth Hamilton and E. E. Constance Jones. Edinburgh, UK: T&T Clark, 1885. Reprinted, Freeport N.Y.: Books for Libraries Press, 1971.

Meinong, Alexius. *Psychologisch-ethische Untersuchungen zur Werttheorie*. Graz, Austria: Leuschner u. Lubensky, 1894.

Perry, Ralph Barton. *General Theory of Value: Its Meaning and Basic Principles Construed in Terms of Interest*. New York: Longmans Green, 1926. Reprinted, Cambridge, Mass.: Harvard University Press, 1950.

Rescher, Nicholas. *Introduction to Value Theory*. Englewood Cliffs, N.J.: Prentice-Hall, 1969.

Stevenson, Charles L. *Ethics and Language*. New Haven, N.J.: Yale University Press, 1944.

Taylor, Paul W. *Normative Discourse*. Englewood Cliffs, N.J.: Prentice-Hall, 1961.

von Wright, G. H. *The Logic of Preference: An Essay*. Edinburgh, UK: Edinburgh University Press, 1963.

Wittgenstein, Ludwig. *Philosophical Investigations*. New York: Macmillan, 1953.

GEORGE ALLAN

VIRTUAL REALITY

Virtual reality is that part of human experience that does not happen in a physical space. Reading a book creates virtual reality, as does participating in an online chat or a telephone conference. These experiences are called "virtual" because the people involved are not actually in the story of the book or in a conference room with other people but physically separated; nonetheless, they participate in the community through thought and imagination and, in some cases, through their eyes, via the monitors, and fingers, via the keyboards.

The term *virtual reality* came into wide use during the 1990s with the increasing popularity of the Internet, and the concept of virtual reality led to many of the metaphors used to describe Internet interactions. A chat room, for example, is not a room, and it does not even have a physical location; it consists entirely of the people who are "meeting" there and interact. They do not meet, of course, but happen to be at their personal computers at the same moment in time. They also do not chat or talk but write messages that appear on others peoples' screens. Keyed graphics called *smileys,* such as :-) and ;-}, convey emotional content. Sometimes people wander off into separate "rooms" to be more "intimate" with a few others instead of sharing their thoughts in "public." These and many other metaphors are used for two reasons. First, humans are physical entities, and, from an evolutionary perspective, everything they did in the past happened in physical time and space. Language arising from this background is naturally physical in its description of human interaction. But once these metaphors are used they also become a selling point for virtual reality because they suggest that virtual reality allows for complete personal interactions.

Despite their obvious popularity, chat rooms and other virtual reality entities raise serious questions. One of the most obvious is the fact that among virtual reality communities there are several churches and prayer groups. The question is, can such spiritual virtual reality communities actually replace mortar and brick churches? Cybercommunities lack the physical space that bodies, together in liturgy and practice, create. Gender, race, and age have no defined roles. In virtual reality, people can lie about themselves and construct different identities. In addition, virtual reality communities give people the freedom to project all their wishes and desires about a "real" community onto the cyber-community because there is no way to know who is there and if the people are actually likeable. But is this community? And where does this wish for clean and perfect relationships come from when everyone knows that real-world relationships are flawed, stressful, full of ambiguities, yet so much fun. Because there is no physical commitment or connection in cyberspace, web communities may be ultimately indifferent and meaningless to the people involved.

The understanding of humankind in recent years has changed from a dualistic, cognition-oriented understanding toward an embodied and social one. The intelligence of humans is not the main characteristic of the species—it is much more the human capacity to connect and to survive in any given environment. Virtual reality, however, is a direct result of the assumption that embodiment and shared physical space are not important for community building because the body is not part of what turns a human into an individual. But if cognitive science theories are correct, then virtual reality spaces lack the required physicality, and relationships in them are incomplete.

See also INFORMATION TECHNOLOGY

Bibliography

Gray, Chris Hables; Figueroa-Sarriera, Heidi J.; and Mentor, Steven; eds. *The Cyborg Handbook*. New York: Routledge, 1996.

Paul, Gregory, and Cox, Earl D. *Beyond Humanity: Cyberevolution and Future Minds*. Rockland, Mass.: Charles River Media, 1996.

Turkle, Sherry. *Life on the Screen*. New York: Simon & Schuster, 1995.

ANNE FOERST

WAVE-PARTICLE DUALITY

The quantum description of matter ascribes a wavelike aspect to particles of matter. In some circumstances, for example in the photoelectric effect, particles behave primarily as if they are mass points. In other circumstances, they display diffraction and interference as if they are waves. The quantum wavelength of a particle is inversely proportional to its mass, and an object's wavelike aspects will be significant whenever its quantum wavelength is larger than its physical size. Therefore, large objects like cars have imperceptible wavelike attributes but subatomic particles, such as neutrons, have significant wavelike aspects. It is more accurate to view the quantum wave aspect as being a wave of information (like a crime wave) or probability than an undulatory quality.

See also PARADOX; PHYSICS QUANTUM

Bibliography

Folse, Henry. *The Philosophy of Niels Bohr: The Framework of Complementarity*. Amsterdam: North Holland. 1985.

Herbert, Nick. *Quantum Reality: Beyond the New Physics*. London: Rider, 1985.

JOHN D. BARROW

WHITEHEAD, ALFRED NORTH

Alfred North Whitehead (1861–1947) believed that the future course of world history depends upon people's decisions as to the relation between science and religion. In fact, the force of religious intuitions and the force of scientific endeavors are the two most powerful forces in history. Whitehead's solution to conflicts between science and religion was to suggest modifications in both science and religion, as each has been traditionally understood, so that an inclusive alternative worldview might be constructed. He turned to speculative philosophy for this constructive task. Whitehead proposed that philosophy attains its chief importance by fusing religion and science into one rational scheme of thought.

Life and influences

Whitehead was born in Ramsgate, England and grew up the son of an Anglican clergyman. His keen intelligence was evident early in life, and, when offered college scholarships to pursue either mathematics or classic literature, he chose the former despite what would be a lifelong fondness for the latter. After a stint as student at Trinity College of Cambridge, England, Whitehead continued on at the school for twenty-five years as fellow and professor. He also took up rigorous theological studies for nearly a decade. As a result of his study, however, he decided to affirm atheism. Whitehead was also elected a fellow of the Royal Society due to his prowess in universal algebra. During this time, he coauthored with fellow philosopher and mathematician Bertrand Russell (1872–1970) one of the most important philosophy books in twentieth century, *Principia Mathematica* (1910–1913).

Following his stint at Trinity, Whitehead moved to London and held positions teaching mathematics at University College London and London's Imperial College of Science and Technology. He served in a number of administrative capacities, including Dean of the Faculty of Science. Whitehead's interest in science resulted in the publication of *Principles of Natural Knowledge* (1919), *The Concept of Nature* (1920), and *The Principle of Relativity* (1922). The insights gained from academic supervision comprise the heart of his influential work pertaining to educational philosophy: *The Organisation of Thoughts* (1917) and *The Aims of Education* (1929).

In 1924, at age sixty-three, Whitehead left London for the United States to teach philosophy at Harvard University in Massachusetts. Whitehead was his most productive as a writer during his Harvard years, and the work he produced provides the basis for how he believed science, religion, and philosophy ought to relate. He wrote his most influential books while at Harvard, including *Science and the Modern World* (1925), *Religion in the Making* (1926), *Adventures of Ideas* (1933), and his magnum opus *Process and Reality* (1929).

Philosophy

Whitehead may have best summarized his overall view of the relationship between science and religion when he wrote, "you cannot shelter theology from science, or science from theology; nor can you shelter either one from metaphysics, or metaphysics from either one of them. There is no shortcut to the truth" (1926, p. 79). The convictions expressed in this statement prompted Whitehead to frame a coherent and logical system of general ideas in terms of which every item of experience could be interpreted. He was insistent that an adequate metaphysics or worldview must account for whatever is found in actual practice, including scientific and religious practice.

Although Whitehead had chosen atheism earlier in life, his stance toward God and religion changed as he attempted to construct an adequate worldview to account for science and religion. Like Aristotle twenty-three hundred years earlier, Whitehead came to postulate the existence of God because he found that the general character of reality requires an all-embracing, purposive, and loving deity.

Whitehead departed from Aristotle, however, in his primary insight that actual existence involves a process of becoming, rather than fixed states of being. Evidently influenced by quantum physics and Buddhism, Whitehead considered these basic units of actual existence to be events or moments of experience rather than bits of unalterable matter. Although the specific makeup of these events differs radically, every event exemplifies the same metaphysical principles.

The process of existence, argues Whitehead, is twofold: It is the becoming of events and the transition from event to event. Each event, occasion of experience, or *actual entity* (he uses these terms interchangeably) exists first as a subject and then as an object. Present events (subjects) are influenced by prior events (objects), and these events, when completed, become objects that exert influence upon subsequent subjects. An *enduring individual* in this process of becoming is a personally ordered chain of events, rather than a single, self-contained mind.

The process of life in which all things flow is a person's first vague intuition. And "the elucidation of meaning involved in the phrase 'all things flow,'" Whitehead argues in light of this intuition, "is one chief task of metaphysics" (1978 [1929], p. 208). Because he considers the flow of events to be primary, Whitehead's thought is often identified as *process philosophy*. This insight corresponds well with the general theory of evolution.

To say, however, that "all things flow" does not mean that all features of reality are changing. The principles of the universe, for instance, are eternally binding and, therefore, never change. Some aspects of God are also unchanging. These principles and aspects, however, are not actual events.

Not only are events the fundamental units of life, each essentially relates to others. When explaining how moments relate, Whitehead spoke of internal and external relatedness. Internal relations develop as each event arises out of its inclusion of prior events. The event begins with a "open window" to the totality of the past. Once the influence from the past has entered, the window closes and the entity forms itself in response to past influences. Whitehead calls this drawing upon the past via relations a *prehension,* and in this activity the production of novel togetherness occurs. The relations that an event has with past events are its internal relations; the relations it will have with events to come are its external relations. In short, interdependence is primary, because all events relate in community.

Whitehead's organismic philosophy of life, which supposes that all events are experiential and relational, presupposes that all events perceive. Perception is not limited to receiving sensory data by means of sensory organs (i.e., eyes, ears, nose). The perception that occurs most frequently is nonsensory, because most events in the universe are not sensory organs. This emphasis upon nonsensory perception, thought Whitehead, serves as a primary basis for overcoming mechanistic and materialistic tendencies in modern science.

The relatedness of all things does not mean that all events are entirely determined by others. Whitehead speculates that all events possess a degree of freedom such that none can be entirely controlled by others. The fact that each moment of experience is essentially free entails that neither the atoms below nor the gods above entirely determine the state of any particular event.

By affirming the necessary freedom of every individual, Whitehead's thought provides a basis for solving the age-old problem of evil. Free creatures, not God, are responsible for the occurrence of genuine evil. God is not culpable for failing to prevent evil because God cannot withdraw, override, or veto the freedom expressed when creatures act in evil ways.

Role of God

Although Whitehead came to speculate that God exists, the vision of God he offers, while congenial with much in sacred scriptures, differs from the visions most philosophers offer. For instance, Whitehead argues that "the divine element in the world is to be conceived as a persuasive agency and not as a coercive agency" (1968 [1933], p. 213). God's inability to coerce, when coercion is defined as *completely* controlling the actions of others, is not a result of divine self-limitation or a moral inability; non-coercion is an eternal law pertaining to all life.

In addition to never controlling individuals entirely, the persuasive God that Whitehead envisions both influences and is influenced by the world. God "adds himself to the actual ground from which every creative act takes its rise," speculates Whitehead, so that "the world lives by its incarnation of God in itself" (1996 [1926], p. 156). Then, "by the reason of the relativity of all things,

there is a reaction of the world on God" (1978 [1929], p. 345). Whitehead's explanation of God's role in this reciprocal relation is oft-quoted: "God is the great companion—the fellow-sufferer who understands" (1978 [1929], p. 351).

The essential relatedness of all actualities implies that God has never been wholly isolated. God relates everlastingly, which implies that some realm of finite actualities or another has always existed (1968 [1933], p. 168). Or, as Whitehead argues, God did not dispose "a wholly derivative world" *ex nihilo* (1968 [1933], p. 216). This relational hypothesis provides a framework for affirming consistently that God expresses love in relationship, while also denying that God ever creates through absolute force. Both notions support a process answer to the problem of evil.

Whitehead suggested a novel scheme for how God influences the world. God offers an initial aim comprised of various possibilities for action to each emerging event. This aim is relevant to each event's particular situation. From the various possibilities in this aim, the event freely chooses what it will be. The fact that God provides an aim to all events is one way Whitehead can speak of God as creator. He did not believe that God wholly decides each aim's contents, however, each aim also contains influences derived from the activity of past creatures. God's persuasive activity includes what Whitehead calls the "graded relevance" of each aim's possibilities. Among all possibilities in an aim, one may be the ideal; the others are graded as to their relevance to that ideal. This scheme provides a basis for affirming that God creatively acts upon both simple and complex individuals: from atoms, genes, cells, and molecules to mice, whales, apes, and humans.

In offering an initial aim to every event, God acts, according to Whitehead, as the "goad towards novelty" (1978 [1929], p. 88). God offers new possibilities for more intense love and beauty when accounting for the past in light of the future. Because these possibilities are offered, a vision of a better way—religiously, scientifically, and aesthetically—is available. Without divine influence, says Whitehead, "the course of creation would be a dead level of ineffectiveness, with all balance and intensity progressively excluded by the cross currents of incompatibility" (1978 [1929], p. 247). Whitehead's belief that God interacts lovingly with creation also presents a crucial underpinning for an adequate ecological ethic.

See also ARISTOTLE; BUDDHISM; DIVINE ACTION; EVIL AND SUFFERING; EVOLUTION; FREEDOM; FREE PROCESS DEFENSE; METAPHYSICS; PANENTHEISM; PHYSICS, QUANTUM; PROCESS THOUGHT

Bibliography

Barbour, Ian G. *Religion in an Age of Science: The Gifford Lectures 1989–91*, Vol. 1. San Francisco: Harper, 1990.

Cobb, John B., Jr. "Alfred North Whitehead." In *Founders of Constructive Postmodern Philosophy: Peirce, James, Bergson, Whitehead, and Hartshorne.* Albany: State University of New York Press, 1993.

Cobb, John B., Jr. *A Christian Natural Theology: Based on the Philosophy of Alfred North Whitehead.* Philadelphia: Westminster, 1965.

Griffin, David Ray. *The Reenchantment of Science: Postmodern Proposals.* Albany: State University of New York Press, 1988.

Griffin, David Ray. *Religion and Scientific Naturalism: Overcoming the Conflicts.* Albany: State University Press of New York, 2000.

Hartshorne, Charles. "Whitehead's Idea of God." *The Philosophy of Alfred North Whitehead,* 2nd edition, ed. Paul Arthur Schilpp. New York: Tudor, 1951.

Jungerman, John A. *World in Process: Creativity and Interconnection in the New Physics.* Albany: State University of New York Press, 2000.

Kraus, Elizabeth M., and Neville, Robert Cummings. *The Metaphysics of Experience: A Companion to Whitehead's Process and Reality.* New York: Fordham University Press, 1998.

McDaniel, Jay B. *Of God and Pelicans: A Theology of Reverence for Life.* Louisville, Ky.: Westminster John Knox, 1989.

Whitehead, Alfred North. *Science and the Modern World.* New York: Macmillan, 1925.

Whitehead, Alfred North. *Religion in the Making* (1926). New York: Macmillan and Fordham University Press, 1996.

Whitehead, Alfred North. *Process and Reality: An Essay in Cosmology* (1929), corrected edition, ed. David Ray Griffin and Donald W. Sherburne. New York: Free Press, 1978.

Whitehead, Alfred North. *Adventures of Ideas* (1933). New York: Free Press, 1968.

THOMAS JAY OORD

WOMANIST THEOLOGY

Alice Walker (b. 1944) coined the term *womanist* in her 1983 book *In Search of Our Mothers' Gardens.* Womanist theology is a form of feminism that focuses on the specific concerns of women of African heritage. It centers around their relationship with God, their commitment to the moral flourishing of their communities, and their past, present, and future struggles for justice. The cultural contexts for womanist reflections are diverse. Although the term originates in the African diaspora, others find the emphasis on communal well-being and empowerment relevant to their own cultural contexts. Although womanism situates itself within a theological context, forays into intersections of science and religion tend to focus on issues of healthcare within African American communities, HIV/AIDS, the effects of biogenetic engineering on the poor, environmental racism, and shifting paradigms of dominance and control emerging from new views of the universe.

See also ECOFEMINISM; FEMINISMS AND SCIENCE; FEMINIST THEOLOGY

Bibliography

Holmes, Barbara A. *Race and Cosmology: An Invitation to View the World Differently.* Harrisburg, Pa.: Trinity Press International, 2002.

Townes, Emilie. *Breaking the Fine Rain of Death: African American Health Issues and a Womanist Ethic of Care.* New York: Continuum Press, 1998.

Walker, Alice. *In Search of Our Mothers' Gardens: Womanist Prose.* New York: Harcourt, 1983.

BARBARA A. HOLMES

WORLDVIEW

There is a fundamental ambiguity in the way the concept of worldview is used within the science/religion discussion. On the one hand, scholars talk about the *scientific worldview,* by which they mean the picture of the universe that emerges if one brings together the different theories of physics, astronomy, biology, sociology, and so on into a systematic whole. On the other hand, some scholars make statements about the imbeddedness of science *within* a particular worldview, for example, within feminism, Christianity, Islam, or naturalism.

If the concept is understood in the second way, it follows that science alone can never provide a worldview, even though science can, of course, contribute to the formation or revision of a worldview. The reason why is that this conception presupposes that science lacks certain features that characterize a worldview. It is a matter of dispute what these features are exactly, but two elements that science seems to lack are values and metaphysics. A worldview in this sense is typically taken to explain who human beings really are, what the world is ultimately like, and what people should do to live a satisfying life. It gives direction and meaning to life and thus provides people with values. But science offers facts and not values. Therefore, it does not qualify as a worldview. Moreover, no scientific discipline can show whether the physical universe is all that there is. If scientists make such an assertion they make a metaphysical rather than a scientific statement.

Theism and naturalism, on the other hand, offer an answer to this kind of question. Theism says that reality consists of God and all that God has made. Naturalism holds that reality consists of nothing but matter in motion. Therefore, theism and naturalism, not science, are worldviews. Some advocates of scientism question this view, arguing that the boundaries of science can be expanded in such a way that it can offer both values and metaphysics. However, this view is highly controversial, lacking scientific consensus. It is therefore better to refer to it as a *scientistic* rather than a *scientific* worldview.

A worldview need not be well-developed or explicit; the worldviews of most people remain simply sets of background assumptions of which they are not fully aware. The function of such a worldview is primarily to help people to deal with their existential concerns, that is, their questions about who they are, why they exist, what the meaning of their life is, and what stance they should take toward the experience of death, suffering, guilt, love, forgiveness, and so forth. A worldview is thus the constellation of beliefs and values that (consciously or unconsciously) guide people in their attempt to deal with their existential concerns. A religious worldview affirms that people could only adequately deal with their existential concerns if they let their lives be transformed or enlightened by God or a divine reality, whereas a secular worldview denies this.

See also PARADIGMS; SCIENTISM; VALUE

Bibliography

Herrmann, Eberhard. *Scientific Theory and Religious Belief: An Essay on the Rationality of Views of Life.* Kampen, Netherlands: Kok Pharos, 1995.

Smart, Ninian. *Worldviews: Crosscultural Explorations of Human Beliefs,* 2nd edition. Englewood Cliffs, N.J.: Prentice Hall, 1995.

Stenmark, Mikael. *Rationality in Science, Religion and Everyday Life: A Critical Evaluation of Four Models of Rationality.* South Bend, Ind.: University of Notre Dame Press, 1995.

MIKAEL STENMARK

XENOTRANSPLANTATION

Xenotransplantation is transplanting an organ or tissue from one species to another. A shortage of human body parts available for *allotransplantation* (transplantation to other humans) has increased interest in this alternative. Since the 1960s, attempts at xenotransplantation have been made using chimpanzee kidneys, baboon hearts and livers, and pig hearts and livers. Present efforts focus on pigs rather than primates, as pigs reach maturity and reproduce quicker than primates, and pigs are not an endangered species. While pig heart valves are used successfully to repair human hearts, xenotransplantation remains in limited clinical trials. The genetic modification of animals has the potential for reducing human rejection and the danger of transmitting dangerous pathogenic agents. Some researchers have suggested that the transplantation of pig organs to humans may be possible within five years.

How religions evaluate the morality of xenotransplantation hinges on views of animals in the created order. For example, Christianity, particularly Roman Catholicism, believes that xenotransplantation can be justified in certain circumstances since humans have a higher dignity than the animals that serve them. Moral limits, however, preclude transplantation of the encephalon and gonads that are linked indissolubly by their function with the personal identity of humans.

See also ANIMAL RIGHTS; BIOTECHNOLOGY; CHRISTIANITY, ROMAN CATHOLIC, ISSUES IN SCIENCE AND RELIGION; CLONING

Bibliography

Clark, M. A. "This Little Piggy Went to Market: The Xenotransplantation and Xenozoonose Debate." *Journal of Law, Medicine, and Ethics* 27 (1999): 137–152.

Cooper, David K. C., and Lanza, Robert P. *Xeno: The Promise of Transplanting Animal Organs into Humans.* New York: Oxford University Press, 2000.

Hanson, M. J. "The Seductive Sirens of Medical Transplantation: The Case of Xenotransplantation." *Hastings Center Report* 25 (1995): 5–6.

International Xenotransplantation Society. Available from http://www.ixa2001chicago.com.

McCarthy, Charles R. "A New Look at Animal-to-Human Organ Transplantation." *Kennedy Institute of Ethics Journal* 6, no. 2 (1996): 183–188.

Pontifical Academy for Life. "Prospects for Xenotransplantation: Scientific Aspects and Ethical Considerations." September 26, 2001. Available from http://www.vatican.va/roman_curia/pontifical_academies/acdlife/.

WHO Electronic Discussion Group (EDG) on International Xenotranplantation Policy Considerations. Available from http://www.who.int/emc/diseases/zoo/meetings/xenodg.html.

DONNA M. MCKENZIE

ZOOLOGY

See LIFE SCIENCES

ANNOTATED BIBLIOGRAPHY

About the Annotated Bibliography

This Annotated Bibliography is intended as a starting point for readers who want to explore some of the themes described in the entries in more detail, or who would like to know more about the religion and science dialogue in general. Without claiming to be exhaustive, the Bibliography contains works that are generally regarded as having had a significant impact on the dialogue. The first three sections contain general introductory, methodological, and historical works. Sections four through twelve contain works on specific scientific and/or religious issues. Most works contain extensive bibliographies which will aid further research.

1. GENERAL INTRODUCTIONS AND TEXTBOOKS

Barbour, Ian G. *Religion and Science: Historical and Contemporary Issues*. San Francisco: HarperSanFrancisco, 1997.

The classic comprehensive introduction to the field. This revised and expanded edition of Barbour's Gifford Lectures deals with most aspects of the modern science and religion dialogue, and offers many reading suggestions. It also contains the famous fourfold typology of relating science and religion: conflict, independence, dialogue, and integration. Though it is mainly intended as an overview of the field, Barbour defends a "theology of nature" position coupled with a cautious use of process philosophy.

Clayton, Philip. *God and Contemporary Science*. Edinburgh: Edinburgh University Press, 1997.

This study in philosophical theology deals with contemporary scientific theories and their ramifications for theological views of God and divine agency. Clayton argues that naturalism can be countered by relating science and religion in a panentheist framework. As such, he argues for an 'emergentist supervenience' model of divine action.

Richardson, W. Mark, and Wildman, Wesley, J., eds. *Religion and Science: History, Method, Dialogue*. New York and London: Routledge, 1996.

This voluminous collection of essays considers the venture of building bridges between science and religion, both historically and methodologically (parts I and II). Part III is a collection of essays by prominent theologians and scientists trying to bring the major contemporary scientific theories into contact with theological doctrines. An extensive thematically structured list of suggested scientific and theological readings concludes this interdisciplinary book.

Southgate, Christopher, ed. *God, Humanity and the Cosmos: A Textbook in Science and Religion*. Harrisburg, Pa: Trinity Press, 1999.

This textbook surveys historical and philosophical aspects of relating science and religion, and highlights many facets of modern scientific theories. It also includes discussions on topics which are often left out, such as the relation between psychology and theology, science and education, Islamic perspectives, and issues of technology and ethics. The individual chapters are clearly structured into many subsections with many cross-references which makes the book usable not only for introductory courses on science and religion but also for self-study.

2. METHODOLOGY OF SCIENCE & RELIGION

Barbour, Ian G. *Myths, Models, and Paradigms: A Comparative Study in Science & Religion*. San Francisco: Harper & Row, 1974.

This book centers around three themes. The first is the different functions and internal logics of scientific and religious language. The second theme concerns the role of models in science and religion and their function for interpreting experience and restructuring our worldview. Thirdly the role of paradigms in science and religion is highlighted. Barbour concludes that both science and religion offer knowledge of reality based on experience. This work also offers the philosophical basics of so-called 'critical realism' in science and religion.

Drees, Willem B. *Religion, Science and Naturalism*. Cambridge: Cambridge University Press, 1996.

In this work, Drees adopts an explicitly naturalistic stance. Many theological issues are considered and critically analyzed according to a extensively outlined naturalist methodology. Drees concludes that a naturalist methodology has serious repercussions for the theological worldview as well as for religious anthropology. Drees sees religion embedded in our evolutionary history and our neurophysiological constitution, and values religious traditions as important for their wisdom and prophetic vision. He also raises the important issue of 'limit questions': the questions that science raises but cannot answer.

Gregersen, Niels H., and Van Huyssteen, J. Wentzel, eds. *Rethinking Theology and Science: Six Models for the Current Dialogue*. Grand Rapids, Mich.: Wm. B. Eerdmans, 1998.

In six essays an equal number of different models for relating theology and science are outlined. Van Huyssteen writes on postfoundationalism; van Kooten Niekerk presents a version of critical realism; Drees outlines naturalism; Herrmann expounds on a nonintegrative pragmatic approach; Watts writes on the complementarity between science and theology; and finally, Gregersen presents a contextual coherence theory that indicates that contact between theology and science takes place on several levels. Every approach tries to absorb the cognitive pluralism and counter relativist currents that threaten the science and religion dialogue.

Murphy, Nancey. *Theology for an Age of Scientific Reasoning*. Ithaca, NY and London: Cornell University Press, 1990.

Murphy's acclaimed book deals with the challenge of skepticism regarding Christian belief. Against the claims of the non- or irrationality of Christian belief over against the rationality of science, Murphy defends the view that religious belief is as rational as science. Murphy refers to Lakatos's methodology of scientific research programs arguing that religious reasoning is similar to scientific procedure. She tests the viability of her proposal by investigating actual theological research programs, such as Pannenberg's and Roman Catholic Modernism, concluding that theology makes claims to knowledge in the same way as science does.

Torrance, Thomas F. *Theological Science*. London: Oxford University Press, 1969.

Theology here is taken by Torrance, influenced by Barth, as the science of God. The methodological and epistemological issues connected with such a concept of theology commit theologians to a dialogue with other sciences and with philosophy, for they all use reason as the basic instrument, be it directed at different subject-matters. Science and theology nowadays share the same problem: how to attain knowledge of what goes beyond ourselves without imposing our presuppositions on reality. This book specifically deals with the methodological issues this problem raises for theology.

3. HISTORY OF SCIENCE & RELIGION

Brooke, John Hedley. *Science and Religion: Some Historical Perspectives*. Cambridge, UK: Cambridge University Press, 1991.

Brooke's work challenges the 'warfare' image of the history of the relation between science and religion by emphasizing contextual shifts. The essays contained in this volume all highlight specific historical periods in which science and religion interacted (such as the age of the Scientific Revolution and the Enlightenment) or specific issues on which science and religions (dis)agreed (such as the clockwork universe, natural theology, and evolutionary theory). Brooke links his historical reflections to the twentieth-century science and religion dialogue. An extensive bibliographical essay concludes this volume.

Funkenstein, Amos. *Theology and the Scientific Imagination: From the Middle Ages to the Seventeenth Century*. Princeton, N.J.: Princeton University Press, 1986.

This study addresses the transition from medieval to modern modes of thought. Funkenstein argues that the divine attributes of omnipresence, omnipotence, and providence contributed to but also underwent reinterpretation because of the emergence of the natural sciences. Due to the resultant theological and scientific changes, there arose in the seventeenth century a new ideal of knowledge: the ideal of knowledge-by-doing or knowledge by construction. Funkenstein argues that these developments eventually lead to the 'de-theologization' of science in Enlightenment thought.

Lindberg, David C., and Numbers, Ronald L., eds. *God & Nature: Historical Essays on the Encounter Between Christianity and Science*. Berkeley, Calif.: University of California Press, 1986.

These essays cover the periods of the Early Church, the Middle Ages and the controversy surrounding Galileo, the seventeenth century Scientific Revolution and the rise of Darwin's evolutionary theory, and contemporary debates concerning Creationism and the relation between present-day protestant theology and science. The essays attempt to counter the 'warfare' thesis, and show that a highly delicate historical account of the interplay between religion and science is possible.

White, Andrew Dickson. *A History of the Warfare of Science with Theology in Christendom*. London and New York: D. Appleton & Co., 1896.

Now generally regarded as one of the founding fathers of the so-called 'warfare'-thesis of religion and science, White sets out to describe the history of the relation between religion and science in terms of an age-old conflict. Evolutionary theory, geography and geology, astronomy, miracles and magic, archeology, anthropology and ethnology, history, meteorology, chemistry and physics, philology, psychology, politics and economy - all these domains are covered in the more than 900 pages of White's account of the battle between the religious and the scientific worldview.

4. PHYSICS & RELIGION

Barrow, John D. and Tipler, Frank J. *The Anthropic Cosmological Principle*. Oxford, UK and New York: Oxford University Press, 1986.

An astronomer and a physicist try to explain the relation between the properties of the universe and the existence of life. Covering the history of design arguments and teleological principles, as well as modern cosmology and astrophysics, the authors argue that modern physics and cosmology indicate that life is not accidental. They claim that modern science contains evidence for both the weak and the strong anthropic principles, stating that there is a close connection between the universe as it is and the emergence of carbon-based observers.

Davies, Paul. *God and the New Physics*. London: J.M. Dent & Sons, 1983.

Davies expounds on "the impact of the new physics on what were formerly religious issues," and concludes that "science offers a surer path than religion in the search of God." This book deals with physical, philosophical, and theological issues such as mind and soul, determinism and free will, and miracles. Davies reworked some of the controversial statements in this work in a sequel *The Mind of God: The Scientific Basis for a Rational World*. (New York etc.: Simon & Schuster, 1992).

Drees, Willem B. *Beyond the Big Bang: Quantum Cosmologies and God*. La Salle, Ill.: Open Court, 1990.

Without too many technicalities, Drees discusses issues at the interface of science and religion, such as: Does Big Bang cosmology have any relation to the Christian doctrine of creation *ex nihilo?* What does quantum cosmology state about 'the beginning' of the universe? Do the 'anthropic principles' have any scientific groundings? And how does eschatology fare in the light of the scientific cosmological futures? Some methodological reflections already foreshadow his naturalist position.

Russell, Robert John; Murphy, Nancey; and Isham, C.J., eds. *Quantum Cosmology and the Laws of Nature: Scientific Perspectives on Divine Action*. 2nd Edition. Berkeley, Calif.: CTNS and Vatican City State: Vatican Observatory, 1999.

A collection of interdisciplinary essays written by leading scientists, theologians, and philosophers of religion on the implications of quantum cosmology and the status of the laws of nature for theological and philosophical issues regarding God's action in the world. The essays are clustered into five sections: the scientific background of quantum cosmology, methodological remarks on relating science and theology, philosophical issues on time and the laws of nature, and two sections on theological implications.

Worthing, Mark William. *God, Creation, and Contemporary Physics*. Minneapolis, Minn.: Fortress Press, 1996.

Worthing's book surveys the links between theories from physics and cosmology and the theological issues of God's existence, creation out of nothing, and divine action. He also describes possible consequences of physical theories for Christian eschatology. The conclusion of the book is that theology cannot, strictly speaking, challenge the scientific conclusions drawn from the new physics, but theology must take notice of the metaphysical and theological implications of these theories.

5. BIOLOGY & RELIGION

Behe, Michael. *Darwin's Black Box: The Biochemical Challenge to Evolution*. New York: The Free Press, 1996.

Behe's book is one of the basic writings of the so-called 'Intelligent Design' movement. Behe argues that evolution takes place on the molecular level where science has shown that 'irreducibly complex' system exist: systems that cannot have evolved, but must have come into existence in one piece. Behe claims that the molecular basis of life is irreducibly complex, and, hence, cannot properly be described by the Darwinian evolutionary theory. Therefore, 'intelligent design' is the only plausible explanation for this irreducible complexity and for life.

Dembski, William A. *Intelligent Design: The Bridge Between Science & Theology*. Downers Grove, Il: Inter-Varsity Press, 1999.

In this book Dembski explains what the Intelligent Design movement is about: a scientific research program, anti-naturalistic, and a theology of divine action. Standing in the tradition of British natural theology,

ID attempts to reinstate design within science, especially in the irreducible complexity of biological sciences. Dembski claims that by referring to empirically detectable signs of intelligent design, theology and science are able to provide epistemic support for each other's claims.

Durant, John, ed. *Darwinism and Divinity: Essays on Evolution and Religious Belief.* Oxford, UK: Basil Blackwell, 1985.

In seven interdisciplinary essays, historians, theologians, anthropologists, sociologists, and philosophers use their expertise to shed some light on the question how evolutionary thought affects religious belief. The essays are written from different perspectives, which results in a kaleidoscope of views instead of a unitary vision. The authors not only consider the impact of evolution on religious thought, but also ask how religion affected evolutionary thinking. Some of the essays deal explicitly with discussions surrounding creationism.

Haught, John F. *God After Darwin: A Theology of Evolution.* Boulder, Colo.: Westview Press, 2000.

According to Haught, the discussions between die-hard evolutionists like Daniel Dennett and Richard Dawkins and Christian apologists all rest on the same mistake: both groups focus too much on static design and (dis)order in the universe. Haught, on the other hand, emphasizes the dynamic aspects of creativity and novelty that emerge in the process of evolution. He shows how these aspects are compatible with a concept of God that is described in partly Teilhardian and partly process-theological terms.

Hefner, Philip. *The Human Factor: Evolution, Culture, and Religion.* Minneapolis, Minn.: Fortress Press, 1993.

This book aims "at a theological anthropology in the light of the natural sciences." Especially noteworthy is Hefner's hypothesis that humans are 'created co-creators' with God, which proved influential in the science and religion dialogue. This hypothesis, emphasizing the potentials of human beings, is the red line of the book. The five parts that make up this book contain theoretical reflections on science and religion, reflections on nature, freedom, culture (including ethics), and connections with theology.

Numbers, Ronald L. *The Creationists.* Berkeley, Calif.: The University of California Press, 1993.

Numbers provides a detailed history of creationist lines of thinking from Darwin on until the renewed interest since the 1960s in the US. He shows that many paradigm shifts have taken place within the creationist framework, specifically with regard to 'catastrophism,' the antiquity of the earth, and the geological interpretations of the Genesis Flood. Numbers also shows how creationism became institutionalized, and how the churches responded to creationist thought, and argues that creationism questions the integrity and meaning of science itself.

Peacocke, Arthur. *God and the New Biology.* London andMelbourne: J.M. Dent & Sons Ltd, 1986.

Peacocke sets out to describe how the perspective of the new biology, with its "increasing apprehension of the labyrinthine complexity of the molecular processes and structures that are involved in the dynamics of a living organism," relates to a new understanding of the interrelations between humans, evolution, and God. Taking the issue of reductionism as his starting point, Peacocke argues that the new biology shows nature to be multi-leveled and hierarchical with new emergent features developing all the time. He also discusses sociobiology and Dawkins' 'selfish gene' idea.

Ruse, Michael. *Can a Darwinian Be a Christian? The Relationship Between Science and Religion.* Cambridge: Cambridge University Press, 2001.

Evolutionary theory meets the Christian religion in this work by an eminent philosopher. The book does not treat the dialogue between science and religion on a general level, but shows how concrete Christian doctrines are confronted by evolutionary thought. Ruse argues against Intelligent Design and Creationism, and argues in favor of social Darwinism and sociobiology. He concludes that nothing precludes a Darwinian to be a Christian, though at times it may be challenging and difficult.

Russell, Robert John; Stoeger, William R.; and Ayala, Francisco J., eds. *Evolutionary and Molecular Biology: Scientific Perspectives on Divine Action.* Berkeley, Calif.: CTNS and Vatican City State: Vatican Observatory, 1999.

A collection of interdisciplinary essays written by leading scientists, theologians, and philosophers of religion on the implications of evolutionary and molecular biology for the concept of divine action. In four sections the authors deal with the scientific background of evolution and molecular biology; the relation between evolution and divine action; religious interpretations of biological themes; and the interrelations between biology, ethics, and the problem of evil.

Ward, Keith. *God, Chance & Necessity.* Oxford: Oneworld, 1996.

Ward argues against the scientist and materialist claims like those of Richard Dawkins, Peter Atkins, and Michael Ruse who see the universe as governed by chance and not by purpose. Ward takes their claims seriously, but shows how these scientist claims ultimately point in the direction of God's existence as the best available explanation. Though the book focuses on (neo-)Darwinian evolutionary theory, Ward also touches upon cosmology, the problem of entropy and emergence, and the mystery of consciousness.

6. MATHEMATICS, COMPUTER SCIENCE & RELIGION

Gell-Mann, Murray. *The Quark and the Jaguar: Adventures in the Simple and the Complex.* London: Little, Brown and Company, 1994.

Gell-Mann, a Nobel Prize-winning theoretical physicist, explores the relationships between various scientific concepts of simplicity and complexity. The central focus of the book is the notion of complex adaptive systems: systems that evolve and learn by acquiring information. Gell-Mann's account covers many terrains: quantum mechanics and the fundamental laws of physics, information theory, biological evolution, human creative thinking, and ecology.

Gregersen, Niels Henrik, ed. *From Complexity to Life: On the Emergence of Life and Meaning.* Oxford/New York: Oxford University Press, 2002.

In the three parts that make up this book the link between complexity and information, the origin of life, and the nature of the universe is investigated. Complexity scientists, theologians, and philosophers of religion explore questions of defining complexity, the nature and role of information in physics and biology, and philosophical and religious perspectives on the meaning of emergence and complexity.

Herzfeld, Noreen L. *In Our Image: Artificial Intelligence and the Human Spirit.* Minneapolis, Minn.: Fortress Press, 2002.

This book charts some of the consequences of the sciences of Artificial Intelligence for our idea of what it means to be human, and how AI affects the phrase that we are created in God's image. Dealing with these and related issues, Herzfeld develops a model of relationality: "The way we define God's image in our human nature or our image in the computer has implications, not only for how we view ourselves but also for how we relate to God, to one another, and to our own creations."

Puddefoot, John. *God and the Mind Machine: Computers, Artificial Intelligence and the Human Soul.* London: SPCK, 1996.

Issues surrounding computers, life, intelligence, and the human soul are the focus of this book. It addresses the question of how to relate theology to issues concerning computer science and Artificial Intelligence. This book addresses the growing anxiety among religious believers that developments in computer science and Artificial Intelligence will take away the soul. Puddefoot argues that these scientific developments might be seen as part of God's purpose with the universe. Though Puddefoot draws no definite conclusions, his study does give impetus to further explorations and reflections.

Russell, Robert John; Murphy, Nancey; and Peacocke, Arthur R., eds. *Chaos and Complexity: Scientific Perspectives on Divine Action.* Berkeley, Calif.: CTNS & Vatican City State: Vatican Observatory, 1995.

A collection of essays of eminent scientists, theologians, and philosophers of religion on the implications of chaos and self-organization in physical, chemical, and biological systems for philosophical and theological issues regarding divine action in the world. The first section contains two introductory essays on the scientific aspects of chaos and complexity. The second relates chaos and complexity to the philosophy of life. The third and fourth sections link chaos and complexity to divine action and explore alternative approaches of divine action. The whole constitutes a detailed overview of the contemporary reception of the sciences of nonlinear systems in theological reflection.

Smith, Peter. *Explaining Chaos.* Cambridge: Cambridge University Press, 1998.

This volume is a mildly technical introduction to the concepts of chaos theory and its philosophical implications. It is especially noteworthy that Smith makes a distinction between the mathematics of chaos and its empirical applications. Fractals, the problem of predictability and explanation, the difference between chaos and randomness, and the definition of chaos - these are only a few of the many issues that Smith covers.

7. THE HUMAN SCIENCES & RELIGION

d'Aquili, Eugene and Newberg, Andrew B. *The Mystical Mind: Probing the Biology of Religious Experience.* Minneapolis, Minn.: Fortress Press, 1999.

D'Aquili and Newberg attempt to integrate theology and neuroscience by exploring "the issue of how 'ultimate being' is perceived and experienced by the human brain and mind." The authors introduce basic concepts from theology and neuroscience, and explore the role of the brain and mind in myth-making, ritual and liturgy, meditation, near-death experiences and mysticism. Both Eastern and Western religious traditions are taken into account. Finally, they try to integrate their findings into a phenomenological 'neurotheology.'

Austin, James H. *Zen and the Brain: Toward an Understanding of Meditation and Consciousness.* Cambridge, Mass.: MIT Press, 1998.

Meditation and neurology are brought together in an attempt to unravel the mystery of consciousness and enlightenment or 'peak' experiences. Austin takes Zen meditation as his starting point, and describes the physiological mechanisms involved. Thereafter he summarizes some of the latest developments in brain research and defines the usual states of consciousness and their alternative expressions. Finally alternate meditative states of consciousness as well as enlightenment experiences are investigated.

Brown, Warren S.; Murphy, Nancey; and Malony, Newton H., eds. *Whatever Happened to the Soul? Scientific and Theological Portraits of Human Nature*. Minneapolis, Minn.: Fortress Press, 1998.

This interdisciplinary volume contains ten essays by scientists and theologians on scientific and theological aspects of human nature. Special focus is on the idea of the soul. Many authors adopt the position of 'nonreductive physicalism,' a holistic or monistic view over against a dualist view of mind and brain. From this perspective the soul is described as "a functional capacity of a complex physical organism."

Mithen, Steven. *The Prehistory of Mind: The Cognitive Origins of Art, Religion and Science*. New York: Thames and Hudson, 1996.

Mithen's book is a mixture of an archeological account of the prehistoric roots of our minds, connected to the emergence of art and religion, and a study in the philosophy of mind, seeing in the archeological data evidence for the modularity of the human brain. Mithen argues there is a common origin to art, religion, and science in the prehistoric usage of the mind, which led, through a series of evolutionary phases of specialization and collaboration, to our modular minds.

Palmer, Michael. *Freud and Jung on Religion*. London/New York: Routledge, 1997.

Today's psychology is still very much indebted to the two founding fathers of twentieth-century psychology, Sigmund Freud and Karl Gustav Jung. Their relation to religion is often interpreted in ambiguous fashion: Freud as a reductionist enemy of religion, and Jung as a New Age enthusiast. In this volume, Palmer goes back to the basics of Freud's and Jung's own writings on the psychology of religion, linking their claims on religion to their psychological theories, and drawing comparisons between their respective positions whilst critically evaluating their claims.

Peters, Ted. *Playing God? Genetic Determinism and Human Freedom*. New York and London: Routledge, 1997.

Thinking about genetics is closely bound to problems of determinism and human freedom. According to Peters, a cultural expression of this is the 'gene myth,' which asserts that everything that makes us distinctively human is genetically determined. Peters confronts this myth with the theological view of humans as future-oriented and as co-creative with God. This view will lead to a healthy ethics for guiding genetic research which should be used "to relieve human suffering and to make this a better world in which to live."

Rolston, Holmes, III. *Genes, Genesis and God: Values and their Origins in Natural and Human History*. Cambridge: Cambridge University Press, 1999.

Based on Rolston's Gifford Lectures, this study explores the connections between religion, ethics, and biological accounts of genetic influences. Rolston strongly argues against sociobiological accounts that reduce religion and ethics to biological features. He interprets evolutionary history as the genesis and history of natural values, which are conserved and transmitted by science, religion, and ethics. He claims that the sociobiological reductionists miss an important point by misunderstanding how these values are transmitted and shared. As such, Rolston assigns a prominent role to culture, and accordingly links 'nurture' intimately with 'nature.'

Russell, Robert John; Murphy, Nancey; Meyering, Theo C.; and Arbib, Michael A. eds. *Neuroscience and the Person: Scientific Perspectives on Divine Action*. Berkeley, Calif.: CTNS and Vatican City State: Vatican Observatory, 1999.

Another collection of essays written by scientists, philosophers, and theologians ranging the broad terrain of the cognitive neurosciences and their implications for philosophy, theology, and models of divine action. Many essays revolve around the issues of the sense of self and soul, the person, and religious anthropology. One can find also philosophical accounts on the relation between mind and brain, theories of supervenience, emergence, and Artificial Intelligence.

8. FEMINIST APPROACHES TO RELIGION & SCIENCE

Haraway, Donna J. *Modest Witness, Second Millennium. FemaleMan© Meets OncoMouse™: Feminism and Technoscience*. New York and London: Routledge, 1997.

A study on the many facets of technoscience and their implications for our view of the world, and for feminism in particular. Haraway argues that the information sciences and the technological applications for the life sciences are changing our view of reality and of ourselves, and she specifically explores the idea of 'cyborgs,' beings that are part human part machine. She further reflects on the changing values and ethical aspects of technoscience.

Harding, Sandra. *Whose Science? Whose Knowledge? Thinking from Women's Lives*. Cornell: Cornell University Press, 1991.

A variety of contemporary voices from many different perspectives criticizes mainstream science and technology. This study links the feminist criticisms on Western science, technology, and epistemology to these other perspectives. Two red lines run through the ten essays contained in this book. First, the evaluation of interrelations between science, models of knowledge and the Western society and culture, and the creation of 'others' which are outside the mainstream society or culture. Secondly, Harding tries to show how feminisms are influenced by and influencing other liberatory movements.

Tuana, Nancy. *The Less Noble Sex: Scientific, Religious, and Philosophical Conceptions of Women's Nature.* Bloomington/Indianapolis: Indiana University Press, 1993.

Tuana argues that religion and philosophy have affected and have been influenced by scientific theories of women's nature and her inferiority to man. The book gives a historical account of these matters from the classical period until the nineteenth century. The central claim is that the belief "that woman is less than man … is more than simple bias, easily amenable to revision. It is part of our inherited metaphysics." Exposing metaphysical assumption will benefit critical reexamination and openness to alternatives.

Wertheim, Margaret. *Pythagoras' Trousers: God, Physics, and the Gender Wars.* New York: Norton, 1997.

Wertheim explores the history of the interconnections between science and the wider cultural sphere. Her claim is that the relation between science and religion is more intimate than is often thought. Under the influence of the idea of a heavenly realm of mathematics, scientists, and especially physicists, received in our Western society a priest-like status. As Wertheim argues, this 'priestly' nature of science is also largely responsible for the masculine character of many sciences, and for the difficulties that women experience when they want to participate in this culture.

9. PHILOSOPHY, SCIENCE & RELIGION

Clayton, Philip. *Explanation from Physics to Theology: An Essay in Rationality and Religion.* New Haven and London: Yale University Press, 1989.

Does religion give explanations similar to scientific explanations? To find an answer to this question, Clayton investigates the nature and justification of explanatory claims in both the natural and the social sciences, and argues that when the concept of explanation is not reduced to merely scientific explanation, religious experiences and beliefs can appropriately be said to function as explanations. The upshot is that the function of religious and scientific explanations are comparable.

Pannenberg, Wolfhart. *Theology and the Philosophy of Science.* Philadelphia: Westminster Press, 1976.

This volume explicitly addresses the issue whether or not theology is a science. Pannenberg gives detailed expositions of theology's struggles with Logical Positivism, and Positivism's struggle with the critical rationalism of Popper. He also considers the relation between the natural and social sciences, and the role of hermeneutics. Ultimately, Pannenberg argues that theology is a science: the 'science of God,' whilst doctrines could be considered as hypotheses.

Stenmark, Mikael. *Rationality in Science, Religion, and Everyday Life: A Critical Evaluation of Four Models of Rationality.* Notre Dame, Ind.: University of Notre Dame Press, 1995.

In this study, Stenmark distinguishes four models of rationality and discusses what these models entail especially for science, religion, and our everyday life. Instead of employing an abstract model of rationality and attempting to incorporate these three areas, Stenmark opts to start with rationality as practice-oriented and as mirroring actual human practices. This leads him to his 'presumptionist' model of rationality: in both science and religion it is rational to accept a belief unless there are good reasons to abandon it.

Stenmark, Mikael. *Scientism: Science, Ethics and Religion.* Aldershot etc.: Ashgate, 2001.

In the first chapter, Stenmark provides an impressive overview of the different kinds of 'scientism,' basically the view that there is nothing "outside the domain of science nor any area of human life to which science cannot successfully be applied." In subsequent chapters Stenmark attempts to debunk scientistic claims with regard to knowledge and reality, morality and ethics, and religion. He concludes that scientism is a metaphysical belief akin to religious belief, and urges scientists to become more conscious of the limitations of the scientific enterprise.

van Huyssteen, J. Wentzel. *The Shaping of Rationality: Toward Interdisciplinarity in Theology and Science.* Grand Rapids, Mich.: William B. Eerdmans Publishing Company, 1999.

Van Huyssteen explores possibilities of interdisciplinary dialogue between theology and science based on mutual respect and understanding. He tries to steer away from both extremes of modernist foundationalism and postmodernist relativism by developing a *postfoundationalist* position which emphasizes contextuality, embedded experience, and the 'transversal' potentiality of rationality to reach beyond the confines of the local community. Van Huyssteen emphasizes the specific rationality of theology over against scientistic, foundationalist, and relativist tendencies in modern philosophy of science and the broader culture.

10. THEOLOGY & THE SCIENCES

Allen, Diogenes. *Christian Belief in a Postmodern World: The Full Wealth of Conviction.* Louisville, Ky.: Westminster John Knox Press, 1989.

Allen is of the opinion that the Enlightenment has expelled God from the world, while faith has been reduced to either fideism of relativism. However, now that we have seen the decline of the Enlightenment project, there may be new possibilities for faith to experience God. In an attempt at rediscovering the riches of the Christian faith, Allen describes how the order of nature can be seen as a witness to God's existence. He also highlights the reasonability of faith and revelation, divine action, and the issue of other faiths.

Nasr, Seyyed Hossein. *Religion and the Order of Nature*. New York and London: Oxford University Press, 1996.

Although the focus of this work is mainly on Western religious interpretations of nature and the interplay between religion, science, and philosophy, Nasr explicitly invokes other religious traditions as well, especially the Islamic tradition. In a blend of historical, philosophical, and religious writing, Nasr tries to indicate how the different religious traditions embody wisdom that can help overcome the contemporary ecological crises, while establishing a new religious worldview based on the re-sacralization of nature.

Peacocke, Arthur. *Theology for a Scientific Age: Being and Becoming - Natural, Divine and Human*. London: SCM Press, 1993.

In this book, based on his Gifford Lectures, Peacocke explores the implications of the sciences for theological doctrine. Focusing on the concept of God, God's interaction with the world, and God's communication with humanity through Jesus Christ, he constructs a panentheist framework in which the world is seen as a many-leveled emergent whole governed by the dynamic interplay of chance and necessity.

Peters, Ted. *God as Trinity: Relationality and Temporality in Divine Life*. Louisville, Ky.: Westminster/John Knox Press, 1993.

The Christian doctrine of the Trinity is explored in relation to some contemporary issues in theology and science. Peters gives an introduction to 'Trinity Talk,' and addresses some contemporary moral and theological issues. He also gives an overview of the trinitarian views of several twentieth-century theologians. Finally, relations to philosophy and science, especially regarding temporality, are explored.

Polkinghorne, John, ed. *The Work of Love: Creation as Kenosis*. Grand Rapids, Mich.: William B. Eerdmans and London: SPCK, 2001.

'Kenosis' or the self-limitation of God has increasingly gained attention. It refers to the idea that God voluntarily limited his power so as to allow for freedom for finite creatures. In the essays collected in this volume, eleven well-known theologians explore this notion, especially in connection with the doctrine of creation, the relation between humans and nature, divine action, and our scientific worldview.

Polkinghorne, John, and Welker, Michael, eds. *The End of the World and the Ends of God: Science and Theology on Eschatology*. Harrisburg, Pa.: Trinity Press International, 2000.

The contributions in this interdisciplinary volume center around the question how our contemporary culture influences and is influenced by theological ideas about the end of the world. The essays are clustered in four sections as reflections on eschatological themes from the natural sciences, the cultural sciences and ethics, biblical studies, and from systematic theology. Some central themes are the relation between scientific cosmology and eschatology, the role of culture and the church as cultural space, the concept of time and the future, eschatological themes in the Bible, and the issue of life after death.

Polkinghorne, John. *The Faith of a Physicist: Reflections of a Bottom-Up Thinker*. Minneapolis, Minn.: Fortress Press, 1996.

Structured according to the Nicene Creed, Polkinghorne's Gifford Lectures explores "to what extent we can use the search for motivated understanding, so congenial to the scientific mind, as a route to being able to make the substance of Christian orthodoxy our own." Polkinghorne discusses how science bears upon specific theological doctrines like creation, christology, pneumatology, and eschatology.

Qadir, C.A. *Philosophy and Science in the Islamic World*. New York: Croom Helm, 1988.

Historically speaking, the Western civilization owes much to Islamic influences, due to the translations of Greek and Arabic texts on science and philosophy. In this work, Qadir narrates the emergence, rise, decline, and the rediscovery of Islamic philosophy and science. He argues that the Islamic perspective emphasizes the wholeness and oneness of the cosmos and of our knowledge. In the final three chapters, the contemporary rediscovery of the Islamic potentials concerning philosophy, science, and technology in Muslim countries is described.

Samuelson, Norbert. *Judaism and the Doctrine of Creation*. Cambridge: Cambridge University Press, 1994.

Expounding historical, religious, and philosophical aspects of some Jewish perspectives on the doctrine of creation, Samuelson discusses the interrelations between the Hebrew scriptures, Greek and Jewish philosophy, and contemporary physics. Some reflections can be found on Rosenzweig's philosophy, the limits of human reason and religious faith, the character of religious belief, the relevance of scientific models to religious doctrine, and the nature of the relationship between God and the universe.

Ward, Keith. *Religion & Creation*. Oxford: Clarendon Press, 1996.

This book contains a thorough analysis and comparison by a Christian theologian of the doctrine of creation and the notion of God in four scriptural traditions, and its interpretation by eminent twentieth-century theologians within those traditions. Ward concludes that there are many fruitful comparisons to be made regarding the properties which are ascribed to God in the different traditions. In the final part of the book, Ward makes explicit "a specifically Christian doctrine of God as Trinity, in the light of the new perspective on the universe which modern cosmology provides."

11. SCIENCE & DIVINE ACTION

Polkinghorne, John. *Science and Providence: God's Interaction with the World*. Boston: Shambala, 1989.

In this book, Polkinghorne addresses issues surrounding the question how we can reconcile the scientific worldview with the Christian's belief in a personal and caring God. Through exploring the relation between embodiment and action, Polkinghorne arrives at a model of divine action wherein God is seen to interact with the world by top-down action. The reference to chaos theory, which he explored further in many subsequent writings, has become the hallmark of Polkinghorne's theology of divine action.

Morris, Thomas V., ed. *Divine and Human Action: Essays in the Metaphysics of Theism*. Ithaca, NY and London: Cornell University Press, 1988.

The twelve diverse essays collected in this volume all revolve around the theological, philosophical, and metaphysical issues surrounding the relation and interaction of God with the created world and its inhabitants. These issues include divine causality and the natural world, providence, creaturely freedom and the role of chance, and the nature and properties of God. As the title indicates, the essays particularly address the traditional theist idea of God.

Tracy, Thomas F., ed. *The God Who Acts: Philosophical and Theological Explorations*. University Park, Pa: The Pennsylvania State University Press, 1994.

This collection of essays of renowned philosophers and theologians deals explicitly with the moral implications and difficulties surrounding divine action. The essays focus on two themes. First particular divine action is considered, especially related to the problem of evil. Secondly, the attention turns to universal divine action in connection with creation and human freedom.

Ward, Keith. *Divine Action*. London: Collins, 1990.

Ward tackles in clear arguments many difficult issues connected with the concept of divine action, such as the order of the universe, miracles, the problem of evil, and prayer. He argues that science has declared the death of the closed universe. Our universe turns out to be emergent and open, and God is personally and continually active in it, though his influence is undetectable for creatures. The life, death, and resurrection of Jesus of Nazareth constitutes "a definite embodiment of God's own activity for human redemption, which is the matrix for interpreting the Divine activity everywhere."

Wiles, Maurice. *God's Action in the World: The Bampton Lectures for 1986*. London: SCM Press, 1986.

In this work the famous though controversial 'single act' theory of divine action is expounded. Wiles shows how evil and suffering pose insurmountable problems for any interventionist view of divine action. This leads him to propose the idea that "the whole process of bringing into being of the world, which is still going on, needs to be seen as one action of God." Arguing from this model he deals with problems of evil, providence and Christology.

12. SCIENCE, RELIGION, & ETHICS

Barbour, Ian G. *Ethics in an Age of Technology: The Gifford Lectures, 1989-91, Vol. 2*. San Francisco: HarperCollins, 1992.

In this second volume of Gifford Lectures, Barbour addresses the ethical issues related to our use of applied science and technology. The book is structured in three parts. The first part deals with the different views on technology, human, and environmental values. In the second part, three 'critical' technologies, agriculture, energy, and computers are explored. In the third part, reflecting on the future use and development of technology, Barbour makes clear how the values discussed in the former two parts are relevant for technological policy decisions.

Murphy, Nancey, and Ellis, George F.R. *On the Moral Nature of the Universe: Theology, Cosmology, and Ethics*. Minneapolis, Minn.: Fortress Press, 1996.

How do science, theology, and ethics relate to each other? And does our understanding of the universe have any ethical implications? These are the questions that are explored in this study by a theologian and a cosmologist. Taking the integrity of the natural order as a starting point, the authors argue that God's action entails refusal to violate that order. This 'kenotic' view of God's action then is taken as having moral implications for a self-renunciatory ethic, "according to which one must renounce self-interest for the sake of the other, *no matter what the cost to oneself*."

Rolston, Holmes, III. *Environmental Ethics: Duties to and Values in the Natural World*. Philadelphia: Temple University Press, 1988.

Rolston defends the view that humans have to respond to and are responsible for nature. As such, he develops a theory of naturalist environmental ethics based on duties and values, which also seeks to optimize human fitness on earth and to do this in a moral manner. This theory is then applied to social, public, and business policy making. Many examples help to elucidate Rolston's points.

TAEDE A. SMEDES

INDEX

Page numbers in **boldface** indicate the main article on a subject.

mind–body problem and, 567–568, 571

mind interaction with. *See* Mind–brain interaction

moral behavior and, 616

multiple coupling complexity of, 152

neural Darwinism and, 610

neuron formation and, 613

neuropsychology and, 610, 707

neurosciences and, 610–616

placebo effect and, 677

reductionism and, 398

regulatory functions of, 614

religious experience areas of, 308, 309–310, 314, 615–616, 617, 707, 726

self–organization of, 798

self–referential system theory and, 153

self–transcendence and, 799–800

specialized regions of, 612, 615

venticular theory and, 611

See also Nervous system; Neural networks; Neurons

Brain damage, 614, 615

Brain death, 523

Brain imaging. *See* Neuroimaging

Brain tumors, 615

Braithwaite, Richard B., 650

Branching time, 899–900

Brandom, Robert B., 903

Brazil, Lutheran churches in, 127

Breathing techniques, 833

Brentano, Franz, 570, 920

Breuil, Abbé, 31

Brewster, David, 122

Bridgebuilding (periodical), 767

Bridgewater Treatises, 103, 104, 105, 660

Brief History of Time, A (Hawking), 175, 825

Brillouin, Leon, 457

Britain. *See* Great Britain

British Association for the Advancement of Science, 120, 754

British Science and Religion Forum, 767

Brno monastery, 557–558

Broad, C. D., 153, 398

Broca, Paul, 612, 615

Broca's area, 615

Brock, Tim Clutton, 809

Broglie, Louis de, 542, 560, 570, 672, 673

Broglie–Bohm theory, 673, 675

Brooke, John, 105–106, 165–166, 344, 768, 774

Brooks, Rodney, 34, 160

Broome, Arthur, 12

Brown, Delmar, 804

Brown, Donald, 22

Brown, Frederick, 778

Brown, Herbert Charles, 493

Brown, L. B., 697

Brown, Louise, 731–732

Brown, Michael Stuart, 494

Brown, Warren, 773, 827

Browne, Thomas, 905

Brown University, 815

Bruce, Donald, 366

Brumbaugh, Robert, 447

Brunel University, 159

Bruning, Bernard, 45

Brunner, Emil, 249

Brunner, John, 777, 778

Bruno, Giordano, 255

Bryan, William Jennings, 122, 785–786

Bryn Mawr College, 159

Buber, Martin, 794

Bucaille, Maurice, 466–467

Bucer, Johannes, 136

Büchner, Ludwig, 252, 541

Bucke, Richard, 307

Buckland, William, 90

Buckley, Michael, 140

Bucknell University, 241

Buddha. *See* Siddhartha Gautama

Buddhaghosa, 77, 94, 799

Buddhism, **74–75**, 106, 107

animal rights and, 12, 419

anthropocentrism and, 19

beliefs and doctrines of, 76–77, 81–82, 85, 107, 184–185, 274–275, 717, 773, 869, 880, 881

causation and, 93–94

compassion as central of, 8, 12, 78, 82, 83, 84, 184, 185

consciousness and, 158, 160, 162

death perspective of, 78, 79, 84, 204–205

divine presence and, 744

empiricism and, 260

environmentalism of, 240

Four Noble Truths of, 74, 94, 107, 274, 869

free will and, 338

hermeneutics and, 395

holism and, 763

human nature and, 436

idealism and, 159

imagination and, 447

impermanence and, 77, 81, 82, 83, 85, 514

Japanese Shinto and, 803

liberation (spiritual) and, 74, 274, 513, 514, 515–516

medicine and, 78–79, 82, 83, 84–85, 553, 830

mysticism and, 308, 309, 586, 587, 588, 589, 799

pantheism and, 645

quantum theory analogies with, 78, 675–676

quantum vacuum state and, 712

reincarnation belief and, 717

self in, 93–94, 436, 514, 793, 794, 799

self–transcendence and, 799

semiotics and, 802–803

sin perspective in, 805

soul and, 820

spiritual definition of, 829

systems theory analogy with, 854

technology and, 869, 871

theistic beliefs contrasted with, 880

theodicy and, 880

theology and, 883

theories of religion and, 728

time and, 897

transmigration and, 82–83, 901

ultimate in, 915

values of, 915, 916

as Whitehead influence, 826

Buddhism, contemporary issues in science and religion, **75–81**, 774

abortion and, 3

biotechnology and, 78–79, 79, 86

cognitive sciences and, 79, 160

environmentalism and, 78, 86, 241–242

as science fiction theme, 778

scientific method and, 77–78

Buddhism, history of science and religion, **81–86**

causation and, 91–92

cosmology and, 75, 76, 82–83, 117, 774

creator belief and, 184–185

Daoism contrasted with, 107

relationship with science, 82–86, 515–516

value and, 915

Buddhism and Ecology: The Interconnection of Dharma and Deeds (Tucker and Williams), 78

Bullinger, Heynrich, 136

Bultmann, Rudolf, 129, 222, 417, 448, 757

Burbank, Luther, 65

Burckhardt, Titus, 468

Burhoe, Ralph, 284, 345, 596, 753

Buri, Fritz, 447

Buridan, John, 124

Burkert, Walter, 738–739

Burks, A. W., 46

Burn treatment, stem cells and, 367

Burtt, E. A., 752

Bush, George W., 368

Business ethics, 239

Butler, Joseph (Bishop Butler), 441, 650

M

N

Sociobiology *(continued)*
  genetic adaptation and, 226
  genetic determinism and, 359,
    363, 364, 761, 796, 810, 812
  genetic fitness and, 334
  Gould's critique of, 385
  hermeneutics and, 93
  human evolution and, 288, 364,
    379
  human moral standards and, 438,
    811
  imago dei belief and, 379
  interpretations of, 810
  memes theory and, 289, 290,
    556–557
  naturalized epistemology and,
    599
  reciprocal altruism and, 808–809
  science–religion conflict model
    and, 761, 768
  scientific materialism and, 761
  selfish gene concept and,
    795–796, 806
Sociobiology: The New Synthesis
  (Wilson), 809
Sociology, **814–818**
  altruism and, 8, 9
  autopoiesis and, 46, 47
  coining of term, 814
  consciousness studies and, 158,
    163
  first academic course in, 815
  functionalism in, 343–344, 729
  metanarrative and, 691
  modernity and, 581
  mystical traditions and, 587
  of religious experience, 311
  rituals and, 738, 739
  science–religion studies and, 758
  social constructivism and, 654
  sociobiology and, 810
  spirituality and, 839
  theories of religion and, 727–729
  value concept in, 914
Sociology of knowledge, 817–818
Sociology of religion, 814, 817, 818
Sociology of Religion (Weber), 246
Sociology of science, 818
Sociology of scientific knowledge
  studies (SSK), 782
Socrates, 567, 679–680
Socratic method, 544
Soffer, Olga, 30
Software
  artificial life and, 37
  Cartesian dualism and, 8
Sokal, Alan, 782
Solaris (Lem), 778
Solar system, 101
  Copernican, 179, 350
  cyclical seasonal rites and,
    820–821
  divine action and, 219

  end–time beliefs and, 264
  extraterrestrial life search and,
    317
  Galileo's telescopic observations
    of, 350
  General Theory of Relativity and,
    718
  gravitation and, 388, 389, 664,
    665
  scientific cosmology and, 170,
    182
  See also Earth; Planetary system;
    Sun
Sola scriptura doctrine, 885
Soleveitchik, Joseph, 485–486
Somatic cell nuclear transfer, 732,
    733–734, 735
  as cloning, 146, 365–366, 367,
    368, 425, 732, 733–734
  stem cell regenerative therapy
    and, 66, 69, 146, 424, 425, 735,
    841–842
Somatic nervous system, 430
"Some Protestant Reflections"
  (Meilaender), 842
Song Dynasty, 112, 117
Sonograms, 402
Sophia (wisdom), 415, 560
Sorbonne. *See* University of Paris
Soskice, Janet Martin, 560, 736
Soteriology, 415
Soul, **818–820**
  ancient conceptions of, 517, 518,
    519, 567, 818, 819
  animals and, 10, 11, 89–90, 231,
    437, 539–540, 813, 818, 918
  artificial intelligence and, 35
  Augustine's view of, 44, 45, 568
  Avicenna's view of, 50
  behaviorism versus, 59
  Buddhism and, 93–94
  Cartesian view of, 89–90
  Christian concept of, 519–520
  cloning and, 366
  contemporary popular culture
    meaning of, 820
  creationism and, 187
  dualism and, 229–231, 414, 572,
    763
  emergence and, 162
  empiricism and, 261
  evil and suffering and, 276
  God and, 379
  hardware–software distinction
    and, 8
  Hindu *atman* as, 204, 405, 406,
    409, 436, 567, 799, 869
  imago dei and, 449–450, 793
  immortality of. *See* Life after
    death
  incarnations of, 567
  Islamic concept of, 794, 820
  Judaic concept of, 517–518, 820

  karma and, 76, 77, 79, 185,
    275–276
  materialistic views of, 539, 540,
    541
  mind–body dualism and,
    567–568
  natural theology and, 601
  neurotheology and, 617
  New Age notion of, 521
  Newton's mortalist view of, 620
  Plato's view of, 124, 230, 437,
    518, 544, 601, 679, 680, 681,
    818, 819, 820
  reincarnation and, 276, 680
  self concept and, 793–794
  sin and, 805
  spirit and, 826–827
  status in heaven of, 520
  transmigration of, 204, 901
Soulé, Michael E., 235
Soul retrieval, 833
Sources of the Self, The (Taylor),
  793
*South African Science and Religion
  Forum* (newsletter), 767
South America. *See* Latin America
South Asian religions. *See*
  Buddhism; Hinduism
Southern Baptist Convention, 734,
    842
Southern Sociological Society, 817
Southgate, Christopher, 755, 772,
    773–774
Space
  ancient chaos concept and, 98
  expansion of cosmic, 721
  fields and, 664
  God's omnipresence and, 622
  Newton's concept of, 372
  noncommutative, 373, 389
  See also Absolute space; Space
    and time
Space and time, **820–825**
  anthropic coincidences and, 15,
    214
  black holes and, 71
  cellular automata and, 45, 46
  common sense notions of, 721,
    824
  creatio continua and, 183, 184
  creatio ex nihilo and, 184
  curvature of, 332, 389, 718
  Einstein's relativity theories and,
    171–172, 251, 372, 373,
    389–390, 664, 667, 717,
    719–722, 747, 824, 894
  Euclidean assumptions on, 824
  expanding universe and, 99
  as fields, 332, 542
  fourth dimension and, 824, 894
  God's omnipresence and,
    628–629, 770
  gravity and, 332, 333